The Civil War Archive

THE HISTORY OF THE CIVIL WAR IN DOCUMENTS

The Civil War Archive

THE HISTORY OF THE CIVIL WAR IN DOCUMENTS

EDITED BY HENRY STEELE COMMAGER
REVISED AND EXPANDED BY ERIK BRUUN

BLACK DOG
& LEVENTHAL
PUBLISHERS
NEW YORK

Published by Black Dog & Leventhal Publishers, Inc.
151 West 19ᵗʰ Street, New York, NY 10011

Distributed by Workman Publishing Company
708 Broadway, New York, NY 10003

Designed by Dutton & Sherman. Printed in the United States of America.

ISBN 1-57912-110-1

h g f e d c b

The civil war archive : the history of the Civil War in documents / edited by H.S. Commager ; revised and expanded by Erik Bruun
        p. cm.
    Rev. ed. of: The Bluc and the Gray. 1950.
    Includes bibliographical references and index.
    ISBN 1-57912-110-1
    1. United States—History—Civil War, 1861–1865—Personal narratives. 2. United States—History—Civil War, 1861-1865—Sources. I. Commager, Henry Steele, 1902- II. Bruun, Erik. III. Blue and the Gray.

E464.C45 2000
973.7'8—dc21
                                            00-024688

A Lou Reda/Mary Commager Book

CONTENTS

PREFACE   23
Erik Bruun

FOREWORD   25
Douglas Southall Freeman

INTRODUCTION   29
Henry Steele Commager

I. DARKENING CLOUDS   39

1. ABRAHAM LINCOLN IS NOMINATED   39
   IN THE WIGWAM
   Murat Halstead

2. "FIRST GALLANT SOUTH   42
   CAROLINA NOBLY MADE
   THE STAND"
   A. South Carolina Ordinance of   42
      Secession
   B. South Carolina Declaration of   42
      Causes of Secession

3. "SHE HAS LEFT US IN PASSION   43
   AND PRIDE"
   Oliver Wendell Holmes

4. LINCOLN REFUSES TO COMPROMISE   44
   ON SLAVERY
   Abraham Lincoln
   A. Letter to E. B. Washburne   44
   B. Letter to James T. Hale   45
   C. Letter to W. H. Seward   45

5. MAYOR FERNANDO WOOD RECOMMENDS   45
   THE SECESSION OF NEW YORK
   Fernando Wood

6. LINCOLN IS INAUGURATED   47
   A. Herndon Describes the Inauguration   47
      William H. Herndon
   B. The Public Man Attends the Inauguration   48
      The "Public Man"

7. "WE ARE NOT ENEMIES BUT FRIENDS"   50
   Abraham Lincoln

8. MR. LINCOLN HAMMERS OUT   51
   A CABINET
   Thurlow Weed

9. SEWARD TRIES TO TAKE CHARGE   52
   OF THE LINCOLN ADMINISTRATION
   A. Memorandum from Secretary Seward   53
      W. H. Seward
   B. Reply to Secretary Seward's Memorandum   53
      Abraham Lincoln

10. THE CONFEDERACY ORGANIZES   54
    AT MONTGOMERY
    T. C. DeLeon

11. CONSTITUTION OF THE   56
    CONFEDERATE STATES OF AMERICA

12. A WAR CLERK DESCRIBES DAVIS   58
    AND HIS CABINET
    J. B. Jones

13. SAM HOUSTON REFUSES TO GO 59
WITH HIS STATE
Sam Houston

14. INAUGURAL ADDRESS OF 61
JEFFERSON DAVIS
Jefferson Davis

II. THE CONFLICT 65
PRECIPITATED

1. MRS. CHESNUT WATCHES THE 65
ATTACK ON FORT SUMTER
Mary Boykin Chesnut

2. ABNER DOUBLEDAY DEFENDS 69
FORT SUMTER
Abner Doubleday

3. "THE HEATHER IS ON FIRE" 71
A. An Indiana Farm Boy Hears the News 72
Theodore Upson
B. "There Is But One Thought—The Stars 72
and Stripes"
Horace Binney
C. "One Great Eagle Scream" 74
Jane Stuart Woolsey

4. "THE SPIRIT OF VIRGINIA CANNOT 75
BE CRUSHED"
John Tyler and Julia Tyler

5. "I AM FILLED WITH HORROR 77
AT THE CONDITION OF OUR
COUNTRY"
Jonathan Worth

6. A NORTHERN DEMOCRAT URGES 78
PEACEFUL SEPARATION
J. L. O'Sullivan

7. "THE RACE OF PHILIP SIDNEYS 79
IS NOT EXTINCT"
John Lothrop Motley

8. THE SUPREME COURT UPHOLDS 80
THE CONSTITUTION
Robert Grier

III. THE GATHERING OF 83
THE HOSTS

1. "OUR PEOPLE ARE ALL UNITED" 84
Henry William Ravenel

2. SOUTHERN LADIES SEND THEIR 85
MEN OFF TO WAR
Mary A. Ward

3. THE NORTH BUILDS A VAST 87
ARMY OVERNIGHT
Edward Dicey

4. NORTHERN BOYS JOIN THE RANKS 89
A. Warren Goss Enlists in the Union Army 89
Warren Lee Goss
B. Lieutenant Favill Raises a Company and 90
Gets a Commission
Josiah M. Favill
C. "We Thought the Rebellion Would Be 92
Over Before Our Chance Would Come"
Michael Fitch

5. BALTIMORE MOBS ATTACK 93
THE SIXTH MASSACHUSETTS
Frederic Emory

6. FRANK WILKESON GOES SOUTH 96
WITH BLACKGUARDS, THIEVES,
AND BOUNTY JUMPERS
Frank Wilkeson

7. SUPPLYING THE CONFEDERACY 98
WITH ARMS AND AMMUNITION
E. P. Alexander

8. HOW THE ARMY OF NORTHERN 99
VIRGINIA GOT ITS ORDNANCE
William Allan

9. SECRETARY BENJAMIN RECALLS 101
THE MISTAKES OF THE
CONFEDERATE CONGRESS
Judah P. Benjamin

10. NORTHERN ORDNANCE 102
Comte de Paris

IV. BULL RUN AND THE PENINSULAR CAMPAIGN   105

1. A Confederate Doctor Describes the Victory at First Bull Run   106
   J. C. Nott

2. "Bull Run Russell" Reports the Rout of the Federals   108
   William Howard Russell

3. Stonewall Jackson Credits God with the Victory   112
   Thomas J. Jackson

4. "The Capture of Washington Seems Inevitable"   113
   Edwin M. Stanton

5. McClellan Opens the Peninsular Campaign   113
   George B. McClellan

6. General Wool Takes Norfolk   115
   Egbert L. Viele

7. The Army of the Potomac Marches to Meet McClellan   117
   Sallie Putnam

8. R. E. Lee Takes Command   117
   Evander M. Law

9. "Beauty" Stuart Rides Around McClellan's Army   119
   John Esten Cooke

10. Oliver Norton Fights Like a Madman at Gaines' Mill   123
    Oliver W. Norton

11. The End of Seven Days   125
    A. The Federals Are Forced Back at White Oak Swamp   125
       Thomas L. Livermore
    B. Captain Livermore Fights at Malvern Hill   126
       Thomas L. Livermore

12. Richard Auchmuty Reviews the Peninsular Campaign   128
    Richard Auchmuty

V. STONEWALL JACKSON AND THE VALLEY CAMPAIGN   131

1. Dick Taylor Campaigns with Jackson in the Valley   132
   Richard Taylor

2. Taylor's Irishmen Capture a Battery at Port Republic   138
   Richard Taylor

3. Colonel Wolseley Visits Stonewall Jackson   140
   Lord Wolseley

4. Henry Kyd Douglas Remembers Stonewall Jackson   141
   Henry Kyd Douglas

VI. SECOND BULL RUN AND ANTIETAM   145

1. "Who Could Not Conquer with Such Troops as These?"   146
   Robert L. Dabney

2. Jackson Outsmarts and Outfights Pope at Manassas   147
   John H. Chamberlayne

3. Pope Wastes His Strength on Jackson   149
   David M. Strother

4. Longstreet Overwhelms Pope at Manassas   152
   Alexander Hunter

5. "Little Mac" Is Reappointed to Command   157
   A. "To Fight Is Not His Forte"   157
      Gideon Welles
   B. General Sherman Explains Why He Cannot Like McClellan   158
      William T. Sherman
   C. "Little Mac's A-Coming"   158
      Oliver W. Norton

6. McClellan "Saves His Country" Twice   159
   George B. McClellan

7. McClellan Finds the Lost Order   163
George B. McClellan

8. McClellan Forces Turner's   164
Gap and Crampton's Gap
David M. Strother

9. The Bloodiest Day of the War   166
David M. Strother

10. Hooker Hammers the   170
Confederate Left—in Vain
   A. Wisconsin Boys Are Slaughtered in the   171
     Cornfield
     Rufus R. Dawes
   B. McLaws to the Rescue of Hood   173
     James A. Graham

11. The Desperate Fighting along   175
Bloody Lane
   A. Thomas Livermore Puts on His War Paint   175
     Thomas L. Livermore
   B. General Gordon Is Wounded   177
     Five Times at Antietam
     John B. Gordon

12. "The Whole Landscape   179
Turns Red" at Antietam
David I. Thompson

VII. FREDERICKSBURG AND   183
CHANCELLORSVILLE

1. Lincoln Urges McClellan   184
to Advance
Abraham Lincoln

2. Burnside Blunders at   185
Fredericksburg
   A. The Yankees Attack Marye's Heights   185
     William H. Owen
   B. The Irish Brigade Is Repulsed on Marye's Hill   188
     J. P. Polley
   C. The 5th New Hampshire to the Rescue   189
     John R. McCrillis

3. The Gallant Pelham at   190
Fredericksburg
John Esten Cooke

4. Night on the Field of   192
Fredericksburg
J. L. Chamberlain

5. Lincoln Appoints Hooker   194
to the Command of the Army
Abraham Lincoln

6. Lee Whips Hooker at   195
Chancellorsville
Charles F. Morse

7. Pleasonton Stops the   198
Confederates at Hazel Grove
Alfred Pleasonton

8. Stuart and Anderson Link   200
Up at Chancellorsville
Heros von Borcke

9. Lee Loses His Right Arm   202
James Power Smith

VIII. HOW THE SOLDIERS   205
LIVED: EASTERN FRONT

1. Theodore Winthrop Recalls a   205
Typical Day at Camp Cameron
Theodore Winthrop

2. Abner Small Paints a Portrait   207
of a Private in the Army of
the Potomac
Abner Small

3. Life with the Thirteenth   209
Massachusetts
Charles E. Davis

4. Minutiae of Soldier Life in   212
the Army of Northern Virginia
Carlton McCarthy

5. Inventions and Gadgets Used   216
by the Soldiers
John D. Billings

6. Hardtack and Coffee   217
John D. Billings

7. "Starvation, Rags, Dirt, and Vermin"   220
Randolph Abbott Shotwell

8. Voting in the Field   222

  A. Electioneering in the Camps   222
    James A. Leonard

  B. President Lincoln Needs the Soldier Vote   222
    Abraham Lincoln

9. Red Tape, North and South   223

  A. Dunn Browne Has Trouble with the War Department   223
    Samuel Fiske

  B. A Confederate Lieutenant Complains That Red-Tapeism Will Lose the War   224
    Randolph Abbott Shotwell

10. The Confederates Get Religion   225

  A. Religion in the Confederate Army   225
    Benjamin W. Jones

  B. John Dooley Describes Prayer Meetings   226
    John Dooley

IX. INCIDENTS OF ARMY LIFE: EASTERN FRONT   227

  1. How It Feels to Be under Fire   227
    Frank Holsinger

  2. Fitz John Porter Views the Confederates from a Balloon   229
    George A. Townsend

  3. Stuart's Ball Is Interrupted by the Yankees   231
    Heros von Borcke

  4. Foreigners Fight in the Northern Army   233
    George B. McClellan

  5. With "Extra Billy" Smith at York   235
    Robert Stiles

  6. Blue and Gray Fraternize on the Picket Line   237
    Alexander Hunter

  7. Life with the Mosby Guerrillas   238
    John W. Munson

  8. Rebel and Yankee Yells   240
    J. Harvie Dew

9. Women Among the Ranks   241

  A. Letters of Sarah Rosetta Wakeman, Alias Private Lyons Wakeman   242
    Sarah Rosetta Wakeman

  B. Exploits of Mrs. Major Belle Reynolds   243
    Peoria Daily Transcript

X. FROM FORT DONELSON TO STONES RIVER   245

  1. Grant Wins his Spurs at Belmont   245
    Eugene Lawrence

  2. U. S. Grant Becomes Unconditional Surrender Grant   247
    U.S. Grant

  3. With the Dixie Grays at Shiloh   252
    Sir Henry Morton Stanley

  4. An Illinois Private Fights at the Hornet's Nest   257
    Leander Stillwell

  5. The Orphan Brigade Is Shattered at Stones River   262
    L. D. Young

XI. THE STRUGGLE FOR MISSOURI AND THE WEST   265

  1. Cotton Is King at the Battle of Lexington   265
    Samuel Phillips Day

  2. Guerrilla Warfare in Missouri   268
    William Monks

  3. The Tide Turns at Pea Ridge   270
    Franz Sigel

  4. The Confederates Scatter after Pea Ridge   272
    William Watson

  5. Quantrill and His Guerrillas Sack Lawrence   275
    Gurdon Grovenor

6. COLONEL BAILEY DAMS THE RED RIVER   277
   David D. Porter

7. PRICE INVADES THE NORTH AND   280
   IS DEFEATED AT WESTPORT
   Wiley Britton

XII. HOW THE SOLDIERS   283
LIVED: WESTERN FRONT

1. JOHN CHIPMAN GRAY VIEWS   283
   THE WESTERN SOLDIER
   John Chipman Gray

2. A WISCONSIN BOY COMPLAINS OF THE   284
   HARDSHIPS OF TRAINING
   Chauncey H. Cooke

3. RELIGION AND PLAY IN THE ARMY   285
   OF THE TENNESSEE
   Jenkin Lloyd Jones

4. THE GREAT REVIVAL IN THE ARMY   288
   OF TENNESSEE
   T. J. Stokes

5. FROM REVEILLE TO TAPS   289
   George Ward Nichols

6. AN INDIANA BOY REASSURES HIS   293
   MOTHER ABOUT MORALS IN THE ARMY
   Theodore Upson

7. GRAFT AND CORRUPTION IN THE   294
   CONFEDERATE COMMISSARY
   William Watson

8. THE SOLDIERS GET PAID AND   295
   THE SUTLER GETS THE MONEY
   Charles B. Johnson

9. SONG AND PLAY IN THE ARMY   297
   OF TENNESSEE
   A. Theatricals in the Army   297
       The Southern Illustrated News
   B. Good Cheer in the Ranks   298
       Bromfield Ridley

XIII. INCIDENTS OF ARMY   301
LIFE: WESTERN FRONT

1. MARK TWAIN RECALLS A CAMPAIGN   301
   THAT FAILED
   Mark Twain

2. MAJOR CONNOLLY LOSES FAITH   309
   IN THE CHIVALRY OF THE SOUTH
   James Connolly

3. THE GREAT LOCOMOTIVE CHASE   312
   IN GEORGIA
   William Pittenger

4. A BADGER BOY MEETS THE   319
   ORIGINALS OF UNCLE TOM'S CABIN
   Chauncey H. Cooke

5. THE CONFEDERATES ESCAPE IN THE   320
   TECHE COUNTRY
   W. De Forest

6. GENERAL WILSON RAISES   324
   HIS CAVALRY THE HARD WAY
   James H. Wilson

XIV. THE PROBLEM OF   325
DISCIPLINE

1. THOMAS WENTWORTH HIGGINSON   326
   EXPLAINS THE VALUE OF TRAINED
   OFFICERS
   Thomas W. Higginson

2. "IT DOES NOT SUIT OUR FELLOWS   330
   TO BE COMMANDED MUCH"
   Charles F. Johnson

3. CONDUCT UNBECOMING AN OFFICER   331
   Robert C. Murphy, William S. Rosecrans and
   Ulysses S. Grant

4. A CAMP OF SKULKERS AT   333
   CEDAR MOUNTAIN
   George A. Townsend

5. "THE ARMY IS BECOMING AWFULLY   333
   DEPRAVED"
   Charles W. Wills

6. ROBERT GOULD SHAW COMPLAINS   335
THAT WAR IS A DIRTY BUSINESS
Robert Gould Shaw

7. THE YANKEE INVADERS PILLAGE AND BURN 336
A. "The Soldiers Delight   337
in Destroying Everything"
Francis Edwin Pierce

B. The Yankees Sack Sarah Morgan's Home 337
Sarah Morgan Dawson

C. Grierson's Raiders on a Rampage   340
Elizabeth Jane Beach

D. "Oh, Earth, Behold the Monster!"   342
Henrietta Lee

8. PUNISHMENTS IN THE UNION AND   343
CONFEDERATE ARMIES
A. Punishments in the Army of the Potomac 344
Frank Wilkeson

B. Punishments in the Army of   345
Northern Virginia
John Dooley

9. EXECUTING DESERTERS   346
A. General Sheridan Executes Two   346
Deserters at Chattanooga
Washington Gardner

B. Executing Deserters from the   347
Confederate Army
Spencer Glascow Welch

10. GENERAL LEE DISCUSSES THE   347
PROBLEM OF DISCIPLINE
A. The Need for Punishment as a Deterrant 348
Robert E. Lee

B. "We Cannot Escape the Disgrace that   349
Attends these Evildoers"
Robert E. Lee

11. SEX IN THE CIVIL WAR   350
Unidentified Sanitary Commission officer

XV. GREAT BRITAIN AND   351
THE AMERICAN CIVIL WAR

1. HENRY RAVENEL EXPECTS FOREIGN   352
INTERVENTION
Henry William Ravenel

2. *Blackwood's Edinburgh Magazine*   352
REJOICES IN THE BREAK-UP OF
THE UNION
Blackwood's Edinburgh Magazine

3. GEORGE TICKNOR EXPLAINS THE   354
WAR TO HIS ENGLISH FRIENDS
George Ticknor

4. CAPTAIN WILKES SEIZES MASON   356
AND SLIDELL
D. Macneill Fairfax

5. "SHALL IT BE LOVE, OR HATE, JOHN?"   358
Russell Lowell

6. PALMERSTON AND RUSSELL   360
DISCUSS INTERVENTION
Lord John Russell and Viscount Palmerston

7. "AN ERROR, THE MOST SINGULAR   362
AND PALPABLE"
William E. Gladstone

8. THE ENGLISH PRESS CONDEMNS THE   363
EMANCIPATION PROCLAMATION
The Times

9. MANCHESTER WORKINGMEN   365
STAND BY THE UNION
A. "We Are Truly One People"   365
Manchester Workingmen

B. "An Instance of Sublime Christian   366
Heroism"
Abraham Lincoln

10. RICHARD COBDEN REJOICES IN THE   367
EMANCIPATION PROCLAMATION
Richard Cobden

11. ENGLISH ARISTOCRATS ORGANIZE FOR   368
SOUTHERN INDEPENDENCE
Southern Independence Association of London

12. "THE REASONS WHY GREAT BRITAIN   370
IS AVERSE TO RECOGNISE US"
The Southern Illustrated News

13. MINISTER ADAMS POINTS OUT   371
THAT THIS IS WAR
Charles Francis Adams

Contents

XVI. SONGS THE SOLDIERS SANG   373

1. DIXIE   373
   Dan D. Emmett

2. THE BONNIE BLUE FLAG   374
   Harry McCarthy

3. JOHN BROWN'S BODY   375
   Thomas B. Bishop (?)

4. ALL QUIET ALONG THE POTOMAC   375
   Ethel Lynn Beers

5. MARCHING ALONG   376
   William Batchelder Bradbury

6. MARYLAND! MY MARYLAND!   377
   James R. Randall

7. THE BATTLE HYMN OF THE REPUBLIC   377
   A. Writing "The Battle Hymn of the Republic"   378
   Julia Ward Howe
   B. The Battle Hymn of the Republic   378
   Julia Ward Howe
   C. "The Battle Hymn of the Republic" in Libby Prison   379
   Laura E. Richards and Maud Howe Elliot

8. WE ARE COMING, FATHER ABRAHAM   379
   James Sloan Gibbons

9. THE BATTLE-CRY OF FREEDOM   380
   George P. Root

10. TRAMP, TRAMP, TRAMP   381
    George P. Root

11. JUST BEFORE THE BATTLE, MOTHER   381
    George F. Root

12. TENTING TONIGHT   382
    Walter Kittredge

13. MARCHING THROUGH GEORGIA   382
    Henry Clay Work

14. MISTER, HERE'S YOUR MULE   383
    A. Mister, Here's Your Mule   383
    Author Unknown
    B. Do They Miss Me in the Trenches   384
    J.W. Naff
    C. We Are the Boys of Potomac's Ranks   384
    Author Unknown
    D. Goober Peas   385
    A. Pender
    E. Grafted into the Army   385
    Henry Clay Work

15. LORENA   386
    H. D. L. Webster (?)

16. WHEN JOHNNY COMES MARCHING HOME   387
    Patrick S. Gilmore (?)

XVII. POEMS OF THE CIVIL WAR   389

1. POET LAUREATE OF THE SOUTH   389
   Henry Timrod
   A. Ethnogenesis   389
   B. Carolina   391
   C. Ode   391

2. THE DEATH OF SLAVERY   392
   William Cullen Bryant

3. BARBARA FRIETCHIE   393
   John Greenleaf Whittier

4. "OH, MOTHER, LOOK DOWN FROM HEAV'N ON ME"   394
   A. The Drummer Boy of Shiloh   394
   Will "Shakespeare" Hays
   B. Little Giffen   395
   Francis Orrery Ticknor
   C. Killed at the Ford   395
   Henry Wadsworth Longfellow
   D. Vigil Strange I Kept on the Field One Night   396
   Walt Whitman
   E. Come Up From the Fields Father   396
   Walt Whitman
   F. Dirge for a Soldier   397
   George Henry Boker

5. THE HONORED GENERAL   398
   A. Lee to the Rear   398
   John Reuben Thompson
   B. Robert E. Lee   399
   Julia Ward Howe

6. O CAPTAIN! MY CAPTAIN!   399
   Walt Whitman

7. DRIVING HOME THE COWS   400
Kate Putnam Osgood

8. THE ARTILLERYMAN'S VISION   401
Walt Whitman

9. THE CONQUERED BANNER   402
Abram Joseph Ryan

10. THE BLUE AND THE GRAY   402
Francis Miles Finch

XVIII. GETTYSBURG   405

1. GENERAL LEE DECIDES TO   406
TAKE THE OFFENSIVE
Robert E. Lee

2. GENERAL LEE INVADES PENNSYLVANIA   407
William S. Christian

3. THE ARMIES CONVERGE ON GETTYSBURG   408
Henry J. Hunt

4. BUFORD AND REYNOLDS HOLD UP   411
THE CONFEDERATE ADVANCE
Joseph G. Rosengarten

5. A BOY CANNONEER DESCRIBES   413
HARD FIGHTING ON THE FIRST DAY
Augustus Buell

6. THE STRUGGLE FOR LITTLE ROUND TOP   417
    A. General Warren Seizes Little Round Top   417
      Porter Farley
    B. Colonel Oates Almost Captures Little   419
    Round Top
      William C. Oates
    C. The 20th Maine Saves Little Round Top   422
      Theodore Gerrish

7. HIGH TIDE AT GETTYSBURG   424
    A. Alexander Gives the Signal to Start   425
      E.P. Alexander
    B. Armistead Falls Beside the Enemy's Battery   428
      James Longstreet
    C. "The Crest Is Safe"   429
      Frank A. Haskell
    D. "All This Will Come Right in the End"   433
      A.J. Fremantle

8. GENERAL LEE OFFERS TO RESIGN   435
AFTER GETTYSBURG
Robert E. Lee and Jefferson Davis

9. "BELLS ARE RINGING WILDLY"   437
William Thompson Lusk

10. A FAR FROM GLORIOUS FOURTH   437
George E. Pickett

11. "A NEW BIRTH OF FREEDOM"   438
Abraham Lincoln

XIX. VICKSBURG AND PORT HUDSON   439

1. "ONWARD TO VICKSBURG"   440
Charles E. Wilcox

2. A UNION WOMAN SUFFERS   445
THROUGH THE SIEGE OF VICKSBURG
Anonymous

3. HOTEL DE VICKSBURG   449
The Southern Illustrated News

4. VICKSBURG SURRENDERS   450
U.S. Grant

5. GENERAL BANKS TAKES PORT   454
HUDSON
    A. Eating Mules at Port Hudson
      Anonymous   454
    B. Blue and Gray Fraternize after the   455
    Surrender of Port Hudson
      Anonymous

6. "THE FATHER OF WATERS AGAIN   455
GOES UNVEXED TO THE SEA"
Abraham Lincoln

7. GENERAL MORGAN INVADES   456
THE NORTH
    A. Morgan's Cavalrymen Sweep   456
    Through Kentucky
      Colonel Alston
    B. Morgan's Raid Comes to an Inglorious End   459
      James B. McCreary

XX. PRISONS, NORTH AND SOUTH   461

1. ABNER SMALL SUFFERS IN   461
   DANVILLE PRISON
   Abner Small

2. SUFFERING IN ANDERSONVILLE   463
   PRISON
   Eliza F. Andrews

3. THE BRIGHT SIDE OF LIBBY PRISON   464
   Frank E. Moran

4. THE AWFUL CONDITIONS AT FORT   466
   DELAWARE
   Randolph Abbott Shotwell

5. THE PRIVATIONS OF LIFE IN ELMIRA   469
   PRISON
   Marcus B. Toney

XXI. BEHIND THE LINES: 473
THE NORTH

1. WASHINGTON AS A CAMP   473
   Noah Brooks

2. WALT WHITMAN LOOKS AROUND   475
   IN WARTIME WASHINGTON
   Walt Whitman

3. MATTHEW BRADY'S "THE DEAD   477
   AT ANTIETAM"
   The New York Times

4. ANNA DICKINSON SEES THE   480
   DRAFT RIOTS IN NEW YORK CITY
   Anna E. Dickinson

5. THE ARMY OF LOBBYISTS AND   483
   SPECULATORS
   Régis de Trobriand

6. CHARLES A. DANA HELPS STOP   484
   FRAUDS IN THE WAR DEPARTMENT
   Charles A. Dana

7. COLONEL BARKER OUTWITS   486
   BOUNTY JUMPERS AND BROKERS
   L.C. Baker

8. DOINGS IN NEVADA   489
   Mark Twain

9. CONFEDERATE PLOTS AGAINST   490
   THE NORTH
   A. A Confederate Plan to Seize Johnson's   490
      Island Is Frustrated
      H.B. Brown
   B. Confederates Raid Vermont   491
      John W. Headley
   C. The Confederates Attempt to Burn   493
      New York
      John W. Headley

10. WAR WEARINESS   495
    A. A Sense of Infinite Weariness   495
       Nathaniel Hawthorne
    B. New-Jersey Peace Resolutions   496
       New-Jersey State Legislature
    C. Protest of the New-Jersey Soldiers   497
       Camp of the Eleventh New-Jersey Volunteers

11. ELECTION OF 1864   498
    Henry Brook Adams

XXII. BEHIND THE LINES: 499
THE SOUTH

1. A WAR CLERK SUFFERS SCARCITIES   499
   IN RICHMOND
   J.B. Jones

2. MR. EGGLESTON RECALLS WHEN   503
   MONEY WAS PLENTIFUL
   George C. Eggleston

3. JEWS IN THE CONFEDERACY   505
   Rabbi Maximilian Michelbacher

4. PARTHENIA HAGUE TELLS HOW   507
   WOMEN OUTWITTED THE BLOCKADE
   Parthenia A. Hague

5. THE CONFEDERATES BURN   509
   THEIR COTTON
   Sarah Morgan Dawson

6. "THE YANKEES ARE COMING"   510
   Mary A. Ward

7. "THE LIVES WHICH WOMEN HAVE   512
   LEAD SINCE TROY FELL"
   Julia LeGrand

8. "They Must Reap the Whirlwind" 513
William T. Sherman

9. "I Do Want to See You So Much" 513
Loulie Gilmer

10. "They Are Intelligent on All 514
Subjects but that of Negro
Slavery, on This They Are Mad."
Geographical Reader of the Dixie Children

11. Resistance at Home 515
A. President Davis Quells a Food Riot in 515
Richmond
J.B. Jones
B. Deaths From Starvation Have Absolutely 516
Occurred
Randolph County Citizens

12. Georgia's Governor Laments 517
Davis' Despotism
Joseph E. Brown

13. Peace at Any Price 518
Jonathan Worth

14. "The Man Who Held His Con- 519
science Higher Than Their Praise"
Petigru Monument

XXIII. HOSPITALS, SURGEONS, 521
AND NURSES

1. George Townsend Describes 521
the Wounded on the Peninsula
George A. Townsend

2. The Sanitary Commission to 524
the Rescue
Katharine Wormeley

3. Clara Barton Surmounts the 526
Faithlessness of Union Officers
Clara Barton

4. Susan Blackford Nurses the 527
Wounded at Lynchburg
Susan Blackford

5. Cornelia Hancock Nurses 528
Soldiers and Contrabands
Cornelia Hancock

6. The Ghastly Work of the 531
Field Surgeons
A. The Heartlessness of the Surgeons 531
Samuel Edmund Nichols
B. The Horrors of the Wilderness 532
Augustus C. Brown

7. Hospital Sketches 533
Louisa May Alcott

8. The Regimental Hospital 536
Charles B. Johnson

XXIV. THE AFRICAN-AMERICAN 539
EXPERIENCE

1. "You Debauched a Young Negro Girl" 540
Charles Colcock Jones

2. No Choice But Escape 541
A. "The Alligators Preferred Dog Flesh 541
to Personal Flesh"
Octave Johnson
B. Confederate Officer Tracks Down 541
Runaway Slaves
Samuel E. Hope

3. The Proclamation and the 542
Negro Army
Frederick Douglass

4. Black Soldiers Serve Bravely 543
A. "Unequaled Coolness and Bravery" 544
Elias D. Strunke
B. Silencing the "Jeers and Taunts" 544
James S. Brisbin

5. Thomas Wentworth Higginson 546
Celebrates Life in a Black Regiment
Thomas W. Higginson

6. Standing Up for the Rights 549
of Black Soldiers
A. "Are We Soldiers, or Are We Labourors?" 550
James Henry Gooding, James W. Grace
B. Hannah Johnson to Abraham Lincoln 551
Hannah Johnson
C. Black Regiment Petitions Government 552
for Redress
Richard Etheredge and Wm. Benson

7. Hardships of an Unequal Freedom   553

   A. Contrabands Experience Hardships   553
      Committee, Samuel Sawyer, Pearl P. Ingall,
      J. G. Forman

   B. "A Sense of Disgust Must Be Awakened"   554
      S.R. Curtis

8. The Fate of Black Soldier—   554
   And Those Left Behind

   A. "The Whole Government Gives   555
      Cheer to Me"
      Spotswood Rice

   B. "I Am in Too Much Trouble"   556
      Martha Glover

   C. "I Wish That His Back Had Been
      as Deeply Scarred"   556
      General Edward A. Wild

9. "If We Are Regarded as   557
   Evil Here"
   Edward A. Wild

10. "A Great Desire for Knowledge"   558
    Charlotte Forten

11. Tennessee Petition   559
    Colored Citizens of Nashville

XXV. A WAR FOR EMANCIPATION   565

   1. Slavery, the Cornerstone of the   566
      Confederacy
      Alexander Stephens

   2. "This Imbecile Pro-slavery   567
      Government Does Try Me So"
      Lydia Maria Child

   3. The Problem of Contrabands   568

      A. General Butler's "Contrabands"   568
         Benjamin F. Butler

      B. Frémont's Proclamation on Slaves   569
         J.C. Frémont

   4. Messages to Congress on   570
      Compensated Emancipation

      A. The Gradual Abolishment of Slavery   570
         Abraham Lincoln

      B. "We Cannot Escape History"   571
         Abraham Lincoln

   5. "My Paramount Object is to   573
      Save the Union"

      A. "The Prayer of Twenty Millions"   574
         Horace Greeley

      B. "I Would Save the Union"   574
         Abraham Lincoln

   6. Lincoln Becomes the   575
      Great Emancipator

      A. Secretary Chase Recalls a Famous   575
         Cabinet Meeting
         Salmon P. Chase

      B. "Forever Free"   577
         Abraham Lincoln

   7. Reactions to the Emancipation   577
      Proclamation

      A. The Day of Jubilee Comes   578
         Frederick Douglass

      B. Illinois State Legislature Opposes   579
         Emancipation Proclamation
         Illinois State Legislature

      C. Kentucky Union Officer Objects to   579
         Emancipation
         Marcellus Mundy

      D. Jefferson Davis Replies to the   580
         Emancipation Proclamation
         Jefferson Davis

      E. A Note on the Emancipation   581
         Proclamation
         The Southern Illustrated News

   8. A War for Liberty   581
      David Porter

   9. Arming Slaves for the   582
      Confederate Army
      18th Virginia Infantry Regiment

   10. "Abolitionists Were the   582
       Only Traitors"

       A. "The Country Was Formed for the   582
          White, Not for the Black Man"
          John Wilkes Booth

       B. Emancipation Arrives in Texas   583
          Anonymous

   11. "The Work of the   584
       Abolitionists Is Not Done"
       Frederick Douglass

XXVI. THE COAST AND INLAND WATERS   *587*

1. THE *Merrimac* AND THE *Monitor*   *588*

   A. The *Minnesota* Fights for Her Life in Hampton Roads   *588*
    Captain Van Brunt

   B. The *Monitor* Repels the *Merrimac*   *590*
    S.D. Green

2. COMMODORE FARRAGUT CAPTURES NEW ORLEANS   *592*
   George H. Perkins

3. NEW ORLEANS FALLS TO THE YANKEES   *594*

   A. Julia LeGrand Describes the Surrender of New Orleans   *594*
    Julea LeGrand

   B. General Butler Outrages the Moral Sentiment of the World   *595*
    Benjamin F. Butler

   C. Palmerston Protests Butler's Proclamations   *595*
    Viscount Palmerston

   D. "A More Impudent Proceeding Cannot Be Discovered"   *596*
    Benjamin Moran

4. ELLET'S STEAM RAMS SMASH THE CONFEDERATE FLEET AT MEMPHIS   *597*
   Alfred W. Ellet

5. ATTACK AND REPULSE AT BATTERY WAGNER   *600*
   New York Tribune

6. FARRAGUT DAMNS THE TORPEDOES AT MOBILE BAY   *602*
   John C. Kinney

7. LIEUTENANT CUSHING TORPEDOES THE *Albermarle*   *608*
   W.B. Cushing

8. THE CONFEDERATES REPULSE AN ATTACK ON FORT FISHER   *610*
   William Lamb

9. "IT BEAT ANYTHING IN HISTORY"   *613*
   Augustus Buell

XXVII. THE BLOCKADE AND THE CRUISERS   *617*

1. THE UNITED STATES NAVY BLOCKADES THE CONFEDERACY   *618*
   Horatio L. Wait

2. THE *Robert E. Lee* RUNS THE BLOCKADE   *622*
   John Wilkinson

3. THE *Rob Roy* RUNS THE BLOCKADE OUT OF HAVANA   *624*
   William Watson

4. BLOCKADE-RUNNERS SUPPLY CHARLESTON   *627*
   W.F.G. Peck

5. CONFEDERATE PRIVATEERS HARRY NORTHERN MERCHANTMEN   *628*

   A. The *Ivy* Prowls Outside New Orleans   *628*
    M. Repard

   B. The *Jefferson Davis* Takes a Prize off Delaware   *629*
    Captain Fitfield

6. THE *Georgia* FIRES THE *Bold Hunter*   *629*
   James M. Morgan

7. THE *Kearsarge* SINKS THE *Alabama* OFF CHERBOURG   *631*
   John McIntosh Kell

XXVIII. CHICKAMAUGA AND CHATTANOOGA   *635*

1. THE FEDERALS OPPOSE HOOD WITH DESPERATION   *636*
   James R. Carnahan

2. THOMAS STANDS LIKE A ROCK AT CHICKAMAUGA   *638*

   A. Longstreet Breaks the Federal Line   *639*
    Daniel H. Hill

   B. Thomas Holds the Horseshoe Ridge   *640*
    Gates P. Thruston

3. CHATTANOOGA UNDER SIEGE   *642*
   W.F.G. Shanks

4. Hooker Wins the "Battle Above the Clouds"   645
Joseph G. Fullerton

5. The Army of the Cumberland Carries Missionary Ridge   647
    A. "First One Flag, Then Another, Leads"   647
    William A. Morgan
    B. "Amid the Din of Battle 'Chickamauga' Could Be Heard"   649
    James Connolly

6. "The Disaster Admits of No Palliation"   652
Braxton Bragg

7. Burnside Holds Out at Knoxville   653
Henry S. Burrage

XXIX. ATLANTA AND THE MARCH TO THE SEA   657

1. General Sherman Takes Command   658
John Chipman Gray

2. Sherman Marches from Chattanooga to Atlanta   659
William T. Sherman

3. Johnston Halts Sherman at New Hope Church   661
Joseph E. Johnston

4. Joe Johnston Gives Way to Hood   663
    A. President Davis Removes General Johnston before Atlanta   663
    Jefferson Davis
    B. General Johnston Justifies Himself   664
    Joseph E. Johnston

5. Hardee Wins and Loses the Battle of Atlanta   665
Richard S. Tuthill

6. "You Might as Well Appeal Against the Thunder-Storm"   668
William T. Sherman

7. Child's Diary of the Atlanta Siege   669
Carrie Berry

8. Sherman Marches from Atlanta to the Sea   671
William T. Sherman

9. Sherman's "Bummers"   674
    A. A Good Word for the Bummers   674
    Henry O. Dwight
    B. "We Were Proud of Our Foragers"   674
    Daniel Oakey

10. "The Heavens Were Lit Up with Flames from Burning buildings"   675
Dolly Summer Lunt

11. Eliza Andrews Comes Home Through the Burnt Country   677
Eliza F. Andrews

12. The Burning of Columbia   679
    A. "A Scene of Shameful Confusion"   679
    George Ward Nichols
    B. Major Hitchcock Explains the Burning of Columbia   680
    Henry Hitchcock

13. General Sherman Thinks His Name May Live   681
William T. Sherman

XXX. THE WILDERNESS   683

1. U.S. Grant Plans His Spring Campaign   684
U.S. Grant

2. Colonel Porter Draws a Portrait of General Grant   685
Horace Porter

3. Private Goss Describes the Battle of the Wilderness   687
Warren Lee Goss

4. "Texans Always Move Them"   691
Anonymous

5. "Their Dead and Dying Piled Higher Than the Works"   692
Robert Stiles

6. Spotsylvania and the Bloody Angle   694
Horace Porter

7. "These Men Have Never   696
Failed You on Any Field"
John B. Gordon

8. Grant Hurls His men to   699
Death at Cold Harbor
William C. Oates

XXXI. THE SIEGE OF PETERSBURG   701

1. Grant's Army Crosses the James   702
U.S. Grant

2. Beauregard Holds the Lines   703
at Petersburg
G.T. Beauregard

3. "A Hurricane of Shot and Shell"   706
Augustus C. Brown

4. The Mine and the Battle of   708
the Crater
John S. Wise

5. Lee Stops Hancock at the   711
Gates of Richmond
Richard W. Corbin

6. The Iron Lines of Petersburg   712
Luther Rice Mills

XII. THE VALLEY IN 1864   715

1. V.M.I. Boys Fight at New Market   715
John S. Wise

2. General Hunter Devastates   719
the Valley
John D. Imboden

3. General Ramseur Fights and   721
Dies for His Country
S.D. Ramseur

4. Early Surprises the Federals   726
at Cedar Creek
S.E. Howard

5. Sheridan Rides Down the   728
Valley Pike to Victory and Fame
P.H. Sheridan

6. "The Valley Will Have Little in   731
It for Man or Beast"
P.H. Sheridan

XXXIII. LEE AND LINCOLN   733

1. Robert E. Lee Goes with   734
His State
   A. "My Relatives, My Children, My Home"   734
   Robert E. Lee
   B. "I Never Desire Again to Draw My Sword"   734
   Robert E. Lee

2. "A Splendid Specimen of an   735
English Gentleman"
Lord Wolseley

3. "It Is Well War Is So Terrible,   736
Or We Should Get Too Fond of It"
W.N. Pendleton

4. Dr. Parks's Boy visits Lee's   737
Headquarters
Leighton Parks

5. "A Sadness I Had never   740
Before Seen upon His Face"
John B. Imboden

6. Lee and Traveller Review   741
the Army of Northern Virginia
Robert E. Lee, Jr.

7. "He Looked as Though He   742
Was the Monarch of the World"
William C. Oates

8. "The Field Resounded with   742
Wild Shouts of Lee, Lee, Lee"
J. Catlett Gibson

9. Lee Bids Farewell to the   744
Army of Northern Virginia
Robert E. Lee

10. Nathaniel Hawthorne Calls   744
on President Lincoln
Nathaniel Hawthorne

11. John Hay Lives with "The Tycoon"   746
in the White House
John Hay

12. "We Shall Nobly Save or Meanly   747
Lose the Last, Best Hope of Earth"
Abraham Lincoln

13. Lincoln's Condolence Letters   748
Abraham Lincoln

14. Lincoln and Hay Follow   749
the Election Returns
John Hay

15. Lincoln Replies to a Serenade   751
Abraham Lincoln

16. Lincoln Visits the Colored   752
Soldiers at City Point
Horace Porter

17. "With Malice Toward None"   753
Abraham Lincoln

18. Lincoln Is Assassinated   754
Gideon Welles

**XXXIV. THE SUNSET OF THE   757
CONFEDERACY**

1. Thomas Annihilates Hood   758
at Nashville
James H. Wilson

2. "The Last Chance of the   762
Confederacy"
Alexander C. McClurg

3. "Now Richmond Rocked in   766
Her High Towers to Watch the
Impending Issue"
George A. Townsend

4. "The Most Superb Soldier in   769
All the World" Falls at Five Forks
William Gordon McCabe

5. The Confederates Abandon   770
Richmond
A. "A Great Burst of Sobbing All Over   770
the Church"
Constance C. Harrison
B. "The Poor Colored People Thanked   772
God that Their Sufferings Were Ended"
R.B. Prescott

C. Night Came and with It Came   774
Sorrow and Sadness
Frances Caldern de la Barca Hunt

6. The White Flag at Appomattox   775
J.L. Chamberlain

7. General Lee Surrenders   779
at Appomattox
Charles Marshall

8. "The Whole Column Seemed   782
Crowned with Red"
J.L. Chamberlain

9. The Last Will and Testament   784
of J. Reb
John Wise

10. The Stars and Stripes Are   785
Raised over Fort Sumter
Mary Cadwalader Jones

11. "Bow Down, Dear Land, for   786
Thou Hast Found Release"
James Russell Lowell

**APPENDIX A:
RECONSTRUCTING THE NATION   787**

1. The Destruction of the South   788
A. Prominent Citizens Became Piesellers   788
Myrta Lockett Avary
B. "In the Heart of Destruction"   790
Sidney Andrews

2. "Education Must Become Universal"   791
Congressional Report on the Freedmen's Bureau

3. First Reconstruction Act   795
U.S. Congress

4. Constitutional Amendments   796
A. Thirteenth Amendment   797
B. Fourteenth Amendment   797
C. Fifteenth Amendment   798

5. "The End of the White   798
Man's Government"
The New Orleans Tribune

6. Black Parliament in South
   Carolina   799
   James S. Pike

7. "A Full Pardon"   802
   Andrew Johnson

8. The Ku Klux Klan   802
   A. "I Shook Hands with Bob 'fore They   802
      Hung Him"
      Ben Johnson

   B. Frankfort, Kentucky,   803
      Congessional Petition
      Colored Citizens of Frankfort and Vicinity

9. "We Had Only Our Ignorance"   806
   Anonymous

10. "The Uneducated Negro   809
    Was Too Weak"
    Daniel Chamberlain

11. "A General Reestablishment   810
    of Order"
    Rutherford B. Hayes

APPENDIX B:
DOCUMENTS OF LASTING   813
INFLUENCE

1. Homestead Act   813
   U.S. Congress

2. Pacific Railway Act   814
   U.S. Congress

3. Morrill Act   816
   U.S. Congress

4. West Virginia Becomes A State   817
   People of Virginia

5. Ousting the French   818
   from Mexico
   A. Seward to Adams   819
      W.H. Seward

   B. House Resolution on French   820
      Intervention In Mexico
      U.S. Congress

   C. Seward to Motley   820
      W.H. Seward

6. Ex Parte Merryman   821
   Roger B. Taney

7. Ex Parte Milligan   824
   David Davis

Bibliography   829

Index   847

LIST OF MAPS

THE CIVIL WAR, 1861-65	68
THE FIRST BATTLE OF BULL RUN	109
THE PENINSULAR CAMPAIGN	114
BATTLEFIELDS OF THE SEVEN DAYS	118
THE VALLEY OF VIRGINIA	133
SECOND BATTLE OF BULL RUN	153
ANTIETAM	172
BATTLE OF FREDERICKSBURG	187
THE SEAT OF THE WAR IN VIRGINIA	193
THE CAMPAIGNS IN TENNESSEE AND KENTUCKY	247
PLAN OF THE BATTLE OF SHILOH	258
THE STRATEGIC POSITION OF MISSOURI	269
THE SEAT OF THE WAR IN PENNSYLVANIA AND MARYLAND	410
THE BATTLE OF GETTYSBURG	418
THE VICKSBURG CAMPAIGN	441
CHARLESTON HARBOR	601
THE BLOCKADED COAST	619
CHATTANOOGA AND ITS APPROACHES	643
FROM CHATTANOOGA TO ATLANTA	661
SAVANNAH TO BENTONVILLE	678
THE WILDERNESS	695
DEFENSES OF RICHMOND AND PETERSBURG	704
FRANKLIN AND NASHVILLE	759
PETERSBURG TO APPOMATTOX	777

PREFACE

Updating a book of such lasting importance as *The Blue and The Gray* is an intimidating task. Fifty years after its intial publication, Henry Steele Commager's classic compilation of documents is a staple among Civil War aficionados. Its eloquence, both in the words of the participants of the Civil War and in Commager's commentary, remains unparalleled.

Accordingly, the goal in this updated version is not to alter or revise Commager's work, but rather to supplement it. A very light hand has been applied to Commager's text. The only changes to his original writing pertain to logistical alterations made necessary by the addition of new documents. Commager's commentaries remain as authoritative today as they were in 1950.

But since then, much has changed in the way we view history. Even the most progressive historians (of which Commager was one) did not devote much attention to some aspects of history that now are considered vital to a complete study the past. Archivists have chronicled tens of thousands of documents that have surfaced since *The Blue and the Gray* was first published. In 1976, The Freedmen and Southern Society Project began a major undertaking to collect the writings of African Americans during the Civil War, adding long-neglected voices to the historical record. Individual

historians have also culled archives to examine overlooked elements of the conflict and to bring new information to the public.

New scholarship and interpretations have altered the way we look at the Civil War. African-American history, issues pertaining to the home front, the effect of the war on ordinary people's lives and the lasting impact of the war (particularly in the wake of the Civil Rights Movement) have emerged as more vital aspects of Civil War history than they were fifty years ago.

This new edition seeks to fill the gaps that have emerged as the interpretation of history has evolved. The criteria for new documents are similar to those outlined by Commager, but with the twin goals of expanding participants to include former slaves, black soldiers, children and others involved in the war, and exploring issues that are perhaps more relevant today than they were fifty years ago. Almost no new documents directly related to battlefield activities have been added.

About one third of the added documents have been integrated into Commager's original thirty chapters. Three new chapters and two appendices have been added. "The African American Experience" delves into the Civil War experiences of slaves and freedmen. Commager's original work did not include a single document written or told by an African-American man or woman. Yet one of the Civil War's greatest impacts was ending slavery and changing the course of African-American history.

The chapter "War for Emancipation" explores in depth the path toward ending slavery. Although Commager touches upon this topic in the original edition, the magnitude of the subject invites a more thorough investigation. The path toward emancipation set the parameters for the national debate on civil rights that continues to this day.

Similarly, Reconstruction represented a continuation of many of those same issues. Just as Commager started *The Blue and The Gray* with documents about the conflict between North and South immediately prior to the outbreak hostilities, it seemed appropriate to add a section at the end exploring the resolution of some of the central conflicts of the war. Hence, an appendix with documents about Reconstruction has been added.

In the original edition, Commager included a spattering of poems and mentioned several that were not included in the text. It seems appropriate that in an updated and expanded version, those poems and others be included. The poems of the Civil War, even the mediocre ones, express the pathos of war in ways that narratives rarely achieve.

Finally, a second appendix has been added with documents marking events that occurred as a direct result of the war and influenced the course of American history. Although less dramatic than battlefield heroics, some of the indirect impacts of the Civil War—escalating the settlement of the West, the defining of American liberties, the creation of West Virginia, and others—remain with us today.

One's respect for Commager's original work is only magnified by the process of adding new documents. The task of selecting the right documents, placing them in the appropriate place, and crafting a narrative is a surprisingly difficult one. There are thousands of documents to select from and so many ways to piece them together. This edition could not have been completed without the extraordinary assistance of several people who eased that process. J.P. Leventhal first conceived the idea of publishing an updated and expanded version of *The Blue and The Gray*. Michael Driscoll's astute judgment as editor kept the revisions focused and his attention to detail headed off many potential blunders. Editorial assistant Hadar Makov chased down many bits and pieces of information, corrected gaffes, and helped sift through many of the finer parts of the book. In other words, she did the important but tedious jobs that do not attract headline coverage, but make everyone else involved look better than they might otherwise appear. Copy editor Stephanie Finnegan did yeoman's work sifting through the pages of added material, picking off mistakes and corralling meandering words. Finally, Mary Commager provided much appreciated support in this venture, placing the original work in the hands of virtual strangers. The goal of this project was to enhance the stature of Commager's original work. Hopefully that has been at least partially realized.

ERIK BRUUN

FOREWORD

Many hands filled the storehouse from which Henry Steele Commager drew the treasures that appear in the fascinating pages of this long-desired collection. Some survivors wrote of the eighteen-sixties because they had tarnished reputations to repolish or grudges to satisfy. Other participants set down the history of their old Regiment to please comrades who met annually at a G.A.R. encampment or at a Confederate reunion to live again in memory their great hours. In a few instances, most notably that of General Grant, memoirs were prepared because the public literally demanded them. Hundreds of books and brochures were the work of those who sought, consciously or otherwise, to associate them selves with the mighty men and the decisive conflict of their generation. The failure of some Southern writers to find a publisher was responsible for the private printing of numerous books and for the allegation, never justified, that the North would not give Southern writers a hearing. One forgotten phase of this had its origin in the persistent effort of certain schoolbook publishers to procure the "adoption" in the South of texts on American history written in partisan spirit for Northern readers. This salesmanship was met repeatedly with pleas for the establishment in Richmond, Atlanta or New Orleans of a publishing house that would be "fair to the South." Where a

response was made to this appeal, the fruit sometimes was a test as extreme as the one that provoked it. A long-popular Southern school history contained 590 pages, of which more than 200 were devoted to the preliminaries of the War between the States and to the events of that struggle. A study of the disputes of the eighteen nineties involving rival books of this type would startle a generation that assumes an author's non-partizan approach as a matter of course.

Many contrasts are offered in the literature of the American war of 1861-65, and most notably in what Mr. Commager remarks in his introduction— that "the Confederate narratives seem to be of a higher literary quality than the Federal." This is meant, of course, to be subject at the outset to qualification as respects some notable books. The list of Union brigade histories, for example, may contain no single volume better than Caldwell's charming story of Gregg's South Carolinians; but Mr. Commager most surely is correct in saying that Charles E. Davis's account of the Thirteenth Massachusetts is definitely the most interesting regimental history on either side.

If there is general, or average superiority in Southern memoirs and personal narratives, this doubtless is due to a number of circumstances that raise no questions of rival "cultures." Nearly always there is glamor to a "lost cause." Cromwell's body on the Tyburn gallows, "Bonnie Prince Charlie" in exile, and Bonaparte dying of cancer at Longwood never fail to arouse sympathy the Puritan Revolution, the Jacobite cause and Napoleonic imperialism cannot stir. It manifestly has been so with the South which had, in addition, a most unusual number of picturesque leaders. These men possessed the "color" and the peculiarities that inspire the *causerie de bivouac* the Little Corporal said every general should provide if he wished to be successful. Lee had a magnificence that awed his soldiers, who seldom cheered him; when Stonewall Jackson came in sight, riding awkwardly on a poor horse, the rebel yell nearly always would be raised. He fired the imagination of his troops as Lee never did until the *post-bellum* years. Albert Sidney Johnston, Forrest, Morgan, "Jeb" Stuart—these, too, were men to arouse enthusiasms that echoed in the memoirs of their followers. The North had soldiers and seamen of like appeal, but somehow the memory of nearly all these leaders was forgotten in the changes of population incident to the Westward movement and to expanded immigration. Static Southern society had longer memory.

Besides this, the South chanced to produce early a "war book" that set a standard which perhaps was considered representative, though actually it could not be maintained. This was Lieutenant General Richard Taylor's *Destruction and Reconstruction*, parts of which appeared in *The North American Review* in January-April 1878, the year before the memoirs were published in book form. Anyone reading that superb narrative would get an exalted conception of the literary skill of Southern military writers, a conception not borne out by later works of other authors. This is not derogatory because Taylor's book remains to this day the most exciting narrative of its kind by an American commander. It would be difficult to find anywhere a better told story of a military movement than Taylor's account of "Stonewall" Jackson's Valley Campaign of 1862 (Vol. I p. 150ff).

If these and other circumstances bear out Mr. Commager's statement regarding the excellence of some Confederate narratives, fair play requires a Southerner to put the emphasis on that word *narratives*. There certainly is not a like superiority in the poetry. Thomas DeLeon remarked in his *Four Years in Rebel Capitals* that he had accumulated 1,900 wartime poems of the South, and later added greatly to his list: "There were battle odes, hymns, calls to arms, paeans and dirges and prayers for peace—many of them good, few of them great; and the vast majority, alasl wretchedly poor."

DeLeon could have carried his scrutiny of Southern literature twenty years further and would have found few Confederate poems besides those of the Catholic priest, Father Abram Joseph Ryan, that voiced impressively the full emotion of the Southern people. Frequently Theodore O'Hara's "The Bivouac of the Dead" is put forward with Father Ryan's "Conquered Banner," but O'Hara wrote in 1847 of the Kentuckians killed in the Battle of Buena Vista. It is a singular fact that John R. Thompson's verses on the Confederacy, though written, as it were, to the pulsing of the guns on the Richmond defenses, seldom reached the level of his best work. Simms, Hayne, Lanier, Timrod, Randall—none of these wrote of "the war" as their admirers might have expected. No theme seemed to elicit their finest utterance, not even "Marse Robert" himself. Lee remains the demigod of the South and has there a place even Washington does not hold, but where may be found a poem on Lee that anyone would wish to make a permanent part of one's mental acquisition? In contrast, Lowell outdid himself in the "Harvard Commemoration Ode"; Whitman's "O Captain! My Captain!" and his "When Lilacs Last in the Dooryard Bloomed" are among the author's most successful works; and as Mr. Commager says, the North produced the "one great battle hymn of our literature."

Perhaps the most remarkable feature of the 300 and more articles reproduced in this notable collection is the humor that runs through nearly all of them and particularly through those of Southern origin. Doubtless there was an Erich Remarque somewhere on the Rappahannock front; letters written home by Billy Yank and Johnny Reb contained the usual number of complaints and requests; but when the column was in motion, there were more jests than oaths on the lips of the soldiers. Laughter was the medicine for most of the ills visible to the men next in line, though fear and rebellious wrath and homesickness might be gnawing at the heart.

Good cheer was not unnatural in the Union Regiments after July 1863, but its persistence until the autumn of 1864 in most of the Southern forces, and particularly in the Army of Northern Virginia, is a phenomenon of morale. The same thing may be said of the attitude of the men toward the manifest inferiority of Southern military equipment. The gray coats laughed at their wagons and their harness, their tatters and their gaping shoes. Again and again this stirs one who opens these volumes at random and reads the first paragraph on which the eye falls: were these men mocking death as a foe long outwitted, or were they assuming a heroism they did not possess? Were they valiant or merely pretending? It scarcely seemed to matter where some of them were or what they were doing: they laughed their way from Manassas to Appomattox and even through the hospitals. Except for the military prisons, the Confederates, for instance, could have had few places of darker tragedy, written in tears and anguish, than Chimborazo Hospital in Richmond, where as many as 7,000 soldiers sometimes suffered together; yet it was life there that Mrs. Phoebe Pember described in some of the most humorous writing of the war.

These Confederate soldiers and nurses and citizens of beleaguered towns had one inspiration that twentieth-century America has not credited to them—the vigorous Revolutionary tradition. The men who fought at Gettysburg were as close in time to the turning point of that earlier struggle, the Trenton-Princeton campaign of 1777, as readers of 1950 are to the *dies irae* described by Colonel

Frank Haskell in his famous account of the repulse of Pickett's charge. Many men in the ranks, North and South, had seen old soldiers of the Continental Army; thousands had heard stories of the sacrifices of 1777 and of the hunger and nakedness at Valley Forge. From its very nature, freedom was born in travail. Ignorant men sensed this vaguely, if at all; the literate reread William Gordon and Washington Irving and steeled themselves to like hardship. To some of the commanders, and above all to Lee, there daily was an inspiring analogy between the struggle of the Confederacy and that of Revolutionary America under the generalship of Lee's great hero, Washington. Many another Southern soldier told himself the road was no more stony than the one that had carried his father and his grandfather at last to Yorktown. If independence was to be the reward, patience, good cheer and the tonic of laughter would bring it all the sooner.

Those Confederates believed they were as good judges of humor as, say, of horses; and both they and their adversaries in blue regarded themselves as strategists or, at least, as competent critics of strategy. Quick to perceive the aim of the marches they were called upon to make, they discussed by every campfire and on every riverbank the shrewdness or the blunders of the men who led them. After the manner of youth in every land and of every era, they made heroes of the officers they admired and they denounced the martinets, but, in time, most of them learned from their discussion and, considering the paucity of their information, came to broad strategical conclusions their seniors would not have been ashamed to own.

Many of the diarists and letter writers were observant, too, and not infrequently recorded important fact no officer set down in any report. If some of these writers let their vanity adorn their tale, the majority were of honest mind. One somewhat renowned *post-bellum* lecturer who should have been an invaluable witness, progressively lost the truth of his narrative as he made it more and more dramatic and egocentric, but he did not have many fellow offenders outside the ranks of those known and branded prevaricators who bored their comrades of the U.C.V. or the G.A.R. as they told how "they won" the battle or the war. On the other hand, Mr. Commager quotes in these pages several veterans who wrote long after the conflict, without access to records, and yet were so astonishingly accurate that any psychologist, chancing on their memoirs, will wish he might have studied in person the mentality of the authors.

These men and women had no literary inhibitions other than those of a decency that is to be respected both for it self and for the contrasts it suggests with certain later writing on war and warriors. If, incidentally, the restraint and modesty of most of the soldiers' letters of the eighteen-sixties were Victorian, then so much the better for Victorianism. This apart, every man felt free to write of anything—and considered himself as competent as freo with the result that the source materials of the conflict are opulently numerous and almost bewilderingly democratic. Private Casler may dispute in a footnote the pronouncements of the learned Dr. Dabney on the strategy of "Old Jack"; the testimony of a boy who saw Grant once only may be preferred to that of a corps commander who conferred so often with "Unconditional Surrender" that, in retrospect, he confused the details of the various interviews.

Historically, then, it may be hoped that one result of the appearance of this book will be the use of other authorities than the few, such as "Rebel War Clerk" Jones and Mrs. Chesnut, for example, who have been overworked and, on some subjects, have been uncritically cited. The student will find that new witnesses have been made available, and that stirring tales have been assembled and prefaced sagely by an editor whose knowledge of the literature of 1861-65 is unexcelled. Henry Steele Commager has the admiration as well as the personal affection of all students who appreciate the catholicity of his scholarship and the penetrating justice of his judgment. Had members of his profession been asked by the publishers to name the individual best equipped to present "a history of the Civil War in the words of those who fought it," their choice would have been the man who flawlessly has rendered here that welcome service to the American people.

DOUGLAS SOUTHALL FREEMAN
Westbourne,
Richmond, Virginia,
August 14, 1950

INTRODUCTION

We have fought six major wars in the last century or so, and four since Appomattox, but of them all it is the Civil War that has left the strongest impression on our minds, our imagination, and our hearts. It is the Civil War songs that we sing—who does not know "Marching Through Georgia" or "Tramp, Tramp, Tramp" or "Dixie"?—and that war gave us the one great battle hymn of our literature. It furnished our best war poetry, both at the time and since; no other war has produced anything as good as "Drum Taps" or the "Harvard Commemoration Ode," nor has any other been celebrated by an epic poem comparable to Stephen Benét's *John Brown's Body*. It has inspired more, and better, novels than any other of our wars and occasionally it excites even Hollywood to rise above mediocrity. It has furnished our standards of patriotism, gallantry, and fortitude; it has given us our most cherished military heroes—Lee and Jackson, Grant and Sherman, and Farragut, and a host of others, and it has given us, too, our greatest national hero and our greatest sectional one, Lincoln and Lee. No other chapter in our history has contributed so much to our traditions and our folklore. The very words—whether they are Civil War or War between the States— conjure up for us a hundred images: Jackson standing like a stone wall; U. S. Grant becoming Unconditional Surrender Grant; Lee astride

Traveller, "It is well war is so terrible, or we should get too fond of it"; Barbara Frietchie waving her country's flag; A. P. Hill breaking through the wheat fields at Antietam; Thomas standing like a rock at Chickamauga; Pickett's men streaming up the long slope of Cemetery Ridge; Farragut lashed to the mast at Mobile Bay, "Damn the torpedoes, full steam ahead"; the Army of the Cumberland scrambling up the rugged heights of Missionary Ridge; Hood's Texans forcing Lee to the rear before they would close the gap at Spotsylvania; Sheridan dashing down the Winchester Pike; Lincoln pardoning the sleeping sentinels, reading Artemus Ward to his Cabinet, dedicating thc battlefield of Gettysburg; Grant and Lee at Appomattox Court House.

It was, in many respects, a curious war, one in which amenities were often preserved. It could not begin until high-ranking officers of the army and navy had been permitted to resign and help organize a rebellion. Southerners tolerated outspoken Unionists, like Petigru or Botts; Northerners permitted Vallandigham to campaign openly against the war, and at the crisis of the conflict almost two million of them voted for a party that had formally pronounced the war a failure. Journalists seemed to circulate at will, and Northern papers had correspondents in the South while Confederates got much of their information about Federal army movements from the Northern newspapers. There was an immense amount of trading back and forth, some of it authorized or at least tolerated by the governments, and Sherman could say that Cincinnati furnished more supplies to the Confederacy than did Charleston. Officers had been trained in the same schools and fought in the same armies and most of them knew one another or knew of one another; Mrs. Pickett tells us that when her baby was born Grant's staff celebrated with bonfires. There was a great deal of fraternization both among soldiers and civilians. Pickets exchanged tobacco, food, and news; if Yankee officers did not marry Southern beauties as often as novelists imagined, there was at least some basis for the literary emphasis on romance. Confederates cheered Meagher's Irish Brigade as it charged up Marye's Heights, and the Yankees almost outdid the Confederates in admiration for Jackson and Pelham. There were plenty of atrocity stories, but few atrocities. There was a good deal of pillaging and vandalism—as in all wars—but little of that systematic destruction we know from two world wars or from the war in Vietnam. On the whole, civilians were safe; there were crimes against property but few against persons, and women everywhere were respected. When Butler affronted the ladies of New Orleans he was transferred to another command, and Sherman engaged in a wordy correspondence with the mayor of Atlanta seeking to justify what he thought a military necessity. Whether Sherman burned Columbia is still a matter of controversy; the interesting thing is that there should be a controversy at all. Both peoples subscribed to the same moral values and observed the same standards of conduct. Both displayed that "decent respect to the opinions of mankind" to which Jefferson had appealed three quarters of a century earlier. Both were convinced that the cause for which they fought was just—and their descendants still are.

Nor did the war come to an end, psychologically or emotionally, with Appomattox. Politicians nourished its issues; patriotic organizations cherished its memories; scholars re fought its battles with unflagging enthusiasm. No other war has started so many controversies and for no other do they flourish so vigorously. Every step in the conflict, every major political decision, every campaign, almost every battle, has its own proud set of controversies, and of all the military figures only Lee stands above argument and debate. Was the election of Lincoln a threat to the South, and was secession justified? Was secession a revolutionary or a constitutional act, and was the war a rebellion or an international conflict? Was the choice of Davis a mistake, and did Davis interfere improperly in military affairs? Should the Confederacy have burned its cotton, or exported it? Was the blockade a success, and if so at what point? Should Britain have recognized the Confederacy, or did she go too far toward the assistance of the South as it was? Who was responsible for the attack on Fort Sumter, Lincoln or Beauregard, and was the call for 75,000 men an act of aggression? Was Jackson late at Seven Days? Was Grant surprised at Shiloh? Did the radicals sabotage McClellan's Peninsular campaign? Who was responsible for the disaster of Second Bull Run and was Fitz John Porter a marplot or a scapegoat? Should Lee have persisted in his offensive of the autumn of 1862 even after the discovery of the Lost Order? Should McClellan have renewed battle after Antietam? Why did Pemberton fail to link up with Johnston outside Vicksburg and why did Johnston fail to relieve Pemberton? Would Gettysburg have been different had Jackson been there, or had Longstreet seized Little Round Top on the morning of the second day, or had Pickett been properly supported on the third? Who was responsible for the Confederate failure at Stones River and who for the debacle of Missionary Ridge, and why did Davis keep Bragg in command so long? Could Johnston have saved Atlanta, and did Hood lose it? Was Hood's Tennessee campaign strategically sound but tactically mismanaged, or was it the other way around? Was Lee deceived during those critical June days when Grant flung his army across the James? And why did the Federals fail to break through the thin lines of Petersburg? Who burned Columbia, and was Sherman's theory of war justified? What really happened at Five Forks, and would the outcome have been different had Pickett been more alert? What explains the failure to have supplies at Amelia Court House and could Lee have made good his escape and linked up with Johnston had the supplies been there? Could the Confederacy ever have won the war, or was defeat foredoomed; if defeat was not foredoomed what caused it? These and a thousand other questions are still avidly debated by a generation that has already forgotten the controversies of the Spanish War and the First World War.

Nor is it by chance that the cause lost on the battlefield should be celebrated in story and in history, or that victors and vanquished alike, should exalt its heroism and cherish its leaders. Lee is only less of a hero than Lincoln, and the Federal Army boasts no figure so glamorous as Stonewall Jackson. Novelists have been kinder to the Confederacy than to the Union, and so, too, in our own day, the moving pictures and television. There is no literary monument to any Union general comparable to that erected to Lee by Douglas Freeman, and for a generation Northern historians found themselves apologizing for Appomattox.

From the point of view of the student of military history, too, the Civil War is inexhaustibly interesting, and it is no wonder that English, French, and German strategists and historians have assiduously studied its battles and campaigns. It was, in a sense, the last of the old wars and the first of the new. It had many of the characteristics of earlier wars—the chivalry that animated officers and men, and the mutual esteem in which the combatants held each other, for example; the old-fashioned weapons and tactics such as sabers and cavalry charges; the woeful lack of discipline; the pitiful inadequacy of medical and hospital services, of what we would now call service of supply, of any provision for welfare and morale; the almost total

absence of any proper Intelligence service or adequate staff work, and the primitive state of maps; the casual and amateur air that pervaded it all. But it was, too, in many and interesting respects, a modern war, one that anticipated the "total" wars of the twentieth century. It was the first in which the whole flation was involved, and it is probable that a larger proportion of the population, North as well as South, was actually in uniform than in any previous war of modern history. It was the first in which there was an even partial control of the economy—this largely in the South rather than in the more fortunate North. It was the first in which a large-scale blockade was a really effective if not indeed a decisive weapon. It was the first in which the railroad and the telegraph played a major role. It involved almost every known form of warfare: large-scale battles, guerrilla fighting, trench warfare, sieges and investments, bold forays into enemy country and large-scale invasions, amphibious warfare along coastal and inland waters, blockade, privateering, surface and sub-surface naval war, the war of propaganda and of nerves. It produced in Lee one of the supreme military geniuses of history, in Farragut one of the great naval captains; in Grant a major strategist; in Sherman, Thomas Jackson, A. P. Hill, and Joseph E. Johnston captains whose tactics are still worthy of study; in Thomas a master of artillery; in Forrest and Stuart, Buford, Sheridan and Wilson, cavalry leaders whose exploits have rarely been surpassed.

Every war dramatizes the ordinary and accentuates the characteristic; more than any other in which we have ever been engaged the Civil War brought out in sharp relief those qualities that we think of as distinctively American. The American was practical, experimental, inventive, intelligent, self-reliant, opportunistic, energetic, careless, undisciplined, amateurish, equalitarian, sentimental, humorous, generous and moral. He believed that the civil was superior to the military even in war, and that privates were as good as officers, that it was wrong to begin a war or to fight in a cause that was not just, that a war should be fought according to rules, and that moral standards should obtain in war as in peace. Most of these qualities and principles were carried over from the civil to the military arena.

Thus the war discovered a people wholly unprepared, and never willing to prepare, either materially or psychologically. Neither side ever really organized for war; neither ever used the whole of its resources—though the South came far closer to this than the North; neither accepted the iron discipline which modern war imposes. The war required the subordination of the individual to the mass, of the particular to the general interest, and of the local to the central government; but both Federals and Confederates indulged their individual ism in the army and out, rejected military standards and discipline, selected officers for almost any but military reasons, pursued local and state interest at the expense of the national. The war required organization and efficiency, but both sides conducted the war with monumental inefficiency—wit ness the shambles of conscription, or of the procurement of ordnance or of finances. The war required the husbanding of resources, but both sides wasted their resources, human and material—witness the medical services, or desertion, or the indulgence of business as usual, especially in the North.

The Americans were an educated, informed, self-reliant and resourceful people, and the Civil War armies probably boasted the highest level of intelligence of any armies in modern history up to that time. It took foreigners to remark this quality, however; Americans themselves took it for granted. Everyone, as both Dicey and Trollope remarked in wonder, read newspapers, followed political debates, and had opinions on the war, slavery, politics, and everything else; almost everyone—as an editor knows—kept a diary or a journal. Resourcefulness was almost their most striking quality. This resourcefulness appeared in Grant, who kept at it until he had found the road to Vicksburg; it appeared in Lee, who was able to adjust his plans to his shifting opponents, and to count on the understanding and co-operation of his lieutenants; it appeared in the engineers, who built dams and bridges, laid railroad tracks—or tore them up—solved problems of transport and supply that appeared insoluble; it appeared in the privates of both armies, who improvised breastworks or camp shelters, foraged for food and supplies, chose their own officers, voted in the field, provided their own newspapers, theatricals, and religious services, and often fought their own battles with such weapons as they could piece together. It appeared, too, in civilians, especially in the South, who managed somehow to improvise most of the weapons of war and the essentials of domestic economy, to make do with such labor and such materials as they had, and to hold society together through four years of strife and want.

Thus the conduct of the war confounded both the critics and the prophets. It was thought a people as unmilitary as the Americans could not fight a long war, or would not—but they did. It was thought that an agricultural South could not produce the materiel of war, but no single Southern de-feat could be ascribed to lack of arms or equipment. It was supposed that neither side could finance a major war, but both managed somehow, and though Confederate finances were a shambles the North emerged from the conflict richer than she had entered it. To blockade thousands of miles of coast line, to invade an area of continental dimensions—these had never been done successfully in modern times, but the Union did them. Curiously, Europe was not convinced; the same basic errors of judgment that distinguished England and France during the Civil War reappeared in Germany in 1917 and in Germany, Italy, and France in 1940.

The Americans were a good-natured people, easygoing and careless, and in a curious sense these qualities carried over even into war. Lincoln set the tone here, for the North—Lincoln, who somehow managed to mitigate the wrath of war and his own melancholy with his humor, and who never referred to the Confederates as rebels; and Lee for the South, Lee, who always called the enemy "those people." Relations between the two armies were often good-natured: the very names the combatants had for each other, Johnny Reb and Billy Yank, testified to this. Only occasionally were relations between these enemies who so deeply respected each other exacerbated by official policy or by the prejudices of an officer. The soldiers themselves—boys for the most part, for it was a boys' war—were high-spirited and amiable, and endured endless discomforts and privations with good humor. Their good humor emerged in their songs—"Goober Peas," "Mister, Here's Your Mule," "Grafted into the Army," "We are the Boys of Potomac's Ranks"—their stories, their camp fire jokes, so naive and innocent for the most part; it spilled over into their letters home and into the diaries and journals they so assiduously kept. There was bitterness enough in the war, especially for the South and for the women of the South, but probably no other great civil war was attended by so little bitterness during the conflict, and no other recorded so many acts of kindness and civility between enemies; cer tainly no other was so magnanimously concluded. Read over, for example, that moving account of the surrender at Appomattox by Joshua Chamberlain:

> Before us in proud humiliation stood the embodiment of manhood: men whom neither toils and sufferings, nor the fact of death, nor disaster, nor hopelessness could bend from their resolve; standing before us now, thin, worn, and famished, but erect, and with eyes looking level into ours, waking memories that bound us together as no other bond;—was not such manhood to be welcomed back into a Union so tested and assured?. . . How could we help falling on our knees, all of us together, and praying God to pity and for give us all!

The Americans thought themselves a moral people and carried their ordinary moral standards over into the conduct of war. They thought aggressive warfare wrong except against Indians—and the war could not get under way until Beauregard had

fired on Fort Sumter; Southerners insisted that the firing was self-defense against Yankee aggression. Every war is barbarous, but—the conduct of Sherman, Hunter, and Sheridan to the contrary notwithstanding—there was less barbarism in the Civil than in most other wars, certainly less than in our own current wars. Both peoples, as Lincoln observed, read the same Bible and prayed to the same God; both armies were devout; leaders on both sides managed to convince themselves that they stood at Armageddon and battled for the Lord. When the end came there was no vengeance and no bloodshed; this was probably the only instance in modern history where rebel lion was crushed without punishing its leaders.

Above all, the generation that fought the war had that quality which Emerson ascribed pre-eminently to the English—character. It is an elusive word, as almost all great words are elusive—truth, beauty, courage, loyalty, honor—but we know well enough what it means and know it when we see it. The men in blue and in gray who marched thirty miles a day through the blistering heat of the Bayou Teche, went without food for days on end, shivered through rain and snow in the mountains of Virginia and Tennessee, braved the terrors of hospital and prison, charged to almost certain death on the crest of Cemetery Ridge, closed the gap at the Bloody Angle, ran the batteries of Vicksburg and braved the torpedoes of Mobile Bay, threw away their lives on the hills outside Franklin for a cause they held dear—these men had character. They knew what they were fighting for, as well as men ever know this, and they fought with a tenacity and a courage rarely equaled in history. So, too, their leaders, civil and military. It is, in last analysis, grandeur of character that assures immortality to Lincoln as to Lee, and it is character, too, we admire in Grant and Jackson, Sherman and Thomas, the brave Reynolds and the gallant Pelham, and a thousand others. Winston Churchill tells us, in his account of Pearl Harbor, that there were some in England who feared the consequences of that fateful blow and doubted the ability of

Americans to stand up to the test of modern war. "But I had studied the American Civil War," he says, "fought out to the last desperate inch," and "I went to bed and slept the sleep of the saved and thankful."

But it is a veteran of the war itself who paid the finest tribute to his comrades in blue and in gray. "Through our great good fortune," said Justice Oliver Wendell Holmes—and he spoke for his whole generation—

> in our youth our hearts were touched with fire. It was given us to learn at the outset that life is a profound and passionate thing. While we are permitted to scorn nothing but indifference, and do not pretend to undervalue the worldly rewards of ambition, we have seen with our own eyes, beyond and above the gold fields, the snowy heights of honor, and it is for us to bear the report to those who come after us.

What I have tried to do in these volumes is very simple, but the execution of the task has been far from simple. I have tried to present a well-rounded—I cannot call it complete—history of the Civil War in the words of those who fought it. From the three hundred-odd narratives which are presented here there will emerge, I hope, a picture of the war that is authentic, coherent, and interesting. All depends, to be sure, on the selection and the editing of the material, and it is relevant therefore to say something about the principles that have governed that selection and about editorial practices.

Only those who have worked in the rich fields of Civil War history know how apparently inexhaustible the material is, and how unorganized. Only the Puritan Revolution and the French Revolutionary and Napoleonic wars boast a comparable literature, and even here the literature is not really comparable. For the American Civil War affected the whole population and, as Edward Dicey remarked in astonishment, it was a highly literate population. Almost everyone could write, and almost everyone, it seems, did. Surely no other chapter of modern history has been so faithfully or

so elaborately recorded by ordinary men and women; in the American Civil War Everyman was, indeed, his own historian. A disproportionate body of the available material is, to be sure, from officers or from statesmen, these were the more articulate members of the population and those who could better arrange for the publication of what they wanted to say. But to a remarkable degree the privates kept records, and so too did the folks back home. Their reminiscences, recollections, and journals are to be found not in the handsomely published volumes from the great publishing houses, but in the pages of regimental histories, of state, local, and patriotic historical societies, of magazines that printed letters from veterans or from their families. The richness of this literature is the delight and the despair of every student.

My point of departure has not, however, been literature but history. My concern has been the particular battle or campaign, the particular military or social institution, and I have worked out from these to the available literature, selecting not primarily what was interesting for its own sake, or dramatic or eloquent, but what illuminated the subject and the problem. I do not mean to imply that I have been immune to the purely literary appeal, or to the appeal of drama or of personality. Needless to say it is not for authenticity alone that I have preferred Haskell's to a score of other accounts of Pickett's charge, or Chamberlain's to a dozen others of the surrender at Appomattox.

I have tried to cover the whole war; not only the military, which has attracted disproportionate attention, and the naval but the economic, social, political, and diplomatic as well. The war was not all fighting; it was public opinion, it was the draft, it was prison and hospital, ordnance and supplies, politics and elections, religion, and even play. Approximately half the material in these volumes records the actual fighting; another half is devoted to the other aspects of the war. I have tried to hold even the balance between Union and Confederate, the East and the West, the military and the civil, and to give some representation to women and to foreign observers. I cannot suppose that I have wholly succeeded in all this, for the available material has not always lent itself to a balanced picture. As every student knows, good battle accounts are voluminous but accounts of Intelligence or ordnance or supply or the roles of the Blacks, North and South, are meager, and there are at least two capital descriptions of fighting for every one of politics or diplomacy or even of social conditions. Nor is the balance between the material available from officer and private really even. Almost every leading officer wrote his reminiscences or at least contributed them to the *Battles and Leaders* series and the temptation to draw on these magisterial accounts has been irresistible. Nor do I feel unduly apologetic about drawing on Grant and Sherman, Longstreet and others; think what we would give for the war memoirs of R. E. Lee!

Even in the matter of proper representation from Federal and Confederate participants and from the East and the West I have not been entirely a free agent. There are considerably more Union than Confederate narratives—quite naturally, considering the relative numbers involved and the mechanics and economy of publishing. Again, the literature on the fighting in the East, especially in Northern Virginia, is far more voluminous and more interesting than that on the fighting in the West, the reasons for this are not wholly clear, but the fact will not, I think, be disputed by any student of the war and it is one to which an editor must accommodate himself as best he can.

There are, of course, many gaps in these volumes, and these will doubtless pain some readers. Those whose grand fathers were wounded at Perryville will object, quite properly, that that battle is neglected; others whose forebears fought at Fort Pillow will wonder why the massacre is not included; students of economic or social history will doubt less feel that these important subjects have been slighted, while military historians, alive to the importance in our own day of Intelligence or logistics, will feel that the fighting war has been overemphasized. In extenuation I can only plead

the obvious. Some of the gaps in these volumes are dictated by considerations of space, others by availability of material. I could not put in everything; I could not even put in everything that was important. That is part of the story. The other part is that many of the things that interest us most did not appear to interest the generation that fought the war—or that read about it. There are descriptions enough of food and cooking, but no systematic account of the services of supply. There must be a hundred narratives of prison life and prison escape for every one of the organization and administration of prisons. If there is any good analysis of what we now call Intelligence, outside voluminous official correspondence, I do not know it.

I have tried in every case to get actual participants and observers to contribute to this cooperative history. Most of the contributors were participants in the physical sense; they experienced what Oliver Wendell Holmes called "the crush of Arctic ice." Others, and among them some of the most sagacious, were "behind the lines": poets who interpreted the significance of the war; diplomats who pleaded their country's cause abroad; women who lived "the lives which women have lead since Troy fell"; surgeons who treated the wounded and chaplains who comforted the dying. All these were participants even though they may not have held a musket, and all have something to tell us of the war.

It would be naive for me, or for the reader, to suppose that the accounts here reproduced are in every case authentic, or that even the most authentic are wholly reliable. Most of those who claimed to be participants undoubtedly were so, but it would strain our imagination to suppose that all of our reporters actually witnessed everything they described. As every student of evidence knows, people do not always see what they think they see and they do not remember what they saw. There are doubtless many instances where soldiers, writing fifteen or twenty years after the event, deluded them selves, as well as their readers. They embroidered on their original stories; they incorporated into their accounts not only what they had experienced but what they had heard or read elsewhere; they went back and consulted official records and doctored their manuscripts. Soldiers whose companies did not actually get into a battle appear, in written recollections, in the thick of it; hangers-on, who have entertained their friends with the gossip of the capital for years, remember through the haze of time that they themselves directed great affairs of state.

All this is a commonplace of historical criticism, and there is no wholly effective safeguard against it. Diaries, journals, and letters are obviously to be preferred to later recollections, but there is no guarantee that diaries and letters conform to the strictest standards of accuracy and objectivity, or that they come to us untouched by the editorial pen, while many volumes of reminiscences, otherwise suspect for age, are based on diaries and letters and have claims on our confidence. Official reports are doubtless more reliable than merely personal accounts, but even official reports were often written months after the event and colored by imagination or wishful thinking, and there is no sound reason for sup posing that the average officer, writing an official report, really knew the whole of what he was writing about.

We must keep in mind, too, that the Civil War was a far more casual affair than more recent wars. There was no proper organization for keeping records or for writing history. Even the most elementary facts are in dispute, and the statistical picture is a chaos. We do not know the numbers of those who fought on either side, or of those who took part in particular battles, or of casualties, and Confederate figures in these fields are mostly guesswork. Take so simple a matter as executions. Our literature tells us of innumerable executions. But Phisterer, author of a statistical hand book of the war, gives us three widely varying official figures, and historians who have gone into the matter accept none of them. Or take the matter of desertion. Both Ella Lonn and Fred Shannon have dealt with this at length, but about the best they can do for us is to give broad estimates. For what was

desertion, after all? Were those who failed to register for conscription deserters, or those who having registered failed to show up? Were bounty jumpers deserters, and how often should one of them be counted? Were those who went home to visit their wives or to help get in the crops, and later returned to the army, deserters? Or what shall we say of the blockade? Was it ever really effective? How many blockade-runners were there, and how many of them got through the blockade? With the most elementary facts of the war in this state of confusion it is perhaps excessive to strain overmuch at discrepancies in accounts of the conduct of a company or a regiment in a particular battle.

Something should be said about the principles governing the reproduction of source material in these volumes. There has been no tinkering with the text except in three very minor details. First, in some instances where paragraphs seemed intolerably long, they have been broken up. Second, while I have faithfully indicated all omissions within any excerpt I have not thought it necessary to put the customary dots at the beginning and end of excerpts: these can usually be taken for granted. Third, in deference to modern usage I have capitalized the word Negro wherever it appears. Aside from these insignificant modifications the text appears here as it appears in the original source to which credit is given in the bibliography.

That authors themselves, or editors—often devoted wives or daughters—have sometimes tinkered with the text is, however, painfully clear. There is no protection against this, and nothing to be done about it short of going back to the original manuscript where that is available; ordinarily it is not available. And this leads me to a more important matter. Not only have I not presumed to correct spelling or punctuation, I have not attempted to correct factual statements or misstatements. To have done so would have involved both me and the reader in a wilderness of controversy. There are, after all, hundreds of histories that attempt to set the facts straight. Careful readers will therefore note many glaring errors in these accounts. Almost every soldier, for example, consistently exaggerated enemy strength, and enemy losses, and two accounts of the same battle will confidently submit wholly inconsistent statistical information. The reader must keep in mind that our contributors are not writing as scholarly historians. They are giving their story from their own point of view—a point of view at once circumscribed and biased. They are not only limited in their knowledge; they are often ignorant, prejudiced, and vain. Sometimes they are on the defensive; sometimes they are repeating rumor and gossip; sometimes they are yielding to the temptation of the purple passage; sometimes they are trying to make a good impression on the folks back home, or on posterity. The reader is warned: they are not always to be trusted. But there are some consolations and some safeguards. As we give both Federal and Confederate accounts the errors often cancel out. The vainglorious give themselves away, and so too the ignorant and the timid, while those who write with an eye on the verdict of history proclaim that fact in every line.

An enterprise of this nature, stretching over more than a decade, naturally incurs a great many debts and obligations. I could not have completed this work without the help of the staff of the Columbia University Library, who endured with patience and good humor continuous raids upon their collections and who co-operated generously in making their Civil War collection one of the best in the country. I am indebted, too, to libraries and librarians elsewhere: the Library of Congress, the New York Public Library, the libraries of Harvard University, the University of Virginia, the University of North Carolina, New York University, the University of California, to name but a few. To my graduate students who have helped in the arduous work of tracking down elusive books, transcribing and photostating, I am deeply indebted, and especially to Mrs. Elizabeth Kelley Bauer, Mr. Wilson Smith, and Mr. Leonard Levy. The editorial and production departments of The Bobbs-Merrill Company have co-operated far beyond the call of duty, and I owe a great deal to the sagacious judgment of Mr. Laurance Chambers, the astute editorial eye of Miss Judith Henley, the imaginative co-operation of Mr. Walter Hurley. To the many publishers, historical societies, university presses, and private individuals who have so generously given me permission to reproduce material in their control I am deeply grateful. To my wife, who magnanimously permitted the Yankees to win an occasional victory in these pages, my debt is, of course, beyond expression.

HENRY STEELE COMMAGER
Williamsville, Vermont
August, 1950
Amherst, Massachusetts
February, 1971

I

DARKENING CLOUDS

With the deeper causes of the Civil War we are not concerned, nor with the question which has commanded so much speculation, whether the war was a repressible or an irrepressible conflict. What is certain is that the leaders of the Deep South had convinced themselves, by December 1860, that separation was essential to the preservation of the "peculiar institution," and to the social and economic prosperity of their section. Whether these views fairly represented majority opinion, even in the Deep South, we do not and cannot know; all we can say is that there were substantial elements in every Southern state which did not subscribe to them and even larger elements which opposed secession. Unionist sentiment was particularly strong in the border states—Maryland, Virginia, Kentucky, Tennessee, and Missouri, and in North Carolina which had never been so deeply committed to slavery or the plantation system as other Southern states.

The political machinery of most Southern states was in the hands of the secessionists; this was particularly the case in South Carolina, least democratic of states in its political organization. With the triumph of the Republicans in the November elections—a triumph which was far from giving that party a complete control of the government however—Southern hotheads decided to act, and South Carolina led the way. There were frantic efforts at compromise, North and South, but all foundered. One reason for their failure was the unwillingness or inability of Lincoln to accept any compromise which extended the area open to slavery; an other was the conviction of Southern extremists that separation was inevitable and that compromise, on no matter what terms, would leave the South in a relatively weaker position for the future. So while Buchanan vacillated and the North marked time, the Deep South seceded and organized as an independent nation. With the secession of Virginia, in April, the capital was moved to Richmond and a permanent government established.

Meantime Lincoln, too, had organized his Cabinet—a Cabinet of all factions rather than all talents—and in his Inaugural Address appealed to "my countrymen, one and all" to sink their differences in a common patriotism. The appeal was in vain.

I.I

ABRAHAM LINCOLN IS NOMINATED IN THE WIGWAM

It was the nomination and subsequent election of the "Black Republican," Lincoln, that precipitated secession and, in the end, war. Lincoln actually represented no immediate threat to the South, but many leading Southerners were convinced that Republican control of the Presidency and of Congress would, in the end, doom the "peculiar institution" of slavery and that separation was "now or never."

The story of Lincoln's nomination is here told by Murat Halstead, one of the most brilliant journalists of the day and long editor of the *Cincinnati Commercial*.

Third day [May 18, 1860].—After adjournment on Thursday (the second day) there were few men in Chicago who believed it possible to prevent the nomination of Seward. His friends had played their game to admiration and had been victorious on every preliminary skirmish. When the platform had been adopted, inclusive of the Declaration of Independence, they felt themselves already exalted upon the pinnacle of victory. They rejoiced exceedingly, and full of confidence, cried in triumphant tones, "Call the roll of states." But it was otherwise ordered. The opponents of Mr. Seward left the wigwam that evening thoroughly disheartened. Greeley was, as has been widely reported, absolutely "terrified." The nomination of Seward in defiance of his influence would have been a cruel blow. He gave up the ship. . . .

The New Yorkers were exultant. Their bands were playing and the champagne flowing at their headquarters as after a victory.

But there was much done after midnight and before the convention assembled on Friday morning. There were hundreds of Pennsylvanians, Indianians, and Illinoisians who never closed their eyes that night. I saw Henry S. Lane at one o'clock, pale and haggard, with cane under his arm, walking as if for a wager, from one caucus room to another, at the Tremont House. He had been toiling with desperation to bring the Indiana delegation to go as a unit for Lincoln. And then in connection with others he had been operating to bring the Vermonters and Virginians to the point of deserting Seward.

The Seward men generally abounded in confidence Friday morning. The air was full of rumors of the caucusing the night before, but the opposition of the doubtful states to Seward was an old story; and after the distress of Pennsylvania, Indiana and Company on the subject of Seward's availability had been so freely and ineffectually expressed from the start, it was not imagined their protests would suddenly become effective. The Sewardites marched as usual from their headquarters at the Richmond House after their magnificent band, which was brilliantly uniformed—epaulets shining on their shoulders and white and scarlet feathers waving from their caps—marched under the orders of recognized leaders, in a style that would have done credit to many volunteer military companies. They were about a thousand strong, and protracting their march a little too far, were not all able to get into the wigwam. This was their first misfortune. They were not where they could scream with the best effect in responding to the mention of the name of William H. Seward.

When the convention was called to order, breathless attention was given the proceedings. There was not a space a foot square in the wigwam unoccupied. There were tens of thousands still outside, and torrents of men had rushed in at the three broad doors until not another one could squeeze in.

Everybody was now impatient to begin the work. Mr. Evarts of New York nominated Mr. Seward. Mr. Judd of Illinois nominated Mr. Lincoln.

Everybody felt that the fight was between them and yelled accordingly.

The applause when Mr. Evarts named Seward was enthusiastic. When Mr. Judd named Lincoln, the response was prodigious, rising and raging far beyond the Seward shriek.

Presently, upon Caleb B. Smith seconding the nomination of Lincoln, the response was absolutely terrific. It now became the Seward men to make another effort, and when Blair of Michigan seconded his nomination,

> At once there rose so wild a yell,
> Within that dark and narrow dell;
> As all the fiends from heaven that fell
> Had pealed the banner cry of hell.

The effect was startling. Hundreds of persons stopped their ears in pain. The shouting was absolutely frantic, shrill and wild. No Comanches, no panthers, ever struck a higher note or gave screams with more infernal intensity. Looking from the stage over the vast amphitheater, nothing was to be seen below but thousands of hats—a black, mighty swarm of hats—flying with the velocity of hornets over a mass of human heads, most of the mouths of which were open. Above, all around the galleries, hats and handkerchiefs were flying in the tempest together. The wonder of the thing was that the Seward outside pressure should, so far from New York, be so powerful.

Now the Lincoln men had to try it again, and as Mr. Delano of Ohio on behalf "of a portion of the delegation of that state" seconded the nomination of Lincoln, the uproar was beyond description. Imagine all the hogs ever slaughtered in Cincinnati giving their death squeals together, a score of big steam whistles going (steam at a hundred and sixty pounds per inch), and you conceive something of the same nature. I thought the Seward yell could not be surpassed, but the Lincoln boys were clearly ahead and, feeling their victory, as there was a lull in the storm, took deep breaths all round and gave a concentrated shriek that was positively awful, and accompanied it with stamping that made every plank and pillar in the building quiver.

Henry S. Lane of Indiana leaped upon a table, and swinging hat and cane, performed like an acrobat. The presumption is he shrieked with the rest, as his mouth was desperately wide open; but no one will ever be able to testify that he has positive knowledge of the fact that he made a particle of noise. His individual voice was lost in the aggregate hurricane.

The New York, Michigan, and Wisconsin delegations sat together and were in this tempest very quiet. Many of their faces whitened as the Lincoln yawp swelled into a wild hosanna of victory.

The convention now proceeded to business. The most significant vote was that of Virginia, which had been expected solid for Seward, and which now gave him but eight and gave Lincoln fourteen. The New Yorkers looked significantly at each other as this was announced. Then Indiana gave her twenty-six votes for Lincoln. This solid vote was a startler. The division of the first vote caused a fall in Seward stock. It was seen that Lincoln, Cameron, and Bates had the strength to defeat Seward, and it was known that the greater part of the Chase vote would go for Lincoln.

The convention proceeded to a second ballot. Every man was fiercely enlisted in the struggle. The partisans of the various candidates were strung up to such a pitch of excitement as to render them incapable of patience, and the cries of "Call the roll" were fairly hissed through their teeth. The first gain for Lincoln was in New Hampshire. The Chase and the Fremont vote from that state were given him. His next gain was the whole vote of Vermont. This was a blighting blow upon the Seward interest. The New Yorkers started as if an Orsini bomb had exploded. And presently the Cameron vote of Pennsylvania was thrown for Lincoln, increasing his

strength forty-four votes. The fate of the day was now determined. New York saw "checkmate" next move and sullenly proceeded with the game, assuming unconsciousness of her inevitable doom. On this ballot Lincoln gained seventy-nine votes. Seward had one hundred and eighty-four and a half votes, Lincoln one hundred and eighty-one. . . .

While this [the third] ballot was taken amid excitement that tested the nerves, the fatal defection from Seward in New England still further appeared, four votes going over from Seward to Lincoln in Massachusetts. The latter received four additional votes from Pennsylvania and fifteen additional votes from Ohio. It was whispered about: "Lincoln's the coming man—will be nominated this ballot." When the roll of states and territories had been called, I had ceased to give attention to any votes but those for Lincoln and had his vote added up as it was given. The number of votes necessary to a choice were two hundred and thirty three, and I saw under my pencil as the Lincoln column was completed the figures 231 1/2—one vote and a half to give him the nomination. In a moment the fact was whispered about. A hundred pencils had told the same story. The news went over the house wonderfully, and there was a pause. There are always men anxious to distinguish them selves on such occasions. There is nothing that politicians like better than a crisis. I looked up to see who would be the man to give the decisive vote. In about ten ticks of a watch, Cartter of Ohio was up. I had imagined Ohio would be slippery enough for the crisis. And sure enough! Every eye was on Cartter, and everybody who understood the matter at all knew what he was about to do. He said: "I rise (eh), Mr. Chairman (eh), to announce the change of four votes of Ohio from Mr. Chase to Mr. Lincoln." The deed was done. There was a moment's silence. The nerves of the thousands, which through the hours of suspense had been subjected to terrible tension, relaxed, and as deep breaths of relief were taken, there was a noise in the wigwam like the rush of a great wind in the van of a storm—and in another breath, the storm was there. There were thousands cheering with the energy of insanity.

A man who had been on the roof and was engaged in communicating the results of the ballotings to the mighty mass of outsiders now demanded, by gestures at the skylight over the stage, to know what had happened. One of the secretaries, with a tally sheet in his hands, shouted: "Fire the salute! Abe Lincoln is nominated!"

The city was wild with delight. The "Old Abe" men formed processions and bore rails through the streets. Torrents of liquor were poured down the hoarse throats of the multitude. A hundred guns were fired from the top of the Tremont House.

I left the city on the night train on the Fort Wayne and Chicago road. The train consisted of eleven cars, every seat full and people standing in the aisles and corners. I never before saw a company of persons so prostrated by continued excitement. The Lincoln men were not able to respond to the cheers which went up along the road for "Old Abe." They had not only done their duty in that respect, but exhausted their capacity. At every station where there was a village, until after two o'clock, there were tar barrels burning, drums beating, boys carrying rails, and guns, great and small, banging away. The weary passengers were allowed no rest, but plagued by the thundering jar of cannon, the clamor of drums, the glare of bonfires, and the whooping of the boys, who were delighted with the idea of a candidate for the Presidency who thirty years ago split rails on the Sangamon River—classic stream now and forevermore—and whose neighbors named him "honest."

—HALSTEAD, *Caucuses of 1860*

I.2

"First Gallant South Carolina Nobly Made the Stand"

Immediately upon the election of Lincoln the legislature of South Carolina called a convention to meet on December 17 to consider the question of secession. The convention met first at Columbia, then adjourned to Charleston, where, on December 20, it voted unanimously for secession, issuing at the same time a Declaration of Causes which emphasized above all the threat to slavery. By February 1861, six other states had joined South Carolina—Mississippi, Florida, Alabama, Georgia, Louisiana, and Texas—and delegates from these states shortly met at Montgomery, Alabama, to organize the Confederate States of America, draw up a Constitution, and name Jefferson Davis of Mississippi as provisional President.

A. South Carolina Ordinance of Secession

December 20, 1860
An Ordinance to Dissolve the Union between the State of South Carolina and other States united with her under the compact entitled the Constitution of the United States of America:

We, the people of the State of South Carolina, in Convention assembled, do declare and ordain, and it is hereby declared and ordained, that the ordinance adopted by us in Convention, on the 23d day of May, in the year of our Lord 1788, whereby the Constitution of the United States of America was ratified, and also all Acts and parts of Acts of the General Assembly of this State ratifying the amendments of the said Constitution, are hereby repealed, and that the union now subsisting between South Carolina and other States under the name of the United States of America is hereby dissolved.

B. South Carolina Declaration of Causes of Secession

December 24, 1860
The people of the State of South Carolina in Convention assembled, on the 2d day of April, A.D. 1852, declared that the frequent violations of the Constitution of the United States by the Federal Government, and its encroachments upon the reserved rights of the States, fully justified this State in their withdrawal from the Federal Union; but in deference to the opinions and wishes of the other Slaveholding States, she forbore at that time to exercise this right. Since that time these encroachments have continued to increase, and further forbearance ceases to be a virtue.

And now the State of South Carolina having resumed her separate and equal place among nations, deems it due to herself, to the remaining United States of America, and to the nations of the world, that she should declare the immediate causes which have led to this act. . . .

We affirm that these ends for which this Government was instituted have been defeated, and the Government itself has been destructive of them by the action of the nonslaveholding States. Those States have assumed the right of deciding upon the propriety of our domestic institutions; and have denied the rights of property established in fifteen of the States and recognized by the Constitution; they have denounced as sinful the institution of Slavery; they have permitted the open establishment among them of societies, whose avowed object is to disturb the peace of and eloin the property of the citizens of other States. They have encouraged and assisted thousands of our slaves to leave their homes; and those who remain, have been incited by emissaries, books, and pictures, to servile insurrection.

For twenty-five years this agitation has been steadily in creasing, until it has now secured to its aid the power of the common Government. Observing the *forms* of the Constitution, a sectional party has found within that article establishing the Executive Department, the means of subverting the Constitution itself. A geographical line has been drawn across the Union, and all the States north of that line have united in the election of a man to the high office of President of the United States whose opinions and purposes are hostile to Slavery. He is to be intrusted with the administration of the common Government, because he has declared that "Government cannot endure permanently half slave, half free," and that the public mind must rest in the belief that Slavery is in the course of ultimate extinction.

This sectional combination for the subversion of the Constitution has been aided, in some of the States, by elevating to citizenship persons who, by the supreme law of the land, are incapable of becoming citizens; and their votes have been used to inaugurate a new policy, hostile to the South, and destructive of its peace and safety.

On the 4th of March next this party will take possession of the Government. It has announced that the South shall be excluded from the common territory, that the Judicial tribunal shall be made sectional, and that a war must be waged against Slavery until it shall cease throughout the United States.

The guarantees of the Constitution will then no longer exist; the equal rights of the States will be lost. The Slave holding States will no longer have the power of self-government, or self-protection, and the Federal Government will have become their enemy.

Sectional interest and animosity will deepen the irritation; and all hope of remedy is rendered vain, by the fact that the public opinion at the North has invested a great political error with the sanctions of a more erroneous religious belief.

We, therefore, the people of South Carolina, by our delegates in Convention assembled, appealing to the Supreme Judge of the world for the rectitude of our intentions, have solemnly declared that the Union heretofore existing between this State and the other States of North America is dissolved, and that the State of South Carolina has resumed her position among the nations of the world, as a separate and independent state, with full power to levy war, conclude peace, contract alliances, establish commerce, and to do all other acts and things which independent States may of right do.

—MOORE, ed., *The Rebellion Record*

———————— I.3 ————————

"SHE HAS LEFT US IN PASSION AND PRIDE"

Although Oliver Wendell Holmes published his first volume of poems in 1836 he devoted himself, for the next twenty years, almost entirely to medicine, serving as professor of anatomy and dean of the Harvard Medical School. With the founding of the *Atlantic Monthly* in 1857 he came into his own as essayist and poet. To this magazine he contributed *The Autocrat of the Breakfast Table* and *The Professor at the Breakfast Table,* and in it appeared many of his best known poems. It was to the

Atlantic, too, that he contributed his famous "My Hunt after the Captain"—the story of his search for his son, wounded at Antietam.

This poem is notable chiefly for its expression in poetry of what Lincoln said in his First Inaugural Address.

Brother Jonathan's Lament for Sister Caroline

She has gone,—she has left us in passion and
    pride,—
Our stormy-browed sister, so long at our side!
She has torn her own star from our firmament's glow,
And turned on her brother the face of a foe!

O Caroline, Caroline, child of the sun,
We can never forget that our hearts have been
    one,—
Our foreheads both sprinkled in Liberty's name,
From the fountain of blood with the finger of flame!

You were always too ready to fire at a touch;
But we said, "She is hasty,—she does not mean
    much."
We have scowled, when you uttered some turbulent
    threat;
But Friendship still whispered, "Forgive and forget!"

Has our love all died out? Have its altars grown cold?
Has the curse come at last which the fathers
    foretold?
Then Nature must teach us the strength of the chain
That her petulant children would sever in vain.
They may fight till the buzzards are gorged with
    their spoil,
Till the harvest grows black as it rots in the soil,
Till the wolves and the catamounts troop from
    their caves,
And the shark tracks the pirate, the lord of
    the waves:

In vain is the strife! When its fury is past,
Their fortunes must flow in one channel at last,
As the torrents that rush from the mountains
    of snow
Roll mingled in peace through the valleys below.

Our Union is river, lake, ocean, and sky:
Man breaks not the medal, when God cuts the die!
Though darkened with sulphur, though cloven
    with steel,
The blue arch will brighten, the waters will heal!

O Caroline, Caroline, child of the sun,
There are battles with Fate that can never be won!
The starfowering banner must never be furled,
For its blossoms of light are the hope of the world!

Go, then, our rash sister! afar and aloof,
Run wild in the sunshine away from our roof;
But when your heart aches and your feet have
    grown sore,
Remember the pathway that leads to our door!

—HOLMES, *Poems*
March 25, 1861

I.4

LINCOLN REFUSES TO COMPROMISE ON SLAVERY

Secession brought frantic efforts to find some compromise which might restore the Union and avoid the danger of a brothers' war. The most prominent of these proposals was the Crittenden Compromise which provided for the extension of the Missouri Compromise line of 36°-30' westward to California—a proposal which would have opened new territory in the West to slavery. It was on this issue that Lincoln, who was otherwise conciliatory, ref used to yield . E. B. Washburne was a representative from the Galena district of Illinois, a friend of both Lincoln and Grant, and one of four brothers who were in Congress—the others all spelled their name without the final "e." James T. Hale was a representative from Pennsylvania. Seward, Lincoln's principal rival for the Republican nomination, had already accepted Lincoln's offer to make him Secretary of State.

A. Letter to E. B. Washburne

(Private and Confidential)
Springfield, Ill., December 13, 1860
Hon. E. B. Washburne.
My Dear Sir:—Yours of the 10th is received.
Prevent, as far as possible, any of our friends from

demoralizing themselves and our cause by entertaining propositions for compromise of any sort on "slavery extension." There is no possible compromise upon it but which puts us under again, and leaves all our work to do over again. Whether it be a Missouri line or Eli Thayer's popular sovereignty, it is all the same. Let either be done, and immediately filibustering and extending slavery recommences. On that point hold firm, as with a chain of steel.

Yours as ever,

A. Lincoln.

B. Letter to James T. Hale

(Confidential)

Springfield, Illinois, January 11, 1861

My Dear Sir: Yours of the 6th is received. I answer it only because I fear you would misconstrue my silence. What is our present condition? We have just carried an election on principles fairly stated to the people. Now we are told in advance the Government shall be broken up unless we surrender to those we have beaten, before we take the offices. In this they are either attempting to play upon us or they are in dead earnest. Either way, if we surrender, it is the end of us and of the Government. They will repeat the experiment upon us *ad libitum*. A year will not pass till we shall have to take Cuba as a condition upon which they will stay in the Union. They now have the Constitution under which we have lived over seventy years, and acts of Congress of their own framing, with no prospect of their being changed; and they can never have a more shallow pretext for breaking up the Government, or extorting a compromise, than now. There is in my judgment but one compromise which would really settle the slavery question, and that would be a prohibition against acquiring any more territory.

C. Letter to W. H. Seward

(Private and Confidential)

Springfield, Illinois, February 1, 1861

My Dear Sir:. . . I say now. . . as I have all the while said, that on the territorial question—that is, the question of extending slavery under the national auspices—I am inflexible. I am for no compromise which assists or permits the extension of the institution on soil owned by the nation. And any trick by which the nation is to acquire territory, and then allow some local authority to spread slavery over it, is as obnoxious as any other. I take it that to effect some such result as this, and to put us again on the highroad to a slave empire, is the object of all these proposed compromises. I am against it. As to fugitive slaves, District of Columbia, slave trade among the slave States, and whatever springs of necessity from the fact that the institution is amongst us, I care but little, so that what is done be comely and not altogether outrageous. Nor do I care much about New Mexico, if further extension were hedged against.

—*Complete Works of Abraham Lincoln*

--- I.5 ---

Mayor Fernando Wood Recommends the Secession of New York

The idea of secession was not limited to the South. Once South Carolina and her fellow Southern states left the Union, it did not take long for other communities to consider the possibilities of breaking away from the United States. New York City, in particular, believed that its contributions to the national wealth far outweighed the benefits the nation had imparted to it.

With heavy investments in the South and the textile industries, the financial and commercial interests of New York City opposed Abraham Lincoln's war policy. New York's leading politicians urged Lincoln to pursue a moderate policy. Even the radical New York Tribune editor Horace Greeley suggested letting the "erring sisters go in peace."

Mayor Fernando Wood of New York City recommended on January 6, 1861, that the city consider independence from the state and the Union. Although the proposal was never seriously pursued, the threat of cities and states throughout the country breaking away weighed heavily on Lincoln, who was determined to keep the Union intact.

To the Honorable the Common Council:

Gentlemen: We are entering upon the public duties of the year under circumstances as unprecedented as they are gloomy and painful to contemplate . . .

It would seem that a dissolution of the Federal Union is inevitable. . . .

If these forebodings shall be realized, and a separation of the States shall occur, momentous considerations will be presented to the corporate authorities of this city. We must provide for the new relations which will necessarily grow out of the new condition of public affairs.

It will not only be necessary for us to settle the relations which we shall hold to other cities and States, but to establish if we can, new ones with a portion of our own State. Being a child of the Union, having drawn our sustenance from its bosom, and arisen to our present power and strength through the vigor of our mother—when deprived of her maternal advantages, we must rely upon our own resources and assume a position predicated upon the new phase which public affairs will present, and upon the inherent strength which our geographical, commercial, political, and financial preeminence imparts to us.

With out aggrieved brethren of the Slave States, we have friendly relations and a common sympathy. We have not participated in the warfare upon their constitutional rights or their domestic institutions. . . . Our ships have penetrated to every clime, and so have New York capital, energy, and enterprise found their way to every State, and, indeed, to almost every county and town of the American Union. If we have derived sustenance from the Union, so have we in return disseminated blessings for the common benefit of all. Therefore, New York has a right to expect, and should endeavor to preserve a continuance of uninterrupted intercourse with every section.

It is, however, folly to disguise the fact that, judging from the past, New York may have more cause of apprehension from the aggressive legislation of our own State than from external dangers. We have already suffered largely from this cause. For the past five years, our interests and corporate rights have been repeatedly trampled upon. Being an integral portion of the State, it has been assumed, and in effect tacitly admitted on our part

by nonresistance, that all political and governmental power over us rested in the State Legislature. Even the common right of taxing ourselves for our own government, has been yielded, and we are not permitted to do so without this authority. . . .

Thus it will be seen that the political connection between the people of the city and the State has been used by the latter to our injury. The Legislature, in which the present partizan majority has the power, has become an instrument by which we are plundered to enrich their speculators, lobby agents, and Abolition politicians. . . .

How we shall rid ourselves of this odious and oppressive connection, it is not for me to determine. It is certain that a dissolution cannot be peacefully accomplished, except by the consent of the Legislature itself. Whether this can be obtained or not, is, in my judgement, doubtful. Deriving so much advantage from its power over the city, it is not probable that a partizan majority will consent to a separation—and the resort to force by violence and revolution must not be thought of for an instant. We have been distinguished as an orderly and law-abiding people. Let us do nothing to forfeit this character, or to add to the present distracted condition of public affairs.

Much, no doubt, can be said in favor of the justice and policy of a separation. . . . Why should not New York city, instead of supporting by her contribution in revenue two-thirds of the expenses of the United States, become also equally independent? As a free city, with but nominal duty on imports, her local Government could be supported without taxation upon her people. Thus we could live free from taxes, and have cheap goods nearly duty free. In this she would have the whole and united support of the Southern States, as well as all the other States to whose interests and rights under the Constitution she has always been true.

It is well for individuals or communities to look every danger squarely in the face and to meet it calmly and bravely. As dreadful as the severing of the bonds that have hitherto united the States has been in contemplation, it is now apparently a stern and inevitable fact. We have now to meet it with all the consequences, whatever they may be. If the Confederacy is broken up, the government is dissolved, and it behooves every distinct community, as well as every individual, to take care of themselves.

When Disunion has become a fixed and certain fact, why may not New York disrupt the bands which bind her to a venal and corrupt master—to a people and a party that have plundered her revenues, attempted to ruin her commerce, taken away the power of self-government, and destroyed the Confederacy of which she was the proud Empire City? Amid the gloom which the present and prospective condition of things must cast over the country, New York, as a Free City, may shed the only light and hope of a future reconstruction of our once blessed Confederacy.

But I am not prepared to recommend the violence implied in these views. In stating this argument in favor of freedom "peaceably if we can, forcibly if we must," let me not be misunderstood. The redress can be found only in appeals to the magnanimity of the people of the whole State. The events of the past two months have no doubt effected a change in the popular sentiment of the State and National politics. This change may bring us the desired relief, and we may be able to obtain a repeal of the law to which I have referred, and a consequent restoration of our corporate rights.

—Fernando Wood, Mayor

1.6

Lincoln is Inaugerated

On February 11 Lincoln left Springfield for Washington, planning to make a number of speeches en route. Because of threats of assassination, which his friends took seriously, the last stage of the trip, from Philadelphia to Washington, was made in complete secrecy.

Two descriptions are here given of the Inauguration—one from Herndon; another, from the mysterious Public Man whose identity—if indeed he ever existed—is still a secret. Frank Maloy Anderson, the most careful student of the "Public Man," concludes that the "Diary" itself was a fabrication, and that the author of the fabrication was probably Samuel Ward. Herndon's book was not published until a decade after the appearance, in the *North American Review,* of the "Diary of a Public Man," and it may have been from this "Diary" that Herndon took his story of Douglas holding Lincoln's hat at the Inauguration. Whether the story is true or not, it belongs to the folklore of our history.

A. Herndon Describes the Inauguration

Having at last reached his destination in safety, Mr. Lincoln spent the few days preceding his inauguration at Willard's Hotel, receiving an uninterrupted stream of visitors and friends. In the few unoccupied moments allotted him, he was carefully revising his inaugural address. On the morning of the 4th of March he rode from his hotel with Mr. Buchanan in an open barouche to the Capitol. There, slightly pale and nervous, he was introduced to the assembled multitude by his own friend Edward D. Baker, and in a fervid and impressive manner delivered his address. At its conclusion the customary oath was administered by the venerable Chief Justice Taney, and he was now clothed with all the powers and privileges of Chief Magistrate of the nation. He accompanied Mr. Buchanan to the White House and here the historic bachelor of Lancaster bade him farewell, bespeaking for him a peaceful, prosperous, and successful administration.

One who witnessed the impressive scene left the following graphic description of the inauguration and its principal incidents: "Near noon I found myself a member of the motley crowd gathered about the side entrance to Willard's Hotel. Soon an open barouche drove up, and the only occupant stepped out. A large, heavy, awkward-moving man, far advanced in years, short and thin gray hair, full face, plentifully seamed and wrinkled, head curiously inclined to the left shoulder, a low-crowned, broad-brimmed silk hat, an immense white cravat like a poultice, thrusting the old fashioned standing collar up to the ears, dressed in black throughout, with swallow-tail coat not of the newest style. It was President Buchanan, calling to take his successor to the Capitol. In a few minutes he reappeared, with Mr. Lincoln on his arm; the two took seats side-by-side, and the carriage rolled away, followed by a rather disorderly and certainly not very imposing procession.

"I had ample time to walk to the Capitol, and no difficulty in securing a place where everything could be seen and heard to the best advantage. The attendance at the inauguration was, they told me, unusually small, many being kept away by anticipated disturbance, as it had been rumored—truly, too—that General Scott himself was fearful of an outbreak, and had made all possible military preparations to meet the emergency. A square platform had been built out from the steps to the eastern portico, with benches for distinguished spectators on three sides. Douglas, the only one I recognized, sat at the extreme end of the seat on the right of the narrow passage leading from the steps.

"There was no delay, and the gaunt form of the president elect was soon visible, slowly making his way to the front. To me, at least, he was completely metamorphosed—partly by his own fault, and partly through the efforts of injudicious friends and ambitious tailors. He was raising (to gratify a very young lady, it is said) a crop of whiskers, of the blacking-brush variety, coarse, stiff, and ungraceful; and in so doing spoiled, or at least seriously impaired, a face which, though never handsome, had in its original state a peculiar power and pathos. On the present occasion the whiskers were reinforced by brand-new clothes from top to toe; black dresscoat, instead of the usual frock, black cloth or satin vest, black pantaloons, and a glossy hat evidently just out of the box. To cap the climax of novelty, he carried a huge ebony cane, with a gold head the size of an egg. In these, to him, strange habiliments, he looked so miserably uncomfortable that I could not help pitying him.

"Reaching the platform, his discomfort was visibly in creased by not knowing what to do with hat and cane; and so he stood there, the target for ten thousand eyes, holding cane in one hand and hat in the other, the very picture of helpless embarrassment. After some hesitation he pushed the cane into a corner of the railing, but could not find a place for the hat except on the floor, where I could see he did not like to risk it. Douglas, who fully took in the situation, came to the rescue of his old friend and rival, and held the precious hat until the owner needed it again; a service which, if predicted two years before, would probably have astonished him.

"The oath of office was administered by Chief Justice Taney, whose black robes, attenuated figure, and cadaverous countenance reminded me of a galvanized corpse. Then the President came forward, and read his inaugural address in a clear and distinct voice. It was attentively listened to by all, but the closest listener was Douglas, who leaned forward as if to catch every word, nodding his head emphatically at those passages which most pleased him. There was some applause, not very much nor very enthusiastic.

"I must not forget to mention the presence of a Mephistopheles in the person of Senator Wigfall, of Texas, who stood with folded arms leaning against the doorway of the Capitol, looking down upon the crowd and the ceremony with a contemptuous air, which sufficiently indicated his opinion of the whole performance. To him the Southern Confederacy was already an accomplished fact. He lived to see it the saddest of fictions."

—WEIK, *Herndon's Lincoln*

B. The Public Man Attends the Inauguration

Washington, March 4th.—I am sure we must attribute to the mischievous influence of the Blairs the deplorable display of perfectly unnecessary, and worse than unnecessary, military force which marred the inauguration today, and jarred so scandalously upon the tone of the inaugural. Nothing could have been more ill-advised or more ostentatious than the way in which the troops were thrust everywhere upon the public attention, even to the roofs of the houses on Pennsylvania Avenue, on which little squads of sharp shooters were absurdly stationed. I never expected to experience such a sense of mortification and shame in my own country as I felt today, in entering the Capitol through hedges of marines armed to the teeth.—, of Massachusetts, who felt as I did—indeed, I have yet to find a man who did not—recalled to me, as we sat in the Senate-chamber, the story of old Josiah Quincy, the President of Harvard College, who, having occasion to visit the Boston court house during one of the fugitive-slave excitements in that city, found the way barred by an iron chain. The sentinels on duty recognized him, and stooped to raise the chain, that he might pass in, but the old man indignantly refused, and turned away, declaring that he would never pass into a Massachusetts court-house by the favor of armed men or under a chain.

It is really amazing that General Scott should have consented to preside over such a pestilent and foolish parade of force at this time, and I can only attribute his doing so to the agitation in which he is kept by the constant pressure upon him from Virginia, of which I heard only too much to-day from—, who returned yesterday from Richmond. Fortunately, all passed off well, but it is appalling to think of the mischief which might have been done by a single evil disposed person to-day. A blank cartridge fired from a window on Pennsylvania Avenue might have disconcerted all our hopes, and thrown the whole country into inextricable confusion.

That nothing of the sort was done, or even so much as attempted, is the most conclusive evidence that could be asked of the groundlessness of the rumors and old women's tales on the strength of which General Scott has been led into this great mistake. Even without this the atmosphere of the day would have been depressing enough. It has been one of our disagreeable, clear, windy, Washington spring days. The arrangements within the Capitol were awkward, and very ill attended to. No one was at his ease Neither Mr. Buchanan nor Mr. Lincoln appeared to advantage. Poor Chief-Justice Taney could hardly speak plainly, in his uncontrollable agitation.

I must, however, except Senator Douglas, whose conduct can not be over-praised. I saw him for a moment in the morning, when he told me that he meant to put himself as prominently for-ward in the ceremonies as he properly could, and to leave no doubt on any one's mind of his determination to stand by the new Administration in the performance Or its first great duty to maintain the Union. I watched him carefully. He made his way not without difficulty—for there was literally no sort of order in the arrangements—to the front of the throng directly beside Mr. Lincoln, when he prepared to read the address. A miserable little rickety table had been provided for the President, on which he could hardly find room for his hat, and Senator Douglas, reaching forward, took it with a smile and held it during the delivery of the address. It was a trifling act, but a symbolical one, and not to be forgotten, and it attracted much attention all around me.

Mr. Lincoln was pale and very nervous, and did not read his address very well, which is not much to be wondered at under all the circumstances. His spectacles troubled him, his position was crowded and uncomfortable, and, in short, nothing had been done which ought to have been done to render the performance of this great duty either dignified in its effect or, physically speaking, easy for the President.

The great crowd in the grounds behaved very well, but manifested little or no enthusiasm, and at one point in the speech Mr. Lincoln was thrown completely off his balance for a moment by a crash not far in front of him among the people, followed by something which for an instant looked like a struggle. I was not undisturbed myself, nor were those who were immediately about me; but it appeared directly that nothing more serious had happened than the fall from a breaking bough of a spectator who had clambered up into one of the trees.

Mr. Lincoln's agitation was remarked, and I have no doubt must have been caused by the impressions which the alarmists have been trying so sedulously to make on his mind, and which the exaggerated preparations of General Scott to-day are but too likely to have deepened.

—Rice, ed., "The Diary of a Public Man"

I.7

"WE ARE NOT ENEMIES BUT FRIENDS"

In his eloquent and moving Inaugural Address, Lincoln insisted that the Union is perpetual and secession unconstitutional and void, and asserted that the government was determined to maintain its authority. At the same time he argued the physical impossibility of separation and urged the Southern people to return to their old place in the American household. The moving final paragraph was probably Seward's contribution.

That there are persons in one section or another who seek to destroy the Union at all events and are glad of any pre text to do it, I will neither affirm nor deny; but if there be such, I need address no word to them. To those, however, who really love the Union may I not speak?

Before entering upon so grave a matter as the destruction of our national fabric, with all its benefits, its memories, and its hopes, would it not be wise to ascertain precisely why we do it? Will you hazard so desperate a step while there is any possibility that any portion of the ills you fly from have no real existence? Will you, while the certain ills you fly to are greater than all the real ones you fly from—will you risk the commission of so fearful a mistake?. . .

Physically speaking, we cannot separate. We cannot re move our respective sections from each other, not build an impassable wall between them. A husband and wife may be divorced and go out of the presence and beyond the reach of each other, but the different parts of our country cannot do this. They cannot but remain face to face, and intercourse, either amicable or hostile, must continue between them. Is it possible, then, to make that intercourse more advantageous or more satisfactory after separation than be fore? Can aliens make treaties easier than friends can make laws? Can treaties be more faithfully enforced between aliens than laws can among friends? Suppose you go to war, you cannot fight always; and when, after much loss on both sides, and no gain on either, you cease

fighting, the identical old questions as to terms of intercourse are again upon you.

This country, with its institutions, belongs to the people who inhabit it. Whenever they shall grow weary of the existing government, they can exercise their constitutional right of amending it or their revolutionary right to dismember or overthrow it. . . .

Why should there not be a patient confidence in the ultimate justice of the people? Is there any better or equal hope in the world? In our present differences is either party with out faith of being in the right? If the Almighty Ruler of nations, with His eternal truth and justice, be on your side of the North, or on yours of the South, that truth and that justice will surely prevail by the judgment of this great tribunal of the American people.

By the frame of the government under which we live, this same people have wisely given their public servants but little power for mischief; and have, with equal wisdom, pro vided for the return of that little to their own hands at very short intervals. While the people retain their virtue and vigilance, no administration, by any extreme of wickedness or folly, can very seriously injure the government in the short space of four years.

My countrymen, one and all, think calmly and well upon this whole subject. Nothing valuable can be lost by taking time. If there be an object to hurry any of you in hot haste to a step which you would never take deliberately, that object will be frustrated by taking time; but no good object can be frustrated by it. Such of you as are now dissatisfied still have the old Constitution unimpaired, and, on the sensitive point, the laws of your own framing under it, while the new administration will have no immediate power, if it would, to change either. If it were admitted that you who are dissatisfied hold the right side in the dispute, there still is no single good reason for precipitate action. Intelligence, patriotism, Christianity, and a firm reliance on Him who has never yet forsaken this favored land, are still competent to adjust in the best way all our present difficulty.

In your hands, my dissatisfied fellow countrymen, and not in mine, is the momentous issue of
civil war. The government will not assail you. You
can have no conflict without being yourselves the
aggressors. You have no oath registered in heaven to
destroy the government, while I shall have the most
solemn one to "preserve, protect, and defend" it.

I am loath to close. We are not enemies, but
friends. We must not be enemies. Though passion
may have strained, it must not break, our bonds of
affection. The mystic cords of memory, stretching
from every battlefield and patriot grave to every
living heart and hearthstone all over this broad
land, will yet swell the chorus of the Union when
again touched, as surely they will be, by the better
angels of our nature.

—Lincoln, "First Inaugural Address"

———————— I.8 ————————

Mr. Lincoln Hammers
out a Cabinet

Because Lincoln was the first President elected by the Republican
party, he faced peculiar difficulties in making up his Cabinet. It
seemed wise to unite the party by giving places to as many of the
principal Republican leaders as possible, whether their views
agreed with his or not. He therefore selected two former
Democrats, Salmon P. Chase of Ohio and Gideon Welles of
Connecticut, and three former Whigs, the radical antislavery
leader, William H. Seward of New York, a moderate Missourian,
F:dward Bates, and Caleb Smith of Indiana. The weakest appointment, as time proved, was a practical politician whose political
affiliations had been varied—Simon Cameron of Pennsylvania.

Thurlow Weed, who here describes Lincoln's troubles, was
editor of the *Albany Evening Journal* and a political boss who,
Henry Adams thought, was a "model of political management
and patient address."

Mr. Lincoln remarked, smiling, that he supposed I
had had some experience in cabinet-making; that
he had a job on hand, and as he had never learned
that trade, he was disposed to avail himself of the
suggestions of friends. Taking up his figure, I replied
that though never a boss cabinet maker, I had as a
journeyman been occasionally consulted about

state cabinets, and that although President Taylor
once talked with me about reforming his cabinet, I
had never been concerned in or presumed to meddle with the formation of an original Federal cabinet, and that he was the first President elect I had
ever seen. The question thus opened became the
subject of conversation at intervals during that and
the following day. I say at intervals, because many
hours were consumed in talking of the public men
connected with former administrations, interspersed, illustrated, and seasoned pleasantly with
Mr. Lincoln's stories, anecdotes, etc. And here I
feel called upon to vindicate Mr. Lincoln, as far as
my opportunities and observation go, from the frequent imputation of telling indelicate and ribald
stories. I saw much of him during his whole presidential term, with familiar friends and alone, when
he talked without restraint, but I never heard him
use a profane or indecent word or tell a story that
might not be repeated in the presence of ladies.

Mr. Lincoln observed that the making of a
cabinet, now that he had it to do, was by no means
as easy as he had supposed; that he had, even
before the result of the election was known, assuming the probability of success, fixed upon the two
leading members of his cabinet, but that in looking
about for suitable men to fill the other departments, he had been much embarrassed, partly from
his want of acquaintance with the prominent men
of the day, and partly, he believed, that while the
population of the country had immensely
increased, really great men were scarcer than they
used to be. He then inquired whether I had any
suggestions of a general character affecting the
selection of a cabinet to make. I replied that, along
with the question of ability, integrity, and experience, he ought, in the selection of his cabinet, to
find men whose firmness and courage fitted them
for the revolutionary ordeal which was about to
test the strength of our government, and that in
my judgment it was desirable that at least two
members of his cabinet should be selected from
slave-holding States. He inquired whether, in the
emergency which I so much feared, they could be
trusted, adding that he did not quite like to hear

Southern journals and Southern speakers insisting that there must be no "coercion"; that while he had no disposition to coerce anybody, yet after he had taken an oath to execute the laws, he should not care to see them violated. I remarked that there were Union men in Maryland, Virginia, North Carolina, and Tennessee, for whose loyalty, under the most trying circumstances and in any event, I would vouch. "Would you rely on such men if their states should secede?" "Yes, sir; the men whom I have in my mind can always be relied on." "Well," said Mr. Lincoln, "let us have the names of your white crows, such ones as you think fit for the cabinet." I then named Henry Winter Davis, of Maryland; John M. Botts, of Virginia; John A. Gilmer, of North Carolina; and Bailey Peyton, of Tennessee.

As the conversation progressed, Mr. Lincoln remarked that he intended to invite Governor Seward to take the State and Governor Chase the Treasury Department, re marking that, aside from their long experience in public affairs and their eminent fitness, they were prominently before the people and the convention as competitors for the Presidency, each having higher claims than his own for the place which he was to occupy. On naming Gidcon Welles as the gentleman he thought of as the representative of New England in the cabinet, I remarked that I thought he could find several New England gentlemen whose selection for a place in his cabinet would be more acceptable to the people of New England. "But," said Mr. Lincoln, "we must remember that the Republican party is constituted of two elements, and that we must have men of Democratic as well as of Whig antecedents in the cabinet."

Acquiescing in this view, the subject was passed over. And then Mr. Lincoln remarked that Judge Blair had been suggested. I inquired, "What Judge Blair?" and was answered, "Judge Montgomery Blair." "Has he been suggested by any one except his father, Francis P. Blair, Sr.?" "Your question," said Mr. Lincoln, "reminds me of a story," and he proceeded with infinite humor to tell a story, which I would repeat if I did not fear that its spirit and effect would be lost. I finally remarked that if we were legislating on the question, I should move to strike out the name of Montgomery Blair and insert that of Henry Winter Davis. Mr. Lincoln laughingly replied, "Davis has been posting you up on this question. He came from Maryland and has got Davis on the brain. Maryland must, I think, be like New Hampshire, a good state to move from." And then he told a story of a witness in a neighboring county, who, on being asked his age, replied, "Sixty." Being satisfied that he was much older, the judge repeated the question, and on receiving the same answer, admonished the witness, saying that the court knew him to be much older than sixty. "Oh," said the witness, "you're thinking about that fifteen year that I lived down on the eastern shore of Maryland; that was so much lost time, and don't count." This story, I perceived, was thrown in to give the conversation a new direction. It was very evident that the selection of Montgomery Blair was a fixed fact, and although I subsequently ascertained the reasons and influences that controlled the selection of other members of the cabinet, I never did find out how Mr. Blair got there.

—*The Autobiography of Thurlow Weed*

I.9

SEWARD TRIES TO TAKE CHARGE OF THE LINCOLN ADMINISTRATION

Like William Pitt, a century earlier, Seward was convinced that only he could save his country. As Gideon Welles observed, "Seward liked to be called premier." His "Thoughts for the President's Consideration" were intended to establish his dominance over Lincoln. Seward's proposal to substitute a series of foreign wars for a domestic one revealed, however, a lack of judgment that has never been satisfactorily explained. Lincoln's reply was a masterly rebuke, but one which did not alienate the self-confident secretary. It made clear, however, that Lincoln was going to run his own administration.

A. Memorandum from Secretary Seward

April 1, 1861

Some Thoughts for the President's Consideration

First. We are at the end of a month's administration, and yet without a policy either domestic or foreign.

Second. This, however, is not culpable, and it has even been unavoidable. The presence of the Senate, with the need to meet applications for patronage, have prevented attention to other and more grave matters.

Third. But further delay to adopt and prosecute our policies for both domestic and foreign affairs would not only bring scandal on the administration, but danger upon the country.

Fourth. To do this we must dismiss the applicants for office. But how? I suggest that we make the local appointments forthwith, leaving foreign or general ones for ulterior and occasional action.

Fifth. The policy at home. I am aware that my views are singular, and perhaps not sufficiently explained. My system is built upon this idea as a ruling one, namely, that we must

CHANGE THE QUESTION BEFORE THE PUBLIC FROM ONE UPON SLAVERY, OR ABOUT SLAVERY, for a question upon UNION OR DISUNION:

In other words, from what would be regarded as a party question, to one of patriotism or union.

The occupation or evacuation of Fort Sumter, although not in fact a slavery or a party question, is so regarded. Witness the temper manifested by the Republicans in the free States, and even by the Union men in the South.

I would therefore terminate it as a safe means for changing the issue. I deem it fortunate that the last administration created the necessity.

For the rest, I would simultaneously defend and reinforce all the ports in the gulf, and have the navy recalled from foreign stations to be prepared for a blockade. Put the island of Key West under martial law.

This will raise distinctly the question of union or disunion. I would maintain every fort and possession in the South.

FOR FOREIGN NATIONS

I would demand explanations from Spain and France, categorically, at once.

I would seek explanations from Great Britain and Russia, and send agents into Canada, Mexico, and Central America to rouse a vigorous continental spirit of independence on this continent against European intervention.

And, if satisfactory explanations are not received from Spain and France.

Would convene Congress and declare war against them.

But whatever policy we adopt, there must be an energetic prosecution of it.

For this purpose it must be somebody's business to pursue and direct it incessantly.

Either the President must do it himself, and be all the while active in it, or

Devolve it on some member of his cabinet. Once adopted, debates on it must end, and all agree and abide.

It is not in my especial province;

But I neither seek to evade nor assume responsibility.

B. Reply to Secretary Seward's Memorandum

Executive Mansion, April 1, 1861

My *dear Sir*: Since parting with you I have been considering your paper dated this day, and entitled "Some Thoughts for the President's Consideration." The first proposition in it is, "*First*, We are at the end of a month's administration, and yet without a policy either domestic or foreign."

At the beginning of that month, in the inaugural, I said: "The power confided to me will be used to hold, occupy, and possess the property and places belonging to the government, and to collect the duties and imposts." This had your distinct approval at the time; and, taken in connection with the order I immediately gave General Scott, directing him to employ every means in his power to strengthen and hold the forts, comprises the exact domestic policy you now urge, with the single exception that it does not propose to abandon Fort Sumter.

Again, I do not perceive how the reinforcement of Fort Sumter would be done on a slavery or a party issue, while that of Fort Pickens would be on a more national and patriotic one.

The news received yesterday in regard to St. Domingo certainly brings a new item within the range of our foreign policy; but up to that time we have been preparing circulars and instructions to ministers and the like, all in perfect harmony, without even a suggestion that we had no foreign policy.

Upon your closing propositions—that "whatever policy we adopt, there must be an energetic prosecution of it.

"For this purpose it must be somebody's business to pursue and direct it incessantly.

"Either the President must do it himself, and be all the while active in it, or

"Devolve it on some member of his cabinet. Once adopted, debates on it must end, and all agree and abide"—I remark that if this must be done, I must do it. When a general line of policy is adopted, I apprehend there is no danger of its being changed without good reason, or continuing to be a subject of unnecessary debate; still, upon points arising in its progress I wish, and suppose I am entitled to have the ad vice of all the cabinet.

Your obedient servant,
A. Lincoln
—*Complete Works of Abraham Lincoln*

I.10

THE CONFEDERACY ORGANIZES AT MONTGOMERY

On February 4, 1861, a convention, with representatives from six Southern states, met at Montgomery, Alabama, to organize the government of the Confederacy. This convention drew up a Constitution, chose a provisional President and Vice-President, and acted as a legislature pending the election of a regular Congress.

Thomas Cooper DeLeon, who here describes the political atmosphere of the temporary capital, was a litterateur of some prominence in his day who served in the Confederate Army throughout the war; his brother, David C. DeLeon, was Surgeon General of the Confederacy.

Montgomery, like Rome, sits on seven hills. The city is picturesque in perch upon bold, high bluffs, which, on the city side, cut sheer down to the Alabama river; here, seemingly scarce more than a biscuit-toss across. From the opposite bank spread great flat stretches of marsh and meadowland, while on the other side, behind the town, the formation swells and undulates with gentle rise. As in most southern inland towns, its one great artery, Main street, runs from the river bluffs to the Capitol, perched on a high hill a full mile away. This street, wide and sandy, was in the cradle days badly paved, but rather closely built up.

Nor was the Capitol a peculiarly stately pile, either in size or architectural effect. Still it dominated the lesser structures, as it stared down the street with quite a Roman rigor. The staff upon its dome bore the flag of the new nation, run up there shortly after the Congress met by the hands of a noted daughter of Virginia. Miss Letitia Tyler was not only a representative of proud Old Dominion blood, but was also granddaughter of the ex-President of the United States, whose eldest son, Robert, lived in the new Capital. All Montgomery had flocked to Capitol Hill in holiday attire; bells rang and cannon boomed, and the throng—including all members of the government—stood bareheaded as the fair Virginian threw that flag to the breeze. Then a poet-priest—who later added the sword to the quill—spoke a solemn benediction on the people, their flag and their cause; and a shout went up from every throat that told they meant to honor and strive for it; if need be, to die for it. . . .

On the whole, the effect of Montgomery upon the newly arrived was rather pleasing, with a something rather provincial, quite in keeping with its location inland. Streets, various in length, uncertain in direction and impractical as to pavement, ran into Main street at many points; and most of them were closely built with pretty houses, all of them surrounded by gardens and many by handsome grounds. Equidistant from the end of Main street and from each other, stood, in these cradle days, the two hotels of which the Capital could boast. Montgomery Hall, of bitter memory—like the much-sung "Raven of Zurich," for uncleanliness of nest and length of bill—had been the resort of country merchants, horse and cattle-men; but now the Solon of the hour dwelt therein, with the possible hero of many a field. The Exchange—of rather more pretentions and vastly more comfort—was at that time in the hands of a northern firm, who "could keep a hotel." The latter was political headquarters—the President, the Cabinet and a swarm of the possible great residing there.

Montgomery was Washington over again; only on a smaller scale, and with the avidity and agility in pursuit of the spoils somewhat enhanced by the freshness of scent.

"The President is at this house?" I queried of the ex member of Congress next me at dinner. "But he does not appear, I suppose?"

"Oh, yes; he's waiting here till his house is made ready. But he doesn't have a private table; takes his meals like an everyday mortal, at the ladies' ordinary."

He had scarcely spoken when Mr. Davis entered by a side door and took his seat, with only an occasional stare of earnest, but not disrespectful, curiosity from the more recent arrivals.

Even in the few weeks since I had seen him there was a great change. He looked worn and thinner; and the set expression of the somewhat stern features gave a grim hardness not natural to their lines. With scarcely a glance around, he returned the general salutations, sat down absently and was soon absorbed in conversation with General Cooper, who had recently resigned the adjutant-generalship of the United States army and accepted a similar post and brigadier's commission from Mr. Davis . . .

Little ceremony, or form, hedged the incubating government; and perfect simplicity marked every detail about Mr. Davis. His office, for the moment, was one of the parlors of the hotel. Members of the Cabinet and high officials came in and out without ceremony, to ask questions and receive very brief replies; or for whispered consultation with the President's private secretary, whose desk was in the same room. Casual visitors were simply announced by an usher, and were received whenever business

did not prevent. Mr. Davis' manner was unvarying in its quiet and courtesy, drawing out all that one had to tell, and indicating by brief answer, or criticism, that he had extracted the pith from it. At that moment he was the very idol of the people; the grand embodiment to them of their grand cause; and they gave him their hands unquestioning, to applaud any move soever he might make. And equally unthinking as this popular manifestation of early hero-worship was the clamor that later floated into Richmond on every wind, blaming the government—and especially its head—for every unto ward detail of the facile descent to destruction.

A better acquaintance with the Confederate Capital impressed one still more with its likeness to Washington toward the end of the session; but many features of that likeness were salient ones, which had marred and debased the older city. The government just organizing, endless places of profit, of trust, or of honor, were to be filled; and for each and every one of them was a rush of justling and almost rapid claimants. The skeleton of the regular army had just been articulated by Congress, but the bare bones would soon have swelled to more than Falstaffian proportions, had one in every twenty of the ardent aspirants been applied as matter and muscle. The first "gazette" was watched for with straining eyes, and naturally would follow aching hearts; for disappointment here first sowed the dragon's teeth that were to spring into armed opponents of the unappreciative power.

The whole country was new. Everything was to be done—to be made; and who was so capable for both, in their own conceit, as that swarm of worn-out lobbymen and contractors who, having thoroughly exploited "the old concern," now gathered to gorge upon the new. And by the hundred flocked hither those unclean birds, blinking bleared eyes at any chance bit, whetting foul bills to peck at carrion from the departmental sewer. Busy and active at all hours, the lobby of the exchange, when the crowd and the noise rose to the flood at night, smacked no little of pandemonium. Every knot of men had its grievance; every flag in the pavement was a rostrum. Slowness of organization, the weak ness of Congress, secession of the border states, personnel of the Cabinet and especially the latest army appointments—these and kindred subjects were canvassed with heat equaled only by ignorance. Men from every section of the South defended their own people in highest of keys and no little temper; startling measures for public safety were offered and state secrets openly discussed in this curbstone congress; while a rank growth of newspaper correspondents, with "the very latest," swelled the hum into a veritable Babel. And the most incomprehensible of all was the diametric opposition of men from the same neighborhood, in their views of the same subject. Often it would be a vital one, of doctrine, or of policy; and yet these neighbors would antagonize more bitterly than would men from opposite parts of the confederation.

—DeLeon, *Four Years in Rebel Capitals*

I.11

Constitution of the Confederate States of America

The fledgling Confederacy hastily prepared a new constitution for its breakaway government during the winter of 1861. Ratified days after Lincoln's inauguration, the Confederate Constitution relied heavily on the United States Constitution of 1787, with some critical modifications reflecting Southerners' misgivings of the political structure they had abandoned. The basic structure of government remained the same with a bicameral legislature, president and judicial system all performing approximately the same duties as the U.S. government. Guarantees of individual liberties (except for slaves) were retained as constitutional rights. The ban on importing slaves was also kept. Whole sections of the U.S. Constitution pertaining to basic operations of the government were simply lifted for the Confederate version.

But major changes were made. As the preamble states, the source of the national government's authority would lie with the states. States became responsible for financing the central government, thus weakening the national government's ability to act. Congress was assigned the constitutional duty to protect the institution of slavery within the Confederacy and its territo-

ries. Slaves were to be considered by the legal system as property. The president was given the right to make line-item vetoes and control of budgetary appropriations.

Paradoxically, the desire to bolster states' rights—which led to secession—hindered the Confederacy's ability to wage war as states were often at odds with each other and the central government. Whereas Lincoln consolidated and strengthened central authority (for which he was sharply criticized) to wage war, President Jefferson Davis of the Confederacy did not have the same political levers.

We the people of the Confederate States, each state acting in its sovereign and independent character, in order to from a permanent government, establish justice, insure domestic tranquillity, and secure the blessings of liberty to ourselves and our posterity—invoking the favor and guidance of Almighty God—do ordain and establish this Constitution for the Confederate States of America.

Article I. Section 1. All legislative powers herein delegated shall be vested in Congress of the Confederate States, which shall consist of a Senate and House of Representatives.

Section 2. (1) The House of Representatives shall be . . . chosen every second year by the people of the several States; and the electors of each State shall be citizens of the Confederate States, and have the qualifications requisite for electors of the most numerous branches of the State Legislature; but no person of foreign birth, not a citizen of the Confederate States, shall be allowed to vote for any officer, civil, or political, State or Federal. . . .

(2) Representatives and direct taxes shall be apportioned among the several States which may be included within this Confederacy, according to their respective numbers, which shall be determined by adding to the whole number of free persons, including those bound to service for a term of years, and excluding Indians not taxed, three-fifths of all slaves. The actual enumeration shall be made within three years after the first meeting of the Congress of the Confederate States, and within every subsequent term of ten years, in such manner as they shall by law direct. The number of Representatives shall not exceed one for every fifty

thousand, but each State shall have at least one Representative; and until such enumeration shall be made the State of South Carolina shall be entitled to choose six; the State of Georgia ten; the State of Alabama nine; the State of Florida two; the State of Mississippi seven; the State of Louisiana six; and the State of Texas six.

Section 9. (1) The importation of negroes of the African race, from any foreign country, other than the slaveholding States or Territories of the United States of America, is hereby forbidden; and Congress is required to pass such laws as shall effectually prevent the same.

(2) Congress shall have the power to prohibit the introduction of slaves from any State not a member, or Territory not belonging to, this Confederacy. . . .

Article IV. Section 2. (1) The citizens of each State shall be entitled to all the privileges and immunities of citizens of the several States, and shall have the right of transit and sojourn in any State of this Confederacy, with their slaves and other property; and the right of property in said slaves shall not be thereby impaired.

(3) No slave or other person held to service or labor in any State or Territory of the Confederate States, under the laws thereof, escaping or [un]lawfully carried into another, shall, in consequence of any law or regulation therein, be discharged from such service or labor; but shall be delivered up on claim of the party to whom such slaves belongs, or to whom such service or labor may be due. . . .

Section 3. (3) The Confederate States may acquire new territory; and Congress shall have power to legislate and provide governments for the inhabitants of all territory belonging to the Confederate States, lying without the limits of the several States, and may permit them, at such times, and in such manner as it may by law provide, to form States to be admitted into the Confederacy. In all such territory, the institution of negro slavery, as it now exists in the Confederate States, shall be recognized and protected by Congress and by the territorial government; and the inhabitants of the several Confederate States and Territories shall

have the right to take to such territory any slaves lawfully held by them in any of the States or Territories of the Confederate States. . . .

Article V. Section 1. (1) Upon the demand of any three States, legally assembled in their several Conventions, the Congress shall summon a Convention of all the States, to take into consideration such amendments to the Constitution as the said States shall concur in suggesting at the time when the said demand is made; and should any of the proposed amendments to the Constitution be agreed on by the said Convention—voting by States—and the same be ratified by the Legislatures of two-thirds thereof—as the one or the other mode of ratification may be proposed by the general convention—they shall thenceforward form a part of this Constitution. But no State shall, without its consent, be deprived of its equal representation in the Senate. . .

Article VII. 1. The ratification of the conventions of five States shall be sufficient for the establishment of this Constitution between the States so ratifying the same.

2. When five States shall have ratified this Constitution in the manner before specified, the Congress, under the provisional Constitution, shall prescribe the time for holding the election of president and Vice-President, and for the meeting of the electoral college, and for counting the votes and inaugurating the President. They shall also prescribe the time for holding the first election of members of Congress under this Constitution, and the time for assembling the same. Until the assembling of such Congress, the Congress under the provisional Constitution shall continue to exercise the legislative powers granted them; not extending beyond the time limited by the Constitution of the Provisional Government.

Adopted unanimously by the Congress of the Confederate States of South Carolina, Georgia, Florida, Alabama, Mississippi, Louisiana, and Texas, sitting in convention at the capitol, in the city of Montgomery, Alabama, on the Eleventh day of March, in the year Eighteen Hundred and Sixty-One.

—CONFEDERATE CONGRESS

A War Clerk Describes Davis
And His Cabinet

Some of the appointments to the Confederate Cabinet posts excited a good deal of surprise; even more astonishment was excited by the failure of Davis to invite to his official family men like Robert Barnwell Rhett of South Carolina and William L. Yancey of Alabama—men who for more than a decade had been leaders in the secession movement.

John Beauchamp Jones, who has been called the "Confederate Pepys," was an author and journalist of some note who obtained a position as clerk in the War Department in order to keep "a diary of the transactions of the government."

May 17th, 1861.—Was introduced to the President to day. He was overwhelmed with papers and retained a number in his left hand, probably of more importance than the rest. He received me with urbanity, and while he read the papers I had given him, as I had never seen him before, I endeavored to scrutinize his features, as one would naturally do, for the purpose of forming a vague estimate of the character and capabilities of the man destined to perform the leading part in a revolution which must occupy a large space in the world's history. His stature is tall, nearly six feet; his frame is very slight and seemingly frail, but when he throws back his shoulders he is as straight as an Indian chief. The features of his face are distinctly marked with character, and no one gazing at his profile would doubt for a moment that he beheld more than an ordinary man. His face is handsome, and [on] his thin lip often basks a pleasant smile. There is nothing sinister or repulsive in his manners or appearance, and if there are no special indications of great grasp of intellectual power on his fore head and on his sharply-defined nose and chin, neither is there any evidence of weakness or that he could be easily moved from any settled purpose. I think he has a clear perception of matters demanding his cognizance, and a nice discrimination of details. As a politician he attaches the utmost importance to

consistency—and here I differ with him. I think that to be consistent as a politician is to change with the circumstances of the case. When Calhoun and Webster first met in Congress, the first advocated a protective tariff and the last opposed. This was told me by Mr. Webster himself, in 1842, when he was Secretary of State; and it was confirmed by Mr. Calhoun in 1844, then Secretary of State himself. Statesmen are the physicians of the public weal, and what doctor hesitates to vary his remedies with the new phases of disease?

When the President had completed the reading of my papers, and during the perusal I observed him make several emphatic nods, he asked me what I wanted. I told him I wanted employment with my pen, perhaps only temporary employment. I thought the correspondence of the Secretary of War would increase in volume, and another assistant besides Major Tyler would be required in his office. He smiled and shook his head, saying that such work would be only temporary indeed; which I construed to mean that even he did not then suppose the war to assume colossal proportions.

May 20th.—Mr. Walker, the Secretary of War, is some forty-seven or -eight years of age, tall, thin, and a little bent not by age, but by study and bad health. He was a successful lawyer and, having never been in governmental employment, is fast working himself down. He has not yet learned how to avoid unnecessary labor, being a man of the finest sensibilities, and exacting with the utmost nicety all due deference to the dignity of his official position. He stands somewhat on ceremony with his brother officials and ac cords and exacts the etiquette natural to a sensitive gentle man who has never been broken on the wheel of office. I predict for him a short career. The only hope for his continuance in office is unconditional submission to the President, who, being once Secretary of War of the United States, is familiar with all the wheels of the department. But soon, if I err not, the President will be too much absorbed in the fluctuations of momentous campaigns to give much of his attention to any one of the departments. Nevertheless Mr. Walker, if he be an apt scholar, may learn much before that day; and Congress may simplify his duties by enacting a uniform mode of filling the offices in the field. The applications now give the greatest trouble, and the disappointed class give rise to many vexations.

May 21st.—Being in the same room with the Secretary and seen by all his visitors, I am necessarily making many new acquaintances; and quite a number recognize me by my books which they have read. Among this class is Mr. Benjamin, the Minister of Justice. . . . Mr. Benjamin is of course a Jew, of French lineage, born I believe in Louisiana, a lawyer and politician. His age may be sixty, and yet one might suppose him to be less than forty. His hair and eyes are black, his forehead capacious, his face round and as intellectual as one of that shape can be; and Mr. Benjamin is certainly a man of intellect, education, and extensive reading, combined with natural abilities of a tolerably high order. Upon his lip there seems to bask an eternal smile; but if it be studied, it is not a smile—yet it bears no unpleasing aspect.

May 22nd.—Today I had, in our office, a specimen of Mr. Memminger's oratory. He was pleading for an installment of the claims of South Carolina on the Confederacy; and Mr. Walker, always hesitating, argued the other side, merely for delay. Both are fine speakers, with most distinct enunciation and musical voices. The demand was audited and paid, amounting to, I believe, several hundred thousand dollars.

And I heard and saw Mr. Toombs today, the Secretary of State. He is a portly gentleman, but with the pale face of the student and the marks of a deep thinker. To gaze at him in repose, the casual spectator would suppose, from his neglect of dress, that he was a planter in moderate circumstances and of course not gifted with extraordinary powers of intellect; but let him open his mouth, and the delusion vanishes. At the time alluded to he was surrounded by the rest of the cabinet, in our office,

and the topic was the policy of the war. He was for taking the initiative and carrying the war into the enemy's country. And as he warmed with the subject, the man seemed to vanish, and the genius alone was visible. . . . These little discussions were of frequent occurrence; and it soon became apparent that the Secretary of War was destined to be the most important man among the cabinet ministers. His position afforded the best prospect of future distinction—always provided he should be equal to the position and his administration attended with success. I felt convinced that Toombs would not be long chafing in the cabinet but that he would seize the first opportunity to repair to the field.

—JONES, A *Rebel War Clerk's Diary at the Confederate States' Capital*

I.13

SAM HOUSTON REFUSES TO GO WITH HIS STATE

Not everyone in the South, however, was enamored with the new Confederate nation. Pockets of Unionist sentiment remained. One of the strongest voices against secession belonged to Governor Sam Houston of Texas, who represented a large minority of residents who opposed disunion.

Sam Houston had given much of his life to the service of Texas and the United States. Born in Virginia during the administration of George Washington, Houston served under Andrew Jackson in the War of 1812. Houston served a brief term as governor of Tennessee, and on at least two occasions lived with Cherokee Indians. In 1832, Jackson sent Houston to Texas to negotiate a treaty with the Indians.

Once in Texas, he threw his lot in with that territory, then under Mexican control. As commander in chief of the victorious Texan army, he helped Texas gain its independence. Houston was elected the first president of the Republic of Texas and strongly advocated for Texan admittance into the Union. He was the first senator from Texas after it was admitted. In 1859, Houston was elected governor.

Houston declared, "I am for the Union without any 'if' in the case," even preferring that Texas become an independent republic rather than join the Confederacy. Houston proposed a convention of Southern states to discuss conciliation, but the former firebrand for Texan independence was ignored. Texas voted for secession, and soon afterward, an oath of loyalty was required of all Texas authorities. Houston issued the following proclamation against it.

In an act of high drama, Houston was called three times at the statehouse to stand and take the oath. Whittling throughout the proceedings, Houston refused to answer to his name. He resigned as governor and returned to his home in Huntsville, Texas. Despite his objections to secession, Houston would not turn against his beloved state. He declined an offer of soldiers from Abraham Lincoln to keep his governorship.

Fellow Citizens: When on account of the election of Mr. Lincoln to the Presidency of the United States, I was urged to call the Legislature, I refused to do so until such time as I believed the public interests required it. To all I said, that if the people desired the Legislature to be called, I would not stand in their way. When satisfied that the necessity existed, I called it together, and upon the assembling urged upon it the importance of immediate action in reference to your relations with the United States and with respect to the Frontier and the Treasury.

In the meantime, the Convention had been called, which assembled on the 28th of January. That convention, besides being revolutionary in its character, did not receive the sanction of a majority of the people. As the representative of a minority, however large, it could not claim the right to speak for the people. It was without the pale of the Constitution, and was unknown to the laws which I had sworn to support. While sworn to support the Constitution, it was my duty to stand aloof from all revolutionary schemes calculated to subvert the Constitution. The people who were free from such solemn obligations, might revolutionize and absolve me from mine, my oath only having reference to my acts in the capacity of their Chief Executive; but as a sworn officer, my duty was too plain to be misunderstood. Because others more lightly regarded the bond they made with Heaven, furnished me no excuse, if my conscience condemned the act. If I had believed that the time had come for revolution, I should have thrown off the burden of an official oath, resigned my office, and

as one of the people, a free and independent citizen, have aided to arouse my countrymen to action. I believed that the Constitution and laws would provide a remedy and therefore I was not ready for revolution. . . .

The Legislature refused to submit the question of our relations with the United States Government to a direct vote of the people; but authorized the Convention to do so. The Legislature having recognized the Convention so far, I was willing to sanction the act, because I saw that in no other way would the people get an opportunity to express their will. I did so, protesting against the assumption of any other powers on the part of the Convention. I knew full well the designs of the leaders of that movement. I saw that in their hands, neither Constitution or Laws would be sacred; and I put upon record my refusal to sanction any attempt on their part, to touch the character of your liberties or infringe upon the rights secured to you by men who framed the State Constitution. . . .

This Constitution has deprived the people of a right to know its doing by holding its sessions in secret. It has appointed military officers and agents under its assumed authority. It has declared by ordinance, that the people of Texas ratify the Constitution of the Provisional Government of the Confederate States, and has changed the State Constitution and established a TEST OATH of allegiance to the Confederate States, requiring all persons now in office to take the same, or suffer the penalty of removal from office; and actuated by a spirit of petty tyranny, has required the Executive and a portion of the other officers at the seat of Government to appear at its bar at a certain hour and take the same. It has assumed to create organic laws and to put the same in execution. It has overthrown the theory of free government, by combining in itself all the Departments of Government, and exercising the powers belonging to each. Our fathers have taught us that freedom requires that these powers shall not be all lodged in, and exercised by any one body. Whenever it is so, the people suffer under a despotism.

Fellow-Citizens, I have refused to recognize this Convention. I believe that it has derived none of the powers which it has assumed either from the people or from the Legislature. I believe it guilty of an usurpation, which the people cannot suffer tamely and preserve their liberties. I am ready to lay down my life to maintain the rights and liberties of the people of Texas. I am ready to lay down the office rather than yield to usurpation and degradation.

I have declared my determination to stand by Texas in whatever position she assumes. Her people have declared in favor of a separation from the Union. I have followed her banners before, when an exile from the land of my fathers. I went back into the Union with the people of Texas. I go out from the Union with them; and though I see only gloom before me, I shall follow the "Lone Star" with the same devotion as of yore. . . .

You have withdrawn Texas from her connection with the United States. Your act changes the character of the obligation I assumed at the time of my inauguration. As Your Chief Executive, I am no longer bound to support the Constitution of the United States. . . .

I love Texas too well to bring civil strife and bloodshed upon her. To avert this calamity, I shall make no endeavor to maintain my authority as Chief Executive of this State, except by the peaceful exercise of my functions. When I can no longer do this, I shall calmly withdraw from the scene, leaving the Government in the hands of those who have usurped its authority; but still claiming that I am its Chief Executive. . . .

I PROTEST IN THE NAME OF THE PEOPLE OF TEXAS AGAINST ALL THE ACTS AND DOINGS OF THIS CONVENTION, AND I DECLARE THEM NULL AND VOID! I solemnly protest against the act of its members who are bound by no other than themselves, in declaring my office vacant, because I refuse to appear before it and take the oath prescribed.

—Sam Houston

I.14

Inaugural Address of Jefferson Davis

Jefferson Davis was appointed the president of the Confederacy on February 18, 1861, during the constitutional convention in Alabama. A regular election held in accordance with the Confederate Constitution, in October 1861, led to his election for a six-year term as president. His inaugural address on February 22, 1862, articulated the causes of the war, which in retrospect seemed all the more legitimate one year into the new nation's life.

Davis recalled the major accomplishments of the government, and the patriotic ideals and vision of the Confederacy. Although the South had suffered some military setbacks, the optimism of Davis's address reflected the continued sense of promise that marked the early stages of the war.

Fellow Citizens: On this the birthday of the man most identified with the establishment of American independence, and beneath the monument erected to commemorate his heroic virtues and those of his compatriots, we have assembled to usher into existence the permanent government of the Confederate States. Through this instrumentality, under the favor of Divine Providence, we hope to perpetuate the principles of our Revolutionary fathers. The day, the memory, and the purpose seem fitly associated.

It is with mingled feelings of humility and pride that I appear to take, in the presence of the people and before high heaven, the oath prescribed as a qualification for the exalted station to which the unanimous voice of the people has called me. Deeply sensible of all that is implied by this manifestation of the people's confidence, I am yet more profoundly impressed by the vast responsibility of the office and humbly feel my own unworthiness . . .

When a long course of class legislation, directed not to the general warfare but to the aggrandizement of the Northern section of the Union, culminated in a warfare on the domestic institutions of the Southern states—when the dogmas of a sectional party, substitutes for the provisions of the constitutional compact, threatened to destroy the sovereign rights of the states—six of those states, withdrawing from the Union, confederated together to exercise the right and perform the duty of instituting a government which would better secure the liberties for the preservation of which that Union was established.

Whatever of hope some may have entertained that a returning sense of justice would remove the danger with which our rights were threatened, and render it possible to preserve the Union of the Constitution, must have been dispelled by the malignity and barbarity of the Northern states in the prosecution of the existing war. The confidence of the most hopeful among us must have been destroyed by the disregard they have recently exhibited for all the time-honored bulwarks of civil and religious liberty.

Bastilles filled with prisoners, arrested without civil processor indictment duly found; the writ of habeas corpus suspended by executive mandate; a state legislature controlled by the imprisonment of members whose avowed principles suggested to the federal executive that there might be another added to the list of seceded states; elections held under threats of a military power; civil officers, peaceful citizens, and gentlewomen incarcerated for opinion's sake—proclaimed the incapacity of our late associates to administer a government as free, liberal, and humane as that established for our common use.

For proof of the sincerity of our purpose to maintain our ancient institutions, we may point to the Constitution of the Confederacy and the laws enacted under it, as well as to the fact that through all the necessities of an unequal struggle there has been no act on our part to impair personal liberty or the freedom of speech, of thought, or of the press. The courts have been open, the judicial functions fully executed, and every right of the peaceful citizen maintained as securely as if a war of invasion had not disturbed the land.

The people of the states now confederates became convinced the government of the United States had fallen into the hands of a sectional majority, who would pervert that most sacred of all trusts to the destruction of the rights which it was pledged to protect. They believed that to remain longer in the Union would subject them to a continuance of a disparaging discrimination, submission to which would be inconsistent with their welfare and intolerable to a proud people. They therefore determined to sever its bonds and establish a new confederacy for themselves. . . .

The first year in our history has been the most eventful in the annals of this continent. A new government has been established, and its machinery put in operation over an area exceeding seven hundred thousand square miles. The great principles upon which we have been willing to hazard everything that is dear to man have made conquests for us which could never have been achieved by the sword. Our Confederacy has grown from six to thirteen states; and Maryland, already united to us by hallowed memories and material interests, will, I believe, when able to speak with unstifled voice, connect her destiny with the South.

Our people have rallied with unexampled unanimity to the support of the great principles of constitutional government, with firm resolve to perpetuate by arms the right which they could not peacefully secure. A million of men, it is estimated, are now standing in hostile array and waging war along a frontier of thousands of miles. Battles have been fought, sieges have been conducted, and although the contest is not ended, and the tide for the moment is against us, the final result in our favor is not doubtful. . . .

This great strife has awakened in the people the highest emotions and qualities of the human soul. It is cultivating feelings of patriotism, virtue, and courage. Instances of self-sacrifice contending are rife throughout the land. Never has a people evinced a more determined spirit than that now animating men, women, and children in every part of our country. Upon the first call, the men fly to arms; and wives and mothers send their husbands and sons to battle without a murmur of regret. . . .

It is a satisfaction that we have maintained the war by our unaided exertions. We have neither asked nor received assistance from any quarter. Yet the interest involved is not wholly our own. The world at large is concerned in opening our markets to its commerce. When the independence of the Confederate States is recognized by the nations of the earth, and we are free to follow our interests and inclinations by cultivating foreign trade, the Southern states will offer to manufacturing nations the most favorable markets which ever invited their commerce. Cotton, sugar, tobacco, provisions, timber, and naval stores will furnish attractive exchanges. . . .

The tyranny of an unbridled majority, the most odious and least responsible form of despotism, has denied us both the rights and the remedy. Therefore we are in arms to renew such sacrifices as our fathers made to the holy cause of constitutional liberty. At the darkest hour of our struggle the provisional gives place to the permanent government. After a series of successes and victories, which covered our arms with glory, we have recently met

with serious disasters. But in the heart of a people resolved to be free, these disasters tend but to stimulate to increased resistance.

To show ourselves worthy of the inheritance bequeathed to us by the patriots of the Revolution, we must emulate that heroic devotion which made reverse to them but the crucible in which their patriotism was refined.

With confidence in the wisdom and virtue of those who will share with me the responsibility and aid me in the conduct of public affairs; securely relying on the patriotism and courage of the people, of which the present war has furnished so many examples, I deeply feel the weight of the responsibilities I now, with unaffected diffidence, am about to assume; and fully realizing the inequality of human power to guide and to sustain, my hope is reverently fixed on Him whose favor is ever vouchsafed to the cause which is just. With humble gratitude and adoration, acknowledge the Providence which has so visibly protected God! I trustingly commit myself, and prayerfully invoke Thy blessing on my country and its cause.

—JEFFERSON DAVIS

THE CONFLICT
PRECIPITATED

Why did the Montgomery government permit the bombardment of Fort Sumter? It is almost a principle of American history that the "other side" must strike the first blow, and that Americans must fight only in defense of their nation and their principles. That was why Polk was so concerned to prove that "American blood had been shed on American soil." Yet at Sumter the South struck the first blow, thus forfeiting, in some part at least, the moral advantage of being the defender rather than the aggressor. From the Confederate point of view, to be sure, the North had already taken the offensive by the occupation of Sumter and by the effort to reprovision it, but this point of view was a bit astigmatic. Clearly the attack on the old flag would arouse and unite the North as would nothing else, and clearly, too, it would precipitate war.

There was, however, one consideration that the Confederates could not afford to overlook. Two days before the bombardment of Sumter Roger Pryor, of Virginia, had put the matter succinctly. "I tell you, gentlemen, what will put Virginia in the Southern Confederacy in less than an hour by Shrewsbury clock—strike a blow." His timing was a bit off, but his argument was sound. Only by striking a blow could the Confederacy be sure of bringing in Virginia—and other wavering states.

Once the war was on, North and South rallied to their causes and their flags. At first unity seemed to obtain, on both sides; only after it became clear that the war would not be over in three months did dissatisfaction appear. There was, in fact, little real unity on either side, and far less real enthusiasm for war than patriotic orators pretended, or than some historians have recorded. Large segments of opinion in the North were opposed to holding the Union together by coercion. Large segments in the South still cherished the old Union and looked upon the war as a slaveholders' fight. Antiwar and disunion sentiment was to be

found almost everywhere in the North, but more strongly in the Middle West than in New England; antiwar and Unionist sentiment in the South was controlled largely by geography: the western counties of Virginia seceded from the state and joined the Union, Maryland, Kentucky and Missouri stayed in the Union, and eastern Tennessee was predominantly Unionist in sentiment.

We shall see, later, something of the consequences of antiwar and Copperhead sentiment in the North, of Union ism and State rights in the South. An appreciation of the importance of these attitudes should not, however, blind us to the fact that the majority, in both sections, believed passionately in and fought loyally for their cause.

II.I

MRS. CHESNUT WATCHES
THE ATTACK ON
FORT SUMTER

When South Carolina seceded, Major Robert Anderson, commanding the Federal forces in Charleston, secretly moved his garrison from Fort Moultrie to Fort Sumter. The question whether his little force should be withdrawn or supported agitated the closing weeks of the Buchanan and the opening weeks of the Lincoln administration. While the fate of Fort Sumter was being discussed, the Confederacy took over all but four of the forts, arsenals, and military posts in the South. Against the advice of some members of his Cabinet, Lincoln finally decided not to reinforce but to provision the fort, and this decision precipitated the crisis, and the war. On April 11 General Beauregard, who was in

command of Confederate forces in Charleston, acting on somewhat ambiguous instructions from Montgomery, demanded an
immediate surrender of the fort; when this was refused
Confederate batteries opened fire on the Stars and Stripes at
dawn of the twelfth, and the war was on. Mary Boykin Chesnut,
whose *Diary* gives us a lively ac count of life in the Confederacy,
was the wife of ex-Senator Chesnut of South Carolina. She tells us
here* of the excitement in Charleston when Sumter was attacked.

April 8th, 1861.—Allen Green came up to speak
to me at dinner in all his soldier's toggery. It sent a
shiver through me. Tried to read Margaret Fuller
Ossoli, but could not. The air too full of war news,
and we are all so restless.

Went to see Miss Pinckney, one of the last of
the old world Pinckneys. Governor Manning
walked in, bowed gravely, and seated himself by
me. Again he bowed low in mock-heroic style and
with a grand wave of his hand said, "Madam, your
country is invaded." When I had breath to speak I
asked, "What does he mean?" He meant this: There
are six men-of-war outside the bar. Talbot and
Chew have come to say that hostilities are to
begin. Governor Pickens and Beauregard are holding a council of war. Mr. Chesnut then came in and
confirmed the story. Wigfall next entered in boisterous spirits and said, "There was a sound of revel-
ry by night." In any stir of confusion my heart is apt
to beat so painfully. Now the agony was so stifling I
could hardly see or hear. The men went off almost
immediately. And I crept silently to my room,
where I sat down to a good cry.

Mrs. Wigfall came in, and we had it out on the
subject of civil war. We solaced ourselves with
dwelling on all its known horrors, and then we
added what we had a right to expect with Yankees
in front and Negroes in the rear. "The slaveowners
must expect a servile insurrection, of course," said
Mrs. Wigfall, to make sure that we were unhappy
enough. Suddenly loud shouting was heard. We ran
out. Cannon after cannon roared. We met Mrs.
Allen Green in the passageway, with blanched

cheeks and streaming eyes. Governor Means rushed
out of his room in his dressing gown and begged us
to be calm. "Governor Pickens," said he, "has
ordered, in the plenitude of his wisdom, seven cannon to be fired as a signal to the Seventh
Regiment. Anderson will hear as well as the
Seventh Regiment. Now you go back and be quiet;
fighting in the streets has not begun yet."

So we retired. Doctor Gibbes calls Mrs. Allen
Green, Dame Placid. There was no placidity today,
with cannon bursting and Allen on the island. No
sleep for anybody last night. The streets were alive
with soldiers, men shouting, marching, singing.
Wigfall, the stormy petrel, is in his glory, the only
thoroughly happy person I see. Today things seem
to have settled down a little. One can but hope
still. Lincoln or Seward has made such silly
advances and then far sillier drawings back. There
may be a chance for peace after all. Things are happening so fast. My husband has been made an aide-
de-camp to General Beauregard.

Three hours ago we were quickly packing to go
home. The convention has adjourned. Now he tells
me the attack on Fort Sumter may begin tonight;
depends upon Anderson and the fleet outside. . . .

Mrs. Hayne called. She had, she said, but one
feeling—pity for those who are not here. Jack
Preston, Willie Alston, "the take-life-easys," as they
are called, with John Green, "the big brave," have
gone down to the islands—volunteered as privates.
Seven hundred men were sent over. Ammunition
wagons were rumbling along the streets all night.
Anderson is burning blue lights, signs and signals
for the fleet out side, I suppose.

Today at dinner there was no allusion to things
as they stand in Charleston harbor. There was an
undercurrent of intense excitement. There could
not have been a more brilliant circle. In addition
to our usual quartet, Judge Withers, Langdon
Cheves, and Trescott, our two-ex-governors dined
with us, Means and Manning. These men all talked
so delightfully. For once in my life I listened. That
over, business began in earnest. Governor Means
has rummaged a sword and red sash from somewhere and brought it for Colonel Chesnut, who

---

* From: *A Diary from Dixie* by Mary B. Chestnut. Copyright,
  1905, D. Appleton & Company. Reprinted by permission of
  the publishers, Appleton-Century-Crofts, Inc.

had gone to demand the surrender of Fort Sumter. And now, patience—we must wait.

Why did that green goose Anderson go into Fort Sumter? Then everything began to go wrong. Now they have intercepted a letter from him, urging them to let him surrender. He paints the horrors likely to ensue if they will not. He ought to have thought of all that before he put his head in the hole.

12th.—Anderson will not capitulate. Yesterday's was the merriest, maddest dinner we have had yet. Men were audaciously wise and witty. We had an unspoken foreboding that it was to be our last pleasant meeting. Mr. Miles dined with us today. Mrs. Henry King rushed in saying: "The news, I come for the latest news! All the men of the King family are on the island," of which fact she seemed proud.

While she was here our peace negotiator or envoy came in—that is, Mr. Chesnut returned. His interview with Colonel Anderson had been deeply interesting, but Mr. Chesnut was not inclined to be communicative. He wanted his dinner. He felt for Anderson and had telegraphed to President Davis for instructions—what answer to give Anderson, etc. He has now gone back to Fort Sumter with additional instructions. When they were about to leave the wharf, A. H. Boykin sprang into the boat in great excitement. He thought himself ill-used, with a likelihood of fighting and he to be left behind?

I do not pretend to go to sleep. How can I? If Anderson does not accept terms at four, the orders are he shall be fired upon. I count four, St. Michael's bells chime out, and I begin to hope. At half past four the heavy booming of a cannon. I sprang out of bed, and on my knees prostrate I prayed as I never prayed before.

There was a sound of stir all over the house, pattering of feet in the corridors. All seemed hurrying one way. I put on my double gown and a shawl and went too. It was to the housetop. The shells were bursting. In the dark I heard a man say, "Waste of ammunition." I knew my husband was rowing a boat somewhere in that dark bay. If

Anderson was obstinate, Colonel Chesnut was to order the fort on one side to open fire. Certainly fire had begun. The regular roar of the cannon, there it was. And who could tell what each volley accomplished of death and destruction?

The women were wild there on the housetop. Prayers came from the women and imprecations from the men. And then a shell would light up the scene. Tonight they say the forces are to attempt to land. We watched up there, and everybody wondered that Fort Sumter did not fire a shot. . . .

We hear nothing, can listen to nothing; boom, boom, goes the cannon all the time. The nervous strain is awful, alone in this darkened room. "Richmond and Washington ablaze," say the papers—blazing with excitement. Why not? To us these last days' events seem frightfully great. We were all women on that iron balcony. Men are only seen at a distance now. Stark Means was leaning over and looking with tearful eyes, when an unknown creature asked, "Why did he take his hat off?" Mrs. Means stood straight up and said, "He did that in honor of his mother; he saw me." She is a proud mother and at the same time most unhappy. Her lovely daughter Emma is dying in there, before her eyes, of consumption. At that moment I am sure Mrs. Means had a spasm of the heart.

13th.—Nobody has been hurt after all. How gay we were last night! Reaction after the dread of all the slaughter we thought those dreadful cannon were making. Not even a battery the worse for wear. Fort Sumter has been on fire. Anderson has not yet silenced any of our guns. So the aides, still with swords and red sashes by way of uniform, tell us. But the sound of those guns makes regular meals impossible. None of us goes to table. Tea trays pervade the corridors, going everywhere. Some of the anxious hearts lie on their beds and moan in solitary misery. Mrs. Wigfall and I solace ourselves with tea in my room. These women have all a satisfying faith. "God is on our side," they say. When we are shut in Mrs. Wigfall and I ask, "Why?" "Of course, He hates the Yankees," we are told, "You'll think that well of Him."

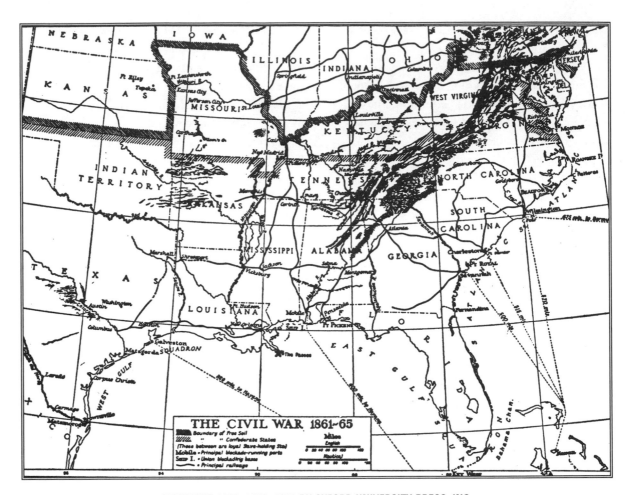

Not by one word or look can we detect any change in the demeanor of these Negro servants. Lawrence sits at our door, sleepy and respectful, and profoundly indifferent. So are they all, but they carry it too far. You could not tell that they even heard the awful roar going on in the bay, though it has been dinning in their ears night and day. People talk before them as if they were chairs and tables. They make no sign. Are they stolidly stupid? or wiser than we are; silent and strong, biding their time?. . .

15th.—I did not know that one could live such days of excitement. Some one called: "Come out! There is a crowd coming." A mob it was, indeed, but it was headed by Colonels Chesnut and Manning. The crowd was shouting and showing these two as messengers of good news. They were escorted to Beauregard's headquarters. Fort Sumter

had surrendered! Those upon the housetops shouted to us, "The fort is on fire." That had been the story once or twice before.

When we had calmed down, Colonel Chesnut, who had taken it all quietly enough, if anything more unruffled than usual in his serenity, told us how the surrender came about. Wigfall was with them on Morris Island when they saw the fire in the fort; he jumped in a little boat and, with his handkerchief as a white flag, rowed over. Wigfall went in through a porthole. When Colonel Chesnut arrived shortly after and was received at the regular entrance, Colonel Anderson told him he had need to pick his way warily, for the place was all mined. As far as I can make out the fort surrendered to Wigfall. But it is all confusion. Our flag is flying there. Fire engines have been sent for to put out the fire. Everybody tells you half of something and then rushes off to tell something else or to hear the last news.

In the afternoon Mrs. Preston, Mrs. Joe Heyward, and I drove out around the battery. We were in an open carriage. What a changed scene—the very liveliest crowd I think I ever saw, everybody talking at once. All glasses were still turned on the grim old fort.

—CHESNUT, *A Diary from Dixie*

ABNER DOUBLEDAY DEFENDS FORT SUMTER

A New Yorker by birth and a West Point graduate who had fought in the Mexican War, Captain Abner Doubleday was second in command at Fort Sumter when it was captured by the Confederates in 1861. He served gallantly throughout the rest of the war, fighting at Antietam, at Fredericksburg, at Chancellorsville, and at Gettysburg, and rose to the rank of major general. His other claim to fame is as the "father" of baseball.

About 4 A.M. on the 12th I was awakened by some one groping about my room in the dark and calling out my name. It proved to be Anderson, who came to announce to me that he had just received a dispatch from Beauregard, dated 3:20 A.M., to the effect that he should open fire upon us in an hour. Finding it was determined not to return the fire until after breakfast, I remained in bed. As we had no lights, we could in fact do nothing before that time except to wander around in the darkness and fire without an accurate view of the enemy's works.

As soon as the outline of our fort could be distinguished, the enemy carried out their program. It had been arranged, as a special compliment to the venerable Edmund Ruffin, who might almost be called the father of secession, that he should fire the first shot against us from the Stevens battery on Cummings Point. Almost immediately afterward a ball from Cummings Point lodged in the magazine wall and by the sound seemed to bury itself in the masonry about a foot from my head, in very unpleasant proximity to my right ear. This is the one that probably came with Mr. Ruffin's compliments. In a moment the firing burst forth in one continuous roar, and large patches of both the exterior and interior masonry began to crumble and fall in all directions. The place where I was had been used for the manufacture of cartridges, and there was still a good deal of powder there, some packed and some loose. A shell soon struck near the ventilator, and a puff of dense smoke entered the room, giving me a strong impression that there would be an immediate explosion. Fortunately, no sparks had penetrated inside.

Nineteen batteries were now hammering at us, and the balls and shells from the ten-inch columbiads, accompanied by shells from the thirteen-inch mortars which constantly bombarded us, made us feel as if the war had commenced in earnest.

When it was broad daylight, I went down to breakfast. I found the officers already assembled at one of the long tables in the mess hall. Our party were calm and even somewhat merry. We had retained one colored man to wait on us. He was a spruce-looking mulatto from Charleston, very active and efficient on ordinary occasions, but now completely demoralized by the thunder of the guns and crashing of the shot around us. He leaned back against the wall, almost white with fear, his eyes closed, and his whole expression one of perfect despair. Our meal was not very sumptuous. It consisted of pork and water, but Doctor Crawford triumphantly brought forth a little farina which he had found in a corner of the hospital.

When this frugal repast was over, my company was told off in three details for firing purposes, to be relieved afterward by Seymour's company. As I was the ranking officer, I took the first detachment and marched them to the casemates which looked out upon the powerful ironclad battery of Cummings Point.

In aiming the first gun fired against the rebellion I had no feeling of self-reproach, for I fully believed that the contest was inevitable and was not of our seeking. . . .

Our firing now became regular and was answered from the rebel guns which encircled us on the four sides of the pentagon upon which the fort was built. The other side faced the open sea. Showers of balls from ten-inch columbiads and forty-two-pounders and shells from thirteen-inch mortars poured into the fort in one incessant stream, causing great flakes of masonry to fall in all directions. When the immense mortar shells, after sailing high in the air, came down in a vertical direction and buried themselves in the parade ground, their explosion shook the fort like an earthquake. . . .

The firing continued all day without any special incident of importance and without our making much impression on the enemy's works. They had a great advantage over us as their fire was concentrated on the fort which was in the center of the circle, while ours was diffused over the circumference. Their missiles were exceedingly destructive to the upper exposed portion of the work, but no essential injury was done to the lower casemates which sheltered us.

From 4 to 6:30 A.M. [April 13] the enemy's fire was very spirited. From 7 to 8 A.M. a rainstorm came on, and there was a lull in the cannonading. About 8 A.M. the officers' quarters were ignited by one of Ripley's incendiary shells or by shot heated in the furnaces at Fort Moultrie. The fire was put out, but at 10 A.M. a mortar shell passed through the roof and lodged in the flooring of the second story, where it burst and started the flames afresh. This too was extinguished, but the hot shot soon followed each other so rapidly that it was impossible for us to contend with them any longer. It became evident that the entire block, being built with wooden partitions, floors, and roofing, must be consumed, and that the magazine, containing three hundred barrels of powder, would be endangered; for even after closing the metallic door sparks might penetrate through the ventilator. The floor was covered with loose powder where a detail of men had been at work manufacturing cartridge bags out of old shirts, woolen blankets, etc.

While the officers exerted themselves with axes to tear down and cut away all the woodwork in the vicinity, the soldiers were rolling barrels of powder out to more sheltered spots and were covering them with wet blankets. The labor was accelerated by the shells which were bursting around us, for Ripley had redoubled his activity at the first signs of a conflagration. We only succeeded in getting out some ninety-six barrels of powder, and then we were obliged to close the massive copper door and await the result. A shot soon after passed through the intervening shield, struck the door, and bent the lock in such a way that it could not be opened again. We were thus cut off from our supply of ammunition but still had some piled up in the vicinity of the guns. Anderson officially reported only four barrels and three cartridges as on hand when we left.

By 11 A.M. the conflagration was terrible and disastrous. One fifth of the fort was on fire, and the wind drove the smoke in dense masses into the angle where we had all taken refuge. It seemed impossible to escape suffocation. Some lay down close to the ground, with handkerchiefs over their mouths, and others posted themselves near the embrasures, where the smoke was somewhat lessened by the draught of air. Every one suffered severely. I crawled out of one of these openings and sat on the outer edge, but Ripley made it lively for me there with his case shot which spattered all around. Had not a slight change of wind taken place, the result might have been fatal to most of us.

Our firing having ceased and the enemy being very jubilant, I thought it would be as well to show them that we were not all dead yet, and ordered the gunners to fire a few rounds more. I heard afterward that the enemy loudly cheered Anderson for his persistency under such adverse circumstances.

The scene at this time was really terrific. The roaring and crackling of the flames, the dense masses of whirling smoke, the bursting of the enemy's shells and our own which were exploding in the burning rooms, the crashing of the shot, and the sound of masonry falling in every direction, made the fort a pandemonium. When at last nothing was left of the building but the blackened walls and smoldering embers, it became painfully evident that an immense amount of damage had been done. There was a tower at each angle of the fort. One of these, containing great quantities of shells upon which we had relied, was almost completely shattered by successive explosions. The massive wooden gates studded with iron nails were burned, and the wall built behind them was now a mere heap of debris, so that the main entrance was wide open for an assaulting party. The sally ports were in a similar condition, and the numerous windows on the gorge side which had been planked up had now become all open entrances.

About 12:48 P.M. the end of the flagstaff was shot down and the flag fell. . . .

About 2 P.M. Senator Wigfall, in company with W. Gourdin Young, of Charleston, unexpectedly made his appearance at one of the embrasures, having crossed over from Morris Island in a small boat rowed by Negroes. He had seen the flag come down, and supposed that we had surrendered in consequence of the burning of the quarters. An artilleryman serving his gun was very much astonished to see a man's face at the entrance and asked him what he was doing there. Wigfall replied that he wished to see Major Anderson. The man, however, refused to allow him to enter until he had surrendered himself as a prisoner and given up his sword. . . . Wigfall, in Beauregard's name, offered Anderson his own terms, which were the evacuation of the fort, with permission to salute our flag and to march out with the honors of war with our arms and private baggage, leaving all other war material behind. As soon as this matter was arranged, Wigfall returned to Cummings Point.

All of the preliminaries having been duly adjusted, it was decided that the evacuation should take place the next morning. Our arrangements were few and simple, but the rebels made extensive preparations for the event in order to give it the

greatest eclat and gain from it as much prestige as possible. The population of the surrounding country poured into Charleston in vast multitudes to witness the humiliation of the United States flag. We slept soundly that night for the first time, after all the fatigue and excitement of the two preceding days.

The next morning, Sunday, the 14th, we were up early, packing our baggage in readiness to go on board the transport. The time having arrived, I made preparations, by order of Major Anderson, to fire a national salute to the flag. . . .

The salute being over, the Confederate troops marched in to occupy the fort. The Palmetto Guard, Captain Cuthbert's company, detailed by Colonel De Saussure, and Captain Hollinquist's Company B, of the regulars, detailed by Colonel Ripley, constituted the new garrison under Ripley. Anderson directed me to form the men on the parade ground, assume command, and march them on board the transport.

I told him I should prefer to leave the fort with the flag flying and the drums beating "Yankee Doodle," and he authorized me to do so. As soon as our tattered flag came down and the silken banner made by the ladies of Charleston was run up, tremendous shouts of applause were heard from the vast multitude of spectators; and all the vessels and steamers, with one accord, made for the fort.

—DOUBLEDAY, *Reminiscences of Forts Sumter and Moultrie*

II.3

"THE HEATHER IS ON FIRE"

Before the attack on Fort Sumter there had been a strong current of opinion in the North which urged that the "erring sisters" be allowed to "depart in peace." When Beauregard fired on the flag the whole North was aroused and, for the moment, appeared to be unified in its determination to put down rebellion.

The three excerpts given here describe the response of the North as seen and interpreted by an Indiana farm boy, a Philadelphia lawyer, and a New York girl.

A. An Indiana Farm Boy Hears the News

April, 1861

Father and I were husking out some corn. We could not finish before it wintered up. When William Cory came across the field (he had been down after the Mail) he was excited and said, "Jonathan the Rebs have fired upon and taken Port Sumpter." Father got white and couldn't say a word.

William said, 'The President will soon fix them. He has called for 75,000 men and is going to blocade their ports, and just as soon as those fellows find out that the North means business they will get down off their high horse."

Father said little. We did not finish the corn and drove to the barn. Father left me to unload and put out the team and went to the house. After I had finished I went in to dinner. Mother said, "What is the matter with Father?" He had gone right upstairs. I told her what we had heard. She went to him. After a while they came down. Father looked ten years older. We sat down to the table. Grandma wanted to know what was the trouble. Father told her and she began to cry. "Oh my poor children in the South! Now they will suffer! God knows how they will suffer! I knew it would come! Jonathan I told you it would come!"

"They can come here and stay," said Father.

"No they will not do that. There is thier home. There they will stay. Oh to think that I should have lived to see the day when Brother should rise against Brother."

She and Mother were crying and I lit out for the barn. I do hate to see women cry.

We had another meeting at the school house last night; we are raising money to take care of the families of those who enlist. A good many gave money, others subscribed. The Hulper boys have enlisted and Steve Lampman and some others. I said I would go but they laughed at me and said they wanted men not boys for this job; that it would all be over soon; that those fellows down South are big bluffers and would rather talk than fight. I am not so sure about that. I know the Hale boys would fight with thier fists at any rate and I believe they would fight with guns too if needs be. I remember how Charlie would get on our Dick and ride on a galop across our south field cutting mullin heads with his wooden sword playing they were Indians or Mexicans (his father was in the Mexican War), and he looked fine. To be sure there was no danger but I feel pretty certain he could fight. May be it won't be such a picnic as some say it will. There has been a fight down in Virginia at Big Bethel. Al Beechers Nephew was in it and wrote to his Uncle and he read the letter in his store. I could not make out which side whipped but from the papers I think the Rebels had the best of it. Mother had a letter from the Hales. Charlie and his Father are in thier army and Dayton wanted to go but was too young. I wonder if I were in our army and they should meet me would they shoot me. I suppose they would.

—WINTHER, ed., *Journal of Theodore Upson*

B. "There is But One Thought— The Stars and Stripes"

Horace Binney to Sir J.T. Coleridge,

Philadelphia, 27 May, 1861

. . . The assault upon Fort Sumter started us all to our feet, as one man; all political division ceased among us from that very moment. Private relations with the South have been put aside, no doubt with great regret. There is among us but one thought, one object, one end, one symbol,—the Stars and Stripes. We are to a great degree at present, and will shortly be throughout, an armed nation. We have the whole naval power of the country. We have nearly all its money at command. We know that we shall be both de graded and ruined unless this government is maintained; and we are not so much embittered at this time (as we hope we shall continue) as to be unable to make the combat as respectable in point of humanity as war between public belligerents can be.

Most of the seceded slave States are much divided. Eastern Tennessee, Northern Alabama, Western Virginia, are wholly in favour of the Union. Kentucky has expressly refused to go out. Tennessee is still balancing; Missouri cannot go. Maryland, now that her mob has been suppressed, speaks and acts the language of Union, and she is encouraged to it by the presence of Pennsylvania forces in Baltimore and overhanging her western counties, which at the same time are known to be faithful, thoroughly Union. It is the slave-selling and slave-working parts of the South that have alone desired to break away,—by no means all of these, nor any considerable part of them but through delusion, venality, or terror. How can the North and West withhold their effort to suppress the terror which has enchained so many? It is their sacred duty under the Constitution. We have, therefore, both duty and right to confirm us in the effort. It will, I have no doubt whatever, be strenuously made. We have no reason to doubt, from either the purposes we entertain, or the motives which actuate us, or the means we shall apply, that God will help us.

Some of the writers for the English press have but an imperfect knowledge of the necessities of the free States when they argue that the slave States should be allowed to depart and make another nation. We are large enough, they say,—and that is true enough, though nothing to the purpose. The North and West cannot conquer them. That also may be true, and yet nothing to the purpose. They will conquer the North and West and destroy the Union, if they can bring about what these writers recommend. Consider, Louisiana and Florida were purchased to make the union of the West with the Atlantic States possible. They hold the Gulf of Mexico and the river Mississippi under their control, if they are left as they claim to be. Texas bounds us and turns us in to the South on the western side of the Gulf. Our intercourse with the Pacific States, all faithful to the Union, lies over the Isthmus of Darien. How can any part of the West continue in union with the North, or the Pacific be united to the Atlantic States, if an independent power holds this control?

The question for negotiation is, Which shall be the master of the gates of entrance and exit to the North and West? Was such a question ever settled by negotiation? The States on the Mississippi and the Gulf must be in union with the North and West, or be commanded by them, or the West must

fly from the North. This is an old question. I heard it argued in 1797, when we had Spain to deal with in regard to these waters; and not a man South or North but held the opinion I express. It was from our weakness then that we did not conquer them, and to this single end—of maintaining our Union—we bought them afterwards, which was better; but their importance to the Union of North and West is just what it was. Great Britain knew what their value to the Union was, when her forces endeavoured to seize New Orleans in 1815.

In fine, my dear sir, I do not say we can conquer. I do say that mere conquest would be an absurdity in our relations if we could achieve it; for the Southern States would become Territories again, if anything, and go into the old connection, to go into revolt a second time. But we may subdue the revolutionary violence which has got the upper hand; we may hearten the friends of the Union in those parts to vindicate their own rights in the Union; and if we cannot do this, we may detach Louisiana, Florida, and the river portions of Mississippi, and Arkansas. If we do not, then I admit our dream of union and our national existence in its present form is gone. And such a shame, dishonour, degradation, in the sight of all the world! God forbid that we should live to see it! Three hundred and fifty thousand masters of slaves—not more—breaking down the power and hopes of twenty millions of freemen, for the most part the descendants of Englishmen! You recollect Cowley's burst, in regard to Cromwell's usurpation:

> "Come the eleventh plague, rather than this should be,
> Come sink us rather in the sea.
> * * * * * * * *
> In all the chains we ever bore,
> We griev'd, we sigh'd, we wept, we never blush'd before."

This has been a long ramble, my dear sir. I have no time to make it shorter, for I am deep in a commission to provide for the poor families of the mechanics who have become volunteers.

—Binney, *The Life of Horace Binney*

C. "One Great Eagle Scream"

Jane Stuart Woolsey to a Friend in Paris.

8 Brevoort Place, Friday, May 10, 1861

I am sure you will like to hear what we are all about in these times of terrible excitement, though it seems almost impertinent to write just now. Everything is either too big or too little to put in a letter. . . . So it will be best perhaps not to try to give you any of my own "views" except, in deed, such views of war as one may get out of a parlor window. Not, in passing, that I haven't any! We all have views now, men, women and little boys,

"Children with drums
Strapped round them by the fond paternal ass,
Peripatetics with a blade of grass
Betwixt their thumbs,"—

from the modestly patriotic citizen who wears a postage stamp on his hat to the woman who walks in Broadway in that fearful object of contemplation, a "Union bonnet," composed of alternate layers of red, white and blue, with streaming ribbons "of the first." We all have our views of the war question and our plans of the coming campaign. An acquaintance the other day took her little child on some charitable errand through a dingy alley into a dirty, noisy, squalid tenement house. "Mamma," said he, "isn't this South Carolina?"

Inside the parlor windows the atmosphere has been very fluffy, since Sumter, with lint-making and the tearing of endless lengths of flannel and cotton bandages and cutting out of innumerable garments. How long it is since Sumter! I suppose it is because so much intense emotion has been crowded into the last two or three weeks, that the "time before Sumter" seems to belong to some dim antiquity. It seems as if we never were alive till now; never had a country till now. How could we ever have laughed at Fourth-of-Julys? Outside the parlor windows the city is gay and brilliant with excited crowds, the incessant movement and music of marching regiments and all the thousands of flags, big and little, which suddenly came

fluttering out of every window and door and leaped from every church tower, house-top, staff and ship-mast. It seemed as if everyone had in mind to try and make some amends to it for those late grievous and bitter insults. You have heard how the enthusiasm has been deepening and widening from that time.

A friend asked an Ohio man the other day how the West was taking it. "The West?" he said, "the West is all one great Eagle-scream!" A New England man told us that at Concord the bells were rung and the President's call read aloud on the village common. On the day but one after that reading, the Concord Regiment was marching into Fanueil Hall. Somebody in Washington asked a Massachusetts soldier: "How many more men of your state are coming?" "All of us," was the answer. One of the wounded Lowell men crawled into a machine shop in Baltimore. An "anti-Gorilla" citizen, seeing how young he was, asked, "What brought you here fighting, so far away from your home, my poor boy?" "It was the stars and stripes," the dying voice said. Hundreds of such stories are told. Everybody knows one. You read many of them in the papers. In our own little circle of friends one mother has sent away an idolized son; another, two; another, four. One boy, just getting over diphtheria, jumps out of bed and buckles his knapsack on. One throws up his passage to Europe and takes up his "enfield." One sweet young wife is packing a regulation valise for her husband today, and doesn't let him see her cry. Another young wife is looking fearfully for news from Harper's Ferry, where her husband is ordered. He told me a month ago, *before Sumter*, that no Northman could be found to fight against the South. One or two of our soldier friends are surgeons or officers, but most of them are in the ranks and think no work too hard or too mean, so it is for The Flag. Captain Schuyler Hamilton was an aid of General Scott's in Mexico, and saw service there, but he shouldered his musket and marched as a private with the Seventh. They wanted an officer when he got down there, and took him out of the ranks, but it was all the same to him; and so on, indefinitely.

The color is all taken out of the "Italian Question." Garibaldi indeed! "Deliverer of Italy!" Every mother's son of us is a "Deliverer." We women regretfully "sit at home at ease" and only appease ourselves by doing the little we can with sewing machines and patent bandage-rollers. Georgy, Miss Sarah Woolsey and half a dozen other friends earnestly wish to join the Nurse Corps, but are under the required age. The rules are stringent, no doubt wisely so, and society just now presents the unprecedented spectacle *of* many women trying to make it believed that they are over thirty!

The Vermont boys passed through this morning, with the "strength of the hills" in their marching and the green sprigs in their button-holes. The other day I saw some companies they told me were from Maine. They looked like it—sun browned swingers of great axes, horn-handed "breakers of the glebe," used to wintering in the woods and getting frost bitten and having their feet chopped off and conveying huge fleets of logs down spring-tide rivers in the snow and in the floods.—The sound of the drum is never out of our ears.

Never fancy that we are fearful or gloomy. We think we feel thoroughly that war is dreadful, especially war with the excitement off and the chill on, but there are so many worse things than gun-shot wounds! And among the worst is a hateful and hollow peace with such a crew as the "Montgomery mutineers." There was a dark time just after the Baltimore murders, when communication with Washington was cut off and the people in power seemed to be doing nothing to re-establish it. It cleared up, however, in a few days, and now we don't feel that the "social fabric"—I believe that is what it is called—is "falling to pieces" at all, but that it is getting gloriously mended. So, "Republicanism will wash"—is washed already in the water and the fire of this fresh baptism, "clothed in white samite, mystic, wonderful," and has a new name, which is *Patriotism.*

—Bacon and Howland, eds., *Letters of a Family During the War*

"The Spirit of Virginia Cannot Be Crushed"

Virginia, where the tradition of nationalism was strong, hesitated to join the seceding states, but the attack on Fort Sumter and Lincoln's proclamation call for 75,000 troops—together with geographical necessity—finally drew her into the Confederacy. On April 17, 1861, a convention voted for secession, 103 to 46, and this vote was ratified a month later by a popular vote of 96,750 to 32,134. Most of the minority vote came from the western counties, which shortly seceded and established the state of West Virginia.

The hopes and fears of Virginians are well illustrated by former President Tyler who, as President of the Peace Convention, labored for compromise but who, like Lee, went with his state when the die was cast. Mrs. Tyler, his second wife, was from New York.

John Tyler to Mrs. Tyler.

Richmond, April 17 [18], 1861
Well my dearest one, Virginia has severed her connection with the Northern hive of abolitionists, and takes her stand as a sovereign and independent State. By a large vote she decided on yesterday, at about three o'clock, to resume the powers she had granted to the Federal government, and to stand before the world clothed in the full vestments of sovereignty. The die is thus cast, and her future in the hands of the god of battle. The contest into which we enter is one full of peril, but there is a spirit abroad in Virginia which cannot be crushed until the life of the last man is trampled out. The numbers opposed to us are immense; but twelve thousand Grecians conquered the whole power of Xerxes at Marathon, and our fathers, a mere handful, overcame the enormous power of Great Britain.

The North seems to be thoroughly united against us. The *Herald* and the *Express* both give way and rally the hosts against us. Things have gone to that point in Philadelphia that no one is safe in the expression of a Southern sentiment. . . At Washington a system of martial law must have been established. The report is that persons are not permitted to pass through the city to the South. . . .

Two expeditions are on foot—the one directed against the Navy Yard at Gosport, the other Harper's Ferry. Several ships are up the river at the Navy Yard, and immense supplies of guns and powder; but there is no competent leader, and they have delayed it so long that the government has now a very strong force there. The hope is that Pickens will send two thousand men to aid in capturing it. From Harper's Ferry nothing is heard. The city is full of all sorts of rumors. To-morrow night is now fixed for the great procession; flags are raised all about town.

Your devoted,
J. Tyler.

Mrs. John Tyler to her mother.

Richmond, June 16, 1861

More and more we have the *realization* of war; from day to day the people, the entire people, are making up their minds to it, until every family of high and low degree are seeing their male members don the soldier's dress and shoulder their musket to go forth for the protection of their invaded firesides. It makes the heart beat and the eyes fill to witness such noble resolution and bravery on the part of all, but in particular on the part of those who, bred in ease and luxury, still cheerfully accept every and any hard ship that comes with a soldier's life, whether as officers or in the ranks, for the latter are thick with accomplished gentle men, than permit the unresisted invasion of their dearest rights. The men have become heroes—*all,* from youths of seventeen to those far advanced in years; but one common feeling swells their bosoms, deep indignation against those who should have been their best friends, and not their worst enemies. An unlawful war has been waged against them and if the possession of every warrior trait will enable them to "conquer a peace," there will soon be one for us. Every way I turn I see an acquaintance and friend, either in the flannel shirt of a private, or in the braided jacket of the zouave, or the plumed cap of the cav-

alry officer. It is women and children only that are not in arms *all ready* for a moment's notice. A large body of noble, brave Marylanders have found it impossible to *wait,* and have resigned with a feeling of relief their homes to *fight* side by side with their Southern brethren. By all sorts of stratagems they are slipping over fully armed, and joining their companions without delay.

Subjugate or *bring to terms* such a people! Little do you *dream* at the North of what stuff they are made. Why, even Gardie and Alex, mourn that they cannot at once be of them; they are *fired up* with enthusiasm for what they consider such a sacred cause as the defense of their soil from the wicked and cruel invader. It is a thrilling, melting sight to see the entrances into the city of troops by the trains from all parts of the Southern country, coming as they ap pear to feel, to the *rescue of old Virginia.* The fatigue of travel makes no impression upon them, and they joyfully march off to their encampments, apparently congratulating themselves they are so near the scene of action. "Still they come."

At church to-day Gen. Davis was introduced to me. He mentioned that Mrs. D. and himself would be to see me to morrow. He is a splendid man, fine manners, and the bearing of one good and great. Gen. Lee called upon us after church; rather grayer than when I last met him, some years ago, but still the elegant officer, looking animated and full of vigor. He spoke very calmly and indifferently of the desecra tion of his home at Arlington, and the flight of his invalid wife. She has moved out of the way of the enemy twice, and now she says *they will have to take her*—she will move no more. The General laughed, as he repeated what she said, but added, as her health was much affected by rheumatism, it was quite a trial to her to be deprived of her home.

And now adieu, dear Mamma. Continue perfectly at ease about me. All I ask is, take care of yourself, and don't get sick.

Your affectionate daughter,
Julia.

—TYLER, *Letters and Times of the Tylers*

"I Am Filled with Horror at the Condition of Our Country"

Nowhere in the Confederacy was Union sentiment stronger than in North Carolina, which was the last state to secede. The despair of Southern Unionists, faced as they were with hostility from both sides, can be read in the correspondence of Jonathan Worth, later governor of his state.

Jonathan Worth to Dr. C. W. Woolen.

Asheboro, May 17, 1861

I am filled with horror at the condition of our country. According to my notions o£ Government, there is much that is wrong on both sides. The Abolitionists of the Free States ought not to have agitated the slavery question at all, even conceding that their feeling is right. It only tends to make the treatment of slaves more vigorous and to en courage bitterness between the two sections. When it was seized upon as a party question it was easy to see it must soon become sectional. . . .

I have always regarded the dissolution of the Union as the greatest misfortune which could befall the whole nation and the whole human race. Hence I have abhorred the agitation of the slavery question as tending to this result. Acting on that conviction I have used all the efforts in my power to stay what I regarded as the madness of both sections, and in the immediate sphere of my influence have impressed my views upon others. My immediate constituents sustained me with greater unanimity than did the constituents of any other representative. I was the first public man in the State to call on the people to vote down the Convention on the 28th Feb., on the ground that the calling of it would tend to a dissolution of the Union. Everybody attributed to me a larger share of the credit or discredit of defeating the call of a Convention than to any other man in the State. I regarded the result in N. C. and Tenn. as arresting the march of madness. Union men had gained

strength up to the proclamation of Lincoln. If he had withdrawn the garrison of Fort Sumter on the principle of a military necessity and in obedience in what seemed to be the will of Congress in refusing to pass the force bill, this State and Tenn. and the other slave States which had not passed the ordinance of Secession, would have stood up for the Union. In the feverish state of the popular mind, if he be a man of good sense, he knew he would crush the Union men in the Slave States by the policy he adopted. All of us who had stood by the Union, felt that he had abandoned us and surrendered us to the tender mercies of Democracy & the Devil. He must have known that he was letting loose on us a torrent to which we could oppose no resistance.

It may be said, theoretically, that this should not have been the effect. Statesmen should have common sense. All sensible men knew it would be the effect. We are still at a loss to determine whether he is an old goose, as well as each of his advisers, thinking to preserve the Union by his course, or whether he became apprehensive that the Union men were about to gain strength enough in the South to stay Secession and he desired to drive us all into rebellion, in order to make a crusade against slavery and desolate our section. In the former case he is a fool: in the latter—a devil. He could have adopted no policy so effectual to destroy the Union. Since the issue of that great proclamation, it is unsafe for a union man in even N. C. to own he is for the Union. The feeling is to resist to the death. Union men feel that just as they had got so they could stand on their legs, Lincoln had heartlessly turned them over to the mercy of their enemies. We feel that his co-operation with the Secessionists left us no alternative but to take arms against our neighbors, or to defend ourself against his aggression.

I am still a Union man, but for military resistance to Lincoln, believing that Lincoln and his cabinet have acted on their mistaken impression that their policy was the best for the preservation of the Union, and that they do not in tend to proclaim servile insurrection. If the latter is the design the South can be conquered only by extermination. If his purpose be, as he says, to respect property and discountenance rebellion or insurrection among our servile population, and our people become satisfied of this, many of our people will not willingly take arms.

I see no hope of any good and stable government except in the United government we are pulling down. It can not be united by war. If peace be immediately made, it will soon re-unite, with an anti-secession clause.

Write me again soon. The Quakers here will not believe your statements as to your Quakers volunteering and the floating of the Stars and Stripes over a Quaker Church.

—HAMILTON, ed., *The Correspondence of Jonathan Worth*

II.6

A NORTHERN DEMOCRAT URGES PEACEFUL SEPARATION

Peace sentiment was to be found in the North as well as the South; many whose loyalty to the Union was beyond question were nevertheless in favor of letting the seceding states go in peace. Much of the antiwar sentiment, how ever, was inspired by distaste for Lincoln and for "black Republicanism." The attitude here expressed took extreme form in copperheadism, or in the activities of such organizations as the Knights of the Golden Circle.

John L. O'Sullivan was a distinguished lawyer, editor and journalist who is credited with the authorship of the phrase "manifest destiny"; he had been appointed Minister to Portugal by President Pierce and after his term ran out lingered on in Lisbon, Paris and London. Tilden was a leading Northern democrat and, in 1876, candidate for the Presidency.

J. L. O'Sullivan to S. J. Tilden.

Lisbon, May 6, 1861

My Dear Tilden,—The heart-breaking news has just reached us here, first of the attack and capture of Sumter, for which the signal was so madly and so wickedly given by the administration (dominated, evidently, by the war portion of that party) in its despatch of reinforcements; and, secondly, of

Lincoln's declaration of war by his proclamation for 75,000 volunteers for the recapture of all the Southern forts, that is, for the invasion of the South—an act followed of course, by secession of Virginia, and soon to be followed, I have no doubt, by that of all or nearly all the border States. Also the telegraph tells of a Massachusetts regiment resisted in an (insane) attempt to force a passage through Baltimore. Gracious God, that we should have lived to see such things! You can better judge, than I could describe, my affliction. At first it drew from me convulsions of tears. . . .

What doom is sufficient for the mad authors of all this! By that I mean, for 9/10 of the crime, the ultra portion of the Republican party. The papers say that there is a common enthusiasm of all parties at the North for the support of the admn. I may stand alone, but I do not share this. I am extremely anxious to hear from you. Do write me your views. I chafe terribly under the impossibilities which alone prevent my hastening home. Not only have I not the means, but I cannot leave my debts here, when a short, prolonged stay will probably assure me the means of paying them. Then I shall come, to do my best in the fight at home for *peaceful* separation if reunion has become indeed impossible.

What will New York do? I trust devoutly that if any troops march from our State southward they may consist only of Republicans. My hope now is that the North will at last realize the mad horror of the whole thing, and that a cloud of witnesses will arise to protest against its being carried further. Thus far the country has drifted along, both sides standing obstinate to the consistency of their opposite *theories*. But surely all, should now agree to pause and hold back! But the Republican leaders, I fear, will now move heaven and hell to push and drag the North to sustain them in the position to which they have brought things. And I fear much from the fighting character of our people. I dread the next news. If Maryland goes with Virginia, there will probably be dreadful fighting for the possession of Washington, unless the wise and patriotic like you can stop it.

We are exemplifying the fable of the dispute between the head and the tail of the snake for the right to lead. The Democratic party is the natural and the only possible government of our Democratic confederation. It alone has ever understood the idea of State rights. The tail has taken its turn of leadership and you see to what a pass it has brought the country.

Were it not for the immediate question of fighting to grow out of the question of the possession of Washington, I should say it were best that the border States should now all go at once, so as to make the North feel the absurdity of further prosecution of war. But reunion is now, I fear, scarcely to be hoped for!

Ever yours,
J. L. O'Sullivan.

—BIGELOW, ed., *Letters and Literary Memorials of Samuel J. Tilden*

—————————— II.7 ——————————

"THE RACE OF PHILIP SIDNEYS IS NOT EXTINCT"

From his diplomatic post in Vienna the historian Motley watched with mounting anxiety the progress of the war. This letter to his old friend Dr. Holmes suggests something of the pride of the Boston aristocracy whose sons fought for the Union as the aristocrats of Virginia and South Carolina fought for independence.

The Wendell Holmes who had been wounded at Ball's Bluff was the later Justice of the U. S. Supreme Court, who said, "The generation that carried on the war has been set apart by its experience. Through our great good fortune our hearts were touched with fire."

John Lothrop Motley to Dr. O. W. Holmes.

Vienna, November 14th, 1861
My Dear Holmes,—Your letter of October 8th awaited me here. I need not tell you with what delight I read it, and with what gratitude I found you so faithful to the promises which we exchanged on board the *Europa*. . . . As soon as I read your letter I sat down to reply, but I had scarcely written

two lines when I received the first telegram of the Ball's Bluff affair. I instantly remembered what you had told me—that Wendell "was on the right of the advance on the Upper Potomac, the post of honour and danger," and it was of course impossible for me to write to you till I had learned more, and you may easily conceive our intense anxiety. The bare brutal telegram announcing a disaster arrives always four days before any details can possibly be brought. Well, after the four days came my London paper; but, as ill luck would have it, my American ones had not begun to arrive. At last, day before yesterday, I got a New York *Evening Post*, which contained Frank Palfrey's telegram. Then our hearts were saddened enough by reading, "Willie Putnam, killed; Lee, Revere, and George Perry, captured;" but they were relieved of an immense anxiety by the words, "O. W. Holmes, jun., slightly wounded."

Poor Mrs. Putnam! I wish you would tell Lowell (for to the mother or father I do not dare to write) to express the deep sympathy which I feel for their bereavement, that there were many tears shed in our little household in this distant place for the fate of his gallant, gentle-hearted, brave spirited nephew. I did not know him much—not at all as grown man—but the name of Willie Putnam was a familiar sound to us six years ago on the banks of the Arno, for we had the pleasure of passing a winter in Florence at the same time with the Putnams, and I knew that that studious youth promised to be all which his name and his blood and the influences under which he was growing up entitled him to become. We often talked of American politics I mean his father and mother and ourselves—and I believe that we thoroughly sympathized in our views and hopes. Alas, they could not then foresee that that fair-haired boy was after so short a time destined to lay down his young life on the Potomac, in one of the opening struggles for freedom and law with the accursed institution of slavery! Well, it is a beautiful death—the most beautiful that man can die. Young as he was, he had gained name and fame, and his image can never be associated in the memory of the hearts which mourn for him except with ideas of honor, beauty, and purity of manhood.

After we had read the New York newspaper, the next day came a batch of Boston dailies and a letter from my dear little Mary. I seized it with avidity and began to read it aloud, and before I had finished the first page it dropped from my hand and we all three burst into floods of tears. Mary wrote that Harry Higginson. of the 2nd, had visited the camp of the 20th, and that Wendell Holmes was shot through the lungs and not likely to recover. It seemed too cruel, just as we had been informed that he was but slightly wounded. After the paroxysm was over, I picked up the letter and read a rather important concluding phrase of Mary's statement, viz., "But this, thank God, has proved to be a mistake." I think if you could have been clairvoyant, and looked in up on our dark little sitting-room of the Archduke Charles Hotel, fourth storey, at that moment, you could have had proof enough, if you needed any fresh ones, of the strong hold that you and yours have on all our affections. There are very many youths in that army of freedom whose career we watch with intense interest; but Wendell Holmes is ever in our thoughts side by side with those of our own name and blood.

I renounce all attempt to paint my anxiety about our affairs. I do not regret that Wendell is with the army. It is a noble and healthy symptom that brilliant, intellectual, poetical spirits like his spring to arms when a noble cause like ours inspires them. The race of Philip Sidneys is not yet extinct, and I honestly believe that as much genuine chivalry exists in our Free States at this moment as there is or ever was in any part of the world, from the Crusaders down. I did not say a word when I was at home to Lewis Stackpole about his plans—but I was very glad when he wrote to me that he had accepted a captaincy in Stevenson's regiment. I suppose by this time that they are in the field. . . .

Nobody on this side the Atlantic has the faintest conception of our affairs. Let me hear from time to time, as often as you can, how you are impressed by the current events, and give me details of such things as immediately interest you. Tell me all about Wendell. How does your wife stand her trials? Give my love to her and beg her to keep a brave heart. *Haec olim meminisse juvabit.* And how will those youths who stay at home "account themselves accursed they were not there," when the great work has been done, as done it will be! Of that I am as sure as that there is a God in heaven.

—CURTIS, ed., *The Correspondence of John Lothrop Motley*

II.8

THE SUPREME COURT UPHOLDS THE CONSTITUTION

Was the rebellion a war? Could the President proclaim a blockade, raise troops, and exercise, generally, war powers, without a recognition of a state of war by the Congress? These questions were not entirely in the realm of speculation. Alleging that only Congress could declare war, that there had been no such declaration or even recognition of war by Congress, that a blockade is an instrument of war, and that the Presidential proclamation of the blockade was therefore illegal, a group of owners of ships seized as prizes for trying to run the blockade sued for recovery of their property.

Justice Grier, in his decision in the so-called Prize Cases, recognized the existence of a state of war, sustained the blockade, and denounced the illegality of secession. But it was a close thing. Astonishing at it seems, today, four judges dissented.

Mr. Justice Grier:

Let us inquire whether, at the time this blockade was instituted, a state of war existed which would justify a resort to these means of subduing the hostile force.

War has been well defined to be, "That state in which a nation prosecutes its right by force."

The parties belligerent in a public war are independent nations. But it is not necessary, to constitute war, that both parties should be acknowledged as independent nations or sovereign States. A war may exist where one of the belligerents claims sovereign rights as against the other.

Insurrection against a government may or may not culminate in an organized rebellion, but a civil war always be gins by insurrection against the lawful authority of the government. A civil war is never solemnly declared; it be comes such by its accidents—the number, power, and organization of-the persons who originate and carry it on. When the party in rebellion occupy and hold in a hostile manner a certain portion of territory; have declared their in dependence; have cast off their allegiance; have organized armies; have commenced hostilities against their former Sovereign, the world acknowledges them as belligerents, and the contest a war. They claim to be in arms to establish their liberty and independence, in order to become a sovereign State, while the sovereign party treats them as insurgents and rebels who owe allegiance, and who should be punished with death for their treason. . . .

As a civil war is never publicly proclaimed, *eo nomine* against insurgents. its actual existence is a fact in our domes tic history which the court is bound to notice and to know. . . .

This greatest of civil wars was not gradually developed by popular commotion, tumultuous assemblies, or local unorganized insurrections. However long may have been its previous conception, it nevertheless sprung forth suddenly from the parent brain, a Minerva in the full panoply of war. The President was bound to meet it in the shape it presented itself, without waiting for Congress to baptize it with a name; and no name given to it by him or them could change the fact.

It is not the less a civil war, with belligerent parties in hostile array, because it may be called an "insurrection" by one side, and the insurgents be considered as rebels or traitors. It is not necessary that the independence of the revolted province or State be acknowledged in order to constitute it a party belligerent in a war according to the law of nations. Foreign nations acknowledge it as war by a declaration of neutrality. The condition of neutrality cannot exist unless there be two belligerent parties. . . .

After such an official recognition by the sovereign, a citizen of a foreign State is estopped to deny the existence of a war, with all its consequences, as regards neutrals. They can not ask a court to affect a technical ignorance of the existence of a war, which all the world acknowledges to be the greatest civil war known in the history of the human race, and thus cripple the arm of the government and paralyze its power by subtile definitions and ingenious sophisms.

The law of nations is also called the law of nature—it is founded on the common consent as well as the common sense of the world. It contains no such anomalous doctrine as that which this court are now for the first time desired to pronounce, to wit: That insurgents who have risen in rebellion against their sovereign, expelled her courts, established a revolutionary government, organized armies, and commenced hostilities, are not enemies because they are traitors; and a war levied on the government by traitors, in order to dismember and destroy it, is not a war because it is an "insurrection."

—*Prize Cases*, 67 United States Supreme Court Reports 635 (1863)

III

THE GATHERING OF
THE HOSTS

Looking back on four years of war Lincoln said, in his memorable Second Inaugural Address, "Neither party expected for the war the magnitude or the duration which it has already attained. Each looked for an easier triumph, and a result less fundamental and astounding."

Certainly neither side was prepared for a long war or even for a hard one. Northerners could hardly believe that the South would actually fight; Southerners deluded themselves that Yankee traders and workingmen were unwilling to fight. The North had a regular army of some 16,000, but with secession many of these resigned to go with their states; the South had no army, though as early as February 28 the President had been authorized to accept such state troops as were offered.

The firing on Fort Sumter inspired widespread enthusiasm in the South; in the North it inspired not so much enthusiasm as sober loyalty to the flag and the Union. Everywhere, North and South, boys and men rallied to the colors; everywhere great crowds assembled to see the new recruits march off to some near-by camp, proud of their improvised uniforms, happily unaware of what lay ahead.

> North and South they assembled, one cry and the other cry.
> And both are ghosts to us now, old drums hung up on
>   a wall,
> But they were the first hot wave of youth too-ready to die,
> And they went to war with an air, as if they went to a ball.
> Dress-uniform boys who rubbed their buttons brighter
>   than gold,
> And gave them to girls for flowers and raspberry lemonade,

> Unused to the sick fatigue, the route-march made in
>   the cold,
> The stink of the fever camps, the tarnish rotting the
>   blade.[*]

By act of March 8, 1861, the Confederate Congress created an army of seven regiments with enlistments for from three to five years. Two months later the President was authorized to accept the services of all volunteers who presented themselves. For the most part, however, the Confederacy raised its army through the states; some states even provided for conscription, on their own. As volunteering proved inadequate, the Confederate government adopted conscription; an act of April l6, 1862, made all men between the ages of 18 and 35 subject to draft, and these age limits were later broadened to embrace a11 between 17 and 50.

On April l5, 1861, Lincoln called for 75,000 three-months volunteers, assigning quotas to each state and Territory. The method of raising companies was left pretty much to the states and localities. The initiative was usually taken by local leaders who undertook to recruit companies—and get themselves elected to captaincies or lieutenancies. When an appropriate number of volunteers had been pledged (many deserted to other companies), the governor of the state would enroll the company in the state militia and assume appropriate expenses. Such matters as providing uniforms arms, equipment, even provisions, were handled haphazardly, sometimes these things were provided by rich men who raised the companies, sometimes by community effort, but usually by the states.

The first call for troops proved inadequate and on May 3 the President called for an additional 500,000; actually 700,000 were raised under this call. Thereafter came a series of calls for varying numbers and for varying periods of service. Altogether the

---

[*] From *John Brown's Body* in *The Selected Works of Stephen Vincent Benét*, published by Rinehart and Company, Inc. Copyright 1927, 1928 by Stephen Vincent Benét.

states were required to raise 2,763,670 troops, and furnished 2,772,408, but this figure includes re enlistments. Perhaps two thirds of these actually served in the army.

This is as good a place as any to deal with the vexatious question of numbers in the Union and Confederate armies. Let it be said at once that the statistics for the Union armies are confusing and unreliable, and that there are no satisfactory statistics whatever for the Confederate armies. A number of considerations enter into even the most elementary computations. There is, for example, the problem of differing periods of service. In both armies service varied from three months to three years, or the duration of the war: obviously a soldier in for four years counts more than one in for three or six months. There is the difficult question of desertion, or failure to report (which was technical desertion); this ran as high as ten per cent in both armies. There is the problem of re-enlistment, and of bounty jumping. There is the problem of the wounded and the sick; these were in the army, but were of course inevectives.

Frederick Phisterer, statistician of the Union armies, gives a total of 2,772,408 furnished by the states and Territories, or credited to them; reducing this to a three-year-service standard he arrives at the figure 2,320,272. Thomas Livermore, whose Numbers and Losses is perhaps more reliable, estimates total enlistments of 2,898,304 of whom some 230,000 failed to serve, for one reason or another. Reducing this figure to a three-years-service equivalent—and taking in to account desertion—he gives a total of 1,556,678 for the Union armies. Estimates of the numbers in the Confederate Army run all the way from a low of 600,000 to a high of 1,500,000. Livermore's estimate of the number equivalent to three-years service is 1,082,119—perhaps as good as any.

Far more illuminating are the numbers actually on the rolls at any one time: this gives a much truer index of relative numbers. The simplest thing here is to reproduce the table which Livermore worked out for Official Records:

		Union	Confederate
July	1861	186,751	112,040
Jan.	1862	575,917	351,418
Mar.	1862	637,126	401,395
Jan.	1863	918,121	446,622
Jan.	1864	860,737	481,180
Jan.	1865	959,460	445,203

Two conclusions emerge from these figures. First that a relatively much higher proportion of Southern than Northern men served in the army. Second that, given the requirements of offensive warfare, of invasion, and of maintaining long lines of communication, the North had far less effective numerical superiority than the bare figures would suggest.

"Our People Are All United"

A member of a great Huguenot family of South Carolina, Henry William Ravenel is remembered for his career as one of the leading American botanists and for his charming and illuminating *Journal,* from which this account of the impact of the war is taken.

[April 18, 1861] . . . This morning Mr. Cornish called to see us. One of the remarkable features of the times is that men of all classes & conditions, of all occupations & professions are of one mind. We have students of Divinity & ministers of the Gospel in the ranks with musket on their shoulders doing battle for their country. Some have gone as chaplains & followed their companies into camp. 1411 give us their prayers & cheer us onward with words of approval. The ablest vindication of our institution of domestic slavery has only lately been published in New York from the pen of Dr. Seabury, a distinguished minister of the Prot. Epis. Church. The war feeling has been nourished & stimulated at the North by the intense hatred of disappointed politicians & mad fanatics, who would consummate their hellish purposes upon us through a sea of blood if possible. The collision which has just taken place, from their determined purpose to hold a fort in our waters & thus subject us to a humiliating position, will probably raise a fury of excitement & bring over many to their side, who think their Govt. should be sustained in war, right or wrong;—but we have great numbers of staunch friends, who will be heard in time, as soon as the first paroxysm is over. Old memories of former party attachments, personal intercourse with Southerners, connections by friendships & blood, & above all, self interest will bring about a reaction & sober second thought will give them time for consideration, & to mature a public feeling there, which even those who are thirsting for our blood, will have to respect. . . .

Th. 25 . . . The New York Herald speaks of raising 500000 men & speedily conquering a peace.

Easier said than done. We can do the same if necessary & fighting for our liberty & our homes, we have no doubt of the issue. All good men should ardently desire a return of peace, but it must be upon terms honorable to us & our rights. I fear the Northern people have an impression that we are unable to cope with them, from inferiority in numbers, want of necessary means; & that our slave population is an element of weakness. It may be necessary therefore that they should be disabused of such impressions, & learn to appreciate & understand us better. If we must pass through the terrible ordeal of War to teach them this lesson, so be it. It may be best in the end. We put our trust in the God of battles & the impartial Dispenser of Justice, & are willing to abide the issue. Our people are all united & stand up as one man in defence of their country. Our Negroes are contented & loyal. The old & the infirm who have not yet gone out to battle are ready to take their places in the ranks when their services are needed. Our women & children all enthusiastic for the common defence, 'Can such a population be subjugated?'. . .

M. 29 . . . We have never sought to assail the Northern people in any way—we have only asked to be let alone. We have been satisfied, in the sight of God & of our approving conscience, that our institutions were sanctioned by justice & religion, that mutual benefits were secured to both races inhabiting our Southern states—that our very existence as a people was staked upon its preservation;—& that it has the sanction of natural, as well as revealed religion. They have re fused to permit us to remain in peace with them, & now that we have decided as a last effort of self preservation to establish a governt. for ourselves, they insolently threaten us with subjugation. We have desired to separate from them in peace, & have offered to negotiate on friendly terms the manner of separation. They have rejected all our overtures & have answered us with insult & defiance. They appeal to arms. We will meet them, putting our trust in Him who is the father of us all & in whose hands are the destinies of his people.

—CHILDS, ed., *The Private Journal of Henry William Ravenel*

SOUTHERN LADIES SEND THEIR MEN OFF TO WAR

Here is an unpretentious recollection of the impact of secession and war on a Georgia community. The enthusiasm of the women of the South for the war was remarked by countless contemporaries and has served as a theme for countless novels and stories. What Mrs. Ward says of the situation in Rome might have been said with equal truth about almost every other Southern community—"if the Southern men had not been willing to go I reckon they would have been made to go by the women."

Mrs. Ward was a Georgia matron of twenty when the war came; these recollections were given verbally to a Congressional committee investigating labor relations in the South. Douglas Freeman calls them "one of the most remarkable of all the women's commentaries on the war."

Well, it was pretty hard for any one in private life, especially for a lady, to realize or appreciate the imminent danger that existed up to the very breaking out of the war, up to the time that the troops were ordered out. Discussions about the state of the country and about the condition of public affairs and the causes for war were frequent, of course, and I think I may safely say that in those discussions the women of the South without exception all took the secession side. There were a great many men in the Southern homes that were disposed to be more conservative and to regret the threatened disruption of the Union, but the ladies were all enthusiastically in favor of secession. Their idea was to let war come if it must, but to have the matter precipitated and get through with it, because this feeling of apprehension and this political wrangling had been continued for many years previous, and we felt that we in the South were strong in our own resources, and in fact we knew very little of the resources of the North compared with those of the South. My mother was a Northern woman and she always regarded the threat of war with the greatest apprehension and fear, because, as she said, she knew more about the resources of the North than others did, more than I did, for instance, or the other people of my age. But the women of the South generally were altogether in favor of secession and of the war, if there had to be a war, and if the Southern men had not been willing to go I reckon they would have been made to go by the women.

The day that Georgia was declared out of the Union was a day of the wildest excitement in Rome. There was no order or prearrangement about it all, but the people met each other and shook hands and exchanged congratulations over it and manifested the utmost enthusiasm. Of course a great many of the older and wiser heads looked on with a great deal of foreboding at these rejoicings and evidences of delight, but the general feeling was one of excitement and joy.

Then we began preparing our soldiers for the war. The ladies were all summoned to public places, to halls and lecture-rooms, and sometimes to churches, and everybody who had sewing-machines were invited to send them; they were never demanded because the mere suggestion was all sufficient. The sewing-machines were sent to these places and ladies that were known to be experts in cutting out garments were engaged in that part of the work, and every lady in town was turned into a seamstress and worked as hard as anybody could work; and the ladies not only worked themselves but they brought colored seamstresses to these places, and these halls and public places would be just filled with busy women all day long.

But even while we were doing all these things in this enthusiastic manner, of course there was a great deal of the pathetic manifested in connection with this enthusiasm, be cause we knew that the war meant the separation of our soldiers from their friends and families and the possibility of their not coming back. Still, while we spoke of these things we really did not think that there was going to be actual war. We had an idea that when our soldiers got upon the ground and showed, unmistakably, that they were really ready and willing to fight—an idea that then, by some sort of hocus pocus, we didn't know what, the whole trouble would be declared at an end. Of course we were not fully conscious of that feeling at the time, but that the feeling existed was beyond doubt from the great disappointment that showed itself afterwards when things turned out differently. We got our soldiers ready for the field, and the Governor of Georgia called out the troops and they were ordered out, five companies from Floyd County and three from Rome. They were ordered to Virginia under the command of General Joseph E. Johnston. The young men carried dress suits with them and any quantity of fine linen. . . .

Every soldier, nearly, had a servant with him, and a whole lot of spoons and forks, so as to live comfortably and elegantly in camp, and finally to make a splurge in Washington when they should arrive there, which they expected would be very soon indeed. That is really the way they went off; and their sweethearts gave them embroidered slippers and pin-cushions and needle-books, and all sorts of such little et ceteras, and they finally got off, after having a very eloquent discourse preached to them at the Presbyterian church, by the Presbyterian minister, Rev. John A. Jones. I remember his text very well. It was, "Be strong and quit yourselves like men." I don't know that I have had occasion to think of that sermon for years, but although this occurred more than twenty years ago, I remember it very distinctly at this moment. Then the choir played music of the most mournful character—"Farewell," and "Good Bye," and all that, and there was just one convulsive sob from one end of the church to the other, for the congregation was composed of the mothers and wives and sisters and daughters of the soldiers who were marching away.

The captain of the Light Guards, the most prominent company, a company composed of the *elite* of the town, had been married on the Thursday evening before this night of which I am speaking. He was a young Virginian. His wife came of very patriotic parents, and was a very brave woman herself. She came into the church that day with her husband, and walked up the aisle with him. She had on a brown traveling-dress, and a broad scarf crossed on her dress, and, I think, on it was inscribed, "The Rome Light Guards," and there was a pistol on one side and a dagger on the other. This lady went to the war with her husband, and staid there through the whole struggle, and never came home until the war was over.

—Testimony of Mrs. Mary A. Ward

III.3

THE NORTH BUILDS A VAST ARMY OVERNIGHT

The United States was notoriously unprepared for war, and the temper of the people—in the North even more than in the South—was pacific. Many foreign critics doubted that a nation without military traditions or a military caste could organize for war. Edward Dicey, a liberal English journalist and scholar, spent six months in the United States in the midst of the Civil War and, after his return, hastened to publish a book giving his country-men a better appreciation of the Union cause. Another Englishman, the novelist Anthony Trollope, who visited the United States during these years, was similarly impressed by the might of the North.

Surely no nation in the world has gone through such a baptism of war as the people of the United States underwent in one short year's time. With the men of the Revolution the memories of the revolutionary wars had died out. Two generations had passed away to whom war was little more than a name. The Mexican campaign was rather a military demonstration than an actual war, and the sixteen years which had elapsed since its termination form a long period in the life of a nation whose whole existence has not completed its first century. Twenty months ago there were not more than 12,000 soldiers in a country of 31,000,000. A soldier was as rare an object throughout America as in one of our country hamlets. I recollect a Northern lady telling me that, till within a year before, she could not recall the name of a single person whom

she had ever known in the army, and that now she had sixty friends and relatives who were serving in the war; and her case was by no means an uncommon one.

Once in four years, on the fourth of March, two or three thousand troops were collected in Washington to add to the pomp of the Presidential inauguration; and this was the one military pageant the country had to boast of. Almost in a day this state of things passed away. Our English critics were so fond of repeating what the North could not do—how it could not fight, nor raise money, nor conquer the South—that they omitted to mention what the North *had* done. There was no need to go farther than my windows at Washington to see the immensity of the war. It was curious to me to watch the troops as they came marching past. Whether they were regulars or volunteers, it was hard for the unprofessional critic to discern; for all were clad alike, in the same dull, grey-blue overcoats, and most of the few regular regiments were filled with such raw recruits that the difference between volunteer and regular was not a marked one.

Of course it was easy enough to pick faults in the aspect of such troops. As each regiment marched or rather waded through the dense slush, and mud which covered the roads, you could observe many inaccuracies of military attire. One man would have his trousers rolled up almost to his knees; another would wear them tucked inside his boots; and a third would appear with one leg of his trousers hanging down, and the other gathered tightly up. It was not unfrequent, too, to see an officer with his epaulettes sewed on to a common plain frock-coat. Then there was a slouching gait about the men, not soldierlike to English eyes. They used to turn their heads round when on parade, with an indifference to rule which would drive an old drill-sergeant out of his senses. There was an absence, also, of precision in the march. The men kept in step; but I always was at a loss to discover how they ever managed to do so. The system of march, it is true, was copied rather from the French than the English or Austrian fashion; but

still it was something very different from the orderly disorder of a Zouave march. That all these, and a
score of similar irregularities, are faults, no one—an
American least of all—would deny. But there are
two sides to the picture.

One thing is certain, that there is no physical
degeneracy about a race which could produce such
regiments as those which formed the army of the
Potomac. Men of high stature and burly frames
were rare, except in the Kentucky troops; but, on
the other hand, small, stunted men were almost
unknown. I have seen the armies of most
European countries; and I have no hesitation in
saying that, as far as the average raw material of
the rank and file is concerned, the American army
is the finest.

The officers are, undoubtedly, the weak point
of the system. They have not the military air, the
self-possession which long habit of command alone
can give; while the footing of equality on which
they inevitably stand with the volunteer privates,
deprives them of the esprit de corps belonging to a
ruling class. Still they are active, energetic, and
constantly with their troops.

Wonderfully well equipped too, at this period
of the war, were both officers and men. Their
clothing was substantial and fitted easily, their arms
were good, and the military arrangements were as
perfect as money alone could make them.

It was remarkable to me how rapidly the new
recruits fell into the habits of military service. I
have seen a Pennsylvanian regiment, raised chiefly
from the mechanics of Philadelphia, which, six
weeks after its formation, was, in my eyes, equal to
the average of our best-trained volunteer corps, as
far as marching and drill-exercise went. Indeed, I
often asked myself what it was that made the
Northern volunteer troops look, as a rule, so much
more soldier-like than our own. I suppose the reason is, that across the Atlantic there was actual
war, and that at home there was at most only a
parade. I have no doubt that, in the event of civil
war or invasion, England would raise a million volunteers as rapidly as America has done—more
rapidly she could not; and that, when fighting had

once begun, there would only be too much of grim
earnestness about our soldiering; but it is not want
of patriotism to say that the American volunteers
looked to me more businesslike than our own. At
the scene of war itself there was no playing at soldiering. No gaudy uniforms or crack companies, no
distinction of classes. From every part of the North;
from the ports of New York and Boston; from the
homesteads of New England; from the mines of
Pennsylvania and the factories of Pittsburgh; from
the shores of the great lakes; from the Mississippi
valley; and from the far-away Texan prairies, these
men had come to fight for the Union. It is idle to
talk of their being attracted by the pay alone. Large
as it is, the pay of thirteen dollars a month is only
two dollars more than the ordinary pay of privates
in the Federal army during peace times. Thirteen
shillings a week is poor pay for a labouring man in
America, even with board, especially during this
war, when the wages of unskilled labour amounted
to from twenty to thirty shillings a week. . . .

The bulk of the native volunteers consisted of
men who had given up good situations in order to
enlist, and who had families to support at home;
and for such men the additional pay was not an
adequate inducement to incur the dangers and
hardships of war. Of course, wherever there is an
army, the scum of the population will always be
gathered together; but the average morale and
character of the couple of hundred thousand
troops collected round Washington was extremely
good. There was very little outward drunkenness,
and less brawling about the streets than if half a
dozen English militia regiments had been quartered there. The number of papers purchased daily
by the common soldiers, and the amount of letters
which they sent through the military post, was
astonishing to a foreigner, though less strange
when you considered that every man in that army,
with the exception of a few recent immigrants,
could both read and write. The ministers, also, of
the different sects, who went out on the Sundays
to preach to the troops, found no difficulty in
obtaining large and attentive audiences.

—DICEY, *Six Months in the Federal States*

III.4

Northern Boys Join the Ranks

We have here three brief accounts of the process of recruiting companies. Warren Goss of the 2nd Massachusetts Artillery contributes the first; he fought through most of the campaigns in the East, was twice captured and exchanged, and lived to write a number of livelyy books on the war.

Josiah Favill, who got himself a commission as a lieutenant, rose to be brevet colonel before the end of the war; his diary is one of the better accounts of the war in the East.

The third, and the most realistic of them all, is from the pen of Michael Fitch, of the 6th (later the 21st) Wisconsin Volunteers; Fitch was brevetted out as a colonel at the end of the war.

A. Warren Goss Enlists in the Union Army

Before the war had really begun I enlisted. I had read the papers, and attended flag-raisings, and heard orators declaim of "undying devotion to the Union." One speaker to whom I listened declared that "human life must be cheapened," but I never learned that he helped on the work experimentally. When men by the hundred walked soberly and deliberately to the front and signed the enlistment papers, he didn't show any inclination that way. As I came out of the hall with conflicting emotions, feeling as though I should have to go finally or forfeit my birthright as an American citizen, one of the orators who stood at the door, glowing with enthusiasm and patriotism, and shaking hands effusively with those who enlisted, said to me:

"Did you enlist?"

"No," I said, "Did you?"

"No; they won't take me. I have got a lame leg and a widowed mother to take care of."

Another enthusiast I remember, who was eager to enlist—others. He declared the family of no man who went to the front should suffer. After the war he was prominent among those in our town who at town meeting voted to refund the money to such as had expended it to procure substitutes during the war. He has, morever, been fierce and uncompro-

mising toward the ex-Confederates since the war closed, and I have heard him repeatedly express the wish that all the civil and general officers of the late Confederacy might be court-martialled and shot.

I was young, but not unobserving, and did not believe, from the first, in a sixty days' war; nor did I consider ten dollars a month and the promised glory, large pay for the services of an able-bodied young man. Enlistment scenes are usually pictured as entirely heroic, but truth compels me to acknowledge that my feelings were mixed. At this moment I cannot repress a smile of amusement and pity for that young recruit—myself.

It was the news that the Sixth Massachusetts Regiment had been mobbed by roughs on their passage through Baltimore which gave me the war fever. When I read Governor Andrews' pathetic telegram to have the hero martyrs "preserved in ice and tenderly sent forward," somehow, though I felt the pathos of it, I could not reconcile myself to the ice. Ice in connection with patriotism did not give me agreeable impressions of the war, and when I came to think of it, the stoning of the heroic "sixth" didn't suit me; it detracted from my desire to die a soldier's death. I lay awake all night thinking it over, with the "ice" and "brickbats" before my mind. However, the fever culminated that night, and I resolved to enlist.

"Cold chills" ran up and down my back as I got out of bed after the sleepless night, and shaved, preparatory to other desperate deeds of valor. I was twenty years of age, and when anything unusual was to be done, like fighting or courting, I shaved. With a nervous tremor convulsing my whole system, and my heart thumping like muffled drum beats, I stood before the door of the recruiting office and before turning the knob to enter, read and re-read the advertisement for recruits posted thereon, until I knew all its peculiarities. The promised chances for "travel and promotion" seemed good, and I thought I might have made a mistake in considering war so serious after all. "Chances for travel." I must confess now, after four years of soldiering, that the "chances for travel" were no myth. But "promotion" was a little uncertain and slow.

I was in no hurry to open the door. Though determined to enlist I was half inclined to put it off awhile; I had a fluctuation of desires; I was faint-hearted and brave; I wanted to enlist,—and yet Here I turned the knob, and was relieved. I had been more prompt, with all my hesitation, than the officer in his duty; he wasn't in.

Finally he came and said: "What do you want, my boy?"

"I want to enlist," I responded, blushing deeply with upwelling patriotism and bashfulness. Then the surgeon came to strip and examine me. In justice to myself, it must be stated that I signed the rolls without a tremor. It is common to the most of humanity, I believe, that when confronted with actual danger, men have less fear than in its contemplation.

My first uniform was a bad fit; my trousers were too long by three or four inches; the flannel shirt was coarse and unpleasant, too large at the neck and too short elsewhere. The forage cap was an ungainly bag with pasteboard top and leather visor; the blouse was the only part which seemed decent; while the overcoat made me feel like a little nib of corn amid a preponderance of husk. Nothing except "Virginia mud" ever took down my ideas of military pomp quite so low.

After enlisting I didn't seem of so much consequence as I expected. There was not so much excitement on account of my military appearance as I deemed justly my due. I was taught my facings, and at the time I thought the drill-master needlessly fussy about shouldering, ordering, and presenting arms. At this time men were often drilled in company and regimental evolutions long before they learned the manual of arms, because of the difficulty of obtaining muskets. These we obtained at an early day, but we would willingly have resigned them after carrying them for a few hours. The musket, after an hour's drill, seemed heavier and less ornamental than it had looked to be. The first day I went out to drill, getting tired of doing the same

things over and over, I said to the drill-sergeant: "Let's stop this fooling and go over to the grocery."

His only reply was addressed to the corporal: "Corporal, take this man out and drill him like hell."; and the corporal did. I found that suggestions were not as well appreciated in the army as in private life, and that no wisdom was equal to a drill-master's. "Right face," "Left wheel," and "Right, oblique, march."

It takes a raw recruit some time to learn that he is not to think or suggest, but obey. Some never do learn. I acquired it at last, in humility and mud, but it was tough. Yet I doubt if my patriotism, during my first three weeks' drill, was quite knee high. Drilling looks easy to a spectator, but it isn't. . . . After a time I cut down my uniform so that I could see out of it, and conquered the drill sufficiently to see through it. Then the word came: On to Washington!. . .

We bad adieu to our friends with heavy hearts, for lightly as I may seem to treat the subject, it was no light thing for a boy of twenty to start out for three years into the unknown dangers of a civil war. Our mothers—God bless them!—had brought us something good to eat,—pies, cakes, doughnuts, and jellies. Our young ladies, (sisters, of course) brought an invention, generally made of leather or cloth, containing needles, pins, thread, buttons, and scissors, so that nearly every recruit had an embryo tailor's shop—with the goose outside. One old lady, in the innocence of her heart, brought her son an umbrella. We did not see anything particularly laughable about it at the time, but our old drill-sergeant did.

—Goss, *Recollections of a Private*

B. Lieutenant Favill Raises a Company and Gets a Commission

As soon as I was mustered out of service with the Seventy-First regiment I lost no time in seeking for a commission, fully determined to return to the field, but not as a private soldier. I soon found that commissions were to be obtained only by securing a certain number of men to enlist, and so after apply-

ing to various organizations in every state of for
mation, all with the same results, in connection
with an ex Danish officer, Julius Ericcson, living in
Brooklyn, I set to work to raise the requisite number of men to secure the prize.

New York and Brooklyn were transformed
into immense recruiting camps. In all the public
squares and parks hundreds of tents were erected,
covered with flags and immense colored bills, on
which the advantage of the various branches of
the service were fully stated. There were bands of
music and scores of public speakers, all engaged by
patriotic citizens, to stimulate the military ardor of
the other fellow, and get him to enlist for three
years.

We soon found a great change had come over
the spirit of the people since the departure of the
military regiments in April. Then, everybody
wanted to go; now, apparently, most people wanted to stay at home. We put up a wall tent in the
New York City Hall Park, and another at the
junction of the Atlantic and Flatbush Avenues,
Brooklyn, in an open lot. The captain and I took
turns in attendance in New York, while John
Ericcson, the captain's eldest son, who was to go
out as orderly sergeant, was put in charge of the
Brooklyn tent. We got some immense posters
printed, and among other inducements offered by
our company was the experience of the future officers, one gained in a foreign service, the other on
the field of Bull Run. Notwithstanding these
seeming advantages, our best efforts, and the
prodigious enthusiasm of the times, recruiting
proved very slow. I coaxed one man into enlisting, through my knowledge of the Crimean War,
one Stuart, a fine six-foot Englishman who had
served in the Crimean War and had been a soldier
in the British army almost all his life. He took
hold with a will, and we put him in charge of the
tent as second sergeant.

As the recruiting proved so slow at home, it
was decided to send me, at the expense of the
State, to Oswego, N. Y., and there I promptly
repaired; advertised in both the daily papers, setting

forth the advantages of a metropolitan regiment.
While there I enjoyed the brief distinction of being
the only man in town who had been at Bull Run,
and in consequence, was feted and honored as an
exceptional personage.

With the assistance of a young man named
Hamilton, native there, I actually obtained some
twenty-nine or thirty men, and was just upon the
point of starting with them to New York, when
they deserted in a body, and went over to one of
the local organizations. Disgusted, I returned immediately, and in a few days afterwards went to
Poughkeepsie, and remained there for two weeks,
but succeeded in getting only about half a dozen
men, mostly from Wappingers Falls. I was taken,
while in that place, with a severe attack of fever
and ague and was almost shaken to pieces.

Considering the ground no longer profitable I
returned home, and found we had already got more
than the number required by the State, to muster
us into its service, with a captain and first lieutenant; and so, on the 23rd of September, 1861, we
marched our company of recruits to the state arsnal
on Elm Street, where they were stripped naked,
examined by a surgeon, and all of them passed as
able bodied men. Then the mustering officer called
the roll, and every man in succession stepped one
pace to the front, took the oath of allegiance to the
State, and swore to serve as a soldier for three
years, or during the war. Immediately afterwards, in
compliance with the state law a very perfunctory
election of officers took place, in the presence of
the mustering officer; and Julius Ericcson was
declared duly elected captain and I the first lieutenant of the new company. The muster roll was
made out, signed by the mustering officer, and we
were at last in the service of the State; legally held
for duty, and under pay. Before leaving the arsenal,
the company was furnished with uniforms, underclothing, haversacks, canteens, and blankets, and at
once divested themselves of their citizen garb, and
emerged from the arsenal, looking something like
real soldiers.

—FAVILL, *The Diary of a Young Officer*

C. "We Thought the Rebellion Would Be Over Before Our Chance Would Come"

The region in northwestern Wisconsin, bounded on the west and northwest by the Mississippi and the St. Croix rivers, and contiguous thereto, in 1861 was sparsely settled. There was no railroad. Transportation was made either by steamboat on the water or by horses on the land. These factors made the raising of a volunteer company for service, an arduous task. When Mr. Lincoln made the first call for seventy-five thousand volunteers, the quota of Wisconsin was one regiment. At least, only one regiment of three months' men left the state under that call. That regiment, I believe, was largely made up of militia companies that had been previously organized and equipped. Yet active recruiting commenced at once all over the state in the latter part of April, 1861. I presume every company that was recruited in any part of the state at that time, made effort to get into that three months' regiment. The sentiment then was quite universal that three months would close the war. Hence, whoever failed to become a part of the first regiment would see no service and receive no military glory.

A mass meeting was held at once in our town, Prescott, Pierce County. Several addresses were made. Patriotism was effervescent, and thirty young men signed the roll of the Prescott Guards. We at once notified the Governor that we would like to be a part of the troops about to be called. But at that time, as we were informed, enough companies had been offered to fill four regiments. As only one regiment was called for three months, our little squad out on the northwestern border had very little show. This did not discourage this little patriotic band. They began drilling every day, studied the tactics, erected a liberty pole mounted by a bayonet, pointing south, with the stars and stripes floating from its top. The fiery spirit of '76, as we understood it, was thoroughly aroused. By April 30th, a full company was enlisted.

Daniel J. Dill, a prominent merchant who had military tastes and who afterwards became captain of the company, went up the river to Hastings, Minnesota, and down the river to various towns, in pursuit of recruits. Rollin P. Converse and myself took a pair of horses and a buggy and started into the back country. That ride across the prairie and through the woods for several days, was novel and exceedingly interesting. We visited, not only the towns, but every farm. At one town, I think River Falls, we met recruiting officers from Hudson, the county seat of the adjoining county of St. Croix, on the same errand. We held a joint meeting at night at which several addresses were made.

We found western pioneer hospitality everywhere. Every rugged backwoodsman, whether American, German or Norwegian, was full of patriotism. Indignation at the firing on Fort Sumter was genuine and universal. The roads, especially through the woods, were in a wretched condition. It rained, and the mud was frightful. One evening in a lonely spot in the primeval forest, a singletree of the buggy broke. But there stood, by the side of the road, a sturdy pioneer with an axe on his shoulder. In five minutes he had cut a hickory withe, twisted it into a pliable rope, tied it around the broken tree in the most skilful manner, and sent us on our way rejoicing, with a buggy stronger than it was before. Wherever we stopped over night the host would refuse pay for our entertainment. The mother and daughters would look after our comfort, even drying our apparel when wet with rain. Everywhere we were bidden Godspeed in our patriotic efforts.

How many recruits we procured on this trip, I have now forgotten. But some walked to Prescott for miles to enlist. The muster rolls of the company show that almost every township in Pierce County was represented among its members. There were no better soldiers in the army than many of these backwoods farmer boys. A number of them never returned. We had some enlistments from far up the St. Croix River among the lumbermen and loggers. Captain Dill was successful in getting recruits from Hastings, Menominee and other towns. A. C. Ellis, a bright-eyed boy with curly black hair brought quite a number from Menominee.

Before the first of May, between ninety and one hundred had taken the oath of service and allegiance to the United States. I administered the oath to each one who signed the enlistment. D. J. Dill was elected captain. Two alleged Mexican war veterans were made lieutenants. I was appointed first sergeant. The Governor was notified that we were ready for service. But, not only the first, but the second, third, fourth and fifth regiments of volunteer infantry were organized at Madison without our company being assigned. There was great uncertainty for some time after this about being called into service. The men went back to their homes, and some of them enlisted in other companies. We thought the rebellion would be over before our chance would come. However, by May 10th, we were informed that we were the sixth company in the sixth regiment.

—FITCH, *Echoes of the Civil War*

III.5

BALTIMORE MOBS ATTACK THE SIXTH MASSACHUSETTS

Massachusetts, which had been preparing since January, was the first state to respond to the President's call to arms. On April 16 the state militia began to muster at Boston, and on the following day the famous 6th Massachusetts started its historic trip to Washington. There was no through rail road connection to the capital at that time; the 6th, which reached Baltimore on the morning of April 19 had to ride on horsecars, or walk, from the Philadelphia, Wilmington and Baltimore Railroad station to the Baltimore and Ohio Railroad station. Seven companies managed to get through on horse cars; then a mob of Southern sympathizers erected street barricades to block the passage of the remaining four. The militia fought its way through, but at the cost of four killed and 36 wounded; the mob casualties are unknown.

"The excitement is fearful," the Governor of Maryland wired the President. "Send no more troops here." To avoid a repetition of the riot the Maryland authorities burned down the railroad bridges connecting Baltimore with Philadelphia and Harrisburg.

This Baltimore fracas excited, among other things, "Maryland! My Maryland!"

Early on the morning of April 19th, 1861, a train of thirty-five cars left the Broad and Washington avenue depot, Philadelphia, having on board twelve hundred troops from Boston, Lowell, and Acton, Massachusetts, and known as the Sixth Massachusetts Regiment, under the command of Colonel Edward F. Jones, a gallant soldier and courteous gentleman; and a regiment, one thousand strong, from Philadelphia, under the command of Colonel William F. Small. Nothing was known in Baltimore of their departure from Philadelphia, but about eleven o'clock it became noised abroad that a large force of Federal soldiers had arrived at President street depot. This depot is in the southeastern portion of the city, and is connected with the Baltimore and Ohio depot, which is situated in the southwestern section, by a line of rail along Pratt street—a leading thoroughfare—and some minor streets. It was necessary for the troops, on disembarking at President street depot, either to march to the Baltimore and Ohio depot or to be drawn thither in the cars by horses. The news of the arrival of the troops spread like wildfire, and in a comparatively short time an immense crowd gathered on Pratt street, with the intention of preventing the passage of the troops. While waiting for the appearance of the soldiers the crowd kept itself up to the requisite pitch of indignation and enthusiasm by "groaning" for Lincoln, Hicks, and the Federal Government, and by cheering Jefferson Davis and the Southern Confederacy.

The first intimation had by the city authorities that the troops were about to enter the city was received by Mayor Brown about ten o'clock. Mr. Brown at once repaired to the office of the Police Commissioners, but found that the Marshal of Police had already gone to Camden station, where he had concentrated his men by request of the railroad authorities. The Mayor at once followed him to Camden station, and on arriving there found him posted with his men prepared to put down any attack. Unfortunately the mob had gathered not at Camden station but on Pratt street, at a point a short distance west of the depot where the troops were disembarking. Pratt street is a narrow thoroughfare, and easily capable of defense. The strategical position of the mob was excellent as they proceeded to fortify it.

About half-past eleven o'clock a car drawn by horses was seen approaching, and was greeted by the mob with cheers for the South. The car, and eight others which followed, were, however, permitted to pass without any molestation, except the usual taunts and gibes at the occupants. A trivial accident, which happened to the tenth car, let loose all the elements of disorder in the mob, and precipitated the fatal conflict. As this car neared Commerce street the brake was accidentally thrown out of gear, and the car stopped. The crowd took advantage of the mishap at once, and began to attack the occupants with stones. Windows were broken, and a few of the soldiers were hurt, but not seriously. Finally the driver of the car became frightened, lost his head, and, having attached his team to the other end of the car, started to haul it back to the depot. The mob followed the car, stoning it all the while, but the driver having urged the horses to a run, succeeded in distancing them. A large portion of the mob, however, followed it into the depot.

The section of the mob which remained at the bridge on Pratt street then, under the advice of their leaders, many of whom, as I have said, were well known citizens of Baltimore, began to build a barricade, Paris fashion. They commenced by digging up the paving stones and the railroad track for a distance of some fifty yards. The stones were piled up with the iron rails, the bridges over the gutters were torn up, and eight large anchors which were found on the wharf near by were placed on the barricade. A car loaded with sand attempted to pass, but was seized by the rioters, who backed it up to the barricade, and emptied the sand on the pile of stones and anchors. A large number of Negroes were working on the wharves at the time. These were ordered to quit work, which they did with alacrity, and were directed by the rioters to assist them on the barricade. . . .

In the meantime, the commander of the Massachusetts troops, finding that the cars would not be permitted to pass through, decided to disembark his men and force a passage on foot through the mob. When this determination was announced, some confederates of the Pratt street rioters at once communicated the news to them. It was also rumored that the troops had decided to go by a different route to Camden station. A portion of the rioters at once started to head them off, while the main body maintained its position on Pratt street. A large crowd assembled at the depot during the disembarkation of the troops, and here several exciting, but not very sanguinary, encounters occurred between Unionists and secessionists in the crowd. As the troops descended from the cars they were hooted, jeered, and twitted. They succeeded, however, in forcing their way to the footway, which extends for several hundred yards along the outer edge of the depot, where they formed in double file and awaited the orders of their officers.

At this point a man appeared bearing a Confederate flag at the head of about one hundred rioters. His appearance was the signal for wild cheering. A rush for the flag was made by several Northern sympathizers in the crowd, and the flag-staff was broken. One of these men was caught by the flagbearer who, with his companions, throttled, and would have killed him, but for the interference of the police, who succeeded in bearing him away. The shreds of the flag were caught up and tied to the flag-staff. On being raised again they were saluted with an outburst of cheering.

The men surrounding the flag then began to taunt the troops, and declared that they would be forced to march behind it to the Camden depot. Colonel Jones gave the order to march, and the troops started. The men surrounding the flag, however, planted themselves directly in front of the soldiers and refused to yield an inch. The troops wheeled about, but found themselves surrounded on all sides, and were unable to move in any direction. Several of the soldiers were hustled away from their comrades, and would have been roughly used by the crowd but for the police, who succeeded, with great difficulty, in rescuing them. The troops again endeavored to force a passage, and this time, with the assistance of the police, they succeeded. As they started, however, the Confederate flag was borne to the front, and they were compelled to march for several squares behind this flag. Too much praise cannot be given to the commander or men for their admirable self-control during this trying episode.

The presence of the Confederate flag was the immediate cause of the sanguinary street fight and loss of life which followed. Several Northern sympathizers in the mob, exasperated at the triumph of the flag-bearer and his friends, made another dash for the flag, but were defeated and pursued. Some of them took refuge in the ranks of the soldiers. This exasperated the citizens against the soldiers, and a savage attack upon the latter was made with stones and other missiles. One of the soldiers, William Patch, was struck in the back with a large paving-stone, and fell to the ground. His musket was seized, and the poor wretch was brutally beaten by the rioters before the police could rescue him. When Patch was seen to fall Colonel Jones gave the order "double quick" to his men, and the whole column started off at a run, ducking and dipping to avoid the stones. At this the crowd set up a yell of derision and started after them full tilt. Two soldiers were knocked down, while running, but managed to make their escape—one of them with the assistance of the police.

While the foregoing events were transpiring in and near President street depot, an immense concourse of people had gathered at the barricade. When the troops appeared in full run a great shout was raised, and the head of the column was greeted with a shower of paving-stones. The troops faltered, and finally, in the face of a second shower of stones, came to a dead halt. The patience of their commander was at last exhausted. He cried out in a voice, which was heard even above the yells of the

mob, "Fire!" The soldiers leveled their pieces and the mob seemed to pause, as if to take breath. The soldiers fired. A young man, named F. X. Ward, now a well-known lawyer of this city, fell pierced by a ball. A hoarse yell of fear and rage went up from the mob, but it did not give way. The troops fired again and again, and the crowd wavering, they rushed upon them with fixed bayonets and forced a passage over the barricade.

A scene of bloody confusion followed. As the troops retreated, firing, the rioters rushed upon them only to be re pulsed by the line of bayonets. Some of the rioters fought like madmen. Finally, the mob, exasperated by their failure to prevent the passage of the troops, made a desperate rush upon them, and one young man, who was in the front rank of the rioters, was forced close upon the soldiery. One of the soldiers raised his gun, took deliberate aim at the rioter and fired. The cap exploded, but the gun failed to go off. The rioter rushed forward, seized the gun, wrested it by an almost super-human effort from the soldier's grasp, and plunged the bayonet through the man's shoulder.

During the firing a number of the rioters fell, killed and wounded. At the intersection of Charles and Pratt streets, Andrew Robbins, a soldier from Stoneham, Massachusetts, was shot in the neck by a rioter. He was carried into a drug store near by, and was protected from the mob. At Howard street a strong force of rioters from Camden station met the troops and refused to yield. The soldiers fired again and the mob gave way. The soldiers again started at the double quick and reached Camden station without further trouble. Thirteen cars were drawn out, and the soldiers left the depot amid the hisses and groans of the multitude.

One of the most remarkable features of the riot was the persistency and courage with which the mob hung on to the troops, in spite of the continued firing. Another remarkable feature was the extraordinary coolness and forbearance of the troops.

—FREDERIC EMORY, "The Baltimore Riots"

FRANK WILKESON GOES SOUTH WITH BLACKGUARDS, THIEVES, AND BOUNTY JUMPERS

Joining the army and entraining for the battle front was not all a matter of cheers and flag-waving. As the going got tougher and the government resorted increasingly to bounties, a regular system of bounty jumping sprang up, and the army had to take drastic measures to see to it that men who enlisted for bounties actually stayed in the army.

Frank Wilkeson, who found himself in the bad company which he here describes so graphically, was a Buffalo boy who later became lieutenant in the 4th United States Artillery and, after the war, worked on the staffs of the *New York Sun* and the *New York Times*.

The war fever seized me in 1863. All the summer and fall I had fretted and burned to be off. That winter, and before I was sixteen years old, I ran away from my father's high lying Hudson River valley farm. I went to Albany and enlisted in the Eleventh New York Battery, then at the front in Virginia, and was promptly sent out to the penitentiary building.

There, to my utter astonishment, I found eight hundred or one thousand ruffians, closely guarded by heavy lines of sentinels, who paced to and fro, day and night, rifle in hand, to keep them from running away. When I entered the barracks these recruits gathered around me and asked, "How much bounty did you get?" "How many times have you jumped the bounty?" I answered that I had not bargained for any bounty, that I had never jumped a bounty, and that I had enlisted to go to the front and fight. I was instantly assailed with abuse. Irreclaimable blackguards, thieves, and ruffians gathered in a boisterous circle around me and called me foul names. I was robbed while in these barracks of all I possessed—a pipe, a piece of tobacco, and a knife.

I remained in this nasty prison for a month. I became thoroughly acquainted with my comrades. A recruit's social standing in the barracks was determined by the acts of villainy he had performed, supplemented by the number of times he had jumped the bounty. The social standing of a hard-faced, crafty pick-pocket, who had jumped the bounty in say half a dozen cities, was assured. He shamelessly boasted of his rascally agility. Less active bounty-jumpers looked up to him as to a leader. He commanded their profound respect. When he talked, men gathered around him in crowds and listened attentively to words of wisdom concerning bounty-jumping that dropped from his tobacco-stained lips. His right to occupy the most desirable bunk, or to stand at the head of the column when we prepared to march to the kitchen for our rations, was undisputed.

If there was a man in all that shameless crew who had enlisted from patriotic motives, I did not see him. There was not a man of them who was not eager to run away. Not a man who did not quake when he thought of the front. Almost to a man they were bullies and cowards, and almost to a man they belonged to the criminal classes. . . .

On my urgent solicitation Major Van Rensselaer promised to ship me with the first detachment of recruits going to the front. One cold afternoon, directly after the ice had gone out of the Hudson River, we were ordered out of the barracks. We were formed into ranks, and stood in a long, curved line 1,000 rascals strong. We were counted, as was the daily custom, to see if any of the patriots had escaped. Then, after telling us to step four paces to the front as our names were called, the names of the men who were to form the detachment were shouted by a sergeant, and we stepped to the front, one after another, until 600 of us stood in ranks. We were marched to the barracks, and told to pack our knapsacks as we were to march at once.

The 400 recruits who had not been selected were carefully guarded on the ground, so as to prevent their mingling with us. If that had happened, some of the recruits who had been chosen would have failed to appear at the proper time. The idea was that if we were kept separate, all the men in the barracks, all outside of the men grouped under guard, would have to go. Before I left the barracks I saw the guards roughly haul straw-littered, dust-coated men out of mattresses, which they had cut open and crawled into to hide. Other men were jerked out of the water-closets. Still others were drawn by the feet from beneath bunks. One man, who had burrowed into the contents of a water-tight swill-box, which stood in the hall and into which we threw our waste food and coffee slops, was fished out, covered with coffee grounds and bits of bread and shreds of meat, and kicked down stairs and out of the building. Ever after I thought of that soldier as the hero of the swill-tub.

Cuffed, prodded with bayonets, and heartily cursed, we fell into line in front of the barracks. An officer stepped in front of us and said in a loud voice that any man who at tempted to escape would be shot. A double line of guards quickly took their proper positions around us. We were faced to the right and marched through a room, where the men were paid their bounties. Some men received $500, others less; but I heard of no man who received less than $400. I got nothing.

As the men passed through the room they were formed into column by fours. When all the recruits had been paid, and the column formed, we started to march into Albany, guarded by a double line of sentinels. Long before we arrived at State Street three recruits attempted to escape. They dropped their knapsacks and fled wildly. Crack! crack! Crack! a dozen rifles rang out, and what had been three men swiftly running were three bloody corpses. The dead patriots lay by the roadside as we marched by. We marched down State Street, turned to the right at Broadway, and marched down that street to the steamboat landing.

Previous to my enlistment I had imagined that the population of Albany would line the side-walks to see the defenders of the nation march proudly by, bound for the front, and that we would be cheered, and would unbend sufficiently to accept floral offerings from beautiful maidens. How was it? No exultant cheers arose from the column. The people who saw us did not cheer.

The faces of the recruits plainly expressed the profound disgust they felt at the disastrous outcome of what had promised to be a remunerative financial enterprise. Small boys derided us. Mud balls were thrown at us. One small lad, who was greatly excited by the unwonted spectacle, rushed to a street corner, and after placing his hands to his mouth, yelled to a distant and loved comrade: "Hi, Johnnie, come see de bounty-jumpers!" He was promptly joined by an exasperating, red-headed, sharp-tongued little wretch, whom I desired to destroy long before we arrived at the steamboat landing. Men and women openly laughed at us. Fingers, indicative of derision, were pointed at us. Yes, a large portion of the populace of Albany gathered together to see us; but they were mostly young males, called gutter-snipes. They jeered us, and were exceedingly loth to leave us. It was as though the congress of American wonders were parading the streets preparatory to aerial flights under tented canvas.

Once on the steamboat; we were herded on the lower deck, where freight is usually carried, like cattle. No one dared to take off his knapsack for fear it would be stolen. Armed sentinels stood at the openings in the vessel's sides out of which gangplanks were thrust. Others were stationed in the bows; others in the dark, narrow passage-ways where the shaft turns; still others were on the decks. We were hemmed in by a wall of glistening steel. "Stand back, stand back, damn you!" was the only remark the alert-eyed, stern-faced sentinels uttered, and the necessity of obeying that command was impressed on us by menacing bayonets. Whiskey, guard eluding whiskey, got in. Bottles, flasks, canteens, full of whiskey, circulated freely among us, and many men got drunk. There was an orgie on the North River steamer that night, but comparatively a decent one.

In spite of the almost certain death sure to ensue if a man attempted to escape, two men jumped overboard. I saw one of these take off his knapsack, loosen his overcoat and then sit down on his knapsack. He drew a whiskey flask from an inner pocket and repeatedly stimulated his courage. He watched the guards who stood by the opening in the vessel's side intently. At last they turned their heads for an instant. The man sprang to his feet, dropped his overcoat and ran to the opening and jumped far out into the cold waters of the river. Above us, in front of us, at our sides, behind us, wherever guards were stationed, there rifles cracked. But it was exceeding dark on the water, and I believe that the deserter escaped safely. Early in the morning, before it was light, I again heard firing. I was told that another recruit had jumped overboard and had been killed.

—WILKESON, *Recollections of a Private Soldier*

III·7

SUPPLYING THE CONFEDERACY WITH ARMS AND AMMUNITION

The industrial development of the South was in its infancy at the time of secession, and the Confederacy experienced greatest difficulty in supplying itself with the munitions for modern warfare. Edward P. Alexander, from whose entrancing *Memoirs* this passage is taken, had been an instructor at West Point where he perfected the system of military signals used by both armies during the war. President Davis appointed him Chief of Ordnance of the Army of Northern Virginia, and he served later as chief artillerist in Long street's corps.

On the day after Bull Run I was appointed Chief of Ordnance of Beauregard's corps, and within a few days Johnston extended my office over the whole army, which, about this period, took the name ever afterwards used,—"The Army of Northern Virginia." The enemy, about the same time, adopted their equally well-known title, "The Army of the Potomac."

My new duties largely absorbed my time, but I remained in charge of the signal service, the work being now confined to sending instructed parties to all parts of the Confederacy where they might be of use. During the fall a "Department of Signals" was organized in Richmond, and the charge of it, with the rank of colonel, was offered me, but declined,

as I was unwilling to leave the field. As head of a department I was soon made Major, and, later, Lieutenant Colonel of Artillery. Col. William Norris of Baltimore be came Chief Signal Officer.

Briefly, my duties embraced the supply of arms and ammunition to all troops in the field,—infantry, artillery, and cavalry. I organized the department, with an ordnance officer or sergeant in every regiment, from whom I received weekly statements showing the arms and ammunition on hand in cartridge boxes and regimental wagons. Reserve storehouses were provided at the nearest railroad points, and reserve trains for brigades and divisions, to run between the store houses and the troops. For emergency, under my own control was held a train of ammunition and battery wagons equipped with tools and expert mechanics for all sorts of repairs from a broken mainspring to a spiked fieldpiece. I was fortunate in securing for superintendent of this train, Maj. George Duffy, an expert from Alexandria, who became an institution in the army, and remained with it throughout the war.

In its early stages we had great trouble with the endless variety of arms and calibres in use, scarcely ten per cent of them being the muzzle-loading rifle musket, calibre .58, which was then the regulation arm for United States infantry. There were several breech-loading small-arms manufactured at the North, but none had secured the approval of the United States Ordnance Department, although many of them would have made more formidable weapons than any muzzle-loaders.

The old idea was still widely entertained that, because the percentage of hits is always small, the fire of infantry should not be rapid, lest the men waste too much ammunition. After a year or two some of the best breech-loaders got admission among cavalry regiments, and common sense and experience gradually forced a recognition of the value of a heavy fire. By 1864, the Spencer breech-loading carbine had been adopted as the regulation arm for the Federal cavalry, and by the fall of that year brigades of infantry began to appear with it. . . .

There is reason to believe that had the Federal infantry been armed from the first with even the breech-loaders avail able in 1861 the war would have been terminated within a year.

The old smooth-bore musket, calibre .69, made up the bulk of the Confederate armament at the beginning, some of the guns, even all through 1862, being old flint-locks. But every effort was made to replace them by rifled muskets captured in battle, brought through the blockade from Europe, or manufactured at a few small arsenals which we gradually fitted up. Not until after the battle of Gettysburg was the whole army in Virginia equipped with the rifled musket. In 1864 we captured some Spencer breech-loaders, but we could never use them for lack of proper cartridges.

Our artillery equipment at the beginning was even more inadequate than our small-arms. Our guns were principally smooth-bore 6-Prs. and 12-Prs. howitzers, and their ammunition was afflicted with very unreliable fuses. Our arsenals soon began to manufacture rifled guns, but they always lacked the copper and brass, and the mechanical skill necessary to turn out first-class ammunition. Gradually we captured Federal guns to supply most of our needs, but we were handicapped by our own ammunition until the close of the war.

No department of our government deserves more credit than our Ordnance Bureau in Richmond under Gen. Josiah Gorgas, for its success in supplying the enormous amount of ordnance material consumed during the war. Although always economical of ammunition, yet we never lost any action from the lack of it. We were, however, finally very near the end of our resources, in the supply of one indispensable article. To make percussion caps nitric acid, mercury, and copper were required. Our Nitre and Mining Bureau had learned to make saltpetre from caves, and the earth under old barns and smoke houses, and from all kinds of nitrogenous waste material. From the saltpetre our chemists could make nitric acid. Our quicksilver came from Mexico, but after the fall of Vicksburg we were cut off from it, and about the

same time our supply of sheet copper was exhausted. The chemists found out a mixture of chlorate of pot ash and sulphuret of antimony which they could use in place of fulminate of mercury; and we collected all the turpentine and apple-brandy stills in the country and sent them to Richmond to be cut up and rerolled into copper strips.

From this copper and the above chemical mixture all the caps were made which we used during the last year of the war, but at its close the copper stills were exhausted. It is hard to imagine what we would then have done had not the surrender at Appomattox relieved the quandary.

—ALEXANDER, *Military Memoirs of a Confederate*

III.8

HOW THE ARMY OF NORTHERN VIRGINIA GOT ITS ORDNANCE

Almost wholly without industries, and cut off from Europe by the blockade, the Confederacy had to get its arms and equipment as best it could. Some ordnance was seized when the Confederate states seceded; some was imported before the blockade became effective; some was smuggled in from the North; substantial quantities were captured f rom the enemy or "gleaned" on the battlefield.

Colonel William Allan, from whose reminiscences this excerpt is taken, was Chief of Ordnance of the Second Army Corps and author of an invaluable history of the campaign in the Shenandoah Valley and of the Army of Northern Virginia.

The troops at this time [1863] were armed in a heterogeneous fashion. Many of the men had smooth bore muskets, calibre .69. Others had rifled muskets, calibre .54, and others still had Springfield-muskets, calibre .58. There were some other arms, as, for instance, some Belgian rifles, calibre .70, but the three kinds I have mentioned were the principal kinds in the hands of the infantry in January, 1863. We were all anxious to replace the smooth bores with rifles, and especially with calibre .58, which was the model the Confederate as well as the Federal Government had adopted. The battlefields of the preceding summer had enabled many commands to exchange their smooth bores for Springfield muskets, but as nine-tenths of the arms in the Confederacy at the beginning of the war had been smooth bore muskets, it required time and patience to effect a complete re-arming. This was finally done in the Second corps at Chancellorsville, but in the winter of 1862-'63, there was often found in the same brigade the three kinds of arms above enumerated, and the same wagon often carried the three kinds of ammunition required. During this winter it was found difficult to obtain arms as fast as we needed them for the new men, and of course we were very glad to take what the department could furnish. Between the first of January and the first of May, General Jackson's corps grew from about twenty-three thousand muskets to thirty-three thousand. These ten thousand arms we obtained from Richmond in small quantities, and they were of different calibres, but the corps was fully armed when it went to Chancellorsville. After that battle the men all had muskets, calibre .58, and henceforth but one sort of ammunition was needed.

Our artillery armament was even more heterogeneous. Six pounder guns, howitzers, some Napoleons, three-inch rifles, ten-pounder Parrotts, and a few twenty-pounder Parrotts were in our corps, besides, probably, some other odd pieces. I remember a Blakely gun or two and a Whitworth, the latter used both at Chancellorsville and Gettysburg. Our batteries had been greatly improved by a number of guns captured from the enemy. We especially valued the three-inch rifles, which became the favorite field piece. During the winter of 1862-'63, the artillery was first thoroughly organized under General Pendleton as chief. Batteries were detached from brigades, and were organized into battalions, containing four batteries, usually of four guns each. A number of these battalions were assigned to each corps under the chief of artillery of that corps, while a number of others constituted the general reserve, of which General Pendleton took immediate oversight. All that our supplies admitted was done to thoroughly equip

these batteries during the winter, and they were ready for action when the campaign opened. A train of wagons was organized to carry the reserve ammunition for the artillery, and this was placed in charge of the artillery ordnance officer of the corps, and, besides this, there was a reserve train for the army under the direct orders of the chief ordnance officer of the army. . . .

Gleaning the battlefields was one of the important duties of the field ordnance officers. They were directed to save everything which could be made of use. Of course they took care of the good arms and good ammunition, but they had to preserve no less carefully all damaged arms, gun barrels, wasted ammunition, of which the lead was the valuable consideration, bayonets, cartridge-boxes, &c. After Chancellorsville and the gathering which had been done during the battle, an ordnance officer of the Second corps was sent to the field with power to call upon a neighboring brigade for as large details as he wished, and he spent a week in gathering the debris of the battle and sending it to Guiney's Station or Hamilton's Crossing, whence it was shipped to Richmond. My recollection is that over twenty thousand stand of damaged arms were sent in this way to the arsenal, besides a considerable quantity of lead, &c. After the first day at Gettysburg the battlefield was gleaned, and such material as we had transportation for sent back. . . .

In the winter of 1864 it was impossible to obtain an adequate quantity of horseshoes and nails from the ordnance department. The cavalry, which had been with General Early during that fall, had seen severe service, and it was absolutely necessary, in reference to the future, to procure in some way a supply of horseshes and nails during the winter. We had to depend upon ourselves. I determined to establish, if possible, twenty forges in Waynesboro', Augusta county, Virginia, and have blacksmiths detailed from the army to make shoes and nails. We sent through the country and got such blacksmith tools as we were able to find. I think I got some, too, from Richmond, from the ordnance department. There was no difficulty in getting good blacksmiths out of the army. A number of men were put to work, and horseshoes and nails began to accumulate. We soon ran out of iron, however, and found that the department at Richmond could not fully supply our wants. There was a fine lot of iron at Columbia furnace, near Mount Jackson, which was at this time in the debatable ground between the two armies. This iron was of fine quality, suitable for casting cannon as well as any other purpose. The commander of the arsenal informed me that if I could manage to get this to Richmond he would give me back in bars as much as I needed for horseshoes and nails. Trains of wagons were sent after it from Staunton, and these trains were protected by cavalry, which General Early sent for the purpose, and they returned in safety with the iron, which was promptly shipped to Richmond.

From this time forward our forges were fully supplied, and I think when Sheridan overhauled and dispersed our forces at Waynesboro', at the beginning of March, 1865, we had manufactured some twenty thousand pounds of horseshoes and nails. They were loaded upon the cars, which were gotten through the tunnel, but were captured by some of Sheridan's people at or near Greenwood depot.

—ALLAN, "Reminiscences of Field Ordnance Service"

III.9

SECRETARY BENJAMIN RECALLS THE MISTAKES OF THE CONFEDERATE CONGRESS

The Confederate government was no more ready for war than was the Union government, and confusion and mismanagement attended the beginnings of that conflict on both sides. More serious even than incompetence and shortsightedness, as events were to prove, was that jealousy between state and federal governments to which Secretary Benjamin here refers.

Benjamin himself, whom we have already met in the pages of Jones's Diary, was successively Attorney General, Secretary of War, and Secretary of State of the Confederacy, and probably the ablest and most trusted of President Davis's advisers. This letter was written after the war to Charles Marshall, an aide-de-camp of Lee.

As soon as war became certain, every possible effort was made by the President and his advisers to induce Congress to raise an army enlisted "for the war." The fatal effects of enlistments for short terms, shown by the history of the War of Independence against England, were invoked as furnishing a lesson for our guidance. It was all in vain. The people as we were informed by the members would not volunteer for the war, but they would rise in mass as volunteers for twelve months. We did not wish them to rise in mass nor in great numbers for any such short term, for the reason that *we could not arm them*, and their term of service would expire before we could equip them. I speak from memory as to numbers, but only a moderate force was raised (all that we could provide with arms) for twelve months service, and thus a *provisional* army was formed, but the fatal effect of the short term of service, combined with the painful deficiency of supplies, were felt long before the end of the year. While the Northern States after the Battle of Manassas were vigorously engaged in preparing for an overwhelming descent upon Virginia, our own army was falling to pieces. . .

The representatives of the people could not be persuaded to pass measures unpalatable to the people; and the unthinking multitude upon whose *voluntary* enlistments Congress forced us to depend were unable to foresee or appreciate the dangers of the policy against which we protested. It was only the imminent danger of being left without *any* army by the return home in mass of the first levy of twelve-month volunteers that drove Congress into passing a law for enlistments for the war, and in order to induce the soldiers under arms to re-enlist we were driven to the fatal expedient of granting them not only bounties but furloughs to return from Virginia to their homes in the far South, and if our actual condition had been at all suspected by the enemy they might have marched through Virginia with but the faintest show of resistance.

As to supplies of munitions I will give a single instance of the straits to which we were reduced. I was Secretary of War *ad interim* for a few months, during which Roanoke Island, commanded by General Wise, fell into the hands of the enemy. The report of that General shows that the capture was due in great measure to the persistent disregard by the Secretary of War of his urgent demands for munitions and supplies. Congress appointed a committee to investigate the conduct of the Secretary. I consulted the President whether it was best for the country that I should submit to unmerited censure or reveal to a Congressional Committee our poverty and my utter inability to supply the requisitions of General Wise, and thus run the risk that the fact should become known to some of the spies of the enemy of whose activity we were well assured. It was thought best for the public service that I should suffer the blame in silence and a report of censure on me was accordingly made by the Committee of Congress.

The *dearth* even of powder was so great that during the descent of the enemy on Roanoke, General Wise having sent me a despatch that he was in instant need of ammunition, I ordered by telegraph General Huger at Norfolk to send an immediate supply; this was done but accompanied by a despatch from General Huger protesting against this exhausting of his small store, and saying that it was insufficient to defend Norfolk for a day. General Lee was therefore ordered to send a part of his very scanty supply to Norfolk, General Lee being in his turn aided by a small cargo of powder which had just run into one of the inlets on the coast of Florida

Another terrible source of trouble, disorganization and inefficiency was the incurable jealousy in many states of the General Government. Each State has its own mode of appointing officers, generally by election. Until disaster forced Congress to pass the Conscription law, all that we could do was to get laws passed calling for certain quotas of troops from the states, and in order to prevent attempts made to create officers of higher rank than the Confederate officers, who would thus have been placed under the orders of ram militia generals, we resorted to the expedient of refusing to receive any higher organisation than a regiment. But the troops being State troops officered by the State officers, the army was constantly scandalized by electioneering to replace regimental officers, and Confederate Commanders were without means of enforcing discipline and efficiency except through the cumbrous and most objectionable expedient of Courts Martial. Another fatal defect was that we had no power to consolidate regiments, battalions, and companies. If a company was reduced to five men or a regiment to fifty, we had no power to remedy this. The message of the President of the 12th of August, 1862, showed the fatal effects of our military system, and a perusal of that message will shed a flood of light on the actual position of things and the hopeless helplessness to which the Executive was reduced by the legislation of Congress and the States. When I look back on it all, I am lost in amazement that the struggle could have been so prolonged, and one of the main, if not the main source of strength and encouragement to the Executive was the genius, ability, constancy, fidelity, and firmness of General Lee.

—Sir Frederick Maurice, ed.,
An Aide-de-Camp of Lee

III.10

Northern Ordnance

The North, with its highly developed arms industries, and with easy access to Britain, had no difficulty supplying its armies with whatever weapons were needed, yet the supply of small arms did not meet requirements until the war was a year old. Altogether some four million muskets were issued to Union soldiers, but less than eight thousand cannon.

The Comte de Paris, from whose compendious history of the Civil this extract is taken, served, with his brother the Duc de Chartres, on McClellan's staff, fighting at Yorktown and Gaines' Mill.

The task of supplying the Federal troops with arms and ammunition, which developed upon the ordnance department, was the most difficult of all. In fact, both the government armories and private manufactories were insufficient to meet the demand, and it required time to establish additional ones. The wonderful machines by which the most complicated rifles now in use throughout Europe are constructed almost without the aid of man are of American invention, and have given a well-deserved reputation to the expansion rifles manufactured at the government armory in Springfield. But this establishment had only the capacity for producing from ten to twelve thousand yearly, and the supply could not be increased except by constructing new machines. The private workshops were equally insufficient; the Federal factory at Harper's Ferry had been destroyed by fire, and the dépôts were empty. It was important, however, to supply the most pressing of all the wants of the soldier, that of having a weapon in his hands.

During the first year of the war the ordnance department succeeded in furnishing the various armies in the field, not counting what was left at the dépôts, one million two hundred and seventy-six thousand six hundred and eighty-six portable firearms (muskets, carbines, and pistols), one thousand nine hundred and twenty-six field- or siege-guns, twelve hundred pieces for batteries in position, and two hundred and fourteen million cartridges for small-arms and cannon. But it was obliged to apply to Europe for muskets and ammunition; this was the only war commodity that America procured in considerable quantities from the Old World, and it was this supply which proved to be the most defective. Agents without either experience or credit, and sometimes unscrupulous, bought in every part of Europe, on account of the Federal government, all the muskets they could pick up, without any regard to their quality or price. The English and Belgian manufactories not being able to satisfy their demands fast enough, they procured from the little German states all

their old-fashioned arms, which those states hastened to get rid of at a price which enabled them to replace them with needle-guns. In short, the refuse of all Europe passed into the hands of the American volunteers.

A portion of the muskets being unfit for use, the few that were serviceable had to be kept for the soldiers doing guard duty in each company. The calibres were all mixed up; conical balls were issued for the large German smooth-bore muskets, while the old American cartridge, containing one ball and four buckshot, was given to those who had the good fortune to possess a mini-rifle. The defective armament of the infantry would have been sufficient to delay the opening of the campaign for several months. In order to remedy this it was found necessary, in the first instance, to classify the calibres of the muskets by regiments, then gradually to throw aside the most worthless. After a while the American factories, both national and private, were able to furnish a sufficient quantity of new arms to justify this process.

While willing to encourage private enterprise to a great extent, the Federal government determined to control it; and in order to avoid being at its mercy, it largely extended its own establishments. Thus, in 1862, the Springfield manufactory delivered two hundred thousand rifles, while in the year 1863, during which there were manufactured two hundred and fifty thousand there, the importation of arms from Europe by the Northern States ceased altogether. The rifle which bore the name of the Federal manufactory had the advantage of not requiring heavy charges, of giving a great precision of aim at a distance of from six to seven hundred metres, and of being easily loaded and managed. It was therefore introduced throughout the army as fast as the ordnance department was able to meet the demands that were made for that arm from every quarter.

But, at the same time, a great number of new inventions were tried upon a scale which enabled the authorities to test their merits. Some were even adopted by whole regiments of cavalry; and the practice of breech-loading, which was common to all the systems, contributed greatly to their efficiency in the numerous engagements in which those regiments had to fight on foot. With the exception of this mode of loading, they differed greatly in their construction; it would be impossible for us to describe all, for there were no less than eleven of the first class. We shall only mention two belonging to the class called repeating-rifles—that is to say, arms which fire a certain number of shots without being reloaded. The Colt rifle is a long-barrelled revolver with five or six chambers, and the ball is forced into seven grooves forming a spiral which grows more and more contracted. This heavy weapon was formidable in practiced hands, but it required consideable time to reload it. The second was the Spencer rifle, an excellent arm, the use of which became more and more extended in the Federal army. The butt is pierced, in the direction of the length, by a tube containing seven cartridges, which are deposited successively, after each fire, in the chamber, replacing in turn those which, when discharged, are thrown out by a very simple mechanism. This magazine, entirely protected, is very easily recharged. Many extraordinary instances have been cited of successful personal defence due to the rapidity with which this arm can be fired, and some Federal regiments of infantry which made a trial of it were highly pleased with the result. Most of these rifles were of two models—one for the use of the infantry, the other, lighter and shorter, for the cavalry.

The *matériel* of the artillery, which had to be created, was as extensive as the armament of the infantry, and its construction was also new to American manufactories. Nevertheless, the great workshops for smelting iron and steel were so rapidly transformed into cannon foundries that the ordnance department was not obliged to depend on Europe for a supply.

At the time when the war broke out none of the systems of rifle cannon invented a few years before had ever been adopted, or even seriously experimented upon, by the officers of the regular army. But the latter, while adhering to the brass smooth-bore cannon, had studied these different inventions, and did not conceal their preference for the rifled system, by which the ball, like the minie bullet, inserted through the mouth of the cannon, is driven into the grooves under the pressure of the gases which propel it forward. The impression obtained from these inquiries in common was never forgotten by the officers who were placed in positions of command in the two hostile armies, and notwithstanding the diversity of details, the guns of those two armies always bore a strong family resemblance. But nothing could limit the fertility of inventors stimulated by the war.

—Comte De Paris, *History of the Civil War in America*

IV

BULL RUN AND THE PENINSULAR CAMPAIGN

After the attack on Fort Sumter and the secession of Virginia, both sides marked time. Neither was eager to assume the offensive, and neither was prepared to do so.

Conscious that it could never hope to muster the numerical or material strength of the North, the Confederacy preferred to exploit the great advantages of defensive operations and of interior lines of communication. Nor was there, from the larger political or diplomatic point of view, anything to be gained by invading the North. The Confederacy was merely asking to be let alone. It wanted to go its way in peace; if the North would not permit this it was prepared to fight. But it rested its hopes of victory not in conquest of the North but in wearing down the Northern will to fight, and in foreign intervention.

The North, on the other hand, could not escape the offensive. Its military task was to invade and conquer the South. This required an altogether more elaborate military organization than it was possible to create in a few months. It meant not only a large army—one necessarily much larger than the Confederate—but a permanent one; three-months militiamen would be worse than useless for an invasion. It meant building up immense quantities of war materiel, developing and maintaining long lines of communication, imposing a blockade on the South, wresting major ports and rivers from Southern control. It meant, in short, a military effort on a scale unprecedented in modern history.

General Scott's original plan was to make the major offensive down the Mississippi—a plan which had much to commend it. Circumstances, however—the proximity of the two capitals to each other, and of the first armies that were organized—dictated that Virginia should be the first and for long the major theater of the war. It is important therefore that we get clearly in mind the geography of that theater in so far as it controlled military operations.

Just a hundred miles separated the two capitals, Washington and Richmond. Between them lay four great rivers—the James, the York, the Rappahannock, and the Potomac—and many lesser streams such as the Chickahominy, the North and South Anna, and Bull Run. The ground between these two cities, and particularly from the Rappahannock to the James, was low, swampy, covered with woods and underbrush; the roads were deep in mud in winter and spring. To the west lay a series of hills and mountains, notably the Blue Ridge and the Shenandoah. The great Valley between these ranges ran northeast and southwest. Its mouth came out on the Potomac, that is to say on the Baltimore and Ohio Railroad and the Chesapeake and Ohio Canal—just fifty miles from Washington, and opened up into the rich Maryland and Pennsylvania country just across the Potomac. Thus the Confederates could use the Valley for striking into the heart of the North, cutting communications with Washington, and threatening that city. But to the Federals the Valley was of little value. If they succeeded in fighting their way up it to Staunton they were as far from Richmond as ever.

Thus while Washington was vulnerable to attack from both south and west, an attack on Richmond presented formidable difficulties. There were two possible approaches to Richmond: the direct approach by land, southward through Fredericksburg; the approach by sea to the Peninsula and up the Peninsula to the capital city. There was a variation on these, or a combination of them, that Grant finally used: a movement southward by land, across the James, and to Petersburg, and an attack on the rear of the city.

During May both governments tried to organize armies chiefly for defensive purposes. By the beginning of June Davis had one army of about 22,000 men under Beauregard at Manassas Junction, an important railroad center some 25 miles southwest of Washington; and a smaller force of about 11,000 under Joseph E. Johnston at Winchester, in the Valley. General Scott, the aged veteran of the War of 1812 and the Mexican War, had assembled a force of some 35,000, under McDowell, in and around Centerville, Virginia, and a force of about 12,000 under the veteran General Patterson at Harpers Ferry. Here at once we see the advantages that the Confederacy enjoyed in its interior lines. Johnston and Beauregard were only a few hours apart, by rail; Patterson and McDowell were days apart.

Scott had no intention of launching an offensive with his three-months militia, but public opinion called loudly for action. On June 24, McDowell submitted his plan for an offensive; it was approved and early in July he began to move on Beauregard. Meantime, however, everything depended on Patterson holding Johnston in the Valley. This he failed to do, with results that were disastrous for the Union cause. The result was the defeat at First Bull Run.

That story and its sequel are told in the following accounts. The direct overland approach having failed, McClellan tried the approach by sea and up the Peninsula. That, too, failed, but whether through the incompetence of the Federal commander, or the interference in his plans by the administration, or the genius of Lee will ever remain a subject of debate.

IV. I

A CONFEDERATE DOCTOR DESCRIBES THE VICTORY AT FIRST BULL RUN

The first major engagement of the war came when public opinion forced an advance on Richmond before the raw Union army was ready for fighting. Union troops, under Mc Dowell, outnumbered the Confederates under Beauregard, but the success of the Union advance depended on the ability of General Patterson to prevent the Confederate General J. E. Johnston from bringing a force of some 9,000 men from the Shenandoah Valley. In this Patterson failed, and on July 20 the vanguard of Johnston's forces began to arrive at Manassas Junction. Before dawn on Sunday, July 21, 1861, Mc Dowell attacked and by three o'clock that afternoon seemed to have carried the day. Then additional Confederate reinforcements threw themselves on the weary Federals and drove them back across the Bull Run. Soon the reverse became a disorderly retreat. Bull Run or First Manassas as it is known in the South—proved a costly victory, for it created a sense of overconfidence in the South while it spurred the North on to more determined efforts.

Richmond, July 23, 1861

Dear Harleston: I have seen the great and glorious battle of Manassas, which brought a nation into existence, and the scene was grand and impressive beyond the power of language. We foresaw the action several days ahead—the enemy were known to be advancing in immense masses from Arlington towards Fairfax, and the master stroke was at once made, to order Johnston down from Winchester, by forced marches, before Patterson could get down on the other side. Johnston's troops marched all twenty-six miles, then crowded into the railroad, came down in successive trains, without sleeping or eating, (15,000,) and arrived, many of them, while the battle was raging.

I got to Manassas the morning of the day previous to the fight; and knowing well both Generals Beauregard and Johnston, and their staff officers, I went immediately to headquarters. . . . General Beauregard determined to attack them in several columns at once the next morning, so as to cut them up before Patterson could arrive—but our scouts came early in the morning, informing the generals that the enemy had been in motion since two hours before day, which set tled the question as to their intention to make the attack. Beauregard, who had studied the whole ground around—knew every hill, ravine, and pathway—had made all the necessary arrangements and planned the battle. Not knowing at what point of a semicircle of ten miles around Manassas the enemy would attack, his forces had to be scattered in such a way as to guard all points, prevent a flank movement on either side, and guard his intrenchments and supplies in the centre.

We got up in the morning at daylight, took a cup of coffee and remained quietly laughing and talking at head-quarters, while the scouts were passing in and out bringing news from the enemy. At a quarter past six in the still, bright morning, we heard the first deep-toned sound of cannon on the centre of our line, about three miles off. We waited till nine for further information, and at nine the generals ordered to horse, and away we dashed to the hill overlooking the point at which cannon, like minute guns, had continued slowly to fire. The enemy could not see any of our troops, but were firing at the dust kicked up along the road, which they saw above the low trees. We were for some time at the point they were firing at, and some twenty or thirty balls of their rifled cannons whizzed through the air above us, and I felt very forcibly the remark of Cuddy to his mother Mause, that "a straggling bullet has nae discretion" and might take my head off as well as that of anybody else.

The firing at this point kept up slowly from a quarter past six till eleven, when we heard a gun fire on the extreme left of the semicircle, and we were then satisfied that the firing in front was a mere feint. In a few minutes the cannon firing came in rapid succession, as if one battery was answering another. The generals then ordered "to horse" again, and away we rode to the seat of battle, about three miles off. When we arrived on the top of a hill, in an old field, we could get glimpses of the fight through the woods. The cannons were roaring and the musketry sounded like a large bundle of fire crackers, and the constant roaring of the big guns, the sharp sound of rifled cannons, Minie rifles and muskets, with the bursting of shells, made one feel that death was doing his work with fearful rapidity.

The enemy had concentrated all his forces on this one point while ours were scattered around a half circle of ten miles, and the few regiments who received the first onset were most terribly cut up. It was far greater odds than human nature could stand, the regiments were torn to pieces, driven back, and so overwhelmed by numbers that I feared the day was lost. At this stage of the game the enemy was telegraphing to Washington that the battle had been won, and secession was about to be crushed. My heart failed me as I saw load after load of our poor wounded and dying soldiers brought and strewed on the ground, along the ravine where I was at work. Dr. Fanthray, who belonged to General Johnston's staff, and myself were just get-

ting fully to work, when an old surgeon, whom I do not know, came to us and said the enemy were carrying every thing before them, and ordered us to fall back to another point with the wounded, as they were turning our flank, and the battle would soon be upon us. Accordingly the wounded were taken up and we fell back, but after following the ambulances for a mile, we found that they were to be taken all the way to Manassas—about four miles—where there were hospitals and surgeons to receive them, and we returned to our position near the battle.

At this juncture I saw our reinforcements pouring in with the rapidity and eagerness of a fox chase, and was satisfied that they would drive every thing before them. No one can imagine such a grand, glorious picture as these patriots presented, rushing to the field through the masses of wounded bodies which strewed the roadside as they passed along. For half a mile behind me the road passed down a gradual slope, and through an old field, as I looked back, I could see a regiment of infantry coming in a trot, with their bright muskets glittering in the sun; then would come a battery of artillery, each gun carriage crowded with men and drawn by four horses in full gallop. Next came troops of cavalry, dashing with the speed of Murat; after these followed, with almost equal speed, wagons loaded with ammunition, &c., screaming all the while, "push ahead boys," "pitch into the d—d "Yankees," "drive them into the Potomac."

"This kept up from about mid-day till dark, and I felt as if the Alps themselves could not withstand such a rush. The cannon and small-arms were roaring like a thunder storm as they rushed to the battle-field. One regiment, which had been driven back by overwhelming numbers, was now supported and I soon perceived that the firing was getting further off, as I had expected, and I knew that the "pet lambs" now could only be saved by their superior heels. About this time, too, the last of General Johnston's command arrived on the cars, opposite the battle-ground, to the number of some three or four thousand, and although they had been two nights with out sleep, they jumped from the cars and cut across to the field.

By this time we had collected about 15,000 against their 35,000, and, from all accounts, no red fox ever made tracks, so fast as did these cowardly wretches. They were all fresh and better accoutred in every respect than our men, one half or more of whom had to make forced marches to get at them. They had selected their position coolly and deliberately in the morning, while ours were scattered over ten miles and had to run through the mid-day sunshine. If our men had been equally fresh they would have gone straight into their intrenchments at Arlington. But I will not speculate on the future and weary you with details which really will reach you through print long before this.

—Letter of Dr. J. C. Not

IV.2

"Bull Run Russell" Reports the Rout of the Federals

The English journalist William Howard Russell arrived in America in 1861 with a great and merited reputation as war correspondent, and soon began sending the *London Times* shrewd and outspoken accounts of American men and affairs. His description of the Federal demoralization after First Bull Run aroused a good deal of criticism, but all the evidence shows that it was by no means exaggerated.

July 20th, 1861.—The great battle which is to arrest rebellion or to make it a power in the land is no longer distant or doubtful. McDowell has completed his reconnaissance of the country in front of the enemy, and General Scott anticipates that he will be in possession of Manassas tomorrow night. . . .

Some senators and many congressmen have already gone to join McDowell's army or to follow in its wake in the hope of seeing the Lord deliver the Philistines into his hands. . . . Every carriage, gig, wagon, and hack has been engaged by people going out to see the fight. The price is enhanced by

mysterious communications respecting the horrible slaughter in the skirmishes at Bull Run. The French cooks and hotel keepers, by some occult process of reasoning, have arrived at the conclusion that they must treble the prices of their wines and of the hampers of provisions which the Washington people are ordering to comfort themselves at their bloody Derby. . . .

It was a strange scene before us. From the hill a densely wooded country, dotted at intervals with green fields and cleared lands, spread five or six miles in front, bounded by a line of blue and purple ridges, terminating abruptly in escarpments toward the left front and swelling gradually to wards the right into the lower spines of an offshoot from the Blue Ridge Mountains. On our left the view was circumscribed by a forest which clothed the side of the ridge on which we stood and covered its shoulder far down into the plain. A gap in the nearest chain of the hills in our front was pointed out by the bystanders as the Pass of Manassas by which the railway from the West is carried into the plain, and still nearer at hand before us is the junction of that rail with the line from Alexandria and with the railway leading south ward to Richmond. The intervening space was not a dead level; undulating lines of forest marked the course of the streams which intersected it and gave by their variety of color and shading an additional charm to the landscape which, in closed in a framework of blue and purple hills, softened into violet in the extreme distance, presented one of the most agreeable displays of simple pastoral woodland scenery that could be conceived.

But the sounds which came upon the breeze and the sights which met our eyes were in terrible variance with the tranquil character of the landscape. The woods far and near echoed to the roar of cannon, and thin, frayed lines of blue smoke marked the spots whence came the muttering sound of rolling musketry; the white puffs of smoke burst high above the treetops, and the gunners' rings from shell and howitzer marked the fire of the artillery.

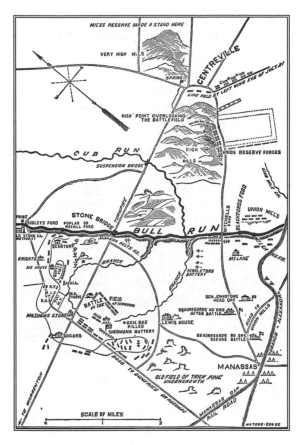

THE FIRST BATTLE OF BULL RUN

Clouds of dust shifted and moved through the forest, and through the wavering mists of light blue smoke and the thicker masses which rose commingling from the feet of men and the mouths of cannon, I could see the gleam of arms and the twinkling of bayonets.

On the hill beside me there was a crowd of civilians on horseback and in all sorts of vehicles, with a few of the fairer, if not gentler, sex. A few officers and some soldiers, who had straggled from the regiments in reserve, moved about among the spectators and pretended to explain the movements of the troops below, of which they were profoundly ignorant . . .

The spectators were all excited, and a lady with an opera glass who was near me was quite beside herself when an unusually heavy discharge roused the current of her blood—"That is splendid. Oh, my! Is not that first-rate? I guess we will be in

Richmond this time tomorrow." These, mingled with coarser exclamations, burst from the politicians who had come out to see the triumph of the Union arms. . . .

Loud cheers suddenly burst from the spectators as a man dressed in the uniform of an officer, whom I had seen riding violently across the plain in an open space below, galloped along the front, waving his cap and shouting at the top of his voice. He was brought up, by the press of people round his horse, close to where I stood. "We've whipped them on all points," he cried. "We have taken all their batteries. They are retreating as fast as they can, and we are after them." Such cheers as rent the welkin! The congressmen shook hands with each other and cried out: "Bully for us! Bravo! Didn't I tell you so?" The Germans uttered their martial cheers, and the Irish hurrahed wildly. At this moment my horse was brought up the hill and I mounted and turned toward the road to the front . . .

I had ridden between three and a half and four miles, as well as I could judge, when I was obliged to turn for the third and fourth time into the road by a considerable stream which was spanned by a bridge, toward which I was threading my way, when my attention was attracted by loud shouts in advance and I perceived several waggons coming from the direction of the battlefield, the drivers of which were endeavoring to force their horses past the ammunition carts going in the contrary direction near the bridge; a thick cloud of dust rose behind them, and running by the side of the waggons were a number of men in uniform whom I supposed to be the guard. My first impression was that the waggons were returning for fresh supplies of ammunition. But every moment the crowd increased; drivers and men cried out with the most vehement gestures: "Turn back! Turn back! We are whipped." They seized the heads of the horses and swore at the opposing drivers. Emerging from the crowd, a breathless man in the uniform of an officer, with an empty scabbard dangling by his side, was cut off by getting between my horse and a cart for a moment. "What is the matter, sir? What is all this about?" "Why, it means we are pretty badly whipped, that's the truth," he gasped, and continued.

By this time the confusion had been communicating itself through the line of waggons toward the rear, and the drivers endeavored to turn round their vehicles in the narrow road, which caused the usual amount of imprecations from the men and plunging and kicking from the horses.

The crowd from the front continually increased, the heat, the uproar, and the dust were beyond description, and these were augmented when some cavalry soldiers, flourishing their sabers and preceded by an officer, who cried out, "Make way there—make way there for the General," attempted to force a covered waggon, in which was seated a man with a bloody handkerchief round his head, through the press.

I had succeeded in getting across the bridge, with great difficulty, before the waggon came up, and I saw the crowd on the road was still gathering thicker and thicker. Again I asked an officer, who was on foot with his sword under his arm, "What is all this for?" "We are whipped, sir. We are all in retreat. You are all to go back." "Can you tell me where I can find General McDowell?" "No! nor can any one else. . . ."

In a few seconds a crowd of men rushed out of the wood down toward the guns, and the artillerymen near me seized the trail of a piece and were wheeling it round to fire when an officer or sergeant called out: "Stop! stop! They are our own men"; and in two or three minutes the whole battalion came sweeping past the guns at the double and in the utmost disorder. Some of the artillerymen dragged the horses out of the tumbrils, and for a moment the confusion was so great I could not understand what had taken place; but a soldier whom I stopped said, "We are pursued by their cavalry; they have cut us all to pieces."

Murat himself would not have dared to move a squadron on such ground. However, it could not be doubted that some thing serious was taking place; and at that moment a shell burst in front of the house, scattering the soldiers near it, which was followed by another that bounded along the road; and in a few minutes more out came another regiment from the wood, almost as broken as the first. The scene on the road had now assumed an aspect which has not a parallel in any description I have ever read. Infantry soldiers on mules and draft horses with the harness clinging to their heels, as much frightened as their riders; Negro servants on their masters' chargers; ambulances crowded with unwounded soldiers; waggons swarming with men who threw out the contents in the road to make room, grinding through a shouting, screaming mass of men on foot who were literally yelling with rage at every halt and shrieking out: "Here are the cavalry! Will you get on?" This portion of the force was evidently in discord.

There was nothing left for it but to go with the current one could not stem. I turned round my horse. . . . I was unwillingly approaching Centerville in the midst of heat, dust, confusion, imprecations inconceivable. On arriving at the place where a small rivulet crossed the road the throng in creased still more. The ground over which I had passed going out was now covered with arms, clothing of all kinds, accouterments thrown off and left to be trampled in the dust under the hoofs of men and horses. The runaways ran along side the waggons, striving to force themselves in among the occupants, who resisted tooth and nail. The drivers spurred and whipped and urged the horses to the utmost of their bent. I felt an inclination to laugh which was overcome by disgust and by that vague sense of something extraordinary taking place which is experienced when a man sees a number of people acting as if driven by some unknown terror. As I rode in the crowd, with men clinging to the stirrup leathers or holding on by anything they could lay hands on, so that I had some apprehension of being pulled off, I spoke to the men and asked them over and over again not to be in such a hurry. "There's no enemy to pursue you. All the cavalry in the world could not get at you." But I might as well have talked to the stones. . . .

It never occurred to me that this was a grand debacle. All along I believed the mass of the army was not broken and that all I saw around was the result of confusion created in a crude organization by a forced retreat, and knowing the reserves were at Centerville and beyond, I said to myself, "Let us see how this will be when we get to the hill.". . .

I was trotting quietly down the hill road beyond Centerville when suddenly the guns on the other side or from a battery very near opened fire, and a fresh outburst of artillery sounded through the woods. In an instant the mass of vehicles and retreating soldiers, teamsters, and civilians, as if agonized by an electric shock, quivered throughout the tortuous line. With dreadful shouts and cursings the drivers lashed their maddened horses and, leaping from the carts, left them to their fate and ran on foot. Artillerymen and foot soldiers and Negroes, mounted on gun horses with the chain traces and loose trappings trailing in the dust, spurred and flogged their steeds down the road or by the side paths. The firing continued and seemed to approach the hill, and at every report the agitated body of horsemen and waggons was seized, as it were, with a fresh convulsion.

Once more the dreaded cry: "The cavalry! cavalry are coming!" rang through the crowd, and looking back to Centerville, I perceived coming down the hill, between me and the sky, a number of mounted men who might at a hasty glance be taken for horsemen in the act of sabering the fugitives. In reality they were soldiers and civilians, with, I regret to say, some officers among them, who were whipping and striking their horses with sticks or whatever else they could lay hands on. I called out to the men who were frantic with terror beside me, "They are not cavalry at all; they're your own men"—but they did not heed me. A fellow who was shouting out, "Run! run!" as loud as he could beside me, seemed to take delight in creating alarm; and as he was perfectly collected as far as I could judge, I said: "What on earth are you running for? What are you afraid of?" He was in the roadside below me and, at once turning on me and

exclaiming, "I am not afraid of you," presented his piece and pulled the trigger so instantaneously that had it gone off I could not have swerved from the ball. As the scoundrel deliberately drew up to examine the nipple, I judged it best not to give him another chance and spurred on through the crowd, where any man could have shot as many as he pleased without interruption. The only conclusion I came to was that he was mad or drunken. When I was passing by the line of the bivouacs a battalion of men came tumbling down the bank from the field into the road with fixed bayonets, and as some fell in the road and others tumbled on top of them, there must have been a few ingloriously wounded.

22d.—I awoke from a deep sleep this morning about six o'clock. The rain was falling in torrents and beat with a dull, thudding sound on the leads outside my window; but louder than all came a strange sound as if of the tread of men, a confused tramp and splashing and a murmuring of voices. I got up and ran to the front room, the windows of which looked on the street, and there, to my intense surprise, I saw a steady stream of men covered with mud, soaked through with rain, who were pouring irregularly, without any semblance of order, up Pennsylvania Avenue toward the Capitol. A dense stream of vapor rose from the multitude, but looking closely at the men, I perceived they belonged to different regiments, New Yorkers, Michiganders, Rhode Islanders, Massachusetters, Minnesotans, mingled pellmell together. Many of them were without knapsacks, crossbelts, and firelocks. Some had neither greatcoats nor shoes; others were covered with blankets. Hastily putting on my clothes, I ran downstairs and asked an officer who was passing by, a pale young man who looked exhausted to death and who had lost his sword. for the empty sheath dangled at his side, where the men were coming from. "Where from? Well, sir, I guess we're all coming out of Virginny as far as we can, and pretty well whipped too." "What! the whole army, sir?" 'That's more than I know. They may stay that like. I know I'm going home. I've had enough of fighting to last my lifetime."

The news seemed incredible. But there before my eyes were the jaded, dispirited, broken remnants of regiments passing onward, where and for what I knew not, and it was evident enough that the mass of the grand army of the Potomac was placing that river between it and the enemy as rapidly as possible. "Is there any pursuit?" I asked of several men. Some were too surly to reply; others said, "They're coming as fast as they can after us"; others, "I guess they've stopped it now—the rain is too much for them." A few said they did not know and looked as if they did not care. . . .

The rain has abated a little, and the pavements are densely packed with men in uniforms, some with, others without, arms, on whom the shopkeepers are looking with evident alarm. They seem to be in possession of all the spirit houses. Now and then shots are heard down the street or in the distance, and cries and shouting, as if a scuffle or a difficulty were occurring. Willard's is turned into a barrack for officers and presents such a scene in the hall as could only be witnessed in a city occupied by a demoralized army. There is no provost guard, no patrol, no authority visible in the streets. General Scott is quite overwhelmed by the affair and is unable to stir. General McDowell has not yet arrived. The Secretary of War knows not what to do, Mr. Lincoln is equally helpless, and Mr. Seward, who retains some calmness, is, notwithstanding his military rank and militia experience, without resource or expedient. There are a good many troops hanging on about the camps and forts on the other side of the river, it is said; but they are thoroughly disorganized and will run away if the enemy comes in sight without a shot, and then the capital must fall at once. Why Beauregard does not come I know not, nor can I well guess. I have been expecting every hour since noon to hear his cannon. Here is a golden opportunity. If the Confederates do not grasp that which will never come again on such terms, it stamps them with mediocrity.

—Russell, *My Diary North and South*

Stonewall Jackson Credits God with the Victory

First Bull Run gave the Confederacy one of its greatest heroes. When on the morning of that battle the bluecoats were having the Confederates back across the Warrenton turnpike, Thomas J. Jackson's brigade stood firm. "Look at Jackson," cried General Bee to his troops. "There he stands like a stonewall." Courage was common enough in the Confederate command; Jackson was soon to reveal other military qualities of a high order. His letter to his wife, written two days after the battle, shows that devoutness which was just as characteristic ot the man as was courage.

Manassas, July 23d 1861

My Precious Pet,—Yesterday we fought a great battle and gained a great victory, for which all the glory is due to *God alone*. Although under a heavy fire for several continuous hours, I received only one wound, the breaking of the longest finger of my left hand; but the doctor says the finger can be saved. It was broken about midway between the hand and knuckle, the ball passing on the side next the fore finger. Had it struck the centre, I should have lost the finger. My horse was wounded, but not killed. Your coat got an ugly wound near the hip, but my servant, who is very handy, has so far repaired it that it doesn't show very much. My preservation was entirely due, as was the glorious victory, to our God, to whom be all the honor, praise and glory. The battle was the hardest that I have ever been in, but not near so hot in its fire. I commanded the centre more particularly, though one of my regiments extended to the right for some distance. There were other commanders on my right and left. Whilst great credit is due to other parts of our gallant army, God made my brigade more instrumental than any other in repulsing the main attack. This is for your information only—say nothing about it. Let others speak praise, not myself.

—M. Jackson, *Life and Letters of General Thomas J. Jackson*

IV.4

"THE CAPTURE OF WASHINGTON SEEMS INEVITABLE'

After Bull Run the Confederates could have advanced on Washington; had they moved promptly they could probably have taken the city. But political and diplomatic considerations suggested that such an offensive would be inadvisable. The people of Washington, however, were for a time a-tremble for their safety.

Edwin M. Stanton—who had the jitters easily—had been Attorney General under Buchanan and was shortly to be appointed Secretary of War by Lincoln.

Washington, July 26, 1861

Dear Sir: . . . The dreadful disaster of Sunday can scarcely be mentioned. The imbecility of this Administration culminated in that catastrophe—an irretrievable misfortune and national disgrace never to be forgotten are to be added to the ruin of all peaceful pursuits and national bankruptcy as the result of Lincoln's "running the machine" for five months. You perceive that Bennett is for a change of the Cabinet, and proposes for one of the new Cabinet Mr. Holt. . . . It is not unlikely that some change in the War and Navy Departments may take place, but none beyond these two departments until Jefferson Davis turns out the whole concern.

The capture of Washington seems now to be inevitable during the whole of Monday and Tuesday it might have been taken without any resistance. The rout, overthrow, and utter demoralization of the whole army is complete. Even now I doubt whether any serious opposition to the entrance of the Confederate forces could be offered. While Lincoln, Scott, and the Cabinet are disputing who is to blame, the city is unguarded and the enemy at hand. General McClellan reached here last evening. But, if he had the ability of Caesar, Alexander, or Napoleon, what can he accomplish? Will not Scott's jealousy, Cabinet intrigues, Republican interference, thwart him at every step? While hoping for the best, I can not shut my eyes against the dangers that beset the Government, and especially this city. It is certain

that Davis was in the field on Sunday, and the Secessionists here assert that he headed in person the last victorious charge. General Dix is in Baltimore. After three weeks' neglect and insult he was sent there. The warm debate between Douglas's friend Richardson and Kentucky Burnett has attracted some interest, but has been attended with no bellicose result.

Since this note was commenced, the morning paper has come in, and I see that McClellan did *not* arrive last night, as I was informed he had. General Lee was after him, but will have to wait awhile before they can meet.

Yours truly,
Edwin M. Stanton.
His Excellency, James Buchanan
—RICE, ed., "A Page of Political Correspondence"

IV.5

McClellan Opens the Peninsular Campaign

After Bull Run, McClellan was appointed commander of all land forces around Washington and, in a short time, replaced the aged Scott as commander in chief of the United States Army.

George B. McClellan is doubtless the most controversial military figure of the Civil War. We meet him first as he embarks on the campaign that is to reduce Richmond, destroy Johnston's army, and end the war; we shall meet him again. With an army almost twice as strong as Johnston's, he was reluctant to take the offensive, and while the North clamored for action, he stayed in and around Washington. Finally on January 27, 1862, President Lincoln issued War Order No. I positively ordering an advance on or before February 22, but McClellan ignored this as well as subsequent orders. Early in March McClellan decided to shift his army to Urbana, on the south bank of the Rappahannock, but when Johnston moved his forces south of the Rappahannock this shift of base became pointless. On March 17 McClellan embarked his army for Fortress Monroe, and on April 4 began a snail-like advance up the Peninsula toward Yorktown, investing the ground as he went. Johnston withdrew from Yorktown to Williamsburg, and there, on May 5, the blue and the gray locked in battle. Although McClellan claimed a victory, his losses were 50 per cent higher than Johnston's. This letter to his wife reveals his characteristic self-confidence and vanity.

Williamsburg, May 6, 1862—
I telegraphed you this morning that we had gained a
battle. Every hour in importance is proved to be
greater. On Sunday I sent Stoneman in pursuit with
the cavalry and four batteries of horse-artillery. He
was supported by the divisions of Hooker, Smith,
Couch, Casey, and Kearny, most of which arrived
on the ground only yesterday. Unfortunately I did
not go with the advance myself, being obliged to
remain to get Franklin and Sedgwick started up the
river for West Point. Yesterday I received pressing
messages from Smith and others begging me to go
to the front. I started with half a dozen aides and
some fifteen orderlies, and found things in a bad
state. Hancock was engaged with a vastly inferior
force some two miles from any support. Hooker
fought nearly all day without assistance, and the
mass of the troops were crowded together where
they were useless. I found everybody discouraged,
officers and men; our troops in wrong positions, on
the wrong side of the woods; no system, no co-operation, no orders given, roads blocked up.

As soon as I came upon the field the men
cheered like fiends, and I saw at once that I could
save the day. I immediately reinforced Hancock and
arranged to support Hooker, advanced the whole
line across the woods, filled up the gaps, and got
everything in hand for whatever might occur. The
result was that the enemy saw that he was gone if he
remained in his position, and scampered during the
night. His works were very strong, but his loss was
very heavy. The roads are in such condition that it is
impossible to pursue except with a few cavalry.

It is with the utmost difficulty that I can feed
the men, many of whom have had nothing to eat for
twenty-four hours and more. I had no dinner yesterday, no supper; a cracker for breakfast, and no dinner
yet. I have no baggage; was out in the rain all day
and until late at night; slept in my clothes and boo
and could not even wash my face and hands. I, however, expect my ambulance up pretty soon, when I
hope for better things. I have been through the hospitals, where are many of our own men and of the
rebels. One Virginian sent for me this morning and

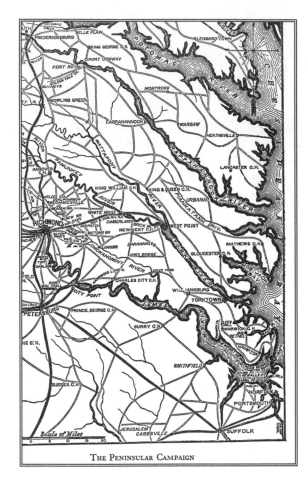

THE PENINSULAR CAMPAIGN

THE PENINSULAR CAMPAIGN

told me that I was the only general from whom they
expected any humanity. I corrected this mistake.

This is a beautiful little town; several very old
houses and churches, pretty gardens. I have taken
possession of a very fine house which Joe Johnston
occupied as his headquarters. It has a lovely flower-
garden and conservatory. If you were here I should
be much inclined to spend some weeks here.

G. W. was one of the whipped community, also
Joe Johnston, Cadmus Wilcox, A. P. Hill, D. H.
Hill, Longstreet, Jeb Stuart, Early (badly wounded);
and many others that we know. We have all their
wounded; eight guns so far. In short, we have given
them a tremendous thrashing, and I am not at all
ashamed of the conduct of the Army of the
Potomac.

—Letter to his wife, in *McClellan's Own Story*

IV.6

GENERAL WOOL TAKES NORFOLK

Johnston's withdrawal from Yorktown exposed Norfolk to capture, and on May 9 the Confederates blew up the crippled *Merrimac* and abandoned the city which they had held since the beginning of the war. General Wool who "captured" Norfolk had been a major in the War of 1812 and a general in the Mexican War, and was 77 at the outbreak of the Civil War. The happily named Egbert Ludovicus Viele was a brigadier general of volunteers; after the war he projected a plan for subways for New York City and served as commissioner of parks.

No time was lost on the following morning in reembarking the troops for the purpose of marching on Norfolk by the rear. At the last moment General Wool, with much emotion begged the Secretary (Chase) to allow him to command the troops. The Secretary had decided to relieve him of the command of the expedition on account of his advanced age, but finally reversed his decision with the remark that he could not inflict sorrow upon gray hairs. . . .

Starting at once to the front with our escort, we had not gone very far before it became evident that a great deal of confusion existed in the command—in fact, that there was no organization, and an utter absence of definite instructions or orders of any kind. Overtaking a regiment that was scattered along the road—most of the men lying down wherever any shade could be found, as the day was intensely warm—Mr. Chase inquired of the colonel to whose command he belonged and what his orders were. He replied that he had no idea who was his commander, that some said Weber and some said Mansfield. He had received no orders except that when he landed he was told to take a certain road, and he thought he would wait to see what was to be done next. Overtaking another regiment a mile or two beyond, the secretary received the same answers. Going on still farther, we came upon General Mansfield and his staff, who had dismounted in the shade near a

spring of cool water. Farther still, another straggling regiment was found; yet no one had any orders or instructions. Suddenly the booming of cannon was heard immediately in front, and as no artillery had been landed by us, it was evident that the firing proceeded from the enemy. Straggling soldiers now came running toward us with exaggerated rumors of the enemy being in force, burning the bridges, and contesting with artillery the passage of the streams that crossed the road. The ridiculousness of the situation would have been amusing if it had not been for the serious aspect that it was gradually assuming. Two regiments of cavalry had been embarked and two batteries of artillery; yet not a horse or a gun had been sent to the front. Four regiments of infantry were marching along, uncertain what road to take and unassigned to any brigade; two brigadier generals and their staffs, without orders and without commands, were sitting by the roadside waiting for something to turn up. This was the situation with the enemy firing in front.

Secretary Chase took it all in at a glance and rose at once to the necessities of the occasion. Tearing some leaves from his memorandum book, he directed me to send one of our escort back to General Wool with a written requisition for artillery and cavalry. This brought the general to the front with two pieces of artillery and some mounted troops. As he rode up, Mr. Chase expressed to him in very strong language his astonishment at the condition of things. General Wool replied by saying that he presumed General Mansfield had felt some delicacy in assuming command over General Weber and that General Weber had hesitated to act while General Mansfield was so near.

"Talk of delicacy," exclaimed the Secretary, "with the enemy firing in front! What absurdity! Let General Mansfield go to the rear and bring up reinforcements, and that will settle all questions of delicacy." This brought about a prolonged discussion between Generals Wool and Mansfield, which was carried on at a short distance from the rear under the shade of a large sycamore tree. Losing all patience, the Secretary exclaimed, "Two cackling hens!" and turning to me with a voice and manner that would have become Wellington or Soul, he said: "Sir! I order you in the name of the President of the United States to take command of these troops and march them upon Norfolk."

An infantry regiment was deployed at double-quick as skirmishers in advance, and the other regiments were soon moving rapidly down the Norfolk road. They had proceeded some distance before General Wool was aware of the movement. He was not long in overtaking us, however, and on his demand for an explanation from me Mr. Chase assumed the responsibility, after which we proceeded harmoniously toward our destination. At the extreme limits of the city and before the formidable line of intrenched works was reached, a large deputation headed by the mayor and municipal councils made its appearance with a flag of truce and per formed a most skillful ruse to gain time for the Confederates to secure their retreat from the city. The mayor, with all the formality of a medieval warden, appeared with a bunch of rusty keys and a formidable roll of papers which he proceeded to read with the utmost deliberation previous to delivering the "keys of the city." The reading of the documents—which embraced a large portion of the history of Virginia, the causes that led to the war, the peculiar position of the good citizens of Norfolk, and in short a little of every thing that could have the remotest bearing upon the subject and exhaust the longest possible space of time in reading—was protracted until nearly dark.

In the meantime the Confederates were hurrying with their artillery and stores over the ferry to Portsmouth, cutting the water pipes and flooding the public buildings, setting fire to the navy yard, and having their own way generally, while our General was listening in the most innocent and complacent manner to the long rigmarole so ingeniously prepared by the mayor and skillfully interlarded with fulsome personal eulogium upon himself. . . .

And now another well-devised plan presented itself in the shape of a number of carriages which the mayor particularly desired should be used by the officers in taking possession of the city, the troops in the meanwhile to remain where they were. Falling readily into this second little trap, the General accepted and we were driven to the city hall, where some more rusty keys were produced and more formal speeches were made. A collection of several thousand people, some of them in butternut and gray, assembled in front of the building. While the General and mayor were going through their high formalities, Mr. Chase asked for a pen and a piece of paper and wrote an order assigning the command of the city to myself as military governor, which General Wool signed at his direction. Then, bidding me goodbye, he took the General by the arm and departed, leaving me the solitary occupant of the city hall, without a soldier within two miles and with not even an aide-de-camp to assist me. Fortunately an enterprising newspaper correspondent had followed the carriages on foot, and him I appointed an aide and dispatched for the troops. By the time the troops arrived the moon had risen, and by its light they were placed in position. A regiment dispatched to the navy yard was too late to res cue it from almost complete destruction, but it cut off the *Merrimac* from any supplies from either side of the river.

It was long after midnight before the final disposition of troops was made, and this had hardly been accomplished when, with a shock that shook the city and with an ominous sound that could not be mistaken, the magazine of the *Merrimac* was exploded, the vessel having been cut off from supplies and deserted by the crew; and thus this most formidable engine of destruction that had so long been a terror not only to Hampton Roads but to the Atlantic coast went to her doom.

—VIELE, "A Trip with Lincoln, Chase and Stanton"

The Army of the Potomac Marches to Meet McClellan

By the end of May McClellan had worked his way slowly and painfully up the Peninsula, and was within sight—and sound—of Richmond. The Federals outnumbered the Confederates probably by a ratio of five to three, but as new regiments and companies swarmed in to the defense of the beleaguered capital the opposing forces became more nearly equal. At this time the Confederate army north of Richmond was called the Army of the Potomac; this is not to be confused with the Federal army of the same name.

Sallie Putnam, from whose delightful reminiscences of Richmond during the war this excerpt is taken, was one of the Virginia gentry who stayed on in the city throughout the war.

The day of the passage of the Army of the Potomac through Richmond will long be remembered by those who were in the city. It was known that they were on their way to the Peninsula, and for days they had been expected to march through the streets of the capital. The greatest interest and excitement prevailed. The morning was bright and beautiful in the early spring, balmy with the odors of the violet and the hyacinth, and the flaunting narcissus, the jonquil, and myriads of spring flowers threw on their parti-colored garments to welcome the army of veterans as they passed.

From an early hour until the sun went down in the West the steady tramp of the soldier was heard on the streets. Continuous cheers went up from thousands of voices; from every window fair heads were thrust, fair hands waved snowy handkerchiefs, and bright eyes beamed "Welcome!" Bands of spirit-stirring music discoursed the favorite airs—Dixie's Land, My Maryland, the Bonny Blue Flag, and other popular tunes—and as the last regiments were passing we heard the strains of "Good-Bye," and tears were allowed to flow, and tender hearts ached as they listened to the significant tune. Soldiers left the ranks to grasp the hands of friends in passing, to receive some grateful refreshment, a small bouquet, or a whispered congratulation. Officers on horseback raised their hats, and some of the more gallant ventured to waft kisses to the fair ones at the doors and windows. We shall never forget the appearance of General Longstreet, the sturdy fighter, the obstinate warrior, as he dashed down Main Street surrounded by his splendid staff.

Through other streets poured our cavalry, under their gallant chieftain, the pink of Southern chivalry,—the gay, rollicking, yet bold, daring and venturous "Jeb." Stuart. As we saw him then, sitting easily on his saddle, as though he was born to it, he seemed every inch the cavalier. His stout yet lithe figure, his graceful bearing, his broad, well-formed chest and shoulders, on which was gracefully poised his splendid head, his bright, beaming countenance, lighted up with a smile as pleasant as a woman's, his dark red hair and flowing beard, with his lower limbs encased in heavy cavalry boots, made up the *tout ensemble* of this brave son of Maryland. His genial temperament made him the idol and companion of the most humble of his men, and his deeds of daring and heroic courage made him respected as their leader.

As they swept through our streets on that beautiful morning, with their horses in good order, their own spirits buoyant and cheerful, many of them wearing in their caps bouquets of the golden daffodils of early spring, cheered on by the ringing sounds of the bugle, we thought never to see them pass again with worn-out horses and weary, listless spirits, as they spurred on their broken-down steeds; but so it was . . .

—[Sallie Putnam], *Richmond during the War*

R. E. Lee Takes Command

After First Bull Run Joseph E. Johnston was assigned to command the Confederate armies in northern Virginia, and in July 1861 appointed general—fourth in rank in the whole Confederacy. When McClellan got himself entangled in the swamps of the Chickahominy, Johnston moved out to meet him.

The Battle of Seven Pines, or Fair Oaks, which came on May 31 and June 1, was, in Freeman's phrase, "a battle of strange errors." Badly fought on both sides, it was at best indecisive. though Confederate losses ran to almost eight thousand, and Union to less than six thousand, the Confederates claimed a victory. General Johnston was severely wounded on the battlefield and Davis turned to Lee—who then held the ambiguous position of "general in charge of military operations under the direction of the President"—and assigned him the command. That very day he baptized the army by the name it was to make immortal, "The Army of Northern Virginia."

General Evander M. Law, who tells us here how Lee appeared when he took command during the Battle of Seven Pines, was a South Carolinian who was teaching at an Alabama military academy when the war broke out. He raised a company from his own school and took it to Virginia. He served all through the war in the East until wounded at Cold Harbor.

It was not until the 24th of May that McClellan's army was in position along the east bank of the Chickahominy and the struggle for Richmond itself began. The Federal army, holding the line of the Chickahominy from Mechanicsville to Bottom's bridge, at once commenced the construction of military bridges between those points, and before the end of May McClellan's left wing was advanced by throwing the two corps of Heintzelman and Keyes across the river. The latter took position and entrenched on a line running in front of "Seven Pines" on the Williamsburg road, with its right extending across the York River Railroad in front of Fair Oaks station. Heintzelman was placed in supporting distance in the rear, near Savage's station. McClellan's outposts were now within five miles of Richmond. Almost near enough to realize President Lincoln's suggestion, when he inquired by telegraph on May 26th, "Can you get near enough to throw shells into the city?" This amiable desire was not destined to be gratified, for during the afternoon and night of the 30th of May a heavy rain-storm occurred, flooding the low grounds of the Chickahominy and threatening the destruction of the military bridges constructed by the Federal army. The two wings were to a certain extent isolated, and General Johnston took advantage of this condition of affairs to attack Keyes' corps near Seven Pines on the 31st of

BATTLEFIELDS OF THE SEVEN DAYS

May. This corps was assailed by D. H. Hill's division and thoroughly routed. Heintzelman came to its support, but by this time the divisions of Longstreet and G. W. Smith had united in the attack with D. H. Hill, and this corps fared little better than that of Keyes. By the most strenuous exertions Sumner's Federal corps was thrown across the almost ruined bridges, during the afternoon and night of the 31st, and this timely reinforcement, together with the intervention of night, saved the left wing of McClellan's army from destruction.

The tardy movements of some of the Confederate commanders on the extreme right delayed the attack several hours beyond the time when it should have been made, and this delay was fatal to the complete success of General Johnston's plans. While G. W. Smith's division, to which I was attached, was warmly engaged near the junction of the "Nine Mile" road and the York River Railroad, General Johnston rode up and gave me an order as to the movements of my command. Night was rapidly approaching, and he seemed anxious to urge forward the attack with all possible speed so as to clear the field of the enemy before night. He was moving with the troops and personally directing the advance, when he received a severe wound in the shoulder and was compelled to relinquish the command. The Confederates had been checked on their left wing by the arrival of Sumner's corps, and the fighting ceased just after dark. It was renewed on our right wing on the morning of the 1st of June without advantage to either side, and by 2 o'clock P.M. the battle was over, without having accomplished the purpose for which it was fought.

General G. W. Smith, an officer of acknowledged ability, succeeded General Johnston in command of the Confederate army on the night of the 31st of May. But during the after noon of the next day, June 1st, he in turn relinquished the command to General Lee, under orders from President Davis. Our right wing was at once withdrawn from its advanced position, and Smith's division on the left followed the next day. As I was standing near the Nine Mile road a day or two after the battle, General Lee passed along the road accompanied by two staff officers. I had never seen him before, and he was pointed out by some one near me. I observed the new commander of the "Army of Northern Virginia" very closely and with a great deal of interest. General Johnston was universally beloved and possessed the unbounded confidence of the army, and the commander who succeeded him must be "every inch a man" and a soldier to fill his place in their confidence and affection. General Lee had up to this time accomplished nothing to warrant the belief in his future greatness as a commander. He had made an unsuccessful campaign in Western Virginia the year before, and since that time had been on duty first at Charleston and then

in Richmond. There was naturally a great deal of speculation among the soldiers as to how he would "pan out." The general tone, however, was one of confidence, which was in variably strengthened by a sight of the man himself. Calm, dignified, and commanding in his bearing, a countenance strikingly benevolent and self-possessed, a clear, honest eye that could look friend or enemy in the face; clean-shaven, except a closely-trimmed mustache which gave a touch of firmness to the well-shaped mouth; simply and neatly dressed in the uniform of his rank, felt hat, and top boots reaching to the knee; sitting his horse as if his home was in the saddle; such was Robert E. Lee as he appeared when he assumed command of the army of "Northern Virginia" in the early days of June, 1862, never to relinquish it for a day, until its colors were furled for ever at Appomattox.

—Law, "The Fight for Richmond"

IV.9

"BEAUTY" STUART RIDES AROUND MCCLELLAN'S ARMY

Although heavily outnumbered Lee planned to seize the offensive and destroy McClellan's army or drive it off the Peninsula. In preparation for the offensive he sent J. E. B. (Beauty) Stuart out to reconnoiter the Federal position, especially between the Chickahominy and the Totopotomy. Stuart set out on June 12 with some 1,000 cavalrymen, made the called-for reconnaissance, and then, instead of turning back, decided to ride 150 miles around McClellan's whole army.

This account of the last part of the ride is by the famous Virginia novelist and historian who fought all through the war with Stuart, John Esten Cooke.

The gayest portion of the raid now began. From this moment it was neck or nothing, do or die. We had one chance of escape against ten of capture or destruction.

Stuart had decided upon his course with that rapidity, good judgment, and decision, which were the real secrets of his splendid effiency as a leader of cavalry, in which capacity I believe that he has never been surpassed, either in the late war or any other. He was now in the very heart of the enemy's citadel, with their enormous masses upon every side. He had driven in their advanced force, passed within sight of the white tents of General McClellan's headquarters, burned their camps, and ascertained all that he wished. How was he to return? He could not cross the Pamunkey, and make a circuit back; he had no pontoons. He could not return over the route by which he had advanced. As events afterward showed, the alarm had been given, and an overpowering force of infantry, cavalry, and artillery had been rapidly moved in that direction to intercept the daring raider. Capture stared him in the face, on both of these routes—across the Pamunkey, or back as he came; he must find some other loophole of escape.

Such was the dangerous posture of affairs, and such was the important problem which Stuart decided in five minutes. He determined to make the complete circuit of McClellan's army; and crossing the Chickahominy below Long Bridge, re enter the Confederate lines from Charles City. If on his way he encountered cavalry he intended to fight it; if a heavy force of infantry barred his way he would elude, or cut a path through it; if driven to the wall and debarred from escape he did not mean to surrender. A few days afterward I said to him:

"That was a tight place at the river, General. If the enemy had come down on us, you would have been compelled to have surrendered."

"No," was his reply; "one other course was left."

"What was that?"

"To die game."

And I know that such was his intention. When a commander means to die game rather than surrender he is a dangerous adversary. . .

Everywhere the ride was crowded with incident. The scouting and flanking parties constantly picked up stragglers, and overhauled unsuspecting wagons filled with the most tempting stores. In this manner a wagon, stocked with champagne and every variety of wines, belonging to a General of the Federal army, fell a prey to the thirsty graybacks. Still they pressed on. Every moment an attack was expected in front or rear. Colonel Will. T. Martin commanded the latter. "Tell Colonel Martin," Stuart said to me, "to have his artillery ready, and look out for an attack at any moment." I had delivered the message and was riding to the front again, when suddenly a loud cry arose of "Yankees in the rear!" Every sabre flashed, fours were formed, the men wheeled about, when all at once a stunning roar of laughter ran along the line; it was a *canard*. The column moved up again with its flanking parties well out. The men composing the latter were, many of them, from the region, and for the first time for months saw their mothers and sisters. These went quite wild at sight of their sons and brothers. . . .

The column was now skirting the Pamunkey, and a detachment hurried off to seize and burn two or three transports lying in the river. Soon a dense cloud rose from them, the flames soared up, and the column pushed on. Everywhere were seen the traces of flight—for the alarm of "hornets in the hive" was given. Wagons had turned over, and were abandoned—from others the excellent army stores had been hastily thrown. This writer got a fine red blanket, and an excellent pair of cavalry pantaloons, for which he still owes the United States. Other things lay about in tempting array, but we were approaching Tunstall's, where the column would doubtless make a charge; and to load down a weary horse was injudicious. The advance guard was now in sight of the railroad. There was no question about the affair before us. The column must cut through, whatever force guarded the railroad; to reach the lower Chickahominy the guard here must be overpowered. Now was the time to use the artillery, and every effort was made to hurry it forward. But alas! it had got into a tremendous mudhole, and the wheels were buried to the axle. The horses were lashed, and jumped, al most breaking the traces; the drivers swore; the harness cracked—but the guns did not move.

"Gat! Lieutenant," said a sergeant of Dutch origin to the brave Lieutenant McGregor, "it can't be done. But just put that keg on the gun, Lieutenant," pointing, as he spoke, to a keg of whiskey in an ambulance, the spoil of the Federal camp, "and tell the men they can have it if they pull through!"

McGregor laughed, and the keg was quickly perched on the gun. Then took place an exhibition of herculean muscularity which would have delighted Guy Livingston. With eyes fixed ardently upon the keg, the powerful cannoneers waded into the mudhole up to their knees, seized the wheels of gun and caisson loaded down with ammunition, and just simply lifted the whole out, and put them on firm ground. The piece whirled on—the keg had been dismounted—the cannoneers revelled in the spoils they had earned.

Tunstall's was now nearly in sight, and that good fellow Captain Frayser, afterward Stuart's signal officer, came back and reported one or two companies of infantry at the rail road. Their commander had politely beckoned to him as he reconnoitred, exclaiming in wheedling accents, full of Teutonic blandishment, "Koom yay!" But this cordial invitation was disregarded; Frayser galloped back and reported, and the ringing voice of Stuart ordered "Form platoonsl draw sabre! charge!" At the word the sabres flashed, a thundering shout arose, and sweeping on in column of platoons, the gray people fell upon their blue adversaries, gobbling them up, almost without a shot. . . .

The men swarmed upon the railroad. Quick axes were applied to the telegraph poles, which crashed down, and Redmond Burke went in command of a detachment to burn a small bridge on the railroad near. Suddenly in the midst of the tumult was heard the shrill whistle of a train coming from the direction of the Chickahominy. Stuart quickly drew up his men in a line on the side of the road, and he had no sooner done so than the train came slowly round a wooded bend, and bore down. When within two hundred yards it was ordered to halt, but the command was not obeyed. The engineer crowded on all steam; the train rushed on, and then a thundering volley was opened upon the "flats" containing officers and men. The engineer was shot by Captain Parley, of Stuart's staff, and a number of the soldiers were wounded. The rest threw themselves upon their faces; the train rushed headlong by like some frightened monster bent upon escape, and in an instant it had disappeared.

Stuart then reflected for a single moment. The question was, should he go back and attack the White House, where enormous stores were piled up? It was tempting, and he afterwards told me he could scarcely resist it. But a considerable force of infantry was posted there; the firing had doubtless given them the alarm; and the attempt was too hazardous. The best thing for that gray column was to set their faces toward home, and "keep moving," well closed up both day and night, for the lower Chickahominy. Beyond the railroad appeared a world of wagons, loaded with grain and coffee standing in the road abandoned. Quick work was made of them. They were all set on fire, and their contents destroyed. Prom the horse-trough of one I rescued a small volume bearing on the fly-leaf the name of a young lady of Williamsburg. I think it was a volume of poems— poetic wagondrivers!

These wagons were only the "vaunt couriers"—the advance guard—of the main body. In a field beyond the stream thirty acres were covered with them. They were all burned. The roar of the soaring flames was like the sound of a forest on fire. How they roared and crackled! The sky overhead, when night had descended, was bloody-looking in the glare. . . .

Pushing on by large hospitals which were not interfered with, we reached at midnight the three or four houses known as Talleysville; and here a halt was ordered to rest men and horses, and permit the artillery to come up. This pause was fatal to a sutler's store from which the owners had fled. It was remorselessly ransacked and the edibles consumed. This historian ate in succession figs, beef-tongue, pickle, candy, tomato catsup, preserves, lemons, cakes, sausages, molasses, crackers, and canned meats. In presence of these attractive commodities, the spirits of many rose. Those who in the morning had made me laugh by saying, "General Stuart is going to get his command destroyed—this movement is mad," now regarded Stuart as the first of men; the raid was a feat of splendour and judicious daring which could not fail in terminating successfully. Such is the difference in the views of the military machine, unfed and fed. . . .

The column. . . began to move on the road to Porge Bridge. The highway lay before us, white in the unclouded splendour of the moon. The critical moment was yet to come. Our safety was to turn apparently on a throw of the dice, rattled in the hand of Chance. The exhaustion of the march now began to tell on the men. Whole companies went to sleep in the saddle, and Stuart himself was no exception. He had thrown one knee over the pommel of his saddle, folded his arms, dropped the bridle, and—chin on breast, his plumed hat drooping over his forehead—was sound asleep. His sure footed horse moved steadily, but the form of the General tottered from side to side, and for miles I held him erect by the arm. The column thus moved on during the remainder of the night, the wary advance guard encountering no enemies and giving no alarm. At the first streak of dawn the Chickahominy was in sight, and Stuart was spurring forward *to the ford*.

It was impassable! The heavy rains had so swollen the waters that the crossing was utterly impracticable! Here we were within a few miles of McClellan's army, with an enraged enemy rushing on our track to make us rue the day we had "circumvented" them, and inflicted on them such injury and insult; here we were with a swollen and impassable stream directly in our front—the angry waters roaring around the half-submerged trunks of the trees—and expecting every instant to hear the crack of carbines from the rear-guard indicating the enemy's approach! The "situation" was not pleasing. I certainly thought that the enemy would be

upon us in about an hour, and death or capture would be the sure alternative. This view was general. I found that cool and resolute officer, Colonel William H. F. Lee, on the river's bank. He had just attempted to swim the river, and nearly drowned his horse among the tangled roots and snags. I said to him:

"What do you think of the situation, Colonel?"

"Well, Captain," was the reply, in the speaker's habitual tone of cheerful courtesy, "I think we are caught."

The men evidently shared this sentiment. The scene upon the river's bank was curious. The men lay about in every attitude, half-overcome with sleep, but holding their bridles, and ready to mount at the first alarm. Others sat their horses asleep, with drooping shoulders. Some gnawed crackers; others ate figs, or smoked, or yawned. Things looked "blue," and the colour was figuratively spread over every countenance. When this writer assumed a gay expression of countenance, laughed, and told the men it was "all right," they looked at him as sane men regard a lunatic! The general conviction evidently was that "all right" was the very last phrase by which to describe the situation.

There was only one man who never desponded, or bated one "jot or tittle of the heart of hope." That was Stuart. . . . He said a few words to Colonel Lee, found the ford impassable, and then ordering his column to move on, galloped down the stream to a spot where an old bridge had formerly stood. Reaching this point, a strong rear-guard was thrown out, the artillery placed in position, and Stuart set to work vigorously to rebuild the bridge, determined to bring out his guns or die trying.

The bridge had been destroyed, but the stone abutments remained some thirty or forty feet only apart, for the river here ran deep and narrow between steep banks. Between these stone sentinels, facing each other, was an "aching void" which it was necessary to fill. Stuart gave his personal superintendence to the work, he and his staff labouring with the men. A skiff was procured; this was affixed by a rope to a tree, in the mid-current just above the abutments, and thus a movable pier was secured in the middle of the stream. An old barn was then hastily torn to pieces and robbed of its timbers; these were stretched down to the boat, and up to the opposite abutment, and a foot-bridge was thus ready. Large numbers of the men immediately unsaddled their horses, took their equipments over, and then returning, drove or rode their horses into the stream, and swam them over. In this manner a considerable number crossed; but the process was much too slow. There, besides, was the artillery, which Stuart had no intention of leaving. A regular bridge must be built without a moment's delay, and to this work Stuart now applied himself with ardour.

Heavier blows resounded from the old barn; huge timbers approached, borne on brawny shoulders, and descending into the boat anchored in the middle of the stream, the men lifted them across. They were just long enough; the ends rested on the abutments, and immediately thick planks were hurried forward and laid crosswise, forming a secure footway for the cavalry and artillery horses. Standing in the boat beneath, Stuart worked with the men, and as the planks thundered down, and the bridge steadily advanced, the gay voice of the General was heard humming a song. He was singing carelessly, although at every instant an overpowering force of the enemy was looked for, and a heavy attack upon the disordered cavalry.

At last the bridge was finished; the artillery crossed amid hurrahs from the men, and then Stuart slowly moved his cavalry across the shaky footway. . . . The hoofs clattered on the hasty structure, the head of the column was turned toward the ford beyond, the last squadron had just passed, and the bridge was being destroyed, when shots resounded on the opposite bank of the stream, and Colonel Rush thundered down with his "lancers" to the bank. He was exactly ten minutes too late. Stuart was over with his artillery, and the swollen stream barred the way, even if Colonel Rush thought it prudent to "knock up against" the one thousand five hundred crack cavalry of Stuart. His

men banged away at Colonel Lee, and a parting salute whizzed through the trees as the gray column slowly disappeared. . . .

—COOKE, *Wearing of the Gray*

IV. 10

OLIVER NORTON FIGHTS LIKE A MADMAN AT GAINES' MILL

With the information which Stuart was able to bring him, with large reinforcements from Georgia and the Carolinas, and with the aid of Jackson, who had just concluded his whirlwind campaign in the Valley, Lee was now prepared to initiate his campaign against the Federals. Summoning Jackson from the Valley, Lee planned to concentrate most of his forces north of the Chickahominy and roll up the Union flank. Jackson was unaccountably late, but the attack came off, almost as planned, on June 26—the first of the famous Seven Days battles.

After his initial attack at Mechanicsville, Lee struck east ward to Gaines' Mill, in the second of the Seven Days battles. Although McClellan's forces greatly outnumbered Lee's, so faulty were the Union general's tactics that Lee was able to throw some 57,000 troops against scarcely half that number under the unfortunate Fitz-John Porter. Porter put up a magnificent resistance, but by sundown of June 27 the Federal ranks were broken and the Federals retreated across the Chickahominy.

The selection given here describes the fighting as seen by an ordinary soldier, Oliver Norton, who answered Lincoln's first call for volunteers, fought through the entire war, first as a private in the 83rd Regiment, Pennsylvania Volunteers, then as a first lieutenant of the 80th United States Colored Troops. He participated in as many as 26 battles and skirmishes. He here describes how he was wounded three times within a few moments.

Camp near James River, July 4, 1862
Dear Friends at Home:—

I sent a few words to you yesterday just to relieve your suspense, and to-day I will write a little more, though, in the present condition of my mind and body, worn out by fatigue and exposure, you cannot expect much but a disconnected letter. The papers will have told you of the strategic movement of McClellan's army, its causes and its complete success. All that remains for me to write, and all that I can be expected to know is where the Eighty-third went and what it did.

The fight on the right began on Thursday, the 26th of June, and we took all on our backs and went out that after noon but did no fighting. Friday morning at daylight we fell back to a position on a stream near Gaines' Mill. The rebels soon followed, feeling their way along, and at about 2 o'clock the fighting became general along the whole line. Our brigade formed the left flank of the line and lay nearest the river. The Eighty-third was posted in a deep gully, wooded, and with the stream I mentioned running in front of us. We built a little breastwork of logs and had a good position. On the hill behind us the Forty-fourth and Twelfth New York and the Sixteenth Michigan were posted. When the rebels made the first attack, we could not fire a shot, the hill concealing them from us, and so we lay still while the buliets of two opposing lines whistled over our heads. They were repulsed, but only to pour in new troops with greater vigor than before.

Suddenly I saw two men on the bank in front of us gesticulating violently and pointing to our rear, but the roar of battle drowned their voices. The order was given to face about. We did so and tried to form in line, but while the line was forming, a bullet laid low the head, the stay, the trust of our regiment—our brave colonel, and before we knew what had happened the major shared his fate. We were then without a field officer, but the boys bore up bravely. They rallied round the flag and we advanced up the hill to find ourselves alone. It appears that the enemy broke through our lines off on our right, and word was sent to us on the left to fall back. Those in the rear of us received the order but the aide sent to us was shot before he reached us and so we got no orders. Henry and Denison were shot about the same time as the colonel. I left them together under a tree.

I returned to the fight, and our boys were dropping on all sides of me. I was blazing away at the rascals not ten rods off when a ball struck my gun just above the lower band as I was capping it, and cut it in two. The ball flew in pieces and part went by my head to the right and three pieces struck just below my left collar bone. The deepest one was not over half an inch, and stopping to open my coat I pulled them out and snatched a gun from Ames in Company H as he fell dead. Before I had fired this at all a ball clipped off a piece of the stock, and an instant after, another struck the seam of my canteen and entered my left groin. I pulled it out, and, more maddened than ever, I rushed in again. A few minutes after, another ball took six inches off the muzzle of this gun. I snatched another from a wounded man under a tree, and, as I was loading kneeling by the side of the road, a ball cut my rammer in two as I was turning it over my head. Another gun was easier got than a rammer so I threw that away and picked up a fourth one. Here in the road a buckshot struck me in the left eyebrow, making the third slight scratch I received in the action. It exceeded all I ever dreamed of, it was almost a miracle.

Then came the retreat across the river; rebels on three sides of us left no choice but to run or be killed or be taken prisoners. We left our all in the hollow by the creek and crossed the river to Smith's division. The bridge was torn up and when I came to the river I threw my cartridge box on my shoulder and waded through. It was a little more than waist deep. I stayed that night with some Sherman boys in Elder Drake's company in the forty-ninth New York.

Sunday night we lay in a cornfield in the rain, without tent or blanket. Monday we went down on the James river, lying behind batteries to support them. Tuesday the same six days exposed to a constant fire of shot and shell, till almost night, when we went to the front and engaged in another fierce conflict with the enemy. Going on to the field, I picked up a tent and slung it across my shoulder. The folds of that stopped a ball that would have passed through me. I picked it out, put it in my pocket, and, after firing sixty rounds of my own and a number of a wounded comrade's cartridges, I came off the field unhurt, and ready, but not anxious, for another fight.

—NORTON, *Army Letters*

IV.11

The End of Seven Days

Lee's success at Gaines' Mill forced McClellan to shift his base from White House on the Pamunkey to Harrison's Landing on the James—a shift which he made with great skill. As soon as Lee discovered that his opponent was heading for the James, he set his troops the task of turning the retreat into a rout. In this he was, however, unsuccessful. The Confederate attacks at Savage's Station and Frayser's Farm, on June 29 and 30, were uncoordinated and without strategic value. During the night of the twenty-ninth McClellan retreated across the White Oak Swamp, a swampy tributary of the Chickahominy. Longstreet and A. P. Hill attacked him there, on the thirtieth, but Jackson failed to get into the fight; once more it was inconclusive and the Federals managed to get away to the heights of Malvern Hill.

The final attack at Malvern Hill, on July 1, was likewise a failure—again chiefly because of Lee's failure to bring all his available troops into battle. While Confederate losses in the Seven Days campaign were heavier than the Union, the campaign must be accounted a Confederate success because it achieved its object of relieving pressure on Richmond and persuaded the administration to abandon the Peninsula.

Thomas Livermore, from whose fascinating wartime reminiscences these excerpts are taken, was a boy of seventeen when the war broke out, studying at Lombard College, Illinois. He hurried east to get into the fighting, found the 1st New Hampshire Infantry encamped in Maryland, and enlisted; he ended the war as colonel of the 18th New Hampshire Volunteers.

A. The Federals Are Forced Back at White Oak Swamp

The sun rose and darted his fiery rays upon us, and as most of us had eaten, we stuck our rifles up by the bayonets, fastened our blankets in the locks, and lay down in their shade to shun the scorching rays, and sleep. The dust of the barren plain was a sweet couch, and the stifling heat which enveloped us could not prevent profound sleep. A few, perhaps, bestirred thmselves to complete the breakfasts which had been begun at our first halt when we had crossed the bridge, but there seemed to be a soothing quiet around us, and we could praise the economy of Nature which made the pleasure of sleep so intense as to requite us almost for our labors and deprivations before. What I thought or

dreamed of I do not know, but suddenly, whatever visions of peace hovered around me were dispelled by the thunders of artillery, the shriek of shells, and the horrid humming of their fragments. Hell seemed to have opened upon us. In a twinkling every man was on his feet, the blankets were slung over our shoulders, and the men were in their places, shrinking under the storm, perhaps, but steady and prepared for action. The rebels had planted a large number of cannon on the other side of the swamp, and having pointed them at the host which lay on the plain had fired them all at once.

And what a scene it was! As far as the eye could see the tired troops were springing to arms; batteries were whirling into position or hurrying out of reach with horses on the gallop; wagons drawn by teams of frightened mules, driven by frantic drivers, rattled away to the woods; the teams of six mules which belonged to a pontoon train which were sur prised watering at the swamp, fled up the hill and away, leaving their boats; stragglers and noncombatants of all kinds fled in all directions from the fire; while the air was filled with clouds of dust and wreaths of smoke which spread out from the fierce clouds, breathing fire of bursting shells, and the ear was dimmed! with explosions, shouts, and a storm of other noises.

The—New York Volunteers was said to have run away when the first shell burst in front of it, and—battery, also of New York, I think, disgraced itself in like manner. But the rest of the troops quickly formed lines of battle, and when we in a very few minutes had reached our position and lair, down in line with our faces to the enemy, order had come out of chaos. Near us, in front and rear and right, the troops of our own division lay in parallel lines; on other parts of the plain Smith's division and Naglee's brigade were in similar order, and a few rods in front the welcome sight of Hazzard's battery of our corps, firing with rapidity at the enemy, greeted our eyes. The enemy's fire was unremitting, and from noon until nearly dark we endured the slow torture of seeing our comrades killed, mangled, and torn around us, while we could not fire a shot, as our business was to lie and wait to repel attacks and protect our batteries. With every discharge of the enemy's guns, the shells would scream over our heads and bury themselves in the woods beyond, burst over us and deal death in the ranks, or ricochet over the plain, killing whenever they struck a line.

The—New York Volunteers in changing position either attempted to escape to the rear or mistook its colonel's orders and retreated right down toward us. General Caldwell, who was near, galloped to our rear and cried out, "5th New Hampshire, rise up!" and we rose, leveled our bayonets, and received the—at their points. This was a decisive barrier to further retreating, and after a little confusion they went back and behaved themselves. We were pleased to have rebuked this cowardice, but were sorry for Colonel—, who was a brave man.

The shot hit some of our men and scattered their vitals and brains upon the ground, and we hugged the earth to escape this horrible fate, but nothing could save a few who fell victims there. I saw a shot strike in the 2d Delaware, a new regiment with us, which threw a man's head perhaps twenty feet into the air, and the bleeding trunk fell over toward us. The men seemed paralyzed for a moment, but presently gathered up the poor fellow's body in a blanket and carried it away. I do not know that I have ever feared artillery as I did then, and I can recollect very well how close I lay to the ground while the messengers of death, each one seemingly coming right into us, whistled over us. . . .

I had just reached my place, when the order was given to rise up and face about. A cannon shot came quicker than the wind through my company, and close by me. Tibbetts fell and Nichols fell. We reached the line designated with a few hasty steps, and resumed our line with faces to the front. Nichols got up, and came back to the captain and said, "Captain, I am wounded and want to go to the rear." The poor fellow held up one arm with the other hand, for it dangled only by a strip of flesh. Some men went forward and hastily gathered up Tibbetts in a blanket and bore him away; the shot had gone through his body. We felt a little safer now. Hazzard's battery withdrew, cut to pieces, and with Captain Hazzard mortally wounded; and for a short time it seemed as if the rebels would fire unmolested, but Pettit galloped up with his battery of 10-pounder Parrotts and went into action, and then iron *did fly*, and the rebels had their hands full. Captain Keller sat up on a knapsack in front of us and gave warning when the shells were coming, and perhaps saved lives by it; anyhow it was a brave thing to do.

It was not a long time before we perceived that Captain Pettit's fire was getting too hot for the rebels, and they only fired at intervals; and at last Pettit would hold up until they fired, when he would fire his whole battery at them, and as his shells went screaming over the tops of the trees to where the smoke was seen, our hearts bounded, for we perceived that their range was almost perfect; the rebels grew timid, and finally toward night they ceased firing, and we felt grateful to Pettit for it.

Once during the afternoon we saw a battery heavily engaged on our side close to the swamp on the right, and I think that we heard in that direction the rattle of musketry, perhaps where the rebels were attempting a crossing. The portion of the pontoon train which was left on the plain was set fire to in the afternoon, and the smoke and flames added to the infernal aspect of affairs. If ever stillness and rest were appreciated, I think it was on the verge of that evening, and even the dusty plain must have assumed a lovely hue when it was no longer disturbed by ricocheting shot.

—LIVERMORE, *Days and Events*

B. Captain Livermore Fights at Malvern Hill

This was the morning of July 1, and we were on Malvern Hill. The army had retreated during the day before and that night, and on this morning were placed in position to meet the advancing enemy again, and I have an indistinct recollection of seeing General McClellan on the field that morning, but he went on board a gunboat soon after and stayed until late in the day. The sun rose as hot as ever and again prostrated some of the men.

Presently a battery appeared in our front and opened fire on us at the distance of perhaps three quarters of a mile. As we lay directly on the crest of the hill, we presented a fair mark and our quarters were decidedly uncomfortable.

Ammunition was sent to us, and I was ordered to distribute it. As I was performing the work, or about that time, a cannon shot took off the foot of a man lying near by, and I was glad when I could lie down again.

The slow hours dragged along until the middle of the afternoon, when the battle opened in earnest on our left far down in front. Cannon and muskets roared and rattled, the blue smoke made the air heavy, and cheers and yells made the heavens ring. We did not remain long in suspense; an order came to move, and setting our faces to the fighting ground, we shook from our feet the dust of that ground where we were fired at without the privilege of a return fire. We moved down the hill, in front of the woods, and into a road, and marched toward the left flank. On our right was a wheatfield and beyond it another field. Through this last one, as we passed it, the shot came whirling over and through our ranks, spending their force in the woods, where they cracked and crashed through limbs, trunks, and foliage. Our men in the line of battle cheered and cheered again, and our hearts bounded to think that we had met with a success. A color sergeant, with his colors all torn, came by us and reported victory. We filed into the field on our right and moved forward. But I must not omit to mention that while we marched by the flank a shot crashed through the ranks of the 61st New York which led us. Captain—fell and cried out in mortal agony, "One man! two men! three men! carry me off the field!" The pitying men sprang forward and raised him up gently to find that the shot had only taken off his coat-tail.

As I have said, we formed line on our right and moved forward. At this time Colonel Barlow, of the 61st New York, was with General Caldwell, and seemed to be maneuvering the brigade for him and in a very cool manner. We moved forward, and as we neared the fight could see our men crouching behind the fences and hedges, firing with a will. The rest of the brigade moved away from us, where I knew not, and we halted behind what was, I think, West's house by the Quaker road. Here we lay down for a few minutes in peace, but very soon a rebel battery close in front opened on us with fury. Some of our officers had got into an outbuilding just in front of us for shelter, but a shell came right in among them and they left. General Howe, a fine looking man, whose command was near by, rode up and ordered Captain Sturtevant to move over to the right and support one of our batteries. In order to do this the quickest way, we had to move directly in front of the rebel battery within not more than four hundred yards, over an open plain with no obstacle between us.

The general rode away, and Captain Sturtevant, who was honest and brave, but a little wanting in decision, got up and, beginning scratching his leg, said, "There! I am ordered to go and support that battery. If I go clear out of range I shall be too long, and if I go across we shall go right into the fire of the rebels; I don't know what to do!"

Perhaps my boldness arose from having been placed in command of "I" Company that day, its officers being absent; but whatever might be the cause, I said to him, "Well, Captain, we might just as well go across under fire as to lie here, for we shall get killed here; so let us go!"

'That's so," said he; "rise up, men! Forward, march!"—and away we went on the double-quick; and then how the rebel battery did pepper us! Shells flew all around us, and the wonder was that more were not hurt. I turned my head to the left and saw the battery and the gunners, springing to their work amid the smoke. I saw one pull the string, saw the flash of the piece, heard the roar, and the whiz of the shell, heard it burst, heard the humming of the fragments, and wondered if I was to be hit, and quicker than a flash something stung my leg on the calf, and I limped out of the Tanks, a wounded man. My first impulse was to go to the rear, but the plain for a quarter of a mile was dotted with dust raised by the flying pieces and ricocheting shot, and I concluded that if I could, 't were better to stay at the front than to be killed going to the rear. So I stooped down, opened the ragged hole in my trousers leg, and saw no blood, but the form of a piece of shell two or three inches long, printed in a cruel bruise on my leg; then I limped to the regiment, which had halted and lain down. I took my place, and was so vexed with pain that I swore at a Frenchman in my company roundly for being out of his place, and then commenced behaving myself. The same shell wounded two or three others, I believe.

We lay just behind the crest of a gentle slope and in front of some trees. In front of us first came the open field and then some woods. The rebel battery had been silenced somehow, but sharpshooters in the farther woods shot at us with uncomfortable precision. The battery on our left threw shell into the woods and I imagine made hot quarters for the sharpshooters. In the course of an hour my leg had swelled badly, and my lameness was such that I could hardly step otherwise than on my toes. It was a matter of honor and pride with me to stay with the regiment as long as I could, but Captain Sturtevant and Captain Cross both urged me to go to the hospital, for (they said) we were liable to move on the enemy at any moment, and as I seemed to grow lamer, I might be in such a plight that I should give out in a bad place and lose my life or be taken prisoner. The force of these arguments was evident, and at length I hobbled away. I passed some of the Third Corps in a field where the wheat was stacked in many piles, and reached the road on which we had marched down, and then climbed the hill and searched for the hospital. I met a good-looking Negro man in my wanderings, and with an eye to business engaged him as a servant, his former employer, a captain in our army, having been killed that day, he said.

At length I found a building which looked like a church, in the darkness which had now settled on the field, around which great numbers of our wounded lay among the trees, groaning and complaining bitterly, and it was a scene of utter misery. I groped around carefully among the prostrate men, who were agonized if any one stepped too close to them, and sat down by a tree. Beside me a groaning man proved to be Second Lieutenant Lawrence, of our regiment, who dolefully informed me that he was very badly wounded in the ankle, but who really, as I learned afterwards, had nothing but a contusion. He was the color sergeant who was promoted to second lieutenant at Camp California, and never rejoined the regiment for duty. How it transpired I do not recollect, but I found our own regimental hospital wagon in the woods, and got my leg bound up, and then lay down in company with some of our men to sleep.

—LIVERMORE, *Days and Events*

IV.12

RICHARD AUCHMUTY REVIEWS THE PENINSULAR CAMPAIGN

A member of one of the most distinguished of New York families, Richard Auchmuty was practicing architecture in New York, in the office of the famous Renwick, when the war broke out. He was commissioned a captain in the V Corps of the Army of the Potomac, and fought gallantly through all the campaigns in Virginia to Gettysburg. Invalided out he took work in the War Department, and participated in the defense of Washington at the time of Early's raid in 1864. After the war Auchmuty devoted himself to architecture and philanthropy.

Harrison's Landing, James River, Saturday, July 5, 1862

My Dear Mother,—

I sincerely thank God that I have passed unhurt through the horrors of the last ten days. I am, of course, worn out with fatigue, but am otherwise well.

I see by the *Times* of the 4th, that you are still but slightly informed of what has been going on here. The correspondents mostly wrote from the steamboats on the Pamunkey.

The army is too immense for one person to have a clear idea of what is going on all along the line. I will confine myself to the right wing, which was supposed to be sufficient to protect the rear.

McClellan undoubtedly meant to swing the army around until it rested on the James; but the fate of war had, in the end, more to do with it than he. On Thursday [June 26], about five o'clock, while enjoying a dinner of lamb and green peas, an order came to send a brigade to assist McCall near Mechanicsville. Butterfield's brigade was on an expedition to the rear, Martindale's somewhere else, and Griffin's (he had taken command that day of the Seconds alone remained. We went with them about four miles, and got in a very heavy cannonading, the rebels having crossed the Chickahominy at that point. This lasted until about 9 P.M. The cannonading was the loudest I have heard, batteries being planted for nearly a mile; and after dark it became more terrible than by day. The Fourth Michigan came to close quarters with the Fourteenth Louisiana and Sixty-sixth Virginia, losing fifty men. The rest of our division suffered but slightly. At eight o'clock Morrell left me with Weedon and went to look after Martindale. I lay on one of the guncarriages and got a nap of two hours.

At 2 A.M., an order came to fall back to our old camp near Gaines' Mills (Camp New Bridge); I went after Griffin, and by daylight we were on our way back, the rebels shelling the road. At Gaines' Mills we had breakfast, and heard that our camp was to be abandoned for a better position. Most of the supplies had been sent over the Chickahominy during the night; those remaining were burned.

At 9 A.M., on Friday, the 27th, we crossed the mill-dam and broke down the bridge, the rebel scouts coming in sight. The men were posted in order of battle, and lay down to rest. The sun was extremely hot. Morrell's division was posted along

a wooded ravine, with an open field rising behind them. In the ravine ran a creek, draining the mill-dam. I did not see the posifion of the right of the line. Behind us, in reserve, was McCall's division.

About twelve, the artillery commenced, and the skirmish ers, who were in a field beyond the ravine, returned. Musketry began on the right, and gradually worked down to us. About one o'clock hell itself seemed to break loose on our division. First Martindale's, then Griffin's, and then Butterfield's brigades, caught a storm of shot, shell, and musketry, which made the trees wave like a hurricane. The enemy would bring a large number of guns to bear on one point, and then advance a whole brigade on one of our regiments. Three times they did this, each attack lasting about half an hour. After each attack, reenforcements went in, but our men still formed the front line. At six came the fourth at tack, more fearful than any. The right wing had gradually fallen back, until our line was thus:

Suddenly a rush of men, horses, and guns passed over the field, the line was broken, the battle was lost. A line was attempted further back, but it broke at once and all moved towards the bridge. A line of fresh troops being formed near the bridge, the men halted, and the officers tried to collect the regiments, or even the brigades, together. Darkness coming on, the firing ceased, and the men were sent over the bridge in good order. The last passed about 6 A.M., destroying it after them.

I got a cup of coffee, and slept on the ground for two or three hours at daylight. At one o'clock we were told to move to Savage Station, about three miles, but marched eight miles to White Oak Swamp. There we had a beautiful camp and a good night's rest. We were around the house of a Mr. Brilton. The next morning McClellan and his staff took breakfast with us. Everything looked so pretty and peaceful there, that I left my horse that had been shot at Gaines' Mills with him, but the next day the whole army swept over his place and destroyed everything. The rear guard was attacked, a fight took place, and his house was burned to the ground.

That day (Sunday) we were posted ready for an attack, and at night commenced to make for the James River. The night was an awful one, as dark as pitch, with constant alarms that the cavalry were upon us, when all would be confusion. To add to our troubles, it was found that our corps had gone by the wrong road, which made it 10 A.M. before we reached the James.

We lay down in a wheat field till one o'clock (on Monday), when heavy firing began, and we were sent to the front. The enemy shelled us from the woods without doing much harm. In the meantime McCall and Heintzelman suffered terribly and fell back to our line.

We were encamped at a lovely place—an old picturesque brick house, surrounded by splendid white oak trees, on a terrace as fine as Hyde Park, overlooking the river. This terrace, instead of following the river, came abruptly around at right angles to it, overlooking the fields and woods, which were humming and crashing under the shells from the gun boats. Towards the enemy the ground sloped gradually down, rising again in wooded hills, first occupied by Heintzelmann and now by the enemy.

The men slept that night in order of battle. I got about an hour, on the floor of the old house. At daybreak things were gotten ready, and at 8 A.M. the enemy opened. The day was clear and cool. The Second Brigade was posted around two sides of the front. At 5 P.M. the enemy advanced in great force on the Fourteenth New York and Sixty-

second Pennsylvania, and much the same scene as at Gaines' Mills was gone through, excepting that the men stood like heroes.

At 6.30 things looked very black. Then up came Porter, who took command in person, with Meagher's Irish brigade. As they passed to the front, Colonel Cass, of the Ninth Massachusetts, was being brought back, his jaw shattered by a ball. As they recognized a fellow-countryman, they gave a yell that drowned the noise of the guns. They moved to the front, and Porter sent for a battery of thirty-two pounders, something very unusual in a field fight. This turned the enemy back. They said they lay down trembling with fright as the immense shells roared through the woods. At nine the firing ceased on our side, the rebels having stopped about an hour before.

We had repulsed their attack, and remained masters of the field, but, great God! what a field it was. To the surprise of all came the order to retreat. The troops could not stand another such attack, no reenforcements having come.

I took part of the Second Brigade with me, and after showing them the way, went back for our light wagon, which I got in a battery, and rushed through, riding in it myself. This retreat was a regular stampede, each man going off on his own hook, guns in the road at full gallop, teams on one side in the fields, infantry on the other in the woods. At daybreak came rain in torrents, and the ground was ankle deep in mud. This was Wednesday. I found shelter in a quartermaster's tent, and lay down to rest.

Your affectionate son,
R.T.A.

—E.S.A., ed. *Letters of Richard Tylden Auchmuty*

STONEWALL JACKSON AND THE VALLEY CAMPAIGN

Jackson's Valley campaign has long been regarded as one of the most brilliant in the history of modern warfare; perhaps no other in American warfare, unless it is Lee's campaign at Second Manassas or Grant's below Vicksburg, has been so assiduously studied abroad. The grand strategy of the Valley campaign was Lee's and, to some extent, Joe Johnston's; but the tactics were Jackson's—and the resolute spirit that gave them meaning. The strategy of the Valley campaign was essentially simple, though the campaign itself is one of the most confusing, in detail, in the history of the war. That strategy was to prevent McDowell from joining McClellan on the Peninsula, to frighten Washington into scattering its effective forces on offensive-defensive operations, and to defend Richmond from the west. All these purposes it attained.

After his brilliant performance at Bull Run Jackson had been made a major general and assigned command in the Shenandoah Valley. Only a familiarity with the geography of the Valley will make clear the details of the campaign, and that requires a careful study of the map. It is sufficient to note here that the Valley between the Blue Ridge and the Shenandoah mountains was divided by the Massanuteen Tange, thus making in effect two valleys—the Luray to the east and the Shenandoah to the west. At the head, or southern end, of the Valley was Staunton, connected by railroad with Richmond; midway down the Valley was Strasburg on the Manassas Gap Railroad which also connected with Richmond; at the mouth, or northern end, was Harpers Ferry. Jackson knew the Valley intimately, had a small and mobile force, and interior lines of communication. The Valley campaign, as he conducted it, was a military chess game; his objective not so much to defeat the enemy as to distract, confuse, check, and eventually checkmate them.

Altogether, even with the forces of Ewell and Edward Johnson that were added to his command, Jackson had only some 18,000 men. Against these were Frémont, in the west

with 15,000, and Banks, at Winchester with over 20,000, while McDowell on the Rappahannock stood ready to send reinforcements if needed. Jackson knew that he could not defeat all these forces, but he hoped to prevent them from combining, and to hold them in the Valley while Johnston and Lee dealt with McClellan.

In March 1862 Banks advanced from Harpers Ferry to Winchester. Jackson fell back, to Strasburg and then to Mount Jackson on the western edge of the Massanuttens. Supposing that he had driven Jackson from the Valley Banks prepared to move east to McDowell. This was what Jackson had to prevent. First he sent his cavalry leader Ashby to strike Shields at Winchester; then he himself moved down to Kernstown to join in the attack. Banks brought up his full forces, repulsed Jackson, and threw him back to Mount Jackson. It was a defeat, but it served its purpose. Banks was back in the Valley in full strength; McDowell was held on the Rappahannock ready to go to his aid. Moving swiftly up the Valley Jackson crossed over westward at Staunton, surprised and defeated Fremont at the Battle of McDowell, then hurried back down the Valley and burst on the astonished Banks at Front Royal (May 23). Banks retreated to Winchester where Jackson struck and scattered his forces. Panic-stricken, Washington detached 20,000 from McDowell's command and hurried them to the Valley.

Jackson meantime doubled on his tracks and retired up the Valley to Port Republic. His plan was to hold Frémont at Cross Keys with Ewel's division while he dealt with Shields. The plan worked out, and with the twin battles of Cross Keys and Port Republic the Valley campaign came to an end. A week later Jackson was on his way east to join Lee in the Peninsular campaign. In three months he had immobilized a good part of the Union army, defeated Milroy, Banks, Shields and Frémont, and proved the value of the Valley as a threat to Washington and the North.

V. I

Dick Taylor Campaigns with Jackson in the Valley

"An iron sabre vowed to an iron Lord," Stephen Vincent Benét calls Jackson, and the phrase suggests something of that Covenanter quality which Jackson, more than any other Civil War general, indubitably had. Both of his wives were daughters of Presbyterian ministers, and he himself was so devout that he would neither march nor fight on the Sabbath if he could avoid it. He regarded himself as an instrument of the Lord, and to the Lord he gave credit for every victory.

Richard Taylor, from whose recollections this and the following selection are taken, was the son of President Zachary Taylor, and a Louisiana planter and politician of wealth and prominence. Commissioned colonel of the 9th Louisiana Infantry, Taylor fought through the whole of the war—in the Valley, at Eleven Days, on the Red River, and in Hood's Tennessee campaign, rising to the rank of lieutenant general. He was a man of unusual intellectual attainments—he had studied at Edinburgh and Paris as well as at Harvard and Yale and his volume of reminiscences is one of the most enchanting of all Civil War books. His account of the Valley campaign during May and June of 1862 tells the story in sufficient detail.

Ewell's division reached the western base of Swift Run Gap on a lovely spring evening, April 30, 1862, and in crossing the Blue Ridge seemed to have left winter and its rigors behind. Jackson, whom we moved to join, had suddenly that morning marched toward McDowell, some eighty miles west, where, after uniting with a force under General Ed ward Johnson, he defeated the Federal general Milroy. Some days later he as suddenly returned. Meanwhile we were ordered to remain in camp on the Shenandoah near Conrad's store, at which place a bridge spanned the stream.

The great Valley of Virginia was before us in all its beauty. Fields of wheat spread far and wide, interspersed with woodlands, bright in their robes of tender green. Wherever appropriate sites existed, quaint old mills, with turning wheels, were busily grinding the previous year's harvest; and grove and eminence showed comfortable homesteads. The soft vernal influence shed a languid grace over the scene. The theatre of war in this region was from Staunton to the Potomac, one hundred and twenty miles, with an average width of some twenty-five miles; and the Blue Ridge and Alleghanies bounded it east and west. Drained by the Shenandoah with its numerous affluents, the surface was no where flat, but a succession of graceful swells, occasionally rising into abrupt hills. . . . Frequent passes or gaps in the mountains, through which wagon roads had been constructed, afforded easy access from east and west; and pikes were excellent, though unmetaled roads became heavy after rains.

But the glory of the Valley is Massanutten. Rising abruptly from the plain near Harrisonburg, twenty-five miles north of Staunton, this lovely mountain extends fifty miles, and as suddenly ends near Strasburg. Parallel with the Blue Ridge, and of equal height, its sharp peaks have a bolder and more picturesque aspect, while the abruptness of its slopes gives the appearance of greater altitude. Midway of Massanutten, a gap with good road affords communication between Newmarket and Luray. The eastern or Luray valley, much narrower than the one west of Massanutten, is drained by the east branch of the Shenandoah, which is joined at Front Royal, near the northern end of the mountain, by its western affluent, whence the united waters flow north, at the base of the Blue Ridge, to meet the Potomac at Harper's Ferry.

The inhabitants of this favored region were worthy of their inheritance. The north and south were peopled by scions of old colonial families, and the proud names of the "Old Dominion" abounded. In the central counties of Rockingham and Shenandoah were many descendants of German Settlers. These were thrifty, substantial Farmers, and, like their kinsmen of Pennsylvania, expressed their opulence in huge barns and fat cattle. The devotion of all to the Southern cause was wonderful. Jackson, a Valley man by reason of his residence at Lexington, south of Staunton, was their hero and idol. The women sent husbands, sons, lovers, to battle as cheerfully as to marriage feasts.

No oppression, no destitution could abate their zeal. Upon a march I was accosted by two elderly sisters, who told me they had secreted a large quantity of bacon in a well on their estate, hard by. Federals had been in possession of the country, and, fearing the in discretion of their slaves, they had done the work at night with their own hands, and now desired to *give* the meat to their people. Wives and daughters of millers, whose husbands and brothers were in arms, worked the mills night and day to furnish flour to their soldiers. To the last, women would go distances to carry the modicum of food between themselves and starvation to a suffering Confederate. . . .

While in camp near Conrad's store, the 7th Louisiana, Colonel Hays, a crack regiment, on picket down stream, had a spirited affair, in which the enemy was driven with the loss of a score of prisoners. Shortly after, for convenience of supplies, I was directed to cross the river and camp some miles to the southwest. The command was in superb condition, and a four-gun battery from Bedford county, Virginia, Captain Bowyer, had recently been added to it. The four regiments, 6th, 7th, 8th, and 9th Louisiana, would average above eight hundred bayonets. . . . The 6th, Colonel Seymour, recruited in New Orleans, was composed of Irishmen, stout, hardy fellows, turbulent in camp and requiring a strong hand, but responding to kindness and justice, and ready to follow their officers to the death. The 9th, Colonel Stafford, was from North Louisiana. Planters or sons of planters, many of them men of fortune, soldiering was a hard task to which they only became reconciled by reflecting that it was "niggering" in gentlemen to assume voluntarily the discharge of duties and then shirk. The 8th, Colonel Kelly, was from the Attakapas—"Acadians," the race of which Longfellow sings in "Evangeline." A homeloving, simple people, few spoke English, fewer still had ever before moved ten miles from their natal *cabanas*; and the war to them was "a liberal education," as was the society of the lady of quality to honest Dick Steele. They had all the light gayety of

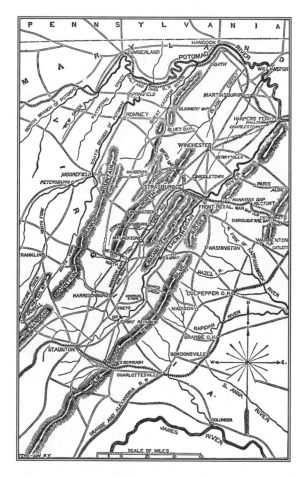

THE VALLEY OF VIRGINIA

the Gaul, and, after the manner of their ancestors, were born cooks. A capital regimental band accompanied them, and whenever weather and ground permitted, even after long marches, they would waltz and "polk" in couples with as much zest as if their arms encircled the supple waists of the Celestines and Melazies of their native Teche. The Valley soldiers Were largely of the Presbyterian faith, and of a solemn, pious demeanor, and looked askant at the caperings of my Creoles, holding them to be "devices and snares.". . .

At nightfall of the second day in this camp, an order came from General Jackson to join him at Newmarket, twenty odd miles north; and it was stated that my division commander, Ewell, had been apprised of the order. Our position was near a pike leading south of west to Harrisonburg, whence, to gain Newmarket, the great Valley pike ran due north. . . . Early dawn saw us in motion, with lovely weather, a fairish road, and men in high health and spirits.

Later in the day a mounted officer was dispatched to report our approach and select a camp, which proved to be beyond Jackson's forces, then lying in the fields on both sides of the pike. Over three thousand strong, neat in fresh clothing of gray with white gaiters, bands playing at the head of their regiments, not a straggler, but every man in his place, stepping jauntily as on parade, though it had marched twenty miles and more, in open column with arms at "right shoulder shift," and rays of the declining sun flaming on polished bayonets, the brigade moved down the broad, smooth pike, and wheeled on to its camping ground. Jackson's men, by thousands, had gathered on either side of the road to see us pass. Indeed, it was a martial sight, and no man with a spark of sacred fire in his heart but would have striven hard to prove worthy of such a command.

After attending to necessary camp details, I sought Jackson, whom I had never met . . . The mounted officer who had been sent on in advance pointed out a figure perched on the topmost rail of a fence overlooking the road and field, and said it was Jackson. Approaching, I saluted and declared my name and rank, then waited for a response. Before this came I had time to see a pair of cavalry boots covering feet of gigantic size, a mangy cap with visor drawn low, a heavy, dark beard, and weary eyes—eyes I afterward saw filled with intense but never brilliant light. A low, gentle voice inquired the road and distance marched that day.

"Keazletown road, six and twenty miles."

"You seem to have no stragglers."

"Never allow straggling."

"You must teach my people; they straggle badly." A bow in reply. Just then my creoles started their band and a waltz. After a contemplative suck at a lemon, "Thoughtless fellows for serious work" came forth. I expressed a hope that the work would not be less well done because of the gayety. A

return to the lemon gave me the opportunity to retire. Where Jackson got his lemons "no fellow could find out," but he was rarely without one. To have lived twelve miles from that fruit would have disturbed him as much as it did the witty Dean.

Quite late that night General Jackson came to my camp fire, where he stayed some hours. He said we would move at dawn, asked a few questions about the marching of my men, which seemed to have impressed him, and then remained silent. If silence be golden, he was a "bonanza." He sucked lemons, ate hard-tack, and drank water, and praying and fighting appeared to be his idea of the "whole duty of man."

In the gray of the morning, as I was forming my column on the pike, Jackson appeared and gave the route—north—which, from the situation of its camp, put my brigade in advance of the army. After moving a short distance in this direction, the head of the column was turned to the east and took the road over Massanutten gap to Luray. Scarce a word was spoken on the march, as Jackson rode with me. From time to time a courier would gallop up, report, and return to ward Luray. An ungraceful horseman, mounted on a sorry chestnut with a shambling gait, his huge feet with outturned toes thrust into his stirrups, and such parts of his countenance as the low visor of his shocking cap failed to conceal wearing a wooden look, our new commander was not prepossessing. That night we crossed the east branch of the Shenandoah by a bridge, and camped on the stream, near Luray. Here, after three long marches, we were but a short distance below Conrad's store, a point we had left several days before. I began to think that Jackson was an unconscious poet, and, as an ardent lover of nature, desired to give strangers an opportunity to admire the beauties of his Valley. It seemed hard lines to be wandering like sentimental travelers about the country, instead of gaining "kudos" on the Peninsula.

Off the next morning, my command still in advance, and Jackson riding with me. The road led north between the east bank of the river and the western base of the Blue Ridge. Rain had fallen and softened it, so as to delay the wagon trains in rear. Past midday we reached a wood extending from the mountain to the river, when a mounted officer from the rear called Jackson's attention, who rode back with him. A moment later, there rushed out of the wood to meet us a young, rather well-looking woman, afterward widely known as Belle Boyd. Breathless with speed and agitation, some time elapsed before she found her voice. Then, with much volubility, she said we were near Front Royal, beyond the wood; that the town was filled with Federals, whose camp was on the west side of the river, where they had guns in position to cover the wagon bridge, but none bearing on the railway bridge below the former; that they believed Jackson to be west of Massanutten, near Harrisonburg; that General Banks, the Federal commander, was at Winchester, twenty miles northwest of Front Royal, where he was slowly concentrating his widely scattered forces to meet Jackson's advance, which was expected some days later.

All this she told with the precision of a staff officer making a report, and it was true to the letter. Jackson was possessed of these facts before he left Newmarket, and based his movements upon them; but, as he never told anything, it was news to me, and gave me an idea of the strategic value of Massanutten—pointed out, indeed by Washington before the Revolution. There also dawned on me quite another view of our leader than the one from which I had been regarding him for two days past.

Convinced of the correctness of the woman's statements, I hurried forward at "a double," hoping to surprise the enemy's idlers in the town, or swarm over the wagon bridge with them and secure it. Doubtless this was rash, but I felt immensely "cocky" about my brigade, and believed that it would prove equal to any demand. Before we had cleared the wood Jackson came galloping from the rear, followed by a company of horse. He ordered me to deploy my leading regiment as skirmishers on both sides of the road and con tinue the advance, then passed on. We speedily came in sight of Front

Royal, but the enemy had taken the alarm, and his men were scurrying over the bridge to their camp, where troops could be seen forming.

The situation of the village is surpassingly beautiful. It lies near the east bank of the Shenandoah, which just below unites all its waters, and looks directly on the northern peaks of Massanutten. The Blue Ridge, with Manassas Gap, through which passes the railway, overhangs it on the east; distant Alleghany bounds the horizon to the west; and down the Shenandoah, the eye ranges over a fertile, well-farmed country. Two bridges spanned the river—a wagon bridge above, a railway bridge some yards lower. A good pike led to Winchester, twenty miles, and another followed the river north, whence many cross-roads united with the Valley pike near Winchester. The river, swollen by rain, was deep and turbulent, with a strong current. The Federals were posted on the west bank, here somewhat higher than the opposite, and a short distance above the junction of waters, with batteries bearing more especially on the upper bridge.

Under instructions, my brigade was drawn up in line, a little retired from the river, but overlooking it—the Federals and their guns in full view. So far, not a shot had been fired. I rode down to the river's brink to get a better look at the enemy through a field-glass, when my horse, heated by the march, stepped into the water to drink. Instantly a brisk fire was opened on me, bullets striking all around and raising a little shower-bath. Like many a foolish fellow, I found it easier to get into than out of a difficulty. I had not yet led my command into action, and, remembering that one must "strut" one's little part to the best advantage, sat my horse with all the composure I could muster. A provident camel, on the eve of a desert journey, would not have laid in a greater supply of water than did my thoughtless beast. At last he raised his head, looked placidly around, turned, and walked up the bank.

This little incident was not without value, for my men welcomed me with a cheer; upon which, as if in response, the enemy's guns opened, and, having the range, inflicted some loss on my line. We had no guns to reply, and, in advance as has been mentioned, had outmarched the troops behind us. Motionless as a statue, Jackson sat his horse some few yards away, and seemed lost in thought. Perhaps the circumstances mentioned some pages back had obscured his star; but if so, a few short hours swept away the cloud, and it blazed, Sirius like, over the land. I approached him with the suggestion that the railway bridge might be passed by stepping on the cross ties, as the enemy's guns bore less directly on it than on the upper bridge. He nodded approval.

The 8th regiment was on the right of my line, near at hand; and dismounting, Colonel Kelly led it across under a sharp musketry fire. Several men fell to disappear in the dark water beneath; but the movement continued with great rapidity, considering the difficulty of walking on ties, and Kelly with his leading files gained the opposite shore. Thereupon the enemy fired combustibles previously placed near the center of the wagon bridge. The loss of this structure would have seriously delayed us, as the railway bridge was not floored, and I looked at Jackson, who, nearby, was watching Kelly's progress. Again he nodded, and my command rushed at the bridge. Concealed by the cloud of smoke, the suddenness of the movement saved us from much loss; but it was rather a near thing. My horse and clothing were scorched, and many men burned their hands severely while throwing brands into the river. We were soon over, and the enemy in full flight to Winchester, with loss of camp, guns, and prisoners.

Just as I emerged from flames and smoke, Jackson was by my side. How he got there was a mystery, as the bridge was thronged with my men going at full speed; but smoke and fire had decidedly freshened up his costume. . . .

Late in the night Jackson came out of the darkness and seated himself by my camp fire. He mentioned that I would move with him in the morning, then relapsed into silence. I fancied he looked at me kindly, and interpreted it into an approval of the conduct of the brigade. The events of the day, anticipations of the morrow,. . . drove away sleep, and I watched Jackson. For hours he sat silent and motionless, with eyes fixed on the fire. I took up the idea that he was inwardly praying, and he remained through the night.

Off in the morning, Jackson leading the way, my brigade, a small body of horse, and a section of the Rockbridge (Virginia) artillery forming the column. Major Wheat, with his battalion of "Tigers," was directed to keep close to the guns. Sturdy marchers, they trotted along with the horse and artillery at Jackson's heels, and after several hours were some distance in advance of the brigade, with which I remained.

A volley in front, followed by wild cheers, stirred us up to a "double," and we speedily came upon a moving spectacle. Jackson had struck the Valley pike at Middletown, twelve miles south of Winchester, along which a large body of Federal horse, with many wagons, was hastening north. He had attacked at once with his handful of men, overwhelmed resistance, and captured prisoners and wagons. The gentle Tigers were looting right merrily, diving in and out of wagons with the activity of rabbits in a warren; but this occupation was abandoned on my approach, and in a moment they were in line, looking as solemn and virtuous as deacons at a funeral. Prisoners and spoil were promptly secured. . . .

At dusk we overtook Jackson, pushing the enemy with his little mounted force, himself in advance of all. I rode with him, and we kept on through the darkness. There was not resistance enough to deploy infantry. A flash, a report, and a whistling bullet from some covert met us, but there were few casualties. I quite remember thinking at the time that Jackson was invulnerable, and that persons near him shared that quality. An officer, riding hard, overtook us, who proved to be the chief quartermaster of the army. He reported the wagon trains far behind, impeded by a bad road in Luray Valley.

"The ammunition wagons?" sternly.

"All right, sir. They were in advance, and I doubled teams on them and brought them through."

"Ah!" in a tone of relief.

To give countenance to this quartermaster, if such can be given of a dark night, I remarked jocosely: "Never mind the wagons. There are quantities of store in Winchester, and the General has invited me to breakfast there to-morrow."

Jackson, who had no more capacity for jests than a Scotchman, took this seriously, and reached out to touch me on the arm. In fact, he was of Scotch-Irish descent, and his unconsciousness of jokes was *de race*. Without physical wants himself, he forgot that others were differently constituted, and paid little heed to commissariat; but woe to the man who failed to bring up ammunition! In advance, his trains were left far behind. In retreat, he would fight for a wheelbarrow.

Some time after midnight, by roads more direct from Front Royal, other troops came on the pike, and I halted my jaded people by the roadside, where they built fires and took a turn at their haversacks.

Moving with the first light of morning, we came to Kerns town, three miles from Winchester, and the place of Jackson's fight with Shields. Here heavy and sustained firing, artillery and small arms, was heard. A staff officer approached at full speed to summon me to Jackson's presence and move up my command. A gallop of a mile or more brought me to him. Winchester was in sight, a mile to the north. To the east Ewell with a large part of the army was fighting briskly and driving the enemy on to the town. On the west a high ridge, overlooking the country to the south and southeast, was occupied by a heavy mass of Federals with guns in position. Jackson was on the pike, and near him were several regiments lying down for shelter, as the fire from the ridge was heavy and searching. A Virginian battery, Rockbridge artillery, was fighting at a great disadvantage, and already much cut up. Poetic authority asserts that "Old Virginny never

tires," and the conduct of this battery justified the assertion of the muses. With scarce a leg or wheel for man and horse, gun or caisson, to stand on, it continued to hammer away at the crushing fire above.

Jackson, impassive as ever, pointed to the ridge and said, "You must carry it." I replied that my command would be up by the time I could inspect the ground, and rode to the left for that purpose. A small stream, Abraham's creek, flowed from the west through the little vale at the southern base of the ridge, the ascent of which was steep, though nowhere abrupt. At one point a broad, shallow, trough-like depression broke the surface, which was further interrupted by some low copse, outcropping stone, and two fences. On the sum mit the Federal lines were posted behind a stone wall, along a road coming west from the pike. Worn somewhat into the soil, this road served as a countersink and strengthened the position. Further west, there was a break in the ridge, which was occupied by a body of horse, the extreme right of the enemy's line.

There was scarce time to mark these features before the head of my column appeared, when it was filed to the left, close to the base of the ridge, for protection from the plunging fire. Meanwhile, the Rockbridge battery held on man fully and engaged the enemy's attention. Riding on the flank of my column, between it and the hostile line, I saw Jackson beside me. This was not the place for the commander of the army, and I ventured to tell him so, but he paid no attention to the remark. We reached the shallow depression spoken of, where the enemy could depress his guns, and his fire be came close and fatal. Many men fell, and the whistling of shot and shell occasioned much ducking of heads in the column. This annoyed me no little, as it was but child's play to the work immediately in hand. Always an admirer of delightful "Uncle Toby," I had contracted the most villainous habit of his beloved army in Flanders, and, forgetting Jack son's presence, ripped out, "What the h— are you dodging for? If there is any more of it, you will be halted under this fire for an hour."

The sharp tones of a familiar voice produced the desired effect, and the men looked as if they had swallowed ramrods but I shall never forget the reproachful surprise expressed in Jackson's face. He placed his hand on my shoulder, said in a gentle voice, "I am afraid you are a wicked fellow," turned, and rode back to the pike.

The proper ground gained, the column faced to the front and began the ascent. At the moment the sun rose over the Blue Ridge, without cloud or mist to obscure his rays. It was a lovely Sabbath morning, the 25th of May, 1862. The clear, pure atmosphere brought the Blue Ridge and Alleghany and Massanutten almost overhead. Even the cloud of murderous smoke from the guns above made beautiful spirals in the air, and the broad fields of luxuriant wheat glistened with dew. . . .

As we mounted we came in full view of both armies, whose efforts in other quarters had been slackened to await the result of our movement. I felt an anxiety amounting to pain for the brigade to acquit itself handsomely; and this feeling was shared by every man in it. About half way up, the enemy's horse from his right charged; and to meet it, I directed Lieutenant-Colonel Nicholls, whose regiment, the 8th, was on the left, to withhold slightly his two flank companies. By one volley, which emptied some saddles, Nicholls drove off the horse, but was soon after severely wounded. Progress was not stayed by this incident. Closing the many gaps made by the fierce fire, steadied the rather by it, and preserving an alignment that would have been creditable on parade, the brigade, with cadenced step and eyes on the foe, swept grandly over copse and ledge and fence, to crown the heights from which the enemy had melted away. Loud cheers went up from our army, prolonged to the east, where warm hearted Ewell cheered himself hoarse, and led forward his men with renewed energy. In truth, it was a gallant feat of arms, worthy of the pen of him who immortalized the charge of the "Buffs" at Albuera.

Breaking into column, we pursued closely. Jackson came up and grasped my hand, worth a thousand words from another, and we were soon in the streets of Winchester, a quaint old town of some five thousand inhabitants. There was a little fighting in the streets, but the people were all abroad—certainly all the women and babies. They were frantic with delight, only regretting that so many "Yankees" had escaped, and seriously impeded our movements.

A buxom, comely dame of some five and thirty summers, with bright eyes and tight ankles, and conscious of these advantages, was especially demonstrative, exclaiming, "Oh!—you are too late—too late!"

Whereupon, a tall creole from the Teche sprang from the ranks of the 8th regiment, just passing, clasped her in his arms, and imprinted a sounding kiss on her ripe lips, with *"Madame! je n'arrive jamais trop tard."* A loud laugh followed, and the dame, with a rosy face but merry twinkle in her eye, escaped.

—TAYLOR, *Destruction and Reconstruction*

V.2

TAYLOR'S IRISHMEN CAPTURE A BATTERY AT PORT REPUBLIC

The climax of the Valley campaign came on June 8 and 9 with the battles of Cross Keys on the north and Port Republic on the south bank of the Shenandoah. Confronted by two armies—one under Frémont, the other under Shields—Jackson, instead of retreating, struck each of them separately. At Cross Keys, on June 8, Ewell checked Fremont while on the following day Ewell and Taylor broke the strongly entrenched Union line at Port Republic, and forced the enemy back to Conrad's Store, some five miles down the river. It was, as Jackson said, a "delightful excitement."

Ewell, in immediate charge at Cross Keys, was ready early in the morning of the 8th, when Fremont attacked. The ground was undulating, with much wood, and no extended view could be had. In my front the attack, if such it could be called, was feeble in the extreme—an affair of skirmishers, in which the enemy yielded to the slightest pressure.

A staff officer of Jackson's, in hot haste, came with orders from his chief to march my brigade double-quick to Port Republic. Elzey's brigade, in second line to the rear, was asked to take my place and relieve my skirmishers; then, advising the staff officer to notify Ewell, whom he had not seen, we started on the run, for such a message from Jackson meant business. Two of the intervening miles were quickly passed, when another officer appeared with orders to halt.

In half an hour, during which the sound of battle at Cross Keys thickened, Jackson came. . . . He had passed the night in the village, with his staff and escort. Up as usual at dawn, he started alone to recross the bridge, leaving his people to follow. The bridge was a few yards below the last house in the village, and some mist overhung the river. Under cover of this a small body of horse, with one gun, from Shields's forces, had reached the east end of the bridge and trained the gun on it. Jackson was within an ace of capture. As he spurred across, the gun was fired on him, but without effect, and the sound brought up staff and escort, when the horse retired north. This incident occasioned the order to me. After relating it (all save his own danger), Jackson passed on to Ewell. Thither I followed, to remain in reserve until the general forward movement in the afternoon, by which Fremont was driven back with loss of prisoners. We did not persist far, as Shields's force was near upon us.

From Ewell I learned that there had been some pretty fighting in the morning, though less than might have been expected from Fremont's numbers. I know not if the presence of this commander had a benumbing influence on his troops, but certainly his advanced cavalry and infantry had proved bold and enterprising.

In the evening we moved to the river and camped. Winder's and other brigades crossed the bridge, and during the night Ewell, with most of the army, drew near, leaving Trimble's brigade and the horse at Cross Keys. No one apprehended

another advance by Fremont. The following morning, Sunday, June 9, my command passed the bridge, moved several hundred yards down the road, and halted. Our trains had gone east over the Blue Ridge. The sun appeared above the mountain while the men were quietly breakfasting. Suddenly, from below, was heard the din of battle, loud and sustained, artillery and small arms. The men sprang into ranks, formed column, and marched, and I galloped forward a short mile to see the following scene:

From the mountain, clothed to its base with undergrowth and timber, a level—clear, open, and smooth—extended to the river. This plain was some thousand yards in width. Half a mile north, a gorge, through which flowed a small stream, cut the mountain at a right angel. The northern shoulder of this gorge projected farther into the plain than the southern, and on an elevated plateau of the shoulder were placed six guns, sweeping every inch of the plain to the south. Federal lines, their right touching the river, were advancing steadily, with banners flying and arms gleaming in the sun. A gallant show, they came on. Winder's and another brigade, with a battery, opposed them. This small force was suffering cruelly, and its skirmishers were driven in on their thin supporting line. As my Irishmen predicted, "Shields's boys were after fighting." Below, Ewell was hurrying his men over the bridge, but it looked as if we should be doubled up on him ere he could cross and develop much strength.

Jackson was on the road, a little in advance of his line, where the fire was hottest, with reins on his horse's neck, seemingly in prayer. Attracted by my approach, he said, in his usual voice, "Delightful excitement." I replied that it was pleasant to learn he was enjoying himself, but thought he might have an indigestion of such fun if the six-gun battery was not silenced. He summoned a young officer from his staff, and pointed up the mountain.

The head of my approaching column was turned short up the slope, and speedily came to a path running parallel with the river. We took this path, the guide leading the way. From him I learned that the plateau occupied by the battery had been used for a charcoal kiln, and the path we were following, made by the burners in hauling wood, came upon the gorge opposite the battery. Moving briskly, we reached the hither side a few yards from the guns. Infantry was posted near, and riflemen were in the undergrowth on the slope above. Our approach, masked by timber, was unexpected. The battery was firing rapidly, enabled from elevation to fire over the advancing lines. The head of my column began to deploy under cover for attack, when the sounds of battle to our rear appeared to recede, and a loud Federal cheer was heard, proving Jackson to be hard pressed.

It was rather an anxious moment, demanding instant action. Leaving a staff officer to direct my rear regiment—the 7th, Colonel Hays—to form in the wood as a reserve, I ordered the attack, though the deployment was not completed, and our rapid march by a narrow path had occasioned some disorder. With a rush and shout the gorge was passed and we were in the battery. Surprise had aided us, but the enemy's infantry rallied in a moment and drove us out. We returned, to be driven a second time. The riflemen on the slope worried us no little, and two companies of the 9th regiment were sent up the gorge to gain ground above and dislodge them, which was accomplished. The fighting in and around the battery was hand to hand, and many fell from bayonet wounds. Even the artillerymen used their rammers in a way not laid down in the Manual, and died at their guns. As Conan said to the devil, "'Twas claw for claw." I called for Hays, but he, the promptest of men, and his splendid regiment, could not be found. Something unexpected had occurred, but there was no time for speculation. With a desperate rally, in which I believe the drummer-boys shared, we carried the battery for the third time, and held it.

Infantry and riflemen had been driven off, and we began to feel a little comfortable, when the enemy, arrested in his advance by our attack, appeared. He had countermarched, and, with left near the river, came into full view of our situation. Wheeling to the right, with colors advanced, like a solid wall he marched straight upon us. There seemed noting left but to set our backs to the mountain and die hard. At the instant, crashing through the underwood, came Ewell, outriding staff and escort. He produced the effect of a reenforcement, and was welcomed with cheers. The line before us halted and threw forward skirmishers. A moment later, a shell came shrieking along it, loud Confederate cheers reached our delighted ears, and Jackson, freed from his toils, rushed up like a whirlwind, the enemy in rapid retreat. We turned the captured guns on them as they passed, Ewell serving as a gunner.

Though rapid, the retreat never became a rout. Fortune had refused her smiles, but Shields's brave "boys" preserved their organization and were formidable to the last; and had Shields himself, with his whole command, been on the field, we should have had tough work indeed.

Jackson came up, with intense light in his eyes, grasped my hand, and said the brigade should have the captured battery. I thought the men would go mad with cheering, especially the Irishmen. A huge fellow, with one eye closed and half his whiskers burned by powder, was riding cock-horse on a gun, and, catching my attention, yelled out, "We told you to bet on your boys."

—TAYLOR, *Destruction and Reconstruction*

V.3

COLONEL WOLSELEY VISITS STONEWALL JACKSON

Fresh from campaigns in the Crimea, India and China, Colonel Garnet Wolseley—later Lord Wolseley—was ordered to Canada as quartermaster general in December 1861. In August of the next year he applied for leave of absence and, without the approval of his superiors, made his way into the Confederate States and visited scenes of recent battles, and the headquarters of Lee and Jackson. Already favorable to the Confederate cause, his enthusiasm was confirmed by what he saw. His account of his month's visit to Confederate Headquarters, which appeared anonymously in *Blackwood's Magazine,* aroused widespread interest in Britain and America.

Upon leaving, we drove to Bunker's Hill, six miles nearer Martinsburg, at which place Stonewall Jackson, now of world wide celebrity, had his headquarters. With him we spent a most pleasant hour, and were agreeably surprised to find him very affable, having been led to expect that he was silent and almost morose. Dressed in his grey uniform, he looks the hero that he is; and his thin compressed lips and calm glance, which meets yours unflinchingly, give evidence of that firm ness and decision of character for which he is so famous. He has a broad open forehead, from which the hair is well brushed back; a shapely nose, straight, and rather long; thin colourless cheeks, with only a very small allowance of whisker; a cleanly-shaven upper lip and chin; and a pair of fine greyish-blue eyes, rather sunken, with overhanging brows, which intensify the keenness of his gaze, but without imparting any fierceness to it. Such are the general characteristics of his face; and I have only to add, that a smile seems always lurking about his mouth when he speaks; and that, though his voice partakes slightly of that harshness which Europeans unjustly attribute to *all* Americans, there is much unmistakable cordiality in his manner: and to us he talked most affectionately of England, and of his brief but enjoyable sojourn there.

The religious element seems strongly developed in him; and though his conversation is perfectly free from all puritanical cant, it is evident that he is a person who never loses sight of the fact that there is an omnipresent Deity ever presiding over the minutest occurrences of life, as well as over the most important.

Altogether, as one of his soldiers said to me in talking of him, "he is a glorious fellow!" and, after I left him, I felt that I had at last solved the mystery of Stonewall Bridge, and discovered why it was that it had accomplished such almost miraculous feats. With such a leader men would go anywhere, and face any amount of difficulties; and for my self, I believe that, inspired by the presence of such a man, I should be perfectly insensible to fatigue, and reckon upon success as a moral certainty.

Whilst General Lee is regarded in the light of infallible Jove, a man to be reverenced, Jackson is loved and adored with all that childlike and trustful affection which the ancients are said to have lavished upon the particular deity presiding over their affairs. The feeling of the soldiers for General Lee resembles that which Wellington's troops entertained for him—namely, a fixed and unshakable faith in all he did, and a calm confidence of victory when serving under him. But Jackson, like Napoleon, is idolised with that intense fervour which, consisting of mingled personal attachment and devoted loyalty, causes them to meet death for his sake, and bless him when dying.

—[Wolseley], "A Month's Visit to Confederate Headquarters"

V.4

Henry Kyd Douglas Remembers Stonewall Jackson

Henry Kyd Douglas, whose reminiscences give us the liveliest and fullest picture of Jackson that we have from any con temporary, was practicing law in St. Louis when the war broke out. Hastening home he enlisted as a private in the 2nd Virginia Regiment—part of the Stonewall Brigade. He was later aide-de-camp to Jackson, and fought with him until his death at Chancellorsville. Douglas rose to be brigadier general—the youngest in either army, it is said—and his brigade fired the last shot and was the last to surrender at Appomattox.

In face and figure Jackson was not striking. Above the average height, with a frame angular, muscular, and fleshless, he was, in all his movements from riding a horse to handling a pen, the most awkward man in the army. His expression was thoughtful, and. as a result I fancy of his long ill health, was generally clouded with an air of fatigue. His eye was small, blue, and in repose as gentle as a young girl's. With high, broad, forehead, small sharp nose, thin, pallid lips generally tightly shut, deep-set eyes, dark, rusty beard, he was certainly not a handsome man. His face in tent or parlor, softened by his sweet smile, was as different from itself on the battlefield .IS a little lake in summer noon differs from the same lake when frozen. Walking or riding the General was ungainly: his main object was to get over the ground. He rode boldly and well, but not with grace or ease; and "Little Sorrel" was as little like a Pegasus as he was like an Apollo. He was not a man of style. General Lee, on horse back or off, was the handsomest man I ever saw. It was said of Wade Hampton that he looked as knightly when mounted as if he had stepped out from an old canvas, horse and all. John C. Breckinridge was a model of manly beauty, John B. Gordon, a picture for the sculptor, and Joe Johnston looked every inch a soldier. None of these things could be said of Jackson.

The enemy believed he never slept. In fact he slept a great deal. Give him five minutes to rest, he could sleep three of them. Whenever he had nothing else to do he went to sleep, especially in church. He could sleep in any position, in a chair, under fire, or on horseback. Being a silent man, he gave to sleep many moments which other men gave to conversation. And yet he was never caught "napping."

He was quiet, not morose. He often smiled, rarely laughed. He never told a joke but rather liked to hear one, now and then. He did not live apart from his personal staff, although they were nearly all young; he liked to have them about, especially at table. He encouraged the liveliness of their conversation at meals, although he took little part in it. His own words seemed to embarrass him, unless he could follow his language by action. As he never told his plans, he never discussed them. He didn't offer advice to his superiors, nor ask it of his subordinates. Reticent and self-reliant he believed "he walks with speed who walks alone." The officer next in command often and very justly

complained of this risky reticence; but Jackson is reported to have said, "If my coat knew what I intended to do, I'd take it off and throw it away." Such reticence at times was neither judicious nor defensible; but luck saved him from evil consequences. . . .

On the battlefield where Longstreet's doughty men were confronting a stubborn foe and A. P. Hill, as usual, was doing his share of the fighting, soldiers heard the cannonade and were encouraged in their hot work. Soon came to them a sharper and more earnest clamor, and there was such a rattle and roar of musketry as I never heard before or after. A staff officer dashed along Longstreet's wearied lines, crying out, "Stonewall's at them!" and was answered with yell after yell of joy, which added a strange sound to the din of battle. The battle was on in earnest; skirmishing died away and was succeeded by the crash of line meeting line.

General Jackson mounted his gaunt sorrel (not "Little Sorrel") and leaving his position moved more to the front. At that moment someone handed him a lemon—a fruit of which he was specially fond. Immediately a small piece was bitten out of it and slowly and unsparingly he began to extract its flavor and its juice. From that moment until darkness ended the battle, that lemon scarcely left his lips except to be used as a baton to emphasize an order. He listened to Yankee shout or Rebel yell, to the sound of musketry advancing or receding, to all the signs of promise or apprehension, but he never for an instant lost his interest in that lemon and even spoke of its excellence. His face, nevertheless, was calm and granite-like. His blue eye was restful and cold, except when now and then it gave, for a moment, an ominous flash. His right hand lay open and flat on his thigh, but now and then was raised into the air as was his habit—a gesture which the troops learned to believe was as significant as the extended arm of Aaron. But the lemon was not abandoned.

The moment came when it was taken from his mouth with an impatient jerk. A wild yell came from the battlefield which attracted his attention. Pendleton came up and said it was from the Stonewall Brigade, for he had just seen Winder taking them in. He drew the lemon away abruptly and said, "We shall soon have good news from that charge. Yes, they are driving the enemy!" and he lifted up his yellow banner, as if in triumph. When I last saw that lemon, it was torn open and exhausted and thrown away, but the day was over and the battle was won. . .

The 6th of July [1862] was a very warm day. The General had returned from his morning ride to the front and was trying to make himself comfortable. Headquarters were in bivouac. He seated himself at the foot of a large tree to take a nap—he could always go to sleep when he had nothing else to do. After a very short rest he aroused himself and asked me if I had a novel. I did not have one, nor did any of the staff, as all books had been left in the vicinity of Mechanicsville with the wagons. He said he had not read a novel for a long time before the war. Hugh McGuire, a clerk at Headquarters, afterwards Captain in T. L. Rosser's Cavalry Brigade, handed me a yellow-back novel of the sensational type, saying he had picked it up on the battlefield. It looked like literary trash, and it was—sensational and full of wood cuts. I handed it to the General, who looked at it with a smile, seated himself again at the foot of the tree, and began to read it. He gave his whole attention to it, as if it was a duty not to give it up, and waded on through it. Now and then his features would relax and smile, but he did not take his eyes from the book. He did not speak a word but kept on until he had finished it; fortunately, it was a small paper volume of large print. He then returned it with thanks, saying it had been a long time since he had read a novel and it would be a long time until he read another. This was the only book not strictly military or religious that I ever saw him attempt to read in the army.

On the 8th of July [1862] the Army of Northern Virginia began to move back to the vicinity of Richmond. When Jack son's command

started he and his staff remained behind until some time after the rest of the army had gone. It was after dark when he started and about midnight when he reached his Headquarters. He was riding along at ten or eleven o'clock with his drowsy staff, nodding on "Little Sorrel," as was his custom, and trusting to that intelligent beast not to give him a fall. More than once did we see his head nod and drop on his breast and his body sway a little to one side or the other, expecting to see him get a tumble; but he never got it. On this occasion our sleepy cavalcade at different times passed small squads of soldiers in fence corners before blazing fires, roasting green corn and eating it. Passing one of these, our staggering leader was observed by one of those thirsty stragglers, who was evidently delighted at the sight of a drunken cavalryman. Perhaps encouraged with the hope of a drink ahead, the ragged Reb jumped up from his fire andj brandishing a roasting-ear in his hand, sprang into the road and to the head of the General's horse, with, "Hello! I say, old fellow, where the devil did you get your licker?"

The General suddenly woke up and said, "Dr. McGuire, did you speak to me? Captain Pendleton, did you? Somebody did," and reined up his horse.

The soldier got a look at him and took in the situation; he saw whom he had thus spoken to. "Good God! it's Old Jack!" he cried, and with several bounds and a flying leap he cleared the road, was over the fence, and disappeared in the dark.

As soon as the staff could recover from their laughter, McGuire explained the situation to the General, who was much amused. He immediately rode up to the fence, dismounted, and took half an hour's nap. Then he roused himself, said he felt better, and we went on to Headquarters. . . .

Under orders from General Lee, General Jackson left his camp at Richmond for Gordonsville about the 14th of July. General John Pope, Commander of the Army of Virginia, was gathering his forces for an advance from the vicinity of Washington. He had settled himself "in the saddle" and from that contracted Headquarters had fulminated his celebrated proclamation in the shape of a general order, for which he was afterward ridiculed by the pen and punished by the sword. Believing that Jackson was not likely to be scared by so much military fustian, General Lee sent him to look after his advancing Hannibal. The General went on in advance and we were soon far ahead of troops and wagon trains on the road to Ashland.

About sundown of the first day, we were driven temporarily into a blacksmith shop for shelter from a rain storm, and from there sent out to seek shelter for the night. We found it in a most hospitable house where a plentiful supper, good rooms, and pleasant beds were made doubly enjoyable by the easy and sincere hospitality of host and hostess. The next morning we were in Ashland early and had sundry invitations to breakfast. The General seemed in excellent humor and unusually talkative. While waiting for breakfast he sat in the parlor, amused himself and others as well by his attempts to be playful with a prattling little girl who was running about the room, and then again listened with most respectful attention to a young lady who was at the piano, giving us such songs and instrumental music as she thought to our taste. Now the General had the least possible knowledge of music and, as was said of him, he had so little of it in his soul, that he was necessarily "fit for treason, strategy and spoils." Still it was a matter of amazement to his staff, when he said with much politeness to the young lady, "Miss—, won't you play a piece of music they call 'Dixie'? I heard it a few days ago and it was, I thought, very beautiful."

The young lady was nonplussed and answered, "Why, General, I just sang it a few minutes ago—it is about our oldest war song."

"Ah, indeed, I didn't know it."

He had heard it a thousand times. Perhaps he thought he would startle the young lady with his knowledge of music; if so, he succeeded. . . .

One night, after the middle of it, General Stuart came riding into our Headquarters, accompanied by his artillery pet, Captain John Pelham, the "boy Major," as he was afterwards called, or "the gallant Pelham," as General Lee named him at Fredericksburg. . . . Everyone had gone to rest. Stuart went directly to General Jackson's tent; Pelham came into mine. The General was asleep and the cavalry chief threw himself down by his side, taking off nothing but his sabre. As the night became chilly, so did he, and unconsciously he began to take possession of blankets and got between the sheets. There he discovered himself in the early morn in the full panoply of war, and he got out of it. After a while, when a lot of us were standing by a blazing log-fire before the General's tent, he came out for his ablutions.

"Good morning, General Jackson," said Stuart, "how are you?"

Old Jack passed his hands through his thin and uncombed hair and then in tones as nearly comic as he could muster he said, "General Stuart, I'm always glad to see you here. You might select better hours sometimes, but I'm always glad to have you. But, General"—as he stooped and rubbed himself along the legs—"you must not get into my bed with your boots and spurs on and ride me around like a cavalry horse all night!"

—Douglas, *I Rode with Stonewall*

VI

SECOND BULL RUN AND ANTIETAM

The Peninsular campaign was indecisive. Lee had saved Richmond, but at heavy cost, and McClellan was at Harrison's Landing preparing to renew the contest. But Lincoln and Nalleck, who in July had been appointed Military Adviser to the President, had different plans. They had lost confidence in McClellan and wanted to try a different commander; they decided that the scattered armies in Virginia ought to be consolidated into one great fighting force. First the armies of the Valley were consolidated under John Pope, who had won a somewhat dubious reputation in the West; then Burnside was ordered north from Fortress Monroe to Falmouth; finally McClellan was directed to bring his great army to Alexandria and unite with Pope.

There was only one serious flaw in this plan: it ignored Lee and the Army of Northern Virginia. While the Union commanders were carrying through these complicated operations, Lee determined to strike. His forces were so small that he could not hope to contest with a united Federal army but he could strike the scattered armies singly. And for this he had the great advantage of inferior lines of communication.

Leaving only a few brigades to protect Richmond Lee started his army toward the Valley. There was a sharp fight at Cedar Mountain near Culpeper Courf House, where Jackson inflicted heavy losses on the hapless Banks. Then while Pope was trying to concentrate his forces along the Rapidan, Jackson swung around his rear and on August 26 destroyed Pope's headquarters and supply depots at Manassas Junction. Pope fatuously supposed that he had Jackson in a trap and hurried to close it. Jackson marched west to Grove ton and invited the attack of Pope's forces. On August 29 Pope finally caught up with Stonewall and all day long wore out his army in desperate assaults on lackson's iron lines. Meanwhile Longstreet was hurrying up the valley between the Blue Ridge and the Bull Run

Mountains. On the twenty ninth he turned east, forced Thoroughfare Gap—which Pope had left practically undefended—and the next day struck Pope's left flank, rolled it up, and sent the whole army reeling toward Bull Run.

The battle ended in a cloud of recriminations, and no wonder. Porter's corps had stood idle the whole afternoon of the twenty-ninth; Banks's 6,500 men had taken no part in the fight; McClellan, at near-by Alexandria, had failed to get any part of his large army to Pope in time to do any good. Porter was later made the scapegoat for all this tragedy of errors, but the real failure was Pope's and McClellan's.

On August 3 Pope withdrew to the defenses of Washington, and two days later McClellan supplanted him as commander of the Army of the Potomac. Lee now determined to carry the war to the North. He knew that his army was in no condition to wage an aggressive campaign, but he hoped that an invasion of the North might be effected without any major battle and that it might accomplish many things. He hoped to cut the B. & O. and possibly the Pennsylvania Railroad, thus temporarily isolating Washington; to reprovision his troops—many of them without shoes; to relieve pressure on Virginia; to bring foreign recognition.

In the first week of September, then, Lee's butternuts were splashing across the fords of the Potomac onto the shores of Maryland. "Virginia shall not call in vain," James Randall had written in the song that every Southerner was singing, but it did: Lee lost more soldiers by straggling and desertion than he gained. His ultimate objective was probably Harrisburg and he planned originally to move his army north between the Catoctin and South Mountains into Pennsylvania. To make sure of his communications he detached half his force under Jackson to take Harpers Ferry. Thus by September 13 his meager force—some 50,000 at most—was badly scattered.

At this juncture fate intervened. Lee's famous Order 191 detailing the entire plan of the campaign fell into McClellan's hands. That general moved with what was for him admirable rapidity. He was convinced that Lee had an army of 120,000 men, so he observed his customary caution, but at least he did go forward. The first clashes came on September 14 at South Mountain and Crampton's Gap. Both were Federal victories, but they did not come in time to save Harpers Ferry, which fell on the morning of the fifteenth, the Confederates bagging 11,000 prisoners and an immense body of equipment.

With his rear safe Lee moved back to Sharpsburg, entrenching his army along the little Antietam creek, his flanks resting on two bends of the Potomac. He had only 18,000 men, McClellan was hot on his trail with 70,000, and prudence would have dictated a retreat. But McClellan did not attack, and the next day Jackson came up, raising Lee's forces to about 40,000: A. P. Hill was still at Harpers Ferry. The great battle came the next day and was, perhaps, the most hotly contested of the whole war. All day long the mighty hosts in blue hurled themselves on the thin gray lines, first on Jackson on the left; then on Hill at the center; then on Longstreet on the right. Again and again it seemed as if the Confederates would be overwhelmed and destroyed, but each time they managed to hang on and to inflict such losses that the final blow was suspended. When night fell McClellan still had not used his reserves, Lee had held his lines, and the battle could fairly be called a draw. Federal losses in killed and wounded were 14,000, Confederate over 11,000.

VI.I

"Who Could Not Conquer with Such Troops as These?"

Reinforced by A. P. Hill's division, Jackson started toward the Valley on August 7. On the ninth he reached Cedar Mountain, south of Culpeper, and there ran into Banks. Banks attacked, won some initial success, and was then thrown back and overwhelmed by superior numbers. Finding the whole of Pope's army in front of him, on the Rapidan line, Jackson fell back toward Gordonsville. After some maneuvering for position, Lee decided to send Jackson around Pope's army, and it is one phase of this great swinging movement that Robert Dabney here describes.

A distinguished clergyman and college professor, Dabney was a major on Jackson's staff and later wrote a biography of his idolized hero.

While the enemy was thus deluded with the belief that the race up the Rappahannock was ended, and

that he now had nothing more to do than to hold its northern bank at this place, General Jackson was preparing, under the instructions of the Commander-in-Chief, for the most adventurous and brilliant of his exploits. This was no less than to separate himself from the support of the remainder of the army, pass around Pope to the westward, and place his *corps* between him and Washington City, at Manassa's Junction. To effect this, the Rappahannock must be passed on the upper part of its course, and two forced marches made through the western quarters of the county of Fauquier, which lie between the Blue Ridge and the subsidiary range of the Bull Run Mountains. Having made a hasty and imperfect issue of rations, Jackson disembarrassed himself of all his trains, save the ambalances and the carriages for the ammunition, and left Jeffersonton early on the morning of August 25th. Marching first westward, he crossed the two branches of the Rappahannock, passed the hamlet of Orlean, and paused at night, after a march of twenty-five miles, near Salem, a village upon the Manassa's Gap Railroad. His troops had been constantly marching and fighting since the 20th; many of them had no rations, and subsisted upon the green corn gathered along the route; yet their indomitable enthusiasm and devotion knew no flagging. As the weary column approached the end of the day's march, they found Jackson, who had ridden forward, dismounted, and standing upon a great stone by the road-side.

His sun-burned cap was lifted from his brow, and he was gazing toward the west, where the splendid August sun was about to kiss the distant crest of the Blue Ridge, which stretched far away, bathed in azure and gold; and his blue eye, beaming with martial pride, returned the rays of the evening with almost equal brightness. His men burst forth into their accustomed cheers, forgetting all their fatigue at his inspiring presence; but, deprecating the tribute by a gesture, he sent an officer to request that there should be no cheering, inasmuch as it might betray their presence to the enemy. They at once repressed their applause, and passed the word down the column to their comrades: "No cheering, boys; the General requests it." But as they passed him, their eyes and gestures, eloquent with suppressed affection, silently declared what their lips were forbidden to utter. Jackson turned to his Staff, his face beaming with delight, and said: "Who could not conquer, with such troops as these?". . .

On the morning of the 26th, he turned eastward, and passing through the Bull Run Mountains, at Thoroughfare Gap, proceeded to Bristoe Station, on the Orange Railroad, by another equally arduous march. At Gainsville, he was joined by Stuart, with his cavalry, who now assumed the duty of guarding his right flank, and watching the main army of Pope, about Warrenton. As the Confederates approached Bristoe Station, about sunset, the roar of a railroad train proceeding eastward, was heard, and dispositions were made to arrest it, by placing the brigade of Hays, under Colonel Forno, across the track. The first train broke through the obstructions placed before it, and escaped. Two others which followed it were captured, but were found to contain nothing.

The *corps* of Jackson, had now marched fifty miles in two days. The whole army of Pope was interposed between it and its friends. They had no supplies whatever, save those which they might capture from the enemy. But they were between that enemy and his capital, and were cheered by the hope of inflicting a vital blow upon him before he escaped. This movement would be pronounced wrong, if judged by a formal and common-place application of the maxims of the military art. But it is the very prerogative of true genius to know how to modify the application of those rules according to circumstances. It might have been objected, that such a division of the Confederate army into two parts, subjected it to the risk of being beaten in detail; that while the Federal commander detained and amused one by a detachment, he would turn upon the other with the chief weight of his forces, and crush it into fragments. Had Pope been a Jackson, this danger would have been real; but because Pope was but Pope, and General Lee had a Jackson to execute the bold conception, and a

Stuart to mask his movement during its progress, the risk was too small to forbid the attempt. The promptitude of General Stuart in seizing the only signal station whence the line of march could possibly be perceived, and the secrecy and rapidity of General Jackson in pursuing it, with the energy of his action when he had reached his goal, ensured the success of the movement.

—DABNEY, *Life and Campaigns of Lt. Gen. Thomas J. Jackson*

VI.2

JACKSON OUTSMARTS AND OUTFIGHTS POPE AT MANASSAS

Jackson's plans worked out to perfection. While Pope's forces were scattered over a wide area between the Catharpin and the Cedar Run rivers, Jackson circled around through Thoroughfare Gap, captured Pope's headquarters at Manassas Junction, swung northward to Groveton and westward to Gainesville. Pope ordered his forces to concentrate at Manassas, then set out in pursuit of the elusive Jackson, wearying his men with marches and countermarches and his commanders with orders that were confusing and contradictory. On August 29 Pope's army finally converged on Jackson between Groveton and Sudley Springs and exhausted itself in savage piecemeal attacks on Stonewall's line. Meantime Longstreet was swinging through Thoroughfare Gap ready to pounce on Pope's flank.

The "rebel lieutenant" of this narrative is John Hampden Chamberlayne, a young graduate of the University of Virginia who fought through the whole war to Petersburg, then made his way west hoping to find an army that would continue the fighting.

Frederick City, Md., Saturday,
Sept. 6 [1862]

My Dear Mother:

I am brimful of matter as an egg of meat. Let me try to outline our progress since my last letter—date not remembered—from Raccoon Ford—you bearing in mind that I am in A. P. Hill's division, in Jackson's corps—that corps consisting of Jackson's own division, Ewell's and Hill's. You will not think me egotistical for speaking of this corps and of the corps of Hill's divison, for of them I know most, and in truth their share was, to me at least, the most memorable in the almost incredible campaign of the last fortnight.

Crossing Raccoon Ford, Jackson in front—remember, Jackson, so used, includes Hill, Ewell, and the Stonewall division—General Lee, without much opposition, reached Rappahannock River, a few miles above Rappahannock station, where a part of Longstreet's troops had a sharp fight. On Friday Evening, August twenty-second, Jackson bivouacked in Culpeper, opposite Warrenton Springs, and the same evening threw over two of Ewell's brigades. The river rose and destroyed the bridge. Saturday the bridge was rebuilt, and that night the two brigades, after some sharp fighting, were with drawn.

On Monday morning the enemy appeared in heavy force, and the batteries of Hill's division were put in position and shelled their infantry. They retired the infantry, and bringing up a large number of batteries, threw a storm of shot and shell at us—we not replying. They must have exploded several thousand rounds, and in all, so well sheltered were we, our killed did not reach twenty. That evening Jackson's whole force moved up to Jefferson, in Culpeper County, Longstreet close to him. The enemy was completely deceived, and concluded that we had given the thing up.

Now comes the great wonder. Starting up the bank of the river on Monday, the twenty-fifth, we marched through Amosville, in Rappahannock County—still further up, crossed the Rappahannock within ten miles of the Blue Ridge, marched across open fields, by strange country paths and comfortable homesteads, by a little town in Fauquier, called Orleans, on and on, as if we would never cease—to Salem, on the Manassas Gap Railroad, reaching there after midnight. Up again by day-dawn, and still on, along the Manassas Gap road, meeting crowds—all welcoming, cheering, staring with blank amazement. So all day Tuesday, through White Plains, Haymarket, Thoroughfare Gap, in Bull Run Mountains, Gainesville, to Bristow station, on the Orange and Alexandria Rail road—making the difference from Amosville to Bristow (between forty-five and fifty miles) within the forty-eight hours. We burned up at Bristow two or three railway-trains, and moved up to Manassas Junction on Wednesday, taking our prisoners with us. Ewell's division brought up the rear, fighting all the way a force Pope had sent up from Warrenton, supposing us a cavalry party.

Upon reaching Manassas Junction, we met a brigade—the first New-Jersey—which had been sent from Alexandria on the same supposition. They were fools enough to send a flag demanding our surrender at once. Of course we scattered the brigade, killing and wounding many, and among them the Brigadier-General (Taylor,) who has since died. At the Junction was a large depot of stores, five or six pieces of artillery, two trains containing probably two hundred large cars loaded down with many millions of quartermaster and commissary stores. Beside these, there were very large sutlers' depots, full of everything; in short, there was collected there, in the space of a square mile, an amount and variety of property such as I had never conceived of, (I speak soberly.) 'Twas a curious sight to see our ragged and famished men helping themselves to every imaginable article of luxury or necessity, whether of clothing, food, or what not. For my part, I got a tooth-brush, a box of candles, a quantity of lobster salad, a barrel of coffee, and other things which I forget. But I must hurry on, for I have not time to tell the hundredth part, and the scene utterly beggars description.

A part of us hunted that New-Jersey brigade like scattered partridges over the hills just to the right of the battle-field of the eighteenth of July, 1861, while the rest were partly plundering, partly fighting the forces coming on us from Warrenton. Our men had been living on roasted corn since crossing the Rappahannock, and we had brought no wagons, so we could carry little away of the riches before us. But the men could eat for one meal at least. So they were marched up, and as much of every thing eatable served out as they could carry. To see a starving man eating lobster salad and drinking Rhine wine, barefooted and in tatters, was curious; the whole thing was incredible.

Our situation now was very critical. We were between Alexandria and Warrenton—between the hosts of McClellan and Pope with over eighteen thousand jaded men, for the corps had not more than that. At nightfall, fire was set to the depot, storehouses, the loaded trains, several empty trains, sutlers' houses, restaurants, every thing. As the magnificent conflagration began to subside, the Stonewall or First division of Jackson's corps moved off toward the battle field of Manassas, the other two divisions to Centreville, six miles distant.

As day broke, we came in sight of Centreville, rested a few hours, and toward evening the rearguard of the corps crossed Bull Run at Stone Bridge—the scene of the great slaughter of last year—closely pursued by the enemy. A part of the force came up the Warrenton turnpike, and in a furious action of two hours—the last two daylight hours of Thursday, August twenty-eighth—disputed the possession of a ridge running from Sudley Church Ford to the Warrenton turnpike. We drove them off, and on Friday morning we held the ridge, in front of which runs an incomplete railroad cut and embankment. Now, we had made a circuit from the Gap in Bull Run Mountains around to the Junction and Centerville, breaking up the railroad and destroying their stores, and returned to within six miles of the Gap, through which Longstreet must come. The enemy disputed his passage and delayed him till late in the day, and, meanwhile, they threw against our corps, all day long, vast masses of troops—Sigel's, Banks's, and Pope's own division. We got out of ammunition; we collected more from cartridge-boxes of fallen friend and foe; that gave out, and we charged with never-failing yell and steel. All day long they threw their masses on us; all day they fell back shattered and shrieking. When the sun went down, their dead were heaped in front of the incomplete railway, and we sighed with relief, for Longstreet could be seen coming into position on our right. The crisis was over; Longstreet never failed yet; but the sun went down so slowly. . . .

I am proud to have borne my humble part in these great operations—to have helped, even so lit-

tle, to consummate the grand plan, whose history will be a text-book to all young soldiers, and whose magnificent success places Lee at the side of the greatest captains, Hannibal, Caesar, Eugene, Napoleon. I hope you have preserved my letters in which I have spoken of my faith in Lee. He and his round table of generals are worthy the immortality of Napoleon and his Marshals. He moves his agencies like a god—secret, complicated, vast, resistless, complete.

—[CHAMBERLAYNE], "Narrative by a Rebel Lieutenant"

VI.3

POPE WASTES HIS STRENGTH ON JACKSON

Had Pope been able to employ all of his available forces, or had he employed what he had properly, he might have driven Jackson from the field on August 29, or overwhelmed him. But Porter's corps, near Bristoe, failed for some reason to get into the fight; Sigel, Reynolds, Heintzelman and Reno attacked separately, McDowell came late. The result was a repulse for the Federals. Pope should have realized that Longstreet was coming up on his flank, and retired to some defensive position where he could have awaited help from McClellan. Instead he elected to renew the battle on the following day.

This account of the fighting on the twenty-ninth is from the pen of David Strother, a Virginia litterateur who went with the Union, served on the states of Banks, McClellan, Pope and Hunter, and ended the war with a brigadier generalship. While his account is in diary form, there is some doubt that it was actually written up from day to day, and some of his statements are probably inaccurate.

August 29, Friday.—Clear and warm. At three o'clock this morning I was aroused by Colonel Ruggles in person to carry written orders to General Fitz-John Porter, supposed to be lying at Manassas Junction, or alternatively at Bristoe. . . . Porter's orders are to move his Corps OQ Centreville without delay.

I started with an orderly. It was pitchy dark— so dark that I couldn't see my horse's ears—and I presently found I had wandered from the road. The orderly knew nothing, or was stupid from sleepiness, so that in endeavoring to retrieve I found myself entangled in thickets, and then wandering through the half-decayed villages of log-huts built by the rebels during their first occupation. As I got out of one of these desolate encampments I fell into another, and began to suspect I was wandering in circles, which frequently happens to people bewildered or benighted. I at length dismounted, and feeling the road got out into the open plain, where the still smouldering fires of the recent destruction served to guide me. I found no troops here, and it was broad daylight when I reached Porter's quarters at Bristoe. Entering his tent I found the handsome General lying on his cot, covered with a blanket of imitation leopard skin.

At his request I lit a candle and read the message, then handed it to him. While he coolly read it over I noted the time by his watch, which marked five o'clock and twenty minutes precisely. He then proceeded to dress himself, and continued to question me in regard to the location of the different commands and the general situation. As I was but imperfectly informed myself I could only give vague and general replies to his queries. We believed Jackson separated from the main army of Lee by a day's march at least—and General Pope desired to throw all his disposable force upon him and crush him before Lee came up. The troops were immediately ordered to cook breakfast and prepare for the march.

Meanwhile the head-quarters breakfast had been served, and I sat down with the Staff officers to partake. The General, who was busy writing dispatches on the corner of the same table, looked up and asked, How do you spell "chaos?" I spelled the word letter by letter c-h-a-o-s. He thanked me, and observed, smiling, that, by a singular lapse of memory, he often forgot the spelling of the most familiar words. . . .

I immediately took leave and started back to general head quarters. The road was now lined with wagons, stragglers, and droves of cattle, all moving northward. From time to time at long intervals the cannon sounded, but no heavy firing yet. Arrived at Bull Run I found our camp broken up; that the enemy had developed in great force near Centre ville, and I must seek the General in that direction. Riding rapidly forward I found the General and Staff grouped around a house on the heights of Centreville, observing a fight which was going on some five or six miles distant in the direction of the old Bull Run battlefield. The fight was evidently thickening and extending, as could be seen by the white cumulus clouds hanging over the batteries, and the long lines of thinner smoke rising above the tree-tops.

We could furthermore see the moving dust-clouds, indicating the march of supporting columns all converging to ward the centre of action. The line of the Bull Run Mountains was visible beyond and from Thoroughfare Gap, which appeared to the right of the battle-cloud. We could see the dust and reciprocal artillery-fire of our retreating and the enemy's advancing forces. Between eleven and twelve o'clock I was standing with Colonel Beckwith and commenting on these movements, when I learned that this was probably Longstreet's command forcing back Ricketts's Division from the Gap, which he had attempted to hold. I was afterward informed it was an artillery duel between the cavalry forces of Stuart and Buford . . .

As we approached the field the pounding of the guns was tremendous, but as we were ascending the last hill that rose between us and the magnificent drama, and just beginning to snuff the sulphurous breath of battle, a Staff officer from Sigel (I think) rode up to General Pope and reported that the ammunition was failing. Immediately the General turned to me: "Captain, ride back to Centreville and hurry up all the ammunition you can find there!" I felt for a moment disgusted and mutinous, but I could not dispute the importance of my mission, so I sullenly drew rein and galloped back over the hot and dusty road. Amidst the vast accumulation of vehicles and baggage-trains at Centreville I should have had great difficulty in finding the wagons I was in search of, had I not fortunately fallen in with Lieutenant Colonel Myers, of M'Dowell's Corps, who seemed to be al ways on hand in an emergency.

With his assistance in a marvelously short time I got between twenty-five and thirty wagons started in the proper direction: and then, by his invitation, stopped to swallow a cup of coffee and a hasty lunch. Observing a considerable body of well-equipped troops lying here apparently idle, I expressed astonishment, and inquired the cause of it. The answer was expressed evasively, but with some bitterness: "There are officers here to-day who would be doing themselves far more credit by marching to the battlefield than by lying idle and exciting disaffection by doubts, sneering criticism, and open abuse of the Commander-in-Chief."

I followed my wagons until I had got them clear of Centreville and in a full trot down the turnpike; I then dug spurs into my mare's flanks, and in the shortest time possible re turned to the great centre of interest. I found the General and Staff grouped around a large pine-tree which stood solitary on the crest of an open hill, overlooking our whole line of battle. The summit immediately in our front was occupied by a line of batteries, some thirty or forty pieces, blazing and fuming like furnaces. Behind these a fine brigade of Reno's command lay resting on their arms. To their right stood Heintzelman, with the divisions of Hooker and Kearney, whose musketry kept up a continuous roar. Supporting the left of this line of guns was Sigel, also sharply engaged with small-arms. On an open bluff still further to the left, and on the opposite side of the valley traversed by the Warrenton turnpike, lay Schenck's Division, which had been a good deal cut up, and was not actively engaged at this moment. The dry grass which covered the hill he occupied had taken fire, and was burning rapidly, occasionally obscuring that portion of the field with its smoke. Beyond him, on the extreme left of our line, General Reynolds, with the Pennsylvania Reserves, lay masked from the enemy by a wood. The enemy's position can only be known by the smoke of his guns, for all his troops and batteries are concealed by the wood. He occupies strong lines on a plateau and along an unfinished railroad embankment, which is equal to a regularly intrenched line. He fights stubbornly, and has thus far resisted all our efforts to dislodge him. The General relies on the advance of M'Dowell and Porter to crush him, and we are in momentary expectation of hearing their guns. The shot and shells of the enemy directed at the batteries in our front render this position rather uncomfortable, as they are. continually screeching over our heads, or plowing the gravelly surface with an ugly rasping whir, that makes one's flesh creep. . . .

Our efforts to carry the wood in front having thus far failed, I was sent to General Reno with orders that he should throw forward the division lying in reserve to support the attack of Heintzelman's troops. The order was promptly and gallantly executed, the troops moving in beautiful order and with admirable spirit. I accompanied the advance until they passed our guns beyond the summit, and remained there admiring until the troops, moving down a fine open slope, reached the edge of the wood. The enemy was pelting away industriously from his wooded strong-hold, and the air was lively with singing bullets. For half an hour or more the roar of musketry was unceasing. At length Reno in person re ported to the General, and stated that he had failed to carry the wood. Simultaneously with his return our position was so sharply raked with shot and shell that the General with drew a short distance to the right, establishing himself on the verge of a wood. . . .

It was now about four o'clock when General Phil Kearney came in and received orders to attack and carry the disputed position at all hazards. He rode off promising to do so. While he was forming his troops for the advance it was thought necessary to pound the position with artillery. Reno, who was riding beside the Commanding General, remarked, "The wood is filled with the wounded of both armies." The Commander replied, "And yet the safety of this army and the nation demands their sacrifice, and the lives of thousands yet unwounded." After a moment's hesitation the necessity of the order was acquiesced in, and forty guns were opened upon the fatal wood. The artillerymen worked with a fiendish activity, and the sulphurous clouds which hung over the field were tinged with a hot coppery hue by the rays of the declining sun. Meanwhile Kearney had gone in, and the in cessant roar of musketry resembled the noise of a cataract.

An hour later Kearney again appeared, and informed the General that the coveted position was carried. I stood beside him as he gave in his report, and while elated with the tidings he communicated, admired the man as the finest specimen of the fighting soldier I had ever seen. With his small head surmounted by the regulation forage-cap, his thin face with its energetic beck, his colorless eyes, glaring as it were with a white heat, his erect figure with the empty coat sleeve pinned across his breast, down to the very point of his sabre, whose ragged leathern scabbard stuck out like a gaff, he looked the game-cock all over. His very voice had the resolute guttural cluck which characterizes that gallant fowl. . . .

Meanwhile M'Dowell in person arrived on the field, and reported the approach of his command. It is a relief to see him here, although it is too late for him to accomplish any thing decisive. While exchanging greetings with me M'Dowell looked toward the west, where the radiance of a rich golden sunset was breaking through the grim battle-clouds, illuminating the mingled glories and horrors of the hard-fought field. "Look," said he, "what a dramatic and magnificent picture! How tame are all Vernet's boasted battle-pieces in comparison with such a scene as this! Indeed, if an artist could successfully represent that effect it would be criticised as unreal and extravagant."

I warmed toward a man who amidst the dangers and responsibilities of the occasion could mark its passing beauties and sublimities. At this point the two Generals, with their aids and escort, rode to the front to inspect the situation. . . . The battery was still working rapidly, and the enemy fighting back with equal spirit, when one of the guns burst, throwing off a heavy fragment of the muzzle, which described an arc immediately over the heads of the line of officers and fell with a thud, just clearing the last man and horse; two feet lower and it would have swept off the whole party. I had

remarked since we came over that the ammunition used seemed miserably and dangerously defective; nearly all the shells bursting prematurely, and several so close to the muzzles of the pieces as to endanger the artillery men. . . .

We remained on this hill until after sunset, when the firing gradually ceased. When it beeame quite dark there was a beautiful pyrotechnical display about a mile distant on our left, and near the Warrenton turnpike, occasioned by a collision of King's Division of M'Dowell's Corps with the enemy's right. The sparkling lines of musketry shone in the darkness like fire-flies in a meadow, while the more brilliant flashes of artillery might have been mistaken for swamp meteors. This show continued for an hour, the advancing and receding fires indicating distinctly the surging of the battle tide; and all this time not the slightest sound either of small-arms or artillery was perceptible. It seemed at length that the fire of the enemy's line began to extend and thicken, while ours wavered and fell back, but still continued the contest. Between eight and nine o'clock it ceased entirely, and we returned to our head-quarters station, where we picketed our horses and prepared to pass the night beside a camp-fire.

—STROTHER, "Personal Recollections of the War"

VI·4

LONGSTREET OVERWHELMS POPE AT MANASSAS

Both Jackson and Pope were exhausted on the evening of the twenty-ninth. Jackson, however, knew that Longstreet was at hand; Pope merely hoped that Franklin and Sumner were on the way from Alexandria. But Pope had deluded himself that Jackson was whipped and in full retreat, he had finally brought up Porter's corps, and he refused to credit the information that Longstreet was through Thoroughfare Gap and on the battlefield. He therefore determined to renew the fight the next day. Later he gave a somewhat different explanation. "I felt it my duty," he said, "not withstanding the desperate condition of my command from great fatigue, from want of provisions and forage, and from the small hope I had of any effective assistance from Alexandria, to hold my position at all hazards and under all privations." The battle was renewed early on the afternoon of the thirtieth, Porter assaulting Jackson furiously. Just when this fighting was at its height Longstreet, whose forces were stretched out at almost a right angle to Jackson's, moved forward with his whole line and overwhelmed Porter and Reynolds.

The story is told here by Alexander Hunter, a private in the 17th Virginia—part of Hood's division. That division had made an initial thrust at the Federal lines on the night of the twenty-ninth, and on the thirtieth it led the attack.

The rapid pounding of the artillery caused us to hurry through the morning meal, almost before the sun rose above the hill, and we pushed for Thoroughfare Gap to rejoin the regiment. We knew by instinct that there would be a battle that day; for there was blood upon the moon . . . Never had life seemed more worth living than on a morning such as this; never existence sweeter; never Death so loath the dying.

Long streams of soldiers were wending their way to the front. The troops seemed everywhere; they filled the railroad track as far as the eye could reach; they emerged from the narrow gap in the mountain and spread out over the fields and meadows; they wound along the base of the hills, and marched in a steady tramp over the dusty highways; following a dozen different routes, but each face turned directly or obliquely northward. Ordnance wagons were being pushed rapidly ahead; batteries were taking position, staff officers were riding at a gallop, as if seconds and minutes were golden. In short, all fighting material was pushing to the van and all the peacefully inclined were valiantly seeking the rear. By a law as fixed as that which bound the Stoics, as unalterable as those which govern the affinities of the chemical world, this separation of the two types ever occurred on the eve of battle. An instant sifting of wheat from the tares took place quietly but surely in every company, and the mass of men so lately mingled became as incapable of mixture as oil and water.

The great receding tide at full ebb sank back toward the Gap; the mighty army of the backsliders whom naught could hinder, non-combatants, camp

SECOND BATTLE OF BULL RUN

darkies, shirking soldiers playing possum, and camp followers. Warm work was expected and all this genus, like war-horses, "sniffed danger from afar.". . .

It was this crowd belonging to the wagon-train or detailed for work such as blacksmithing, using every artifice to avoid the marching and fighting, which hung on the army like barnacles on a staunch ship's bottom, impeding its course and weighting it down. It was the impedimenta that flocked to the battle-field as soon as the shot and shell ceased firing, and despoiled and stripped friend and foe alike dead or wounded, it mattered not, though they never killed or ill treated the injured or maimed.

Reaching the Gap we found that the brigade had passed through. Following hard upon the track, our little squad after an hour's march caught up and took its place in rank.

The men were in a fearful humor, grumbling at their luck and cursing the commissary. They had ample cause; not a single ration had been issued to the troops for several days and the soldiers were savage from hunger. . . .

The forenoon had passed and the sound of hostile cannon was breaking the silence in our front while a battle was being fought on our left. . . .

"Fall in!" the officers shouted, and the men sprang to their feet, the line was dressed, and the brigade headed to the front to take position. On the way we were halted, and every soldier was compelled to strip for the fight by discard ing his blanket,—if he had one, which was not often—oil cloth or overcoat. All these were deposited in a large pile, and guards set over them, looking very much as if we did not intend to retreat. Cartridge-boxes were filled with forty rounds, and in our haversacks we carried twenty more, making sixty rounds per man.

Soon the crack of the skirmisher's rifles were heard, then the artillery opened, and the purple-colored smoke drifted like mist from lowland marshes, across the valley.

"Forward! Guide to the colors! March!"

Across that level plateau the First Brigade moved, the flower of Virginia in its ranks, the warm blood rushing in its veins as it did in warrior ancestors centuries ago. It was a glorious and magnificent display, the line keeping perfect time, the colors showing red against the azure sky. There was no cheering, only the rattling of the equipments and the steady footfalls of the men who trod the earth with regular beat. As the brigade swept across the plain it was stopped by a high Virginia snake fence; hundreds of willing hands caught the rails, tossed them aside, and then instinctively touching each other's elbows, the ranks were dressed as if by magic.

The first shell now shrieked over us. Another burst not ten feet from the ground directly over the heads of our forces. The long chain kept intact, though close to the spot where the explosion occurred; the links vibrated and oscillated for a moment, then grew firm again and pressed onward.

How the shells rained upon us now; a Yankee six-gun battery, on a hill about half a mile off,

turned its undivided attention upon us and essayed to shatter the advancing line. It did knock a gap here and there, but the break was mended almost as soon as broken, and the living wall kept on. Shells were bursting everywhere, until it seemed as if we were walk ing on torpedoes. They crackled, split and exploded all around, throwing dirt and ejecting little spirits of smoke that for a moment dimmed the sky.

Colonel Marye dismounted, drew his sword from the scab bard, and looking the beau ideal of a splendid soldier, placed himself at the head of his men. He stopped for a moment and pointed his sword with an eloquent and vivid gesture toward the battery on the hill. A cheer answered him, and the line instinctively quickened its pace. Though the shells were tearing through the ranks, the men did not falter. One man's resonant voice was sounding above the din, exercising a magical influence; one man's figure strode on in front and where he led, his men kept close behind. We followed unwaveringly our colonel over the hill, down the declivity, up the slope, straight across the plain toward the battery, with even ranks, though the balls were tearing a way through flesh and blood. The brigade stretched out for several hundred yards, forming, as they marched, a bow with concave toward the enemy. The Seventeenth was on the right of the line, and the other regiments dressed by our colors as we bore right oblique toward the battery, which was now hidden by a volleying fume that settled upon the crest.

Still the advance was not stayed nor the ranks broken. We neared the Chinn House, when suddenly a long line of the enemy rose from behind an old stone wall and poured straight in our breasts a withering volley at pointblank distance. It was so unexpected, this attack, that it struck the long line of men like an electric shock. Many were falling killed or wounded, and but for the intrepid coolness of its colonel, the Seventeenth would have retired from the field in disorder. His clear, ringing voice was heard, and the wavering line reformed. A rattling volley answered the foe, and for a minute or two the contest was fiercely waged. Then the colonel fell with his knee frightfully shattered by a Minie-ball. Once down, the calm, reassuring tones heard no longer, the line broke. Now individual bravery made up for the disaster. The officers surged ahead with their swords waving in the air, cheering on the men, who kept close to their heels, loading and firing as they ran. The line of blue was not fifty yards distant and every man took a sure, close aim before his finger pressed the trigger. It was a decisive fight of about ten minutes, and both sides stood up gamely to their work. Our foes were a Western regiment from Ohio, who gave and received and asked no odds. The left of our brigade having struck the enemy's right and doubled it up, now sent one volley into their flank.

In a moment the blue line quivered and then went to pieces. Officers and men broke for the rear, one regimental colors captured by Jim Coleman, of the Seventeenth. In a few moments there were none left except the dead and wounded.

There was hardly a breathing spell, only time indeed to take a full draught from the canteen, transfer the cartridges from the haversacks to the cartridge-box, and the enemy was upon us with a fresh line.

We were now loading and firing at the swiftly approaching enemy, who were about two hundred yards distant, advancing straight towards us and shouting with their steady hurrah, so different from the Rebel yell. It was a trying moment and proved the metal of the individual man. Some ran, or white with fear cowered behind the Chinn House, while others hid in a long gulley near by; others yet stood in an irregular form and loaded and fired, unmindful of the dust and noise of the hurtling shell and screaming shot. . . .

The brigade was scattered everywhere now. For an hour they had fired as fast as the cartridges could be rammed home. When the Union troops came up to retake the Chinn House, our men began to give ground. On came the Yankees in splendid style, with the Stars and Stripes waving and their line capitally dressed. It was a perfect advance, and some of us forgot to fire our muskets while watching them. In their front line was a little

drummer beating a *pas de charge*, the only time we ever heard the inspiriting sound on the battle field. The dauntless little fellow was handling his sticks lustily, too, for the roll of the drum was heard above the noise of the guns.

It was high time to be leaving, we thought, and now our men were turning to fire one good shot before heeling it to the rear, when right behind us there came with a rush and a vim a fresh Rebel brigade aiming straight for the Yankees. They ran over us and we joined their lines. Not a shot was fired by them in response to the fusilade of musketry that was raining lead all around. Every man with his head bent sideways and down, like people breasting a hailstorm, for soldiers always charge so, and the Gray and the Blue met with a mighty shock. A tremendous sheet of flame burst from our line; the weaker side went to the ground in a flash, and with a wild yell the Gray swept on toward the six-gun battery that had been sending forth a stream of death for the past hour. We could only see the flashes of light through the dense smoke.

The line stopped a moment at the foot of the hill to allow itself to catch up. It was late in the evening and the battle was raging in all its deadliest fury. On our right, on our left, in the front, in the rear, from all directions came the warring sound of cannon and musketry. We could see nothing but smoke, breathe nothing except the fumes of burning powder, feel nothing save the earth jarred by the concussion of the guns, hear nothing but the dire, tremendous clamor and blare of sound swelling up into a vast volume of fire. How hot it was! The clothes damp with perspiration, the canteens empty, throats parched with thirst, faces blackened by powder, the men mad with excitement.

The left of the line came up and then some one asked:

"Whose brigade is this?"

"Hood's," was the answer.

Then burst a ringing cry, "Forward, Texans!"

The line sprang like a tightly-bent bow suddenly loosened, and rushed up the hill in a wild, eager dash—a frenzied, maddening onset up the hill through the smoke, nearer and nearer to the guns.

When about a hundred yards from them the dense veil lifted, floated upward and softly aside, and discovered to us that the battery had ceased firing. We could see the muzzles of the guns, their sullen black mouths pointing at us, and behind them the gunners, while from the center of the battery was a flag that lay drooping upon its staff. It was for a second only, like the rising of the curtain for a moment on a hideous tableau, only to be dropped as the eye took in the scene in all its horrors, yet it impressed itself, that vivid picture, brief as it was, upon mind, heart and brain.

At once came a noise like a thunder shock, that seemed as if an earthquake had riven the place. The ground trembled with the concussion. The appalling sound was heard of iron grapeshot tearing its way through space and through bodies of bone, flesh and blood.

Mercifully for us, but not intended by our foes, the guns were elevated too high, or it would have been simply annihilation; for when those six guns poured their volley into the charging lines they were loaded to the muzzle with grape, and the distance was only about pistol shot. Of course the execution was fearful, and for a second the line was stupefied and nearly senseless from the blow. The ground was covered with victims and the screams of the wounded rose high above the din and were awful to hear.

The advance was not stayed long.

"Forward; boys! Don't stop now! Forward, Texans!" and with a cry from every throat the Southerners kept on, officers and men together without form or order, the swiftest runners ahead, the slowest behind, 'tis true, but struggling desperately to better their time. Up! Still up! until we reached the crest! As the Yankees pulled the lanyards of the loaded pieces our men were among them. A terrific shock. A lane of dead in front. Those standing before the muzzles were blown to pieces like captured Sepoy rebels. I had my hand on the wheel of one cannon just as it fired, and I fell like one dead, from the concussion. There was

a frenzied struggle in the semi-darkness around the guns, so violent and tempestuous, so mad and brain-reeling that to recall it is like fixing the memory of a horrible, blood-curdling dream. Every one was wild with uncontrollable delirium.

Then the mists dissolved and the panting, gasping soldiers could see the picture as it was. The battery had been captured by the Texans and every man at the pieces taken prisoner. Many were killed by a volley that we had poured into them when only a few paces distant, and a large proportion wounded. The few who escaped unhurt stood in a group, so blackened with powder that they ceased to look like white men. These soldiers had nobly worked their guns and had nothing to be ashamed of. All that men could do they had done. . .

Just as the day was drawing to a close a mighty yell arose, a cry from twice ten thousand throats, as the Rebel re serves, fresh from the rear, rushed resistlessly to the front. Never did mortal eyes behold a grander sight; not even when MacDonald put his columns in motion at Wagram or Ney charged the Russian center at Borodino.

It was an extended line, reaching as far as the eye could see, crescent in form, and composed of many thousand men. It was, in fact, a greater part of Longstreet's corps. The onset was thrilling in the extreme, as the men swept grandly forward, the little battle-flags with the Southern cross in the center fluttering saucily and jauntily aloft, while the setting sun made of each bayonet and musket-barrel a literal gleam of fire that ran along the chain of steel in a scintillating flame. As they swept over the plain they took up all the scattered fighting material, and nothing was left but the wounded which had sifted through, and the dead.

Then ensued the death struggle, a last fearful grappling in mortal combat. The enemy threw forward all their reserves to meet the shock, and for the space of fifteen minutes the commotion was terrible. Bursts of sound surpassed every thing that was ever he2rd or could-be conceived. The baleful flashes of the cannon, darting out against the dusky horizon, played on the surface of the evening clouds like sharp, vivid lightning. Long lines of musketry vomited through the plain their furious volleys of pestilential lead, sweeping scores of brave soldiers into the valley of the Shadow of Death.

At last the enemy staggered, wavered, broke and fled in utter rout. Where Longstreet was dealing his heavy blows, they were throwing away their knapsacks and rushing madly for the rear. Only one final stand was made by a brigade in the woods close by; but as the long gray line closed in on each flank they threw down their arms and surrendered with but few exceptions; those few, as they ran, turned and fired.

On the hill, which had been occupied by the Washington Artillery of eighteen guns in the earlier part of the day, the eye took in a dim and fast-fading yet extended view of the whole surrounding country. A vast panorama stretched out on an open plain with patches of wood here and there on its surface, and with but two or three hills in the whole range of sight to break the expanded level. It was unutterably grand. Jackson could be seen swinging his left on his right as a pivot, and Longstreet with his entire corps in the reverse method. The whole Yankee army was in retreat, and certainly nothing but darkness prevented it from be coming *une affaire flambée*.

—HUNTER, *Johnny Reb and Billy Yank*

VI.5

"LITTLE MAC" IS REAPPOINTED TO COMMAND

Pretty clearly neither the army nor public opinion would tolerate Pope after the fiasco of Second Bull Run. On September 5 Lincoln relieved him of command and, over vigorous opposition from his Cabinet, reappointed McClellan to command of the now reunited Army of the Potomac.

McClellan is the most controversial military figure of the Civil War and, after more than a hundred years, the controversy still rages. Lee was supposed to have characterized him as the ablest of his opponents, but it is highly doubtful that he ever did so, and if he did the characterization was palpable nonsense. That McClellan was an able organizer, a close student of war, and beloved by his troops, few will deny. On the other hand his timidity, vacillation, procrastination and sensitiveness, his persecution mania, his arrogance toward Lincoln, and his monumental egotism, suggest a psychopathic personality. To an almost total want of real military ability he united a vaulting ambition; discredited on the field of battle he sought compensation in politics, and his career is a standing warning against the mixture of the military and the civil.

The three following selections present varying views of McClellan. The first is from the acid but honest pen of Gideon Welles; the second from General Sherman; and the third the same Norton whose account of the Seven Days fighting we have already read. It is important to note the dates of the observations. Welles wrote just after Pope's debacle and just before McClellan was reappointed to command; Sherman two years after McClellan's final dismissal; Norton at the height of McClellan's popularity.

A. "To Fight is Not His Forte"

September 3, 1862

McClellan is an intelligent engineer and officer, but not a commander to lead a great army in the field. To attack or advance with energy and power is not in him; to fight is not his forte. I sometimes fear his heart is not earnest in the cause; yet I do not entertain the thought that he is unfaithful. The study of military operations interests and amuses him. It flatters him to have on his staff French princes and men of wealth and position; he likes show, parade, and power. Wishes to outgeneral the Rebels, but not to kill and destroy them. In a conversation which I had with him in May last at Cumberland on the Pamunkey, he said he desired of all things to capture Charleston; he would demolish and annihilate the city. He detested, he said, both South Carolina and Massachusetts, and should rejoice to see both States extinguished. Both were and always had been ultra and mischievous, and he could not tell which he hated most. These were the remarks of the General-in-Chief at the head of our armies then in the field, and when as large a proportion of his troops were from Massachusetts as from any State in the Union. . . .

I cannot relieve my mind from the belief that to him, in a great degree, and to his example, influence, and conduct, are to be attributed some portion of our late reverses, more than to any other person on either side. His reluctance to move or to have others move, his inactivity, his detention of Franklin, his omission to send forward supplies unless Pope would send a cavalry escort from the battle-field, and the tone of his conversation and dispatches, all show a moody state of feeling. The slight upon him and the generals associated with him, in the selection of Pope, was injudicious, impolitic, wrong perhaps, but is no justification for their withholding one tithe of strength in a great emergency, where the lives of their countrymen and the welfare of the country were in danger. The soldiers whom McClellan has commanded are doubtless attached to him. They have been trained to it, and he has kindly cared for them while under him. With partiality for him they have imbibed his prejudices, and some of the officers have, I fear, a spirit more factious and personal than patriotic.

—*Diary of Gideon Welles*

B. General Sherman Explains Why He Cannot Like McClellan

To his wife

Gaylesville, Ala., October 27, 1864

You ask my opinion of McClellan. I have been much amused at similar inquiries of John and others in answer to a news paragraph that I pledged ninety-nine votes of the hundred to McClellan. Of course this is the invention of some knave. I never said such thing. I will vote for nobody, because I am not entitled to vote. Of the two, with the inferences to be drawn at home and abroad, I would prefer Lincoln, though I know that McClellan, Vallandigham or even Jeff Davis if President of the U.S. would prosecute the war, and no one with more vigor than the latter.

But at the time the howl was raised against McClellan I knew it was in a measure unjust, for he was charged with delinquencies that the American people are chargeable for. Thus, how unjust to blame me for any misfortune now when all the authorities and people are conspiring to break up the Army till the election is over. Our armies vanish before our eyes and it is useless to complain because the election is more important than the war. Our

armies are merely paper armies. I have 40,000 Cavalry on paper but less than 5,000 in fact. A like measure runs through the whole, and so it was with McClellan. He had to fight partly with figures.

Still I admit he never manifested the simple courage and manliness of Grant, and he had too much staff, too many toadies, and looked too much to No. 1. When I was in Kentucky he would not heed my counsels, and never wrote me once, but since I have gained some notoriety at Atlanta and the papers announced, as usually falsely, that I was for him, he has written me twice and that has depreciated him more in my estimation than all else. He cannot be elected. Mr. Lincoln will be, but I hope it will be done quick, that voters may come to their regiments and not give the Rebels the advantage they know so well to take.

I believe McClellan to be an honest man as to money, of good habits, decent, and of far more than average intelligence, and therefore I never have joined in the hue and cry against him. In revolutions men fall and rise. Long before this war is over, much as you hear me praised now, you may hear me cursed and insulted. Read history, read Coriolanus, and you will see the true measure of popular applause. Grant, Sheridan and I are now the popular favorites, but neither of us will survive this war. Some other must rise greater than either of us, and he has not yet manifested himself.

—HOWE, ed., *Home Letters of General Sherman*

C. "Little Mac's A-Coming"

Harrison's Landing, James River, Va.,
Sunday, July 13, 1862

Dear Brother and Sister:—

We had a review by moonlight a few nights ago. "Old Abe" was down here to see the army, and he did not get round to us till 9 o'clock at night, but it was beautiful moonlight, and as he went galloping past, riding beside "Little Mac," everyone could tell him by his "stovepipe hat" and his unmilitary acknowledgment of the cheers which everywhere greeted him. His riding I can compare to nothing else than a pair of tongs on a chair back, but notwithstanding his grotesque appearance, he has the respect of the army.

But the man in the army is "Little Mac." No general could ask for greater love and more unbounded confidence than he receives from his men, and the confidence is mutual. He feels that he has an army he can depend on to do all that the same number of men can do anywhere. He is everywhere among "his boys," as he calls them, and everywhere he is received with the most unbounded enthusiasm.

He was here yesterday about noon. The boys were getting dinner or lounging about under the trees, smoking, reading or writing, when we heard a roar of distant cheers away down the road a mile or more. "Little Mac's a-coming" was on every tongue. "Turn out the guard—General McClellan," called the sentry on the road. The guard paraded and the men flocked to the roadside. He came riding along on his "Dan Webster," by the way as splendid a horse as you ever saw. He rode slowly, looking as jovial and hearty as if he could not be more happy. Up go the caps, and three rousing cheers that make the old woods ring, greet the beloved leader of the Army of the Potomac. He raises his cap in graceful acknowledgement of the compliment, and so he passes along. Those cheers always give notice of his approach. He speaks an occasional encouraging word, and the men return to their occupations more and more devoted to the flag and their leader.

But what have they to say to the men who have been using their influence to prevent his being reinforced, to se cure his defeat, and in some way to so prolong the war as to make the abolition of slavery a military necessity? Curses loud and deep are heaped on such men. Old Greeley would not live twenty-four hours if he should come here among the army. I used to be something of an abolitionist myself, but I've got so lately that I don't believe it is policy to sacrifice everything to the nigger. Such a policy as Greeley advocates, of letting this army be defeated for the purpose of making the people see that slavery must be abolished before we could end the war, I tell you is "played out." Ten thousand men have been sacrificed to that idea now, and the remainder demand that some other policy be adopted hence forth.

We want that three hundred thousand men raised and sent down here immediately. We want them drafted if they won't volunteer. We want the men who have property to furnish the government with the means to carry on the war. We want such a force sent here that the whole thing can be finished up by fall. We've been fooling about this thing long enough, and now we want a change. No more playing at cross purposes by jealous generals, no more incompetent or traitorous officials. The army demands and the people demand such a vigorous prosecution of the war as shall give some hope of ending it some time or other. McClellan must be reinforced sufficiently to enable him to do something more than keep at bay three times his force. That will never conquer the South. We must take the offensive and destroy their army and take their capital. When this is done, the clouds will begin to break.

—NORTON, *Army Letters*

VI.6

MCCLELLAN "SAVES HIS COUNTRY" TWICE

But let McClellan speak for himself. We give here excerpts from his letters to his wife. These letters, it will be seen, begin with the Peninsular campaign and carry through the Antietam campaign to McClellan's dismissal from the command of the Army of the Potomac. As they are valuable primarily for their rejection of McClellan's character rather than for their analysis of military operations, we print them as a unit even though this violates chronology.

April 8, 1862, 8 A.M.—

I have raised an awful row about McDowell's corps. The President very coolly telegraphed me yesterday that he thought I had better break the enemy's lines at once. I was much tempted to reply that he had better come and do it himself.

April 11, 1862—

Don't worry about the wretches; they have done nearly their worst, and can't do much more. I am sure that I will win in the end, in spite of all their rascality. History will present a sad record of these traitors who are willing to sacrifice the country and its army for personal spite and personal aims. The people will soon understand the whole matter.

July 17, 1862, A.M.—

You do not feel one bit more bitterly towards those people than I do. I do not say much about it, but I fear they have done all that cowardice and folly can do to ruin our poor country, and the blind people seem not to see it. It makes my blood boil when I think of it. I cannot resign so long as the fate of the Army of the Potomac is entrusted to my care. I owe a great duty to this noble set of men, and that is the only feeling that retains me. I fear that my day of usefulness to the country is past—at least under this administration. I hope and trust that God will watch over, guide, and protect me. I accept most resignedly all He has brought upon me. Perhaps I have really brought it on myself; for while striving conscientiously to do my best, it may well be that I have made great mistakes that my vanity does not permit me to perceive. When I see so much self-blindness around me I cannot arrogate to myself greater clearness of vision and self examination.

I *did* have a terrible time during that week [the Seven Days], for I stood alone, without any one to help me. I felt that on me rested everything, and I felt how weak a thing poor, mortal, erring man is! I felt it sincerely, and shall never, I trust, forget the lesson; it will last me to my dying days. I am very well now, perfectly well, and ready for any amount of fatigue that can be imagined.

July 18, 1862, 9:00 P.M.—

I am inclined now to think that the President will make Halleck commander of the army and that the first pretext will be seized to supersede me in com-

mand of this army. Their game seems to be to withhold reinforcements, and then to relieve me for not advancing, well knowing that I have not the means to do so. If they supersede me in the command of the Army of the Potomac I will resign my commission at once. If they appoint Halleck commanding general I will remain in command of this army as long as they will allow me to, provided the army is in danger and likely to play an active part. I cannot remain as a subordinate in the army I once commanded any longer than the interests of my own Army of the Potomac require. I owe no gratitude to any but my own soldiers here; none to the government or to the country. I have done my best for the country; I expect nothing in return; they are my debtors, not I theirs.

If things come to pass as I anticipate I shall leave the service with a sad heart for my country, but a light one for myself. But one thing keeps me at my work—love for my country and my army. Surely no general had ever better cause to love his men than I have to love mine.

July 20, 1862, P.M.—

Which despatch of mine to Stanton do you allude to? The telegraphic one in which I told him that if I saved the army I owed no thanks to any one in Washington, and that he had done his best to sacrifice my army? It was pretty frank and quite true. Of course they will never forgive me for that. I knew it when I wrote it; but as I thought it possible that it might be the last I ever wrote, it seemed better to have it exactly true. The President, of course, has not replied to my letter, and never will. His reply may be, however, to avail himself of the first opportunity to cut my head off. I see it reported in this evening's paper that Halleck is to be the new general-in-chief. Now let them take the next step and relieve me, and I shall once more be a free man. . . .

Later.—I believe it is now certain that Halleck is commander-in-chief. . . I am content. I have not disgraced my name, nor will my child be ashamed of her father. Thank God for that! I shall try to get something to do which will make you comfortable—

and it will be most pleasant and in the best taste for me that we should lead here after a rather quiet and retired life. It will not do to parade the tattered remnants of my departed honors to the gaze of the world. Let us try to live for each other and our child, and to prepare for the great change that sooner or later must overtake us all.

I have had enough of earthly honors and place. I believe I can give up all and retire to privacy once more, a better man than when we gave up our dear little home with wild ideas of serving the country. I feel that I have paid all that I owe her. I am sick and weary of all this business. I am tired of serving fools. God help my country! He alone can save it. It is grating to have to serve under the orders of a man whom I know by experience to be my inferior. But so let it be. God's will be done! All will turn out for the best. My trust is in God, and I cheerfully submit to His will.

August 22, 1862, 10 A.M. (Fort Monroe)—

I think they are all pretty well scared in Washington, and probably with good reason. I am confident that the disposition to be made of me will depend entirely upon the state of their nerves in Washington. If they feel safe there I will, no doubt, be shelved; perhaps placed in command here *vice* Gen. Dix. I don't care what they do; would not object to being kept here for a while, because I could soon get things in such condition that I could have you here with me.

Their sending for me to go to Washington only indicates a temporary alarm. If they are at all reassured you will see that they will soon get rid of me. I shall be only too happy to get back to quiet life again; for I am truly and heartily sick of the troubles I have had, and am not fond of being a target for the abuse and slander of all the rascals in the country. Well, we will continue to trust in God and feel certain that all is for the best. It is often difficult to under stand the ways of Providence; but I have faith enough to believe that nothing is done without some great purpose.

September 5, 1862, 11 A.M.—

Again I have been called upon to save the country. The case is desperate, but with God's help I will try unselfishly to do my best, and, if He wills it, accomplish the salvation of the nation. My men are true and will stand by me till the last. I still hope for success, and will leave nothing undone to gain it. How weary I am of this struggle against adversity! But one thing sustains me—that is, my trust in God. I know that the interests at stake are so great as to justify His interference; not for me, but for the innocent thousands, millions rather, who have been plunged in misery by no fault of theirs. It is probable that our communications will be cut off in a day or two, but don't be worried. You may rest assured that I am doing all I can for my country, and that no shame shall rest upon you, wilfully brought upon you by me. . . . My hands are full, so is my heart.

September 8, 1862, camp near Rockville—

You don't know what a task has been imposed upon me! I have been obliged to do the best I could with the broken and discouraged fragments of two armies defeated by no fault of mine. Nothing but a desire to do my duty could have induced me to accept the command under such circumstances. Not feeling at all sure that I could do anything, I felt that under the circumstances no one else *could* save the country, and I have not shrunk from the terrible task.

McDowell's own men would have killed him had he made his appearance among them; even his staff did not dare to go among his men. I can afford to forgive and forget him. I saw Pope and McDowell for a few moments at Upton's Hill when I rode out to meet the troops and assume command. I have not seen them since; I hope never to lay eyes on them again. Between them they are responsible for the lives of many of my best and bravest men. They have done all they could (unintentionally, I hope) to ruin and destroy the country. I can never forgive them that. Pope has been foolish enough to try to throw the blame of his defeat on the Army of the Potomac. He would have been wiser to have accepted his defeat without complaint.

I will probably move some four or five miles further to the front tomorrow, as I have ordered the whole army forward. I expect to fight a great battle and to do my best at it. I do not think secesh will catch me very badly.

September 20, 1862, 9 A.M.,
camp near Sharpsburg—

The battle of Wednesday [Antietam] was a terrible one. I presume the loss will prove not less than 10,000 on each side. Our victory was complete, and the disorganized rebel army has rapidly returned to Virginia, its dreams of "invad ing Pennsylvania" dissipated for ever. I feel some little pride in having, with a beaten and demoralized army, defeated Lee so utterly and saved the North so completely. Well, one of these days history will, I trust, do me justice in deciding that it was not my fault that the campaign of the Peninsula was not successful. . . .

Since I left Washington, Stanton has again asserted that I, not Pope, lost the battle of Manassas No. 2!. . . I am tired of fighting such disadvantages, and feel that it is now time for the country to come to my help and remove these difficulties from my path. If my countrymen will not open their eyes and assist themselves they must pardon me if I decline longer to pursue the thankless avocation of serving them.

September 20, 1862, 9 P.M.,
camp near Sharpsburg—

I feel that I have done all that can be asked in twice saving the country. If I continue in its service I have at least the right to demand a guarantee that I shall not be interfered with. I know I cannot have that assurance so long as Stanton continues in the position of Secretary of War and Halleck as general-in-chief. I can retire from the service for sufficient reasons without leaving any stain upon my reputation. I feel now that this last short campaign is a sufficient legacy for our child, so far as honor is concerned. . . .

You should see my soldiers *now!* You never saw anything like their enthusiasm. It surpasses anything you ever imagined. . . . My tent is filled quite to overflowing with trophies in the way of captured secesh battle-flags. We have more than have been taken in all battles put together, and all sorts of inscriptions on them.

November 7, 1862, 11:30 P.M.
(camp near Rectorton)—

Another interruption—this time more important. It was in the shape of Burnside, accompanied by Gen. Buckingham, the secretary's adjutant-general. They brought with them the order relieving me from the command of the Army of the Potomac, and assigning Burnside to the command. No cause is given. I am ordered to turn over the command immediately and repair to Trenton, N. J., and on my arrival there to report by telegraph for further orders. . . .

Of course I was much surprised; but as I read the order in the presence of Gen. Buckingham I am sure that not the slightest expression of feeling was visible on my face, which he watched closely.

They have made a great mistake. Alas for my poor country! I know in my inmost heart she never had a truer servant. I have informally turned over the command to Burnside, but shall go to-morrow to Warrenton with him, and perhaps remain a day or two there in order to give him all the information in my power. . . .

Do not be at all worried—I am not. I have done the best I could for my country; to the last I have done my duty as I understand it. That I must have made many mistakes I cannot deny. I do not see any great blunders; but no one can judge of himself. Our consolation must be that we have tried to do what was right; if we have failed it was not our fault.

—Letters of MCCLELLAN to his wife,
in *McClellan's Own Story*

VI·7

McClellan Finds the Lost Order

Almost before Pope had carried out his retirement to Washington, Lee had started his army northward into Maryland. There were large strategic, and even political, purposes in this campaign, but there were practical purposes too—a chance to get food for soldiers and forage for animals. McClellan learned almost at once of Lee's advance, but did not know what his ultimate objectives would be. When news came that Lee was across the Potomac McClellan edged ahead to head him off, reaching Frederick, Maryland, on the twelfth. The next day he had the great good fortune to learn the whole of Lee's plans.

Mystery still surrounds the loss of Special Order 191. That it was picked up at Frederick, Maryland, by Private Mitchell of the 27th Indiana on September 13 and delivered promptly to McClellan's headquarters is clear, but who was responsible for its loss is not known. Lee learned that the Order was in McClellan's hands sometime the next day. To what extent the disclosure of his plans forced Lee to change them is not wholly clear. According to Colonel Allan, historian of the Army of Northern Virginia Lee said in 1868 that "had the Lost Dispatch not been lost. . . I would have had all my troops reconcentrated on Md. side, stragglers up, men rested, and intended then to attack McClellan hoping the best results from state of my troops and those of the enemy."

On the 13th an order fell into my hands, issued by General Lee, which fully disclosed his plans, and I immediately gave orders for a rapid and vigorous forward movement.

The following is a copy of the order referred to:
"Special Orders No. 191.
"Headquarters Army of Northern Virginia,
"September 9, 1862.
"The army will resume its march to-morrow, taking the Hagerstown road. General Jackson's command will form the advance, and, after passing Middletown, with such portions as he may select, take the route towards Sharpsburg, cross the Potomac at the most convenient point, and, by Friday night, take possession of the Baltimore and Ohio railroad, capture such of the enemy as may be at Martinsburg, and intercept such as may attempt to escape from Harper's Ferry.

"General Longstreet's command will pursue the same road as far as Boonsboro', where it will halt with the reserve, supply and baggage trains of the army.

"General McLaws, with his own division and that of Gen eral R. H. Anderson, will follow General Longstreet; on reaching Middletown, he will take the route to Harper's Ferry, and, by Friday morning, possess himself of the Maryland heights, and endeavor to capture the enemy at Harper's Ferry and vicinity.

"General Walker, with his division, after accomplishing the object in which he is now engaged, will cross the Potomac at Cheek's ford, ascend its right bank to Lovettsville, take possession of Loudon heights, if practicable, by Friday morning; Keys's ford on his left, and the road between the end of the mountain and the Potomac on his right. He will, as far as practicable, co-operate with General McLaws and General Jackson in intercepting the retreat of the enemy.

"General D. H. Hill's division will form the rear guard of the army, pursuing the road taken by the main body. The reserve artillery, ordnance and supply trains, &c., will precede General Hill.

"General Stuart will detach a squadron of cavalry to ac company the commands of Generals Longstreet and Mc Laws, and, with the main body of the cavalry, will cover the route of the army, and bring up all stragglers that may have been left behind.

"The commands of Generals Jackson, McLaws, and Walker, after accomplishing the objects for which they have been detached, will join the main body of the army at Boonsboro' or Hagerstown.

"Each regiment on the march will habitually carry its axes in the regimental ordnance wagons, for use of the men at their encampments, to procure wood, &c.

"By command of General R. E. Lee.
"R. H. Chilton,
"Assistant Adjutant General."
—*Letter of the Secretary of War*

VI.8

McClellan Forces Turner's Gap and Crampton's Gap

As the Lost Order tells, Lee divided his little army, sending Jackson with some 25,000 men to seize Harpers Ferry. Alive to the danger of being cut off from Jackson, now that McClellan knew his plans, Lee turned westward toward Sharpsburg, leaving only token forces to hold back the Federals. Moving with unwonted celerity McClellan pushed after the Confederates. The armies were separated by two low lying ranges, South Mountain and Elk's Ridge; the easiest roads through these were at Turner's Gap and Crampton's Gap. The Confederates put up a stiff resistance at both places, but were brushed aside.

Here is David Strother, whom we have already met at Manassas, telling how these fights looked from McClellan's headquarters. His comments on Maryland's reaction to the invasion are especially perspicacious.

September 13, Saturday.—Fair and pleasant. Making an early start we entered Frederick City about ten o'clock A.M., and were welcomed with a spontaneous ovation that stirred every soul to its depths. The whole city was fluttering with national flags; while the streets through which we passed, from the sidewalks to the house-tops, shone with happy human faces. It seemed as if the whole population had turned out, wild with joy. Handkerchiefs fluttered and flowers showered upon the moving troops; and when the Commander and Staff appeared the crowd became so demonstrative that we were forcibly brought to a halt. The officers of the Staff received their due share of the floral honors, but the General and horse were absolutely covered with wreaths and bouquets; while old men, women, and children crowded around, anxious to touch his hand, or by some word or act to testify their enthusiasm for the leader of the National power.

As soon as the General could release himself from this pleasing but rather embarrassing position he rode to Burn side's head-quarters on the Baltimore turnpike, and then dismounting entered the General's tent. While waiting outside I fell into conversation with a cavalry officer, who narrated the following incident of the occupation which took place on yesterday: Our advanced cavalry met that of the enemy in the streets and drove them through the town. Being reinforced the enemy returned, driving our men back as rapidly as they had advanced. Meanwhile a section of artillery had been unlimbered and posted to support the cavalry, the guns charged with canister and the gunners with the lanyards taut, ready to open at command. As our squadrons rushed back in disordered flight a stupid trooper rode between the gunner and the piece, thus drawing the friction primer and discharging the gun full in the faces of our men, killing two outright and wounding half a dozen. Our infantry having arrived in the mean time, the rebels abandoned the town, retiring westward by the Hagerstown road. While the Commander tarried with General Burnside I rode into the city again, accompanied by some young Staff officers, and hoping to meet some former acquaintance among the citizens. . . .

Lee entered Maryland evidently indulging in the belief that the State would rise and welcome the Southern army. His proclamation was plausibly framed to engage the good will of the inhabitants, and the conduct of his troops as constrainedly regular as was possible under the circumstances. The observation of a few days was sufflcient to disenchant him. In the districts which he visited the mass of the population was of undoubted and uncompromising loyalty. Yet the open defiance and hatred of this class was not so discouraging as the coldness and even terror with which the Maryland secessionists regarded their ragged and needy liberators. In truth, the spirit of rebellion which had boiled over scalding hot in April, 1861, had by this time simmered down to a tepid sentimentalism which manifested itself in weak social snobbery, silly songs, intriguing, speculating, and blockade-running. There were, indeed, some more daring spirits left, who, in spite of the Federal martial law, would on occasions drink themselves drunk to the success of "the good cause," and hurrah for Jeff Davis at the risk of a night in the guard-house. But that living, practical faith which is willing to undergo hard knocks for opinion's sake, and take pay in Confederate promises, is totally lacking in Maryland. In brief, except a few young Hotspurs attracted by the love of adventure, and a few cock-eyed politicians who have compromised themselves unwittingly, rebel Maryland seems to prefer the sideboard to the field, and from all accounts Lee will lose two by desertion where he gains one by recruiting. . .

September 14, Sunday.—Pleasant. On rising this morning I heard cannon sounding to the westward, and evidently nearer to us than Harper's Ferry. I also observed our columns moving in the same direction, and winding over the Catoctin Ridge, which divides Frederick from the Middle town Valley. We were presently in the saddle; and on ar riving at the summit of the mountain with one accord drew rein to admire the scene which presented itself. The Valley of the Catoctin, which lay beneath us like a map unrolled, is one of the most fertile and best improved districts in Maryland. As far as the eye can reach, north and southward, it is dotted with handsome farm-houses, and pretty thriving villages, and checkered with cultivated fields and scraps of woodland, enlivened by silvery streams and traversed by fine public roads. The western horizon is limited by a mountain range which rises abruptly to the height of a thousand feet. This ridge, about four miles distant, is a continuation of the Great Blue Ridge of Virginia, here called the South Mountain, and within sight is crossed by two great highways—the national turnpike passing over Turner's Gap immediately in front of us, and a less important road passing at Crampton's Gap opposite Burkittsville, about five miles to the southward and leading directly to Maryland Heights and Harper's Perry. Prom both these passes we could hear the sullen booming of the guns, and see the white wreaths of smoke rolling up the blue face of the mountain. Across the lovely valley, by every road and pathway, our columns of horses foot, and artillery were moving, all centring toward the defiant batteries.

Comprehending the beauty and thrilling interest of the scene at a glance, the Commander rode rapidly forward to Middletown, where he stopped at Burnside's quarters, located in an orchard at the eastern end of the village. . . .

About two o'clock P.M. it was ascertained that the passage of South Mountain would cost us a battle; and following the Commander through Middletown we rode forward about two miles, and ascending a spur of the mountain took a position between two of our batteries. Prom this point we had as comprehensive a view of the position as could be conveniently obtained. The windings of the main turnpike through cleared fields were visible from the valley to the summit; but the flanking roads and positions to the right and left of the turnpike were a good deal obscured by forest which covered the ridge continuously. By both these flanking roads our columns were already ascending to the attack—that on the left commanded by Reno, while Hooker led the forces on the right. At the same time Gibbon's Brigade was advanced on the national turnpike in the centre to amuse the enemy with a feint attack. Generals Cox and Wilcox with their brigades had already made a lodgment on the left summit, and the continuous peals of musketry from that quarter showed that they were stoutly resisted. Sturgis was ordered forward to support them; and as his glittering column was seen ascending the steep road Reno, who had been riding with McClellan, started forward, saying, "I must see to this matter in person."

There is nothing like the master's eye "when work is to be done," and for an hour after Reno's departure the redoubled roar of musketry proved the truth of the proverb. In time the sounds waxed fainter and fainter, the line of white smoke disappeared over the crest, and then news came that the position was carried and the enemy retreating.

Simultaneously with this action the column under Hooker, supported by Meade, was seen crawling up the rocky and difficult ascent on the right. Slowly trailing across the open ground, now entering a piece of wood, and again emerging on the upper side, winding over spurs and up ravines, the march resembled the course of a black serpent with glittering scales stealing upon its prey.

At length we had a glimpse of Hooker's command in some open ground on the summit, moving in column of companies, and heading in toward the Gap. They presently disappeared in the wood, and then came the distant muttering of musketry, which continued with little intermission until after dark, and always approaching the Gap. As Hooker moved in from the exterior position on the right, we could discern a dense and continuous column of the enemy moving to meet him by a road diverging from the National turnpike at the Summit House. This we ascertained was Longstreet's reinforcing column, and it seemed a heavy one; but after a short time it was seen retiring by the same route. All the while the batteries posted on the different eminences were unremitting in their activity, but so broken and densely wooded was the field that comparatively little artillery was used, and that probably with but little effect.

From the position of the Staff we also had a good view of Franklin's operations at Burkittsville and Crampton's Gap, between three and four miles distant, and as matters in our immediate proximity seemed to promise a fortunate conclusion, we found leisure at intervals to turn our glasses in that direction. From the summit the enemy's guns were working industriously, no batteries replying from our side, but the line of musketry smoke was evidently advancing up the as cent, and that indicated a victory there.

About sunset it was understood that both our flanking columns had established themselves solidly in positions commanding the main pass. The enemy had contested the ground with the greatest obstinacy, making repeated and determined efforts to recover what they had lost, but all in vain. As they still maintained a defiant attitude, Gibbon was ordered to advance on the centre, and carry the main road. This he did in gallant style, deploying his lines on either side of the turn pike, and moving a section of artillery on the road. His advance was difficult and slow, as the enemy had greatly the advantage of position, and disputed every step with bitter tenacity. This fight took place after dark, and the General-in Chief, riding to an adjacent knoll,

continued to overlook the sparkling combat until after nine o'clock. About that time the fires died away, Gibbon having advanced apparently about half-way up the mountain. . . .

General McClellan occupied a room in which was a table, two or three chairs, and a couple of tallow-candles, without other furniture or embellishment. Here, surrounded by the officers of his Staff and the chiefs of the army, he discussed the events of the day. We had carried all our points, and inflicted heavy loss on the enemy, capturing between one and two thousand prisoners. . . .

It seems that we have spent the day manoeuvring and studying the ground. I don't like the delay. We should have attacked on sight, Monday evening, or this morning at all risks. We might then have got Lee at a disadvantage. But while we take time to concentrate he will do the same or escape. If he is here to-morrow it will be because he feels quite confident of his game. We are entirely too methodical.

—STROTHER, "Personal Recollections of the War"

VI.9

THE BLOODIEST DAY OF THE WAR

With the loss of the passes through South Mountain and the major part of his army still tied down at Harpers Ferry, Lee decided to recross the Potomac and stand on the defensive. Then on September 15 he got word that Harpers Ferry had fallen and that Jackson was on his way. Lee decided to go ahead with his original plan; by the night of the fifteenth he had three of his divisions in place along the Antietam, and next day Jackson came up and took place alongside them. That day, too, McClellan brought up his mighty host—twice the force that Lee commanded—but did not offer battle.

A word about the terrain and the disposition of the contending forces. Sharpsburg stands in a great bend in the Potomac; the little Antietam flows below the town, winding through woods, orchards and fields of grain. Lee ranged his divisions between the Antietam and the town, Jackson on the left, D. H. Hill at the center, Longstreet on the right, Walker's division in reserve. It was, strategically, about as bad a position as an army could take. Both flanks were vulnerable, and if McClellan could roll up the right flank he would interpose his army between Lee and Virginia. Mc Clellan's forces straddled .the Antietam, Hooker, Sumner and Franklin on the right, across the stream, and Burnside on the left, east of the stream, with Porter in reserve.

The battle itself was a piecemeal affair, fought not by armies or even by corps, but by divisions and brigades. At no time did McClellan launch a concerted assault on the Confederate line or use his reserves; instead he wasted his superior strength in a series of fragmentary attacks. While there was some fighting all along the line most of the day, there were in fact three major and separate battles: first, Hooker's attack on the Confederate left; second, Sumner's drive on the Confederate center; third, Burnside's struggle to get across the river and his assault on the Confederate right. All three were partially successful, none was followed through to that complete success which would have destroyed Lee's army and might have spelled the end of the Confederacy.

Antietam was not a decisive battle—but it might have been. A signal victory by Lee would not have altered the military situation, for the Confederate commander could not have followed up victory. But a victory by McClellan would have cut Lee off from his base, or destroyed him and exposed Richmond to imminent capture. McClellan, to be sure, claimed a victory but, as the historian Major Steele observes, "it is hard to say which should reflect least credit upon the Union commander, not to have defeated Lee's army, or not to have destroyed it if he defeated it. Truth to tell, McClellan did neither."

We begin our story of the battle with a general view—a sort of headquarters view—by Colonel Strother, who had the confidence of McClellan.

September 17, Wednesday. . . . At Newcomer's I found the Commander-in-Chief, surrounded by a number of sub ordinate generals, planning and receiving orders. Thus far the great argument had been opened and conducted solely by those stately and bombastic orators—the cannon. The dispute presently assumed a closer and more conversational tone as the angry chattering of the musketry prevailed. About half past seven o'clock this had swelled to an ominous roar, accompanied by repeated and triumphant cheers. The General-in-Chief, followed by all his attendants, hurried to a bluff just behind the house, whence they had a splendid view of Hooker's advance driving the enemy before them in rapid and disordered flight.

Horses were forthwith ordered, and we rode rapidly across to a commanding knoll on the eastern side of the Sharpsburg turnpike, about the cen-

tre of our line of battle, and nearly opposite the town of Sharpsburg, whose locality was indicated by the belfry of a small church which peered above the opposite hill. This was the same point from which the General reconnoitred the enemy on Monday afternoon, and afforded the most comprehensive view of the field that could be had from any single point.

Our order of battle, as detailed to me by McClellan on yesterday afternoon, was as follows: Our right wing under Sumner was established across the Antietam, and would swing round, closing in upon the enemy's left and forcing it back upon the centre, thus cutting off the roads to Hagerstown and Williamsport. Our left, under Burnside, was ordered to force the passage of the Antietam at a stone bridge a mile below the central turnpike, and driving the enemy's right back on Sharpsburg, would bar his retreat toward Antietam Ford on the Potomac and Harper's Ferry, thus (to use the General's own words) pinching him up in a vice. Our centre was refused, and lay behind the stream ready to act as circumstances might require. . . .

The enemy's lines, occupying the ridge which conceals Sharpsburg from us, and thence westward along the Hagers town pike and the wood behind the Dunker church, are only iridicated by the smoke of his guns and an occasional horse man showing himself over the summit to reconnoitre. Meanwhile Sumner had crossed and taken full possession of the position in front of the Dunker church, driving the enemy back into the wood. Several brigades, which I understood to be Richardson's Division, advanced to a position still nearer the centre, confronting the enemy between the Dunker church and the town. To meet them the enemy's lines moved out into the open ground and opened fire, when a portion of our troops broke in confusion and ran down the road toward the central bridge. In a few moments, however, they were rallied, and returned to their positions, showing great steadiness for the rest of the day. The rebel line also stood as straight and firm as a stone-wall, although under a heavy fire both of artillery and musketry. I saw the shells strike them frequently, and when there appeared symptoms of wavering I could see the officers collaring the men and forcing them back to their places.

Our troops fought splendidly, and made several advances at a run, but the force seemed entirely too light and too much isolated to effect any decisive purpose. They did their part, however, and gave their *vis-a-vis* full occupation. A portion of Sumner's advance had pushed forward nearly to the line of fence in front of the Dunker church; but they seemed to be so cut up and reduced in numbers that they took shelter behind a slope in the field, and only kept up a light skirmishing against the wood.

During these operations the clamor of the artillery along the whole line of battle (several miles in extent) was incessant. We could hear the distant muttering of musketry from the flanks, but Sumner's movement had evidently come to a stand. This produced a lull in the battle within our sight, and I had leisure to remark upon the head-quarters group immediately about me. In the midst was a small redan built of fence-rails, behind which sat General Fitz John Porter, who, with a telescope resting on the top rail, studied the field with unremitting attention, scarcely leaving his post during the whole day. His observations he communicated to the commander by nods, signs, or in words so low-toned and brief that the nearest by-standers had but little benefit from them. When not engaged with Porter, McClellan stood in a soliderly attitude intently watching the battle and smoking with the utmost apparent calmness; conversing with surrounding officers and giving his orders in the most quiet under-tones. General Marcy, his Chief of Staff, was always near him, and through him orders were usually given to the aides-de-camp to be transmitted to distant points of the field. Several foreign officers of the French, Prussian, and Sardinian service were present. Every thing was as quiet and punctilious as a drawing-room ceremony.

While the activity of the infantry within sight seemed to have been temporarily suspended, the thunder of between two and three hundred pieces of artillery still kept up the continuity of the battle. The shells had set fire to several barns, which were in full blaze, while at intervals I recognized from among the enemy's guns the sudden spring of that tall mushroom-shaped cloud which indicates the explosion of a caisson or ammunition-wagon, showing that our artillery was doing good work.

Franklin's Corps having arrived on the field he is ordered to fill a gap between Sumner and Hooker, occasioned by the rapid advance of the latter doubling back the enemy's left. Shortly after this order was sent I observed a sudden movement from the line of wood behind the Dunker church, and in a moment, as it appeared, the whole field in front was covered with masses of the enemy, formed in columns of grand divisions, advancing at a run, with arms at right shoulder shift, and yelling like demons. I could see the heads of four columns, which seemed to be composed of a brigade each; but the extreme left of the movement was masked by a wood and the smoke of a burning farm-house. The attack was evidently made to recover the wood and position from which they had been driven by Hooker at the commencement of the fight.

The rush of this fiery avalanche swept away the feeble remnant of Sumner's command as the flame of a torch scatters the swarms of blue flies from the shambles. As these, in their disordered and more rapid flight, unmasked the front of the rebel advance there was a swell in the chorus of the battle so vast and voluminous that it seemed as if heaven and earth vibrated with the stunning roar. Cannon and musketry mingled in a tonic outpouring that exceeded in grandeur all sounds I ever heard, except, perhaps, Niagara. The check of pulsation produced by this sudden apparition was relieved by an officer, who whispered: "That's Franklin. Hear him!"

The rebel columns had swept on, disappearing entirely in the dust raised by their own movement through the trampled field, the rolling smoke of the burning houses, and the sulphurous cloud which rose like a snowy mountain over the assailed position. We could distinctly see Sumner's debris rallying behind the wood, forming in line, and returning to the combat. Higher and higher rolled the white clouds, steady and unbroken; the roar of ordnance continued for twenty minutes or more, when, emerging from the smoke, flying in the wildest disorder, thinned and scattered, we saw the enemy returning to the wood from which he had advanced. Shot and shell followed with vengeful rapidity, and anon our ordered lines were seen sweeping over the disputed field to resume their position in front of the Dunker church. As the smoke and dust disappeared I was astonished to observe our troops moving along the front and passing over what appeared to be a long, heavy column of the enemy without paying and discovered this to be actually a column of enemy's dead and wounded lying along a hollow road—afterward known as Bloody Lane. Among the prostrate mass I could easily distinguish the movements of those endeavoring to crawl away from the ground; hands waving as if calling for assistance, and others struggling as if in the agonies of death.

I was standing beside General McClellan during the progress and conclusion of this attack. The studied calmness of his manner scarcely concealed the underlying excitement, and when it was over he exclaimed: "By George, this is a magnificent field, and if we win this fight it will cover all our errors and misfortunes forever!"

"General," I said, "fortune favors the bold; hurl all our power upon them at once, and we will make a glorious finish of the campaign and the war."

"Colonel," said he, "ride forward to Pleasonton and tell him to throw a couple of squadrons forward on the Sharpsburg road, as far as they can go, to find out what is there."

I surmise, from this order, the General had suspected the enemy's line immediately in front of our centre was weak. I rode down the turnpike, leaving Porterstown to the left, and near the central bridge found General Pleasonton, to whom I delivered the message. He responded promptly by throwing forward two horse-batteries, which took position across the Antietam on either side of the turnpike.

Thus far we had heard nothing and seen no results from Burnside's wing. The General was impatient, and frequently asked: "What is Burnside about? Why do we not hear from him?" During the morning he sent several messengers to hasten his movements;

but we only heard vaguely that he had not yet affected a crossing and could not carry the bridge.

Meanwhile the news from the right showed that matters were taking an unfavorable turn there. Hooker was wounded and withdrawn from the field. Mansfield was killed, and a number of other valuable general officers *hors de combat*. Our right wing seemed to have spent its aggressive power, and held its ground because the enemy was equally incapable of aggression.

About one o'clock we had news that Burnside had carried the bridge; but there seemed to be a lull in the battle along the whole line from right to left. An aid was wanted to carry another urgent message to Burnside. General Marcy asked me if I was ready for the service. I promptly led up my mare, but the General observing that she was sweltering from my recent ride, called Colonel Key, whose horse was fresh, and asked him to ride over to General Burnside's position and ascertain what was the cause of the delay. I was extremely anxious to see what was going on there, and begged to be permitted to carry the message, but Key would not yield. He returned with the information that Burnside had effected a crossing and thought he could hold the bridge.

The Commander-in-Chief replied, "He should be able to do that with five thousand men; if he can do no more I must take the-remainder of his troops and use them else where in the field.". . .

As the afternoon wore away, and while the Commanding General was absent, the fires of death were rekindled along the whole line. Since the overwhelming repulse by Franklin of the enemy's powerful attacking column he seemed to have yielded the contested ground on the right, and to have fallen back to a more sheltered line between the Dunker church and the town. Yet, though his infantry was less demonstrative, his artillery appeared to be stronger and more active than during the forenoon. About this time we witnessed one of the handsomest exhibitions of gallantry which occurred during the day. A battery of ours was seen entering the field in the vicinity of Richardson's Division; moving at a walk and taking position, apparently in advance of our line, it opened fire at short range, and maintained its ground for half an hour under the concentrated fire of at least forty guns of the enemy. As they moved in with the utmost deliberation I saw a number of shells strike and overthrow men and horses, and during the combat the battery sometimes appeared covered with the smoke and dust of the enemy's bursting shells. Unable to sustain the unequal contest they at length withdrew to shelter, and then we saw parties returning to the ground to bring off the wounded in blankets and to remove the limbers of two guns the horses of which had been killed. This, I afterward ascertained, was Graham's Battery United States Artillery, and I was further informed by Lieutenant Elder, who commanded a section in the action, that in half an hour they lost eleven men and seventeen horses. The affair was observed from head-quarters with the greatest interest, and elicited the warmest commendation, especially from the foreign officers on the ground.

At length, about four o'clock in the afternoon, the cumulating thunder on the left announced that Burnside's advance had at least commenced (three hours too late). The advance was distinctly visible from our position, and the movement of the dark columns, with arms and banners glittering in the sun, following the double line of skirmishers, dashing forward at a trot, loading and firing alternately as they moved, was one of the most brilliant and exciting exhibitions *of* the day. As this splendid advance seemed to be carrying every thing before it our attention was withdrawn to the right by the appearance of large bodies of the enemy with glittering arms and banners moving up the Hagerstown road toward the Dunker church with the apparent intention of renewing the attack in that direction. In a short time, however, this menacing cloud was dispelled by the concentrated fire of forty-two guns which Franklin had in position.

Meanwhile Burnside's attack had carried the height over looking Sharpsburg on the left, having driven the enemy and captured the guns, but a counter attack on his troops, exhausted with their victory, sent them streaming down the hill again,

and the last rays of the setting sun shone upon the bayonets of the enemy crowning the hill from which ours had just been driven. At this crisis the General, followed by his whole retinue, rode forward to a bluff nearer the scene of action. It was nearly dark when we reached the point, yet the sullen boom of an occasional gun, and the sparkling lines of musketry on a line about midway between Sharpsburg and the Antietam, showed that ours still held on to a portion of the field they had wrested from the enemy. About this time Burnside's messenger, asking for reinforcements, arrived. It was too late to repair errors or initiate any new movement, and they were not sent.

By eight o'clock the wailing cries of the wounded and the glare of the burning buildings alone interrupted the silence and darkness which reigned over the field of the great battle. The General then led us back to the headquarters camp, established in the rear of Keedysville, where, forgetting the events of the day for the time, we supped heartily and slept profoundly.

—Strother, "Personal Recollections of the War"

VI.10

HOOKER HAMMERS THE CONFEDERATE LEFT—IN VAIN

The Federal attack was launched at sunrise as Doubleday and Ricketts, of Hooker's corps, moved with great elan on Jackson's line stretching at almost a right angle from the Dunker Church through the West Woods toward the Potomac. Stuart opened with artillery; Jackson moved Lawton's Georgians into a field of corn, head-high; and the lines held. Hooker sent in reserves, and Jackson called on Hood to go to the rescue. The fighting raged for an hour; then Hood sent his famous message, "Tell General Jackson unless I get reinforcements I must be forced back, but I am going on while I can." Reinforcements came—from Early and finally from McLaws, who had come up just that morning. But the Federal attack, too, was reinforced. Mansfield's corps—now under Williams—entered the battle, drove the Confederates back through the savage cornfield, and captured the Dunker Church. A counter-attack by McLaws recaptured it. By nine o'clock both sides were exhausted, and the fighting on the left died down. When a brother officer asked Hood, "Where is your division?" he answered, "Dead on the field."

Those who actually participated in fighting of this kind could give only their own experience and that of their company or regiment. Here are a Federal and a Confederate account of the fighting through the cornfield and for the Dunker Church. Major Rufus R. Dawes was with the 6th Wisconsin; James Graham a captain in the 27th North Carolina, one of the regiments that was rushed to the rescue of Hood.

A. Wisconsin Boys Are Slaughtered in the Cornfield

Our lines on the left now came sweeping forward through the corn and the open fields beyond. I ordered my men up to join in the advance, and commanded: "Forward—guide left—march!" We swung away from the turnpike, and I sent the sergeant-major to Captain Kellogg, commanding the companies on the turnpike, with this order: "If it is practicable, move forward the right companies, aligning with the left wing." Captain Kellogg said: "Please give Major Dawes my compliments, and say it is impracticable; the fire is murderous."

As we were getting separated, I directed Sergeant Huntington to tell Captain Kellogg that he could get cover in the corn, and to join us, if possible. Huntington was struck by a bullet, but delivered the order. Kellogg ordered his men up, but so many were shot that he ordered them down again at once. While this took place on the turn-pike, our companies were marching forward through the thick corn, on the right of a long line of battle. Closely following was a second line. At the front edge of the cornfield was a low Virginia rail fence. Before the corn were open fields, beyond which was a strip of woods surrounding a little church, the Dunkard church. As we appeared at the edge of the corn, a long line of men in butternut and gray rose up from the ground. Simultaneously, the hostile battle lines opened a tremendous fire upon each other. Men, I can not say fell; they were knocked out of the ranks by dozens. But we jumped over the fence, and pushed on, loading, firing, and shouting as we advanced. There was, on the part of the men, great hysterical excitement, eagerness to go forward, and

a reckless disregard of life, of everything but victory. Captain Kellogg brought his companies up abreast of us on the turn pike.

The Fourteenth Brooklyn Regiment, red legged Zouaves, came into our line, closing the awful gaps. Now is the pinch. Men and officers of New York and Wisconsin are fused into a common mass, in the frantic struggle to shoot fast. Every body tears cartridges, loads, passes guns, or shoots. Men are falling in their places or running back into the corn. The soldier who is shooting is furious in his energy. The soldier who is shot looks around for help with an imploring agony of death on his face. After a few rods of advance, the line stopped and, by common impulse, fell back to the edge of the corn and lay down on the ground behind the low rail fence.

Another line of our men came up through the corn. We all joined together, jumped over the fence, and again pushed out into the open field. There is a rattling fusilade and loud cheers. "Forward" is the word. The men are loading and firing with demoniacal fury and shouting and laughing hysterically, and the whole field before us is covered with rebels fleeing for life, into the woods. Great numbers of them are shot while climbing over the high post and rail fences along the turnpike. We push on over the open fields half way to the little church. The powder is bad, and the guns have become very dirty. It takes hard pounding to get the bullets down, and our firing is becoming slow. A long and steady line of rebel gray, unbroken by the fugitives who fly before us, comes sweeping down through the woods around the church. They raise the yell and fire. It is like a scythe running through our line. "Now, save, who can." It is a race for life that each man runs for the cornfield. A sharp cut, as of a switch, stings the calf of my leg as I run. Back to the corn, and back through the corn, the headlong flight continues.

At the bottom of the hill, I took the blue color of the state of Wisconsin, and waving it, called a rally of Wisconsin men. Two hundred men gathered around the flag of the Badger state. Across the

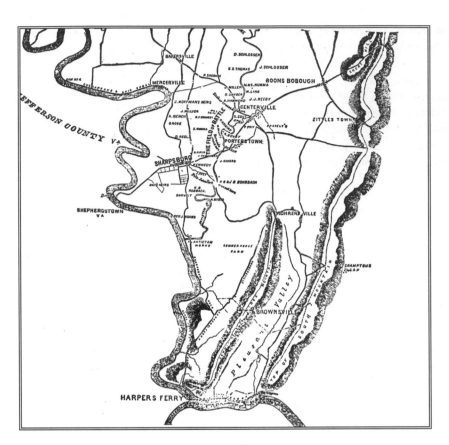

ANTIETAM

turnpike just in front of the hay stacks, two guns of Battery "B," 4th U. S. artillery were in action. The pursuing rebels were upon them. General John Gibbon, our brigade commander, who in regular service was captain of this battery, grimed and black with powder smoke in himself sighting these guns of his old battery, comes running to me, "Here, major move your men over, we must save these guns." I commanded "Right face, forward march," and started ahead with the colors in my hand into the open field, the men following. As I entered the field, a report as of a thunderclap in my ear fairly stunned me. This was Gibbon's last shot at the advancing rebels. The cannon was double charged with canister. The rails of the fence flew high in the air.

A line of union blue charged swiftly forward from our right across the field in front of the battery, and into the corn-field. They drove back the rebels who were firing upon us. It was our own gallant 19th Indiana, and here fell dead their leader, Lieutenant Colonel A. F. Bachman; but the youngest captain in their line, William W. Dudley, stepped forward and led on the charge.

I gathered my men on the turnpike, reorganized them, and reported to General Doubleday, who was himself there. He ordered me to move back to the next woods in the rear, to remain and await instruction. Bullets, shot, and shell, fired by the enemy in the corn-field, were still flying thickly around us, striking the trees in this woods, and cutting off the limbs. I placed my men under the best shelter I could find, and here we figured up, as nearly as we could, our dreadful losses in the battle. Three hundred and fourteen officers and men had marched with us into battle. There had been killed and wounded, one hundred and fifty-two. Company "C" under Captain Hooe, thirty-five men, was not in the fight in front of the corn-field. That company was on skirmish duty farther to our right. In this service they lost two men. Of two hundred and eighty men who were at the cornfield and turnpike, one hundred and fifty were killed or wounded. This was the most dreadful slaughter to which our regiment was subjected in the war. We were joined in the woods by Captain Ely, who reported to me, as the senior officer present, with the colors and eighteen men of the second Wisconsin. They represented what remained for duty of that gallant regiment.

—Dawes, *Service with the Sixth Wisconsin Volunteers*

B. McLaws to the Rescue of Hood

Before day on the morning of 17 September, 1862, we were moved and placed in line of battle on the extreme right of the Confederate lines, our left resting upon the yard of a man whose name I did not learn, who, to prevent our getting water, broke off his pump-handle and destroyed his pump, so that we were compelled to fill our canteens from a mud hole in his stable lot or do without water. Most of us filled from this mud-hole, and I can testify that, while not as fresh and sweet as some I have seen, yet in the heat and strife of that day its filth was almost forgotten and it served very well to quench thirst. We remained in this position till about 8:30 o'clock A.M., when we were ordered to the left centre. After double-quicking one and a half or two miles we were placed in line about one mile to the left of the town of Sharpsburg.

The Twenty-seventh North Carolina infantry, Colonel John R. Cooke, and the Third Arkansas, Captain Ready commanding, were detached from the rest of the division and fought as a little brigade by themselves under the command of Colonel Cooke of the Twenty-seventh North Carolina; Colquitt's Georgia Brigade being some 500 yards to our right, and the rest of our division about the same distance to our left. Forming in a corn field we advanced under a heavy fire of grape and canister at a quick step, up a little rise, and halted at a rail fence, our right considerably advanced. Captain Greenough's battery, attached to General Kershaw's Brigade was placed on our left, but was soon withdrawn. After holding this position for half an hour or more our front was changed; the left retiring about ten steps and the right thrown back considerably, so as to be upon a line with the other troops.

In the meantime we had suffered heavily and, I think indicted equally as much damage upon the enemy. The Yankees getting possession of a piece of woods upon our left, Companies F, K, and G, the three left companies of the Twenty-seventh, were directed to center their fire upon that point; and right well did they do their work, as it appeared upon an examination of the field next day that the enemy were piled two or three deep in some places. About 1 o'clock P.M., the enemy having retired behind the hill upon which they were posted, and none appearing within range in our front, Colonel Cooke ordered us to fall back some twenty steps in the corn field and lie down, so as to draw them on; he in the meantime, regardless of personal danger from sharpshooters, remained at the fence beside a small hickory tree.

After remaining there some twenty minutes the enemy attempted to sneak up a section of artillery to the little woods on our left. Colonel Cooke, watching the movement, ordered the four left companies of the Twenty-seventh North Carolina up to the fence and directed them to fire upon this artillery. At the first fire, before they had gotten into position, nearly every horse and more than half the men fell, and the infantry line which had moved up to support them showed evident signs of wavering. Colonel Cooke seeing this, and having received orders to charge if opportunity offered, ordered a charge. Without waiting a second word of command both regiments leaped the fence and "went at them" and soon we had captured these guns and had the troops in front of us in full retreat. A battery posted near a little brick church upon a hill (the Dunkard church, so often referred to in accounts of this battle, which was situated on the "Hagerstown Pike" and just to our left and front), was playing sad havoc with us, but thinking that would be taken by the troops upon our left, who we supposed were charging with us, we still pursued the flying foe. Numbers of them surrendered to us and they were ordered to the rear. Two or three hundred took shelter behind a lot of haystacks, and fastening white handkerchiefs to their muskets and bayonets, held them out offering to surrender.

We pushed on, and soon wheeling to the right drove down their line, giving them an enfilade fire, and succeeded in breaking six regiments, which fled in confusion. Only one Federal regiment, that I saw, left the field in anything like good order. After pushing on in this way, we found ourselves opposed by a body of the enemy behind a stone wall in a corn field. Stopping to contend with these we found that we were almost out of ammunition; the cartridges which we had captured on the field, and of these there was a large quantity, not fitting our guns.

Colonel Cooke, learning this fact, and seeing that we were not supported in our charge, ordered us to fall back to our original position. This, of course, was done at double quick. As we returned we experienced the perfidy of those who had previously surrendered to us and whom we had not taken time to disarm. They, seeing that we were not supported, attempted to form a line in our rear and in a few minutes would have done so. As it was, we had to pass between two fires, a part of the troops having been thrown back to oppose our movement on their flank and these supposed prisoners having formed on the other side. A bloody lane indeed it proved to us. Many a brave man lost his life in that retreat. At some points the lines were not sixty yards distant on either side of us. Arriving at our original position both regiments halted and were soon reformed.

In this retreat we were very materially aided and protected by Cobb's Brigade, then commanded by Colonel William MacRae, of the Fifteenth North Carolina Regiment . . .

As soon as the regiments could reform behind their rail fence, they opened fire with the few cartridges they had left and soon checked the advance of the enemy who did not come beyond the line which they had occupied in the morning. In a short while all our ammunition was exhausted. Colonel Cooke sent courier after courier for ammunition, but still none was sent. Four or five times during the after noon General Longstreet sent couriers telling Colonel Cooke to hold the position at all hazards, that "it was the key to the whole line." Colonel Cooke's reply was always, "Tell General Longstreet to send me some ammunition. I have not a cartridge in my command, but will hold my position at the point of the bayonet."

The rail fence, which was our only protection, was riddled with bullets and torn with shot and shell and our men were falling fast, but still the Twenty-seventh North Carolina and the Third Arkansas flinched not. Imbued with the courage of their commander, they stood firm to their post.

For about two hours and a half they held the position literally without a cartridge. . . . Between 4 and 5 o'clock in the afternoon we were relieved (I think by the Third North Carolina and a Louisiana regiment), and were moved about a mile to the rear to get ammunition and fresh water. After resting about half an hour we were marched again to the front and placed in position just behind and in support of the troops who had relieved us. Here we were subjected to a severe shelling, but had no chance to return the fire. The day had been a long one, but the evening seemed longer; the sun seemed almost to go backwards, and it appeared as if night would never come. As soon as it became dark we were moved to the left, rejoined our division, and with them bivouacked upon the battlefield.

The regiment entered the battle with 325 officers and men and lost in killed and wounded 203, about 63. per cent. One company (G) went in 30 strong and had but five left at the end of the day. Another (Company E), with an average company and a full compliment of officers, lost its Captain, First Lieutenant and Second Lieutenant killed, and two thirds of its men killed or wounded.

—Graham, "Twenty Seventh Regiment"

VI.11

The Desperate Fighting along Bloody Lane

The second part of the battle came at the Confederate center, and almost by accident. About nine in the morning Sumner's corps had moved out to support Hooker. French's division went astray, and struck at the Confederate line as it curved eastward from the Dunker Church. Here D. H. Hill stood behind a sunken lane that was that day to be rebaptized "bloody." French was shortly joined by Richardson's division. Outnumbered, Hill put up a savage resistance. "The combat that took place," writes the historian Ropes, "was beyond question one of the most sanguinary and desperate in the whole war." When the Federals succeeded in enfilading the lane, the Confederates withdrew, leaving a yawning hole between the left and the center. It was a crucial moment for the Confederacy; General Alexander later wrote that Lee's army was ruined and the end of the Confederacy was in sight." Now was the moment for McClellan to hurl in his reserves—Franklin's VI Corps, which had scarcely seen action, and Porter's V. McClellan did nothing. The attack ebbed away, the Confederates rallied, and the line held .

We have included two accounts of this fight at the center. The first is from Thomas Livermore of the 18th New Hampshire; we have met him before and he needs no further introduction. The second is by the famous John B. Gordon, who rose to be lieutenant general by the end of the war and was subsequently Senator from Georgia and commander in chief of the Confederate Veterans.

A. Thomas Livermore Puts on His War Paint

The events of a battle in which the troops maneuver a good deal are almost always confused in one's memory, and I am not exactly certain of the order in which I place events, nor of the duration of the various struggles here, but they are related as now pictured on my mind. I believe that while we fired by file a little before we advanced across the road, yet that we did not meet with great opposition

here, probably because the Irish regiment we relieved had done considerable toward using up the line we first dealt with. At any rate, we swept forward, and as we were advancing (either now or previously across the sward) I heard old General Richardson cry out, "Where's General ?" I looked over my right shoulder and saw that gallant old fellow advancing on the right of our line, almost alone, afoot and with his bare sword in his hand, and his face was as black as a thunder cloud; and well it might be, for some of our own men, turning their heads toward him, cried out, "Behind the haystack!" and he roared out, "God damn the field officers!" I shall never cease to admire that magnificent fighting general who advanced with his front line, and with his sword bare and ready for use, and his swarthy face burning eye, and square jaw, though long since lifeless dust, are dear to me.

We swept on over the road into the cornfield, taking prisoner the broken remnants of the line which had opposed, now crouching in the corn before us, and down into a ravine, to the foot of the slope on which the rebel batteries stood, and not more than two hundred yards from them; all the time being pelted with canister from the battery in our front, which hurtled through and tore down even the slender cornstalks. . . . The rebels then attempted to send a line of battle down the slope to meet us under cover of the artillery fire, but by this time we had advanced beyond the range of the batteries on the right, and my impression is that either on account of the depth of the ravine we were in or because of the advancing rebel line being in the way, the pieces of the battery in our front were not depressed enough to hurt us, and we gave our undivided attention to this advancing line. We were fresh, and opened a withering, *literally* withering, fire on the rebels; for although they may have started in regular order, yet before they got to the foot of the slope there was no semblance of a line, and the individuals of what had been the line, either by reason of invincible bravery, or for the purpose of gaining shelter, ran forward scatteringly in the face of our fire, with heads down as if before a storm, to a fence which was a few yards in front of us, but did not form a line which annoyed us, that I recollect.

In my opinion here was a glorious chance to win the victory. We seemed to have penetrated to the right flank of the enemy, no infantry appeared to turn our left flank at this juncture, and no battery opened on our left front and the line which the rebels sent down in our front was broken by a regiment of 300 men or less. Of course, I don't know what troops there were in reserve behind the rebel line at this point, but from all that I have learned I see no reason to doubt that if the prolongation of our line to the left, which we ended, had been continued by one division, we should have turned the right of the left wing of this rebel army.

But, however triumphant our advance had been, it seems that Colonel Cross found that he was not only in advance of the line on his right, but that there was an interval between his right and its left on the same alignment; so to avoid the catastrophe which such a position might bring upon us, he moved us to the right and rear until at length we found ourselves in the vicinity of the sunken road again with our line intact. The rebels followed this movement closely with an advance of a formidable line of battle, which we met with a rapid fire, but the rebels now attempted a maneuver, which was the very one I have suggested we might have accomplished, that is, the flanking of our left. We were very busily engaged in the corn when some one on the left detected this movement of the enemy around our left, which was concealed from the most of us by the corn. Colonel Cross convinced himself that this was the case when he in some way changed our front "to the left and rear" so as to confront the rebel line squarely. . . .

And then we filed to the left . . . and outflanking the rebel line in turn poured such a fire into it as to drive it off. As I was near the right of the line I did not see how much the rebels outflanked us, nor did I see how much we outflanked them, and was very busily occupied with the rebels in my own front.

At this time we were subjected to a most terrible fire of artillery, and I recollect one shell or case shot which burst in the middle of "G," the color company, and killed and wounded eight men and tore a great hole in one of our flags, and our regiment, already weakened, was fast losing men from its ranks. At this trying time the rebel infantry advanced for the third time against us, when the colonel moved us into the sunken road and there we planted ourselves for the last struggle.

On looking around me I found that we were in the old, sunken road mentioned several times before, and that the bed of it lay from one to three feet below the surface of the crest along which it ran. In this road there lay so many dead rebels that they formed a line which one might have walked upon as far as I could see, many of whom had been killed by the most horrible wounds of shot and shell, and they lay just as they had been killed apparently, amid the blood which was soaking the earth. It was on this ghastly flooring that we kneeled for the last struggle. The rebels advanced through the corn, firing, the artillery played upon us without mercy, and now we were harder pressed than ever before, with no help at hand from the reserves which we could see. The battle still raged on our right, and it seemed useless to expect aid from that quarter; this is retrospective, however, and I am not aware that we thought of or prayed for help.

As the rebel advance became apparent, we plied the line with musketry with all our power, and no doubt with terrible effect, but they still advanced. A color-bearer came for ward within fifteen yards of our line, and with the utmost desperation waved a rebel flag in front of him. Our men fairly roared, "Shoot the man with the flag!" and he went down in a twinkling and the flag was not raised in sight again. As the fight grew furious, the colonel cried out, "Put on the war paint"; and looking around I saw the glorious man standing erect, with a red handkerchief, a conspicuous mark, tied around his bare head and the blood from some wounds on his forehead streaming over his face, which was blackened with powder. Taking the cue somehow we rubbed the torn end of the cartridges over our faces, streaking them with powder like a pack of Indians, and the colonel, to complete the similarity, cried out, "Give 'em the war whoop!" and all of us joined him in the Indian war whoop until it must have rung out above all the thunder of the ordnance. I have sometimes thought it helped to repel the enemy by alarming him to see this dev-ilish-looking line of faces, and to hear the horrid whoop; and at any rate, it reanimated us and let him know we were unterrified.

Added to the inspiration of these devices, a stream of shouts, curses, and appeals to "Fire! Fire! Fire faster!" came from our mouths, and while with our first advance into the cornfield my contempla-tion of death in the abstract had given place to inflicting it in reality, at this time my spirits became fairly boisterous between firing, shouts, and the smell of powder smoke and all. The dead rebel whom I knelt on held in his hands a "Belgian rifle" (a poor enough arm, but worth something in a pinch like this), and although it was my duty to tend solely to my men's behavior, yet as they were each one of them doing their best, and the cap on this rifle denoted that it was loaded, I took it out of his hands, and discharged it at his living comrades, and liking the work I looked around for another piece to discharge, when Colonel Cross, who was omnipresent, omniscient, and omnipotent in the fight, cried out sharply, "Mr. Livermore, tend to your company!" and I quenched my aspirations and thenceforward watched my men. . . .

Among the incidents I remember on this day were these. I saw a private of the 61st New York, who was mounted for some reason, with a brilliant red shirt on, riding to and fro along the infantry line when the musketry was hottest, and he being the only mounted man in his vicinity was espe-cially conspicious, and I learned that he was doing his best to encourage the men. I was told, too, that a woman, who followed the Irish Brigade as laundress or nurse, went up with it, and standing with it in the fight, swung her bonnet around and cheered on the men; and that Colonel Barlow, of

the 61st New York, tired of seeing his drummers shrink from their duty, tied them to his waist with his sash and led them under fire. A rebel in flying before our advance was killed as he was climbing over a fence and remained fixed upon it, and through mistake or rage our men had shot or bay-oneted him many times.

—LIVERMORE, *Days and Events*

B. General Gordon is Wounded Five Times at Antietam

Vigorously following up the success achieved at South Mountain, McClellan, on the 16th day of September, 1862, marshalled his veteran legions on the eastern hills bordering the Antietam. On the opposite slopes, near the picturesque village of Sharpsburg, stood the embattled lines of Lee. As these vast American Armies, the one clad in blue and the other in gray, stood contemplating each other from the adjacent hills, flaunting their defi-ant banners, they presented an array of martial splendor that was not equalled, perhaps, on any other field. It was in marked contrast with other battle-grounds. On the open plain, where stood these hostile hosts in long lines, listening in silence for the signal summoning them to battle, there were no breastworks, no abatis, no intervening woodlands, nor abrupt hills, nor hid ing-places, nor impassable streams. The space over which the assaulting columns were to march, and on which was soon to occur the tremendous struggle, consist-ed of smooth and gentle undulations and a narrow valley covered with green grass and growing corn. From the position assigned me near the centre of Lee's lines, both armies and the entire field were in view. . . .

On the elevated points beyond the narrow val-ley the Union batteries were rolled into position, and the Confederate heavy guns unlimbered to answer them. For one or more seconds, and before the first sounds reached us, we saw the great vol-umes of white smoke rolling from the mouths of McClellan's artillery. The next second brought the roar of the heavy discharges and the loud explo-sions of hostile shells in the midst of our lines, inaugurating the great battle. The Confederate batteries promptly responded; and while the artillery of both armies thundered, McClellan's compact columns of infantry fell upon the left of Lee's lines with the crushing weight of a land-slide. The Confederate battle line was too weak to withstand the momentum of such a charge. Pressed back, but neither hopelessly broken nor dismayed, the Southern troops, enthused by Lee's presence, reformed their lines, and, with a shout as piercing as the blast of a thousand bugles, rushed in counter-charge upon the exulting Federals, hurled them back in confusion, and recovered all the ground that had been lost. Again and again, hour after hour, by charges and counter-charges, this portion of the field was lost and recovered, until the green corn that grew upon it looked as if it had been struck by a storm of bloody hail.

Up to this hour not a shot had been fired in my front. There was an ominous lull on the left. From sheer exhaustion, both sides, like battered and bleeding athletes, seemed willing to rest. General Lee took advantage of the respite and rode along his lines on the right and centre. He was accompanied by Division Commander General D. H. Hill. With that wonderful power which he possessed of divining the plans and purposes of his antagonist, General Lee had decided that the Union commander's next heavy blow would fall upon our centre, and those of us who held that important position were notified of this conclusion. We were cautioned to be prepared for a determined assault and urged to hold that centre at any sacrifice, as a break at that point would endanger his entire army. My troops held the most advanced position on this part of the field, and there was no supporting line behind us. It was evident, therefore, that my small force was to receive the first impact of the expected charge and to be subjected to the deadliest fire. To comfort General Lee and General Hill, and especially to make, if possible, my men still more resolute of purpose, I called aloud to these officers as they rode away: "These men are going to stay here, General, till the sun goes down or victory is won." Alas! many of the brave fellows are there now.

General Lee had scarcely reached his left before the predicted assault came. The day was clear and beautiful, with scarcely a cloud in the sky. The men in blue filed down the opposite slope, crossed the little stream (Antietam), and formed in my front, an assaulting column four lines deep. The front line came to a "charge bayonets," the other lines to a "right shoulder shift." The brave Union commander, superbly mounted, placed himself in front, while his band in rear cheered them with martial music. It was a thrilling spectacle. The entire force, I concluded, was composed of fresh troops from Washington or some camp of instruction. So far as I could see, every soldier wore white gaiters around his ankles. The banners above them had apparently never been discolored by the smoke and dust of battle. Their gleaming bayonets flashed like burnished silver in the sun light. With the precision of step and perfect alignment of a holiday parade, this magnificent array moved to the charge, every step keeping time to the tap of the deep-sounding drum. As we stood looking upon that brilliant pageant, I thought, if I did not say, "What a pity to spoil with bullets such a scene of martial beauty!" But there was nothing else to do. . . .

My extraordinary escapes from wounds in all the previous battles had made a deep impression upon my comrades as well as upon my own mind. So many had fallen at my side, so often had balls and shells pierced and torn my clothing, grazing my body without drawing a drop of blood, that a sort of blind faith possessed my men that I was not to be killed in battle. This belief was evidenced by their constantly repeated expressions: "They can't hurt him." "He's as safe one place as another." "He's got a charmed life."

If I had allowed these expressions of my men to have any effect upon my mind the impression was quickly dissipated when the Sharpsburg storm came and the whizzing Minies, one after another, began to pierce my body.

The first volley from the Union lines in my front sent a ball through the brain of the chivalric Colonel Tew, of North Carolina, to whom I was talking, and another ball through the calf of my right leg. On the right and the left my men were falling under the death-dealing crossfire like trees in a hurricane. The persistent Federals, who had lost so heavily from repeated repulses, seemed now determined to kill enough Confederates to make the debits and credits of the battle's balance-sheet more nearly even. Both sides stood in the open at short range and without the semblance of breast-works, and the firing was doing a deadly work. Higher up in the same leg I was again shot; but still no bone was broken. I was able to walk along the line and give encouragement to my resolute rifle-men, who were firing with the coolness and steadi-ness of peace soldiers in target practice. When later in the day the third ball pierced my left arm, tear-ing asunder the tendons and mangling the flesh, they caught sight of the blood running down my fingers, and these devoted and big-hearted men, while still loading their guns, pleaded with me to leave them and go to the rear, pledging me that they would stay there and fight to the last. I could not consent to leave them in such a crisis. The sur-geons were all busy at the field-hospitals in the rear, and there was no way, therefore, of stanching the blood, but I had a vigorous constitution, and this was doing me good service.

A fourth ball ripped through my shoulder, leaving its base and a wad of clothing in its track. I could still stand and walk, although the shocks and loss of blood had left but little of my normal strength. I remembered the pledge to the comman-der that we would stay there till the battle ended or night came. I looked at the sun. It moved very slowly; in fact, it seemed to stand still.

I thought I saw some wavering in my line, near the extreme right, and Private Vickers, of Alabama, volunteered to carry any orders I might wish to send. I directed him to go quickly and remind the men of the pledge to General Lee, and to say to them that I was still on the field and intended to stay there. He bounded away like an Olympic racer; but he had gone less than fifty yards when he fell, instantly killed by a ball through his head. I then attempted to go myself, although I was bloody and faint, and my legs did not bear me steadily. I had

gone but a short distance when I was shot down by a fifth ball, which struck me squarely in the face, and passed out, barely missing the jugular vein. I fell forward and lay unconscious with my face in my cap; and it would seem that I might have been smothered by the blood running into my cap from this last wound but for the act of some Yankee, who, as if to save my life, had at a previous hour during the battle, shot a hole through the cap, which let the blood out.

I was borne on a litter to the rear, and recall nothing more till revived by stimulants at a late hour of the night.

—GORDON, *Reminiscences of the Civil War*

VI.12

"THE WHOLE LANDSCAPE TURNS RED" AT ANTIETAM

The third, and what should have been the most important, bat-tle came on the Confederate right. Burnside was massed east of the Antietam; a thin line of Confederates under Longstreet were ranged on the hills along the western side of the stream. The first efforts to get across what came to be known as Burnside's Bridge were repulsed by Toombs. Not until one o'clock was the bridge carried; not until almost four did Burnside finally launch a full-scale attack. It was irresistible. The Federals swept up the hill, pushed the butternuts back onto the Cemetery and into Sharpsburg, and threatened disas-ter to the whole Confederate army.

Then came one of the dramatic moments of the war. Jackson had left A P. Hill at Harpers Ferry with about 2,500 men. Early on the seventeenth Hill had started for Sharpsburg, a 15-mile hike which involved fording the Potomac. Just as Burnside broke the Confederate line, Hill's men came up on the double-quick from Shepardstown, and sounding the rebel yell burst on the triumphant Federals, hurled them back down the hill, and saved the day. That was the end. The next day Lee stood his ground; then he slipped away, across the Potomac and into Virginia.

David Thompson, who here recalls the fighting across the Burnside Bridge, was a member of the 9th New York Volunteers.

About noon the battle began afresh. This must have been Franklin's men of the Sixth Corps, for the firing was nearer, and they came up behind the center. Suddenly a stir beginning far up on the right, and running like a wave along the line, brought the regiment to its feet. A silence fell on every one at once, for each felt that the momentous "now" had come. Just as we started I saw, with a little shock, a line officer take out his watch to note the hour, as though the affair beyond the creek were a business appointment which he was going to keep.

When we reached the brow of the hill the fringe of trees along the creek screened the fighting entirely, and we were deployed as skirmishers under their cover. We sat there two hours. All that time the rest of the corps had been moving over the stone bridge and going into position on the other side of the creek. Then we were ordered over at a ford which had been found below the bridge, where the water was waist-deep. One man was shot in mid-stream. At the foot of the slope on the opposite side the line was formed and we moved up through the thin woods. Reaching the level we lay down behind a battery which seemed to have been disabled. There, if anywhere, I should have remembered that I was soaking wet from my waist down. So great was the excitement, however, that I have never been able to recall it. Here some of the men, going to the rear for water, discovered in the ashes of some hay-ricks which had been fired by our shells the charred remains of several Confederates. After long waiting it became noised along the line that we were to take a battery that was at work several hundred yards ahead on the top of a hill. This narrowed the field and brought us to consider the work before us more attentively.

Right across our front, two hundred feet or so away, ran a country road bordered on each side by a snake fence. Beyond this road stretched a plowed field several hundred feet in length, sloping up to the battery, which was hidden in a cornfield. A stone fence, breast-high, inclosed the field on the left, and behind it lay a regiment of Confederates, who would be directly on our flank if we should attempt the slope. The prospect was far from

encouraging, but the order came to get ready for the attempt.

Our knapsacks were left on the ground behind us. At the word a rush was made for the fences. The line was so disordered by the time the second fence was passed that we hurried forward to a shallow undulation a few feet ahead, and lay down among the furrows to re-form, doing so by crawling up into line. A hundred feet or so ahead was a similar undulation to which we ran for a second shelter. The battery, which at first had not seemed to notice us, now, apprised of its danger, opened fire upon us. We were getting ready now for the charge proper, but were still lying on our faces. Lieutenant-Colonel Kimball was ramping up and down the line. The discreet regiment behind the fence was silent. Now and then a bullet from them cut the air over our heads, but generally they were reserving their fire for that better shot which they knew they would get in a few minutes. The battery, however, whose shots at first went over our heads, had depressed its guns so as to shave the surface of the ground. Its fire was beginning to tell. I remember looking behind and seeing an officer riding diagonally across the field—a most inviting target—instinctively bending his head down over his horse's neck, as though he were riding through driving rain. While my eye was on him I saw, between me and him, a rolled overcoat with its straps on bound into the air and fall among the furrows. One of the enemy's grape-shot had plowed a groove in the skull of a young fellow and had cut his overcoat from his shoulders. He never stirred from his position, but lay there face downward—a dreadful spectacle. A moment after, I heard a man cursing a comrade for lying on him heavily. He was cursing a dying man.

As the range grew better, the firing became more rapid, the situation desperate and exasperating to the last degree. Human nature was on the rack, and there burst forth from it the most vehement, terrible swearing I have ever heard. Certainly the joy of conflict was not ours that day. The suspense was only for a moment, however, for the order to charge came just after. Whether the regiment was thrown into disorder or not, I never knew. I only remember that as we rose and started all the fire that had been held back so long was loosed. In a second the air was full of the hiss of bullets and the hurtle of grape-shot. The mental strain was so great that I saw at that moment the singular effect mentioned, I think, in the life of Goethe on a similar occasion—the whole landscape for an instant turned slightly red. I see again as I saw it then in a flash, a man just in front of me drop his musket and throw up his hands, stung into vigorous swearing by a bullet behind the ear. Many men fell going up the hill, but it seemed to be all over in a moment, and I found myself passing a hollow where a dozen wounded men lay— among them our sergeant-major, who was calling me to come down. He had caught sight of the blanket rolled across my back, and called me to unroll it and help to carry from the field one of our wounded lieutenants.

When I returned from obeying this summons the regiment (?) was not to be seen. It had gone in on the run, what there was left of it, and had disappeared in the cornfield about the battery. There was nothing to do but lie there and await developments. Nearly all the men in the hollow were wounded, one man—a recruit named Devlin, I think—frightfully so, his arm being cut short off. He lived a few minutes only. All were calling for water, of course, but none was to be had.

We lay there till dusk, perhaps an hour, when the fighting ceased. During that hour, while the bullets snipped the leaves from a young locust-tree, growing at the edge of the hollow and powdered us with the fragments, we had time to speculate on many things—among others, on the impatience with which men clamor, in dull times, to be led into a fight. We heard all through the war that the army "was eager to be led against the enemy." It must have been so, for truthful correspondents said so, and editors confirmed it. But when you came to hunt for this particular itch, it was always the next regiment that had it. The truth is, when bullets are whacking against tree-trunks and solid shot are cracking skulls like egg-shells, the consuming passion in the breast of the average man is to get out of the way. Between the physical fear of going forward and the moral fear of turning back, there is a predicament of exceptional awkwardness from which a hidden hole in the ground would be a wonderfully welcome outlet.

Night fell, preventing further struggle. Of 600 men of the regiment who crossed the creek at 3 o'clock that afternoon, 45 were killed and 176 wounded. The Confederates held possession of that part of the field over which we had moved, and just after dusk they sent out detachments to collect arms and bring in prisoners. When they came to our hollow all the unwounded and slightly wounded there were marched to the rear—prisoners of the 15th Georgia. We slept on the ground that night without protection of any kind; for, with a recklessness quite common throughout the war, we had thrown away every incumbrance on going into the fight.

—THOMPSON, "With Burnside at Antietam"

VII

FREDERICKSBURG AND CHANCELLORSVILLE

McClellan had won a technical victory at Antietam, and Lincoln took advantage of it to issue his preliminary Emancipation Proclamation. But once again "Little Mac" had the slows. On October 6 Halleck ordered him "to cross the Potomac and give battle to the enemy," but McClellan procrastinated. While he delayed Stuart rode with impunity around his army. Finally, on November 2, McClellan succeeded in getting his army across the Potomac; five days later Lincoln relieved him from command and appointed General Ambrose Burnside—who gave his name to sideburns—to his place. A second-rate officer with little to recommend him, Burnside was ambitious to succeed where so many had failed. Noting that Lee's forces were widely scattered, he proposed to drive south through Fredericksburg to Richmond before Lee could collect an army to oppose him. Moving with laudable celerity Burnside concentrated his "Grand Divisions" at Falmouth, just north of Fredericksburg on the Rappahannock. But alas there were no pontoons, and while the army marked time Jackson joined Lee at Fredericksburg and the Confederates dug in.

Properly defended, Fredericksburg was well-nigh impregnable, and with Lee in command of over 75,000 men and 306 guns there was no doubt that it would be properly defended. The town lay on a bend of the broad Rappahannock; behind it were a series of low-lying hills from Marye's Heights southward to Prospect Hill, along the base of which ran the tiny Massapomax River. It was along these heights that the Confederates were entrenched, Jackson commanding the left, on Marye's Heights, and Longstreet the right. In front of Marye's Heights ran a drainage ditch, and at the base of Marye's Hill— a knoll at the southern end of the Heights—was a sunken road with a stone retaining wall which offered almost perfect protection to infantry. It was against this position that Burnside hurled his army, in vain.

Fredericksburg ended in a bloody repulse. Burnside blamed his subordinates, and demanded that the President dismiss them or him. Lincoln dismissed him, and—somewhat reluctantly, as his letter reveals—appointed in his place "Fighting Joe" Hooker, whom Burnside had declared to be "unfit to hold an important commission during a crisis like the present." It was, perhaps, the one time when Burnside's judgment proved sound.

Hooker took command of an army that had been defeated but was far from demoralized, and that was far larger than Lee's; when Longstreet was sent south of the James to find provisions and forage for men and horses, Hooker outnumbered Lee by at least two to one.

Hooker's strategy was admirable. Leaving Sedgwick with 40,000 men at Fredericksburg, he planned to move up the Rappahannock, cross over through the Wilderness, catch Lee in a giant pincers movement, and overwhelm him. If Lee chose to stand and fight at Fredericksburg, Hooker could strike him from the rear; if he moved into the Wilderness to grapple with Hooker, Sedgwick could sweep down on Richmond. By the end of April Hooker had completed the reorganization and rebuilding of his army, and on the twenty seventh his advance guard began fording the Rappahannock. By the thirtieth the whole army, except for a reserve corps, was across and prepared to move on Lee.

But once again, as we shall see, Lee outgeneraled and out - fought his adversary, using on Hooker the strategy that Hooker had planned to use on him. Instead of being himself caught in a pincers, he caught Hooker in a pincers, rolled him up on both flanks, and pushed him back to the edge of the river; then he turned on the hapless Sedgwick and sent him, too, hurtling back across the river. It was a great victory, in some ways the most spectacular of Lee's career, but it was bought at a great price: Jackson.

Lincoln Urges McClellan to Advance

McClellan's conduct of the Antietam campaign seemed to vindicate his reappointment to the command of the armies. Once that battle was over, however, he fell back into his old habits of delay. On October 1 Lincoln went personally to view the situation and on his return to Washington formally ordered McClellan "to cross the Potomac and give battle to the enemy." Even this categorical demand was disregarded. The following letter, characteristically patient and reasonable, was sent a week later. McClellan met it with the plea that his cavalry was broken down—a reply which drew from Lincoln the memorable report, "Will you pardon me for ask ing what the horses of your army have done since the battle of Antietam that fatigues anything?" Finally on October 26 McClellan got under way, but when he permitted Lee to interpose his army between Richmond and the Federal forces, Lincoln removed him.

Few generals, it is safe to say, ever did more to merit dismissal. The Democrats sought to make a martyr out of McClellan, nominating him for the Presidency in 1864 on a platform which called the war a failure and demanded a cessation of hostilities. McClellan repudiated this plank in the platform but accepted the nomination; fortunately for the Union he was defeated that November.

To General G. B. McClellan.

Executive Mansion, Washington,
October 13, 1862

My Dear Sir:—You remember my speaking to you of what I called your over-cautiousness. Are you not over cautious when you assume that you cannot do what the enemy is constantly doing? Should you not claim to be at least his equal in prowess, and act upon the claim?

As I understand, you telegraphed General Halleck that you cannot subsist your army at Winchester unless the rail road from Harper's Ferry to that point be put in working order. But the enemy does now subsist his army at Winchester, at a distance nearly twice as great from railroad transportation as you would have to do, without the railroad last named. He now wagons from Culpepper Court-House. which is just about twice as far as you would have to do from Harper's Ferry. He is certainly not more than half as well provided with wagons as you are. I certainly should be pleased for you to have the advantage of the railroad from Harper's Ferry to Winchester; but it wastes all the remainder of autumn to give it to you, and, in fact, ignores the question of *time*, which cannot and must not be ignored.

Again, one of the standard maxims of war, as you know, is "to operate upon the enemy's communications as much as possible, without exposing your own." You seem to act as if this applies *against you*, but cannot apply in your *favor*. Change positions with the enemy, and think you not he would break your communication with Richmond within the next twenty-four hours? You dread his going into Pennsylvania. But if he does so in full force, he gives up his communications to you absolutely, and you have nothing to do but to follow and ruin him; if he does so with less than full force, fall upon and beat what is left behind all the easier.

Exclusive of the water line, you are now nearer to Richmond than the enemy is, by the route that you *can* and he *must* take. Why can you not reach there before him, unless you admit that he is more than your equal on a march? His route is the arc of a circle, while yours is the chord. The roads are as good on yours as on his.

You know I desired, but did not order, you to cross the Potomac below instead of above the Shenandoah and Blue Ridge. My idea was, that this would at once menace the enemy's communications, which I would seize if he would permit. If he should move northward, I would follow him closely, holding his communications. If he should prevent our seizing his communications, and move toward Richmond, I would press closely to him, fight him if a favorable opportunity should present, and at least try to beat him to Richmond on the inside track. I say "try;" if we never try, we shall never succeed. If he makes a stand at Winchester, moving neither north or south, I would fight him there, on the idea that if we cannot beat him when he bears the wastage of coming to us, we never can when we bear the wastage of going to him. This proposition is a simple truth, and is too important to be lost sight of for a moment. In coming to us he tenders us an advantage which we should not waive. We should not so operate as to merely drive him away. As we must beat him somewhere or fail finally, we can do it, if at all, easier near to us than far away. If we cannot beat the enemy where he now is, we never can, he again being within the intrenchments of Richmond . . .

It is all easy if our troops march as well as the enemy, and it is unmanly to say they cannot do it. This letter is in no sense an order.

Yours truly,

A. Lincoln.

—War of the Rebellion . . . Official Records

VII.2

BURNSIDE BLUNDERS AT FREDERICKSBURG

We have here three accounts of Fredericksburg—Confederate and Union. Each tells its own story, and it is unnecessary to recapitulate that story here, but we may give something of the setting of the battle. It was on December 10 that Burnside began laying five pontoon bridges across the Rappahannock. Confederate sharpshooter interfered effectively with this undertaking and Burnside attempted to drive them out first by a heavy bombardment of the town itself, then by sending four companies of Federal sharpshooters across in boats to hold down the Confederate fire. By the twelfth two of the "Grand Divisions" were across the river—Sumner's in Fredericksburg itself and Franklin's to the south. On the morning of the thirteenth the attack began, all along the line.

It was the attack on the Confederate left, on Marye's Hill, that proved most costly to the Union army. All through the deadly afternoon of December 13 Burnside hurled his men against the sunken road and the stone walls and the artillery of the Confederates, and when in the end darkness all upon the battlefield Union losses had mounted to over 6,000.

The first account here is by one of the defenders, William Owen of the Washington Artillery of New Orleans. Few of those who have left us records had a more varied experience than this Louisianian who fought in the Virginia campaigns to 1863, then went west, took part in the ChickamaugaChattanooga campaign,

and then returned east to fight in the Wilderness and at Petersburg.

The second is from the pen of the effervescent J. B. Polley, who fought with Hood's Texans—and whose figures are dramatic rather than accurate; the third by Corporal—later Captain—John McCrillis of the 5th New Hampshire Volunteers, one of the regiments that suffered most heavily in the attack on Marye's Hill.

A. The Yankees Attack Marye's Heights

On the night of the 10th of December [1862] we, of the New Orleans Washington Artillery, sat up late in our camp on Marye's Heights, entertaining some visitors in an improvised theater, smoking our pipes, and talking of home. A final punch having been brewed and disposed of, everybody crept under the blankets and was soon in the land of Nod.

In an hour or two we were aroused by the report of a heavy gun. I was up in an instant, for if there should be another it would be the signal that the enemy was preparing to cross the river. Mr. Florence, a civilian in the bivouac, bounced as if he had a concealed spring under his blanket, and cried out, "Wake up! wake up! what's that?"

The deep roar of the second gun was heard, and we knew what we had to do. It was 4 o'clock. Our orders were that upon the firing of these signal guns we should at once take our places in the redoubts prepared for us on Marye's Hill, and await developments. "Boots and saddles" was sounded, and the camp was instantly astir, and in the gray of the morning we were on the Plank road leading up the hill. The positions reached, . . . without delay the men made the redoubts as snug as possible, and finding the epaulements not to their liking, went to work with pick and shovel throwing the dirt a little higher, and fashioning embrasures to fire through. The engineers objected, and said they were "ruining the works," but the cannoneers said, "We have to fight here, not you; we will arange them to suit ourselves." And General Longstreet approvingly said, "If you save the finger of a man's hand, that does some good." A dense fog covered the country, and we could not discern what was going on in the town.

The morning of the 12th was also foggy, and it was not until 2 P.M. that it cleared off, and then we could see the Stafford Heights, across the river, densely packed with troops. At 3 P.M. a heavy column moved down toward one of the bridges near the gas-works, and we opened upon it, making some splendid practice and apparently stirring them up prodigiously, for they soon sought cooler localities. While our guns were firing, the enemy's long range batteries on the Stafford Heights opened upon us, as much as to say, "What are you about over there?" We paid no attention to their inquiry, as our guns could not reach them.

At dawn the next morning, December 13th, in the freshand nipping air, I stepped upon the gallery overlooking the heights back of the little old-fashioned town of Fredericksburg. Heavy fog and mist hid the whole plain between the heights and the Rappahannock, but under cover of that fog and within easy cannon-shot lay Burnside's army. Along the heights, to the right and left of where I was standing, extending a length of nearly five miles, lay Lee's army.

The bugles and the drum corps of the respective armies were now sounding reveille, and the troops were preparing for their early meal. All knew we should have a battle to-day and a great one, for the enemy had crossed the river in immense force, upon his pontoons during the night. On the Confederate side all was ready, and the shock was awaited with stubborn resolution. Last night we had spread our blankets upon the bare floor in the parlor of Marye's house, and now our breakfast was being prepared in its fire-place, and we were impatient to have it over. After hastily dispatching this light meal of bacon and corn-bread, the colonel, chief bugler, and I (the adjutant of the battalion) mounted our horses and rode out to inspect our lines . . . and found everything ready for instant action . . .

At 12 o'clock the fog had cleared, and while we were sitting in Marye's yard smoking our pipes, after a lunch of hard crackers, a courier came to Colonel Walton, bearing a dispatch from General Longstreet for General Cobb, but, for our information as well, to be read and then given to him. It was as follows: "Should General Anderson, on your left, be compelled to fall back to the second line of heights, you must conform to his movements." Descending the hill into the sunken road, I made my way through the troops, to a little house where General Cobb had his headquarters, and handed him the dispatch. He read it carefully, and said, "Well! if they wait for me to fall back, they will wait a long time."

Hardly had he spoken, when a brisk skirmish fire was heard in front, toward the town, and looking over the stone wall we saw our skirmishers falling back, firing as they came; at the same time the head of a Federal column was seen emerging from one of the streets of the town. They came on at the double-quick, with loud cries of "Hi! Hi! Hi!" which we could distinctly hear. Their arms were carried at "right shoulder shift," and their colors were aslant the shoulders of the color-sergeants. They crossed the canal at the bridge, and getting behind the bank to the low ground to deploy, were almost concealed from our sight. It was 12:30 P.M, and it was evident that we were now going to have it hot and heavy.

The enemy, having deployed, now showed himself above the crest of the ridge and advanced in columns of brigades, and at once our guns began their deadly work with shell and solid shot. How beautifully they came off. Their bright bayonets glistening in the sunlight made the line look like a huge serpent of blue and steel. The very force of their onset leveled the broad fences bounding the small fields and gar dens that interspersed the plain. We could see our shells bursting in their ranks, making great gaps; but on they came, as though they would go straight through and over us. Now we gave them canister, and that staggered them. A few more paces onward and the Georgians in the road below us rose up, and, glancing an instant along their rifle barrels, let loose a storm of

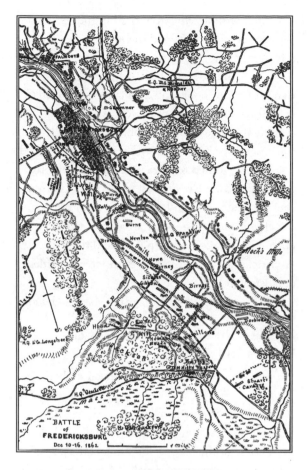

BATTLE OF FREDERICKSBURG

Cooke's brigade of Ransom's division was now placed in the sunken road with Cobb's men. At 2 P.M. other columns of the enemy left the crest and advanced to the attack; it appeared to us that there was no end of them. On they came in beautiful array and seemingly more determined to hold the plain than before; but our five was murderous, and no troops on earth could stand the *feu d'enfer* we were giving them. In the foremost line we distinguished the green flag with the golden harp of old Ireland, and we knew it to be Meagher's Irish brigade. The gunners of the two rifle pieces, Corporals Payne and Hardie, were directed to turn their guns against this column; but the gallant enemy pushed on beyond all former charges, and fought and left their dead within five and twenty paces of the sunken road.

Our position on the hill was now a hot one, and three regiments of Ransom's brigade were ordered up to reenforce the infantry in the road. We watched them as they came marching in line of battle from the rear, where they had been lying in reserve. They passed through our works and rushed down the hill with loud yells, and then stood shoulder to shoulder with the Georgians. The 25th North Carolina regiment, crossing Miller's guns, halted upon the crest of the hill, dressed its line, and fired a deadly volley at the enemy at close range, and then at the command "Forward!" dashed down the hill. It left dead men on Miller's redoubt, and he had to drag them away from the muzzles of his guns.

At this time General Cobb fell mortally wounded, and General Cooke was borne from the field, also wounded. Among other missiles a 3-inch rifle-ball came crashing through the works and fell at our feet. Kursheedt picked it up and said, "Boys, let's send this back to them again"; and into the gun it went, and was sped back into the dense ranks of the enemy.

General Kershaw now advanced from the rear with two regiments of his infantry, to reenforce the men in the sunken road, who were running short of ammunition, and to take command.

lead into the faces of the advance brigade. This was too much; the column hesitated, and then, turning, took refuge behind the bank.

But another line appeared from behind the crest and advanced gallantly, and again we opened our guns upon them, and through the smoke we could discern the red breeches of the "Zouaves," and hammered away at them especially. But this advance, like the preceding one, although passing the point reached by the first column, and doing and daring all that brave men could do, recoiled under our canister and the bullets of the infantry in the road, and fell back in great confusion. Spotting the fields in our front, we could detect little patches of blue—the dead and wounded of the Federal infantry who had fallen facing the very muzzles of our guns.

The sharp-shooters having got range of our embrasures, we began to suffer. Corporal Ruggles fell mortally wounded, and Perry, who seized the rammer as it fell from Ruggles's hand, received a bullet in the arm. Rodd was holding "vent," and away went his "crazy bone." In quick succession Everett, Rossiter, and Kursheedt were wounded. Falconer in passing in rear of the guns was struck behind the ear and fell dead. We were now so short-handed that every one was in the work, officers and men putting their shoulders to the wheels and running up the guns after each recoil. The frozen ground had given way and was all slush and mud. We were compelled to call upon the infantry to help us at the guns. Eshleman crossed over from the right to report his guns nearly out of ammunition; the other officers reported the same. They were reduced to a few solid shot only. It was now 5 o'clock, P.M., and there was a lull in the storm. The enemy did not seem inclined to renew his efforts, so our guns were withdrawn one by one, and the batteries of Woolfolk and Moody were substituted.

The little whitewashed brick-house to the right of the redoubt we were in was so battered with bullets during the four hours and a half engagement that at the close it was transformed to a bright brick-dust red. An old cast-iron stove lay against the house, and as the bullets would strike it it would give forth the sound of "bing! bing!" with different tones and variations. During the hottest of the firing old Mr. Florence, our non-combatant friend, was peering around the end of the house (in which, by the way, our wounded took refuge), looking out to see if his son, who was at the gun, was all right. A cannon-ball struck the top of the work, scattering dirt all over us and profusely down our necks, and, striking the end of the house, carried away a cart-load of bricks, just where Mr. Florence had been looking an instant before. We thought surely he had met his fate, but in a moment we were pleased to see his gray head "bob up serenely," determined to see "what was the gage of the battle."

After withdrawing from the hill the command was placed in bivouac, and the men threw themselves upon the ground to take a much-needed rest. We had been under the hottest fire men ever experienced for four hours and a half, and our loss had been three killed and twenty-four wounded. Among them was Sergeant John Wood, our leading spirit in camp theatricals, who was severely injured and never returned to duty. One gun was slightly disabled, and we had exhausted all of our canister, shell and case shot, and nearly every solid shot in our chests. At 5:30 another attack was made by the enemy, but it was easily repulsed, and the battle of Fredericksburg was over, and Burnside was baffled and defeated.

—Owen, "A Hot Day on Marye's Heights"

B. The Irish Brigade is Repulsed on Marye's Hill

Camp near Fredericksburg, Va.,
Dec. 20, 1862

At nine o'clock on the morning. . . the battle began in earnest. On the top of the hill, and close to the edge of the bluff, there was a battery, and behind the stone fence crouched Cobb's brigade of Georgians—one of the regiments being the gallant Eighteenth, which, when in our brigade, complimented us by its willingness to be known as the Third Texas. . . . To assault this position was a desperate undertaking. . . . Even Irish hearts had to be tempered for the ordeal, and to this end it was necessary not only to appeal to their love for "ould Ireland" but to imbue them with a supplemental fictitious courage. Only when a sprig of arbor vitae, stolen from the deserted yards of the town, was pinned upon their caps to remind them of the shamrock of their native Isle, their throats moistened liberally and their canteens filled with liquor, did they become ready to move forward as an initiatory forlorn hope. . . .

Between the last houses of the town proper and the stone fence stretched a piece of level open ground about two hundred yards wide. Entering this, the Federals halted a second or two to reform their lines; and then, some shouting "Erin go bragh," and others the Yankee huzzah, they rushed impetuously forward against a storm of grape and canister that, as long as the guns on the hilltop could be sufficiently depressed, tore great gaps in their ranks. But, wavering not, they closed together and rushed onward until within fifty yards of the stone fence, when in one grand, simultaneous burst of light, sound, and death, came the blinding flash, the deafening roar, the murderous destruction of two thousand well-aimed rifles, the wild, weird, blood-curdling Confederate yell, and two thousand Irishmen sank down wounded or dead, and a cowed and demoralized remnant sought safety in inglorious flight.

Seven assaults were made on the stone fence during the day, and five thousand men were sent to eternity before Burnside convinced himself that the position was impregnable. Only two regiments of our division were engaged in any undertaking that might be called a battle. These were the Fifty-seventh and Fifty-fourth North Carolina regiments composed of conscripts—young men under twenty and old men—all dressed in homespun, and presenting to the fastidious eyes of us veterans a very unsoldierly appearance. But we judged hastily. Ordered to drive the enemy back, they not only charged with surprising recklessness, but kept on charging until, to save them from certain capture, General Hood peremptorily recalled them. As they passed our brigade on their return, one old fellow halted, wiped the powder grime from his weather-beaten face with the sleeve of his coat, and wrathfully exclaimed, "Durn ole Hood, anyhow! He jes' didn't have no bus'ness ter stop us when we'uns was a-whippin' the durn blue-bellies ter h-ll an' back, an' eff we'uns hadder bin you Texicans, he'd never o' did it."

—Polley, *A Soldier's Letters to Charming Nellie*

C. The 5th New Hampshire to the Rescue

On the 13th at 12:30 P.M., the order was given for the Second Corps to assault the rebel position. In less than thirty minutes French's Division was dri-ven back, shattered and broken with a loss of about one-half its number killed and wounded. The brigades of Zook and Meagher advance and are broken, and lose more than one-half their men.

At this time, and during the operations of the Irish Brigade, General Hancock sat upon his horse in our immediate front, cool and collected. All at once his voice is heard above the cannon's roar. How well I remember the precise words; they have been ringing in my ears ever since: 'General Caldwell, you will forward your brigade at once; the Irish Brigade is suffering severely.' Then comes the quick and impetuous command of Colonel Cross: 'Attention! Every man is expected to do his duty to-day. If I fall never mind me. Fix bayonets! No man to fire a shot until he is inside the rebel lines. Shoulder arms! Trail arms! Forward, march!' Each man firmly grasps his musket, and the lines move for ward into that rain of death, and the last march of many, this side of the eternal camping-ground, begins.

The artillery fire seemed to increase, shells bursting over head and in the ranks, the solid shot crashing through that on-sweeping line of blue, opening large gaps which were quickly closed up again to have, the next moment, that crimson swath again cut through. Now we are in range of their infantry behind a stone wall, when a stream of fire and a shower of leaden hail causes the line to disappear like dew before a morning sun. 'Close in on the colors!' is the order heard above the din of battle. 'Steady! Forward!' rose in trumpet tones from lips that were the next moment hushed in death. The colors go down, only to be again upborne by some brave spirit who in his turn slept the sleep that knows no waking.

The line has now reached the brick house. Every man belonging to the color guard of the Fifth is dead or wounded. Colonel Cross is severely wounded; no man dares to leave the ranks to assist him. Major Sturtevant, Captains Perry, Murray and Moore, Lieutenants Ballou, Nettleton and Little are killed. Beyond the brick house extends a close board fence, parallel to the stone wall. We have now reached the fence, the point beyond which no previous line had been able to go. The dead and dying lay in a windrow along this fence. With the butts of our muskets we knocked the boards off in several places. Sergeant George S. Gove of Company K, with the colors, dashed on toward the rebel line.

At the fence all formation of the line of battle was lost. Beyond this point we saw no officers, neither did we receive any orders. At about twenty-five yards from the stone wall, Gove halted. I was the first man on his left; next on my left was Foss of Company E. Gove and Foss were the only two men standing. All the others, who were not shot down, fell down of their own accord. I asked them to lay down. Gove made no reply, while Foss said he would stand up until he was hit. Hardly had Foss said this before he was shot through the hip. At the same instant I heard Gove call my name. I looked, and he was down. I started to go to him when I was struck with a piece of shell in the left arm above the elbow, cutting a piece out of my overcoat, blouse and shirt, rendering my arm useless. I managed to get to Gove. He told me that he was shot through, and that I must save the colors and not mind anything about him. I rolled him over as carefully as I could, and gathered the tattered folds about the staff.

The fire of the enemy had slackened considerably. At this time there was no one in sight to my right or left, except the dead or wounded. Fixing my eye on an opening in the fence, I made a break for the rear, out to the brick house, where there were hundreds of men huddled. A shell dropped in their midst, killing and wounding a great many. I decided to go on to the rear. Arriving at the place where we came into line near the canal, I found a few of our own regiment and one officer. By his orders we fell back into the city.

Of the 5,500 men of Hancock's Division, 2,000 were killed and wounded. The Fifth went into action with 249 officers and men. Out of nineteen commissioned officers, seven were killed and ten wounded. Total loss, killed and wounded, 180.

—McCrillis in Child, *A History of the Fifth New Hampshire Volunteers*

VII·3

The Gallant Pelham at Fredericksburg

The Confederate artillery took a heavy toll of the Federals at Fredericksburg, and much of the credit for its performance went to "the gallant Pelham." This "boy major," as he was known, was one of the most romantic figures in the Army of Northern Virginia. Resigning from West Point in 1861 he entered the Confederate Army as a lieutenant, was assigned to the horse artillery, fought effectively in the Seven Days campaign, at Second Manassas and Antietam, and was promoted to a majority in 1862, at the age of twenty-one. Handsome, chivalrous, and courageous, he was one of the most widely admired officers in the army. Stuart named his daughter "Virginia Pelham," Lee characterized him as "the gallant Pelham" and recommended his promotion to a lieutenant colonelcy. When he was killed at Kelly's Ford, in March 1863, the whole South mourned.

This account is from the pen of the romantic novelist, John Esten Cooke.

He was ever by the guns which were under the hottest fire; and, when the enemy shifted their fire to other portions of the field, he proceeded thither, riding at full speed, and directed the fresh batteries in person. His men will remember how cheering and inspiring was his presence with them—how his coolness steadied them in the most exciting moments—and his brave cheerful voice was the herald of success. "He was the bravest human being I ever saw in my life," said one of his officers whom I conversed with recently; and all who have seen him under fire will bear similar testimony. His coolness had something heroic in it. It never deserted him, or was affected by those chances of battle which excite the bravest. He saw guns shattered and dismounted, or men torn to pieces, without exhibiting any signs of emotion. His nature seemed strung and every muscle braced to a pitch which made him rock; and the ghastliest spectacle of blood and death left his soul unmoved—his stern will unbent.

That unbending will had been tested often, and never had failed him yet. At Manassas, Williamsburg, Cold Harbour, Groveton, Oxhill, Sharpsburg, Shepherdstown, Kearneysville, Aldie, Union, Upperville, Markham, Barbee's, Hazel River, and Fredericksburg—at these and many other places he fought his horse artillery, and handled it with heroic coolness. One day when I led him to speak of his career, he counted up something like a hundred actions which he had been in—and in every one he had borne a prominent part. Talk with the associates of the young leader in those hard fought battles, and they will tell you a hundred instances of his dauntless courage. At Manassas he took position in a place so dangerous that an officer, who had followed him up to that moment, rode away with the declaration that "if Pelham was fool enough to stay there, *he was not.*"

But General Jackson thanked him, as he thanked him at Cold Harbour, when the brave young soldier came back covered with dust from fighting his Napoleon—the light of victory in his eyes. At Markham, while he was fighting the enemy in front, they made a circuit and charged him in the rear; but he turned his guns about, and fought them as before, with his "Napoleon detachment" singing the loud, triumphant *Marseillaise,* as that same Napoleon gun, captured at Seven Pines, and used at Fredericksburg, drove them back. All that whole great movement was a marvel of hard fighting, however, and Pelham was the hero of the stout, close struggle. Any other chief of artillery might have sent his men in at Fredericksburg and elsewhere, leaving the direction of the guns to such officers as the brave Captain Henry; but this did not suit the young chieftain. He must go himself with the one gun sent forward, and beside that piece he remained until it was ordered back—directing his men to lie down, but sitting his own horse, and intent solely upon the move-

ments and designs of the enemy, wholly careless of the "fire of hell" hurled against him. . . .

The work done by Pelham on the great day of Fredericksburg is a part of history now. All know how stubbornly he stood on that day—what laurels encircled his young brow when night at last came. This was the climax of his fame—the event with which his name will be inseparably connected. With one Napoleon gun, he opened the battle on the right, and instantly drew upon himself the fire, at close range, of three or four batteries in front, and a heavy enfilading fire from thirty-pound Parrots across the river. But this moved him little. That Napoleon gun was the same which he had used at the battle of Cold Harbour—it was taken from the enemy at Seven Pines—and, in the hands of the young officer, it had won a fame which must not be tarnished by defeat! Its grim voice must roar, however great the odds; its reverberating defiance must roll over the plain, until the bronze war-dog was silenced.

So it roared on steadily with Pelham beside it, blowing up caissons, and continuing to tear the enemy's ranks. General Lee was watching it from the hill above, and exclaimed, with eyes filled with admiration, "It is glorious to see such courage in one so young!" It was glorious indeed to see that one gun, placed in an important position, hold its ground with a firmness so unflinching. Not until his last round of ammunition was shot away did Pelham retire; and then only after a peremptory order sent to him. He afterwards took command of the entire artillery on the right, and fought it until night with a skill and courage which were admirable. He advanced his guns steadily, and at nightfall was thundering on the flank of the retreating enemy, who no longer replied. No answering roar came back from those batteries he had fought with his Napoleon so long; he had triumphed. That triumph was complete, and placed for ever upon record when the great Commander-in-Chief, whom he loved and admired so ardently, gave him the name in his report of "the gallant Penham."

—Cooke, *Wearing of the Gray*

VII.4

NIGHT ON THE FIELD OF FREDERICKSBURG

Here is a description of the dreadful night of December 13-14, from the pen of one of the most gifted of all the chroniclers of the war, General Joshua L. Chamberlain, colonel of the 20th Maine Volunteers. A professor at Bowdoin College, Chamberlain enlisted in 1862, received the Congressional Medal of Honor for his defense of Little Round Top, was promoted to brevet major general, was six times wounded, and was selected to receive the surrender of the Confederates at Appomattox. Later he was four times governor of Maine, and president of Bowdoin College. We shall meet him against Gettysburg and at Appomattox.

The desperate charge was over. We had not reached the enemy's fortifications, but only that fatal crest where we had seen five lines of battle mount but to be cut to earth as by a sword-swoop of fire. We had that costly honor which sometimes falls to the "reserve"—to go in when all is havoc and confusion, through storm and slaughter, to cover the broken and depleted ranks of comrades and take the battle from their hands. Thus we had replaced the gallant few still struggling on the crest, and received that withering fire, which nothing could withstand, by throwing ourselves flat in a slight hollow of the ground, within pistol shot of the enemy's works; and, mingled with the dead and dying that strewed the field, we returned the fire till it reddened into night, and at last fell away through darkness into silence.

But out of that silence from the battle's crash and roar rose new sounds more appalling still; rose or fell, you knew not which, or whether from the earth or air; a strange ventriloquism, of which you could not locate the source, a smothered moan that seemed to come from distances beyond reach of the natural sense, a wail so far and deep and wide, as if a thousand discords were flowing together into a keynote weird, unearthly, terrible to hear and bear, yet startling with its nearness; the writhing concord broken by cries for help, pierced by shrieks of paroxysm; some begging for a drop of water; some

calling on God for pity; and some on friendly hands to finish what the enemy had so horribly begun; some with delirious, dreamy voices murmuring loved names, as if the dearest were bending over them; some gathering their last strength to fire a musket to call attention to them where they lay helpless and deserted; and underneath, all the time, that deep bass note from closed lips too hopeless or too heroic to articulate their agony.

Who could sleep, or who would? Our position was isolated and exposed. Officers must be on the alert with their command. But the human took the mastery of the official; sympathy of soldiership. Command could be devolved; but pity, not. So with a staff officer I sallied forth to see what we could do where the helpers seemed so few. Taking some observations in order not to lose the bearing of our own position, we guided our steps by the most piteous of the cries. Our part was but little; to relieve a painful posture; to give a cooling draught to fevered lips; to compress a severed artery, as we had learned to do, though in bungling fashion; to apply a rude bandage, which yet might prolong the life to saving; to take a token or farewell message for some stricken home; it was but little, yet it was an endless task. We had moved towards the right and rear of our own position—the part of the field immediately above the city. The farther we went the more the need deepened, and the calls multiplied. Numbers half wakening from the lethargy of death, or of despair, by sounds of succor, begged us to take them quickly to a surgeon; and when we could not do that, imploring us to do the next most merciful service and give them quick dispatch out of their misery. Right glad were we when, after midnight, the shadowy ambulances came gliding along, and the kindly hospital stewards, with stretchers and soothing appliances, let us feel that we might return to our proper duty.

And now we were aware of other figures wandering, ghostlike, over the field. Some on errands like our own, drawn by compelling appeals; some seeking a lost comrade, with uncertain steps amidst the unknown, and ever and anon bending down to

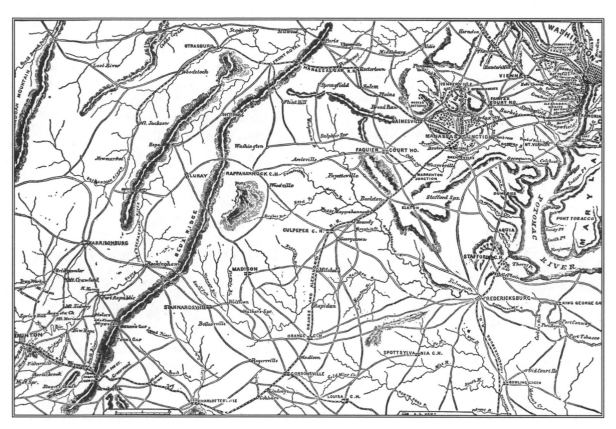

THE SEAT OF THE WAR IN VIRGINIA

scan the pale visage closer, or, it may be, by the tight of a brief match, whose blue, flickering flame scarcely can give the features a more recognizable or more human look; some man, desperately wounded, yet seeking, with faltering step, before his fast ebbing blood shall have left him too weak to move, some quiet or sheltered spot out of sound of the terrible appeals he could neither answer nor endure, or out of reach of the raging battle coming with the morning; one creeping, yet scarcely moving, from one lifeless form to another, if, perchance, he might find a swallow of water in the canteen still swung from the dead soldier's side; or another, as with just returning or just remaining consciousness, vainly striving to rise from a mangled heap, that he may not be buried with them while yet alive; or some man, yet sound of body, but pacing feverishly his ground because in such a bivouac his spirit could not sleep. And so we picked our way

back, amidst the stark, upturned faces, to our little living line.

The night chill had now woven a misty veil over the field. Fortunately, a picket fence we had encountered in our charge from the town had compelled us to abandon our horses, and so had saved our lives on the crest; but our overcoats had been strapped to the saddles, and we missed them now. Most of the men, however, had their overcoats or blankets—we were glad of that. Except the few sentries along the front, the men had fallen asleep—the living with the dead. At last, outwearied and depressed with the desolate scene, my own strength sunk, and I moved two dead men a little and lay down between them, making a pillow of the breast of a third. The skirt of his overcoat drawn over my face helped also to shield me from the bleak winds. There was some comfort even in this companionship. But it was broken sleep. The deepening chill drove many forth to take the garments of those who could no longer need them, that they might keep themselves alive. More than once I was startled from my unrest by some one turning back the coat skirt from my face, peering, half vampire-like, to my fancy, through the darkness, to discover if it too were of the silent and unresisting; turning away more disconcerted at my living word than if a voice had spoken from the dead.

Having held our places all the night, we had to keep to them all the more closely the next day, for it would be certain death to attempt to move away. As it was, it was only by making breastworks and barricades of the dead men that covered the field that we saved any alive. We did what we could to take a record of these men. A testament that had fallen from the breast pocket of the soldier who had been my pillow, I sent soon after to his home—he was not of my command—and it proved to be the only clue his parents ever had to his fate.

The next midnight, after thirty-six hours of this harrowing work, we were bidden to withdraw into the town for refreshment and rest. But neither rest nor motion was to be thought of till we had paid fitting honor to our dead. We laid them on the spot which they had won, on the sheltered edge of the crest, and committed their noble forms to the earth, and their story to their country's keeping.

> We buried them darkly, at dead of night,
> The sod with our bayonets turning.

Splinters of boards torn by shot and shell from the fences we had crossed served as headstones, each name hurriedly carved under brief match lights, anxiously hidden from the foe. It was a strange scene around that silent and shadowy sepulture. "We will give them a starlight burial," it was said; but heaven ordained a more sublime illumination. As we bore them in dark and sad procession, their own loved North took up the escort and lifting all her glorious lights led the triumphal march over

the bridge that spans the worlds—an aurora borealis of marvelous majesty! fiery lances and banners of blood and flame, columns of pearly light, garlands and wreaths of gold, all pointing upward and beckoning on. Who would not pass on as they did, dead for their country's life, and lighted to burial by the meteor splendors of their native sky?

—CHAMBERLAIN, "Night on the
Field of Fredericksburg"

--------- VII.5 ---------

LINCOLN APPOINTS HOOKER TO THE COMMAND OF THE ARMY

After Fredericksburg Burnside prepared an order dismissing Hooker and three other general officers, and relieving Franklin and four other officers from duty. This he laid before Lincoln with the choice of accepting it or dismissing him. Inevitably Lincoln relieved Burnside from command and—less inevitably—appointed Hooker to his p1ace. A West Pointer, with experience in the Florida campaign and the Mexican War, Hooker had been appointed brigadier general of volunteers in 1861 and had fought in the Peninsular and the Antietam campaigns. Like Pope he was given to boasting. "My plans are perfect," he said shortly after his appointment to the top command. "May God have mercy on General Lee for I will have none." Lincoln, as this famous letter reveals, was not so sure.

Executive Mansion, Washington, D. C.
January 26, 1863

Major-General Hooker:
General:

I have placed you at the head of the Army of the Potomac. Of course I have done this upon what appears to me to be sufficient reasons, and yet I think it best for you to know that there are some things in regard to which I am not quite satisfied with you. I believe you to be a brave and skillful soldier, which, of course, I like. I also believe you do not mix politics with your profession, in which you are right. You have confidence in yourself, which is a valuable, if not an indispensable, quality.

You are ambitious, which, within reasonable bounds, does good rather than harm; but I think that during General Burnside's command of the army you have taken counsel of your ambition, and thwarted him as much as you could, in which you did a great wrong to the country and to a most meritorious and honorable brother officer. I have heard, in such a way as to believe it, of your recently saying that both the Army and the Government needed a dictator. Of course, it was not for this, but in spite of it, that I have given you the command. Only those generals who gain successes can set up dictators. What I now ask of you is military success, and I will risk the dictatorship. The Government will support you to the utmost of its ability, which is neither more nor less than it has done or will do for all commanders. I much fear that the spirit which you have aided to infuse into the army, of criticizing their commander and withholding confidence from him, will now turn upon you. I shall assist you as far as I can to put it down. Neither you nor Napoleon, if he were alive again, could get any good out of an army while such a spirit prevails in it. And now beware of rashness. Beware of rashness, but with energy and sleepless vigilance go forward and give us victories.

Yours, very truly,

A. Lincoln.

—*War of the Rebellion . . . Official Records*

——— VII.6 ———

LEE WHIPS HOOKER AT CHANCELLORSVILLE

By the end of April Hooker had what he called "the finest army on the planet." Certainly it was the largest and best-equipped that had ever been seen in America. Against Hooker's force of some 130,000 men Lee could muster less than 60,000, for Longstreet's corps was south of the James. No wonder Hooker was sure of victory. "The enemy must either ingloriously fly, or come out from behind his defenses and give us battle on our own ground where certain destruction awaits him," he said in an order to his troops. First he sent Stoneman off on a raid designed to disorganize Lee's communications and threaten

Richmond. Then, leaving Sedgwick at Fredericksburg, he moved the rest of his vast army up the Rappahannock and Rapidan, crossed at Kelly's Ford, and on April 30 reached Chancellorsville in the heart of the Wilderness. He failed however to catch Lee by surprise and when Slocum's corps moved down the Plank Road toward Fredericksburg, the next day, it ran into the well-entrenched Confederates. Instead of joining battle Hooker mysteriously withdrew his forces to Chancellorsville, giving the initiative over to Lee, who promptly seized and exploited it.

We begin with a general account of the battle. Charles Morse here recounts the errors of judgment that led to Federal defeat. A colonel of the 2nd Massachusetts Infantry, Morse fought in Virginia through the first two years of the war, then in Tennessee and the Carolinas.

Stafford C.H., May 7, 1863

I am going to give you without any introduction, a history of this last campaign against Richmond by the army under the great Joe Hooker. I believe I have seen it and judged it fairly.

On Monday, April 27th, our corps broke camp early in the morning and marched to Hartwood Church, ten miles; there it went into camp for the night. The Eleventh and Fifth Corps also came up there and camped in our vicinity; next morning, we all moved and camped that night near Kelly's Ford. A pontoon bridge was thrown across and the Eleventh was over before daylight Wednesday; the other corps followed rapidly and the advance began towards the Rapidan. The Eleventh and Twelfth marched on the road to Germana Ford, the Fifth on the road to Ely's Ford; all three of the corps were under command of General Slocum. I was detailed, the morning of the advance, as Aide to General Slocum, and another officer was made Acting Provost Marshal. All the companies of the Second Massachusetts were sent to the Regiment. We skirmished all the way to Germana Ford; there we met quite a determined resistance; our cavalry was drawn in and the Second Massachusetts and the Third Wisconsin sent forward to clear the way; they drove everything before them and, by their heavy fire, forced the rebels at the Ford to surrender (about one hundred officers and men). We lost in this skirmish about a dozen killed and wounded.

General Slocum now determined to cross the Rapidan, though there was no bridge and the ford was almost impassable. . . . At about noon [April 30], we arrived at Chancellorsville, and found the Fifth Corps already there. We had a small cavalry skirmish,. . . but besides that, nothing of importance occurred during that day; the troops were formed in line of battle, but were not attacked. Up to this time you see everything had gone well and success seemed certain.

Towards night [April 30], General Hooker arrived with his staff, and we heard of the crossing at the U. S. Ford of the Second, Third and First Corps. All the headquarters were in the vicinity of the Chancellor House, a large, fine brick mansion. General Hooker took supper with General Slocum; he didn't seem to be able to express his gratification at the success of General Slocum in bringing the three corps up so rapidly. Then, in the most extravagant, vehement terms, he went on to say how he had got the rebels, how he was going to crush them, annihilate them, etc.

The next morning at ten, the Fifth and Twelfth Corps advanced in order of battle on two parallel roads; we soon met the enemy and skirmished for about two miles, when they ap peared in considerable force and the battle began. We were in a splendid position and were driving the enemy when an order came to General Slocum to retire his command to its former position. No one could believe that the order was genuine, but almost immediately, another of General Hooker's staff brought the same order again. Now, perhaps, you don't know that to retire an army in the face of an enemy when you are engaged is one of the most difficult operations in war; this we had to do. I carried the order to General Geary to retire his division in echelon by brigades, and stayed with him till the movement was nearly completed. It was a delicate job; each brigade would successively bear the brunt of the enemy's attack. Before the last brigades of the Fifth and Twelfth Corps were in position, the enemy made a furious attack on the Chancellor House; luckily we had considerable

artillery concentrated there and they were driven back. The next attack was on our corps, but the enemy was severely repulsed. This about ended the fighting on Friday; we lost, I suppose, about five hundred men.

During the night, the men were kept at work digging trenches and throwing up breastworks of 10gs. Our head-quarters were at Fairview, an open piece of ground rising into quite a crest in the centre. Skirmishing began at daylight next morning [May 2] and continued without much result to either side, tilt afternoon, when the enemy began to move, in large force, towards our right, opposite General Howard, Eleventh Corps. This corps was in a fine position in intrenchments, with almost open country in front of them, the right resting on Hunting Creek. At about four P.M. the Third Corps, General Sickles, was moved out to the right of the Twelfth and advanced towards Fredericksburgh. The order then came to General Slocum that the enemy were in full retreat, and to advance his whole tine to capture att he could of prisoners, wagons, etc. Our right, General Williams' Division, advanced without much trouble, driving the enemy before it, but the Second Division had hardly got out of the trenches before it was attacked with great determination, yet it steadily retained its position.

At about five P.M. a tremendous and unceasing musketry fire began in the direction of the Eleventh Corps. As it was necessary to know what was going on there in order to regulate the movements of the Twelfth Corps, General Slocum and the rest of us rode for our lives towards this new scene of action. What was our surprise when we found that instead of a fight, it was a complete Bull Run rout. Men, horses, mules, rebel prisoners, wagons, guns, etc. etc. were coming down the road in terrible confusion, behind them an unceasing roar of musketry. We rode until we got into a mighty hot fire, and found that no one was attempting to make a stand, but every one running for his life. Then General Slocum dispatched me to General Hooker to explain the state of affairs, and three other staff officers to find General Williams and order him back to his trenches with all haste.

I found General Hooker sitting atone on his horse in front of the Chancellor House, and delivered my message, he merely said, "Very good, sir." I rode back and found the Eleventh Corps still surging up the road and still this terrible roar behind them. Up to this time, the rebels had received no check, but now troops began to march out on the plank road and form across it, and Captain Best, Chief of Artillery of our corps, had on his own responsibility gathered together all the batteries he could get hold of, and put them in position (forty-six guns in alt) on Fairview, and had begun firing at the rate of about one hundred guns a minute, into the rebels. This, in my opinion, saved our army from destruction. . . .

The artillery men were hard at work all night, throwing up traverses to protect their guns, and about two in the morning we all lay down on the ground and slept until about four, when daylight [May 3] began to appear. Our right was now formed by the Third, Fifth and First Corps, about five hundred yards in the rear of our first position. The rebels began the attack as soon as there was light enough, from the left of our First Division to about the right of the Third Corps. General Birney's Division of the Third Corps was out in front of General Williams; his men behaved badly, and after a slight resistance, fell back into our lines, losing a battery.

The rebels now charged down our First Division, but were met with such a deadly fire that they were almost annihilated. Their second line was then sent in, but met the same fate, and their third and last line advanced. Our men now had fired more than forty rounds of cartridges and were getting exhausted. General Slocum sent almost every one of his staff officers to General Hooker, stating his position and begging for support; Hooker's answer was, "I can't make men or ammunition for General Slocum."

Meantime, Sickles' Corps was holding its own on the right of ours, but it was rapidly getting into the same condition as the Twelfth. The rebels were driven back every time they advanced, and we were taking large numbers of prisoners and colors. All this time while our infantry was fighting so gallantly in front, our battery of forty-six guns was firing incessantly. The rebels had used no artillery until they captured the battery from Birney, when they turned that on us, making terrible destruction in General Geary's line. General Meade, Fifth Corps, now went to Hooker and entreated that he might be allowed to throw his corps on the rebel flank, but General Hooker said, "No, he was wanted in his own position." On his own responsibility General Meade sent out one brigade, which passed out in the rear of the enemy's right, recaptured a battery, three hundred of our men who were prisoners, and four hundred of the rebels, and took them safely back to their corps.

It was now after seven o'clock. Our men had fired their sixty rounds of cartridges and were still holding their position; everything that brave men could do, these men had done, but now nothing was left but to order them to fall back and give up their position to the enemy. This was done in good order and they marched off under a heavy fire to the rear of our batteries. The rebels, seeing us retreating, rushed forward their artillery and began a fearful fire. I found I could be useful to Captain Best, commanding our artillery, so I stayed with him. I never before saw anything so fine as the attack on that battery; the air was full of missiles, solid shot, shells, and musket balls. I saw one solid shot kill three horses and a man, another took a leg off one of the captains of the batteries. Lieutenant Crosby of the Fourth Artillery was shot through the heart with a musket ball; he was a particular friend of Bob Shaw and myself; he lived just long enough to say to Captain Best, "Tell father I die happy."

The rebels came up to the attack in solid masses and got within three hundred yards, but they were slaughtered by the hundreds by the case-shot and canister, and were driven back to the woods. Still not an infantry man was sent to the support of the guns. More than half the horses were killed or wounded; one caisson had blown up, another had been knocked to pieces; in ten minutes more the guns would have been isolated. They, too, therefore, were ordered to retire, which they did without losing a gun. You see, now our centre was broken, everything was being retired to our second line, the rebel artillery was in position, their line of battle steadily advancing across our old ground. This fire of the batteries was concentrated on the Chancellor House, Hooker's original headquarters, and it was torn almost to pieces by solid shot and was finally set on fire by a shell.

The army was now put in position in the second line; the centre was on a rising piece of ground and protected by a battery of forty or fifty guns . . . You can easily see that, if the enemy once forced our right or left, our communications would at once be cut and all possibility of retreat prevented. Late that night we lay down close beside the Rappahannock. By three o'clock next morning we were awakened by a heavy artillery fire and shells bursting over us. Our guns replied and kept at it for about an hour, when the enemy's batteries were silenced. We now mounted our horses and rode along the lines to look at our position; we found that it was a very strong one and capable of being made very much more so. . . .

I doubt if ever in the history of this war, another chance will be given us to fight the enemy with such odds in our favor as we had last Sunday, and that chance has been worse than lost to us. I don't believe any men ever fought better than our Twelfth Corps, especially the First Division; for two hours, they held their ground without any support, against the repeated assaults of the enemy; they fired their sixty rounds of cartridges and held their line with empty muskets until ordered to fall back. The old Second, of course, did splendidly, and lost heavily . . . Our colors got thirty holes in them and the staff (the third one) was smashed to pieces.

—Morse, *Letters Written During the Civil War*

VII.7

PLEASONTON STOPS THE CONFEDERATES AT HAZEL GROVE

Early on May 2 Lee sent Jackson with the bulk of the army along the Plank Road and through the Wilderness to Hooker's rear. Although Hooker was repeatedly warned of this movement, he fatuously insisted that the Confederates were retreating, and took no precautions. On the afternoon of the second Jackson swept out of the woods and fell on Howard's corps and on Sickles. Pleasonton hurried up his cavalry, collected scattered elements of infantry and artillery, and made a stand that may have saved the army from destruction.

General Pleasonton was a West Pointer with long military experience in the Mexican, Sioux and Seminole wars, who commanded the Union cavalry at Gettysburg and was later transferred to the Trans-Mississippi theater.

On arriving at Hazel Grove, about one mile from Chancellorsville, I found that General Sickles was moving two of the divisions of the Third Corps in the direction of Catherine Furnace, and shortly after he became engaged there with a strong rearguard. Hazel Grove was the highest ground in the neighborhood and was the key of our position, and I saw that if Lee's forces gained it the Army of the Potomac would be worsted.

General Sickles wanted some cavalry to protect his flanks, and I gave him the 6th New York. This left me with only the 8th and 17th Pennsylvania regiments and Martin's New York battery of horse artillery. I posted this command at the extreme west of the clearing, about two hundred yards from the woods in which the Eleventh Corps was encamped. This position at Hazel Grove was about a quarter of a mile in extent, running nearly north-east and south-west, but was in no place farther than two hundred yards from the woods, and on the south and east it sloped off into a marsh and a creek. It commanded the position of the army at Fairview and Chancellorsville and enfiladed our line. The moving out to the Furnace of the two divisions of the Third Corps left a gap of about a mile from Hazel Grove to the right of the Twelfth Corps. Shortly after General Sickles had been engaged at the Furnace, he sent me word that the enemy were giving way and cavalry could be used to advantage in pursuit. Before moving my command I rode out to the Furnace to comprehend the situation. It was no place for cavalry to operate, and as I could hear spattering shots going more and more toward the north-west, I was satisfied that the enemy were not retreating.

I hastened back to my command at Hazel Grove; when I reached it, the Eleventh Corps to our rear and our right was in full flight, panic-stricken beyond description. We faced about, having then the marsh behind us. It was an ugly marsh, about fifty yards wide, and in the stampede of the Eleventh Corps, beef cattle, ambulances, mules, artillery, wagons, and horses became stuck in the mud, and others coming on crushed them down, so that when the fight was over the pile of debris in the marsh was many feet high. I saw that something had to be done, and that very quickly, or the Army of the Potomac would receive a crushing defeat. The two cavalry regiments were in the saddle, and as I rode forward Major Keenan of the 8th Pennsylvania came out to meet me, when I ordered him to take the regiment, charge into the woods, which, as we had previously stood, were to our rear, and hold the enemy in check until I could get some guns into position. He replied, with a smile at the size of the task, that he would do it, and started off immediately. Thirty men, including Major Keenan, Captain Arrowsmith, and Adjutant Haddock, never came back.

I then directed Captain Martin to bring his guns into battery, load with double charges of canister, and aim them so that the shot would hit the ground half-way between the guns and the woods. I also stated that I would give the order to fire. Just then a handsome young lieutenant of the 4th U. S. Artillery, Frank B. Crosby (son of a distinguished lawyer of New York City), who was killed the next day, galloped up and said, "General, I have a battery of six guns; where shall I go? what shall I do?" I

told him to place his battery in line on the right of Martin's battery, and gave him the same instructions I had given Martin as to how I wanted him to serve his guns. These 2 batteries gave me 12 guns, and to obtain more I then charged 3 squadrons of the 17th Pennsylvania Cavalry on the stragglers of the Eleventh Corps to clear the ground, and with the assistance of the rest of the regiment succeeded in placing 10 more pieces of artillery in line. The line was then ready for Stonewall Jackson's onset. It was dusk when his men swarmed out of the woods for a quarter of a mile in our front (our rear ten minutes before). They came on in line five and six deep, with but one flag—a Union flag dropped by the Eleventh Corps.

I suspected deception and was ready for it. They called out not to shoot, they were friends; at the same time they gave us a volley from at least five thousand muskets. As soon as I saw the flash I gave the command to fire, and the whole line of artillery was discharged at once. It fairly swept them from the earth; before they could recover themselves the line of artillery had been loaded and was ready for a second attack. After the second discharge, suspecting that they might play the trick of having their men lie down, draw the fire of the artillery, then jump up and charge before the pieces could be reloaded, I poured in the canister for about twenty minutes, and the affair was over. . . .

For half an hour General Jackson had the Army of the Potomac at his mercy. That he halted to re-form his troops in the woods, instead of forging ahead into the clearing, where he could reform his troops more rapidly, and where he could have seen that he was master of the situation, turned out to be one of those fatalities by which the most brilliant prospects are sacrificed. When he advanced upon the artillery at Hazel Grove Jackson had another opportunity to win, if his infantry had been properly handled. The fire of his infantry was so high it did no harm; they should have been ordered to fire so low as to disable the cannoneers at the guns. Had his infantry fire been as effective as that of our artillery, Jackson would have carried the position. The artillery fire was effective because I applied to it that principle of dynamics in which the angle of incidence is equal to the angel of reflection,—that is to say, if the muzzle of a gun is three feet from the ground and it is discharged so that the shot will strike the ground at a distance of one hundred yards, it will glance from the earth at the same angle at which it struck it, and in another one hundred yards will be three feet from the ground. I knew my first volley must be a crushing one, or Jackson, with his superior numbers, would charge across the short distance which separated us and capture the artillery before the guns could be reloaded.

—PLEASONTON, "The Successes and Failures of Chancellorsville"

VII.8

STUART AND ANDERSON LINK UP AT CHANCELLORSVILLE

The timely employment of artillery, the coming of darkness, and the wounding of Jackson combined to save the Federals on the second day. Early next morning Lee renewed the attack on both flanks, Stuart on the right, Anderson at the center, and McLaws on the left. Stuart quickly seized Hazel Grove and pushed on ahead to take Chancellorsville itself; at about noon his line linked up with Anderson's, and the Federals were hemmed in on three sides. Hooker had been injured that morning by a falling brick; perhaps that is why he failed to put in his reserves or to get Sedgwick's attack under way in time to afford any effective relief. Sedgwick had, to be sure, swept the thin Confederate line of Marye's Heights, but when Lee sent McLaws to Early's aid Sedgwick found himself encircled just as Hooker was encircled, and retired across the Rappahannock. The Federals, still twice as strong as Lee, stood their ground on May 4, but next day withdrew across the river.

Heros von Borcke, a Prussian nobleman and professional soldier, here tells the story of the third day.

The enemy, fully three times our number, occupied a piece of wood extending about two miles from our immediate front towards the plateau and open fields round Chancellorsville, a village consisting of only a few houses. The Federals had made good use of their time, having thrown up in the wood during the night three successive lines of breastworks, constructed of strong timber, and on the plateau itself, occupied by their reserves, had erected a regular line of redoubts, mounted by their numerous artillery, forty pieces of which were playing on the narrow plank-road. . . .

All our divisions now moving forward, the battle soon be came general, and the musketry sounded in one continued roll along the lines. Nearly a hundred hostile guns opening fire at the same time, the forest seemed alive with shot, shell, and bullets, and the plank-road, upon which, as was before mentioned, the fire of forty pieces was concentrated, was soon enveloped in a cloud of smoke from the bursting of shells and the explosion of caissons. This road being our principal line of communication, and crowded therefore with ambulances, ammunition-trains, and artillery, the loss of life soon became fearful, and dead and dying men and animals were strewing every part of it. How General Stuart, and those few staff-officers with him who had to gallop to and fro so frequently through this *feu infernal*, escaped unhurt, seems to me quite miraculous. . . .

Stuart was all activity, and wherever the danger was greatest there was he to be found, urging the men forward, and animating them by the force of his example. The shower of missiles that hissed through the air passed round him unheeded; and in the midst of the hottest fire I heard him, to an old melody, hum the words, "Old Joe Hooker get out of the Wilderness."

After a raging conflict, protracted for several hours, during which the tide of battle ebbed and flowed on either side we succeeded in taking the advanced works, and driving the enemy upon their third line of intrenchments, of a still stronger character than those before it. This partial success was only gained with a sad sacrifice of life, while countless numbers were seen limping and crawling to the rear. The woods had caught fire in several places from the explosion of shells—the flames spreading principally, however, over a space of several acres in extent where the ground was thickly covered with dry leaves; and here the conflagration progressed with the rapidity of a prairie-fire, and a large number of Confederate and Federal wounded thickly scattered in the vicinity, and too badly hurt to crawl out of the way, met a terrible death. The heartrending cries of the poor victims, as the flames advanced, entreating to be rescued from their impending fate—entreaties which it was impossible to heed in the crisis of the battle, and amidst duties on which the lives of many others depended seem still in my ears.

Among the heart-sickening scenes of this terrible conflict which are still vivid in my memory, is one no lapse of time can ever efface, and in contemplating which I scarcely could check the tears from starting to my eyes. Riding to the front, I was hailed by a young soldier, whose boyish looks and merry songs on the march had frequently attracted my attention and excited my interest, and who was now leaning against a tree, the life-blood streaming down his side from a mortal wound, and his face white with the pallor of approaching death. "Major," said the poor lad, "I am dying, and I shall never see my regiment again, but I ask you to tell my comrades that the Yankees have killed but not conquered me." When I passed the place again half an hour afterwards I found him a corpse. Such was the universal spirit of our men, and in this lay the secret of many of our wonderful achievements.

The enemy had in the meanwhile been strongly rein forced, and now poured forth from their third line of intrenchments a fire so terrible upon our advancing troops that the first two divisions staggered, and, after several unsuccessful efforts to press onward, fell back in considerable confusion. In vain was it that our officers used every effort to bring them forward once more; in vain even was it that Stuart, snatching the battle-flag of one of our brigades from the hands of the colour-bearer and waving it over his head, called on them as he rode forward to follow him. Nothing could induce them again to face that tempest of bullets, and that devastating hurricane of grape and canister vomited at close range from more than sixty pieces of artillery, and the advantages so dearly gained seemed about to be lost. At this critical moment, we suddenly heard the yell of Rodes's division behind us, and saw these gallant troops, led by their heroic general, charge over the front lines, and fall upon the enemy with such impetus that in a few minutes their works were taken, and they were driven in rapid flight from the woods to their redoubts on the hills of Chancellorsville.

A slight pause now intervened in the conflict, both sides, after the terrible work of the last few hours, being equally willing to draw breath awhile; and this gave us an opportunity to re-form our lines and close up our decimated ranks. The contest, meanwhile, was sustained by the artillery alone, which kept up a heavy cannonade; and the nature of the ground being now more favourable, most of our batteries had been brought into action, while from a hill on our extreme right, which had only been abandoned by the enemy after the charge of Rodes's division, twenty 12-pounder Napoleons played with a well-directed flank-fire upon the enemy's works, producing a terrible effect upon their dense masses.

About half-past ten we had news from General Lee, in forming us that, having been pressing steadily forward the entire morning, he had now, with Anderson's and M'Laws's divisions, reached our right wing. I was at once despatched by Stuart to the Commander-in-Chief to report the state of affairs, and obtain his orders for further proceedings. I found him with our twenty-gun battery, looking as calm and dignified as ever, and perfectly regardless of the shells bursting round him, and the solid shot ploughing up the ground in all directions. General Lee expressed himself much satisfied with our operations, and intrusted me with orders for Stuart, directing a general attack with his whole force, which was to be supported by a charge of Anderson's division on the left flank of the enemy.

With renewed courage and confidence our three divisions now moved forward upon the enemy's strong position on the hills, encountering as we emerged from the forest into the open opposite the plateau of Chancellorsville, such a storm of canister and bullets, that for a while it seemed an impossibility to take the heights in the face of it. Suddenly we heard to our right, piercing the roar and tumult of the battle, the yell of Anderson's men, whom we presently beheld hurled forward in a brilliant charge, sweeping everything before them. Short work was now made of the Federals, who, in a few minutes, were driven from their redoubts, which they abandoned in disorderly flight, leaving behind them cannons, small-arms, tents, and baggage in large quantities, besides a host of prisoners, of whom we took 360 in one redoubt.

A more magnificent spectacle can hardly be imagined than that which greeted me when I reached the crest of the plateau, and beheld on this side the long lines of our swiftly advancing troops stretching as far as the eye could reach, their red flags fluttering in the breeze, and their arms glittering in the morning sun; and farther on, dense and huddled masses of the Federals flying in utter rout towards the United States Ford, whilst high over our heads flew the shells which our artillery were dropping amidst the crowd of the retreating foe. The Chancellorsville House had caught fire, and was now enveloped in flames, so that it was with difficulty that we could save some portion of the Federal wounded lying there, to the number of several hundreds, the majority of whom perished. . . The flight and pursuit took the direction of United States Ford, as far as about a mile beyond Chancellorsville, where another strong line of intrenchments offered their protection to the fugitives, and heavy reserves of fresh troops opposed our further advance.

—Von Borcke, *Memoirs of the Confederate War for Independence*

VII.9

Lee Loses His Right Arm

Chancellorsville was a dearly bought victory; Confederate casualties were 13,156, of whom almost eleven thousand were killed and wounded. Irreparable was the loss of Stonewall Jackson, wounded by his own men. To Chaplain Lacy

Lee said, "Give him my affectionate regards, and tell him to make haste and get well and come back to me as soon as he can. He has lost his left arm; but I have lost my right arm." But pneumonia and other complications set in and the mighty Stonewall "passed over the river."

The Reverend James Power Smith, who here describes the wounding of Jackson, was Jackson's aide-de-camp.

When Jackson had reached the point where his line now crossed the turnpike, scarcely a mile west of Chancellorsville, and not half a mile from a line of Federal troops, he had found his front line unfit for the farther and vigorous advance he desired, by reason of the irregular character of the fighting, now right, now left, and because of the dense thickets, through which it was impossible to preserve alignment. Division commanders found it more and more difficult as the twilight deepened to hold their broken brigades in hand. Regretting the necessity of relieving the troops in front, General Jackson had ordered A. P. Hill's division, his third and reserve line, to be placed in front.

While this change was being effected, impatient and anxious, the general rode forward on the turnpike, followed by two or three of his staff and a number of couriers and signal sergeants. He passed the swampy depression and began the ascent of the hill toward Chancellorsville, when he came upon a line of the Federal infantry lying on their arms. Fired at by one or two muskets (two musket-balls from the enemy whistled over my head as I came to the front), he turned and came back toward his line, upon the side of the road to his left.

As he rode near to the Confederate troops, just placed in position and ignorant that he was in the front, the left company began firing to the front, and two of his party fell from their saddles dead—Captain Boswell, of the Engineers, and

Sergeant Cunliffe, of the Signal Corps. Spurring his horse across the road to his right, he was met by a second volley from the right company of Pender's North Carolina brigade. Under this volley, when not two rods from the troops, the general received three balls at the same instant. One penetrated the palm of his right hand and was cut out that night from the back of his hand. A second passed around the wrist of the left arm and out through the left hand. A third ball passed through the left arm half-way from shoulder to elbow. The large bone of the upper arm was splintered to the elbowjoint, and the wound bled freely. His horse turned quickly from the fire, through the thick bushes which swept the cap from the general's head, and scratched his forehead, leaving drops of blood to stain his face.

As he lost his hold upon the bridle-rein, he reeled from the saddle, and was caught by the arms of Captain Wilbourn, of the Signal Corps. Laid upon the ground, there came at once to his succor General A. P. Hill and members of his staff. The writer reached his side a minute after, to find General Hill holding the head and shoulders of the wounded chief. Cutting open the coat-sleeve from wrist to shoulder, I found the wound in the upper arm, and with my handkerchief I bound the arm above the wound to stem the flow of blood. Couriers were sent for Dr. Hunter McGuire, the surgeon of the corps and the general's trusted friend, and for an ambulance. Being outside of our lines, it was urgent that he should be moved at once. With difficulty litter-bearers were brought from the line near by, and the general was placed upon the litter and carefully raised to the shoulder, I myself bearing one corner.

A moment after, artillery from the Federal side was opened upon us; great broadsides thundered over the woods; hissing shells searched the dark thickets through, and shrapnels swept the road along which we moved. Two or three steps farther, and the litter-bearer at my side was struck and fell, but, as the litter turned, Major Watkins Leigh, of Hill's staff, happily caught it. But the fright of the men was so great that we were obliged to lay the litter and its burden down upon the road. As the litter-bearers ran to the cover of the trees, I threw myself by the general's side and held him firmly to the ground as he attempted to rise. Over us swept the rapid fire of shot and shell— grape-shot striking fire upon the flinty rock of the road all around us, and sweeping from their feet horses and men of the artillery just moved to the front.

Soon the firing veered to the other side of the road, and I sprang to my feet, assisted the general to rise, passed my arm around him and with the wounded man's weight thrown heavily upon me, we forsook the road. Entering the woods, he sank to the ground from exhaustion, but the litter was soon brought, and again rallying a few men, we essayed to carry him farther, when a second bearer fell at my side. This time, with none to assist, the litter careened, and the general fell to the ground, with a groan of deep pain. Greatly alarmed, I sprang to his head, and, lifting his head as a stray beam of moonlight came through clouds and leaves, he opened his eyes and wearily said: "Never mind me, Captain, never mind me." Raising him again to his feet, he was accosted by Brigadier-General Pender: "Oh, General, I hope you are not seriously wounded. I will have to retire my troops to re-form them, they are so much broken by this fire." But Jackson, rallying his strength, with firm voice said: "You must hold your ground, General Pender; you must hold your ground, sir!" and so uttered his last command on the field.

Again we resorted to the litter, and with difficulty bore it through the bush, and then under a hot fire along the road. Soon an ambulance was reached, and stopping to seek some stimulant at Chancellor's (Dowdall's Tavern), we were found by Dr. McGuire, who at once took charge of the wounded man. Passing back over the battle-field of the afternoon, we reached the Wilderness store, and then, in a field on the north, the field-hospital of our corps under Dr. Harvey Black. Here we found a tent prepared, and after midnight the left arm was amputated near the shoulder, and a ball taken from the right hand.

All night long it was mine to watch by the sufferer, and keep him warmly wrapped and undisturbed in his sleep. At 9 A.M., on the next day, when he aroused, cannon firing again filled the air, and all the Sunday through the fierce battle raged, General J. E. B. Stuart commanding the Confederates in Jackson's place. A dispatch was sent to the commanding general to announce formally his disability,—tidings General Lee had received during the night with profound grief. There came back the following note:

> "GENERAL: I have just received your note, informing me that you were wounded. I cannot express my regret at the occurrence. Could I have directed events, I should have chosen, for the good of the country, to have been disabled in your stead. I congratulate you upon the victory which is due to your skill and energy. Most truly yours, R. E. LEE, GENERAL."

When this dispatch was handed to me at the tent, and I read it aloud, General Jackson turned his face away and said, "General Lee is very kind, but he should give the praise to God."

The long day was passed with bright hopes for the wounded general, with tidings of success on the battle-field, with sad news of losses, and messages to and from other wounded officers brought to the same infirmary.

On Monday the general was carried in an ambulance, by way of Spotsylvania Court House, to most comfortable lodging at Chandlerss, near Guinea's Station, on the Richmond, Fredericksburg and Potomac railroad. And here, against our hopes, notwithstanding the skill and care of wise and watchful surgeons, attended day and night by wife and friends, amid the prayers and tears of all the Southern land, thinking not of himself, but of the cause he loved, and for the troops who had followed him so well and given him so great a name, our chief sank, day by day, with symptoms of pneumonia and some pains of pleurisy, until, at 3:15 P.M. on the quiet of the Sabbath afternoon, May 10th, 1863, he raised himself from his bed, saying, "No, no, let us pass over the river, and rest under the shade of the trees"; and, falling again to his pillow, he passed away, "over the river, where, in a land where warfare is not known or feared, he rests forever 'under the trees.'"

—SMITH, "Stonewall Jackson's Last Battle"

VIII

HOW THE SOLDIERS LIVED:
EASTERN FRONT

The Union and Confederate armies were haphazardly raised, badly organized, poorly trained, inadequately fed, clothed and housed, and almost wholly without comforts, sports, entertainments or proper medical care. Whether a regiment was well or badly trained, disciplined, and cared for depended largely on its officers and to some extent on the initiative and enterprise of the men themselves. Regiments camped where they could, foraged for fuel and often for food, and depended on their own resources, on the sutlers, and on friends and relatives, for amusement and for luxuries. The Civil War armies were youthful, high-spirited, sentimental, and for the most part moral. They endured what seem to us wholly unnecessary hardships—heavy woolen clothing in the summertime, for example, or leaky tents or maggoty food—but they managed to enjoy themselves, indulged in rough sports and horseplay, fixed up their winter quarters with "all the comforts of home," sang romantic songs, enjoyed religious services and revivals, and generally acted like civilians on a picnic—when the enemy permitted!

Most of these items tell their own story; few need explanatory introductions. Some describe various aspects of camp life—clothing, housing, marching, work and play. Others deal more specifically with the everlasting problem of food, with religion, politics, red tape, corruption, and morale. Some of them are by men who for one reason or another distinguished themselves—in soldiering, in literature, in politics—or merely by writing a memorable memoir. Others are by men whom it has not been possible to rescue from obscurity. The notes win serve as introductions to the writers rather than to the subjects—which explain themselves.

VIII.1

THEODORE WINTHROP RECALLS A TYPICAL DAY AT CAMP CAMERON

Lawyer, novelist, and professional traveler, Theodore Winthrop is probably best remembered for his two volumes of sketches: *The Canoe and the Saddle* and *Life in the Open Air;* his novels, *Cecil Dreeme* and *John Brent,* are universally unread. At the beginning of the war he enlisted in the 7th New York. He was killed in a charge at the Battle of Great Bethel, June 1861.

Boom! I would rather not believe it; but it is—yes, it is—the morning gun, uttering its surly "Hullo!" to sunrise. Yes,—and, to confirm my suspicions, here rattle in the drums and pipe in the fifes, wooing us to get up, *get up,* with music too peremptory to be harmonious.

I rise up *sur mon séant* and glance about me. I, Private W., chance, by reason of sundry chances, to be a member of a company recently largely recruited and bestowed all to gether in a big marquee. As I lift myself up, I see others lift themselves up on those straw bags we kindly call our mattresses. The tallest man of the regiment, Sergeant K., is on one side of me. On the other side I am separated from two of the fattest men of the regiment by Sergeant M., another excellent fellow, prime cook and prime forager.

We are all presently on our pins,—K. on those lengthy continuations of his, and the two stout gentlemen on their stout supporters. The deep sleepers are pulled up from those abysses of slumber where they had been choking, gurgling, strangling, death-rattling all night. There is for a moment a sound of legs rushing into pantaloons and arms plunging into jackets.

Then, as the drums and fifes whine and clatter their last notes, at the flap of our tent appears our orderly—and fierce in the morning sunshine gleams his moustache,—one month's growth this blessed day. "Fall in, for roll-call!" he cries, in a ringing voice. The orderly can speak sharp, if need be.

We obey. Not "Walk in!" "March in!" "Stand in!" is the order; but "Fall in!" as sleepy men must. Then the orderly calls off our hundred. There are several boyish voices which reply, several comic voices, a few mean voices, and some so earnest and manly and alert that one says to himself, "Those are the men for me, when work is to be done!" I read the character of my comrades every morning in each fellow's monosyllable "Here!"

When the orderly is satisfied that not one of us has run away and accepted a Colonelcy from the Confederate States since last roll call, he notifies those unfortunates who are to be on guard for the next twenty-four hours of the honor and responsibility placed upon their shoulders. Next he tells us what are to be the drills of the day. Then, "Right face! Dismissed! Break ranks! March!"

With ardor we instantly seize tin basins, soap, and towels, and invade a lovely oak-grove at the rear and left of our camp. Here is a delicious spring into which we have fitted a pump. The sylvan scene becomes peopled with "National Guards Washing,"—a scene meriting the notice of Art as much as any "Diana and her Nymphs." But we have no Poussin to paint us in the dewy sunlit grove. Few of us, indeed, know how picturesque we are at all times and seasons.

After this *beau idéal* of a morning toilet comes the anteprandial drill. Lieutenant W. arrives, and gives us a little appetizing exercise in "Carry arms!" "Support arms! "By the right flank, march!" "Double quick!"

Breakfast follows. My company messes somewhat helter skelter in a big tent. We have very tolerable rations. Some times luxuries appear of potted meats and hermetical vegetables, sent us by the fond New-Yorkers. Each little knot of fellows, too, cooks something savory. Our table-furniture is not elegant, our plates are tin, there is no silver in our forks; but à *la guerre, comme à la guerre*. Let the scrubs grow! Lucky fellows, if they suffer no worse hardships than this!

By and by, after breakfast, come company drills, bayonet practice, battalion drills, and the heavy work of the day. Our handsome Colonel, on a nice black nag, manoeuvres his thousand men of the line-companies on the parade for two or three hours. Two thousand legs step off accurately together. Two thousand pipe-clayed cross-belts—whitened with infinite pains and waste of time, and offering a most inviting mark to a foe—restrain the beating bosoms of a thousand braves, as they—the braves, not the belts—go through the most intricate evolutions unerringly. Watching these battalion movements, Private W., perhaps, goes off and inscribes in his journal—"Any clever, prompt man, with a mechanical turn, an eye for distance, a notion of time, and a voice of command, can be a tactician. It is pure pedantry to claim that the manoeuvring of troops is difficult; it is not difficult, if the troops are quick and steady. But to be a general, with patience and purpose and initiative,—ah!" thinks Private W., "for that purpose you must have the man of genius; and in this war he already begins to appear out of Massachusetts and elsewhere."

Private W. avows without fear that about noon, at Camp Cameron, he takes a hearty dinner, and with satisfaction. Private W. has had his feasts in cot and chateau in Old World and New. It is the conviction of said private that no-where and no-when has he expected his ration with more interest, and remembered it with more affection, than here.

In the middle hours of the day, it is in order to get a pass to go to Washington, or to visit some of the camps, which now, in the middle of May, begin to form a cordon around the city. . . Our capital seems arranged by nature to be protected by fortified camps on the circuit of its hills. It may be made almost a Verona, if need be. Our brother regiments have posts nearly as charming as our own, in these fair groves and on these fair slopes on either side of us.

In the afternoon comes target practice, skirmishing-drill, more company- or recruit drill, and at half past five our evening parade. Let me not forget tent-inspection, at four, by the officer of the day, when our band plays deliciously.

At evening parade all Washington appears. A regiment of ladies, rather indisposed to beauty, observe us. Sometimes the Dons arrive,—Secretaries of State, of War, of Navy,—or military Dons, bestriding prancing steeds, but bestriding them as if " 'twas *not* their habit often of an afternoon." All which,—the bad teeth, pallid skins, and rustic toilets of the fair, and the very moderate horsemanship of the brave,—privates, standing at ease in the ranks, take note of, not cynically, but as men of the world.

Wondrous gymnasts are some of the Seventh, and after evening parade they often give exhibitions of their prowess to circles of admirers. Muscle has not gone out, nor nerve, nor activity, if these athletes are to be taken as the types or even as the leaders of the young city-bred men of our time. All the feats of strength and grace of the gymnasiums are to be seen here, and show to double advantage in the open air.

Then comes sweet evening. The moon rises. It seems always full moon at Camp Cameron. Every tent becomes a little illuminated pyramid. Cooking-fires burn bright along the alleys. The boys lark, sing, shout, do all these merry things that make the entertainment of volunteer service. The gentle moon looks on, mild and amused, the fairest lady of all that visit us.

At last when the songs have been sung and the hundred rumors of the day discussed, at ten the intrusive drums and scolding fifes get together and stir up a concert, always premature, called tattoo. The Seventh Regiment begins to peel for bed; at all events, Private W. does; for said W. takes, when he can, precious good care of his cuticle, and never yields to the lazy and unwholesome habit of soldiers,—sleeping in the clothes. At taps—half past ten—out go the lights. If they do not, presently comes the sentry's peremptory command to put them out. Then, and until the dawn of another day, a cordon of snorers inside of a cordon of sentries surrounds our national capital. The outer cordon sounds its "All's well"; and the inner cordon, slumbering, echoes it.

And that is the history of any day at Camp Cameron. It is monotonous, it is not monotonous, it is laborious, it is lazy, it is a bore, it is a lark, it is half war, half peace, and totally attractive, and not to be dispensed with from one's experience in the nineteenth century.

—WINTHROP, *Life in the Open Air, and Other Papers*

VIII.2

ABNER SMALL PAINTS A PORTRAIT OF A PRIVATE IN THE ARMY OF THE POTOMAC

Abner Small, whose diary, *The Road to Richmond,* is one of the best of Civil War sources, enlisted as a private in the 16th Maine Volunteers, fought through all the campaigns until 1864, was captured at Petersburg and imprisoned in Libby prison. He was later appointed historian of his regiment.

Portrait of a private.—The ideal picture of a soldier makes a veteran smile. Be a man never so much a man, his importance and conceit dwindle when he crawls into an unteaseled shirt, trousers too short and very baggy behind, coat too long at both ends, shoes with soles like firkin covers, and a cap as shapeless as a feed bag. Let me recall how our private looked to me in the army, in the ranks, a position he chose from pure patriotism. I can see him exactly as I saw him then. He is just in front of me trying to keep his balance and his temper, as he spews from a dry mouth the infernally fine soil of Virginia and with his hands—he hasn't a handkerchief—wipes the streaks of dirty sweat that make furrows down his unshaven face. No friend of civilian days would recognize him in this most unattractive and disreputable-looking fellow, bowed under fifty-eight pounds of army essentials, and trying to suck a TD.

His suit is a model one, cut after the regulation pattern, fifty thousand at a time, and of just two sizes. If he is a small man, God pity him; and if he is a big man, God pity him still more for he is an object of ridicule. His forage cap, with its leather visor, when dry curls up, when wet hangs down, and usually covers one or both ears. His army brogans, nothing can ever make shine or even black. Perhaps the coat of muddy blue can be buttoned in front, and it might be lapped and buttoned behind. The tailor never bushels army suits, and he doesn't crease trousers, although he is always generous in reenforcing them with the regulation patch.

The knapsack (which is cut to fit, in the engraving) is an unwieldy burden with its rough, coarse contents of flannel and sole leather and sometimes twenty rounds of ammunition extra. Mixed in with these regulation essentials, like beatitudes, are photographs, cards, huswife, Testament, pens, ink, paper, and oftentimes stolen truck enough to load a mule. All this is crowned with a double wool blanket and half a shelter tent rolled in a rubber blanket. One shoulder and the hips support the "commissary department"—an odorous haversack, which often stinks with its mixture of bacon, pork, salt junk, sugar, coffee, tea, desiccated vegetables, rice, bits of yesterday's dinner, and old scraps husbanded with miserly care against a day of want sure to come.

Loaded down, in addition, with a canteen, full cartridge box, belt, cross belt, and musket, and tramping twenty miles in a hurry on a hot day, our private was a soldier, but not just then a praiser of the soldier's life. I saw him multiplied by thousands.

A photograph of any one of them, covered with yellow dust or mosaics of mud, would have served any relation, North or South, and ornamented a mantel, as a true picture of "Our Boy.". . .

Beans.—Long, weary marches were patiently endured if in the distant perspective could be seen the company bean-hole, and no well-disciplined New England regiment would be in camp thirty minutes without the requisite number. When we went into bivouac, every cook would have one dug and a fire over it before the companies broke to the rear and stacked arms. In the early morning I would hang around a particular hole, and ask Ben to just h'ist the cover and let me get a sniff for an appetizer; and how Ben would roll his orbs, till only the whites were visible, and say, "Golly, Adjutant, dem yalla-eyes don' got dere kivers off yet; you'll just natchely have to wait a while!" But many's the time we would have to "git up and git," eating our beans half-cooked, and then would come an internal disturbance—not that infernal demon, dyspepsia, of civil life, but an almighty bellyache that would double a man up and send him into line at "Surgeon's Call."

Desiccated vegetables.—Too many beans with salt junk demanded an antiscorbutic, so the government advertised proposals for some kind of vegetable compound in portable form, and it came—tons of it—in sheets like pressed hops. I suppose it was healthful, for there was variety enough in its composition to satisfy any condition of stomach and bowels. What in Heaven's name it was composed of, none of us ever discovered. It was called simply "desiccated vegetables." Ben once brought in just before dinner a piece with a big horn button on it, and wanted to know "if dat 'ere was celery or cabbage?" I doubt our men have ever forgotten how a cook would break off a piece as large as a boot top, put it in a kettle of water, and stir it with the handle of a hospital broom. When the stuff was fully dissolved, the water would remind one of a dirty brook with all the dead leaves floating around promiscuously. Still, it was a substitute for food. We ate it, and we liked it, too.

—SMALL, *The Road to Richmond*

VIII.3

LIFE WITH THE THIRTEENTH MASSACHUSETTS

The 13th Massachusetts was organized in Boston shortly after the attack on Fort Sumter and, after brief training at Fort Independence, left for New York in July 1861. The story of the march southward to the fields of battle is told in these pages of diaries put together by the regimental historian, Charles E. Davis. The regiment fought in the Valley campaign, at Antietam, Chancellorsville, Gettysburg, and Petersburg. Davis himself was wounded and imprisoned at Manassas. It is no exaggeration to say that this is on the whole the most interesting of all the many regimental histories.

1861. Thursday, Aug. 1, Hagerstown: After tents were pitched some of the men turned in and went to sleep, though the novelty of the thing was too great for most of us, who straggled back into town. During the day one of the boys brought in a Virginia paper in which it was stated that one "Southerner could lick five Northern mudsills." It was not so very comforting to feel that we were to be killed off in blocks of five. Nothing was said to us on the 16th of July, the date of our muster-in, about this wholesale slaughter. There was a kind of airy confidence as well as contemptuousness about the statement that made our enlistment look a little less like a picnic than when we marched down Broadway. It was hard to realize that we had come so far from home merely to solve a problem in mathematics, yet so it seemed to the writer of that philippic.

Some time during the night an alarm was sounded by the beating of the "long roll," and we were ordered into line to drive the terrible foe, who was thought, even then, to be in our midst. Immediately everything was excitement and confusion. We can afford to laugh now, but then it was terribly serious, and no doubt we did some silly things; but it should be borne in mind that this was very early in the war. When it was discovered, as it shortly was, that all this excitement was caused by a pig who strolled into camp and was mistaken by the officer of the guard for the rebel army, many of us were imbued with a courage we hardly felt

before. There was little sleep during the balance of the night, as the matter had to be discussed and talked about, as most things were in the rank and file of the Thirteenth, particularly when it related to the foolishness of an officer.

Although orders awaited us, on our arrival in Hagerstown, to march to Harper's Ferry, we were delayed on account of the bad condition of the roads from recent rains. This kind of consideration went out of fashion very soon after, we are sorry to say.

About sunset we struck tents and marched to Boonesboro', fourteen miles, arriving there at the witching hour of night when it is said churchyards yawn. We were led into an empty corral, lately occupied by mules, to bivouac for the night.

Ordinarily a mule-yard would not be considered a desirable place in which to spend the night, but it was midnight, and we were weary with marching, and worn out with excitement and loss of sleep. This was our fifth night from home. The first night was spent on a Sound steamer, the second on our way to Philadelphia, the third *en route* to Hagerstown, and the fourth in driving pigs out of camp, so that this old mule-yard, as far as we could see it, appeared the most delightful place in the world. At eighteen to twenty years of age little time is wasted in seeking sleep. It comes quickly and takes entire possession of your soul and body, and all we did was to drop in our tracks, making no inquiries about camp or picket guard, but let Morpheus lead us to the land of pleasant dreams. This being our first bivouac, occurrences made a deeper impression than at any time afterward. When reveille was sounded, and our eyes opened to the bright sunlight, we looked about to see where we were and who were near us. The bright red blankets of the regiment made the place look attractive. Many of the boys were still stretching themselves into activity, while others were examining their bed to account for sundry pains in the body from neglect to brush the stones aside when they laid down. How we all laughed when we saw where we were! Many and many a time while sitting round a camp fire have we recalled this night in the mule-yard.

Saturday, Aug. 3: A very hot day. Shortly after breakfast we left for Pleasant Valley, sixteen miles, where we arrived in the afternoon, and where we bivouacked for the night. A good many of the men were overcome by the heat, and didn't reach camp until after dark. The size of the knapsack was too heavy for men unused to carrying such a weight. It must be reduced, and there were no more Bibles. Just what to throw away it was difficult to decide, as many of the articles we carried were connected by association with those we held most dear. Some of the boys had dressing-cases among their luxuries. They hated to dispense with them, but it had to be done.

Among the articles provided us by the State were "havelocks," commonly used in hot countries by the English army. The havelock was named after Sir Henry Havelock, a distinguished English general. It is made of white linen, to be worn on the head as a protection from the rays of the sun. As it was made sufficiently large to cover the neck and shoulders, the effect, when properly adjusted, was to deprive the wearer of any air he might other vise enjoy. An English man would melt in his boots before he would give up a custom enjoyed by his grandfather. Not so a Yankee. The motive which prompted the State to supply them was a good one, as was also the suggestion that prompted their immediate transfer to the plebeian uses of a dish-cloth or a coffee strainer, which suggestion was universally adopted,—a dish cloth or coffee-strainer being the only things in the world, apparently, we were unprovided with.

Friday, Aug. 23: While at Sandy Hook we received the hats and uniform coats issued to us by the State, and which were forwarded by express. The coat was much too heavy, with the thermometer in the eighties. It was made with long skirts, and when fitting the wearer was not a bad-appearing garment; but as very few of them did fit, our personal appearance was not improved. They were made large in front, to meet an abnormal expansion of chest. Until we grew to them, it was a handy place to stow some of the contents of our knapsack.

The hats were neither useful nor ornamental. They were made of black felt, high-crowned, with a wide rim turned up on one side, and fastened to the crown by a brass shield representing an eagle with extended wings, apparently screaming with holy horror at so base an employment. On the front of the crown was a brass bugle containing the figure 13. Now it so happened that the person who selected the sizes was under the impression that every man from Massachusetts had a head like Daniel Webster—a mistake that caused most of us much trouble, inasmuch as newspapers were in great demand to lessen the diameter of the crown. Those of us who failed to procure newspapers made use of our ears to prevent its falling on our shoulders. As will be seen later on, they mysteriously disappeared. . . .

September 13: A man in one of the Connecticut regiments was shot today for sleeping on guard. It was not pleasant to feel that a quiet nap, on picket, might be followed by death, so we swore off sleeping while on guard.

It was at Darnestown that we were first made acquainted with an article of food called "desiccated" vegetables. For the convenience of handling, it was made in to large, round cakes about two inches thick. When cooked, it tasted like herb tea. From the flow of language which followed, we suspected it contained powerful stimulating properties. It be came universally known in the army as "desecrated" vegetables, and the aptness of this term would be appreciated by the dullest comprehension after one mouthful of the abominable compound. It is possible that the chaplain, who over heard some of the remarks, may have urged its discontinuance as a ration, inasmuch as we rarely, if ever, had it again.

[1862]. Wednesday, March 12: The rattle of drums and the sweet singing of birds announced that morn was here. The army was to move on Winchester at once, so we hastily cooked our coffee, and as quickly as possible ate our breakfast. There was no time to spare, as orders to "fall in" were heard in every direction. Orders were received for the Thirteenth to take the advance of the column as skirmishers. Winchester was four miles away occupied by 25,000 troops under Stonewall Jackson, and well-fortified by earthworks. As soon as we were out of the woods the regiment was deployed as skirmishers, and marched in that order in quick time across fields, over fences and stone walls, fording brooks or creeks, preserving distances and line as well as we could under such disadvantages.

The sensations we experienced on this bright, beautiful morning are not likely to be forgotten. It was very warm, and the march a hard one, because the line was irregularly obstructed. That is to say, while one part would be marching on the smooth surface of the ground, another part might be climbing a fence or wading a brook. To keep the line tolerably straight under such exasperating circumstances was very trying and perspiring work. In addition to this we were, for the first time, in line of battle, and in plain sight of the rest of the division, who were watching our movements as they followed in close column.

Situated as we were, there was no opportunity for obeying, without disgrace, those instincts of discretion which are said to be the better part of valor, and which prompt human nature to seek safety in flight. Those of us who omitted to sneak away before the line was formed, but who afterward showed such ingenuity and skill in escaping the dangers of battle, found no chance open for skulking on this occasion. Yes! like other regiments, we had our percentage of men who dared to run away, that they might live to fight some other, far distant day.

We saw those dreaded earthworks a long time before we reached them, and wondered at the enemy's silence, but concluded they were reserving their fire until we should be close enough for the greatest execution. Whatever the boys felt, there was no faltering or wavering. Within a short distance of the earthworks we formed in close order, and with a yell and a rush we bounded over them to find, after all our fears and anticipations, they were empty. We were soon formed in line, and marched, in columns of companies, into town, being the first Union regiment that entered Winchester. We felt proud enough at our bloodless victory.

We had hardly entered the main street of the town when General Jackson and Colonel Ashby were discovered on horseback, in front of the Taylor House, waving an adieu with their hats. An

order was immediately given to fire, but we were not quick enough to do them harm or retard their flight. This was a daring thing to do, though common enough with such men as Jackson and Ashby.

We marched down the main street, the band playing patriotic airs, while the people scanned our appearance to see what a Yankee looked like. Some who were prepared to scoff could get no farther than "How fat they are!"

After the companies were assigned to quarters the officers met at the Taylor House, and dined on the meal provided for Jackson and his staff.

Tuesday, July 22: In passing through towns and villages, and even on the high-roads, we naturally attracted a good deal of attention. We frequently noticed among the crowds so gathered, the scowling faces of women, who, upon learning we were from Massachusetts, saluted us as "Niggerlovers," and other opprobrious epithets, while it occasionally happened that by grimaces only could they express the intensity of their feelings. . . .

The remarks we heard from the bystanders as we marched along often became by-words in the regiment. We were no exception to the generality of mankind, of liking to see a pretty face, even if it did belong to a woman of "secesh" sentiments. When the boys at the head of the column discovered a pretty girl, if she was on the right side of the road, "*guide right*" would be passed along the line; and "*guide left*" if on the left side of the road. By this ingenious device we were enabled to direct our eyes where we would receive the largest return for our admiration. . .

Various were the devices adopted by the boys to relieve the monotony of weary marches. On these occasions, as conversation was allowed, stories were told, gossip repeated, discussions carried on, and criticisms made on the acts of public men, as well as on the merits of our commanders. An occasional silence would be broken by the starting of a familiar song, and very soon the whole regiment would join in the singing. Sometimes it would be a whistling chorus, when all would be whistling. Toward the end of a day, however, so tired we were all, that it was difficult to muster courage for these diversions, then our only reliance for music would be the band. When a temporary halt was granted, it was curious to see how quickly the boys would dump themselves over on their backs at the side of the road as soon as the word was given, looking like so many dead men. There was one thing we were thankful to the colonel for, and that was his freedom from nonsense on such occasions. No "right facing," no "right-dressing," no "stacking arms," to waste valuable minutes, but "get all the rest you can, boys," and when the order was given to "forward," each man took his place in line without confusion or delay. . . .

It would often occur, when we were tired and dusty from a long day's march, "Old Festive" would ride by, when suddenly you would hear sung:

"Saw my leg off,
Saw my leg off,
Saw my leg off—
Short!!!

There was another man in the regiment who contributed a large share of fun for the amusement of others, and that was the "Medicine man"—the man who honored the doctor's sight-drafts for salts, castor-oil, etc., delicacies intended for the sick, but greatly in demand by those who wished to rid themselves of unpleasant duties. He was the *basso profundo* of the glee club, and could gaze without a tremor at the misery of a man struggling with castor-oil, while at the same time encouraging him to show his gratitude at the generosity of the Government by drinking the last drop. "Down with it, my boy, the more you take the less I carry."

Saturday, Aug. 9: The last place to look for a stock company would be among a regiment of soldiers. After being deprived of camp kettles, mess pans, etc., each man was obliged to do his own cooking, as already stated, in his tin dipper, which held about a pint. Whether it was coffee, beans, pork, or anything depending on the services of a fire to make it palatable, it was accomplished by the aid of the dipper only. Therefore any utensil like a frying-pan was of incalculable service in preparing a meal. There were so few of these in the regiment, that only men of large means, men who

could raise a dollar thirty days after a paymasters visit, could afford such a luxury.

In one instance the difficulty was overcome by the formation of a joint-stock company, composed of five stockholders, each paying the sum of twenty cents toward the purchase of a frying-pan, which cost the sum of one dollar. The par value of each share was therefore twenty cents. It was understood that each stockholder should take his turn at carrying the frying-pan when on a march, which responsibility entitled him to its first use in halting for the night. While in camp, it passed from one to the other each day in order of turn. It was frequently loaned for a consideration, thereby affording means for an occasional dividend among the stockholders. The stock advanced in value until it reached as high as forty cents per share, so that a stockholder in the "Joint Stock Frying Pan Company" was looked upon as a man of consequence. Being treated with kindness and civility by his comrades, life assumed a roseate hue to the shareholders in this great company, in spite of their deprivations. It was flattering to hear one's self mentioned in terms of praise by some impecunious comrade who wished to occupy one side of it while you were cooking.

On this particular morning, when we started out, expecting shortly to be in a fight, the stock went rapidly down, until it could be bought for almost nothing. As the day progressed, however, there was a slight rise, though the market was not strong. When the order was given to leave knapsacks, it necessarily included this utensil, and so the "Joint Stock Frying Pan Company" was wiped out.

—Davis, *Three Years in the Army*

VIII.4

Minutiae of Soldier Life in the Army of Northern Virginia

To an extraordinary degree—or what to us now seems an extraordinary degree—the Civil War soldier, North and South, was on his own. He often supplied his own uniform and his own arms;

often he had to depend upon his own ingenuity, or that of his company, for food. He depended almost wholly upon himself for entertainment. He was—like American soldiers in all wars—an individualist. He regarded all regulations with distaste, avoided regimentation, tried to live his own life as much as he could.

Of all the many accounts of life in the Confederate armies, that of Carlton McCarthy is the best—the best because the most detailed. McCarthy was a private in the famous Richmond Howitzers.

The volunteer of 1861 made extensive preparations for the field. Boots, he thought, were an absolute necessity, and the heavier the soles and longer the tops the better. His pants were stuffed inside the tops of his boots, of course. A double-breasted coat, heavily wadded, with two rows of big brass buttons and a long skirt, was considered comfortable. A small stiff cap, with a narrow brim, took the place of the comfortable "felt," or the shining and towering tile worn in civil life.

Then over all was a huge overcoat, long and heavy, with a cape reaching nearly to the waist. On his back he strapped a knapsack containing a full stock of underwear, soap, towels, comb, brush, looking-glass, tooth-brush, paper and envelopes, pens, ink, pencils, blacking, photographs, smoking and chewing tobacco, pipes, twine string, and cotton strips for wounds and other emergencies, needles and thread, but tons, knife, fork, and spoon, and many other things as each man's idea of what he was to encounter varied. On the outside of the knapsack, solidly folded, were two great blankets and a rubber or oil-cloth. This knapsack, etc., weighed from fifteen to twenty-five pounds, sometimes more. All seemed to think it was impossible to have on too heavy clothes, or to have too many conveniences, and each had an idea that to be a good soldier he must be provided against every possible emergency.

In addition to the knapsack, each man had a haversack, more or less costly, some of cloth and some of fine morocco, and stored with provisions always, as though he expected any moment to receive orders to march across the Great Desert, and supply his own wants on the way. A canteen was considered indispensable, and at the outset it was thought prudent to keep it full of water. Many,

expecting terrific hand-to-hand encounters, carried revolvers, and even bowie knives. Merino shirts (and flannel) were thought to be the right thing, but experience demonstrated the contrary. Gloves were also thought to be very necessary and good things to have in winter time, the favorite style being buck gauntlets with long cuffs.

In addition to each man's private luggage, each mess, generally composed of from five to ten men, drawn together by similar tastes and associations, had its outfit, consisting of a large camp chest containing skillet, frying pan, coffee boiler, bucket for lard, coffee box, salt box, meal box, your box, knives, forks, spoons, plates, cups, etc., etc. These chests were so large that eight or ten of them filled up an army wagon, and were so heavy that two strong men had all they could do to get one of them into the wagon. In addition to the chest each mess owned an axe, water bucket, and bread tray. Then the tents of each company, and little sheet-iron stoves, and stove pipe, and the trunks and valises of the company officers, made an immense pile of stuff, so that each company had a small wagon train of its own.

All thought money to be absolutely necessary, and for a while rations were disdained and the mess supplied with the best that could be bought with the mess fund. Quite a large number had a "boy" along to do the cooking and washing. Think of it! a Confederate soldier with a body servant all his own, to bring him a drink of water, black his boots, dust his clothes, cook his corn bread and bacon, and put wood on his fire. Never was there fonder admiration than these darkies displayed for their masters. Their chief delight and glory was to praise the courage and good looks of "Mahse Tom," and prophesy great things about his future. Many a ringing laugh and shout of fun originated in the queer remarks, shining countenance, and glistening teeth of this now forever departed character.

It is amusing to think of the follies of the early part of the war, as illustrated by the outfits of the volunteers. They were so heavily clad, and so burdened with all manner of things, that a march was torture, and the wagon trains were so immense in proportion to the number of troops, that it would have been impossible to guard them in an enemy's country. Subordinate officers thought themselves entitled to transportation for trunks, mattresses, and folding bedsteads, and the privates were as ridiculous in their demands.

Thus much by way of introduction. The change came rapidly, and stayed not until the transformation was complete. Nor was this change attributable alone to the orders of the general officers. The men soon learned the inconvenience and danger of so much luggage, and, as they became more experienced, they vied with each other in reducing themselves to light-marching trim.

Experience soon demonstrated that boots were not agreeable on a long march. They were heavy and irksome, and when the heels were worn a little one-sided, the wearer would find his ankle twisted nearly out of joint by every unevenness of the road. When thoroughly wet, it was a laborious undertaking to get them off, and worse to get them on in time to answer the morning roll-call. And so, good, strong brogues or brogans, with broad bottoms and big, fat heels, succeeded the boots, and were found much more comfortable and agreeable, easier put on and off, and altogether the more sensible.

A short-waisted and single-breasted jacket usurped the place of the longtailed coat, and became universal. The enemy noticed this peculiarity, and called the Confederates gray jackets, which name was immediately transferred to those lively creatures which were the constant admirers and inseparable companions of the Boys in Gray and in Blue.

Caps were destined to hold out longer than some other uncomfortable things, but they finally yielded to the demands of comfort and common sense, and a good soft felt hat was worn instead. A man who has never been a soldier does not know, nor indeed can know, the amount of comfort there is in a good soft hat in camp, and how utterly useless is a "soldier hat" as they are generally made. Why the Prussians, with all their experience, wear their heavy, unyielding helmets, and the French their little caps, is a mystery to a Confederate who has enjoyed the comfort of an old slouch.

Overcoats an inexperienced man would think an absolute necessity for men exposed to the rigors of a northern Virginia winter, but they grew scarcer and scarcer; they were found to be a great inconvenience. The men came to the conclusion that the trouble of carrying them on hot days outweighed the comfort of having them when the cold day arrived. Besides they found that life in the open air hardened them to such an extent that changes in the temperature were not felt to any degree. Some clung to their overcoats to the last, but the majority got tired lugging them around, and either discarded them altogether, or trusted to capturing one about the time it would be needed. Nearly every overcoat in the army in the latter years was one of Uncle Sam's captured from his boys.

The knapsack vanished early in the struggle. It was inconvenient to "change" the underwear too often, and the disposition not to change grew, as the knapsack was found to gall the back and shoulders, and weary the man before half the march was accomplished. The better way was to dress out and out, and wear that outfit until the enemy's knapsacks, or the folks at home supplied a change. Certainly it did not pay to carry around clean clothes while waiting for the time to use them.

Very little washing was done, as a matter of course. Clothes once given up were parted with forever. There were good reasons for this: cold water would not cleanse them or destroy the vermin, and hot water was not always to be had. One blanket to each man was found to be as much as could be carried, and amply sufficient for the severest weather. This was carried generally by rolling it lengthwise, with the rubber cloth outside, tying the ends of the roll together, and throwing the loop thus made over the left shoulder with the ends fastened together hanging under the right arm.

The haversack held its own to the last, and was found practical and useful. It very seldom, however, contained rations, but was used to carry all the articles generally carried in the knapsack; of course the stock was small. Somehow or other, many men managed to do without the haversack, and carried absolutely nothing but what they wore and had in their pockets.

The infantry threw-away their heavy cap boxes and cartridge boxes, and carried their caps and cartridges in their pockets. Canteens were very useful at times, but they were as a general thing discarded. They were not much used to carry water, but were found useful when the men were driven to the necessity of foraging, for conveying buttermilk, cider, sorghum, etc., to camp. A good strong tin cup was found better than a canteen, as it was easier to fill at a well or spring, and was serviceable as a boiler for making coffee when the column halted for the night.

Revolvers were found to be about as useless and heavy lumber as a private soldier could carry, and early in the war were sent home to be used by the women and children in protecting themselves from insult and violence at the hands of the ruffians who prowled about the country shirking duty.

Strong cotton was adopted in place of flannel and merino, for two reasons: first, because easier to wash; and second, because the vermin did not propagate so rapidly in cotton as in wool. Common white cotton shirts and drawers proved the best that could be used by the private soldier.

Gloves to any but a mounted man were found useless, worse than useless. With the gloves on, it was impossible to handle an axe, buckle harness, load a musket, or handle a rammer at the piece. Wearing them was found to be simply a habit, and so, on the principle that the less luggage the less labor, *they* were discarded.

The camp-chest soon vanished. The brigadiers and major generals, even, found them too troublesome, and soon they were left entirely to the quartermasters and commissaries. One skillet and a couple of frying pans, a bag for flour or meal, another bag for salt, sugar, and coffee, divided by a knot tied between served the purpose as well. The skillet passed from mess to mess. Each mess generally owned a frying pan, but often one served a company. The oil-cloth was found to be as good as the wooden tray for making up the dough. The water bucket held its own to the last!

Tents were *rarely seen*. All the poetry about the *"tented field"* died. Two men slept together, each having a blanket and an oil-cloth; one oil-cloth went next to the ground. The two laid on this, covered themselves with two blankets, protected from the rain with the second oil-cloth on top, and slept very comfortably through rain, snow or hail, as it might be.

Very little money was seen in camp. The men did not expect, did not care for, or often get any pay, and they were not willing to deprive the old folks at home of their little supply, so they learned to do without any money.

When rations got short and were getting shorter, it be came necessary to dismiss the darkey servants. Some, how ever, became company servants, instead of private institutions, and held out faithfully to the end, cooking the rations away in the rear, and at the risk of life carrying them to the line of battle to their "young mahsters."

Reduced to the minimum, the private soldier consisted of one man, one hat, one jacket, one shirt, one pair of pants, one pair of drawers, one pair of shoes, and one pair of socks. His baggage was one blanket, one rubber blanket, and one haversack. The haversack generally contained smoking tobacco and a pipe, and a small piece of soap, with temporary additions of apples, persimmons, blackberries, and such other commodities as he could pick up on the march.

The company property consisted of two or three skillets and frying pans, which were sometimes carried in the wag on, but oftener in the hands of the soldiers. The infantry men generally preferred to stick the handle of the frying pan in the barrel of a musket, and so carry it.

The wagon trains were devoted entirely to the transportation of ammunition and commissary and quartermaster's stores, which had not been issued. Rations which had become company property, and the baggage of the men, when they had any, was carried by the men themselves. If, as was sometimes the case, three days' rations were issued at one time and the troops ordered to cook them, and be prepared to march, they did cook them, *and eat them if* possible, *so* as to avoid the labor of carrying them. It was not such an undertaking either, to eat three days' rations in one, as frequently none had been issued for more than a day, and when issued were cut down one half.

The infantry found out that bayonets were not of much use, and did not hesitate to throw them, with the scabbard, away.

The artillerymen, who started out with heavy sabres hanging to their belts, stuck them up in the mud as they marched, and left them for the ordnance officers to pick up and turn over to the cavalry.

The cavalrymen found sabres very tiresome when swung to the belt, and adopted the plan of fastening them to the saddle on the left side, with the hilt in front and in reach of the hand. Finally sabres got very scarce even among the cavalrymen, who relied more and more on their short rifles.

No soldiers ever marched with less to encumber them, and none marched faster or held out longer.

The courage and devotion of the men rose equal to every hardship and privation, and the very intensity of their sufferings became a source of merriment. Instead of growling and deserting, they laughed at their own bare feet, ragged clothes and pinched faces; and weak, hungry, cold, wet, worried with vermin and itch, dirty, with no hope of reward or rest, marched cheerfully to meet the well-fed and warmly clad hosts of the enemy.

—McCarthy, *Detailed Minutiae of Soldier Life*
in the Army of Northern Virginia

VIII.5

Inventions and Gadgets
Used by the Soldiers

Civil War soldiers, like their successors in the First and Second World Wars, were endlessly resourceful. They had to be. Their resourcefulness appeared not only in such contrivances as those here described, but in the creation of new weapons and new techniques of warfare.

John D. Billings, whose *Hardtack and Coffee* is one of the most entertaining of all Civil War books, was a member of the 10th Massachusetts battery of light artillery.

One of the first products of their genius which I recall was a combination *knife-fork-and-spoon* arrangement, which was peddled through the state camping-grounds in great numbers and variety. Of course every man must have one. So much convenience in so small a compass must be taken advantage of. It was a sort of soldier's trinity, which they all thought that they understood and appreciated. But I doubt whether this invention, on the average, ever got beyond the first camp in active service.

I still have in my possession the remnants of a *water-filterer* in which I invested after enlistment. There was a metallic mouth-piece at one end of a small gutta-percha tube, which latter was about fifteen inches long. At the other end of the tube was a suction-chamber, an inch long by a half-inch in diameter, with the end perforated, and containing a piece of bocking as a filter. Midway of the tubing was an air-chamber. The tubing long since dried and crumbled away from the metal. It is possible that I used this instrument half a dozen times, though I do not recall a single instance, and on breaking camp just before the Gettysburg Campaign, I sent it, with some other effects, northward.

I remember another filterer, somewhat simpler. It consisted of the same kind of mouth-piece, with rubber tubing attached to a small conical piece of pumice stone, through which the water was filtered. Neither of these was ever of any practical value.

There was another invention that must have been sufficiently popular to have paid the manufacturer a fair rate on his investment, and that was the steel-armor enterprise. There were a good many men who were anxious to be heroes, but they were particular. They preferred to be *live* heroes. They were willing to go to war and Sight as never man fought before, if they could only be insured against bodily harm. They were not willing to assume all the risks which an enlistment involved, without securing something in the shape of a drawback.

Well, the iron tailors saw and appreciated the situation and sufferings of this class of men, and came to the rescue with a vest of steel armor, worth, as I remember it, about a dozen dollars, and greaves. The latter, I think, did not find so ready a market as the vests, which were comparatively common. These ironclad warriors admitted that when panoplied for the fight their sensations were much as they might be if they were dressed up in an old-fashioned air-tight stove; still, with all the discomforts of this casing, they felt a little safer with it on than off in battle, and they reasoned that it was the right and duty of every man to adopt all honorable measures to assure his safety in the line of duty.

This seemed solid reasoning, surely; but, in spite of it all, a large number of these vests never saw Rebeldom. Their owners were subjected to such a storm of ridicule that they could not bear up under it. It was a stale yet common joke to remind them that in action these vests must be worn be hind. Then, too, the ownership of one of them was taken as evidence of faint-heartedness. Of this the owner was often reminded; so that when it came to the packing of the knapsack for departure, the vest, taking as it did considerable space, and adding no small weight to his already too heavy burden, was in many cases left behind. The officers, whose opportunity to take baggage along was greater, clung to them longest; but I think that they were quite generally abandoned with the first important reduction made in the luggage. . . .

Then there were fancy patent-leather haver-sacks, with two or three compartments for the assortment of rations, which Uncle Sam was expected to furnish. But those who invested in them were somewhat disgusted at a little later stage of their service, when they were ordered to throw away all such "high-toned" trappings and adopt the regulation pattern of painted cloth. This was a bag about a foot square, with a broad strap for the shoulder, into which soldiers soon learned to bundle all their food and table furniture, which . . . after a day's hard march were always found in such a delightful hodge-podge. . . .

The Turkish fez, with pendent tassel, was seen on the heads of some soldiers. Zouave regiments wore them. They did very well to lie around camp in, and in a degree marked their owner as a some-what conspicuous man among his fellows, but they were not tolerated on line; few of them ever sur-vived the first three months' campaigning.

And this recalls the large number of the sol-diers of '62 who did not wear the forage cap fur-nished by the government. They bought the "McClellan cap," so called, at the hatters' instead, which in most cases faded out in a month. This the government caps did not do, with all their awkward appearance. They may have been coarse and unfashionable to the eye, but the colors would stand. Nearly every man embellished his cap with the number or letter of his company and regiment and the appropriate emblem. For infantry this emblem is a bugle, for artillery two crossed can-nons, and for cavalry two crossed sabres.

—BILLINGS, *Hardtack and Coffee*

VIII.6

HARDTACK AND COFFEE

Here is the invaluable John Billings again, giving us what appears to be a wholly faithful account of eating—and not eat-ing—in the Army of the Potomac.

I will now give a complete list of the rations served out to the rank and file, as I remember them. They were salt pork, fresh beef, salt beef, rarely ham or bacon, hard bread, soft bread, potatoes, an occa-sional onion, flour, beans, split pease, rice, dried apples, dried peaches, desiccated vegetables, coffee, tea, sugar, molasses, vinegar, candles, soap, pepper, and salt.

It is scarcely necessary to state that these were not all served out at one time. There was but one kind of meat served at once, and this . . . was usually pork. When it was hard bread, it wasn't *soft* bread or flour, and when it was pease or beans it wasn't rice.

Here is just what a single ration comprised, that is, what a soldier was entitled to have in one day. He should have had twelve ounces of pork or bacon, *or* one pound four ounces of salt or fresh beef; one pound six ounces of soft bread or flour, *or* one pound of hard bread, *or* one pound four ounces of corn meal. With every hundred such rations there should have been distributed one peck of beans or pease; ten pounds of rice or hominy; ten pounds of green coffee, *or* eight pounds of roasted and ground, *or* one pound eight ounces of tea; fifteen pounds of sugar; one pound four ounces of candles; four pounds of soap; two quarts of salt; four quarts of vinegar; four ounces of pepper; a half bushel of potatoes when practicable, and one quart of molasses. Desiccated potatoes or desiccated compressed vegetables might be substituted for the beans, pease, rice, hominy, or fresh potatoes. Vegetables, the dried fruits, pickles, and pickled cabbage were occasionally issued to prevent scurvy, but in small quantities.

But the ration thus indicated was a camp ration. Here is the *marching* ration: one pound of hard bread; three-fourths of a pound of salt pork, or one and one-fourth pounds of fresh meat; sugar, coffee, and salt. The beans, rice, soap, candles, etc., were not issued to the soldier when on the march, as he could not carry them; but, singularly enough, as it seems to me, unless the troops went into camp before the end of the month, where a regular depot of supplies might be established from which the other parts of the rations could be issued, they were *forfeited,* and *reverted to the government*—an injustice to the rank and file, who, through no fault of their own, were thus cut off from a part of their allowance at the time when they were giving most liberally of their strength and perhaps of their very heart's blood . . .

I will speak of the rations more in detail, beginning with the hard bread, or, to use the name by which it was known in the Army of the Potomac, *Hardtack.* What was hardtack? It was a plain flour-and-water biscuit. Two which I have in my possession as mementos measure three and one-eighth by two and seven-eighths inches, and are nearly half an inch thick. Although these biscuits were furnished to organizations by weight, they were dealt

out to the men by number, nine constituting a ration in some regiments, and ten in others; but there were usually enough for those who wanted more, as some men would not draw them. While hardtack was nutritious, yet a hungry man could eat his ten in a short time and still be hungry. . . .

For some weeks before the battle of Wilson's Creek, Mo., where the lamented Lyon fell, the First Iowa Regiment had been supplied with a very poor quality of hard bread (they were not then [1861] called hard*tack*). During this period of hardship to the regiment, so the story goes, one of its members was inspired to produce the following touching lamentation:—

Let us close our game of poker,
Take our tin cups in our hand,
While we gather round the cook's tent door,
Where dry mummies of hard crackers
Are given to each man;
O hard crackers, come again no morel

Chorus:
'Tis the song and sigh of the hungry,
"Hard crackers, hard crackers, come again no morel
Many days have you lingered upon our stomachs sore,
O hard crackers, come again no morel"

There's a hungry, thirsty soldier
Who wears his life away,
With torn clothes, whose better days are o'er;
He is sighing now for whiskey,
And, with throat as dry as hay,
Sings, "Hard crackers, come again no morel"
                                        Chorus.

'Tis the song that is uttered
In camp by night and day,
'Tis the wail that is mingled with each snore,
'Tis the sighing of the soul
For spring chickens far away,
"O hard crackers, come again no morel"
                                        Chorus.

When General Lyon heard the men singing these stanzas in their tents, he is said to have been moved by them to the extent of ordering the cook to serve up corn-meal mush, for a change, when the song received the following alteration:—

But to groans and to murmurs
There has come a sudden hush,
Our frail forms are fainting at the door;
We are starving now on horse-feed
That the cooks call mush
O hard crackers, come again once morel

Chorus:
It is the dying wail of the starving,
Hard crackers, hard crackers, come again once more;
You were old and very wormy, but we pass your
    failing o'er.
O hard crackers, come again once morel

The name hardtack seems not to have been in general use among the men in the Western armies.

But I now pass to consider the other bread ration—the *loaf* or *soft bread*. Early in the war the ration of flour was served out to the men uncooked; but as the eighteen ounces allowed by the government more than met the needs of the troops, who at that time obtained much of their living from outside sources . . . it was allowed, as they innocently supposed, to be sold for the benefit of the Company Fund, al ready referred to. Some organizations drew, on the requisition, ovens, semi-cylindrical in form, which were properly set in stone, and in these regimental cooks or bakers baked bread for the regiment. But all of this was in the tentative period of the war. As rapidly as the needs of the troops pressed home to the government, they were met with such despatch and efficiency as circumstances would permit. For a time, in 1861, the vaults under the broad terrace on the western front of the Capitol were converted into bakeries, where sixteen thousand loaves of bread were baked daily. The chimneys from the ovens pierced the terrace where now the freestone pavement joins the grassy slope, and for months smoke poured out of these in dense black volumes. The greater part of the loaves supplied to the Army of the Potomac up to the summer of 1864 were baked in Washington,

Alexandria, and at Fort Monroe, Virginia. The ovens of the latter place had a capacity of thirty thousand loaves a day. But even with all these sources worked to their uttermost, brigade commissaries were obliged to set up ovens near their respective depots, to eke out enough bread to fill orders. These were erected on the sheltered side of a hill or woods, then enclosed in a stockade, and the whole covered with old canvas. . . .

I began my description of the rations with the bread as being the most important one to the soldier. Some old veterans may be disposed to question the judgment which gives it this rank, and claim that *coffee*, of which I shall speak next, should take first place in importance. . . .

It would have interested a civilian to observe the manner in which this ration was served out when the army was in active service. It was usually brought to camp in an oat sack, a regimental quartermaster receiving and apportioning his among the ten companies, and the quartermaster-sergeant of a battery apportioning his to the four or six detachments. Then the orderly-sergeant of a company or the sergeant of a detachment must devote himself to dividing it. One method of accomplishing this purpose was to spread a rubber blanket on the ground—more than one if the company was large,—and upon it were put as many piles of the coffee as there were men to receive rations; and the care taken to make the piles of the same size to the eye, and to keep the men from growling, would remind one of a country physician making his powders, taking a little from one pile and adding to another. The sugar which always accompanied the coffee was spooned out at the same time on another blanket. When both were ready, they were given out, each man taking a pile, or, in some companies, to prevent any charge of unfairness or in justice, the sergeant would turn his back on the rations, and take out his roll of the company. Then, by request, some one else would point to a pile and ask, "Who shall have this?" and the sergeant, without turning, would call a name from his list of the company or detachment, and the person thus called would appropriate the pile specified. This process would be continued until the last pile was disposed of. There were other plans for distributing the rations; but I have described this one because of its being quite common.

The manner in which each man disposed of his coffee and sugar ration after receiving it is worth noting. Every soldier of a month's experience in campaigning was provided with some sort of bag into which he spooned his coffee; but the *kind of* bag he used indicated pretty accurately, in a general way, the length of time he had been in the service. For example, a raw recruit just arrived would take it up in a paper, and stow it away in that well known receptacle for all eatables, the soldier's haversack, only to find it a part of a general mixture of hard-tack, salt pork, pepper, salt, knife, fork, spoon, sugar, and coffee by the time the next halt was made. A recruit of longer standing, who had been through this experience and had begun to feel his wisdom-teeth coming, would take his up in a bag made of a scrap of rubber blanket or a *poncho;* but after a few days carrying the rubber would peel off or the paint of the *poncho* would rub off from contact with the greasy pork or boiled meat ration which was its travelling companion, and make a black, dirty mess, besides leaving the coffee-bag unfit for further use. Now and then some young soldier, a little starchier than his fellows, would bring out an oil-skin bag lined with cloth, which his mother had made and sent him; but even oil-silk couldn't stand everything, certainly not the peculiar inside furnishings of the average soldier's haversack, so it too was not long in yielding. But your plain, straightforward old veteran, who had shed all his poetry and romance, if he had ever possessed any, who had roughed it up and down "Old Virginny," man and boy, for many months, and who had tried all plans under all circumstances, took out an oblong plain cloth bag, which looked as immaculate as the every-day shirt of a coal-heaver, and into it scooped without ceremony both his sugar and coffee, and stirred them thoroughly together. . . .

The coffee ration was most heartily appreciated by the soldier. When tired and foot-sore, he would drop out of the marching column, build his little camp-fire, cook his mess of coffee, take a nap behind the nearest shelter, and when he woke, hurry on to overtake his company. Such men were sometimes called stragglers; but it could, obviously, have no offensive meaning when applied to them. Tea was served so rarely that it does not merit any particular description. In the latter part of the war, it was rarely seen outside of hospitals.

One of the most interesting scenes presented in army life took place at night when the army was on the point of bivouacking. As soon as this fact became known along the column, each man would seize a rail from the nearest fence, and with this additional arm on the shoulder would enter the proposed camping-ground. In no more time than it takes to tell the story, the little camp-fires, rapidly increasing to hundreds in number, would shoot up along the hills and plains, and as if by magic acres of territory would be luminous with them. Soon they would be surrounded by the soldiers, who made it an almost invariable rule to cook their coffee first, after which a large number, tired out with the toils of the day, would make their supper of hardtack and coffee, and roll up in their blankets for the night. If a march was ordered at midnight, unless a surprise was intended, it must be preceded by a pot of coffee; if a halt was ordered in mid-forenoon or afternoon, the same dish was inevitable, with hardtack accompaniment usually. It was coffee *at* meals and *between* meals; and men going on guard or coming off guard drank it at all hours of the night, and to-day the old soldiers who can stand it are the hardest coffee-drinkers in the community, through the schooling which they received in the service.

—Billings, *Hardtack and Coffee*

VIII.7

"Starvation, Rags, Dirt, and Vermin"

At school in Pennsylvania when the war broke out, Randolph Shotwell left at once for his native Virginia, determined to join the first Confederate outfit that he found. He served through the whole of the war, until 1864, when he was captured; we shall read later his bitter description of conditions in Federal prisons. After the war he went into journalism in North Carolina, and was active, for a time, in the Ku Klux Klan and in politics. The conditions which he describes so vividly were not characteristic of the whole of the Confederate Army, but were doubtless to be found quite commonly toward the end of the war when the whole economic machinery of the South seemed to be breaking down.

Our Quarter Master's department. . . really did a great deal more to break down the army than to keep it up. I mean that their shortcomings, their negligence, improvidence, and lack of energy counterbalanced their services. It is a well-known fact, and a most disgraceful one, that when General Lee crossed the Potomac fully *ten thousand* of his men were *barefooted, blanketless,* and *hatless!* The roads were lined with stragglers limping on swollen and blistered feet, shivering all night, (for despite the heat of the day the nights were chilly), for want of blankets; and utterly devoid of underclothes—if indeed they possessed so much as one shirt!

And the lack of proper equipment gradually made itself felt on the *morale* of the men. In the earlier stages of the war when our men were well dressed and cleanly every company having its wagon for extra baggage enabling the private soldier to have a change of clothing and necessary toilet articles—the men retained much of their individuality as citizen-soldiers, volunteering to undergo for a time, the privations and perils of army life, but never forgetting that they were *citizens* and *gentlemen,* with a good name and reputation for gentlemanliness to maintain. Hence, when in battle array, these gallant fellows, *each had a pride in bearing himself bravely;* and when the hour of conflict arrived they rushed upon the foe with an impetuosity and fearlessness that amazed the old army officers; and caused foreign military men to declare them the best fighters in the world. After a while the spirit of the men became broken. Constant marching and fighting were sufficient of themselves to gradually wear out the army; but it was more undermined by the continu-

al neglect and ill-provision to which the men were subjected.

Months on months they were without a change of underclothing, or a chance to wash that they had worn so long, hence it became actually coated with grease and dust, moistened with daily perspiration under the broiling sun.

Pestiferous vermin swarmed in every camp, and on the march—an indescribable annoyance to every well-raised man yet seemingly uneradicable. Nothing would destroy the little pests but *hours of steady boiling,* and of course, we had neither kettles, nor the time to boil them, if we had been provided with ample means.

As to purchasing clothes, the private soldiers did not have an opportunity of so doing once in six months, as their miserable pittance of $12 per month was generally withheld that length of time, or longer—(I only drew pay *three* times in *four years,* and after the first year, I could not have bought a *couple of shirts* with a *whole month's pay.*) Naturally fastidious in tastes, and habituated to the strictest personal cleanliness and neatness, I chafed from morning till night at the insuperable obstacles to decency by which I was surrounded, and as a consequence there was not one time in the whole four years of the war that I could not have blushed with mortification at meeting with any of my old friends.

It is impossible for such a state of things to continue for years without breaking down one's self-respect, wounding his *amour propre,* stirring his deepest discontent, and very materially impairing his efficiency as a soldier.

Starvation, rags, dirt, and vermin may be borne *for a time* by the neatest of gentlemen; but when he has become habituated to them, he is no longer a gentleman. The personal pride which made many a man act the *hero* during the first year of the war was gradually worn out, and undermined by the open, palpable neglect, stupidity, and indifference of the authorities until during the last year of the war, the hero became a "shirker," and finally a "deserter."

—SHOTWELL, "Three Years in Battle"

VIII.8

VOTING IN THE FIELD

The problem of the soldier vote agitated the Civil War as it did World War II. The Republican party was particularly eager to provide opportunity for soldiers to go home to vote or machinery for voting in the field. Both methods were widely used in the state elections of 1863 and the Presidential election of 1864. The Wisconsin soldier vote—which James Leonard describes—was decisive in the election of a chief justice. That the soldier vote was decisive in the 1864 election, too, is generally conceded. Thousands of soldiers were furloughed home at voting time. Lincoln wrote to Sherman, for example, that it might be well to let Indiana's soldiers "or any part of them go home and vote at the state elections," and so enthusiastically did Sherman act on the suggestion that the 19th Vermont Volunteers found themselves voting in the Indiana elections—which the Republicans carried. Some states—New York, for example, and Ohio—arranged for voting in the field, and the overwhelming majority of these votes went to Lincoln. The most careful student of the subject concludes that "without the soldiers' vote in six crucial states, Lincoln would have lost the election."

A. Electioneering in the Camps

Camp near White Oak Church, May 14, 1863 Let me state a simple instance as regards myself and the late election that took place in Co. A for Chief Justice of Wisconsin The morning of election day the Captain and Lieutenants asked me and the Orderly our opinion in regard to holding an election, The Captain was rather against it, fearing that very few of the boys would vote as was the case last fall, I almost sided with him but I and the Orderly both advised to open a poll, and take what votes could be got, He finally consented to commence on the condition that I would act as runner and speak to, or rather electioneer the boys in the company, I declined at first, advising the selection of some one who as I thought had more influence than myself. Finally however I consented just to satisfy the Captain and Lieutenant but satisfied in my own mind that I could accomplish but little I went to work and first brought up all those whom I knew to be sure and then I set at those who were a little wavering or careless and by some talking got them up, then I went at those who are true Union men but still cling

to party, all that was needed with them, was to satisfy them that Mr. Cothren was a Copperhead and we had the papers to do that The result was that 53 votes were polled every man in the company voting who was old enough, save one before the polls were opened I would not have believed that 30 votes could be obtained unless he set some one to work who had more influence than me, I wish though that I could have more influence in the temperance cause here Whiskey rations are occasionally dealt out now and I am the only one in our Co who does not use his ration, it is rather embarrassing to be thus the odd member of a family with the rest joking you on the matter, but I have withstood these temptations thus far and I hope by the sustaining grace of God to hold out firm to the end.

—JAMES A. LEONARD, "Letters of a
Fifth Wis. Volunteer"

B. President Lincoln Needs the Soldier Vote

To GENERAL W. T. SHERMAN

Executive Mansion, Washington,
September 19, 1864

Major-General Sherman:

The State election of Indiana occurs on the 11th of October, and the loss of it, to the friends of the Government would go far toward losing the whole Union cause. The bad effect upon the November election, and especially the giving the State government to those who will oppose the war in every possible way, are too much to risk if it can be avoided. The draft proceeds, notwithstanding its strong tendency to lose us the State. Indiana is the only important State voting in October whose soldiers cannot vote in the field. Anything you can safely do to let her soldiers, or any part of them, go home and vote at the State election will be greatly in point. They need not remain for the Presidential election, but may return to you at once. This is in no sense an order, but is merely intended to impress you with the importance to the Army itself of your doing all you safely can, yourself being the judge of what you can safely do.

Yours truly,
A. Lincoln.

—*The Complete Works of Abraham Lincoln*

VIII.9

Red Tape, North and South

It is the complaint of soldiers and civilians alike that every war is cursed by red tape. The Civil War was no exception; indeed, in some respects, it was the worst administered of all American wars.

Samuel Fiske—or Dunn Browne as he was known—was a Massachusetts clergyman who enlisted in the 14th Connecticut Volunteers, became a captain, fought at Chancellorsville and Gettysburg, spent two weeks in Libby prison, was exchanged, and killed in the Wilderness. During the war he contributed a series of letters to the Springfield Republican; these were published posthumously as *Dunn Browne's Experiences in the Army*. It is interesting to note that Randolph Shotwell's complaints about red-tapism in the Confederacy parallel those of Samuel Fiske.

A. Dunn Browne Has Trouble with the War Department

Judge of this other case I will relate: about a fair specimen of my experience. An errand at the adjutant-general's office. Went up at ten o'clock. Found a fat doorkeeper. Asked him if I could see any of the assistant adjutant generals or their clerks. No: couldn't see anybody on business till eleven o'clock. Departed. Came back at eleven. found a long string of people passing in slowly to one of the rooms. Took my turn. Got a word at last with the clerk. Found it wasn't his specialty to answer questions of the sort I asked him. Was referred by him to another clerk who perhaps could. Went to another room. Stopped by a doorkeeper. At last, permitted to enter, after some other people had come out. Stated my case to the clerk at the desk: "Pay of certain officers of my regiment stopped by order from your office near four months since. No reason assigned. No notice given. Come to you for reason."

"Why don't you send up your request through the proper military channels, sir?"

"Request was so sent up eight weeks ago, enclosing a precise copy of the order issued from your own office to the paymaster. Instead of looking in your own office to find the reason of your own order, you sent our request over to the paymaster-general, asking him why the order was issued. He sent it back indorsed with the statement, that no such order of stoppage was recorded in the pay-department. This you sent back to us 'through the regular channel' as eminently satisfactory. So it would be, only the paymaster, having your positive order not to pay us, and no order countermanding it, refuses to come down with the greenbacks. Another paper came up to you from us several weeks ago, and has not been heard from. This is the progress of eight weeks through the regular channel."

"Why don't you ask the paymaster to find out about the matter?"

"We have done so. He says he has been repeatedly to your office, which, of course, is the only place where information can be obtained, and is unable to get any satisfactory reply."

"Why don't you go to the ordnance and quartermasters departments, and see if your accounts are all right there?"

"We have done so, and find it a reasonable certainty that no stoppages against us have been ordered there. Moreover, they would not stop through your department. The order came from you. You had a precise copy of it sent you with our application. Where could we apply for information as to the reason of your acts save to you?"

"Very well: we'll try to look it up."

"But, sir, if you would let a clerk look at your orders of that date, and answer us to-day, we can perhaps get our pay; otherwise we shall not have access to the paymaster again for two or three months."

The clerk, utterly disgusted at such pertinacity, dismisses us with an appointment to call again at two o'clock. He will see what he can do for us. Call again at two o'clock. Doorkeeper refuses to let us in. No person seen on business after two o'clock. Finally work our way through with the plea of the special appointment. Find, of course, that nothing has been done. "What shall be our next course?"

"Oh! send up another paper through the regular channel."

—[Samuel Fiske], *Mr. Dunn Browne's Experiences in the Army*

B. A Confederate Lieutenant Complains that Red-Tapeism Will Lose the War

Red Tapeism at Richmond threatens to work our everlasting ruin. Some of our junior officers say that anyone under the rank of Brigadier-General can rarely gain so much as access to the Departments, and even the Brigadiers got but little attention if they happen to be out of favor with the "parlour Cabinet" at the Executive Mansion. The President now has *six* aides, ranking as colonels, and decked in all the bravery of gold lace, and feathers, to someone of whom the "commoner," or "common soldier" must make the *"grande salaam,"* and have his plea for audience first *"vised"* by the popinjay before he may approach the "magic circle" within which is his Supreme Excellency—"clothed with the divinity which doth hedge" a *"servant of the people."*

All members of this noble Court are beginning to "feel their dignity" in the same manner. Secretary of the Treasury Memminger, (said to be a born *Hessian)* whose chief duties consist in writing his autograph upon unlimited quantities of half-worthless "bank-notes" "so-called," has adopted a set of rules governing all applicants for permission to inter view his Royalty. A favorite clerk named Jacques—is posted in the ante-chamber to scrutinize all callers, and *vise* the talismanic bit of cardboard which shall be your "Open Sesame," to audience with his secretaryship. *Some* gentlemen are not willing to be catechized by Jacques as to their business, wishes, etc., consequently retire enraged at the Royal customs of our not too firmly established *Republic.*

Oh! that Mr. Davis could see and realize, the fallacy of undermining our cause by wearying the people with red tape regulations, and nice points of etiquette, instead of showing common fraternity and sympathy with one and all, the poorest and most tiresome citizen as well as the epauletted Major General.

General Winder rules Richmond like a military Camp; nay, not like a well-disciplined camp, for his rule gives annoyance merely to honest men and faithful soldiers, while permitting the city to be over-run by rogues, spies, speculators, foreigners, blockade runners, and fellows of that ilk. His police force is mainly composed of ex-"Plugs" and "Roughs" from Baltimore and Washington, who care little for the cause, and less for honesty, so that it is a matter of common notoriety that any one who has a hundred or two hundred in greenbacks, or a less sum in specie, can not only travel over the whole South—spying out the weakness of the land—but pass through the "underground road" to the North whenever so minded.

Whereas veteran soldiers—armed with furlough, or special order from their general—must lose a day or two—at their own expense—kicking their heels at the doors of the Pass Port Bureau, awaiting the convenience of some dandified clerk within. Is it any wonder that the veteran grows *soured,* and in telling his family, or his comrades in camp how he had been treated sows the seeds for discontent, and ultimate desertion?

How sad to see the enthusiasm and energies of a great people gradually relaxing under the ill-shaped, negligent, insensate policy of the appointed agents for the administration of the government!

I verily believe if we shall ultimately fail in our efforts to secure independence (which God forbid!) the causes of such failure will be found in the fact that all our great military and civil leaders have become infatuated with the idea that success is assured, and that they can conduct the war as if we were an old established nation, or as France and England would conduct it. They do not seem at all aware that if once the spirit and faith of *the people is* broken all will be lost.

Instances of mismanagement by the Red Tapeists are coming to light by every mail. The great "Flour Contract" of Secretary Randolph, giving Crenshaw, Haxall, and Company, an exclusive monopoly of the flour furnishing business is causing much comment. Aside from the reports of undue influences in the execution of the original contract, it is evident that the monopoly thus created is working injury to the people. Flour is now $40, a barrel in Richmond, and cornmeal $3.50 a bushel, and no doubt these prices will be considered *cheap* before spring.

"Crenshaw Mills," by the terms of the contract are allowed the preference in the use of the railways in the shipment of grain, so that while the depots are full of goods and flour only $8.00 per barrel in the upper valley, the people of Richmond must pay four times that amount or starve!

The Government seems to have less discretion and good judgment than would be found in "an old field school" debating society. Thus, for instance, when we lay at Manassas and Centreville last year, and could easily have drawn supplies from the rich regions of Loudon, Farquier, Warren, and from the valley, via the Manassas and Strasburg Railroad—all our rations and stock-provender was hauled all the way from Richmond—to which it must first have been hauled—merely because Red-Tapeism had its "system" and wanted a "regular issue," and to have things done "through proper channels," and as the result the fine resources of the region referred to, were left untouched to be gathered by the marauders of Pope, Fremont, Banks and Sigel, while that portion of Virginia which should have been reserved to feed the besieged city nine months later, was drained of its provisions to ship to an army surrounded by adjacent supplies!. . .

I haven't a doubt of Mr. Davis' patriotism, or his intention to do *right*, but he is dreadfully mistaken in his selection of Cabinet officers, and in his whole civil policy of administration. . . . I am more and more convinced that our chief chance of success lies in a short, sharp, aggressive warfare.

—SHOTWELL, "Three Years in Battle"

VIII.10

THE CONFEDERATES GET RELIGION

The generation that fought the war, North and South alike, was a deeply religious one. Chaplains were customarily attached to regiments of both armies, and numerous preachers visited the troops with or without official status. One of the most interesting features of the history of the Confederacy was the series of revivals that swept the armies, both East and West, throughout the war. There were a few revivals in the winter of 1861-62, but the "great revival" came in the Army of Northern Virginia in the winter and spring of 1863 and spread to the armies of the West. The Reverend John W. Jones, whose Christ in the Camp is perhaps the best history of this great

revival, estimates that no less than 150,000 soldiers "got religion" that year. What is equally interesting is that the religious revival affected the leaders of the Confederacy as well as the rank and file. It was at this time that Jefferson Davis, Generals Bragg, Ewell, Hood, Hardee, and Joseph E. Johnston all entered the church. It is entirely possible that General Lee's deep piety played a role here.

The two brief excerpts given here describe the great revival of 1863 in the Army of Northern Virginia. Benjamin W. Jones was a private in the 3rd Virginia Infantry Regiment; John Dooley a Virginia boy who left Georgetown College in 1862 to enlist in the famous 1st Virginia Infantry—a regiment whose history dated from 1661. We shall meet him again.

A. Religion in the Confederate Army

Camp Roper, Va, Feby. 20, 1863

My dear Friend:

I hear that a great religious spirit and revival is spreading throughout Lee's army, and some of the other armies of the South, and there are some evidences of it here, and in other camps about Richmond. Old professors that had become lukewarm in their zeal, are arousing to a sense of their duty, and many of the openly sinful are growing more temperate and reverent in their conversation and regard for religious things. There is less of cursing and profligacy and much less of card playing in our Company now than formerly. The voice of prayer is often heard in camp among the men, and many commands now have regular, or at least, occasional, preaching. Many ministers have gone out as evangelists to the armies, and some have gone into the ranks as private soldiers, or have become regular chaplains in some command. Their example and teaching are exerting a wide-spread and salutary influence. Rev. J. W. Ward, of Isle of Wight, has preached to our Company once recently, and other ministers hold meetings near us occasionally.

Almost nightly now, before the tattoo is sounded, we hear the voice of song in our camp, religious and revival songs and hymns. There are several men here who sing well, and these assemble together and pass an hour or two together at night very pleasantly. Sergeant N. B. Pond's tent is headquarters for these exercises, and doubtless, to some extent, this method of praise and prayer is doing good here and toning down some of the rougher vices of the men. May it lead finally to a great out-pouring of the Holy Spirit upon all the armies, and all the people of all the South. A soldier may fight and be a religious and God-fearing man, too.

But let me tell you of a little incident that has really taken place in our camp lately—one of the little comedies, not altogether innocent, but wholly harmless, that are occasionally happening and which serve as safety-valves to let off the superfluous steam engendered by the life of confinement and idleness in camp.

One of the songs that were being sung quite frequently, almost nightly in fact, by our religious choir was that somewhat eccentric refrain:

"Scotland's burning! Scotland's burning!
Cast on water! Cast on water!"

and so some of the prankish set among our boys conceived the idea of turning a little joke on the men in Sergeant Pond's tent. As a few of the tents had been fixed up with rude dirt chimneys for fireplaces, and Sergeant Pond's was one of these, it gave the boys a fine chance to play their game. And so, one night, one of the smallest among the men, with a bucket of water in hand, was lifted up by a big, strong fellow to the top of the little stick chimney. And just as the choir rang out the alarm,

"Scotland's burning!
Cast on water!"

the little fellow on the chimney cast his bucket of water down upon the fire inside, which deluged the whole fireplace, put out the fire, and scattered the embers in every direction.

Of course, too, it put a sudden stop to the song, and sent the men quickly out of the tent after the offenders. But not in time to discover who they were. Before they were fairly out of the tent, the boys had gained their own bunks, and were enjoying the fun at a distance.

The choir soon saw the joke, and, as they could do no more, submitted quietly. But it is presumed that nothing more will be heard of "Scotland's burning" for some time.

With a prayer for your continued safety and welfare at home, I remain,
Your friend, B.

—Jones, *Under the Stars and Bars*

B. John Dooley Describes Prayer Meetings

Perhaps this is the night for prayer meeting, for the parsons, taking advantage of this period of calm, are indefatigable in their efforts to draw the soldiers together to sing psalms and assist at prayer. Hundreds and thousands respond to their call and the woods resound for miles around with the unscientific but earnest music of the rough veterans of Lee's army. In doleful contrast to the more enlivening notes of the initiated, the chorus of the 'Mourners' ' may often be recognized; for conversions among the non-religious members of the army of Lee are of daily occurrence, and when they establish themselves upon the 'Mourners' Bench, it is evident to all how deep and loud is their repentance. There is something very solemn in these immense choruses of earnest voices, and there are, I am sure, hundreds of these honest soldiers truly sincere in believing that they are offering their most acceptable service to God.

Some of the parsons or chaplains are very zealous and persevering in assembling the soldiers to prayer; especially the chaplain of the eleventh Va. and the seventh. The latter is held in high esteem by all, whether members of religion or not; for, they say, in times of action, he is as bold as the bravest and is to be seen in the first and fiercest battles, consoling and assisting the wounded. 'Florence McCarthy' of Richmond, chaplain of the 7th inf., is also distinguished for his preaching and zeal among the soldiers. They say he told his congregation the other day that when they heard the doors and windows of the church slamming while the minister of God was preaching, they might be sure that the devil was at work trying to hinder the faithful from listening to the divine word. Some might very naturally presume from this that his Satanic Majesty was most at large during the blustering month of March than at any other time in the year.

—Durkin, ed., *John Dooley, Confederate Soldier*

IX

INCIDENTS OF ARMY LIFE: EASTERN FRONT

The war was not all fighting, and the fighting was not all in the pitched battles that have been commemorated in history. Judge Oliver Wendell Holmes liked to say that war was an organized bore, but it was Holmes, too, who observed that "accidents may call up the events of the war. You see a battery of guns go by at a trot and for a moment you are back at the White Oak Swamps, or Antietam, or on the Jerusalem Road. You hear a few shots fired in the distance, and for an instant your heart stops as you say to yourself, The Skirmishers are at it, and listen for the long roll of fire from the main line." For most of the soldiers, boys from farms and villages who had lived quietly and simply, the war was exciting enough, and most of the veterans came to look back on the war with pride and nostalgia—witness the enthusiastic reunions of the GAR and the Confederate Veterans. It was filled with minor adventures—scouting, foraging, the picket line, the forced march; it was memorable for good fellowship and lasting friendship; it had humor as well as pathos and tragedy; it was a microcosm of life.

What we have here is a series of incidents, episodes and experiences that illustrate the vicissitudes of fighting. Some of the circumstances here set forth were peculiar, but that, too, was typical: it was not only (as Winston Churchill said of World War I) a "very dangerous war," it was, in many respects, a very odd war—a war where enemies fraternized between battles, where newspapers kept correspondents in enemy capitals, where the line between regulars and guerillas was tenuous; where foreigners with strange names were always turning up as observers, or sometimes in uniform, where soldiers were expected to take care of themselves and to exercise their ingenuity; where there was opportunity for play and high jinks as well as for fighting.

No collection of excerpts can describe the whole of these varied experiences; all we can hope to do is to submit some that

are illustrative and that suggest the dangers and adventures and vicissitudes of the war. There is little continuity in this series of incidents, and we shall content ourselves with notes on the authors and on those episodes which may have some more general significance.

IX.I

HOW IT FEELS TO BE UNDER FIRE

It must not be forgotten that both Federal and Confederate armies were made up largely of volunteers who had never before had experience in battle, and that only a small proportion even of the Regular Army had ever been under fire. Frank Holsinger, who here recalls what it was like to be under fire, was a captain of the 19th U. S. Colored Infantry who was given brevet rank of major at the end of his service, and settled later in Kansas.

The influence of a courageous man is most helpful in battle. Thus at Antietam, when surprised by the Sixth Georgia Regiment, lying immediately behind the fence at the celebrated cornfield, allowing our regiment to approach within thirty feet, and then pouring in a volley that decimated our ranks fully one-half; the regiment was demoralized. I was worse—I was stampeded. I did not expect to stop this side of the Pennsylvania line. I met a tall, thin young soldier, very boyish in manner, but cool as a cucumber, his hat off, which he was lustily swinging, who yelled: "Rally, boys, rally! Die like men; don't run like dogs!" Instantly all fear vanished. "Why can I not stand and take what this boy can?" I commenced loading and firing, and from this on I was as comfortable as I had been in more pleasant places.

How natural it is for a man to suppose that if a gun is discharged, he or some one is sure to be hit. He soon finds, however, that the only damage done, in ninety-nine cases out of a hundred, the only thing killed is the powder! It is not infrequently that a whole line of battle (this among raw troops) will fire upon an advancing line, and no perceptible damage ensue. They wonder how men can stand such treatment, when really they have done no damage save the terrific noise incident to the discharge. To undertake to say how many discharges are necessary to the death of a soldier in battle would be presumptuous, but I have frequently heard the remark that it took a man's weight in lead to kill him.

In presentiments of death I have no confidence. While I have seen men go into battle predicting truthfully their own death, yet I believe it is the belief of nine out of ten who go into battle that that is their last. I have never gone into battle that I did not expect to be killed. I have seen those who had no thought of death coming to them killed outright. Thus Corporal George Horton, wounded at South Mountain, wrapped his handkerchief around his wounded arm and carried the colors of our regiment to Antietam. Being asked why he did not make the best of it and go to the hospital, that he was liable to be killed, he answered, "The bullet has not been moulded to kill me." Alas, he was killed the next day.

My sensations at Antietam were a contradiction. When we were in line "closed *en masse*," passing to the front through the wood at "half distance," the boom of cannon and the hurtling shell as it crashed through the trees or exploding found its lodgment in human flesh; the minies sizzing and savagely spotting the trees; the deathlike silence save the "steady men" of our officers. The shock to the nerves were indefinable—one stands, as it were, on the brink of eternity as he goes into action. One man alone steps from the ranks and cowers behind a large tree, his nerves gone; he could go no farther. General Meade sees him, and, calling a sergeant, says, "Get that man in ranks." The sergeant responds, the man refuses; General Meads rushes up with, "I'll move him!" Whipping out his saber, he deals the man a blow, he falls— who he was, I do not know. The general has no time to tarry or make inquiries. A lesson to those witnessing the scene. The whole transaction was like that of a panorama. I felt at the time the action was cruel and needless on the part of the general. I changed my mind when I became an officer, when with sword and pistol drawn to enforce discipline by keeping my men in place when going into the conflict.

When the nerves are thus unstrung, I have known relief by a silly remark. Thus at Antietam, when in line of battle in front of the wood and exposed to a galling fire from the cornfield, standing waiting expectant with "What next?" the minies zipping by occasionally, one making the awful *thud* as it struck some unfortunate. As we thus stood listlessly, breathing a silent prayer, our hearts having ceased to pulsate or our minds on home and loved ones, expecting soon to be mangled or perhaps killed, some one makes an idiotic remark; thus at this time it is Mangle, in a high nasal twang, with "D——d sharp skirmishing in front." There is a laugh, it is infectious, and we are once more called back to life.

The battle when it goes your way is a different proposition. Thus having reached the east wood, each man sought a tree from behind which he not only sought protection, but dealt death to our antagonists. They halt, also seeking protection behind trees. They soon begin to retire, falling back into the corn-field. We now rush forward. We cheer; we are in ecstasies. While shells and canister are still resonant and minies sizing spitefully, yet I think this one of the supreme moments of my existence. . . .

The worst condition to endure is when you fall wounded upon the field. Now you are helpless. No longer are you filled with the enthusiasm of battle. You are helpless—the bullets still fly over and about you—you no longer are able to shift your position or seek shelter. Every bullet as it strikes near you is a new terror. Perchance you are enabled to take out your handkerchief, which you raise in supplication to the enemy to not fire in your direction and to your friends of your helplessness. This is a trying moment. How slowly times flies! Oh, the agony to the poor wounded man, who alone can ever know its horrors! Thus at Bermuda Hundreds, November 28th, being in charge of the picket-line, we were attacked, which we repulsed and were rejoiced, yet the firing is maintained. I am struck in the left forearm, though not disabled; soon I am struck in the right shoulder by an explosive bullet, which is imbedded in my shoulder strap. We still maintain a spiteful fire. About 12 M. I am struck again in my right forearm, which is broken and the main artery cut; soon we improvise a tourniquet by using a canteen-strap and with a bayonet the same is twisted until blood ceases to flow. To retire is impossible, and for nine weary hours, or until late in the night, I remain on the line. I am alone with my thoughts; I think of home, of the seriousness of my condition; I see myself a cripple for life—perchance I may not recover; and all the time shells are shrieking and minie bullets whistling over and about me. The tongue becomes parched, there is no water to quench it; you cry, "Water! water!" and pray for night, that you can be carried off the field and to the hospital, and there the surgeons' care—maimed, crippled for life, perchance die. These are your reflections. Who can portray the horrors coming to the wounded?

The experiences of a man under fire differ materially between his first and subsequent engagements. Why? Because of discipline. "Familiarity with death begets contempt" is an old and true saying. With the new troops, they have not been called on to train or restrain their nerves. They are not only nervous, but they blanch at the thought of danger. They want education. What to them, on joining the service, was a terrible mental strain, is soon transformed into in difference. It is brought about by discipline.

—HOLSINGER, "How Does One Feel Under Fire?"

IX.2

FITZ JOHN PORTER VIEWS THE CONFEDERATES FROM A BALLOON

The use of balloons for observation dates back to the 1790s, but the Civil War was the first war in which they were generally used for military purposes. At the outbreak of the war Thaddeus Lowe was authorized to create an aeronautic service; he built five balloons which were used during the Peninsular and later campaigns. Lowe was the first person in America to take photographs from a balloon. Fitz John Porter, whose ascent is here described, is the general whose career was ruined by charges of disobedience at Second Bull Run; his long struggle to win vindication ended favorably in 1886.

On the 11th of April [1862] at five o'clock, an event at once amusing and thrilling occurred at our quarters. The commander-in-chief had appointed his personal and confidential friend, General Fitz John Porter, to conduct the siege of Yorktown. Porter was a polite, soldierly gentleman, and a native of New Hampshire, who had been in the regular army since early manhood. He fought gallantly in the Mexican war, being thrice promoted and once seriously wounded, and he was now forty years of age,—handsome, enthusiastic, ambitious, and popular. He made frequent ascensions with Lowe and learned to go aloft alone. One day he ascended thrice, and finally seemed as cosily at home in the firmament as upon the solid earth. It is needless to say that he grew careless, and on this particular morning leaped into the car and demanded the cables to be let out with all speed. I saw with some surprise that the flurried assistants were sending up the great straining canvas with a single rope attached. The enormous bag was only partially inflated, and the loose folds opened and shut with a crack like that of a musket. Noisily, fitfully, the yellow mass rose into the sky, the basket rocking like a feather in the zephyr; and just as I turned aside to speak to a comrade, a sound came from overhead, like the explosion of a shell, and something striking me across the face laid me flat upon the ground.

Half blind and stunned, I staggered to my feet, but the air seemed full of cries and curses. Opening my eyes ruefully, I saw all faces turned upwards, and when I looked above,—the balloon was adrift.

The treacherous cable, rotted with vitriol, had snapped in twain; one fragment had been the cause of my downfall, and the other trailed, like a great entrail, from the receding car, where Fitz John Porter was bounding upward upon a Pegasus that he could neither check nor direct.

The whole army was agitated by the unwonted occurrence. From battery No. 1, on the brink of the York, to the mouth of Warwick river, every soldier and officer was absorbed. Far within the Confederate lines the confusion extended. We heard the enemy's alarm-guns, and directly the signal flags were waving up and down our front.

The General appeared directly over the edge of the car. He was tossing his hands frightenedly, and shouting some thing that we could not comprehend.

"O—pen—the—valve!" called Lowe, in his shrill tones; "climb—to—the—netting—and—reach—the—valve—rope."

"The valve!—the valve!" repeated a multitude of tongues, and all gazed with thrilling interest at the retreating hulk that still kept straight upward, swerving neither to the east nor the west.

It was a weird spectacle,—that frail, fading oval, gliding against the sky, floating in the serene azure, the little vessel swinging silently beneath, and a hundred thousand martial men watching the loss of their brother in arms, but powerless to relieve or recover him. Had Fitz John Porter been drifting down the rapids of Niagara, he could not have been so far from human assistance. But we saw him directly, no bigger than a child's toy,

clambering up the netting and reaching for the cord.

"He can't do it," muttered a man beside me; "the wind blows the valve-rope to and fro, and only a spry, cool-headed fellow can catch it."

We saw the General descend, and appearing again over the edge of the basket, he seemed to be motioning to the breathless hordes below, the story of his failure. Then he dropped out of sight, and when we next saw him, he was reconnoitring the Confederate works through a long black spy-glass. A great laugh went up and down the lines as this cool procedure was observed, and then a cheer of applause ran from group to group. For a moment it was doubtful that the balloon would float in either direction; it seemed to falter, like an irresolute being, and moved reluctantly south eastward, towards Fortress Monroe. A huzza, half uttered, quivered on every lip. All eyes glistened, and some were dim with tears of joy. But the wayward canvas now turned due westward, and was blown rapidly toward the Confederate works. Its course was fitfully direct, and the wind seemed to veer often, as if contrary currents, conscious of the opportunity, were struggling for the possession of the daring navigator. The south wind held mastery for awhile, and the balloon passed the Federal front amid a howl of despair from the soldiery. It kept right on, over sharpshooters, rifle pits, and outworks, and finally passed, as if to deliver up its freight, directly over the heights of Yorktown.

The cool courage, either of heroism or despair, had seized upon Fitz John Porter. He turned his black glass upon the ramparts and masked cannon below, upon the remote camps, upon the beleaguered town, upon the guns of Gloucester Point, and upon distant Norfolk. Had he been reconnoitring from a secure perch at the tip of the moon, he could not have been more vigilant, and the Confederates probably thought this some Yankee device to peer into their sanctuary in despite of ball or shell. None of their great guns could be brought to bear upon the balloon; but there were some discharges of musketry that appeared to have no effect, and finally even these demonstrations ceased. Both armies in solemn silence were gazing aloft, while the imperturbable mariner continued to spy out the land.

The sun was now rising behind us, and roseate rays struggled up to the zenith, like the arcs made by showery bombs. They threw a hazy atmosphere upon the balloon, and the light shone through the network like the sun through the ribs of the skeleton ship in the *Ancient Mariner*. Then, as all looked agape, the air-craft "plunged, and tacked, and veered," and drifted rapidly toward the Federal lines again.

The allelujah that now went up shook the spheres, and when he had regained our camp limits, the General was seen clambering up again to clutch the valve-rope. This time he was successful, and the balloon fell like a stone, so that all hearts once more leaped up, and the cheers were hushed. Cavalry rode pell-mell from several directions, to reach the place of descent, and the General's personal staff galloped past me like the wind, to be the first at his debarkation. I followed the throng of soldiery with due haste, and came up to the horsemen in a few minutes. The balloon had struck a canvas tent with great violence, felling it as by a bolt, and the General, unharmed, had disentangled himself from innumerable folds of oiled canvas, and was now the cynosure of an immense group of people. While the officers shook his hands, the rabble bawled their satisfaction in hurrahs, and a band of music marching up directly, the throng on foot and horse gave him a vociferous escort to his quarters.

—TOWNSEND, *Campaigns of a Non-Combatant*

IX.3

STUART'S BALL IS INTERRUPTED BY THE YANKEES

We have met both Von Borcke and Stuart before and know that they are good company. Von Borcke's Memoirs first appeared in *Blackwood's Magazine* and did much to popularize the Southern cause and leader in Britain. The Memoirs give us, with John Esten Cooke's *Wearing of the Gray*, the best of all pictures of "Beauty" Stuart.

We were indulging in the dreamy sentiment natural to the hour, when the gay voice of Stuart broke in—"Major, what a capital place for us to give a ball in honour of our arrival in Maryland! don't you think we could manage it?" To this there was a unanimous response in the affirmative, which was especially hearty on the part of the ladies. It was at once agreed that the ball should be given. I undertook to make all necessary arrangements for the illumination and decoration of the hall, the issuing of the cards of invitation, &c., leaving to Stuart the matter of the music, which he gladly consented to provide.

A soldier's life is so uncertain, and his time is so little at his own disposal, that in affairs of this sort delays are always to be avoided; and so we determined on our way home, to the great joy of our fair companions, that the ball should come off on the following evening.

There was great stir of preparation at headquarters on the morning of the 8th. Invitations to the ball were sent out to all the families in Urbana and its neighbourhood, and to the officers of Hampton's brigade. The large halls of the Academy were aired and swept and festooned with roses, and decorated with battle flags borrowed from the different regiments. At seven in the evening all was complete, and already the broad avenue was filled with our fair guests, proceeding to the scene of festivity according to their social rank and fortune— some on foot, others in simple light "rockaways," others again in stately family coaches, driven by fat Negro coachmen who sat upon the box with great dignity. Very soon the sound of distant bugles announced the coming of the band of the 18th Mississippi Infantry, the Colonel and Staff of the regiment, who had been invited as an act of courtesy, leading the way, and the band playing in excellent style, the well-known air of Dixie. Amid the loud applause of the numerous invited and uninvited guests, we now made our grand *entrée* into the large hall, which was brilliantly lighted with tallow candles.

As master of the ceremonies, it was my office to arrange the order of the different dances, and I had decided upon a polka as the best for an animated beginning. I had selected the New York Rebel as the queen of the festival, and had expected to open the ball with her as my partner, and my surprise was great indeed when my fair friend gracefully eluded my extended arms, and with some confusion explained that she did not join in round dances, thus making me uncomfortably acquainted for the first time with the fact that in America, and especially in the south, young ladies rarely waltz except with brothers or first cousins, and indulge only in reels and contredances with strangers.

Not to be baffled, however, I at once ordered the time of the music to be changed, and had soon forgotten my disappointment as to the polka in a very lively quadrille. Louder and louder sounded the instruments, quicker and quicker moved the dancers, and the whole crowded room, with its many exceedingly pretty women and its martial fig ures of officers in their best uniforms, presented a most striking spectacle of gaiety and enjoyment.

Suddenly enters an orderly covered with dust, and reports in a loud voice to General Stuart that the enemy have surprised and driven in our pickets and are attacking our camp in force, while at the same moment the sound of shots in rapid succession is distinctly borne to us on the midnight air.

The excitement which followed this announcement I can not undertake to describe. The music crashed into a *concordia discors*. The officers rushed to their weapons and called for their horses, panic-stricken fathers and mothers endeavoured in a frantic way to collect around them their bewildered children, while the young ladies ran to and fro in most admired despair. General Stuart maintained his accustomed coolness and composure. Our horses were immediately saddled, and in less than five minutes we were in rapid gallop to the front. Upon arriving there we found, as is usually the case in such sudden alarms, that things were by no means so desperate as they had been represented.

Colonel Baker, with the splendid 1st North Carolina regiment, had arrested the bold forward movement of the Yankees. Pelham, with his guns in favourable position, was soon pouring a rapid fire upon their columns. The other regiments of the command were speedily in the saddle. The line of battle having been formed, Stuart gave the order for a general attack, and with great rage and fury we precipitated ourselves upon the foe, who paid, with the loss of many killed and wounded, and a considerable number of prisoners for their unmannerly interruption of our social amusement. They were pursued in their headlong flight for several miles by the 1st North Carolina, until, a little past midnight, they got quite out of reach, and all was quiet again.

It was about one o'clock in the morning when we got back to the Academy, where we found a great many of our fair guests still assembled, awaiting with breathless anxiety the result of the conflict. As the musicians had never dispersed, General Stuart ordered them again to strike up; many of our pretty fugitives were brought back by young officers who eagerly volunteered for that commendable purpose; and as everybody was determined that the Yankees should not boast of having completely broken up our party, the dancing was resumed in less than half an hour, and kept up till the first glimmer of dawn. At this time the ambulances laden with the wounded of last night's engagement were slowly approaching the Academy, as the only building at Urbana that was at all suited to the purposes of an hospital. Of course the music was immediately stopped and the dancing ceased, and our lovely partners in the quadrille at once became "ministering angels" to the sufferers.

—Von Borcke, *Memoirs of the Confederate War for Independence*

IX.4

FOREIGNERS FIGHT IN THE NORTHERN ARMY

The Civil War, like the Revolution, attracted soldiers of fortune and ardent partisans from abroad. Literally dozens of more or less distinguished foreigners served in the Con federate ranks; somewhat fewer were attracted to the Union cause. Most of the visiting warriors preferred to stay in the East, in the armies of Northern Virginia or of the Potomac. Many foreign visitors—the Comte de Paris, Fremantle, Wolseley, Estvan, Trobiand, and others—wrote up their wartime experiences, and we have drawn on these from time to time. This account is taken from *McClellan's Own Story.*

The most entertaining of my duties were those which sometimes led me to Blenker's camp, whither Franklin was always glad to accompany me to see the "circus," or "opera," as he usually called the performance. As soon as we were sighted, Blenker would have the "officer's call" blown to assemble his polyglot collection, with their uniform as varied and brilliant as the colors of the rainbow. Wrapped in his scarlet-lined cloak, his group of officers ranged around him, he would receive us with the most formal and polished courtesy. Being a very handsome and soldierly-looking man himself, and there being many equally so among his surroundings, the tableau was always very effective, and presented a striking contrast to the matter-of-fact way in which things were managed in the other divisions.

In a few minutes he would shout, *"Ordinanz numero eins!"* whereupon champagne would be brought in great profusion, the bands would play, sometimes songs be sung. It was said, I know not how truly, that Blenker had been a non-commissioned officer in the German contingent serving under King Otho of Greece.

His division was very peculiar. So far as "the pride, pomp, and circumstance of glorious war" were concerned, it certainly outshone all the others. Their drill and bearing were also excellent; for all the officers, and probably all the men, had served in Europe. I have always regretted that the division was finally taken from me and sent to Fremont. The officers and men were all strongly attached to me; I could control them as no one else could, and they would have done good service had they remained in Sumner's corps. The regiments were all foreign and mostly of Germans; but the most remarkable of all was the Garibaldi regiment. Its colonel, D'Utassy, was a Hungarian, and was said to have been a rider in Franconi's Circus, and terminated his public American career in the Albany Penitentiary. His men were from all known and unknown lands, from all possible and impossible armies: Zouaves from Algiers, men of the "Foreign Legion," Zephyrs, Cossacks, Garibaldians of the deepest dye, English deserters, Sepoys, Turcos, Croats, Swiss, beer-drinkers from Bavaria, stout men from North Germany, and no doubt Chinese, Esquimaux, and detachments from the army of the Grand Duchess of Gerolstein.

Such a mixture was probably never before seen under any flag, unless, perhaps, in such bands as Holk's Jagers of the Thirty Years' War, or the free lances of the middle ages.

I well remember that in returning one night from beyond the picket-lines I encountered an outpost of the Garibaldians. In reply to their challenge I tried English, French, Spanish, Italian, German, Indian, a little Russian and Turkish; all in vain, for nothing at my disposal made the slightest impression upon them, and I inferred that they were perhaps gypsies or Esquimaux or Chinese.

Mr. Seward's policy of making ours "a people's war," as he expressed it, by drumming up officers from all parts of the world, sometimes produced strange results and brought us rare specimens of the class vulgarly known as "hard cases." Most of the officers thus obtained had left their own armies for the armies' good, although there were admirable and honorable exceptions, such as Stahl, Willich, Rosencranz, Cesnola, and some others. Few were of the slightest use to us, and I think the reason why the German regiments so seldom turned out well was that their officers were so often men without character.

Soon after General Scott retired I received a letter from the Hungarian Klapka informing me that he had been approached by some of Mr. Seward's agents to get him into our army, and saying that he thought it best to come to a direct understanding with myself as to terms, etc. He said that he would require a bonus of $100,000 in cash and a salary of $25,000 per annum; that on his first arrival he would consent to serve as my chief of staff for a short time until he acquired the language, and that he would then take my place of general commanding-in-chief. He failed to state what provision he would make for me, that probably to depend upon the impression I made upon him.

I immediately took the letter to Mr. Lincoln, who was made very angry by it, and, taking possession of the letter, said that he would see that I should not be troubled in that way again.

Cluseret—afterwards Minister of War under the Commune—brought me a letter of introduction from Garibaldi, recommending him in the highest terms as a soldier, man of honor, etc. I did not like his appearance and declined his services; but without my knowledge or consent Stanton appointed him a colonel on my staff. I still declined to have anything to do with him, and he was sent to the Mountain Department, as chief of staff, I think. . . .

Of a different order were the French princes who formed part of my military family from September 20, 1861, to the close of the Seven Days. They served as captains, declining any higher rank, though they had fully earned promotion before the close of their connection with the army. They served precisely as the other aides, taking their full share of all duty, whether agreeable or disagreeable, dangerous or the reverse. They were fine young fellows and good soldiers, and deserved high credit in every way.

Their uncle, the Prince de Joinville, who accompanied them as a mentor, held no official position, but our relations were always confidential and most agreeable. The Duc de Chartres had received a military education at the military school at Turin; the Comte de Paris had only received instruction in military matters from his tutors. They had their separate establishment, being accompanied by a physician and a captain of *chasseurs-à-pied*. The latter was an immense man, who could never, under any circumstances, be persuaded to mount a horse: he always made the march on foot.

Their little establishment was usually the jolliest in camp, and it was often a great relief to me, when burdened with care, to listen to the laughter and gayety that resounded from their tents. They managed their affairs so well that they were respected and liked by all with whom they came in contact. The Prince de Joinville sketched admirably and possessed a most keen sense of the ridiculous, so that his sketch-book was an inexhaustible source of amusement, because everything ludicrous that struck his fancy on the march was sure to find a place there. He was a man of far more than ordinary ability and of excellent judgment. His deafness was, of course, a disadvantage to him, but his admirable qualities were so marked that I became warmly attached to him, as, in fact, I did to all the three, and I have good reason to know that the feeling was mutual.

Whatever may have been the peculiarities of Louis Philippe during his later life, it is very certain that in his youth, as the Duc de Chartres, he was a brave, dashing, and excellent soldier. His sons, especially the Ducs d'Orléans, d'Aumale, Montpensier, and the Prince de Joinville, showed the same characteristics in Algiers and elsewhere; and I may be permitted to say that my personal experience with the three members of the family who served with me was such that there could be no doubt as to their courage, energy, and military spirit. The course pursued by the Prince de Joinville and the Duc de Chartres during the fatal invasion of France by the Germans was in perfect harmony with this. Both sought service, under assumed names, in the darkest and most dangerous hours of their country's trial. The duc served for some months as Capt. Robert le

Fort, and under that name, his identity being known to few if any beyond his closest personal friends, gained promotion and distinction by his gallantry and intelligence.

—*McClellan's Own Story*

IX·5

WITH "EXTRA BILLY" SMITH AT YORK

After Chancellorsville Lee planned once again to move into Pennsylvania, in part to bring the war home to the North, in part to find food for his soldiers and forage for his horses. Early in June the Army of Northern Virginia was on the move, Ewell's corps swinging through the Valley and crossing the upper Potomac near Sharpsburg. Ewell had been authorized by Lee, not only to find flour and horses but, if possible, to capture Harrisburg. On June 27 he reached Carlisle; the same day Early moved out from Gettysburg to York, levying a $28,000 contribution on that town.

It was here that Stiles—whose *Four Years* is a minor classic—heard "Extra Billy" Smith haranguing the natives. This "Extra Billy" was one of the fabulous characters of the Confederacy. He had received this curious name a generation earlier when, as local postmaster, he collected so much "extra" money for deliveries. Later he was elected Governor of Virginia; went out to California where he took a prominent part in Democratic politics; returned to Virginia and served as Congressman for the decade before the war; and at the age of sixty-five offered his services to the Confederacy. Appointed brigadier general, he refused that rank and took, instead, the colonelcy of the 49th Virginia Infantry. Serving with distinction, and with reckless daring, he was promoted to major general but resigned in 1864 to accept once again the Governorship of his state.

Robert Stiles was a major of the famous Richmond Howitzers.

Things were not likely to be dull when our old friend "Extra Billy" was about;. . . in fact there was apt to be "music in the air" whenever he was in charge. On the occasion below described, the old Governor seemed to be rather specially concerned about the musical part *of* the performance.

We were about entering the beautiful Pennsylvania town of York, General Smith's brigade in the lead. Under these conditions, feeling sure there was likely to be a breeze stirring about the head of the column, I rode forward so as to be near the General and not miss the fun. As we approached, the population seemed to be very generally in the streets, and I saw at a glance that the old Governor had blood in his eye. Turning to Fred, his aide,—who was also his son, and about the strongest marked case of second edition I ever saw,—he told him to "go back and look up those tooting fellows," as he called the brigade band, "and tell them first to be sure their drums and horns are all right, and then to come up here to the front and march into town tooting 'Yankee Doodle' in their very best style."

Fred was off in a jiffy, and soon here came the band, their instruments looking bright and smart and glistening in the June sunlight—playing, however, not "Yankee Doodle," but *Dixie*," the musicians appearing to think it important to be entirely impartial in rendering these national airs, and therefore giving us "Dixie" by way of prelude to "Yankee Doodle."

When they got to the head of the column and struck up "Yankee Doodle," and the Governor, riding alone and bare headed in front *of* his staff, began bowing and saluting first one side and then the other, especially every pretty girl he saw, with that manly, hearty smile which no man or woman ever doubted or resisted—the Yorkers seemed at first astounded, then pleased. Finally, by the time we reached the public square they had reached the point of ebullition, and broke into enthusiastic cheers as they crowded about the head of the column actually embarrassing its progress, till the old Governor,—the "Governor-General," we might call him,—nothing loth, acceded to the half suggestion and called a halt, his brigade stacking arms and constituting, if not formally organizing, themselves and the people of York into a political meeting.

It was a rare scene—the vanguard of an invading army and the invaded and hostile population hobnobbing on the public green in an enthusiastic public gathering. The General did not dismount, but from the saddle he made a rattling, humorous speech which both the Pennsylvanians and his own brigade applauded to the echo. He said substantially:

"My friends, how do you like this way of coming back into the Union? I hope you like it; I have been in favor of it for a good while. But don't misunderstand us. We are not here with any hostile intent—unless the conduct of your side shall render hostilities unavoidable. You can see for yourselves we are not conducting ourselves like enemies today. We are not burning your houses or butchering your children. On the contrary, we are behaving ourselves like Christian gentlemen, as we are.

"You see, it was getting a little warm down our way. We needed a summer outing and thought we would take it at the North, instead of patronizing the Virginia springs, as we generally do. We are sorry, and apologize that we are not in better guise for a visit of courtesy, but we regret to say our trunks haven't gotten up yet; we were in such a hurry to see you that we could not wait for them. You must really excuse us.

"What we all need, on both sides, is to mingle more with each other, so that we shall learn to know and appreciate each other. Now here's my brigade—I wish you knew them as I do. They are such a hospitable, wholehearted, fascinating lot of gentlemen! Why, just think of it—of course this part of Pennsylvania is ours to-day; we've got it, we hold it, we can destroy it, or do what we please with it. Yet we sincerely and heartily invite you to stay. You are quite welcome to remain here and to make yourselves entirely at home—so long as you behave yourselves pleasantly and agreeably as you are doing now. Are we not a fine set of fellows? You must admit that we are."

At this point my attention was called to a volley of very heated profanity poured forth in a piping, querulous treble, coming up from the rear, and being mounted and located where I commanded a view of the road I saw that the second brigade in column, which had been some distance in the rear, had caught up and was now held up by our public meeting, which filled and obstructed the entire street.

Old Jube (Early), who had ridden forward to ascertain the cause of the deadlock, was fairly blistering the air about him and making furious but for the time futile efforts to get at Extra Billy, who in plain sight and not far off, yet blissfully unconscious of the presence of the major-general and of his agreeable observations and comments, was still holding forth with great fluency and acceptability.

The jam was solid and impervious. As D. H. Hill's report phrased it, "Not a dog, no, not even a sneaking exempt, could have made his way through," and at first and for some time Old Jube couldn't do it, and no one would help him. But at last officers and men were compelled to recognize the division commander, and he made his way so far that, by leaning forward, a long stretch, and a frantic grab, he managed to catch General Smith by the back of his coat collar. Even Jube did not dare curse the old General in an offensive way, but he did jerk him back and around pretty vigorously and half screamed:

"General Smith, what the devil are you about? stopping the head of this column in the cursed town?"

With unruffled composure the old fellow replied:

"Having a little fun, General, which is good for all of us, and at the same time teaching these people something that will be good for them and won't do us any harm."

Suffice it to say the matter was amicably arranged and the brigade and its unique commander moved on, leaving the honest burghers of York wondering what manner of men we were. I should add that General Early had the greatest regard and admiration for General Smith, which indeed he could not well avoid, in view of his intense patriotic devotion and his other sterling and heroic qualities. I have seldom heard him speak of any other officer or soldier in the service, save of course Lee and Jackson, in such exalted terms as of the old "Governor-General."

—STILES, *Four Years Under Marse Robert*

IX.6

BLUE AND GRAY FRATERNIZE ON THE PICKET LINE

The bitterness which characterizes any civil war was ameliorated by friendliness among the soldiers on opposite sides. This friendliness was found among the officers, many of whom belonged to the West Point fraternity or had fought together in Mexican and Indian wars; it was found, no less pervasively, among the rank and file, who, for the most part, respected each other and fought without animosity. Civil War narratives are filled with examples of fraternization across picket lines, the exchange of tobacco and food, acts of courtesy and friendliness.

Alexander Hunter, whose *Johnny Reb and Billy Yank* is one of the liveliest of descriptions of life in the ranks, was a college boy who joined the 17th Virginia Regiment at the outbreak of the war.

It was the latter part of August [1863]; orders were given to be prepared to go on picket early in the morning; and until a late hour the men were busy cooking rations and cleaning equipments.

Before the mists had been chased by the rising sun, the company in close column of fours marched down the road. Men and animals were in perfect condition, brimful of mettle and in buoyant spirits.

The route lay along the banks of the river, upon the winding course of which, after several hours' riding, the regiment reached its destination and relieved the various pickets. A sergeant and squad of men were left at each post, the company being spread out several miles on the river banks to act as videttes, whose duty it was to watch the enemy on the other side of the Rappahannock.

The next day our squad, Sergeant Joe Reid in command, sauntered down the bank, but seeing no one we lay at length under the spreading trees, smoking as solemnly and meditatively as the redoutable Wilhelmus Kraft and all the Dutch Council, over the affairs of state.

The Rappahannock, which was at this place about two hundred yards wide, flowing slowly oceanward, its bosom reflecting the roseate-hued morn, was as lovely a body of water as the sun ever shone upon. The sound of the gentle ripple of its waves upon the sand was broken by a faint "halloo" which came from the other side.

"Johnny Reb; I say, J-o-h-n-n-y R-e-b, don't shoot!"

Joe Reid shouted back, "All right!"

"What command are you?"

The spoken words floated clear and distinct across the water, "The Black Horse Cavalry. Who are you?"

"The Second Michigan Cavalry."

"Come out on the bank," said our spokesman, "and show yourselves; we won't fire."

"On your honor, Johnny Reb?"

"On our honor, Billy Yank."

In a second a large squad of blue-coats across the way advanced to the water's brink. The Southerners did the same; then the former put the query.

"Have you any tobacco?"

"Plenty of it," went out our reply.

"Any sugar and coffee?" they questioned.

"Not a taste nor a smell."

"Let's trade," was shouted with eagerness.

"Very well," was the reply. "We have not much with us, but we will send to Fredericksburg for more, so meet us here this evening."

"All right," they answered; then added, "Say, Johnny, want some newspapers?"

"Y-e-s!"

"Then look out, we are going to send you some."

"How are you going to do it?"

"Wait and see."

The Rebs watched the group upon the other side curiously, wondering how even Yankee ingenuity could devise a way for sending a batch of papers across the river two hundred yards wide, and in the meantime each man had his own opinion.

"They will shoot arrows over," said Martin.

"Arrows, the devil!" replied the sergeant; "there never was a bow bent which could cast an arrow across this river."

"Maybe they will wrap them around a cannon ball and shoot them across; we'd better get away from here," hastily answered a tall, slim six-footer, who was rather afraid of big shots.

A roar of laughter followed this suggestion, but the originator was too intent on his own awakened fears to let the slightest movement of the enemy pass unscanned. Eagerly he watched while the others were having all the fun at his expense. Presently he shouted:

"Here they come!" and then in a tone of intense admiration, "I'll be doggoned if these Yanks are not the smartest people in the world."

On the other side were several miniature boats and ships—such as schoolboys delight in—with sails set; the gentle breeze impelled the little crafts across the river, each freighted with a couple of newspapers. Slowly, but surely, they headed for the opposite bank as if some spirit Oberon or Puck sat at the tiller; and in a few minutes had accomplished their voyage and were drawn up to await a favorable wind to waft them back.

Drawing lots, Joe Boteler, who found luck against him, started to town, with a muttered curse, to buy tobacco, leaving his comrades to seek some shady spot, and with pipes in our mouths sink deep in the latest war news from the enemy's standpoint, always interesting reading.

It was a cloudless day,—a day to dream,—and with a lazy *sans souci* manner and half-shut eyes, enjoy to the soul the deep loveliness of the scene which lay around us like some fair creation of the fancy, listening the while to the trills of the blue-bird which sat on the top of a lofty tree industriously practicing his notes like a prima donna getting a new opera by heart.

Joe returned in the evening with a box of plug tobacco about a foot square; but how to get it across was the question. The miniature boats could not carry it, and we shouted over to the Yanks that we had about twenty pounds of cut plug, and asked them what we must do? They hallooed back to let one of us swim across, and declared that it was perfectly safe. We held a council of war, and it was found that none of the Black Horse could swim beyond a few rods. Then I volunteered. Having

lived on the banks of the Potomac most of my life, I was necessarily a swimmer.

Sergeant Reid went to a house not far off and borrowed a bread trough, and placing it on a plank, the box of tobacco was shipped, and disrobing I started, pushing my queer craft in front of me. As I approached the shore the news of my coming had reached camp, and nearly all the Second Michigan were lined up along the bank.

I felt a little queer, but I had perfect faith in their promise and kept on without missing a stroke until my miniature scow grounded on the beach. The blue-coats crowded around me and gave me a hearty welcome, and relieving the trough of its load, heaped the craft with offerings of sugar, coffee, lemons, and even candy, till I cried out that they would sink my transport. I am sure they would have filled a rowboat to the gunwhale had I brought one.

There was no chaffing or banter, only roistering welcomes.

Bidding my friends the enemy good-by, I swam back with the precious cargo, and we had a feast that night.

—HUNTER, *Johnny Reb and Billy Yank*

IX.7

LIFE WITH THE MOSBY GUERRILLAS

There is a Robin Hood quality about the Mosby Guerrillas. Mosby himself had served as cavalryman under Stuart in the Peninsular campaign, at Manassas and Antietam, but in January 1863 he set up on his own with a band of some three hundred free spirits, harrying the Federals north of the Rappahannock and, later, in the Valley. While the Federals regarded Mosby's men as outlaws, they operated under a Confederate "partisan ranger" law which made them subject to the same regulations as other soldiers, but permitted them almost complete freedom of action. When, on one occasion, Sheridan executed some of his men, Mosby hung seven prisoners in reprisal. At the close of the war the Mosby Guerrillas consisted of eight companies, well mounted and equipped; Mosby himself had been promoted to a colonelcy.

John Munson, from whose recollections this excerpt has been taken, was himself one of the Mosby Guerrillas.

The life led by Mosby's men was entirely different from that of any other body of soldiers during the war. His men had no camps nor fixed quarters, and never slept in tents. They did not even know anything about pitching a tent. The idea of making coffee, frying bacon, or soaking hardtack was never entertained. When we wanted to eat we stopped at a friendly farm house, or went into some little town and bought what we wanted. Every man in the Command had some special farm he could call his home.

The people in that part of the state which was designated "Mosby's Confederacy," embracing in a general way the counties of Fauquier and Loudoun, were loyal to the South, though frequently outside the lines of the Southern army, and they were glad to have Mosby's men among them, not only to show their sympathy with the South, but also to have the protection which the presence of the Partisans afforded them.

During the war all local government in that country was suspended. There were no courts nor court officers. The people looked to Mosby to make the necessary laws and to enforce them, and no country before, during or since the war was ever better governed. Mosby would not permit any man to commit a crime, or even a misdemeanor, in his domain. One of our men, in a spirit of deviltry, once turned over an old Quaker farmer's milk cans, and when Mosby heard of it he ordered me to take the man over to the army, which was then near Winchester, and turn him over to General Early, with the message that such a man was not fitted to be a Guerrilla.

As a Command we had no knowledge of the first principles of cavalry drill, and could not have formed in a straight line had there ever been any need for our doing so. We did not know the bugle-calls, and very rarely had roll-call. Our dress was not uniform in make or color; we did not address our officers, except Mosby, by their titles; in fact, we did not practice anything usually required of a soldier; and yet withal there was not another body of men in the army under better or more willing control of

their leader. Two things were impressed upon us well, however; to obey orders, and to fight. . . .

Each of Mosby's men was armed with two muzzle-loading Colt's army revolvers of forty-four caliber. They were worn in belt holsters. Some few who could afford it, or who had succeeded in capturing extra pistols or who wanted to gratify a sort of vanity, wore an extra pair in their saddle-holsters or stuck into their boot legs. These weapons were extremely deadly and effective in the hand-to-hand engagements in which our men indulged. Long and frequent practice had made every man in the Command a good shot, and each was as sure with his revolver as every cow-boy is with his six-shooter. As a general thing our real fights were fast and furious and quickly over, one or the other side withdrawing at a dead run when the pistols were empty . . .

"Something gray" was the one requisite of our dress and the cost of it mattered little. Much of it was paid for by Uncle Sam out of the money we got from him directly and indirectly. Like gamblers we took chances with fate. We had ups and downs; but after our successful raids we were the best dressed, best equipped, and best mounted Command in the Confederate army. There were meek and lowly privates among us, of whom it might truly be said that Solomon in all his glory was not arrayed as one of these. Union army sutlers supplied us with a varied assortment of luxuries, and I cannot recall an instance when we rejected what they had on hand on over-hauling their stock, or when we threatened to take our trade to some competitor. . . .

Some of the Command were extremely fastidious in the matter of dress and affected gold braid, buff trimmings, and ostrich plumes in their hats. After the "greenback raid" when we captured General Sheridan's paymasters with a hundred and seventy thousand dollars in crisp new Government notes, each man received as his share more than twenty-one hundred dollars. The result was that all had clothes and accoutrements such as had never gladdened their hearts be fore. At all times, whether things went well or ill, the Guerrillas were as vain a lot of dandies as one would wish to see; blithe in the face of danger, full of song and story, indifferent to the events of tomorrow, and keyed up to a high pitch of anticipation; mingled with this was the pride that goes hand in hand with repeated victories and the possession of spoils. . . .

Whenever we made a successful raid, we made it a point to repay the farmers and country people whose bounty we enjoyed, in live stock and supplies. The return from a sutler's raid was a holiday occasion,, for everybody got some thing. On one occasion we captured about two hundred and fifty fat cattle from General Sheridan's supply train, and we gave our country friends half of them, dividing them among all the people living within range.

On one occasion, we got into some sutler's stores at Duffield depot on the Baltimore & Ohio Railroad and the goods were so tempting that I concluded to carry an assortment back to our lady hostess and her household. I loaded up a sack with all sorts of useful and ornamental goods, and fastened it to my saddle securely. Then, going back into the store and looking around, I spied some hoop-skirts which the sutler had no doubt bought for some special order from an army officer's wife. I took these and strapped them to my saddle. Then I made another and final round of the store, and began stuffing my many pockets with notions, such as buttons, hair pins, thread, hooks and eyes, and the like; finally I found a lot of papers of needles, and I thrust a handful of these into my trousers' pocket.

Just then some one poked his head into the door and cried:

"The Yankees are coming."

We made a break for our horses and galloped away with our plunder, and our prisoners; keeping up a pretty fast gait for some miles for fear our burdens would slacken the usual speed we practiced when we were retreating. I had not gone a mile before my papers of needles began to come undone in my pocket, and at every jump of my horse a newly re leased needle would remind me that I had captured it, until at the end of our run I had dozens

of needle marks on my anatomy, and two or three points were left inside, to work upward or downward, or out, as they severally saw fit.

I recollect that I delivered all my presents safely to my kind friends, except needles, and I made no deference to these in my account of the raid. In all my later raids on sutler's stores I contented myself with things that were not likely to prove troublesome, or stick into me, such as boots, and gloves, and furnishing goods; but I ignored needles.

—MUNSON, *Reminiscences of a Mosby Guerrilla*

IX.8

REBEL AND YANKEE YELLS

We hear a great deal about the Rebel Yell, though no two people seem agreed on just what it was, or even on its origin. It has been variously described as "more overpowering than the cannon's roar" and "a mingling of Indian whoop and wolf-howl" it was probably born of the hunting field. There is far less information on the Yankee Yell; this was undoubtedly something that varied greatly from army to army.

Harvie Dew was a member of the 9th Virginia Cavalry, attached to Stuart.

That there existed a marked difference between the yells of the opposing armies during our late war was a recognized fact, and a frequent source of comment. The notes and tones peculiar to each of them were well defined, and led to their designation as the "Yankee" and the "Rebel" yells. . . .

The Federal, or "Yankee," yell, compared with that of the Confederate, lacked in vocal breadth, pitch, and resonance. This was unquestionably attributable to the fact that the soldiery of the North was drawn and recruited chiefly from large cities and towns, from factory districts, and from the more densely settled portions of the country.

Their surroundings, their circumstances of life and employment, had the effect of molding the character and temperament of the people, and at the same time of restraining their vocal development. People living and working in close proximity to one another have no absolute need for loud or strained vocal efforts, and any screaming or prolonged call ing becomes seriously annoying to neighbors. Consequently, all such liberties or inconsiderate indulgences in cities, towns, etc., have long ago been discouraged by common consent. . . .

To afford some idea of the difference between these "yells," I will relate an incident which occurred in battle on the plains at Brandy Station, Virginia, in the fall of 1863. Our command was in full pursuit of a portion of Kilpatrick's cavalry. We soon approached their reserves (ours some distance behind), and found ourselves facing a battery of artillery with a regiment of cavalry drawn up on each side. A point of woods projected to the left of their position. We were ordered to move by the right flank till the woods protected us from the battery, and then, in open field, within a few hundred yards of the enemy, we were ordered to halt and right dress.

In a moment more one of the Federal regiments was ordered to charge, and down they came upon us in a body two or three times outnumbering ours. Then was heard their peculiar characteristic yell—"Hoo-ray! Hoo-ray! Hoo-ray!" etc. (This yell was called by the Federals a "cheer," and was intended for the word "hurrah," but that pronunciation I never heard in a charge. The sound was as though the first syllable, if heard at all, was "hoo," uttered with an exceedingly short, low, and indistinct tone, and the second was "ray," yelled with a long and high tone slightly deflecting at its termination. In many instances the yell seemed to be the simple interjection "heigh," rendered with the same tone which was given to "ray.")

Our command was alone in the field, and it seemed im possible for us to withstand the coming shock; but our commander, as brave an officer as ever drew a saber, frequently repeated, as the charging column approached us, his precautionary orders, to "Keep steady, boys! Keep steady!" and so we remained till the Federals were within a hundred yards of us. Then, waving his sword in air, he gave the final order, loud enough to be heard the field over: "Now is your time, boys! Give them the saber! Charge them, men! Charge!"

In an instant every voice with one accord vigorously shouted that "Rebel yell," which was so often heard on the field of battle. "Woh-who-ey! who-ey! who-ey! Woh-who ey! who-ey!" etc. (The best illustration of this "true yell" which can be given the reader is by spelling it as above, with directions to sound the first syllable "woh" short and low, and the second "who" with a very high and prolonged note deflecting upon the third syllable "ey.")

A moment or two later the Federal column wavered and broke. In pursuit we chased them to within twenty feet of their battery, which had already begun to retreat. The second regiment to the right and rear of the battery then charged upon us, and for a moment we were forced back; but by that time our reserves were up, and we swept the field.

—Dew, "The Yankee and Rebel Yells"

IX.9

WOMEN AMONG THE RANKS

At least 400 women served as soldiers in the Union and Confederate armies during the Civil War. Cloaked by bulky male clothing, closely clipped hair, and male aliases, women entered the army for many reasons, including patriotism, the love of adventure or the desire to stay close to a husband or loved one.

Amazingly enough, many women went undetected for years at a time. Physical examinations and boot camps were often cursory or nonexistent. Most soldiers lived outdoors, allowing women to avoid close scrutiny. The presence of so many adolescent boys in the military meant that it was not at all uncommon to have beardless youths among the ranks.

Women were most often discovered when they became ill or were wounded. At least six pregnant women hid their gender and their condition until they delivered their babies. Colonel Eliejah H. C. Cavins, of Indiana, wrote home that "a corporal was promoted to sergeant for gallant conduct at the battle of Fredericksburg—since which time the sergeant has become the mother of a child. What use have we for women, if soldiers in the army can give birth to children? It is said that the sergeant and his Capt. occupied the same tent, they being intimate friends." One of the most famous female soldiers was "Albert"

Cashier of the 95th Illinois Volunteer Infantry whose true identity as Jennie Hodgers was not revealed until 1911.

Many women fought in several battles. "Hundreds of women marched steadily up to the mouth of a hundred cannon pouring out fire and smoke, shot and shell, mowing down the advancing hosts like grass; men, horses, and colors going down in confusion, disappearing in clouds of smoke; the only sound, the screaming of shells, the crackling musketry, the thunder of artillery," wrote Susan B. Anthony, Elizabeth Cady Stanton and Matilda Gage in their book *History of Women Suffrage*, "through all this women were sustained by the enthusiasm born of love of country and liberty."

Lauren Cook Burgess, a female Civil War reenactor, has documented 135 women who enlisted in Civil War armies. When Burgess was "discovered" in 1989 to be a woman, the National Park Service attempted to banish her from reenactments, citing the need to keep the events authentic. Burgess, however, filed a successful discrimination lawsuit. She has accomplished significant research to prove that women did actually serve as frontline soldiers.

Burgess edited the first published letters of a female Civil War soldier, Sarah Rosetta Wakeman, a private in the 153rd Regiment, New York State Volunteers. Three of her letters to back home follow. Wakeman may have disguised herself as a man to earn more money to assist her debt-ridden father on an upstate New York farm, Burgess hypothesizes. Wakeman fought in two battles during the Red River Campaign of 1864 and died of illness that spring.

Newspapers frequently wrote about women's contributions to the military effort. A series of short articles from the *Peoria Daily Transcript* about Belle Reynolds, who accompanied her husband's military unit, follow, as well.

A. Letters of Sarah Rosetta Wakeman, Alias Private Lyons Wakeman

Alexandria
Nov. 24, 1862

My Dear Father and mother and sister and brothers, one in all,

I receive your letter on Sunday the 23. I was very glad to hear from you and learn that you were all well. I am well and enjoy good health. Our Regiment is in Camp at Alexandria, Va. We have had no fighting yet. We have to guard the City and stand on picket. I stood on my post all last night. When i left you i went to Binghamton. I saw you there. I meet you coming home from meeting. I went to work with Stephen Saldon the next day. I work half a month for 4$ in money. I

was only 7 miles from Binghamton up the river. I didn't go to the fair. When i got done [with] work I went on the canal to work. I agreed to run 4 trips from Binghamton to Utica for 20$ in money, but this load of coal was going to Canajoharie, Montgomery Co.

When I got there i saw some soldiers. They wanted I should enlist and so i did. I got 100 and 52$ in money. I enlisted for 3 years or soon [as] discharged. All the money I send you i want you should spend it for the family in clothing or something to eat. Don't save it for me for i can get all the money i want. If i ever return i shall have money enough for my self and to divide with you.

If you want to save anything to remember me by, keep that spotted calf and if i ever return i want you to let me have her again. Tell Robert to give her a few oats this winter and I will pay him for doing so. Tell Celestia that I will send her my likeness as soon as I can. Mother, i will tell you where my little Chest is. It is upstairs over the bedroom in the garret. Let Robert go and climb up by the stove pipe hole and he will find it on the left hand side toward the road up in the corner. I want you should keep all my things for me for i believe that God will spare my life and that I shall see you all again face to face before i die. Father, if you will send me some postage stamps I will be very thankful for them. I want to drop all old affray and I want you do to do the same and when i come home we will be good friends as ever.

Good-by for the present
Sarah Rosetta Wakeman
Direct your letter to Alexandria, VA., R. L. Wakeman in the care of
Capt. McLaughlin

Tell Mary i thank her for that card and I send her this little knife.

Father, you needn't be a feared to write any[thing] private to me for I can read all you can write. I suppose you thought that I would have to get Somebody to read it for me but I read it all my self
Rosetta Wakeman

Dear Father and Mother,

I receive you letter last night. I was glad to hear from you all once more. I am well and I feel thankful to god that he has spared my life and kept me in good health until the present time, and glad to hear that you have bought out that Cider mill in Church hollow and got it home. When I get my pay I will send you what money I can Spare if it ain't but a little. Tell mother I will send her that ring that I Showed to Henry Austin.

Our regiment expect to Stay here this winter. I would like to have you Send me a small box with iron hinges on it and a lock and key. Put the key inSide of the box and Screw the Cover on and when I get the box I Can draw the Screw and open the box and get the key. Then if I have anything, my goods friends won't Steal it. If you are a mind to Send me a piece of butter and Some Cakes, I will be very thankful to you.

Is Fon aliving with you yet or not? Please let me know. When I think of home it Seems like a dream to me, but Still I know there is such a place as home that I left one year ago. It is but one Chance to ten that I ever Shall meet you again in this world. There is a good many temptations in the army. I got led away into this world So bad that I sinned a good deal. But I now believe that God Spirit has been aworking with me, and 'til that I was aComing back to Him again, and I hope and pray that I never shall be led away like it again. I have a hope that if I never meet you again in this world that I Shall meet you in paradise where parting will be no more.

I got a letter from Frank a few days ago. He is not but a little ways from Alexandria. Some of our men have Stood guard where Frank is. Good-by for this time from,
Rosetta Wakeman

I thank you for the Stamps. Don't you ever ask me to lend you some money again in this world. If you do I won't send it to you.

Dear Father and Mother,

I receive you kind and welcome letter today. I am well and tough as a bear this winter. I receive a letter from Frank today. He is well at the time the letter was wrote.

As for my Coming home on a furlough this winter I don't know whether I can or not. There has a good many of our men has been home on a furlough. You needn't send me any box for I can get along without one just as well as not. . . .

I don't care anything about Coming home for I [am] aShamed to Come, and I sometimes think that I never will go home in the world. I have enjoyed myself the best since I have been gone away from home than I ever did before in my life. I have had plenty of money to spend and a good time asoldier[ing]. I find just as good friends among Strangers as I do at home.

We haven't seen any snow here yet but it rains here today.

I sometimes think that I will re-enlist for five years and get my eight hundred dollars bounty. I Can do that if I am a mind to. What do you think about that?

I Can't think of any more to write. So good-by from your
Edwin R. Wakeman
or Rosetta Wakeman

B. Exploits of Mrs. Major Belle Reynolds

An Unprecedented Military Appointment

Governor Yates has paid a rather unusual but well-merited compliment to Mrs. Reynolds, wife of Lieut. Reynolds, of Co. A, 17th Ill., and a resident of this city. Mrs. Reynolds has accompanied her husband through the greater part of the campaign through which the 17th has passed, sharing with him the dangers and privations of a soldier's life. She was present at the battle of Pittsburgh Landing, and like a ministering angel, attended to the wants of as many of the wounded and dying soldiers as she could thus winning the gratitude and esteem of the brave fellows by whom she was surrounded.

Gov. Yates, hearing of her heroic and praiseworthy conduct, presented her with a commission as Major in the army, the document conferring the well-merited honor being made out with all due formality, and having attached the great seal of the State. Probably no lady in America will ever again have such a distinguished military honor conferred upon her. Mrs. Reynolds is now in this city, and leaves to join her regiment in a day or two.

—*Peoria Daily Transcript*, April 22, 1862

Major Belle Reynolds

The editor of the Bloomington Pantagraph had the pleasure of a trip down the Tennessee with Mrs. Major Belle Reynolds, and gives his impressions of that lady. The editor evidently expected to find Mrs. Reynolds an Amazon, and therein was disappointed. He says: "She is a young lady of dignified manners, apparently wearing her honors meekly, and by no means evidences in personal appearance, that inflexible will, and energy of character, for which she is so meritously celebrated."

—*Peoria Daily Transcript*, May 19, 1862

Mrs. Major Belle Reynolds again—an Unexpected Family Difficulty

Our now rather celebrated fellow-townswoman, Mrs. Major Reynolds, has, it appears, met with a little domestic trouble growing out of her recent military appointment, which was altogether unlooked for by herself or friends. Still, when we remember the conjugal injunction imposed upon her sex, and by which "honor and obedience" to their liege lords are so imperatively commanded, there is no room for wonder that her gallant husband should feel that his "rights" were being invaded. The correspondent of the Cincinnati times tells the story, and, we give it for what it is worth, merely remarking that we think it a lengthy attempt to perpetrate a small joke. The Times correspondent says:

"I am sorry to inform you that there is at present some apprehension of a domestic difficulty, originating out of the late commission of a female to the rank of Major in the United States army.

The worthy lady, whose bravery and Samaritan kindness to our wounded soldiers on the battle-field of Shiloh, has won her the love and esteem of an appreciating public, and who has been promoted to rank by a grateful Government, is, I fear about to fall victim to that most dreaded of delusions—jealousy. This lady is at present holding her headquarters on board one of the hospital steamers now lying at Pittsburg Landing, anxiously awaiting for the expected battle, to again render that comfort and aid known only to exist in the presence of angels and the attentions of lovely women.

But what is most unhappy in the case of this lady-Major, is that her once adoring and loving husband, who now holds the rank of Lieutenant, insists on being made a Colonel, and gives as a reason that his wife now commands him, from the virtue of her rank—being a Major—and that this is directly contrary to the original understanding existing between them at the day of their nuptials. From this protest of the Lieutenant, I fear that all law-abiding wives will hold up their hands and exclaim, "Oh! the brute."

—*Peoria Daily Transcript*, May 22, 1862

X

FROM FORT DONELSON TO STONES RIVER

While the war in the East surged back and forth between Washington and Richmond, the Chesapeake Bay and the Valley, the war in the West raged and burned over an enormous territory, from Missouri to the Gulf, from the Alleghenies to the Mississippi, with great outcroppings in Missouri, Arkansas, Louisiana, and even in Texas and New Mexico. Nor is it to be forgotten that the heaviest blows of the war in the East were directed, in the end, from the Western theater, Sherman carrying the war to Georgia and the Carolinas.

Not only were the geographical circumstances of the war in the West profoundly different from those in the East, the strategic objectives, too, were different. The objectives of fighting in Virginia and Maryland were the capture of the rival capitals and the destruction of the rival armies. The war in the West was of necessity directed to different ends. There was, first, the control of the belt of border states—Kentucky and Missouri—and of eastern Tennessee, heavily Unionist in sentiment and commanding the approaches to the East and the South. There was, second, control of the great arteries of commerce: the Mississippi, the Cumberland, Tennessee, and Red rivers, and the railroads which connected the deep South with the Atlantic coast, the border states with the Gulf. The greatest strategical objective was, of course, control of the Mississippi River, and the separation of the Trans-Mississippi West from the rest of the Confederacy. Almost all the major battles of the Western theater involved some strategic point on some river or railroad: Fort Donelson, Island No. 10, Shiloh, Murfreesboro, Vicksburg, Port Hudson, Chattanooga, and others. The otherwise confusing cavalry raids, too, fall into a logical pattern when we see them against the background of lines of communication; and the cavalry leaders of the Western armies—men like Forrest and Morgan and Grierson—played a very different role from Eastern cavalry leaders like Stuart and Buford.

Most of the campaigns of the West involved control of rivers or railroads. There was one prolonged campaign for the control of the Mississippi—a campaign that began with the minor Battle of Belmont and was concluded with the fall of Port Hudson. A second was directed to the first Confederate line of defense—the line stretching from Columbus to Forts Henry and Donelson and to Bowling Green. A third was directed to the second Confederate line of defense—Memphis to Corinth to Chattanooga. The fourth major campaign—that of Chickamauga and Chattanooga—was for the gateway.

X.I

GRANT WINS HIS SPURS AT BELMONT

Grant was working in his father's store in Galena, Illinois, when the war broke out. A West Pointer, he had made a good record in the Mexican War, and then seen service on distant frontier posts until, in 1854, he had resigned from the army, probably under pressure. With the outbreak of the war he applied for appointments from the Governor of Illinois and probably from the Governor of Ohio, tried to get an appointment under McClellan, who ignored him, and worked in the state adjutant general's office. His application to the adjutant general at Washington was ignored. Finally, in June, Governor Yates appointed him colonel of an unruly regiment, the 21st Illinois. Two months later, somewhat to his surprise, he was made brigadier general.

After whipping his regiment into shape Grant took it to Missouri, then under the command of John C. Fremont, whose only claim to military ability was his record as an explorer.

Fremont was trying, with no great success, to hold Missouri for the Union. Meantime Pillow had built up a strong force at Columbus, just south of Cairo; from Columbus he could not only block the Mississippi but threaten Paducah at the mouth of the Tennessee, Cairo at the junction of the Ohio and the Mississippi, or advance into Missouri to support the Confederates there. To forestall these moves Grant fortified Cairo, then pounced on Paducah; then he asked and obtained permission to make a demonstration against Columbus. Lacking strength for a direct attack he selected instead the little village of Belmont, opposite the great fort, where Pillow had a force of some 2,500 men. Belmont was a minor affair, and it was not very clearly a victory, but it brought Grant recognition.

Autumn glided away; the leaves were dropping along the banks of the Potomac and the Ohio; the fairest season of the year would soon be gone. It was a period of disaster and inaction. . . . Grant meantime was busily employed in drilling new troops at Cairo, and probably in wondering why they were not made use of. He always believed that where both sides are equally undisciplined the most active would be the most successful. He saw Columbus grow into an impregnable fortress under the care of Pillow and Polk; he heard that the Tennessee and the Cumberland were to be closed by new fortifications; and he asked his superior officer at St. Louis, Fremont, to be allowed to take Columbus (September 10) while it was yet assailable. At length (November 1, 1861) he received orders to make a demonstration against the fortress, to prevent the enemy from sending reinforcements to their general, Price, in Missouri. Grant resolved finally to turn the movement into an actual attack on Belmont.

Columbus rises on a high bluff above the Mississippi on the Kentucky shore. It was now so strongly fortified as to be quite impregnable; armies might have wasted their strength against its lofty bluff for months without result; its long range of heavy cannon closed up the navigation of the river; and a large force of the enemy filled its walls. But it was Belmont, a post on the opposite side of the Mississippi, under the guns of Columbus, that Grant meant to threaten or assail. Here a considerable force of rebels had formed their camp, defend-

ed by rough lines of felled trees and the fire of Columbus; and it was here that the reinforcements were chiefly ferried over the river to aid Price in Missouri. Grant's aim was to destroy their camp, disperse their troops, and then return to Cairo. He would thus practice his new levies, and at the same time alarm the enemy.

No sooner did the brave Western soldiers at Cairo learn that a real attack was to be made than all was exultation and excitement. They rejoiced to be relieved from the dull monotony of camp-life, and to test their courage in the fierce trial of actual combat. Grant ordered General Smith from Paducah to make a demonstration against Columbus, to employ the enemy's attention on that side of the river, while he himself set out for Missouri. His troops, it should be remembered, were all untried men. His two chief commanders, Logan and M'Clernand, had never heard a shot fired in actual battle, and Grant stood alone in the midst of a brave but inexperienced army. His force numbered about thirty-one hundred men.

After several feints he landed his troops from transports at Hunter's Point, in Missouri, and marched at once against Belmont, about three miles below. The enemy were soon found, and the brave troops, advancing as skirmishers, threw themselves against the rude defenses; the officers behaved like veterans, always in the front of the battle; the soldiers climbed, crept, or sprang over the strong abatis; the enemy were slowly driven back to the shore. Pillow, who had crossed over with reinforcements from Columbus, was forced to give way, and the disordered and broken force, larger in numbers than the assailants, took refuge under the river bank and the fire of Columbus.

A strange scene followed. Grant's troops, carried away by the joy of the moment, having taken several hundred prisoners and the enemy's camp, broke into disorder. Speeches were delivered by excited orators; the captured camp was plundered; in the midst of their enemies the inexperienced soldiers believed themselves secure. Grant ordered the camp to be set on fire to drive the troops to

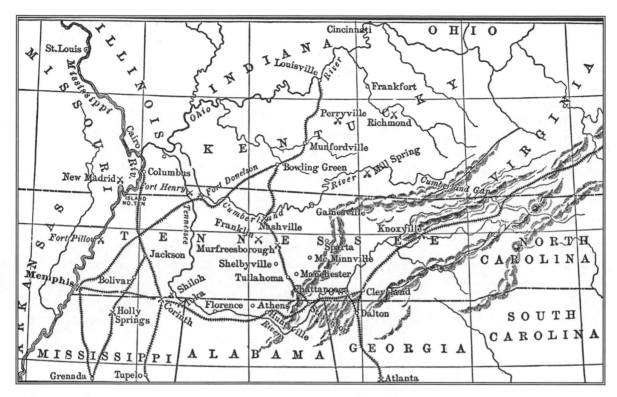

THE CAMPAIGNS IN TENNESSEE AND KENTUCKY

their ranks, and suddenly the heavy guns of Columbus opened upon the Union army. Meanwhile large bodies of rebels had crossed the river, and with the aid of Pillow's men had surrounded their late victors.

A startled aid-de-camp, riding up to Grant, exclaimed in alarm, "General, we are surrounded!"

"Well," said he, "we must cut our way out as we cut our way in."

His calmness reassured his little army, and with Grant, M'Clernand, and Logan at their head, they broke through the enemy's line and passed in good order to the landing. Here the whole force was safely embarked, with but slight loss. Grant acted as his own rear-guard, was the last man on the shore, and at one time found himself not more than one hundred and fifty feet from a line of the enemy. He paused a moment to survey them, then turned his-horse's head, rode slowly away, and finally broke into a gallop as he approached the river. He made his way with difficulty upon one of the transports,

and then the little flotilla moved on under a heavy fire of musketry from the shore. By five o'clock the last vessel was beyond reach of the enemy, and the successful expedition arrived safely at Cairo.

—Eugene Lawrence, "Grant on the Battle-Field"

X.2

U. S. Grant Becomes Unconditional Surrender Grant

Grant had already forestalled a Confederate advance down the Tennessee to the Ohio by seizing Paducah. Now he proposed to General Halleck, who had succeeded the incompetent Fremont, an attack on the bastions of Forts Henry and Donelson. The reduction of these forts would not only clear two great rivers, the Tennessee and the Cumberland, but cut the Confederate line of defense from Columbus to Bowling Green, Kentucky, and force the Confederates to retire from Kentucky to Tennessee. After a good deal of prodding Halleck authorized a joint attack on the forts by Grant and Commodore Foote, the latter to blast the forts from his gunboats. Early in February 1862 Grant's army of 17,000 men advanced on Fort Henry. Meantime the gunboats had already reached the fort, which was promptly abandoned, its small defending force marching overland to the much larger and stronger Fort Donelson.

Here is Grant's own story of how he forced the surrender of this fort. As he makes clear, the surrender was quite unnecessary; the Confederates could have withstood a long siege, or they could have fought their way out—as Forrest did. The capture of these two forts, coming on the heels of the Belmont affair, gave Grant a national reputation and brought him a major generalship.

I was very impatient to get to Fort Donelson because I knew the importance of the place to the enemy and sup posed he would reinforce it rapidly. I felt that 15,000 men on the 8th would be more effective than 50,000 a month later. I asked Flag-officer Foote, therefore, to order his gunboats still about Cairo to proceed up the Cumberland River and not to wait for those gone to Eastport and Florence; but the others got back in time and we started on the 12th [February 1862]. I had moved McClernand out a few miles the night before so as to leave the road as free as possible. . . .

I started from Fort Henry with]15,000 men, including eight batteries and part of a regiment of cavalry, and, meeting with no obstruction to detain us, the advance arrived in front of the enemy by noon. That afternoon and the next day were spent in taking up ground to make the investment as complete as possible. General Smith had been directed to leave a portion of his division behind to guard forts Henry and Heiman. He left General Lew. Wallace with 2,500 men. With the remainder of his division he occupied our left, extending to Hickman creek. McClernand was on the right and covered the roads running south and south-west from Dover. His right extended to the backwater up the ravine opening into the [Cumberland] south of the village. The troops were not intrenched, but the nature of the ground was such that they were just as well protected from the fire of the enemy as if rifle-pits had been thrown up. Our line was generally along the crest of ridges. The artillery was

protected by being sunk in the ground. The men who were not serving the guns were perfectly covered from fire on taking position a little back from the crest. The greatest suffering was from want of shelter. It was midwinter and during the siege we had rain and snow, thawing and freezing alternately. It would not do to allow camp-fires except far down the hill out of sight of the enemy, and it would not do to allow many of the troops to remain there at the same time. In the march over from Fort Henry numbers of the men had thrown away their blankets and overcoats. There was there fore much discomfort and absolute suffering.

During the 12th and 13th, and until the arrival of Wallace and Thayer on the 14th, the National forces, composed of but 15,000 men, without intrenchments, confronted an in trenched army of 21,000 without conflict further than what was brought on by ourselves. Only one gunboat had arrived. There was a little skirmishing each day, brought on by the movement of our troops in securing commanding positions; but there was no actual fighting during this time except once, on the 13th, in front of McClernand's command. That general had undertaken to capture a battery of the enemy which was annoying his men. Without orders or authority he sent three regiments to make the assault. The battery was in the main line of the enemy, which was de fended by his whole army present. Of course the assault was a failure, and of course the loss on our side was great for the number of men engaged. In this assault Colonel William Morrison fell badly wounded. Up to this time the surgeons with the army had no difficulty in finding room in the houses near our line for all the sick and wounded; but now hospitals were overcrowded. Owing, however, to the energy and skill of the surgeons the suffering was not so great as it might have been. The hospital arrangements at Fort Donelson were as complete as it was possible to make them, considering the inclemency of the weather and the lack of tents, in a sparsely settled country where the houses were generally of but one or two rooms.

On the return of Captain Walke to Fort Henry on the 10th, I had requested him to take the vessels that had accompanied him on his expedition up the Tennessee, and get possession of the Cumberland as far up towards Donelson as possible. He started without delay, taking, however, only his own gunboat, the *Carondelet*, towed by the steamer *Alps*. Captain Walke arrived a few miles below Donelson on the 12th, a little after noon. About the time the advance of troops reached a point within gunshot of the fort on the land side, he engaged the water batteries at long range. On the 13th I informed him of my arrival the day before and of the establishment of most of our batteries, requesting him at the same time to attack that day so that I might take advantage of any diversion. The attack was made and many shots fell within the fort, creating some consternation, as we now know. The investment on the land side was made as complete as the number of troops engaged would admit of. . . .

The plan was for the troops to hold the enemy within his lines, while the gunboats should attack the water-batteries at close quarters and silence his guns if possible. Some of the gunboats were to run the batteries, get above the fort and above the village of Dover. I had ordered a reconnaissance made with the view of getting troops to the river above Dover in case they should be needed there. That position attained by the gunboats it would have been but a question of time—and a very short time, too—when the garrison would have been compelled to surrender.

By three in the afternoon of the 14th Flag-officer Foote was ready, and advanced upon the water batteries with his entire fleet. After coming in range of the batteries of the enemy the advance was slow, but a constant fire was delivered from every gun that could be brought to bear upon the fort. I occupied a position on shore from which I could see the advancing navy. The leading boat got within a very short distance of the water battery, not further off I think than two hundred yards, and I soon saw one and then an other of them dropping down the river, visibly disabled. Then the whole fleet followed and the engagement was closed for the day. The gunboat which Flag-officer Foote was on, besides having been hit about sixty times, several of the shots passing through near the water-line, had a shot enter the pilot-house which killed the pilot, carried away the wheel, and wounded the flag-officer himself. The tiller-ropes of another vessel were carried away, and she, too, dropped helplessly back. Two others had their pilot-houses so injured that they scarcely formed a protection to the men at the wheel.

The enemy had evidently been much demoralized by the assault, but they were jubilant when they saw the disabled vessels dropping down the river entirely out of the control of the men on board. Of course I only witnessed the falling back of our gunboats and felt sad enough at the time over the repulse. Subsequent reports, now published, show that the enemy telegraphed a great victory to Richmond. The sun went down on the night of the 14th of February, 1862, leaving the army confronting Fort Donelson anything but comforted over the prospects. The weather had turned intensely cold; the men were without tents and could not keep up fires where most of them had to stay; and, as previously stated, many had thrown away their overcoats and blankets. Two of the strongest of our gunboats had been disabled, presumably beyond the possibility of rendering any present assistance. I retired this night not knowing but that I would have to intrench my position, and bring up tents for the men or build huts under the cover of the hills.

On the morning of the 15th, before it was yet broad day, a messenger from Flag-officer Foote handed me a note, expressing a desire to see me on the flag-ship and saying that he had been injured the day before so much that he could not come himself to me. I at once made my preparations for starting. . . .

When I reached the fleet I found the flag-ship was anchored out in the stream. A small boat, however, awaited my arrival and I was soon on board with the flag-officer. He explained to me in short the condition in which he was left by the engagement of the evening before, and suggested that I should intrench while he turned to Mound City with his disabled boats, expressing at the time the belief that he could have the necessary repairs made and be back in ten days. I saw the absolute necessity of his gunboats going into hospital, and did not know but I should be forced to the alternative of going through a siege. But the enemy relieved me from this necessity.

When I left the National line to visit Flag-officer Foote I had no idea that there would be any engagement on land unless I brought it on myself. The conditions for battle were much more favorable to us than they had been for the first two days of the investment. From the 12th to the 14th we had but 15,000 men of all arms and no gunboats. Now we had been reinforced by a fleet of six naval vessels, a large division of troops under General L. Wallace and 2,500 men brought over from Fort Henry belonging to the division of C. F. Smith. The enemy, however, had taken the initiative. Just as I landed I met Captain Hillyer of my staff, white with fear, not for his personal safety, but for the safety of the National troops. He said the enemy had come out of his lines in full force and attacked and scattered McClernand's division, which was in full retreat. The roads, as I have said, were unfit for making fast time, but I got to my command as soon as possible. The attack had been made on the National right. I was some four or five miles north of our left. The line was about three miles long. In reaching the point where the disaster had occurred I had to pass the divisions of Smith and Wallace. I saw no sign of excitement on the portion of the line held by Smith; Wallace was nearer the scene of conflict and had taken part in it. He had, at an opportune time, sent Thayer's brigade to the support of Mc Clernand and thereby contributed to hold the enemy within his lines.

I saw everything favorable for us along the line of our left and center. When I came to the right appearances were different. The enemy had come out in full force to cut his way out and make his escape. McClernand's division had to bear the brunt of the attack from this combined force. His men had stood up gallantly until the ammunition in their cartridge-boxes gave out. There was abundance of ammunition near by lying on the ground in boxes, but at that stage of the war it was not all of our commanders of regi-

ments, brigades, or even divisions, who had been educated up to the point of seeing that their men were constantly supplied with ammunition during an engagement. When the men found themselves without ammunition they could not stand up against troops who seemed to have plenty of it. The division broke and a portion fled, but most of the men, as they were not pursued, only fell back out of range of the fire of the enemy. It must have been about this time that Thayer pushed his brigade in between the enemy and those of our troops that were without ammunition. At all events, the enemy fell back within his intrenchments and was there when I got on the field.

I saw the men standing in knots talking in the most excited manner. No officer seemed to be giving any directions. The soldiers had their muskets, but no ammunition, while there were tons of it close at hand. I heard some of the men say that the enemy had come out with knapsacks, and haversacks filled with rations. They seemed to think this indicated a determination on his part to stay out and fight just as long as the provisions held out. I turned to Colonel J. D. Webster, of my staff, who was with me, and said: "Some of our men are pretty badly demoralized, but the enemy must be more so, for he has attempted to force his way out, but has fallen back: the one who attacks first now will be victorious and the enemy will have to be in a hurry if he gets ahead of me." I determined to make the assault at once on our left. It was clear to my mind that the enemy had started to march out with his entire force, except a few pickets, and if our attack could be made on the left before the enemy could redistribute his forces along the line, we would find little opposition except from the intervening abatis. I directed Colonel Webster to ride with me and call out to the men as we passed: "Fill your cartridge-boxes, quick, and get into line; the enemy is trying to escape, and he must not be permitted to do so." This acted like a charm. The men only wanted someone to give them a command. We rode rapidly to Smith's quarters, when I explained the situation to him and directed him to charge the enemy's works in his front with his whole division, saying at the same time that he would find nothing but a very thin line to contend with. The general was off in an incredibly short time, going in advance himself to keep his men from firing while they were working their way through the abatis intervening between them and the enemy. The outer line of rifle-pits was passed, and the night of the 15th General Smith, with much of his division, bivouacked with the lines of the enemy. There was now no doubt but that the Confederates must surrender or be captured the next day. . . .

A council of war was held by the enemy at which all agreed that it would be impossible to hold out longer. General Buckner, who was third in rank in the garrison but much the most capable soldier, seems to have regarded it a duty to hold the fort until the general commanding the department, A. S. Johnston, should get back to his headquarters at Nashville. Buckner's report shows, however, that he considered Donelson lost and that any attempt to hold the place longer would be at the sacrifice of the command. Being assured that Johnston was already in Nashville, Buckner too agreed that surrender was the proper thing. Floyd turned over the command to Pillow, who declined it. It then devolved upon Buckner, who accepted the responsibility of the position. Floyd and Pillow took possession of all the river transports at Dover and before morning both were on their way to Nashville, with the brigade formerly commanded by Floyd and some other troops, in all about 3,000. Some marched up the east bank of the Cumberland; others went on the steamers. During the night Forrest also, with his cavalry and some other troops, about a thousand in all, made their way out, passing between our right and the river. They had to ford or swim over the back-water in the little creek just south of Dover.

Before daylight General Smith brought to me the following letter from General Buckner:

> Headquarters, Fort Donelson,
> February 16, 1862
>
> Sir:—In consideration of all the circumstances governing the present situation of affairs at this station, I propose to the Commanding Officer of the Federal forces the appointment of Commissioners to agree upon terms of capitulation of the forces and fort under my command, and in that view suggest an armistice until 12 o'clock to-day.
>
> I am, sir, very respectfully,
> Your ob't se'v't,
> S. B. BUCKNER
> Brig. Gen. C.S.A.

To this I responded as follows:

> Headquarters Army in the Field,
> Camp near Donelson,
> February 16, 1862
>
> General S.B. Buckner,
> Confederate Army.
> Sir:—Yours of this date, proposing armistice and appointment of Commissioners to settle terms of capitulation, is just received. No terms except an unconditional and im mediate surrender can be accepted. I propose to move immediately upon your works.
>
> I am, sir, very respectfully,
> Your ob't se'v't,
> U. S. GRANT
> Brig. Gen.

To this I received the following reply:

> Headquarters, Dover, Tennessee,
> February 16, 1862
>
> To Brig. Gen'l U. S. Grant,
> U.S. Army.
> Sir:—The distribution of the forces under my command, incident to an unexpected change of commanders, and the overwhelming force under your command, compel me, not withstanding the brilliant success of the Confederate arms yesterday, to accept the ungenerous and unchivalrous terms which you propose.
>
> I am, sir,
> Your very ob't se'v't,
> S.B. BUCKNER
> *Brig. Gen. C.S.A.*

. . . I had been at West Point three years with Buckner and afterwards served with him in the army, so that we were quite well acquainted. In the course of our conversation, which was very friendly, he said to me that if he had been in command I would not have got up to Donelson as easily as I did. I told him that if he had been in command I should not have tried in the way I did: I had invested their lines with a smaller force than they had to defend them, and at the same time had sent a brigade full 5,000 strong, around by water; I had relied very much upon their commander to allow me to come safely up to the outside of their works.

—*Personal Memoirs of U.S. Grant*

X.3

WITH THE DIXIE GRAYS AT SHILOH

The fall of Forts Henry and Donelson forced the Confederates back on their second line of defense. Johnston with drew to Murfreesboro, in Tennessee, and prepared to fall back to Corinth. Polk gave up Columbus but was ordered to hold on to New Madrid and Island No. 10 in the great bend of the Mississippi at the juncture of Missouri, Arkansas, Kentucky and Tennessee. On March 3 General Pope advanced on New Madrid with 20,000 men; by cutting off access to it he succeeded in starving it into submission in ten days.

As there was no direct approach to Island No. 10 by land, Pope cut a channel through the great bend north of the island and ferried his army to Point Pleasant below the Island. Meantime Commodore Foote's gunboats ran the batteries of the island. Isolated, the Confederates tried to evacuate their forts, but were cut off and forced to surrender 7,000 men and 123 heavy guns on April 7.

After this debacle, the Confederates formed a line of defense stretching from Memphis through Corinth to Chattanooga. Johnston collected some 40,000 troops here, and awaited the arrival of Van Dorn with another 20,000 from the west. Halleck, now in command of the entire Western theater, directed Grant and Buell to advance to Savannah on the Tennessee River about 30 miles northeast of Corinth. Grant's army began to arrive at Savannah on March 11, and within a week he had some 35,000 men at and around Savannah and

Pittsburg Landing, a few miles below on the western side of the river. Buell, however, made a leisurely advance from Nashville, taking 22 days to cover 135 miles.

All unsuspecting of danger, Grant's army was scattered over a large irregular quadrangle heavily wooded and cut by many gullies and ravines. Early on the morning of April 6 Johnston struck the Federal outposts, drove them in, and pushed on to the main attack. Although taken by surprise, the Federals rallied and fought back with great courage and pertinacity. The fighting raged for over 12 hours, the Confederates steadily pushing back the Union right flank and driving toward Pittsburg Landing on the left flank.

During the afternoon, when the situation looked desperate for the Federals, advance detachments of Lew Wallace's division and of Buell's reached the field of battle, and the gunboats joined in the fray. By nightfall victory rested with the Confederates, but they had succeeded neither in destroying Grant's army nor in capturing Pittsburg Landing, and they had lost their leader, the brilliant and beloved Albert Sidney Johnston. By the next day the whole situation was reversed. Grant had 25,000 fresh men to throw into the battle; the Confederates were exhausted, and on the defensive. There was some sharp fighting on the seventh, but the Con federates withdrew and Grant failed to pursue. By the time he did get ready to pursue, the Confederate army had retired to Corinth. Shiloh was, with Antietam, the bloodiest day of the war, and the hardest fought. Union losses were over 13,000—of whom some 2,500 were prisoners; Confederate losses over 10,500.

This account of Shiloh is by young Henry M. Stanley, later the world-famous Sir Henry Stanley. Born in Wales as John Rowlands 19 years earlier, he had shipped as a cabin boy to Louisiana, where he was adopted by a New Orleans merchant, Henry Morton Stanley, whose name he took. In 1861 he enlisted in the Dixie Grays. Captured at Shiloh he endured the discomforts of Camp Douglas prison, enlisted briefly in the Federal artillery, was discharged, and returned to England, only to come back to the United States and enlist in the Union Navy. Later he returned to England and to an illustrious career in journalism and exploration.

On April 2, 1862, we received orders to prepare three days' cooked rations. Through some misunderstanding, we did not set out until the 4th; and, on the morning of that day, the 6th Arkansas Regiment of Hindman's brigade, Hardee's corps, marched from Corinth to take part in one of the bloodiest battles of the West. We left our knapsacks and tents behind us. After two days of marching, and two nights of bivouacking and living on cold rations, our spirits were not buoyant at dawn of Sunday, the 6th April, as they ought to have been for the serious task before us. . .

At four o'clock in the morning, we rose from our damp bivouac, and, after a hasty refreshment, were formed into line. We stood in rank for half an hour or so, while the military dispostions were being completed along the three mile front. Our brigade formed the centre; Cleburne's and Gladden's brigades were on our respective flanks.

Day broke with every promise of a fine day. Next to me, on my right, was a boy of seventeen, Henry Parker. I remember it because, while we stood-at-ease, he drew my attention to some violets at his feet, and said, "It would be a good idea to put a few into my cap. Perhaps the Yanks won't shoot me if they see me wearing such flowers, for they are a sign of peace."

"Capital," said I, "I will do the same."

We plucked a bunch, and arranged the violets in our caps. The men in the ranks laughed at our proceedings, and had not the enemy been so near, their merry mood might have been communicated to the army.

We loaded our muskets, and arranged our cartridge pouches ready for use. Our weapons were the obsolete flintlocks, and the ammunition was rolled in cartridge-paper, which contained powder, a round ball, and three buckshot. When we loaded we had to tear the paper with our teeth, empty a little powder into the pan, lock it, empty the rest of the powder into the barrel, press paper and ball into the muzzle, and ram home. Then the Orderly-sergeant called the roll, and we knew that the Dixie Greys were present to a man. . .

Before we had gone five hundred paces, our serenity was disturbed by some desultory firing in front. It was then a quarter-past five. "They are at it already," we whispered to each other. "Stand by, gentlemen,"—for we were all gentle men volunteers at this time,—said our Captain L. G. Smith. Our steps became unconsciously brisker, and alertness was noticeable in everybody. The firing continued at intervals, deliberate and scattered, as at target practice. We drew nearer to the firing, and soon a sharper rattling of musketry was heard. "That is the enemy waking up," we said. Within a few minutes, there was another exlosive burst of musketry, the air was pierced by many missiles, which hummed and pinged sharply by our ears, pattered through the tree tops, and brought twigs and leaves down on us. "Those are bullets," Henry whispered with awe.

At two hundred yards further, a dreadful roar of musketry broke out from a regiment adjoining ours. It was followed by another further off, and the sound had scarcely died away when regiment after regiment blazed away and made a continuous roll of sound. "We are in for it now," said Henry. . . .

"Forward, gentlemen, make ready!" urged Captain Smith. In response, we surged forward, for the first time marring the alignment. We trampled recklessly over the grass and young sprouts. Beams of sunlight stole athwart our course. Nothing now stood between us and the enemy.

"There they are!" was no sooner uttered, than we cracked into them with levelled muskets. "Aim low, men!" commanded Captain Smith. I tried hard to see some living thing to shoot at, for it appeared absurd to be blazing away at shadows. But, still advancing, firing as we moved, I, at last, saw a row of little globes of pearly smoke streaked with crimson, breaking-out with spurtive quickness, from a long line of blue figures in front; and simultaneously, there broke upon our ears an appalling crash of sound, the series of fusillades following one another with startling suddenness, which suggested to my somewhat moidered sense a mountain upheaved, with huge rocks tumbling and thundering down a slope, and the echoes rumbling and receding through space. Again and again, these loud and quick explosions were repeated, seemingly with increased violence, until they rose to the highest pitch of fury, and in unbroken continuity. All the world seemed involved in one tremendous ruin!. . .

Though one's senses were preternaturally acute, and engaged with their impressions, we plied our arms, loaded, and fired, with such nervous haste as though it depended on each of us how soon this fiendish uproar would be hushed.

My nerves tingled, my pulses beat double-quick, my heart throbbed loudly, and almost painfully; but, amid all the excitement, my thoughts, swift as the flash of lightning, took all sound, and sight, and self, into their purview. I listened to the battle raging far away on the flanks, to the thunder in front, to the various sounds made by the leaden storm. I was angry with my rear rank, because he made my eyes smart with the powder of his musket; and I felt like cuffing him for deafening my ears! I knew how Captain Smith and Lieutenant Mason looked, how bravely the Dixie Greys' banner ruffled over Newton Story's head, and that all hands were behaving as though they knew how long all this would last. Back to myself my thoughts came, and, with the whir ring bullet, they fled to the blue-bloused ranks afront. They dwelt on their movements, and read their temper, as I should read time by a clock. Through the lurid haze the contours of their pink faces could not been seen, but their gappy, hesitating, incoherent, and sensitive line revealed their mood clearly.

We continued advancing, step by step, loading and firing as we went. To every forward step, they took a backward move, loading and firing, as they slowly withdrew. Twenty thousand muskets were being fired at this stage, but, though accuracy of aim was impossible, owing to our labouring hearts, and the jarring and excitement, many bullets found their destined billets on both sides.

After a steady exchange of musketry, which lasted some time, we heard the order: "Fix Bayonets! On the double-quick!" in tones that thrilled us. There was a simultaneous bound forward, each soul doing. his best for the emergency The Federals appeared inclined to await us; but, at this juncture, our men raised a yell, thousands responded to it, and burst out into the wildest yelling it has ever been my lot to hear. It drove all sanity and order from among us. It served the double purpose of relieving pent-up feelings, and transmitting encouragement along the attacking line. I rejoiced in the shouting like the rest. It reminded me that there were about four hundred companies like the Dixie Greys, who shared our feelings. Most of us, engrossed with the musket-work, had forgotten the fact; but the wave after wave of human voices, louder than all other battle-sounds together, penetrated to every sense, and stimulated our energies to the utmost.

"They fly!" was echoed from lip to lip. It accelerated our pace, and filled us with a noble rage. Then I knew what the Berserker passion was! It deluged us with rapture, and transfigured each Southerner into an exulting victor. At such a moment, nothing could have halted us.

Those savage yells, and the sight of thousands of racing figures coming towards them, discomfited the blue-coats; and when we arrived upon the place where they had stood, they had vanished. Then we caught sight of their beautiful array of tents, before which they had made their stand, after being roused from their Sunday-morning sleep, and huddled into line, at hearing their pickets challenge our skirmishers. The half-dressed dead and wounded showed what a surprise our attack had been. We drew up in the enemy's camp, panting and breathing hard. Some precious minutes were thus lost in recovering our breaths, indulging our curiosity, and reforming our line. Signs of a hasty rouse to the battle were abundant. Military equipments, uniform-coats, half-packed knapsacks, bedding, of a new and superior quality, littered the company streets.

Meantime, a series of other camps lay behind the first ar ray of tents. The resistance we had met, though comparatively brief, enabled the brigades in rear of the advance camp to recover from the shock of the surprise; but our delay had not been long enough to give them time to form in proper order of battle. There were wide gaps between their divisions, into which the quick-flowing tide of elated Southerners entered, and compelled them to fall back lest they should be surrounded. Prentiss's brigade, despite their most desperate efforts, were thus hemmed in on all sides, and were made prisoners.

I had a momentary impression that, with the capture of the first camp, the battle was well-nigh over; but, in fact, it was only a brief prologue of the long and exhaustive series of struggles which took place that day.

Continuing our advance, we came in view of the tops of another mass of white tents, and almost at the same time, were met by a furious storm of bullets, poured on us from a long line of blue-coats, whose attitude of assurance proved to us that we should have tough work here. But we were so much heartened by our first success that it would have required a good deal to have halted our advance for long. Their opportunity for making a full impression on us came with terrific suddenness. The world seemed bursting into fragments. Cannon and musket, shell and bullet, lent their several intensities to the distracting uproar. If I had not a fraction of an ear, and an eye inclined towards my Captain and Company, I had been spell-bound by the energies now opposed to us. I likened the cannon, with their deep bass, to the roaring of a great herd of lions; the ripping, cracking musketry, to the incessant yapping of terriers; the windy whisk of shells, and zipping of minie bullets, to the swoop of eagles, and the buzz of angry wasps. All the opposing armies of Grey and Blue fiercely blazed at each other.

After being exposed for a few seconds to this fearful downpour, we heard the order to "Lie down, men, and continue your firing!" Before me was a prostrate tree, about fifteen inches in diameter, with a narrow strip of light between it and the ground. Behind this shelter a dozen of us flung ourselves. The security it appeared to offer restored me to my individuality. We could fight, and think, and observe, better than out in the open. But it was a terrible period! How the cannon bellowed, and their shells plunged and bounded, and flew with screeching hisses over us! Their sharp rending explosions and hurtling fragments made us shrink and cower, despite our utmost efforts to be cool and collected. I marvelled, as I heard the unintermitting patter, snip, thud, and hum of the bullets, how anyone could live under this raining death. I could

hear the balls beating a merciless tattoo on the outer surface of the log, pinging it vivaciously as they flew off at a tangent from it, and thudding into something or other, at the rate of a hundred a second. One, here and there, found its way under the log, and buried itself in a comrade's body. One man raised his chest, as if to yawn, and jostled me. I turned to him, and saw that a bullet had gored his whole face, and penetrated into his chest. Another ball struck a man a deadly rap on the head, and he turned on his back and showed his ghastly white face to the sky.

"It is getting too warm, boys!" cried a soldier, and he uttered a vehement curse upon keeping soldiers hugging the ground until every ounce of courage was chilled. He lifted his head a little too high, and a bullet skimmed over the top of the log and hit him fairly in the centre of his fore head, and he fell heavily on his face. But his thought had been instantaneously general; and the officers, with one voice, ordered the charge; and cries of "Forward, forward!" raised us, as with a spring, to our feet, and changed the complexion of our feelings. The pulse of action beat feverishly once more; and, though overhead was crowded with peril, we were unable to give it so much attention as when we lay stretched on the ground. . . .

Our progress was not so continuously rapid as we desired, for the blues were obdurate; but at this moment we were gladdened at the sight of a battery galloping to our assistance. It was time for the nerve-shaking cannon to speak. After two rounds of shell and canister, we felt the pressure on us slightly relaxed; but we were still somewhat sluggish in disposition, though the officers' voices rang out imperiously. Newton Story at this juncture strode forward rapidly with the Dixies' banner, until he was quite sixty yards ahead of the foremost. Finding himself alone, he halted; and turning to us smilingly said, "Why don't you come on, boys? You see there is no danger!" His smile and words acted on us like magic. We raised the yell, and sprang lightly and hope fully towards him. "Let's give them hell, boys!" said one. "Plug them plum-centre, every time!"

It was all very encouraging, for the yelling and shouting were taken up by thousands. "Forward, forward; don't give them breathing time!" was cried. We instinctively obeyed, and soon came in clear view of the blue-coats, who were scornfully unconcerned at first; but, seeing the leaping tide of men coming on at a tremendous pace, their front dissolved, and they fled in double-quick retreat. Again we felt the "glorious joy of heroes." It carried us on exultantly, rejoicing in the spirit which recognises nothing but the prey. We were no longer an army of soldiers, but so many schoolboys racing, in which length of legs, wind, and condition tell.

We gained the second line of camps, continued the rush through them, and clean beyond. It was now about ten o'clock. My physical powers were quite exhausted, and, to add to my discomfiture, something struck me on my belt clasp, and tumbled me headlong to the ground. I could not have been many minutes prostrated before I recovered from the shock of the blow and fall, to find my clasp deeply dented and cracked. My company was not in sight. I was grateful for the rest, and crawled feebly to a tree, and plunging my hand into my haversack, ate ravenously. Within half an hour, feeling renovated, I struck north in the direction which my regiment had taken, over a ground strewn with bodies and the debris of war.

The desperate character of this day's battle was now brought home to my mind in all its awful reality. While in the tumultuous advance, and occupied with a myriad of exciting incidents, it was only at brief intervals that I was conscious of wounds being given and received; but now, in the trail of pursuers and pursued, the ghastly relics appalled every sense. I felt curious as to who the fallen Greys were, and moved to one stretched straight out. It was the body of a stout English Sergeant of a neighbouring company, the members of which hailed principally from the Washita Valley. . . .

Close by him was a young Lieutenant, who, judging by the new gloss on his uniform, must have been some father's darling. A clean bullet-hole through the centre of his forehead had instantly ended his career. A little further were some twenty bodies, lying in various postures, each by its own pool of viscous blood, which emitted a peculiar scent, which was new to me, but which I have since learned is inseparable from a battle-field. Beyond these, a still larger group lay, body overlying body, knees crooked, arms erect, or widestretched and rigid according as the last spasm overtook them. The company opposed to them must have shot straight. . . .

It was the first Field of Glory I had seen in my May of life, and the first time that Glory sickened me with its repulsive aspect, and made me suspect it was all a glittering lie. . . . Under a flag of truce, I saw the bearers pick up the dead from the field, and lay them in long rows beside a wide trench; I saw them laid, one by one, close together at the bottom. . . .

I overtook my regiment about one o'clock. . . . The enemy resolutely maintained their ground, and our side was pre paring for another assault. The firing was alternately brisk and slack. We lay down, and availed ourselves of trees, logs, and hollows, and annoyed their upstanding ranks; battery pounded battery, and meanwhile we hugged our resting places closely. Of a sudden, we rose and raced towards the position, and took it by sheer weight and impetuosity. About three o'clock, the battle grew very hot. The enemy appeared to be more concentrated, and immovably sullen. Both sides fired better as they grew more accustomed to the din; but, with assistance from the reserves, we were continually press ing them towards the river Tennessee, without ever retreating an inch.

About this time, the enemy were assisted by the gun boats, which hurled their enormous projectiles far beyond us; but, though they made great havoc among the trees, and created terror, they did comparatively little damage to those in close touch with the enemy.

The screaming of the big shells, when they first began to sail over our heads, had the effect of reducing our fire; for they were as fascinating as they were distracting. But we became used to them . . .

As it drew near four o'clock . . . several of our company lagged wearily behind, and the remainder showed, by their drawn faces, the effects of their efforts. Yet, after a short rest, they were able to make splendid spurts. As for myself, I had only one wish, and that was for repose. The long-continued excitement, the successive tautening and relaxing of the nerves, the quenchless thirst, made more intense by the fumes of sulphurous powder, and the caking grime on the lips caused by tearing the paper cartridges, and a ravening hunger, all combined, had reduced me to a walking automaton, and I earnestly wished that night would come. . . .

Finally, about five o'clock, we assaulted and captured a large camp; after driving the enemy well away from it; the front line was as thin as that of a skirmishing body, and we were ordered to retire to the tents.

An hour before dawn, I awoke and, after a hearty replenishment of my vitals with biscuit and molasses, I conceived myself to be fresher than on Sunday morning. While awaiting day-break, I gathered from other early risers their ideas in regard to the events of yesterday. They were under the impression that we had gained a great victory, though we had not, as we had anticipated, reached the Tennessee River. Van Dorn, with his expected reinforcements for us, was not likely to make his appearance for many days yet; and, if General Buell, with his 20,000 troops, had joined the enemy during the night, we had a bad day's work before us. We were short of provisions and ammunition, General Sidney Johnston, our chief Commander, had been killed; but Beauregard was safe and unhurt, and, if Buell was absent, we would win the day.

At daylight I fell in with my Company, but there were only about fifty of the Dixies present.Regiments were hurried into line, but, even to my inexperienced eyes, the troops were in ill-condition for repeating the efforts of Sunday. . . . In consequence of our pickets being driven in on us, we were moved forward in skirmishing order. With my musket on the trail I found myself in active motion, more active than otherwise I would have been, perhaps, because Captain Smith had said, "Now, Mr. Stanley, if you please, step briskly forward!" This singling-out of me wounded my *amour-propre*, and sent me forward like a rocket. In a short time, we met our opponents in the same formation as our selves, and advancing most resolutely. We threw ourselves behind such trees as were near us, fired, loaded, and darted forward to another shelter. Presently, I found myself in an open grassy space, with no convenient tree or stump near; but, seeing a shallow hollow some twenty paces ahead, I made a dash for it, and plied my musket with haste.

I became so absorbed with some blue figures in front of me, that I did not pay sufficient heed to my companion greys. Seeing my blues in about the same proportion, I assumed that the greys were keeping their position, and never once thought of retreat. However, as, despite our firing, the blues were coming uncomfortably near, I rose from my hollow; but, to my speechless amazement, I found myself a solitary grey, in a line of blue skirmishers! My companions had retreated! The next I heard was, "Down with that gun, Secesh, or I'll drill a hole through you! Drop it, quick!"

Half a dozen of the enemy were covering me at the same instant, and I dropped my weapon, incontinently. Two men sprang at my collar, and marched me, unresisting, into the ranks of the terrible Yankees. I *was a prisoner!*

—*The Autobiography of Sir Henry Morton Stanley*

X.4

AN ILLINOIS PRIVATE FIGHTS AT THE HORNET'S NEST

The hottest fighting in the Battle of Shiloh—and some of the hottest of the whole war—was at the so-called Hornet's Nest, at the center of the Union line. Here Hulbert, W.H.L. Wallace, and Prentiss held out for hours against a series of savage attacks. In the end Wallace was killed, and only a fragment of his regiments succeeded in fighting their way out.

Leander Stillwell, who here tells us how thrilling it was to see the battle flags of the 36th Indiana come on the field, was an

Illinois boy who enlisted at St. Louis in 1862, fought at Shiloh, Corinth, and Vicksburg, and later in Arkansas and Tennessee. His recollections, though written years after the war, are based on letters and diaries.

[April 6, 1862]

We had "turned out" about sunup, answered to roll-call, and had cooked and eaten our breakfast. We had then gone to work, preparing for the regular Sunday morning inspection, which would take place at nine o'clock. The boys were scattered around the company streets and in front of the company parade grounds, engaged in polishing and brightening their muskets, and brushing up and cleaning their shoes, jackets, trousers, and clothing generally.

It was a most beautiful morning. The sun was shining brightly through the trees, and there was not a cloud in the sky. It really seemed like Sunday in the country at home.

During week days there was a continual stream of army wagons going to and from the landing, and the clucking of their wheels, the yells and oaths of the drivers, the cracking of whips, mingled with the braying of mules, the neighing of the horses, the commands of the officers engaged in drilling the men, the incessant hum and buzz of the camps, the blare of bugles, and the roll of drums,—all these made up a prodigious volume of sound that lasted from the coming up to the going-down of the sun. But this morning was strangely still. The wagons were silent, the mules were peacefully munching their hay, and the army teamsters were giving us a rest. I listened with delight to the plaintive, mournful tones of a turtle-dove in the woods close by, while on a dead limb of a tall tree right in the camp a wood-pecker was sounding his "long roll" just as I had heard it beaten by his Northern brothers a thousand times on the trees in the Otter Creek bottom at home.

Suddenly, away off on the right, in the direction of Shiloh church, came a dull, heavy "Pum!" then another, and still another. Every man sprung to his feet as if struck by an electric shock, and we looked inquiringly into one another's faces. "What

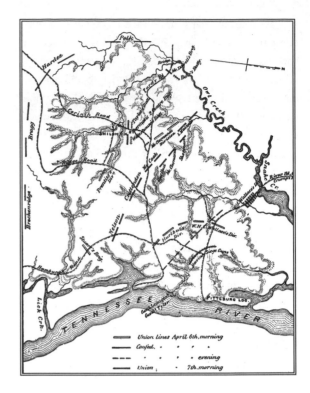

BATTLE OF SHILOH

is that?" asked every one but no one answered. Those heavy booms then came thicker and faster, and just a few seconds after we heard that first dull, ominous growl off to the southwest, came a low, sullen, continuous roar. There was no mistaking that sound. That was not a squad of pickets emptying their guns on being relieved from duty; it was the continuous roll of thousands of muskets, and told us that a battle was on.

What I have been describing just now occurred during a few seconds only, and with the roar of musketry the long roll began to beat in our camp. Then ensued a scene of desperate haste, the like of which I certainly had never seen before nor ever saw again. I remember that in the midst of this terrible uproar and confusion, while the boys were buckling on their cartridge boxes, and before even the companies had been formed, a mounted staff officer came galloping wildly down the line from the right. He checked and whirled his horse sharply around right in our company street, the iron bound hoofs of his steed crashing among the tin plates lying in a little pile where my mess had eaten its breakfast that morning. The horse was flecked with foam and its eyes and nostrils were red as blood. The officer cast one hurried glance around him, and exclaimed: "My God! this regiment not in line yet! They have been fighting on the right over an hour!" And wheeling his horse, he disappeared in the direction of the colonel's tent . . .

Well, the companies were formed, we marched out on the regimental parade ground, and the regiment was formed in line. The command was given: "Load at will; load!" We had anticipated this, however, as the most of us had instinctively loaded our guns before we had formed company. All this time the roar on the right was getting nearer and louder. Our old colonel rode up close to us, opposite the center of the regimental line, and called out, "Attention, battalion!" We fixed our eyes on him to hear what was coming. It turned out to be the old man's battle harangue.

"Gentlemen," said he, in a voice that every man in the regiment heard, "remember your State, and do your duty to day like brave men."

That was all. . . . Immediately after the colonel had given us his brief exhortation, the regiment was marched across the little field I have before mentioned, and we took our place in line of battle, the woods in front of us, and the open field in our rear. We "dressed on" the colors, ordered arms, and stood awaiting the attack. By this time the roar on the right had become terrific. The Rebel army was unfolding its front, and the battle was steadily advancing in our direction. We could begin to see the blue rings of smoke curling upward among the trees off to the right, and the pungent smell of burning gun-powder filled the air. As the roar came travelling down the line from the right it reminded me (only it was a million times louder) of the sweep of a thunder-shower in summer-time over the hard ground of a stubble-field.

And there we stood, in the edge of the woods, so still, waiting for the storm to break on us. . . . The time we thus stood, waiting the attack, could not have exceeded five minutes. Suddenly, oblique-

ly to our right, there was a long, wavy flash of bright light, then another, and another! It was the sunlight shining on gun barrels and bayonets— and—there they were at last! A long brown line, with muskets at a right shoulder shift, in excellent order, right through the woods they came.

We began firing at once. From one end of the regiment to the other leaped a sheet of red flame, and the roar that went up from the edge of that old field doubtless advised General Prentiss of the fact that the Rebels had at last struck the extreme left of his line. We had fired but two or three rounds when, for some reason—I never knew what,—we were ordered to fall back across the field, and did so. The whole line, so far as I could see to the right, went back. We halted on the other side of the field, in the edge of the woods, in front of our tents, and again began firing. The Rebels, of course, had moved up and occupied the line we had just abandoned. And here we did our first hard fighting during the day. Our officers said, after the battle was over, that we held this line an hour and ten minutes. How long it was I do not know. I "took no note of time."

We retreated from this position as our officers afterward said, because the troops on our right had given way, and we were flanked. Possibly those boys on our right would give the same excuse for their leaving, and probably truly, too. Still, I think we did not fall back a minute too soon. As I rose from the comfortable log from behind which a bunch of us had been firing, I saw men in gray and brown clothes, with trailed muskets, running through the camp on our right, and I saw something else, too, that sent a chill all through me. It was a kind of flag I had never seen before. It was a gaudy sort of thing, with red bars. It flashed over me in a second that that thing was a Rebel flag. It was not more than sixty yards to the right. The smoke around it was low and dense and kept me from seeing the man who was carrying it, but I plainly saw the banner. It was going fast, with a jerky motion, which told me that the bearer was on a double-quick. About that time we left. We observed no kind of order in leaving; the main thing was to get out of there as quick as we could. I ran down our company street, and in passing the big Sibley tent of our mess I thought of my knapsack with all my traps and belongings, including that precious little packet of letters from home. I said to myself, "I will save my knapsack, anyhow;" but one quick backward glance over my left shoulder made me change my mind, and I went on. I never saw my knapsack or any of its contents afterwards.

Our broken forces halted and re-formed about half a mile to the rear of our camp on the summit of a gentle ridge, covered with thick brush. I recognized our regiment by the little gray pony the old colonel rode, and hurried to my place in the ranks. Standing there with our faces once more to the front I saw a seemingly endless column of men in blue, marching by the flank, who were filing off to the right through the woods, and I heard our old German adjutant, Cramer, say to the colonel, "Dose are de troops of Sheneral Hurlbut. He is forming a new line dere in de bush." I exclaimed to myself from the bottom of my heart, "Bully for General Hurlbut and the new line in the bush! Maybe we'll whip 'em yet." I shall never forget my feelings about this time. I was astonished at our first retreat in the morning across the field back to our camp, but it occurred to me that maybe that was only "strategy" and all done on purpose; but when we had to give up our camp, and actually turn our backs and run half a mile, it seemed to me that we were forever disgraced, and I kept thinking to myself: "What will they say about this at home?"

I was very dry for a drink, and as we were doing nothing, just then, I slipped out of ranks and ran down to the little hollow in our rear, in search of water. Finding a little pool, I threw myself on the ground and took a copious draught. As I rose to my feet, I observed an officer about a rod above me also quenching his thirst, holding his horse meanwhile by the bridle. As he rose I saw it was our old adjutant. At no other time would I have dared accost him unless in the line of duty, but the situation made me bold.

"Adjutant," I said, "What does this mean—our having to run this way? Ain't we whipped?"

He blew the water from his mustache, and quickly answered in a careless way: "Oh, no; dat is all ride. We yoost fall back to form on the reserve. Sheneral Buell vas now crossing der river mit 50,000 men, and vill be here pooty quick; and Sheneral Lew Vallace is coming up from Crump's Landing mit 15,000 more. Ve vips 'em; ve vips 'em. Go to your gompany.". . . But as the long hours wore on that day, and still Buell and Wallace did not come, my faith in the adjutant's veracity became considerably shaken.

It was at this point that my regiment was detached from Prentiss' division and served with it no more that day. We were sent some distance to the right to support a battery, the name of which I never learned. It was occupying the summit of a slope, and was actively engaged when we reached it. We were put in position of about twenty rods in the rear of the battery, and ordered to lie flat on the ground. The ground sloped gently down in our direction, so that by hugging it close, the rebel shot and shell went over us.

It was here, at about ten o'clock in the morning, that I first saw Grant that day. He was on horseback, of course, accompanied by his staff, and was evidently making a personal examination of his lines. He went by us in a gallop, riding between us and the battery, at the head of his staff. The battery was then hotly engaged; shot and shell were whizzing overhead, and cutting off the limbs of trees, but Grant rode through the storm with perfect indifference, seemingly paying no more attention to the missiles than if they had been paper wads.

We remained in support of this battery until about 2 o'clock in the afternoon. We were then put in motion by the right flank, filed to the left, crossed the left-hand Corinth road; then we were thrown into the line by the command: "By the left flank, march." We crossed a little ravine and up a slope, and relieved a regiment on the left of Hurlbut's line. This line was desperately engaged, and had been at this point, as we afterwards learned, for fully four hours. I remember as we went up the slope and began firing, about the first thing that met my gaze was what out West we would call a "windrow" of dead men in blue; some doubled up face downward, others with their white faces upturned to the sky, brave boys who had been shot to death in "holding the line." Here we stayed until our last cartridge was shot away. We were then relieved by another regiment. We filled our cartridge boxes again and went back to the support of our battery. The boys laid down and talked in low tones. Many of our comrades alive and well an hour ago, we had left dead on that bloody ridge. And still the battle raged. From right to left, everywhere, it was one never-ending, terrible roar, with no prospect of stopping.

Somewhere between 4 and 5 o'clock, as near as I can tell, everything became ominously quiet. Our battery ceased firing; the gunners leaned against the pieces and talked and laughed. Suddenly a staff officer rode up and said something in a low tone to the commander of the battery, then rode to our colonel and said something to him. The battery horses were at once brought up from a ravine in the rear, and the battery limbered up and moved off through the woods diagonally to the left and rear. We were put in motion by the flank and followed it. Everything kept so still, the loudest noise I heard was the clucking of the wheels of the gun-carriages and caissons as they wound through the woods. We emerged from the woods and entered a little old field. I then saw at our right and front lines of men in blue moving in the same direction we were, and it was evident that we were falling back.

All at once, on the right, the left, and from our recent front, come one tremendous roar, and the bullets fell like hail. The lines took the double-quick towards the rear. For awhile the attempt was made to fall back in order, and then everything went to pieces. My heart failed me utterly. I thought the day was lost. A confused mass of men and guns, caissons, army wagons, ambulances, and all the debris of a beaten army surged and crowded along the narrow dirt road to the landing, while that pitiless storm of leaden hail came crashing on us from the rear. It was undoubtedly at this crisis in our affairs that the division of General Prentiss was captured. . . .

It must have been when we were less than half a mile from the landing on our disorderly retreat before mentioned, that we saw standing in line of battle, at ordered arms, extending from both sides of the road until lost to sight in the woods, a long well-ordered line of men in blue. What did that mean? and where had they come from? I was walking by the side of Enoch Wallace, the orderly sergeant of my company. . . . Even he, in the face of this seemingly ap palling state of things, had evidently lost heart.

I said to him: "Enoch, what are those men there for?"

He answered in a low tone: "I guess they are put there to hold the Rebels in check till the army can get across the river."

And doubtless that was the thought of every intelligent soldier in our beaten column. And yet it goes to show how little the common soldier knew of the actual situation. We did not know then that this line was the last line of battle of the "Fighting Fourth Division" under General Hurlbut; that on its right was the division of McClernand, the Fort Donelson boys; that on its right, at right angles to it, and, as it were, the refused wing of the army, was glorious old Sherman, hanging on with a bulldog grip to the road across Snake Creek from Crump's Landing by which Lew Wallace was coming with 5,000 men. In other words, we still had an unbroken line confronting the enemy, made up of men who were not yet ready, by any manner of means, to give up that they were whipped . . .

Well, we filed through Hurlbut's line, halted, re-formed, and faced to the front once more. We were put in place a short distance in the rear of Hurlbut, as a support to some heavy guns. It must have been about five o'clock now. Suddenly, on the extreme left, and just a little above the landing, came a deafening explosion that fairly shook the ground beneath our feet, followed by others in quick and regular succession. The look of wonder and inquiry that the soldiers' faces wore for a moment disappeared for one of joy and exultation as it flashed across our minds that the gunboats had at last joined hands in the dance, and were pitching big twenty-pound Parrott shells up the ravine in front of Hurlbut, to the terror and discomfiture of our adversaries.

The last place my regiment assumed was close to the road coming up from the landing. As we were lying there I heard the strains of martial music and saw a body of men marching by the flank up the road. I slipped out of ranks and walked out to the side of the road to see what troops they were. Their band was playing "Dixie's Land," and playing it well. The men were marching at a quick step, carrying their guns, cartridge-boxes, haversacks, canteens, and blanket-rolls. I saw that they had not been in the fight, for there was no powder-smoke on their faces. "What regiment is this?" I asked of a young sergeant marching on the flank. Back came the answer in a quick, cheery tone. "The 36th Indiana, the advance guard of Buell's army."

I did not, on hearing this, throw my cap into the air and yell. That would have given those Indiana fellows a chance to chaff and guy me, and possibly make sarcastic remarks, which I did not care to provoke. I gave one big, gasping swallow and stood still, but the blood thumped in the veins of my throat and my heart fairly pounded against my little infantry jacket in the joyous rapture of this glorious intelligence. Soldiers need not be told of the thrill of unspeakable exultation they have all felt at the sight of armed friends in danger's darkest hour. Speaking for myself alone, I can only say, in the most heart-felt sincerity, that in all my obscure military career, never to me was the sight of reinforcing legions so precious and so welcome as on that Sunday evening when the rays of the descending sun were flashed back from the bayonets of Buell's advance column as it deployed on the bluffs of Pittsburg Landing.

—Stillwell, *The Story of a Common Soldier of Army Life in the Civil War*

X.5

The Orphan Brigade is Shattered at Stones River

After Shiloh Braxton Bragg was appointed to command the Army of Tennessee. When Halleck detached Buell for an advance on Chattanooga, Bragg took some 40,000 men and got there before him. From September through December 1863 there was confused marching and countermarching through central Kentucky and Tennessee. One detachment of Bragg's army, under Kirby Smith, reached Frankfort, Kentucky, and inaugurated a secession government in that state. Buell advanced on the Confederates there, and on October 8 struck them at Perryville; the battle was a draw but the Confederates retired into East Tennessee and then to Murfreesboro, on the Stones River, not far from Nashville. Meantime Rosecrans had supplanted Buell in command of the newly organized army of the Cumberland. He built up supplies at Nashville and, when he was ready, moved out to fight Bragg.

The two armies met December 31, outside Murfreesboro, and one of the most bitterly contested battles of the war ensued. It was, in a sense, another Shiloh. Bragg got the jump on Rosecrans, smashed his right flank, and rolled him up against Stones River. Just as disaster threatened the whole Federal army Thomas turned his artillery on the enemy and held him in check. The next day the Confederates renewed the battle, but the most desperate effort came on the third day, January 2, when the misguided Bragg ordered Breckinridge to attack the Union left.

Lieutenant L. D. Young of the 4th Kentucky "Orphan Brigade" tells the story of the futile attack.

Captain Bramblett with two of his lieutenants, myself one of them, crawled through the weeds a distance of several hundred yards to a prominent point of observation from which through his field glass and even the naked eye we could see the enemy's concentrated forces near and above the lower ford on the opposite side of the river, his artillery being thrown forward and nearest to the river. His artillery appeared to be close together and covering quite a space of ground; we could not tell how many guns, but there was quite a number. The infantry was seemingly in large force and extended farther down toward the ford.

Captain Bramblett was a man of no mean order of military genius and information, and after looking at, and studying the situation in silence for some minutes, he said to us boys, "that he believed Rosecrans was setting a trap for Bragg." Continuing, he said, "If he means to attack us on this side, why does he not reinforce on this side? Why concentrate so much artillery on the bluff yonder? He must be expecting us to attack that force yonder, pointing to Beatty's position on the hill North of us, and if we do, he will use that artillery on us as we move to the attack." At another time during the afternoon I heard him while discussing the situation with other officers of the regiment use substantially the same argument. I accompanied Captain Bramblett to General Breckinridge's headquarters and heard him make substantially in detail a report containing the facts above recited. . . .

General Breckinridge, to thoroughly and unmistakably understand the situation and satisfy himself, in company with one or two of his staff examined the situation as best he could and I presume reached the same conclusion, and when he (Breckinridge) repaired to Bragg's headquarters and vouchsafed this information and suggested the presumptive plan of the enemy, Bragg said: "Sir, my information is different. I have given the order to attack the enemy in your front and expect it to be obeyed."

What was General Breckinridge to do but attempt to carry out his orders, though in carrying out this unwise and ill conceived order it should cost in one hour and ten minutes 1,700 of as brave and chivalrous soldiers as the world ever saw. What a terrible blunder, what a bloody and useless sacrifice!. . .

How was this wicked and useless sacrifice brought about? "That subordinate must always obey his superior"—is the military law. In furtherance of Bragg's order we were assembled about three o'clock on the afternoon of January 2, 1863 (Friday, a day of ill luck) in a line North of and to the right of Swain's hill, confronting Beatty's and Growes' brigades, with a battery or two of artillery as support. They being intended for the bait that had been thrown across the river at the lower ford, and

now occupied an eminence some three-quarters of a mile to the right-front of the Orphan's position on Swain's hill.

This was the force, small as it was that Bragg was so anxious to dislodge. Between the attacking line and federal position was a considerable scope of open ground, fields and pastures, with here and there a clump of bushes or briars, but the entire space was in full view of and covered by the enemy's batteries to the left of the line on the opposite side of the river previously referred to. If the reader will only carry these positions in his eye, he can readily discover the jaws of the trap in this murderous scheme.

A more imposing and thoroughly disciplined line of soldiers never moved to the attack of an enemy than responded to the signal gun stationed immediately in our rear, which was fired exactly at four o'clock. Every man vieing with his fellowman, in steadiness of step and correct alignment, with the officers giving low and cautionary commands, many knowing that it was their last hour on earth, but without hesitating moved forward to their inevitable doom and defeat. We had gotten only fairly started, when the great jaws of the trap on the bluff from the opposite side of the river were sprung, and bursting shells that completely drowned the voice of man were plunging and tearing through our columns, ploughing up the earth at our feet in front and behind, everywhere. But with steadiness of step we moved on. Two companies of the Fourth regiment, my own and adjoining company, encountered a pond, and with a dexterous movement known to the skilled officer and soldier was cleared in a manner that was perfectly charming, obliquing to the right and left into line as soon as passed.

By reason of the shorter line held by the enemy, our line, which was much longer and the colors of each of our battalions being directed against this shorter line, caused our lines to interlap, making it necessary, in order to prevent confusion and crowding, that some of the regiments halt, until the others had passed forward out of the way. When thus halted they would lie down in order to shield them selves from the enemy infantry fire in front, who had by this time opened a lively fusillade from behind-their temporary works.

While lying on the ground momentarily . . . a shell exploded right in the middle of the company, almost literally tearing it to pieces. When I recovered from the shock the sight I witnessed was appalling. Some eighteen or twenty men hurled in every direction, including my dear friend, Lieut. George Burnley of Frankfort. But these circumstances were occurring every minute now while the battle was raging all around and about us. Men moved intuitively—the voice being silenced by the whizzing and bursting shells. On we moved, Beatty's and Growes' lines giving way seemingly to allow the jaws of the trap to press with more and ever increasing vigor upon its unfortunate and discomfited victims. But, on we moved, until the survivors of the decoy had passed the river and over the lines stationed on the other side of the river, when their new line of infantry opened on our confused and disordered columns another destructive and ruinous fire.

Coupled with this condition and correlative to it, a battery of Growes and a part of their infantry had been cut off from the ford and seeing our confused condition, rallied, re formed and opened fire on our advanced right now along the river bank. Confronted in front by their infantry, with the river intervening; swept by their artillery from the left and now attacked by both infantry and artillery by an oblique fire from the right, we found ourselves in a helpless condition, from which it looked like an impossibility to escape; and but for the fact that two or three batteries had been ordered into position to check the threatened advance of the enemy and thereby distract their attention, we doubtless would have fared still worse.

We rallied some distance to the right of where we started and found that many, very many, of our noblest, truest and best had fallen. Some of them were left on the field, among whom was my military preceptor, advisor and dear friend, Captain Bramblett, who fell into the hands of the enemy and who died a few days after in Nashville. I shall never forget our parting, a moment or two before he received his wound—never forget the last quick glance and the circumstances that called it forth. He was a splendid soldier and his loss grieved me very much. Many another gallant Kentuckian, some of our finest line and field officers, were left on the field, a sacrifice to stupidity and revenge. Thirty-seven per cent in one hour and ten minutes—some say one hour—was the frightful summary. Among the first of these was the gallant and illustrious Hanson, whose coolness and bearing was unsurpassed and whose loss was irreparable. He with Breckinridge, understood and was fully sensible of—as indicated by the very seriousness of his countenance—the unwisdom of this move and as shown in their protest to Bragg. What a pity that a strict observance of military rule compelled it to be obeyed against his mature military mind and judgment, causing the loss of such a magnificent soldier and gentleman—uselessly and foolishly.

Contemplating this awful sacrifice, as he rode by the dead and dying in the rear of our lines, General Breckinridge, with tears falling from his eyes, was heard to say in tones of anguish, "My poor Orphans! My poor Orphans!" little thinking that he was dedicating to them a name that will live through out the annals of time and crown the history of that dear little band with everlasting immortality.

—YOUNG, *Reminiscences of a Soldier in the Orphan Brigade*

— XI —

THE STRUGGLE FOR
MISSOURI AND THE WEST

The war in the Trans-Mississippi West has been unjustly neglected by historians. The outcome of the war was decided, to be sure, in the East—at Gettysburg and Vicksburg, at Chattanooga and Atlanta and the Wilderness—yet the fighting in the West profoundly influenced the course of these Eastern campaigns, and some of these campaigns, in turn, were directed to the severance of the Confederacy along the Mississippi River.

It was Missouri that was crucial. Had that state gone with the Confederacy the consequences would have been grave and might have been decisive. It outflanked Illinois and the Northwest; controlled the Mississippi; conditioned the fighting in Kentucky and Tennessee. And there was, from the beginning, a likely chance that Missouri would throw in its lot with the Confederacy, or yield to Confederate invasion. It was a slave state; a substantial part of its population was of Southern origin; its government was in the hands of Confederate sympathizers. Fortunately northern Missouri and the large German population were pro-Union; fortunately, too, the powerful Blair family was unalterably opposed to secession.

But at the beginning it was touch and go, and indeed it remained that until the war was well under way. Prompt action saved the St. Louis arsenal for the Union; prompt action, too, prevented Governor Jackson from using Camp Jackson as a rallying center for a secession movement. Meantime the Confederate forces grew apace, and in the fighting of the first year the Confederates had the best of it. Not until the Battle of Pea Ridge, in Arkansas, was Missouri safe for the Union, and even after that Sterling Price and Ben McCulloch, the bold Confederate leaders, tried one invasion after another. Even as late as summer of 1864 there was a major battle along the Missouri-Kansas boundary line at Westport, the "Gettysburg of the West." Meantime Missouri was the scene of the most desperate guerrilla and partisan fighting of the war: no other theater of the war could confess anything like the Lawrence and Baxter Springs massacres.

Much of the fighting in Arkansas was part of the Missouri campaign, and Arkansas, too, saw bitter guerrilla warfare. The campaigns along the Red River were part of the larger campaign for the control of the Mississippi. As the Federals closed both the lower and the upper portions of the Mississippi, the only major route from the West to the eastern Confederacy was the Red River, and the Confederate forces in Louisiana threatened New Orleans, Baton Rouge, and even the Vicksburg expedition, from the Red River valley. There was, as we shall see, a good deal of marching and some fighting in the Bayou Teche country west of New Orleans.

Even the Far West boasted its campaigns. The Confederacy obtained substantial supplies through Mexico, and in the fall and winter of 1863 Banks had occupied Brownsville at the mouth of the Rio Grande and a number of harbors along the coast to Corpus Christi. In distant New Mexico, too, there was a campaign which ended disastrously for Confederate arms.

In a sense all the miscellaneous fighting over this vast area constitutes one great campaign for the control of the West and of the supplies and men that might come from the West to the East. At the risk therefore of cutting across or violating chronology, we present the various segments of the Trans-Mississippi fighting geographically rather than chronologically.

— XI. I —

COTTON IS KING AT THE
BATTLE OF LEXINGTON

On June 12, 1861, Governor Jackson of Missouri abandoned his pretense of neutrality and declared openly for the Confederacy, calling for 50,000 volunteers to defend the state against the

Federal invaders. Not that many were forthcoming, but Sterling Price gathered an army of perhaps 10,000, and was shortly reinforced from Arkansas by Ben McCulloch, a famous Texas Ranger. Nathaniel Lyon moved speedily to get control of the state capital, Jefferson City! then sent General Franz Sigel after Price. The two small armies met at Carthage, on the edge of the Ozarks, and Sigel was roundly beaten. Lyon himself came up to take command, followed the Confederates to Wilson's Creek, and—though outnumbered almost two to one—attacked them, August 10, 1861. The gallant Lyon was killed, and his beaten army fell back on Rolla, which had direct railroad connections with St. Louis. The Confederates marched north to the Missouri, by-passed Jefferson City, and attacked a small force of Federals at Lexington. It was another Confederate victory. After that the incompetent Frémont was removed from command in the West, and the Union organized its strength to drive the Confederates out of Missouri.

This story of the Battle of Lexington is told by an Englishman, Samuel P. Day, correspondent for the *London Morning Herald*.

The Union forces, under Colonel Mulligan . . . had for some time previous occupied the town of Lexington, around which they had erected defences. On the night of the 11th September [1861] the attack was initiated by an advance party of Confederate troops, who appeared in front of the Federal entrenchments, when a sharp action took place. Four cannons were planted, so as to command the different points, including the entire semi-circle of the Federal position, and a falling fire was kept up in addition to an incessant discharge of musketry. The Confederates rendered themselves almost invisible, being concealed in the adjacent corn-fields and woods; so the attacked party had no other means of doing execution among them, than by firing in the neighbourhood of the localities designated by the cannon smoke, and now and again taking aim at the sharp-shooters who had ventured out of ambush. . .

On the morning of Wednesday the 17th, the Confederates, under General Price, opened fire from all their batteries, and kept pouring in a shower of iron hail the entire day upon the enemy's entrenchments; while the practice of the sharp-shooters was excellent, as has been acknowledged by the enemy himself. Some time

after the siege had commenced, with a praiseworthy humanity General Price sent a flag of truce to Colonel Mulligan, demanding a surrender, and informing him, that as the force he commanded was so superior as to render it useless for him to contend, he had no desire to fight for the sake of shedding blood. He proposed, moreover, to allow the Federal forces to march out of the town under arms, taking their property and baggage with them. All that General Price required was the position; and, this yielded, General Mulligan was free to go with his command wherever he pleased. Half-way between the lines both Generals met, attended by their respective Staff-officers. General Mulligan was obstinate, and would not accept the liberal proposition made to him. They separated, however, in a seemingly friendly manner, and with mutual expressions of regret that the fortunes of war had made their interest so antagonistic and deadly.

During the afternoon of the 18th a hand-to-hand conflict took place, which was but of short duration, when the Con federate troops attacked and carried a portion of the works. Advancing in a strong and steady line up a slope, after slight opposition they caused the Montgomery Guards to break from their entrenchments and retire in disorder before their approach. A murderous volley was then poured into the dispersed ranks, inflicting the heaviest loss that had been experienced since the opening of the siege. Colonel Mulligan endeavoured to rally his men for a charge, but few of them responded to his call.

Hot shot and shell kept pouring into the town, one ball having fired the College building, in which the Federal provisions had been collected. Nevertheless, the troops succeeded in saving the stores and extinguishing the conflagration. From eight o'clock until midnight was occupied by both belligerents in burying their dead. When the truce had expired, the cannonade opened again with additional vigour on the Confederate side, which the enemy did not reply to until the morning. So soon as daybreak had revealed localities sufficiently to afford correct aim, the cannonading became more furious still. The firing on both sides was continuous and furious, and nothing could be heard save the heavy boom of artillery and the sharp clank of musketry.

The ingenuity of the Southerners was conspicuously manifested by the invention of a moving breast-work of cotton bales, which received the Federal shot harmlessly, and completely protected the troops from injury. The effect created by this novel appliance of warfare may be estimated by the following account furnished by the Correspondent of a Northern journal:—

"At this juncture our men discovered, with no little dismay, an engine of war. which was being brought to bear upon them, threatening the very consequences which they dreaded most: a safe approach or the enemy, and an ultimate charge in force over the entrenchments. The rebels presented a strong breast-work of hemp-bales, which appeared like a moving barrier, impenetrable to bullets or cannon shot, and swarming with men in the rear. It was about twenty rods in length, and the height of two bales of hemp. The bales were placed with the ends facing our fortifications, affording a thickness of about six feet. This immense breast-work commenced moving forward, not by detachments or singly, but in one vast body, unbroken and steady, as though it slid along the ground at its own volition. It advanced steadily over the smooth surface, parting to pass trees, and closing up again, as impenetrable as a rock. Behind it were hundreds of men pushing and urging with levers, while others held the bales steadily to their places, and others still, whose numbers were almost indefinite, firing between the crevices and over the top at our soldiers.

"Our men looked at the moving monster in astonishment. It lay like a large serpent, winding over the hills and hollows, apparently motionless, yet moving broadside on, to envelop and destroy them in its vast folds. In vain the cannon were turned upon it. The heavy bales absorbed the shot harmlessly, or quietly resumed the positions from which they were displaced, seemingly moving without hands, but in reality controlled by strong arms, which were unseen. In vain the musket bullets rained upon it in unremitting showers. The thousands that it concealed were safe from such puny assaults, and slowly gliding along, they waited with eagerness the time when their position should warrant them in bursting through its walls and storming up to the intrenchments. Our brave soldiers could only watch it with keen anxiety, and wait for the fearful result."

After having been desperately attacked upon various sides, and finding it useless to resist, about four o'clock on the afternoon of Wednesday, Major Becker, who commanded the Home Guards, crawled out to an advanced breast-work, and ran up a white flag.

The Home Guards deserted their trenches at the order of Major Becker, and rushed into the inner fortification, where they again raised the white flag, and kept it flying. Immediately upon this the Confederates ceased firing, and the garrison was thrown into the greatest confusion. Word was passed around that a surrender had been made, and the men left their entrenchments in disorder to ascertain the truth. Consternation reigned in all directions—Colonel Mulligan, it is said, being on the opposite side, and nobody present to assume control. Word was sent to him, and he ordered the flag down; but the Captains, who by this time realized their true position, and saw nothing but death or surrender before them, implored him to save the men.

Meanwhile the hemp breast-works had moved up under cover of the general confusion, until they had got within a few yards of the Federal entrenchments. The Confederate forces advanced, and everything indicated that the moment had arrived when the crowning assault was to be attempted. In this emergency Colonel Mulligan ordered his men to lay down their arms, and an officer was dispatched to General Price with a flag of truce.

—DAY, *Down South*

XI.2

Guerrilla Warfare in Missouri

This long succession of Confederate victories heartened Southern sympathizers not only in Missouri but in Kansas and Arkansas as well. Guerrilla bands harried Union sympathizers everywhere, and some of them were not too careful whom they attacked; from Kansas came the Jay Hawkers—a term applied indiscriminately to Unionists and Confederates—to join in the civil war.

This account of guerrilla warfare comes from Colonel Monks and describes conditions in Ozark County, on the Arkansas border, in 1862.

The rebels being encouraged by the late victory, determined to rid the country of all Union men at once. About that time about 350 men, mostly from Oregon country, commanded by two very prominent men, made a scout into Ozark county, Mo. On reaching the North Fork of White River they went into camp at what was known as Jesse James' mill. The owner, a man of about 55 or 60 years of age, as good a man as resided in Ozark county, was charged with grinding corn for Union men and their families; at the time he and a man by the name of Brown were cutting saw logs about two miles from home in the pinery. They went out and arrested them, arrested an old man by the name of Russell and several others, carried them to a man's house, who was a Union man, and had fled to prevent arrest. They took Brown and James about 300 yards from the house, procured a rope, hunted a long limb of a tree, rolled a big rock up to the tree where the first rope was tied to the limb, placed the noose about James' neck, stood him on the rock, rolled the rock out from under him and left him swinging, rolled the rock to the next rope, stood Brown on it, placed the noose around his neck, rolled the rock out and left Brown swinging in the air, went to the third rope, placed Russell on the rock, and just as they aimed to adjust the noose, word came that the home guards and Federals were right upon them in considerable force. They fled, leaving Russell standing

upon the rock and both Brown and James dangling in the air.

Every Union man now having fled in fear of his life, the next day the wives of Brown and James, with the help of a few other women, buried them as best they could. They dug graves underneath the swinging bodies, laid bed clothing in the graves and cut them loose. The bodies fell into the coffinless graves and the earth was replaced. So the author is satisfied that the bones of these men still remain in the lonely earth underneath where they met their untimely death with no charge against them except that they had been feeding Union men, with no one to bury them but their wives and a few other women who aided. . . .

A short time after this hanging there was a man by the name of Rhodes, who resided at the head of Bennett's Bayou in Howell County. He was about eighty years of age and had been a soldier under General Jackson. His head was perfectly white and he was very feeble. When he heard of the hanging of Brown and James he said openly that there was no civil war in that, and that the men who did it were guilty of murder.

Some two weeks from the date of the hanging of Brown and James, about twenty-five men, hearing of what he had said, organized themselves and commanded by Dr. Nunly and William Sapp, proceeded to the house of Rhodes, where he and his aged wife resided alone, calling him out and told him they wanted him to go with them. His aged wife came out, and being acquainted with a part of the men, and knowing that they had participated in the hanging and shooting of a number of Union men, talked with them and asked: "You are not going to hurt my old man?" They said: "We just want him to go a piece with us over here." Ordering the old man to come along, they went over to a point about a quarter of a mile from the house and informed him of what he had said. There they shot him, cut his ears off and his heart out. Dr. Nunly remarked that he was going to take the heart home with him, pickle it and keep it so people could see how a black Republican's heart looked.

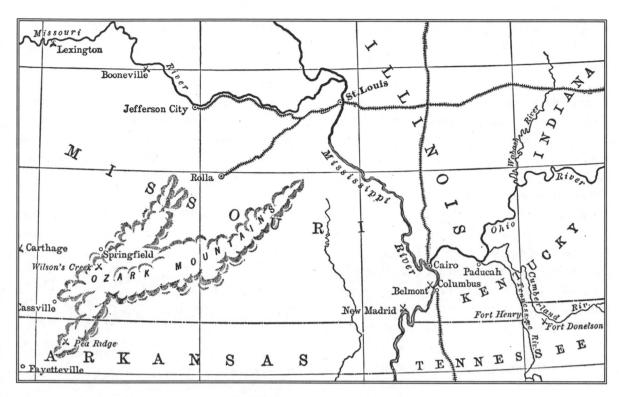

THE STRATEGIC POSITION OF MISSOURI

In the meantime, Rhodes not having returned home, and not a single Union man left in the country that Mrs. Rhodes could get to look after him, and having heard when they reached Joseph Spears' that the old man was not with them, although very feeble, she still continued the search; on the second day, about fifty yards from the road and about a quarter of a mile from home, she heard hogs squealing and grunting as though they were eating something. She proceeded to the place and found the hogs were just about to commence eating the remains of her husband. The Union men having fled, she notified some of the neighbors, and the women came in and helped dress the body and buried him the best they could.

There never was a man arrested by the Confederate authorities, or a single word of condemnation uttered, but as far as could be heard there was general approval. It was said that the means were desperate, but that was the only way to get rid of the men and strike terror to them so they could neither give aid nor countenance to the lop-eared Dutch. . . .

After they had hung, shot, and captured and driven from the country all of the Union men, they called a public meeting for the purpose of taking into consideration what should be done with the families of the Union men, which meeting had a number of preachers in it. After discussing the premises, they arrived at the conclusion that if they let the families of the Union men, who had escaped and gone into the Federal lines, remain, they would return and bring in the lop-eared Dutch. They didn't believe that both parties could ever live together, and as they now had the country completely rid of the Union men, they would force their families to leave. They at once appointed men, among whom were several preachers, to go to each one of the Union families and notify them that they would not be allowed to remain; because if they let them stay, their men would be trying to come back, and they didn't believe both parties could live together. They stated at the same time that they were really sorry for the women and children, but nobody was to blame but their husbands and sons, who had cast their lot with the lop-eared Dutch. Also, as they had taken up arms against the Confederate States, all the property they had, both real and personal, was subject to confiscation and belonged to the Confederate authorities; but they would allow them to take enough of their property to carry them inside the lines of the lop-eared Dutch, where they supposed their men were and where they could care for them.

They said they might have a reasonable time to make preparations to leave the country, and if they didn't leave, they would be forced to do so, if they had to arrest them and carry them out.

The wildest excitement then prevailed among the women and children. They had no men to transact their business and make preparations to leave. Little had they thought, while they were chasing, arresting, hanging and shooting their men, that they, too, would become victims of the rebel hatred and be forced to leave house and home, not knowing where their men were or whether they were dead or alive. All they knew of their whereabouts was, that those who escaped arrest had left their homes, aiming to reach the nearest Federal lines.

Women were at once dispatched to reach the nearest Federal lines, if possible, and inform them of the Confederate order, and procure help to take them out. Their homes and houses were being continually raided by small bands of Confederates roaming over the country, claiming that they were hunting Union men, taking all classes of property that they might see proper to take, without any restraint whatever.

The suffering that followed the women and children is indescribable. They had to drive their own teams, take care of the little ones, travel through the storms, exposed to it all without a man to help them, nor could they hear a single word of comfort spoken by husband, son or friend. On reaching the Federal lines, all vacant houses and places of shelter were soon filled, and they were known and styled as refugees. Many of them went into soldier huts, where the soldiers had wintered and covered the tops of their huts with earth. They had to leave home with a small amount of rations, and on the road the rebels would stop them and make them divide up the little they had started with, and reaching the Federal lines they would be almost destitute of food and many of them very scantily clothed.

—MONKS, "A History of Southern Missouri and Northern Arkansas"

— XI.3 —

THE TIDE TURNS AT PEA RIDGE

Halleck was now in command in the West. In December he sent Pope out with greatly strengthened forces to restore Union-control of northern and central Missouri. Price had retreated to Springfield; he now moved southward to Arkansas where he was joined by Ben McCulloch with a force that included some 5,000 Indians from the Five Civilized Nations. Their combined force numbered over 20,000, and was under the command of General Van Dorn. After him went General Samuel Curtis. The two armies met at Pea Ridge, Arkansas, at the southernmost tip of the Ozarks. With almost a two-to-one superiority Van Dorn thought it safe to divide his army and try an attack from front and rear. The attempt miscarried. While the Confederate left flank was successful, the right under McCulloch was thrown back with heavy loss. The next day, March 8, 1862, Curtis extended his line around both Confederate flanks, enfiladed the Confederates with artillery fire, and forced them to retreat. It was a decisive victory; thereafter Missouri was safe for the Union.

General Franz Sigel, who tells this story, was one of the noble band of '48ers who had fought for liberalism in Germany. He fled to Switzerland and later to England, and came to the United States in 1852. The outbreak of the war found him director of public schools of St. Louis; he was appointed general of the 2nd Missouri Brigade, fought at Pea Ridge, and went with Pope to Virginia. After the war Sigel moved to New York City, where he had a long and distinguished career as editor.

It was a little after 6 o'clock in the morning [March 8] when I sent out Colonel Osterhaus with Captain Asmussen of my staff to reconnoiter the ground on which I intended to deploy, and to find the nearest road leading to it. The 44th Illinois followed the two officers for the purpose of marking the right of the position to be taken, but with orders to keep concealed as much as possible, and not to enter into an engagement unless attacked. Half an hour later, I was standing in front of my tent, ready to mount, and anxiously awaiting the return of the staff-officers, when suddenly a few cannonshots in our front, from Davidson's Union battery, announced the conflict. At this moment General Curtis, to whom I had sent word during the night where my two divisions were assembling, and that they would be ready for action in the morning, rode toward me from the direction where the firing had begun, and, somewhat excitedly, said: "General, I have opened the battle; it will be a hard fight; Davis is already there. Please bring your troops in line as quickly as possible."

I confess that I did not understand the reason why a cannonade was commenced on our side when we were not ready to meet a counter-attack of the enemy with a good chance of success, the more so, as I had been out in our front before General Curtis met me, and had found that our line was weak, stretched out in an open field, the Telegraph road obstructed by artillery, ammunition-wagons, and other vehicles, and that there was no room to deploy my divisions, except behind the first line and masked by it; nor on the left, unless immediately exposed to and raked by the fire of the enemy, whose batteries were supposed to be posted in the margin of the woods, whence they could reach my troops at point-blank range. I explained this to General Curtis, made him acquainted with the object in view, told him that I expected Colonel Osterhaus and Captain Asmussen back every moment, and finally asked him to give me ten minutes' time to wait for them, when I would move immediately to the position selected and commence the attack. Even if our troops on the right should be compelled to yield, it could only be momentarily, as the enemy would

have to direct his whole attention to my attack on his flank and rear. I never felt more relieved than when General Curtis, evidently encouraged by this proposition, said: "Well, General, do what you propose." I must add here that I had not seen General Curtis during the night and before I met him near my tent; he could, therefore, not have been fully aware of what I had experienced in my position away from him on the left, and what my intention was to do in the morning, although I had sent Captain Asmussen to his head quarters to report to him, receiving, however, no orders from him in return. After our conversation, which lasted only a few minutes, the two officers came back in all haste, and reported that they had found an excellent position; that no enemy was in sight, and that Colonel Knobelsdorff, with his regiment, was posted as directed. General Curtis declared himself satisfied and rode off, but scarcely had he left me when the cannonade in front became very brisk, some of the hostile missiles bursting over our heads.

I mounted, told Colonel Osterhaus to take charge of our column and move it to the position to be occupied; then, accompanied by Captain Asmussen, I rode to the front, where Davis's division had formed into line, to see what was going on. I found one of our batteries hotly engaged, but compelled to withdraw, which exposed the infantry on the right to an enfilading fire, and also forced it to change its position. One of the regiments—I think it was the 22d or the 8th Indiana—was thrown into momentary disorder by this surprise, and the men fell back toward an eminence on the right of the road on which I was halting. I assisted their brave commander to rally them, which did not take long, and spoke a few words to them, saying that if the right could hold out for half an hour, assistance would come, and all would be well. Meanwhile another regiment had formed on the left, the battery had taken position again and was sup ported by four other guns (of White's brigade), farther to the left, diverting the enemy's fire.

The line stood firm, and as no hostile infantry appeared, I took leave of the commander of the "Indiana boys," and hastened to my own troops. I reached the head of the column when it was just debouching from the woods, and the first battery that arrived took position on the left of the 44th Illinois, which was kneeling behind a fence. In about 15 minutes the First Division (Osterhaus's) was formed into line, with the artillery in the intervals between the infantry, the Second Division in reserve, about 250 paces behind our right, with General Asboth at its head, who, in spite of his wound received on the 7th, was again in the saddle. Our position, in full view of the open fields, which sloped gently down toward the long skirt of woods, where the enemy's artillery and infantry were posted, was excellent, and allowed the full development of our forces. The enemy's batteries received us well, but many of their shots were either aimed too high, or struck the ground and were buried a short distance in front of us. When well in action, we advanced slowly from position to position, at the same time contracting our line, the infantry following, rising quickly, and as soon as they had reached a new position lying down again. . . .

It was now a little after 11 o'clock; most of the enemy's batteries (about fifty guns) were silenced one after an other, by our concentric fire; his infantry, not venturing out of the woods into the open fields, was now treated with a shower of shell and shrapnel. Opposite our extreme left, how ever, near Elkhorn Tavern, Van Dorn made a determined effort to hold the high spur of hills, the top of which was crowned and protected by rocks and bowlders. Some of Price's infantry had already taken possession of it, and a battery was being placed in position, when Hoffmann's and Elbert's batteries were ordered to direct their fire against them chiefly with solid shot. Not more than fifteen minutes elapsed before the enemy evacuated this last stronghold, while our infantry on the left—the 36th Illinois, and the 2d, 3d, and 17th Missouri—rushed up the steep hill and forced the remnants of the enemy's troops down into Cross Timber Hollow. Almost simultaneously the 12th Missouri, the 25th and the 44th Illinois advanced in double-quick from the center and right into the woods, engaged the enemy's infantry, drove it back, and one of our regiments (the 12th Missouri) captured the "Dallas Battery." On the extreme right, where General Curtis had directed the movements of the troops, Davis's division and a part of Carr's, assisted by Hayden's and Jones's batteries (the latter commanded by Lieutenant David), pushed forward against the left wing of the enemy and forced it to leave the field. The army of Van Dorn and Price, including about two thirds of McCulloch's troops under Churchill and Greer, and one-third of Pike's Indian Brigade, all of whom had joined Price during the night, were now in precipitate retreat in all directions, pursued by the First and Second Divisions as far as Keetsville, 9 miles to the north, and by a cavalry force under Colonel Bussey with 2 mountain howitzers to the south-west beyond Bentonville. So ended the battle of Pea Ridge, and our little army, instead of being "beaten and compelled to surrender," had gained a decisive victory.

—SIGEL, "The Pea Ridge Campaign"

XI.4

THE CONFEDERATES SCATTER AFTER PEA RIDGE

Confederate losses at Pea Ridge had been shattering; the losses on the retreat were doubtless as heavy. Alarmed at the situation in western Tennessee and in Mississippi, the Confederate government ordered Van Dorn to transfer his army to Memphis. This put an effective end to the formal fighting in Arkansas; guerrilla warfare continued.

William Watson, who here tells us something of the re treat and disintegration of Confederate forces after Pea Ridge, was a Scotsman engaged in business at Baton Rouge. He enlisted in the Confederate Army; fought in the Missouri and Arkansas campaigns and at Corinth; was mustered out and re-enlisted; was captured and exchanged. Later he was active in blockade-running. His *Life in the Confederate Army* is one of the liveliest accounts of the nonmilitary aspects of the war in the West.

We had now the march before us, and we must undertake it, without provisions, without tents or cooking utensils, with out blankets or overcoats, and our thin clothing now worn and ragged. I have never seen or read either in newspaper or history any details of this miniature Moscow retreat. It was, perhaps, one of those black or blurred pages in history that is unreadable, and is best to be torn out.

We proceeded to scramble along the best way we could, wading through creeks and rivers and scrambling over rocks and through brushwood. At night we kindled large fires and took off our wet clothes, wrung the water out of them, and dried them the best way we could. Occasionally we passed a small settlement from which the inhabitants had fled, but everything had been carried away by Price's army. In the gardens we sometimes found the remains of some turnips or onions, which were eagerly dug out of the ground with our sabres and eaten raw. Everything like military order of march was at an end, but the battalions and companies kept in their places, and discipline was still maintained, although to leave the line in search of something to eat could no longer be strictly forbidden. Several times it was found that we had taken the wrong road and had to turn back. Some times we passed through rather better tracts of country which had been settled, but the few settlers had all fled from their homes and the houses were deserted, and everything in the shape of food had been taken by Price's troops. . . .

About the seventh night we halted on the sloping banks of a creek which ran at the bottom of a pretty deep valley. On the near side of the creek there was abundance of dry grass, making a fine place to bivouac; and, what was better, the weather had suddenly changed, and the afternoon and evening were warm and sultry. We expected to get some sleep to-night if the pangs of hunger would allow us. How the other companies were faring we were not sure, but sup posed they had just their little chances same as ourselves.

Notwithstanding the wretchedness of our condition, there was throughout the whole of this trying campaign still kept up a continual animation by light merry-making. Joking was always the order of the day. The most disagreeable and trying privations were alleviated and smoothed over by turning them into a cause for laughter. If some became sullen and desponding, there were always some spirits who could by some comical expressions raise the merry laugh and incite good humour, and put animation into the men. . . .

When daylight came, and we were about to proceed on our march, we found we were in something of a fix.

Our line of march was across the creek, and we had not followed the rules, which was that a creek should always be crossed and the troops to bivouac on the far side. This rule had been departed from at this time, because on the far side of the creek there was not for some distance any suitable place for bivouacing, besides creeks here were so plentiful, and had to be crossed so often, that if we got on the far side we were not far from the near side of another. However, in this case the meaning or object of the rule was very well demonstrated.

The creek, by the sudden storm, was swollen to a great extent, so that it was impossible to cross, and we could not proceed; and if the enemy had been harassing our rear we would have been in the same position as the Israelites at the Red Sea. What was now to be done? No other route was possible; we were pressed by starvation, and no food was to be obtained in the neighbourhood. It would be at least two days before the creek was passable, and if more rain fell it was quite uncertain when we might get across. There was only the remnant or wreck of the 2nd brigade here, but who was in command of it, or whether it had any commander, we did not know, every regiment seeming to act for itself, and every company to act for itself.

After a consultation among the officers of our regiment, it was agreed that the regiment should separate and each company act for itself, and get along the best way they could to Van Buren, and there join again.

Each company then started to shift for itself as they best could. The novelty of the thing was pleasing, as they were now comparatively free. Our company, amounting in the aggregate to 32, proceeded by itself. We had two axes which we carried along for cutting wood for fires, etc., but that was all the company property we had beyond our arms. We proceeded along the creek to see if there was any possibility of finding a place where we might effect a crossing by felling trees so as to fall across it.

We had some splendid fellows for such an emergency, who could handle the axe as well as the rifle, one of whom we called Canada, as he was a native of that country.

Some gigantic trees grew along the edge of the creek in some places, and soon one of them fell across the stream, but it went whirling away with the roaring torrent as if it had been chips. Another and another was cut, but all were carried away.

At length we came to a place where the creek was narrow and the banks high, but there did not seem to be any tree large enough and sufficiently near the bank to fall across, and at this narrow part all were eagerly looking for a tree that would, if felled, span the creek.

"Here, sergeant! here, sergeant," cried Tim D., in great ecstasy, "here is a fine one."

I hastened to where he was. "Where is it?" said I.

"Over yonder," said he, pointing to a tree on the opposite side of the creek, "if we could only manage to get over to cut it."

"You confounded fool," said I, "if we could only manage to get over to it, it would be of no use to us, because we would not want it."

"What is that?" cried some one.

"Oh, it is one of Tim's bulls," said I. "He proposes that we cross the river first, and then cut a tree on the other side."

"Throw him in the river!" cried two or three of the boys.

"Well, now, that was not what I said at all," cried Tim. "I said, There is a fine tree over there, and if some of yees would go over and cut it, we would all get over; and if you would just come and see the tree, you would say yourself that it was a splendid one."

"Then, go over and cut it;" cried two or three of the boys.

At that time Lieutenant G. and Canada, the axe-man, came up; we looked across at the tree and pondered. "Well, certainly, if any one was on that side to cut that tree it would just fall across and make a splendid badge. I wonder if there could be no means of getting one man across to cut it."

There was a place a little farther down, where the stream ran through a narrow chasm, where the banks were high on each side, and not quite 30 feet from bank to bank, but there were no trees near the place. It was suggested that we might get one of the tall ash trees, which grew higher up the bank, and carry it down, and raise it on end and let it fall across, and if it did not break it would be strong enough for some active fellow to straddle over upon, and then we could throw him over the axe to cut the tree.

"The very thing!" cried Canada, "and I will volunteer to cross on it." And he was off at once to select a suitable ash tree.

One was soon cut down and trimmed, and all hands carried it to the place, and a hole was dug in the ground with our sabres to put the thick end into, while the men got about it, and with the aid of long forked sticks got it raised to the perpendicular, and it was thrown across, and landed successfully on the other side.

The roaring torrent below looked rather trying to the nerves.

"Here, Tim," cried some of the boys, "go over now and cut the tree."

Tim said he would go, but, as he was no axe-man, he could not cut the tree.

"Then stand aside, you useless bog-trotter."

The end of the tree was firmly bedded, and held tight to keep it from rolling, while Canada straddled across, like Blondin, crossing Niagara Falls on the tight rope. He landed safely on the other side, amidst the cheers of the boys; while another immediately crossed after him, and we threw them over the two axes. Of course, they cried back in a joke, pretending to bid us goodbye, as they were going to proceed on and leave us, but we could not hear them for the roaring of the torrent.

They both set to work with a will and the tree, a very large one, soon fell across the creek, forming an excellent bridge, and in a few minutes all had scrambled over.

We ascended the banks on the opposite side, where we looked back and saw some of the other companies along on the banks, vainly searching for a place to cross. We gave a loud cheer to attract their attention. There was soon a commotion among them, and a cry of—"Hilloa, the rifles are over!"

We pointed in the direction of where we had crossed, that they might see our bridge and make use of it, and we proceeded on our way.

"Now, don't yees see," said Tim D., "that I was right after all; you talk about bulls and bog-trotters, but if it had not been for me you would all have been left behind."

"Why, what did you do?"

"Well, it was my tree that was the right tree, and if it had not been the right tree you might all have been drowned in the river, and then you would have said that I had been right.". . .

We now got on to the regular road, and the track of an army was now only too plainly visible every house was deserted, and everything in the shape of food or forage was carried away, and a good deal of property seemed to have been wantonly destroyed.

We saw some stragglers on the road before us, and we hastened to overtake them, thinking that they might be a part of our regiment, or perhaps Lieutenant G.'s party. When we overtook them we found them to be mostly of our regiment, but not more than a dozen in all, and among them were two of our company, from Lieutenant G.'s party.

Upon inquiring how it was with the party, and why they were separated from it, they said that Lieutenant G. had heard something about some of the missing from our company, and that our 2nd lieutenant, B., was lying very ill somewhere, and some others were also in distress, and he was going to try to render them assistance; and that he had told these two to go and see if they could meet with our party, and tell us not to wait for them, but to push on to Van Buren.

The effects of an army passing over a country distracted by war were now clearly to be seen. Be that army friend or foe, it passes along like a withering scourge, leaving only ruin and desolation behind.

We found it needless to attempt to procure anything like food on the way, and it was only a loss of time and strength going off the road to look for it. We therefore resolved to push on and reach Van Buren as soon as possible, as the road was now plain before us.

At length we drew near to the place. The poor fellows were brightened up with hope, but they were in a sorry plight. They were actually staggering from want and fatigue. Their shoes were worn off their feet, from passing over rocks and boulders, and through creeks. Their clothes were in rags from scrambling through the woods and briars, and burnt in holes from crouching too close to the camp fires in their broken slumbers. Their eyes were bleared and blood shot from want of sleep and the smoke of the woodfires, and their bodies were emaciated by hunger. But now their difficulties were overcome, and their privations supposed to be at an end for the time at least.

It was about three o'clock in the afternoon when we entered Van Buren.

—WATSON, *Life in the Confederate Army*

XI.5

QUANTRILL AND HIS GUERRILLAS SACK LAWRENCE

William C. Quantrill is probably the most unsavory figure of the Civil War. Born in Ohio, he moved to Kansas in 1857, where he lived something of a Jekyll-Hyde life, teaching school as William Quantrill, gambling and stealing—and perhaps murdering—as Charley Hart. With the outbreak of the war he raised an irregular band of Confederate sympathizers in the border country of Kansas and Missouri, fought at Lexington, and then embarked upon a career of guerrilla warfare. The Federal government declared him an outlaw, but the Confederates mustered him into service and commissioned him captain. In August 1863 he rode into Lawrence, Kansas, at the head of some 450 men, killed upward of 150 men, women, and children, pillaged the town and left it in ashes. Two months later he repeated this exploit at Baxter Springs, Missouri. All efforts to capture him were vain; in 1865 he appeared in Kentucky, but there he was surprised and fatally wounded.

This story of the infamous Lawrence massacre is by one of the few men who escaped, Gurdon Grovenor.

The raid occurred on the morning of Aug. 21st, 1863. It was a clear, warm, still morning, in the midst of one of the hot, dry, dusty spells of weather common in Kansas in the month of August. The guerrillas reached Lawrence just be fore sunrise after an all night's ride from the border of Missouri. Myself and family were yet in bed and asleep. They passed directly by our house, and we were awakened by their yelling and shouting.

I thought at first that the noise came from a company of colored recruits who were camped just west of our house; thought that they had got to quarrelling among themselves. I got up and went to the window to see what was the matter, and as I drew aside the curtain the sight that met my eyes was one of terror—one that I never shall forget. The bushwhackers were just passing by my house. There were 350 of them, all mounted and heavily armed; they were grim and dirty from their night's ride over the dusty roads and were a reckless and bloodthirsty set of men. It was a sight we had somewhat anticipated, felt that it might come, and one that we had dreaded ever since the commencement of the war. I turned to my wife and said: "The bushwhackers are here."

They first made for the main street, passing up as far as the Eldridge House to see if they were going to meet with any opposition, and when they found none they scattered out all over town, killing, stealing and burning. We hastily dressed ourselves and closed up the house tightly as possible and began to talk over what was best to do. My first thought was to get away to some hiding place, but on looking out there seemed no possibility of

that as the enemy were everywhere, and I had a feeling that I ought not to leave my family, a young wife and two children, one a babe of three months old, and so we sat down and awaited developments. We saw men shot down and fires shooting up in all directions.

Just on the north of our house, a half a block away and in full view was a camp of recruits twenty-two in all, not yet mustered into service and unarmed. They were awakened by the noise, got up and started to run but were all shot down but five. I saw this wholesale shooting from my window, and it was a sight to strike terror to a stouter heart than mine. But we had not long to wait before our time came. Three of the guerrillas came to the house, stepped up on the front porch, and with the butt of a musket smashed in one of the front windows; my wife opened the door and let them in. They ransacked the house, talked and swore and threatened a good deal, but offered no violence. They set the house on fire above and below, took such things as they fancied, and left. After they had gone I put the fire out be low, but above it had got too strong a hold, and I could not put it out.

Not long after a single man rode up to the front gate; he was a villainous looking fellow, and was doubly villainous from too much whiskey. He saw me standing back in the hall of the house, and with a terrible oath he ordered me to come out. I stepped out on the piazza, and. he leveled his pistol at me and said; "Are you union or secesh?"

It was my time of trial; my wife with her little one in her arms, and our little boy clinging to her side, was standing just a little ways from me. My life seemingly hung on my answer, my position may be imagined but it cannot be described. The thought ran through me like an electric shock, that I could not say that I was a secessionist, and deny my loyalty to my country; that I would rather die than to live and face that disgrace; and so I answered that I was a union man. He snapped his pistol but it failed to fire. I stepped back into the house and he rode around to the north door and met me there, and snapped his pistol at me again, and this time it failed. Was there a providence in this?

Just then a party of a half dozen of the raiders came riding towards the house from the north, and seeing my enemy, hallooed to him "Don't shoot that man." They rode up to the gate and told me to come there; I did so and my would be murderer came up to me and placed the muzzle of his revolver in my ear. It was not a pleasant place to be in, but the leader of the new crowd told him not to shoot, but to let me alone until he could inquire about me, so he asked me if I had ever been down in Missouri stealing niggers or horses; I told him "No that I never had been in Missouri, except to cross the state going and coming from the east." This seemed to be satisfactory so he told my old enemy to let me alone and not to kill me. This seemed to make him very angry, and he cursed me terribly, but I ventured to put my hand up and push away his revolver. The leader of the party then told me if I did not expect to get killed, I must get out of sight, that they were all getting drunk, and would kill everybody they saw; I told him that that was what I had wanted to do all the morning, but I could not; "Well," he says, "you must hide or get killed." And they all rode away.

After they had gone I told my wife that I would go into the cellar, and stay until the fire reached me, and if any more of the raiders inquired for me to tell them that I had been taken a prisoner and carried off. Some years ago I read an article in the Sunday School Times, saying that a lie under any circumstances was a sin. I thought then that I should like to see that writer try my experiences at the time of the raid and see what he would think then; I did not feel my lie a sin then and never have since.

The cellar of my house was under the ell and the fire was in the front and in the upper story. There was an outside bulk-head door, where I knew I could get out after the fire had reached the floor above me. I had not been in the cellar long before my wife came and said they had just killed my neighbor across the street.

Soon after the notorious Bill Anderson, passing by the house, saw my wife standing in the yard, stopped and commenced talking with her; told her how many men he had killed that morning, and inquiring where her husband was; she told him that he had been taken prisoner and carried away—was it my wife's duty to tell him the truth, tell him where I was and let him come and shoot me as he would a dog, which he would have done? Awhile after my wife came and said she thought the raiders had all gone, and so I came out of my prison just as the fire was eating through the floor over my head, thankful that I had passed through that dreadful ordeal and was safe.

Such was my experience during those four or five terrible hours. Our home and its contents was in ashes, but so thankful were we that my life was spared that we thought but little of our pecuniary loss. After the raiders had left and the people could get out on the street, a most desolate and sickening sight met their view. The whole business part of the town, except two stores, was in ashes. The bodies of dead men, some of them partly burned away, were laying in all directions. A large number of dwellings were burned to the ground, and the moaning of the grief stricken people was heard from all sides. Gen. Lane, who was in the city at the time, told me that he had been over the battle-ground of Gettysburg a few days before, but the sight was not so sickening as the one which the burned and sacked city of Lawrence presented. The exact number killed was never known, but it was about 150, many of them of the best citizens.

—GROVENOR in *Quantrill and the Border Wars*

XI.6

COLONEL BAILEY DAMS THE RED RIVER

Early in 1864 General Halleck projected an elaborate plan for crushing remaining Confederate resistance in Arkansas and Louisiana. Banks was ordered to move up the Red River to Alexandria, where he would be joined by General Steele, coming down from Arkansas.

Together they were to advance on Shreveport and crush the Confederate forces under Kirby Smith and Taylor. The whole expedition was to be supported by a flotilla of gunboats and transports.

From the beginning things went wrong. Taylor dug in at Mansfield, and repulsed a Federal attack with heavy loss. Taylor in turn advanced, only to be repulsed. But Banks decided to retreat to Alexandria. Meantime however the spring floods had not materialized and the Red River, already low, threatened to fall so low that the fleet would be isolated.

At this juncture Colonel Bailey, chief engineer for the defenses of New Orleans and in the Port Hudson campaign, saved the day by constructing a series of wing dams which got the boats over the falls at Alexandria. For this service Bailey was promoted to a brigadier generalship. After the war he went to Missouri, was elected sheriff of his county, and was murdered by two bushwhackers whom he had arrested.

The story of this exploit is here told by Admiral Porter in a report to Secretary of the Navy Gideon Welles.

Mississippi Squadron, Flagship Black Hawk,
Mouth Red River, May 16th, 1864.

Sir: I have honor to inform you that the vessels lately caught by low water above the falls at Alexandria, have been released from their unpleasant position. The water had fallen so low that I had no hope or expectation of getting the vessels out this season, and, as the army had made arrangement to evacuate the country, I saw nothing before me but the destruction of the best part of the Mississippi squadron.

There seems to have been an especial Providence looking out for us in providing a man equal to the emergency. Lieut.-Col. Bailey, Acting Engineer of the 19th Army Corps, proposed a plan of building a series of dams across the rocks at the falls, and raising the water high enough to let the vessels pass over. This proposition looked like madness, and the best engineers ridiculed it; but Col. Bailey was so sanguine of success that I requested to have it done, and he entered heartily into the work. Provisions were short and forage was almost out, and the dam was promised to be finished in ten days or the army would have to leave us. I was doubtful about the time, but I had no doubt about the ultimate success, if time would only permit. Gen. Banks placed at the disposal of Col. Bailey all the forces he required, consisting of some three thousand men and two or three hundred wagons. All the neighboring stream-mills were torn down for material; two or three regiments of Maine men were set to work felling trees, and on the second day after my arrival in Alexandria, from Grand Ecore, the work had fairly begun.

Trees were falling with great rapidity, teams were moving in all directions, bringing in brick and stone; quarries were opened; flat-boats were built to bring stone down from above, and every man seemed to be working with a vigor I have seldom seen equalled, while perhaps not one in fifty believed in the undertaking. These falls are about a mile in length, filled with rugged rocks, over which at the present stage of water it seemed to be impossible to make a channel.

The work was commenced by running out from the left bank of the river a tree dam, made of the bodies of very large trees, brush, brick, and stone, cross-tied with heavy timber, and strengthened in every way which ingenuity could devise This was run out about three hundred feet into the river; four large coal barges were then filled with brick and sunk at the end of it. From the right bank of the river, cribs filled with stone were built out to meet the barges, all of which were successfully accomplished, notwithstanding there was a current running of nine miles an hour, which threatened to sweep every thing before it.

It will take too much time to enter into the details of this truly wonderful work; suffice it to say that the dam had nearly reached completion in eight days' working time, and the water had risen sufficiently on the upper falls to allow the *Fort Hindman*, *Osage*, and *Neosho*, to get down and be ready to pass the dam. In another day it would have been high enough to enable all the other vessels to pass the upper falls. Unfortunately, on the morning of the 9th inst., the pressure of water became so great that it swept away two of the stone-barges which swung in below the dam on one side. Seeing this unfortunate accident, I jumped on a horse and rode up to where the upper vessels were anchored, and ordered the *Lexington* to pass the upper falls if possible, and immediately attempt to go through the dam. I thought I might be able to save the four vessels below, not knowing whether the persons employed on the work would ever have the heart to renew the enterprise.

The *Lexington* succeeded in getting over the upper falls just in time, the water rapidly falling as she was passing over. She then steered directly for the opening in the dam, through which the water was rushing so furiously that it seemed as if nothing but destruction awaited her. Thousands of beating hearts looked on anxious for the result.

The silence was so great as the *Lexington* approached the dam that a pin might almost have been heard to fall. She entered the gap with a full head of steam on, pitched down the roaring torrent, made two or three spasmodic rolls, hung for a moment on the rocks below, was then swept into deep water by the currents, and rounded to safely into the bank.

Thirty thousand voices rose in one deafening cheer, and universal joy seemed to pervade the face of every man present. The *Neosho* followed next— all her hatches battened down, and every precaution taken against accident. She did not fare as well as the *Lexington*, her pilot having become frightened as he approached the abyss, and stopped her engine when I particularly ordered a full head of steam to be carried. The result was that for a moment her hull disappeared from sight, under the water. Every one thought she was lost. She rose, however, swept along over the rocks with the current, and fortunately escaped with only one hole in her bottom, which was stopped in the course of an hour. The *Hindman* and *Osage* both came through beautifully without touching a thing, and I thought if I was only fortunate enough to get my large vessels as well over the falls my fleet once more would do good service on the Mississippi.

The accident to the dam, instead of disheartening Col. Bailey, only induced him to renew his exertions, after he had seen the success of getting four vessels through. The noble hearted soldiers, seeing their labor of the last eight days swept away in a moment, cheerfully went to work to repair

damages, being confident now that all the gunboats would be finally brought over. The men had been working for eight days and nights, up to their necks in water, in the broiling sun, cutting trees and wheeling bricks, and nothing but good humor prevailed among them. On the whole, it was very fortunate the dam was carried away, as the two barges that were swept away from the centre swung around against some rocks on the left and made a fine cushion for the vessels, and prevented them, as it afterward appeared, from running on certain destruction.

The force of the water and the current being too great to construct a continuous dam of six hundred feet across the river in so short a time, Col. Bailey determined to leave a gap of fifty-five feet in the dam, and build a series of wing dams on the upper falls. This was accomplished in three days' time, and on the 11th instant the *Mound City*, the *Carondelet*, and *Pittsburgh* came over the upper falls, a good deal of labor having been expended in hauling them through, the channel being very crooked, scarcely wide enough for them. Next day the *Ozark*, *Louisville*, *Chillicothe*, and two tugs also succeeded in crossing the upper falls.

Immediately afterward the *Mound City*, *Carondelet*, and *Pittsburgh* started in succession to pass the dam, all their hatches battened down and every precaution taken to prevent accident.

The passage of these vessels was a most beautiful sight, only to be realized when seen. They passed over without an accident except the unshipping of one or two rudders. This was witnessed by all the troops, and the vessels were heartily cheered when they passed over. Next morning at ten o'clock, the *Louisville*, *Chillicothe*, *Ozark*, and two tugs passed over without any accident except the loss of a man, who was swept off the deck of one of the tugs. By three o'clock that afternoon, the vessels were all coaled, ammunition replaced, and all steamed down the river with the convoy of transports in company. A good deal of difficulty was anticipated in getting over the bars in lower Red River—depth of water reported only five feet; gunboats were drawing six. Providentially, we had a rise from the back water of the Mississippi—that river being very high at that time—the back water extending to Alexandria, one hundred and fifty miles distant, enabling it to pass all the bars and obstructions with safety.

Words are inadequate to express the admiration I feel for the ability of Lieut.-Col. Bailey. This is without doubt the best engineering feat ever performed. . .

I have the honor to be, very respectfully, your obedient servant,

David D. Porter, Rear-Admiral.
—Letter from DAVID D. PORTER
to Gideon Welles

XI. 7

PRICE INVADES THE NORTH AND IS DEFEATED AT WESTPORT

Early in 1864 General Banks moved north on Shreveport but was stopped by General Taylor at Mansfield. At the Battle of Sabine Crossing, April 8, 1864, Banks was repulsed, and retreated toward the Mississippi, harassed by Kirby Smith.

As Banks moved toward the Mississippi, General Steele, who had earlier advanced from Little Rock, fell back on that city. Swollen rivers delayed his retreat, and at the end of April 1864 the forces of Price and Kirby Smith caught up with him at Jenkins's Ferry on the Saline River. The Confederates were repulsed, and Steele made good his retirement. Emboldened by their success, however, the Confederates decided to launch another offensive into Missouri.

Wiley Britton of the 6th Kansas Cavalry—later the historian of the fighting in the Trans-Mississippi area—here tells the story of the confused fighting of the last six months, culminating in the smashing Union victory at Westport.

After the battle of Jenkins's Ferry [April 30, 1864], instead of making preparations to attack the Federal forces at Little Rock and Fort Smith, Price commenced organizing his forces for an expedition into Missouri, to be led by him in person. The Confederate troops under Cooper, Maxey, and Gano, in the Indian Territory and western Arkansas, were to make demonstrations against Fort Smith and Fort Gibson, and the line of com-

munication between those points and Kansas, while another part of the Confederate army was to threaten Little Rock. Price's army for the invasion of Missouri numbered some 15,000 men and 20 pieces of artillery before crossing the Arkansas River, and consisted of three divisions, commanded by Generals Fagan, Marmaduke, and Shelby. These troops were mostly veterans, having been in active service since the first year of the war.

About the 1st of September, while strong demonstrations were being made against Fort Smith and Little Rock, Price, with his army, crossed the Arkansas River about half-way between those points at Dardanelle, and marched to the northern part of the State without opposition, and, in fact, without his movements being definitely known to General Rosecrans, who then commanded the Department of the Missouri at St. Louis. When the Confederate forces entered Missouri they were met by detachments of the State militia, who captured several Confederate prisoners, from whom it was ascertained that the invading force was much larger than had been supposed, and that Price was marching direct for St. Louis. Rosecrans at once commenced collecting his forces to meet and check the enemy. General Thomas Ewing, Jr., was in command of the District of South-east Missouri. Pilot Knob, near Iron Mountain, was a post of importance, with fortifications of considerable strength, and was on Price's direct line of march to St. Louis, which was only eighty-six miles distant.

Finding that General Price was certainly advancing toward St. Louis, Ewing, in order to defend Pilot Knob, drew in the detachments of his command stationed at different points in south-east Missouri. As the Federal forces around and in the vicinity of St. Louis were considered inadequate to defend the city against the reported strength of Price's veteran army, on the request of Rosecrans General A. J. Smith's veteran division of the Army of the Tennessee, 4500 strong, passing up the Mississippi River to join Sherman's army, was detained at Cairo to assist in checking the advance of the Confederate army.

Price arrived before Pilot Knob in the afternoon of September 26th, and skirmished until night with detachments of Federal cavalry, which had been thrown out to meet his advance. Ewing had 1051 men at that post, which were only enough to man the works. Having got his troops and artillery all up, Price opened the attack on the fort at day light on the 27th, and kept it up all day with great resolution. But Ewing's well-served artillery of eleven pieces and his thousand small-arms repulsed every assault made by the Confederates. When night came, however, Ewing was satisfied that he could not hold out another day against the superior attacking force, and he determined to evacuate the fort. Shortly after midnight his troops marched out, and a few moments later his magazine was blown up, and the ammunition which could not be taken along was destroyed. Ewing then marched with his force and joined the troops engaged in the defense of St. Louis and of Jefferson City. On hearing the explosion of the magazine, Price suspected the retreat of the garrison, and immediately ordered his generals to start in pursuit. Continuing his march north with his army he came up and attacked the defenses of St. Louis some miles south of the city, but was repulsed by General A. J. Smith's veterans and other troops, and then changed his line of march and moved westward toward Jefferson City, the State capital.

While Price's plans were not definitely known, his movements indicated that he would endeavor to take Jefferson City. But Rosecrans determined not to allow the State capital to fall into the hands of the invader, and not only called out the enrolled militia of central Missouri for its defense, but also ordered General John B. Sanborn, commanding the District of South-west Missouri at Springfield, and General John McNeii, commanding the District of Rolla, to march to its defense with their available forces, with the least possible delay. General E. B. Brown and General Clinton B. Pisk, commanding districts in central and north Missouri, were also directed to bring forward to Jefferson City all the State militia that could be spared from their respec-

tive districts. General Price moved forward and attacked the capital, but as he was closely pursued by the Federal forces from St. Louis he was soon driven off, and continued his march westward up the south side of the Missouri River.

His next objects were understood to be the capture of Kansas City, and Fort Leavenworth, Kansas, and more particularly the invasion and desolation of Kansas. He con scripted and pressed into service every man and youth found at home able to bear arms. Major-General S. R. Curtis, commanding the Department of Kansas and the Indian Territory, the moment he was advised of the approaching storm, began collecting all his forces along the eastern border of the State south of Kansas City, and urged Governor Carney, of Kansas, to call out the militia to cooperate with the volunteers in resisting the threatened invasion. In response to the governor's call, twenty-four regiments of militia were hastily organized, and took position along the eastern line of the State. Early in these preparatory operations for the defense of the border, Major-General George Sykes, commanding the District of South Kansas, was, at his own request, relieved, and Major-General James G. Blunt was placed in command. As soon as information was received that Price had been driven from Jefferson City and was moving west ward, Curtis and Blunt took the field in person to direct the operations of their forces in defense of the border. Blunt took the available force of the volunteers and several sections of artillery, and moved down to Lexington, some forty miles, to meet and hold the enemy as long as possible, so that Rosecrans's forces in pursuit from St. Louis and Jefferson City, under Generals Alfred Pleasonton and A. J. Smith, could come up and attack Price in the rear.

On the afternoon of October 20th Price's advance under Shelby came within sight of Lexington on the south side of the city. Sharp fighting at once commenced between the opposing forces, and lasted until night, when Blunt, having ascertained the strength of the enemy, fell back to Little Blue River, a few miles east of Independence, to form a new line of battle. As this stream was fordable at different points above and below where the Independence and Lexington road crossed it, Blunt's forces, under Colonel Thomas Moon light were obliged, on the 21st, to abandon the position taken up behind it after an engagement with Shelby's division, lasting several hours, and fall back behind the Big Blue River, a few miles west of Independence. Here a new line of battle was formed with all Curtis's available troops, including most of the Kansas State militia, who had consented to cross the State line into Missouri. Curtis and Blunt determined to hold Price's army east of the Big Blue as long as practicable in the hope of receiving assistance from Rosecrans, who, it was thought, was following close upon the rear of the Confederate army.

While Curtis's forces were thus fighting and skirmishing with the enemy over nearly every foot of the ground from Lexington to Big Blue, Pleasonton's provisional cavalry division of Rosecrans's army was marching day and night from Jefferson City to overtake the invading force. On the 22d, just as Curtis's troops were being driven from the line of the Big Blue back upon the State line and Kansas City, Pleasonton's cavalry came up and attacked the rear of Price's army, east of Independence, and routed it and drove it in great disorder through the town. Pleasonton at once sent a messenger to Curtis, announcing his presence upon the field. The night of the 22d

Price's army encamped on the west side of the Big Blue, just south of Westport. Pleasonton's cavalry encamped that night around and in the neighborhood of Independence, east of the Big Blue. Curtis's forces were encamped from Kansas City to Westport and along the State line west of Westport.

At daylight on the 23d the columns of Pleasonton began to move west, and those of Curtis to move south, and in a short time afterward they became warmly engaged with the Confederates, who were drawn up in the line of battle two and a half miles south of Westport. The opposing armies fought over an area of five or six square miles, and at some points the fighting was furious. At times there were as many as forty or fifty guns throwing shot and shell and grape and canister. About the middle of the afternoon Price's lines began to give way, and by sundown the entire Confederate army was in full retreat southward along the State line, closely pursued by the victorious Federal forces. . . .

The "Price raid," as it was called in the West, was the last military operation of much consequence that took place in Missouri and Arkansas. It is certain that Price lost more than he gained in war material and that the raid did not tend to strengthen the Confederate cause in the West.

—BRITTON, "Resume of Military Operations in Arkansas and Missouri"

XII

HOW THE SOLDIERS LIVED:
WESTERN FRONT

On the whole Americans were the same, East and West, the Army of Tennessee much like the Army of Northern Virginia, the Army of the Cumberland much like the Army of the Potomac. Not only this but the troops were, in fact, very mixed; Illinois and Minnesota, Texas and Alabama regiments fought in Virginia. But the Western armies were made up, almost wholly, from the region west of the Alleghenies, though this was less true of the Confederate than of the Union armies. There were, however, minor differences.

There was probably a larger proportion of foreign-born soldiers in the Union armies in the West—Germans and Scandinavians particularly. The war in this theater was some what more of a real civil war: in Missouri and Arkansas, in Kentucky and particularly in Tennessee, the division of Union and Confederate sentiment ran right through society. In the East only Maryland had regiments in both armies; but the Army of the Tennessee (Union) included a "1st Alabama" cavalry brigade, while there were many Kentucky and Missouri regiments in the Confederate ranks.

A third difference was imposed by geography and grand strategy. The Western armies f ought over an enormous territory, and it is suggestive that there are half a dozen accounts of the hardships of long marches from the West for every one from the East. Cavalry played, perhaps, a larger role—not the cavalry charge but the long raids and the harassment of lines of communication. Climate and geography permitted more winter campaigns. The necessity of co-operating with the navy for control of the Mississippi, the Tennessee and the Cumberland, and the Red rivers made operations more nearly a joint affair, and there are examples even of amphibious operations.

Yet on the whole the excerpts we give here need little elaboration. Life in camp; the forced march; religion and play; relations with civilians; the roles of the commissary and of the sutler—these things were pretty much the same East as West, and North as South. It will be sufficient to introduce some of the chroniclers themselves.

XII. 1

JOHN CHIPMAN GRAY VIEWS THE WESTERN SOLDIER

Member of a distinguished Massachusetts family, and graduate off the Harvard Law School, Gray enlisted in the 41st Massachusetts Volunteers in 1862 and fought for a year in the Valley and the Peninsular campaigns. In 1863 he was appointed assistant judge advocate and the following year judge advocate, assigned to the Department of the South. All through the war he corresponded with his law school friend, John Codman Ropes—future historian of the Civil War—and this letter, so Eastern in its point of view, is part of that correspondence.

> On Board Steamboat 'Bostona No. 2'
> White River, Arkansas, July 24, 1864

My Dear John,—

With regard to the general appearance of the Westerners, it is not so different from our own as I had supposed, but certain it is that discipline is most astonishingly lax. We came up from New Orleans to Memphis with veterans of the 49th Indiana Regiment going home on furlough. They were on terms of great familiarity with their officers, eating, drinking and playing cards with them; yet I must say a finer, cleaner, more orderly and well behaved set of men I never saw; the bar was open all the time and was always filled with men and officers, but I did not see an officer or man drunk and in deed in all my boating on these rivers, I have seen but two men at all affected by liquor, though this may be in some measure due to the exceeding weakness of the tipple concocted at the bar. Other western troops that I have seen have not been so clean and good looking as these Indiana men, but the same lack of discipline exists in all. This is carried to so great an extent that General Gordon, whom you will not suppose to be lax in this respect, says he thinks it very doubtful whether it would be worth while to attempt to impart a severer discipline to troops who have been brought up as these have for more than three years. In Memphis there was a sentry whom I had to pass daily, he was always seated in an arm-chair, his gun rested on the wall near his side, he was often reading, and had another chair by him for the convenience of any friend who might like to stop and chat a while. This is no solitary instance, I might tell you of a dozen things as strange.

Our white troops manage to get along though indifferently, on account of the individual character of the men, but I cannot conceive that the Negro troops commanded by officers taken from the ranks of white regiments, and with men taken from the lowest state of degradation can be anything but a burden to the Government and all the Negro troops I have seen in the West (not many to be sure) have been squalid and miserable in the extreme, very different in look from some of the fine Massachusetts and Maryland Regiments that I have seen in the Department of the South.

The run of officers and citizens that one meets in the towns and on the boats is much less rough than I had anticipated, and I have never seen officials more civil and accommodating than the Captains and Clerks of the river boats. My prejudices against the West have been materially lessened by the experience I have had.

There has been and is undoubtedly an immense deal of contraband cotton dealing and other trading, and almost every commanding officer is accused of having a hand in it. The army accuse the navy and the navy accuse the army. The profligacy too in all the large towns in this region is great. Partly from natural causes and partly from want of the means of life, the prostitution in all this region is astonishing. General Steele at Little Rock lives quite like an Eastern Prince with his harem, wines, dogs, horses, equipages and everything in great style. There is something al most romantic in the existence of all these appliances of luxury and civilization in a little town in the midst of a howling wilderness of bloodthirsty enemies.

—Ford, ed., *War Letters of John Chipman Gray and John Codman Ropes*

XII.2

A Wisconsin Boy Complains of the Hardships of Training

A farm boy from the Wisconsin frontier, Chauncey Cooke was barely sixteen when he went to La Crosse to enlist in the 25th Wisconsin Infantry. He was with Pope in the abortive Sioux campaign of 1862; then in the following year his regiment was sent south, where it fought through the Vicksburg and subsequent campaigns. His letters home have an unpretentious and authentic quality that commends them to the historian of the war. This letter—not the last that we shall read describes training at a camp outside Madison.

Madison, Wis. Dec. 25th, 1862
Co. G., 25th Regt.

Dear Mother:

You see my paper don't have the regulation picture on it of Soldiers in file or in battle array. I am tired of such flummery. The meaning of the whole thing is to make money for the inventor and not for the soldier. We are told that the life of the Nation is at stake, and every fellow that enlists offers himself as a martyr to save his country. I was thinking these things over last, about 2 P.M. in the morning when I was nearly froze and the relief guard came around and I was off duty to go to my tent and get some sleep. It seems like foolery to the common soldier that for two hours we must stand in a temperature of 30 or 40 degrees when we are a thousand miles from the enemy. I had to walk and walk to keep from freezing. The mercury was down near 40 below zero and the guard house where we sat down between reliefs or lay down was little better than out of doors.

The health of our Regiment is none too good. One man dies on an average every day. As I write this letter the drum is beating. The food we get is to blame for our bad health. The boys threaten a riot every day for the bad beef and spoilt bread issued to us and all this in our home state of Wisconsin.

I went to meeting yesterday both morning and evening. In the morning at the Baptist, in the evening at the Episcopal church. The preacher discussed the state of the Union. I thot he talked a bit like a traitor. He was sorry the states should go to war over the question of slavery. He hoped the Union would be preserved and he thot Uncle Tom's Cabin was much to blame for the war. Capt. Dorwin said the preacher ought to live in South Carolina.

There is talk that we will get pay tomorrow. I have sent a record of our company home. Hope you got it. I shall send you a lot of clothing just before we leave.

From your son,
Chauncey

—COOKE, "Letters of a Badger
Boy in Blue"

XII.3

RELIGION AND PLAY IN THE ARMY OF THE TENNESSEE

There is nothing dramatic or stirring about this simple chronicle of daily life in camp. Jenkin Jones was another of the many Wisconsin boys who fought in the Army of the Tennessee. Born in Wales he had been brought to this country as a baby; enlisted, at nineteen, in the 6th Wisconsin Battery; fought at Corinth, Vicksburg, Chattanooga, and in Georgia. After the war Jones became a prominent Unitarian preacher and editor. His diary is one of the most revealing about soldier life in the Western theater.

Huntsville [Alabama], Sunday, Jan 17, 1864. A pleasant day. Meeting was announced to be had at 2 P.M. in the Presbyterian Church. Obtained permission and went down, but found none, it being held at 6 P.M. Walked over town. Visited the waterworks of the city, which is the largest of the the kind South, with the exception of one at Columbia, S. C. A large stream gushes out of the solid rock under the court house, which is dammed about four feet and propels a large water wheel which works a powerful force pump that forces water all over the city, furnishing a hydrant at every corner. Pump is enclosed in a neat stone house. Returned to camp for supper and evening roll-call, then we walked back again. The church was very neat and filled with soldiers, but one woman in the audience. Chaplain of 18th Wisconsin officiated, of the Calvinistic school, and but ill agreed with my views, but it seemed good to be once more listening to an earnest speaker and hear the old-fashioned tunes swell in the bass voices that filled the room. Returned to camp, if not better, a more thoughtful man. It was the second sermon I have listened to since leaving home, and in common with all soldiers, I have acquired a careless and light way of passing time.

Sunday, Feb. 7. Rough night for the guard. Rainy and cold. The countersign "Vicksburg" which gave rise to musings which aided in forgetting time. Relieved at 9 A.M. Attended church in company with Griff, E. W. and D. J. D. Service was held in the Methodist, Presbyterian and Episcopal churches at the same hour (10 A.M.) Curiosity prompted to attend the latter, an elegant furnished church of unique construction, Gothic style, poorly arranged for sound. The civilians were apparently of the aristocratic class, mostly women, equalling the military in numbers. The white-robed minister was a young intelligent Irishman, I should judge. A good choir with the deep-toned organ opened the service with fitting music, after which prayers were read and ceremonies performed for nearly an hour and a half, which to me was mere mockery of religion, reading their desires to God from an established formula, but careful always to omit the prayer for the President of the U. S. A. It was not worship. Ah no! the heart was cold. It was but Phariseeical affectations. A short sermon on charity was read at the close. Very good, the effect of which was tested by passing the plates which were returned well laden with "soldier green backs." The money of that government they will not pray for is very acceptable.

I returned to camp, although not pleased with the exercise, yet I trust, benefited. The solemn notes of the organ had awakened feelings that are too apt to lie dormant in the soldier's breast, those that raise the mind above the din of common life, and look to a future of immortality, purity, which all hope to obtain ere long. "Heaven is my home."

Saturday, Feb. 20. As soon as breakfast was over I hitched a new team and drove out to a confiscated fence, a mile off, for a load of lumber, as the two Hungerfords were desirous of coming in with us, and we must build a larger one [hut]. After we were all loaded, a guard commanded us to unload, but after some talk allowed us to leave in quiet with our lumber. Tore down our "humble cot" and six of us went to work in earnest to erect a more commodious one. Had no tent. Built it entirely of lumber. Had it almost completed by night. Was quite tired, with a settled cold on my lungs, almost sick.

Friday, March 4. Evie Evans and myself went to the city on pass. Visited the Christian Commission rooms. Bought stamps. Also went to the colored school under charge of Chaplain of 17th Colored. Had school-teachers, being volunteers from the ranks, teaching the little woolyheads their "A. B. C.'s." One class of youngsters was taught by a large Negro. A class of young ladies was reading in the *Second Reader*. All seemed attentive and anxious to receive the instruction but poorly imparted to them. Harnesses were opened and distributed to the platoons. I was given one set. No horses.

Sunday, March 13. A delightful Sabbath morning. T. J. Hungerford very sick, heavy fever and

hard breathing. Afraid he is going to have a fever. Bathed him, towels kept around him, and all we can do for him is done gladly. After in spection 8 A.M. attended Sabbath school and meeting at the Methodist Church. . . . The minister preached from the 35th and 36th verses of the fourth chapter of St. John, a discourse filled with hell fire and eternal misery, with but little consolation to the many bereaved mothers and sisters present who had lost their all in the Confederate army. Al though enemies, I could but feel for their distressing sobs, that were audible all over the room. In the afternoon the day was so cheering that I could not resist the temptation of another walk to town, where in a crowded house of soldiers and citizens I listened to an excellent practical sermon on the ten virgins, wise and foolish.

Tuesday, March 29. Our camp was visited today by Mother Bickerdyke with four mule teams loaded with good things from the North for the soldiers. Left us three barrels of potatoes, turnips, carrots, etc., one barrel of sourkraut with one of dried apples. *Noble woman. I* still remember with gratitude the motherly interest she took in my welfare while lying in the hospital at Corinth. Here again she comes with that which she has gathered by her own labor in the North, not leaving it to be wholly absorbed by surgeons, directors and officers, as is too often the case with sanitary goods. She comes along in a mule wagon and delivers it herself to the "good boys" as she terms us, without seeking the officers. She drew a large crowd around her soon. Her glowing, welcoming face, filled with cordiality, had a magnetic influence upon the hearts of all, such a contrast to the haughty, disdainful looks we are accustomed to receive from women in general. May God bless her noble, self-sacrificing spirit, is the soldier's prayer.

Monday, April 4. A cloudy rainy day. Orders given us at 8 A.M. to put our tents in order preparatory to an inspection by medical director. All filth to be removed. Dirty clothes were washed, etc. In the evening the artillery boys listened to a stirring speech on the parade ground by Rev. Collins, chaplain 57th Illinois, a spicy and able speaker. Kept the crowd laughing much of the time, at the same time encouraging and instructing each one in the duty of the hour, and had a good effect. Sold several tracts.

Monday, April 11. Spent the day in the usual way. Two hours' gun drill in the morning, then game of ball; an hour company drill in the afternoon; a game or two of chess, then parade 4 P.M.; reading, writing, the remainder of the time till retreat at 8 P.M. when I made down my cot. In the quiet of alone I lay down, a few yearning thoughts of home, mother, etc. and all is oblivion till reveille calls me forth from the land of nod. A little after noon we were startled by a terrible explosion near the depot. A caisson of the Illinois Battery had exploded while returning from drill, killing six cannoneers instantly and wounding two. A very sad affair. Bodies torn to shreds.

Sunday, April 17. A beautiful and holy Sabbath morning. Warmed even the coldest heart to softness and filled the thoughtful mind with piety, though to many imperceptibly. Knapsack inspection at 8 A.M. Afterwards D. J. D. Griff and myself attended Sabbath school taught by a chaplain. The presiding elder of the Methodist church was sick, and to my astonishment the Yankee chaplain was invited to preach, which he did very fittingly, delivering an excellent sermon from Romans 8th chapter, XV verse. Went down in the afternoon to witness the baptizing at the Methodist church, but we were too late. Visited the new font that is going up, and caught in heavy rain storm before we got back.

Sunday, April 24. Awoke to hear the rain pattering thick and fast on the pine boards overhead. At first I was dis satisfied with the anticipation of a wet day with mud—very blue, but at the thought of yesterday's dusty ordeal I could but say "blessed be the rain that clears the atmosphere and makes all nature look more pleasing when it ceases." Cleared off into a most delightful day by 9 A.M., and I listened to a thorough scientific sermon from Dr. Ross upon technical points, existence of evil. His argu-

ments were very concise and binding. Although differing in opinion I received many new ideas. He is one of the leading Southern clergy and formerly a rabid secessionist, and to-day he touched upon the war, but so nicely that it could not displease any of his audience which was composed of the two extremes, viz: Yankee soldiers and secesh women. He sat way up, he said, upon his faith in God, "looking down upon the struggle with as much composure as though they were but the convulsions of so many pigmies—God would do it right." Just found it out I suppose.

Monday, May 2. A cold, windy day for this time of the year. At night a fire was very comfortable. Expect to move camp nearer to town soon so as to shorten the picket line. The left wing of the 1 6th Corps under Dodge was moving in all day. Stood on the roadside most of the after noon, the first time we were ever permitted to see a moving column without ourselves forming a part of it. 26th Wisconsin passed. Many of our boys found acquaintances and friends. In the same Brigade was a regiment of Yanks all the way from Jersey, regular blue-blooded Yankees. Made a strange appearance in their leggins and yellow tassels. Physically made a poor comparison by the side of our sturdy Western boys.

Tuesday, May 10. . . . All the Negroes in town pressed in and put to work. Twenty of us detailed with Corporal Ferris to load a train with 3 by 8 stuff for gun platforms to obtain which we had to tear down an old machine shop. Returned and unloaded by noon.

All the details marched up in line to McBride's headquarters, where whiskey rations were freely issued to all that wanted, many of the most greedy drinking in several different details. After this issue the Captain mounted a table and read a dispatch from Sherman by telegraph, of glorious news from Grant. Whips Lee and in full pursuit. Butler in Petersburg within ten miles of Richmond. The news and whiskey brought forth thundering acclamations from the soldiers. After stating the importance of the immediate completion of the works, we were dismissed for dinner and started home. Deplorable sight. The intemperate indulgence by those but little used to the poison, caused a large portion of them to be beastly drunk, and our march through town was filled with demoniac yells, tumbling in the mud and mire. I felt ashamed to be seen in the crowd. Such mistaken kindness tends to demoralize the army as well as to increase the hatred of our enemy. Many of the boys had to be carried to their tents, and were unable to return to the work in the afternoon. Rained heavy all the afternoon. Worked hard. After night a terrible thunder storm deluged our camp, water standing in one of the tents eighteen inches deep. Our floor was all afloat, and we had to climb into our bunks to keep dry. Dry land could not be seen. Much noise and fun in order to forget the disagreeable in the humorous.

—Jones, *An Artilleryman's Diary*

XII.4

The Great Revival in the Army of Tennessee

In 1863 and 1864 the Army of Tennessee, like the army of Northern Virginia, was swept by a "great revival." Officers and men alike were baptized, and piety spread—per haps with despair. These letters are from the Reverend T. J. Stokes, a member—probably chaplain—of the 10th Texas. Mrs. Gay, who reproduces them in her charming Life in Dixie, lived in Decatur, Georgia.

Near Dalton, April 5th, 1864. We have had for some weeks back very unsettled weather, which has rendered it very disagreeable, though we haven't suffered; we have an old tent which affords a good deal of protection from the weather. It has also interfered some with our meetings, though there is preaching nearly every night that there is not rain. Brother Hughes came up and preached for us last Friday night and seemed to give general satisfaction. He was plain and practical, which is the only kind of preaching that does good in the army. He promised to come back again. I

like him very much. Another old brother, named Campbell, whom I heard when I was a boy, preached for us on Sabbath evening. There was much feeling, and at the close of the services he invited mourners to the anxious seat, and I shall never forget that blessed half-hour that followed; from every part of that great congregation they came, many with streaming eyes; and, as they gave that old patriarch their hands, asked that God's people would pray for them. Yes, men who never shrank in battle from any responsibility, came forward weeping. Such is the power of the Gospel of Christ when preached in its purity. Oh, that all ministers of Christ could, or would, realize the great responsibility resting upon them as His ambassadors.

Since my return we have established a prayer-meeting in our company, or, rather, a kind of family service, every night after roll call. There is one other company which has prayer every night. Captain F. is very zealous. There are four in our company who pray in public—one sergeant, a private, Captain P. and myself. We take it time about. We have cleared up a space, fixed a stand and seats, and have a regular preaching place. I have never seen such a spirit as there is now in the army. Religion is the theme. Everywhere, you hear around the camp-fires at night the sweet songs of Zion. This spirit pervades the whole army. God is doing a glorious work, and I believe it is but the beautiful prelude to peace. I feel confident that if the enemy should attempt to advance, that God will fight our battles for us, and the boastful foe be scattered and severely rebuked.

I witnessed a scene the other evening, which did my heart good—the baptism of three men in the creek near the encampment. To see those hardy soldiers taking up their cross and following their Master in His ordinance, being buried with Him in baptism, was indeed a beautiful sight. I really believe, Missouri, that there is more religion now in the army than among the thousands of skulkers, exempts and speculators at home. There are but few now but who will talk freely with you upon the subject of their soul's salvation. What a change, what a change! when one year ago card playing and profane language seemed to be the order of the day. Now, what is the cause of this change? Manifestly the working of God's spirit. He has chastened His people, and this manifestation of His love seems to be an earnest of the good things in store for us in not a far away future. "Whom the Lord loveth He chasteneth, and scourgeth every son whom He receiveth." Let all the people at home now, in unison with the army, humbly bow, acknowledge the afflicting hand of the Almighty, ask Him to remove the curse upon His own terms, and soon we will hear, so far as our Nation is concerned, "Glory to God in the highest, on earth peace, good will toward men!"

Your affectionate brother,
T. J. Stokes

In Camp, Near Dalton, Ga., April 18, 1864. The good work still goes on here. Thirty-one men were baptized at the creek below our brigade yesterday, and I have heard from several other brigades in which the proportion is equally large (though the thirty-one were not all members of this brigade). Taking the proportion in the whole army as heard from (and I have only heard from a part of one corps), there must have been baptized yesterday 150 persons—maybe 200. This revival spirit is not confined to a part only, but pervades the whole army. . . . Brother Hughes was with us the other night, but left again the next morning. The old man seemed to have much more influence in the army than young men. I have preached twice since writing to you, and the Spirit seemed to be with me. . . . Many presented themselves, and I could hear many among them, with sobs and groans, imploring God to have mercy upon them; and I think the Lord did have mercy upon them, for when we opened the door of the church six united with us. Every Sabbath you may see the multitude wending their way to the creek to see the solemn ordinance typical of the death, burial and resurrection of our Savior. . . .

If this state of things should continue for any considerable length of time we will have in the Army of Tennessee an army of believers. Does the history of the world record any where the like? Even Cromwell's time sinks into insignificance. A revival so vast in its proportions, and under all the difficulties attending camp life, the bad weather this spring, and innumerable difficulties, is certainly an earnest of better, brighter times not far in the future.

Near Dalton, May 5th, 1864. The great revival is going on with widening and deepening interest. Last Sabbath I saw eighty-three immersed at the creek below our brigade. Four were sprinkled at the stand before going down to the creek, and two down there, making an aggregate within this vicinity of eighty-nine, while the same proportion, I suppose, are turning to God in other parts of the army, making the grand aggregate of many hundreds. Yesterday I saw sixty-five more baptized, forty more who were to have been there failing to come because of an order to be ready to move at any moment. They belong to a more distant brigade. . . . If we do not move before Monday, Sabbath will be a day long to be remembered—"the water will," indeed, "be troubled." Should we remain three weeks longer, the glad tidings may go forth that the Army of Tennessee is the army of the Lord. But He knoweth best what is for our good, and if he sees proper can so order His providence as to keep us here. His will be done.

—GAY, *Life in Dixie during the War*

XII.5

FROM REVEILLE TO TAPS

Most of the accounts of marching emphasize its hardships. Here is a simple factual account of how an army on the march spends its day. The auspices were, of course, favor able, for this is Sherman's army marching through Georgia. A young man of twenty-four or five when he joined the army, George Ward Nichols had already lived a busy life. Born in Maine and educated in Boston, he had worked as a journalist, taken part in the struggle for free Kansas, studied art in France, and become art editor on the *New York Evening Post*. Shortly after the outbreak of the war, he joined Fremont's staff; then went as provost marshal to Wisconsin; and ended up as aide-de-camp to General Sherman. His *Story of the Great March* from which this excerpt is taken was one of the most popular of all postwar books, published in England and translated into many European languages. After the war Nichols had a long and distinguished career promoting art and music in Cincinnati.

Among the most characteristic features of the soldier's life is the important step of breaking camp, which is at once the close of a season of monotonous inactivity and the preliminary stage of a phase of exciting adventure. The same general details are on such occasions observed throughout the entire army, differing slightly in some of the corps, when the division which was in the centre or rear marches first, taking the place of the division which was in advance the day before.

The order of march is issued by the army commanders the preceding night, from them to the corps commanders, and then passed along until every soldier, teamster, and camp-follower knows that an early start is to be made. "The second division will be on the Milledgeville road promptly at five o'clock" reads an order, by way of instance.

At three o'clock the watch-fires are burning dimly, and, but for the occasional neighing of horses, all is so silent that it is difficult to imagine that twenty thousand men are within a radius of a few miles. The ripple of the brook can be distinctly heard as it breaks over the pebbles, or winds petulantly about the gnarled roots. The wind sweeping gently through the tall pines overhead only serves to lull to deeper repose the slumbering soldier, who in his tent is dreaming of his far-off Northern home.

But in an instant all is changed. From some commanding elevation the clear-toned bugle sounds out the *reveille*, and another and another responds, until the startled echoes double and treble the clarion calls. Intermingled with this comes the beating of drums, often rattling and jarring on unwilling ears. In a few moments the peaceful quiet is replaced by noise and tumult, arising from hill and dale, from field and forest. Camp-fires, hitherto extinct or smouldering in dull gray ashes, awaken to new life and brilliancy, and send forth their sparks high into the morning air. Although no gleam of sunrise blushes in the east, the harmless flames on every side light up the scene, so that there is no disorder or confusion.

The aesthetic aspects of this sudden change do not, how ever, occupy much of the soldier's time. He is more practical ly engaged in getting his breakfast ready. The potatoes are frying nicely in the well-larded pan; the chicken is roasting delicately on the red-hot coals, and grateful fumes from steaming coffee-pots delight the nostrils. The animals are not less busy. An ample supply of corn and huge piles of fodder are greedily devoured by these faithful friends of the boys in blue, and any neglect is quickly made known by the pawing of neighing horses and the fearful braying of the mules. Amid all is the busy clatter of tongues and tools—a Babel of sound, forming a contrast to the quiet of the previous hour as marked as that between peace and war.

Then the animals are hitched into the traces, and the droves of cattle relieved from the night's confinement in the corral. Knapsacks are strapped, men seize their trusty weapons, and as again the bugles sound the note of command, the soldiers fall into line and file out upon the road, to make another stage of their journey—it may be to win fresh laurels in another victory, or perhaps to find a rest which shall only be broken by the *reveille* of the last trump.

A day's march varies according to the country to be traversed or the opposition encountered. If the map indicates a stream crossing the path, probably the strong party of mounted infantry or of cavalry which has been sent forward the day before has found the bridges burned, and then the pontoons are pushed on to the front. If a battle is anticipated, the trains are shifted to the rear of the centre. Under any circumstances, the divisions having the lead move unencumbered by wagons, and in close fighting trim. The ambulances following in the rear of the division are in such close proximity as to be available if needed. In the rear of each regiment follow the pack-mules, laden with every kind of camp baggage, including blankets, pots, pans, kettles, and all the kitchen-ware needed for cooking. Here will be found the led horses, and with them the Negro servants, who form an important feature of the *ménage*.

Having placed the column upon the road, let us now follow that long line of muskets gleaming in the rays of the morning sunlight, and ride, heedless of the crack of the rifles, to the head of the column. The advance are driving a squad of Rebel cavalry before them so fast that the march is not in the least impeded. The flankers spread out, on a line parallel to the leading troops, for several hundred yards, more or less, as the occasion may require. They search through the swamps an forests, ready for any concealed

foe, and anxiously looking out for any line of works which may have been thrown up by the enemy to check our progress. Here the General of the division, if a fighting man, is most likely to be found; his experienced eye noting that there is no serious opposition, he orders up a brigade or another regiment, who, in soldier's phraseology, send the Rebel rascals "kiting," and the column moves on. A large plantation appears by the road-side. If the "bummers" have been ahead, the chances are that it has been visited, in which event the interior is apt to show evidences of confusion; but the barns are full of corn and fodder, and parties are at once detailed to secure and convey the prize to the road-side. As the wagons pass along they are not allowed to halt, but the grain or fodder is stuffed into the front and rear of the vehicles as they pass, the unhandy operation affording much amusement to the soldiers, and not unfrequently giving them a poor excuse for swearing as well as laughing.

When the treasure-trove of grain, and poultry, and vegetables has been secured, one man is detailed to guard it until the proper wagon comes along. Numbers of these details will be met, who, with proper authority, have started off early in the morning, and have struck out miles away from the

flank of the column. They sit upon some cross-road, surrounded with their spoils—chickens, turkeys, geese, ducks, pigs, hogs, sheep, calves, nicely-dressed hams, buckets full of honey, and pots of fresh white lard. . . .

There is a halt in the column. The officer in charge of the pioneer corps, which follows the advance guard, has discovered an ugly place in the road, which must be "corduroyed" at once, before the wagons can pass. The pioneers quickly tear down the fence near by and bridge over the treacherous place, perhaps at the rate of a quarter of a mile in fifteen minutes, If rails are not near, pine saplings and split logs supply their place. Meanwhile the bugles have sounded, and the column has halted. The soldiers, during the temporary halt, drop out of line on the road-side, lying upon their backs, supported by their still unstrapped knapsacks. If the halt is a long one, the different regiments march by file right, one behind the other, into the fields, stacking their muskets, and taking their rest at ease, released from their knapsack.

These short halts are of great benefit to the soldier. He gains a breathing-spell, has a chance to wipe the perspiration from his brow and the dust out of his eyes, or pulls off his shoes and stockings to cool his swollen, heated feet, though old campaigners do not feel the need of this. He munches his bit of hard bread, or pulls out a book from his pocket, or oftener a pipe, to indulge in that greatest of luxuries to the soldier, a soothing, refreshing smoke. Here may be seen one group at a brook-side, bathing their heads and drinking; and another, crowded round an old song-book, are making very fair music. One venturesome fellow has kindled a fire, and is brewing a cup of coffee. All are happy and jolly; but when the bugle sounds "fall in," "attention," and "forward," in an instant every temporary occupation is dropped, and they are on the road again.

This massing of brigades and wagons during a halt is a proper and most admirable arrangement. It keeps the column well closed up; and if a brigade or division has by some means been delayed, it has the opportunity to overtake the others. The 20th Corps manage this thing to perfection.

A great many of the mounted officers ride through the fields, on either side of the line of march, so as not to interfere with the troops. General Sherman always takes to the fields, dashing through thickets or plunging into the swamps, and, when forced to take the road, never breaks into a regiment or brigade, but waits until it passes, and then falls in. He says that they, and not he, have the right to the road.

Sometimes a little creek crosses the path, and at once a foot-bridge is made upon one side of the way for those who wish to keep dry-shod; many, however, with a shout of derision, will dash through the water at a run, and then they all shout the more when some unsteady comrade misses his footing and tumbles in at full length. The unlucky wight, however, takes the fun at his expense in the best of humor. Indeed, as a general rule, soldiers are good-humored and kind-hearted to the last degree. I have seen a soldier stand at a spring of water for ten minutes, giving thirsty comers cool draughts, although it would delay him so that he would have to run a quarter of a mile or more to overtake his company. The troops, by the way, kept their ranks admirably during this Georgia campaign. Occasionally, however, they would rush for a drink of water, or for a bee-hive which they would despoil of its sweets with a total disregard of the swarm of bees buzzing about their ears, but which, strange to say, rarely stung.

But the sun has long since passed the zenith, the droves of cattle which have been driven through the swamps and fields are lowing and wandering in search of a corral, the soldiers are beginning to lag a little, the teamsters are obliged to apply the whip oftener, ten or fifteen miles have been traversed, and the designated halting-place for the night is near. The column must now be got into camp.

Officers ride on in advance to select the ground for each brigade, giving the preference to slopes in the vicinity of wood and water. Soon the troops file out into the woods and fields, the leading division pitching tents first, those in the rear marching on yet farther, ready to take their turn in the advance the next day.

As soon as the arms are stacked, the boys attack the fences and rail-piles, and with incredible swiftness their little shelter-tents spring up all over the ground. The fires are kindled with equal celerity, and the luxurious repast prepared, while "good digestion waits on appetite, and health on both." After this is heard the music of dancing or singing, the pleasant buzz of conversation, and the measured sound of reading. The wagons are meanwhile parked and the animals fed. If there has been a fight during the day, the incidents of success or failure are recounted; the poor fellow who lies wounded in "the anguish-laden ambulance" is not forgotten, and the brave comrade who fell in the strife is remembered with words of loving praise.

By-and-by the tattoo rings out on the night air. Its familiar sound is understood. "Go to rest, go to rest," it says, as plainly as organs of human speech.

Shortly after follows the peremptory command of "Taps." "Out lights, out lights, out lights!" The soldier gradually disappears from the camp-fire. Rolled snugly in his blanket, the soldier dreams again of home, or revisits in imagination the battlefields he has trod. The animals, with dull instinct, lie down to rest, and with dim gropings of consciousness ruminate over "fresh fields and pastures new." The fires, neglected by the sleeping men, go out, gradually flickering and smouldering, as if unwilling to die.

All is quiet. The army is asleep. Perhaps there is a brief interruption to the silence as some trooper goes clattering down the road on an errand of speed, or some uneasy sleeper turns over to find an easier position. And around the slumbering host the picket-guards keep quiet watch, while constant, faithful hearts in Northern and Western homes pray that the angels of the Lord may encamp around the sleeping army.

—NICHOLS, *The Story of the Great March*

XII.6

An Indiana Boy Reassures His Mother About Morals in the Army

Theodore Upson was barely seventeen when he enlisted in the 100th Regiment of Indiana Volunteers. Brought up in a strict Presbyterian household, he was much concerned to reassure his parents about such matters as drinking, swearing, and gambling. On the whole the morals of both armies were remarkably good. There was comparatively little drunken ness and, by modern standards, little gambling. While there was a great deal of pillaging, especially among the invaders, crimes against persons were rare and sex offenses almost unknown. Young Upson fought at Vicksburg and Chattanooga and was with Sherman in his March to the Sea.

Bellefont, Ala., April 2, 1864

Dear Mother—

I have had several letters from the home people asking me about drinking in the Army, and Father has written me saying he hopes I am not getting to be a d[r]unkard as he hears many of the soldiers are. I think you good people at home must imagine we keep a barell of whisky on tap all of the time. Now for the truth about this and other things that are told about our boys. There is some drinking in the Army, I am sorry to say, but it is the exception rather than the rule. Some of our officers may take a social glass when they get together at times but few if any of them drink to excess, and I think drinking among the officers is less now than ever before. Good officers know that when wine is in, wit is out. They know too that the men distrust and have no confidence in an intemperate officer, in fact will make fun of him. And an officer whose men make fun of him had better resign as some *have done*, for his usefulness is at-an end. I know what I am talking about for I have been around Head Quarters enough to have learned the habits of our Generals. Grant does not drink at all; Sherman but little, if any; I don't think any. Howard never; McPherson, I think, never; Logan is

no tippler; and in our Division and Brigade officers all, or nearly all, are total abstainers.

As to the rank and file hardly a man is a drinker. It is not so easy for a soldier to get liquor as most people seem to think. First, he has to have an order from a commissioned officer. Not so easy to get as the officers do not want thier men to drink. Next, it takes money which the men are often without. Another thing, good hard experience has taught them that liquor is no good, that they need clear heads and sound bodies to stand the strain and hardships of Army life. A soldier must be above all temperate in all things.

As to profanity a good many of the boys do use swear words, some liberaly, some not at all. But this is a strenuous life. Men will do here what they would not do at home and I know this. Profanity is not deep nor vicious. Let a Chaplain come along who the men respect and the most of them will be gaurded in thier talk. Why? Because all the time thier better selves are lying dormant and under different conditions would assert themselves. We have a good many men, Uncle Aaron Woflord, for instance, who set a good quiet example which is respected, to say the least, by the roughest.

As to gambling, there is very little of it. The men play cards a good deal, it is true, sometimes for small stakes, but it is for amusement alone. No gambling about it. A real gambler would not be held in any respect by the men.

As to other vices, I think I am safe in saying that you might search the world over and not find as clean a lot of men as comprise the Army today. I do not say it has always been so, but the men who compose the great Army to which I have the honor to belong have passed through the trials and temptations of the soldiers life and now are like gold—cleared of its dross. And when this war is ended and what are left of this Army return to civil life, you will see that they will be accepted as among the best and highest of ideal American citizens. All the roughness will fall away and they will be shining lights in thier chosen walks of life. As for myself, I am too proud to dabble in mud and mire.

So do not worry, Father mine, I am not going to the dogs; neither are any of the other boys you know.

I have at one time mentioned our excellent Chaplain, Rev John A Brouse, father of Captain Charles Brouse, who was so teribly wounded at Mission Ridge. Chaplain Brouse is a valient soldier, not only of the Cross, but also of this war. He never seems to think of himself and was right on the firing line helping care for the wounded and saying words of comfort to the dying. A noble man is Chaplain Brouse and the boys love him as a Father. There is also a Chaplain of the 90 Ill, a Catholic Preist, who is greatly loved and respected by all of the men of his and other Regiments. So you see this war is breaking down the barriers between beliefs and creeds as well as doing many other things you may think more or less desirable. And another thing I know you will find it hard to understand, money has but little value with the boys now. They all seem to think the pittance paid them by the Government is an incident of the service, that they are giving this part of their lives for a principle and do not expect to gain any personal profit from it in any way.

—WINTHER, ed., *Journal of Theodore Upson*

XII.7

GRAFT AND CORRUPTION IN THE CONFEDERATE COMMISSARY

Complaints against the commissary were ardent, on both sides. The simple fact was that there was no such organization of the commissary department, during the Civil War, as we are familiar with from the First and Second World Wars. Nor was there any adequate check on the food and drink that went through the commissary, or on the activities of the sutlers.

This picture of graft in the Confederate commissary is doubtless accurate enough for Watson's particular outfit, but it is by no means a faithful picture of conditions generally in the Confederate armies. We have already met the irrepressible Watson on the retreat from Pea Ridge.

The army was furnished, through the quarter master's department, with quarters, whether houses or tents, camp equipage, arms, ammunition, accoutrements, and clothing, and all means of transport. These the department obtained from contractors, and the shocking quality of the materials furnished showed corruption to a great extent. The soldier, of course, knew nothing about the contracts, and in the South they had always the excuse that good materials were not to be got; but the things which mostly affected the soldier personally were shoes and clothing, and these, to a great extent, they managed to provide for themselves, or they were sent to them by their friends at home.

The system pursued by the commissaries, even making allowance for the difficulties they were subject to, were simply disgraceful. I do not exaggerate when I say that on an average from every requisition of rations said to be issued to the troops, the commissary took off one-third and sold it, putting the proceeds in his pocket. The cause of this peculation lay greatly in the system of management. I might say that the system, as it then existed, was such that even a man of the most sterling integrity, and of honest and upright principles, if appointed commissary of a regiment on active service could hardly after six months, remain an honest man. If so, he would deserve the greatest credit for it.

The system was this: The commissary received a supply of provisions from the depot. He got with it an invoice detailing quantity and price. From these he issued to the noncommissioned officers and soldiers, on requisitions signed by the orderly-sergeants and captains of companies. He sold for money to all officers and men pertaining to the army. He had to account for the amount of the consignment (losses and casualties excepted) by money and requisitions. The practice was this: An orderly sergeant made out a requisition for his company—say for 100 men for one day—flour, 100 lb.; beef, pork, or bacon, 75 lb.; coffee, seven lb.; sugar, 14 lb.; rice or pease, six lb.; soap, two lb.; salt, pepper, vinegar, etc. This requisition was signed by the captain, and men were detailed to go to the commissary store to draw these rations. The commissary takes the requisition and calls his assistant, and says to the men, "Well, you can get three-quarter ration of flour, half ration of pork, half ration of coffee, and half ration of sugar, and that is all." The men would grumble and say, "We only got half rations yesterday," "Can't help it, I am short of provisions, and there are other companies to serve as well as you, and all must get their share." He then sticks the requisition on the file, and his assistant weighs out the rations. "Will we get the back rations when the supplies come up?" some mischievous young rascal would say as he dodged behind a barrel. The commissary would put his hand on his revolver, but restrain himself, and pretend to take no notice of a thing so absurd, and buries his face in his book, while he credits himself with full rations issued to 100 men as per requisition, while his assistant and the men would laugh at the audacity of the offender, "no back rations" being the commissary's watch word, and, what was more strange, no requisition would be received unless it was made out for the full amount.

Thus the commissary had a voucher for and was credited with supplying a full requisition when he had only supplied a small part of it, and he had the rest to sell for his own benefit. I have frequently known instances of a company, after giving the full requisition and being supplied with half rations on the grounds that provisions were scarce, getting one of the army waggon drivers, and giving him money to go to the commissary store and purchase four or five pounds of coffee, or other necessaries, which had been kept off them, which he would obtain for money without the least trouble, and this system was carried on quite openly. I more than once nearly got into serious difficulty by insisting on marking on the requisition the actual quantity of provisions delivered.

In the post-commissaries and depots there was another system of peculation.

In these depots there were immense stocks of provisions stored for army use. These were periodically inspected by officers, generally of the sinecure kind appointed through favour for such purposes,

and there was always a consider able quantity marked "condemned" as being unfit for use. The ceremony of inspecting was generally done in this way: The inspecting officers would come to the depot, where they would be met by the post-commissary, who would receive them in the most friendly manner, and conduct them into the large stores. On each side along the wall would be piled up on the top of each other with their ends exposed, a great many barrels of beef, pork, flour, biscuit, etc.

"These," says the commissary, "are what I have myself picked out as being bad. Those on this side are good, but you can inspect for yourself. Cooper, open one or two of these barrels." The cooper opens a barrel which of course had been already selected. The unsavoury brine spurts out. The officers stand back to save their handsome uniforms. Other barrels are examined of flour, biscuit, etc., similarly selected. Then all on that side, the bulk of which were probably the best provisions, are ordered to be marked condemned. The officers would take a list of the numbers to make their report, and then go and inspect the hospital stores of wines, brandies, etc., of which they would ac knowledge they were better judges. A few days' notice would then be given of a sale of "condemned army stores" and they would be auctioned off for a mere trifle. The commissary of course has an agent present who knew what lots to purchase.

Thus it was said large quantities of the very best stores were often marked "Condemned" and sold off at a mere trifle, the commissary having an agent on the ground to buy them in.

—Watson, *Life in the Confederate Army*

XII.8

The Soldiers Get Paid and the Sutler Gets the Money

By European standards the United States paid its soldiers well; by American standards the pay was shockingly low. At the beginning of the war it was 11 dollars a month for privates, plus a clothing allowance; this was raised to 13 and then to 16 dollars, but the depreciation of money meant that the purchasing value of this pay actually declined during the war. It should be remembered, however, that soldiers' pay was supplemented by Federal and state bounties. The pay of Confederate soldiers was even lower, and the rapid depreciation of Confederate currency meant that most soldiers were fighting without pay.

Not only was Civil War pay low, but soldiers were expected to supply most of the services and comforts that the government furnished in later wars. Thus they had to do their own wash, or find some camp hanger-on to do it; they supplemented their food by private purchases; they even bought their own stoves. Sutlers, who supplied luxuries to the soldiers—tobacco, fruit, cheese, and sometimes liquor—held a semiofficial position. In an effort to regulate them, Congress provided that a board of officers should fix the prices charged, and that no sutler might take a lien on more than one sixth of a soldier's pay in any one month, but these provisions were generally ignored.

At intervals, various in duration, we were visited by the paymaster, who paid us what was coming from the Government. A paymaster had the rank of Major in the regular army. To us in the field he always came with his "strong box" conveyed in an ambulance, or army wagon, and well guarded by a troop of cavalry with loaded carbines in their hands. Reaching a particular regiment he would go over the amount due each man, as reported by the Adjutant, and, if this was found correct, the specified sum would be put in a pay envelope; then the men would be formed in line, and when the name of a given soldier was called he would step forward and receive his money, which was always in currency or "greenbacks." Even small fractional amounts were paid in paper money, as neither gold, silver, nor even copper was in circulation.

The paymaster always had on a bright, new uniform, his linen was immaculate, and his boots never failed to be glossy black. In all this he presented a striking contrast to the other officers in active service in the field.

The more thrifty among the soldiers sent, by far, the greater part of their pay home. In most instances this was done through express companies which followed us in the field, and were new institutions to practically all of us. The prudent soldier, if so disposed, had opportunity to lay by substantially all his wages, which, in the early part of the war, was for

the private soldier $13 per month, but later was advanced to $16. The ration furnished by the Government was ample, and so was the clothing allowed each man. Indeed, some of the more thrifty did not use all that was allowed in this way, and consequently received commutation in the way of small, but by no means, intangible amounts of money.

As said above, a few men sent their pay home to almost the last cent. In contrast to these of the more thrifty there was a pitiful minority who had squandered their last far thing in a few hours after being paid off. How? Some of them in gambling with cards, some of them at dice, and others by indulging in what was called "chuck-a-luck." This last was a game of chance, with the *chances* very greatly against the poor soldier victim on the outside.

Not a few "blew-in" all they had received from the pay master at the Sutler's tent. The Sutler was the recognized regimental merchant. After securing the consent of the commanding offlcer the Sutler proceeded to lay in a stock of such things as he thought the men would need in the field, and in amount about what could be loaded in a wagon.

His stock included such articles as tobacco, cigars, lemons, oranges, apples, candy, raisins, soda crackers, cakes, canned fruits of various kinds, loaf sugar, mackerel, salt fish, bacon, ginger ale, "pop" and other "soft" drinks. Nearly all these articles were outside the soldier's rations, and were hence, by him, regarded as luxuries which the more provident refused to buy.

Arrived in camp the Sutler transferred his goods to a strong tent of proper size, which through the day, was open in front and, at which, was a wide transverse board which served the double purpose of counter and showcase. The sides of the tent came well down and were securely fastened. The Sutler always slept in his tent and in the midst of his stock. However, sometimes a thief would take advantage of the darkness to rip a hole in the sides of the tent and make a hasty dash for whatever he might be able to lay his hands on.

That the Sutler's prices were always high, and sometimes even exorbitant, can well be imagined.

But to make a good profit he had to mark his goods high, for he necessarily incurred great risk. In the field he was in danger of capture. Then, when the regiment had orders to move on short notice, he had to pack his stock hurriedly and often put it "pell-mell" in a wagon for transfer to the next camping place. Furthermore, unless quickly turned some of his goods would grow stale on his hands. One article of this nature was butter, which not infrequently became so rancid as to be wholly unusable.

As to the Sutler himself, he might be long or short. He might be a blonde or brunette. He might be a native or foreigner. But one thing he was always sure to be, namely, "on the make." At the time the average regiment was organized those who joined it were actuated by motives more or less mixed in character. But with the Sutler it was different, for his sole motive was gain.

An "easy-mark" for the Sutler was the financial "tender foot," the "live-to-day-and-starve-tomorrow" man who was in every regiment, in every company, and indeed, in practically every squad. And no sooner had this "come-easy-go easy" specimen received his pay than he forthwith went to the Sutler's tent and proceeded to get "outside" a good deal that, for the man's good, had far better have been left on the shelves.

But not only would these "easy-goers" get rid of their money, but oftentimes the stuff they ate would make them sick. Indeed, in every regiment more than one death could primarily be attributed to certain articles in the Sutler's tent.

—Charles Beneulyn Johnson, *Muskets and Medicine*

XII.9

SONG AND PLAY IN THE ARMY OF TENNESSEE

The periods covered by an article in *The Southern Illustrated News* and a passage by Bromfield Ridley were in the last year of the war. Although prospects for the Confederacy were dimming,

camp morale among Southern soldiers could be quite good. Amusements for soldiers were rarely provided by the government or national agencies. Men in the armies usually found ways of their own to provide entertainment.

Bands were not widespread, but individual musicians and informal groups often played in military camps. Performances by amateur theater groups were occasionally staged, such as the one described below in the spring of 1864.

By the time of Ridley's description, the Army of the Tennessee had been driven out of South Carolina and into North Carolina. In the midst of this scene of disaster, Ridley took the opportunity to recall some of the more cheerful aspects of army life. What he recorded is of interest alike to students of social history and of the American language. Ridley was a first lieutenant, attached to the staff of General A. P. Stewart.

A. Theatricals in the Army

Camp Gregg's Brigade, Field's division,
Zollicoffer, East Tennessee,
April 15, 1864

Mr. Editor: As a portion of your valuable journal is devoted to the drama, I take the liberty to ask a small space therein, in order to bring before the public an enterprise in this far-famed corner of the Confederacy—vulgarly called "East Tenn."

I dare say a majority of your readers will be surprised to learn that the drama (not Ogden's legitimate) is prospering among Longstreet's war-worn veterans. Such is the case, however, as I shall soon show. Mrs. Bailey, a member of the *quondam* "Bailey Troupe," being on a visit to her husband, leader of the 3d Arkansas band, kindly tendered her efforts toward relieving the dull monotony of camp life. Thereupon, Mr. J. A. Bailey, calling to his assistance his brother, Geo. A. Bailey, together with several members of "Hood's Minstrels," determined to give a theatrical performance. "Where there's a will there's a way;" and despite the weather—April weather—lack of conveniences, &c., they at once set to work to extemporize a *stage* under the broad canopy of Heaven.

The spot selected for this model "temple of the Muses" is, as the accompanying drawing shows, a natural amphitheatre, close to the track of the East Tenn. & Va. Railroad, and about one mile from Zollicoffer. The *stage* consisted of planks used for shipping horses on the cars, and was kindly furnished by an obliging quartermaster. The *infernal regions* from which "Banquo Ghost" issues forth to astonish "Macbeth," were, of course, omitted. The back scenery was formed by a tent-fly from General Anderson's headquarters; the ladies' dressing-room, to the left, by a wall-tent, captured at Lenoir Station, from Burnside & Co., and the gentlemen's *ditto*, by a so-called A tent. As to boxes, parquette, reserved seats, and other modern improvements, our opera-house was almost destitute; a dozen or so of benches, borrowed from a neighboring church, supplying the whole. In fact, "standing seats" were found more convenient, and the hill in front served as an admirable substitute for these sometimes indispensable articles.—Tallow candles, screened by a board as reflector, supplied the place of footlights; but "pale-faced Luna," who was expected to shed her benign rays over the assembled multitude, deemed it proper to hide her features behind a veil of sable clouds, and the audience was thus thrown into darkness. I am thus explicit in detailing the minutiae of this novel theatre as I consider it important for future reference as a guide to all who intend to seek "pleasure under difficulties."

The first performance was given on the 5th April, and commenced at the hour usually designated as "early candle light," the band of the 3d Arkansas playing the overture—"La Sonnambula."

The programme opened with, "The Soldier Boy's Courtship," Mr. George A. Bailey (soldier boy) being *the* character par excellence; his side-splitting humor convulsing the "house," and instituting him, at once, the favorite.—"The Soldier Lad I Adore," was sung by Mrs. Bailey, with exquisite taste and feelings and failed not to carry every heart with it. "Highland Fling," danced by Mr. D. Stretter, of "Hood's Minstrels," in Ethiopian costume, (female) was executed to perfection—so much so, that no one would have imagined the little drummer of the 4th Texas to be sailing under false colors. Mrs. Bailey followed in that charming ballad, "Annie of the Vale," in which, if possible, she surpassed her first effort. Mr. George A. Bailey,

who has already proved himself complete master of the humorous, appeared next, with unbounded success in the execution of a comic hornpipe; in fact, we have seen but few to equal him, and still fewer to surpass him. The farce of "Lucy Long," in which "Hood's Minstrels" appeared as a body was well rendered. Messrs. Chandler and Jett brought out the negro's character in a manner which might make the "Buckley's" look to their laurels. Albert Pike's "Fine Arkansas Gentleman" was sung next by Mr. G. A. Bailey, and here again his well-modulated voice, comic gestures, and inimitable performance carried the audience by *storm*, as we soldiers say. The performance concluded with "P. T. Barnum's ball," the principal character (negro Pete) being sustained by Mr. Jett, in his usual excellent style. His dance with the soldier, (Mr. G. B.) especially, was most humorous, and brought down the "house" as well as himself, for he was skillfully tripped by his nimble antagonist. Such, Mr. Editor, was one of our most pleasant nights in camp, and we do not think that this performance has ever been equalled in the army.

The performers, each and all, deserve the thanks of their fellow-soldiers, and especially Mrs. Bailey, who, by her fine acting and vocal powers, elevated the whole affair to the rank of a first class entertainment.

All hails to the Messrs. Baileys and Hood's Minstrels.—Long may they meet the plaudits with which they were greeted is the wish of one who, with many others, varied camp life by a pleasant evening among the Muses.

—*The Southern Illustrated News*

B. Good Cheer in the Ranks

One night, one of Colonel McLemore's captains formed a line of battle by saying, "Boys, you can't see me, but dress up on my voice." Colonel Anderson would say, "Dress up on my friend Brit." These things got to be by-words in those commands. Instead of "Blow the Bugle," it was "Toot the Dinner Horn." That takes me to some of our greenhorns in the drill. When we first started, a fellow in East Tennessee began drilling his company thus: "Men, tangle in fours! By move forward! Put! Wheel into line! By turn around! Git!" A Middle Tennessee captain, wanting his company to cross a creek on a log, said: "Attention, company! In one rank to walk a log! Walk a log! March!"

It carried you back to old times to hear the guards around a regiment halloo out, "T-w-e-l-v-e o'-c-l-o-c-k and a-l-l-'s well!" The rude and untrained soldier would play on that and say: "T-w-e-l-v-e o'-c-l-o-c-k, and sleepy as h—l!" When a soldier goes out foraging it is called going on a "lark;" when he goes stealing, it is "impressing it into service;" when a Quartermaster wants to shield his rascality, he has a favorite abstract called "L," which is used, and means "Lost in the service;" when a squad runs from the enemy, it is "Skedadling;" the ricochetting of a cannon ball is "Skiugling"—words whose origin began with the war. Let a stranger or soldier enter camp and call for a certain company—say, Company F. Some soldier will say, "Here's Company F!" By the time he can get there, another will cry out at the far part of the regiment, "Here's Company F!" Then the whole command will take up the refrain, until the poor fellow in vexation will sulk away. Let an old soldier recognize a passing friend, and say, "How are you Jim?" a marching division will keep it up, with "How are you, Jim?" until the poor fellow swoons.

In the army we have some of the finest mimics in the world. Let one cackle like a hen, and the monotony of camp is broken by the encore of "S-h-o-o!" Then other cacklers take it up, until it sounds like a poultry yard stirred up over a mink or a weasel. Let one bray like an ass, others take it up until the whole regiment will personate the sound, seemingly like a fair ground of asses. As mimics they are perfect; as musicians, also. I met one once who said, "If you will give me a jigger, I'll give you some chin music." He put his hands to his chin, and with his teeth made a sound like rattling bones, keeping time to his pat and song. Some of the finest singers I ever heard were soldiers and some of the best acting I ever saw was done by

them. In camp it is so delightful to hear the brass band dispensing music in the sweetest strains. Near Atlanta, a Dutch battery entertained us every fifteen minutes, and whilst we kept our eyes open to the music of the shells from far away would beat upon our ears the music of the enemy's brass bands; our bands would tunc up and make us oblivious to the roar of that old battery. I tried once in the progress of the battle to assimilate it to music. The sound of the minnie ball—Zip! Zip!—I dubbed the soprano; the roar of the musketry, the alto; the lingering sound of battle, the tenor; the artillery, the basso. Now, intersperse it with the interlude of an old Rebel yell, and you've got it.

As to wit and sarcasm you hear in camp, I'd defy the world to beat it. Anyone attempting to be consequential, or unnatural, is the character to work on, and the gravest of the Chaplains cannot look upon their ridicule without smiling. A psalm-singing soldier one day gave out a distich for song, to sing to the long meter hymn of St. Thomas. Some blasphemous fellow changed it to

"The possum am a cunning fowl,
He climbs upon a tree."

The regiment broke out with the chorus.

"Rye-straw! Rye-straw! Rye-straw!"
"And when he wraps his tail 'round a limb,
He turn and looks at me."
"Rye-straw! Rye-straw! Rye-straw! Rye-straw!"

This is shocking to us now, but when you reflect upon the idea that in their daily walk the soldiers had no way of entertainment, it was excusable to find some means of pastime and of keeping cheerful, if sacrilege is pardonable.

Some of the parodies on our Southern songs should be remembered. I copy a verse to the tune of "My Maryland." (If you know the tune, sing it.)

Old Stonewall Jackson's in the field,
Here's your mule, Oh, here's your mule!

And he has the boys that will not yield,
Here's your mule, Oh, here's your mule!

And when you hear the old may pray,
You may be sure that on next day,
The very Devil will be to pay—
Here's your mule, Oh, here's your mule!

And now since my native place is Old
Jefferson, Tennessee, within a stone's throw of the
battlefield of Murfreesboro (Stone's river), I think
of the devastation and desolation created there by
war. I will give a verse of my parody that I used to
sing, as I rode along in Ward's regiment, Morgan's
cavalry.

Also to enjoy it sing it as you read.

The Yankee's heel is on the street,
Jefferson, Old Jefferson!
I hear the tramp of the vandal's feet,
Jefferson, Old Jefferson!
Hark! I hear a rooster squall,
The vandal takes them hen and all,
And makes the men and women bawl,
Jefferson, Old Jefferson!

One more on the Happy Land of Canaan, and
I am done. (If you know the tune sing it.)

I will sing you a song, as the ladies pass along,
All about the times we are gaming; aha!
I will sing it in rhymes, and suit it to the times,
And we'll call it the "Happy Land of Canaan."
                                        —Chorus.

Oh me! Oh my! The pride of our Southern boys
        am coming; aha!
So it's never mind the weather, but get over double
        trouble,
For I'm bound for the Happy Land of Canaan.

In the Harper's Ferry section, there was an
        insurrection,
Old John Brown thought the niggers would sustain
        him, aha!
But old Governor Wise put his specks upon his
        eyes,
And sent him to the Happy Land of Canaan.
                                        —Chorus.

Old John Brown is dead, and the last words
        he said,
"Don't keep me here a long time remaining;" aha!
So we led him up a slope, and hung him on a rope,
And sent him to the Happy Land of Canaan.
                                        —Chorus.

—RIDLEY, *Battles and Sketches
of the Army of Tennessee*

XIII

INCIDENTS OF ARMY LIFE: WESTERN FRONT

Fundamentally, as we have already observed, the war in the East and in the West was pretty much the same. The same soldiers fought, the same officers commanded; the same weapons and techniques were used. Differences were imposed by considerations of geography rather than by social or psychological considerations. Thus warfare in the West was more mobile, more fluid. Armies fought over vast areas and army corps and divisions were shifted back and forth from Missouri to Mississippi to Tennessee. Occasionally—as with Rosecrans' army at Murfreesboro, between Stones River and the Tullahoma campaigns—the Western armies did stay put for some length of time, but normally they were on the move. The soldiers got a chance to see more varied types of society and economy than in the fighting in Virginia.

There was another difference—in degree rather than in kind, to be sure. As has been mentioned, the fighting in the West was more nearly a civil war than was the fighting in the East. Family fought against family, brother against brother. The pillaging was about as bad in the East as in the West, but there was nothing in the East so savage as the guerrilla warfare in Missouri, nor was there anything like the bitter ness in West Virginia that was found in eastern Tennessee.

Because of these circumstances of geography and history there is, about the fighting in the West, a more personal and perhaps a more casual character than i• to be found else where. Thus Mark Twain tells us how uncertain he and his friends were whether they were Confederates or Unionists. Thus there seemed to be—perhaps it is an illusion—a more personal quality about the cavalry fighting; Forrest and Morgan roamed pretty much where they would; Grierson seemed to be on his own; Wilson raised his cavalry his own way.

It is perhaps not too bold a generalization to say that the warfare in Virginia approached more nearly the traditional warfare of the Old World, while the warfare in the West kept a bit more its casual independence and almost its frontier character.

XIII. I

MARK TWAIN RECALLS A CAMPAIGN THAT FAILED

As a young man of twenty-two Mark Twain was apprenticed to a river pilot—the most glorious of all professions, he thought—and four years on the river gave him the material for *Life on the Mississippi.* The Civil War closed the river to ordinary steamboat traffic, and he returned to his boyhood town, Hannibal, Missouri. There he joined a volunteer company of a dozen or so, which, according to his own story, was ready to fight on either side. "Out West," he wrote, "there was a good deal of confusion in men's minds during the first months of the great trouble. . . . It was hard for us to get our bearings." His campaign came to an inglorious end when he sprained an ankle falling out of a barn hayloft. One of the "Marion Rangers," Absalom Grimes, later became a famous Confederate scout. As Mark Twain himself says, this is not an unfair picture of what went on in the border states during the early months of the war.

You have heard from a great many people who did something in the war; is it not fair that you listen a little moment to one who started out to do something in it, but didn't? Thousands entered the war, got just a taste of it, and then stepped out again, permanently. These, by their very numbers, are respectable, and are therefore entitled to a sort of voice,—not a loud one, but a modest one; not a boastful one, but an apologetic one. They ought not to be allowed much space among better people—people who did something—I grant that; but they ought at least to be allowed to state why they didn't do anything, and also to explain the process by which they didn't do anything. Surely this kind of light must have a sort of value.

Out West there was a good deal of confusion in men's minds during the first months of the great trouble—a good deal of unsettledness, of leaning first this way, then that, then the other way. It was hard for us to get our bearings. I call to mind an instance of this. I was piloting on the Mississippi when the news came that South Carolina had gone out of the Union on the 20th of December, 1860. My pilot-mate was a New Yorker. He was strong for the Union; so was I. But he would not listen to me with any patience; my loyalty was smirched, to his eye, because my father had owned slaves. I said, in palliation of this dark fact, that I had heard my father say, some years before he died, that slavery was a great wrong, and that he would free the solitary Negro he then owned if he could think it right to give away the property of the family when he was so straitened in means. My mate retorted that a mere impulse was nothing—any body could pretend to a good impulse; and went on decrying my Unionism and libeling my ancestry. A month later the secession atmosphere had considerably thickened on the Lower Mississippi, and I became a rebel; so did he. We were together in New Orleans, the 26th of January, when Louisiana went out of the Union. He did his full share of the rebel shouting, but was bitterly opposed to letting me do mine. He said that I came of bad stock—of a father who had been willing to set slaves free. In the following summer he was piloting a Federal gun-boat and shouting for the Union again, and I was in the Confederate army. I held his note for some borrowed money. He was one of the most upright men I ever knew; but he repudiated that note without hesitation, because I was a rebel, and the son of a man who owned slaves.

In that summer—of 1861—the first wash of the wave of war broke upon the shores of Missouri. Our State was invaded by the Union forces. They took possession of St. Louis, Jefferson Barracks, and some other points. The Governor, Claib Jackson, issued his proclamation calling out fifty thousand militia to repel the invader.

I was visiting in the small town where my boyhood had been spent—Hannibal, Marion County. Several of us got together in a secret place by night and formed ourselves into a military company. One Tom Lyman, a young fellow of a good deal of spirit but of no military experience, was made captain; I was made second lieutenant. We had no first lieutenant; I do not know why; it was long ago. There were fifteen of us. By the advice of an innocent connected with the organization, we called ourselves the Marion Rangers, I do not remember that any one found fault with the name. I did not; I thought it sounded quite well. The young fellow who proposed this title was perhaps a fair sample of the kind of stuff we were made of. He was young, ignorant, good-natured, well-meaning, trivial, full of romance, and given to reading chivalric novels and singing forlorn love ditties. He had some pathetic little nickel-plated aristocratic instincts, and detested his name, which was Dunlap; detested it, partly because it was nearly as common in that region as Smith, but mainly because it had a plebeian sound to his ear. So he tried to ennoble it by writing it in this way: *d'Unlap.* That contented his eye, but left his ear unsatisfied, for people gave the new name the same old pronunciation—emphasis on the front end of it. He then did the bravest thing that can be imagined,—a thing to make one shiver when one remembers how the world is given to resenting shams and affectations; he began to write his name so: *d'Un Lap.* And he waited patiently through the long storm of mud that was flung at this work of art, and he had his reward at last; for he lived to see that name accepted, and the emphasis put where he wanted it, by people who had known him all his life, and to whom the tribe of Dunlaps had been as familiar as the rain and the sunshine for forty years. . . .

That is one sample of us. Another was Ed Stevens, son of the town jeweler,—trim-built, handsome, graceful, neat as a cat; bright, educated, but given over entirely to fun. There was nothing serious in life to him. As far as he was concerned, this military expedition of ours was simply a holiday. I should say that about half of us looked upon it in the same way; not consciously, perhaps, but unconsciously. We did not think; we were not capable of it. As for myself, I was full of unreasoning joy to be done with turning out of bed at midnight and four in the morning, for a while; grateful to have a change, new scenes, new occupations, a new interest. In my thoughts that was as far as I went; I did not go into the details; as a rule one doesn't at twenty four. . . .

These samples will answer—and they are quite fair ones. Well, this herd of cattle started for the war. What could you expect of them? They did as well as they knew how, but really what was justly to be expected of them? Nothing, I should say. That is what they did.

We waited for a dark night, for caution and secrecy were necessary; then, toward midnight, we stole in couples and from various directions to the Griffith place, beyond the town; from that point we set out together on foot. Hannibal lies at the extreme south-eastern corner of Marion County, on the Mississippi River; our objective point was the hamlet of New London, ten miles away, in Ralls County.

The first hour was all fun, all idle nonsense and laughter. But that could not be kept up. The steady trudging came to be like work; the play had somehow oozed out of it; the stillness of the woods and the somberness of the night began to throw a depressing influence over the spirits of the boys, and presently the talking died out and each person shut himself up in his own thoughts. During the last half of the second hour nobody said a word.

Now we approached a log farm-house where, according to report, there was a guard of five Union soldiers. Lyman called a halt; and there, in the deep gloom of the overhanging branches, he began to whisper a plan of assault upon that house, which made the gloom more depressing than it was

before. It was a crucial moment; we realized, with a cold suddenness, that here was no jest—we were standing face to face with actual war. We were equal to the occasion. In our response there was no hesitation, no indecision: we said that if Lyman wanted to meddle with those soldiers, he could go ahead and do it; but if he waited for us to follow him, he would wait a long time.

Lyman urged, pleaded, tried to shame us, but it had no effect. Our course was plain, our minds were made up: we would flank the farm-house—go out around. And that is what we did.

We struck into the woods and entered upon a rough time, stumbling over roots, getting tangled in vines, and torn by briers. At last we reached an open place in a safe region, and sat down, blown and hot, to cool off and nurse our scratches and bruises. Lyman was annoyed, but the rest of us were cheerful; we had flanked the farm-house, we had made our first military movement, and it was a success; we had nothing to fret about, we were feeling just the other way. Horse-play and laughing began again; the expedition was become a holiday frolic once more.

Then we had two more hours of dull trudging and ultimate silence and depression; then, about dawn, we straggled into New London, soiled, heel-blistered, fagged with our little march, and all of us except Stevens in a sour and raspy humor and privately down on the war. We stacked our shabby old shot-guns in Colonel Ralls's barn, and then went in a body and breakfasted with that veteran of the Mexican war. Afterwards he took us to a distant meadow, and there in the shade of a tree we listened to an old-fashioned speech from him, full of gunpowder and glory, full of that adjective piling, mixed metaphor, and windy declamation which was regarded as eloquence in that ancient time and that remote region; and then he swore us on the Bible to be faithful to the State of Missouri and drive all invaders from her soil, no matter whence they might come or under what flag they might march. This mixed us considerably, and we could not make out just what service we were embarked in; but Colonel Ralls, the practiced politician and phrase-juggler, was not similarly in doubt; he knew quite clearly that he had invested us in the cause of the Southern Confederacy. He closed the solemnities by belting around me the sword which his neighbor, Colonel Brown, had worn at Buena Vista and Molino del Rey; and he accompanied this act with another impressive blast.

Then we formed in line of battle and marched four miles to a shady and pleasant piece of woods on the border of the far-reaching expanses of a flowery prairie. It was an enchanting region for war—our kind of war.

We pierced the forest about half a mile, and took up a strong position, with some low, rocky, and wooded hills behind us, and a purling, limpid creek in front. Straightway half the command were in swimming, and the other half fishing. The ass with the French name gave this position a romantic title, but it was too long, so the boys shortened and simplified it to Camp Ralls.

We occupied an old maple-sugar camp, whose half-rotted troughs were still propped against the trees. A long corn crib served for sleeping quarters for the battalion. On our left, half a mile away, was Mason's farm and house; and he was a friend to the cause. Shortly after noon the farmers began to arrive from several directions, with mules and horses for our use, and these they lent us for as long as the war might last, which they judged would be about three months. The animals were of all sizes, all colors, and all breeds. They were mainly young and frisky, and nobody in the command could stay on them long at a time; for we were town boys, and ignorant of horsemanship. The creature that fell to my share was a very small mule, and yet so quick and active that it could throw me without difficulty; and it did this whenever I got on it. Then it would bray—stretching its neck out, laying its ears back, and spreading its jaws till you could see down to its works. It was a disagreeable animal, in every way. If I took it by the bridle and tried to lead it off the grounds, it would sit down and brace back, and no one could budge it. However, I was not entirely

destitute of military resources, and I did presently manage to spoil this game; for I had seen many a steamboat aground in my time, and knew a trick or two which even a grounded mule would be obliged to respect. There was a well by the corn-crib; so I substituted thirty fathom of rope for the bridle, and fetched him home with the windlass.

I will anticipate here sufficiently to say that we did learn to ride, after some days' practice, but never well. We could not learn to like our animals; they were not choice ones, and most of them had annoying peculiarities of one kind or another. Stevens's horse would carry him, when he was not noticing, under the huge excrescences which form on the trunks of oak-trees, and wipe him out of the saddle; in this way Stevens got several bad hurts. Sergeant Bowers's horse was very large and tall, with slim, long legs, and looked like a railroad bridge. His size enabled him to reach all about, and as far as he wanted to, with his head; so he was always biting Bowers's legs. On the march, in the sun, Bowers slept a good deal; and as soon as the horse recognized that he was asleep he would reach around and bite him on the leg. His legs were black and blue with bites. This was the only thing that could ever make him swear, but this always did; whenever the horse bit him he always swore, and of course Stevens, who laughed at everything, laughed at this, and would even get into such convulsions over it as to lose his balance and fall off his horse; and then Bowers, already irritated by the pain of the horse-bite, would resent the laughter with hard language, and there would be a quarrel; so that horse made no end of trouble and bad blood in the command.

However, I will get back to where I was—our first after noon in the sugar-camp. The sugar-troughs came very handy as horse-troughs, and we had plenty of corn to fill them with. I ordered Sergeant Bowers to feed my mule; but he said that if I reckoned he went to war to be dry-nurse to a mule, it wouldn't take me very long to find out my mistake. I believed that this was insubordination, but I was full of uncertainties about everything military, and so I let the thing pass, and went and ordered Smith, the blacksmith's apprentice, to feed the mule; but he merely gave me a large, cold, sarcastic grin, such as an ostensibly seven-year-old horse gives you when you lift his lip and find he is fourteen, and turned his back on me. I then went to the captain, and asked if it was not right and proper and military for me to have an orderly. He said it was, but as there was only one orderly in the corps, it was but right that he himself should have Bowers on his staff. Bowers said he wouldn't serve on anybody's staff; and if anybody thought he could make him, let him try it. So, of course, the thing had to be dropped; there was no other way.

Next, nobody would cook; it was considered a degradation; so we had no dinner. We lazied the rest of the pleasant afternoon away, some dozing under the trees, some smoking cob-pipes and talking sweethearts and war, some playing games. By late suppertime all hands were famished; and to meet the difficulty all hands turned to, on an equal footing, and gathered wood, built fires, and cooked the meal. Afterward everything was smooth for a while; then trouble broke out between the corporal and the sergeant, each claiming to rank the other. Nobody knew which was the higher office; so Lyman had to settle the matter by making the rank of both officers equal. The commander of an ignorant crew like that has many troubles and vexations which probably do not occur in the regular army at all. However, with the song-singing and yarn-spinning around the camp fire, everything presently became serene again; and by and by we raked the corn down level in one end of the crib, and all went to bed on it, tying a horse to the door, so that he would neigh if any one tried to get in.

We had some horsemanship drill every forenoon; then, afternoons, we rode off here and there in squads a few miles, and visited the farmers' girls, and had a youthful good time, and got an honest good dinner or supper, and then home again to camp, happy and content.

For a time, life was idly delicious, it was perfect; there was nothing to mar it. Then came some

farmers with an alarm one day. They said it was rumored that the enemy were advancing in our direction, from over Hyde's prairie. The result was a sharp stir among us, and general consternation. It was a rude awakening from our pleasant trance. The rumor was but a rumor—nothing definite about it; so, in the confusion, we did not know which way to retreat. Lyman was for not retreating at all, in these uncertain circumstances; but he found that if he tried to maintain that attitude he would fare badly, for the command were in no humor to put up with insubordination. So he yielded the point and called a council of war—to consist of himself and the three other officers; but the privates made such a fuss about being left out, that we had to allow them to be were already present. I mean we had to allow them to remain, for they present, and doing the most of the talking too. The question was, which way to retreat; but all were so flurried that nobody seemed to have even a guess to offer. Except Lyman. He explained in a few calm words, that inasmuch as the enemy were approaching from over Hyde's prairie, our course was simple: all we had to do was not to retreat *toward* him; any other direction would answer our needs perfectly. Everybody saw in a moment how true this was, and how wise; so Lyman got a great many compliments. It was now decided that we should fall back on Mason's farm.

It was after dark by this time, and as we could not know how soon the enemy might arrive, it did not seem best to try to take the horses and things with us; so we only took the guns and ammunition, and started at once. The route was very rough and hilly and rocky, and presently the night grew very black and rain began to fall; so we had a troublesome time of it, struggling and stumbling along in the dark; and soon some person slipped and fell, and then the next person behind stumbled over him and fell, and so did the rest, one after the other; and then Bowers came with the keg of powder in his arms, whilst the command were all mixed together, arms and legs, on the muddy slope; and so he fell, of course, with the keg, and this started the whole detachment down the hill in a body, and they landed in the brook at the bottom in a pile, and each that was undermost pulling the hair and scratching and biting those that were on top of him; and those that were being scratched and bitten scratching and biting the rest in their turn, and all saying they would die before they would ever go to war again if they ever got out of this brook this time, and the invader might rot for all they cared, and the country along with him—and all such talk as that, which was dismal to hear and take part in, in such smothered, low voices, and such a grisly dark place and so wet, and the enemy may be coming any moment.

The keg of powder was lost, and the guns too; so the growling and complaining continued straight along whilst the brigade pawed around the pasty hillside and slopped around in the brook hunting for these things; consequently we lost considerable time at this; and then we heard a sound, and held our breath and listened, and it seemed to be the enemy coming, though it could have been a cow, for it had a cough like a cow; but we did not wait, but left a couple of guns behind and struck out for Mason's again as briskly as we could scramble along in the dark. But we got lost presently among the rugged little ravines, and wasted a deal of time finding the way again, so it was after nine when we reached Mason's stile at last; and then before we could open our mouths to give the countersign, several dogs came bounding over the fence, with great riot and noise, and each of them took a soldier by the slack of his trousers and began to back away with him. We could not shoot the dogs without endangering the persons they were attached to; so we had to look on, helpless, at what was perhaps the most mortifying spectacle of the civil war. There was light enough, and to spare, for the Masons had now run out on the porch with candles in their hands. The old man and his son came and undid the dogs without difficulty, all but Bowers's; but they couldn't undo his dog, they didn't know his combination; he was of the bull kind, and seemed to be set with a Yale time lock; but they got

him loose at last with some scalding water, of which Bowers got his share and returned thanks. Peterson Dunlap afterwards made up a fine name for this engagement, and also for the night march which preceded it, but both have long ago faded out of my memory.

We now went into the house, and they began to ask us a world of questions, whereby it presently came out that we did not know anything concerning who or what we were running from; so the old gentleman made himself very frank, and said we were a curious breed of soldiers, and guessed we could be depended on to end up the war in time, because no government could stand the expense of the shoe-leather we should cost it trying to follow us around. "Marion *Rangers!* good name, b'gosh!" said he. And wanted to know why we hadn't had a picket-guard at the place where the road entered the prairie, and why we hadn't sent out a scouting party to spy out the enemy and bring us an account of his strength, and so on, before jumping up and stampeding out of a strong position upon a mere vague rumor—and so on and so forth, till he made us all feel shabbier than the dogs had done, not half so enthusiastically welcome. So we went to bed shamed and low-spirited; except Stevens. Soon Stevens began to devise a garment for Bowers which could be made to automatically display his battle-scars to the grateful, or conceal them from the envious, according to his occasions; but Bowers was in no humor for this, so there was a fight, and when it was over Stevens had some battle-scars of his own to think about.

Then we got a little sleep. But after all we had gone through, our activities were not over for the night; for about two o'clock in the morning we heard a shout of warning from down the lane, accompanied by a chorus from all the dogs, and in a moment everybody was up and flying around to find out what the alarm was about. The alarmist was a horseman who gave notice that a detachment of Union soldiers was on its way from Hannibal with orders to capture and hang any bands like ours which it could find, and said we had no time to lose. Farmer Mason was in a flurry this time, himself. He hurried us out of the house with all haste, and sent one of his Negroes with us to show us where to hide ourselves and our tell-tale guns among the ravines half a mile away. It was raining heavily.

We struck down the lane, then across some rocky pasture land which offered good advantages for stumbling; consequently we were down in the mud most of the time, and every time a man went down he blackguarded the war, and the people that started it, and everybody connected with it, and gave himself the master dose of all for being so foolish as to go into it. At last we reached the wooded mouth of a ravine, and there we huddled ourselves under the streaming trees, and sent the Negro back home. It was a dismal and heart-breaking time. We were like to be drowned with the rain, deafened with the howling wind and the booming thun der, and blinded by the lightning. It was indeed a wild night. The drenching we were getting was misery enough, but a deeper misery still was the reflection that the halter might end us before we were a day older. A death of this shame ful sort had not occurred to us as being among the possibilities of war. It took the romance all out of the campaign, and turned our dreams of glory into a repulsive nightmare. As for doubting that so barbarous an order had been given, not one of us did that.

The long night wore itself out at last, and then the Negro came to us with the news that the alarm had manifestly been a false one, and that breakfast would soon be ready. Straightway we were lighted-hearted again, and the world was bright, and life as full of hope and promise as ever—for we were young then. . . .

The mongrel child of philology named the night's refuge Camp Devastation, and no soul objected. The Masons gave us a Missouri country breakfast, in Missourian abundance, and we needed it: hot biscuits; hot "wheat bread" prettily criss-crossed in a lattice pattern on top; hot corn pone; fried chicken, bacon, coffee, eggs, milk, buttermilk, etc.-,—and the world may be confidently challenged to furnish the equal to such a breakfast, as it is cooked in the South.

We staid several days at Mason's. . . . At last it was with something very like joy that we received news that the enemy were on our track again. With a new birth of the old warrior spirit, we sprang to our places in line of battle and fell back on Camp Ralls.

Captain Lyman had taken a hint from Mason's talk, and he now gave orders that our camp should be guarded against surprise by the posting of pickets. I w-as ordered to place a picket at the forks of the road in Hyde's prairie. Night shut down black and threatening. I told Sergeant Bowers to go out to that place and stay till midnight; and, just as I was expecting, he said he wouldn't do it. I tried to get others to go, but all refused. Some excused themselves on account of the weather; but the rest were frank enough to say they wouldn't go in any kind of weather. This kind of thing sounds odd now, and impossible, but there was no surprise in it at the time. On the contrary, it seemed a perfectly natural thing to do. There were scores of little camps scattered over Missouri where the same thing was happening. These camps were composed of young men who had been born and reared to a sturdy independence, and who did not know what it meant to be ordered around by Tom, Dick, and Harry, whom they had known familiarly all their lives, in the village or on the farm. It is quite within the probabilities that this same thing was happening all over the South. . . .

It was quite the natural thing. One might justly imagine that we were hopeless material for war. And so we seemed, in our ignorant state; but there were those among us who afterward learned the grim trade; learned to obey like machines; became valuable soldiers; fought all through the war, and came out at the end with excellent records. One of the very boys who refused to go out on picket duty that night, and called me an ass for thinking he would expose himself to danger in such a foolhardy way, had become distinguished for intrepidity before he was a year older.

I did secure my picket that night—not by authority, but by diplomacy. I got Bowers to go, by agreeing to ex change ranks with him for the time being, and go along and stand the watch with him as his subordinate. We staid out there a couple of dreary hours in the pitchy darkness and the rain, with nothing to modify the dreariness but Bowers's monotonous growlings at the war and the weather; then we began to nod, and presently found it next to impossible to stay in the saddle; so we gave up the tedious job, and went back to the camp without waiting for the relief guard. We rode into camp without interruption or objection from anybody, and the enemy could have done the same, for there were no sentries. Everybody was asleep; at midnight there was nobody to send out another picket, so none was sent. We never tried to establish a watch at night again, as far as I remember, but we generally kept a picket out in the daytime.

In the camp the whole command slept on the corn in the big corn-crib; and there was usually a general row before morning, for the place was full of rats, and they would scramble over the boys' bodies and faces, annoying and irritating everybody; and now and then they would bite some one's toe, and the person who owned the toe would start up and magnify his English and begin to throw corn in the dark. The ears were half as heavy as bricks, and when they struck they hurt. The persons struck would respond, and inside of five minutes every man would be locked in a death-grip with his neighbor. There was a grievous deal of blood shed in the corn-crib, but this was all that was spilt while I was in the war.

The rest of my war experience was a piece with what I have already told of it. We kept monotonously falling back upon one camp or another, and eating up the country. I marvel now at the patience of the farmers and their families. They ought to have shot us; on the contrary, they were as hospitably kind and courteous to us as if we had deserved it. In one of these camps we found Ab Grimes, an Upper Mississippi pilot, who afterwards became famous as a daredevil rebel spy, whose career bristled with desperate ad ventures. The look and style of his comrades suggested that they had not come into the war to play, and their deeds made good the conjecture later. They were fine horsemen and good revolver-shots; but their favorite arm was the lasso. Each had one at his pommel, and could snatch a man out of the saddle with it every time, on a full gallop, at any reasonable distance.

In another camp the chief was a fierce and profane old blacksmith of sixty, and he had furnished his twenty recruits with gigantic home-made bowie-knives, to be swung with the two hands, like the *machetes* of the Isthmus. It was a grisly spectacle to see that earnest band practicing their murderous cuts and slashes under the eye of that remorseless old fanatic.

The last camp which we fell back upon was in a hollow near the village of Florida, where I was born—in Monroe County. Here we were warned, one day, that a Union colonel was sweeping down on us with a whole regiment at his heels. This looked decidedly serious. Our boys went apart and consulted; then we went back and told the other companies present that the war was a disappointment to us and we were going to disband. They were getting ready, themselves, to fall back on some place or other, and were only waiting for General Tom Harris, who was expected to arrive at any moment; so they tried to persuade us to wait a little while, but the majority of us said no, we were accustomed to falling back, and didn't need any of Tom Harris's help; we could get along perfectly well without him—and save time too. So about half of our fifteen, including myself, mounted and left on the instant; the others yielded to persuasion and staid—staid through the war.

An hour later we met General Harris on the road, with two or three people in his company—his staff, probably, but we could not tell; none of them were in uniform; uniforms had not come into vogue among us yet. Harris ordered us back; but we told him there was a Union colonel coming with a whole regiment in his wake, and it looked as if there was going to be a disturbance; so we had concluded to go home. He raged a little, but it was of no use; our minds were made up. We had done our share; had killed one man, exterminated one army, such as it was; let him go and kill the rest, and that would end the war. I did not see that brisk young general again until last year; then he was wearing white hair and whiskers.

In time I came to know that Union colonel whose coming frightened me out of the war and crippled the Southern cause to that extent—General Grant. I came with in a few hours of seeing him when he was as unknown as 1 was myself; at a time when anybody could have said, "Grant?—Ulysses S. Grant? I do not remember hearing the name before." It seems difficult to realize that there was once a time when such a remark could be rationally made; but there was, and I was within a few miles of the place and the occasion too, though proceeding in the other direction.

The thoughtful will not throw this war-paper of mine lightly aside as being valueless. It has this value: it is a not unfair picture of what went on in many and many a militia camp in the first months of the rebellion, when the green recruits were without discipline, without the steadying and heartening influence of trained leaders; when all their circumstances were new and strange, and charged with exaggerated terrors, and before the invaluable experience of actual collision in the field had turned them from rabbits into soldiers. If this side of the picture of that early day has not before been put into history, then history has been to that degree incomplete, for it had and has its rightful place there. There was more Bull Run material scattered through the early camps of this country than exhibited itself at Bull Run. And yet it learned its trade presently, and helped to fight the great battles later. I could have become a soldier myself, if I had waited. I had got part of it learned; I knew more about retreating than the man that invented retreating.

—MARK TWAIN, "The Private History
of a Campaign That Failed"

XIII.2

MAJOR CONNOLLY LOSES FAITH IN THE CHIVALRY OF THE SOUTH

One of the best of all Civil War commentators, Major James A. Connolly was an Illinois lawyer who in 1862 raised a company which promptly elected him captain. Later he was made major in the 123rd Illinois Infantry and at the end of the war had been promoted to lieutenant colonel. After Chickamauga he was assigned as division inspector in the XIV Army Corps, and went with Sherman to the sea and beyond. He wrote of his Civil War diary that "like an old army ambrotype it may not be a delight, but it is a true picture just as it was taken in the stirring days." We shall turn to him again for lively pictures of the battlefield. After the war Connolly was U. S. Attorney for the Southern District of Illinois and a member of Congress. He tells us here of a holiday trip from Cairo up the Ohio and the Cumber land to Port Donelson shortly after its capture.

March 10th, '62

Dear———:

The Cumberland was on a regular bender. We passed several small villages, completely inundated; some of the houses floating off and others stationary with nothing but the chimneys visible.

In the villages built higher up on the bluffs everything appeared like a Sunday; no smoke visible, except from an occasional chimney—no doors open—no signs of life—no citizens except occasionally a solitary butternut as the soldiers called them. Most of the farm houses along the river are built of logs in very primitive style, and nearly every one we saw was surrounded by water, so that their occupants had to go around the premises in rude canoes made of logs. It is probable that I am prejudiced, but I certainly thought I never saw such miserable looking creatures as inhabit the banks of the Cumberland, and their habitations looked more wretched than themselves. We frequently sailed so close to farm houses that we could easily hold conversation with the occupants, and wherever a man appeared the soldiers in variably made him swing his hat, the boys consoling them selves with the idea that the swinging of the hat was an evidence of respect for the Union and for "Yankee" soldiers. One instance I recollect, where we must have sailed through the door yard of a cabin (if cabins have such things in Dixie,) the inmates were assembled on the rude porch, five dirty children, three dirty, tangle haired, parchment faced women, sans crinoline, sans shoes, sans stockings,—half a dozen dogs of low degree, and one middle-aged, lantern jawed, long haired butternut clad concern such as they called a man in Dixie.

As we neared the cabin the soldier boys called out "swing your hat and hurrah for the Union, old butternut;" no response from butternut who leans lazily against his porch, and throws a sullen, defiant look toward the passing steamer; that don't suit the boys; they never pass a native without making him do some reverence toward the Union, so they hail him again, still he is silent; then the boys clamor to have the boat stopped; they want to "clean him out," "set his cabin adrift," "take him in out of the wet," and all such expressions are heard amongst the soldiers, but one cool fellow picks up his musket as the boat is just opposite the cabin, and pointing it at the butternut, takes aim at him; butternut darts within the cabin door amid the shouts of the soldiers, and the women follow him; in an instant out comes a woman with a dirty white rag which she swings lustily, and after a swing or two of the rag out comes the man again, and swinging his slouch hat vigorously, gives three rousing yells; the boys conclude they have converted him—made a Union man of him, so they gave him three such cheers as a regiment of Western boys can give when they are in good humor, and they sail on satisfied, to produce similar conversions on all refractory butternuts they meet. The last I saw of the cabin, as we turned a bend in the river, the man was swinging his hat and the women white rags at a steamer loaded with soldiers just behind us.

We passed several double log houses that were probably the residences of well to do farmers, judg-

ing alone from the number of "niggers" around. In every instance the blacks would manifest the most extravagant delight; jumping up and down, clapping their hands, the little nigs rolling and tumbling on the ground, performing as many antics as so many monkeys. We passed several large iron works surrounded by the little cabins of the operatives, and generally one large fine brick mansion—the residence, probably of the manager. But all was silent—no smoke curling from the chimneys—sounds of machinery hushed—the operatives scattered on battle fields, within prison walls, and in rude graves, the children of these iron villages orphaned and with the taint of treason on their lives—the mothers widowed and the proprietors ruined. The banks of the Cumberland are desolated, not by "Yankee invaders" but by the mad folly of the inhabitants; they had been traitors all the way up the river, and their newborn respect for the Union was only begotten by the thunder of Grant's guns at Fort Donelson My faith in the superior chivalry of the South is gone. It is mere gasconade. They boast of their chivalry and courage, but so did Don Quixote and the renowned Jack Falstaff. Their boasted chivalry will in the end avail no more than the chivalry of Lilliput in the grasp of Gulliver. Many of them no doubt had been Union men at the commencement of the struggle, but the slow progress of the Union army led them to believe rebellion would triumph and so their want of faith in the old Union led them to embrace the rebel cause.

They thought they won the race at "Bull Run," but that proved only to be "false start." We steamed on up the river, the same appearance of desolation on every hand, the same sport with the soldiers and "butternuts" on the banks, the some deserted villages and jubilant darkies, until the word passed around, "Three miles to Fort Donelson." Then came a scene of excitement, all crowding to the bow of the boat, every eye strained to catch the first glimpse of the rebel stronghold. We turn a bend in the river and the fort is in view, the stars and stripes floating over it. A cheer bursts from the soldiers on board, the band strikes up the "Star Spangled Banner" and we sail gaily over the same waters that our gunboats breasted a few days before in a murderous hail of rebel shot and shell. We passed the batteries and went up the river about half a mile to the landing at the village of Dover. I was soon ashore and wandering through the city of tents, in search of my home company. I found it in about an hour, and was soon surrounded by the company answering inquiries about home, the wounded, etc. They had supper before I found them, but a fire was soon lighted, some coffee made, some fat pork fried, and with the ground for my table and seat, a tin pan full of fried pork, a tin cup full of coffee and plenty of "hard tack," I ate a hearty supper. . . .

The battle was fought in dense timber, on very high hills and deep ravines, and nearly the whole of the fighting was done by the enemy outside of their entrenchments. The lines of the battle extended over a space of three or four miles, and the whole distance is thickly strewn with the pits of the dead. . . .

I saw a great many taken up. I saw one pit containing five opened and the dead taken out to be sent home. They lay there side by side, with uniform and cartridge box on, just as they fell, covered over with blankets and the dirt thrown in on them. From the best estimate I could make I should say there were 500 of our men buried on the field and at least an equal number of rebels; and I should think there were 1,500 of our men wounded so as to be obliged to go into hospital, and probably 500 more who were wounded, but not seriously enough to go into hospital. A very small proportion of our wounded, however, will, for most of their wounds are from buckshot and are not very serious . . . . A great many horses were lying on the field, just where they fell, scattered all over the field, singly, by twos, threes and fours. Frozen pools of blood were visible on every hand, and I picked up over twenty hats with bullet holes in them and pieces of skull, hair and blood sticking to them inside.

The ground was strewn with hats, caps, coats, pants, canteens, cartridge boxes, bayonet scabbards, knapsacks, rebel haversacks filled with biscuits of their own making, raw pork, broken guns, broken bayonets, dismounted cannon, pieces of exploded shells, six and twelve-pound balls, and indeed all sorts of things that are found in an army. There was such a profusion of everything that I scarcely could determine what to take as a memento of that terrible field, which is probably the only one I shall ever have a chance to see. You can form no conception of what a battlefield looks like. No pen and ink description can give you anything like a true idea of it. The dead were buried from two to two and a half feet deep; the rebels didn't bury that deep and some had their feet protruding from the graves. . . .

The ignorance of many of the rebels surprised me and I should not have believed it had I not talked with them my self. Some of them told me, and they seemed to be honest in it, that they thought they had been fighting for the Union; others told me they thought our army was coming down there to carry off all the "niggers;" they told me they thought none but abolitionists were in our army, and that they were surprised when they found there were more Demo crats than abolitionists in it. An amusing incident occurred at the Fort in a conversation between an Illinoisan and a Mississippi captain. The Mississippian remarked that they could whip the New England Yankees every time, and went on to speak of the New England Yankee as a dried up, bloodless specimen of humanity, without courage or physical power, and without a single idea higher than money. The Illinoisan heard him through and then pointing to a Federal captain standing in sight, about 6 feet 3 in height and weighing at least two hundred pounds, remarked: "There is a New England Yankee, born and raised in the state of Maine, and he was among the first men who climbed over your breastworks and ran over your guns." The Mississippian changed the topic of conversation speedily.

—"Major Connolly's Letters to his Wife"

XIII.3

The Great Locomotive
Chase in Georgia

General Ormsby Mc. Mitchel, who organized this locomotive
raid, was one of the most remarkable minor figures of the war.
Born in Kentucky and a graduate of West Point, Mitchel was a
combination engineer, philosopher, and astronomer—chief engineer for the Little Miami Railroad, professor of philosophy and
astronomy at Cincinnati College with the largest telescope on
the continent. Appointed brigadier at the outbreak of the war he
served in the Department of Ohio and later under Buell in
Tennessee and Alabama. Quarreling with Buell he resigned late
in 1862 but was transferred, instead, to Hilton Head, South
Carolina, where he contracted yellow fever and died.

The locomotive raid was designed to disrupt Confederate
communications far behind the lines. William Pittenger of the
2nd Ohio Volunteers was a member of the "Andrews Raiders"
who carried out this assignment. Twenty-two of the raiders were
captured and of these eight were hanged and eight escaped.
Pittenger later became a Methodist minister.

The railroad raid to Georgia, in the spring of
1862, has always been considered to rank high
among the striking and novel incidents of the
civil war. At that time General O. M. Mitchel,
under whose authority it was organized, commanded Union forces in middle Tennessee, consisting of a division of Buell's arrny. The
Confederates were concentrating at Corinth,
Mississippi, and Grant and Buell were advancing
by different routes toward that point. Mitchel's
orders required him to protect Nashville and the
country around, but al lowed him great latitude in
the disposition of his division, which, with
detachments and garrisons, numbered nearly seventeen thousand men. His attention had long
been strong ly turned toward the liberation of east
Tennessee, which he knew that President Lincoln
also earnestly desired, and which would, if
achieved, strike a most damaging blow at the
resources of the rebellion. . . . He determined,
therefore, to press into the heart of the enemy's
country as far as possible, occupying strategical
points before they were adequately defended and

assured of speedy and powerful reinforcement.
To this end his measures were vigorous and well
chosen.

On the 8th of April, 1862,. . . he marched
swiftly south ward from Shelbyville, and seized
Huntsville in Alabama on the 11th of April, and
then sent a detachment westward over the
Memphis and Charleston Railroad to open railway
communication with the Union army at Pittsburg
Landing. Another detachment, commanded by
Mitchel in person, advanced on the same day seventy miles by rail directly into the enemy's territory,
arriving unchecked with two thousand men within
thirty miles of Chattanooga,—in two hours' time
he could now reach that point,—the most important position in the West. Why did he not go on?
The story of the rail road raid is the answer. The
night before breaking camp at Shelbyville, Mitchel
sent an expedition secretly into the heart of
Georgia to cut the railroad communications of
Chattanooga to the south and east. The fortune of
this attempt had a most important bearing upon his
movements, and will now be narrated.

In the employ of General Buell was a spy named
James J. Andrews, who had rendered valuable services in the first year of the war, and had secured the
full confidence of the Union commanders. In
March, 1862, Buell had sent him secretly with eight
men to burn the bridges west of Chattanooga; but
the failure of expected cooperation defeated the
plan, and Andrews, after visiting Atlanta, and
inspecting the whole of the enemy's lines in that
vicinity and northward, had returned, ambitious to
make another attempt. His plans for the second raid
were submitted to Mitchel, and on the eve of the
movement from Shelbyville to Huntsville Mitchel
authorized him to take twenty-four men, secretly
enter the enemy's territory, and, by means of capturing a train, burn the bridges on the northern part of
the Georgia State Railroad, and also one on the East
Tennessee Railroad where it approaches the Georgia
State line, thus completely isolating Chattanooga,
which was virtually ungarrisoned.

The soldiers for this expedition, of whom the

writer was one, were selected from the three Ohio regiments belonging to General J. W. Sill's brigade, being simply told that they were wanted for secret and very dangerous service. So far as known, not a man chosen declined the perilous honor. Our uniforms were exchanged for ordinary Southern dress, and all arms except revolvers were left in camp. On the 7th of April, by the roadside about a mile east of Shelbyville, in the late evening twilight, we met our leader. Taking us a little way from the road, he quietly placed before us the outlines of the romantic and adventurous plan, which was: to break into small detachments of three or four, journey eastward into the Cumberland Mountains, then work southward, traveling by rail after we were well within the Con federate lines, and finally, the evening of the third day after the start, meet Andrews at Marietta, Georgia, more than two hundred miles away. When questioned, we were to profess ourselves Kentuckians going to join the Southern army.

On the journey we were a good deal annoyed by the swollen streams and the muddy roads consequent on three days of almost ceaseless rain. Andrews was led to believe that Mitchers column would be inevitably delayed; and as we were expected to destroy the bridges the very day that Huntsville was entered, he took the responsibility of sending word to our different groups that our attempt would be postponed one day—from Friday to Saturday, April 12. This was a natural but a most lamentable error of judgment.

One of the men detailed was belated, and did not join us at all. Two others were very soon captured by the enemy; and though their true character was not detected, they were forced into the Southern army, and two reached Marietta, but failed to report at the rendezvous. Thus, when we assembled very early in the morning in Andrews's room at the Marietta Hotel for final consultation before the blow was struck we were but twenty, including our leader. All preliminary difficulties had been easily overcome, and we were in good spirits. But some serious obstacles had been

revealed on our ride from Chattanooga to Marietta the previous evening. The railroad was found to be crowded with trains, and many soldiers were among the passengers. Then the station—Big Shanty—at which the capture was to be effected had recently been made a Confederate camp.

To succeed in our enterprise it would be necessary first to capture the engine in a guarded camp with soldiers standing around as spectators, and then to run it from one to two hundred miles through the enemy's country, and to deceive or overpower all trains that should be met—a large contract for twenty men. Some of our party thought the chances of success so slight, under existing circumstances, that they urged the abandonment of the whole enterprise. But Andrews declared his purpose to succeed or die, offering to each man, however, the privilege of withdrawing from the attempt—an offer no one was in the least disposed to accept. Final instructions were then given, and we hurried to the ticket-office in time for the northward-bound mail train, and purchased tickets for different stations along the line in the direction of Chattanooga.

Our ride, as passengers, was but eight miles. We swept swiftly around the base of Kenesaw Mountain, and soon saw the tents of the Confederate forces camped at Big Shanty gleam white in the morning mist. Here we were to stop for breakfast, and attempt the seizure of the train. The morning was raw and gloomy, and a rain, which fell all day, had already begun. It was a painfully thrilling moment. We were but twenty, with an army about us, and a long and difficult road before us, crowded with enemies. In an instant we were to throw off the disguise which had been our only protection, and trust to our leader's genius and our own efforts for safety and success. Fortunately we had no time for giving way to reflections and conjectures which could only unfit us for the stern task ahead.

When we stopped, the conductor, the engineer, and many of the passengers hurried to breakfast, leaving the train unguarded. Now was the moment of action. Ascertaining that there was nothing to prevent a rapid start, Andrews, our two engineers, Brown and Knight, and the firemen hurried forward, uncoupling a section of the train consisting of three empty baggage or box-cars, the locomotive, and the tender. The engineers and the firemen sprang into the cab of the engine, while Andrews, with hand on the rail and foot on the step, waited to see that the remainder of the party had gained entrance into the rear box-car. This seemed difficult and slow, though it really consumed but a few seconds, for the car stood on a considerable bank, and the first who came were pitched in by their comrades, while these in turn dragged in the others, and the door was instantly closed. A sentinel, with musket in hand, stood not a dozen feet from the engine, watching the whole proceeding; but before he or any of the soldiers or guards around could make up their minds to interfere all was done, and Andrews, with a nod to his engineer, stepped on board. The valve was pulled wide open, and for a moment the wheels slipped round in rapid, ineffective revolutions; then, with a bound that jerked the soldiers in the box-car from their feet, the little train darted away, leaving the camp and the station in the wildest uproar and confusion. The first step of the enterprise was triumphantly accomplished.

According to the time-table, of which Andrews had secured a copy, there were two trains to be met. These presented no serious hindrance to our attaining high speed, for we could tell just where to expect them. There was also a local freight not down on the time-table, but which could not be far distant. Any danger of collision with it could be avoided by running according to the schedule of the captured train until it was passed; then at the highest possible speed we could run to the Oostenaula and Chickamauga bridges, lay them in ashes, and pass on through Chattanooga to Mitchel at Huntsville, or wherever eastward of that point he might be found, arriving long before the close of the day. It was a brilliant prospect, and so far as human estimates can deter-

mine it would have been realized had the day been Friday instead of Saturday. On Friday every train had been on time, the day dry, and the road in perfect order. Now the road was in disorder, every train far behind time, and two "extras" were approaching us. But of these unfavorable conditions we knew nothing, and pressed confidently forward.

We stopped frequently, and at one point tore up the track, cut telegraph wires, and loaded on cross-ties to be used in bridge-burning. Wood and water were taken without difficulty, Andrews very cooly telling the story to which he adhered throughout the run—namely, that he was one of General Beauregard's officers, running an impressed powder train through to that commander at Corinth. We had no good instruments for track-raising, as we had intended rather to depend upon fire; but the amount of time spent in taking up a rail was not material at this stage of our journey, as we easily kept on the time of our captured train. There was a wonderful exhilaration in passing swiftly by towns and stations through the heart of an enemy's country in this manner. It possessed just enough of the spice of danger, in this part of the run, to render it thoroughly enjoyable. The slightest accident to our engine, however, or a miscarriage in any part of our program, would have completely changed the conditions.

At Etowah we found the "Yonah," an old locomotive owned by an iron company, standing with steam up; but not wishing to alarm the enemy till the local freight had been safely met, we left it unharmed. Kingston, thirty miles from the starting-point, was safely reached. A train from Rome, Georgia, on a branch road, had just arrived and was waiting for the morning mail—our train. We learned that the local freight would soon come also, and, taking the side-track, waited for it. When it arrived, however, Andrews saw, to his surprise and chagrin, that it bore a red flag, indicating another train not far behind. Stepping over to the conductor, he boldly asked: "What does it mean that the road is blocked in this manner when I have orders to take this powder to Beauregard without a minute's delay?" The answer was intersting, but not reassuring: "Mitchel has captured Huntsville, and is said to be coming to Chattanooga, and we are getting everything out of there." He was asked by Andrews to pull his train a long way down the track out of the way, and promptly obeyed.

It seemed an exceedingly long time before the expected "extra" arrived, and when it did come it bore another red flag. The reason given was that the 'local," being too great for one engine, had been made up in two sections, and the second section would doubtless be along in a short time. This was terribly vexatious; yet there seemed nothing to do but to wait. To start out between the sections of an extra train would be to court destruction. There were already three trains around us, and their many passengers and others were all growing very curious about the mysterious train, manned by strangers, which had arrived on the time of the morning mail. For an hour and five minutes from the time of arrival at Kingston we remained in this most critical position. The sixteen of us who were shut up tightly in a box-car,—personating Beauregard's ammunition,—hearing sounds out side, but unable to distinguish words, had perhaps the most trying position. Andrews sent us, by one of the engineers, a cautious warning to be ready to fight in case the uneasiness of the crowd around led them to make any investigation, while he himself kept near the station to prevent the sending off of any alarming telegram. So intolerable was our suspense, that the order for a deadly conflict would have been felt as a relief. But the assurance of Andrews quieted the crowd until the whistle of the expected train from the north was heard; then as it glided up to the depot, past the end of our sidetrack, we were off without more words.

But unexpected danger had arisen behind us. Out of the panic at Big Shanty two men emerged, determined, if possible, to foil the unknown captors of their train. There was no telegraph station, and no locomotive at hand with which to follow; but

the conductor of the train, W. A. Fuller, and Anthony Murphy, foreman of the Atlanta railway machine shops, who happened to be on board of Fuller's train, started on foot after us as hard as they could run. Finding a hand-car they mounted it and pushed forward till they neared Etowah, where they ran on the break we had made in the road, and were precipitated down the embankment into the ditch. Continuing with more caution, they reached Etowah and found the "Yonah," which was at once pressed into service, loaded with soldiers who were at hand, and hurried with flying wheels toward Kingston. Fuller prepared to fight at that point, for he knew of the tangle of extra trains, and of the lateness of the regular trains, and did not think we should be able to pass.

We had been gone only four minutes when he arrived and found himself stopped by three long, heavy trains of cars, headed in the wrong direction. To move them out of the way so as to pass would cause a delay he was little inclined to afford—would, indeed, have almost certainly given w the victory. So, abandoning his engine, he with Murphy ran across to the Rome train, and, uncoupling the engine and one car, pushed forward with about forty armed men. As the Rome branch connected with the main road above the depot, he encountered no hindrance, and it was now a fair race. We were not many minutes ahead.

Four miles from Kingston we again stopped and cut the telegraph. While trying to take up a rail at this point we were greatly startled. One end of the rail was loosened, and eight of us were pulling at it, when in the distance we distinctly heard the whistle of a pursuing engine. With a frantic effort we broke the rail, and all tumbled over the embankment with the effort. We moved on, and at Adairsville we found a mixed train (freight and passenger) waiting, but there was an express on the road that had not yet arrived. We could afford no more delay, and set out for the next station, Calhoun, at terrible speed, hoping to reach that point before the express, which was behind time, should arrive. The nine miles which we had to travel were left behind in less than the same number of minutes. The express was just pulling out, but, hearing our whistle, backed before us until we were able to take the side-track. It stopped, however, in such a manner as completely to close up the other end of the switch. The two trains, side by side, almost touched each other, and our precipitate arrival caused natural suspicion. Many searching questions were asked, which had to be answered before we could get the opportunity of proceeding. We in the box-car could hear the altercation, and were almost sure that a fight would be necessary before the conductor would consent to "pull up" in order to let us out. Here again our position was most critical, for the pursuers were rapidly approaching.

Fuller and Murphy saw the obstruction of the broken rail in time, by reversing their engine, to prevent wreck, but the hindrance was for the present insuperable. Leaving all their men behind, they started for a second footrace. Before they had gone far they met the train we had passed at Adairsville, and turned it back after us. At Adairsville they dropped the cars, and with locomotive and tender loaded with armed men, they drove forward at the highest speed possible. They knew that we were not many minutes ahead, and trusted to overhaul us before the express train could be safely passed.

But Andrews had told the powder story again with all his skill, and added a direct request in peremptory form to have the way opened before him, which the Confederate conductor did not see fit to resist; and just before the pursuers arrived at Calhoun we were again under way. Stopping once more to cut wires and tear up the track, we felt a thrill of exhilaration to which we had long been strangers. The track was now clear before us to Chattanooga; and even west of that city we had good reason to believe that we should find no other train in the way till we had reached Mitchel's lines. If one rail could now be lifted we would be in a few minutes at the Oostenaula bridge; and that burned,

the rest of the task would be little more than simple manual labor, with the enemy absolutely powerless. We worked with a will.

But in a moment the tables were turned. Not far behind we heard the scream of a locomotive bearing down upon us at lightning speed. The men on board were in plain sight and well armed. Two minutes—perhaps one—would have removed the rail at which we were toiling; then the game would have been in our own hands, for there was no other locomotive beyond that could be turned back after us. But the most desperate efforts were in vain. The rail was simply bent, and we hurried to our engine and darted away, while remorselessly after us thundered the enemy.

Now the contestants were in clear view, and a race followed unparalleled in the annals of war. Wishing to gain a little time for the burning of the Oostenaula bridge, we dropped one car, and, shortly after, another; but they were "picked up" and pushed ahead to Resaca. We were obliged to run over the high trestles and covered bridge at that point without a pause. This was the first failure in the work assigned us.

The Confederates could not overtake and stop us on the road; but their aim was to keep close behind, so that we might not be able to damage the road or take in wood or water. In the former they succeeded, but not in the latter. Both engines were put at the highest rate of speed. We were obliged to cut the wire after every station passed, in order that an alarm might not be sent ahead; and we constantly strove to throw our pursuers off the track, or to obstruct the road permanently in some way, so that we might be able to burn the Chickamauga bridges, still ahead. The chances seemed good that Fuller and Murphy would be wrecked. We broke out the end of our last box-car and dropped crossties on the track as we ran, thus checking their progress and getting far enough ahead to take in wood and water at two separate stations. Several times we almost lifted a rail, but each time the coming of the Confederates within rifle-range compelled us to desist and speed on. Our worst hindrance was the rain. The previous day (Friday) had been clear, with a high wind, and on such a day fire would have been easily and tremendously effective. But to day a bridge could be burned only with abundance of fuel and careful nursing.

Thus we sped on, mile after mile, in this fearful chase, round curves and past stations in seemingly endless perspective. Whenever we lost sight of the enemy beyond a curve, we hoped that some of our obstructions had been effective in throwing him from the track, and that we should see him no more; but at each long reach backward the smoke was again seen, and the shrill whistle was like the scream of a bird of prey. The time could not have been so very long, for the terrible speed was rapidly devouring the distance; but with our nerves strained to the highest tension each minute seemed an hour. On several occasions the escape of the enemy from wreck was little less than miraculous. At one point a rail was placed across the track on a curve so skilfully that it was not seen till the train ran upon it at full speed. Fuller says that they were terribly jolted, and seemed to bounce altogether from the track, but lighted on the rails in safety. Some of the Confederates wished to leave a train which was driven at such a reckless rate, but their wishes were not gratified.

Before reaching Dalton we urged Andrews to turn and attack the enemy, laying an ambush so as to get into close quarters, that our revolvers might be on equal terms with their guns. I have little doubt that if this had been carried out it would have succeeded. But either because he thought the chance of wrecking or obstructing the enemy still good, or feared that the country ahead had been alarmed by a telegram around the Confederacy by the way of Richmond, Andrews merely gave the plan his sanction without making any attempt to carry it into execution.

Dalton was passed without difficulty, and beyond we stopped again to cut wires and to obstruct the track. It happened that a regiment was encamped not a hundred yards away, but they did not molest us. Fuller had written a despatch to

Chattanooga, and dropped a man with orders to have it forwarded instantly, while he pushed on to save the bridges. Part of the message got through and created a wild panic in Chattanooga, although it did not materially influence our fortunes. Our supply of fuel was now very short, and without getting rid of our pursuers long enough to take in more, it was evident that we could not run as far as Chattanooga.

While cutting the wire we made an attempt to get up another rail; but the enemy, as usual, were too quick for us. We had no tool for this purpose except a wedge-pointed iron bar. Two or three bent iron claws for pulling out spikes would have given us such incontestable superiority that, down to almost the last of our run, we should have been able to escape and even to burn all the Chickamauga bridges. But it had not been our intention to rely on this mode of obstruction—an emergency only rendered necessary by our unexpected delay and the pouring rain.

We made no attempt to damage the long tunnel north of Dalton, as our enemies had greatly dreaded. The last hope of the raid was now staked upon an effort of a kind different from any that we had yet made, but which, if successful, would still enable us to destroy the bridges nearest Chattanooga. But, on the other hand, its failure would terminate the chase. Life and success were put upon one throw.

A few more obstructions were dropped on the track, and our own speed increased so that we soon forged a considerable distance ahead. The side and end boards of the last car were torn into shreds, all available fuel was piled upon it, and blazing brands were brought back from the engine. By the time we approached a long, covered bridge a fire in the car was fairly started. We uncoupled it in the middle of the bridge, and with painful suspense waited the issue. Oh for a few minutes till the work of conflagration was fairly begun! There was still steam pressure enough in our boiler to carry us to the next wood-yard, where we could have replenished our fuel by force, if necessary, so as to run as near to

Chattanooga as was deemed prudent. We did not know of the telegraph message which the pursuers had sent ahead. But, alas! the minutes were not given. Before the bridge was extensively fired the enemy was upon us, and we moved slowly onward, looking back to see what they would do next. We had not long to conjecture. The Confederates pushed right into the smoke, and drove the burning car before them to the next side-track.

With no car left, and no fuel, the last scrap having been thrown into the engine or upon the burning car, and with no obstruction to drop on the track, our situation was indeed desperate. A few minutes only remained until our steed of iron which had so well served us would be powerless.

But it might still be possible to save ourselves. If we left the train in a body, and, taking a direct course toward the Union lines, hurried over the mountains at right angles with their course, we could not, from the nature of the country, be followed by cavalry, and could easily travel—athletic young men as we were, and fleeing for life—as rapidly as any pursuers. There was no telegraph in the mountainous districts west and northwest of us, and the prospect of reaching the Union lines seemed to me then, and has always since seemed, very fair. Confederate pursuers with whom I have since conversed freely have agreed on two points— that we could have escaped in the manner here pointed out, and that an attack on the pursuing train would likely have been successful. But Andrews thought otherwise, at least in relation to the former plan, and ordered us to jump from the locomotive one by one, and, dispersing in the woods, each endeavor to save himself. Thus ended the Andrews railroad raid.

It is easy now to understand why Mitchel paused thirty miles west of Chattanooga. The Andrews raiders had been forced to stop eighteen miles south of the same town, and no flying train met him with the expected tidings that all railroad communications of Chattanooga were destroyed, and that the town was in a panic and undefended. He dared advance no farther without heavy reinforcements from Pittsburg Landing or the north; and he probably believed to the day of his death, six months later, that the whole Andrews party had perished without accomplishing anything.

A few words will give the sequel to this remarkable enterprise. There was great excitement in Chattanooga and in the whole of the surrounding Confederate territory for scores of miles. The hunt for the fugitive raiders was prompt, energetic, and completely successful. Ignorant of the country, disorganized, and far from the Union lines, they strove in vain to escape. Several were captured the same day on which they left the cars, and all but two within a week. Even these two were overtaken and brought back when they supposed that they were virtually out of danger. Two of those who had failed to be on the train were identified and added to the band of prisoners.

Now follows the saddest part of the story. Being in citizens' dress within an enemy's lines, the whole party were held as spies, and closely and vigorously guarded. A court martial was convened, and the leader and seven others out of the twenty-two were condemned and executed. The remainder were never brought to trial, probably because of the advance of Union forces, and the consequent confusion into which the affairs of the departments of east Tennessee and Georgia were thrown. Of the remaining fourteen, eight succeeded by a bold effort—attacking their guard in broad daylight—in making their escape from Atlanta, Georgia, and ultimately in reaching the North. The other six who shared in this effort, but were recaptured, remained prisoners until the latter part of March, 1863, when they were exchanged through a special arrangement made with Secretary Stanton. All the survivors of this expedition received medals and promotion. The pursuers also received expressions of gratitude from their fellow-Confederates, notably from the governor and the legislature of Georgia.

—PITTENGER, "The Locomotive
Chase in Georgia"

XIII.4

A Badger Boy Meets the Originals of *Uncle Tom's Cabin*

Here is our old friend Chauncey Cooke again—the Wisconsin boy who enlisted at sixteen, fought the Sioux Indians, and then was sent to Kentucky to take part in the campaign against Bragg. It is not to be supposed that all Union soldiers saw the Negroes through the eyes of Harriet Beecher Stowe; many of them—like Colonel Niebling—were bitterly hostile to emancipation.

Columbus, Ky., March 5th, 1863
25th Wis. Vol Infantry

Dear Folks at Home:

I sent you a letter a day or two ago and maybe I will hear from you soon. I hope I shall. I am well and we are hearing and seeing things and the days are not so heavy as at Madison. The weather is fine—most of the time warm and clear.

We drill every day, do police work, cleaning round the camp, and take a stroll now and then back in the country, far as the pickets will let us. We are really in the "Sunny South." The slaves, contrabands, we call them, are flocking into Columbus by the hundred. General Thomas of the regular army is here enlisting them for war. All the old buildings on the edge of the town are more than full. You never meet one but he jerks his hat off and bows and shows the whitest teeth. I never saw a bunch of them together, but I could pick out an Uncle Tom, a Quimbo, a Sambo, a Chloe, an Eliza, or any other character in *Uncle Tom's Cabin.* The women take in a lot of dimes washing for the soldiers, and the men around picking up odd jobs. I like to talk with them. They are funny enough, and the stories they tell of slave life are stories never to be forgotten. Ask any of them how he feels and the answer nearly always will be, "Sah, I feels might good, sah," or "God bress you, massa, I'se so proud I'se a free man." Some are leaving daily on up-river boats for Cairo and up the Ohio River. The Ohio has always been the river Jordan to the slave. It has been the dream of his life even to look upon the Ohio River.

The government transports returning from down river points where they had been with troops or supplies would pick up free men on every landing and deliver them free of charge at places along the Ohio and upper Mississippi points.

The slaves are not all black as we in the North are apt to suppose. Some of them are quite light. Those used as house servants seem to have some education and don't talk so broad. A real pretty yellow girl about 18 was delivering some washing to the boys yesterday. She left her master and mistress in December and came to Columbus. In answer to the questions of the boys she said she left home because her mistress was cross to her and all other servants since Lincoln's emancipation. She said her mother came with her. One of the boys asked her why her father did not come with her. She said, "My father hain't no colored man, he's a white man." When the boys began to laugh she picked up her two-bushel basket of clothes, balanced it on her head, and went her way. That girl must have made fifty stops among the tents leaving her basket of clothes. I wonder if she heard the same dirty talk in each of them. The talk wasn't clean, but some of us who tho't so just let it pass and kept still. . . .

Your son,
Chauncey

Columbus, Ky., March 21st., 1863
25th Wisconsin Vol.

Dear Mother:

After drill went out in the edge of the woods. Its more peaceful and homelike than the racket of the camp. I can see the picket guard beyond me slowly pacing his beat. There is no enemy about but the discipline and regulations are just as rigid as they are in Georgia. No white man can come within the picket line except he has the password. A Negro is allowed to come in. We are afraid that the whites may be spies, we know the blacks are our friends.

The health of the regiment is good save a few cases of bowel trouble. The boys call it the Kentucky quickstep. There is more sickness among the poor lazy blacks. They are filling all the vacant houses and even sleeping under the trees, so anxious are they to get near "de Lincoln soldiers." They live on scraps and whatever they can pick up in camp and they will shine our shoes or do any camp work for an old shirt or cast-off coat. They had a revival meeting at the foot of the bluff last night and such shouting and singing and moaning. It was Massa Lincoln was a savior that came after two hundred years of tribulation in the cotton fields and cane. They had long known that something was going to happen because so many times their massa had visitors and they would tell the servants to stay in their cabins and not come to the "big house" until they were called. Then some of the house servants would creep round under the windows and hear the white folks talking about war and that the slaves were going to be free. And when the one that was sent to listen would come back and tell the others, they would get down on their knees and pray in whispers and give thanks to the Lord. Everything with the darkies is Lord, Lord. Their faith that the Lord will help them has held out more than 200 years.

I sometimes wonder if the Lord is not partial to the white race and rather puts it onto the black race because they are black. We sometimes get terribly confused when we try to think of the law of Providence. This black race for instance, they can't talk ten words about slavery and old Massa and old Missus, but they get in something about "de blessed Lord and de lovely Jesus" and yet in this land of Washington, God has permitted them to be bought and sold like our cattle and our hogs in the stockyards for more than 200 years.

I listened for two hours this morning to the stories of a toothless old slave with one blind eye who had come up the river from near Memphis. He told me a lot of stuff. He said his master sold his wife and children to a cotton planter in Alabama to pay his gambling debts, and when he

told his master he couldn't stand it, he was tied to the whipping post stripped and given 40 lashes. The next night he ran to the swamps. The bloodhounds were put on his track and caught him and pulled him down. They bit him in the face and put out his eye and crushed one of his hands so he could not use it. He stripped down his pants and showed me a gash on one of his hips where one of the hounds hung unto him until he nearly bled to death. This happened in sight of Nashville, the capitol of Tennessee. I told this to some of the boys and they said it was all bosh, that the niggers were lying to me. But this story was just like the ones in Uncle Tom's Cabin, and I believe them. And father knows of things very much like this that are true.

I will write you again soon,
Your son
Chauncey
—Cooke, "Letters of a Badger Boy in Blue"

XIII.5

The Confederates Escape in the Teche Couniry

Before he could support Grant in the Vicksburg-Fort Hudson campaign General Banks, who had replaced Butler in New Orleans, felt that he had to dispose of the Confederate forces in the Teche country west of the city, a country of bayous, lakes, and swamps. In January 1863 Banks organized the first of his expeditions against General Taylor's miscellaneous forces, but this petered out. A second advance took place in April and met with some success. It is this advance that is recorded here. Later that summer General Taylor, whom we have already met in the Valley campaign, and his subordinate Mouton struck back, recovering the whole Teche country up to the gates of New Orleans. The fall of Port Hudson released large forces for a counterattack, however, and Taylor retreated to the Red River country.

The novelist and historian John De Forest tells the story.

The Teche country was to the war in Louisiana what the Shenandoah Valley was to the war in Virginia. It was a sort of back alley, parallel to the main street wherein the heavy fighting must go on;

and one side or the other was always running up or down the Teche with the other side in full chase after it. There the resemblance ends, for the Teche country is a long flat, hemmed in by marshes and bayous, which, as everybody but a blind man can see, is a very different thing from a rolling valley bordered by mountains. . . .

My first adventure in this region was in January, 1863. Weitzel dashed up to the confluence of the Teche and Atchafalaya with five or six regiments, scared Mouton out of his position there, smashed the Confederates' new ironclad gun boat *Cotton,* and returned next morning. Although pestered with cold and hunger, our march homeward was as hilarious as a bacchanal procession. It was delightful to have beaten the enemy, and it was delightful to be on the way back to our comfortable quarters. The expedition was thus brief because it had fulfilled its object, which was to weaken the Con federate naval power on the Teche, and thus enable Banks to take the back alley in his proposed advance on Port Hudson.

But why should he go by the back alley of the Teche instead of by the main street of the Mississippi? Because it was necessary to destroy the army of Mouton, or, at least, to drive it northward as far as possible, in order to incapacitate it from attacking New Orleans while we should be engaged with the fortress of the bluffs. The story ran in our brigade that this sensible plan originated in the head of our own commandant, Weitzel. I believed it then, and I have learned no better since, although I can affirm nothing. The reader will please to remember that there is a great deal of uncertainty in war, not only before but after.

About the middle of April, 1863, I was once more at the confluence of the Teche and the Atchafalaya. This time Mouton was there in strong force, posted behind entrenchments which seemed to me half a mile in length, with an impassable swamp on his right and armored gunboats on his left. Banks's army was far superior in numbers and, supported as it was by a sufficient fleet of gunboats, could doubtless have carried the position; but the

desirable thing to do was of course, not so much to beat Mouton as to bag him, and so finish the war in this part of Louisiana. Accordingly, by mysterious waterways of which I know nothing, Grover's division was transported to Irish Bend, in Mouton's rear, while Emory's and Weitzel's divisions should amuse him in front.

And here I am tempted . . . to describe this same amusement. The first part of the joke was to push up Weitzel's brigade to draw the enemy's fire. In a single long line, stretching from the wood on the left well toward the river on the right, the brigade advanced directly toward the enemy's works, prostrating or climbing fences, and struggling amid horrible labyrinths of tangled sugar cane. Rush through a mile of Indian corn, taking the furrows diagonally, then imagine yourself three times as tired and breathless as you are, and you will form some conception of what it is to move in line through a canefield. At first you valiantly push aside the tough green obstacles; then you ignominiously dodge under or around them; at last you fall down with your tongue out. The ranks are broken; the regiment tails off into strings, the strongest leading; the ground is strewn with panting soldiers; the organization disappears.

The cane once passed, stragglers began to come up and find their places; the ranks counted off anew while advancing, and we had once more a regiment. Now we obtained a full view of the field of projected amusement. Before us lay a long and comparatively narrow plain, bounded by forests rising out of swamps, and decorated by a long low earthwork, a third of a mile ahead of us, and barely visible to the naked eye. Away to our right were two half-demolished brick sugar-houses, near which there was a scurrying of dust to and fro, bespeaking a skirmishing of cavalry. Otherwise the scene was one of perfect quietness and silence and desertion.

Of a sudden *bang, bang, bang,* roared an unseen battery, and *jiz, jiz, jiz,* screeched the shells over our heads. Evidently the enemy was too much amused to keep his mouth shut. Then our own batteries joined in with their *bang, bang, bang, jiz, jiz, jiz,* and for twenty minutes or more it was as disgusting as a Fourth of July. The shelling did not hurt us a bit, and consequently did not scare us much, for we were already accustomed to this kind of racket, and only took it hard when it was mingled with the cries of the wounded. I never assisted, as the French phrase it, at a noisier or a more harmless bout of cannonading. Not a man in my regiment was injured, although the shells hummed and cracked and fought each other in flights over our heads, dotting the sky with the little globes of smoke which marked their explosions, and sending buzzing fragments in all directions.

Meantime our point was gained; the enemy had defined his position. There was a battery in the swampy wood on his right, which would enfilade an attacking column, while on his left the same business would be performed by his armored gunboats in the Teche. Now came an order to take the brigade to the rear. A greenhorn of an aide, shrieking with excitement, galloped up to our commander and yelled: "Colonel, double-quick your men out of range. Double-quick!"

I remember the wrath with which I heard this order. Run? Be shot if I would run or let a man of my company run. The regiment, hearing the command, had faced about and was going to the rear at a pace which threatened confusion and panic. I rushed through the ranks, drew my sword, ordered, threatened, and brought my own company from a double-quick down to the ordinary marching step. Every other officer, from the colonel downward, instinctively did the same; and the regiment moved off in a style which we considered proper for the Twelfth Connecticut.

That night we bivouacked with mosquitoes, who drew more blood than the cannonade of the afternoon. Next morning the heavy guns of the opposing gunboats opened a game of long bowls, in which the Parrotts of the Twenty-first Indiana took a part, sending loud-whispering shells into the farthest retreats of the enemy. At ten, the whole army, three lines deep and stretching across the river—a fine martial spectacle—advanced slowly through the canefields toward the entrenchments. Marching in my preferred position, in the front rank of my company and next to the regimental colors, I felt myself to be an undesirably conspicuous person, as we came out upon the open ground in view of the enemy, and received the first discharge of their artillery. It is a grand thing to take the lead in battle, but all the same it is uncomfortable. The first cannon shot which I noticed struck the ground sixty or eighty feet in front of our color guard, threw up the ploughed soil in a little cloud, leaped a hundred feet behind the regiment, and went bounding off to the rear.

"That's bad for the fellows behind us," I said to my men, with that smile which a hero puts on when he makes the best he can of battle, meantime wishing himself at home.

The next shot struck within thirty feet of the line, and also went jumping and whistling rearward. They were evidently aiming at the colors, and that was nearly equivalent to aiming at me.

"You'll fetch him next time," I thought, grimly; and so, doubtless, thought hundreds of others, each for himself.

But at this moment one of our own batteries opened with great violence and evidently shook the nerves of the enemy's gunners, for their next shot screeched over the colors and first struck the ground far in rear of the regiment, and thereafter they never recovered their at first dangerously accurate range. Now came an order to the infantry to halt and lie down, and no veteran will need to be told that we obeyed it promptly. I never knew that order to be disregarded on a field of battle, not even by the most inexperienced and subordinate of troops, unless, indeed, they were already running.

The battle of Camp Beaseland was an artillery duel of fifteen or twenty pieces on a side, lasting hotly from eleven in the morning till six in the evening, with a dash of infantry charging and heavy musketry on either flank, and a dribble of skirmishing along the whole line. Where we were, it was all artillery and skirmishing, noisy and lively enough, but by no means murderous. Bainbridge's regular battery on our right pitched into a Louisiana battery on our left front, and a little beyond it a battery of the Twenty-first Indiana pounded away at the Confederate gunboats and at an advanced earth work. The loud metallic spang of the brass howitzers, the dull thud of the iron Parrotts, and the shrieking and cracking of the enemy's shells made up a *charivari* long to be remembered.

Meantime, companies moved out here and there from the line of infantry, deployed as skirmishers, advanced to within two or three hundred yards of the breastworks, and opened fire. This drew the Rebel musketry and made things hotter than ever. The order to lie low passed along, and we did the best we could with the cane-hills, wishing that they were bigger. As I lay on my side behind one of these six-inch fortifications, chewing the hardtack which was my only present creature comfort, several balls cut the low weeds which overhung me. Yet, notwithstanding the stunning racket and the quantity of lead and iron flying about, our loss was very small.

Nor could the enemy have suffered more severely, except on our left. There the Seventy-fifth and 114th New York, drawn up in the swampy wood which at that point separated the two armies, repulsed with a close volley of musketry a swarm of Texans who attempted to ford the morass and turn our flank. There, too, the heaviest fire of our batteries was concentrated and made havoc, as I afterward heard, of the enemy's artillery. An officer of one of our skirmishing companies, whose position enabled him to see this part of the enemy's line, assured me, with a jocose exaggeration founded on fact, that "the air was full of horses' tails and bits of harness." But, in a general way, there was very little slaughter for the amount of powder expended. We were not fighting our hardest; we were merely amusing the enemy. The only serious work done was to smash one or two of his gunboats. Meanwhile, it was hoped that Grover was gaining Mouton's rear and so posting himself as to render escape impossible.

An officer, major of a Texas regiment, as I was told by prisoners, attracted the notice of both armies by riding from left to right of the enemy's position in full view of our line. He was behind the entrenchment, it is true, but that was little more than a rifle pit and hardly concealed the legs of his horse. He was undoubtedly a staff officer engaged in carrying orders to the battery in the wood. As he came back on his perilous mission every skirmisher fired at him, and many men in the line of battle added their bullets to the deadly flight which sought his life, while all our brigade watched him with breathless interest. Directly in front of me the horse reared; the rider dismounted and seemed to examine him; then, remounting, cantered a few yards; then leaned backwards and slid to the ground. Away went the horse, wildly, leaving his gallant master dead.

About five o'clock an order arrived to move out of range of fire. The skirmishers came in; the men rose and took their places in line; and we marched slowly back to our position of the morning. During the night we fought mosquitoes not with the idea of amusing them, but in deadly earnest. During the night, also, the colonel in charge of the pickets, a greenhorn of some nine-months' regiment, distinguished himself by an exhibition of the minimum of native military genius. Early in the morning he reported to Weitzel that the enemy had vacated their position.

"How do you know?" demanded the startled general.

"I heard their artillery going off about two o'clock."

"Good God, sir! why didn't you inform me of it immediately?"

"Why, General, I thought you wanted them to clear out; and I didn't like to disturb you after such a hard day's work."

Thus collapsed the plan by which we were to stick like a burr to the enemy and pitch into his rear whenever he should attempt to force his way through Grover.

—De Forest, "Forced Marches"

XIII.6

GENERAL WILSON RAISES HIS CAVALRY THE HARD WAY

This entertaining episode is from the closing chapter of the war in the West. After Sherman launched his March to the Sea he sent General Thomas to Nashville to collect an army that would hold Tennessee against Hood. The troubles General Wilson had getting horses for his cavalry suggest how that army was improvised.

We will meet James Harrison Wilson again and need not pause here for a lengthy introduction. Only twenty-four when the war broke out, he had a meteoric rise, ending the war with the rank of major general. He was, by general agreement, with Sheridan the most brilliant cavalry commander in the Union armies.

While Hood was advancing from the Tennessee and I had nominally six divisions of cavalry, my actual force with the colors in front of Hood did not exceed five thousand fighting men. Until the movement began I remained at Nashville, engaged night and day in perfecting the paper work, in gathering horses, arms, and equipments, and in making ready for the campaign which was soon to burst upon us. Generally, the supply departments responded promptly to my call, but horses, our greatest want, were scarce, and with the higher requirements and closer inspections I had myself prescribed a few months before, and the advance in price which had naturally followed the advance in quality, the western horse contractors found it impossible to supply our demands. The War Department itself seemed to despair, and while Stanton appeared willing to do what he could, he finally lost patience and his good sense besides, and telegraphed Thomas that if he waited for Wilson to remount his cavalry he would wait "till the crack of doom." But as this was after I had asked and he had granted permission to impress horses from the people wherever they could be found south of the Ohio River, his pes-

simistic assertion was shortly shown to be both unjust and unfounded.

This arbitrary measure was entirely without precedent within our lines, but it was carried ruthlessly into effect while the contending armies were facing each other in front of Nashville. Within seven days after the Secretary's authority came to hand seven thousand horses were obtained in middle and western Kentucky and our mounted force was thereby increased to twelve thousand, nine thousand of which were actually assembled at Edgefield or within supporting distance. The quartermasters to whom this duty was assigned gave vouchers in proper form for every horse taken and it is believed that no permanent loss or injury was inflicted upon the loyal people.

Every horse and mare that could be used was taken. All street-car and livery stable horses, and private carriage- and saddle-horses, were seized. Even Andrew Johnson, the vice president-elect, was forced to give up his pair. A circus then at Nashville lost everything except its ponies; even the old white trick horse was taken but it is alleged that the young and handsome equestrienne, who claimed him, succeeded in convincing my adjutant general that the horse was unfit for cavalry service. Be this as it may, a clean sweep was made of every animal that could carry a cavalry-man and the result is shown by the fact that although two brigades of three thousand men were sent to Kentucky in pursuit of Lyon's Confederate cavalry, about ten thousand well mounted men crossed the Cumberland on the night of December 12 [1864] and marched out against the enemy on the morning of the 15th, as soon as the thaw made it possible to move at all.

The great victory which resulted from turning the enemy's flank shows how important the measure was in making the cavalry the tremendous factor it became, not only in that battle but in the campaign which wound up the war.

—WILSON, *Under the Old Flag*

XIV

THE PROBLEM OF
DISCIPLINE

Why should discipline have been a problem in the Civil War? There are a number of reasons for this, and not all of them are discreditable. Americans had never taken kindly to discipline, either in peace or in war. In civil life every man thought himself as good as his neighbor—even if that neighbor happened to be a merchant or a physician, a mayor or a Congressman—and this attitude was carried over into the armies. There was no military tradition in America, and little understanding of the value of rules and of discipline. This was the first major war in which Americans had ever been engaged, and it was the first to levy on the whole population. From 3,500,000 to 4,000,000 men fought, at one time or another, in Union or Confederate armies— an astonishingly high percentage of the total population of 31,000,000—and all but a handful of these were wholly without previous military experience.

These considerations suggest that the problem of discipline would have been difficult in the best of circumstances; it was aggravated by the policies of Federal and Confederate governments. There was, for example, no trained officer class, and neither government did anything effective either to use such materiel as was available or to train officers. At the outbreak of the war the Regular Army consisted of 16,367 officers and men; there were, in addition, a number of graduates of West Point or of the Citadel and the Virginia Military Institute who were available. This nucleus of Regular Army and veterans might have been sufficient to provide officers for the volunteers of 1861 and 1862; by the time of the draft the war had produced a crop of competent officers. But the government did not follow the policy of breaking up the Regular Army, nor did the Confederacy use its officer material to best advantage. Most of the field and many of the general officers were appointed by state governors, usually on political grounds; a great many of these, especially in the North, earned their

appointments by raising their own regiments or companies. Lower officers were customarily elected by the rank and file. Most of the officers were totally ignorant of the rules of warfare, of military tactics, and of the requirements of discipline. Some learned quickly; others never learned.

One result of this situation was widespread insubordination, downright disobedience, and a staggeringly high rate of desertion. It was not that the typical American was either disorderly or disobedient; it was rather that while willing enough to fight, he saw no reason for observing discipline when there was no fighting at hand. He had little respect for officers, as such, and many of these were not deserving of respect. He was unfamiliar with the requirements of camp sanitation; saw no harm in straggling; was inclined to regard most regulations as something between a joke and a nuisance. Circumstances, as well as the inevitable opportunities and temptations of war, encouraged him to foraging and pillaging.

Punishment for insubordination varied greatly from army to army, from regiment to regiment, and from time to time. Many officers were lax disciplinarians because they curried favor with their men; in the long run the men respected more the strict disciplinarians. Military courts—often drum head courts—dealt with more serious cases. The penalty for desertion, or for sleeping on sentry duty, was death, but this extreme penalty was rarely inflicted. Statistics for the Confederacy are wholly wantng; those for the Union are inadequate and misleading. While there are numerous accounts of executions and numerous accounts, too, of last-minute reprieves, the surgeon general's office gives total executions as 121; when we recall that there were well over 200,000 desertions from the Union Army, and that some 75,000 of these were arrested during the last two years of the war, we realize how feeble was the machinery of enforcement and discipline.

The excerpts which follow are designed to show some of the varied aspects of the problem of discipline: the causes of soldier discontent, the manifestations of that discontent in insubordination and desertion, the ravages of pillaging, the methods of punishment, and the impression that the conduct and misconduct of the Civil War soldiers made on thoughtful observers.

XIV.I

THOMAS WENTWORTH HIGGINSON EXPLAINS THE VALUE OF TRAINED OFFICERS

Higginson himself was an amateur—a Unitarian clergyman who had helped raise and train a Massachusetts regiment and then found himself colonel of the 1st South Carolina colored regiment, where his chief problems were in the realm of training, discipline, sanitation, the commissary, and so forth. This essay on the problem of command—one of the very best in our literature—appeared within a few months of Higginson's retirement from the army.

Now that three years have abolished many surmises, and turned many others into established facts, it must be owned that the total value of the professional training has proved far greater, and that of the general preparation far less, than many intelligent observers predicted. The relation between officer and soldier is something so different in kind from anything which civil life has to offer, that it has proved almost impossible to transfer methods or maxims from the one to the other. If a regiment is merely a caucus, and the colonel the chairman,—or merely a fire-company, and the colonel the foreman,—or merely a prayer-meeting, and the colonel the moderator,—or merely a bar-room, and the colonel the landlord,—then the failure of the whole thing is a foregone conclusion.

War is not the highest of human pursuits, certainly; but an army comes very near to being the completest of human organizations, and he alone succeeds in it who readily accepts its inevitable laws, and applies them. An army is an aristocracy, on a three-years' lease, supposing that the period of enlistment. No mortal skill can make military

power effective on democratic principles. A democratic people can perhaps carry on a war longer and better than any other; because no other can so well comprehend the object, raise the means, or bear the sacrifices. But these sacrifices include the surrender, for the time being, of the essential principle of the government. Personal independence in the soldier, like personal liberty in the civilian, must be waived for the preservation of the nation. With shipwreck staring men in the face, the choice lies between despotism and anarchy, trusting to the common sense of those concerned, when the danger is over, to revert to the old safeguards. It is precisely because democracy is an advanced stage in human society, that war, which belongs to a less advanced stage, is peculiarly inconsistent with its habits. Thus the undemocratic character, so often lamented in West Point and Annapolis, is in reality their strong point. Granted that they are no more appropriate to our stage of society than are revolvers and bowie-knives, that is precisely what makes them all serviceable in time of war. War being exceptional, the institutions which train its officers must be exceptional likewise.

The first essential for military authority lies in the lower of command,—a power which it is useless to analyze, for it is felt instinctively, and it is seen in its results. It is hardly too much to say, that, in military service, if one has this power, all else becomes secondary; and it is perfectly safe to say that without it all other gifts are useless. Now for the exercise of power there is no preparation like power, and nowhere is this preparation to be found, in this community, except in regular army-training. Nothing but great personal qualities can give a man by nature what is easily acquired by young men of very average ability who are systematically trained to command.

The criticism habitually made upon our army by foreign observers at the beginning of the war continues still to be made, though in a rather less degree,—that the soldiers are relatively superior to the officers, so that the officers lead, perhaps, but do not command them. The reason is plain. Three years are not long enough to overcome the settled habits of twenty years. The weak point of our volunteer service invariably lies here, that the soldier, in nine cases out of ten, utterly detests being commanded, while the officer, in his turn, equally shrinks from commanding. War, to both, is an episode in life. not a profession, and therefore military subordination, which needs for its efficiency to be fixed and absolute, is, by common consent, reduced to a minimum. The white American soldier, being, doubtless, the most intelligent in the world, is more ready than any other to comply with a reasonable order, but he does it because it is reasonable, not because it is an order. With advancing experience his compliance increases, but it is still because he better and better comprehends the reason. Give him an order that looks utterly unreasonable—and this is sometimes necessary,—or give him one which looks trifling, under which head all sanitary precautions are yet to apt to rank, and you may, perhaps, find that you still have a free and independent citizen to deal with, not a soldier. *Implicit* obedience must be admitted still to be a rare quality in our army; nor can we wonder at it.

In many cases there is really no more difference between officers and men, in education or in breeding, than if the one class were chosen by lot from the other; all are from the same neighborhood, all will return to the same civil pursuits side by side; every officer knows that in a little while each soldier will again become his client or his customer, his constituent or his rival. Shall he risk offending him for life in order to carry out some hobby of stricter discipline? If this difficulty exist in the case of commissioned officers, it is still more the case with the non-commissioned, those essential intermediate links in the chain of authority. Hence the discipline of our soldiers has been generally that of a town meeting or of an engine-company, rather than that of an army; and it shows the extraordinary quality of the individual men, that so much has been accomplished with such a formidable defect in the organization. Even granting that there has been a great and constant improvement,

the evil is still vast enough. And every young man trained at West Point enters the service with at least this advantage, that he has been brought up to command, and has not that task to learn.

He has this further advantage, that he is brought up with some respect for the army-organization as it is, with its existing rules, methods, and proprieties, and is not, like the newly commissioned civilian, desposed in his secret soul to set aside all its proprieties as mere "pipe-clay," its rnethods as "old-fogyism," and its rules as "red-tape." How many good volunteer officers will admit, if they speak candidly, that on entering the service they half believed the "Army Regulations" to be a mass of old-time rubbish, which they would gladly reedit, under contract, with immense improvements, in a month or two,—and that they finally left the service with the conviction that the same book was a mine of wisdom, as yet but half explored!

Certainly, when one thinks for what a handful of an army our present military system was devised, and with what an admirable elasticity it has borne this sudden and stupendous expansion, it must be admitted to have most admirably stood the test. Of course, there has been much amendment and alteration needed, nor is the work done yet; but it has mainly touched the details, not the general principles. The system is wonderfully complete for its own ends, and the more one studies it the less one sneers. Many a form which at first seems to the volunteer officer merely cumbrous and trivial he learns to prize at last as almost essential to good discipline; he seldom attempts a short cut without finding it the longest way, and rarely enters on that heroic measure of cutting red-tape without finding at last that he has en tangled his own fingers in the process.

More thorough training tells in another way. It is hard to appreciate, without the actual experience, how much of military life is a matter of mere detail. The maiden at home fancies her lover charging at the head of his company, when in reality he is at that precise moment endeavoring to convince his company-cooks that salt-junk needs five hours' boiling, or is anxiously deciding which pair of worn-out trousers shall be ejected from a drummer-boy's knapsack. Courage is, no doubt, a good quality in a soldier, and luckily not often wanting; but, in the long run, courage depends largely on the haversack. Men are naturally brave, and when the crisis comes, almost all men will fight well, if well commanded. As Sir Philip Sidney said, an army of stags led by a lion is more formidable than an army of lions led by a stag. Courage is cheap; the main duty of an officer is to take good care of his men, so that every one of them shall be ready, at a moment's notice, for any reasonable demand.

A soldier's life usually implies weeks and months of waiting, and then one glorious hour; and if the interval of leisure has been wasted, there is nothing but a wasted heroism at the end, and perhaps not even that. The penalty for misused weeks, the reward for laborious months, may be determined within ten minutes.

Without discipline an army is a mob, and the larger the worse; without rations the men are empty uniforms; without ammunition they might as well have no guns; without shoes they might almost as well have no legs. And it is in the practical appreciation of all these matters that the superiority of the regular officer is apt to be shown. . . .

Military glory may depend on a thousand things,—the accident of local position, the jealousy of a rival, the whim of a superior. But the merit of having done one's whole duty to the men whose lives are in one's keeping, and to the nation whose life is staked with theirs,—of having held one's command in such a state, that, if at any given moment it was not performing the most brilliant achievement, it might have been,—this is the substantial triumph which every faithful officer has always within reach.

Now will any one but a newspaper flatterer venture to say that this is the habitual standard in our volunteer service? Take as a test the manner in which official inspections are usually regarded by a regimental commander. These occasions are to him what examination's by the School Committee are to a public-school teacher. He may either deprecate and dodge them, or he may manfully welcome them as the very best means of improvement for all under his care. Which is the more common view? What sight more pitiable than to behold an officer begging off from inspection because he has just come in from picket, or is just going out on picket, or has just removed camp, or was a day too late with his last requisition for cartridges?

No doubt it is a trying ordeal to have some young regular army lieutenant ride up to your tent at an hour's notice, and leisurely. devote a day to probing every weak spot in your command,—to stand by while he smells at every camp kettle, detects every delinquent gun-sling, ferrets out old shoes from behind the mess-bunks, spies out every tent-pole not labelled with the sergeant's name, asks to see the cash-balance of each company-fund, and perplexes your best captain on forming from two ranks into one by the left flank. Yet it is just such unpleasant processes as these which are the salvation of an army; these petty mortifications are the fulcrum by which you can lift your whole regiment to a first-class rank, if you have only the sense to use them. So long as no inspecting officer needs twice to remind you of the same thing, you have no need to blush. But though you be the bravest of the brave, though you know a thousand things of which he is utterly ignorant, yet so long as he can tell you one thing which you ought to know, he is master of the situation. He may be the most conceited little popinjay who ever strutted in uniform; no matter; it is more for your interest to learn than for his to teach. Let our volunteer officers, as a body, once resolve to act on this principle, and we shall have such an army as the world never saw. But nothing costs the nation a price so fearful, in money or in men, as the false pride which shrinks from these necessary surgical operations, or regards the surgeon as a foe. . . .

In those unfortunate early days, when it seemed to most of our Governors to make little difference whom they commissioned, since all were alike untried, and of two evils it was natural to choose that which would produce the more agreeable consequences at the next election-time,—in those days of darkness many very poor officers saw the light. Many of these have since been happily discharged or judiciously shelved. The trouble is, that those who remain are among the senior officers in our volunteer army, in their respective grades. They command posts, brigades, divisions. They preside at court-martials. Beneath the shadow of their notorious incompetency all minor evils may lurk undetected. To crown all, they are, in many cases, sincere and well-meaning men, utterly obtuse as to their own deficiencies, and manifesting (to employ a witticism coeval with them selves) all the Christian virtues except that of resignation.

The present writer has beheld the spectacle of an officer of high rank, previously eminent in civil life, who could only vindicate himself before a court-martial from the ruinous charge of false muster by summoning a staff-officer to prove that it was his custom to sign all military papers without looking at them. He has seen a lieutenant tried for neglect of duty in allowing a soldier under his command, at an important picket-post, to be found by the field-officer of the day with two inches of sand in the bottom of his gun,—and pleading, in mitigation of sentence, that it had never been the practice in his regiment to make any inspection of men detailed for such duty. That such instances of negligence should be tolerated for six months in any regiment of regulars is a thing almost inconceivable, and yet in these cases the regiments and the officers had been nearly three years in service. . . .

The glaring defect of most of our volunteer regiments, from the beginning to this day, has lain in slovenliness and remissness as to every department of military duty, except the actual fighting and dying. When it comes to that ultimate test, our men usually endure it so magnificently that one is tempted to overlook all deficiencies on intermediate points. But they must not be overlooked, because they create a fearful discount on the usefulness of our troops, when tried by the standard of regular armies. I do not now refer to the niceties of dress-parade or the courtesies of salutation: it has long since been tacitly admitted that a white American soldier will not present arms to any number of rows of buttons, if he can by any ingenuity evade it; and to shoulder arms on passing an officer is something to which only Ethiopia or the regular army can attain. Grant, if you please, (though I do not grant,) that these are merely points of foolish punctilio. But there are many things which are more than punctilio, though they may be less than fighting.

The efficiency of a body of troops depends, after all, not so much on its bravery as on the condition of its sick-list. A regiment which does picket-duty faithfully will often avoid the need of duties more terrible. Yet I have ridden by night along a chain of ten sentinels, every one of whom should have taken my life rather than permit me to give the countersign without dismounting, and have been required to dismount by only four, while two did not ask me for the countersign at all, and two others were asleep. I have ridden through a regimental camp whose utterly filthy condition seemed enough to send malaria through a whole military department, and have been asked by the colonel, almost with tears in his eyes, to explain to him why his men were dying at the rate of one a day. The latter was a regiment nearly a year old, and the former one of almost two years' service, and just from the old Army of the Potomac.

The fault was, of course, in the officers. The officer makes the command, as surely as, in educational matters, the teach er makes the school. There is not a regiment in the army so good that it could not be utterly spoiled in three months by a poor commander, nor so poor that it could not be altogether transformed in six by a good one. The difference in material is nothing,—white or black, German or Irish; so potent is military machinery that an officer who knows his business can make good soldiers out of almost anything, give him but a fair chance. The difference between the present Army of the Potomac and any previous one,—the reason why we do not daily hear, as in the early campaigns, of irresistible surprises, overwhelming numbers, and masked batteries,—the reason why the present movements are a tide and not a wave,—is not that the men are veterans, but that the officers are. There is an immense amount of perfectly raw material in General Grant's force, besides the colored regiments, which in that army are all raw, but in which the Copperhead critics have such faith they would gladly select them for dangers fit for Napoleon's Old Guard. But the newest recruit soon grows steady with a steady corporal at his elbow, a well-trained sergeant behind him, and a captain or a colonel whose voice means something to give commands.

—HIGGINSON, "Regular and Volunteer Officers"

XIV.2

"IT DOES NOT SUIT OUR FELLOWS TO BE COMMANDED MUCH"

The major difficulty in discipline was with the officers. Captains and lieutenants were customarily elected by the men; as this letter tells, they could be dismissed by the men, too.

Charles Johnson was a Swedish-born boy who enlisted in the Hawkins Zouaves—a New York regiment—and fought through the Peninsular, the Roanoke, and the Antietam campaigns. This letter was written from Fort Clark, near Hampton, Virginia.

Monday, October 28th [1861]
Our Company seems to be not only unfortunate in the choice of officers, but. in the officers chosen for us as well. Captain Coppault, certainly a splendid drillmaster and with every outward appearance of a soldier, turns out a failure in the field, and has resigned. Lieutenant Russell is not much better, and perhaps ought to resign. Flemming is the best of men, but too good a fellow for a disciplinarian, and our First Sergeant is so ridiculously boyish that

all his discipline loses its effect. Second Sergeant Peret, the slave of a clique which runs the Company, dares not say his soul is his own, and not an intelligent officer in our tribe, except it be Corporal Davis of the Color Guard, and he, being an artist who cares nothing for this military business except for the subjects it furnishes his pencil, is neither appreciated nor understood. And now we are to have one Barnard for our Captain. This man, for shooting a subordinate in the First New York Volunteers, had to fly for his life, but instead of resigning, he was transferred to this Regiment. Colonel Hawkins refused to recognize him, however, and he is, in consequence thereof, under arrest. Lieutenant-Colonel Betts has assigned Barnard to our Company to fill the vacancy caused by the resignation of Captain Coppault.

It does not suit the temper of our fellows to be commanded much, anyway; and for one of our own Regiment even, unless he carried a pretty strong hand, it might be an unpleasant task to take hold of Company I, and that being the case, the feeling of the Company as a whole can easily be imagined. The idea of being controlled by a man for whom most of us felt an abhorrence, seemed entirely intolerable. This feeling, sharpened by the notion that we would be submitting to another indignity put upon us, assisted by the contemptuous opinion we held of Barnard as to his bravery, combined to give the Captain a reception such as perhaps no other officer had ever before had from his subordinates. A variety of insults were heaped upon him openly, the moment he entered our quarters, and last Thursday, when he came out to take command, the Company refused to a man to obey his orders. And this, too, after he had made a speech to the effect that the insulting remarks he had heard must be stopped, and that he would shoot another man under the same circumstances, etc.; but all in vain—our boys insisted that they did not know him and would not obey, and he was obliged to retire, leaving the command to Lieutenant Russell.

During that day he was burned in effigy, a caricature was made on his tent, and a variety of greater indignities suggested, should he ever attempt to take command. On Dress Parade, a general order was read assigning him to our Company with every circumstance of name and rank, which only served to exasperate our men the more. Russell did all he could in a few remarks, laying down the law, but his little speech was instantly followed by three cheers for Russell and three groans for Barnard, and that night the Company's quarters seemed a perfect bedlam, so that the poor man dared not step out of his tent. This was the last of Captain Barnard. In the morning, the Major sent in a request that the Company cease their demonstrations, as Captain Barnard had already sent in his resignation.

—JOHNSON, *The Long Roll*

XIV.3

CONDUCT UNBECOMING AN OFFICER

It was not just enlisted men who presented problems of discipline. In both armies, officers disobeyed orders, became drunk on duty, exhibited cowardice and brutish behavior and conducted themselves in ways dangerous to their men and sometimes themselves. In recent years, Thomas P. and Beverly Lowry have undertaken a systematic study of surviving court-martial records in the Union army. Surprisingly, they discovered that the rate of court-martials for colonels and lieutenant colonels was five times greater than for enlisted men.

Records reveal that scores of higher echelon officers were guilty of stealing military supplies, insulting their commanding and subordinate officers, being so drunk that they fell off horses, keeping women in their quarters, abusing men with excessive punishment, disobeying orders and other acts that did not reflect conduct becoming an officer.

Both armies were staffed by amateurs in a very deadly business heavily influenced by politics. In many cases, Civil War officers had no military background. They gained their commissions through political appointments. Untrained in warfare, they were often not equipped to deal with the challenges of military life and combat. Officers were also subject to rivalries within the ranks, making them more vulnerable to charges of misconduct by rival officers. Finally, the responsibilities of leadership and having to order men to their likely deaths were greater than some men could handle.

In the case below, Colonel Robert C. Murphy, of Wisconsin, was accused by General William Rosecrans of cowardice in the face of the enemy at the Battle of Iuka in September 1862. Rosecrans and Murphy sent a flurry of telegrams to each other on September 12. Rosecrans urged Murphy to hold his position, stating at one point: "For God's sake, don't skedaddle any more. Look at your orders." Rosecrans arrested Murphy after the battle and had him tried for cowardice. The court-martial board found Murphy not guilty, much to Rosecrans's annoyance.

But three months later General Grant summarily relieved Murphy of his duties because of very similar circumstances at Holly Springs, Mississippi. Arrested in his nightclothes while hiding under his bed, Murphy regretted his conduct. "My fate is most mortifying," he said. "I have wished a hundred times today that I had been killed."

The said Colonel R. C. Murphy, 8th Wisconsin Volunteer Infantry, at Iuka, in the State of Mississippi on the 14th day of September, 1862, when threatened with an attack by the enemy, did omit and refuse to give the enemy battle, and run away from the enemy and withdraw his troops from the town Iuka, and hastily retreat with his troops before an inferior force of the enemy, and did continue to retreat with haste to the town of Farmington, without making a stand or attempting to check the pursuit of the enemy.

The said Col. R. C. Murphy, having been placed in command of the town of Iuka, Mississippi, then occupied by United States troops as a military post, by his commanding officer Brig. Gen. W. S. Rosecrans, with orders to hold the same until the commissary and Hospital Stores had been removed, did disobey said orders, and did shamefully abandon said post, and withdraw the troops under his command from said post, before said Commissary and Hospital Stores had been removed, and did neglect to destroy said stores, but abandoned them to fall into the hands of the enemy.

—Indictment of Colonel R. C. Murphy

On September 12th , at 12:00 o'clock M [noon], I entered Iuka with the 8th Wisconsin, seven companies of the 5th Minnesota, one section of Dee's Battery and three companies of cavalry. Five companies of cavalry were left behind by mistake and joined me on the morning of the 13th. During the day of the 12th, I examined roads and placed the 8th Wisconsin and Dee's section on the hill, the 5th Minnesota in the town and the cavalry on the roads leading south and southwest. On the evening of the 12th, I received a series of telegrams from headquarters, which led me to believe that an attack was expected at any moment on Corinth and that General Rosecrans thought we were under strength.

On the morning of the 13th, my pickets were driven in and captured, but we drove them back. We took two prisoners who told us that this was an advanced force of 2,000 Confederates. Now our telegraph was out and the railroad was blocked. I sent couriers and telegraph repairmen, but never saw them again. I saw many enemy signal rockets. A courier that I sent to the garrison at Burnsville returned at 8:00 P.M. and told me there was not a single Union soldier there. I was now cut off and surrounded by a superior force. At 9:00 P.M., I notified Captains Simmons and Mott to prepare the stores for destruction. I awaited orders to hold Iuka, *at all costs*. I sent orders to destroy the stores at daylight and evacuate the town. Captain Webster, then commanding the cavalry, was ordered to form a rear guard and to burn our supplies as we moved out.

When we were four miles out of the town, enemy forces in superior numbers pressed our rear and my cavalry came up informing me that they had been surprised and unable to burn the stores. As we neared Burnsville, I deployed my forces. . . but found no enemy at Burnsville. My scouts reported sharpshooters in Burnsville. We turned towards Farmington. A few enemy shot at us from a swamp. Captain Webster asked me to move my columns losing a wagon or a man. One of my men who had been wounded in the initial skirmish and released by the Confederates reported that the enemy was at least 3,000 cavalry and believed that I had 17,000 men.

—Colonel Robert C. Murphy

The General Commanding, with much regret, feels compelled to disapprove the findings of the Court. The evidence shows fully the abandonment of the post and public stores without pressure from the enemy. It shows a rapid retreating march, without the show of anything deserving the name of pursuit. The forming of a line of battle, faced to the rear, without a shadow to justify it. It shows a colonel in command of a covering column, retreating without feeling of the enemy's advance, which had subsequently to be done; leaving to fall into the hands of the rebels, public stores which he was bound by the first principle of military caution to have seen destroyed, and that he could have remained three hours later to accomplish this without seeing a Rebel infantry soldier to interfere with him. But when seven miles distant, and behind a defile, he forms a line of battle faced, not toward, but from the defile, and pressed forward to Farmington, some ten miles, leaving at Burnsville, without heed or notice, the telegraph operator and two companies of sharpshooters, for a garrison to meet the enemy from whom he was retreating.

The General Commanding, having himself a high personal and official regard for Colonel Murphy, considers that to pass over such conduct with nothing but the announcement of an honorable acquittal, would be to sanction that which would ruin the service. Colonel Murphy is released from arrest and will report to Brigadier General [David] Stanley for duty. The General Court-martial, of which Brigadier General J. McArthur is president, is dissolved.

—Brigadier General William S. Rosecrans

Colonel R. C. Murphy of the 8th regiment Wisconsin Infantry Volunteers, having, while in command of the post at Holly Springs, Mississippi, neglected and failed to exercise the usual and ordinary precautions to guard and protect the same, having after repeated and timely warning of the approach of the enemy, failed to make any preparations or defense, or show any disposition to do so, and having with a force amply sufficient to have repulsed the enemy and protected the public stores entrusted to his care, disgracefully permitted him to capture the post and destroy the stores—and the movement of troops in the face of an enemy rendering it impractical to convene a court martial for his trial, is therefore dismissed [from] the service of the United States to take effect from the 20th day of December, 1862, the date of his cowardly and disgraceful conduct.

—General Ulysses S. Grant

XIV.4

A Camp of Skulkers at Cedar Mountain

There were various kinds and degrees of desertion: failure to report for the draft, bounty jumping, outright desertion, and skulking and straggling to avoid battle.

George Alfred Townsend, whom we have met once before, here describes a camp of skulkers hiding in the woods during the Battle of Cedar Mountain—or, as it is sometimes called, Slaughter Mountain—of August 9, 1862. This was one of the minor engagements preceding the Second Manassas campaign; partly because Banks and McDowell were unable to bring up their full forces, it was a victory for Jackson.

Beyond this the way was comparatively clear; but as I knew that other guards held the road further on, I passed to the right, and with the hope of finding a rill of water, went across some grass fields, keeping toward the low places. The fields were very still, and I heard only the subdued noises wafted from the road; but suddenly I found myself surrounded by men. They were lying in groups in the tall grass, and started up suddenly, like the clansmen of Roderick Dhu. At first I thought myself a prisoner, and these some cunning Confederates, who had lain in wait. But, to my surprise, they were Federal uniforms, and were simply skulkers from various regiments, who had been hiding here during the hours of battle. Some of these miserable wretches asked me the particulars of the fight, and when told of the defeat, mut-

tered that they were not to be hood-winked and slaughtered.

"I was sick, anyway," said one fellow, "and felt like droppin' on the road."

"I didn't trust my colonel," said another; "he ain't no soldier."

"I'm tired of the war, anyhow," said a third, "and my time's up soon; so I shan't have my head blown off."

As I progressed, dozens of these men appeared; the fields were strewn with them; a true man would rather have been lying with the dead on the field of carnage, than here, among the craven and base. I came to a spring at last, and the stragglers surrounded it in levies. One of them gave me a cup to dip some of the crystal, and a prayerful feeling came over me as the cooling draught fell over my dry palate and parched throat. Regaining the road, I encountered reinforcements coming rapidly out of Culpepper, and among them was the 9th New York. My friend, Lieutenant Draper, recognized me, and called out that he should see me on the morrow, if he was not killed meantime. Culpepper was filling with fugitives when I passed up the main street, and they were sprinkled along the sidewalks, gossiping with each other. The wounded were being carried into some of the dwellings, and when I reached the Virginia Hotel, many of them lay upon the porch. I placed my blanket on a clean place, threw myself down exhaustedly, and dropped to sleep directly.

—Townsend, *Campaigns of a Non-Combatant*

XIV.5

"The Army is Becoming Awfully Depraved"

Away from home, in the enemy's country, and without any inbred sense of discipline or firm officers, many of the soldiers were, indeed, "awfully depraved." Depravity ran the gamut from drunkenness and profanity to theft, pillaging, and murder.

Charles Wills, whose moral sense was deeply affronted by what he saw, was an Illinois boy of twenty-one when he enlisted as a private in the 8th Illinois Infantry. Before the end of the war he had been promoted to lieutenant colonel. He fought in Missouri, Tennessee, and Alabama, and was with Sherman in the March to the Sea. His letters are filled with accounts of immorality and pillaging in the army.

Provost Marshal's Office, Waterford, Miss.,
December 12, '62

From captain of the provost guard I have been changed to provost marshal. I had charge of two companies, doing the guard duty for the provost of our division until yesterday; the division was ordered forward to Oxford, except our regiment, which was left to guard the railroad between this point and the Tallahatchie river. Headquarters being here, Colonel Dickerman appointed me provost and sent my company to guard a bridge one and one-half miles south of this place. My business is to attend to all prisoners, deal with citizens (administer oaths, take paroles, etc.), give all passes for citizens and soldiers leaving, have charge of all soldiers straggling from their regiments, issue permits to sutlers, etc., and overlook the cotton trade. Altogether, quite enough for any one man to attend to.

The little advantage of having a comfortable house to live in, etc., is worth something; but I kind o' feel as if I would rather be with my company. Another regiment came in to night, 12th Indiana, and we may possibly be relieved to morrow. Shall be glad if we can only get with our division again. General Lanman has again taken command of our division, and although we know nothing against McKean, yet we know so much good of Lanman, that we're much pleased. Eight of our companies are guarding bridges, so we only have two here. Confound this railroad guarding; I'm down on it. 'Tis more dangerous than regular soldiering, harder work, and no shadow of a chance for glory. There's a smart chance of fun in my present business, particularly in the citizens branch thereof.

It would have furnished you with amusement enough for a month, could you have heard an old lady talk who visited me to-day. She was a F. F. and

blooded, O Lord! We let all come within the lines; but before they can pass out, an oath or parole is required of them. How they squirm! Rebels, though they are, 'tis shocking and enough to make one's blood boil to see the manner in which some of our folks have treated them. Trunks have been knocked to pieces with muskets when the women stood by, offering the keys, bureau drawers drawn out, the contents turned on the floor, and the drawer thrown through the window, bed clothing and ladies' clothing carried off and all manner of deviltry imaginable perpetrated. Of course the scoundrels who do this kind of work would be severely punished if caught, but the latter is almost impossible. Most of the mischief is done by the advance of the army, though, God knows, the infantry is bad enough. The d—d thieves even steal from the Negroes (which is lower business than I ever thought it possible for a white man to be guilty of) and many of them are learning to hate the Yankees as much as our "Southern Brethern" do.

The army is becoming awfully depraved. How the civilized home folks will ever be able to live with them after the war, is, I think, something of a question. If we don't degenerate into a nation of thieves, 'twill not be for lack of the example set by a fair sized portion of our army. Do you remember that I used to write that a man would no sooner lose his morality in the army than at home? I now respectfully beg to recall the remark.

Scottsboro, Ala., January 5, 1864

It's all over now, the mounting part has "played" and that string will not probably be harped on again for this brigade to dance to. I think that today, Sherman, Logan or Ewing would not trust a detachment of this brigade on sorebacked mules if they had only three legs. This little squad of 500 men in the two months they have been mounted have committed more devilment than two divisions of regular cavalry could in five years. Everything you can think of, from shooting Negroes, or marrying these simple country women, down to stealing babies' diapers. From taking $2,700.00 in gold, to snatching a brass ring off the finger of the woman who handed a drink of water. From taking the last "old mar' " the widow had to carry her grist to mill, to robbing the bed of its cord, for halters, and taking the clothes line and bedclothing "to boot." I'll venture that before we were dismounted, not a well-rope, tracechain, or piece of cord of any kind strong enough to hold a horse could be found in the districts through which we have foraged.

I want you to understand that my command is not responsible for the heavy devilment. I have steadily discountenanced it, and watched my men carefully. I am willing to be responsible for all they did, and will probably have a chance, as I understand a board of inquiry sits on the subject shortly. Some of the officers will, I think, have cause to wish they were never mounted; and to think that "Mission Ridge" would have been preferable to the duty they have been on.

—Wills, *Army Life of an Illinois Soldier*

XIV.6

Robert Gould Shaw Complains that War is a Dirty Business

Robert Gould Shaw, member of a prominent Massachusetts merchant family, was a lieutenant in the 2nd Massachusetts Volunteers when the famous 54th Massachusetts colored regiment was formed; he volunteered for service. and was appointed colonel. His regiment saw duty of the coast of Florida and Georgia and then in the heroic attack on Battery Wagner, where Shaw lost his life. Although only a minor figure in the war he has had raised to him two noble memorials—St. Gaudens' great Shaw Memorial overlooking Boston Common, and William Vaughn Moody's "Ode in Time of Hesitation."

St. Simon's Island [Georgia], June 9th, 1863
We arrived at the southern point of this island at six this morning. I went ashore to report to Colonel Montgomery, and was ordered to proceed

with my regiment to a place called Pike's Bluff, on the inner coast of the island, and en camp. We came up here in another steamer, the *Sentinel,* as the *De Molay is* too large for the inner waters, and took possession of a plantation formerly owned by Mr. Gould.

On Wednesday, a steamboat appeared off our wharf, and Colonel Montgomery hailed me from the deck with, "How soon can you get ready to start on an expedition?"

I said, "In a half an hour," and it was not long before we were on board, with eight companies, leaving two for camp-guard.

We steamed down by his camp, where two other steamers, with five companies from his regiment, with two sections of Rhode Island artillery, joined us. A little below there we ran aground and had to wait until midnight for flood-tide, when we got away once more.

At 8 A.M. we were at the mouth of the Altamaha river, and immediately made for Darien. We wound in and out through the creeks, twisting and turning continually, often heading in directly the opposite direction from that which we intended to, and often running aground, thereby losing much time. Besides our three vessels, we were followed by the gunboat *Paul Jones.*

On the way up, [Colonel] Montgomery threw several shells among the plantations, in what seemed to me a very brutal way, for he didn't know how many women and children there might be.

About noon, we came in sight of Darien, a beautiful little town. Our artillery peppered it a little, as we came up, and then our three boats made fast to the wharves, and we landed the troops. The town was deserted, with exception of two white women and two Negroes.

Montgomery ordered all the furniture and movable property to be taken on board the boats. This occupied some time; and, after the town was pretty thoroughly disembowelled, he said to me, "I shall burn this town." He speaks always in a very low tone, and has quite a sweet smile when addressing you. I told him "I did not want the responsibility of it;" and he was only too happy to take it all on his shoulders. So the pretty little place was burnt to the ground, and not a shed remained standing—Montgomery firing the last buildings with his own hand. One of my companions assisted in it, because he ordered them out, and I had to obey. You must bear in mind, that not a shot had been fired at us from this place, and that there were evidently very few men left in it. All the inhabitants (principally women and children) had fled on our approach, and were, no doubt, watching the scene from a distance. Some of our grapeshot tore the skirt of one of the women whom I saw. Montgomery told her that her house and property should be spared; but it went down with the rest.

The reasons he gave me for destroying Darien were, that the Southerners must be made to feel that this was a real war, and that they were to be swept away by the hand of God, like the Jews of old. In theory, it may seem all right to some, but when it comes to being made the instrument of the Lord's vengeance, I myself don't like it. Then he says "We are outlawed, and, therefore, not bound by the rules of regular warfare." But that makes it none the less revolting to wreak our vengeance on the innocent and defenceless.

By the time we had finished this dirty piece of business, it was too dark to go far down the narrow river, where our boat sometimes touched both sides at once: so we lay at anchor until daylight, occasionally dropping a shell at a stray house. The *Paul Jones* fired a few guns as well as we.

I reached camp at about 2 P.M., to-day, after as abominable a job as I ever had a share in.

Remember not to breathe a word of what I have written about this raid, for I have not yet made up my mind what I ought to do. Besides my own distaste for this barbarous sort of warfare, I am not sure that it will not harm very much the reputation of black troops and of those connected with them. For myself, I have gone through the war so far without dishonor, and I do not like

to degenerate into a plunderer and robber—and the same applies to every officer in my regiment. . . .

All I complain of is wanton destruction. After going through the hard campaigning and hard fighting in Virginia, this makes me very much ashamed of myself, Montgomery, from what I have seen of him, is a conscientious man, and really believes what he says, "that he is doing his duty to the best of his knowledge and ability." There are two courses only for me to pursue: to obey orders and say nothing, or to refuse to go on any more such expeditions, and be put under arrest, probably court-martialed, which is a serious thing.

—POST, ed., *Soldiers' Letters from Camp, Battle-Field and Prison*

XIV.7

THE YANKEE INVADERS PILLAGE AND BURN

With the exception of Lee's two invasions north of the Potomac, Morgan's abortive raid into Indiana, Early's thrust toward Washington, and the fighting in Missouri, the war was fought entirely in the South. This meant not only the devastation and ruin that inevitably accompany the bombardment of cities, pitched battles, the encampment and marching of hostile armies, but destruction and pillaging. Pillaging is to be distinguished from organized and systematic destruction such as that carried out by Sheridan and Hunter in the Valley of Virginia and by Sherman in his March to the Sea; the first was an expression of individual lawlessness, the second systematic and authorized. From the point of view of the victims, to be sure, it made little difference whether their houses were sacked out of motives of high strategy or of wantonness: the result was the same. Pillaging was sometimes inspired by greed, sometimes by the kind of brutal destructiveness familiar to us from the Second World War, sometimes by bitterness and hatred. Some officers made sincere efforts to prevent or at least to control pillaging; others appear to have connived at it. That it was a violation of the rules of war and destructive of discipline is too obvious for emphasis.

The four excerpts which follow speak for themselves, and it will be sufficient to say a word about the circumstances and the authors.

Francis Pierce, who describes the looting of Fredericksburg—already battered by artillery—was a member of the 108th New York Volunteers.

Sarah Morgan we shall meet again; her lively description of the sacking of the Judge Thomas Gibbes Morgan house in Baton Rouge, Louisiana, is something of a classic.

General Grierson's great raid of 1863, commemorated elsewhere, was merely one of a series by that dashing cavalry officer; the intrepid Elizabeth Beach gives us an incident from one of his raids of the following year.

Henrietta Lee, a descendant of Richard Henry Lee and close relative to Robert E. Lee, wrote a scathing letter to Hunter, who had ordered the destruction of her house in the Valley Campaign of 1864. Hunter had also played a role in the plundering described earlier in this chapter by Colonel Shaw. Hunter was Montgomery's commanding officer. Shaw amended his views of Montgomery. In a letter written shortly afterward, Shaw described Montgomery as being "gentlemanly" and worthy of respect. Montgomery had laid the countryside in ruins as part of his duty "that the South be devastated with fire & sword." Interestingly, Shaw had few kind words to say of Hunter, a fellow ardent abolitionist. Shaw wrote that he was "glad" when Hunter was relieved of command and that "he does not impress one as being a man of power."

A. "The Soldiers Delight in Destroying Everything"

Fredericsburgh [was] given up to pillage and destruction. Boys came into our place *loaded* with *silver* pitchers, *silver* spoons, silver lamps and castors etc. Great 3 story brick houses furnished magnificently were broken into and their contents scattered over the floors and trampled on by the muddy feet of the soldiers. Splended alabaster vases and pieces of statuary were thrown at 6 and 700 dollar mirrors. Closets of the very finest china ware were broken into and their contents smashed onto the Moor and stamped to pieces. Finest cut glass ware goblets were hurled at nice plate glass windows, beautifully embroidered window curtains torn down, rosewood pianoes piled in the street and burned or soldiers would get on top of them and dance and kick the keyboard and internal machinery all to pieces—little table ornaments kicking in every direction—wine cellars broken into and the soldiers drinking all they could and then opening the faucets and let the rest run out—boys go to a

barrel of flour and take a pailful and use enough to make one batch of pancakes and then pour the rest in the street everything turned up side down. The soldiers seemed to delight in destroying everything. Libraries worth thousands of dollars were overhauled and thrown on the floor and in the streets—Ed I can't begin to *describe* the scenes of destruction. It was so throughout the whole city and from its appearance very many wealthy families must have inhabited it.

—McKelvey, ed., "Civil War Letters of Francis Edwin Pierce"

B. The Yankees Sack Sarah Morgan's Home

August 13th, 1862.—I am in despair. Miss Jones, who has just made her escape from town, brings a most dreadful account. She, with seventy-five others, took refuge at Doctor Enders', more than a mile and a half below town, at Hall's. It was there we sent the two trunks containing Father's papers and our clothing and silver. Hearing that guerrillas had been there, the Yankees went down, shelled the house in the night, turning all those women and children out, who barely escaped with their clothing, and let the soldiers loose on it. They destroyed everything they could lay their hands on, if it could not be carried off; broke open armoires, trunks, sacked the house, and left it one scene of devastation and ruin. They even stole Miss Jones's braid! She got here with nothing but the clothes she wore.

This is a dreadful blow to me. Yesterday I thought myself beggared when I heard that our house was probably burnt, remembering all the clothing, books, furniture, etc., that it contained; but I consoled myself with the recollection of a large trunk packed in the most scientific style, containing quantities of nightgowns, skirts, chemises, dresses, cloaks—in short, our very best—which was in safety. Winter had no terrors when I thought of the nice warm clothes; I only wished I had a few of the organdy dresses I had packed up before wearing. And now? It is all gone, silver, Father's law papers, without which we are beggars, and clothing! Nothing left!

August 25th.—About twelve at night.—Sleep is impossible after all that I have heard; so, after vainly endeavoring to follow the example of the rest and sleep like a stoic, I have lighted my candle and take to this to induce drowsiness.

Just after supper, when Anna and I were sitting with Mrs. Carter in her room, I talking as usual of home and saying I would be perfectly happy if Mother would decide to remain in Baton Rouge and brave the occasional shellings, I heard a well-known voice take up some sentence of mine from a dark part of the room; and, with a cry of surprise, I was hugging Miriam until she was breathless. Such a forlorn creature!—so dirty, tired, and fatigued as to be hardly recognizable. We thrust her into a chair and made her speak. She had just come with Charlie, who went after them yesterday, and had left Mother and the servants at a kind friend's on the road. I never heard such a story as she told. I was heartsick, but I laughed until Mrs. Badger grew furious with me and the Yankees and abused me for not abusing them.

She says when she entered the house she burst into tears at the desolation. It was one scene of ruin. Libraries emptied, china smashed, sideboards split open with axes, three cedar chests cut open, plundered, and set up on end; all parlor ornaments carried off; her desk lay open with all letters and notes well thumbed and scattered around, while Will's last letter to her was open on the floor, with the Yankee stamp of dirty fingers. Mother's portrait, half cut from its frame, stood on the floor. Margaret, who was present at the sacking, told how she had saved Father's. It seems that those who wrought destruction in our house were all officers. One jumped on the sofa to cut the picture down (Miriam saw the prints of his muddy feet) when Margaret cried: "For God's sake, gentlemen, let it be! I'll help you to anything here. He's dead, and the young ladies would rather see the house burn than lose it!"

"I'll blow your damned brains out," was the "gentleman's" answer as he put a pistol to her head, which a brother officer dashed away, and the pic-

ture was abandoned for finer sport. All the others were cut up in shreds.

Upstairs was the finest fun. Mother's beautiful mahogany armoire, whose single door was an extremely fine mirror, was entered by crashing through the glass, when it was emptied of every article and the shelves half split and half thrust back crooked. Letters, labeled by the boys private, were strewn over the floor; they opened every armoire and drawer, collected every rag to be found, and littered the whole house with them, until the wonder was where so many rags had been found. Father's armoire was relieved of everything, Gibbes's handsome Damascus sword with the silver scabbard included. All his clothes, George's, Hal's, Jimmy's, were appropriated. They entered my room, broke that fine mirror for sport, pulled down the rods from the bed, and with them pulverized my toilet set, taking also all Lydia's china ornaments I had packed in the washstand. The debris filled my basin and ornamented my bed. My desk was broken open. Over it were spread all my letters and private papers, a diary I kept when twelve years old, and sundry tokens of dried roses, etc., which must have been very funny, they all being labeled with the donor's name and the occasion. Fool! how I writhe when I think of all they saw; the invitations to buggy rides, concerts, "compliments of," etc.! Lilly's sewing machine had disappeared, but as Mother's was too heavy to move, they merely smashed the needles.

In the pillaging of the armoires they seized a pink flounced muslin of Miriam's, which one officer placed on the end of a bayonet and paraded round with, followed by the others who slashed it with their swords, crying: "I have stuck the damned Secesh! That's the time I cut her!" and continued their sport until the rags could no longer be pierced. One seized my bonnet, with which he decked himself, and ran in the streets. Indeed, all who found such rushed frantically around town, by way of frolicking, with the things on their heads. They say no frenzy could surpass it. Another snatched one of my calico dresses and a pair of vases that Mother had when she was married, and was about to decamp when a Mrs. Jones jerked them away and carried them to her boardinghouse, and returned them to Mother the other day. Blessed be Heaven! I have a calico dress! Our clothes were used for the vilest purposes and spread in every corner, at least those few that were not stolen.

Aunt Barker's Charles tried his best to defend the property. "Ain't you 'shamed to destroy all dis here that belongs to a poor widow lady who's got two daughters to support?" he asked of an officer who was foremost in the destruction.

"Poor? Damn them! I don't know when I have seen a house furnished like this! Look at that furniture! They poor!" was the retort, and thereupon the work went bravely on of making us poor indeed.

It would have fared badly with us had we been there. The servants say they broke into the house, crying: "Where are those damned Secesh women? We know they are hid in here, and we'll make them dance for hiding from federal officers!" And they could not be convinced that we were not there until they had searched the very garret. Wonder what they would have done? Charles caught a Captain Clark in the streets, when the work was almost over, and begged him to put an end to it. The gentleman went readily, but though the devastation was quite evident, no one was to be seen, and he was about to leave when, insisting that there was some one there, Charles drew him into my room, dived under the bed, and drew from thence a Yankee captain by one leg, followed by a lieutenant, each with a bundle of the boys' clothes which they instantly dropped, protesting they were only looking around the house. The gentleman captain carried them off to their superior.

Ours was the most shockingly-treated house in the whole town. We have the misfortune to be equally feared by both sides, because we will blackguard neither. So the Yankees selected the only house in town that sheltered three forlorn women, to wreak their vengeance on. From far and near,

strangers and friends flocked in to see the ravages committed. Crowds rushed in before, crowds came in after, Miriam and Mother arrived, all apologizing for the intrusion, but saying they had heard it was a sight never before seen. So they let them examine to their hearts' content, and Miriam says the sympathy of all was extraordinary. A strange gentleman picked up a piece of Mother's mirror, which was as thick as his finger, saying: "Madame, I should like to keep this as a memento. I am about to travel through Mississippi and, having seen what a splendid piece of furniture this was and the state your house is left in, should like to show this as a specimen of Yankee vandalism.". . .

Thursday, August 28th—I am satisfied. I have seen my home again. Tuesday I was up at sunrise, and my few preparations were soon completed, and before any one was awake I walked over to Mr. Elder's, through mud and dew, to meet Charlie. Fortunate was it for me that I started so early, for I found him hastily eating his breakfast and ready to leave. He was very much opposed to my going, and for some time I was afraid he would force me to remain, but at last he consented, perhaps because I did not insist; and with wet feet and without a particle of breakfast, I at length found myself in the buggy on the road home.

Our house could not be reached by the front; so we left the buggy in the back yard, and running through the lot without stopping to examine the storeroom and servants' rooms that opened wide, I went through the alley and entered by the front door.

Fortunate was it for this record that I undertook to describe the sacking only from Miriam's account. If I had waited until now, it would never have been mentioned; for as I looked around, to attempt such a thing seemed absurd. I stood in the parlor in silent amazement, and in answer to Charlie's "Well?" I could only laugh. It was so hard to realize. As I looked for each well-known article, I could hardly believe that Abraham Lincoln's officers had really come so low down as to steal in such a wholesale manner. . . .

Bah! What is the use of describing such a scene? Many suffered along with us, though none so severely. Indeed, the Yankees cursed loudly at those who did not leave anything worth stealing. They cannot complain of us on that score. All our handsome Brussels carpets, together with Lydia's fur, were taken, too. What did they not take? In the garret, in its darkest corner, a whole gilt-edged china set of Lydia's had been overlooked; so I set to work and packed it up, while Charlie packed her furniture in a wagon to send to her father.

—Sarah Dawson, A *Confederate Girl's Diary*

C. Grierson's Raiders on a Rampage

New Albany Miss. July 29th 1864
Dear Father & Mother

I am seated once more to write to you all. . . . I went up to Mr. Hills in the evening to see Gen. Grearson, and asked him to place a guard at my house, told him that his men were searching all over my house and tearing up every thing. Told him that they had already got all I had to eat, that I only asked protection that night, for myself and children. he said certainly he would send me a guard, and if I would treat him right he would protect me until they left. So he sent one of his body guard, and we rested quietly that night. I treated him very kindly, made him a good pallet in the passage and we were not bothered with any other Yankees that night. They all left next morning, so I thought I had got off tolerably well.

I talked with Greaerson about half an hour. he treated me very politely, but I dont think he has much feeling. You ought to have seen how grand him and his staff looked. There were five of them, him and his adjutant sergeon and two others. They were sitting in Mrs Hills passage *dressed into fits*, with three or four bottles of champaign, and boxes of segars setting around them. They asked me a great many questions about my husband. I told them the truth, told them he had gone off to save his horse, that he had lost four horses by them. he says has he a fine horse now. I told him yes that he could not practice medicine on a sorry one, that

good horses were scarce in this country now, and he had got him a good one, and went off to keep them from getting him. Oh! he says he had as well stay at home, we would not bother him nor his horse either. I told him that I knew better than that, that he had been taken once, and his horse every time. . . .

Well next morning Mr Hill got on his horse, came down here and asked Asa to go up and see Luly. They concluded they would then ride up towards Ellistown, and see what the Yankees done up there the night before. They rode up to Mr Hills hitched their horses at the gate, and went in to see the child. Asa put medicine in his pocket for her, and left his saddle bags on his horse, something he very seldom ever does. They had not been in there more than five minutes, before the Yankees came *tearing* down the lane from Langstons right up to Hills house. Mr Hill and Asa broke to run as hard as they could. Mrs. Hill screamed at them to stop they would shoot them. Mr. Hills stopped. They were so close by, but Asa put out and never looked back, untill he was out of hearing. Says he forgot he ever had the rheumatism, he went through the back yard, and horse lot. The Yankees never saw him at all. he did not pretend to go towards his horse. That would have been going right into the Yankees. They were riding round the corner before they knew they wer[e] in ten miles of them. They rode up and took the horses first thing. The one that got Asa's horse says, well I have got a fine horse, rode off saddle-bags, and all. Asa says he would not mind loosing the saddle-bags much, if they had not have had his surgical instruments in them. They cant be replaced. Mr Hill went back in the house and staid untill they left. That was not till next day. They did not bother him.

They staid here all that day, camped in the same place that night, and left next day, but they ruined us all before they left. I cant begin to tell you what they done to other people, it would take so long but will *try* and tell you how they treated us, they came here thicker than they did before if possible. *All day* working like ants, all over the house up stairs and down, in every hole and corner, searching & peeping every where, carried off every irish potatoe beet onion beans, even took time to pick pans of beans took my pillow cases to put them in took towels one new table cloth all my knives but 3 some of my dishes and every pan they could find. Took my shears Asas hatchet. Tore my house all to pieces, it would take me a week to mess it up like they did, pulled all our dirty clothes out of the closets, and examined them. Took all Asa's clothes they could find. Worked here all day I reckon two hundred had been up stairs looked around and came down I followed after them, untill I was nearly broke down, *scared* nearly to death for fear they would find my things that were hid for I knew that was *my all*, provision clothes bed-clothes blankets and every thing was in there, after awhile about a dozen of the infantry came in, and up stairs they went to searching all about, commenced looking under the floor I had a few things hid under their, they commenced pulling them out, pulled out medicine tobacco cards and other little things, but did not seem to want any thing but the tobacco.

After awhile one *rascal* went up in the corner and in stooping to put his hand under the floor, put it against the planks, and they slipped a little. he pulled them off, and says, by george, boys here is the place, they just ripped the planks off and in they went. One says run down and guard the door, dont let another fellow come up, we'll divide the things amongst us. I had in there, meat, flour sugar, coffee, molasses, lard & salt. All of Asas good clothes, Sarahs mine and the childrens. We all had new shoes in there that we had not worn, in a pillow case. They pulled them all out and looked at them. I stood over them and as they would pull out the shoes & clothes, I would grab them and tell them that they could not have them, but every time they came to anything of Asa's they *would* take it. Took his over coat, a pair of new blue jeans pants, three pair of summer pants all his drawers except the ones he had on, one shirt, a new silk handkerchief. So you know he is very near without clothes. They did not take any of my clothes,

except pocket handkerchiefs. Sarah & me both had some new handkerchiefs, they got them all, and would have taken our dresses, if we had not fought over them so, as they pulled them out, I would take them from them, and throw them to Sarah, she would sit down on them, untill she had a large pile under her, she said she would fight over them a long time before they got them. They took two of her dresses, that were left hanging in her room, and Melia's white embroidered dress it was hanging in one of Sarahs. They were taken while we were up stairs *fighting* over the others. We dont know who took them, every room was full at once, we could not watch them all. They were old dresses of Sarahs she hid all her best onces, her pink flounce and dark striped skirt. I hate their taking Melia's, very much, because it came from where it did. I gave Sarah my purple flounce muslin in the place of the one she lost. I have not had it on in three summers. They took one of my best quilts, and three nice blankets but I stole one of them from him after he had got it. he laid it down by him to divide the provision. I slipped up behind him and got it, there was such confusion amongst them he never discovered it.

They left me nothing to eat at all. Took *every solitary* thing I had, except one jar of lard and my salt. There was not even a grain of corn on the place to make hominy after they were gone, and we had enough of every thing to last us till christmas. I hated their taking my chickens and groceries worse than any thing else. I knew we could get meat and bread as soon as they left, but the other things cannot be replaced without sending to Memphis, and we have no cotton. We were living well, but will have to live on meat & bread after this, and we may not be able to get that all the time. They killed all of Asa's hogs for next years meat, but we happened to save our cows. They killed nearly everybodys cows & calves around here but ours. We have two good cows with young calves. They happened not to come up untill very late. We turned them in the yard and kept them there. My calves were in the orchard.

They started to shoot them several times, but I ran after them and begged them not to kill them. Told them they had taken everything I had to eat, but if they would leave the calves that we could live on milk & bread.

Mr Bond milked fifteen cows. They killed every cow and calf he had he now has no cow at all. They nearly ruined him, burned 40 bags of cotton, and killed all his stock took every thing he had in the house to eat, and *every* Negro he had, went with them. Mrs Bond has all her work to do.

They treated Mr Hill in the same manner took & killed nearly every thing he had. They had a little provision hid that they did not find. Every one of his Negroes went with them there is not a Negro on his place large nor small. Mrs Hill has all her work to do. . . .

Well I will quit writing about the Yankees. I know you are all tired of it. I have not told you half that I could tell you. I must tell you though about their finding Mr Bells money. Mrs Bell heard they were coming, and went and buried the money in the corner of a fence. Not a living soul knew where she put it, they went there and dug it up. They had 25 dollars in gold, 15 greenback, and 100 Confederate.

I must tell you of another thing too, how bad we were scared, after the Yankees had been gone about five days, the news came here, that they had sent all the Negroes & waggons on to Memphis, and they were coming back burning every house they passed, turning the people out of doors. We heard one evening that they would be here next morning, and burn us out, heard it from several different sources. Every body went to work, bundling up their clothes, to try & save some. We tied up a bundle apiece, to carry of[f] when they set the house on fire, Asa put on his best clothes that were left, took his account books, and left. You would have laughed to seen us next morning. Sarah May Jones me and Kitsy, all had a string of clothes tied under our hoops. Mr Flournoy worked all night carrying things of[f] in the woods, they did not come back though we soon heard it was all false. . . .

You must all write to me as soon as you get this. I would have written sooner, but have not had energy enough to write a letter since the Yankees left untill now. They turned over my molasses, up stairs, spilt all over the house up stairs & down, and I did not have it scoured up in a week, so you see I did not care much for anything. I have got over that now, we are all in good spirits again. . . .

This leaves us all well, children are getting along well and growing fast. Clara's school is broken up, the teacher cant get board. All send love to you

Your affectionate daughter

E. J. Beach

—Smith, ed., "The Yankees in New Albany"

D. "Oh, Earth, Behold the Monster!"

Jefferson County, Virginia
July 20, 1864

General Hunter:

Yesterday your underling, Captain Martindale, of the First New York Cavalry, executed your infamous order and burned my house. You have had the satisfaction ere this of receiving from him the information that your orders were fulfilled to the letter; the dwelling and every out-building, seven in number, with their contents being burned. I, therefore, a helpless woman whom you have cruelly wronged, address you, a Major-General of the United States army, and demand why this was done? What was my offence? My husband was absent, in exile. He had never been a politician or in any way engaged in the struggle now going on, his age preventing. This fact your chief of staff, David Strother, could have told you. The house was built by my father, a Revolutionary soldier, who served the whole seven years for your independence. There was I born; there the sacred dead repose. It was my house and my home, that has your niece, (Miss Griffith), who has tarried among us all this horrid war up to the present time, met with all kindness and hospitality at my hands. Was it for this that you turned me, my young daughter, and little son out upon the world without a shelter? Or was it because my husband is the grandson of the Revolutionary patriot and "rebel," Richard Henry Lee, and the near kinsman of the noblest of Christian warriors, the greatest of generals, Robert E. Lee. Heaven's blessing be upon his head forever. You and your Government have failed to conquer, subdue, or match him; and disappointment, rage, and malice find vent on the hopeless and inoffensive.

Hyena-like, you have torn my heart to pieces! For all hallowed memories clustered around that homestead, and demon-like, you have done it without even the pretext of revenge, for I never saw or harmed you. Your office is not to lead, like a brave man and soldier, your men to fight in the ranks of war, buy your work has been to separate yourself from all danger, and with your incendiary band steal unaware upon helpless women and children, to insult and destroy. Two fair homes did you ruthlessly lay in ashes, giving not a moment's warning to the startled inmates of your wicked purpose; turning mothers and children out of doors, you are execrated by your own men for the cruel work you give them to do.

In the case of Colonel A. R. Boteler, both father and mother were far away. Any heart but that of Captain Martindale (and yours) would have been touched by that little circle, compromising a widowed daughter just risen from her bed of illness, her three fatherless babies—the oldest not five years old—and her heroic sister. I repeat, any man would have been touched at that sight but captain Martindale. One might as well hope to find mercy and feeling in the heart of a wolf bent on his prey of young lambs, as to search for such qualities in his bosom. You have chosen well your agents for such deeds, and doubtless will promote him.

A colonel of the Federal army has stated that you deprived forty of your officers of their commands because they refused to carry on your malignant mischief. All honor to their names for this, at least! They are men; they have human hearts and blush for such a commander!

I ask who that does not wish infamy and disgrace attached to him forever would serve you?

Your name will stand on history's page as the Hunter of weak women, and innocent children the Hunter to destroy defenceless villages and refined and beautiful homes—to torture afresh the agonized hearts of widows; the Hunter of Africa's poor sons and daughters, to lure them on to ruin and death of soul and body; the Hunter with the relentless heart of a wild beast, the face of a fiend and the form of a man. Oh, Earth, behold the monster! Can I say, "god forgive you?" No prayer can be offered for you. Were it possible for human lips to raise your name heavenward, angels would thrust the foul thing back again, and demons claim their own. The curses of thousands, the scores of manly and upright, and the hatred of the true and honorable, will follow you and yours through all time, and brand your name infamy! Infamy!

Again, I demand why you have burned my home? Answer as you must answer before the Searcher of all hearts, why have you added this cruel, wicked deed to your many crimes?

—HENRIETTA LEE

XIV.8

PUNISHMENTS IN THE UNION AND CONFEDERATE ARMIES

Punishments varied greatly from regiment to regiment and from army to army. Much depended on the character of the commanding officers; much, too, on the circumstances in which the offenses were committed. As might be expected, too, the attitude of the soldiers toward the punishment of their comrades varied considerably. Companies that were badly officered, or that had suffered from a poorly managed commissary, or from other forms of mistreatment and neglect, generally sympathized with the culprits. Some times the punishments were brutal; generally they were merely humiliating. Although flogging had been forbidden by law before the Civil War, it is evident that the practice continued in both armies.

We have already met both our reporters: Frank Wilkeson, who went south with bounty jumpers; and the effervescent John Dooley of the 1st Virginia Infantry.

A. Punishments in the Army of the Potomac

The discipline throughout the Army of the Potomac during the winter of 1863-64 was necessarily severe. The ranks of the original volunteers, the men who sprang to arms at the tap of the northern war-drum had been shot to pieces. Entire platoons had disappeared. Regiments that had entered the great camps of instruction formed around Washing ton in 1861-62 a thousand men strong, had melted before the heat of Confederate battle-fire till they numbered three hundred, two hundred, and as low as one hundred and fifty men. During the winter of 1863-64 these regiments were being filled with bountyjumpers, and these men had to be severely disciplined, and that entailed punishment. There was no longer the friendly feeling of cordial comradeship between the enlisted men and their officers, which was one of the distinguishing characteristics of the volunteer troops. The whole army was rapidly assuming the character and bearing of regular troops, and that means mercenaries. The lines drawn between the recruits of 1863-64 and their officers were well marked and they were rigid. The officers were resolute in their intention to make the recruits feel the difference in their rank. Breaches of army discipline were promptly and severely punished. . . .

The punishments inflicted on the enlisted men were various, and some of them were horribly brutal and needlessly severe; but they apparently served their purpose, and the times were cruel, and men had been hardened to bear the suffering of other men without wincing. One punishment much affected in the light artillery was called "tying on the spare wheel." Springing upward and rearward from the centre rail of every caisson was a fifth axle, and on it was a spare wheel. A soldier who had been insubordinate was taken to the spare wheel and forced to step upon it. His legs were drawn apart until they spanned three spokes. His arms were stretched until there were three or four spokes between his hands. Then feet and hands were firmly bound to the felloes of the wheel. If the soldier was to be punished moderate-

ly he was left, bound in an upright position on the wheel for five or six hours. If the punishment was to be severe, the ponderous wheel was given a quarter turn after the soldier had been lashed to it, which changed the position of the man being punished from an upright to a horizontal one. Then the prisoner had to exert all his strength to keep his weight from pulling heavily and cuttingly on the cords that bound his upper arm and leg to the wheel. I have frequently seen men faint while undergoing this punishment, and I have known men to endure it for hours without a murmur, but with white faces, and set jaws and blazing eyes. To cry out, to beg for mercy, to protest, ensured additional discomfort in the shape of a gag, a rough stick, being tied into the suffering man's mouth. Tying on the spare wheel was the usual punishment in the artillery service for rather serious offences; and no man wanted to be tied up but once. . . .

To be bucked and gagged? Yes, that was severe, but not dangerous. It was highly disagreeable and painful, too, if prolonged, and at all times calculated to make a man's eyes stick out of his head as lobster's eyes do. And then the appearance of a man while undergoing the punishment was highly discreditable. The soldier about to be bucked and gagged, generally a drunken or noisy soldier, was forced to sit on the ground; his knees were drawn up to his chin, then his hands were drawn forward to his shins, and there they were securely bound together. A long stick was then thrust under his knees and over his arms. A gag was then securely bound in his mouth. The soldier who was bucked and gagged could not hurt himself or any one else. He could not speak, but he could make inarticulate sounds indicative of his suffering, and he invariably made them before he was released.

Daily many men were tied up by the thumbs, and that was far from pleasant. The impudent bounty-jumper who had stood on his toes under a tree for a couple of hours to keep his weight off of his thumbs, which were tied to a limb over his head, was exceedingly apt to heed the words of his officers when next they spoke to him. The bounty-jumper lacked the moral qualities which could be appealed to in an honest endeavor to create a soldier out of a ruffian; but his capacity to suffer physically was unimpaired, and that had to be played upon.

Then there was the utterly useless and shoulder-chafing punishment of carrying a stick of cordwood. The stick that one picked up so cheerfully, and stepped off with so briskly, and walked up and down before a sentinel with so gayly in the early morning, had an unaccountable property of growing heavier and heavier as the sun rose higher and higher. One morning at ten o'clock I dropped a stick that did not weigh more than twelve pounds at sunrise. I sat down by it and turned it over and over. It had not grown, but I was then willing to swear that it had gained one hundred and eighty pounds in weight during the time I had carried it.

—WILKESON, *Recollections of a Private Soldier*

B. Punishments in the Army of Northern Virginia

I would like to tell you how breakers of discipline are treated. All prisoners of the Regt. are consigned to the guard house and if they prove refractory are liable to be bucked or gagged. Some times refractory members of companies are sent to the guard house under condemnation either to be bucked or gagged or perhaps to wear a barrel shirt.

'Bucking' is making the culprit sit in a doubled up posture, clasping his knees with his hands, and whilst his knees almost touch his chin a long stick is inserted between his arms and underneath his knee joints. 'Gagging' is more severe, and is performed by placing a bayonet in the culprit's mouth and fixing it there by tying behind the head strings or cord attached to either end of the implement of torture. Frequently however a stick is used in place of the bayonet on account of the severity of the former instrument. Should the condemned resist or become very insolent, he is shown no mercy until he evinces some marks of

repentance and future subordination. Usually neither of these two punishments lasts more than from an hour to two hours.

The barrel shirt punishment is generally inflicted upon such as have been guilty of some petty or shameful misdemeanors and have been sentenced by a court martial to this ignominious and ludicrous mode of expiation. The barrel shirt is simply a flour barrel minus both head and bottom, with two holes made in the staves. The culprit is clothed with this staving garment, thrusts his arms through the holes, gets its chin over the rim, and has to walk up and down a given space under guard for as many hours during the day as are appointed by his sentence. He finds it quite embarrassing and his legs are at a loss how to proceed. I have never seen any one hung up by the thumbs, which punishment, they say, is very frequent in the Yankee army. I have seen however what may be thought a novel punishment for an offense by no means unusual. Some of the men being caught in the act of straggling from their regiments were brought back and made to march in a circle, like horses working a threshing machine, at the same time having billets of wood tied to their ankles in order to impede their progress. But this novelty I have seen but once. . . .

This evening (March 9, 1863) our Brigade is ordered out to witness a horrible sight. One of the 24th Va. Infantry be ing tried by court martial for cowardice at the battle of Sharpsburg is condemned to be whipped publicly and then dishonorably dismissed from the service. The brigade is to be present at this degrading punishment.

We are all drawn up in line and the poor man is tied to a pole about fifty yards in front of us. His hands are stretched above his head and his shirt stripped to the waist. The executioner then steps forward and with several heavy switches, the executioner being likewise a criminal who is to earn his release from punishment by inflicting this disgrace on his fellow man.

The word being given, the executioner began his disgusting work, the wretched man wincing and his flesh shrinking neath every blow which one after another were delivered in quick succession until 39 were rec'd. by the culprit. In truth it is a horrid sight, and the executioner was so overcome by his feelings that as soon as his work was done his eyes filled with tears and he wept—he wept! This horrible event transpired without the loss of blood to any one, and the wretched creature (or happy individual, had he truly a craven heart) pockets his dishonorable discharge and leaves for parts unknown.

—DURKIN, ed., *John Dooley, Confederate Soldier*

XIV.9

EXECUTING DESERTERS

Desertion was the bane of both Union and Confederate armies. The total number of desertions assumed almost astronomical proportions. There was a total of some 260,000 desertions from the ranks in the Union armies, of whom possibly 60,000 returned to service; in addition there were 160,000 who failed to appear when drafted and qualified technically as deserters. The figures for the Confederate Army are unsatisfactory, but desertion here probably ran to about 10 per cent.

The pattern of desertion varied North and South. A large proportion of Confederate desertions was probably absence without leave—soldiers going home to help get in the crops, or to visit their families. While there was widespread evasion of the draft, in the South, much of this was under the masquerade of legality and was connived at by state authorities. Many Confederate deserters, too, were Union sympathizers who had been pressed into Confederate service: this was particularly true in the border states. There are comparatively few examples of Union soldiers deserting to the enemy; toward the end of the war many Confederates went over to the other side. Yet notwithstanding all the temptations and opportunities to desert, Confederate desertions were proportionately slightly lower than Federal.

The penalty for desertion was death, but this penalty was rarely imposed. Statistics here, too, are unreliable, but it is probable that not one deserter in 500 paid the extreme penalty. Clearly both armies would have been better for more effective punishments here. As executions were in fact rare it is sufficient to confine ourselves to a single witness from each army describing these tragic incidents of war.

A. General Sheridan Executes Two Deserters at Chattanooga

Chattanooga, Tennessee, November 14, 1863
My dear Friend—

This town is suffering severely on account of its rebellious sentiments. Since our army came back from the Chickamauga field the town has been pretty roughly handled by the 'merciless Yankees.' Many of the finest residences, particularly those on the more commanding points have been torn down and 'Yankee forts' erected in their stead. Generally where the buildings have been torn down the owners had gone south among their friends. I think they will be somewhat disappointed when they return and find their beautiful homes among the things that were. But 'the way of the transgressor is hard,' at least it seems so in this case.

I witnessed a painful sight this afternoon—the shooting of two federal soldiers. As it may be of interest I will give you a description of it. The two men belonged to Illinois regiments: one to the 44th and the other to the 88th, both of our division, which as you know is commanded by General Sheridan. The men had been tried for desertion, found guilty and sentenced to be shot. One brigade of the division under arms, with colors flying and band playing formed about noon in nearly a hollow square with one side entirely open. Thousands of soldier spectators gathered about those who stood under arms. About one P.M. a solemn procession composed of two details of infantry, one in front of the prisoners and one in the rear, marched into the inclosure. Behind the first company and immediately in front of the prisoners their coffins were borne each upon the shoulders of four men. In the rear of the doomed men marched the second company with their rifles at the right shoulder shift and bayonets fixed. A band playing a solemn tune marched with slow and measured step in front of the little procession. General Sheridan and staff were present. All were mounted and all in full uniform. The General had a broad yellow sash over his shoulder drawn across his breast and down under his sword belt. He sat motionless upon his big black horse which stood just a little in front of the other horsemen. When the procession arrived at the open side of the square it was halted, the coffins were placed upon the ground, when the prisoners knelt and the chaplain prayed. They then arose, apparently very calm, and sat erect each upon his coffin. A bandage was then bound over the eyes of each. A platoon of soldiers with loaded rifles stood a few paces in front. There was a strange silence for a moment and then the voice of command rang out. "Ready!" "Aim!" "Fire!" And each of the prisoners fell back over his coffin, dead.

It was hard to see men thus killed by their own comrades but you have no idea how many have deserted, encouraged by friends at home to do the disgraceful act. Sad as the scene this afternoon was, it will have a wholesome effect upon the whole division.

Truly yours, W. G.

—"Civil War Letters of Washington Gardner"

B. Executing Deserters From the Confederate Army

Camp near Rappahannock River, Va.,
March 5, 1863

A man was shot near our regiment last Sunday for desertion. It was a very solemn scene. The condemned man was seated on his coffin with his hands tied across his breast. A file of twelve soldiers was brought up to within six feet of him, and at the command a volley was fired right into his breast. He was hit by but one ball, because eleven of the guns were loaded with powder only. This was done so that no man can be certain that he killed him. If he was, the thought of it might always be painful to him. I have seen men marched through the camps under guard with boards on their backs which were labeled, "I am a coward," or "I am a thief," or "I am a shirker from battle," and I saw one man tied hand and foot astride the neck of a cannon and exposed to view for sixteen hours. These severe punishments seem necessary to preserve discipline.

Camp near Orange Court House, Va.,
September 27, 1863

We had nine more military executions in our division yesterday—one man from Thomas' Brigade, one from Scales' and seven from Lane's. Colonel Hunt was a member of the court-martial which sentenced them, and he tells me that one of the men from Lane's Brigade was a brother of your preacher, and that the two looked very much alike. He said he was a very intelligent man, and gave as his reason for deserting that the editorials in the Raleigh "Standard" had convinced him that Jeff Davis was a tyrant and that the Confederate cause was wrong. I am surprised that the editor of that miserable little journal is allowed to go at large. It is most unfortunate that this thing of shooting men for desertion was not begun sooner. Many lives would have been saved by it, because a great many men will now have to be shot before the trouble can be stopped. . . .

I must close, as a doctor has just come for me to go with him to assist in dissecting two of the men who were shot yesterday.

—WELCH, *A Confederate Surgeon's
Letters to his Wife*

XIV. 10

GENERAL LEE DISCUSSES THE PROBLEM OF DISCIPLINE

Lee was as gentle as any warrior in history, but he was a professional soldier and a firm disciplinarian. From long experience in the Mexican War, on the border, and as Superintendent of the United States Military Academy, he knew that failure to enforce rules or to maintain discipline leads to demoralization and penalizes the innocent instead of the guilty.

In this letter to President Davis Lee discusses the question of amnesty for deserters and touches on one of the problems which most harassed him. It is worth remembering that when he wrote it the Army of Northern Virginia had been reduced to some 70,000 men and was facing Grant's army of almost twice that size; had the Confederate government been able to round up deserters—many of them hiding behind state exemptions and writs of habeas corpus—he might have brought his army up to a strength sufficient to defeat Grant.

Eight months later, disciplinary problems within Lee's army had deteriorated along with the increasingly difficult scenario that his men confronted. The combination of shortages of food and supplies within the Confederacy and the bloody military campaigns of 1864 had taken their toll. Supplies became scarcer. Soldiers turned to scrounging as an acceptable means of sustenance. Inevitably, some soldiers overstepped their bounds. On December 12, 1864, Lee ordered a crackdown to impose strict discipline among his ranks.

A. The Need for Punishment as a Deterrant

HD QRS ARMY N. VA.

13th April 1864

His Excy Jefferson Davis,
Presdt. Confed. States,
Richmond,
Mr. President,

. . . I am satisfied that it would be impolitic and unjust to the rest of the army to allow previous good conduct alone to atone for an offence most pernicious to the service, and most dangerous as an example. In this connection, I will lay before your Excellency some facts that will assist you in forming your judgment, and at the same time, present the opinions I have formed on the subject of punishment in the army. In reviewing Court Martial cases, it has been my habit to give the accused the benefit of all extenuating circumstances that could be allowed to operate in their favor without injury to the service. In addition to those parties whose sentences I have remitted altogether or in part, or whom, when capitally convicted, I have recommended to pardon or commutation of punishment, I have kept a list during the past winter of certain offenders, whose cases while they could not be allowed to go unpunished altogether, without injury to the service, had some extenuating features connected with them. I confirmed the sentences, and all of them have undergone a part of their punishment, but recently I remitted the remainder in the order of which I enclose a copy.

Beyond this, I do not think it prudent to go, unless some reason be presented which will enable me to be lenient with out creating a bad precedent, and encouraging others to be come offenders. I have arrived at this conclusion from experience. It is certain that a relaxation of the sternness of discipline as a mere act of indulgence, unsupported by good reasons, is followed by an increase in the number of offenders. The escape of one criminal encourages others to hope for like impunity, and that encouragement can be given as well by a repetition of a general act of amnesty or pardon, as by frequent exercise of clemency towards individuals. If the convicted offenders alone were concerned, there would be no objection to giving them another trial, as we should be no worse off if they again deserted than before. But the effect of the example is the chief thing to be considered, and that it is injurious, I have no doubt. Many more men would be lost to the service if a pardon be extended in a large number of cases than would be restored to it by the immediate effects of that action.

The military executions that took place to such an extent last autumn, had a very beneficial influence, but in my judgment, many of them would have been avoided had the infliction of punishment in such cases uniformly followed the commission of the offence. But the failure of courts to convict or sentence to death, the cases in which pardon or commutation of punishment had been granted upon my recommendation, and the instances in which the same indulgence was extended by your Excellency upon grounds made known to you by others, had somewhat relaxed discipline in this respect, and the consequences became immediately apparent in the increased number of desertions. I think that a return to the current policy would inevitably be attended with like results. Desertion and absence without leave are nearly the only offences ever tried by our Courts. They appear to be almost the only vices in the army. Not withstanding the executions that have recently taken place, I fear that the number of those who have escaped punishment in some one of the ways above mentioned has had a bad effect already. The returns for the month of March show

5474 men absent without leave, and 322 desertions during the month. There have been 62 desertions within the present month specially reported, but the whole number I fear considerably exceeds that some of the large number absent without leave, are probably sick men who have failed to report, and some of the deserters are probably absent with out leave, but the number is sufficiently great to show the necessity of adhering to the only policy that will restrain the evil, and which I am sure will be found truly merciful in the end. Desertions and absence without leave not only weaken the army by the number of offenders not reclaimed, but by the guards that must be kept over those who are arrested. I think therefore that it would not be expedient to pardon & return to duty any of those now under sentence, or release those under charges, except for good cause shown.

I have the honour to be
With great respect
Your obt. servt.
R. E. Lee
Genl.
—Freeman, ed., *Lee's Confidential Dispatches*

B. "We Cannot Escape the Disgrace that Attends these Evildoers"

Headquarters Army of Northern Virginia
12th December, 1864

General Orders, No. 71

The General Commanding has heard with pain and mortification that outrages and depredations amounting in some cases to flagrant robbery, have been perpetrated upon citizens living within the lines, and near the camps of the army. Poor and helpless persons have been stripped of the means of subsistence and suffered violence by the hands of those upon whom they had a right to rely for protection. In one instance an atrocious murder was perpetrated upon a child by a band of ruffians whose supposed object was plunder.

The General Commander is well aware that the great body of the army which so unselfishly devotes itself to the defence of the country, regards

these of
comm
name
esca
exc
to
th
c

su
feel that the ex
themselves. The aid of all su
confidently invoked to remove this stain ...
fair name of the army. Let each man guard its honor as zealously as his own, regarding those who bring reproach upon it, as enemies of his own reputation, and remembering that to withhold information that might lead to the detection of these criminals is to become morally a participant of their guilt.

The attention of officers is particularly directed to this subject. Their responsibility is greatest, for upon their care and vigilance necessarily depend, in a great degree, the prevention and detection of unlawful acts by these men.

Those commanding regiments, companies, or in charge of camps, hospitals, or detachments, will be required to account for all who fail to attend the roll calls under existing orders, or for such of their officers and men as may be arrested absent from their commands without proper authority, by the guards and pickets of the army.

Corps commanders will habitually keep out patrols to arrest all who are improperly absent and to protect the persons and property of those residing in the vicinity of their commands. When arrested the parties, themselves, and the officers responsible for their conduct will be brought to trial without delay.

By command of General Lee.

—W. H. Taylor

XIV.11

... N THE CIVIL WAR

... come as a surprise that the men who fought the ... also engaged in sex while away from home in the ... of their country. The average soldier was a 26-year-old ... Removed from normal society, he was almost always ... exclusively in the company of other men. Opportunities for social engagement with women were extremely limited. As a result, it was not at all uncommon for soldiers to seek out prostitutes.

Although prostitution was commonplace during the Civil War—as it has been throughout military history—it is a part of the war that has often been overlooked. However, research by Thomas P. Lowry, a Civil War historian and medical doctor, has revealed information that Victorian morals and national sentiment preferred not to discuss. The Union army treated nearly 250,000 reported cases of venereal disease. Records in the Confederate army are not known, but there is evidence that it had a similar caseload.

While military leaders such as Robert E. Lee and Stonewall Jackson were well-known and admired for their moral restraint, both armies accepted prostitution as part of military life. The Union army, in fact, organized legal prostitution in Tennessee during 1863. In some military units, half the men suffered from venereal disease. What righteous citizens of the day would call "moral depravity" did, in truth, exist. In some instances it ran rampant, as this 1864 letter describing City Point, Virginia, from an officer in the Sanitary Commission attests.

But now to the evils of this place. There is a whole city of whores. Yes, father, a whole city. They have laid out a village to the east of where the railroad bends to the docks. Streets, signs and even corduroy sidewalks with drain gutters. Of course, it was all built with Army supplies and by the very men for free that they have extracted their sinful wages from. These whores do pay the Negroes fair wages for whatever work they do, but so much more than we can that the blacks prefer to work for them to us. Our older workers here say that I must accept this evil. They fear it is here yet to the end. I found that my conscience would not let it go unchallenged from me. I determined to see the place for myself, and to protest to General Grant in person. There were three parallel streets about four blocks each long. Each block there are about ten structures on either side. They are for the most part one-storied, northern log or clapboard make. The number of rooms are different. How many, I am not sure, since I have not been in any. For the most part, they do not cook inside but have tents with Negroes behind or on the side of them, with pine or evergreen boughs covering. They, like the rebels, seem to separate the officers from the men. They will not do double duty. To each their own. Most of the officers ones have fine horses, saddles, furniture, et cetera, all from our supply houses. The [enlisted] men ones have things in equality from the storehouse. At pay time, the lines before these houses are appalling and men often fight each other for a place. The average charge is three dollars and on paydays some make as much as $250 to $300. Though between pay periods, it is said that they will take their time and do many special things and charge accordingly. Some of these hussies, during their indisposed periods sell their services to the men to write letters for them to their loved ones back home. How foul. A mother, wife or sweetheart receiving a mistle penned by these soiled hands. I have not yet been able to reach Grant to protest these matters. Though he has ordered our men not to rape the rebel women, under penalty of death, two have been so executed since I have been here. I have talked with Bowers and he tries to defend the village as necessary in view of that order. Think of it, Father, he implies are devoted soldiers would become rapers and satyrs if not for these creatures.

—UNIDENTIFIED SANITARY COMMISSION OFFICER

XV

GREAT BRITAIN AND THE
AMERICAN CIVIL WAR

The Civil War was not fought in isolation; the greatest civil war that the Western world had known could not be a purely domestic affair. The issues that were involved, or that seemed to be involved, deeply affected European peoples and nations, and America, in turn, was affected by European attitudes and policies. Yet Britain and Europe were from the first confused about the Civil War. Was the South fighting for self-determination—or for slavery? Was the North fighting for empire—or for freedom? Official declarations of policy, North and South, did little to clarify the situation. Confusion extended even to the legal realm. Was the war in fact a war, in the legal sense? If so it was entirely proper to recognize the belligerency of the Confederacy. The official Northern position was that the struggle was not a war at all, but a domestic insurrection; yet Lincoln proclaimed a blockade, which is an instrument of war, and recognized in fact, if not in law, the belligerency of the South.

Just as in the American Revolution the role of France was of crucial importance to those fighting for independence, so in the Civil War the role of Britain was crucial. Southerners were ever conscious of that earlier chapter in American history, and the hopes of the South were fixed, from the be ginning, on Britain and on France—which would presumably follow the British lead. It was not merely that Southerners thought that they had a good cause and one that would inevitably appeal to the British who, in the words of Henry Adams, "took naturally to rebellion—when foreign." Nor was it merely that they could count on the sympathy of the British upper classes, whose general social system was far closer to that of the South than to that of the more equalitarian North. There were practical considerations as well. Politically—so it was assumed by Southerners—Britain would prefer to see the United States split into two nations, for the United States was a potential rival, and American democracy a potential threat to the British social and economic system. Economically—again so it was assumed—the British would inevitably favor the creation in

America of a nation dedicated to free trade. Finally—and this was the trump card—Cotton was King. English spindles depended on Southern cotton; without it the textile mills would shut down, England would lose her markets, unemployment and political disorder would spread. In sheer self-defense Britain would have to recognize the South and break the blockade.

Breaking the blockade would, almost inevitably, mean war. With England, and doubtless France, as allies how could the Confederacy fail to win!

Thus the stakes were high. But Britain, too, knew that the stakes were high. Would she allow the sympathies of her upper classes to dictate her policy? Would she be so affected by the blockade as to intervene in self-defense? Would she risk war with her American cousins—war which would ally her, willy-nilly, with a slave power?

In Britain itself the Civil War divided classes as had no other foreign conflict in her history—not even the French Revolution. On the whole, and with important exceptions, the upper classes were pro-Southern, the middle and working classes pro-Northern. The English aristocracy saw in the American conflict a chance to humiliate an upstart nation whose democratic and equalitarian practices they detested; the middle and working classes saw the struggle as one for the vindication of democracy and—after the Emancipation Proclamation—of freedom. The intellectuals were sharply divided. Some, like Acton, for example, saw the American war as a chapter in the great history of freedom, and sup ported the South as the champion of self-determination. Others, like Leslie Stephen and John Stuart Mill, saw it, too, as a struggle for freedom, but thought of freedom for the Negro. The most influential spokesmen for the North were, however, liberal statesmen and publicists like Cobden, Bright, and Forster, men who were convinced that the progress of democracy in Britain was intimately bound up with the triumph of the Union.

Both the Union and the Confederate governments made strenuous efforts to win English support: propaganda techniques were as skillfully developed during the Civil War as during the World Wars. Lincoln sent over such spokesmen—and spokeswomen—as Henry Ward Beecher and Harriet Beecher Stowe and the egregious Robert Walker; the Confederacy sent over a number of accredited agents, like James Mason and Pierre Rost and John Peyton, or Captain Bullock, who was to arrange for building ships, or Henry Hotze, who established and edited the Index, a newspaper devoted to presenting the Southern cause.

On the whole the official English policy was correct, but the expression of that policy was often discourteous. Thus, though the British position in the *Trent* affair was technically correct, the manner of stating that position was arrogant, and the widespread demand for war over what was at worst a minor mistake was unpardonable. Nor were the British themselves guiltless of infractions of international law—witness the subsequent *Alabama* award. Even more deplorable, from the point of view of the future relations of the two great English-speaking peoples, was the persistent expression of sympathy for the South and hostility to the North in such great papers as the *Times* and the *Standard,* and the almost scurrilous attacks on the North in such magazines as the *Edinburgh, Blackwood's,* the *Quarterly, Punch* and the *Saturday Review.* In short the English aristocracy, the press, the Established Church, and even the universities appeared to be pro-Southern. It took a long time for Americans to forget this.

XV. I

HENRY RAVENEL EXPECTS FOREIGN INTERVENTION

Here is the way the recognition situation looked to a thoughtful Southern observer, and the way it looked to most Southerners.

Ravenel, the reader will recall, was a South Carolina planter who had won distinction as one of the leading American botanists.

M[onday] 8. [April 1861]—The great European powers, as far as we may judge from their leading papers, seem inclined to favour the new Confederacy.

Old prejudices against our misunderstood domestic institution of African servitude (it is the *word* "slavery" that has blinded their eyes) are giving way before the urgent calls of *Self Interest,* & we only need that they should become more intimately acquainted with it, to disipate their mistaken

notions. In addition to their requiring the produce of the Cotton States to keep their manufacturers in motion, & furnish food & employment to their operatives, new complications have arisen which are favourable to their friendly recognition of our independence. The United States have lately increased their Tariff so high on many articles of European manufacture, as to amount almost to prohibition; whilst the Confederate States have lessened theirs from the old standard, & have it in contemplation to reduce still more. The case then stands thus: We furnish what is absolutely essential to their commercial & manufacturing prosperity, & we alone—We offer them a market for their goods on better terms than heretofore. We invite their vessels to do our carrying trade, or at any rate throw open the door of competition to them, which has been hitherto open only to U. S. vessels. On the other hand the United States, now that the Cotton States have seceded, can furnish but little toward supplying their wants with cotton—They have in addition imposed such a tariff, as to cut off trade in a great measure. The

U. S. are mainly a manufacturing & commercial nation, & must necessarily come into competition with them. In a word, what the U. S. have lost by our withdrawal from the Union, they have gained. They know too that we are an agricultural people, & will never compete with them in manufactures & commerce, but will always be their best customers.

These various reasons which lie on the surface, & which they already understand, must have their effect. Self Interest is the ruling power among nations, no less than among individuals.

—OLDS, ed., *The Private Journal of Henry William Ravenel*

XV.2

Blackwood's Edinburgh Magazine REJOICES IN THE BREAK-UP OF THE UNION

Most of the English press was implacably hostile to the North. This hostility did not always carry with it friendship to the South.

Sometimes it was merely a general hostility to everything American—American republicanism, democracy, business, manners, and leaders. *Blackwood's Edinburgh Magazine,* which contained some of the best reporting on the war, was from the beginning critical of the Federal government. As was the English practice at the time, the articles are unsigned; this one appeared in October 1861.

Our constitution has fulfilled its most important and most delicate office—that of bringing the best of the spirit and intellect of the nation to the service of the state. . . .

It is notorious that this end has not been fulfilled by the American constitution. Nor was it rational to expect that it should be. Statesmanship is born of the collision of great principles or of important interests. No such result can be produced where power is all on one side. When the people have everything, they need no champions. Therefore, in America, patriotism means flattery of the people; party spirit is the spirit of rapine; and debates, instead of eliciting wisdom and truth, are the ignoble squabbles of mediocrities. Where, in American history for the last forty years—that is to say, ever since the impulse of the Revolution died out—are we to look for her great statesmen? Yet in that period there is no great nation in Europe that has not produced men who have secured an enduring fame by their assertion of great principles, or by the influence they have exerted on the destinies of nations. And it is not true, as has been said, and quoted with applause, that the nation is happiest which has no history, for such happiness is stagnation or worse. The spirit that presides over the public life of America has made itself felt over the whole nation. The higher minds stand aloof from politics, as Bayard would turn from a modern prizering. The meed for which he had been used to contend with noble knights—the smiles of ladies, the favo'ur of anointed kings, and immortal honour—is now a bag of coin handed to the victor in a pothouse. So the best Americans either betake themselves to other pursuits, or roam disconsolately over the world, where they see their equals winning honour in the field from which they are for ever excluded.

That men of this class should countenance the violent measures of the North is at first sight unaccountable. It is difficult to imagine that intellectual men should either be friendly to a system which extends its theory of equality to intellect, and thus neutralises their natural superiority—or should wish to establish, in its grossest form, the supremacy of a numerical majority, by the forcible subjugation of the great minority which constitutes the South. It is quite possible, however, that, while giving their voice to the North, they may neither be friendly to the Union, nor desirous of seeing the South subjugated. They may wish to see the natural aristocracy to which they belong raised to its proper position in the state. They may consider that, by quiet separation, the Union might, with increased compactness and unanimity, rerecover much of its vitality, and that the system they suffer under might be indefinitely prolonged. And they may view the present convulsion of that system as the necessary preliminary of those political changes which, it is natural to suppose, they must ardently desire. To suppose this is not to impugn their patriotism; for if we have made our views clear in this paper, it is evident that they may look on such a crisis as now exists as necessary for the regeneration of their most important institutions. They may therefore accompany the movement with the expectation of finding an opportunity to control it.

But we do not suppose that any men possessing the powers requisite for statesmanship can really believe that, if by force of arms the reluctant South should be dragged back to the Union, the Union will be thereby restored on its original basis. Successful coercion would be a greater revolution than the acknowledgment of secession—this only lops the branches, while that strikes at the root. Nor do we imagine that any such men as these are to be found in the ranks of the Abolition party. Clever people may belong to that party. Mrs Beecher Stowe is a very clever woman, and has written a very clever novel; but she is, by the success of that novel, committed to sentiments more adapted to fiction than to politics. She evidently looks on the South as a vast confederation of

Legrees, keeping millions of virtuous Uncle Toms in horrible subjection; and quotes Mr Wendell Phillipps as if she believed that mischievous monomaniac to be an inspired apostle. But statesmen must ask themselves how the difficulty presented by the condition of the African race would be solved by setting them free. What is to become of the liberated slaves? and how is their labour to be replaced? are questions the very first to be asked, but which we must not expect a crazy Abolitionist to answer. But such considerations do not occur to those enthusiastic philanthropists who testify to their love of the Negro by their hatred of the planter. The destruction of armies, the ravage and ruin of territory, are as nothing, in their heated fancy, compared with the success of their plan. And if secession were accomplished their plan would be at an end, for they would then have no more concern in the liberation of the slaves of the South than in a crusade to set the Georgian and Circassian ladies free from the harems of the Bosphorus. Thus, under present circumstances, their fanaticism has become sanguinary; they are pledged to their course, and will follow it with all the desperate recklessness and tenacity with which weak minds will cling to their only chance of notoriety.

—ANONYMOUS, "Democracy Teaching by Example"

—————— XV.3 ——————

GEORGE TICKNOR EXPLAINS THE WAR TO HIS ENGLISH FRIENDS

The campaign for foreign understanding and sympathy was carried on by private individuals as well as by governments. Here the North doubtless had the best of it, for the intellectual and financial ties between the North and Britain were intimate.

George Ticknor is so well known that he needs little introduction. He had long been a major figure in the intellectual life of New England and, as author of the notable *History of Spanish Literature,* was known everywhere abroad. Like Belmont, and

like his friend Charles Sumner, he was indefatigable in presenting the Union cause to his English and European friends.

To Sir Charles Lyell.

Boston, February 11, 1862

MY DEAR LYELL,—No doubt, I ought to have written to you before. But I have had no heart to write to my friends in Europe, since our troubles took their present form and proportions. . . .

You know how I have always thought and felt about the slavery question. I was never an Abolitionist, in the American sense of the word, because I never have believed that any form of emancipation that has been proposed could reach the enormous difficulties of the case, and I am of the same mind now. Slavery is too monstrous an evil, as it exists in the United States, to be reached by the resources of legislation. . . .I have, therefore, always desired to treat the South with the greatest forbearance, not only because the present generation is not responsible for the curse that is laid upon it, but because I have felt that the longer the contest could be postponed, the better for us. I have hoped, too, that in the inevitable conflict with free labor, slavery would go to the wall. I remember writing to you in this sense, more than twenty years ago, and the results thus far have confirmed the hopes I then entertained. The slavery of the South has made the South poor. The free labor of the North has made us rich and strong.

But all such hopes and thoughts were changed by the violent and unjustifiable secession, a year ago; and, since the firing of the first gun on Fort Sumter, we have had, in fact, no choice. We must fight it out. Of the results I have never doubted. We shall beat the South. But what after that? I do not see. It has pleased God that, whether we are to be two nations, or one, we should live on the same continent side by side, with no strong natural barrier to keep us asunder; but now separated by hatreds which grow more insane and intense every month, and which generations will hardly extinguish. . . .

Our prosperity has entered largely into the prosperity of the world, and especially into that of England and France. You feel it to have been so.

And some persons have been unwise enough to think that your interference in our domes tic quarrel can do good to yourselves, and perhaps to us, by attempting to stop this cruel and wicked war. It is, I conceive, a great mistake. I have believed, since last August, that Prance was urging your government to some sort of intervention,—to break the blockade or to enforce a peace,—but the general opinion here has been that England has been the real mover in the matter, thus engendering a bitter hatred of your people, which the unjustifiable tone of your papers and ours increases and exasperates. All this is wrong, and so far as you are excited by it to intervention, it is most unhappy and portentous. The temptation, no doubt, is strong. It almost always is in the case of civil wars, which, from their very nature, invite interested and neighboring nations to interfere. But how rarely has good come to anybody from such interference. In the present instance I am satisfied that it would only exasperate us, and lead to desperate measures. . . .

As to the present comparative condition of North and South, there can be no question. At Richmond, and else where beyond the Potomac, gold is at forty per cent premi um, coffee and tea at four or five prices, salt as dear. . . . Beef and bread they have in abundance, and so resolute and embittered are they, that they seem content with this. But it cannot be. The women, I hear, in a large part of the South, will not speak to men who stay at home from the army without obvious and sufficient cause. But the suffering is great, however the proud spirit may bear up against it, and they must yield, unless, what is all but incredible, they should speedily gain great military success. . . .

At the North the state of things is very different. There is no perceptible increase of poverty. . . . Nor is any body disheartened. If you were here you would see little change in our modes of life, except that we are all busy and in earnest about the war. . . . This, however, is not to last. The government must either impose taxes heavy enough to sustain its credit, as it ought to have done long ago, and then our incomes will all feel it, or it must rush into a paper currency, and then, of course, prices must rise in proportion, and the whole end in disaster. . . .

A country that has shown the resources and spirit of the North—however they may have been misused, and may continue to be—cannot be ruined by a year or two of ad verse fortune, or even more. Changed it will be, how, or how much, I cannot guess, nor do I find anybody worth listening to that can tell me. But we are young and full of life. Diseases that destroy the old are cast off by the vigor of youth; and, though I may not live to see it, we shall again be strong and have an honored place among the nations. For the South I have no vaticinations. The blackness of thick darkness rests upon them, and they deserve all they will suffer. I admit that a portion of the North, and sometimes the whole North, has been very unjust to them. . . . But it is all no justification of civil war. . . . It is the unpardonable sin in a really free State.

You will, perhaps, think me shabby if I stop without saying anything about the Trent affair, and so I may as well make a clean breast of it. Except Everett, all the persons hereabout in whose judgment I place confidence believed from the first that we had no case. I was fully of that mind. . . .

As to the complaint about our closing up harbors, we are not very anxious. It is a harsh measure, but there are precedents enough for it,—more than there ought to be. But two will fully sustain the mere right. By the treaty of Utrecht you stipulated not only for the destruction of the fortifications of Dunkirk, but for filling up the port; and in 1777 (I think it was that year) you destroyed the entrance to Savannah, so that appropriations were made, not many years ago, by our Congress, to remove the obstructions, although the river, there, has cut out itself a new channel. I do not think that we have closed any but the minor and more shallow channels by the blockade. . . . However, if England and France want a pretext for interfering with us, perhaps this will do as well as any other. No doubt the "Times" at least, will be satisfied with it.

—LIFE, *Letters and Journals of George Ticknor*

XV.4

CAPTAIN WILKES SEIZES MASON AND SLIDELL

It was the *Trent* affair that brought the first, and perhaps the major, crisis in Anglo-American affairs during the war. The story itself is fully told in Lieutenant Fairfax's narrative. What Fairfax does not tell is the story of the impact of the Trent affair on England, and of the subsequent diplomatic controversy.

James Mason and John Slidell were, respectively, Confederate commissioners to Britain and France. Learning that they had left Havana for England, Captain Wilkes stopped the Trent and removed them, without specific instructions from his own government. His act was technically a violation of international law; he should have brought the Trent to an American port where a prize court would have adjudicated the whole case. What he did, however, was what the British themselves had done scores of times in the early years of the century. Nor did the British government at first hold Wilkes's act contrary to international law. As early as November 11, 1861, Palmerston had written the editor of the *Times* that "this American cruiser might, by our own principles of International Law, stop the West India packet, search her, and if the Southern men and their despatches and credentials were found on board, either take them out or seize the packet and carry her back to New York for trial." Yet when Wilkes did just this a wave of anger swept over England, and the government itself was moved to threats. The British government demanded that the United States release the prisoners and apologize for Wilkes's action, and insisted on an immediate answer. Fortunately the Prince Consort toned down Lord Russell's first letter, but even after toning down it bore the appearance of an ultimatum. Meantime orders were issued to hold the fleet in readiness for action, and thousands of soldiers were shipped over to Canada, while the export of war munitions to America was for a time stopped.

Lincoln and Seward were in a dilemma. If they did not satisfy Britain they might find themselves with another war on their hands. If they did public opinion—which had made a hero of Wilke would be outraged. With his customary skill Seward found a solution. He did not apologize, but congratulated England on at last adopting the principles of inter national law for which the United States had long con tended; then he had Mason and Slidell shipped off to England. American public opinion was on the whole pleased; the English were satisfied. In the long run the *Trent* affair cleared the air; like the Venezuela crisis of Cleveland's ad ministration it led both countries to contemplate war and revealed to both that they did not like the prospect. Yet in the lasting sense of resentment which was planted in America, Britain paid a high price for her insistence on a fine point of law.

Donald Macneill Fairfax, who here tells the story of the removal of Mason and Slidell, was executive offcer of the *San Jacinto;* he later fought with Farragut at New Orleans, and off Charleston. In 1880 he was named rear admiral.

In October, 1861, the United States screw-sloop *San Jacinto*, of which Captain Charles Wilkes was commander and the writer was executive officer, on her return from the west coast of Africa, touched at the island of St. Thomas to coal ship. Here for the first time we learned of the presence in those waters of the Confederate cruiser *Sumter* (Captain Raphael Semmes). Captain Wilkes immediately determined to search for the enemy. At Cienfuegos, on the south coast of Cuba, he learned from the United States consul-general at Havana that Messrs. Mason and Slidell, Confederate com mis sioners to Europe, and their secretaries and families had recently reached that port from Charleston en route to England. He immediately put to sea, October 26th, with the purpose of intercepting the blockade runner which had brought them out. The commissioners . . . had run the Union blockade successfully . . . and had arrived . . . at Havana on the 17th. There we ascertained that their plan was to leave on the 7th of November in the English steamer *Trent* for St. Thomas on their way to England, and readily calculated when and where in the Bahama Channel we might intercept them. Meanwhile . . . Captain Wilkes continued his cruise after the *Sumter* along the north coast of Cuba, also running over to Key West in the hope of finding the *Powhatan* or some other steamer to accompany him to the Bahama Channel. . . . Here, 240 miles from Havana, and 90 miles from Sagua la Grande, where the channel contracts to the width of 15 miles, at noon on the 8th of November the *Trent* was sighted . . .

It was evident, even at that early day, that the South had the sympathy of nearly all Europe—particularly of England and France. When Captain Wilkes first took me into his confidence, and told me what he purposed to do, I earnestly reminded him of the great risk of a war with these two

Governments, supported as they were by powerful navies; and when we reached Key West I suggested that he consult with Judge Marvin, one of the ablest maritime lawyers. I soon saw, however, that he had made up his mind to intercept and capture the *Trent* as well as to take possession of the commissioners, and I therefore ceased to discuss the affair. As the next in rank to Captain Wilkes, I claimed the right to board the mail-packet. Captain Wilkes fully expected that I would tender my services for this "delicate duty," and rather left to me the plan of carrying out his instructions. I was impressed with the gravity of my position, and I made up my mind not to do anything unnecessary in the arrest of these gentlemen, or anything that would irritate the captain of the *Trent*, or any of his passengers, particularly the commissioners— lest it might occur to them to throw the steamer on my hands, which would necessitate my taking her as a prize.

As the *Trent* approached she hoisted English colors; where upon our ensign was hoisted and a shot was fired across her bow. As she maintained her speed and showed no disposition to heave to, a shell was fired across her bow which brought her to. Captain Wilkes hailed that he intended to send a boat on board, and I then left with the second cutter.

The manner of heaving the *Trent* to evidently was galling to Captain Moir. When he did stop his steamer, he showed how provoked he was by impatiently singing out through his trumpet, "What do you mean by heaving my vessel to in this manner?" I felt that I must in every way conciliate him when I should get on board. Two boats had been equipped ready to lower and the officers and crews detailed to jump into them. These were not employed until later. The boat I took was a third one, and as the sea was smooth, but a few minutes elapsed before we reached the *Trent*. I instructed the boat's crew to remain alongside for orders, and, board ing the vessel, I was escorted by one of her officers to the upper or promenade deck and was introduced to Captain Moir. . . . I immediately asked if I might see his passenger list,

saying that I had information that Messrs. Mason and Slidell were on board. The mention of Mr. Slidell's name caused that gentleman to come up and say, "I am Mr. Slidell; do you want to see me?" Mr. Mason, whom I knew very well, also came up at the same time, thus relieving me from Captain Moir's refusal, which was very polite but very positive, that I could not under such circumstances be shown any list of passengers. . . . In the briefest time . . . I informed Captain Moir that I had been sent by my commander to arrest Mr. Mason and Mr. Slidell and their secretaries, and send them prisoners on board the United States war vessel near by.

As may readily be understood, when it was known why I had boarded the *Trent*, there was an outburst of rage and indignation from the passengers, who numbered nearly one hundred, many of them Southerners. The captain and the four gentlemen bore themselves with great composure, but the irresponsible lookers-on sang out, "Throw the d—fellow overboard!" I called on Captain Moir to preserve order, but, for the benefit of the excited passengers, I re minded them that our every move was closely observed from the *San Jacinto* by spyglasses (she was within hailing distance), that a heavy battery was bearing upon them, and that any indignity to any of her officers or crew then on board might lead to dreadful consequences. This, together with Captain Moir's excellent commanding manner, had a quieting effect.

During this uproar among the passengers, the officer in charge of the *San Jacinto's* boat, not knowing what it meant, and fearing some ill-treatment of me, hurried up with six or eight of the crew. Captain Moir was the first to see this body of armed men, and remonstrated with me at their appearance on the promenade-deck among his passengers, there being many ladies and children among them. I immediately directed the officer to return to his boat and await my orders. I assured him, amidst the noise of his passengers, that the men had come contrary to my instructions. I was really pleased to find the captain so tenacious of his command, for my mind was possessed with the idea that Mr. Mason or Mr. Slidell, or both, would urge Captain Moir to relinquish his command, making it necessary for me to assume it, as in such event my instructions left no opening for me to decline it.

After order had been restored, we discussed the affair more generally, Captain Moir, however, scarcely joining in the conversation—always dignified and punctilious. . . . I carefully avoided giving offense, and confined myself strictly to the duty which had taken me on board. I was anxious that Mr. Slidell and Mr. Mason should not leave any of their luggage behind. Mrs. Slidell having asked me who commanded the *San Jacinto,* I replied, "Your old acquaintance, Captain Wilkes"; whereupon she expressed surprise that he should do the

very thing the Confederates were hoping for—something to arouse England;. . . "Really," she added, "Captain Wilkes is playing into our hands!". . .

After the first uproar had subsided, I sent the boat to Captain Wilkes to say that these gentlemen were all on board, and had objected to being sent to the *San Jacinto,* and that I must use force to accomplish my orders; I asked for a boat to carry them comfortably on board, another for their baggage, and a third to carry stores, which the pay master's clerk, at Captain Wilkes's order, had already purchased from the steward of the *Trent,* to add to the comfort of the new guests.

When all was ready and the boats were in waiting, I notified both Mr. Mason and Mr. Slidell that the time had come to send them to the *San Jacinto.* They came quietly down to the main-deck, and there repeated that they would not go unless force was used—whereupon two officers, previously instructed, escorted each commissioner to the side, and assisted them into the comfortable cutter sent especially for them. . . .

When all was finished I went on board the *San Jacinto* and reported to Captain Wilkes that I had not taken the *Trent* as a prize, as he had instructed me to do, giving certain reasons, which satisfied him; for he replied, "inasmuch as you

have not taken her, you will let her go" or "proceed on her voyage.". . . The reasons I assigned to Captain Wilkes for my action were: First, that the capture of the *Trent* would make it necessary to put a large prize crew (officers and men) on board, and thus materially weaken our battery for use at Port Royal; secondly, that as there were a large number of women and children and mails and specie bound to various ports, the capture would seriously inconvenience innocent persons and merchants; so that I had determined, before taking her, to lay these matters before him for more serious consideration.

I gave my real reasons some weeks afterward to Secretary Chase, whom I met by chance at the Treasury Department, he having asked me to explain why I had not literally obeyed Captain Wilkes's instructions. I told him that it was because I was impressed with England's sympathy for the South, and felt that she would be glad to have so good a ground to declare war against the United States. Mr. Chase seemed surprised, and exclaimed, "You have certainly relieved the Government from great embarrassment, to say the least."

I returned immediately to the *Trent* and informed Captain Moir that Captain Wilkes would not longer detain him, and he might proceed on his voyage. The steamers soon separated, and thus ended one of the most critical events of our civil war.

—FAIRFAX, "Captain Wilkes's Seizure of Mason and Slidell

XV.5

"SHALL IT BE LOVE, OR HATE, JOHN?"

Few American poets were better known in England, or more respected, than James Russell Lowell. "Jonathan to John"—one of the famous *Biglow Papers*—was Lowel's criticism of the British reaction to the Trent affair, but it covered broad ground. Widely read in America, it long retained its popularity, but needless to say it never achieved a comparable popularity with that people to whom it was directed.

Jonathan to John

It don't seem hardly right, John,
When both my hands was full,
To stump me to a fight, John,—
Your cousin, to, John Bull!
Ole Uncle S. sez he, "I guess
We know it now," sez he,
"The Lion's paw is all the law,
Accordin' to J. B.,
That's fit for you an' me!"

You wonder why we're hot, John?
Your mark wuz on the guns,
The neutral guns, thet shot, John,
Our brothers an' our sons:
Ole Uncle S. sez he, "I guess
There's human blood," sez he,
"By fits an' starts, in Yankee hearts,
Though 't may surprise J. B.
More 'n it would you an' me.". . .

When your rights was our wrongs, John,
You didn't stop for fuss,—
Britanny's trident prongs, John,
Was good 'nough law for us.

Ole Uncle S. sez he, "I guess,
Though physic's good," sez he,
"It doesn't foller thet he can swaller
Prescriptions signed 'J. B.,'
Put up by you an' me."

We own the ocean, tu, John:
You mus'n' take it hard,
Ef we can't think with you, John,
It's jest your own back yard.
Ole Uncle S. sez he, "I guess
Ef *thet's* his claim," sez he,
'The fencin'-stuff '11 cost enough
To bust up friend J. B.,
Ez wal ez you an' me!". . .

We give the critters back, John,
Cos Abram thought 't was right;
It warn't your bullyin' clack, John,

Provokin' us to fight.
Ole Uncle S. sez he, "I guess
We've a hard row," sez he
"To hoe jest now; but thet, somehow,
May happen to J. B.,
Ez wal ez you an' me!"

We ain't so weak an' poor, John,
With twenty million people,
An' close to every door, John,
A school-house an' a steeple.
Ole Uncle S. sez he, "I guess
It is a fact," sez he,
"The surest plan to make a Man
Is, think him so, J. B.,
Ez much ez you or me!". . .

We know we've got a cause, John,
Thet's honest, just, an' true;
We thought 't would win applause, John,
If nowheres else, from you.
Ole Uncle S. sez he, "I guess
His love of right," sez he,
"Hangs by a rotten fibre o' cotton:
There's natur' in J. B.,
Ez wal ez in you an' me!"

The South says, *"Poor folks down!"* John,
An' *"All men up!"* say we,—

White, yaller, black, an' brown, John:
Now which is your idee?
Ole Uncle S. sez he, "I guess
John preaches wal," sez he;
"But, sermon thru, an' come to *du,*
Why, there's the old J. B.
A-crowdin' you an' me!"

Shall it be love, or hate, John?
It's you thet's to decide;
Ain't *your* bonds held by Fate, John,
Like all the world's beside?
Ole Uncle S. sez he, "I guess
Wise men forgive," sez he,
"But not forgit; an' some time yit

Thet truth may strike J. B.,
Ez wal ez you an' me!"

God means to make this land, John,
Clear thru, from sea to sea,
Believe an' understand, John,
The *wuth o'* bein' free.
Ole Uncle S. sez he, "I guess
God's price is high," sez he;
"But nothin' else than wut he sells
Wears long, an' thet J. B.
May larn, like you an' me!"

—LOWELL, *Poems*

xv.6

PALMERSTON AND RUSSELL DISCUSS INTERVENTION

Although the Government had defeated Lindsay's motion, it continued to consider the propriety of an offer of mediation to the American belligerents. By the autumn of 1862 the American situation appeared to justify such a move. McClellan had been defeated on the Peninsula; Lee had whipped Pope at Second Bull Run, and now Lee's victorious hosts were invading the North with every prospect of success. Pressure from Napoleon, too, was mounting. In mid-September 1862 the Prime Minister, the Viscount Palmerston and the Foreign Secretary, Earl Russell, corresponded about the next move. Both appeared to favor mediation. Then came the news of Antietam—a Union victory after all. Palmerston had sober second thoughts, and the mediation movement died as far as the Government was concerned.

Here are the crucial letters that passed between Palmerston and Russell.

94 Piccadilly: September 14, 1862
My dear Russell,—The detailed accounts given in the 'Observer' to-day of the battles of August 29 and 30 between the Confederates and the Federals show that the latter got a very complete smashing; and it seems not altogether unlikely that still greater disasters await them, and that even Washington or Baltimore may fall into the hands of the Confederates.

If this should happen, would it not be time for us to consider whether in such a state of things England and France might not address the contending parties and recommend an arrangement upon the basis of separation?
—Yours sincerely,
PALMERSTON.

Gotha: September 17, 1862
My dear Palmerston,—Whether the Federal army is destroyed or not, it is clear that it is driven back to Washington, and has made no progress in subduing the insurgent States. Such being the case, I agree with you that the time is come for offering mediation to the United States Government, with a view to the recognition of the independence of the Confederates. I agree further, that, in case of failure, we ought ourselves to recognise the Southern States as an independent State. For the purpose of taking so important a step, I think we must have a meeting of the Cabinet. The 23rd or 30th would suit me for the meeting.

We ought then, if we agree on such a step, to propose it first to France, and then, on the part of England and France, to Russia and other powers, as a measure decided upon by us.

We ought to make ourselves safe in Canada, not by sending more troops there, but by concentrating those we have in a few defensible posts before the winter sets in.

J. RUSSELL

Broadlands: September 23, 1862
My dear Russell,—Your plan of proceedings about the mediation between the Federals and Confederates seems to be excellent. Of course, the offer would be made to both the contending parties at the same time; for, though the offer would be as sure to be accepted by the Southerns as was the proposal of the Prince of Wales by the Danish Princess, yet, in the one case as in the other, there are certain forms which it is decent and proper to go through.

A question would occur whether, if the two parties were to accept the mediation, the fact of our mediating would not of itself be tantamount to an acknowledgment of the Confederates as an independent State.

Might it not be well to ask Russia to join England and France in the offer of mediation?. . .

We should be better without her in the mediation, be cause she would be too favourable to the North; but on the other hand her participation in the offer might render the North the more willing to accept it.

The after communication to the other European powers would be quite right, although they would be too many for mediation.

As to the time of making the offer, if France and Russia agree,—and France, we know, is quite ready, and only waiting for our concurrence—events may be taking place which might render it desirable that the offer should be made before the middle of October.

It is evident that a great conflict is taking place to the north-west of Washington, and its issue must have a great effect on the state of affairs. If the Federals sustain a great defeat, they may be at once ready for mediation, and the iron should be struck while it is hot. If, on the other hand, they should have the best of it, we may wait awhile and see what may follow.—Yours sincerely,

Palmerston.

—Walpole, *The Life of Lord John Russell*

October 2

My dear Russell,

I return you Granville's letter which contains much deserving of serious consideration. There is no doubt that the offer of Mediation upon the basis of Separation would be accepted by the South. Why should it not be accepted? It would give the South in principle the points for which they are fighting. The refusal, if refusal there was, would come from the North, who would be unwilling to give up the principle for which they have been fighting so long as they had a reasonable expectation that by going on fighting they could carry their point. The condition of things therefore which would be favourable to an offer of mediation

would be great success of the South against the North. That state of things seemed ten days ago to be approaching. Its advance has been lately checked, but we do not yet know the real course of recent events, and still less can we foresee what is about to follow. Ten days or a fortnight more may throw a clearer light upon future prospects.

As regards possible resentment on the part of the Northerns following upon an acknowledgment of the Independence of the South, it is quite true that we should have less to care about that resentment in the spring when communication with Canada was open, and when our naval force could more easily operate upon the American coast, than in winter when we are cut off from Canada and the American coast is not so safe.

But if the acknowledgment were made at one and the same time by England, France and some other Powers, the Yankees would probably not seek a quarrel with us alone, and would not like one against a European Confederation. Such a quarrel would render certain and permanent that Southern Independence the acknowledgment of which would have caused it.

The first communication to be made by England and France to the contending parties might be, not an absolute offer of mediation but a friendly suggestion whether the time was not come when it might be well for the two parties to consider whether the war, however long continued, could lead to any other result than separation; and whether it might not therefore be best to avoid the great evils which must necessarily flow from a prolongation of hostilities by at once coming to an agreement to treat upon that principle of separation which must apparently be the inevitable result of the contest, however long it may last.

The best thing would be that the two parties should settle details by direct negotiation with each other, though perhaps with the rancorous hatred now existing between them this might be difficult. But their quarrels in negotiation would do us no harm if they did not lead to a renewal of war. An armistice, if not accompanied by a cessation of blockades, would be all in favour of the North, especially if New Orleans remained in the hands of the North.

The whole matter is full of difficulty, and can only be cleared up by some more decided events between the contending armies.

Palmlrston.

—ADAMS, *Great Britain and the American Civil War*

─────── XV.7 ───────

"AN ERROR, THE MOST SINGULAR AND PALPABLE"

The great surprise of the diplomatic battle was Gladstone's Newcastle speech of October 7, 1862. By that time the Cabinet had pretty well decided neither to intervene nor to offer mediation. Gladstone was Chancellor of the Exchequer, and presumably supported the Government policy. Yet at Newcastle he said, "Jefferson Davis and other leaders of the South have made an army; they are making, it appears, a navy; and they have made what is more than either, they have made a nation." By British political standards this was clearly an improper speech to make. A few days later the Home Secretary, Sir George Cornewall Lewis, said at Hereford that the Government did not contemplate any change of policy, thus in effect repudiating Gladstone. Gladstone himself later confessed that this speech was one of the great errors of his career. We give his apology, written in July 1896.[*]

I have yet to record an undoubted error, the most singular and palpable, I may add the least excusable of them all, especially since it was committed so late as in the year 1862, when I had outlived half a century. In the autumn of that year, and in a speech delivered after a public dinner at Newcastle-upon-Tyne, I declared in the heat of the American struggle that Jefferson Davis had made a nation, that is to say, that the division of the American Republic by the establishment of a Southern or secession state was an accomplished fact. Strange to say, this declaration, most unwarrantable to be made by a minister of the crown with no authority

other than his own, was not due to any feeling of partizanship for the South or hostility to the North. The fortunes of the South were at their zenith. Many who wished well to the Northern cause despaired of its success. The friends of the North in England were beginning to advise that it should give way, for the avoidance of further bloodshed and greater calamity. I weakly supposed that the time had come when respectful suggestions of this kind, founded on the necessity of the case, were required by a spirit of that friendship which, in so many contingencies of life, has to offer sound recommendations with a knowledge that they will not be popular. Not only was this a misjudgment of the case, but even if it had been otherwise, I was not the person to make the declaration. I really, though most strangely, believed that it was an act of friendliness to all America to recognise that the struggle was virtually at an end. I was not one of those who on the ground of British interests desired a division of the American Union. My view was distinctly opposite. I thought that while the Union continued it never could exercise any dangerous pressure upon Canada to estrange it from the empire—our honour, as I thought, rather than our interest forbidding its surrender. But were the Union split, the North, no longer checked by the jealousies of slave-power, would seek a partial compensation for its loss in annexing, or trying to annex, British North America. Lord Palmerston desired the severance as a diminution of a dangerous power, but prudently held his tongue.

That my opinion was founded upon a false estimate of the facts was the very least part of my fault. I did not perceive the gross impropriety of such an utterance from a cabinet minister, of a power allied in blood and language, and bound to loyal neutrality; the case being further exaggerated by the fact that we were already, so to speak, under indictment before the world for not (as was alleged) having strictly enforced the laws of neutrality in the matter of the cruisers. My offence was indeed only a mistake, but one of incredible grossness, and with such consequences of offence and alarm attached to it, that my failing to perceive them justly exposed me

---

1 (From Morley: *The Life of William Ewart Gladstone*, Vol. II. Copyright 1903 by The Macmillan Company, 1931 by Mary O. Morley, and used with the permission of The Macmillan Company and Mr. Guy E. Morley.

to very severe blame. It illustrates vividly that incapacity which my mind so long retained, and perhaps still exhibits, an incapacity of viewing subjects all round, in their extraneous as well as in their internal properties, and thereby of knowing when to be silent and when to speak.

I am the more pained and grieved, because I have for the last five-and-twenty years received from the government and people of America tokens of goodwill which could not fail to arouse my undying gratitude. When we came to the arbitration at Geneva, my words were cited as part of the proof of hostile *animus*. Meantime I had prepared a lengthened statement to show from my abundant declarations on other occasions that there was and could be on my part no such *animus*. I was desirous to present this statement to the arbitrators. My colleagues objected so largely to the proceeding that I desisted. In this I think they probably were wrong. I addressed my paper to the American minister for the information of his government, and Mr. Secretary Fish gave me, so far as intention was concerned, a very handsome acquittal.

And strange to say, *post hoc* though perhaps not *propter hoc*, the United States have been that country of the world in which the most signal marks of public honour have been paid me, and in which my name has been the most popular, the only parallels being Italy, Greece, and the Balkan Peninsula

—MORLEY, *The Life of William Ewart Gladstone*

XV.8

THE ENGLISH PRESS CONDEMNS THE EMANCIPATION PROCLAMATION

It is commonly believed that it was the Emancipation Proclamation that turned the tide of opinion in Britain. There is some truth in this, for that proclamation gave the war a new character. It was no longer a war for Union alone or—as the opposition called it—for Empire. Now it was also a war for Freedom. It is of some interest, however, to note that the immediate reaction of a substantial part of the English press was decidedly hostile to the Proclamation and to the policy which it announced.

We include here merely one of the many critical editorials on the Proclamation. This is from the *Times*, the most powerful paper in Britain and perhaps in the world.

It is rarely that a man can be found to balance accurately mischief to another against advantage to himself. President Lincoln is, as the world says, a good-tempered man, neither better nor worse than the mass of his kind—neither a fool nor a sage, neither a villain nor a saint, but a piece of that common useful clay out of which it delights the American democracy to make great Republican personages. Yet President Lincoln has declared that from the 1st of January next to come every State that is in rebellion shall be, in the eye of Mr. Lincoln, a Free State. After that date Mr. Lincoln proposes to enact that every slave in a rebel State shall be for ever after free, and he promises that neither he, nor his army, nor his navy will do anything to repress *any* efforts which the Negroes in such rebel States may make for the recovery of their freedom.

This means, of course, that Mr. Lincoln will, on the 1st of next January, do his best to excite a servile war in the States which he cannot occupy with his arms. He will run up the rivers in his gunboats; he will seek out the places which are left but slightly guarded, and where the women and children have been trusted to the fidelity of coloured domestics. He will appeal to the black blood of the African; he will whisper of the pleasures of spoil and of the gratification of yet fiercer instincts; and when blood begins to flow and shrieks come piercing through the darkness, Mr. Lincoln will wait till the rising flames tell that all is consummated, and then he will rub his hands and think that revenge is sweet. This is what Mr. Lincoln avows before the world that he is about to do.

Now, we are in Europe thoroughly convinced that the death of slavery must follow as necessarily upon the success of the Confederates in this war as the dispersion of darkness occurs upon the rising of the sun; but sudden and forcible emancipation resulting from "the efforts the Negroes may make for their actual freedom" can only be effected by massacre and utter destruction. Mr. Lincoln avows, therefore, that he proposes to excite the Negroes of the Southern plantations to murder the families of their masters while these are engaged in the war. The conception of such a crime is horrible. The employment of Indians sinks to a level with civilized warfare in comparison with it; the most detestable doctrines of Mazzini are almost less atrocious; even Mr. Lincoln's own recent achievements of burning by gunboats the defenceless villages on the Mississippi are dwarfed by this gigantic wickedness. The single thing to be said for it is that it is a wickedness that holds its head high and scorns hypocrisy. It does not pretend to attack slavery as slavery. It launches this threat of a servile rebellion as a means of war against certain States, and accompanies it with a declaration of general protection to all other slavery.

Where he has no power Mr. Lincoln will set the Negroes free; where he retains power he will consider them as slaves. "Come to me," he cries to the insurgent planters, "and I will preserve your rights as slaveholders; but set me still at defiance, and I will wrap myself in virtue, and take the sword of freedom in my hand, and, instead of aiding you to oppress, I will champion the rights of humanity. Here are whips for you who are loyal; go forth and flog or sell your black chattels as you please. Here are torches and knives for employment against you who are disloyal; I will press them into every black hand, and teach their use." Little Delaware, with her 2000 slaves, shall still be protected in her loyal tyranny. Maryland, with her 90,000 slaves, shall "freely accept or freely reject" any project for either gradual or immediate abolition; but if Mississippi and South Carolina, where the slaves rather outnumber the masters, do not repent, and receive from Mr. Lincoln a licence to trade in human flesh, that human flesh shall be adopted by Mr. Lincoln as the agent of his vengeance. The position is peculiar for a mere layman. Mr. Lincoln, by this proclamation, constitutes himself a sort of moral American Pope. He claims to sell indulgences to own votaries, and he offers them with full hands to all who will fall down and worship him. It is his to

bind, and it is his to loose. His decree of emancipation is to go into remote States, where his temporal power cannot be made manifest, and where no stars and stripes are to be seen; and in those distant swamps he is, by a sort of Yankee excommunication, to lay the land under a slavery interdict. . . .

As a proof of what the leaders of the North, in their passion and their despair, would do if they could, this is a very sad document. As a proof of the hopelessness and recklessness which prompt their actions, it is a very instructive document. We gather from it that Mr. Lincoln has lost all hope of preserving the Union, and is now willing to let any quack try his nostrum. As an act of policy it is, if possible, more contemptible than it is wicked. It may possibly produce some partial risings, for let any armed power publish an exhortation to the labouring class of any community to plunder and murder, and there will be some response. It might happen in London, or Paris, or New York. That Mr. Lincoln's emancipation decrees will have any general effect bearing upon the issue of the war, we do not, however, believe. The Negros have already abundantly discovered that the tender mercies of the Northerners are cruelties. The freedom which is associated with labour in the trenches, military discipline, and frank avowals of personal abhorrence momentarily repeated does not commend itself to the Negro nature. General Butler could, if he pleased, tell strange stories of the ill success of his tamperings with the Negroes about New Orleans.

We do not think that even now, when Mr. Lincoln plays his last card, it will prove to be a trump. Powerful malignity is a dreadful reality, but impotent malignity is apt to be a very contemptible spectacle. Here is a would-be conqueror and a would-be extirpator who is not quite safe in his seat of government, who is reduced to such straits that he accepts a defeat as a glorious escape, a capitulation of 8000 men as an unimportant event, a drawn battle as a glorious victory, and the retreat of an invading army which retires laden with plunder and rich in stores as a deliverance. Here is a President who has just, against his will, supplied his antagonists with a hundred and twenty guns and millions of stores, and who is trembling for the very ground on which he stands. Yet, if we judged only by his pompous proclamations, we should believe that he had a garrison in every city of the South. This is more like a Chinaman beating his two swords together to frighten his enemy than like an earnest man pressing on his cause in steadfastness and truth.

—*The Times*, October 7, 1862

XV.9

MANCHESTER WORKINGMEN STAND BY THE UNION

One of the moving and—as it has turned out—one of the historic interchanges of Anglo-American history came when the workingmen of Manchester, most of them thrown out of work by the cotton shortage, addressed a letter to President Lincoln assuring him of their support now that the war was clearly directed to the abolition of slavery. Lincoln's reply was one of his most felicitous efforts.

A. "We Are Truly One People"

December 31, 1862

To Abraham Lincoln, President of the United States:

As citizens of Manchester, assembled at the Free-Trade Hall, we beg to express our fraternal sentiments toward you and your country. We rejoice in your greatness as an outgrowth of England, whose blood and language you share, whose orderly and legal freedom you have applied to new circumstances, over a region immeasurably greater than our own. We honor your Free States, as a singularly happy abode for the working millions where industry is honored. One thing alone has, in the past, lessened our sympathy with your country and our confidence in it—we mean the ascendency of politicians who not merely maintained Negro slavery, but desired to extend and root it more firmly.

Since we have discerned, however, that the victory of the free North, in the war which has so sorely distressed us as well as afflicted you, will strike off the fetters of the slave, you have attracted our warm and earnest sympathy. We joyfully honor you, as the President, and the Congress with you, for many decisive steps toward practically exemplifying your belief in the words of your great founders: "All men are created free and equal." You have procured the liberation of the slaves in the district around Washington, and thereby made the centre of your Federation visibly free. You have enforced the laws against the slave-trade, and kept up your fleet against it, even while every ship was wanted for service in your terrible war. You have nobly decided to receive ambassadors from the Negro republics of Hayti and Liberia, thus forever renouncing that unworthy prejudice which re fuses the rights of humanity to men and women on account of their color. In order more effectually to stop the slave trade, you have made with our Queen a treaty, which your Senate has ratified, for the right of mutual search. Your Congress has decreed freedom as the law forever in the vast unoccupied or half unsettled Territories which are directly subject to its legislative power. It has offered pecuniary aid to all States which will enact emancipation locally, and has forbidden your Generals to restore fugitive slaves who seek their protection. You have entreated the slave-masters to accept these moderate offers; and after long and patient waiting, you, as Commander-in-Chief of the Army, have appointed to-morrow, the first of January, 1863, as the day of unconditional freedom for the slaves of the rebel States.

Heartily do we congratulate you and your country on this humane and righteous course. We assume that you cannot now stop short of a complete uprooting of slavery. It would not become us to dictate any details, but there are broad principles of humanity which must guide you. If complete emancipation in some States be deferred, though only to a predetermined day, still in the interval, human beings should not be counted chattels. Women must have the rights of chastity and maternity, men the rights of husbands, masters the liberty of manumission. Justice demands for the black, no less than for the white, the protection of law—that his voice be heard in your courts. Nor must any such abomination be tolerated as slave-breeding States, and a slave market—if you are to earn the high reward of all your sacrifices, in the approval of the universal brotherhood and of the Divine Father. It is for your free country to decide whether any thing but immediate and total emancipation can secure the most indispensable rights of humanity against the inveterate wickedness of local laws and local executives.

We implore you, for your own honor and welfare, not to faint in your providential mission. While your enthusiasm is aflame, and the tide of events runs high, let the work be finished effectually. Leave no root of bitterness to spring up and work fresh misery to your children. It is a mighty task, indeed, to reorganize the industry not only of four millions of the colored race, but of five millions of whites. Nevertheless, the vast progress you have made in the short space of twenty months fills us with hope that every stain on your freedom will shortly be removed, and that the erasure of that foul blot upon civilization and Christianity—chattel slavery—during your Presidency will cause the name of Abraham Lincoln to be honored and revered by posterity. We are certain that such a glorious consummation will cement Great Britain to the United States in close and enduring regards. Our interests, moreover, are identified with yours. We are truly one people, though locally separate. And if you have any ill-wishers here, be assured they are chiefly those who oppose liberty at home, and that they will be powerless to stir up quarrels between us, from the very day in which your country becomes, undeniably and without exception, the home of the free.

Accept our high admiration of your firmness in upholding the proclamation of freedom.

—MOORE, ed., *The Rebellion Record*

B. "An Instance of Sublime Christian Heroism"

January 19, 1863

To the Working-Men of Manchester:

I have the honor to acknowledge the receipt of the address and resolutions which you sent me on the eve of the new year. When I came, on the 4th of March, 1861, through a free and constitutional election to preside in the Government of the United States, the country was found at the verge of civil war. Whatever might have been the cause, or whosoever the fault, one duty, paramount to all others, was before me, namely, to maintain and preserve at once the Constitution and the integrity of the Federal Republic. A conscientious purpose to perform this duty is the key to all the measures of administration which have been and to all which will hereafter be pursued. Under our frame of government and my official oath, I could not depart from this purpose if I would. It is not always in the power of governments to enlarge or restrict the scope of moral results which follow the policies that they may deem it necessary for the public safety from time to time to adopt.

I have understood well that the duty of self-preservation rests solely with the American people; but I have at the same time been aware that favor or disfavor of foreign nations might have a material influence in enlarging or prolonging the struggle with disloyal men in which the country is engaged. A fair examination of history has served to authorize a belief that the past actions and influences of the United States were generally regarded as having been beneficial toward mankind. I have, therefore, reckoned upon the forbearance of nations. Circumstances—to some of which you kindly allude—induce me especially to expect that if justice and good faith should be practised by the United States, they would encounter no hostile influence on the part of Great Britain. It is now a pleasant duty to acknowledge the demonstration you have given of your desire that a spirit of amity and peace toward this country may prevail in the councils of your Queen, who is respected and esteemed in your own country only more than she is by the kindred nation which has its home on this side of the Atlantic.

I know and deeply deplore the sufferings which the working-men at Manchester, and in all Europe, are called to endure in this crisis. It has been often and studiously represented that the attempt to overthrow this government, which was built upon the foundation of human rights, and to substitute for it one which should rest exclusively on the basis of human slavery, was likely to obtain the favor of Europe. Through the action of our disloyal citizens, the working-men of Europe have been subjected to severe trials, for the purpose of forcing their sanction to that attempt. Under the circumstances, I cannot but regard your decisive utterances upon the question as an instance of sublime Christian heroism which has not been surpassed in any age or in any country. It is indeed an energetic and reinspiring assurance of the inherent power of truth and of the ultimate and universal triumph of justice, humanity, and freedom. I do not doubt that the sentiments you have expressed will be sustained by your great nation; and on the other hand, I have no hesitation in assuring you that they will excite admiration, esteem, and the most reciprocal feelings of friendship among the American people. I hail this interchange of sentiment, therefore, as an augury that whatever else may happen, whatever misfortune may befall your country or my own, the peace and friendship which now exist between the two nations will be, as it shall be my desire to make them, perpetual.

Abraham Lincoln.

—*Complete Works of Abraham Lincoln*

XV.10

RICHARD COBDEN REJOICES IN THE EMANCIPATION PROCLAMATION

Cobden was a leader of the English liberals in the mid-nineteenth century. A wealthy manufacturer, he abandoned business to agitate against the Corn Laws and was chiefly instrumental in obtaining their repeal. In Parliament he proved an eloquent spokesman for liberal and humanitarian causes, strongly opposing the Crimean War, intervention in China, and espousing, like Bright, free trade and electoral reform. Twice offered posts in the Cabinet, he twice refused. Worn out with his public labors Cobden died in 1865, but not before he had rendered signal service to the cause of Anglo-American unity; it is not an accident that the Carnegie Endowment has made Cobden's birthplace, Dunford House, an international shrine.

This letter is addressed to Charles Sumner.

Athenaeum Club, London, 13 Feby., 1863
Private
My dear Sumner.

If I have not written to you before it is not because I have been indifferent to what is passing in your midst. I may say sincerely that my thoughts have run almost as much on American as English politics. But I could do you no service, and shrunk from occupying your overtaxed attention even for a moment. My object in now writing is to speak of a matter which has a practical bearing on your affairs.

You know how much alarmed I was from the first lest our government should interpose in your affairs. The disposition of our ruling class, and the necessities of our cotton trade, pointed to some act of intervention and the indifference of the great mass of our population to your struggle, the object of which they did not foresee and understand, would have made intervention easy indeed popular if you had been a weaker naval power. This state of feeling existed up to the announcement of the President's emancipation Policy. From that moment our old anti-slavery feeling began to arouse itself, and it has been gathering strength ever since. The great rush of the public to all the public meetings called on the subject shows how wide and deep the sympathy for personal freedom still is in the hearts of our people. I know nothing in my political experience so striking as a display of spontaneous public action as that of the vast gathering at Exeter Hall when without one attraction in the form of a popular orator the vast building, its minor rooms and passages and the streets adjoining were crowded with an enthusiastic audience. That meeting has had a powerful effect on our newspapers and politicians. It has closed the mouths of those who have been advocating the side of the South.

And I now write to assure you that any unfriendly act on the part of our government, no matter which of our aristocratic parties is in power, towards your cause is not to be apprehended. If an attempt were made by the government in any way to commit us to the South, a spirit would be instantly aroused which would drive our government from power. This I suppose will be known and felt by the Southern agents in Europe and if communicated to their government must I should think operate as a great discouragement to them. For *I know* that those agents have been incessantly urging in every quarter where they could hope to influence the French and English governments the absolute necessity of *recognition* as a means of putting an end to the war. Recognition of the South, by England, whilst it bases itself on Negro slavery, is an impossibility, unless indeed after the Federal government have recognized the Confederates as a nation.

So much for the influence which your emancipation policy has had on the public opinion of England. But judging from the tone of your press in America it does not seem to have gained the support of your masses. About this however I do not feel competent to offer an opinion. Nor, to confess the truth, do I feel much satisfaction in treating of your politics at all. There appears to me great mismanagement I had almost said incapacity in the management of your affairs, and you seem to be hastening towards financial and economical evils in a manner which fills me with apprehension for the future.

When I met Fremont in Paris two years ago just as you commenced this terrible war I remarked to him that the total abolition of slavery in your northern Continent was the only issue which could justify the war to the civilized world. Every symptom seems to point to this result. But at what a price is the Negro to be emancipated! I confess that if then I had been the arbiter of his fate I should have refused him freedom at the cost of so much white men's blood and women's tears. I do not however blame the North. The South fired the first shot, and on them righteously falls the malediction that "they who take the sword shall perish by the sword."

Believe me,
Yours very truly
R. Cobden

—E. L. PIERCE, contrib., "Letters of Richard
Cobden to Charles Sumner"

XV.11

ENGLISH ARISTOCRATS ORGANIZE FOR SOUTHERN INDEPENDENCE

The mediation crisis or 1862 had been successfully surmounted by Antietam, and by the Emancipation Proclamation. Yet the Confederate cause appeared by no means hopeless, and agitation for some form of intervention persisted. More and more, however, that agitation took on a class character; it was supported by the aristocracy and the great shipbuilders and textile manufacturers. A London Confederate States Aid Association had been organized in 1862, but had died a lingering death. Early in 1863 it was supplanted by a Southern Independence Association, whose Constitution we reproduce here. The most interesting thing about this otherwise curious organization is its list of sponsors. It appealed, as the Index pointed out, to "persons of rank and gentlemen of standing." It was this association that called forth Goldwin Smith's devastating "Letter to a Whig Member," one of the most powerful of all defenses of the Union cause.

Southern Independence Association of London
Public opinion is becoming enlightened upon the disruption of the late United States, and upon the character of the war which has been raging on the American continent for nearly three years. British subjects were at first hardly able to realize a federation of States each in itself possessed of sovereign attributes; while deriving their views of American history from New York and New England, they ascribed the secession of the Southern States to pique at a lost election, and to fear for the continuance of an institution peculiarly distasteful to Englishmen. Assurances were rife from those quarters that the movement was the conspiracy of a few daring men, and that a strong Union sentiment existed in the seceding States, which would soon assert its existence under stress of the war.

Gradually the true causes of the disruption have made themselves more and more manifest. The long-widening and now insuperable divergence of character and interests between the two sections of the former Union has been made palpable by the facts of the gigantic struggle. Their wisdom in council, their endurance in the field, and the universal self-sacrifice which has characterized their public and their private life, have won general sympathy for the Confederates as a people worthy of, and who have earned, their independence.

On the other hand, the favorable judgment which Englishmen had long cherished as a duty towards that portion of the United States which they imagined most to resemble the Mother Country has met with many rude shocks from the spectacles which have been revealed in that land of governmental tyranny, corruption in high places, ruthlessness in war, untruthfulness of speech, and causeless animosity towards Great Britain. At the same time the Southerners, who had been very harshly judged in this country, have manifested the highest national characteristics, to the surprise and admiration of all.

Public men are awakening to the truth that it is both use less and mischievous to ignore the gradual settlement of Central North America into groups of States, or consolidated nationalities, each an independent Power. They feel that the present attempt of the North is in manifest opposition to this law of natural progress, and they see that the South can never be reunited with the North except as a conquered and garrisoned dependency; whilst the Northern States, if content to leave their former partners alone, are still in possession of all the elements of great and growing national power and wealth.

Our commercial classes are also beginning to perceive that our best interests will be promoted by creating a direct trade with a people so enterprising as the Confederates, inhabiting a land so wide and so abundant in the richest gifts of Providence, and anxious to place themselves in immediate connection with the manufacturers and consumers of Europe.

In short, the struggle is now felt to be, according to Earl Russell's pregnant expression, one for independence on the part of the South, and for empire on the part of the North; for an independence, on the one hand, which it is equitable for themselves and desirable for the world they should achieve; for an empire, on the other hand. which is only possible at the price of the first principles of Federal Republicanism, and whose establishment by fire and sword, and at a countless cost of human life on both sides, would be the ruin of the Southern States. These, surely, are reasons which invoke the intervention of other Powers, if intervention be possible, in the cause of common humanity.

Therefore, not in enmity to the North, but sympathizing with the Confederates, the Southern Independence Association of London has been formed, to act in concert with that which is so actively and usefully at work in Manchester. . . .

The Association will also devote itself to the cultivation of friendly feelings between the people of Great Britain and of the Confederate States; and it will, in particular, steadily but kindly represent to the Southern States that recognition by Europe must necessarily lead to a revision of the system of servile labor unhappily bequeathed to them by England, in accordance with the spirit of the age, so as to combine the gradual extinction of slavery with the preservation of property, the maintenance of the civil polity, and the true civilization of the Negro race.

The Most Noble the Marquis of Lothian
The Most Noble the Marquis of Bath
The Lord Robert Cecil, M.P.
The Lord Eustace Cecil
The Right Honourable Lord Wharncliffe
The Right Honourable Lord Campbell
The Hon. C. Fitzwilliam, M.P.
The Honourable Robt. Bourke
Edward Akroyd, Esq., Halifax
Colonel Greville, M.P.
W.H. Gregory, Esq. M.P.
T. C. Haliburton, Esq. M.P.
A.J.B. Beresford Hope, Esq.
W.S. Lindsay, Esq. M.P.
Wm. Scholefield, Esq. M.P.
James Spence, Esq., Liverpool
William Vansittart, Esq. M.P.

—Goldwin Smith, *Letter to a Whig Member*

"THE REASONS WHY GREAT BRITAIN IS AVERSE TO RECOGNISE US"

The fact that Great Britain never did recognize the Confederacy was a tremendous sore point to the South, as this editorial in *The Southern Illustrated News* shows. Southerners simply rejected the issue of slavery as being a central concern for the British, pointing out that it was not an issue that got in the way of its international policy with other slaveholding nations. Instead, the publication asserts that other international issues deflected British support. British fear over the vulnerability of Canada to United States attack and the need to concentrate British attention on European crises, such as the emergence of Italy, the newspaper reasons, prevented intervention on behalf of the South.

A great deal of indignation has been felt and expressed in certain quarters because we have not been acknowledged as an independent nation by Great Britain, and not a little astonishment. For indignation, we cannot but think there is great reason. The old Government of the United States, taking warning from the events of the Revolution, established a rule from which it never departed with respect to such matters. It was to acknowledge the Government *de facto* of every country with which it had political relations. This was a wise rule, instituted by the great Southern Presidents who ruled the destinies of the country for so many years, and made for it all of its history which is not absolutely contemptible. Of late years this has also been the policy of Great Britain, borrowed, no doubt, from the practice of the Unites States, and founded on the plainest dictates of justice and common sense. Great Britain had suffered awfully from having pursued the opposite course, and she seemed to have taken warning from the past. She had entered into a war of five years' standing with France for acknowledging the independence of the thirteen colonies, and had come out of it with a beggared exchequer, a defeated army, and an empire sundered in twain. She had refused to acknowledge the independence of the French Republic, and the

bloodiest and most dangerous war she had ever been engaged in to that time was the consequence. The practice which she borrowed from the United States was a wise and a safe practice. It committed her to no discussion of the right of the government she recognised to rule the country which it professed to rule, and to no interference with the internal affairs of such country. It disclaimed, indeed, all pretension to knowledge upon that head. It merely addressed itself to the Government which it found in power, without asking any questions whatever. Thus, when Louis Phillipe established the throne of July upon the ruins of the throne of the elder Bourbon dynasty, Great Britain at once recognised the new government. When the Orleans dynasty was overthrown, she made haste to acknowledge the Republic. When Louis Napoleon established his Presidency, she did the same thing, as she did likewise when he made himself Emperor. She recognised all the Republics of South America, and the Empire of Iturbide in Mexico, though, to the best of our belief, Spain has never acknowledged their independence to this day. She recognised and assisted to set up Greece. She not only recognised Belgium, but contributed to get prince Leopold made King. But two years ago, when the King of Naples was driven from his throne, she immediately recognised his successor, Victor Emmanuel. The confederate States are the only new power she has refused to recognise, and yet they have manifested a degree of strength greater than all those we have enumerated put together. We have, under these circumstances, we think, some right to be indignant. We have not the smallest right to be astonished.

Great Britain has been trying to bring about the very state of things now existing here ever since the United States became a recognised power of the earth. She never could find it in her heart to forgive the successful revolt of the colonies. During Mr. Madison's first term, disclosures were made to discredit the witness, proved, beyond a doubt, that a deeply laid plot had been concocted by the Government of Canada and certain traitors in New England to separate that part of the country from the Union and annex it to the British Empire. In the war which followed shortly after, the people and press of New England were almost unanimous in favor of Great Britain, and opposed to those whom they ought to have regarded as their countrymen. In latter days England has been jealous of the growing power of the United States to an inordinate degree. She has clearly foreseen that, if they continue united, they must become, before the close of this century the first nation of the world, with an invincible army, a navy that must assume the empire of the seas, and a commerce that must swallow up all the commerce of the Old World. Thus, in addition to the old grudge, she has been stimulated by the fear of losing her position among the powers of the earth. Cost what it might, she has felt that for her greatest of all objects has been to destroy the Union. She has succeeded at last, and it is not wonderful that she should desire to see the war carried on as long as both parties may have the strength to maintain themselves. She feels that intervention would follow recognition, and this she is by no means disposed to undertake, because it might have the effect of shortening the war.

The war in question, besides removing a powerful rival from her path, is useful to her in another respect. If it should last long enough, it may be the means of getting her cotton from India into demand, and it may stimulate the production in Australia. When we consider that cotton constitutes the very basis upon which her enormous power is built, we shall see at once the importance of having it all under her own control. This she hopes to accomplish by destroying the culture in this country, which can only be done by destroying the labor which produces it. The abolition of slavery in her West Indian possessions was but the preliminary step to the abolition of slavery in this country. . . . She cares nothing for the slave in Brazil, where his condition is infinitely worse than it is here, or in Cuba, where it is worse even than it is in Brazil. All her sympathy is reserved for the slave in the southern States of this Confederacy, who cultivates the products of which she wishes to preserve a monopoly.

In addition to these causes, it may be that the British government feels itself in no condition to intervene, because of the present condition in Europe. Affairs are far from satisfactory in Italy, and any moment may witness the outbreak of a general war. As we have already observed, recognition might bring on intervention as a necessary consequence, and intervention would be sure to bring on war. This the British Government will avoid if it can. It already has a most exaggerated opinion of the strength of the Yankee Government, and is evidently very willing—we might almost say afraid—to come into collision with it. A late debate in Parliament plainly revealed an extraordinary degree of alarm on the subject of Canada. Entangled as it already is in a war which it supports with difficulty, the Ministry apparently think Yankeedom yet strong enough to tear that noble province from their grasp.

These, we think are the reasons why Great Britain—meaning the British Government—is averse to recognise us. That the majority of the people sympathise with us, while they detest the Yankees, we do not doubt.

—*The Southern Illustrated News*

XV.13

Minister Adams Points Out That This is War

The last diplomatic crisis between Britain and the United States threatened to be the most serious. As early as 1861 the Confederate government had dispatched Captain Bulloch to England to contract for the construction of commerce-destroyers in British shipyards. English law, and the Proclamation of Neutrality, forbade this, but it was relatively easy to evade the prohibition by juggling the ownership papers.

Thus the Confederates were able to build the *Florida* and the *Alabama* in England; the subsesequent depredations of these ships laid the basis for the *Alabama* claims. That the *Alabama* was being built for the Confederacy was common knowledge, but when Adams protested it, he was met with the assertion that there was no legal proof of Confederate ownership!

Even more serious was the Confederate plan to build ironclad rams in British yards. Contracts for these were placed with the Laird brothers, for delivery in the summer of 1863, and construction was soon under way at Birkenhead. If these should get away the prospects for American commerce were black; there were no United States ships that could stand up to them and, as Captain Gustavus Fox, Assistant Secretary of the Navy, wrote, "it is a question of life and death." Adams took energetic action, laying before Russell evidence of Confederate ownership. Russell was not satisfied, and Adams supplied him with additional evidence, which he found only partly persuasive.

Meantime other influences were more persuasive. One was the Congressional Act of March 1863 authorizing Lincoln to issue letters of marque to merchantmen: the victims would obviously be English vessels. Another was the combination of Gettysburg and Vicksburg.

On September 3 Russell ordered the ironclads to be detained. Adams did not know this, and two days later he sent this famous letter with its somewhat ambiguous threat of war. The letter was not essential, but it helped. In October the ironclads were seized by the British government, and subsequently purchased and commissioned in the British Navy.

This was the last episode that seriously troubled Anglo American relations during the war. The combination of Union success on the battlefields and in the coastal waters and of the Emancipation policy persuaded the British government to a far more friendly attitude toward the North. The one thing that continued to exacerbate the relations of the two countries was the ravages of the cruisers *Alabama, Shenandoah* and *Florida*. After the war (1872) the *Alabama* Claims Commission found the British government remiss in allowing these ships to escape and required Britain to pay the United States damages of fifteen and one-half million dollars.

Legation of the United States, London, September 5, 1863

My Lord,

At this moment, when one of the iron-clad war-vessels is on the point of departure from this kingdom on its hostile errand against the United States, I am honoured with the reply of your Lordship to my notes of the 11th, 16th, and 25th of July and of the 14th of August. I trust I need not express how profound is my regret at the conclusion to which Her Majesty's Government have arrived. I can regard it no otherwise than as practically opening to the insurgents free liberty in this kingdom to execute a policy described in one of their late publications in the following language:—

"In the present state of the harbour-defences of New York, Boston, Portland, and smaller Northern cities, such a vessel as the 'Warrior' would have little difficulty in entering any of those ports, and inflicting a vital blow upon the enemy. The destruction of Boston alone would be worth a hundred victories in the field. It would bring such a terror to the 'blue-noses' as to cause them to wish eagerly for peace, de spite their overweening love of gain which has been so freely administered to since the opening of this war. Vessels of the 'Warrior' class would promptly raise the blockade of our ports, and would, even in this respect, confer advantages which would soon repay the cost of their construction."

It would be superfluous in me to point out to your Lord-ship that this is war. No matter what may be the theory adopted of neutrality in a struggle, when this process is carried on in the manner indicated from a territory and with the aid of the subjects of a third party, that third party, to all intents and purposes, ceases to be neutral. Neither is it necessary to show that any Government which suffers it to be done fails in enforcing the essential conditions of international amity towards the country against whom the hostility is directed. In my belief it is impossible that any nation retaining a proper degree of self-respect could tamely submit to a continuance of relations so utterly deficient in reciprocity. I have no idea that Great Britain would do so for a moment.

After a careful examination of the full instructions with which I have been furnished in preparation for such an emergency, I deem it inexpedient for me to attempt any recurrence to arguments for effective interposition in the present case. The fatal objection of impotency which paralyzes Her Majesty's Government seems to present an insuperable barrier against all further reasoning. Under these circumstances I prefer to desist from communicating to your Lordship even such further portions of my existing instructions as are suited to the case, lest I should contribute to aggravate difficulties already far too serious. I therefore content myself with informing your Lordship that I transmit by the present steamer a copy of your note for the consideration of my Government, and shall await the more specific directions that will be contained in the reply.

Charles Francis Adams

—*State Papers, North America*

XVI

SONGS THE SOLDIERS SANG

It is no accident that the motorized armies of the First and Second World Wars inspired so few songs, and sang so few. The Civil War armies were not mechanized; soldiers marched afoot, and as they marched they sang. No other war has provided us with so many songs, or so many that have retained their popularity for so long—marching songs like "Tramp, Tramp, Tramp," inspirational songs like "The Battle Hymn of the Republic," patriotic songs like "Bonnie Blue Flag," humorous songs like "Goober Peas," sentimental songs like "Lorena."

There was little organized entertainment in the Civil War—the Sanitary Commission had other things to do than entertain soldiers—so the soldiers amused themselves, often by communal singing, and we know that many of these songs were sung around the campfires of Union and Confederate armies. The folks back home sang, too, gathering around the pianos now appearing in increasing numbers in American parlors.

Only a few of these songs—a selection from hundreds—need any explanation. Most of them can be assigned, with some assurance, to particular authors, and sometimes to composers; others are of disputed origin; others still seem to have come spontaneously from the soldiers themselves. Many of them are preserved for us in variant forms.

This selection is designed to suggest what the soldiers, and their families, actually sang. Some songs were popular in particular regions, or with particular armies, or enjoyed only fleeting popularity; others, like "Lorena," seem to have been equally popular North and South, East and West, with soldiers and with civilians.

XVI.1

DIXIE

The most famous and most widely sung of an Civil War Songs, "Dixie" actually antedated the war by two years. Nor was it, originally, a Southern song. It was composed by an Ohioan, Dan Emmett, and first sung in Mechanics' Hall on Broadway in April 1859. The origin of the name "Dixie" is obscure, but it was used by Emmett himself in another song composed shortly before "Dixie Land." The song caught on at once and, with the coming of secession, swept the South, where numerous other—and supposedly more appropriate—words were attached to it. It was played at Davis' inauguration as provisional President in Montgomery, Alabama, in February 1861. Yet it was never wholly a Southern song; it is worth remembering that when Lincoln was serenaded after the surrender of Lee he came out on a White House balcony and asked the band to play "Dixie"—now once again a national tune.

Daniel Decatur Emmett is remembered as "the father of The Negro Ministrelsy." He had composed "Old Dan Tucker" in 1830, at the age of fifteen, and thereafter poured a succession of popular songs for his troupe: "Root, Hog, or Die," "Jordan is a Hard Road to Travel," "High Daddy," and many others well known in their day. He wrote both the words and the music for "Dixie."

I wish I was in de land ob cotton,
Old times dar am not forgotten,
Look away, look away, look away, Dixie Land!
In Dixie Land whar I was born in,

Early on one frosty mornin',
Look away, look away, look away, Dixie Land!

Chorus—Den I wish I was in Dixie
Hooray, hooray!
In Dixie Land I'll take my stan'!
To lib an' die in Dixie
Away, away,
Away down south in Dixie

Away, away,
Away down south in Dixie.

Ole Missus marry "Will-de-Weaber," William was a
    gay deceber
Look away, look away, look away, Dixie Land!
But when he put his arm around 'er
He smiled as fierce as a forty-pounder
Look away, look away, look away, Dixie Land
    —Chorus

His face was sharp as a butcher's cleaber,
But dat did not seem to grieb 'er,
Look away, look away, look away, Dixie Land!
Ole Missus acted de foolish part,
An' died for a man dat broke her heart,
Look away, look away, look away, Dixie Land!
    —Chorus

Now, here's a health to de next ole Missus.
An' all de gals dat want to kiss us,
Look away, look away, look away, Dixie Land!
But if you want to drive 'way sorrow,
Come an' hear dis song to-morrow,
Look away, look away, look away, Dixie Land!
    —Chorus

Dar's buckwheat cakes an' Injun batter,
Makes you fat, or a little fatter!
Look away, look away, look away, Dixie Land!
Den hoe it down and scratch your grabble,
To Dixie's Land I'm bound to trabble,
Look away, look away, look away, Dixie Land!
    —Chorus

—Daniel D. Emmett

—————— XVI.2 ——————

The Bonnie Blue Flag

"The Bonnie Blue Flag" came out of New Orleans. It was written
and first sung by Harry McCarthy, who needed a new song to fill
out an act at the Varieties Theatre, in September 1861; the tune
was that of an old Irish song, "The Jaunting Car." From New
Orleans it spread quickly throughout the South, becoming, in the
end, the most popular of Southern marching songs next to
"Dixie." When Butler was in command in New Orleans he arrested and fined Blackmar, its publisher, and threatened to fine any
one who sang this song, 25 dollars. As with so many Civil War
songs there are many versions, and many variations in the text.

We are a band of brothers, and native to the soil,
Fighting for the property we gained by honest toil;
And when our rights were threatened, the cry rose
    near and far:
Hurrah for the bonnie Blue Flag that bears a single
    star!
Hurrah! hurrah! for the bonnie Blue Flag
That bears a single star.

As long as the Union was faithful to her trust,
Like friends and like brothers, kind were we and
    just;
But now when Northern treachery attempts our
    rights to mar,
We hoist on high the bonnie Blue Flag that bears a
    single star.

First, gallant South Carolina nobly made the stand;
Then came Alabama, who took her by the hand;
Next, quickly Mississippi, Georgia, and Florida—
All raised the flag, the bonnie Blue Flag that bears
    a single star.

Ye men of valor, gather round the banner of the
    right;
Texas and fair Louisiana join us in the fight.
Davis, our loved President, and Stephens, states-
    men are;
Now rally round the bonnie Blue Flag that bears a
    single star.

And here's to brave Virginia! the old Dominion
  State
With the young Confederacy at length has linked
  her fate.
Impelled by her example, now other States prepare
To hoist on high the bonnie Blue Flag that bears a
  single star.

Then here's to our Confederacy; strong we are and
  brave,
Like patriots of old we'll fight, our heritage to save;
And rather than submit to shame, to die we would
  prefer;
So cheer for the bonnie Blue Flag that bears a
  single star.

Then cheer, boys, cheer, raise the joyous shout,
For Arkansas and North Carolina now have both
  gone out;
And let another rousing cheer for Tennessee be
  given,
The single star of the bonnie Blue Flag has grown
  to be
Eleven!
Hurrah! hurrah! for the bonnie Blue Flag
That bears a single star.

— Harry McCarthy

— XVI.3 —

John Brown's Body

This, the most widely sung of Federal songs, is apparently a
genuine folk song. No one knows its precise origin, or its author.
The tune was taken from a Negro melody popular in the Carolina
low country, where it was sung to the refrain

> Say, brothers, will you meet us?
> On Canaan's happy shore?

The words have been assigned to Thomas B. Bishop; the adapta-
tion of the words to the familiar tune to James E. Greenleaf of
the Boston Light Artillery, and to a Mr. Gilmore who played it
before the 12th Massachusetts Volunteers. Perhaps the most
popular variation was "We'll Hang Jeff Davis on a Sour Apple
Tree."

John Brown's body lies a-mould'ring in the grave,
John Brown's body lies a-mould'ring in the grave,
John Brown's body lies a-mould'ring in the grave,
His soul is marching on.

Chorus: Glory! Glory! Hallelujah!
Glory! Glory! Hallelujah!
Glory! Glory Hallelujah!
His soul is marching on.

He's gone to be a soldier in the army of the Lord!
His soul is marching on.—Chorus

John Brown's knapsack is strapped upon his back.
His soul is marching on.—Chorus

His pet lambs will meet him on the way,
And they'll go marching on.—Chorus

They'll hang Jeff Davis on a sour apple tree,
As they go marching on.—Chorus

Now for the Union let's give three rousing cheers,
As we go marching on.
Hip, Hip, hip, hip, Hurrah!—Chorus
— Thomas B. Bishop

— XVI.4 —

All Quiet along the Potomac

Both the author and the composer of this song, so popular with
both armies and both peoples, were New Yorkers. Inspired by
the oft-repeated headline in the newspapers in 1861, "All Quiet
Along the Potomac," with a little notice underneath—"A Picket
Shot"—Ethel Lynn Beers composed this poem and published it
in *Harper's Magazine* in November 1861 under the title "The
Picket Guard." Later it was claimed by the fabulous Major Lamar
Fontaine of the Confederate Army. The music has been credited
to both Henry Coyle and to J. Dayton, both of the 1st
Connecticut Artillery, but it seems clearly to have been com-
posed by the famous poet, journalist, and musician, James
Hewitt—who at the time was drilling recruits in Richmond,
Virginia.

"All quiet along the Potomac," they say,
    "Except now and then a stray picket
Is shot, as he walks on his beat to and fro,
    By a rifleman hid in the thicket.
'Tis nothing—a private or two now and then
    Will not count in the news of the battle;
Not an officer lost—only one of the men,
    Moaning out, all alone, the death-rattle."

All quiet along the Potomac to-night,
    Where the soldiers lie peacefully dreaming;
Their tents in the rays of the clear autumn moon,
    Or the light of the watch-fire, are gleaming.
A tremulous sigh of the gentle night-wind
    Through the forest leaves softly is creeping;
While stars up above, with their glittering eyes,
    Keep guard, for the army is sleeping.

There's only the sound of the lone sentry's tread,
    As he tramps from the rock to the fountain,
And thinks of the two in the low trundle-bed
    Far away in the cot on the mountain.
His musket falls slack; his face, dark and grim,
    Grows gentle with memories tender,
As he mutters a prayer for the children asleep,
    For their mother; may Heaven defend her!

The moon seems to shine just as brightly as then,
    That night, when the love yet unspoken

Leaped up to his lips—when low-murmured vows
    Were pledged to be ever unbroken.
Then drawing his sleeve roughly over his eyes,
    He dashes off tears that are welling,
And gathers his gun closer up to its place,
    As if to keep down the heart-swelling.

He passes the fountain, the blasted pine-tree,
    The footstep is lagging and weary;
Yet onward he goes, through the broad belt of light,
    Toward the shade of the forest so dreary.
Hark! was it the night-wind that rustled the leaves?
    Was it moonlight so wondrously flashing?
It looked like a rifle . . . "Ha! Mary, good-bye!"
    The red life-blood is ebbing and plashing.

All quiet along the Potomac to-night;
    No sound save the rush of the river;
While soft falls the dew on the face of the dead—
    The picket's off duty forever!

                                    —ETHEL LYNN BEERS

XVI.5

MARCHING ALONG

This was a favorite with the soldiers of the Army of the Potomac: the name of the "leader" was changed—pretty frequently as it turned out—to fit the facts. William Bradbury was, in his day, one of the most distinguished of American composers. A student of the great Lowell Mason, he was instrumental in introducing music into the schools, put out a number of singing books, and contributed richly to American psalmody. Among his better known songs are "Just as I Am" and "He Leadeth Me."

The army is gathering from near and from far;
The trumpet is sounding the call for the war;
McClellan's our leader, he's gallant and strong;
We'll gird on our armor and be marching along.

Chorus:
Marching along, we are marching along,
Gird on the armor and be marching along;
McClellan's our leader, he's gallant and strong;
For God and our country we are marching along.

The foe is before us in battle array,
But let us not waver, or turn from the way;
The Lord is our strength, and the Union's our song;
With courage and faith we are marching along.
    —Chorus

Our wives and our children we leave in your care;
We feel you will help them with sorrow to bear:
'Tis hard thus to part, but we hope 't won't be long:
We'll keep up our heart as we're marching along.
    —Chorus

We sigh for our country, we mourn for our dead;
For them now our last drop of blood we will shed;
Our cause is the right one—our foe's in the wrong;

Then gladly we'll sing as we're marching along.
   —Chorus

The flag of our country is floating on high;
We'll stand by that flag till we conquer or die;
McClellan's our leader, he's gallant and strong;
We'll gird on our armor and be marching along.
   —Chorus

        —William Batchelder Bradbury

——— XVI.6 ———

Maryland! My Maryland!

This best known of all state songs was written, appropriate ly enough, by a native of Baltimore. James Ryder Randall had gone to New Orleans in 1859 to clerk in a ship broker's office. The following year he took a position as tutor in English at Poydras College, a Creole school in Pointe Coupee Parish, and he was there when he read the story of the attack on the 6th Massachusetts as it forced its way through Baltimore. That night he wrote "Maryland! My Maryland!" and sent it to the *New Orleans Delta,* where it was printed in the issue of April 26. The Misses Cary of Baltimore adapted the words to the familiar music of "O Tannenbaum," and it became one of the favorite marching songs of the Confederacy.

The despot's heel is on thy shore,
   Maryland!
His torch is at thy temple door,
   Maryland!
Avenge the patriotic gore
That flecked the streets of Baltimore,
And be the battle queen of yore,
   Maryland! My Maryland!

Hark to an exiled son's appeal,
   Maryland!
My mother State! to thee I kneel,
   Maryland!
For life and death, for woe and weal,
Thy peerless chivalry reveal,
And gird thy beauteous limbs with steel,
   Maryland! My Maryland!

Thou wilt not cower in the dust,
   Maryland!

Thy beaming sword shall never rust,
   Maryland!
Remember Carroll's sacred trust,
Remember Howard's warlike thrust,—
And all thy slumberers with the just,
   Maryland! My Maryland!

Come! for thy shield is bright and strong,
   Maryland!
Come! for thy dalliance does thee wrong,
   Maryland!
Come to thine own heroic throng,
Stalking with Liberty along,
And chaunt thy dauntless slogan song,
   Maryland! My Maryland!

Dear Mother! burst the tyrant's chain,
   Maryland!
Virginia should not call in vain,
   Maryland!
She meets her sisters on the plain—
"Sic semper!" 'tis the proud refrain
That baffles minions back again,
   Maryland! My Maryland!

I hear the distant thunder-hum,
   Maryland!
The Old Line's bugle, fife, and drum,
   Maryland !
She is not dead, nor deaf, nor dumb—
Huzza! she spurns the Northern scum!
She breathes! she burns! she'll come! she'll come!
   Maryland! My Maryland!

        —James R. Randall

——— XVI.7 ———

The Battle Hymn of the Republic

It can hardly be doubted that this is the one great song to come out of the Civil War—the one that transcends that particular conflict and embraces every great moral crusade.

Julia Ward Howe was the daughter of a New York banker and the wife of the famous Massachusetts reformer, Samuel Gridley Howe. She early made a name for herself in Boston circles by her essays and poems and by her zealous advocacy of abolition and woman's rights. The following excerpts tell how she came to write the "Battle Hymn," and give a glimpse of the meaning of the song to Union prisoners.

A. Writing "The Battle Hymn of the Republic"

I distinctly remember that a feeling of discouragement came over me as I drew near the city of Washington. I thought of the women of my acquaintance whose sons or husbands were fighting our great battle, the women them selves serving in the hospitals, or busying themselves with the work of the Sanitary Commission. My husband was beyond the age of military service, my eldest son but a stripling; my youngest was a child of not more than two years. I could not leave my nursery to follow the march of our armies; neither had I the practical deftness which the preparing and packing of sanitary stores demanded. Some thing seemed to say to me, "You would be glad to serve, but you cannot help any one; you have nothing to give, and there is nothing for you to do." Yet, because of my sincere desire, a word was given me to say, which did strengthen the hearts of those who fought in the field and of those who languished in the prison.

We were invited one day to attend a review of troops at some distance from the town. While we were engaged in watching the maneuvers, a sudden movement of the enemy necessitated immediate action. The review was discontinued, and we saw a detachment of soldiers gallop to the assistance of a small body of our men who were in imminent danger of being surrounded and cut off from retreat. The regiments remaining on the field were ordered to march to their cantonments. We returned to the city very slowly, of necessity, for the troops nearly filled the road. My dear minister was in the carriage with me, as were several other friends. To beguile the rather tedious drive, we sang from time to time snatches of the army songs so popular at that time, concluding, I think, with:

John Brown's body lies a-moldering in the ground;
His soul is marching on.

The soldiers seemed to like this and answered back, "Good for you!" Mr. Clark said, "Mrs. Hower, why do you not write some good words for that stirring tune?" I replied that I had often wished to do this but had not as yet found in my mind any leading toward it.

I went to bed that night as usual and slept, according to my wont, quite soundly. I awoke in the gray of the morning twilight, and as I lay waiting for the dawn, the long lines of the desired poem began to twine themselves in my mind. Having thought out all the stanzas, I said to myself, "I must get up and write these verses down, lest I fall asleep again and forget them." So with a sudden effort I sprang out of bed and found in the dimness an old stump of a pen which I remembered to have used the day before. I scrawled the verses almost without looking at the paper. I had learned to do this when, on previous occasions, attacks of versification had visited me in the night and I feared to have recourse to a light lest I should wake the baby, who slept near me. I was always obliged to decipher my scrawl before another night should intervene, as it was only legible while the matter was fresh in my mind. At this time, having completed my writing, I returned to bed and fell asleep, saying to myself, "I like this better than most things that I have written."

The poem, which was soon after published in the *Atlantic Monthly* [February 1862], was somewhat praised on its appearance, but the vicissitudes of the war so engrossed public attention that small heed was taken of literary matters. I knew and was content to know that the poem soon found its way to the camps, as I heard from time to time of its being sung in chorus by the soldiers.

—Howe, *Reminiscences*

B. The Battle Hymn of the Republic

Mine eyes have seen the glory of the coming
   of the Lord:
He is trampling out the vintage where the grapes of
   wrath are stored;

He hath loosed the fateful lightning of his terrible
swift sword:
His truth is marching on.

I have seen Him in the watch fires of a hundred
circling camps;
They have builded Him an altar in the evening
dews and damps;
I can read His righteous sentence by the dim and
flaring lamps.
His day is marching on.

I have read a fiery gospel writ in burnished rows
of steel:
"As ye deal with my contemners, so with you my
grace shall deal;
Let the Hero, born of woman, crush the serpent
with his heel,
Since God is marching on."

He has sounded forth the trumpet that shall never
call retreat;
He is sifting out the hearts of men before his judgment seat:
Oh! be swift, my soul, to answer Him! be jubilant,
my feet!
Our God is marching on.

In the beauty of the lilies Christ was born across
the sea,
With a glory in His bosom that transfigures you and
me:
As He died to make men holy, let us die to make
men free,
While God is marching on.

—Julia Ward Howe

C. "The Battle Hymn of the Republic" in Libby Prison

Among the singers of the "Battle Hymn" was Chaplain McCabe, the fighting chaplain of the 122d Ohio Volunteer Infantry. He read the poem in the "Atlantic," and was so struck with it that he committed it to memory before rising from his chair. He took it with him to the front, and in due time to Libby Prison, whither he was sent after being captured at Winchester. Here, in the great bare room where hundreds of Northern soldiers were herded together, came one night a rumor of disaster to the Union arms. A great battle, their jailers told them; a great Confederate victory. Sadly the Northern men gathered together in groups, sitting or lying on the floor, talking in low tones, wondering how, where, why. Suddenly, one of the Negroes who brought food for the prisoners stooped in passing and whispered to one of the sorrowful groups. The news was false: there had, indeed, been a great battle, but the Union army had won, the Confederates were defeated and scattered.

Like a flame the word flashed through the prison. Men leaped to their feet, shouted, embraced one another in a frenzy of joy and triumph; and Chaplain McCabe, standing in the middle of the room, lifted up his great voice and sang aloud,—

"Mine eyes have seen the glory of the coming of
the Lord!"

Every voice took up the chorus, and Libby Prison rang with the shout of "Glory, glory, hallelujah!"

The victory was that of Gettysburg. When, some time after, McCabe was released from prison, he told in Washington, before a great audience of loyal people, the story of his war-time experiences; and when he came to that night in Libby Prison, he sang the "Battle Hymn" once more. The effect was magical; people shouted, wept, and sang, all together; and when the song was ended, above the tumult of applause was heard the voice of Abraham Lincoln, exclaiming, while the tears rolled down his cheeks,—

"Sing it again!"

—Richards and Elliott, *Julia Ward Howe*

——— XVI.8 ———

We Are Coming, Father Abraham

The losses in the Peninsular campaign were so heavy that Lincoln on July 2, 1862, appealed to the states to raise "three hundred thousand more" soldiers. It was in response to this appeal that James Sloan Gibbons, the New York abolitionist, wrote "We Are Coming, Father Abraham"—an assertion which, as it turned out, was overconfident.

Gibbons was a Philadelphia Quaker who in the thirties moved to New York and simultaneously entered banking and reform, becoming one of the staunchest supporters of the American Anti-Slavery Society. During the draft riots of 1863 his house was sacked. The music for this song was composed by Stephen Foster, then living in poverty and obscurity in New York City.

We are coming, Father Abraham, three hundred
    thousand more,
From Mississippi's winding stream and from New
    England's shore;
We leave our ploughs and workshops, our wives
    and children dear,
With hearts too full for utterance, with but a
    silent tear;
We dare not look behind us, but steadfastly before:
We are coming, Father Abraham, three hundred
    thousand more!

If you look across the hill-tops that meet the
    northern sky,
Long moving lines of rising dust your vision may
    descry;
And now the wind, an instant, tears the cloudy
    veil aside,
And floats aloft our spangled flag in glory and in
    pride,
And bayonets in the sunlight gleam, and bands
    brave music pour,
We are coming, Father Abraham, three hundred
    thousand more!

If you look all up our valleys where the growing
    harvests shine,
You may see our sturdy farmer boys fast forming
    into line;
And children from their mother's knees are pulling
    at the weeds,
And learning how to reap and sow against their
    country's needs;
And a farewell group stands weeping at every
    cottage door:
We are coming, Father Abraham, three hundred
    thousand more!

You have called us, and we're coming, by
    Richmond's bloody tide
To lay us down, for Freedom's sake, our brothers'
    bones beside,
Or from foul treason's savage grasp to wrench the
    murderous blade,

And in the face of foreign foes its fragments to
    parade.
Six hundred thousand loyal men and true have
    gone before:
We are coming, Father Abraham, three hundred
    thousand more!

—James Sloan Gibbons

XVI.9

THE BATTLE-CRY OF FREEDOM

This song, like "We are Coming, Father Abraham," was written in response to Lincoln's appeal for troops. George F. Root, who wrote both the words and the music, was, with his friend and colleague Henry Clay Work, the most prolific and successful of Northern Civil War song writers, author of the ever popular "Tramp, Tramp, Tramp," "The Vacant Chair," "Just Before the Battle, Mother," and others. He had taught at the Boston Academy of Music and the New York Normal Institute before going to Chicago, in 1859, to open a music store. "The Battle-Cry of Freedom" was written for a rally at Court House Square in Chicago; the famous Hutchinson family of singers carried it throughout the North.

There were two versions of this song—the so-called "rallying" version and the "battle-song" version. The better known "rallying" song is given here; the first verse of the "battle-song" is as follows:

We are marching to the field, boys, we're going to
    the fight,
Shouting the battle-cry of freedom;
And we bear the glorious stars for the Union and
    the right,
Shouting the battle-cry of freedom.

If we are to believe Mrs. Pickett one version of the song was equally popular in the Confederacy.

Yes, We'll rally round the flag,
Boys, we'll rally once again,

Shouting the battle-cry of Freedom,
We will rally from the hillside, we'll gather from
    the plain,
Shouting the battle-cry of Freedom.

Chorus: The Union forever,
Hurray! boys, Hurrah!
Down with the traitor, up with the star;
While we rally round the flag boys, rally once again,
Shouting the battle-cry of Freedom.

We are springing to the call of our Brothers gone
    before,
Shouting the battle-cry of Freedom;
And we'll fill the vacant ranks with a million
    freemen more,
Shouting the battle-cry of Freedom.—Chorus

We will welcome to our numbers the loyal, true
    and brave,
Shouting the battle-cry of Freedom;
And altho' they may be poor, not a man shall
    be a slave,
Shouting the battle-cry of Freedom.—Chorus

So we're springing to the call from the East and
    from the West,
Shouting the battle-cry of Freedom;
And we'll hurl the rebel crew from the land we
    love the best,
Shouting the battle-cry of Freedom.—Chorus
                                —GEORGE F. ROOT

XVI.10

TRAMP, TRAMP, TRAMP

This song, also by George Root, was even more popular with the soldiers than "The Battle-Cry of Freedom." It is a shining example of the sentimentalism of the Civil War generation, but it is worth noting that it has retained its popularity to this day, largely because of its lively tune.

In the prison cell I sit,
Thinking, mother dear, of you,

And our bright and happy home so far away,
And the tears they fill my eyes,
Spite of all that I can do,
Tho' I try to cheer my comrades and be gay.

Chorus: Tramp, tramp, tramp, the boys are marching,
Oh, cheer up, comrades, they will come,
And beneath the starry flag we shall breathe the
air again,
Of freedom in our own beloved home.

In the battle front we stood
When the fiercest charge they made,
And they swept us off a hundred men or more,
But before we reached their lines
They were beaten back dismayed,
And we heard the cry of vict'ry o'er and o'er.

So within the prison cell
We are waiting for the day
That shall come to open wide the iron door,
And the hollow eye grows bright,
And the poor heart almost gay,
As we think of seeing friends and home once more.
    —Chorus
                                —GEORGE F. ROOT

XVI.11

JUST BEFORE THE BATTLE, MOTHER

Here is another song from the adept pen of George Root. Better than most songs it lent itself to parody, one of the most widely sung of which ran:

Just before the battle, mother,
I was drinking mountain dew.
When I saw the Rebels marching,
To the rear I quickly flew.

It was widely sung in both armies, but appeared to be more popular in the South than in the North.

Just before the battle, mother,

I am thinking most of you;
While upon the field we are watching,
With the enemy in view.
Comrades brave are 'round me lying,
Filled with thoughts of home and God;
For well they know upon the morrow
Some will sleep beneath the sod.

Chorus: Farewell, mother, you may never
Press me to your heart again;
But, oh, you'll not forget me, mother,
If I'm numbered with the slain.

Oh! I long to see you, mother,
And the loving ones at home;
But I'll never leave our banner
'Till in honor I can come.
Tell the enemy around you
That their cruel words, we know,
In every battle kill our soldiers
By the help they give the foe.—Chorus

—GEORGE F. ROOT

XVI.12

TENTING TONIGHT

Like so many Civil War songs this one was almost equally popular on both sides. It was written by a New Hampshire singer, Walter Kittredge, who in 1861 had published a compilation of Union songs. Unable to find a publisher for "Tenting Tonight," he sang it himself in the army, and soon, despite its palpable defeatism, it had immense vogue.

We're tenting tonight on the old camp ground,
Give us a song to cheer our weary hearts,
A song of home, and the friends we love so dear.

Chorus: Many are the hearts that are weary
    tonight,
Wishing for the war to cease;
Many are the hearts looking for the right
To see the dawn of peace.
Tenting tonight, tenting tonight,
Tenting on the old camp ground.

We've been tenting tonight on the old camp
    ground,
Thinking of days gone by, of the loved ones at home
That gave us the hand, and the tear that said
    "goodbye!"
    —Chorus

We are tired of war on the old camp ground,
Many are dead and gone, of the brave and true
Who've left their homes, others been wounded long.
    —Chorus

We've been fighting today on the old camp ground,
Many are lying near; some are dead
And some are dying, many are in tears.

Last Chorus: Many are the hearts that are weary
    tonight,
    Wishing for the war to cease;
    Many are the hearts looking for the right,
    To see the dawn of peace.
    Dying tonight, dying tonight,
    Dying on the old camp ground.

—WALTER KITTREDGE

XVI.13

MARCHING THROUGH GEORGIA

Few other Civil War songs have had the enduring popularity of this, and probably no other has spread so widely over the globe. The Japanese played it when they entered Port Arthur, the British sang it in India, it was included in a British Soldiers' Songbook in the First World War, and was played and sung by British and Americans alike in the Second World War.

Henry Clay Work was the son of an abolitionist who had suffered imprisonment for his work on the underground railway in Illinois; he himself was active not only in antislavery but in temperance work as well, and among his better-known songs is the memorable "Father, Dear Father, Come Home with Me Now."

Bring the good old bugle, boys, we'll sing another
    song—
Sing it with a spirit that will start the world
    along—

Sing it as we used to sing it, fifty thousand
    strong,
While we were marching through Georgia.

Chorus: "Hurrah! Hurrah! we bring the
    jubilee!
Hurrah! Hurrah! the flag that makes you free!"
So we sang the chorus from Atlanta to the sea,
While we were marching through Georgia.

How the darkeys shouted when they heard
    the joyful sound!
How the turkeys gobbled which our commissary
    found!
How the sweet potatoes even started from the
    ground,
While we were marching through Georgia
    —Chorus

Yes, and there were Union men who wept
    with joyful tears,
When they saw the honored flag they had not seen
    for years;
Hardly could they be restrained from breaking forth
    in cheers,
While we were marching through Georgia.
    —Chorus

"Sherman's dashing Yankee boys will never reach
    the coast!"
So the saucy rebels said, and 'twas a handsome
    boast.
Had they not forgot, alas! to reckon with the host,
While we were marching through Georgia?
    —Chorus

So we made a thoroughfare for Freedom and her
    train,
Sixty miles in latitude—three hundred to the
    main;
Treason fled before us, for resistance was in vain,
While we were marching through Georgia.
    —Chorus

            —HENRY CLAY WORK

XVI.14

MISTER, HERE'S YOUR MULE

No introduction is needed for this and the following four items.
They remind us that Americans of the Civil War generation, for
all their sentimentalism, were able to laugh at themselves—and
at others. "Mister, Here's your Mule" was particularly popular in
the Western armies. "Do They Miss Me in the Trenches," written
by J. W. Naff of the 3rd Louisiana Infantry, is a parody on "Do
They Miss Me at Home." The vicissitudes of fighting in the Army
of the Potomac inspired the wry "We Are the Boys of Potomac's
Ranks," rehearsing the defeat of one Union general after another
in the mud and forests of northern Virginia. It was sung to the
tune of "When Johnny Comes Marching Home." The "goober
peas" of Pender's song are, of course, peanuts. "Grafted into the
Army" is something of a take-off both on the draft and on the
boys who tried, in vain, to avoid it.

A. Mister, Here's Your Mule

A farmer came to camp, one day, with milk and
    eggs to sell,
Upon a mule who oft would stray to where no one
    could tell,
The farmer, tired of his tramp, for hours was made a
    fool
By ev'ryone he met in camp, with "Mister, here's
    your mule."

Chorus: Come on, come on, come on, old man,
    and don't be made a fool,
      I'll tell the truth as best I can,
      John Morgan's got your mule.

His eggs and chickens all were gone before the
    break of day,
The mule was heard of all along—that's what the
    soldiers say;
And still he hunted all day long—alas! the witless
    fool—
While ev'ry man would sing the song, "Mister,
    here'syour mule."—Chorus

The soldiers now, in laughing mood, on mischief
    were intent,

They toted muly on their backs, around from tent
  to tent;
Through this hole and that they pushed his head,
  and made a rule
To shout with humorous voices all, "Mister, here's
  your mule."—Chorus

Alas! one day the mule was missed, ah! who could
  tell his fate?
The farmer, like a man bereft, searched early and
  searched late;
And as he passed from camp to camp, with stricken
  face, the fool
Cried out to ev'ryone he met, "Oh, Mister, where's
  my mule?"—Chorus
                                    —Author Unknown

B. Do They Miss Me in the Trenches?

Do they miss me in the trench, do they miss me
When the shells fly so thickly around?
Do they know that I've run down the hill-side
To look for my hole in the ground?
But the shells exploded so near me,
It seemed best for me to run;
And though some laughed as I crawfished,
I could not discover the fun.

I often get up in the trenches,
When some Yankee is near out of sight,
And fire a round or two at him,
To make the boys think that I'll fight.
But when the Yanks commence shelling,
I run to my home down the hill;
I swear my legs never will stay there,
Though all may stay there who will.

I'll save myself through the dread struggle,
And when the great battle is o'er,
I'll claim my full rations of laurels,
As always I've done heretofore.
I'll say that I've fought them as bravely
As the best of my comrades who fell,
And swear most roundly to all others
That I never had fears of a shell.
                                    —J. W. Naff

C. We Are the Boys of Potomac's Ranks

We are the boys of Potomac's ranks,
  Hurrah! Hurrah!
We are the boys of Potomac's ranks,
We ran with McDowell, retreated with Banks,
And we'll all drink stone blind—
Johnny, fill up the bowl.

We fought with McClellan, the Rebs, shakes, and
  fever,
  Hurrah! Hurrah!
We fought with McClellan, the Rebs, shakes, and
  fever,
But Mac joined the navy on reaching James River,
And we'll all drink stone blind—
Johnny, fill up the bowl.

They gave us John Pope, our patience to tax,
  Hurrah! Hurrah!
They gave us John Pope, our patience to tax,
Who said that out West he'd seen naught but *gray
  backs,*
And we'll all drink stone blind—
Johnny, fill up the bowl.

He said his headquarters were in the saddle,
  Hurrah! Hurrah!
He said his headquarters were in the saddle,
But Stonewall Jackson made him skedaddle
And we'll all drink stone blind—
Johnny, fill up the bowl.

Then Mac was recalled, but after Antietam,
  Hurrah! Hurrah!
Then Mac was recalled, but after Antietam
Abe gave him a rest, he was too slow to beat 'em,
And we'll all drink stone blind—
Johnny, fill up the bowl.

Oh, Burnside, then he tried his luck,
  Hurrah! Hurrah!
Oh, Burnside, then he tried his luck,
But in the mud so fast got stuck,
And we'll all drink stone blind—
Johnny, fill up the bowl.

Then Hooker was taken to fill the bill,
  Hurrah! Hurrah!
Then Hooker was taken to fill the bill,
But he got a black eye at Chancellorsville,
And we'll all drink stone blind—
Johnny, fill up the bowl.

Next came General Meade, a slow old plug,
  Hurrah! Hurrah!
Next came General Meade, a slow old plug,
For he let them get away at Gettysburg,
And we'll all drink stone blind—
Johnny, fill up the bowl.
                              —AUTHOR UNKNOWN

D. Goober Peas

Sitting by the roadside on a summer day,
Chatting with my messmates, passing time away,
Lying in the shadow underneath the trees,
Goodness, how delicious, eating goober peas!

Chorus: Peas! Peas! Peas! Peas! eating goober peas!
  Goodness, how delicious, eating goober peas!

When a horseman passes, the soldiers have a rule,
To cry out at their loudest, "Mister, here's your
  mule,"
But another pleasure enchantinger than these,
Is wearing out your grinders, eating goober peas!
    —Chorus

Just before the battle the General hears a row,
He says, "The Yanks are coming, I hear their rifles
  now,"
He turns around in wonder, and what do you think
  he sees?
The Georgia militia eating goober peas!
    —Chorus

I think my song has lasted almost long enough.
The subject's interesting, but the rhymes are
  mighty rough,
I wish this war was over, when free from rags and
  fleas,

We'd kiss our wives and sweethearts and gobble
  goober peas !
    —Chorus
                              —A. PENDER

E. Grafted into the Army

Our Jimmy has gone for to live in a tent,
They have grafted him into the army;
He finally pucker'd up courage and went,
When they grafted him into the army.
I told them the child was too young, alas!
At the captain's fore-quarters, they said he
  would pass—
They'd train him up well in the infantry class—
So they grafted him into the army.

Chorus: Oh, Jimmy farewell!
  Your brothers fell
  Way down in Alabarmy;
  I tho't they would spare a lone widder's heir,
  But they grafted him into the army.

Drest up in his unicorn—dear little chap;
They have grafted him into the army;
It seems but a day since he sot in my lap,
But they grafted him into the army.
And these are the trousies he used to wear—
Them very same buttons—the patch and the
  tear—
But Uncle Sam gave him a bran new pair
When they grafted him into the army.
    —Chorus

Now in my provisions I see him revealed—
They have grafted him into the army;
A picket beside the contented field,
They have grafted him into the army.
He looks kinder sickish—begins to cry—
A big volunteer standing right in his eye!
Oh what if the ducky should up and die,
Now they've grafted him into the army
    —Chorus
                              —HENRY CLAY WORK

XVI.15

LORENA

Almost forgotten now, "Lorena" was the most widely sung and the most popular of Civil War songs, and justly so, for, except for some of Stephen Foster's, no song of this decade had a lovelier melody. As with so many Civil War songs, the origin of "Lorena" is obscure. It has been as signed to one H. D. L. Webster, as early as 1850, but John Wyeth, historian of Forrest and author of *With Sabre and Scalpel,* gives it a different history:

"As we passed a home of the Trappist Brotherhood, Lieutenant Frank Brady entertained us by singing Lorena, a war time poem which had been set to music and was then very popular. He told us that the author of the poem was an inmate of this Trappist home. If this were so, and the self-imprisoned brother heard the sweet voice of the cavalier as he sang 'The Years creep slowly by, Lorena' what sad and tender memories it must have awakened."

The years creep slowly by, Lorena,
The snow is on the grass again;
The sun's low down the sky, Lorena,
The frost gleams where the flowers have been,
But the heart throbs on as warmly now,
As when the summer days were nigh;
Oh, the sun can never dip so low,
Adown affection's cloudless sky.
The sun can never dip so low,
Adown affection's cloudless sky.

A hundred months have passed, Lorena,
Since last I held that hand in mine;
And felt the pulse beat fast, Lorena,
Tho' mine beat faster far than thine.
A hundred months, 'twas flow'ry May,
When up the hilly slope we climbed,
To watch the dying of the day
And hear the distant church bells chime.
To watch the dying of the day
And hear the distant churchbells chime.

We loved each other then, Lorena,
More than we ever dared to tell;

And what we might have been, Lorena,
Had but our lovings prospered well—
But then, 'tis past, the years are gone,
I'll not call up their shadowy forms;
I'll say to them, "lost years, sleep on!
Sleep on! nor heed life's pelting storms."
I'll say to them, "lost years, sleep on!
Sleep onl nor heed life's pelting storms."

The story of that past, Lorena,
Alas! I care not to repeat
The hopes that could not last, Lorena,
They lived, but only lived to cheat.
I would not cause e'en one regret
To rankle in your bosom now;
For "if we *try,* we may forget,"
Were words of thine long years ago.
For "if we *try,* we may forget,"
Were words of thine long years ago.

Yes, these were words of thine, Lorena,
They burn within my memory yet;
They touched some tender chords, Lorena,
Which thrill and tremble with regret.
'Twas not thy woman's heart that spoke;
Thy heart was always true to me;
A duty, stern and pressing, broke
The tie which linked my soul with thee.
A duty, stern and pressing, broke
The tie which linked my soul with thee,

It matters little now, Lorena,
The past is in the eternal Past,
Our heads will soon lie low, Lorena,
Life's tide is ebbing out so fast.
There is a Future! O thank God!
Of life, this is so small a part!
'Tis dust to dust beneath the sod;
But there, *up there,* 'tis heart to heart.
'Tis dust to dust beneath the sod;
But there, *up there,* 'tis heart to heart.

—H. D. L. WEBSTER(?)

XVI.16

When Johnny Comes Marching Home

This song, more commonly associated with the Spanish American War, originated in the Civil War, but just when we do not know. It has been assigned to Father Louis Lambert, "the American Newman," who served as chaplain of the 18th Illinois Infantry, but the better claim seems to be that of the extraordinary Patrick Sarsfield Gilmore, Butler's bandmaster in New Orleans and organizer of the gigantic Peace Jubilee of 1869 which employed a chorus of ten thousand and an orchestra of one thousand pieces. The melody itself has entered deeply into American music: Burnet Tuthill wrote a series of variations on it for piano and wind instruments, and Roy Harris composed his *American Overture* on its theme.

When Johnny comes marching home again,
    hurrah, hurrah!
We'll give him a hearty welcome then,
    hurrah, hurrah!
The men will cheer, the boys will shout,
The ladies they will all turn out,

Chorus: And we'll all feel gay when Johnny comes
        marching home.
    And we'll all feel gay when Johnny comes
        marching home.

The old church bell will peal with joy,
    hurrah, hurrah!
To welcome home our darling boy, hurrah, hurrah!
The village lads and lassies say,
With roses they will strew the way,

Chorus: And we'll all feel gay when Johnny comes
        marching home.

Get ready for the Jubilee, hurrah, hurrah!
We'll give the hero three times three,
    hurrah, hurrah!
The laurel wreath is ready now
To place upon his loyal brow,

Chorus: And we'll all feel gay when Johnny comes
        marching home.

Let love and friendship on that day,
    hurrah, hurrah!
Their choicest treasures then display,
    hurrah, hurrah!
And let each one perform some part,
To fill with joy the warrior's heart,

Chorus: And we'll all feel gay when Johnny
        comes marching home.
    And we'll all feel gay when Johnny comes
        marching home.
                    —Patrick S. Gilmore (?)

XVII

POEMS OF THE CIVIL WAR

The Civil War was a time of great hope, personal anguish, and national pathos. The prose of speeches, frontline dispatches, letters, and newspaper editorials was often inadequate to convey the deep emotional import of the war and its impact on those who took part. Many turned to poetry, whether as an expression of national ambitions or a reflection of deep personal loss.

The quality of Civil War poetry was extremely mixed. It ranged from the sentimental to the patriotic to the profoundly moving to the outright bad. Some have found their way into the anthologies of great American poetry. Two of the greatest American poets—Henry Wadsworth Longfellow and Walt Whitman—applied their words to the Civil War.

Few of the poems in this chapter speak to the issues of the war or the conduct of the military campaigns (although there are many poems about these subjects). Henry Timrod's poems represented the perspective of the new and struggling Confederate nation and Walt Whitman spoke for the North when he wrote "O Captain! My Captain!" shortly after the assassination of Abraham Lincoln.

Poetry, however, was more often best applied to the issues that transcended the political and strategic issues of the day. Most of the poems that follow reveal little about the conduct of the war but they speak volumes on how the war affected the people who took part. For those who lived and died in the Civil War, the conflict was an individual experience, laced by profound emotions. The best of the Civil War poetry speaks to those personal experiences.

XVII.I

POET LAUREATE OF THE SOUTH

Known as the "Poet Laureate of the Confederacy," Henry Timrod threw himself and his words behind the Southern cause. Timrod had studied law as a young man with the Unionist James Louis Petigru and had his first book of poems published in Boston in 1860, but Timrod strongly believed in secession.

Timrod's literary work helped articulate the South's view of itself and its commitment to the Confederacy's most noble virtues. He wrote "Ethnogenesis" during the first Southern Congress in Montgomery in February, 1861, proclaiming "at last we are a nation among nations." The poem "Carolina" reflects the southern view that South Carolina was more a victim than a perpetrator of aggression.

Timrod enlisted briefly in the Confederate Army, but poor health led to his discharge. Illness and poverty afflicted him. He died two years after the Civil War. His "Ode" read at Magnolia Cemetery, Charleston, in April, 1867, was a melancholy companion piece to "Ethnogenesis," marking the demise of the Southern cause.

A. Ethnogenesis

I.

Hath not the morning dawned with added light?
And will not evening call another star
Out of the infinite regions of the night,
To mark this day in Heaven? At last, we are
A nation among nations; and the world
Shall soon behold in many a distant port
    Another Flag, unfurled!
Now, come what may, whose favor need we court?
And, under God, whose thunder need we fear?
    Thank Him who placed us here
Beneath so kind a sky—the very sun
Takes part with us; and on our errands run
All breezes of the ocean; dew and rain
Do noiseless battle for us; and the Year,

And all the gentle daughters in her train,
March in our ranks, and in our service wield
Long spears of golden grain!
A yellow blossom as her fairy shield,
June flings her azure banner to the wind,
While in the order of their birth
His sisters pass, and many an ample field
Grows white beneath their steps, till now, behold
Its endless sheets unfold
THE SNOW OF SOUTHERN SUMMERS! Let the earth
Rejoice! Beneath those fleeces soft and warm
Our happy land shall sleep
In a repose as deep
As if we lay intrenched behind
Whole leagues of Russian ice and Arctic
storm!

II.
And what if, mad with wrongs themselves have
wrought,
In their own treachery caught,
By their own fears made bold,
And leagued with him of old,
Who long since in the limits of the North
Set up his evil throne, and warred with God—
What if, both mad blinded in their rage,
Our foes should fling us down their mortal gage,
And with a hostile step profane our sod!
We shall not shrink, my brothers, but go forth
To meet them, marshalled by the Lord of Hosts,
And overshadowed by the mighty ghosts
Of Moultrie and of Eutaw—who shall foil
Auxiliars such as these? Nor these alone
But every stock and stone
Shall help us: but the very soil,
And all the generous wealth it gives to toil,
And all for which we love our noble land,
Shall fight beside, and through us, sea and strand,
The heart of woman, and her hand,
Tree, fruit, and flower, and every influence,
Gentle, grave, or grand;
The winds of our defence
Shall seem to blow; to us the hills shall lend
Their firmness and their calm;

And in our stiffened sinews we shall blend
The strength of pine and palm!

III.
Nor should we shun the battle-ground,
Though weak as we are strong;
Call up the clashing elements around,
And test the right and wrong!
On one side, creeds that dare to teach
What Christ and Paul refrained to preach;
Codes built upon a broken pledge,
And Charity that whets a poniard's edge;
Fair schemes that leave the neighboring poor
To starve and shiver at the schemer's door,
While in the world's most liberal ranks enrolled,
He turns some vast philanthropy to gold;
Religion, taking every mortal form
But that a pure and Christian faith makes warm,
Where not to vile fanatic passion urged,
Or not in vague philosophies submerged,
Repulsive with a Pharisaic leaven,
And making laws to stay the laws of Heaven!
And on the other, scorn of sordid gain,
Unblemished honor, truth without a stain,
Faith, justice, reverence, charitable wealth,
And, for the poor and humble, laws which give,
Not the mean right to buy the right to live,
But life, and home, and health!
To doubt the end were want of trust in God,
Who, if he has decreed
That we must pass a redder sea
Than that which rang to Miriam's holy glee,
Will surely raise at need
A Moses with his rod!

IV.
But let our fears—if fears we have—be still,
And turn us to the future! Could we climb
Some mighty Alp, and view the coming time,
We should indeed behold a sight to fill
Our eyes with happy tears!
Not for the glories which a hundred years
Shall bring us; not for lands from sea to sea,
And wealth, and power, and peace, though these
shall be;

But for the distant peoples we shall bless,
And the hushed murmurs of a world's distress:
For, to give labor to the poor,
    The whole sad plant o'er,
And save from want and crime the humblest door,
Is one among the many ends for which
    God makes us great and rich!
The hour perchance is not yet wholly ripe
When all shall own it, but the type
Whereby we shall be known in every land
Is that vast gulf which laves our Southern strand,
And through the cold, untempered ocean pours
Its genial streams, that far off Arctic shores
May sometimes catch upon the softened
    breeze
Strange tropic warmth and hints of
    summer seas.

                —HENRY TIMROD

B. Carolina

The despot treads thy sacred sands,
Thy pines give shelter to his bands,
Thy sons stand by with idle hands,
    Carolina!
He breathes at ease thy airs of balm,
He scorns the lances of thy palm;
Oh! Who shall break thy craven calm,
    Carolina!
Thy ancient fame is growing dim,
A spot is on thy garment's rim;
Give to the winds thy battle-hymn,
    Carolina!

Call on thy children of the hill,
Wake swamp and river, coast, and rill,
Rouse all thy strength and all thy skill,
    Carolina!
Cite wealth and science, trade and art,
Touch with they fire the cautious mart,
And pour thee through the people's heart,
    Carolina!
Till even the coward spurns his fears,
And all thy fields, and fens, and meres

Shall bristle like thy palm with spears,
    Carolina!

I hear a murmur as of waves
That grope their way through sunless caves,
Like bodies struggling in their graves,
    Carolina!
And now it deepens; slow and grand
It swells, as, rolling to the land,
An ocean broke upon thy strand,
    Carolina!
Shout! Let it reach the startled Huns!
And roar with all thy festal guns!
It is the answer of thy sons,
    Carolina!

                —HENRY TIMROD

C. Ode

Sleep sweetly in your humble graves,
    Sleep, martyrs of a fallen cause;
Though yet no marble column craves
    The pilgrim here to pause.

In seeds of laurel in earth
    The blossom of your fame is blown,
And somewhere, waiting for its birth,
    The shaft is in the stone!
Meanwhile, behalf the tardy years
    Which keep in trust your storied tombs,
Behold! Your sisters bring their tears,
    And these memorial blooms.

Small tributes! but your shades will smile
    More proudly on these wreaths to-day,
Than when some cannon-moulded pile
    Shall overlook this bay.

Stoop, angels, hither from the skies!
    There is no holier spot of ground
Than where defeated valor lies,
    By mourning beauty crowned.

                —HENRY TIMROD

XVII.2

THE DEATH OF SLAVERY

Northern poets had a very different take on the motivations of the war. William Cullen Bryant, author of "Thatatopsis" and "To a Waterfowl," was one of the leading journalists of his day. As an influential newspaper editor, he was an ardent and vocal abolitionist. Like many of his brethren, Bryant viewed the Civil War as an opportunity to end slavery in the United States once and for all.

"The Death of Slavery" echoes John Brown's last speech before his execution, in which he condemned slavery as a great crime which the nation—and particularly the South—was paying for through the bloody conflict. It was one of many Northern abolitionist poems such as "Formerly a Slave" by Herman Melville, "Boston Hymn" by Ralph Waldo Emerson, "Battle Hymn of the Republic" by Julia Ward Howe, "Battle Cry of Freedom" by George F. Root, and "Laus Deo!" by John Greenleaf Whittier that state emancipation as a war goal.

O thou great Wrong, that, through the slow-paced
 years,
  Didst old thy millions fettered, and didst wield
  The scourge that drove the laborer to the field,
And turn a stony gaze on human tears,
  Thy cruel reign is o'er;
  Thy bondmen crouch no more
In terror at the menace of thine eye;
  For He who marks the bounds of guilty power,
Long-suffering, hath heard the captive's cry,
  And touched his shackles at the appointed hour,
And lo! They fall, and he whose limbs they galled
Stands in his native manhood, disenthralled.

A shout of joy from the redeemed is sent;
  Ten thousand hamlets swell the hymn of
  thanks;
  Our rivers roll exulting, and their banks
Send up hosannas to the firmament!
  Fields where the bondman's toil
  No more shall trench the soil,
Seem now to bask in a serener day;
  The meadow-birds sing sweeter, and the airs
Of heaven with more caressing softness play,
  Welcoming man to liberty like theirs.

A glory clothes the land from sea to sea,
For the great land and all its coasts are free.

Within that land wert thou enthroned of late,
  And they by whom the nation's laws were
  made,
  And they who filled its judgment-seats obeyed
Thy mandate, rigid as the will of Fate.
  Fierce men at thy right hand,
  With gesture of command,
Gave forth the word that none might dare gainsay;
  And grave and reverend ones, who loved the
  not,
Shrank from thy presence, and in blank dismay
  Choked down, unuttered, the rebellious
  thought;
While meaner cowards, mingling with thy train,
Proved, from the book of God, thy right to reign.

Great as thou wert, and feared from shore to shore,
  The wrath of Heaven o'ertook thee in thy
  pride;
  Thou sitt'st a ghastly shadow; by thy side
Thy once strong arms hang nerveless evermore.
  And they who quailed but now
  Before thy lowering brow,
Devote thy memory to scorn and shame,
  And scoff at the pale, powerless thing thou art.
And they who ruled in thine imperial name,
  Subdued, and standing sullenly apart,
Scowl at the hands that overthrew thy reign,
And shattered at a blow the prisoner's chain.
Well was thy doom deserved; thou didst not spare
  Life's tenderest ties, but cruelly didst part
  Husband and wife, and from the mother's heart
Didst wrest her children, deaf to shriek and prayer;
  Thy inner lair became
  The haunt of guilty shame;
Thy lash dropped blood; the murderer, at thy side,
  Showed his red hands, nor feared the
  vengeance due.
Thou didst sow earth with crimes, and, far and wide,
  A harvest of uncounted miseries grew,
Until the measure of thy sins at last
Was full, and then the avenging bolt was cast!

Go now, accursed of God, and take thy place
    With hateful memories of the elder time,
    With many a wasting plague, and nameless
        crime,
And bloody war that thinned the human race;
    With the Black Death, whose way
    Through wailing cities lay,
Worship of Moloch, tyrannies that built
    The Pyramids, and cruel creeds that taught
To avenge a fancied guilt by deeper guilt—
    Death at the stake to those that held them not.
Lo! The foul phantoms, silent in the gloom
Of the flown ages, part to yield thee room.

I see the better years that hasten by
    Carry thee back into that shadowy past,
    Where, in the dusty spaces, void and vast,
The graves of those whom thou hast murdered lie.
    The slave-pen, through whose door
    Thy victims pass no more,
Is there, and there shall the grim black remain
    At which the slave was sold; while at thy feet
Scourges and engines of restraint and pain
    Moulder and rust by thine eternal seat.
There, mid the symbols that proclaim thy crimes,
Dwell thou, a warning to the coming times.
             —William Cullen Bryant

XVII.3

Barbara Frietchie

One of the great patriotic poems of the Civil War, "Barbara Frietchie" celebrated the courage of a ninety-year-old woman who refused to take down her American flag in the face of hostile invading Confederate soldiers. John Greenleaf Whittier was a Quaker and an abolitionist dedicated to the Northern cause. In the poem, Whittier salutes Frietchie's bravery as well as the gallantry of Confederate general Thomas "Stonewall" Jackson—when Frietchie stands steadfast against calls from Confederate troops to lower the Union flag, Jackson vows that any soldier who harms Frietchie "dies like a dog."

    Whittier wrote the poem in 1863. He claimed it was based on a real event. True or not, "Barbara Frietchie" has found a place in many anthologies of American poetry and is memorized by many students. It is one of the best-known American poems.

Up from the meadows rich with corn,
Clear in the cool September morn,

The clustered spires of Frederick stand
Green-walled by the hills of Maryland.

Round about them orchards sweep,
Apple and peach tree fruited deep,

Fair as the garden of the Lord
To the eyes of the famished rebel horde,

On that pleasant morn of the early fall
When Lee marched over the mountain-wall;

Over the mountains winding down,
Horse and foot, into Frederick town.

Forty flags with their silver stars,
Forty flags with their crimson bars,

Flapped in the morning wind: the sun
Of noon looked down, and saw not one.

Up rose old Barbara Frietchie then,
Bowed with her fourscore years and ten;

Bravest of all in Frederick town,
She took up the flag the men hauled down;

In her attic window the staff she set,
To show that one heart was loyal yet.

Up the street came the rebel tread,
Stonewall Jackson riding ahead.

Under his slouched hat left and right
He glanced; the old flag met his sight.

"Halt!"—the dust-brown ranks stood fast.
"Fire!"—out blazed the rifle-blast.

It shivered the window, pane and sash;
It rent the banner with seam and gash.

Quick, as it fell, from the broken staff
Dame Barbara snatched the silken scarf.

She leaned far out on the window will,
And shook it forth with a royal will.

"Shoot, if you must, this old gray head,
But spare your country's flag," she said.

A shade of sadness, a blush of shame,
Over the face of the leader came;

The nobler nature within him stirred
To life at the woman's deed and word;

"Who touches a hair of yon gray head
Dies like a dog! March on!" he said.

All day long through Frederick street
Sounded the tread of marching feet:

All day long that free flag tost
Over the heads of the rebel host.

Ever its torn folds rose and fell
On the loyal winds that loved it well;

And through the hill-gaps sunset light
Shone over it with a warm good night.

Barbara Frietchie's work is o'er,
And the Rebel rides on his raids no more.

Honor to her! And let a tear
Fall, for her sake, on Stonewall's bier.

Over Barbara Frietchie's grave,
Flag of Freedom and Union, wave!

Peace and order and beauty draw
Round thy symbol of light and law;

And ever the stars above look down
On thy stars below in Frederick town!

—John Greenleaf Whittier

XVII.4

"Oh, Mother, Look Down From Heav'n on me"

The sudden and traumatic deaths of young men and boys in battle affected all Americans. The causes of war varied, but the grief was singular and universal, shared by North and South. While newspapers and speechmakers covered the grand sweeping events of the war, poets expressed the great personal losses that individuals suffered. This was a subject that transcended patriotic loyalty.

No poem illustrated this better than Will "Shakespeare" Hays' "The Drummer Boy of Shiloh." Hays wrote the poem shortly after the Battle of Shiloh in 1862. It describes the death of a Yankee drummer boy killed at Shiloh, the bloodiest battle in American history up to that point. Hays, however, does not identify his young hero as being either a Yankee or a Confederate. The sentimental poem, which was set to music, gained wide popularity in both northern and southern states.

The following three poems also speak to the deaths of soldiers in battle. "Little Giffen" by the Southern poet and physician Francis Orrery Ticknor was about a young Confederate soldier wounded at the Battle of Murfreesboro. Ticknor helped restore Giffen's health, but the boy was killed in a later battle. Henry Wadsworth Longellow, America's most popular poet at the time, recounts in "Killed at the Ford" the death of a young man in an isolated incident at the front and its impact for those who survive him. Walt Whitman touches upon a similar theme in "Vigil Strange I Kept on the Field One Night" and "Come Up From The Fields Father." Despite being very pro-Union, the poet and diplomat George Henry Boker laments the loss of life on both sides of the war in "Dirge for a Soldier."

A. The Drummer Boy of Shiloh

Oh Shiloh's dark and bloody ground, the dead and
    wounded lay.
Amongst them was a drummer boy, that beat the
    drum that day.
A wounded soldier raised him up, His drum was by
    his side.
He clasped his hands and raised his eyes and prayed
    before he died:
Look down upon the battle field, Oh Thou, our
    Heav'nly friend,
Have mercy on our sinful souls. The soldiers cried,
    "Amen."

For gather'd round a little group, Each brave man
    knelt and cried.
They listened to the drummer boy who prayed
    before he died.

"Oh, Mother," said the dying boy, "look down from
    Heav'n on me,
Receive me to thy fond embrace, Oh take me
    home to thee.
I've loved my country as my god, To serve them
    both I've tried."
He smiled, shook hands. Death seized the boy who
    prayed before he died.

Each soldier wept then like a child, Stout hearts
    were they and brave.
The flag his winding sheet, God's book the key
    unto his grave.
They wrote upon a simple board these words "This
    is a guide
To those who mourn the drummer boy who prayed
    before he died."
                 —WILL "SHAKESPEARE" HAYS

B. Little Giffen

Out of the focal and foremost fire,
Out of the hospital walls as dire,
Smitten of grape shot and gangrene
(Eighteenth battle and he sixteen)—
Spectre such as you seldom see,
Little Giffen of Tennessee.

"Take him—and welcome!" the surgeons said,
"Little the doctor can help the dead!"
So we took him and brought him where
The balm was sweet on the summer air;
And we laid him down on a wholesome bed—
Utter Lazarus, heel to head!

And we watched the ware with bated breath—
Skeleton Boy against skeleton Death.
Months of torture, how many such!
Weary weeks of the stick and crutch;
And still a glint in the steel blue eye
Told of a spirit that wouldn't die.

And didn't. Nay, more! In death's despite
The crippled skeleton learned to write.
"Dear Mother," at first of course; and then
"Dear Captain," inquiring about "the men."
Captain's answer: Of eighty and five,
Giffen and I are left alive."

Word of gloom from the war one day:
"Johnston's pressed at the front, they say!"
Little Giffen was up and away;
A tear—his first as he bade good-bye,
Dimmed the flint of his steel blue eye.
"I'll write, if spared!" There was news of the fight;
But none of Giffen—he did not write.

I sometimes fancy that, were I king
Of the princely knights of the Golden Ring,
With the song of the minstrel in mine ear,
And the tender legend that trembles here,
I'd give the best, on his bended knee,
The whitest soul of my chivalry,
For Little Giffen of Tennessee.
                 —FRANCIS ORRERY TICKNOR

C. Killed at the Ford

He is dead, the beautiful youth,
The heart of honor, the tongue of truth,
He, the life and light of us all,
Whose voice was blithe as a bugle-call,
Whom all eyes followed with one consent,
The cheer of whose laugh, and whose pleasant
    word,
Hushed all murmurs of discontent.

Only last night, as we rode along,
Down the dark of the mountain gap,
To visit the picket-guard at the ford,
Little dreaming of any mishap,
He was humming the words of some old song:
"Two red roses he had on his cap
And another he bore at the point of his sword."

Sudden and swift a whistling ball
Came out of a wood, and the voice was still;
Something I heard in the darkness fall,

And for a moment my blood grew chill;
I spake in a whisper, as he who speaks
In a room where some one is lying dead;
But he made no answer to what I said.

We lifted him to his saddle again,
And through the mire and the mist and the rain
Carried him back to the silent camp,
And laid him as if asleep on his bed;
And I saw by the light of the surgeon's lamp
Two white roses upon his cheeks,
And one, just over his heart, blood red!

And I saw in a vision how far and fleet
That fatal bullet went speeding forth,
Till it reached a town in the distant North,
Till it reach a house in a sunny street,
Till it reach a heart that ceased to beat
Without a murmur, without a cry;
And a bell was tolled, in that far-off town,
For one who had passed from cross to crown,
And the neighbors wondered that she
    should die.

—Henry Wadsworth Longfellow

D. Vigil Strange I Kept on the Field One Night

Vigil strange I kept on the field one night;
When you my son and my comrade dropt at my
    side that day,
One look I but gave which your dear eyes return'd
    with a look I shall never forget,
One touch of your hand to mine O boy, reach'd up
    as you lay on the ground,
Then onward I sped in the battle, the even-con-
    tested battle,
Till late in the night reliev'd to the place at last
    again I made my way,
Found you in death so cold dear comrade, found
    your body son of responding kisses, (never again
    on earth responding,)
Bared your face in the starlight, curious the scene,
    cool blew the moderate night-wind,
Long there and then in vigil I stood, dimly around
    me the battlefield spreading,

Vigil wondrous and vigil sweet there in the fragrant
    silent night,
But not a tear fell, not even a long drawn-sigh,
    long, long I gazed,
Then on the earth partially reclining sat by your
    side leaning my chin in my hands,
Passing sweet hours, immortal and mystic hours
    with you dearest comrade—not a tear, not a
    word,
Vigil of silence, love and death, vigil for you my
    son and my soldier,
As onward silently stars aloft, eastward new ones
    upward stole,
Vigil final for you brave boy, (I could not save you,
    swift was your death,
I faithfully loved you and cared for you living, I
    think we shall surely meet again,)
Till at latest lingering of the night, indeed just as
    the dawn appear'd,
My comrade I wrapt in his blanket, envelop'd well
    his form,
Folded the blanket well, tucking carefully over
    head and carefully under feet.
And there and then and bathed by the raising sun,
    my son in his grave, in his rude-dug grave I
    deposited,
Ending my vigil strange with that, vigil of night
    and battlefield dim,
Vigil for boy of responding kisses, (never again on
    earth responding,)
Vigil for comrade swiftly slain, vigil I never forget,
    how as day brighten'd,
I rose from the chill ground and folded my soldier
    well in his blanket,
And buried him where he fell.

—Walt Whitman

E. Come Up From the Fields Father

Come up from the fields father, here's a letter from
    our Pete,
And come to the front door mother, here's a letter
    from thy dear son.
Lo, 'tis autumn,
Lo where the trees, deeper green, yellower and
    redder,

Cool and sweeten Ohio's villages with leaves flut-
    tering in the moderate wind,
Where apples ripe in the orchards hang and grapes
    on the trellis'd vines,
(Smell you the smell of the grapes of the vines?
Smell you the buckwheat where the bees were late-
    ly buzzing?)

Above all, lo, the sky so calm, so transparent after
    the rain, and with wondrous clouds,
Below too, all calm, all vital and beautiful, and the
    farm prospers well.
Down in the fields all prospers well,
But now from the fields come father, come at the
    daughter's call,
And come to the entry mother, to the front door
    come right away.

Fast as she can she hurries, something ominous, her
    steps trembling,
She does not tarry to smooth her hair nor adjust
    her cap.
Open the envelope quickly,
O this is not our son's writing, yet his name is sign'd,
O strange hand writes for our dear son, O stricken
    mother's soul!
All swims before her eyes, flashes with black, she
    catches the main words only,
Sentences broken, gunshot wound in the breast,
    cavalry skirmish, taken to hospital,
At present low, but will soon be better.

Ah now the single figure to me,
Amid all teeming and wealthy Ohio with all its
    cities and farms,
Sickly white in the face and dull in the head, very
    faint,
By the jamb of a door leans.

Grieve not so, dear mother, (the just-grown
    daughter speaks through her sobs,
The little sisters huddle around speechless and dis-
    may'd,)
See, dearest mother, the letter says Pete will soon
    be better.

Alas, poor boy, he will never be better, (nor may-be
    needs to be better that brave and simple soul,)
While they stand at home at the door, he is dead
    already,
The only son is dead.

But the mother needs to be better,
She with thin form presently drest in black,
By day her meals untouch'd, then at night fitfully
    sleeping, often waking,
In the midnight waking, weeping, longing with one
    deep longing,
O that she might withdraw unnoticed, silent from
    life escape and withdraw,
To follow, to seek, to be with her dear dead son.
                       —WALT WHITMAN

F. Dirge for a Soldier

Close his eyes; his work is done!
    What to him is friend or foeman,
Rise of moon, or set of sun,
    Hand of man, or kiss of woman?
    Lay him low, lay him low,
    In the clover or the snow!
    What cares he? He cannot know:
        Lay him low!

As man may, he fought his fight,
    Proved his truth by his endeavor;
Let him sleep in solemn night,
    Sleep forever and forever.
    Lay him low, lay him low,
    In the clover or the snow!
    What cares he? He cannot know:
        Lay him low!

Fold him in his country's stars,
    Roll the drum and fire the volley!
What to him are all our wars,
    What but death-bemocking folly?
Lay him low, lay him low,
    In the clover or the snow!
    What cares he? He cannot know:
        Lay him low!

Leave him to God's watching eye;
 Trust him to the hand that made him.
Mortal love weeps idly by:
 God alone has power to aid him.
Lay him low, lay him low,
 In the clover or the snow!
 What cares he? He cannot know:
  Lay him low!

     —George Henry Boker

XVII.5

The Honored General

Civil War poets often wrote of the heroism of soldiers in battle. Perhaps no man received as much praise as Robert E. Lee. John Reuben Thompson, editor and owner of the *Southern Literary Messenger*, wrote of a famous incident during the Battle of the Wilderness in 1864 when Lee attempted to lead his soldiers in a bold charge to prevent their defeat. Despite the general's order, the soldiers refused to make the attack until Lee withdrew to safety, such was their affection for the revered leader. They then went on to charge the Union army and save the day.

 Even the North came to honor Lee. Of all people, Julia Ward Howe (1819-1910) wrote a poem commemorating Lee. Howe, who wrote the inspiring "Battle Hymn of the Republic" urging soldiers to "die to make men free" in battle against Lee's army, penned "Robert E. Lee" as a tribute to the general after the war.

A. Lee to the Rear

Dawn of a pleasant morning in May
Broke through the Wilderness cool and gray;
While perched in the tallest tree-tops, the birds
Were carolling Mendelssohn's "Song without
 Words."

Far from the haunts of men remote,
The brook brawled on with a liquid note;
And Nature, all tranquil and lovely, wore
The smile of the spring, as in Eden of yore.

Little by little, as daylight increased,
And deepened the roseate flush in the East—
Little by little did morning reveal
Two long glittering lines of steel;

Where two hundred thousand bayonets gleam,
Tipped with the light of the earliest beam,
And the faces are sullen and grim to see
In the hostile armies of Grant and Lee.

All of a sudden, ere rose the sun,
Pealed on the silence the opening gun—
A little white puff of smoke there came,
And anon the valley was wreathed in flame.

Down on the left of the Rebel lines,
Where a breastwork stands in a copse of pines,
Before the Rebels their ranks can form,
The Yankees have carried the place by storm.

Stars and Stripes on the salient wave,
Where many a hero has found a grave,
And the gallant Confederates strive in vain
The ground they have drenched with their blood,
 to regain.

Yet louder the thunder of battle roared—
Yet a deadlier fire on the columns poured;
Slaughter infernal rode with Despair,
Furies twain, through the murky air.

Not far off, in the saddle there sat
A gray-bearded man in a black-slouched hat;
Not much moved by the fire was he,
Calm and resolute Robert E. Lee.

Quick and watchful he kept his eye
On the bold Rebel brigades close by—
Reserves that were standing (and dying) at ease,
While the tempest of wrath toppled over the trees.

For still with their loud, deep, bull-dog bay,
The Yankee batteries blazed away,
And with every murderous second that sped
A dozen brave fellows, alas! Fell dead.

The grand old graybeard rode to the space
Where Death and his victims stood face to face,
And silently waved his old slouched hat—
A world meaning there was in that!

"Follow me! Steady! We'll save the day!"
This was what he seemed to say;
And to the light of his glorious eye
The bold brigades thus made reply:

"We'll go forward, but you must go back"—
And they moved not an inch in the perilous track:
"Go to the rear, and we'll send them to hell!"
And the sound of the battle was lost in their yell.

Turning his bridle, Robert Lee
Rode to the rear. Like waves of the sea,
Bursting the dikes in their overflow,
Madly his veterans dashed on the foe.

And backward in terror that foe was driven,
Their banners rent and their columns riven,
Wherever the tide of battle rolled
Over the Wilderness, wood and wold.

Sunset out of a crimson sky
Streamed o'er a field of ruddier dye,
And the brook ran on with a purple stain,
From the blood of ten thousand foeman slain.

Seasons have passed since that day and year—
Again o'er its pebbles the brook runs clear,
And the field in a richer green is drest
Where the dead of a terrible conflict rest.

Hushed is the roll of the Rebel drum,
The sabres are sheathed, and the cannon are dumb;
And Fate, with his pitiless hand, has furled
The flag that once challenged the gaze of the
    world;

But the fame of the Wilderness fight abides;
And down into history grandly rides,
Calm and unmoved as in battle he sat,
The gray-bearded man in the black slouched hat.
                    —JOHN REUBEN THOMPSON

B. Robert E. Lee

A gallant foeman in the fight,
A brother when the fight was o'er,

The hand that led the host with ⌐
The blessed torch of learning bor⌐
Thought may the minds of men ⌐
Love makes the heart of nations ⌐
And so, thy soldier grave beside,
We honor thee, Virginia's son.⌐
                    —JULIA WARD HOWE

——— XVII.6 ———

O CAPTAIN! MY CAPTAIN!

The assassination of Abraham Lincoln at the end of the war was a great shock to the North. After years of bloody conflict, Lincoln's embattled leadership came to a sudden end at Ford's Theater just as the war ended in victory. Tens of thousands of people lined the railroad to mourn Lincoln as the train carrying his body made its way to Springfield, Illinois, for his burial. Hundreds of writers expressed the nation's grief, none more eloquently than Walt Whitman in his poems "O Captain! My Captain!" (included below) and the much longer "When Lilacs Last in the Dooryard Bloom'd."

O Captain! My Captain! our fearful trip is done,
The ship has weather'd every rack, the prize we
    sought is won,
The port is near, the bells I hear, the people all
    exulting,
While follow eyes the steady keel, the vessel grim
    and daring;
But O heart! Heart! Heart!
    O the bleeding drops of red,
            Where on the deck my Captain lies,
                Fallen cold and dead.

O Captain! my Captain! rise up and hear the bells;
Rise up—for you the flag is flung—for you the
    bugle trills,
For you bouquets and ribbon'd wreaths—for you
    the shore a-crowding,
For you they call, the swaying mass, their eager
    faces turning;
Here Captain! dear father!
    The arm beneath your head!
            It is some dream that on the deck,
                You've fallen cold and dead.

XVII. *Poems of the Civil War*

My Captain does not answer, his lips are pale and
    still,
My father does not feel my arm, he has no pulse
    nor will,
The ship is anchor'd safe and sound, its voyage
    closed and done,
From fearful trip the victor ship comes in with
    object won:
Exult O shores, and ring O bells!
    But I with mournful tread,
        Walk the deck my Captain lies,
           Fallen cold and dead.
                —Walt Whitman

XVII.7

DRIVING HOME THE COWS

When the war ended, many families did not know the fate of their
sons, husbands and fathers. It could take weeks, months or even
years for news to get back home. Communication was limited to
word of mouth and the mail, which was notoriously unreliable,
especially in the South. In the confusion of battle, armies often lost
track of their own men and many simply disappeared—it was
often unclear whether as prisoners of war, deserters or fatalities.

The poem "Driving Home the Cows" by Kate Putnam
Osgood addresses the bittersweet experience of one northern
farmer whose three sons went to war.

Out of the clover and blue-eyed grass,
    He turned them into the river-lane;
One after another he let them pass,
    Then fastened the meadow-bars again.
Under the willows, and over the hill,
    He patiently followed their sober pace;
The merry whistle for once was still,
    And something shadowed the sunny face.

Only a boy! And his father had said
    He never could let his youngest go:
Two already were lying dead
    Under the feet of the trampling foe.

But after the evening work was done,
    And the frogs were loud in the meadow-swamp,

Over his shoulder he slung his gun,
    And stealthily followed the foot-path damp,

Across the clover, and through the wheat,
    With resolute heart and purpose grim,
Though cold was the dew on his hurrying feet,
    And the blind bat's flitting startled him.

Thrice since then had the lanes been white,
    And the orchards sweet with apple-bloom;
And now, when the cows came back at night,
    The feeble father drove them home.

For news had come to the lonely farm
    That three were lying where two had lain;
And the old man's tremulous, palsied arm
    Could never lean on a son's again.

The summer day grew cold and late.
    He went for the cows when the work was done:
But down the lane, as he opened the gate,
    He saw them coming, one by one—

Brindle, Ebony, Speckle, and Bess,
    Shaking their horns in the evening wind;
Cropping the buttercups out of the grass—
    But who was it following close behind?

Loosely swung in the idle air
    The empty sleeve of army blue;
And worn and pale, from the crisping hair,
    Looked out a face that the father knew.

For Southern prisons will sometimes yawn,
    And yield their dead until life again;
And the day that comes with a cloudy dawn
    In golden glory must at last wane.

The great tears sprang to their meeting eyes;
    For the heart must speak when the lips are dumb;
And under the silent evening skies,
    Together they followed the cattle home.
                —KATE PUTNAM OSGOOD

XVII.8

THE ARTILLERYMAN'S VISION

Of all the great 19th century American writers, none were touched by the war as deeply as Walt Whitman. In December, 1862, Whitman went to Washington, D.C., in search of his brother, who had been wounded at Fredericksburg. Whitman found his brother, who eventually recovered from his wounds. But Whitman was overwhelmed by what he experienced at the hospitals. He started visiting wounded soldiers, helping to tend to their needs, write letters for them and simply keep them company.

"I have been almost daily calling as a missionary," he wrote, "distributing now & then little sums of money—and regularly letter-paper and envelopes, oranges, tobacco, jellies, &c. &c." Whitman estimated that he made 600 visits to hospitals and convalescent camps.

Whitman wrote articles for newspapers, kept a journal, and wrote many poems about the lives and experiences of the men he tended. Although he once famously wrote "the real war will never get into the books," Whitman published four collections of writings—*Drum-Taps* (1865), *Sequel to Drum-Taps* (1865-66), *Memoranda During the War* (1875-76), and *Specimen Days* (1882-83)—about the Civil War and those who lived it.

In 1888, a friend asked Whitman of his Civil War experiences: "Do you ever go back to those days?" Whitman replied: "I do not need to. I have never left them." As "The Artilleryman's Vision" displays and veterans to the present day attest, the trauma of combat lingers well past war's conclusion.

While my wife at my side lies slumbering, and the
    wars are over long,
And my head on the pillow rests at home, and the
    vacant midnight passes,
And through the stillness, through the dark, I hear,
    I just hear, the breath of my infant,
There in the room as I wake from sleep this vision
    presses upon me;
The engagement opens there and then in fantasy
    unreal,
The skirmishes begin, they crawl curiously ahead, I
    hear the irregular snap! Snap!
I hear the sounds of the different missiles, the short
    t-h-t! t-h-t! of the rifle balls,

I see the shells exploding leaves small white clouds,
    I hear the great shells shrieking as they pass,
The grape like the hum and whirr of wind through
    the trees, (tumultuous now the contest rages,)
All the scenes at the batteries rise in detail before
    me again,
The crashing and smoking, the pride of the men in
    their pieces,
The chief-gunner ranges and sights his piece and
    selects a fuse of the right time,
After firing I see him lean aside and look eagerly
    off to note the effect;
Elsewhere I hear the cry of a regiment charging,
    (the young colonel leads himself this time with
    brandish'd sword,)
I see the gaps cut by the enemy's volley, (quickly
    fill'd up, no delay,)
I breathe the suffocating smoke, then the flat
    clouds hover low concealing all;
Now a strange lull for a few seconds, not a shot
    fired on either side,
Then resumed the chaos louder than ever, with
    eager calls and orders of officers
While some distant part of the field the wind wafts
    to my ears a shout of applause, (some special
    success,)
And ever the sound of the cannon far or near,
    (rousing even in dreams a devilish exultation
    and all the old mad joy in the depth of my
    soul,)
And ever the hastening of infantry shifting posi-
    tions, batteries, cavalry, moving hither and
    thither,
(The falling, dying, I heed not, the wounded drip-
    ping and red I heed not, some to the rear are
    hobbling,)
Grime, hear, rush, aides-de-camp galloping by or on
    a full run,
With the patter of small arms, the warning s-s-t of
    the rifles, (these in my vision I hear or see,)
And bombs bursting in air, and at night the vari-
    color'd rockets.

—WALT WHITMAN

THE CONQUERED BANNER

The end of the Civil War was especially difficult for soldiers of the South. In addition to the trials of war and losses in battle, Southern veterans faced the indignity of defeat. There was little solace in having lost life or limb for a lost cause.

Abram Joseph Ryan was a Catholic priest who served as a chaplain in the Confederate Army. His poem, "The Conquered Banner," became one of the most popular Confederate poems of the war.

Furl that Banner, for 'tis weary;
Round its staff 'tis drooping dreary;
 Furl it, fold it—it is best;
For there's not a man to wave it,
And there's not a sword to save it,
And there's not one left to lave it
In the blood which heroes gave it;
And its foes now scorn and brave it;
 Furl it, hide it—let it rest!

Take that banner down! 'tis tattered;
Broken is its staff and shattered;
And the valiant hosts are scattered,
 Over whom it floated high.
Oh, 'tis hard for us to fold it,
Hard to think there's none to hold it,
Hard that those who once unrolled it
 Now must furl it with a sigh!

Furl that Banner—furl it sadly;
Once ten thousands hailed it gladly,
And ten thousands wildly, madly,
 Swore it should forever wave—
Swore that foeman's swords should never,
Hearts like theirs entwined dissever,
Till that flag should float forever
 O'er their freedom or their grave!

Furl it! For the hands that grasped it,
And the hearts that fondly clasped it,
 Cold and dead are lying low;
And that Banner—it is trailing,

While around it sounds the wailing
 Of its people in their woe.

For, though conquered, they adore it—
Love the cold, dead hands that bore it!
Weep for those who fell before it!
Pardon those who trailed and tore it!
But, oh, wildly they deplore it,
 Now who furl and fold it so!

Furl that Banner! True, 'tis gory,
Yet 'tis wreathed around with glory,
And 'twill live in song and story
 Though its folds are in the dust!
For its fame on brightest pages,
Penned by poets and by sages,
Shall go sounding down the ages—
 Furl its folds though now we must.

Furl that Banner, softly slowly;
Treat it gently, it is holy,
 For it droops above the dead;
Touch it not—unfold it never;
Let it droop there, furled forever—
 For its people's hopes are fled.

—ABRAM JOSEPH RYAN

THE BLUE AND THE GRAY

Francis Miles Finch first published "The Blue and the Gray" in *The Atlantic Monthly* in 1867 as a salve for both North and South. It was inspired by the women of Columbus, Mississippi, who lay flowers on the graves of both Confederate and Union soldiers. Finch, a judge of the New York Court of Appeals, expressed the desire of many Americans after the war to mourn their shared losses and heal the division between North and South. The poem was later included in the 1879 *McGuffey's Reader*. Millions of schoolchildren read and memorized the poem, and it was frequently recited at Memorial Day ceremonies in the years after the war.

By the flow of the inland river,
 Whence the fleets of iron have fled,

Where the blades of the grave-grass quiver,
    Asleep are the ranks of the dead:
Under the sod and the dew,
      Waiting the judgment day;
Under the one, the Blue,
      Under the other, the Gray.

These in the robings of glory,
    Those in the gloom of defeat,
All with the battle-blood gory,
    In the dusk of eternity meet:
Under the sod and the dew,
      Waiting the judgment day;
Under the laurel, the Blue,
      Under the willow, the Gray.

From the silence of sorrowful hours
    The desolate mourners go,
Lovingly laden with flowers
    Alike for the friend and the foe:
Under the sod and the dew,
      Waiting the judgment day;
Under the roses, the Blue,
      Under the lilies, the Gray.

So with an equal splendor,
    The morning sun-rays fall,
With a touch impartially tender,
    On the blossoms blooming for all:
      Under the sod and the dew,
      Waiting the judgment day;

Broidered with gold, the Blue,
      Mellowed with gold, the Gray.

So when the summer calleth,
    On the forest and field of grain,
With an equal murmur falleth
    The cooling drip of the rain:
Under the sod and the dew,
      Waiting the judgment day;
Wet with the rain, the Blue,
      Wet with the rain, the Gray.

Sadly, but not with upbraiding,
    The generous deed was done,
In the storm of the years that are fading
    No braver battle was won:
      Under the sod and the dew,
      Waiting the judgment day;
Under the blossoms, the Blue,
      Under the garlands, the Gray.

No more shall the war cry sever,
    Or the winding rivers be red;
They banish our anger forever
    When they laurel the graves of our dead!
Under the sod and the dew,
      Waiting the judgment day;
Love and tears for the Blue,
      Tears and love for the Gray.

—FRANCIS MULES FINCH

XVIII

GETTYSBURG

The Battle of Gettysburg is commonly regarded as the turning point of the war. In a sense it was. Certainly it was high tide for the Confederacy—had Lee won at Gettysburg he might have gone on to Harrisburg, Philadelphia, Baltimore, or Washington, and while it is almost inconceivable that he could have captured and held any of these cities or transferred the theater of the war permanently to the North, a successful invasion might have had far-reaching consequences. It might have brought that foreign recognition so important to the survival of the Confederacy; it might have strengthened the peace party in the North, The Copperheads, and the draft rioters, and created a widespread demand for a negotiated peace. Needless to say all of these possibilities were in Lee's mind, and in the minds of Confederate leaders, in planning the invasion.

Yet from the strategical point of view Gettysburg was not decisive. It was strategically far less important than Vicksburg, which cleared the Mississippi and cut off the West from the heart of the Confederacy. It is well to remember that there were almost two years of hard fighting ahead, and that in these months the South could still have won the war—won it not by successful invasion or even by overwhelming victories on the battlefield, but by wearing down the Northern will to fight. The draft riots came after Gettysburg; greenbacks and government bonds were lower in 1864 than in 1863; Lincoln thought that he was going to be defeated for reelection in the summer of 1864. It was, after all, the campaigns of 1864 that were decisive— Sherman's capture of Atlanta and the March to the Sea, and the attrition of Lee's forces in the Wilderness.

Yet Gettysburg remains the great battle of the war—the one that everyone knows, the one that had inspired more historical investigation—and more controversy, more fiction and more poetry, than any other; it is wholly appropriate that it gave its name to the most memorable of Lincoln's addresses. The reason

is not hard to find. It was the greatest single battle ever fought in North America, both in numbers actually involved and in casualties. It was marked by some of the hardest fighting in the war, and as long as Americans cherish courage such names as Peach Orchard, Little Round Top, and Cemetery Ridge will quicken their pulses. There were other fights as fierce as that for Culp's Hill— the Bloody Angle for instance; there were other charges as gallant as Pickett's—the Union charge up Missionary Ridge or the Confederate charge at Franklin; there were other battles whose outcome was as uncertain—Shiloh or Antietam; there were other days which exacted heavier casualties than any one day of Gettysburg—Shiloh again. But no other single battle combined so dramatically so many memorable scenes and events.

Gettysburg was, in many respects, a curious battle, but this might be said of most battles. It was, in a sense, an accident: neither Lee nor Hooker wanted to fight at Gettysburg, though once the fighting had begun Meade—who succeeded Hooker— saw the advantages of the Gettysburg terrain for defensive fighting. Neither strategically nor tactically was it a well-fought battle, though Meade, whose task was simpler, appears to better advantage in these matters than Lee. That it was Lee's "worst-fought" battle is generally agreed. He had allowed Stuart to go off on one of his junkets, and was without his eyes. He missed those lieutenants who had brought him victory in the past, especially the in comparable Jackson. Once the battle was joined the Confederates made a series of mistakes—mistakes that in the end proved fateful: the failure to push on and seize Cemetery Hill the first day, to occupy either Big or Little Round Top early on the second day, to attempt a flanking movement around the Union left, the delay in the assault on the third day and the inability to concentrate all available forces for that assault. Meade, too, fought a somewhat disorganized battle. There was confusion on the first day, even in the matter of command; there was a failure to use all potential strength—four of seven Union corps bore the brunt of the battle; there was above all an egregious failure to follow up victory by energetic pursuit.

The literature on Gettysburg is voluminous, and we can only skim its surface. Here are accounts of the preliminary skirmishing in the Valley, the invasion of Maryland and Pennsylvania, the high points of each of the three days of fighting, and the retreat. Wherever possible we have presented Union and Confederate accounts of the same engagements.

—————— XVIII. I ——————

GENERAL LEE DECIDES TO TAKE THE OFFENSIVE

After Fredericksburg and Chancellorsville, Lee decided once more to carry the war to the North. Many considerations led to this resolution, which he urged successfully on Davis and his Cabinet. He wanted to take his army north of the Potomac where he could find provisions for both men and horses. He wanted to get clear of the Wilderness, to where he could maneuver more effectively against the enemy. He hoped that an invasion of the North would encourage Copperheads and the peace movement in that section and that, if successful, it would hasten foreign recognition.

"I considered the problem in every possible phase," he later recalled, "and to my mind, it resolved itself into a choice of one of two things—either to retire to Richmond and stand a siege, which must ultimately have ended in surrender, or to invade Pennsylvania." We can follow, in his letters, the crystallization of his plans.

(Confidential.) HDQRS. Army of Northern Virginia

June 8, 1863

Hon. James A. Seddon
Secretary of War, Richmond, Va.:
Sir:

. . . As far as I can judge, there is nothing to be gained by this army remaining quietly on the defensive, which it must do unless it can be re-enforced. I am aware that there is difficulty and hazard in taking the aggressive with so large an army in its front, intrenched behind a river, where it cannot be advantageously attacked. Unless it can be drawn out in a position to be assailed, it will

take its own time to prepare and strengthen itself to renew its advance upon Richmond, and force this army back within the intrenchments of that city. This may be the result in any event; still, I think it is worth a trial to prevent such a catastrophe. Still, if the Department thinks it better to remain on the defensive, and guard as far as possible all the avenues of approach, and await the time of the enemy, I am ready to adopt this course. You have, therefore, only to inform me.

R. E. LEE,
General.

Headquarters Army of Northern Virginia
June 10, 1863

His Excellency JEFFERSON DAVIS, *Richmond:*

MR. PRESIDENT: . . . Conceding to our enemies the superiority claimed by them in numbers, resources, and all the means and appliances for carrying on the war, we have no right to look for exemptions from the military consequences of a vigorous use of these advantages, excepting by such deliverance as the mercy of Heaven may accord to the courage of our soldiers, the justice of our cause, and the constancy and prayers of our people. While making the most we can of the means of resistance we possess, and gratefully accepting the measure of success with which God has blessed our efforts as an earnest of His approval and favor, it is nevertheless the part of wisdom to carefully measure and husband our strength, and not to expect from it more than in the ordinary course of affairs it is capable of accomplishing. We should not, therefore, conceal from ourselves that our re sources in men are constantly diminishing, and the disproportion in this respect between us and our enemies, if they continue united in their efforts to subjugate us, is steadily augmenting.

The decrease of the aggregate of this army, as disclosed by the returns, affords an illustration of this fact. Its effective strength varies from time to time, but the falling off in its aggregate shows that its ranks are growing weaker and that its losses are not supplied by recruits.

Under these circumstances, we should neglect no honorable means of dividing and weakening our enemies, that they may feel some of the difficulties experienced by ourselves. It seems to me that the most effectual mode of accomplishing this object, now within our reach, is to give all the encouragement we can, consistently with truth, to the rising peace party of the North.

Nor do I think we should, in this connection, make nice distinction between those who declare for peace unconditionally and those who advocate it as a means of restoring the Union, however much we may prefer the former.

We should bear in mind that the friends of peace at the North must make concessions to the earnest desire that exists in the minds of their countrymen for a restoration of the Union, and that to hold out such a result as an inducement is essential to the success of their party.

Should the belief that peace will bring back the Union become general, the war would no longer be supported, and that, after all, is what we are interested in bringing about. When peace is proposed to us, it will be time enough to discuss its terms, and it is not the part of prudence to spurn the proposition in advance, merely because those who wish to make it believe, or affect to believe, that it will result in bringing us back to the Union. We entertain no such apprehensions, nor doubt that the desire of our people for a distinct and independent national existence will prove as steadfast under the influence of peaceful measures as it has shown it self in the midst of war. . . .

I am, with great respect, your obedient servant,
R. E. LEE,
General.

After Chancellorsville both armies marked time for a while. Hooker was too badly hurt to resume the offensive; Lee awaited reinforcement by Longstreet's corps. During May he carried through a reorganization of the command, dividing the army into three corps and appointing A. P. Hill commander of the new corps. Early in June, reinforced by Longstreet and by new recruits and conscripts, he embarked on the most famous of his offensives. Leaving A. P. Hill temporarily at Fredericksburg to tie

down Hooker's vast army, Lee began to move his other two corps into the Valley. Hooker, who suspected that something was up, sent his cavalry under Pleasonton to probe out the Confederates; the clash with Stuart at Brandy Station was the largest cavalry engagement of the war, but ended in a draw.

Meantime Ewell moved down the Valley toward Winchester, which Milroy held with 9,000 men. Warned of the Confederate approach, Milroy decided to stay and fight it out. With an 61an reminiscent of Stonewall Jackson, Ewell struck Milroy on June 14, drove him out of Winchester, bagged over 3,300 prisoners, and sent the Federals scurrying toward Harpers Ferry.

XVIII.2

GENERAL LEE INVADES PENNSYLVANIA

The defeat of Milroy at Winchester and the withdrawal of the Federals from Harpers Ferry to Maryland Heights cleared the Valley; on the seventeenth Ewell forded the Potomac and occupied Hagerstown and Sharpsburg. Meantime Longstreet was swinging up on the east side of the Blue Ridge Mountains while Stuart's cavalry protected the passes on his right. Realizing that Lee had left Richmond practically undefended! Hooker wanted to launch an attack on that city, but was overruled by Lincoln, who insisted that Lee's army and not Richmond was his proper objective. "If the head of Lee's army is at Martinsburg and the tail of it on the plank road between Fredericksburg and Chancellorsville," he wrote, "the animal must be very slim somewhere. Could you not break him" But by that time it was too late to "break him." Ewell was well into Pennsylvania; Longstreet's corps was splashing across the fords of the Potomac; Stuart had repulsed the Federals in several sharp cavalry engagements—Aldie, Middleburg, and Upperville— and was off on his foraging expedition.

This letter from William Christian reveals something of the spirit of Lee's troops as they invaded the North in that fateful June of 1863.

Camp near Greenwood, Pa., June 28, 1863.—My own darling wife: You can see by the date of this that we are now in Pennsylvania. We crossed the line day before yesterday and are resting today near a little one-horse town on the road to Gettysburg, which we will reach tomorrow. We are paying back these people for some of the damage they have done us, though we are not doing them half as bad as they done us. We are getting up all the horses, etc., and feeding our army with their beef and flour, etc., but there are strict orders about the interruption of any private property by individual soldiers.

Though with these orders, fowls and pigs and eatables don't stand much chance. I felt when I first came here that I would like to revenge myself upon these people for the desolation they have brought upon our own beautiful home, that home where we could have lived so happy, and that we loved so much, from which their vandalism has driven you and my helpless little ones. But though I have such severe wrongs and grievances to redress and such great cause for revenge, yet when I got among these people I could not find it in my heart to molest them. They looked so dreadfully scared and talked so humble that I have invariably endeavored to protect their property and have prevented soldiers from taking chickens, even in the main road; yet there is a good deal of plundering going on, confined principally to the taking of provisions. No houses were searched and robbed, like our houses were done by the Yankees. Pigs, chickens, geese, etc., are finding their way into our camp; it can't be prevented, and I can't think it ought to be. We must show them something of war. I have sent out today to get a good horse; I have no scruples about that, as they have taken mine. We took a lot of Negroes yesterday. I was offered my choice, but as I could not get them back home I would not take them. In fact my humanity revolted at taking the poor devils away from their homes. They were so scared that I turned them all loose.

I dined yesterday with two old maids. They treated me very well and seemed greatly in favor of peace. I have had a great deal of fun since I have been here. The country that we have passed through is beautiful, and everything in the greatest abundance. You never saw such a land of plenty. We could live here mighty well for the next twelve months, but I suppose old Hooker will try to put a stop to us pretty soon. Of course we will have to fight here, and when it comes it will be the biggest on record. Our men feel that there is to be no back-out. A defeat here would be ruinous. This

army has never done such fighting as it will do now, and if we can whip the armies that are now gathering to oppose us, we will have everything in our own hands. We must conquer a peace. If we can come out of this country triumphant and victorious, having established a peace, we will bring back to our own land the greatest joy that ever crowned a people. We will show the Yankees this time how we can fight.

Be of good cheer, and write often to your fondly attached husband.

—Letter of WILLIAM S. CHRISTIAN

XVIII.3

THE ARMIES CONVERGE ON GETTYSBURG

"It had not been intended to deliver a general battle so far from our base unless attacked," wrote General Lee later. "But coming unexpectedly upon the whole Federal army, to withdraw through the mountains with our extensive trains would have been difficult and dangerous." This was accurate enough, but not comprehensive. Had Stuart's cavalry been on the job, Lee would have known where the Federal army was, and how widely it was scattered. After being surprised at Brandy Station Stuart was eager to redeem himself and once more suggested riding around the Federal army. On June 22 Lee gave him somewhat ambiguous instructions to "move into Maryland and take position on Ewell's right." This was what Stuart wanted and off he went into Maryland and Pennsylvania. Not until July I did he learn that Lee's army was concentrated around Gettysburg.

Meantime Gordon Meade had supplanted Hooker in command of the Army of the Potomac. As General Hunt makes clear, both Hooker and Meade had hoped to fight behind Pipe Creek, in Maryland, and the seven corps of the army were spread out over a wide area south of Gettysburg. Only Buford's cavalry was in the town, and it was Buford who held up Heth when that general, hearing that there was a supply of shoes at Gettysburg, sent Pettigrew's brigade down the Chambersburg Pike on June 30.

General Hunt, who here recalls the beginnings of the great battle, was a veteran of the Mexican War and of the Peninsular, Antietam, and Fredericksburg campaigns. At this time he was chief of artillery of the Army of the Potomac.

Hearing nothing from Stuart, and therefore believing that Hooker was still south of the Potomac, Lee, on the afternoon of the 28th, ordered Longstreet and A.P. Hill to join Ewell at Harrisburg; but late that night one of Longstreet's scouts came in and reported that the Federal army had crossed the river, that Meade had relieved Hooker and was at Frederick. Lee thereupon changed the rendezvous of his army to Cash town, which place Heth reached on the 29th. Next day Heth sent Pettigrew's brigade on to Gettysburg, nine miles, to procure a supply of shoes. Nearing this place, Pettigrew discovered the advance of a large Federal force and returned to Cashtown. Hill immediately notified Generals Lee and Ewell, informing the latter that he would advance next morning on Gettysburg. Buford, sending Merritt's brigade to Mechanicstown as guard to his trains, had early on the morning of the 29th crossed into and moved up the Cumberland valley via Boonsboro' and Fairfield with those of Gamble and Devin, and on the afternoon of Tuesday, June 30th, under instructions from Pleasonton, entered Gettysburg, Pettigrew's brigade withdrawing on his approach.

From Gettysburg, near the eastern base of the Green Ridge, and covering all the upper passes into the Cumberland valley, good roads lead to all important points between the Susquehanna and the Potomac. It is therefore an important strategic position. On the west of the town, distant nearly half a mile, there is a somewhat elevated ridge running north and south, on which stands the "Lutheran Seminary." The ridge is covered with open woods through its whole length, and is terminated nearly a mile and a half north of the seminary by a commanding knoll, bare on its southern side, called Oak Hill. From this ridge the ground slopes gradually to the west, and again rising forms another ridge about 500 yards from the first upon which, nearly opposite the seminary, stand McPherson's farm buildings. The second ridge is wider, smoother, and lower than the first, and Oak Hill, their inter section, has a clear view of the slopes of both ridges and of the valley between them. West of McPherson's ridge Willoughby Run flows south into Marsh Creek. South of the farm buildings and directly opposite

the seminary, a wood borders the run for about 300 yards, and stretches back to the summit of McPherson's ridge. From the town two roads run: one south-west to Hagerstown via Fairfield, the other north westerly to Chambersburg via Cashtown. The seminary is midway between them, about 300 yards from each. Parallel to and 150 yards north of the Chambersburg pike, is the bed of an unfinished railroad, with deep cuttings through the two ridges. Directly north of the town the country is comparatively flat and open; on the east of it, Rock Creek flows south. On the south, and overlooking it, is a ridge of bold, high ground, terminated on the west by Cemetery Hill and on the east by Culp's Hill, which, bending to the south, extends half a mile or more and terminates in low grounds near Spangler's Spring. Culp's Hill is steep toward the east, is well wooded, and its eastern base is washed by Rock Creek.

Impressed by the importance of the position, Buford, expecting the early return of the enemy in force, assigned to Devin's brigade the country north, and to Gamble's that west of the town; sent out scouting parties on all the roads to collect information, and reported the condition of affairs to Reynolds. His pickets extended from below the Fairfield road, along the eastern bank of Willoughby Run, to the railroad cut, then easterly some 1500 yards north of the town, to a wooded hillock near Rock Creek.

On the night of June 30th Meade's headquarters and the Artillery Reserve were at Taneytown; the First Corps at Marsh Run, the Eleventh at Emmitsburg, Third at Bridgeport, Twelfth at Littlestown, Second at Uniontown, Fifth at Union Mills, Sixth and Gregg's cavalry at Manchester, Kilpatrick's at Hanover. A glance at the map will show at what disadvantage Meade's army was now placed. Lee's whole army was nearing Gettysburg, while Meade's was scattered over a wide region to the east and south of that town.

Meade was now convinced that all designs on the Susquehanna had been abandoned; but as Lee's corps were reported as occupying the country from

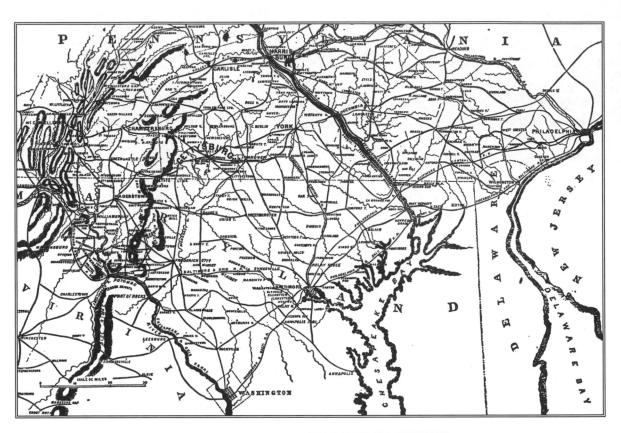

THE SEAT OF THE WAR IN PENNSYLVANIA AND MARYLAND

Chambersburg to Carlisle, he ordered, for the next day's moves, the First and Eleventh corps to Gettysburg, under Reynolds, the Third to Emmitsburg, the Second to Taneytown, the Fifth to Hanover, and the Twelfth to Two Taverns, directing Slocum to take command of the Fifth in addition to his own. The Sixth Corps was left at Manchester, thirty-four miles from Gettysburg, to await orders. But Meade, while conforming to the current of Lee's movement, was not merely drifting. The same afternoon he directed the chiefs of engineers and artillery to select a field of battle on which his army might be concentrated, whatever Lee's lines of approach, whether by Harrisburg or Gettysburg,—indicating the general line of Pipe Creek as a suitable locality. Carefully drawn instructions were sent to the corps commanders as to the occupation of this line, should it be ordered; but it was added that developments might cause the offensive to be assumed from present positions.

These orders were afterward cited as indicating General Meade's intention not to fight at Gettysburg. They were, under any circumstances, wise and proper orders, and it would probably have been better had he concentrated his army behind Pipe Creek rather than at Gettysburg; but events finally controlled the actions of both leaders.

At 8 A.M., July 1st, Buford's scouts reported Heth's advance on the Cashtown road, when Gamble's brigade formed on McPherson's Ridge, from the Fairfield road to the railroad cut, one section of Calef's battery A, 2d United States, near the left his line, the other two across the Chambersburg or Cashtown pike. Devin formed his disposable squadrons from Gamble's right toward Oak Hill, from which he had afterward to transfer them to the north of the town to meet Ewell. As Heth advanced, he threw Archer's brigade to the right, Davis's to the left of the Cashtown pike, with Pelligrew's and Brockerbrough's brigades in support.

The Confederates advanced skirmishing heavily with Buford's dismounted troopers. Calef's battery, engaging double the number of its own guns, was served with an efficiency worthy of its former reputation as "Duncan's battery" in the Mexican war, and so enabled the cavalry to hold their long line for two hours. When Buford's report of the enemy's advance reached Reynolds, the latter, ordering Doubleday and Howard to follow, hastened toward Gettysburg with Wadsworth's small division (two brigades, Meredith's and Cutler's) and Hall's 2d Maine battery. As he approached he heard the sound of battle, and directing the troops to cross the fields toward the firing, galloped himself to the seminary, met Buford there, and both rode to the front, where the cavalry, dismounted, were gallantly holding their ground against heavy odds. After viewing the field, he sent back to hasten up Howard, and as the enemy's main line was now advancing to the attack, directed Doubleday, who had arrived in advance of his division, to look to the Fairfield road, sent Cutler with three of his five regiments north of the rail road cut, posted the other two under Colonel Fowler, of the 14th New York, south of the pike, and replaced Calef's battery by Hall's, thus relieving the cavalry. Cutler's line was hardly formed when it was struck by Davis's Confederate brigade on its front and right flank, where upon Wadsworth, to save it, ordered it to fall back to Seminary Ridge. This order not reaching the 147th New York, its gallant major, Harney, held that regiment to its position until, having lost half its numbers, the order to retire was repeated. Hall's battery was now imperiled, and it withdrew by sections, fighting at close canister range and suffering severely. Fowler thereupon changed his front to face Davis's brigade, which held the cut, and with Dawes's 6th Wisconsin—sent by Doubleday to aid the 147th New York—charged and drove Davis from the field. The Confederate brigade suffered severely, losing all its field-officers but two, and a large proportion of its men killed and captured, being disabled for further effective service that day.

—HUNT, "The First Day at Gettysburg"

BUFORD AND REYNOLDS HOLD UP THE CONFEDERATE ADVANCE

Lee concentrated his army more rapidly than Meade, Hilt pushing on from the west of Gettysburg down the Chambers burg Pike, and Ewell coming down from the north. Only Buford's cavalry division was there to resist the Confederate advance—but that was a formidable force. There was some skirmishing on June 30; the real fighting got under way the next morning when, as we have seen, Buford's cavalrymen, fighting as dismounted troopers, put up a stiff resistance to Heth's and Pender's divisions, giving Reynolds time to hurry up with the I and XI Corps. At about midmorning Wads worth's division took up position on Seminary Ridge, and from there sallied forth to capture a good part of Arthur's brigade. It was at this time that General Reynolds was killed.

Few officers in the Union Army had longer military experience than John Reynolds. He had served with distinction in the Mexican War and in the Mormon and Indian campaigns of the fifties, and the skill with which he commanded his troops at Fredericksburg and Chancellorsville marked him as one of the coming leaders of the Union forces. He was in command of the left wing of the Union army at Gettysburg, and the rapidity with which he brought up his scattered forces and the discernment which led him to order the occupation of Cemetery Hill contributed largely to ultimate Union victory.

Joseph Rosengarten was a major in the Army of the Potomac.

Reynolds knew Buford thoroughly, and knowing him and the value of cavalry under such a leader, sent them through the mountain passes beyond Gettysburg to find and feel the enemy. The old rule would have been to keep them back near the infantry, but Reynolds sent Buford on, and Buford went on, knowing that wherever Reynolds sent him, he was sure to be supported, followed, and secure. It was Buford who first attracted Reynolds' attention to the concentration of roads that gave Gettysburg its strategic importance, and it was Reynolds who first appreciated the strength and value of Cemetery Hill, and the plateau between that point and Round Top, as the stronghold to be secured for the concentration of the scattered corps and as the place where Meade could put his army to meet and overthrow the larger body he was pursuing. Together they found Gettysburg and made it the spot upon which the Union forces won a victory that was bought with his among the precious lives lost there. Buford and Reynolds were soldiers of the same order, and each found in the other just the qualities that were most needed to perfect and complete the task intrusted to them. The brilliant achievement of Buford, with his small body of cavalry, up to that time hardly appreciated as to the right use to be made of them, is but too little considered in the history of the battle of Gettysburg. It was his foresight and energy, his pluck and self-reliance, in thrusting forward his forces and pushing the enemy, and thus inviting, almost compelling their return, that brought on the engagement of the first of July.

Buford counted on Reynolds' support, and he had it fully, faithfully, and energetically. Reynolds counted in turn on having within his reach and at his immediate service at least the three corps that belonged to him, and there can be little question that if they had been up as promptly as he was in answer to Buford's call, the line he had marked out would have been fully manned and firmly held, while Meade's concentration behind Gettysburg would have gone on easily, and the whole of the Army of the Potomac would have done briefly and effectually what was gained only at the end of three days of hard fighting, with varying successes that more than once threatened to turn against us, and the loss on our side would have been so much less that the pursuit of Lee's forces could have been made promptly and irresistibly. It is not, however, given to all men to be of the same spirit, and the three corps that were under Reynolds followed his orders in a very different way from that in which he always did his work. When he got Buford's demand for infantry support on the morning of the first it was just what Reynolds expected, and with characteristic energy, he went forward, saw Buford, accepted at once the responsibility, and returning to find the leading division of the First Corps (Wadsworth's), took it in hand, brought it to the front, put it in position, renewed his orders for the rest of the corps, assigned the positions for the other divisions, sent for his other corps, urged their coming with the greatest speed, directed the point to be held by the reserve, renewed his report to Meade that Buford had found the place for a battle, and that he had begun it, then calmly and coolly hurried some fresh troops forward to fill a gap in his lengthening lines, and as he returned to find fresh divisions, fell at the first onset.

The suddenness of the shock was in itself, perhaps, a relief to those who were nearest to Reynolds. In the full flush of life and health, vigorously leading on the troops in hand, and energetically summoning up the rest of his command, watching and even leading the attack of a comparatively small body, a glorious picture of the best type of military leader, superbly mounted, and horse and man sharing in the excitement of the shock of battle, Reynolds was, of course, a shining mark to the enemy's sharpshooters. He had taken his troops into a heavy growth of timber on the slope of a hill-side, and, under their regimental and brigade commanders, the men did their work well and promptly. Returning to join the expected divisions, he was struck by a Minnie ball, fired by a sharpshooter hidden in the branches of a tree almost over head, and killed at once; his horse bore him to the little clump of trees, where a cairn of stones and a rude mark on the bark, now almost overgrown, still tells the fatal spot. The battle went on in varying fortune, and so long as the influence of his orders that had inspired men and officers could still be felt, all went well; but when the command had been changed by the successive arrival of generals who outranked each other, what there was of plan could hardly be made out, and the troops of the First Corps, without reinforcements and worn out and outnumbered, fell back at first with some show of order, and then as best they could, to find shelter in the lines pointed out by Reynolds for the concentration of his fresh troops. Thus even after his death, his military foresight had provided for the temporary defeat, which prepared the way for the great victory.

It is a striking proof of the discipline he had taught his own corps, that the news of the death, although it spread rapidly and that at a time when the inequality of numbers became apparent, produced no ill effect, led to no disorder, changed no disposition that he had directed, and in itself made the men only the more eager to carry out his orders. At the moment that his body was taken to the rear, for his death was instantaneous, two of his most gallant staff officers, Captain Riddle and Captain Wadsworth, in pursuance of his directions, effected a slight movement which made prisoners of Archer's Brigade, so that the rebel prisoners went to the rear almost at the same time, and their respectful conduct was in itself the highest tribute they could pay to him who had thus fallen.

—ROSENGARTEN, "General Reynolds' Last Battle"

XVIII.5

A BOY CANNONEER DESCRIBES HARD FIGHTING ON THE FIRST DAY

The great battles of the second and third days of Gettysburg have overshadowed the fighting on the first. Had the battle ended with the retreat of the Federals on the afternoon of the first, it would still have gone down in history as one of the hardest fought engagements of the war. The stout resistance of Buford, the charge of Archer's brigade, the sharp fighting along Willoughby's Run, the desperate struggle for the railway cut, the final victorious advance of Pender's and Heth's divisions that hurled the Federals back through Gettysburg to Cemetery and Culp's hills—all these engagements added up to a major battle.

By late afternoon of July I the Union front had collapsed but Schurz and Doubleday managed to retire in good order through Gettysburg and to the hills south of the town. The Confederates had bagged almost 5,000 prisoners and were confidently anticipating another Chancellorsville.

There is no better account of the first day's fighting than that by "cannoneer" Augustus Buell, member of a famous artillery brigade attached to the 1st division of the 1 Corps of the Army of the Potomac.

We were turned out the next morning about daybreak [July 1, 1863], harnessed up, and, after crossing the creek, halted to let the infantry of Wadsworth's Division file by. There was no mistake now. While we stood there watching these splendid soldiers file by with their long, swinging "route step," and their muskets glittering in the rays of the rising sun, there came out of the northwest a sullen "boom! boom! boom!" of three guns, followed almost immediately by a prolonged crackling sound, which, at that distance, reminded one very much of the snapping of a dry brush-heap when you first set it on fire. We soon reasoned out the state of affairs up in front. Buford, we calculated, had engaged the leading infantry of Lee's army, and was probably trying to hold them with his cavalry in heavy skirmish line, dismounted, until our infantry could come up. They said that the enemy had not yet developed more than a skirmish line, because if he had shown a heavy formation Buford would be using his artillery, of which he had two or three batteries, whereas we had thus far heard only the three cannon shots mentioned. These apparently trifling incidents show how the men in our Army were in the habit of observing things, and how unerring their judgment was, as a rule, even in matters of military knowledge far beyond their sphere or control.

But my eyes were riveted on the infantry marching by. No one now living will ever again see those two brigades of Wadsworth's Division— Cutler's and the Iron Brigade—file by as they did that morning. The little creek made a depression in the road, with a gentle ascent on either side, so that from our point of view the column, as it came down one slope and up the other, had the effect of huge blue billows of men topped with a spray of shining steel, and the whole spectacle was calculated to give nerve to a man who had none before. Partly because they had served together a long time, and, no doubt, because so many of their men were in our ranks, there was a great affinity between the Battery and the Iron Brigade, which expressed itself in cheers and good natured chaffing between us as they went by. "Find a good place to camp; be sure and get near a good dry rail fence; tell the Johnnies we will be right along," were the salutations that passed on our part, while the infantry made such responses as "All right; better stay here till we send for you; the climate up there may be unhealthy just now for such delicate creatures as you," and all that sort of thing. It was probably 8 o'clock when the last brigade had passed, and then we got the order to march, moving with Doubleday's Division. As we moved up the road we could see the troops of the next division coming close behind. By this time the lead ing regiments of Wadsworth's infantry had got on the ground, and the sounds of battle were increasing rapidly. . . .

The sounds of the cavalry fight had been distinct ever since we left Marsh Creek—a fitful crackle but now we heard fierce, angry crash on crash, rapidly growing in volume and intensity, signifying that our leading infantry—Cutler's and the Iron Brigade—had encountered the "doughboys" of Lee's advance. It is well known that the men of the Iron Brigade always preferred slouch hats (Western fashion), and seldom or never wore caps. At the time this heavy crashing began we were probably half way up from Marsh Creek, and, as the Battery was marching at a walk, most of us were walking along with the guns instead of riding on the limbers. Among the Cannoneers was a man from the 2d Wisconsin (John Holland) who took great pride in the Iron Brigade. So, when that sudden crash! crash! crash! floated over the hills to our ears, John said, with visible enthusiasm, "Hear that, my son! That's the talk! The old slouch hats have got there, you bet!!"

Now the artillery began to play in earnest, and it was evident that the three batteries which had preceded us were closely engaged, while the musketry had grown from the crackling sound of the skirmishing we had heard early in the morning to an almost incessant crash, which betokened the file firing of a main line of battle. Just before reaching the brow of the hill, south of the town, where we could get our first sight of the battle itself, there

was a provoking halt of nearly half an hour. We could hear every sound, even the yells of the troops fighting on the ridge beyond Gettysburg, and we could see the smoke mount up and float away lazily to the northeastward; but we could not see the combatants. While halted here Doubleday's Division passed up the road, each regiment breaking into double quick as it reached the top of the hill. The Eleventh Corps also began by this time to arrive from Emmittsburg. Finally, when the last of the Second Brigade of Doubleday's (Stone's) had passed, we got the order to advance again, and in two minutes the whole scene burst upon us like the lifting of the curtain in a grand play. The spectacle was simply stupendous. It is doubtful if there was ever a battle fought elsewhere of which such a complete view was possible from one point as we got of that battle when we reached the top of the hill abreast of Round Top. . .

Our guns pointed about due west, taking the Cashtown Pike *en echarpe*. The right half-battery was in line with us on the north side of the cut. Its right gun rested on the edge of a little grove, which extended some distance farther to the right, and was full of infantry (the 11th Pennsylvania) sup porting us. There was also infantry in our rear, behind the crest and in the Railroad Cut (the 6th Wisconsin). One of our squad volunteered the facetious remark that these infantry "were put there to shoot the recruits if they flinched," for which he was rebuked by Corp'l Packard, who told him to "see that he himself behaved as well as the recruits." As Stewart commanded the right half-battery in person, he did not have much to do with us, directly, during the action that followed.

At this time, which was probably about noon, all the infantry of the First Corps, except that massed immediately about our position, together with Hall's, Reynolds's and one of the cavalry horse-batteries—Calef's—had been struggling desperately in the fields in our front, and for a few moments we had nothing to do but witness the magnificent scene. The enemy had some batteries firing down the pike, but their shot—probably canister—did not reach us. In a few minutes they opened with shell from a battery on a high knoll to the north of us (Oak Hill), and, though at long range, directly enfilading our line. But they sent their shells at the troops who were out in advance. We stood to the guns and watched the infantry combat in our front. Over across the creek (Willoughby's) we could see the gray masses of the Rebel infantry coming along all the roads and deploying in the fields, and it seemed that they were innumerable. At this time some 200 or 300 Rebel prisoners passed by our position on their way to our rear. They were a tough-looking set. Some had bloody rags tied round their limbs or heads, where they had received slight wounds.

In the meantime our infantry out in the field toward the creek was being slowly but surely over-powered, and our lines were being forced in toward the Seminary. It was now considerably past noon. In addition to the struggle going on in our immedi-ate front, the sounds of a heavy attack from the north side were heard, and away out beyond the creek, to the south, a strong force could be seen advancing and overlapping our left. The enemy was coming nearer, both in front and on the north, and stray balls began to zip and whistle around our ears with unpleasant frequency. Then we saw the batter-ies that had been holding the position in advance of us limber up and fall back toward the Seminary, and the enemy simultaneously advance his batteries down the road. All our infantry out toward the creek on both sides of the pike began to fall back.

The enemy did not press them very closely, but halted for nearly an hour to reform his lines, which had been very much shattered by the battle of the forenoon. At last, having reformed his lines behind the low ridges in front, he made his appearance in grand shape. His line stretched from the rail road grading across the Cashtown Pike, and through the fields south of it half way to the Fairfield Road—nearly a mile in length. First we could see the tips of their color staffs coming up over the little ridge, then the points of their bayonets, and then the Johnnies themselves, coming on with a steady

tramp, tramp, and with loud yells. It was now apparent that the old Battery's turn had come again, and the embattled boys who stood so grimly at their posts felt that another page must be added to the record of Buena Vista and Antietam. The term "boys" is literally true, because of our gun detachment alone, consisting of a Sergeant, two Corporals, seven Cannoneers and six Drivers, only four had hair on their faces, while the other 12 were beardless boys whose ages would not average 19 years, and who, at any other period of our histo-ry, would have been at school! The same was more or less true of all the other gun detachments. But if boys in years they were, with one or two exceptions not necessary to name, veterans in battle, and braver or steadier soldiers than they were never faced a foe! A glance along our line at that moment would have been a rare study for an artist. As the day was very hot many of the boys had their jackets off, some with sleeves rolled up, and they exchanged little words of cheer with each other as the gray line came on. In quick, sharp tones, like successive reports of a repeating rifle, came Davison's orders: "Load—Canister—Double!" There was a hustling of Cannoneers, a few thumps of the rammer-heads, and then "Ready!—By piece!—At will!—Fire!!" . . .

Directly in our front—that is to say, on both sides of the pike—the Rebel infantry, whose left lapped the north side of the pike quite up to the line of the railroad grading, had been forced to halt and lie down by the tornado of canister that we had given them from the moment they came in sight over the bank of the creek. But the regiments in the field to their right (south side of the pike kept on, and kept swinging their right flanks for-ward as if to take us in reverse or cut us off from the rest of our troops near the Seminary. At this moment Davison, bleeding from two desperate wounds, and so weak that one of the men had to hold him up on his feet (one ankle being totally shattered by a bullet), ordered us to form the half-battery, action left, by wheeling on the left gun as a pivot, so as to bring the half-battery on a line with the Cash town Pike, muzzles facing south, his object being to rake the front of the Rebel line closing in on us from that side.

Of the four men left at our gun when this order was given two had bloody heads, but they were still "standing by," and Ord. Serg't Mitchell jumped on our off wheels to help us. "This is tough work, boys" he shouted, as we wheeled the gun around, "but we are good for it."

And Pat Wallace, tugging at the near wheel, shouted back: "If we ain't, where'll you find them that is!"

Well, this change of front gave us a clean rake along the Rebel line for a whole brigade length, but it exposed our right flank to the raking volleys of their infantry near the pike, who at that moment began to get up again and come on. Then for seven or eight minutes ensued probably the most desperate fight ever waged between artillery and infantry at close range without a particle of cover on either side. They gave us volley after volley in front and flank, and we gave them double canister as fast as we could load. The 6th Wisconsin and 11th Pennsylvania men crawled up over the bank of the cut or behind the rail fence in rear of Stewart's caissons and joined their musketry to our canister, while from the north side of the cut flashed the chainlightning of the Old Man's half-battery in one solid streak!

At this time our left half-battery, taking their first line *en echarpe*, swept it so clean with double canister that the Rebels sagged away from the road to get cover from the fences and trees that lined it. From our second round on a gray squirrel could not have crossed the road alive.

How those peerless Cannoneers sprang to their work! Twenty-six years have but softened in memory the picture of "Old Griff" (Wallace), his tough Irish face set in hard lines with the unflinching resolution that filled his soul, while he sponged and loaded under that murderous musketry with the precision of barrack drill; of the burly Corporal, bareheaded, his hair matted with blood from a scalp wound, and wiping the crimson fluid out of

his eyes to sight the gun; of the steady Orderly Sergeant, John Mitchell, moving calmly from gun to gun, now and then changing men about as one after another was hit and fell, stooping over a wounded man to help him up, or aiding another to stagger to the rear; of the dauntless Davison on foot among the guns, cheering the men, praising this one and that one, and ever and anon profanely exhorting us to "Feed it to 'em, G—d—em; feed it to 'em!" The very guns became things of life not implements, but comrades. Every man was doing the work of two or three. At our gun at the finish there were only the Corporal, No. 1 and No. 3, with two drivers fetching ammunition. The water in Pat's bucket was like ink. His face and hands were smeared all over with burnt powder. The thumbstall of No. 3 was burned to a crisp by the hot vent-field. Between the black of the burnt powder and the crimson streaks from his bloody head, Packard looked like a demon from below! Up and down the line men reeling and falling; splinters flying from wheels and axles where bullets hit; in rear, horses tearing and plunging, mad with wounds or terror; drivers yelling, shells bursting, shot shrieking overhead, howling about our ears or throwing up great clouds of dust where they struck; the musketry crashing on three sides of us; bullets hissing, humming and whistling everywhere; cannon roaring; all crash on crash and peal on peal, smoke, dust, splinters, blood, wreck and carnage indescribable; but the brass guns of Old B still bellowed and not a man or boy flinched or faltered! Every man's shirt soaked with sweat and many of them sopped with blood from wounds not severe enough to make such bulldogs "let go"—bareheaded, sleeves rolled up, faces blackened—oh! if such a picture could be spread on canvas to the life! Out in front of us an undulating field, filled almost as far as the eye could see with a long, low, gray line creeping toward us, fairly fringed with flame! . . .

For a few moments the whole Rebel line, clear down to the Fairfield Road, seemed to waver, and we thought that maybe we could repulse them, single-handed as we were. At any rate, about our fifth or sixth round after changing front made their first line south of the pike halt, and many of them sought cover behind trees in the field or ran back to the rail fence parallel to the pike at that point, from which they resumed their musketry. But their second line came steadily on, and as Davison had now succumbed to his wounds Ord. Serg't Mitchell took command and gave the order to limber to the rear, the 6th Wisconsin and the 11th Pennsylvania having begun to fall back down the railroad track toward the town, turning about and firing at will as they retreated.

—BUELL, *"The Cannoneer"*

XVIII.6

THE STRUGGLE FOR LITTLE ROUND TOP

Gettysburg was won, and lost, on the second day, and the outcome of that day's fighting was determined largely by geography, or by the enterprise of Union commanders in taking advantage of geography. The terrain of the second and third days of the battle is familiar enough. Immediately to the south of Gettysburg lies an irregular string of hills forming, as has often been noted, a giant fishhook almost four miles in length: the eye at Round Top, the shank along Cemetery Ridge, the bend at Cemetery Hill, the barb curving around Culp's Hill. The approach to these hills was everywhere difficult. The slope up to Cemetery Ridge was covered by wheat fields, orchards and patches of woods; the fields in front of the Round Tops, Cemetery and Culp!s hills were littered with boulders and underbrush.

On the afternoon of the first Lee, who saw the strategical importance of Cemetery and Culp's hills, ordered Ewell to seize them "if possible." That evening, before Ewell could carry out these instructions, Wadsworth entrenched himself on Culp's Hill and Steinwehr and Schurz took position on Cemetery Hill; Ewell did not find it possible to advance. Longstreet's corps came up during the night, and Lee planned a general assault on the Union lines early the next morning. But Meade, too, had some appreciation of terrain, and as brigade after brigade marched in during the night and next morning—many of them exhausted with long marches—they were assigned positions an along Cemetery Ridge and Culp's Hill. Not until three o'clock in the afternoon did Longstreet's offensive get under way. By that time the Union positions were bristling with guns and men.

Prompt action might still have given victory to the Confederates. For there was an Achilles' heel in the Union position: the Round Tops. Sickles had been ordered to occupy the Round Tops but had chosen, instead, to probe the ground in front of Little Round Top and there—at the Peach Orchard—ran into Longstreet's corps and suffered severe losses. Meantime the Round Tops were all but undefended. Late in the afternoon Hood, who had begged hard to be allowed to swing south of the Federal position and outflank it—a perfectly feasible plan—started for Little Round Top. Iust in time General Warren discovered its defenseless position and ordered elements of the V Corps to hurry to its defense. There ensued one of the fiercest fights not only of the battle but of the entire war. It was a touch and go affair, but in the end the Federals held the hill.

We give here three accounts of the struggle for Little Round Top. The first is by Captain Porter Farley, a Rochester boy who enlisted in the 140th New York Volunteers, fought through the last years of the war, and later became one of the most distinguished of upstate New York surgeons; it tells how Warren's instant understanding of the importance of Little Round Top came just in time to save the Union position. The second is by William Oates, colonel of the 15th Alabama Infantry and later governor of his state. The third is by Theodore Gerrish of the 20th Maine Volunteers—a regiment which bore the brunt of the fighting.

A. General Warren Seizes Little Round Top

The leading regiments of our brigade were just passing over that slightly elevated ground north of Little Round Top when down its slopes on our left, accompanied by a single mounted officer and an orderly, rode General G. K. Warren, our former brigade commander, then acting as General Meade's chief engineer. Warren came straight toward the head of the regiment, where I was riding with the colonel. He called out to O'Rorke, beginning to speak while still some eight or ten rods from us, that he wanted us to come up there, that the enemy were advancing unopposed up the opposite side of the hill, down which he had just come, and he wanted our regiment to meet them. He was evidently greatly excited and spoke in his usual impulsive style.

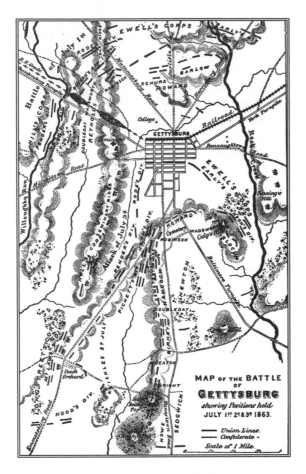

THE BATTLE OF GETTYSBURG

O'Rorke answered, "General Weed is ahead and expects me to follow him."

'Never mind that," said Warren, "bring your regiment up here and I will take the responsibility."

It was a perplexing situation, but without hesitating O'Rorke turned to the left and followed the officer who had been riding with Warren, while Warren himself rode rapidly down the stony hill, whether in the direction from which we had just come or to overtake the rest of our brigade I cannot say, but evidently to find and order up more troops. . .

We turned off the road to our left and rushed along the wooded, rocky, eastern slope of Little Round Top, ascending it while at the same time moving toward its southern extremity. It was just here that some of the guns of Hazlett's battery came rapidly up and plunged directly through our ranks, the horses being urged to frantic efforts by the

whips of their drivers and the cannoniers assisting at the wheels, so great was the effort necessary to drag the guns and caissons up the ragged hillside.

As we reached the crest a never to be forgotten scene burst upon us. A great basin lay before us full of smoke and fire, and literally swarming with riderless horses and fighting, fleeing and pursuing men. The air was saturated with the sulphurous fumes of battle and was ringing with the shouts and groans of the combatants. The wild cries of charging lines, the rattle of musketry, the booming of artillery and the shrieks of the wounded were the orchestral accompaniments of ascene like very hell itself—as terrific as the warring of Milton's fiends in Pandemonium. The whole of Sickles's corps, and many other troops which had been sent to its support in that ill-chosen hollow, were being slaughtered and driven before the impetuous advance of Longstreet. But fascinating as was this terrible scene we had no time to spend upon it. Bloody work was ready for us at our very feet.

Round Top, a conical hill several hundred feet in height, lay just to the south of us, and was separated from Little Round Top, on whose crest we were now moving, by a broad ravine leading down into the basin where the great fight was raging. Right up this ravine, which offered the easiest place of ascent, a rebel force, outflanking all our troops in the plain below, was advancing at the very moment when we reached the crest of the hill. Vincent's brigade of the First division of our corps, had come up through the woods on the left and were just getting into position, and the right of their line had opened fire in the hollow on our left when the head of our regiment came over the hill. As soon as we reached the crest bullets came flying in among us. We were moving with the right in front and not a musket was loaded, a fact which Warren of course knew nothing about when he rushed us up there. The enemy were coming from our right and to face them would bring our file closers in front. The order, "On the right, by file into line," would have brought us into proper position; but there was no time to execute it, not even time to allow the natural impulse which manifest itself on the part of the men to halt and load the instant we received the enemy's fire.

O'Rorke did not hesitate a moment. "Dismount!" he said to me, for the ground before us was too rough to ride over. We sprung from our horses and gave them to the sergeant major. O'Rorke shouted, "Down this way, boys," and following him we rushed down the rocky slope with all the same moral effect upon the rebels, who saw us coming, as if our bayonets had been fixed and we ready to charge upon them. Coming abreast of Vincent's brigade, and taking advantage of such shelter as the huge rocks lying about there afforded the men loaded and fired, and in less time than it takes to write it the onslaught of the rebels was fairly checked, and in a few minutes the woods in front of us were cleared except for the dead and wounded. Such of the rebels as had approached so near as to make escape almost impossible dropped their guns, threw up their hands, and upon a slight slackening of our fire rushed in upon us, and gave themselves up as prisoners, while those not so near took advantage of the chance left them and retreated in disorder.

—FARLEY, "Reminiscences of the 140th New York Volunteers"

B. Colonel Oates Almost Captures Little Round Top

General Law rode up to me as we were advancing, and informed me that I was then on the extreme right of our line and for me to hug the base of Great Round Top and go up the valley between the two mountains, until I found the left of the Union line, to turn it and do all the damage I could, and that Lieutenant-Colonel Bulger would be instructed to keep the Forty-seventh closed to my regiment, and if separated from the brigade he would act under my orders.

Just after we crossed Plum Run we received the first fire from the enemy's infantry. It was Stoughton's Second Regiment United States sharpshooters, posted behind a fence at or near the southern foot of Great Round Top. They reached that position as we advanced through the old field.

No other troops were there nor on that mountain at that time. I did not halt at the first fire, but looked to the rear for the Forty eighth Alabama, and saw it going, under General Law's order, across the rear of our line to the left, it was said, to reenforce the Texas brigade, which was hotly engaged. That left no one in my rear or on my right to meet this foe. They were in the woods and I did not know the number of them.

I received the second fire. Lieutenant-Colonel Feagin and one or two of the men fell. I knew it would not do to go and leave that force, I knew not how strong, in our rear with no troops of ours to take care of them; so I gave the command to change direction to the right. The seven companies of the Forty-seventh swung around with the Fifteenth and kept in line with it. The other three companies of that regiment were sent forward as skirmishers before the advance began. The sharpshooters retreated up the south front of the mountain, pursued by my command.

In places the men had to climb up, catching to the rocks and bushes and crawling over the boulders in the face of the fire of the enemy, who kept retreating, taking shelter and firing down on us from behind the rocks and crags which covered the side of the mountain thicker than grave-stones in a city cemetery. Fortunately they usually overshot us. We could see our foe only as they dodged back from one boulder to another, hence our fire was scattering. As we advanced up the mountain they ceased firing about half way up, divided, and a battalion went around the mountain on each side. Those who went up to the right fired a few shots at my flank. To meet this I deployed Company A, and moved it by the left flank to protect my right, and continued my rugged ascent until we reached the top.

Some of my men fainted from heat, exhaustion, and thirst. I halted and let them lie down and rest a few minutes. . . . I saw Gettysburg through the foliage of the trees. Saw the smoke and heard the roar of battle which was then raging at the Devil's Den, in the peach orchard, up the Emmitsburg road, and on the west and south of the

Little Round Top. I saw from the highest point of rocks that we were then on the most commanding elevation in that neighborhood. I knew that my men were too much exhausted to make a good fight without a few minutes' rest. . . .

When we formed line of battle before the advance began, a detail was made of two men from each of the eleven companies of my regiment to take all the canteens to a well about one hundred yards in our rear and fill them with cool water before we went into the fight. Before this detail could fill the canteens the advance was ordered. It would have been infinitely better to have waited five minutes for those twenty-two men and the canteens of water, but generals never ask a colonel if his regiment is ready to move. The order was given and away we went. The water detail followed with the canteens of water, but when they got into the woods they missed us, walked right into the Yankee lines, and were captured, canteens and all. My men in the ranks, in the intense heat, suffered greatly for water. The loss of those twenty-two men and lack of the water contributed largely to our failure to take Little Round Top a few minutes later. About five minutes after I halted, Captain Terrell, assistant adjutant-general to General Law, rode up by the only path way on the southeast side of the mountain and inquired why I had halted. I told him. He then informed me that General Hood was wounded, Law was in command of the division, and sent me his compliments, said for me to press on, turn the Union left, and capture Little Round Top, if possible, and to lose no time.

I then called his attention to my position. A precipice on the east and north, right at my feet; a very steep, stony, and wooded mountain-side on the west. The only approach to it by our enemy, a long wooded slope on the northwest. Within half an hour I could convert it into a Gibraltar that I could hold against ten times the number of men that I had, hence in my judgment it should be held and occupied by artillery as soon as possible, as it was higher than the other mountain and would command ihe entire field. Terrell replied that probably I was right, but that he had no authority to change or originate orders, which I very well knew; but with his sanction I would have remained at that point until I could have heard from Law or some superior in rank. I inquired for Law. Terrell said that as senior brigadier he was commanding the division, and along the line to the left. He then repeated that General Law had sent him to tell me to lose no time, but to press forward and drive everything before me as far as possible. General Meade did not then know the importance of the Round Tops. . . .

Just as the Forty-seventh companies were being driven back, I ordered my regiment to change direction to the left, swing around, and drive the Federals from the ledge of rocks, for the purpose of enfilading their line, relieving the Forty-seventh— gain the enemy's rear, and drive him from the hill. My men obeyed and advanced about half way to the enemy's position, but the fire was so destructive that my line wavered like a man trying to walk against a strong wind, and then slowly, doggedly, gave back a little; then with no one upon the left or right of me, my regiment exposed, while the enemy was still under cover, to stand there and die was sheer folly; either to retreat or advance became a necessity. The Lieutenant-Colonel, I. B. Feagin, had lost his leg at Plum Run; the heroic Captain Ellison had fallen; while Captain Brainard, one of the bravest and best officers in the regiment, in leading his company forward, fell, exclaiming, "O God! that I could see my mother," and instantly expired. Lieutenant John O. Oates, my dear brother, succeeded to the command of the company, but was pierced through by a number of bullets, and fell mortally wounded. Lieutenant Cody fell mortally wounded, Captain Bethune and several other officers were serious wounded, while the carnage in the ranks was appalling.

I again ordered the advance, and knowing the officers and men of that gallant old regiment, I felt sure they would follow their commander anywhere in the line of duty. I passed through the line waving my sword, shouting, "Forward, men, to the ledge!" and was promptly followed by the command in splendid style. We drove the Federals from their strong defensive position; five times they rallied and charged us, twice coming so near that some of my men had to use the bayonet, but in vain was their effort. It was our time now to deal death and destruction to a gallant foe, and the account was speedily settled. I led this charge and sprang upon the ledge of rock, using my pistol within musket length, when the rush of my men drove the Maine men from the ledge along the line. . . . At this angle and to the southwest of it is where I lost the greatest number of my men. The Twentieth Maine was driven back from this ledge, but not farther than to the next ledge on the mountain-side.

I recall a circumstance which I recollect. I, with my regiment, made a rush forward from the ledge. About forty steps up the slope there is a large boulder about midway the Spur. The Maine regiment charged my line, coming right up in a hand-to-hand encounter. My regimental colors were just a step or two to the right of that boulder, and I was within ten feet. A Maine man reached to grasp the staff of the colors when Ensign Archibald stepped back and Sergeant Pat O'Connor stove his bayonet through the head of the Yankee, who fell dead. I witnessed that incident, which impressed me beyond the point of being forgotten.

There never were harder fighters than the Twentieth Maine men and their gallant Colonel. His skill and persistency and the great bravery of his men saved Little Round Top and the Army of the Potomac from defeat. Great events sometimes turn on comparatively small affairs. My position rapidly be came untenable. The Federal infantry were reported to be coming down on my right and certainly were closing in on my rear, while some dismounted cavalry were closing the only avenue of escape on my left rear. I sent my sergeant major with a request to Colonel Bowles, of the Fourth Alabama, the next in line to the left, to come to my relief. He returned within a minute and reported that none of our troops were in sight, the enemy to be between us and the Fourth Alabama, and swarming the woods south of Little Round Top. The lamented Captain Park, who was after

wards killed at Knoxville, and Captain Hill, killed near Richmond in 1864, came and informed me that the enemy were closing in on our rear. I sent Park to ascertain their number. He soon returned, and reported that two regiments were coming up behind us, and just then I saw them halt behind a fence, some two hundred yards distant, from-which they opened fire on us. These, I have since learned from him, were the battalions of Stoughton's sharpshooters, each of which carried a flag, hence the impression that there were two regiments. They had been lost in the woods, but, guided by the firing, came up in our rear. At Balaklava Captain Nolan's six hundred had cannon to the right of them, cannon to the left of them, cannon in front of them, which volleyed and thundered. But at this moment the Fifteenth Alabama had infantry in front of them, to the right of them, dismounted cavalry to the left of them, and infantry in the rear of them. With a withering and deadly fire pouring in upon us from every direction, it seemed that the regiment was doomed to destruction. While one man was shot in the face, his right hand or left-hand comrade was shot in the side or back. Some were struck simultaneously with two or three balls from different directions. Captains Hill and Park suggested that I should order a retreat; but this seemed impracticable. My dead and wounded were then nearly as great in number as those still on duty. They literally covered the ground. The blood stood in puddles *n some places on the rocks; the ground was soaked with the blood of as brave men as ever fell on the red field of battle.

I still hoped for reenforcements or for the tide of success to turn my way. It seemed impossible to retreat and I there fore replied to my captains, "Return to your companies; we will sell out as dearly as possible."

Hill made no reply, but Park smiled pleasantly, gave me the military salute, and said, "All right, sir."

On reflection a few moments later I saw no hope of success and did order a retreat, but did not undertake to retire in order. I sent Sergeant-Major Norris and had the officers and men advised the best I could that when the signal was given that we would not try to retreat in order, but every one should run in the direction from whence we came, and halt on the top of the Big Round Top Mountain. I found the under taking to capture Little Round Top too great for my regiment unsupported. I waited until the next charge of the Twentieth Maine was repulsed, as it would give my men a better chance to get out unhurt, and then ordered the retreat. . . .

When the signal was given we ran like a herd of wild cattle, right through the line of dismounted cavalrymen. Some of the men as they ran through seized three of the cavalrymen by the collar and carried them out prisoners. As we ran, a man named Keils, of Company H, from Henry County, who was to my right and rear had his throat cut by a bullet, and he ran past me breathing at his throat and the blood spattering. His wind-pipe was entirely severed, but notwithstanding he crossed the mountain and died in the field hospital that night or the next morning.

—OATES, *The War between the Union and the Confederacy*

C. The 20th Maine Saves Little Round Top

At daylight, on the morning of July 2d, we resumed our march, and in a few hours halted within supporting distance of the left flank of our army, about a mile to the right of Little Round Top. The long forenoon passed away, and to our surprise the enemy made no attack. This was very fortunate for our army, as it enabled our men to strengthen our lines of fortifications, and also to obtain a little rest, of which they were in great need. The rebels were also engaged in throwing up rude lines of defenses, hurrying up reinforcements, and in discussing the line of action they should pursue. . . .

The hour of noon passed, and the sun had measured nearly one-half the distance across the western sky, before the assault was made. Then, as suddenly as a bolt of fire flies from the storm cloud, a hundred pieces of rebel artillery open upon our left flank, and under the thick canopy of screaming, hissing, burst-

ing shells, Longstreet's corps was hurled upon the troops of General Sickles. Instantly our commanders discerned the intention of General Lee. It was to turn and crush our left flank, as he had crushed our right at Chancellorsville. It was a terrible onslaught. The brave sons of the South never displayed more gallant courage than on that fatal afternoon of July 2d. But brave Dan Sickles and the old Third corps were equal to the emergency, and stood as immovable against the surging tides as blocks of granite. But a new and appalling danger suddenly threatened the Union army. Little Round Top was the key to the entire position. Rebel batteries planted on that rocky bluff could shell any portion of our line at their pleasure. For some reason Sickles had not placed any infantry upon this important position. A few batteries were scattered along its ragged side, but they had no infantry support.

Lee saw at a glance that Little Round Top was the prize for which the two armies were contending, and with skillful audacity he determined to wrest it from his opponent. While the terrible charge was being made upon the line of General Sickles, Longstreet threw out a whole division, by extending his line to his right, for the purpose of seizing the coveted prize. The danger was at once seen by our officers, and our brigade was ordered forward, to hold the hill against the assault of the enemy. In a moment all was excitement. Every soldier seemed to understand the situation, and to be inspired by its danger. "Fall in! Fall in! By the right flank! Double quick! March!" and away we went, under the terrible artillery fire. It was a moment of thrilling interest. Shells were exploding on every side. Sickles' corps was enveloped in sheets of flame, and looked like a vast windrow of fire. But so intense was the excitement that we hardly noticed these surroundings. Up the steep hillside we ran, and reached the crest. "On the right by file into line," was the command, and our regiment had assumed the position to which it had been assigned. We were on the left of our brigade, and consequently on the extreme left of all our line of battle. The ground sloped to our front and left, and was sparsely covered with a growth of oak trees, which were too small to afford us any protection. Shells were crashing through the air above our heads, making so much noise that we could hardly hear the commands of our officers; the air was filled with fragments of exploding shells and splinters torn from mangled trees; but our men appeared to be as cool and deliberate in their movements as if they had been forming a line upon the parade ground in camp.

Our regiment mustered about three hundred and fifty men. Company B, from Piscataquis county, commanded by the gallant Captain Morrill, was ordered to deploy in our front as skirmishers. They boldly advanced down the slope and disappeared from our view. Ten minutes have passed since we formed the line; the skirmishers must have advanced some thirty or forty rods through the rocks and trees, but we have seen no indications of the enemy; "But look!" "Look!" "Look!" exclaimed half a hundred men in our regiment at the same moment; and no wonder, for right in our front, between us and our skirmishers, whom they have probably captured, we see the lines of the enemy. They have paid no attention to the rest of the brigade stationed on our right, but they are rushing on, determined to turn and crush the left of our line. Colonel Chamberlain with rare sagacity understood the movement they were making, and bent back the left flank of our regiment until the line formed almost a right angle with the colors at the point, all these movements requiring a much less $pace of time than it requires for me to write of them.

How can I describe the scenes that followed? Imagine, if you can, nine small companies of infantry, numbering perhaps three hundred men, in the form of a right angle, on the extreme flank of an army of eighty thousand men, put there to hold the key of the entire position against a force at least ten times their number, and who are desperately determined to succeed in the mission upon which they came. Stand firm, ye boys from Maine, for not once in a century are men permitted to bear such responsibilities for freedom and justice, for God and humanity, as are now placed upon you.

The conflict opens. I know not who gave the first fire, or which line received the first lead. I only know that the carnage began. Our regiment was mantled in fire and smoke. I wish that I could picture with my pen the awful details of that hour,— how rapidly the cartridges were torn from the boxes and stuffed in the smoking muzzles of the guns; how the steel rammers clashed and clanged in the heated barrels; how the men's hands and faces grew grim and black with burning powder; how our little line, baptized with fire, reeled to and fro as it advanced or was pressed back; how our officers bravely encouraged the men to hold on and recklessly exposed themselves to the enemy's fire,—a terrible medley of cries, shouts, cheers, groans, prayers, curses, bursting shells, whizzing rifle bullets and clanging steel. And if that was all, my heart would not be so sad and heavy as I write. But the enemy was pouring a terrible fire upon us, his superior forces giving him a great advantage. Ten to one are fearful odds where men are contending for so great a prize. The air seemed to be alive with lead. The lines at times were 80 near each other that the hostile gun barrels almost touched. As the contest continued, the rebels grew desperate that so insignificant a force should so long hold them in check. At one time there was a brief lull in the carnage, and our shattered line was closed up, but soon the contest raged again with renewed fierceness. The rebels had been reinforced, and were now determined to sweep our regiment from the crest of Little Round Top.

Many of our companies have suffered fearfully. . . . But there is no relief, and the carnage goes on. Our line is pressed back so far that our dead are within the lines of the enemy. The pressure made by the superior weight of the enemy's line is severely felt. Our ammunition is nearly all gone, and we are using the cartridges from the boxes of our wounded comrades. A critical moment has arrived, and we can remain as we are no longer; we must advance or retreat. It must not be the latter, but how can it be the former? Colonel Chamberlain understands how it can be done. The order is given "Fix bayonets!" and the steel shanks of the bayonets rattle upon the rifle barrels. "Charge bayonets, charge!" Every man understood in a moment that the movement was our only salvation, but there is a limit to human endurance, and I do not dishonor those brave men when I write that for a brief moment the order was not obeyed, and the little line seemed to quail under the fearful fire that was being poured upon it. O for some man reckless of life, and all else save his country's honor and safety, who would rush far out to the front, lead the way, and inspire the hearts of his exhausted comrades!

In that moment of supreme need the want was supplied. Lieut. H. S. Melcher, an officer who had worked his way up from the ranks, and was then in command of Co. F, at that time the color company, saw the situation, and did not hesitate, and for his gallant act deserves as much as any other man the honor of the victory on Round Top. With a cheer, and a flash of his sword, that sent an inspiration along the line, full ten paces to the front he sprang—ten paces—more than half the distance between the hostile lines. "Come on! Come on! Come on, boys!" he shouts. The color sergeant and the brave color guard follow, and with one wild yell of anguish wrung from its tortured heart, the regiment charged.

The rebels were confounded at the moment. We struck them with a fearful shock. They recoil, stagger, break and run, and like avenging demons our men pursue. The rebels rush toward a stone wall, but, to our mutual surprise, two scores of rifle barrels gleam over the rocks, and a murderous volley was poured in upon them at close quarters. A band of men leap over the wall and capture at least a hundred prisoners. Piscataquis has been heard from, and as usual it was a good report. This unlooked-for reinforcement was Company B, whom we supposed were all captured.

Our Colonel's commands were simply to hold the hill, and we did not follow the retreating rebels but a short distance. After dark an order came to advance and capture a hill in our front. Through the trees, among the rocks, up the steep hillside, we made our way, captured the position, and also a number of prisoners.

—GERRISH, *Army Life*

XVIII.7

HIGH TIDE AT GETTYSBURG

Both Pickett and Stuart had come up during the afternoon of the second. With his army at full strength, and undaunted by the repulses of the second day's fighting, Lee determined to renew the next morning, Aurling Longstreet and Hill against the Union center on Cemetery Ridge and Ewell against Culp's Hill. Again ill fortune plagued him. Ewell's at tack came off almost as planned, but was thrown back. Longstreet once more had what Lincoln called "the slows," but whether because of natural diffculties of coordinating so many forces for attack or because of reluctance to launch an attack which he disapproved is still a subject of controversy.

Meanwhile two of the greatest artillerists of the war—Alexander and Hunt—made ready. Although the Federals had artillery superiority, Alexander was able to bring over 100 guns to bear on the Union position, while Hunt could not mass more than about 80 on Cemetery Ridge and the Round Tops. At one o'clock the greatest artillery duel ever seen on the continent began, and for 40 minutes the roar of cannon shook the earth. Then—with both sides low on artillery ammunition—silence fell over the battlefield.

Now Pickett and Pettigrew were ready for that famous charge which was to live forever in history. "Up men and to your posts!" cried Pickett. "Don't forget today that you are from old Virginia." And Pettigrew called to Colonel Marshall "Now, Colonel, for the honor of the good Old North State, forward!" Forward they swept, 15,000 men in gray, the colors of 47 regiments fluttering in the breeze, up the long slope of Cemetery Ridge. The Federals, too, were ready, General Gibbon—a Southerner with three brothers in the Confederate ranks—riding up and down encouraging his men to stand firm.

But let our chroniclers tell the great story. They need little introduction. First comes the lionhearted General Alexander, chief of artillery of Longstreet's corps and—as the event proved—a distinguished stylist. Next comes Lee's war horse, James Longstreet, the focal figure in the controversies that raged around Gettysburg for a generation after the battle. We have only one Union historian—but what an historian he is! Frank Haskell had been born in Vermont and educated at Dartmouth; he moved out to Wisconsin and it was there that he joined the famous Iron Brigade, was promoted from lieutenant to colonel, and in time became aide-de-camp to General Gibbon. During the two weeks after the repulse of Pickett's charge he composed a book-length letter to his brother giving a history of the battle. A year later he was killed at Cold Harbor. Haskell's Gettysburg has become a classic of American literature—the only American military account to find its way into the Harvard Classics. Our final account is from the gifted pen of the English observer, Colonel Fremamtle, who tells of the aftermath of the charge and gives us an unforgettable picture of Lee at this crisis of his career.

A. Alexander Gives the Signal to Start

Before daylight on the morning of the 3d I received orders to post the artillery for an assault upon the enemy's position, and later I learned that it was to be led by Pickett's division and directed on Cemetery Hill. Some of the batteries had gone back for ammunition and forage, but they were all brought up immediately, and by daylight all then on the field were posted. Dearing's batallion (with Pickett's division) reported sometime during the morning. The enemy fired on our movements and positions occasionally, doing no great damage, and we scarcely returned a shot. The morning was consumed in waiting for Pickett's division, and possibly other movements of infantry. . . .

About 11 A.M. the skirmishers in A. P. Hill's front got to fighting for a barn in between the lines, and the artillery on both sides gradually took part until the whole of Hill's artillery in position, which I think was 63 guns, were heavily engaged with about an equal number of the enemy's guns for over a half hour, but not one of the 75 guns which I then had in line was allowed to fire a shot, as we had at best but a short supply of ammunition for the work laid out. . . .

Gradually the cannonade just referred to died out as it began, and the field became nearly silent, but writers have frequently referred to "the cannonade preceding the assault" as having begun at 11 o'clock and lasted for some hours, being misled by this affair. About 12 M. General Longstreet told me that when Pickett was ready, he would himself give the signal for all our guns to open (which was to be two guns from the Washington Artillery, near the center of our line, and meanwhile he desired me to select a suitable position for observation, and to take with me one of General Pickett's staff, and exercise my judgment in selecting the moment for Pickett's advance to begin. Complying, I selected

the advanced salient angle of the wood in which Pickett's line was now formed, just on the left flank of my line of 75 guns. While occupying this position and in conversation with General A. R. Wright, commanding a Georgia brigade in A. P. Hill's corps, who had come out there for an observation of the position, I received a note from General Longstreet, which I copy from the original still in my possession, as follows:

HD. QRS., July 3rd, 1863

COLONEL:

If the artillery fire does not have the effect to drive off the enemy or greatly demoralize him so as to make our efforts pretty certain, I would prefer that you should not advise General Pickett to make the charge. I shall rely a great deal on your good judgment to determine the matter, and shall expect you to let General Pickett know when the moment offers.

Respectfully,
J. Longstreet, Lieut.-General.

To Colonel E.P. Alexander, Artillery.

This note at once suggested that there was some alternative to the attack, and placed me on the responsibility of deciding the question. I endeavored to avoid it by giving my views in a note, of which I kept no copy, but of which I have always retained a vivid recollection, having discussed its points with General A. R. Wright as I wrote it. It was expressed very nearly as follows:

General:

I will only be able to judge of the effect of our fire on the enemy by his return fire, for his infantry is but little exposed to view and the smoke will obscure the whole field. If, as I infer from your note, there is any alternative to this attack, it should be carefully considered before opening our fire, for it will take all the artillery ammunition we have left to test this one thoroughly, and, if the result is unfavorable, we will have none left for another effort. And even if this is entirely successful it can only be so at a very bloody cost.

Very respectfully, &c.,

E. P. ALEXANDER, *Colonel Artillery.*

To this note I soon received the following reply:

HD. QTRS., July 3rd, 1863

Colonel:

The intention is to advance the infantry if the artillery has the desired effect of driving the enemy's off, or having other effect such as to warrant us in making the attack. When that moment arrives advise General P., and of course advance such artillery as you can use in aiding the attack.

Respectfully,

J. LONGSTREET, *Lieut.-General, Commanding.*

To Colonel ALEXANDER.

This letter again placed the responsibility upon me, and I felt it very deeply, for the day was rapidly advancing (it was about 12 M., or a little later), and whatever was to be done was to be done soon. Meanwhile I had been anxiously discussing the attack with General A. R. Wright, who said that the difficulty was not so much in *reaching* Cemetery Hill, or taking it—that his brigade had carried it the afternoon before—but that the trouble was to hold it, for the whole Federal army was massed in a sort of horse-shoe shape and could rapidly reinforce the point to any extent, while our long, enveloping line could not give prompt enough support. This somewhat reassured me, as I had heard it said that morning that General Lee had ordered "every brigade in the army to charge Cemetery Hill," and it was at least certain that the question of supports had had his careful attention. Before answering, however, I rode back to converse with General Pickett whose line was now formed or forming in the wood, and without telling him of the question I had to decide, I found out that he was entirely sanguine of success in the charge, and was only congratulating himself on the opportunity. I was convinced that to make any half-way effort would insure a failure of the campaign, and that if our

artillery fire was once opened, after all the time consumed in preparation for the attack, the only hope of success was to follow it up promptly with one supreme effort, concentrating every energy we possessed into it, and my mind was fully made up that if *the artillery opened Pickett must charge.* After the second note from General Longstreet, therefore, and the interview with Pickett, I did not feel justified in making any delay, but to acquaint General Longstreet with my determination. I wrote him a note, which I think I quote verbatim, as follows: "General: When our artillery fire is doing its best I shall advise General Pickett to advance." It was my intention, as he had a long distance to traverse, that he should start not later than fifteen minutes after our fire opened. . . .

It was 1 P.M. by my watch when the signal guns were fired, the field at that time being entirely silent, but for light picket firing between the lines, and as suddenly as an organ strikes up in a church, the grand roar followed from all the guns of both armies. The enemy's fire was heavy and severe, and their accounts represent ours as having been equally so, though our rifle guns were comparatively few and had only very defective ammunition. . . .

I had fully intended giving Pickett the order to advance as soon as I saw that our guns had gotten their ranges, say, in ten or fifteen minutes, but the enemy's fire was so severe that when that time had elapsed I could not make up my mind to order the infantry out into a fire which I did not believe they could face, for so long a charge, in such a hot sun, tired as they already were by the march from Chambersburg. I accordingly waited in hopes that our fire would produce some visible effect, or something turn up to make the situation more hopeful; but fifteen minutes more passed without any change in the situation, the fire on neither side slackening for a moment. Even then I could not bring myself to give a peremptory order to Pickett to advance, but feeling that the critical moment would soon pass, I wrote him a note to this effect: "If you are coming at all you must come immediately or I cannot give you proper support; but the enemy's fire has not slackened materially, and at least 18 guns are still firing from the Cemetery itself."

This note (which, though given from memory, I can vouch for as very nearly verbatim) I sent off at 1:30 P.M., consulting my watch. I afterwards heard what followed its receipt from members of the staff of both Generals Pickett and Longstreet, as follows: Pickett on receiving it galloped over to General Longstreet, who was not far off, and showed it to General L. The latter read it and made no reply. (General Longstreet himself, speaking of it afterwards, said that he knew the charge had to be made, but could not bring himself to give the order.) General Pickett then said: "General, shall I advance?" Longstreet turned around in his saddle and would not answer. Pickett immediately saluted, and said: "I am going to lead my division forward, sir," and galloped off to put it in motion; on which General L. left his staff and rode out alone to my position.

Meanwhile, five minutes after I sent the above note to Pickett, the enemy's fire suddenly slackened materially, and the batteries in the Cemetery were limbered up and were withdrawn. As the enemy had such abundance of ammunition and so much better guns than ours that they were not compelled to reserve their artillery for critical moments (as we almost always had to do), I knew that they must have felt the punishment a good deal, and I was a good deal elated by the sight. But to make sure that it was a withdrawal for good, and not a mere change of position or relieving of the batteries by fresh ones, I waited for five minutes more, closely examining the ground with a large glass. At that time I sent my courier to Pickett with a note: "For God's sake come quick; the 18 guns are gone"; and, going to the nearest guns, I sent a lieutenant and a sergeant, one after the other, with other messages to same effect.

A few minutes after this, Pickett still not appearing, General Longstreet rode up alone, having seen Pickett and left his staff as above. I showed him the situation, and said I only feared I could not give Pickett the help I wanted to, my ammunition being very low, and the seven guns under Richardson having been taken off. General Longstreet spoke up promptly: "Go and stop Pickett right where he is, and replenish your ammunition." I answered, that the ordnance wagons had been nearly emptied, replacing expenditures of the day before, and that not over 20 rounds to the gun were left—too little to accomplish much—and that while this was being done the enemy would recover from the effect of the fire we were now giving him. His reply was: "I don't want to make this charge; I don't believe it can succeed. I would stop Pickett now, but that General Lee has ordered it and expects it," and other remarks, showing that he would have been easily induced, even then, to order Pickett to halt.

It was just at this moment that Pickett's line appeared sweeping out of the wood, Garnett's brigade passing over us. I then left General Longstreet and rode a short distance with General Garnett, an old friend, who had been sick, but, but toned up in an old blue overcoat, in spite of the heat of the day, was riding in front of his line. I then galloped along my line of guns, ordering those that had over 20 rounds left to limber up and follow Pickett, and those that had less to maintain their fire from where they were. I had advanced several batteries or parts of batteries in this way, when Pickett's division appeared on the slope of Cemetery Hill, and a considerable force of the enemy were thrown out, attacking his un protected right flank. Meanwhile, too, several batteries which had been withdrawn were run out again and were firing on him very heavily. We opened on these troops and batteries with the best we had in the shop, and appeared to do them considerable damage, but meanwhile Pickett's division just seemed to melt away in the blue musketry smoke which now covered the hill. Nothing but stragglers came back. As soon as it was clear that Pickett was "gone up," I ceased firing, saving what little ammunition was left for fear of an advance by the enemy. About this time General Lee came up to our guns alone and remained there a half hour or more, speaking to Pickett's men as they came straggling back, and encouraging them to form again in the first cover they could find.

—Letter from General E. P. Alexander
to the Reverend J. Wm. Jones

B. Armistead Falls Beside the Enemy's Battery

The signal guns broke the silence, the blaze of the second gun mingling in the smoke of the first, and salvoes rolled to the left and repeated themselves, the enemy's fine metal spreading its fire to the converging lines, plowing the trembling ground, plunging through the line of batteries, and clouding the heavy air. The two or three hundred guns seemed proud of their undivided honors and organized confusion. The Confederates had the benefit of converging fire into the enemy's massed position, but the superior metal of the enemy neutralized the advantage of position. The brave and steady work progressed. . . .

General Pickett rode to confer with Alexander, then to the ground upon which I was resting, where he was soon handed a slip of paper. After reading it he handed it to me. It read:

"If you are coming at all, come at once, or I cannot give you proper support, but the enemy's fire has not slackened at all. At least eighteen guns are still firing from the cemetery itself.

—ALEXANDER"

Pickett said, "General, shall I advance?"

The effort to speak the order failed, and I could only indicate it by an affirmative bow. He accepted the duty, with seeming confidence of success, leaped on his horse, and rode gaily to his command. I mounted and spurred for Alexander's post. He reported that the batteries he had reserved for the charge with the infantry had been spirited away by General Lee's chief of artillery, that the ammunition of the batteries of position was so reduced that he could not use them in proper support of the infantry. He was ordered to stop the march at once and fill up his ammunition chests. But, alas! there was no more ammunition to be had.

The order was imperative. The Confederate commander had fixed his heart upon the work. Just then a number of the enemy's batteries hitched up and hauled off, which gave a glimpse of unexpected hope. Encouraging messages were sent for the columns to hurry on—and they were then on elastic springing step. The officers saluted as they passed, their stern smiles expressing confidence. General Pickett, a graceful horseman, sat lightly in the saddle, his brown locks flowing quite over his shoulders. Pettigrew's division spread their steps and quickly rectified the alignment, and the grand march moved bravely on. As soon as the leading columns opened the way, the supports sprang to their alignments. General Trimble mounted, adjusting his seat and reins with an air and grace as if setting out on a pleasant afternoon ride. When aligned to their places solid march was made down the slope and past our batteries of position.

Confederate batteries put their fire over the heads of the men as they moved down the slope, and continued to draw the fire of the enemy until the smoke lifted and drifted to the rear, when every gun was turned upon the infantry columns. The batteries that had been drawn off were replaced by others that were fresh. Soldiers and officers began to fall, some to rise no more, others to find their way to the hospital tents. Single files were cut here and there; then the gaps increased, and an occasional shot tore wider openings, but, closing the gaps as quickly as made, the march moved on. . . .

Colonel Latrobe was sent to General Trimble to have his men fill the line of the broken brigades, and bravely they repaired the damage. The enemy moved out against the supporting brigade in Pickett's rear. Colonel Sorrel was sent to have that move guarded, and Pickett was drawn back to that contention. McLaws was ordered to press his left forward, but the direct line of infantry and cross fire of artillery was telling fearfully on the front. Colonel Fremantle ran up to offer congratulations on the apparent success, but the big gaps in the ranks grew until the lines were reduced to half their length. I called his attention to the broken, struggling lines. Trimble mended the battle of the left in handsome style, but on the right the massing of the enemy grew stronger and stronger. Brigadier Garnett was killed; Kemper and Trimble were desperately wounded, Generals Hancock and Gibbon were wounded. General Lane succeeded Trimble and with Pettigrew held the battle of the left in steady ranks.

Pickett's lines being nearer, the impact was heaviest upon them. Most of the field officers were killed or wounded. Colonel Whittle, of Armistead's brigade, who had been shot through the right leg at Williamsburg and lost his left arm at Malvern Hill, was shot through the right arm, then brought down by a shot through his left leg.

General Armistead, of the second line, spread his steps to supply the places of fallen comrades. His colors cut down, with a volley against the bristling line of bayonets, he put his cap on his sword to guide the storm. The enemy's massing, enveloping numbers held the struggle until the noble Armistead fell beside the wheels of the enemy's battery. Pettigrew was wounded but held his command.

General Pickett, finding the battle broken while the enemy was still reinforcing, called the troops off. There was no indication of panic. The broken files marched back in steady step. The effort was nobly made and failed from blows that could not be fended.

—Longstreet, *From Manassas to Appomattox*

C. "The Crest is Safe"

Half-past two o'clock, an hour and a half since the commencement, and still the cannonade did not in the least abate; but soon thereafter some signs of weariness and a little slacking of fire began to be apparent upon both sides. . . . All things must end, and the great cannonade was no exception to the general law of earth. In the number of guns active at one time, and in the duration and rapidity of their fire, this artillery engagement, up to this time, must stand alone and pre-eminent in this war. It has not been often, or many times, surpassed in the battles of the world. Two hundred and fifty guns, at least, rapidly fired for two mortal hours. . . .

At three o'clock almost precisely, the last shot hummed, and bounded and fell, and the cannonade was over. The purpose of General Lee in all this fire of his guns—we know it now, we did not at the time so well—was to disable our artillery and break up our infantry upon the position of the Second Corps, so as to render them less an impediment to the sweep of his own brigades and divisions over our crest and through our lines. . . . There was a pause between acts, with the curtain down, soon to rise upon the great final act, and catastrophe of Gettysburg. We have passed by the left of the Second Division, coming from the First; when we crossed the crest the enemy was not in sight, and all was still—we walked slowly along in the rear of the troops, by the ridge cut off now from a view *of* the enemy on his position, and were returning to the spot where we had left our horses. . . . In a moment afterwards we met Captain Wessels and the orderlies who had our horses; they were on foot leading the horses. Captain Wessels was pale, and he said, excited: "General, they say the enemy's infantry is advancing." We spring into our saddles, a score of bounds brought us upon the all-seeing crest.

To say that men grew pale and held their breath at what we and they there saw, would not be true. Might not six thousand men be brave and without shade of fear, and yet, before a hostile eighteen thousand, armed, and not five minutes' march away, turn ashy white? None on that crest now need be told that *the enemy is advancing.* Every eye could see his legions, an overwhelming resistless tide of an ocean of armed men sweeping upon us! Regiment after regiment and brigade after brigade moved from the woods and rapidly take their places in the lines forming the assault. Pickett's proud division, with some additional troops, hold their right; Pettigrew's (Worth's) their left. The first line at short interval is followed by a second, and that a third succeeds; and columns between support the lines. More than half a mile their front extends; more than a thousand yards the dull gray masses deploy, man touching man, rank pressing rank, and line supporting line. The red flags wave, their horsemen gallop up and down, the arms of eighteen thousand men, barrel and bayonet, gleam in the sun, a sloping forest of flashing steel. Right on they move, as with one soul, in perfect order, without impediment of ditch, or wall or stream, over ridge and slope, through orchard and meadow, and corn-field, magnificent, grim, irresistible.

All was orderly and still upon our crest; no noise and no confusion. The men had little need of commands, for the survivors of a dozen battles knew well enough what this array in front portend-ed, and, already in their places, they would be pre-pared to act when the right time should come. The click of the locks as each man raised the hammer to feel with his fingers that the cap was on the nip-ple; the sharp jar as a musket touched a stone upon the wall when thrust in aiming over it, and the clicking of the iron axles as the guns were rolled up by hand a little further to the front, were quite all the sounds that could be heard. Cap-boxes were slid around to the front of the body; cartridge boxes opened, officers opened their pistol-holsters. Such preparations, little more was needed. The trefoil flags, colors of the brigades and divisions moved to their places in rear; but along the lines in front the grand old ensign that first waved in battle at Saratoga in 1777, and which these people coming would rob of half its stars, stood up, and the west wind kissed it as the sergeants sloped its lance towards the enemy. I believe that not one above whom it then waved but blessed his God that he was loyal to it, and whose heart did not swell with pride towards it, as the emblem of the Republic before that treason's flaunting rag in front.

General Gibbon rode down the lines, cool and calm, and in an unimpassioned voice he said to the men, "Do not hurry, men, and fire too fast, let them come up close before you fire, and then aim low and steadily." The coolness of their General was reflected in the faces of his men. Five minutes has elapsed since first the enemy have emerged from the woods—no great space of time surely, if measured by the usual standard by which men esti-mate duration—but it was long enough for us to note and weigh some of the elements of mighty moment that surrounded us; the disparity of num-bers between the assailants and the assailed; that few as were our numbers we could not be supported or reinforced until support would not be needed or would be too late; that upon the ability of the two

trefoil divisions to hold the crest and repel the assault depended not only their own safety or destruction, but also the honor of the Army of the Potomac and defeat or victory at Gettysburg. Should these advancing men pierce our line and become the entering wedge, driven home, that would sever our army asunder, what hope would there be afterwards, and where the blood-earned fruits of yesterday? It was long enough for the Rebel storm to drift across more than half the space that had at first separated it from us. None, or all, of these considerations either depressed or elevated us. They might have done the former, had we been timid; the latter had we been confident and vain. But, we were there-waiting, and ready to do our duty—that done, results could not dishonor us.

Our skirmishers open a spattering fire along the front, and, fighting, retire upon the main line—the first drops, the heralds of the storm, sounding on our windows. Then the thunders of our guns, first Arnold's then Cushing's and Woodruff's and the rest, shake and reverberate again through the air, and their sounding shells smite the enemy. . . . All our available guns are noy active, and from the fire of shells, as the range grows shorter and shorter, they change to shrap nel, and from shrapnel to can-ister; but in spite of shells, and shrapnel and canis-ter, without wavering or halt, the hardy lines of the enemy continue to move on. The Rebel guns make no reply to ours, and no charging shout rings out to-day, as is the Rebel wont; but the courage of these silent men amid our shots seem not to need the stimulus of other noise.

The enemy's right flank sweeps near Stannard's bushy crest, and his concealed Vermonters rake it with a well-delivered fire of musketry. The gray lines do not halt or reply, but with drawing a little from that extreme, they still move on. And so across all that-broad open ground they have come, nearer and nearer, nearly half the way, with our guns bellowing in their faces, until now a hundred yards, no more, divide our ready left from their advancing right. The eager men there are impatient to begin. Let them. First, Harrow's breastworks flame; then Hall's; then Webb's. As if our bullets were the fire coals that touched off their muskets, the enemy in front halts, and his countless level barrels blaze back upon us. The Second Division is struggling in battle. The rattling storm soon spreads to the right, and the blue trefoils are vieing with the white. All along each hostile front, a thousand yards, with narrowest space between, the volleys blaze and roll; as thick the sound as when a summer hail-storm pelts the city roofs; as thick the fire as when the incessant lightning fringes a summer cloud.

When the Rebel infantry had opened fire our batteries soon became silent, and this without their fault, for they were foul by long previous use. They were the targets of the concentrated Rebel bullets, and some of them had expended all their canister. But they were not silent before Rhorty was killed, Woodruff had fallen mortally wounded, and Cushing, firing almost his last canister, had dropped dead among his guns shot through the head by a bullet. The conflict is left to the infantry alone. . . .

The conflict was trememdous, but I had seen no wavering in all our line. Wondering how long the Rebel ranks, deep though they were, could stand our sheltered volleys, I had come near my destination, when—great heaven! were my senses mad? The larger portion of Webb's brigade—my God, it was true—there by the groups of trees and the angles of the wall, was breaking from the cover of their works, and, without orders or reason, with no hand lifted to check them, was falling back, a fear-stricken flock of confusion! The fate of Gettysburg hung upon a spider's single thread!

A great magnificent passion came on me at the instant, not one that overpowers and confounds, but one that blanches the face and sublimes every sense and faculty. My sword, that had always hung idle by my side, the sign of rank only in every battle, I drew, bright and gleaming, the symbol of command. Was not that a fit occasion, and these fugitives the men on whom to try the temper of the Solinzen steel? All rules and proprieties were forgotten; all considerations of person, and danger and safety despised; for, as I met the tide of these rabbits, the damned red flags of the rebellion began to thicken and flaunt along the wall they had just deserted, and one was already waving over one of the guns of the dead Cushing. I ordered these men to "halt," and "face about" and "fire," and they heard my voice and gathered my meaning, and obeyed my commands. On some unpatriotic backs of those not quick of comprehension, the flat of my sabre fell not lightly, and at its touch their love of country returned, and, with a look at me as if I were the destroying angel, as I might have become theirs, they again faced the enemy.

General Webb soon came to my assistance. He was on foot, but he was active, and did all that one could do to repair the breach, or to avert its calamity. The men that had fallen back, facing the enemy, soon regained confidence in them selves, and became steady. This portion of the wall was lost to us, and the enemy had gained the cover of the reverse side, where he now stormed with fire. But Webb's men, with their bodies in part protected by the abruptness of the crest, now sent back in the enemies' faces as fierce a storm. Some scores of venturesome Rebels, that in their first push at the wall had dared to cross at the further angle, and those that had desecrated Cushing's guns, were promptly shot down, and speedy death met him who should raise his body to cross it again.

At this point little could be seen of the enemy, by reason of his cover and the smoke, except the flash of his muskets and his waving flags. These red flags were accumulating at the wall every moment, and they maddened us as the same color does the bull. Webb's men are falling fast, and he is among them to direct and encourage; but, however well they may now do, with that walled enemy in front, with more than a dozen flags to Webb's three, it soon becomes apparent that in not many minutes they will be overpowered, or that there will be none alive for the enemy to overpower. Webb has but three regiments, all small, the 69th, 71st and 72nd Pennsylvania—the 106th Pennsylvania, except two companies, is not here to-day—and he must have speedy assistance, or this crest will be lost.

Oh, where is Gibbon? where is Hancock?—some general—anybody with the power and the will to support that wasting, melting line? No general came, and no succor! . . . As a last resort I resolved to see if Hall and Harrow could not send some of their commands to reinforce Webb. I galloped to the left in the execution of my purpose, and as I attained the rear of Hall's line, from the nature of the ground and the position of the enemy it was easy to discover the reason and the manner of this gathering of Rebel flags in front of Webb.

The enemy, emboldened by his success in gaining our line by the group of trees and the angle of the wall, was concentrating all his right against and was further pressing that point. There was the stress of his assault; there would he drive his fiery wedge to split our line. In front of Harrow's and Hall's Brigades he had been able to advance no nearer than when he first halted to deliver fire, and these commands had not yielded an inch. To effect the concentration before Webb, the enemy would march the regiment on his extreme right of each of his lines by the left flank to the rear of the troops, still halted and facing to the front, and so continuing to draw in his right, when they were all massed in the position desired, he would again face them to the front, and advance to the storming. This was the way he made the wall before Webb's line blaze red with his battle flags, and such was the purpose there of his thick-crowding battalions.

Not a moment must be lost. Colonel Hall I found just in rear of his line, sword in hand, cool, vigilant, noting all that passed and directing the battle of his brigade. The fire was constantly diminishing now in his front, in the manner and by the movement of the enemy that I have mentioned, drifting to the right.

"How is it going?" Colonel Hall asked me, as I rode up.

"Well, but Webb is hotly pressed and must have support, or he will be overpowered. Can you assist him?"

"Yes."

"You cannot be too quick."

"I will move my brigade at once."

"Good."

He gave the order, and in the briefest time I saw five friendly colors hurrying to the aid of the imperilled three; and each color represented true, battle-tried men, that had not turned back from Rebel fire that day nor yesterday, though their ranks were sadly thinned; to Webb's brigade, pressed back as it had been from the wall, the distance was not great from Hall's right. The regiments marched by the right flank. . . . The movement, as it did, attracting the enemy's fire, and executed in haste, as it must be, was difficult; but in reasonable time, and in order that is serviceable, if not regular, Hall's men are fighting gallantly side by side with Webb's before the all important point.

I did not stop to see all this movement of Hall's, but from him I went at once further to the left, to the 1st brigade. Gen'l Harrow I did not see, but his fighting men would answer my purpose as well. The 19th Me., the 15th Mass., the 32d N. Y. and the shattered old thunderbolt, the 1st Minn.—poor Farrell was dying then upon the ground where he had fallen—all men that I could find I took over to the right at the *double quick*.

As we were moving to, and near the other brigade of the division, from my position on horseback, I could see that the enemy's right, under Hall's fire, was beginning to stagger and to break. "See," I said to the men, "See the *chivalry*! See the gray-backs run!" The men saw, and as they swept to their places by the side of Hall and opened fire, they roared, and this in a manner that said more plainly than words—for the deaf could have seen it in their faces, and the blind could have heard it in their voices—*the crest is safe!*

The whole Division concentrated, and changes of position, and new phases, as well on our part as on that of the enemy. having as indicated occurred, for the purpose of showing the exact present posture of affairs, some further description is necessary. Before the 2d Division the enemy is massed, the main bulk of his force covered by the ground that slopes to his rear, with his front at the stone wall. Between his front and us extends the very apex of the crest. All there are left of the White Trefoil Division—yesterday morning there were three thousand eight hundred, this morning there were less than three thousand—at this moment there are somewhat over two thousand;—twelve regiments in three brigades are below or behind the crest, in such a position that by the exposure of the head and upper part of the body above the crest they can deliver their fire in the enemy's face along the top of the wall.

By reason of the disorganization incidental in Webb's brigade to his men's having broken and fallen back, as mentioned, in the two other brigades to their rapid and difficult change of position under fire, and in all the divisions in part to severe and continuous battle, formation of companies and regiments in regular ranks is lost; but commands, companies, regiments and brigades are blended and intermixed—an irregular extended mass—men enough, if in order, to form a line of four or five ranks along the whole front of the division. The twelve flags of the regiments wave defiantly at intervals along the front, at the stone wall, at unequal distances from ours of forty, fifty or sixty yards, stream nearly double this number of the battle flags of the enemy.

These changes accomplished on either side, and the concentration complete, although no cessation or abatement in the general din of conflict since the commencement had at any time been appreciable, now it was as if a new battle, deadlier, stormier than before, had sprung from the body of the old—a young Phoenix of combat, whose eyes stream lightning, shaking his arrowy wings over the yet glowing ashes of his progenitor. The jostling, swaying lines on either side boil, and roar, and dash their flamy spray, two hostile billows of a fiery ocean. Thick flashes stream from the wall, thick volleys answer from the crest. No threats or expostulation now, only example and encouragement. All depths of passion are stirred, and all combatives fire, down to their deep foundations. Individuality is drowned in a sea of clamor, and timid men, breathing the breath of the multitude, are brave. The frequent dead and wounded lie where they stagger and fall—there is no humanity for them now, and none can be spared to care for them. The men do not cheer or shout; they growl, and over that uneasy sea, heard with the roar of musketry, sweeps the muttered thunder of a storm of growls. Webb, Hall, Devereux, Mallon, Abbott among the men where all are heroes, are doing deeds of note.

Now the loyal wave rolls up as if it would overleap its barrier, the crest. Pistols flash with the muskets. My "Forward to the wall" is answered by the Rebel counter-command, "Steady, men!" and the wave swings back. Again it surges, and again it sinks. These men of Pennsylvania, on the soil of their own homesteads, the first and only to flee the wall, must be the first to storm it. . . . "Sergeant, forward with your color. Let the Rebels see it close to their eyes once be fore they die." The color sergant of the 72d Pa., grasping the stump of the severed lance in both his hands, waved the flag above his head and rushed towards the wall. "Will you see your color storm the wall alone?" One man only starts to follow. Almost half way to the wall, down go color bearer and color to the ground—the gallant sergeant is dead. The line springs—the crest of the solid ground with a great roar, heaves forward its maddened load, men, arms, smoke, fire, a fighting mass. It rolls to the wall—flash meets flash, the wall is crossed—a moment ensues of thrusts, yells, blows, shots, and undistinguishable conflict, followed by a shout universal that makes the welkin ring again, and the 1ast and bloodiest fight of the great battle of Gettysburg is ended and won.

—Haskell, *The Battle of Gettysburg*

D. "All This Will Come Right in the End"

July 3d.—The distance between the Confederate guns and the Yankee position—i.e. between the woods crowning the opposite ridges—was at least a mile, quite open, gently undulating, and exposed to artillery the whole distance. This was the ground which had to be crossed in today's attack. Pickett's division, which had just come up, was to bear the brunt in Longstreet's attack, together with Heth and Pettigrew in Hill's corps. Pickett's division was a weak one (under five thousand), owing to the absence of two brigades.

At noon all Longstreet's dispositions were made; his troops for attack were deployed into line and lying down in the woods; his batteries were ready to open. The General then dismounted and went to sleep for a short time. . . .

Finding that to see the actual fighting it was absolutely necessary to go into the thick of the thing, I determined to make my way to General Longstreet. It was then about two thirty. After passing General Lee and his staff, I rode on through the woods in the direction in which I had left Longstreet. I soon began to meet many wounded men returning from the front; many of them asked in piteous tones the way to a doctor or an ambulance. The farther I got, the greater became the number of the wounded. At last I came to a perfect stream of them flocking through the woods in numbers as great as the crowd in Oxford Street in the middle of the day. Some were walking alone on crutches composed of two rifles, others supported by men less badly wounded than themselves, and others were carried on stretchers by the ambulance corps; but in no case did I see a sound man helping the wounded to the rear unless he carried the red badge of the ambulance corps. They were still under a heavy fire; the shells were continually bringing down great limbs of trees and carrying further destruction amongst this melancholy procession. I saw all this in much less time than it takes to write it, and although astonished to meet such vast numbers of wounded, I had not seen enough to give me any idea of the real extent of the mischief.

When I got close up to General Longstreet, I saw one of his regiments advancing through the woods in good order; so, thinking I was just in time to see the attack, I remarked to the General that "I wouldn't have missed this for anything."

Longstreet was seated at the top of a snake fence at the edge of the wood and looking perfectly calm and unperturbed. He replied, laughing: "The devil you wouldn't! I would like to have missed it very much; we've attacked and been repulsed; look there!"

For the first time I then had a view of the open space between the two positions and saw it covered with Confederates, slowly and sulkily returning toward us in small broken parties, under a heavy fire of artillery. But the fire where we were was not so bad as farther to the rear, for although the air seemed alive with shell, yet the greater number burst behind us. The General told me that Pickett's division had succeeded in carrying the enemy's position and capturing his guns, but after remaining there twenty minutes, *it* had been forced to retire, on the retreat of Heth and Pettigrew on its left. . . .

Soon afterward I joined General Lee, who had in the mean while come to the front on becoming aware of the disaster. If Longstreet's conduct was admirable, that of Lee was perfectly sublime. He was engaged in rallying and in encouraging the broken troops and was riding about a little in front of the wood, quite alone, the whole of his staff being engaged in a similar manner farther to the rear. His face, which is always placid and cheerful, did not show signs of the slightest disappointment, care, or annoyance; and he was addressing to every soldier he met a few words of encouragement, such as: "All this will come right in the end; we'll talk it over afterwards; but in the meantime, all good men must rally. We want all good and true men just now," etc. He spoke to all the wounded men that passed him, and the slightly wounded he exhorted to "bind up their hurts and take up a musket" in this emergency. Very few failed to answer his appeal, and I saw many badly wounded men take off their hats and cheer him.

He said to me, "This has been a sad day for us, Colonel—a sad day; but we can't expect always to gain victories." . . . I saw General Willcox come up to him and explain, almost crying, the state of his brigade. General Lee immediately shook hands with him and said cheerfully: "Never mind, General, all this has been my fault—it is I that have lost this fight, and you must help me out of it in the best way you can."

In this way I saw General Lee encourage and reanimate his somewhat dispirited troops and magnanimously take upon his own shoulders the whole weight of the repulse. It was impossible to look at him or to listen to him without feeling the strongest admiration.

—[FREMANTLE], "The Battle of Gettysburg"

XVIII.8

GENERAL LEE OFFERS TO RESIGN AFTER GETTYSBURG

"It is all my fault," said Lee, on the afternoon of the third. History does not agree with that verdict, bur it was characteristic of Lee that he should shoulder the blame for the failure of the invasion. On August 8 he sent Davis his offer to resign. In his reply Davis referred finely to those "achievements which will make you and your army the subject of history and object of the world's admiration for generations to come."

Camp Orange, August 8, 1863

His Excellency JEFFERSON DAVIS,
President of the Confederate States:

MR. PRESIDENT: Your letters of July 28 and August 2 have been received, and I have waited for a leisure hour to reply, but I fear that will never come. I am extremely obliged to you for the attention given to the wants of this army, and the efforts made to supply them. Our absentees are returning, and I hope the earnest and beautiful appeal made to the country in your proclamation may stir up the virtue of the whole people, and that they may see their duty and perform it. Nothing is wanted but that their fortitude should equal their bravery to insure the success of our cause. We must expect reverses, even defeats. They are sent to teach us wisdom and prudence, to call forth greater energies, and to prevent our falling into greater disasters. Our people have only to be true and united, to bear manfully the misfortunes incident to war, and all will come right in the end.

I know how prone we are to censure and how ready to blame others for the non-fulfillment of our expectations. This is unbecoming in a generous people, and I grieve to see its expression. The general remedy for the want of success in a military commander is his removal. This is natural, and, in many instances, proper. For, no matter what may be the ability of the officer, if he loses the confidence of his troops disaster must sooner or later ensue.

I have been prompted by these reflections more than once since my return from Pennsylvania to propose to Your Excellency the propriety of selecting another commander for this army. I have seen and heard of expression of discontent in the public journals at the result of the expedition. I do not know how far this feeling extends in the army. My brother officers have been too kind to report it, and so far the troops have been too generous to exhibit it. It is fair, how ever, to suppose that it does exist, and success is so necessary to us that nothing should be risked to secure it. I therefore, in all sincerity, request Your Excellency to take measures to supply my place. I do this with the more earnestness be cause no one is more aware than myself of my inability for the duties of my position. I cannot even accomplish what I myself desire. How can I fulfill the expectations of others? In addition I sensibly feel the growing failure of my bodily strength. I have not yet recovered from the attack I experienced the past spring. I am becoming more and more in capable of exertion, and am thus prevented from making the personal examinations and giving the personal supervision to the operations in the field which I feel to be necessary. I am so dull that in making use of the eyes of others I am frequently misled. Everything, therefore, points to the advantages to be derived from a new commander, and I the more anxiously urge the matter upon Your Excellency from my belief that a younger and abler man than myself can readily be attained. I know that he will have as gallant and brave an army as ever existed to second his efforts, and it would be the happiest day of my life to see at its head a worthy leader—one that would accomplish more than I could perform and all that I have wished. I hope Your Excellency will attribute my request to the true reason, the desire to serve my country, and to do all in my power to insure the success of her righteous cause.

I have no complaints to make of any one but myself. I have received nothing but kindness from those above me, and the most considerate attention from my comrades and companions in arms. To Your Excellency I am specially indebted for uniform kindness and consideration. You have done everything in your power to aid me in the work committed to my charge, without omitting anything to promote the general welfare. I pray that your efforts may at length be crowned with success, and that you may long live to enjoy the thanks of grateful people.

With sentiments of great esteem, I am, very respectfully and truly, yours,

R.E. LEE,
General.

RICHMOND, VA., August 11, 1863

General R. E. LEE,
Commanding Army of Northern Virginia:

Yours of 8th instant has been received. I am glad that you concur so entirely with me as to the want of our country in this trying hour, and am happy to add that after the first depression consequent upon our disaster in the west, indications have appeared that our people will exhibit that fortitude which we agree in believing is alone needful to secure ultimate success.

It well became Sidney Johnston, when overwhelmed by a senseless clamor, to admit the rule that success is the test of merit; and yet there has been nothing which I have found to require a greater effort of patience than to bear the criticisms of the ignorant, who pronounce everything a failure which does not equal their expectations or desires, and can see no good result which is not in the line of their own imaginings. I admit the propriety of your conclusions, that an officer who loses the confidence of his troops should have his position changed, whatever may be his ability, but when I read the sentence I was not at all prepared for the application you were about to make. Expressions of discontent in the public journals furnish but little evidence of the sentiment of an army. I wish it were otherwise, even though all the abuse of myself should be accepted as the results of honest observation. I say I wish I could feel that the public journals were not generally partisan nor venal.

Were you capable of stooping to it, you could easily surround yourself with those who would fill the press with your laudations, and seek to exalt you for what you had not done, rather than detract from the achievements which will make you and your army the subject of history and object of the world's admiration for generations to come.

I am truly sorry to know that you still feel the effects of the illness you suffered last spring, and can readily understand the embarrassments you experience in using the eyes of others, having been so much accustomed to make your own reconnaissances. Practice will, however, do much to relieve that embarrassment, and the minute knowledge of the country which you have acquired will render you less dependent for topographical information.

But suppose, my dear friend, that I were to admit, with all their implications, the points which you present, where am I to find that new commander who is to possess the greater ability which you believe to be required? I do not doubt the readiness with which you would give way to one who could accomplish all that you have wished, and you will do me the justice to believe that if Providence should kindly offer such a person for our use, I would not hesitate to avail of his services.

My sight is not sufficiently penetrating to discover such hidden merit, if it exists, and I have but used to you the language of sober earnestness when I have impressed upon you the propriety of avoiding all unnecessary exposure to danger, because I felt our country could not bear to lose you. To ask me to substitute you by some one in my judgment more fit to command, or who would possess more of the confidence of the army, or of the reflecting men of the country, is to demand an impossibility.

It only remains for me to hope that you will take all possible care of yourself, that your health and strength may be entirely restored, and that the Lord will preserve you for the important duties devolved upon you in the struggle of our suffering country for the independence which we have engaged in war to maintain.

As ever, very respectfully and truly, yours,
Jefferson Davis.

—*War of the Rebellion . . . Official Records*

XVIII.9

"BELLS ARE RINGING WILDLY"

The day after Gettysburg was the greatest Fourth of July since the Declaration. Vicksburg had fallen, Lee had been defeated, the Union was safe! So, at least, thought most Northerners, and the North was swept with enthusiasm and jubilation.

William Lusk tells of the reception of the news in Wilmington.

Headquarters Delaware Department,
Wilmington, Del., July 7th, 1863

Dear, dear Cousin Lou:

I said I would write you so soon as the full purport of the good news was ascertained. And now that it has all broken upon us, although my heels are where my head ought to be, I will try and fulfil my engagement as coherently as possible. We have had the dark hour. The dawn has broken, and the collapsed confederacy has no place where it can hide its head. Bells are ringing wildly all over the city. Citizens grin at one another with fairly idiotic delight. One is on the top of his house frantically swinging a dinner bell, contributing thus his share of patriotic clamor to the general ding-dong. Bully for him! How I envy the heroes of Meade's Army. It would be worth while to die, in order that one's friends might say, "He died at Gettysburg." But to live to hear all the good news, and now to learn that Vicksburg has surrendered, is a little too much happiness for poor mortal men. I can laugh, I can cry with joy. All hysterical nonsense is pardonable now. Manassas, twice repeated, Fredericksburg and Chickahominy! Bless them as the cruel training that has made us learn our duties to our country. Slavery has fallen, and I believe Heaven as well as earth rejoices. Providence has tenderly removed that grand old hero, Jackson, before the blow came, that the one good, earnest, misguided man might be spared the sight of the downfall of a cause fanaticism led him to believe was right. . . . These enthusiastic citizens of Wilmington, not content with bell-ringing, have taken to firing cannon, and the boys, to help matters, are discharging pistols into empty barrels. The people in a little semi-slave holding State, when not downright traitors, are noisily, obstreperously loyal, to a degree that New England can hardly conceive of. My letter must be short and jubilant, I cannot do anything long to-day.

Just dance through the house for me, and kiss every one you meet. So I feel now. Goody-bye.

Affec'y.,
Will.

—*War Letters of William Thompson Lusk*

XVIII.10

A FAR FROM GLORIOUS FOURTH

For the Confederacy, the Fourth of July, 1863, was a bitter day for celebration. Perhaps none felt its sting more painfully than Gen. George E. Pickett. Filled with anguish and regret, Pickett wrote this letter to his beloved, La Salle Corbelle, a few days after the battle was concluded and Pickett's division devastated.

Pickett never forgave Lee for ordering his men to their fate on Cemetery Ridge. "That old man had my division slaughtered at Gettysburg," Pickett later said of Lee. Pickett's bitterness led to severe depression after the war. He refused commands offered by the president of the United States and the Khedive of Egypt. Instead, Pickett entered the insurance business.

Headquarters, July 6, 1863

On the Fourth—far from a glorious Fourth to us or to any with love for his fellow-men—I wrote you just a line of heart-break. The sacrifice of life on that blood-soaked field on the fatal third was too awful for the heralding of victory, even for our victorious foe, who, I think, believe as we do, that it decided the fate of our cause. No words can picture the anguish of that roll-call—the breathless waits between the responses. The "Here" of those who, by God's mercy, had miraculously escaped the awful rain of shots and shell was a sob—a gasp—a knell—for the unanswered name of his comrade called before his. There was no tone of thankfulness for having been spared to answer to their names, but rather a toll, and an unvoiced wish that they, too, had been among the missing.

But for the blight to your sweet young life, but for you, only you, my darling, your soldier would rather by far be out there, too, with his brave Virginians—dead.

Even now I can hear them cheering as I gave the order, "Forward"! I can feel their faith and trust in me and their love for our cause. I can feel the thrill of their joyous voices as they called out all along the line, "We'll follow you, Marse George. We'll follow you—we'll follow you." Oh, how faithfully they kept their word—following me on—on—to their death, and I, believing in the promised support, led them on—on—on—Oh, God!

I can't write you a love letter to-day, my Sallie, for with my great love for you and my gratitude to God for sparing my life to devote to you, comes the over-powering thought of those whose lives were sacrificed—of the broken-hearted widows and mothers and orphans. The moans of my wounded boys, the sight of the dead, upturned faces, flood my soul with grief—and here am I whom they trusted, whom they followed, leaving them on that field of carnage—leaving them to the mercy of—and guarding four thousand prisoners across the river back to Winchester. Such a duty for men who a few hours ago covered themselves with glory eternal.

Well, my darling, I put the prisoners all on their honor and gave them equal liberties with my own soldier boys. My first command to them was to go and enjoy themselves the best they could, and they have obeyed my order. To-day a Dutchman and two of his comrades came up and told me they were lost and besought me to help them find their commands. They had been with my men and gotten separated from their own comrades. So I sent out old Floyd off on St. Paul to find out where they belonged and deliver them.

This is too gloomy and too poor a letter for so beautiful a sweetheart, but it seems sacrilegious, almost, to say I love you, with the hearts that are stilled to love on the field of battle.

Your Soldier,

—General George E. Pickett

XVIII.11

"A New Birth of Freedom"

On July 4 Lincoln had announced to the country the victory of the Army of the Potomac, and invoked "the condolences of all for the many gallant fallen." That November part of the battlefield of Gettysburg was made a permanent cemetery for the soldiers who had fallen there. Edward Everett of Massachusetts delivered the principal oration. The superintendent of the enterprise, David Wills, asked Lincoln to make "a few appropriate remarks" and the result was the most memorable of all American addresses.

Fourscore and seven years ago our fathers brought forth on this continent a new nation, conceived in Liberty, and dedicated to the proposition that all men are created equal.

Now we are engaged in a great civil war, testing whether that nation or any nation so conceived and so dedicated can long endure. We are met on a great battlefield of that war. We have come to dedicate a portion of that field as a final resting place for those who here gave their lives that that nation might live. It is altogether fitting and proper that we should do this.

But in a larger sense we cannot dedicate—we cannot consecrate—we cannot hallow—this ground. The brave men, living and dead, who struggled here, have consecrated it, far above our poor power to add or detract. The world will little note nor long remember what we say here, but it can never forget what they did here. It is for us the living, rather, to be dedicated here to the unfinished work which they who fought here have thus far so nobly advanced. It is rather for us to be here dedicated to the great task remaining before us— that from these honored dead we take increased devotion to that cause for which they gave the last full measure of devotion—that we here highly resolve that these dead shall not have died in vain—that this nation, under God, shall have a new birth of freedom—and that government of the people, by the people, for the people, shall not perish from the earth.

—Lincoln, "The Gettysburg Address"

XIX

VICKSBURG AND
PORT HUDSON

The Vicksburg campaign, which lasted from November 1862 to July 1863, was the most confused and confusing of an Civil War campaigns. The confusion, however, is in the tactics rather than in the grand strategy. That strategy was simple enough. It was to clear the Mississippi, thus cutting off the Trans-Mississippi West from the rest of the Confederacy, and opening a channel from the Gulf to the North. By midsummer 1862 these grand objectives had been largely achieved. Farragut had taken New Orleans; Columbus had been evacuated; New Madrid and Island No. 10 had fallen; the Confederates had abandoned Fort Pillow and Memphis. In the thousand-mile stretch from the Gulf to the Ohio, only Vicks burg and Port Hudson were still in Confederate hands.

In June 1862 Farragut had steamed northward toward the gunboat flotilla under Davis; he had been able to run the batteries of Vicksburg, but unable to take the city. Such an operation required a combined land and water attack. Had Halleck moved promptly on Vicksburg after Shiloh he could probably have captured it; he failed to do so and the Confederates, alert to its importance, hastened to reinforce it. As early as October 1862 Grant asked permission to attack Vicksburg, but not until December was that permission granted, and even then it was not clear whether the operation was to be by Grant, Sherman, or McClernand.

The Vicksburg campaign opened in November when Grant established a base at Holly Springs, Mississippi, and prepared to move down the Yazoo on Vicksburg. Forrest attacked Grant's communications and then Van Dorn captured Holly Springs and destroyed his stores, and the plan was abandoned Late the next month Sherman moved down the Mississippi to the mouth of the Yazoo, and up the Yazoo to Chickasaw Bluffs; on December 29 he attacked the Confederates at the Bluffs and was repulsed.

Thus the first attempt to take Vicksburg from the rear—a joint operation by Grant and Sherman ended in failure. It was, as

events were to prove, the sound approach, and had Grant been properly supported it might have worked. Balked in the attempt to take Vicksburg from Memphis, Grant moved his forces to the west side of the Mississippi and began to probe for a crossing. We cannot follow in detail the long and complex story of the effort to find a crossing below Vicksburg and ferry the great army for an attack from the south. Eventually Grant moved his army down a series of rivers and bayous west of the Mississippi—Lake Providence, the Bayou Macon, the Tensas, and the Washita—to Hard Times on the Red River. An attempt to cross at Grand Gulf—about 50 miles below Vicksburg—was frustrated by stiff Confederate opposition. Meantime Porter's gunboats had run the batteries of Vicksburg and steamed south to where Grant's army lay waiting. On April 30 Grant began ferrying his army across the Mississippi at Bruinsburg. Pemberton, now in command at Vicksburg, hurried reinforcements south to Port Gibson, a few miles from Bruinsburg; there was a sharp fight but the Confederates were worsted and retreated. During the next week the whole of Grant's army crossed the river and prepared to move against Vicksburg.

The next two weeks saw a swift development of Grant's campaign, and some of the hottest fighting of the war. Pemberton had some 25,000 men at Vicksburg and along the Vicksburg and Jackson Railway; Joseph E. Johnston had about the same number at and around Jackson. It was Grant's purpose to prevent these two forces from combining, and to defeat them separately. It was a formidable task. He had broken his communications and was forced to live off the country; the terrain—muddy and swampy and with wretched roads—was not favorable to swift movements; if Grant was defeated his army would be lost in enemy territory.

On May 12 Grant moved one wing of his army under McPherson on Jackson, capital of the state and important railroad center. There was a fight at Raymond; the Confederates fell back; and on the fourteenth McPherson defeated Johnston, and seized Jackson. Then the army turned westward to deal with Pemberton. That hapless general, who did everything at the wrong time, had moved out to harry Grant's rear and his nonexistent line of communications. Grant caught him at Champion's Hill on May 15 and defeated him. Pemberton retreated to the Black River, where there was another sharp fight. Once more the Confederates withdrew, this time to the strong works outside Vicksburg. Reluctant to embark on a siege Grant tried, on May 19, to storm the works—and failed. Undaunted he tried another general assault on the twenty-second, only to be repulsed with heavy losses.

Clearly Vicksburg could be taken only by a siege. Methodically Grant collected a large army of some 70,000, over 200 guns, and set about to invest the city. The siege lasted 47 days. Just as Grant was preparing for a final grand attack, Pemberton surrendered. Johnston, who had been preparing to go to Pemberton's aid, fell back with Sherman in pursuit. Port Hudson surrendered on July 9. Once more the Mississippi went unvexed to the sea.

XIX.1

"Onward to Vicksburg"

High on a bluff the guns of Vicksburg commanded the Mississippi approaches from both north and south. As Grant feared to run the batteries he decided to move his army to the western side of the river and attack the great fortress city from the south and rear. A long-drawn-out attempt to by-pass Vicksburg by building a canal across the peninsula. in the great curve of the Mississippi failed when the Confederates planted batteries below the city and commanding the canal. By the end of April, however, Grant had succeeded in getting his army of some 40,000 down the river system to the west of the Mississippi and across to the east side of the Mississippi at Bruinsburg. Now, as Sergeant Charles Wilcox tells us, the cry was "On to Vicksburg!"

The campaign that followed was one of the most brilliant of the war, both in tactics and in strategy. In three weeks Grant's armies won five victories—Port Gibson, Raymond, Jackson, Champion's Hill, and Big Black River; captured the capital of the state; separated the armies of Johnston and Pemberton; and invested Vicksburg.

Charles Wilcox, whose diary tells something of this story, was a student at Illinois State Normal University when the war opened. He enlisted in the 33rd Illinois Volunteers, fought in Missouri, at Vicksburg, and in Louisiana, and ended up as captain of the 92nd Colored Infantry.

Thursday, [April] 23d [1863]—We are jubilant over the success of our boats (transports) which came past Vicksburg last night. Six transports made the attempt and all got past—this side of the battery (rebel) fartherest down the river when one—the *Tigress*—was sunk, it having sprung a leak from the effect of the enemy's fire; the other five came down past Carthage though one (the *Empire City*) being so disabled it floated all the way from Vicksburg. The other four are somewhat injured but will soon be fitted for our use. Talked with several of those who came down on the boats. Only three or four out of the crews of the *six* boats were wounded— none killed—some fatally wounded though. These crews were nearly all soldiers who volunteered their services. . . . The crew of the *Tigress* were all saved. The *Empire City* was under fire one hour and a half; this long time is accounted for by she being totally disabled before she got half way past the batteries.

Some of our baggage came up. Gen. Osterhaus' Division *is* on transports to go and attack Grand Gulf. Our Brigade is ordered to be ready with 3 days cooked rations to march to the support of Osterhaus' Division.

Sunday, [April] 26th . . . Weather cloudy—it commenced-raining about sunset and still continues. The private news is that we march sometime to-night, and are to make the attack upon Grand Gulf sometime to-morrow. The rebels have been, of late, reinforcing their force at that place. O God, protect us.

Monday, [April] 27th—Got orders about noon to embark immediately, which we very soon prepared to do, but did not succeed in getting aboard the boat (*Forest Queen*, the Flag Boat) till after dark. We leave behind everything save the well men with their knapsacks, guns and accoutrements with 80 rounds of ammunition to the man, three days rations in our haversacks, and horses for the main staff officers and their orderlies. Everybody is jolly and each one has a good word of cheer for his friend or comrade all are in a bustle; every one is confident of victory in the coming contest. It rained in the night and some this forenoon; it is very muddy. . . .

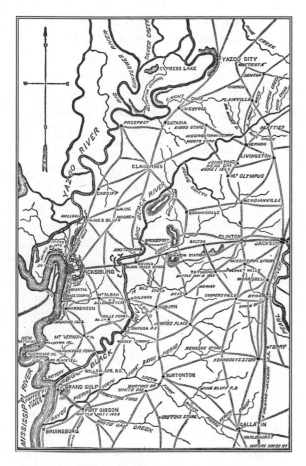

THE VICKSBURG CAMPAIGN

Tuesday, [April] 28th—Did not leave the landing last night as all the boats were not loaded till about eleven o'clock this A.M. Troops are coming in from Milliken's Bend; a part of McPherson's *Corps de Armie is* already here waiting to embark which they will do as soon as the boats can take us down and return. Seven transports and four or five barges, each loaded with a regiment or more, left Perkin's Plantation about noon, we disembarking on the Louisiana side, four or five miles above the fortifications at Grand Gulf, about two o'clock P.M. The rebels' position is in plain view. Judging from appearances they have a strong position. We found six of our gunboats just above Grand Gulf, lying out of reach of the rebels' guns. As the day was closing our gunboats threw three shells into the enemy's position, to learn the range of the guns; the enemy did not reply. The weather is very warm,

sky clear. It is said that the ball opens in the morning. The transportt and barges are all back after more troops. All of Carr's Division and part of Osterhaus' are here. When we were landing there were some Negroes near by who appeared to be very happy indeed upon seeing us. They clapped their hands in joy, prostrated themselves, shook hands with each other, and thanked the Lord as a Negro only can. 'Twas interesting, affecting, and impressive to witness these manifestations of joy. Col. Lippincott, who, until this war has always been a proslavery man, seeing them remarked "I was never more tempted to be an abolitionist." I carry a gun, and have no horse to ride while on this expedition.

Wednesday, [April] 29th—The sun arose throwing an impressive splendor upon the exciting scenes of the early morn. Every boat—transport and barge lies at the landing, about five miles above Grand Gulf, covered till they are black with troops. Every heart here is full of anxiety and emotion; wondering eyes and eyes not altogether tearless, gaze ever and anon upon the *Father of Waters* where lie the formidable fleet of gunboats and rams, transports and barges, the latter heavily loaded with troops whose courage and valor are sufficient when combined with that of the rest of this mighty army, to redeem this lovely valley of the Mississippi from fiends and traitors who are desecrating it.

Now it is 7 1/2 o'clock, A.M. Each gunboat and transport has gotten up full steam. The black smoke curls up from the blacker smoke-pipes, and moves towards the rebels, seeming to tell them of their black deeds and warns them of their portion when we attack them. It is like that which comes from the lower regions, scented with brimstone and issuing as it does from those gunboats, the traitors may well think, as they see it, that that fleet from which it comes has a portion of hell to give them, and that too, ere long, if they do not surrender or run. And now what means that? Every gunboat is steaming up the river. Can it be that the attack is not to be made? Every one is surprised. No; 'tis only the preparation for the attack. They are now "rounding to" and there they go. Thousands of eyes are looking upon. The first gun is fired by the enemy; the *Benton*, I believe, replies. 'Tis 8 o'clock. The contest has fairly begun; every gunboat is engaged. We all know when the enemy fires his heaviest guns as they make a sharper report than any of ours, though we have as large guns as he; this is probably accounted for by ours being on the water.

Eleven o'clock, A.M. Several of the enemy's batteries are silenced. The gunboats ply around and close to his strongest battery which gives them a round every opportunity, but as they near that battery they, one after another, give him broadsides which are terrible and produce a marked effect. The *Benton* "lays off" nearly across the river and just opposite and within good range of this powerful battery; every few minutes she sends an 84 or 64 pounder with nice precision at it; the dust flies and the enemy is quiet for a minute. This boat makes the most of the best shots that are fired. It seems to me that the enemy shoots wildly.

A few minutes after 12 M. The bombardment is over. Every one of the enemy's batteries save one, of three heavy guns are silenced, and we tried in vain to silence it.

The fleet has retired; Gen. Grant who was in a messenger boat during the bombardment, has come ashore. A little while passes and we get orders to start immediately down the levee, past Grand Gulf. The transports are being unloaded. At two P.M. we started for below; all the boats are to run the gauntlet to-night. We are now (evening) three or four miles below the enemy's works, though we only marched about three miles to get from five miles above them. The generals, colonels, and privates all lie down together, one faring no better than another. . . .

Friday, May 1st [1863]—A bright, clear and warm day, with a very slight breeze. This has been a glorious day for the Union, and for the despondent hearts in the North. We have fought a battle and won a complete victory. Having partaken our suppers last evening we again set forth upon our march, the Second Brigade going in the advance on account of our much wearied skirmishers. We came along slowly, carefully feeling our way though the moon shone brightly, and twice dispersing the enemy's pickets, till two o'clock A.M. when we came upon the enemy in force who *saluted us* with several rounds of grape and cannister, though not hurting us very much. . . .

A little after sunrise Major Potter in command of companies A, C, F and G of our regiment was ordered to go out on the road to our left (our line of battle at this time was north and south, facing to the east, and hold it till Gen. Osterhaus could relieve him. I asked permission of the Colonel to go with comp. "A," and carry a gun, but was refused so I had to stay with the regiment to be ready to carry and repeat orders. The Major with his pet soldiers had not gone far ere the enemy opened fire upon him with his cannon. This was really the beginning of the battle. Soon the skirmishers in front come in contact and the roar of musketry is heard. . . . We have not *all* got our positions yet, but the battle commences in earnest, the artillery on both sides firing smartly. The enemy has a cross fire upon us and we double quick into line or cover ourselves under the brow of a ridge of land. Our regiment being divided the six companies are ordered to stay back till the other four companies come up.

And now I see Major Potter with his gallant band coming I tell the fact to Col. Lippincott. He orders me to bring the Major and his command to join the regiment. I go but dear me! how the shells and shot whiz around me. One shell bursts just over me; I shrink and dodge with the flash, but hasten on very soon, and after some difficulty, helping right up capsized caissons and crowding through the excited troops, I find the Major and direct him to the regiment, but on our way the grape, cannister, shells and solid shot drop about us and go over us in storms. I hear a ball whizzing towards me; I fall to the earth for safety and just in time for it to go about three feet over me. It strikes the ground a few yards from me; I dare not turn to look at it, but am up and off.

Now our regiment hastens to its post in the line of battle. Meanwhile the small arms of the other regiments send forth terrible volleys. The line of battle having moved forward it is now just behind the brow of a hill. As our regiment comes up into the line the rebels fire upon it, but our boys pour a deadly fire into them and make them get behind a ridge beyond the one we are on. *"Cease firing"* is ordered; *"Lie down"* follows. Gen. Benton comes along the line and orders us to fix bayonet for he's going to charge. All is quiet for several minutes and then a few rebel sharpshooters fire at our heads and our flags.

When our boys see a rebel they give him a round, the same as they do us.

The 99th Ill, and the 18th and 24th Ind. make a charge, the order don't reach us so we lie quiet. A furious yell is sent up by those who are charging. The rebels break and run but we capture many of them and take two of their cannons. This ends the fight for the forenoon with us, and it is nearly noon now. Osterhaus continues the fight on the left; Hovey's and our Division pursue the rebels that we routed, and we find them, after traveling two miles towards Port Gibson, where they found their reinforcements.

It is a little after noon; again we are thrown into a line of battle, facing as before, to the east, meanwhile the fight is progressing. The enemy masses his troops and try to break our line, but fail. He throws a heavy force upon our right, then centre, and then left. He has but two cannons working upon us and ere night we capture those two. Our artillery fires with powerful effect at them; we have to go over an open field before our musketry can reach them, but there is a ridge, upon which are our cannon, behind which we lie in almost perfect safety. Now we have about 30 pieces of artillery all at work; their booming is not unfamiliar to our ears. With now and then a cessation in firing the battle is thus kept up till night fall when our regiment with some others retires to get a bite to eat, but as soon as we are through eating we return to the field, stack our arms on the line of battle and lie down to sleep, and oh, how thankful

we are, for we have slept but about four hours within the last sixty.

We don't know our whole success, but we know this, that we drove the enemy in every close contact.

Sunday, [May] 3d—Reveille at three and was to march at five A.M. but did not get started till nearer seven. Our Division then moved one mile and a half directly towards Grand Gulf when, finding we could not cross Bayou Perre with our artillery as the enemy had burnt the bridges, we about faced and came back to Port Gibson and then came on seven miles from there towards Rocky Spring, having traveled in all ten miles. Saw about 20000 lbs of bacon and shoulders and hams that the enemy had endeavored to secrete. The enemy evacuated Grand Gulf last night, first spiking the cannons and blowing up two of their magazines, our gunboats making it too unpleasant for them to blow up the third. We are bivouaced in line of battle, and live upon what we can forage. The weather was warm—road very dusty. Carne through a fine tract of country. Negroes are flocking to our lines with mules, horses, and wagons.

Tuesday, [May] 19th—"Onward to Vicksburg" is the cry. Came up within rifle shot of the enemy's works in rear of Vicksburg. The fight began our our right in the morning. It is stated that Sherman has taken Hanes' Bluff and that we therefore have direct communication with the [Yazoo] river and can get ample supplies. We, too, began the fight at about 2 P.M. and continued it till night closed in upon us. Some of our Regt. were wounded by shell from the enemy. The enemy used his cannon freely upon us. We have now completely invested this place and believe we'll take it with the whole garrison within a day or two. Sherman's Corps is on the right, his right resting on the Yazoo River between Haines' Bluff & Vicksburg, McPherson's in the center and McClernand's on the left. Our provisions are cooked in our rear and brought up to us. Our (Division) Hospital is a mile and a half directly in our rear and near the railroad. Smith's Division is just to the right of the railroad, ours just to the left and Osterhaus' to the left of us; Hovey is our reserve. Weather warm.

Friday, [May] 22nd—Now that we have tried to take the enemy's works by storm we suffering terribly and doing the enemy but little harm, we are all—generals and privates—content to lay a regular siege to the place. This has been a sad day for the 33d as well as for this whole army. The army's loss to-day will I think exceed 4000 killed and wounded while the enemy has repulsed us his loss, undoubtedly being trifling. At ten we were all ready for the charge and though not very confident of success we put on an air of confidence. Our Brigade filed down the hollow in which we lay last night till it intersected a larger hollow which we followed up to its head, and then, still marching by the flank, we mounted the ridge within 4 rods of the enemy who poured a deadly fire into us till we reached the opposite side of the ridge. To do this we had to run along the brow of the ridge in a direct line of the enemy's fire, for 15 rods.

Here is where our poor boys suffered terribly, the ridge being covered with the dead and wounded. A part of the Brigade halted and lay down in the wagon road which runs along on the ridge; I was among this lot. We lay there about eight minutes and yet it seemed an age to me, for showers of bullets and grape were passing over me and not a foot above me, and on my right and left were my comrades dying and dead as well as living. What an awful eight minutes that was, we having to lay there not allowed to fire a single shot at the enemy who was sending to eternity by scores our brave boys souls! Oh, how my heart palpitated! It seemed to thump the ground (I lay on my face) as hard as the enemy's bullets. The sweat from off my face run in a stream from the tip ends of my whiskers. God only knows all that passed through my mind. Twice I exclaimed aloud, that my comrades might here *"My God, why don't they order us to charge,"* and then I thought perhaps all of our officers were killed and there was no one to order us forward. I thought of dear friends, of home and of heaven, but never wished, as did some who were near me that, I had never attempted to charge, and, indeed, wished that I had not become a soldier. Some who were wounded groaned and shrieked, others were calm

and resigned. Generally those that were the slightest wounded shrieked the loudest, thinking they were wounded the worst.

One fellow whose performance was the most pleasing thing I saw during the day was wounded slightly just as he got near where I lay. He immediately started to go back, his officers trying in vain to make him stay with us. After stepping a few steps he, it seemed to me, purposely dropped on the ground and then rolled as if the lightning had set him going, clear back into the ravine, a distance of about two and a half rods. Though under such precarious circumstances and in such peril I could not refrain from smiling when seeing the "rolling man."

Receiving orders from Colonel Roe all of our regiment who could arose and made for over the ridge where we could get under cover; meantime Col. Roe fell just before me, wounded in the leg. The regiment was then divided, all of us who lay down in the road being in one place and the rest in another. The right wing of the 8th Ind. soon coming up our little band joined them and we all charged over the railroad where we were again exposed to an awful fire, though but few were hit as we were exposed but a minute. Here on the south side of the railroad we took a position within three rods of one of the enemy's forts upon which the 77th Ill. had its flag planted, and from which it was taken, by the enemy. Here we lay sharpshooting whenever the enemy showed himself, till after dark when we all fell back without molestation to the position we occupied early in the morning. There were only six companies of the 33d in the charge, (three being out sharpshooting and one on provost guard), about one hundred and fifty men. Out of this number there were 76 killed and wounded. Am wearied and can't tell more of the sad tale. The fragment of the regiment is this evening still a unit and if we are attacked to-night we will be able to give the enemy a warm reception, though our hearts are sad.

—ERICKSON, ed., "With Grant at Vicksburg—
From the Civil War Diary of Captain
Charles E. Wilcox"

XIX.2

A UNION WOMAN SUFFERS THROUGH THE SIEGE OF VICKSBURG

After two futile assaults, May 19 and 22, Grant settled down to reducing Vicksburg by siege. While his batteries hurled shells into the beleaguered city, the gunboats attacked it from the river. Pemberton had failed adequately to pro vision the city, and its inhabitants were soon enduring near starvation.

This diary by an unknown Union lady, caught in the siege, tells of the hardships and perils that the civilian inhabitants endured.

March 20.—The slow shelling of Vicksburg goes on all the time, and we have grown indifferent. It does not at present interrupt or interfere with daily avocations, but I suspect they are only getting the range of different points; and when they have them all complete, showers of shot will rain on us all at once. Non-combatants have been ordered to leave or prepare accordingly. Those who are to stay are having caves built. Cave-digging has become a regular business; prices range from twenty to fifty dollars, according to size of cave. Two diggers worked at ours a week and charged thirty dollars. It is well made in the hill that slopes just in the rear of the house, and well propped with thick posts, as they all are. It has a shelf also, for holding a light or water. When we went in this evening and sat down, the earthy, suffocating feeling, as of a living tomb, was dreadful to me. I fear I shall risk death outside rather than melt in the dark furnace. The hills are so honeycombed with caves that the streets look like avenues in a cemetery.

The hill called the Sky-parlor has become quite a fashionable resort for the few upper-circle families left there. Some officers are quartered there, and there is a band and a field glass. Last evening we also climbed the hill to watch the shelling, but found the view not so good as on a quiet hill nearer home. Soon a lady began to talk to one of the officers: "It is such folly for them to waste their ammunition like that. How can they ever take a town that has such advantages for defense and protection as this? We'll just burrow into these hills and let them batter away as hard as they please." . . .

It is strange I have met no one yet who seems to comprehend an honest difference of opinion, and stranger yet that the ordinary rules of good breeding are now so entirely ignored. As the spring comes one has the craving for fresh, green food that a monotonous diet produces. There was a bed of radishes and onions in the garden that were a real blessing. An onion salad, dressed only with salt, vinegar, and pepper, seemed fit for a king; but last night the soldiers quartered near made a raid on the garden and took them all.

April 2.—We have had to move, and thus lost our cave. The owner of the house suddenly returned and notified us that he intended to bring his family back; didn't think there 'd be any siege. The cost of the cave could go for the rent. That means he has got tired of the Confederacy and means to stay here and thus get out of it. . . .

April 28.—I never understood before the full force of those questions—What shall we eat? what shall we drink? and wherewithal shall we be clothed? We have no prophet of the Lord at whose prayer the meal and oil will not waste. Such minute attention must be given the wardrobe to preserve it that I have learned to darn like an artist. Making shoes is now another accomplishment. Mine were in tatters. H. came across a moth-eaten pair that he bought me, giving ten dollars, I think, and they fell into rags when I tried to wear them; but the soles were good, and that has helped me to shoes. A pair of old coat-sleeves saved—nothing is thrown away now—was in my trunk. I cut an exact pattern from my old shoes, laid it on the sleeves, and cut out thus good uppers and sewed them carefully; then soaked the soles and sewed the cloth to them. I am so proud of these home made shoes, think I'll put them in a glass case when the war is over, as an heirloom. . . .

I have but a dozen pins remaining, so many I gave away. Every time these are used they are straightened and kept from rust. All these curious labors are performed while the shells are leisurely screaming through the air; but as long as we are out of range we don't worry. For many nights we have had but little sleep, because the Federal gunboats have been running past the batteries. The uproar when this is happening is phenomenal. The first night the thundering artillery burst the bars of sleep, we thought it an attack by the river. To get into garments and rush up-stairs was the work of a moment. From the upper gallery we have a fine view of the river, and soon a red glare lit up the scene and showed a small boat, towing two large barges, gliding by. The Confederates had set fire to a house near the bank. Another night, eight boats ran by, throwing a shower of shot, and two burning houses made the river clear as day. One of the batteries has a remarkable gun they call "Whistling Dick," because of the screeching, whistling sound it gives and certainly it does sound like a tortured thing. Added to ail this is the indescribable Confederate yell, which is a soul-harrowing sound to hear. . . . Yesterday the *Cincinnati* attempted to go by in daylight, but was disabled and sunk. It was a pitiful sight; we could not see the finale, though we saw her rendered helpless.

May 1, 1863.—It is settled at last that we shall spend the time of siege in Vicksburg. Ever since we were deprived of our cave, I had been dreading that H. would suggest sending me to the country, where his relatives lived. As he could not leave his position and go also without being conscripted, and as I felt certain an army would get between us, it was no part of my plan to be obedient. A shell from one of the practising mortars brought the point to an issue yesterday and settled it. Sitting at work as usual, listening to the distant sound of bursting shells, apparently aimed at the court-house, there suddenly came a nearer explosion; the house shook, and a tearing sound was followed by terrified screams from the kitchen. I rushed thither, but met in the hall the cook's little girl America, bleeding from a wound in the forehead, and fairly dancing with fright and pain, while she uttered fearful yells. I stopped to examine the wound, and her mother bounded in, her black face ashy from terror. "Oh!

Miss V., my child is killed and the kitchen tore up." Seeing America was too lively to be a killed subject, I consoled Martha and hastened to the kitchen. Evidently a shell had exploded just outside, sending three or four pieces through. When order was restored I endeavored to impress on Martha's mind the necessity for calmness and the uselessness of such excitement. Looking round at the close of the lecture, there stood a group of Confederate soldiers laughing heartily at my sermon and the promising audience I had. They chimed in with a parting chorus:

"Yes, it's no use hollerin', old lady." . . .

May 17.—Hardly was our scanty breakfast over this morning when a hurried ring drew us both to the door. Mr. J., one of H.'s assistants, stood there in high excitement. "Well, Mr. L.? they are upon us; the Yankees will be here by this evening."

"What do you mean?"

"That Pemberton has been whipped at Baker's Creek and Big Black, and his army are running back here as fast as they can come, and the Yanks after them, in such numbers nothing can stop them." . . .

What struck us both was the absence of that concern to be expected, and a sort of relief or suppressed pleasure. After twelve some worn-out-looking men sat down under the window.

"What is the news?" I inquired.

"Ritreat, ritreat!" they said, in broken English—they were Louisiana Acadians.

About three o'clock the rush began. I shall never forget that woeful sight of a beaten, demoralized army that came rushing back,—humanity in the last throes of endurance. Wan, hollow eyed, ragged, foot-sore, bloody, the men limped along unarmed, but followed by siege-guns, ambulances, guncarriages, and wagons in aimless confusion. At twilight two or three bands on the court-house hill and other points began playing "Dixie," "Bonnie Blue Flag," and so on, and drums began to beat all about; I suppose they were rallying the scattered army.

May 28.—Since that day the regular siege has continued. We are utterly cut off from the world, surrounded by a circle of fire. Would it be wise like the scorpion to sting our selves to death? The fiery shower of shells goes on day and night. H.'s occupation, of course, is gone; his office closed. Every man has to carry a pass in his pocket. People do nothing but eat what they can get, sleep when they can, and dodge the shells. There are three intervals when the shelling stops, either for the guns to cool or for the gunners' meals, I suppose,—about eight in the morning, the same in the evening, and at noon. In that time we have both to prepare and eat ours. Clothing cannot be washed or anything else done. On the 19th and 22d, when the assaults were made on the lines, I watched the soldiers cooking on the green opposite. The half-spent balls coming all the way from those lines were flying so thick that they were obliged to dodge at every turn. At all the caves I could see from my high perch, people were sitting, eating their poor suppers at the cave doors, ready to plunge in again. As the first shell again flew they dived, and not a human being was visible. The sharp crackle of the musketry firing was a strong contrast to the scream of the bombs. I think all the dogs and cats must be killed or starved: we don't see any more pitiful animals prowling around. . . .

The cellar is so damp and musty the bedding has to be carried out and laid in the sun every day, with the forecast that it may be demolished at any moment. The confinement is dreadful. To sit and listen as if waiting for death in a horrible manner would drive me insane. I don't know what others do, but we read when I am not scribbling in this. H. borrowed somewhere a lot of Dickens's novels, and we reread them by the dim light in the cellar. When the shelling abates, H. goes to walk about a little or get the "Daily Citizen," which is still issuing a tiny sheet at twenty-five and fifty cents a copy. It is, of course, but a rehash of speculations which amuses a half hour. To-day he heard while out that expert swimmers are crossing the Mississippi on logs at night to bring and carry news to Johnston.

I am so tired of corn-bread, which I never liked, that I eat it with tears in my eyes. We are lucky to get a quart of milk daily from a family near

who have a cow they hourly expect to be killed. I send five dollars to market each morning, and it buys a small piece of mule-meat. Rice and milk is my main food; I can't eat the mule-meat. We boil the rice and eat it cold with milk for supper. Martha runs the gauntlet to buy the meat and milk once a day in a perfect terror. The shells seem to have many different names: I hear the soldiers say, "That 's a mortar-shell. There goes a Parrott. That's a rifle shell." They are all equally terrible. A pair of chimney swallows have built in the parlor chimney. The concussion of the house often sends down parts of their nest, which they patiently pick up and reascend with.

Friday, June 5. In the cellar. . . . Yesterday morning a note was brought H. from a bachelor uncle out in the trenches, saying he had been taken ill with fever, and could we receive him if he came? H. sent to tell him to come, and I arranged one of the parlors as a dressing-room for him, and laid a pallet that he could move back and forth to the cellar. He did not arrive, however.

It is our custom in the evening to sit in the front room a little while in the dark, with matches and candle held ready in hand, and watch the shells, whose course at night is shown by the fuse. H. was at the window and suddenly sprang up, crying, "Run!"—"Where?"—"Back!"

I started through the back room, H. after me. I was just within the door when the crash came that threw me to the floor. It was the mose appalling sensation I'd ever known—worse than an earthquake, which I've also experienced. Shaken and deafened, I picked myself up; H. had struck a light to find me. I lighted mine, and the smoke guided us to the parlor I had fixed for Uncle J. The candles were useless in the dense smoke, and it was many minutes before we could see. Then we found the entire side of the room torn out. The soldiers who had rushed in said, "This is an eighty-pound Parrott." . . .

June 7. (In the cellar. There is one thing I feel especially grateful for, that amid these horrors we have been spared that of suffering for water. The weather has been dry a long time, and we hear of others dipping up the water from ditches and mud-holes. This place has two large underground cisterns of good cool water, and every night in my subterranean dressingroom a tub of cold water is the nerve calmer that sends me to sleep in spite of the roar. One cistern I had to give up to the soldiers, who swarm about like hungry animals seeking something to devour. Poor fellows! my heart bleeds for them. They have nothing but spoiled, greasy bacon, and bread made of musty pea-flour, and but little of that. The sick ones can't bolt it. They come into the kitchen when Martha puts the pan of corn-bread in the stove, and beg for the bowl she mixed it in. They shake up the scrapings with water, put in their bacon, and boil the mixture into a kind *of* soup, which is easier to swallow than pea-bread. When I happen in, they look so ashamed of their poor clothes. I know we saved the lives of two by giving a few meals.

To-day one crawled on the gallery to lie in the breeze. He looked as if shells had lost their terrors for his dumb and famished misery. I've taught Martha to make first-rate corn meal gruel, because I can eat meal easier that way than in hoe-cake, and I fixed him a saucerful, put milk and sugar and nutmeg—I've actually got a nutmeg! When he ate it the tears ran from his eyes. "Oh, madam, there was never any thing so good! I shall get better."

June 13.—Shell burst just over the roof this morning. Pieces tore through both floors down into the dining-room. The entire ceiling of that room fell in a mass. We had just left it. Every piece of crockery on the table was smashed up. The "Daily Citizen" to-day is a foot and a half long and six inches wide. It has a long letter from a Federal offlcer, P. P. Hill, who was on the gunboat *Cincinnati*, that was sunk May 27. Says it was found in his floating trunk. The editorial says, "The utmost confidence is felt that we can maintain our position until succor comes from outside. The undaunted Johnston is at hand."

June 18.—To-day the "Citizen" is printed on wallpaper; therefore has grown a little in size. It says, "But a few days more and Johnston will be here"; also that "Kirby Smith has driven Banks

from Port Hudson," and that "the enemy are throwing incendiary shells in."

June 21.—I had gone up-stairs to-day during the inter regnum to enjoy a rest on my bed, and read the reliable items in the "Citizen," when a shell burst right outside the window in front of me. Pieces flew in, striking all around me, tearing down masses of plaster that came tumbling over me. When H. rushed in I was crawling out of the plaster, digging it out of my eyes and hair. When he picked up a piece as large as a saucer beside my pillow, I realized my narrow escape. The window-frame began to smoke, and we saw the house was on fire. H. ran for a hatchet and I for water, and we put it out. Another [shell] came crashing near, and I snatched up my comb and brush and ran down here. It has taken all the afternoon to get the plaster out of my hair, for my hands were rather shaky.

June 25.—A horrible day. The most horrible yet to me, because I've lost my nerve. We were all in the cellar, when a shell came tearing through the roof, burst up-stairs, tore up that room, and the pieces coming through both floors down into the cellar, one of them tore open the leg of H.'s pantaloons. This was tangible proof the cellar was no place of protection from them. On the heels of this came Mr. J. to tell us that young Mrs. P. had had her thigh-bone crushed. When Martha went for the milk she came back horror-stricken to tell us the black girl there had her arm taken off by a shell. For the first time I quailed. I do not think people who are physically brave deserve much credit for it; it is a matter of nerves. In this way I am consitutionally brave, and seldom think of danger till it is over; and death has not the terrors for me it has for some others. Every night I had lain down expecting death, and every morning rose to the same prospect, without being unnerved. It was for H. I trembled. But now I first seemed to realize that something worse than death might come: I might be crippled, and not killed. Life, without all one's powers and limbs, was a thought that broke down my courage. I said to H., "You must get me out of this horrible place; I cannot stay; I know I shall be crippled." Now the regret comes that I lost control, because H. is worried, and has lost his composure, because my coolness has broken down.

July 3.—To-day we are down in the cellar again, shells flying as thick as ever; provisions so nearly gone, except the hogshead of sugar, that a few more days will bring us to starvation indeed. Martha says rats are hanging dressed in the market for sale with mule-meat: there is nothing else. The officer at the battery told me he had eaten one yesterday. We have tried to leave this Tophet and failed, and if the siege continues I must summon that higher kind of courage—moral bravery—to subdue my fears of possible mutilation.

July 4.—It is evening. All is still. Silence and night are once more united. I can sit at the table in the parlor and write. Two candles are lighted. I would like a dozen. We have had wheat supper and wheat bread once more. H. is leaning back in the rocking-chair; he says:

"G., it seems to me I can hear the silence, and feel it, too. It wraps me like a soft garment; how else can I express this peace?"

But I must write the history of the last twenty-four hours. About five yesterday afternoon, Mr. J., H.'s assistant, who, having no wife to keep him in, dodges about at every change and brings us the news, came to H. and said:

"Mr. L., you must both come to our cave to-night. I hear that to-night the shelling is to surpass everything yet. An assault will be made in front and rear. You know we have a double cave; there is room for you in mine, and mother and sister will make a place for Mrs. L. Come right up; the ball will open about seven."

We got ready, shut up the house, told Martha to go to the church again if she preferred it to the cellar, and walked up to Mr. J.'s. When supper was eaten, all secure, and ladies in their cave night toilet, it was just six, and we crossed the street to the cave opposite. As I crossed a mighty shell flew screaming right over my head. It was the last thrown into Vicksburg. We lay on our pallets waiting for the expected roar, but no sound came except the chatter from neighboring caves, and at last we dropped asleep. I woke at dawn stiff. A draft from the funnel-shaped opening had been blowing on me all night. Every one was expressing surprise at the quiet. We started for home and met the editor of the "Daily Citizen." H. said:

"This is strangely quiet, Mr. L."

"Ah, sir," shaking his head gloomily, "I'm afraid (?) the last shell has been thrown into Vicksburg."

"Why do you fear so?"

"It is surrender. At six last evening a man went down to the river and blew a truce signal; the shelling stopped at once."

—Cable, ed., "A Woman's Diary of the Siege of Vicksburg"

XIX.3

Hotel de Vicksburg

For some, humor was the key to surviving the almost unendurable hardships of Vicksburg. After the surrender of the city, Northern newspapers published a "Bill of Fare" discovered in one of the Confederate military camps. *Southern Punch* magazine reprinted the piece for its Confederate audience.

The Chicago Tribune publishes the following bill of fare found in one of the camps at Vicksburg. It is surrounded by an engraving of a mule's head, behind which is a hand brandishing what may be a bowie, or may be a carving knife. *The Tribune* thinks it is a melancholy burlesque. The most melancholy thing about it is the reflection which must suggest to a thoughtful Yankee—if there be such an animal—on the prospect of conquering men who can live and jest on such fare:

Hotel De Vicksburg
Bill of Fare for July, 1863
Soup.
Mule Tail.

Boiled.
Mule bacon with poke greens.
Mule ham canvassed.

Roast.
Mule sirloin.
Mule rump stuffed with rice.

Vegetables.
Peas and Rice.

Entrees.
Mule head stuffed a-la-Mode.
Mule beef jerked a-la-Mexicana.
Mule ears fricasseed a-la-gotch.
Mule side stewed, new style, hair on.
Mule spare ribs plain.
Mule liver, hashed.

Side Dishes.
Mule salad.
Mule hoof soused.
Mule brains a-la-omelette.
Mule kidney stuffed with peas.
Mule tripe fired in pea meal batter.
Mule tongue cold a-la-Bray.

Jellies.
Mule foot.

Pastry.
Pea meal pudding, blackberry sauce.
Cotton-wood berry pies.
China berry tart.

Dessert.
White-oak acorns.
Beech nuts.
Blackberry leaf tea.
Genuine Confederate Coffee.

Liquors.
Mississippi Water, vintage of 1498, superior, $3.00.
Limestone Water, late importation, very fine, $2.75.
Spring Water, Vicksburg brand, $1.50.

Meals at all hours. Gentlemen to wait upon themselves. Any inattention on the part of servants will be promptly reported at the office.

Jeff. Davis & Co., Proprietors.

Card—The proprietors of the justly celebrated Hotel are now prepared to accommodate all who may favor them with a call. Parties arriving by the river, or Grant's inland route, will find Grape, Canister, & Co.'s., carriages at the landing, or any depot on the line of intrenchments. Buck, Ball & Co., take charge of all baggage. No effort will be spared to make the visit of all as interesting as possible.

—*The Southern Illustrated News*

XIX.4

VICKSBURG SURRENDERS

On May 18, 1863, Johnston had ordered Pemberton to abandon Vicksburg and escape, if possible. Pemberton decided that escape was impossible, and retired behind the formidable works of the city. By the end of June it was clear that he could not hold out much longer, and Grant's army was by that time so large that it appeared unlikely that Johnston could break through to his aid. He therefore decided to surrender. That decision was probably inevitable; what inspired a good deal of criticism was the decision to make the formal surrender on July 4. Altogether over 30,000 Confederates were surrendered at Vicksburg—the largest force, it is alleged, in the history of modern warfare up to that time.

General Grant himself here tells the story of the surrender.

On July 1st Pemberton, seeing no hope o£ outside relief, addressed the following letter to each of his four division commanders:

> "Unless the siege of Vicksburg is raised, or supplies are thrown in, it will become necessary very shortly to evacuate the place. I see no prospect of the former, and there are many great, if not insuperable, obstacles in the way of the latter. You are, therefore, requested to inform me with as little delay as possible as to the condition of your troops, and their ability to make the marches and undergo the fatigues necessary to accomplish a successful evacuation."

Two of his generals suggested surrender, and the other two practically did the same; they expressed the opinion that an attempt to evacuate would fail. Pemberton had previously got a message to Johnston suggesting that he should try to negotiate with me for a release of the garrison with their arms. Johnston replied that it would be a confession of weakness for him to do so; but he authorized Pemberton to use his name in making such an arrangement.

On the 3d, about 10 o'clock A.M., white flags appeared on a portion of the rebel works. Hostilities along that part of the line ceased at once. Soon two persons were seen coming toward our lines bearing a white flag. They proved to be General Bowen, a division commander, and Colonel Montgomery, aide-de-camp to Pemberton, bearing the following letter to me:

"I have the honor to propose an armistice for—hours, with the view to arranging terms for the capitulation of Vicksburg. To this end, if agreeable to you, I will appoint three commissioners, to meet a like number to be named by yourself, at such place and hour to-day as you may find convenient. I make this proposition to save the further effusion of blood, which must otherwise be shed to a frightful extent, feeling myself fully able to maintain my position for a yet indefinite period. This communication will be handed you, under a flag of truce, by Major-General John S. Bowen."

It was a glorious sight to officers and soldiers on the line where these white flags were visible, and the news soon spread to all parts of the command. The troops felt that their long and weary marches, hard fighting, ceaseless watching by night and day in a hot climate, exposure to all sorts of weather, to diseases, and, worst of all, to the gibes of many Northern papers that came to them, saying all their suffering was in vain, Vicksburg would never be taken, were at last at an end, and the Union sure to be saved.

Bowen was received by General A. J. Smith, and asked to see me. I had been a neighbor of Bowen's in Missouri, and knew him well and favorably before the war; but his request was refused. He then suggested that I should meet Pemberton. To this I sent a verbal message saying that if

Pemberton desired it I would meet him in front of McPherson's corps, at 3 o'clock that afternoon. I also sent the following written reply to Pemberton's letter:

"Your note of this date is just received, proposing an armistice for several hours, for the purpose of arranging terms of capitulation through commissioners to be appointed, etc. The useless effusion of blood you propose stopping by this course can be ended at any time you may choose, by the unconditional surrender of the city and garrison. Men who have shown so much endurance and courage as those now in Vicksburg will always challenge the respect of an adversary, and I can assure you will be treated with all the respect due to prisoners of war. I do not favor the proposition of appointing commissioners to arrange the terms of capitulation, because I have no terms other than those indicated above."

At 3 o'clock Pemberton appeared at the point suggested in my verbal message, accompanied by the same officers who had borne his letter of the morning. Generals Ord, McPherson, Logan, A. J. Smith, and several officers of my staff accompanied me. Our place of meeting was on a hill-side within a few hundred feet of the rebel lines. Near by stood a stunted oak-tree, which was made historical by the event. It was but a short time before the last vestige of its body, root, and limb had disappeared, the fragments being taken as trophies. Since then the same tree has furnished as many cords of wood, in the shape of trophies, as "The True Cross."

Pemberton and I had served in the same division during a part of the Mexican war. I knew him very well, therefore, and greeted him as an old acquaintance. He soon asked what terms I proposed to give his army if it surrendered. My answer was the same as proposed in my reply to his letter. Pemberton then said, rather snappishly, "The conference might as well end," and turned abruptly as if to leave. I said, "Very well." General Bowen, I saw, was very anxious that the surrender should be consummated. His manners and remarks while Pemberton and I were talking showed this. He now proposed that he and one of our generals should have a conference. I had no objection to this, as nothing could be made binding upon me that they might propose. Smith and Bowen accordingly had a conference, during which Pemberton and I, moving some distance away toward the enemy's lines, were in conversation. After a while Bowen suggested that the Confederate army should be allowed to march out, with the honors of war, carrying their small arms and field artillery. This was promptly and unceremoniously rejected. The interview here ended, I agreeing, however, to send a letter giving final terms by 10 o'clock that night. I had sent word to Admiral Porter soon after the correspondence with Pemberton had commenced, so that hostilities might be stopped on the part of both army and navy. It was agreed on my parting with Pemberton that they should not be renewed until our correspondence should cease.

When I returned to my headquarters I sent for all the corps and division commanders with the army immediately confronting Vicksburg. (Half the army was from eight to twelve miles off, waiting for Johnston.) I informed them of the contents of Pemberton's letters, of my reply, and the sub stance of the interview, and was ready to hear any suggestion; but would hold the power of deciding entirely in my own hands. This was the nearest to a "council of war?" I ever held. Against the general and almost unanimous judgment of the council I sent the following letter:

> "In conformity with agreement of this afternoon I will submit the following proposition for the surrender of the city of Vicksburg, public stores, etc. On your accepting the terms proposed I will march in one division as a guard, and take possession at 8 A.M. to-morrow. As soon as rolls can be made out of our lines, the officers taking with them their side-arms and clothing; and the field, staff, and cavalry officers one horse each. The rank and file will be allowed all their clothing, but no other property. If these conditions are accepted, any amount

of rations you may deem necessary can be taken from the stores you now have, and also the necessary cooking-utensils for preparing them. Thirty wagons also, counting two-horse or mule teams as one, will be allowed to transport such articles as cannot be carried along. The same conditions will be allowed to all sick and wounded officers and soldiers as fast as they become able to travel. The paroles for these latter must be signed, however, whilst officers present are authorized to sign the roll of prisoners."

. . . Late at night I received the following reply to my last letter:

> "I have the honor to acknowledge the receipt of your communication of this date, proposing terms of capitulation for this garrison and post. In the main, your terms are accepted; but, in justice both to the honor and spirit of my troops manifested in the defense of Vicksburg, I have to submit the following amendments, which, if acceded to by you, will perfect the agreement between us. At 10 o'clock A.M. to-morrow I propose to evacuate the works in and around Vicksburg, and to surrender the city and garrison under my command, by marching out with my colors and arms, stacking them in front of my present lines, after which you will take possession. Officers to retain their side-arms and personal property, and the rights and property of citizens to be respected."

This was received after midnight; my reply was as follows:

> "I have the honor to acknowledge the receipt of your communication of 3d July. The amendment proposed by you cannot be acceded to in full. It will be necessary to furnish every officer and man with a parole signed by himself, which, with the completion of the roll of prisoners, will necessarily take some time. Again, I can make no stipulations with regard to treatment of citizens and their private property. While I do not propose to cause them any undue annoyance or loss, I cannot consent to

leave myself under any restraint by stipulations. The property which officers will be allowed to take with them will be as stated in my proposition of last evening; that is, officers will be allowed their private baggage and side arms, and mounted officers one horse each. If you mean by your proposition for each brigade to march to the front of the lines now occupied by it, and stack arms at 10 o'clock A.M., and then return to the inside and there remain as prisoners until properly paroled, I will make no objection to it. Should no notification be received of your acceptance of my terms by 9 o'clock A.M. , I shall regard them as having been rejected, and shall act accordingly. Should these terms be accepted, white flags should be displayed along your lines to prevent such of my troops as may not have been notified from firing upon your men."

Pemberton promptly accepted these terms.

During the siege there had been a good deal of friendly sparring between the soldiers of the two armies, on picket and where the lines were close together. All rebels were known as "Johnnies"; all Union troops as "Yanks." Often "Johnny" would call, "Well, Yank, when are you coming into town?" The reply was sometimes: "We propose to celebrate the 4th of July there." Sometimes it would be: "We always treat our prisoners with kindness and do not want to hurt them"; or, "We are holding you as prisoners of war while you are feeding yourselves." The garrison, from the commanding general down, undoubtedly expected an assault on the 4th. They knew from the temper of their men it would be successful when made, and that would be a greater humiliation than to surrender. Besides it would be attended with severe loss to them.

The Vicksburg paper, which we received regularly through the courtesy of the rebel pickets, said prior to the 4th, in speaking of the "Yankee" boast that they would take dinner in Vicksburg that day, that the best receipt for cooking rabbit was, "First ketch your rabbit." The paper at this time, and for some time previous, was printed on the plain side of wall paper. The last was issued on the 4th and announced that we had "caught our rabbit."

I have no doubt that Pemberton commenced his correspondence on the 3d for the twofold purpose; first, to avoid an assault, which he knew would be successful, and second, to prevent the capture taking place on the great national holiday,—the anniversary of the Declaration of American Independence. Holding out for better terms, as he did, he defeated his aim in the latter particular.

At the 4th, at the appointed hour, the garrison of Vicksburg marched out of their works, and formed line in front, stacked arms, and marched back in good order. Our whole army present witnessed this scene without cheering. . . .

Pemberton says in his report: "If it should be asked why the 4th of July was selected as the day for surrender, the answer is obvious. I believed that upon that day I should obtain better terms. Well aware of the vanity of our foe, I knew they would attach vast importance to the entrance, on the 4th of July, into the stronghold of the great river, and that, to gratify their national vanity, they would yield then what could not be extorted from them at any other time." This does not support my view of his reasons for selecting the day he did for surrendering. But it must be recollected that his first letter asking terms was received about 10 o'clock, A.M., July 3d. It then could hardly be expected that it would take 24 hours to effect a surrender. He knew that Johnston was in our rear for the purpose of raising the siege, and he naturally would want to hold out as long as he could. He knew his men would not resist an assault, and one was expected on the 4th. In our interview he told me he had rations enough to hold out some time—my recollection is two weeks. It was this statement that induced me to insert in the terms that he was to draw rations for his men from his own supplies. . . .

As soon as our troops took possession of the city, guards were established along the whole line of parapet, from the river above to the river below. The prisoners were allowed to occupy their old camps behind the intrenchments. No restraint was put upon them, except by their own commanders. They were rationed about as our own men, and from our supplies. The men of the two armies fraternized as if they had been fighting for the same cause. When they passed out of the works they had so long and so gallantly defended, between lines of their late antagonists, not a cheer went up, not a remark was made that would give pain. I believe there was a feeling of sadness among the Union soldiers at seeing the dejection of their late antagonists.

—U. S. Grant, "The Vicksburg Campaign"

XIX.5

General Banks Takes Port Hudson

Port Hudson, just above Baton Rouge, was the last remaining Confederate fort on the Mississippi. As early as December 1862 Banks had made a demonstration against it, but had not been strong enough to take it. Feeling that he could not undertake a full-scale attack on the fort while the Confederates were in strength in the Bayou Teche and Red River country, Banks undertook several expeditions west of the Mississippi. These were for the most part inconclusive. When Grant succeeded in crossing the river at Bruinsburg, Banks was ordered to co-operate by reducing Port Hudson. He arrived there with some 30,000 men in mid-May. It was the story of Vicksburg over again. Like Grant, Banks launched two futile assaults on the strong works of the fort, then settled down to a siege. By July the defenders of the fort were reduced to eating mules; the surrender of Vicksburg made the Confederate position untenable, and on July 9 General Gardner surrendered.

We have here two accounts of the Port Hudson operations from the pen of an unknown Confederate officer.

A. Eating Mules at Port Hudson

The last quarter ration of beef had been given out to the troops on the 29th of June [1863]. On the 1st of July, at the request of many officers a wounded mule was killed and cut up for experimental eating. All those who partook of it spoke highly of the dish. The flesh of mules is of a darker color than beef, of a finer grain, quite tender and juicy, and has a flavor something between that of beef and venison. There was an immediate demand for this

kind of food, and the number of mules killed by the commissariat daily increased. Some horses were also slaughtered, and their flesh was found to be very good eating, but not equal to mule.

Rats, of which there were plenty about the deserted camps, were also caught by many officers and men and were found to be quite a luxury—superior, in the opinion of those who eat them, to spring chicken; and if a philosopher of the Celestial Empire could have visited Port Hudson at the time, he would have marveled at the progress of the barbarians there toward the refinements of his own people.

Mule meat was regularly served out in rations to the troops from and after the 4th of July, and there were very few among the garrison whose natural prejudices were so strong as to prevent them from cooking and eating their share. The stock of corn was getting very low, and besides that nothing was left but peas, sugar, and molasses. These peas were the most indigestible and unwholesome articles that were ever given to soldiers to eat, and that such a large quantity was left on hand was probably accounted for by the fact that most of the troops would not have them on any consideration. To save corn they were issued out to horses and mules and killed a great many of these animals. All of the horses and mules which were not needed for hauling or other imperative duties had been turned out to graze, where numbers of them were killed or disabled by the enemy's cannonade and rain of Minie balls and the rest nearly starved to death.

The sugar and molasses were put to good use by the troops in making a weak description of beer which was constantly kept at the lines by the barrelful and drunk by the soldiers in preference to the miserable water with which they were generally supplied. This was a very pleasant and healthful beverage and went far to recompense the men for the lack of almost every other comfort or luxury. In the same way, after the stock of tobacco had given out, they substituted sumac leaves, which grew wild in the woods. It had always been smoked by the Indians under the name of killickinnic and when properly prepared for the pipe is a tolerably good substitute for tobacco.

There was a small proportion of the garrison who could not, however, reconcile themselves so easily to the hardships and dangers of the siege. Some one hundred and fifty or more men, almost entirely foreigners of a low class or ignorant conscripts from western Louisiana, men who were troubled with none of that common feeling usually styled patriotism, deserted us for the better-provided commissariats of the enemy, slinking away by couples and squads during the night time. Their loss was not wept over, nor could the information they carried with them concerning our position enable the enemy to capture it.

—*Port Hudson . . . As Sketched from the Diary of an Officer*

B. Blue and Gray Fraternize after the Surrender of Port Hudson

At two o'clock on the morning of the 8th of July [1863] General Gardner sent to General Banks by flag of truce for confirmation of the fall of Vicksburg, which was accorded him. About nine o'clock the same morning he dispatched commissioners to treat for the surrender of the post [Port Hudson]. They did not return until afternoon and then announced that an unconditional surrender of the place and garrison had been agreed upon and that the ceremony would take place at seven o'clock the next morning.

A cessation of hostilities had already taken place, and immediately that it was known that the capitulation had been agreed upon, a singular scene was presented to the observer, particularly upon the extreme right, where the contending parties, almost near enough to clutch each other by the throat, had been engaged in a desperate struggle for the mastery.

Soldiers swarmed from their places of concealment on either side and met each other in the most cordial and fraternal spirit. Here you would see a group of Federal soldiers escorted round our works and shown the effects of their shots and entertained with accounts of such part of the siege operations as they could not have learned before. In the same way our men went into the Federal lines and gazed with curiosity upon the work which had been

giving them so much trouble, escorted by Federal soldiers, who vied with each other in courtesy and a display of magnanimous spirit. The subject of the attack and defense seemed to be a tireless one with both sides, and the conversations that ensued between them were of so cheerful and pleasant a character that one could hardly believe it possible these men had just before been fighting with the ferocity of tigers and striving by every art to slaughter the men they were now fraternizing with.

Not a single case occurred in which the enemy, either officers or privates, exhibited a disposition to exult over their victory, but on the contrary, whenever the subject came up in conversation it elicited from them only compliments upon the kill and bravery of the defense. Nor was their conduct limited to mere expressions. They were liberal in making presents of tobacco and other luxuries, asking of the garrison only such articles as they could retain as relics of the siege. One of their surgeons came in during a heavy rainstorm and brought medicines for our sick, repeating his visit the next morning and bringing a large quantity of quinine, which he dosed out to the fever patients. During the afternoon and evening of the 8th a large number of Federals were within our lines visiting at our camps, whither most of our men had repaired to pack up their little stock of clothing preparatory to an expected departure on the morrow.

—*Port Hudson . . . As Sketched from the Diary of an Officer*

XIX.6

"THE FATHER OF WATERS AGAIN GOES UNVEXED TO THE SEA"

Lincoln had been invited to address a meeting of Union men at Springfield, Illinois; finding it impossible to leave Washington he sent, instead, a long letter to the chairman of the meeting, James Conkling. Most of the letter argued the necessity of emancipation; the concluding paragraphs—some of the most felicitous words Lincoln ever wrote—discussed some of the implications of the war and of victory.

Executive Mansion, Washington,
August 26, 1863

Hon. James C. Conkling
My Dear Sir.

. . . The signs look better. The Father of
Waters again goes unvexed to the sea. Thanks to
the great Northwest for it. Nor yet wholly to them.
Three hundred miles up they met New England,
Empire, Keystone, and Jersey, hewing their way
right and left. The sunny South, too, in more colors than one, also lent a hand. On the spot, their
part of the history was jotted down in black and
white. The job was a great national one; and let
none be banned who bore an honorable part in it.
And while those who have cleared the great river
may well be proud, even that is not all. It is hard to
say that any thing has been more bravely and well
done than at Antietam, Murfreesboro', Gettysburg,
and on many fields of lesser note. Nor must Uncle
Sam's web-feet be forgotten. At all the watery margins they have been present. Not only on the deep
sea, the broad bay, and the rapid river, but also up
the narrow muddy bayou, and wherever the ground
was a little damp, they have been, and made their
tracks. Thanks to all. For the great republic, for the
principle it lives by, and keeps alive—for man's vast
future—thanks to all.

Peace does not appear so distant as it did. I
hope it will come soon, and come to stay; and so
come as to be worth the keeping in all future
time. It will then have been proved that, among
free men, there can be no successful appeal from
the ballot to the bullet; and that they who take
such an appeal are sure to lose their case, and pay
the cost. And then, there will be some black men
who can remember that, with silent tongue, and
clenched teeth, and steady eye, and well-poised
bayonet, they have helped mankind on to this
great consummation; while, I fear, there will be
some white ones, unable to forget that with malignant heart, and deceitful speech, they strove to
hinder it.

Still, let us not be over-sanguine of a speedy
final triumph. Let us be quite sober. Let us diligent-
ly apply the means, never doubting that a just

God, in his own good time, will give us the
rightful result.

Yours very truly
A. Lincoln.

—*Complete Works of Abraham Lincoln*

XIX.7

General Morgan Invades the North

After Stones River (December 31, 1862) General Bragg had fall-
en back on Tullahoma, and then to Chattanooga. To cover his
retreat he ordered General Morgan to raid the railroads in
Kentucky and, if possible, threaten Louisvine. Morgan wanted to
invade Ohio, but to this plan Bragg refused his consent. Starting
out on July 2, 1863—just as Pemberton was getting ready to
surrender Vicksburg—Morgan swept through Kentucky, crossed
the Green River, captured Lebanon, and on July 9 reached the
banks of the Ohio. Contrary to orders he then went ahead with
his own plan of an invasion—with disastrous results.

Morgan himself was one of the most glamorous figures in
the Confederacy. He had fought in the Mexican War and as early
as 1857 had organized the Lexington (Kentucky) Rifles.
Commissioned captain in 1861 he began the series of raids that
were so effective in disrupting Federal communications in the
West. By the time of Shiloh he was a colonel, and in June a
brigadier. With Forrest and Wheeler he was one of the three
great cavalry leaders of the Army of Tennessee. Captured at the
end of this raid Morgan was imprisoned in the Ohio State
Penitentiary; we will read elsewhere how he escaped. In 1864
he was sent to western Virginia to deal with the attack launched
by Averell and Crook, and was killed at Greenville, Tennessee, in
September of that year.

We have here two accounts of the Morgan raid. The first,
by Colonel Alston, Morgan's chief of staff, carries the story up
through July 5, 1863; the second, by Colonel James B.
McCreary, continues the story to its end. McCreary was later
Governor of Kentucky and served for six terms in Congress.

A. Morgan's Cavalrymen Sweep
Through Kentucky

July 1st, 1863.—On the banks of the Cumberland.
The river very high. No boats. General M. obliged
to build a number of boats, which he accomplished
with very little delay, and commenced crossing at
sundown.

July 2d.—Bucksville. He had great difficulty in making the horses swim, but by united and systematic exertion succeeded in getting the entire command of——regiments over by ten A.M., though the command was very much scattered. At eleven o'clock, scouts came into Bucksville and reported the enemy advancing, and within four miles of the town. It was supposed to be only a scouting party, and a portion of Dick Morgan's command was sent out to make a reconnoissance. The report of the scouts of the enemy advancing proved to be correct, and a message was received from Colonel Ward that he was attacked. Colonel Grigsby was sent to reenforce him, and succeeded in driving the Yankees back in great confusion upon their reenforcements. My regiment lost two mortally wounded and two others slightly. Five of the Yankees were known to be killed and a number wounded, with about fifteen prisoners. No tidings heard of the Second brigade until dark, when they arrived and reported that Colonel Johnson, commanding, had experienced great difficulty in crossing, and that in addition to the precipitous banks and absence of all boats or other means of transportation, the enemy were hovering on the river and harassing him as far as they could. He was, however, quite successful in driving them back. Yesterday a young man, calling himself Charles Rogers, dressed in full confederate uniform, came into our lines and expressed a desire to join our command. I suspicioned him, and, after a few questions, I was convinced that he was a spy. I threatened to shoot him, when he confessed that he had been lying, and that his name was Simon Blitz—in fact he convicted himself of being a spy. I hated to shoot him, although he deserved it.

July 3d.—My regiment behaved very gallantly in yesterday's fight with the enemy, frequently having hand-to-hand encounters. To-day we experienced the same difficulty in getting the artillery on, and had to press a number of oxen for the purpose. After two halts for the column to close up, our advance proceeded to Columbia. They were met by detachments from three regiments said to be under command of Colonel Wolford. A brief engagement followed, in which we drove the enemy in great haste through the town, capturing six prisoners, killing two, among them Captain Carter, and wounding three. Our loss was two killed and two wounded, among them Captain Cassel, a most dashing and daring officer, wounded in the thigh. Our men behaved badly at Columbia, breaking open a store and plundering it. I ordered the men to return the goods, and made all the reparation in my power. These outrages are very disgraceful, and are usually perpetrated by men accompanying the army simply for plunder. They are not worth a——, and are a disgrace to both armies. Passed through Columbia, and camped six miles from Green River Bridge.

July 4th.—New-Market, Ky. A day of gloom, deep gloom, to our entire command. How many who rose this morning full of enthusiasm and hope now "sleep the sleep that knows no waking." The sun rose bright and beautiful, the air was cool and balmy, all nature wore the appearance of peace and harmony. While riding along, affected by the stillness of all around, Captain Magennis, the Adjutant-General, rode up and remarked how dreadful to reflect that we were marching on to engage in deadly strife, and how many poor fellows would pass into eternity before the setting of yonder sun. I have no doubt the poor fellow was moved to these reflections by one of those unaccountable presentiments which are so often the harbingers of evil. (Before dark he was a corpse.) About sunrise we drove in the enemy's pickets and were soon near their fortifications, which had been erected to prevent our crossing. General Morgan sent in a flag of truce and demanded the surrender, but the Colonel quietly remarked: "If it was any other day he might consider the demand, but the Fourth of July was a bad day to talk about surrender, and he must therefore decline." This Colonel is a gallant man, and the entire arrangement of his defence entitles him to the highest credit for military skill. We would mark such a man in our army for promotion.

We attacked the place with two regiments, sending the remainder of our force across at another ford. The place was judiciously chosen and skilfully defended, and the result was that we were repulsed with severe loss—about twenty five killed and twenty wounded. . . . Our march thus far has been very fatiguing—bad roads, little rest or sleep, little to eat, and a fight every day. Yet our men are cheerful, even buoyant, and to see them pressing along barefooted, hurrahing and singing, would cause one to appreciate what those who are fighting in a just and holy cause will endure.

About three o'clock, as I rode on about forty yards in advance, I heard the General exclaim something in a very excited tone, which I could not understand, and heard at the same time the report of a pistol. I turned, and, great God! to my horror I saw Captain Magennis falling from his horse, with the blood gushing out of his mouth and breast. His only remark was: "Let me down easy." In another moment his spirit had fled. He was killed by Captain Murphy because Magennis, by the direction of General Morgan, had ordered Murphy to restore a watch taken from a prisoner. Thus was the poor fellow's language of the morning dreadfully realized. I was terribly affected. I had seen blood flow freely on many a battlefield—my friends had been killed in the morning—but this caused a deeper impression and shock than any occurrence I ever witnessed. Truly this has been a sad day. General Morgan looks haggard and weary, but he never despairs. May to-morrow dawn more bright than to-day closes.

July 5th.—Another day of gloom, fatigue, and death. Moved on Lebanon at sunrise—placed our men in line. Sent around Colonel J——with his brigade to the Danville road to cut off reenforcements, which we knew were expected from Danville. I went in with a flag of truce. It was fired on five times. Officer apologized, saying he thought it was a man with a white coat on. Very dangerous mistake, at least for me. Demanded unconditional surrender. Told Colonel Han son we had his reenforcements cut off, and resistance was useless. He refused to surrender, and T then ordered him to send out the non-combatants, as we would be compelled to shell the town. He posted his regiment in the depot and in various houses, by which he was

enabled to make a desperate resistance. After a fight of seven hours, General Morgan, finding the town could be taken in no other way, ordered a charge to be made. This ought to have been done at first, but General Morgan said, when it was urged on him, that he wished to avoid the destruction of private property as much as possible, and he would only permit it as a last and final resort. Colonel Hanson still held out in hopes of receiving reenforcements, and only surrendered after we had fired the buildings in which he was posted. . . .

By this surrender we obtained a sufficient quantity of guns to arm all our men who were without them; also a quantity of ammunition, of which we stood sorely in need. At the order to charge, Duke's regiment rushed forward, and poor Tommy Morgan, who was always in the lead, ran forward and cheered the men with all the enthusiasm of his bright nature. Almost at the first volley he fell back, pierced through the heart. His only words were: "Brother Cally, they have killed me." Noble youth! how deeply lamented by all who knew you! This was a crushing blow to General Morgan, as his affection for his brother exceeded the love of Jonathan to David. It caused a terrible excitement, and the men were in a state of frenzy. It required the utmost energy and promptitude on the part of the officers to prevent a scene of slaughter, which all would deeply have lamented. Our men behaved badly here, breaking open stores and plundering indiscriminately. All that officers could do was done to prevent, but in vain. These occurrences are very disgraceful, and I am truly glad that they form exceptions to the general conduct.

While I was paroling the prisoners, a courier arrived, informing me that the enemy were approaching with two regiments of cavalry and a battery of artillery, and that skirmishing was then going on with our pickets. I was there fore obliged to order the prisoners to Springfield on the double-quick. Soon after we left Lebanon, the hardest rain I ever experienced commenced to fall, and continued till nine o'clock. Arrived at Springfield at dark, when I halted the prisoners in order to parole those who were not paroled at Lebanon, and formally dismissed them. This detained me at Springfield two hours after the command had passed. Wet and chilly, worn out, horse tired and hungry. Stopped to feed her. Falling asleep, was aroused by one of the men. Started on to the command. When I reached the point on the Bards town road where I had expected the Second brigade to en camp, was halted by a party of cavalry. Supposing them to be our own pickets, I rode up promptly to correct them for standing in full view of any one approaching, when lo! to my mortification, I found myself a prisoner. My God! how I hated it, no one can understand.

—"Journal of Lieutenant-Colonel Alston"

B. Morgan's Raid Comes to an Inglorious End

8 July, 1863. The great Ohio River, the dividing line between the North and the South, is reached. The command is crossing. Here I met Capt. Heady. The enemy are pressing us in the rear, and their gunboats kept up a steady fire on the two stern boats, in which Morgan's command is crossing. Thoughts, hopes and anxieties chase each other in wild succession through my mind, but my Regiment is again guarding the rear and vigilance is the price of liberty. At 12 o'clock tonight, it being moonrise, the enemy pressed upon us and drove our pickets in, but again fell back.

July 9. This morning I am left with half of the Regiment one mile from the river as rear guard, and at daylight the Yankees moved down upon me. It was a critical and trying moment. By the interposition of Divine Providence, a heavy fog suddenly, and whilst hot skirmishing was going on, enveloped friends and foes, and the Yankees halted. Under this fog I crossed my command over the river. As I moved up the hills of Indiana, the enemy moved down the hills of Kentucky. We are now fairly into Yankee land. What the result will be God only knows. We attacked Corydon this evening, and, after a tolerable severe fight of two hours, took the place and several hundred prisoners. Thence to Salsberry, where we bivouacked for a few hours.

July 10. Attacked Palmyra and captured a small force of the enemy. Then moved on Salem,

where, after some fighting, a considerable force surrendered to us. Here we destroyed heavy supplies, a depot, and several bridges. Then we captured Canton, tore up the railroad, and tore down the telegraph, and then rapidly moved on, like an irresistible storm, to the vicinity of Vienna, where, for a brief period, we bivouacked. The citizens seemed frightened almost to death, for Federal papers have published the wildest tales about us. The Governors of Indiana and Ohio have ordered out all able-bodied men, and we have already fought decrepit, white-haired age and buoyant, blithe boyhood.

July 11. Marched without any hindrance through Vienna, New Philadelphia, Lexington, and Paris, and came to Vernon, where we found the enemy in great force. The enemy consisted of a large force of Volunteers and Militia. We made a flank movement, tore up all the railroads around Vernon, and then traveled all night to Dupont, where we rested and fed our horses. Like an irresistible avalanche we are sweeping over this country. Man never knows his powers of endurance 'till he tries himself. The music of the enemy's balls is now as familiar and common as the carol of the spring bird which, unknowing of death and carnage around, sings today the same song that gladdened our forefathers.

July 12. We move rapidly through six or seven towns with out any resistance, and tonight lie down for a little while with our bridles in our hands.

July 13. Today we reach Harrison, the most beautiful town I have yet seen in the North—a place, seemingly, where love and beauty, peace and prosperity, sanctified by true religion, might hold high carnival. Here we destroyed a magnificent bridge and saw many beautiful women. From here we moved to Miami Town, where we destroyed another splendid bridge over the Miami River. The bridge at Harrison was across Whitewater River. From Miami Town we passed through the most fertile and lovely region of Ohio. For hours the column moved at full speed, for we were now moving around Cincinnati. County seat after county seat reared it self in stately splendor, now scarcely distinguishable for the clouds of dust. Town after town and city after city are passed. A part of Morgan's command makes a feint on Cincinnati, and we move at this rate a distance of eighty-three miles, and all in sixteen hours. If there be a man who boasts of a march, let him excel this. After this Gilpin race we rested by capturing a train of cars on the Little Miami and a consider able number of prisoners. Then we surrounded Camp Dennison, captured a large train of wagons, and about two hundred mules. From there we moved on Winchester, where we destroyed a fine bridge, and thence to Jackson.

July 15. Today we traveled through several unimportant towns, destroyed one bridge, and bivouacked at Walnut Grove.

July 16. Today we find the first obstruction in our way, consisting of felled trees. The enemy are now pressing us on all sides, and the woods swarm with militia. We capture hundreds of prisoners, but, a parole being null, we can only sweep them as chaff out of our way. Today we crossed the Scioto to Piketon, and, as usual, destroyed the bridge. Thence we moved to Jackson.

July 17. Today we find our road badly blockaded and "axes to the front" is now the common command. We have today passed through many little dutch towns with which this country abounds. Tonight we halt near Pomeroy. The enemy are in considerable force in front. We attacked them and drove them from our front, and then moved rapidly in the direction of Buffington, where we intend to cross.

July 18. All are now on the qui vive, for the Ohio River is full of gunboats and transports, and an immense force of cavalry is hovering in our rear. We reached Buffington to night. All was quiet. A dense fog wrapped this woodland scene. Early in the morn-

ing of the 19th the Yankees guarding the ford were attacked by our force, and driven away and their artillery captured. Immediately after this, and whilst we were trying the river to ascertain if it was fordable, the gun boats steamed up the river. The transports landed their infantry, thousands of cavalry moved down upon us, and the artillery commenced its deadly work. We formed and fought here to no purpose. The river was very full in consequence of a heavy rain away up the river. Shells and minie balls were ricocheting and exploding in every direction, cavalry were charging, and infantry with its slow, measured tread moved upon us, while broadside after broadside was poured upon our doomed command from the gunboats. It seemed as if our comparatively small command would be swallowed up by the innumerable horde. About half of it was here captured or killed. I made my way out by charging through the enemy's lines with about one-half the Regiment, and finally formed a juncture with the remnant of our command under Gen. Morgan, now numbering about 1,200. With these we moved to wards Cheshire, traveling rapidly all night, and passing around the enemy's pickets, over cliffs and ravines, which under ordinary circumstances, would have been considered insurmountable.

July 20. Today reached Cheshire. There Buffington was entrenched to a certain extent. The Yankees pressed us in the rear and fired on us from their gunboats in front, thus forcing us back to a high hill, where, after exhausting our ammunition, we surrendered, 700 men. I saw General Shackelford and arranged the terms of surrender. He allowed all field officers to retain side arms and horses, all other to retain private property. This proposition I announced to all the officers, and all voted to surrender, and thus ended the saddest day of my life.

—McCreary, "The Journal of My Soldier Life"

XX

PRISONS,
NORTH AND SOUTH

It is doubtless the darkest chapter in the history of the war. No other, certainly, reveals so clearly American unreadiness for war or the failure to take in, early enough, its true nature or to anticipate its problems. In a sense the war took both sides by surprise. Neither government was prepared for it, neither anticipated its long duration. There was, consequently, no adequate preparation either for prisoners or for medical services. At the beginning authorities on both sides improvised prisons. The North was fairly well supplied with prisons of a sort—the existing penitentiaries, and military prisons—and others were speedily set up well behind the lines. The South used the meager facilities it already had, took over factories and warehouses, and eventually fell back on open stockades such as the notorious Andersonville.

From the very beginning there were perplexing problems relating to the treatment of prisoners. From the strictly legal point of view all Confederates were rebels—and thus traitors—and subject to the extreme penalty. Circumstances, how ever, forced the Union to recognize the de facto belligerency of the South, and Confederate prisoners were accorded the customary treatment of prisoners of war. There was a brief attempt to make an exception of sailors on privateers—to regard them as pirates—but a threat of reprisal took care of that. Some Southern officers were inclined to regard Negro troops as beyond the pale and there was a gesture of turning them over to state authorities for such treatment as was thought appropriate; this, too, yielded to the threat of reprisal and there is no evidence that Negro prisoners were maltreated. The most serious problem was that of prisoner exchange. Under the cartel of July 1862 both sides agreed to exchange or parole all prisoners within ten days, and if this cartel had been observed it would have eliminated the whole prisoner problem, for captures (up to the very end of the war) were roughly equal. Unfortunately both sides violated the cartel, and in 1863 Grant suspended further

exchange of prisoners—technically on the ground of Confederate violations of the cartel but actually because the Confederacy had more to gain by exchange than the Union.

Conditions in prisons, North and South, were uniformly bad. Most of them were overcrowded; few provided adequate food, shelter or clothing, and the medical and sanitary services were about as bad as they could be. The result was a shockingly high mortality rate. Of 194,743 Union soldiers actually imprisoned, 30,128 died in captivity; of 214,865 Confederate soldiers actually imprisoned, 25,976 died. The different mortality rate was a measure not of wickedness or neglect on the part of the Confederacy but of shortages of food, clothing, medical supplies, and manpower. If approximately one third of all the prisoners at Andersonville died, it must be remembered that the mortality rate in Camp Douglas in Chicago ran as high as 10 per cent a month, at times, while that at such comparatively well built camps as Elmira ran to 5 per cent a month.

XX.1

ABNER SMALL SUFFERS IN
DANVILLE PRISON

Abner Small was a boy in Waterville, Maine, when the war broke out. Enlisting as a private in the 3rd Maine Volunteers he eventually rose to be major of the 16th Maine, whose history he subsequently wrote. He fought through Fredericksburg, Chancellorsville, Gettysburg, and the Wilderness, was captured in August 1864, and imprisoned in Libby and Danville prisons in Virginia, and in Salisbury, North Carolina. His is one of the best, and one of the least embittered, accounts of prison life in the South.

[November 1864]. Our quarters were so crowded that none of us had more space to himself than he actually occupied, usually a strip of the bare, hard floor, about six feet by two. We lay in long rows, two rows of men with their heads to the side walls and two with their heads together along the center of the room, leaving narrow aisles between the rows of feet. The wall spaces were preferred because a man could brace his back there and sit out the long day or the longer night. There was a row of posts down the center of the room, but these were too few and too narrow to give much help; I know, because I had a place by one of them.

I remember three officers, one a Yankee from Vermont, one an Irishman from New York, and one a Dutchman from Ohio, who messed together by the wall opposite me. When they came to Danville they were distinct in feature and personality. They became homesick and disheartened. They lost all interest in everything, and would sit in the same attitude hour after hour and day after day, with their backs against the wall and their gaze fixed on the floor at my feet. It grew upon me that they were gradually being merged into one man with three bodies. They looked just alike; truly, I couldn't tell them apart. And they were dying of nostalgia. . . .

Some of the prisoners played chess, checkers, and backgammon. Captain Conley and I had made a set of checkers in Libby, and we still had them, but the game palled on us. Like the ungodly majority, we killed time and escaped insanity with cards. A few of our associates, pursuing the consolations of religion, found none too much time to study the Scriptures; games had no fascinating power over them. A few others, remembering what they had learned at college, engaged in the study of classical or modern languages. Many tried to read, but reading somehow ceased to be a comfort in prison; at least, that was my experience. Our library, moreover, was a small one; it consisted of a few books and some back numbers of monthlies brought to us by the Reverend Charles K. Hall, a Methodist minister of Danville, who occasionally preached to us.

Many of our comrades developed a wonderful talent at handicraft and made hundreds of orna-
ments from bone and wood. Crosses, rings, and pins were artistically fashioned and most beautifully chased. Busts were carved from bricks taken from the walls. Checkers with monograms and raised figures were cut from bone and bits of wood. Altogether, there was output enough to stock a respectable museum. These objects were not made wholly in the cause of art, nor to while away the time; they were valuable for barter and exchange.

As our money gave out, we sold the things to get more, or swapped articles of value or works of art for necessities. Boots, spurs, watches, rings, jack-knives, buttons, even tooth picks, were commodities of traffic. Boots were a quick commodity and brought high prices in debased rebel currency; but we hated to part with them. Captain Conley's pride in a pair of nice boots lasted until his luxurious habit of smoking demanded a sacrifice. The officer of the guard, an inveterate haggler with the general manner and appearance of a Malay pirate, offered one hundred Confederate dollars and finally a pair of shoes also, for the boots, and the offer was accepted. The cash was paid, and the captain, almost in tears, gave up his fine footwear. After a wait of two weeks there was passed into the prison a package addressed to Captain Conley. "My shoes!" he cried. He tore off the wrapper, and for an hour sat and swore at two old army brogans, of different sizes and both for the same foot. My own boots went for cash the day after Christmas. I fared better than Conley; I got a hundred dollars and a pair of shoes that I could wear.

All sorts of makeshifts were adopted to cover our persons as decency demanded. When I was captured, I was the proud possessor of a new staff uniform ornamented with gold lace. Five months later, my most intimate friends would have failed to recognize me in the ragged tramp who sat naked on the floor at Danville and robbed the ends of his trousers in order to reseat them. It was not until after I was paroled that I took those trousers off; I couldn't have done so before, because after sewing up the legs while I had them on, I couldn't get my feet through.

Although we all became disreputable in appearance, some of us kept up as best we could our proper relations of mutual respect. I am sorry to say that military rank was soon ignored by the majority of officers in Prison No. 3, and that selfish ness and dishonesty added to our cup of humiliation and suffering; yet I know that much should be forgiven in men who had almost lost their natural humanity. Our nerves were worn ragged. The slightest of provocations would cause a quarrel. Two cavalry officers, Captain Harris and Lieutenant McGraw, fought over the possession of a few rusty cans. The captain's shirt was torn to shreds, and since it was the only shirt he had, and the remainder of his wardrobe consisted of a well-ventilated pair of trousers, he was to be pitied. . . .

Life became so unbearable, and the prospects of a general exchange so delusive, that on December 10th about a hundred of the prisoners, the most courageous, or the most wanting in judgment, made an attempt to break prison and escape, and failed miserably. Unaware of the attempt to be made, I, with five others, was walking on the ground floor for exercise when I saw two officers close in on the sentry by the door that opened into the yard, one seizing his gun and the other taking him by the throat to prevent him from giving an alarm. At the same moment another officer tried to choke into silence the sentry by the stairs, but his grip was too weak, and the brave rebel, in spite of threats, shouted, "Turn out the guard!" The cry was at once repeated outside, and muskets were thrust in through the sashless windows. I have outlived the sensation of that moment, but I know that I was never more conscious of being in the presence of death than when I caught a glimpse of eternity in the black muzzle of a gun held within six feet of my breast. The other promenaders were as helplessly exposed, and we all might have been the victims of nervous and frightened sentries, but Colonel Smith came running and shouted, "Cease firing!" He was not quick enough, however, to save the officer who had grappled with the sentry by the stairs. That unfortunate prisoner was shot through the bowels, and his wound was cruelly aggravated

as he made his way up the two flights to the top floor, hurriedly helped along by some of his associates. Colonel Smith came inside, ordered a number of prisoners into close confinement, and told us that a keg of powder was buried under the prison, and that if another attempt to escape should be made, he would blow us all to hell.

—SMALL, *The Road to Richmond*

XX.2

SUFFERING IN ANDERSONVILLE PRISON

Andersonville, in southwestern Georgia, was the largest and the most dreaded of Confederate prisons. The first capture Federals arrived there early in 1864, by midsummer the number of prisoners had increased to some 32,000, and this though the prison was originally designed to accommodate only 10,000. In no other prison were conditions so crowded or so wretched, the prisoners lived in tents on the bare ground or in improvised huts; the food was woefully insufficient; the water polluted: sanitary facilities wholly inadequate. By the end of the war about 50,000, prisoners—all of them privates—had been received at Andersonville, and about one third of these had died. After peace the superintendent, Captain Henry Wirz, was tried for murder and executed.

This account differs from most prison narratives in that it comes from a friendly source. Eliza Andrews was one of that notable galaxy of Confederate woman diarists who tell us so much about social life in the South during the war. After the war she wrote two books on botany and three novels.

January 27, 1865.—While going our rounds in the morning we found a very important person in Peter Louis, a paroled Yankee prisoner, in the employ of Captain Bonham. The captain keeps him out of the stockade, feeds and clothes him, and in return reaps the benefit of his skill. Peter is a French Yankee, a shoemaker by trade, and makes as beautiful shoes as I ever saw imported from France. My heart quite softened toward him when I saw his handiwork, and little Mrs. Sims was so overcome that she gave him a huge slice of her Confederate fruitcake. I talked French with him, which pleased him greatly, and Mett and I engaged him to make us each a pair of shoes. I will feel like a lady once more, with good shoes on my feet. I expect the poor Yank is glad to get away from Anderson on any terms. Although matters have improved somewhat with the cool weather, the tales that are told of the condition of things there last summer are appalling. Mrs. Brisbane heard all about it from Father Hamilton, a Roman Catholic priest from Macon, who has been working like a good Samaritan in those dens of filth and misery. It is a shame to us Protestants that we have let a Roman Catholic get so far ahead of us in this work of charity and mercy. Mrs. Brisbane says Father Hamilton told her that during the summer the wretched prisoners burrowed in the ground like moles to protect themselves from the sun. It was not safe to give them material to build shanties as they might use it for clubs to overcome the guard. These underground huts, he said, were alive with vermin and stank like charnel houses. Many of the prisoners were stark naked, having not so much as a shirt to their backs. He told a pitiful story of a Pole who had no garment but a shirt, and to make it cover him better, he put his legs into the sleeves and tied the tail around his neck. The others guyed him so on his appearance and the poor wretch was so disheartened by suffering that one day he deliberately stepped over the dead line and stood there till the guard was forced to shoot him. But what I can't understand is that a Pole, of all people in the world, should come over here and try to take away our liberty when his own country is in the hands of oppressors. One would think that the Poles, of all nations in the world, ought to sympathize with a people fighting for their liberties.

Father Hamilton said that at one time the prisoners died at the rate of a hundred and fifty a day, and he saw some of them die on the ground without a rag to lie on or a garment to cover them. Dysentery was the most fatal disease, and as they lay on the ground in their own excrements, the smell was so horrible that the good father says he was often obliged to rush from their presence to get a breath of pure air. It is dreadful. My heart aches

for the poor wretches, Yankees though they are, and I am afraid God will suffer some terrible retribution to fall upon us for letting such things happen. If the Yankees ever should come to southwest Georgia and go to Anderson and see the graves there, God have mercy on the land! And yet what can we do? The Yankees themselves are really more to blame than we, for they won't exchange these prisoners, and our poor, hard-pressed Confederacy has not the means to provide for them when our own soldiers are starving in the field. Oh, what a horrible thing war is when stringed of all its pomp and circumstance!

—ANDREWS, *The War-Time Journal of a Georgia Girl*

XX.3

THE BRIGHT SIDE OF LIBBY PRISON

Next to Andersonville Libby was the most famous, or notorious, of Confederate prisons. Originally a vacant warehouse in Richmond, it was taken over by General Winder, provost marshal of the city, and made into a prison for commissioned officers; privates fro•m the Virginia battles were housed at Belle Isle in the James. There were a number of spectacular escapes from Libby, and after the Dahlgren Raid of 1864, designed to free the prisoners, Libby was largely abandoned in favor of prisons farther to the south.

Frank Moran, who here tells something of the brighter side of prison life, was a captain of the 73rd New York Volunteers who was captured at Gettysburg and imprisoned first at Libby and later at Macon, Georgia, and Charleston, South Carolina.

The building had a frontage from east to west of 145 feet, and a depth from north to south of 105 feet. It stood isolated from other buildings, with streets passing its front, rear, and west ends, and with a vacant space on the east of about sixty feet in width. The portion of the building devoted to the use of the prisoners consisted of nine rooms, each 102 feet in length by forty-five feet in breadth. The ceiling was eight feet high, except in the upper rooms, which were higher, better lighted, and better ventilated, owing to the pitch of the roof. Rickety, unbanistered stairs led from the lower to the upper rooms, and all the rooms of the upper floors were connected by doors, leaving free access from one to the other. With the exception of a few rude bunks and tables in the upper and lower west rooms, which were respectively termed "Streight's room" and "Milroy's room," and four long tables in the lower middle or "kitchen room," there was no furniture in the prison. The north windows commanded a partial view of the hilly portion of the city. From the east the prisoners could look off toward the Rocketts and City Point. The south windows looked out upon the canal and James river, with Manchester opposite and Belle Isle, while from the windows of the upper west room could be seen Castle Thunder, Jefferson Davis's mansion, and the Confederate capital.

Libby prison was a vast museum of human character, where the chances of war had brought into close communion every type and temperament; where military rank was wholly ignored, and all shared a common lot. At the time referred to, there were about 1200 Union officers there, of all ranks, and representing every loyal state. They were not men who would have sought each other's society from natural or social affinity, but men who had been involuntarily forced together by the fortunes of war, which, like politics, often "makes strange bedfellows." There were men of all sizes and nationalities. Youth and age, and titled men of Europe, who had enlisted in our cause, might be found among the captives. There were about thirty doctors, as many ministers, a score of journalists and lawyers, a few actors, and a proportionate representation from all trades and professions that engage men in civil life. Among them were travelers and scholars, who had seen the world, and could entertain audiences for hours with narratives of their journeyings; indeed, among the attractions of the prison was the pleasure derived by intimate association with men of bright and cultured minds; men who had often led their squadrons on the tough edge of battle and who in their history pre-

sented the best types of modern chivalry. It was indeed a remarkable gathering and the circumstances are not likely to arise that will reassemble its counterpart again in this generation. All in all, Libby prison, from the vast mixture of its inmates, and from all its peculiar surroundings, was doubtless the best school of human nature ever seen in this country.

It will not seem strange, therefore, that men of such varied talents, tastes, and dispositions, shipwrecked in this peculiar manner, should begin to devise ways and means to turn the tedious hours of prison life to some account. To this end meetings and consultations were held to set on foot amusements and instruction for the prisoners.

A minstrel troupe was organized, and its talent would compare favorably with some professional companies of to-day. A number of musical instruments were purchased, forming a respectable orchestra.

Refreshing music often enlivened the place when the weary-souled prisoner had laid down for the night. If there ever was a time and place when that old melody, "Home Sweet Home," touched the tenderest chords of the soldier's heart, it was on Christmas Eve of 1863, behind the barred windows of Libby prison. Chess, checkers, cards, or such other games occupied much of our time. Some busied themselves with making bone rings or ornaments, many of them carved with exquisite skill. .

At night the prisoners covered the floor completely, lying in straight rows like prostrate lines of battle, and when one rolled over all must necessarily do the same. it was inevitable that among such large numbers there should appear the usual infliction of snorers, whose discord at times drew a terrific broadside of boots, tin cans, and other convenient missiles, which invariably struck the wrong man. Among our number was one officer whose habit of grinding his teeth secured him a larger share of room at night than was commonly allowed to a prisoner, and his comrades hoped that a special exchange might restore him to his family; for certainly he was a man that would be missed wherever he had lodged. On a memorable night when this gentleman was entertaining us with his "tooth solo," one comrade who had been kept awake for the three previous nights, after repeatedly shouting to the nocturnal minstrel to "shut up," arose in wrath, and, picking his steps in the dark among his prostrate comrades, arrived at last near a form which he felt certain was that of the disturber of the peace. With one mighty effort, he bestowed a kick in the ribs of the victim, and hurriedly retreated to his place. Then arose the kicked officer, who was not the grinder at all, and made an address to his invisible assailant, employing terms and vigorous adjectives not seen in the New Testament, vehemently declaring in a brilliant peroration that it was enough to be compelled to spend wakeful nights beside a man who made nights hideous with serenades, without being kicked for him. He resumed his bed amid thunderous applause, during which the grinder was awakened and was for the first time made aware of the cause of the enthusiasm.

The spirit of Yankee enterprise was well illustrated by the publication of a newspaper by the energetic chaplain of a New York regiment. It was entitled *The Libby Prison Chronicle*. True, there were no printing facilities at hand, but, undaunted by this difficulty, the editor obtained and distributed quantities of manuscript paper among the prisoners who were leaders in their several professions, so that there was soon organized an extensive corps of able correspondents, local reporters, poets, punsters, and witty paragraphers, that gave the chronicle a pronounced success. Pursuant to previous announcement, the "editor" on a stated day each week, would take up his position in the center of the upper east room, and, surrounded by an audience limited only by the available space, would read the articles contributed during the week.

"The Prison Minstrels" were deservedly popular. The troupe was organized and governed by strictly professional rules. Nothing but the possession and display of positive musical or dramatic talent could command prominence, and as a natural consequence it was a common occurrence to see a

second lieutenant carrying off the honors of the play, and the colonel of his regiment carrying off the chairs as a "supe." Our elephant, by the way, deserves especial mention, not only because of his peculiar construction, but because both intellectually and physically he differed from all elephants we had previously seen. The animal was composed of four United States officers, which certainly gave him unusual rank. One leg was a major, a second a naval officer, a third a captain of cavalry, and the last leg was by the happy thought of the astute manager an army surgeon. A quantity of straw formed the body; the tusks and trunk were improvised from the meager resources of our "property room." The whole was covered ingeniously by five army blankets. Indeed the elephant, seen by the "footlights" (four candles set in bottles), was pronounced by the critics of *The Libby Prison Chronicle* "*a* masterpiece of stage mechanism."

—MORGAN, "Libby's Bright Side"

XX.4

THE AWFUL CONDITIONS AT FORT DELAWARE

Fort Delaware was the Andersonville of the North—the most dreaded of Northern prisons. Located on an island in the Delaware River, much of it was below water—which was held back by dykes—and the flimsy barracks in which the men lived were cold and damp. Unlike most prisons, Fort Delaware housed both officers and privates. Young Shotwell whom we have met before, was captured on the eve of the battle of Cold Harbor and imprisoned first at Point Lookout and later at Fort Delaware.

July 12, 1864.—I have just witnessed a sight that made my blood boil. When I first arrived here I made the acquaintance of a handsome young officer; Captain William H. Gordon, from West Virginia, a native of Brooke County, not far from Wheeling. After some years' service he went home on furlough and was captured while returning to the Army.

His captors were renegades, Southern born, but wearing Yankee blu; and to furnish an excuse for their malevolent treatment, they charged him with being on a recruiting expedition inside of their lines; just as I was. put in irons as a spy, tho' simply on a legitimate scouting expedition with arms in my hands, and wearing our uniform.

On Saturday, Captain Gordon, and Mr. E. J. Debett, a Democrat, held as a "political prisoner," were marched out of the pen, stripped of their clothes, and dressed in the castoff blue trousers of the Yankees; after which they were put in the "Chain gang," or gang of condemned felons from the Yankee Army, underoing sentence to hard labor for various crimes. Several hundred of this class are on the island; deserters, bounty jumpers, murderers, thieves, etc., all of whom are compelled to haul heavy loads of stone or lumber for the repair of dykes or buildings. In strange contrast of cause and effect, a handsome Gothic Chapel was built for the use of the garrison, by the labor of these miserable malefactors—hardened old sinners, who never before were inside of a church even as workmen. Into such companionship was young Gordon thrust, and today I saw his tall figure clad in shabby rags, and paired with a greasy looking convict, dragging at the rope of a heavy cart together with about fifty other men; while a low-browed brutal looking Yankee, with a long stick or goad, sat atop the load of bricks of granite, and continuously yelled at the team, thus: "Pull, d——n you, pull! What the h——l you hanging back for? Who's that making signs at them windows?" The last speech was meant for Captain Gordon, who as he passed our windows looked up with a sad smile as if to say: "This is hard! but I shall endure to the end." . . .

August 10th.—How strange a thing it is to be hungry! actually craving something to eat, and constantly thinking about it from morning till night, from day to day; for weeks and months!

It did not seem possible for a man thus to worry over lack of nourishment, keeping his mind continually engrossed with anger against those who starve us, and with longing for food, the German philosopher's "earnest aspirations after the unattainable."

For the past month our rations have been six, sometimes four hard crackers and 1/10 of a pound of rusty bacon (a piece the size of a hen's egg) for the twenty-four hours.

But for five days past we have not had a morsel of meat of any kind; the cooks alleging that the supply ran short and "spoiled." (For a fortnight before it ceased to be issued, the rations were so full of worms, and stank so that one had to hold his nose while eating it!) But now we receive none *at all!* Talk about Andersonville! We would gladly exchange rations with the Yankees there!

For my part I cannot swallow very fat meat, or any that is in the very least tainted, so that for a long time I have subsisted on little else than hard tack and water. And such water! There has been no rain for some time; the tanks are no longer adequate for the supply of the pen even when full; therefore the Yankees have a small vessel that is used as a water boat, and is designed to ascend the creek sufficiently far to obtain fresh water. But the boat doesn't go above tide water, hence brings back a brackish *briny* fluid scarcely one whit better than the water from the Delaware, which oozes through the ditches in the pen.

The standing rain water of course breeds a dense swarm of animalculae, and when the hose pipes from the water boat are turned into the tanks the interior sediment is stirred up, and the whole contents become a turgid, salty, jellified mass of waggle tails, worms, dead leaves, dead fishes, and other putrescent abominations, most of which is visibile to the eye in a cup of it.

The *smell* of it is enough to revolt the stomach of a fastidious person; to say nothing of the thought of making one's throat a channel for such stuff. Yet, when the tanks are empty—as they are for half a day once or oftener in the week—the cry for this briny liquid is universal, because it creates a thirst equally as much as it quenches it, but if it were not so, the intense heat which beats upon this flat, parched island would make us swallow soluble salts for temporary relief.

The surface of the Pea Patch being of alluvial mud, becomes very porous and damp in wet weather, but parched and as hard as rock in the long dry season. No shade is there, no elevation, no breeze; only a low, flat, sultry, burning oven! Today the heat is so intense that men by hundreds are seen sweltering on their backs, fairly gasping for breath,- like fish dying on a sand beach.

August 11th:—Shocking reports of the ravage of pestilence both in this pen and the other. I remain so closely in my bunk, or walking to and fro in the yard that I had no idea there was so much sickness prevailing until two cases of smallpox had been taken from my own division.

Horrible to relate, the hospital is full and men are no longer taken out until dying or dead. One of the smallpox cases (since dead I learn) was poor C., who slept directly over my bunk. He was very dirty and annoying while in health, and we had some words about his stepping on my blankets with muddy boots while climbing to his bunk; but after he took the fearful disease I felt sorry for him, and helped to lift him down from his tier and carry him to the gate. Strange to say, I cannot realize the danger, though most of the prisoners are getting nervous. So are the garrison. . . .

Oct. 4th:—The catching and eating of the huge rats which infest the island has become a common thing. It is a curious sight; grown men, whiskered and uniformed officers who have already "set a squadron in the field," lurking, club in hand, near one of the many breathing holes, which the long tailed rodents have cut in the hard earth, patiently awaiting a chance to strike a blow for "fresh meat and rat soup"—for dinner! They generally succeed in getting one or more rats at a sitting. Indeed the surface of the earth in some portions of the yard seems to be honeycombed by these amphibious burrowers, which are not the ordinary house rat, but a larger species of water rat, something like the Norway variety.

They are eaten by fully a score of the officers, and apparently with relish. When deviled or stewed, they resemble young squirrels in *looks. I* have not yet mustered stomach enough to nibble at one—though once—three years ago on the Potomac island—their brethren nibbled at me in no pleasant fashion. The flesh of these rodents is quite white, and when several are on a plate with plenty of dressing, they look so appetizing one cannot help regretting his early mis-education, or prejudice. That our antipathy to rats is all prejudice the rat eaters firmly assert. "Why," quoth one of them—"you eat wagon loads of hogs, and everybody knows a rat is cleaner than a hog. Rats are just as-dainty as squirrels or chickens. Try a piece?" "No, thanks, my 'prejudices' unfortunately, are not yet abated.". . .

Oct. 9th:—Ugh! Fingers are too cold to hold the pen! Dozens of us have lain since breakfast, curled up under our blankets—thinking, thinking, and shivering with intense chilliness; not comfortable a moment in the day!

The wintry blasts sweep up the broad river, and across the flat island, with the keenness of an ocean cyclone; roaring round the prison yard, whistling through thousands of crevices in the open barracks with a chill rasping sound that increases the cold by imagination.

As for comfort, it is out of the question for the well and hearty. How much worse for the sick and debilitated! God help us this dreary winter! I dread to see night come, for then I must surrender the blankets borrowed from my comrades, and I have only half of one to sleep on and half for a covering.

And yet we are much better off than many of the poor fellows in the Privates' Pen! There are ten, or more, thousand men packed into a square of about six acres—thousands of them *barefooted,* not one in twenty supplied with underclothing. Even of those taken out to work the greater number are shoeless and hatless, and yet they gladly consent to go out and drag the heavy stone carts as long as they can stand, simply *for a few extra crusts of bread* to appease their constant, unsatisfied hunger! . . .

Stoves have been put up, one in each shed, but there is not fuel enough furnished to keep up even a semblance of fire more than half the time, and with a crowd of one hundred and ten shivering men to make a double circle around it, there is not much chance for a diffident person to get any where near it.

For three weeks I have not been comfortably warm during the day, nor able to sleep over two hours any night; have not tasted warm food; have not been free from the pangs of actual hunger any moment during the time. Our ration is still three hardtacks at 9 A.M. and three more at 3 P.M. with a morsel of rusty meat, and an occasional gill of rice soup. Stuff at which no ordinary respectable Negro's *dog* would condescend to sniff at, down South.

The hardships that we, officers and gentlemen, *prisoners of war,* not criminals, suffer, and which have tumbled nearly ten thousand Southerners into the pits on yonder Jersey shore, are not *necessary;* are not the result of poverty, blockade, lack of supplies, nor from necessary vigor of discipline to prevent escape. It is sheer cruelty!

—HAMILTON, ed., 'The Papers of Randolph Abbott Shotwell"

XX.5

THE PRIVATIONS OF LIFE IN ELMIRA PRISON

Elmira, opened in May 1864 to relieve pressure on the older prisons, was one of the largest of the Northern prisons, housing, by the end of the war, over 12,000 Confederates. At first the prisoners had only tents; with the coming of winter rude barracks were constructed and as these were equipped with stoves they protected the Southern boys from the worst rigors of an upstate New York winter. A feud between the commandant and the surgeon was partly responsible for bad conditions and a high sickness and mortality rate: altogether some 3,000 of Elmira's inmates died during one year of operation.

Marcus Toney was a Tennessee boy whose *Privations of a Private* is one of the better of the little-known Civil War narratives.

The prison camp contained some forty acres of land about one mile above the city [of Elmira, New York], and near the Chemung River, a beautiful,

clear, limpid mountain stream of very pure water. The stockade that surrounded the camp was much like the one at Point Lookout, but built of heavier material, and the ends of the upright planks going some eighteen inches into the ground. The planks were about sixteen feet high, and nailed to heavy sills, which were supported by large posts set deep in the ground. The stockade was about six teen feet high, and three feet from the top was the parapet walkway or beat of the guards, who were stationed some forty feet apart, and were relieved every two hours by other guards.

Commencing at nine o'clock at night, or taps, they would cry out their posts all through the hours of the night, as "Post No. 1, nine o'clock; all is well" which would be taken up by all posts and repeated all around the stockade. Inside the stockade about fifty feet apart were large coal oil lamps nailed near the center of the stockade, with large reflectors, which were lit after nightfall, and the guards on the parapet would be able to see any one approaching.

The tents in which we slept were struck every morning in order for inspection. The prisoners in one of the tents had a false floor laid and covered with dirt hard packed so it would have the same appearance as the ground floor in the other tents. Under this false floor was one of the prisoners digging day and night. There were six occupants of this particular tent and by making a detail one man was digging, all the time. They were tunneling to get under the fence. The tunnel was only about two feet under the ground and they had to go about sixty feet distance to get under the fence; the only implement they had was a large knife. They had a small box to which was attached a string at both ends and when the fellow at the farther side had filled his box he gave a pull of the string and the other fellow just under the false floor of the tent would pull the box under the floor, pile up the dirt and at night they would remove the false floor, gather the dirt in their hands, fill their haversacks, and scatter the dirt along the new-made streets. When they reached the up right planks of the stockade they had to go over a foot lower than the tunnel in order to get under the end of the planks. Finally the tunnel was completed and one of the boys crawled through poked his head on the outside and came and reported bright moonshine disclosed the camp of the guards under patrol across the street and a number of pieces of artillery in position along the camp; so they waited for the moon to go down before they commenced their underground journey. The plan was that the last of the six to leave should notify as many of the prisoners as he could in order that they might take advantage of it; but only fifteen got out and we heard that they reached Canada in safety. . . .

In a military prison it was very difficult to get information from the outside world. No papers were allowed, and the papers received had been opened and read; if there was any thing contraband, you did not get it. When you wrote a letter it was left unsealed, and when the prison authorities examined it they stamped it "Prisoner's letter, approved," and then sealed and mailed it. Money was contraband of war, for a fellow might bribe his way out; therefore, whenever a remittance came to a prisoner it was turned over to the sutler who opened an account with the owner, and he could purchase all he wished so long as the funds held out; but when money went, a prisoner's credit was non *est*.

Until I reached prison I did not know what a slave to habit man was. I have seen men go hungry a day and save their rations and trade them for tobacco. I have seen a prisoner discharge a quid of tobacco from his mouth and other one pick it up, dry and smoke it. They used the black navy tobacco, sold in prison at the rate of one dollar per pound. They would cut it into little squares; each square would be called a chew, and five chews five cents. We had all kinds of trade and traffics, and tobacco was one of the mediums of exchange. We had many barbers, and they would shave you for five chews of tobacco. When the barber would get more tobacco than he needed, he would sell five chews for a small loaf of bread, valued at five cents, or he could purchase a small piece of meat or a fresh rat each valued at five

cents. These barbers carried square boxes with them, upon which they set their patients; and a fellow would have to be very patient, as they never used a hone or strap except their boots and shoes, and it was hard to tell which was the worst sufferer, the barber or his customer. . . .

Adjoining the cook house was a large shed with tables that would accommodate three hundred men, and there were in the shed about twenty tables which were higher than my waist when standing. . . . Seats were not allowed. The men were marched in in two ranks, and separated at the head of the table, making one rank face the other. Each man had a plate and spoon; in the plate were his bean soup and beans, by the side of his plate was a small piece of light bread, and on the bread a thin ration of salt pork. The rations were thus prepared: a baker who lived outside would come in daily and superintend the baking. In the cook house were a large number of iron kettles or caldrons in which the meat and beans were boiled. I suppose these caldrons would hold fifty gallons. The salt pork was shipped in barrels and rolled up to the caldrons, and with a pitchfork tossed in, then the beans—I have heard the boys say four beans to a gallon of water. Now when this is boiled down it gets very salty, and after three weeks of a diet of this kind a prisoner will commence to get sick. I thought for a while that the government was retaliating on us on account of Andersonville, but I afterwards believed that it was done by the army contractors. . . . I can say without hesitancy that the death rate here was higher than at any other prison North or South. . . .

A prisoner eating this diet will crave any kind of fresh meat. Marching through the camp one day was a prisoner in a barrel shirt, with placard, "I eat a dog"; another one bearing a barrel, with placard, "Dog Eater." The barrel shirt was one of the modes of punishment. The shirt was made by using a whisky or coal oil barrel knocking out one end and in the other boring a hole so as to get his head through, and then putting on a placard to indicate the crime. It appeared that these prisoners had captured a lapdog owned by the baker who came into camp daily to bake the bread. The baker made complaint to Colonel Beall, and said that his wife and children would not have taken one hundred dollars for the dog. As the prisoners had nothing to pay with, they were treated to the barrel shirt. The punishment was a two hours' march followed by a soldier with a boyonet, and they were not allowed much rest till the two hours were completed.

I saw another barrel shirt, "I told a lie." A prisoner did not have much compunction of conscience, especially if he had lied to deceive the commandant, which he conceived to be his religious duty. A prisoner carrying a barrel shirt, "I stole my messmate's rations," was hissed all around the camp; and deservedly so, because a man who would steal from his mess mates in prison deserved the most severe punishment; while the ones who carried the placard, "Dog Eater" had the sympathies of the entire camp, because many of them would have enjoyed a piece of fresh meat. When twitted about it they said: "It was not a common cur, but a Spitz, and tasted like mutton."

On account of the waste from the commissary a great many rodents from Elmira ran into the prison. As there were not any holes in which they could hide it was an easy catch for the boys by knocking them over with sticks, and there was quite a traffic in them. As there was very little currency in prison, tobacco, rats, pickles, pork, and light bread were mediums of exchange. Five chews of tobacco would buy a rat, a rat would buy five chews of tobacco, a loaf of bread would buy a rat, a rat would buy a loaf of bread, and so on.. . . .

The bunks extended the length of the ward on each side, leaving an aisle in the center and two stoves in each ward, and the prisoners were not allowed to get very close to them in zero weather. With an open building, the heat was not very intense. The bunks were three high, and the boys occupying the top bunk had to do some climbing. They were wide enough to sleep two medium-sized men. Each one was al lowed only a pair of blankets, and so had to sleep on the hard board; therefore, in extreme weather four slept in the space of two, using one pair of blankets to sleep on, which gave three for cover. Two of them slept with their heads toward the east, and two with their heads toward the west, and of course had to be on their sides; and when ready to change positions, one would call out, "All turn to the right", and the next call would be, "All turn to the left." The turns had to be made as stated, or there would be collisions. Of course the men did not disrobe in extreme cold weather, and on awakening in the morning their feet would be in each other's faces.

—TONEY, *The Privations of a Private*

XXI

BEHIND THE LINES: THE NORTH

Total war is a twentieth-century concept. The Civil War was very far from a total war, either North or South. Neither side ever mustered its full strength; neither side achieved any thing like the unity we take for granted in our own time. Because the war was f ought almost entirely in the South, and because the Confederacy, as the smaller and weaker of the belligerents, was required to organize a larger part of her resources, the impact of the war on the South was far deeper than it was on the North. To an extraordinary degree life went on, in the North, almost on a peacetime basis. Industry boomed; farmers expanded into the West; immigration kept up and with it city growth; colleges flourished; for the most part there was politics as usual. The war itself was fought haphazardly and inefficiently. The potential man power of the North was never effectively exploited; conscription was long delayed and, when it came, was badly administered. Business as usual was the order of the day, and profits and cost of living soared.

What is perhaps most striking, to the contemporary student, is the pervasiveness in the North of disunity and disloyalty, fraud and corruption, incompetence and confusion in both the civilian and the military. Large segments of the population were unalterably opposed to the war; men like Vallandigham denounced it in language that was treasonable, and organizations like the Knights of the Golden Circle planned revolution, while the draft was sabotaged, bounty jumping was common, and desertion ran to over 10 per cent. Only because the Confederacy was afflicted by comparable disunity and disorganization did the Union eventually triumph.

It would require a whole volume to do justice to this large theme of the Union and the Confederacy—behind the lines. We have, of necessity, contented ourselves here with some of the more interesting and illuminating narratives.

XXI. 1

WASHINGTON AS A CAMP

A political compromise dating back to the beginning of the Republic had located the capitol city on the banks of the Potomac; with Maryland seething with secession sentiment and Virginia in the Confederacy, Washington was from the beginning peculiarly vulnerable, and its defense remained, through out the war, a major strategical consideration. The location of the Confederate capital, too, was dictated by political considerations that deeply and adversely affected military strategy; had the capital remained at Montgomery, the-whole strategy of the war, North and South, might have been different.

Noah Brooks, who here describes the capital as a camp, was a journalist who was in Washington during the war as correspondent of the Sacramento Union; long-standing friend ship with Lincoln gave him access to the White House and to many of the political leaders of the Republic. After the war he served as editor of the *New York Tribune* and the *New York Times*, and wrote a number of juveniles, the best of which are *The Boy Emigrants* and *The Fairport Nine*.

Washington was then a military camp, a city of barracks and hospitals. The first thing that impressed the newly arrived stranger, especially if he came, as I did, from the shores of the Peaceful Sea, where the waves of war had not reached, was the martial aspect of the capital. Long lines of army wagons and artillery were continually rumbling through the streets; at all hours of the day and night the air was troubled by the clatter of galloping squads of cavalry; and the clank of sabers, and the measured beat of marching infantry, were ever present to the ear. The city was under military government and the wayfarer was liable to be halted anywhere in public buildings, or on the outskirts of the city, by an armed sentry, who curtly asked, "What is your business here?" Army blue was the predominating color on the sidewalks, sprinkled here and there with the gold lace of officers. In the galleries of the Senate and House of Representatives, especially during the cold weather,—when the well-warmed Capitol was a convenient refuge for idle people,—great patches of the light blue of military overcoats were to be marked among more somber colors of the groups of visitors.

It was contrary to army regulations to supply soldiers with liquors, and in most bar-rooms cards were conspicuous, bearing the legend, "Nothing sold to soldiers." At some of the drinking-places, as if to soften the severity of the dictum, was displayed an artistically painted group of the three arms of the military service, over which were printed the words, "No liquors sold to."

Now and again, just after some great battle near at hand, like that of Fredericksburg, or Chancellorsville, or Grant's long struggles in the Wilderness, the capital afforded a most distressful spectacle. Then, if at no other time, the home staying citizen realized something of the horrors of war. The Washington hospitals were never empty, but at such times they were crowded with the maimed and wounded, who arrived by hundreds as long as the waves of sorrow came streaming back from the fields of slaughter. One occasionally met a grim procession of the slightly wounded coming up from the railway station at Alexandria or the steamboat landing from Aquia Creek. They arrived in squads of a hundred or more, bandaged and limping, ragged and disheveled, blackened with smoke and powder, and drooping with weakness. They came groping, hobbling, and faltering, so faint and so longing for rest that one's heart bled at the piteous sight. Here and there were

men left to make their way as best they could to the hospital, and who were leaning on the iron railings or sitting wearily on the curbstones; but it was noticeable that all maintained the genuine American pluck in the midst of sorrow and suffering. As a rule, they were silent and unmurmuring; or if they spoke, it was to utter a grim joke at their own expense.

At the height of the war there were twenty-one hospitals in and about Washington. Some were in churches, public halls, the Patent Office, and other public buildings; but many were temporary wooden structures built for this special purpose. One of the representative hospitals was that of Hare wood, erected by the government on the private grounds of W. W. Corcoran, in the outskirts of the city. There was a highly ornamented barn filled with hospital stores, clothing, and sanitary goods. A long row of cattlesheds was boarded in and transformed into a hospital bakery. The temporary buildings constructed by the government were one story high, arranged in the form of a hollow square, row within row, and kept very neat and clean. . . .

Convalescents who had been discharged from the hospitals and who were not fit for military duty were assembled at a rendezvous in Alexandria, known as Camp Convalescent. This camp eventually became so crowded with the vast numbers of those who had been discharged from the hospitals or were stragglers from the army, that its condition was properly characterized as "infamous." More than ten thousand men, some of whom in the depth of winter were obliged to sleep on the cold ground, under canvas shelter and without fire or suitable covering, were massed together there, in the company of healthy reprobates who were "bummers," deserters, and stragglers—the riffraff of the Federal and Confederate armies. There were two of these curious improvised institutions—Camp Convalescent and Camp Straggle both of which were crammed full. . . .

The Washington of the war was a very different city from the present stately capital. Before the war the city was as drowsy and as grass-grown as any old New England town. Squalid Negro quarters hung on the flanks of fine old mansions, and although in the centers of this "city of magnificent distances" there were handsome public buildings, with here and there a statue or some other work of art, the general aspect of things was truly rural. The war changed all that in a very few weeks. Temporary hospitals and other rude shelters arose as if by magic on every hand. The streets were crowded by night and day, and the continual passage of heavily loaded quartermasters' trains, artillery, and vehicles of kinds before unknown in Washington, churned the unpaved streets into muddy thoroughfares in winter, or cut them deep with impalpable dust in summer. It was a favorite joke of Washingtonians that "real estate was high in dry weather, as it was for the most part all in the air."

Over the flats of the Potomac rose the then unfinished white obelisk of the Washington monument, a truncated cone; and in the weather-beaten sheds around its base were stored the carved and ornamented blocks that had been contributed to the structure by foreign governments, princes, potentates, and political and social organizations. On its hill rose the unfinished dome of the Capitol, whose bare ribs were darkly limned against the sky. It was a feeling of pride, or perhaps of some tenderer sentiment, that induced the government to insist that work on the Capitol should go on in the midst of the stress and strain of civil war, just as though nothing had happened to hinder the progress of the magnificent undertaking. It is no metaphor to say that the sound of the workman's hammer never ceased on that building, even in the dark times when it was not certain that "Washington was safe." The completion of the pediments of the House and Senate wings went on without delay during all these perilous times. The colossal statue of Freedom which now adorns the apex of the central dome (designed by Crawford and cast in bronze by Clark Mills) was at first set up on a temporary base in the Capitol grounds, where it was an object of curiosity and interest to visitors. . . .

The frequent appearance in Washington of paroled rebel officers, who usually wore their own uniform with evident pride and pleasure, and sometimes with a swagger, generally threw loyalists into a fever of excitement. More than once I saw ultra-loyal newsboys or boot-blacks throw a lump of mud, or a brickbat, at the passing Confederate. One of these officers, a Lieutenant Garnett, being on parole, sent in his card to Representative Wickliffe, of Kentucky, and was by him introduced upon the floor of the House, where he attracted attention, as well as indignation, from the members present. Presently a wave of excitement seemed to sweep over the galleries, the spectators being visibly affected by the appearance of an officer in full Confederate uniform sitting on one of the sofas of the House of Representatives. This was intensified when a door-keeper spoke to the visitor, who rose from his seat, gave a profound and sweeping bow, and withdrew to the outer corridor. It appeared that the door-keeper had told the Confederate that it was contrary to the rules of the House for him to be present.

—Brooks, "Washington in Lincoln's Time"

XXI.2

Walt Whitman Looks Around in Wartime Washington

Here is another, and very different, impression of wartime Washington, and from an even more famous pen. Walt Whitman was writing for New York and Brooklyn newspapers when, in December 1862, he got word that his young brother George had been wounded at Fredericksburg. He left at once for the front, found his brother at Falmouth, Virginia; and then returned to Washington, where he earned a meager living copying documents and devoted most of his time to visiting wounded soldiers in the Washington hospitals. It was during this experience as a "wound dresser" that—so he always believed—he contracted the infection which later led to paralysis. At the very end of the war Whitman got a clerkship in the Department of the Interior, only to lose it when the Secretary discovered that he was the author of a "scandalous" book—*Leaves of Grass*.

Washington, March 19, 1863

Dear Nat and Fred Gray:

Since I left New York I was down in the Army of the Potomac in front with my brother a good part of the winter, commencing time of the battle of Fredricksburgh—have seen *"war-life,"* the real article—folded myself in a blanket, lying down in the mud with composure—relished salt pork and hard tack—have been on the battlefield among the wounded, the faint and the bleeding, to give them nourishment—have gone over with a flag of truce the next day to help direct the burial of the dead—have struck up a tremendous friendship with a young Mississippi captain (about 19) that we took prisoner badly wounded at Fredricksburgh (he has followed me here, is in the Emory hospital here minus a leg—he wears his confederate uniform, proud as the devil—I met him first at Falmouth, in the Lacy house middle of December last, his leg just cut off, and cheered him up—poor boy, he has suffered a great deal, and still suffers—has eyes bright as a hawk, but face pale—our affection is an affair quite romantic—some times when I lean over to say I am going, he puts his arms around my neck, draws my face down, etc., quite a scene for Rappahannock.—During January came up hither, took a lodging room here. Did the 37th Congress, especially the night sessions the last three weeks, explored the Capitol, meandering the gorgeous painted interminable Senate corridors, getting lost in them (a new sensation, rich and strong, that endless painted interior at night)—got very much interested in some particular cases in Hospitals here—go now steadily to more or less of said Hospitals by day or night—find always the sick and dying soldiers forthwith begin to cling to me in a way that makes a fellow feel funny enough. These Hospitals, so different from all others—there thousands, and tens and twenties of thousands of American young men, badly wounded, all sorts of wounds, operated on, pallid with diarrhoea, languishing, dying with fever, pneumonia, etc., open a new world somehow to me, giving closer insights, new things, exploring deeper mines, than any yet, showing our humanity (I sometimes put myself in fancy in the cot, with typhoid, or under the knife) tried by terrible, fearfullest tests, probed deepest, the living soul's, the body's tragedies, bursting the petty bonds of art. To these, what are your dramas and poems, even the oldest and the fearfullest? Not old Greek mighty ones; where man contends with fate (and always yealds)—not Virgil showing Dante on and on among the agonized and damned, approach what here I see and take part in. For here I see, not at intervals, but quite always, how certain man, our American man—how he holds himself cool and unquestioned master above all pains and bloody mutilations. It is immense, the best thing of all—nourishes me of all men. This then, what frightened us all so long. Why, it is put to flight with ignominy—a mere stuffed scarecrow of the fields. Oh death, where is thy sting? Oh grave, where is thy victory?

In the Patent Office, as I stood there one night, just off the cot-side of a dying soldier, in a large ward that had received the worst cases of Second Bull Run, Antietam, and Fredricksburgh, the surgeon, Dr. Stone (Horatio Stone the Sculptor) told me, of all who had died in that crowded ward the past six months, he had still to find the first man or boy who had met the approach of death with a single tremor or unmanly fear. But let me change the subject—I have given you screed enough about Death and the Hospitals—and too much—since I got started. Only I have some curious yarns I promise you my darlings and gossips, by word of mouth whene'er we meet.

Washington and its points I find bear a second and a third perusal, and doubtless many. My first impressions, architectural, etc., were not favorable: but upon the whole, the city, the spaces, buildings, etc., make no unfit emblem of our country, so far, so broadly planned, everything in plenty, money and materials staggering with plenty, but the fruit of the plans, the knit, the combination yet wanting—Determined to express ourselves greatly in a Capitol but no fit Capitol yet here (time, associations, wanting I suppose) many a hiatus yet—many a thing to be taken down and done over again yet—perhaps an entire change of base—maybe a succession of changes.

Congress does not seize very hard upon me: I studied it and its members with curiosity, and long—much gab, great fear of public opinion, plenty of low business talent, but no masterful man in Congress (probably best so). I think well of the President. He has a face like a Hoosier Michael Angelo, so awful ugly it becomes beautiful, with its strange mouth, its deep cut, crisscross lines, and its doughnut complexion.—My notion is too, that underneath his outside smutched mannerism, and stories from third-class county barrooms (it is his humor), Mr. Lincoln keeps a fountain of first-class practical telling wisdom. I do not dwell on the supposed failures of his government: he has shown, I sometimes think an almost supernatural tact in keeping the ship afloat at all, with head steady, not only not going down, and now certain not to, but with proud and resolute spirit, and flag flying in sight of the world, menacing and high as ever. I say never yet captain, never ruler, had such a perplexing dangerous task as his, the past two years. I more and more rely upon his idiomatic western genius, careless of court dress or court decorum.

Friday morning, 20th—I finish my letter in the office of Major Hapgood, a paymaster, and a friend of mine. This is a large building filled with paymasters' offices, some thirty or forty or more. This room is up on the fifth floor (a most noble and broad view from my window) curious scenes around here—a continual stream of soldiers, officers, cripples, etc., some climbing wearily up the stairs. They seek their pay—and every hour, almost every minute, has its incident, its hitch, its romance, farce or tragedy. There are two paymasters in this room. A sentry at the street door, another halfway up the stairs, another at the chief clerk's door, all with muskets and bayonets—sometimes a great swarm, hundreds around the side walk in front waiting (everybody is waiting for something here). I take a pause, look up a couple of minutes from my

pen and paper—see spread, off there the Potomac, very fine, nothing pretty about it—the Washington monument, not half finished—the public grounds around it filled with ten thousand beeves on the hoof—to the left the Smithsonian with its brown turrets—to the right far across, Arlington Heights, the forts, eight or ten of them—then the long bridge, and down a ways but quite plain, the shipping of Alexandria. Opposite me and in a stone throw is the Treasury Building, and below the bustle and life of Pennsylvania Avenue. I shall hasten with my letter, and then go forth and take a stroll down "the avenue" as they call it here.

Now you boys, don't you think I have done the handsome thing by writing this astoundingly magnificent letter—certainly the longest I ever wrote in my life. Fred, I wish you to present my best respects to your father, Bloom and all; one of these days we will meet, and make up for lost time, my dearest boys.

Walt.

—HALLOWAY, ed., *The Uncollected Poetry and Prose of Walt Whitman*

XXI.3

MATTHEW BRADY'S "THE DEAD AT ANTIETAM"

In late September 1862, Matthew Brady opened an exhibition of Civil War photographs at his New York City gallery. Entitled "The Dead of Antietam," the exhibit was a major development in the history of photojournalism. It featured a series of photographs taken by Brady's assistants, James E. Gibson and Alexander Gardner, in the immediate aftermath of the Battle of Antietam, offering the general public a shocking new view of the harsh realities of combat.

Photography as a technology and an art was barely 20 years old when the war started. Dozens of photographers followed armies to take portraits of soldiers and document their activities. Matthew Brady was the best known of these photographers, though some would say he was as accomplished at spinning publicity as he was at taking photographs. He rarely ventured from his studio, preferring to send his assistants into the field, then often taking credit for their work.

In the mid-19th century, on-location photography was a cumbersome task. Cameras could not capture movement, and subjects had to sit still to avoid blurring the photographic image. Cameras were big and bulky, and photographers had to bring developing equipment in their wagons. They used fragile glass plates (measuring 8 inches by 10 inches) that were shuttled back and forth from the wagon to the camera, then back to the wagon again for developing.

Nevertheless, Brady and other photographers took advantage of this new medium to bring the war home. Pioneering photographers gradually improved their equipment and popularized the technology. As the following review from *The New York Times* documents, photography brought the brutality of war to the home front for the first time, and helped transform the public's perception of war in ways that still resonate today.

Brady's Photographs.
Pictures of the Dead at Antietam.

The living that throng Broadway care little perhaps for the Dead at Antietam, but we fancy they would jostle less carelessly down the great thorough fare, saunter less at their ease, were a few dripping bodies, fresh from the field, laid along the pavement. There would be a gathering up of skirts and a careful picking of way; conversation would be less lively, and the general air of pedestrians more subdued. As it is, the dead of the battle-field come up to us very rarely, even in dreams. We see the list in the morning paper at breakfast, but dismiss its recollection with the coffee. There is a confused mass of names, but they are all strangers; we forget the horrible significance that dwells amid the jumble of type. The roll we read is being called over in Eternity, and pale, trembling lips are answering to it. Shadowy fingers point from the page to a field where even imagination is loth to follow. Each of these little names that the printer struck off so lightly last night, whistling over his work, and that we speak with a clip of the tongue, represents a bleeding, mangled corpse. It is a thunderbolt that will crash into some brain—a dull, dead, remorseless weight that will fall upon some heart, straining it to breaking. There is nothing very terrible to us, however, in the list, though our sensations might be different if the newspaper carrier left the names on the battle-field and the bodies at our doors instead.

We recognize the battle-field as a reality, but it stands as a remote one. It is like a funeral next door. The crape on the bell-pull tells us there is death in the house, and in the close carriage that rolls away with muffled wheels you know there rides a woman to whom the world is very dark now. But you only see the mourners in the last of the long line of carriages—they ride very jollily and at their ease, smoking cigars in a furtive and discursive manner, perhaps, and, were it not for the black gloves they wear, which the deceased was wise and liberal enough to furnish, it might be a wedding for all the world would know. It attracts your attention, but does not enlist your sympathy. But it is very different when the hearse stops at your own door, and the corpse is carried out over your own threshold—you know whether it is a wedding or a funeral then, without looking at the colors of gloves worn. Those who lose friends in battle know what battle-fields are, and our Marylanders, with their door-yards strewed with the dead and dying, and their houses turned into hospitals for the wounded, know what battle-fields are.

Mr. Brady has done something to bring home to us the terrible reality and earnestness of war. If he has not brought bodies and laid them in our door-yards and along the streets, he has done something very like it. At the door of his gallery hangs a little placard, "The Dead of Antietam." Crowds of people are constantly going up the stairs; follow them, and you find them bending over photographic views of that fearful battle-field, taken immediately after the action. Of all objects of horror one would think the battle-field should stand preeminent, that it should bear away the palm of repulsiveness. But, on the contrary, there is a terrible fascination about it that draws one near these pictures, and makes him loth to leave them. You will see hushed, reverend groups standing around these weird copies of carnage, bending down to look in the pale faces of the dead, chained by the strange spell that dwells in dead men's eyes. It seems somewhat singular that the same sun that looked down on the faces of the slain, blistering them, blotting out from the bodies all semblance to humanity, and hastening corruption, should have thus caught their features upon canvas', and give them perpetuity for ever. But so it is.

These poor subjects could not give us the sun sittings, and they are taken as they fell, their poor hands clutching the grass around them in spasms of Pain, or reaching out for help which none gave. Union soldier and Confederate, side by side, here they lie, the red light of battle faded from their eyes but their lips set as when they met in the last fierce charge which loosed their souls and sent them grappling with each other and battling to the very gates of heaven. The ground whereon they lie is torn by shot and shell, the grass is trampled down by the tread of hot, hurrying feet, and little rivulets that can scarcely be of water are trickling along the earth like tears over a mother's face. It is a bleak, barren plain and above it bends an ashen sullen sky; there is no friendly shade or shelter from the noonday sun or the midnight dews; coldly and unpityingly the stars will look down on them and darkness will come with night to shut them in. But there is a poetry in the scene that no green fields or smiling landscapes can possess. Here lie men who have not hesitated to seal and stamp their convictions with their blood,—men who have flung themselves into the great gulf of the unknown to teach the world that there are truths dearer than life, wrongs and shames more to be dreaded than death. And if there be on earth one spot where the grass will grow greener than on another when the next Summer comes, where the leaves of Autumn will drop more lightly when they fall like a benediction upon a work completed and a promise fulfilled, it is these soldiers' graves.

There is one side of the picture that the sun did not catch, one phase that has escaped photographic skill. It is the background of widows and orphans, torn from the bosom of their natural protectors by the red remorseless hand of Battle, and thrown upon the fatherhood of God. Homes have been made desolate, and the light of life in thousands of hearts has been quenched forever. All this desolation imagination must paint—broken hearts cannot be photographed.

These pictures have a terrible distinctness. By the aid of the magnifying-glass, the very features of the slain may be distinguished. We would scarce choose to be in the gallery, when one of the women bending over them should recognize a husband, a son, or a brother in the still, lifeless lines of bodies, that lie ready for the gaping trenches. For these trenches have a terror for a woman's heart, that goes far to outweigh all the others that hover over the battle-field. How can a mother bear to know that the boy whose slumbers she has cradled, and whose head her bosom pillowed until the rolling drum called him forth—whose poor, pale face, could she reach it, should find the same pillow again—whose corpse should be strewn with the rarest flowers that Spring brings or Summer leaves—when, but for the privilege of touching that corpse, of kissing once more the lips though white and cold, of smoothing back the hair from the brow and cleansing it of blood stains, she would give all the remaining years of life that Heaven has allotted her—how can this mother bear to know that in a shallow trench, hastily dug, rude hands have thrown him. She would have handled the poor corpse so tenderly, have prized the boon of caring for it so dearly—yet, even the imperative office of hiding the dead from sight has been done by those who thought it trouble, and were only glad where their work ended.

Have heart, poor mother; grieve not without hope, mourn not without consolation. This is not the last of your boy.

With pealing of trumpets and beating of drums, these trenches shall open—the Son of Man comes. And then is reserved for him that crown which only heroes and martyrs are permitted to wear—a crown brighter than bays, greener and more lasting than laurel.

—*The New York Times*, October 20, 1862

XXI.4

Anna Dickinson Sees the Draft Riots in New York City

The Confederacy had resort to conscription as early as April 1862; not until March 1863 did the Federal Congress enact a conscription act, and it proved so full of loopholes and exemptions as to be practically useless. The act was widely denounced as unconstitutional and despotic, and first attempts to enforce it met with resistance in various Northern cities. By all odds the worst disturbances were the great "draft riots" that swept New York City from the thirteenth to the seventeenth of July. For three or four days New York was in the grip of hoodlums who rioted, pillaged, and burned almost at will; the local authorities were all but helpless and Governor Seymour gave aid and comfort to the rioters by promising to get the obnoxious law repealed. The most disgraceful feature of the riots was the savage attack on Negroes; even the Negro Orphan Asylum was burned down by the mob.

Anna Dickinson, who here describes these outbreaks, was at the time a young woman but already well known as writer and lecturer on antislavery, temperance and woman's rights.

On the morning of Monday, the thirteenth of July [1863], began this outbreak, unparalleled in atrocities by anything in American history and equaled only by the horrors of the worst days of the French Revolution. Gangs of men and boys, composed of railroad employees, workers in machine shops, and a vast crowd of those who lived by preying upon others, thieves, pimps, professional ruffians, the scum of the city, jailbirds, or those who were running with swift feet to enter the prison doors, began to gather on the corners and in streets and alleys where they lived; from thence issuing forth, they visited the great establishments on the line of their advance, commanding their instant close and the companionship of the workmen—many of them peaceful and orderly men—on pain of the destruction of one and a murderous assault upon the other, did not their orders meet with instant compliance.

A body of these, five or six hundred strong, gathered about one of the enrolling offices in the upper part of the city, where the draft was quietly proceeding, and opened the assault upon it by a shower of clubs, bricks, and paving stones torn from the streets, following it up by a furious rush into the office. Lists, records, books, the drafting wheel, every article of furniture or work in the room, was rent in pieces and strewn about the floor or flung into the streets, while the law officers, the newspaper reporters—who are expected to be everywhere—and the few peaceable spectators, were compelled to make a hasty retreat through an opportune rear exit, accelerated by the curses and blows of the assailants.

A safe in the room, which contained some of the hated records, was fallen upon by the men, who strove to wrench open its impregnable lock with their naked hands, and, baffled, beat them on its iron doors and sides till they were stained with blood, in a mad frenzy of senseless hate and fury. And then, finding every portable article destroyed—their thirst for ruin growing by the little drink it had had—and believing, or rather hoping, that the officers had taken refuge in the upper rooms, set fire to the house, and stood watching the slow and steady lift of flames, filling the air with demoniac shrieks and yells, while they waited for the prey to escape from some door or window, from the merciless fire to their merciless hands. One of these, who was on the other side of the street, courageously stepped forward and, telling them that they had utterly demolished all they came to seek, informed them that helpless women and little children were in the house and besought them to extinguish the flames and leave the ruined premises—to disperse or at least to seek some other scene.

By his dress recognizing in him a government official, so far from hearing or heeding his humane appeal, they set upon him with sticks and clubs and beat him till his eyes were blind with blood, and he, bruised and mangled, succeeded in escaping to the handful of police who stood helpless before this howling crew, now increased to thousands. With difficulty and pain the inoffensive tenants escaped from the rapidly-spreading fire, which, having devoured the house originally lighted, swept across the neighboring buildings till the whole block stood a mass of burning flames. The firemen came up tardily and reluctantly, many of them of the same class as the miscreants who surrounded them and who cheered at their approach, but either made no attempt to perform their duty or so feeble and farcical a one as to bring disgrace upon a service they so generally honor and ennoble.

At last, when there was here nothing more to accomplish, the mob, swollen to a frightful size, including myriads of wretched, drunken women and the half-grown vagabond boys of the pavements, rushed through the intervening streets, stopping cars and insulting peaceable citizens on their way, to an armory where were manufactured and stored carbines and guns for the government. In anticipation of the attack, this, earlier in the day, had been fortified by a police squad capable of coping with an ordinary crowd of ruffians, but as chaff before fire in the presence of these murderous thousands. Here, as before, the attack was begun by a rain of missiles gathered from the streets, less fatal, doubtless, than more civilized arms, but frightful in the ghastly wounds and injuries they inflicted. Of this no notice was taken by those who were stationed within. It was repeated. At last, finding they were treated with contemptuous silence and that no sign of surrender was offered the crowd swayed back, then forward, in a combined attempt to force the wide entrance doors. Heavy hammers and sledges which had been brought from forges and workshops, caught up hastily as they gathered the mechanics into their ranks, were used with frightful violence to beat them in at last successfully. The foremost assailants began to climb the stairs but were checked and for the moment driven back by the fire of the officers, who at last had been commanded to resort to their revolvers. A half score fell wounded, and one who had been acting in some sort as their leader—a big, brutal Irish ruffian—dropped dead.

The pause was but for an instant. As the smoke cleared away there was a general and ferocious onslaught upon the armory; curses, oaths, revilings, hideous and obscene blasphemy, with terrible yells and cries, filled the air in every accent of the English tongue save that spoken by a native American. Such were there mingled with the sea of sound, but they were so few and weak as to be unnoticeable in the roar of voices. The paving stones flew like hail until the street was torn into gaps and ruts and every windowpane and sash and doorway was smashed or broken. Meanwhile divers attempts were made to fire the building but failed through haste or ineffectual materials or the vigilant watchfulness of the besieged. In the midst of this gallant defense word was brought to the defenders from headquarters that nothing could be done for their support and that if they would save their lives they must make a quick and orderly retreat. Fortunately there was a side passage with which the mob was unacquainted, and one by one they succeeded in gaining this and vanishing.

The work was begun, continued, gathering in force and fury as the day wore on. Police stations, enrolling offices, rooms or buildings used in any way by government authority or obnoxious as representing the dignity of law, were gutted, destroyed, then left to the mercy of the flames. Newspaper offices whose issues had been a fire in the rear of the nation's armies by extenuating and defending treason and through violent and incendiary appeals stirring up "lewd fellows of the baser sort" to this very carnival of ruin and blood were cheered as the crowd went by. Those that had been faithful to loyalty and law were hooted, stoned, and even stormed by the army of miscreants, who were only driven off by the gallant and determined charge of the police and in one place by the equally gallant and certainly unique defense which came from turning the boiling water from the engines upon the howling wretches, who, unprepared for any such warm reception as this, beat a precipitate and general retreat. Before night fell it was no longer one vast crowd collected in a single section, but great numbers of gatherings, scattered over the whole length and breadth of the city, some of them engaged in actual work of demolition and ruin, others, with clubs and weapons in their hands, prowling round apparently with no definite atrocity to perpetrate, but ready for any iniquity that might offer, and, by way of pastime, chasing every stray police officer or solitary soldier or inoffensive Negro who crossed the line of their vision; these three objects—the badge of a defender of the law, the uniform of the Union army, the skin of a helpless and outraged race—acted upon these madmen as water acts upon a rabid dog.

Late in the afternoon a crowd which could have numbered not less than ten thousand, the majority of whom were ragged, frowzy, drunken women, gathered about the Orphan Asylum for Colored Children—a large and beautiful building and one of the most admirable and noble charities of the city. When it became evident from the menacing cries and groans of the multitude that danger, if not destruction, was meditated to the harmless and inoffensive inmates, a flag of truce appeared, and an appeal was made in their behalf, by the principal, to every sentiment of humanity which these beings might possess—a vain appeal! Whatever human feeling-had ever, if ever, filled these souls was utterly drowned and washed away in the tide of rapine and blood in which they had been steeping themselves. The few officers who stood guard over the doors and manfully faced these demoniac legions were beaten down and flung to one side, helpless and stunned, whilst the vast crowd rushed in. All the articles upon which they could seize—beds, bedding, carpets, furniture, the very garments of the fleeing inmates, some of these torn from their persons as they sped by—were carried into the streets and hurried off by the women and children who stood ready to receive the goods which their husbands, sons, and fathers flung to their care. The little ones, many of them assailed and beaten—all, orphans and caretakers, exposed to every indignity and every danger—driven on to the street, the building was fired. This had been attempted whilst the helpless children, some of them scarce more than babies, were still in their rooms; but this devilish consummation was prevented by the heroism of one man. He, the chief of the fire department, strove by voice and arm to stay the endeavor; and when, overcome by superior numbers, the brands had been lit and piled, with naked hands and in the face of threatened death he tore asunder the glowing embers and trod them underfoot. Again the effort was made and again failed through the determined and heroic opposition of this solitary soul. Then on the front steps, in the midst of these drunken and infuriated thousands, he stood up and be sought them, if they cared nothing for themselves nor for those hapless orphans, that they would not bring lasting disgrace upon the city by destroying one of its noblest charities, which had for its object nothing but good.

He was answered on all sides by yells and execrations and frenzied shrieks of "Down with the nagurs!" coupled with every oath and every curse that malignant hate of the blacks could devise and drunken Irish tongues could speak. It had been decreed that this building was to be razed to the ground. The house was fired in a thousand places, and in less than two hours the walls crashed in, a mass of smoking, blackened ruins, whilst the children wandered through the streets, a prey to beings who were wild beasts in everything save the superior ingenuity of man to agonize and torture his, victims.

Frightful as the day had been, the night was yet more hideous, since to the horrors which were seen was added the greater horror of deeds which might be committed in the darkness—or, if they were seen, it was by the lurid glare of burning buildings, the red flames of which, flung upon the stained and brutal faces, the torn and tattered garments, of men and women who danced and howled around the scene of ruin they had caused, made the whole aspect of affairs seem more like a gathering of fiends rejoicing in pandemonium than aught with which creatures of flesh and blood had to do. . . .

The next morning's sun rose on a city which was ruled by a reign of terror. Had the police possessed the heads of Hydra and the arms of Briareus and had these heads all seen, these arms all fought, they would have been powerless against the multitude of opposers. Outbreaks were made, crowds gathered, houses burned, streets barricaded, fights enacted, in a score of places at once. Where the officers appeared they were irretrievably beaten and overcome, their stand, were it ever so short, but inflaming the passions of the mob to fresh deeds of violence. Stores were closed, the business portion of the city deserted, the large works and factories emptied of men, who had been sent home by their employers or were swept into the ranks of the marauding bands. The city cars, omnibuses, hacks, were unable to run and remained under shelter. Every telegraph wire was cut, the posts torn up, the operators driven from their offices. The mayor, seeing that civil power was helpless to stem this tide, desired to call the military to his aid and place the city under martial law, but was opposed by the Governor—a governor who, but a few days before, had pronounced the war a failure and not only predicted but encouraged this mob rule which was now crushing everything beneath its heavy and ensanguined feet. This man, through almost two days of these awful scenes, remained at a quiet seaside retreat but a few miles from the city. Coming to it on the afternoon of the second day, instead of ordering cannon planted in the streets, giving these creatures opportunity to retire to their homes, and, in the event of refusal, blowing them there by powder and ball, he first went to the point where was collected the chiefest mob and proceeded to address them. Before him stood incendiaries, thieves, and murderers, who even then were sacking dwelling houses and butchering powerless and inoffensive beings. These wretches he apostrophized as "my friends," repeating the title again and again in the course of his harangue, assuring them that he was there as a proof of his friendship, which he had demonstrated by "sending his adjutant general to Washington to have the draft stopped," begging them to "wait for his return," "to separate now as good citizens," with the promise that they "might assemble again whenever they wished to so do"; meanwhile he would "take care of their rights." This model speech was incessantly inter-

rupted by tremendous cheering and frantic demonstrations of delight, one great fellow almost crushing the Governor in his enthusiastic embrace.

His allies in newspaper offices attempted to throw the blame upon the loyal press and portion of the community. This was but a repetition of the cry raised by traitors in arms that the government, struggling for life in their deadly hold, was responsible for the war: "If thou wouldst but consent to be murdered peaceably, there could be no strife."

It was absurd and futile to characterize this new reign of terror as anything but an effort on the part of Northern rebels to help Southern ones at the most critical moment of the war, with the state militia and available troops-absent in a neighboring commonwealth and the loyal people unprepared. These editors and their coadjutors, men of brains and ability, were of that most poisonous growth—traitors to the government and the flag of their country—renegade Americans.

—Anna Dickinson, *What Answer?*

XXI.5

The Army of Lobbyists and Speculators

No one has ever told the full story of graft and corruption in the Civil War, but we know that it was pervasive and constant—far more so in the North than in the South, for the Confederacy offered little opportunity for large-scale corruption. Régis de Trobriand was one of those foreigners whom McClellan saluted in his Story. He was colonel of the 54th New York Volunteers, a French unit raised in the summer of 1861, and fought bravely through the war, winning the brevet rank of major general. His *Four Years with the Army of the Potomac* was based on a diary.

Besides the army formed to act against the enemy, there was another army—of lobbyists, contractors, speculators, which was continually renewed and never exhausted. These hurried to the assault on the treasury, like a cloud of locusts alighting down union the cap;tal to devour the substance of the country. They were everywhere: in the streets, in the hotels, in the offices, at the Capitol, and in the

White House. They continually besieged the bureaus of administration, the doors of the Senate and House of Representatives, wherever there was a chance to gain something.

Government, obliged to ask the aid of private industry, for every kind of supply that the army and navy must have without delay, was really at the mercy of these hungry spoilers, who combined with one another to make the law for the government. From this arose contracts exceedingly burdensome, which impoverished the treasury, to enrich a few individuals.

As a matter of course, these latter classes, strangers to every patriotic impulse, saw in the war only an extraordinary opportunity of making a fortune. Every means for obtaining it was a good one to them; so that corruption played a great part in the business of contracting. Political protection was purchased by giving an interest in the contracts obtained. Now, as these contracts must be increased or renewed, ac cording to the duration of the war, its prolongation became a direct advantage to a certain class of people disposing of large capital and of extended influence. What was the effect on events? It would be difficult to state precisely. But, in any case, this was evidently one of the causes which embarrassed the course of affairs, and delayed, more or less, the reestablishment of the Union.

The government—that is, the people, who, in the end, support the weight of public expenses—was, then, fleeced by the more moderate and robbed by the more covetous. The army suffered from it directly, as the supplies, which were furnished at a price which was much above their value if they had been of a good quality, were nearly all of a fraudulent inferiority. For example, instead of heavy woolen blankets, the recruits received, at this time, light, open fabrics, made I do not know of what different substances, which protected them against neither the cold nor the rain. A very short wear changed a large part of the uniform to rags, and during the winter spent at Tenally-town the ordinary duration of a pair of shoes was no longer than twenty or thirty days.

This last fact, well attested in my regiment, was followed by energetic remonstrances, on account of which the general commanding the brigade appointed, according to the regulations, a special *Board of Inspection,* with the object of obtaining the condemnation of the defective articles. Amongst the members of the board was an officer expert in these matters, having been employed, before the war, in one of the great shoe factories of Massachusetts. The report was very precise. It showed that the shoes were made of poor leather, not having been properly tanned, that the inside of the soles was filled with gray paper, and that the heels were so poorly fastened that it needed only a little dry weather following a few days of rain to have them drop from the shoes. In fine, the fraud was flagrant in every way.

The report was duly forwarded to the superior authorities. Did it have any consideration? I never knew. However, it was necessary to exhaust the stock in hand before obtaining a new supply, and the price charged the soldier was not altered.

—DE TROBRIAND, *Four Years with the Army of the Potomac*

—— XXI.6 ——

CHARLES A. DANA HELPS STOP FRAUDS IN THE WAR DEPARTMENT

Charles A. Dana had gone from Brook Farm to the *New York Tribune* under Greeley, and had become, by the time of the Civil War, one of the most influential of American editors. A disagreement with Greeley led to his resignation in 1862; he was promptly appointed by the War Department a sort of field inspector, attached himself to Grant's headquarters, and did inestimable service to the Union cause by his shrewd championship of Grant and Sherman. In 1863 he became Assistant Secretary of War, dividing his time between Washington and the battle front. After the war he bought the *New York Sun* and lived to become the most powerful editor of his generation. The frauds he recounts here were typical of many that were being perpetrated at the time.

At the time that I entered the War Department for regular duty, it was a very busy place. Mr. Stanton frequently worked late at night, keeping his carriage waiting for him. I never worked at night, as my eyes would not allow it. I got to my office about nine o'clock in the morning, and I stayed there nearly the whole day, for I made it a rule never to go away until my desk was cleared. When I arrived I usually found on my table a big pile of papers which were to be acted on, papers of every sort that had come to me from the different departments of the office.

The business of the War Department during the first winter that I spent in Washington was something enormous. Nearly $285,000,000 was paid out that year (from June, 1863, to June, 1864) by the quartermaster's office, and $221,000,000 stood in accounts at the end of the year awaiting examination before payment was made. We had to buy every conceivable thing that an army of men could need. We bought fuel, forage, furniture, coffins, medicine, horses, mules, telegraph wire, sugar, coffee, flour, cloth, caps, guns, powder, and thousands of other things. Sometimes our supplies came by contract; again by direct purchase; again by manufacture. Of course, by the fall of 1863 the army was pretty well supplied; still, that year we bought over 3,000,000 pairs of trousers, nearly 5,000,000 flannel shirts and drawers, some 7,000,000 pairs of stockings, 325,000 mess pans, 207,000 camp kettles, over 13,000 drums, and 14,830 fifes. It was my duty to make contracts for many of these supplies.

In making contracts for supplies of all kinds, we were obliged to take careful precautions against frauds. I-had a colleague in the department, the Hon. Peter H. Watson, the distinguished patent lawyer, who had a great knack at detecting army frauds. One which Watson had spent much time in trying to ferret out came to light soon after I went into offlce. This was an extensive fraud in forage furnished to the Army of the Potomac. The trick of the fraud consisted in a dishonest mixture of oats and Indian corn for the horses and mules of the army. By changing the proportions of the two sorts of grain, the contractors were able to make a considerable difference in the cost of the bushel, on account of the difference in the weight and price of the grain, and it was difficult to detect the cheat. However, Watson found it out, and at once arrested the men who were most directly involved.

Soon after the arrest Watson went to New York. While he was gone, certain parties from Philadelphia interested in the swindle came to me at the War Department. Among them was the president of the Corn Exchange. They paid me thirty-three thousand dollars to cover the sum which one of the men confessed he had appropriated; thirty-two thousand dollars was the amount restored by another individual. The morning after this transaction the Philadelphians returned to me, demanding both that the villians should be released, and that the papers and funds belonging to them, taken at the time of their arrest, should be restored. It was my judgment that, instead of being released, they should be remanded to solitary confinement until they could clear up all the forage frauds and make complete justice possible. Then I should have released them, but not before. So I telegraphed to Watson what had happened, and asked him to return to prevent any false step.

Now, it happened that the men arrested were of some political importance in Pennsylvania, and eminent politicans took a hand in getting them out of the scrape. Among others, the Hon. David Wilmot, then Senator of the United States and author of the famous Wilmot proviso, was very active. He went to Mr. Lincoln and made such representations and appeals that finally the President consented to go with him over to the War Department and see Watson in his office. Wilmot remained outside, and Mr. Lincoln went in to labor with the Assistant Secretary. Watson eloquently described the nature of the fraud, and the extent to which it had already been developed by his partial investigation. The President, in reply, dwelt upon the fact that a large amount of money had been refunded by the guilty men, and urged the greater question of the safety of the cause and the necessity of preserving united the powerful support which Pennsylvania was giving to the administration in suppressing the rebellion. Watson answered:

"Very well, Mr. President, if you wish to have these men released, all that is necessary is to give the order; but I shall ask to have it in writing. In such a case as this it would not be safe for me to obey a verbal order; and let me add that if you do release them the fact and the reason will necessarily become known to the people."

Finally Mr. Lincoln took up his hat and went out. Wilmot was waiting in the corridor, and came to meet him.

"Wilmot," he said, "I can't do anything with Watson; he won't release them."

The reply which the Senator made to this remark can not be printed here, but it did not affect the judgment or the action of the President.

The men were retained for a long time afterward. The fraud was fully investigated, and future swindles of the kind were rendered impossible. If Watson could have had his way, the guilty parties—and there were some whose names never got to the public—would have been tried by military commission and sternly dealt with. But my own reflections upon the subject led me to the conclusion that the moderation of the President was wiser than the unrelenting justice of the Assistant Secretary would have been.

—DANA, *Recollections of the Civil War*

XXI.7

COLONEL BAKER OUTWITS BOUNTY JUMPERS AND BROKERS

It is difficult to imagine how the enlistment and conscription laws of the Federal government could have been drawn more badly than they were. By the law of July 1861 Congress promised a bounty of $100 for three-year enlistments, and this bounty was later extended to conscripts who agreed to serve for a long term. The act of March 3, 1863, gave a bounty of $300 to three-year enlisters. At the same time many states and localities filled their quotas by offering generous bounties. Altogether, it is estimated, the Federal government paid out some $300,000,000 in bounties, and state and local governments a comparable sum. Inevitably many soldiers en listed just for the bounty, deserted, and re-enlisted elsewhere; some professional bounty jumpers managed to enlist and collect bounty ten or twenty times. Along with bounty jumping went bounty brokers—crooks who recruited men, and then robbed them of their bounties.

Colonel LaFayette C. Baker, who here tells us how he caught bounty jumpers and brokers red-handed, was Chief of the United States Secret Service, notorious alike for his high handed and illegal methods and for his success in feathering his own nest while serving his government. President Johnson dismissed him for maintaining an espionage system in the White House. One historian observes that Baker's "habitual carelessness in mixing truth and fiction was not overcome in his History of the Secret Service," but, however unreliable his general account of his own distinguished services, this story of bounty jumping in January 1865 would seem to be authentic enough.

The great demand for recruits during the war, the large bounties offered for them, and the manifold facilities for fraudulent transactions, presented temptations of great power, even to reputable citizens, to evade the plain letter of the law, and traffic in substitutes, or, by bribery and deception, personally to keep out of the hands of the recruiting officer.

The majority of the officers assigned to recruiting service were guilty of great dereliction of duty, inasmuch as, instead of endeavoring to check the growing evil, they rather pre tended ignorance, or allowed it to pass unnoticed. . . .

The Department at Washington was constantly urging upon me the necessity for forming some plan, which, in a summary and successful manner, would frustrate the designs of these dishonest parties, and bring them to justice. Several attempts had been made for this purpose, but had all proved unsuccessful.

A number of plans were submitted to me, each of which I considered objectionable, on certain accounts. The shortest way to catch these deserters, which was tracking them to their haunts, it would have been folly to pursue, as such a course would result in a general alarm and stampede of the guilty. . . .

I took up my headquarters at the Astor House, and let the brokers know that I was an agent or supervisor for the interior of the State, having several large quotas to fill. I was at once besieged by applications to purchase credits. The third day I purchased sixteen sets of these enlistment-papers; and on the fourth, twenty-two, when a proposition was made by a broker to purchase forged papers, saying, those I had were such, and would answer the same purpose; that so skillfully were they prepared detection was impossible. The offer was accepted, and placed me on the most friendly terms with my associates in business. For a number of days I continued the purchase of spurious papers for less than half the price of the genuine documents. This feature of the swindling came near causing a quarrel among the brokers; some of them insisting that I should not have been informed that I bought forged papers, because I might then have paid full price. The other party contended, that by committing me to the forgery I was secured against betrayal of the cause. The former further claimed, that forged papers were worth as much to me as the genuine. These negotiations were carried on four days, when I decided to arrest the whole company. It will be understood, that the arrest of a single broker in the city would create an alarm, and end the investigation. The greatest strategy-and concealment were therefore indispensible to success. The knowledge of my presence in the metropolis would have defeated my plans. On a certain day I requested nine brokers with whom I had business, to come to my room at the same hour, bringing their papers. I had concealed, in an adjoining room, a number of my assistants. I instructed them that the signal I should use to bring them to my aid, would be a knock on the door of the apartment in which they were placed.

The illustrious nine stood around me, forged papers in hand, eagerly waiting for the checks which would bring the reward of their villainy. To fasten the guilt upon the criminals beyond dispute, I had written receipts for the money to be paid each broker. As they walked up in line, and made

their marks, for most of them could not write, I stepped to the folding-doors and gave the signal. Instantly a detective came in, and I said to my broker-friends: "Gentlemen, this joke has gone far enough; you are my prisoners. I am General Baker, the Chief of the Detective Bureau."

It would be futile for tongue or pen to attempt to describe the effect of my words upon the assemblage before me. The change that passed over it was very marked, and to me, who was the cause of it, irresistibly entertaining. The explosion of a bomb-shell in the battle-ranks could not have startled and dismayed the soldiery more suddenly than this unexpected exposure of their crimes, and the powerful grasp of justice, did the discomfited brokers, who had anticipated a very different fate. . . .

It has been sufficiently demonstrated, by incidents recorded, that monstrous frauds were perpetrated by the manufacture and sale of enlistment papers.

Indeed, it is very evident, from knowledge thus far obtained, that not a small proportion of all such documents, on which credits were given, were forged.

I shall only add to the record a few incidents, which combine in their character both comic and tragic qualities.

I had been told that soldiers would receive the bounty, re enlist the same day, be sent to the Island, and repeat the process the day following. I was, at the time, skeptical respect ing such facility in deception and incredible assurance, and to satisfy myself in regard to the truth of the matter, I dressed myself in the garb of a regular jumper and repaired, February 9th, to a recruiting office in the public square near the Astor House, New York. Assuming the air of a veteran in the business, I asked the officer what he was paying for recruits.

Before the question could be answered, the gentlemanly broker, always at hand, inquired of me my name and place of residence, which I gave him. In a low tone of voice, and with a knowing wink, he said: "Have you been through before in New York?"

I answered: "Not since last fall."

He added: "All right; come inside." And in less time than it has taken to relate the incident, I was one of "Uncle Sam's boys."

My friend gave me one hundred dollars, promising the remainder due me when I should arrive at the Island; then directing me to remain where I was for a while, he left me.

Returning within an hour, he opened the following conversation with me: "Have you ever been on the Island?"

I replied, "Yes."

Evidently enlightened in regard to the matter, he immediately remarked: "You know how to get off, then? When you *do*, come up to Tammany Hall, and I will put you through up town": meaning, of course, he would enlist me again.

While this conversation was passing between us another broker stepped up, and said: "Gentlemen, let us take a drink." We accepted the invitation, and they conducted me across the Park to a saloon, where I saw, at a glance, they were quite at home. Liquor was called for, and while the vender was getting it, one of the brokers quietly stepped behind the bar and addressed some conversation to him.

We then all drank to the success of the Union, or rather, all of us *appeared* to do so.

I raised the glass to my lips, and, unobserved by the rest, poured its contents into my bosom, as I had done many times before when compelled to join the convivial ring. I was convinced that my potation had been drugged. Next followed a proposition to repair to an adjoining room and engage in a game of cards.

We played until I thought it necessary to affect drowsiness and insensibility. My eyes began to close, until at length my head rested on the table in front of me, and my whole appearance indicated to my betrayers my entire helplessness in their hands.

At this juncture one of them left the room, but soon returning, exclaimed, "All right." Immediately I caught the sound of carriage wheels, and, as I anticipated, was carried to the door, and, supported by broker number one, lifted into a vehicle, and

driven rapidly to the Cedar Street rendezvous. My hat was then unceremoniously pushed over my face, and I was hurried into the presence of the recruiting officer in attendance, who asked me, "Do you wish to enlist?"

Number two answered, in a tone to represent my own voice, "Ye-e-s."

I was again declared to be one of the volunteers, taken into another room, and laid on a bench, where I remained an hour, in company with three other recruits, who had been drugged in the same manner, my friends the brokers supposing they had disposed of me.

In the mean time broker number one returned, and said: "Well, old fellow, how do you feel?" to which I replied, "Very sick." Then remarking, "You'll be all right by-and-by," he left me.

I looked about me to judge of the possibility of escape. I saw at once that I could not pass out by the door, as a sentry was stationed there, and came to the conclusion that I would have to try my chances at a window.

I opened one which overlooked a back yard, sprang out, and after walking through a long passage-way, which led me into the open street, I went deliberately to my room in the Astor House.

Here I masked my face, disguised myself anew, and proceeded directly to the office of Mr. Blunt, where I offered myself to the army service, to make my third enlistment for that day.

I was hardly seated, when broker number three approached me, saying: "You want to enlist, do you?"

"Yes, I am thinking of it. What are you paying recruits now?"

"Six hundred dollars. Where are you from?"

"Steuben County. I would like to enlist if I could get a situation as clerk. I can write a pretty good hand, and am hardly able to go into the ranks."

He replied quickly, "Oh, I can fix that all right."

A conversation then followed between him and the recruiting officer, when I was made a soldier of the Union army once more. I was requested to be seated for a few moments. Soon after the broker asked me to take "a glass." I went with him to an old drinking-saloon in Cherry Street, where I found brokers numbers one and two, who immediately recognized me, but expressed no surprise at the meeting. My successful escape from the Cedar Street headquarters convinced my friends that I was an old expert in the tricks of the trade.

Their admiration for me became so great that they received me into full fellowship, regarded me as a shrewd member of the bounty jumping brotherhood, and, after freely discussing their plans and prospects, declared me to be a "perfect trump." Propositions were made to enter into partnership at once.

I was greatly amused while listening to the exploits of each, as he in turn detailed them. One related, that at a certain period he left New York, and having enlisted at Albany, Troy, Utica, Buffalo, and Chicago, returned *via* Elmira, at which place he likewise enlisted. Another had enlisted at every rendezvous from New York to Portland, Maine; while a third boasted of the amounts he had received, and mentioned those paid to recruiting officers, surgeons, brokers, and detectives. The den in which I spent the evening was a favorite haunt of the bounty jumpers. It contained a wardrobe of wearing apparel, consisting of both soldiers' and citizens' outfits. The idea of this I easily comprehended; here the jumpers could assume whatever dress they pleased, to carry out their designs. Three times that night, before two o'clock, I saw the interesting operation performed.

I selected one of my assistants to experiment in this military lottery. He dressed himself in the appropriate apparel, and in one day enlisted three times; he was sent to the Island, bought himself off, and reported for duty the following day.

The scenes described were followed by numberless arrests of bounty brokers, bounty jumpers, and others in the business, and consequently by the disclosures of their crimes, which have since attracted much public attention.

—BAKER, *The Secret Service in the Late War*

XXI.8

DOINGS IN NEVADA

While war raged in the East, miners, prospectors, speculators, ruffians, homesteaders, and a ragtag assortment of adventurers headed westward. Removed from the war, but not unaware of its implications, settlers (most of them sympathetic to the Union cause) continued to seek new opportunities. One of the most important facets of this continued migration was the ongoing excavation of gold and silver mines, which had been inspired by the California gold rush. Mining towns in California and Nevada appeared overnight. The excavation of precious metals helped play a crucial role in the North's ability to finance the war.

At the outset of the war Samuel Clemens joined a Confederate unit in Missouri. When military life did not suit him, he headed West. Clemens tried his hand as a prospector in some of the mining camps, but did not like the backbreaking work. Instead, he on took on the pen name "Mark Twain" and became a newspaper correspondent. He quickly built his reputation as a keen observer with a biting wit. Here he describes the Nevada state convention of 1864.

Carson City, Nevada Territory
January 4, 1864

Editor T. T.: The concentrated wisdom of Nevada Territory (known unto and respected by the nations of the earth as "Washoe") assembled in convention at Carson recently, and framed a constitution. It was an excellent piece of work in some respects, but it had one or two unfortunate defects which debarred it from assuming to be an immaculate conception. The chief of these was a clause authorizing the taxing of the mines. The people will not stand that. There are some 30,000 gold and silver mining incorporations here, or mines, or claims, or which you please, or all, if it suits you better. Very little of the kind of property thus represented is improved yet, or "developed" as we call it; it will take two or three years to get it in a developed and paying condition, and will require an enormous outlay of capital to accomplish such a result. And until it does begin to pay dividends, the people will not consent that it shall be burdened and hindered by taxation. Therefore, I am satisfied they will refuse to ratify our new constitution on the 19th inst.

It had an amusing feature in it, also. That was the Great Seal of the State. It had snow-capped mountains in it; and tunnels and shafts, and pick-axes and quartz-mills, and pack-trains, and mule-teams. These things were good; what there were of them. And it had railroads in it, and telegraphs, and stars, and suspension-bridges, and other romantic fictions foreign to sand and sage-brush. But the richest of it was the motto. It took them thirty days to decide whether it should be "Volens et Potens" (which they said meant "Able and Willing"), or "The Union Must and Shall be preserved." Either would have been presumptuous, and surpassingly absurd just at present. Because we are not able and willing, thus far, to do a great deal more than locate wild-cat mining-claims and reluctantly sell them to confiding strangers at a ruinous sacrifice—of conscience. And if it were left to us to preserve the Union, in case the balance of the country failed in the attempt, I seriously believe we couldn't do it. Possibly, we might make it mighty warm for the Confederacy if it came prowling around here, but ultimately we would have to forsake our high trust, and quit preserving the Union. I am confident of it. And I have thought the matter over a good deal, off and on, as we say in Paris. We have an animal here whose surname is the "jackass rabbit". It is three feet long, has legs liking a counting-house stool, ears of monstrous length, and no tail to speak of it. It is swifter than a greyhound, and as meek and harmless as an infant. I might mention, also, that it is as handsome as most infants; however, it would be foreign to the subject, and I do not know that a remark of that kind would be popular in all circles. Let it pass, then—I will say nothing about it, though it would be a greater comfort to me to do it, if people would consider the source and overlook it. Well, somebody proposed a substitute for that pictorial Great Seal, a figure of a jackass-rabbit reposing in the shade of his native sage-brush, with the motto "Volens enough, but not some d—d Potens". Possibly that had something to do with the rejection of one of the proposed mottoes by the Convention.

—MARK TWAIN

XXI.9

CONFEDERATE PLOTS AGAINST THE NORTH

It was entirely natural that the Confederacy, which was on the defensive militarily, should have sought to attack the Union from behind the lines. For in the end the only hope of Confederate victory—and it was a persistent hope—lay in encouraging discontent and disunity to the point where the Northern people would weary of the war. To this end Confederate secret agents, working closely with such treasonable organizations as the Knights of the Golden Circle and the Sons of Liberty, planned a series of attacks and uprisings in the fall of 1864. The immediate objective was to release Confederate prisoners at such places as Camp Douglas, in Chicago, and Johnson's Island, in Lake Erie, to burn Northern cities, and to distract the strength of the North by border raids; the ultimate purpose was to encourage the peace movement and defeat Lincoln in the 1864 elections. The plan to seize Camp Douglas miscarried and the leaders of the Knights implicated in the plan were captured and tried for treason. A border raid on St. Albans, Vermont, was a minor success. The three plots described in these excerpts were all fiascos.

A. A Confederate Plan to Seize Johnson's Island is Frustrated

On the 20th of September, 1864, the Lake cities were suddenly aroused from their imagined security by the news that a passenger steamer upon Lake Erie had been seized by a squad of Confederates, her crew overpowered, the steamer captured and her course directed to Johnson's Island, with the avowed purpose of rescuing the prisoners confined there and taking them to the Ohio shore, whence it was hoped they might make their way South through the state of Ohio. The plot was carefully planned, and perhaps might have been carried to a successful conclusion had it not been for the abundant precautions taken by the Federal forces.

The steamer, the *Philo Parsons*, left Detroit at her usual hour in the morning, and at the request of one Bennett G. Burleigh, who had come on board the night before stopped at Sandwich in Canada, nearly opposite Detroit, to take on board three friends of Burleigh, one of whom he said was lame and unable to cross the ferry. Proceeding down the river, the steamer stopped at Amherstberg, where sixteen roughish looking men came aboard with an old trunk tied with a rope. They did not seem to be connected with Burleigh, but were supposed to be refugees from the draft returning home; and little attention was paid to them.

Nothing occurred to excite suspicion until the boat was well within American waters, when one Beall, the leader of the gang, while engaged in conversation with the mate in the pilot house, suddenly drew his revolver, and demanded possession of the boat as a Confederate officer. Recognizing the force of this argument, the mate surrendered the wheel. The crew and passengers were overpowered, driven into the cabin, and the old trunk, which proved to be a small arsenal, opened, hatchets and revolvers distributed among the conspirators, and the course of the boat continued toward Sandusky, near which lay Johnson's Island.

But at this point the success of the expedition culminated. Failing to meet a messenger who was to have been sent to meet them at Kelley's Island, on the route of the steamer, or to receive an expected signal, all the conspirators but three mutinied, refused to go further, and returned at top speed to Amherstberg, where the boat was scuttled and abandoned and the conspirators dispersed. Another steamer was captured and scuttled on the Lake. All of the men were arrested, taken before a Justice of the Peace and discharged, although the officers were sufficiently alert to seize certain property which had been landed and detain it for customs dues.

It was fortunate the steamer turned about when she did. The officers of the *Michigan* had been apprised that the raid would be made that day. The *Michigan*, a man-of-war of fifteen guns, lay off the island, cleared for action, her guns shotted, her anchor hove short, and every preparation made to receive the expected guests. The messenger who was sent to Kelley's Island to join the conspirators had already been arrested and put in custody. There was an available force of nine hundred men at the Island to put down any insurrection. That twenty

men, armed only with revolvers and hatchets, should have been able to capture the *Michigan* and release the prisoners was simply preposterous. A single broadside from the *Michigan* would probably have sunk the steamer.

—BROWN, "The Lake Erie Piracy Case"

B. Confederates Raid Vermont

Lieutenant Young, after a conference with Mr. Clay, went into Vermont alone and selected St. Albans for an attack which could be made with the twenty reliable men who were now under his command. By arrangement, his men, two and three in a party, went by different routes and trains so as to arrive all together on the night of the 18th of October, 1864. . . . Every man arrived, and each party found rooms at the several hotels, where they remained most of the time. Lieutenant Young and one or two others went out the next forenoon and located the banks and livery stables.

Promptly at 3 o'clock in the afternoon the little command suddenly rallied and formed in the street, with overcoats off and Confederate uniforms on. Each man wore a pair of navy sixes belted on outside. They proclaimed that they took possession of St. Albans in the name of the Confederate States. . . . All the citizens on the street were ordered to go into the square and remain. This was ridiculed by a number of citizens, when the Confederates began to shoot at men who hesitated to go, and one was wounded. The citizens now realized that the exhibition was not a joke.

The confederates were prepared with fifty four-ounce bottles of Greek Fire each, and while three men went to each bank and secured their money, the others were firing the hotels and other buildings, and securing horses and equipment.

The citizens had been held at bay during the proceedings, which had consumed perhaps three-quarters of an hour. But the city contained about 5,000 inhabitants, and many men began to come into the public square. A number of Federal soldiers appeared among them, and preparations were being made for an attack upon the Confederates, who were not ready to go when a few more horses were equipped.

Suddenly the people began to fire from windows, and three of the Confederates were seriously wounded. A skirmish now ensued, and one citizen was killed. The Confederates dashed their Greek Fire against the houses all about on the square, and began their march to escape, with the citizens and a few soldiers, some in buggies and some on horseback, in pursuit. Lieutenant Young took the road to Shelburne, some eight miles distant, and was beyond reach of the pursuers until at Shelburne he reached a bridge over a river, on which a team was found crossing with a load of hay, for which he was obliged to wait. The pursuers approached, when the Confederates halted and opened fire, at the same time halting the team and turning it upon the bridge set fire to the hay, which fired and destroyed the bridge. The pursuers did not again overtake the Confederates. Lieutenant and his men, however, pushed forward and reached the border line of Canada about nine o'clock that night. The party at once donned their citizens' clothing and abandoned the St. Albans horses on the highway. They then dispersed and proceeded on foot to Canada.

The next forenoon Lieutenant Young learned that several of his men had been arrested at Phillipsburg. He at once decided that this must necessarily compel him to give himself up to the authorities and make the cause of his men his own, since he was the commander, and holding a commission and the authority for the raid.

Young stopped at a farm-house, and leaving his revolvers in an adjoining room, he sat at the only fire, which was in the kitchen, to get warm. To his surprise, about twenty-five people from St. Albans, in pursuit of his party, learning that there was a stranger in the house, suddenly rushed in and reached Young before he could get to his pistols, which they secured. They promptly seized him and at once proceeded to beat him with the pistols and with swords.

The American party now started with Young to return to St. Albans. They could have killed him, but doubtless deemed it important to deliver him alive in St. Albans for several reasons. They put Young in an open wagon with two men on each side and one in his rear, all in the wagon. The men were excited and carried their pistols cocked, badgering him with threats to shoot, while they denounced him in unmeasured terms. Young, however, continued to protest against their proceedings, insisting that they were in violation of British neutrality, but they said they did not care d__n for British law or the British nation. The front gate was some two hundred feet from the house. The road which passed in front of the house led from the United States to Phillipsburg. When they reached the gate to pass out, Young suddenly knocked the men from each side with his arms, seized the reins, and quickly turning the horses, drove toward Phillipsburg. But his captors, who were apparently paralyzed for a moment, soon recovered, and pounced upon him with their pistols and swords. In the midst of the melee, and fortunately for Young, a British officer happened upon the scene. Young told him of his character—that of a Confederate officer on British soil and entitled to protection, that his captors were Americans who proposed to take him without any authority to the United States in violation of British neutrality and in defiance of British law.

The British officer reasoned with the Americans for a time, who were reluctant to listen to argument or to delay their return to St. Albans. The officer, however, told them that others of the raiding party had been arrested and . . . were to be sent to St. Albans the next day. Young's captors then agreed that the officer should take him . . . to Phillipsburg. Here he found five of his comrades under arrest. But it happened that there was no arrangement for the Americans or any one else to carry the prisoners back to St. Albans.

That night Lieutenant Young and his five men were carried to St. Johns, a distance of about twenty miles, and placed in jail. Here a large garrison of British Regulars was stationed, who manifested the warmest friendship for the prisoners.

They went so far as to suggest to Lieutenant Young that he and his men might be rescued. They extended every possible courtesy, and the citizens were likewise friendly and hospitable to the prisoners. Lieutenant Young and his comrades concluded that it would be unwise now to evade the issue and preferred to await their fate in the courts of Canada, since their extradition had been demanded by the Government of the United States.

—JOHN W. HEADLEY, *Confederate Operations in Canada and New York*

C. The Confederates Attempt to Burn New York

At 6 o'clock promptly on the evening of November 25, 1864, our party met in our cottage headquarters, two failing to report.

The bottles of Greek fire having been wrapped in paper were put in our coat pockets. Each man took ten bottles. It was agreed that after our operations were over we should secrete ourselves and meet here the next night at 6 o'clock to compare notes and agree on further plans.

I had rooms at the Astor House, City Hotel, Everett House, and the United States Hotel. Colonel Martin occupied rooms at the Hoffman, Fifth Avenue, St. Denis, and two others. Lieutenant Ashbrook was at the St. Nicholas, La Farge, and several others. Altogether nineteen hotels were fired, namely: Hoffman House, Fifth Avenue, St. Denis, St. James, La Farge, St. Nicholas, Metropolitan, Howard, Tammany, Brandreth's, Gramercy Park, Hanford, New England, Belmont, Lovejoy's, City Hotel, Astor, United States, and Everett.

I reached the Astor House at 7.20 o'clock, got my key, and went to my room in the top story. It was the lower corner front room on Broadway. After lighting the gas jet I hung the bedclothes loosely on the headboard and piled the chairs, drawers of the bureau and washstand on the bed. Then stuffed some newspapers about among the mass and poured a bottle of turpentine over it all. I

concluded to unlock my door and fix the key on the outside, as I might have to get out in a hurry, for I did not know whether the Greek fire would make a noise or not. I opened a bottle carefully and quickly and spilled it on the pile of rubbish. It blazed up instantly and the whole bed seemed to be in flames, before I could get out. I locked the door and walked down the hall and stairway to the office, which was fairly crowded with people. I left the key at the office as usual and passed out.

Across at the City Hotel I proceeded in the same manner. Then in going down to the Everett House I looked over at my room in the Astor House. A bright light appeared within but there were no indications below of any alarm. After getting through at the Everett House I started to the United States Hotel, when the fire bells began to ring up town. I got through at the United States Hotel without trouble, but in leaving my key the clerk, I thought, looked at me a little curiously. It occurred to me that it had been discovered that my satchel had no baggage in it and that perhaps the clerk had it in mind to mention the fact.

As I came back to Broadway it seemed that a hundred bells were ringing, great crowds were gathering on the street, and there was general consternation. I concluded to go and see how my fires were doing. There was no panic at the Astor House, but to my surprise a great crowd was pouring out of Barnum's Museum nearly opposite the Astor. It was now a quarter after nine o'clock by the City Hall tower clock. Presently the alarm came from the City Hotel and the Everett. The surging crowds were frantic. But the greatest panic was at Barnum's Museum. People were coming out and down ladders from the second and third floor windows and the manager was crying out for help to get his animals out. It looked like people were getting hurt running over each other in the stampede, and still I could not help some astonishment for I did not suppose there was a fire in the Museum.

In accordance with our plan I went down Broadway and turned across to the North River wharf. The vessels and barges of every description were lying along close together and not more than twenty yards from the street I picked dark spots to stand in, and jerked a bottle in six different places. They were ablaze before I left. One had struck a barge of baled hay and made a big fire. There were wild scenes here the last time I looked back. I started straight for the City Hall.

There was still a crowd around the Astor House and every where, but I edged through and crossed over to the City Hall, where I caught a car just starting up town. I got off on Bowery street opposite the Metropolitan Hotel to go across and see how Ashbrook and Harrington had succeeded. After walking half a square I observed a man walking ahead of me and recognized him. It was Captain Kennedy. I closed up behind him and slapped him on the shoulder. He squatted and began to draw his pistol, but I laughed and he knew me. He laughed and said he ought to shoot me for giving him such a scare.

We soon related to each other our experience. Kennedy said that after he touched off his hotels he concluded to go down to Barnum's Museum and stay until something turned up, but had only been there a few minutes when alarms began to ring all over the city. He decided to go out, and coming down the stairway it happened to be clear at a turn and the idea occurred to him that there would be fun to start a scare. He broke a bottle of Greek fire, he said, on the edge of a step like he would crack an egg. It blazed up and he got out to witness the result. He had been down there in the crowd ever since and the fires at the Astor House and the City Hotel had both been put out. But he had listened to the talk of the people and heard the opinion expressed generally that rebels were in the city to destroy it. He thought our presence must be known. Harrington had broken a bottle in the Metropolitan Theater at 8 o'clock, just after he fired the Metropolitan Hotel adjoining; and Ashbrook had done likewise in Niblo's Garden Theater adjoining the La Farge Hotel.

We went into the crowd on Broadway and stopped at those places to see what had happened. There was the wildest excitement imaginable. There was all sorts of talk about hanging the rebels to lamp posts or burning them at the stake. Still we discovered that all was surmise apparently. So far as we could learn the programme had been carried out, but it appeared that all had made a failure. It seemed to us that there was something wrong with our Greek fire.

All had observed that the fires had been put out in all the places as easily as any ordinary fire. We came to the conclusion that Longmire and his manufacturing chemist had put up a job on us after it was found that we could not be dissuaded from our purpose.

Martin and I got together as agreed and found lodging about 2 o'clock. We did not awake until 10 o'clock next day. We went into a restaurant on Broadway near Twelfth street for breakfast. It was crowded, but every one was reading a newspaper. After giving our order we got the *Herald*, *World*, *Tribune*, and *Times*, and to our surprise the entire front pages were given up to sensational accounts of the attempt to burn the city. It was plainly pointed out that rebels were at the head of the incendiary work, and quite a list *of* names was given of parties who had been arrested. All our fictitious names registered at the different hotels were given and interviews with the clerks described us all. The clerk of the United States Hotel especially gave a minute description of my personal appearance, clothing, manners and actions. He said I did not eat a meal at the hotel, though I had been there two days as a guest, and had nothing in my black satchel.

It was stated in the papers that the authorities had a full knowledge of the plot and the ring-leaders would be captured during the day. One paper said the baggage of two of them had been secured, and all avenues of escape being guarded the villains were sure to be caught, the detectives having a full knowledge of the rebels and their haunts.

—HEADLEY, *Confederate Operations in Canada and New York*

XXI.10

WAR WEARINESS

Throughout the Civil War, Southern sympathizers and Peace Democrats resisted the war effort. Northern support for the war often ebbed and flowed with the success of the Union army. Early 1863 was a low point in Northern support for the conflict. The devastating loss at the Battle of Fredericksburg was followed by the pointless "Mud March" in which the army of Potomac attempted a failed flanking movement in driving ice storms and rainstorms. Northern soldiers were deserting at a rate of 200 men a day.

Back home, the peace movement flourished. Appalling casualties and military losses fueled discontent. Politics plagued the federal government. The Emancipation Proclamation had infuriated a large proportion of the Union. In states such as Indiana and Illinois, recently elected Democratic legislatures called for an armistice and a repeal of the Emancipation Proclamation. Some newspapers called for soldiers to desert.

"The president tells me that he now fears 'the fire in the rear'—meaning the [Democrats], especially at the Northwest—more than our military chances," Seward wrote. Lincoln's suspension of habeas corpus angered Democrats. Groups began to meet to organize opposition to the war. They were called copperheads, in reference to the poisonous snake. Lincoln had the army arrest the leading Copperhead, Congressman Clement Vallandigham of Ohio, for his statements urging soldiers to desert and suggesting that western states join the Confederacy.

Even some of the most stalwart supporters of the war grew tired of the conflict. Nathaniel Hawthorne, America's leading literary figure, questioned whether union was worth the bloody costs of waging a seemingly endless war. Living in Concord, Massachusetts, one of the most politically charged and pro-war communities in the country, he wrote in a letter to Henry A. Bright, a friend in England, about his aggravations over the conflict. Within a few months, Hawthorne had infuriated his fellow New England literati by dedicating a book to former-President Franklin Pierce, a Peace Democrat and former classmate of Hawthorne's.

The New Jersey Peace Resolutions and the response from soldiers in the field reflect the schism between those who were starting to question the purpose of the war back home and those who remained dedicated to its cause and their fallen comrades on the front lines. Twenty months later New Jersey was one of only three states to vote against Lincoln's reelection as president.

A. A Sense of Infinite Weariness

Concord, March 8, 1863

I ought to be heartily ashamed of my long silence, but in these revolutionary times, it is impossible to be ashamed of anything. When society is about to be overturned from its foundations, the courtesies of life must needs be a little damaged in advance of the general ruin; nor is it easy to write gossiping epistles when an earthquake is shaking one's writing table. So pardon me; and I will be as merciful to you when England is in a similar predicament.

You must not suppose, however, that I make myself very miserable about the war. The play (be it tragedy or comedy) is too long drawn out, and my chief feeling about it now is a sense of infinite weariness. I want the end to come, and the curtain to drop, and then go to sleep. I never did really approve of the war, though you may have supposed so from the violence and animosity with which I controverted your notions about it, when I wrote last. But you are an Englishman, you know, and of course cannot have any correct ideas about our country, and even if you had, a true American is bound not to admit them. The war-party here do not look upon me as a reliably loyal man, and, in fact, I have been publicly accused of treasonable sympathies;—.whereas. I sympathize with nobody and approve of nothing: and if I have any wishes on the subject, it is that New England might be a nation by itself. But, so far as I can judge of the temper of the people, they mean to have re-union; and if they really mean it, it will be accomplished. The North has never yet put out half its means, and there is a great deal of fight left in us yet. . . .

I went to the Club, last Saturday, and met all the usual set, besides some generals and colonels, from the battle-field, war-worn and wounded. The tone of feeling was very patriotic, the mildest men and most abstract philosophers being, as it seemed to me, the most truculent. Emerson is as merciless as a steel bayonet; and I would not give much for a rebel's life if he came within a sword's length of your friend Charles Norton. For Heaven's sake don't tell him what I say, or he will turn his weapon against me.—But, seriously, this Club may fairly be considered as representing the most enlightened public opinion of New England, at least, if not of the whole North; and it is unreservedly and enthusiastically in favor of continuing the war, and steadfastly confident of the result. We had a consultation about establishing a weekly Journal, of a military character, chiefly for the purpose of operating on the minds of the soldiers and sailors; but I doubt whether these poets and philosophers know how to bring their abilities to bear on that class of men. At any rate, I expressed my distrust, and declined having anything to do with it. . . .

—NATHANIEL HAWTHORNE

B. New-Jersey Peace Resolutions

3. Be it Resolved by the Senate and General Assembly of the State of New-Jersey, That this State, in promptly answering the calls made by the president of the United States, at and since the inauguration of the war, for troops and means to assist in maintaining the power and dignity of the Federal government, believed and confided in the professions and declarations of the President of the United States, in his inaugural address, and in the resolutions passed by Congress on the twenty-fifth day of July, 1861, in which, among other things, it was declared "that the war is not waged for conquest or subjugation, or interfering with the rights or established institutions of the States, but to maintain and defend the supremacy of the Constitution, with the rights and eqaulity under it unimpaired, and that as soon as these objects shall be accomplished the war ought to cease;" . . .

4. And be it Resolved, That this State having waited for the redemption of the sacred pledges of the President and Congress with a patience and forbearance only equalled in degree by the unfaltering and unanswering bravery and fidelity of her sons, conceives it to be her solemn duty, as it is her unques-

tioned right, to urge upon the President and Congress, in the most respectful but decided manner, the redemption of the pledges under which the troops of this State entered upon, and to this moment have continued in, the contest;. . .

5. And be it Resolved, That it is the deliberate sense of the people of this State that the war power within the limits of the Constitution is ample for any and all emergencies, and that all assumption of power, under whatever plea, beyond that conferred by the Constitution, is without warrant or authority, and if permitted to continue without remonstrance, will finally encompass the destruction of the liberties of the people and the death of the Republic; and therefore, to the end that in any event the matured and deliberate sense of the people of New-Jersey may be known and declared, we, their representatives in Senate and General Assembly convened, do, in their name and in their behalf, make unto the Federal government this our solemn

Protest

Against a war waged with the insurgent States for their accomplishment of unconstitutional or partisan purposes;

Against a war which has for its object the subjugation of any of the States, with a view to their reduction to territorial condition;. . .

Against the domination of the military over the civil laws in States, Territories, or districts not in a state of insurrection;

Against all arrests without warrant; against the suspension of the writ of habeus corpus in States and Territories sustaining the Federal government, "where the public safety does not require it," and against the assumption of power by any person to suspend such writ, except under the express authority of Congress;

Against the creation of new States by the division of existing ones, or in any other manner not clearly authorized by the Constitution, and against the right of secession as practically admitted by the action of Congress in admitting as a new State a portion of the State of Virginia;

Against the power assumed in the proclamation of the President made January first, 1863, by which all the slaves in certain States and parts of States are for ever set free; and against the expenditures of public moneys for the emancipation of slaves or their support at any time, under any pretence whatever;

Against any and every exercise of power upon the part of the Federal Government that is not clearly given and expressed in the Federal Constitution—reasserting that "the powers not delegated to the United States by the Constitution, nor prohibited by it to the States, are reserved to the States respectively, or to the people.". . .

6. And be it Resolved, That . . . while abating naught in her devotion to the Union of the States and the dignity and power of the Federal Government, at no time since the commencement of the present war has this State been other than willing to terminate peacefully and honorably to all war unnecessary in its origin, fraught with horror and suffering in its prosecution, and necessarily dangerous to the liberties of all in its continuance. . . .

—NEW-JERSEY STATE LEGISLATURE

C. Protest of the New-Jersey Soldiers

Below Falmouth, Va., March 10, 1863

Whereas, The Legislature of our native States, . . . has sought to tarnish its high honor, and bring upon it disgrace, by the passage of resolutions tending to a dishonorable peace with armed rebels seeking to destroy our great and beneficent Government, the best ever designed for the happiness of the many; and

Whereas, We, her sons, members of the Eleventh regiment New-Jersey volunteers, citizens representing every section of the State, have left our homes to endure the fatigues, privations, and dangers incident to a soldiers' life, in order to maintain our Republic in its integrity, willing to sacrifice our lives to that object; fully recognizing the impropriety of a soldier's discussion of the legislative functions of the State, yet deeming it due to ourselves, that the voice of those who offer their all in their country's cause, be heard when weak and wicked men seek its dishonor; therefore,

Resolved, That the Union of the States is the only guarantee for the preservation of our liberty and independence, and that the war for the maintenance of that Union commands now, as it ever has done, our best efforts and our heartfelt sympathy.

Resolved, That we consider the passage, or even the introduction of the so-called Peace Resolutions, as wicked, weak, and cowardly, tending to aid by their sympathy, the rebels seeking to destroy the Republic.

Resolved, That we regard as traitors alike the foe in arms and the secret enemies of our Government, who, at home, foment disaffection and strive to destroy confidence in our legally chosen rulers.

Resolved, That the reports spread broadcast throughout the North, by secession sympathizers, prints, and voices, that the army of which we esteem it a high honor to form a part, is demoralized and clamorous for peace on any terms, are the lying utterances of traitorous tongues, and do base injustice to our noble comrades who have never faltered in the great work, and are now not only willing but anxious to follow their gallant and chivalric leader against the strongholds of the enemy.

Resolved, That we put forth every effort, endure every fatigue, and shrink from no danger, until, under the gracious guidance of a kind Providence, every armed rebel shall be conquered, and traitors at home shall quake with fear, as the proud emblem of our national independence shall assert its power from North to South, and crush beneath its powerful folds all who dared to assail its honor, doubly hallowed by the memory of the patriot dead. . . .

—CAMP OF THE ELEVENTH NEW-JERSEY VOLUNTEERS

XXI.11

Election of 1864

The election of 1864 tested the strength of American democracy and the commitment of the North to continue to wage war. No nation had ever held a free election in the midst of a civil war. The bloody failure of Grant's Virginia campaign to break the South in the spring of 1864, and Sherman's stalled armies outside of Atlanta, Georgia, sapped Northern resolve. The last president to win a second election was Andrew Jackson almost thirty years earlier. The Republican Party was divided over whether to support Lincoln.

Democrats nominated General George B. McClellan whose contempt of Lincoln—whom he referred to as "the original gorilla"—had only increased since his departure from the Army in 1862. Northern soldiers had worshipped McClellan when he commanded the Army. The campaign was one of the nastiest in American history. Republicans accused McClellan and his supporters of treason. Democrats charged Lincoln and the Republicans as being "Negro lovers" bent on blending the black and white races.

In August, Lincoln was convinced he would lose the election "and badly." But Sherman's capture of Atlanta in September, followed by his March to the Sea, and Sheridan's decisive victory at Cedar Creek in the Shenandoah Valley reversed public opinion. Lincoln carried 54 percent of the vote, winning all the states but New Jersey, Delaware, and Kentucky. Lincoln's election eliminated Southern hopes of ending the war through an armistice with the North. The President declared the last Thursday of November as a National Day of Thanksgiving.

The great-grandson and grandson of Presidents John Adams and John Quincy Adams, Henry Brook Adams saw the events of the Civil War in the larger context of history, perhaps none so cogently as the importance of Lincoln's re-election. Rather than seeing democracy as a hindrance to strong government—as most Europeans believed—Adams reasoned in a letter to his brother Charles Francis Adams, Jr., in England that it was the greatest strength of American government.

November 25, 1864

The election is over then, and after all that excitement, worry and danger, behold all goes on as before! It was one of those cases in which life and death seemed to hang on the issue, and the result is so decisive as to answer all our wishes and hopes. It is a curious commentary upon theatrical reasoning as to forms of Government, that this election which ought by all rights to be a defect in the system, and which is universally considered by the admirers of "strong Governments" to be proof of the advantage of their own model, should yet turn out in practice a great and positive gain and a fruitful source of national strength. After all, systems of Government are secondary matters, if you've only get your people behind them. I never yet have felt so proud as now of the great qualities of our race, or so confident of the capacity of men to develop their faculties in the mass. I believe that a new era of the movement of the world will date from that day, which will drag nations up still another step, and carry us out of a quantity of old fogs. Europe has a long way to go yet to catch us up.

—Henry Brook Adams

BEHIND THE LINES:
THE SOUTH

Why did the Confederacy lose the war? Historians are still discussing this engrossing question, and they are still unable to agree on the answer. There is pretty general agreement, though, that the South did not lose the war on the battlefield. To be sure the Confederates were beaten at Vicksburg and Gettysburg, Chattanooga and Atlanta, decimated in the Wilderness, and shattered by Sherman's march from Atlanta to the sea and beyond. But these military defeats—so runs the argument—were consequences, not causes.

The most varied causes are assigned to explain these defeats: the blockade and shortages of essential materials; failure to win the foreign recognition so confidently anticipated; the breakdown of finance and of transportation; the incompetence of the President and of Congress; the disintegrating impact of State rights. Yet had the Confederacy used such resources of man power as it had, it might not have suffered defeat. There was food enough in the Confederacy; finances could have been controlled; the transportation system was not beyond repair; the blockade was not effective until 1863; foreign intervention would have followed upon military success and a statesmanlike policy toward such things as cotton and slavery; State rights denied to the Confederacy resources that promised victory; a wiser government would have made Lee commander in chief and permitted him to control the grand strategy of the war, and so forth. So the argument runs, and most students fall back, in the end, on the vague phrase "breakdown of morale"—a phrase which merely begs the question.

But what an this adds up to is that the Confederate cause was lost in the Confederacy itself—that is, behind the lines. The internal history of the Confederacy thus becomes a matter of paramount interest. This chapter is not designed, primarily, to illuminate the breakdown of the Confederacy, but there can be little doubt that it does so. Successive excerpts describe the inadequacy of food and of other necessities, runaway inflation, the incompetence of the medical services, the short sighted cotton policy, the effectiveness of the blockade, the impact of invasion and of defeat on morale, dissatisfaction with the conduct of the war, the role of State rights, and the growth of defeatism.

XXII. I

A WAR CLERK SUFFERS
SCARCITIES IN RICHMOND

Concentration on staple crops at the expense of grains and dairy products made the agricultural South far from self sufficient, while industrially the South was almost wholly de pendent on the North or on Britain. These basic economic factors, plus state competition for such foodstuffs and industrial products as could be found, contributed largely to the growing shortages that harassed the Confederacy.

After the war was fairly under way the Confederate government tried to meet nearly all its expenses by issues of paper money. This money steadily depreciated in value, so that every new issue was followed by a rise in prices which had to be met, in turn, by another new issue. By the end of 1864 the paper currency in circulation had reached about one billion dollars.

Other factors, too, contributed to inflation: the blockade by shutting off imports from abroad; the breakdown of the transportation system by making it hard to move merchandise; the decline in farm and factory production. All this meant that prices soared, that wages—especially the sorry wages of the soldiers—became almost worthless, and that the poor everywhere and the city-folk suffered sharp hardships.

John Beauchamp Jones, whose *Rebel War Clerk's Diary* we have used before, was an editor and novelist who obtained a clerkship in the War Department for the express purpose of being at the center of things and writing about them. His book, verbose and prejudiced, is an authentic record of day by-day life in the capital.

May 23, 1862.—Oh, the extortioners! Meats of all kinds are selling at fifty cents per pound; butter, seventy-five cents; coffee, a dollar and half; tea, ten dollars; boots, thirty dollars per pair; shoes, eighteen dollars; ladies' shoes, fifteen dollars; shirts, six dollars each. Houses that rented for five hundred dollars last year are a thousand-dollars now. Boarding, from thirty to forty dollars per month. General Winder has issued an order fixing the maximum prices of certain articles of marketing, which has only the effect of keeping a great many things out of market. The farmers have to pay the merchants and Jews their extortionate prices and complain very justly of the partiality of the general. It does more harm than good.

October 1st.—How shall we subsist this winter? There is not a supply of wood or coal in the city—and it is said that there are not adequate means of transporting it hither. Flour at sixteen dollars per barrel and bacon at seventy-five cents per pound threaten a famine. And yet there are no beggars in the streets. We must get a million of men in arms and drive the invader from our soil. We are capable of it, and we must do it. Better die in battle than die of starvation produced by the enemy.

The newspapers are printed on half sheets—and I think the publishers make money; the extras (published almost every day) are sold to the newsboys for ten cents and often sold by them for twenty-five cents. These are mere slips of paper, seldom containing more than a column—which is reproduced in the next issue. The matter of the extras is mostly made up from the Northern papers, brought hither by persons running the blockade. The supply is pretty regular, and dates are rarely more than three or four days behind the time of reception. We often get the first accounts of battles at a distance in this way, as our generals and our government are famed for a prudential reticence.

6th.—. . . This evening Custis and I expect the arrival of my family from Raleigh, N.C. We have procured for them one pound of sugar, eighty cents; four loaves of bread, as large as my fist, twenty cents each; and we have a little coffee, which is selling at two dollars and a half per pound. In the morning some one must go to market, else there will be short commons. Washing is two dollars and a half per dozen pieces. Common soap is worth seventy-five cents per pound.

November 7th.—Yesterday I received from the agent of the City Councils fourteen pounds of salt, having seven persons in my family, including the servant. One pound to each member, per month, is allowed at five cents per pound. The extortionists sell it at seventy cents per pound. One of *them* was drawing for his family. He confessed it but said he paid fifty cents for the salt he sold at seventy cents. Profit ten dollars per bushel! I sent an article today to the *Enquirer*, suggesting that fuel, bread, meat, etc. be furnished in the same manner. We shall soon be in a state of siege.

21st.—Common shirting cotton and Yankee calico that used to sell at twelve and a half cents per yard is now a dollar seventy-five! What a temptation for the Northern manufacturers! What a rush of trade there would be if peace should occur suddenly! And what a party there would be in the South for peace (and unity with Northern Democrats) if the war were waged somewhat differently. The excesses of the Republicans *compel* our people to be almost a unit. This is all the better for us. Still, we are in quite a bad way now, God knows!

Mr. Dargan, M.C., writes to the President from Mobile that the inhabitants of that city are in an awful condition—meal is selling for three dollars and a half per bushel and wood at fifteen dollars per cord—and that the people are afraid to bring supplies, apprehending that the government agents will seize them. The President (thanks to him!) has ordered that interference with domestic trade must not be permitted.

December 1st.—God speed the day of peace! Our patriotism is mainly in the army and among the ladies of the South. The avarice and cupidity of the men at home, could only be excelled by the ravenous wolves; and most of our sufferings are fully deserved. Where a people will not have mercy on one another, how can they expect mercy? They depreciate the Confederate notes by charging from $20 to $40 per bbl. for flour; $3.50 per bushel of meal; $2 per lb. for butter; $20 per cord for wood, etc. When we shall have peace let the extortionists be remembered! let an indelible stigma be branded upon them.

A portion of the people look like vagabonds. We see men and women and children in the streets in dingy and dilapidated clothes; and some seem gaunt and pale with hunger—the speculators, and thieving quartermasters and commissaries only, looking sleek and comfortable. If this state of things continue a year or so longer, they will have their reward. There will be governmental bankruptcy, and all their gains will turn to dust and ashes, dust and ashes!

January 18, 1863.—We are now, in effect, in a state of siege, arid none but the opulent, often those who have defrauded the government, can obtain a sufficiency of food and raiment. Calico, which could once be bought for twelve and a half cents per yard, is now selling at two dollars and a quarter, and a lady's dress of calico costs her about thirty dollars. Bonnets are not to be had. Common bleached cotton shirting brings a dollar and a half per yard. All other dry goods are held in the same proportion. Common tallow candles are a dollar and a quarter per pound; soap, one dollar; hams, one dollar; opossum, three dollars; turkeys, four to eleven dollars; sugar, brown, one dollar; molasses, eight dollars per gallon; potatoes, six dollars per bushel, etc.

These evils might be remedied by the government, for there is no great scarcity of any of the substantials and necessities of life in the country, if they were only equally distributed. The difficulty is in procuring transportation, and the government monopolizes the railroads and canals.

January 30th.—I cut the following from yesterday's *Dispatch:*

"The Results of Extortion and Speculation.—The state of affairs brought about by the speculating and extortion practiced upon the public cannot be better illustrated than by the following grocery bill for one week for a small family, in which the prices before the war and those of the present are compared:

1860		
Bacon, 10 lbs. at 12 1/2¢		$1.25
Flour, 30 lbs. at 5¢		1.50
Sugar, 5 lbs. at 8¢		.40
Coffee, 4 lbs. at 12 1/2¢		.50
Tea (green), 1/2 lb. at $1		.50
Lard, 4 lbs. at 12 1/2¢		.50
Butter, 3 lbs. at 25¢		.75
Meal, 1 pk. at 25¢		.25
Candles, 2 lbs. at 15¢		.30
Soap, 5 lbs. at 10¢		.50
Pepper and salt (about)		.10
Total		S6.55

1863		
Bacon, 10 lbs. at $1		$10.00
Flour, 30 lbs. at 12 1/2¢		3.75
Sugar, 5 lbs. at $1.15		5.75
Coffee, 4 lbs. at $5		20.00
Tea (green), 1/2 lb. at $16		8.00
Lard, 4 lbs. at $1		4.00
Butter, 3 lbs. at $1.75		5.25
Meal, 1 pk. at $1		1.00
Candles, 2 lbs. at $1.25		2.50
Soap, 5 lbs. at $1.10		5.50
Pepper and salt (about)		2.50
Total		$68.25

"So much we owe the speculators, who have stayed at home to prey upon the necessities of their fellow-citizens."

February 11th.—Some idea may be formed of the scarcity of food in this city from the fact that, while my youngest daughter was in the kitchen today, a young rat came out of its hole and seemed to beg for something to eat; she held out some bread, which it ate from her hand, and seemed grateful. Several others soon appeared and were as tame as kittens. Perhaps we shall have to eat them!

18th.—One or two of the regiments of General Lee's army were in the city last night. The men were pale and haggard. They have but a quarter of a pound of meat per day. But meat has been ordered from Atlanta. I hope it is abundant there.

All the necessaries of life in the city are still going up higher in price. Butter, three dollars per pound; beef, one dollar; bacon, a dollar and a quarter; sausage meat, one dollar; and even liver is selling at fifty cents per pound.

By degrees, quite perceptibly, we are approaching the condition of famine. What effect this will produce on the community is to be seen. The army must be fed or disbanded, or else the city must be abandoned. How we, "the people," are to live is a thought of serious concern.

March 30th.—The gaunt form of wretched famine still approaches with rapid strides. Meal is now selling at twelve dollars per bushel and potatoes at sixteen. Meats have almost disappeared from the market, and none but the opulent can afford to pay three dollars and a half per pound for butter. Greens, however, of various kinds, are coming in; and as the season advances, we may expect a diminution of prices. It is strange that on the 30th of March, even in the "sunny South," the fruit trees are as bare of blossoms and foliage as at midwinter. We shall have fire until the middle of May—six months of winter!

I am spading up my garden and hope to raise a few vegetables to eke out a miserable subsistence for my family. My daughter Ann reads Shakespeare to me o' nights, which saves my eyes.

April 17th.—Pins are so scarce and costly that it is now a pretty general practice to stoop down and pick up any found in the street. The boarding-houses are breaking up, and rooms, furnished and unfurnished, are renting out to messes. One dollar and fifty cents for beef leaves no margin for profit even at a hundred dollars per month, which is charged for board, and most of the boarders cannot afford to pay that price. Therefore they take rooms and buy their own scanty food. I am inclined to think provisions would not be deficient to an alarming extent if they were equally distributed. Wood is no scarcer than before the war, and yet thirty dollars per load (less than a cord) is demanded for it and obtained.

August 22nd.—Night before last all the clerks in the city post-office resigned, because the government did not give them salaries sufficient to subsist them. As yet their places have not been filled, and the government gets no letters—some of which lying in the office may be of such importance as to involve the safety or ruin of the government. Tomorrow is Sunday, and of course the mails will not be at tended to before Monday—the letters lying here four days unopened! This really looks as if we had no Postmaster General.

October 22nd.—A poor woman yesterday applied to a merchant in Carey Street to purchase a barrel of flour. The price he demanded was $70.

"My God!" exclaimed she, "how can I pay such prices? I have seven children; what shall I do?"

"I don't know, madam," said he, coolly, "unless you eat your children."

Such is the power of cupidity—it transforms men into demons. And if this spirit prevails throughout the country, a just God will bring calamities upon the land, which will reach these cormorants, but which, it may be feared, will involve all classes in a common ruin.

January 26, 1864.—The prisoners on Belle Isle (8000) have had no meat for eleven days. The Secretary says the Commissary-General informs him that they fare as well as our armies, and so he refused the commissary (Capt. Warner) of the prisoners a permit to buy and bring to the city cattle he might be able to find. An outbreak of the prisoners is apprehended: and if they were to rise, it is feared some of the in habitants of the city would join them, for they, too, have no meat—many of them—or bread either. They believe the famine is owing to the imbecility, or worse of the government. A riot would be a dangerous occurrence now:

the city battalion would not fire on the people—and if they did the army might break up, and avenge their slaughtered kindred. It is a perilous time.

March 18th.—My daughter's cat is staggering to-day, for want of animal food. Sometimes I fancy I stagger myself. We do not average two ounces of meat daily; and some do not get any for several days together. Meal is $50 per bushel. I saw adamantine candles sell at auction to-day (box) at $10 per pound; tallow, $6.50. Bacon brought $7.75 per pound by the 100 pounds.

April 8th.—Bright and warm—really a fine spring day. It is the day of *fasting,* humiliation, and prayer, and all the offices are closed. May God put it into the hearts of the extortioners to relent, and abolish, for a season, the insatiable greed for gain! I paid $25 for a half cord of wood today, new currency. I fear a nation of extortioners are unworthy of independence, and that we must be chastened and purified before success will be vouchsafed us.

What enormous appetites we have now, and how little illness, since food has become so high in price! I cannot afford to have more than an ounce of meat daily for each member of my family of six; and to-day Custis's parrot, which has accompanied the family in all their flights, and, it seems, will *never* die, stole the cook's ounce of fat meat and gobbled it up before it could be taken from him. He is permitted to set at one corner of the table, and has lately acquired a fondness for meat. The old cat goes staggering about from debility, although Fannie often gives him her share. We see neither rats nor mice about the premises now. This is famine. Even the pigeons watch the crusts in the hands of the children, and follow them in the yard. *And, still, there are no beggars.*

August 13th.—Flour is falling: It is now $200 per barrel—$500 a few weeks ago; and bacon is falling in price also, from $11 to $6 per pound. A commission merchant said to me, yesterday, that there was at least eighteen months' supply (for the people) of breadstuffs and meats in the city; and pointing to the upper windows at the corner of

Thirteenth and Cary Streets, he revealed the ends of many barrels piled above the windows. He said that flour had been there two years, held for "still higher prices." Such is the avarice of man. Such is war. And such the greed of extortioners, even in the midst of famine—and famine in the midst of plenty!

—Jones, *A Rebel War Clerk's Diary*

XXII.2

Mr. Eggleston Recalls When Money Was Plentiful

Eggleston's account of the impact of inflation on the life of the South—and especially of Richmond—parallels and supplements that of the Rebel war clerk, but is more genial and optimistic. Certainly his conclusion that municipal regulations wiped out gambling in the Confederate capital is not borne out by other evidence. George Cary Eggleston was, himself, a romantic character. Born in Indiana—brother of that Edward Eggleston who wrote the famous *Hoosier Schoolmaster*—he early inherited a plantation in Amelia County, Virginia, and wholly identified himself with the life of the South. At the outbreak of the war he joined the 1st Virginia Cavalry, fought under Stuart, Fitzhugh Lee, and Longstreet and, for a time, in the South Carolina field artillery.

After the war Eggleston had a long career as journalist and man of letters. He was literary editor of the *New York Evening Post,* served on the staff of the *New York World,* wrote scores of novels and boy's stories, compiled his recollections, and contributed a two-volume *History of the Confederate War* that is still valuable.

The financial system adopted by the Confederate government was singularly simple and free from technicalities. It consisted chiefly in the issue of treasury notes enough to meet all the expenses of the government, and in the present advanced state of the art of printing there was but one difficulty incident to this process; namely, the impossibility of having the notes signed in the Treasury Department as fast as they were needed. There happened, however, to be several thousand young ladies in Richmond willing to accept light and remunerative employment at their homes, and as it was really a matter of small moment whose names the notes bore, they were given out in sheets to these young ladies, who signed and returned them for a consideration. I shall not undertake to guess how many Confederate treasury notes were issued. Indeed, I am credibly informed by a gentleman who was high in office in the Treasury Department that even the secretary himself did not certainly know. The acts of Congress authorizing issues of currency were the hastily formulated thought of a not very wise body of men, and my informant tells me they were frequently susceptible of widely different construction by different officials. However that may be, it was clearly out of the power of the government ever to redeem the notes, and whatever may have been the state of affairs within the treasury, nobody outside its precincts ever cared to muddle his head in an attempt to get at exact figures.

We knew only that money was astonishingly abundant. Provisions fell short sometimes, and the supply of clothing was not always as large as we should have liked, but nobody found it difficult to get money enough. It was to be had almost for the asking. And to some extent the abundance of the currency really seemed to atone for its extreme badness. Going the rounds of the pickets on the coast of South Carolina one day in 1863, I heard a conversation between a Confederate and a Union soldier, stationed on opposite sides of a little inlet, in the course of which this point was brought out.

Union Soldier. Aren't times rather hard over there, Johnny?

Confederate Soldier. Not at all. We've all the necessaries of life.

U.S. Yes, but how about luxuries? You never see any coffee nowadays, do you?

C.S. Plenty of it.

U.S. Isn't it pretty high?

C.S. Forty dollars a pound, that's all.

U.S. Whew! Don't you call that high?

C.S. (after reflecting). Well, perhaps it is a trifle uppish, but then you never saw money so plentiful as it is with us. We hardly know what to do with it and don't mind paying high prices for things we want.

And that was the universal feeling. Money was so easily got and its value was so utterly uncertain that we were never able to determine what was a fair price for anything. We fell into the habit of paying whatever was asked, knowing that tomorrow we should have to pay more. Speculation became the easiest and surest thing imaginable. The speculator saw no risks of loss. Every article of merchandise rose in value every day, and to buy anything this week and sell it next was to make an enormous profit quite as a matter of course. So uncertain were prices, or rather so constantly did they tend upward, that when a cargo of cadet-gray cloths was brought into Charleston once, an officer in my battery, attending the sale, was able to secure enough of the cloth to make two suits of clothes without any expense whatever, merely by speculating upon an immediate advance. He became the purchaser at auction of a case of the goods and had no difficulty, as soon as the sale was over, in finding a merchant who was glad to take his bargain off his hands, giving him the cloth he wanted as a premium. The officer could not possibly have paid for the case of goods, but there was nothing surer than that he could sell again at an advance the moment the auctioneer's hammer fell on the last lot of cloths. . . .

The prices which obtained were almost fabulous, and singularly enough there seemed to be no sort of ratio existing between the values of different articles. I bought coffee at forty dollars and tea at thirty dollars a pound on the same day.

My dinner at a hotel cost me twenty dollars, while five dollars gained me a seat in the dress circle of the theater. I paid one dollar the next morning for a copy of the *Examiner*, but I might have got the *Whig, Dispatch, Enquirer,* or *Sentinel* for half that sum. For some wretched tallow candles I paid ten dollars a pound. The utter absence of proportion between these several prices is apparent, and I know no way of explaining it except upon the theory that the unstable character of the money superinduced a reckless disregard of all value on the part of both buyers and sellers. A facetious friend used to say prices were so high that nobody could see them and that they "got mixed for want of supervision." He held, how ever, that the difference between the old and the new order of things was a trifling one. "Before the war," he said, "I went to market with the money in my pocket and brought back my purchases in a basket; now I take the money in the basket and bring the things home in my pockets.". . .

The effects of the extreme depreciation of the currency were sometimes almost ludicrous. One of my friends, a Richmond lady, narrowly escaped very serious trouble in an effort to practise a wise economy. Anything for which the dealers did not ask an outrageously high price seemed wonderfully cheap always, and she, at least, lacked the self-control necessary to abstain from buying largely whenever she found any thing the price of which was lower than she had supposed it would be. Going into market one morning with "stimulated ideas of prices," as she phrased it, the consequence of having paid a thousand dollars for a barrel of flour, she was surprised to find nearly everything selling for considerably less than she had expected. Thinking that for some unexplained cause there was a temporary depression in prices, she purchased pretty largely in a good many directions, buying, indeed, several things for which she had almost no use at all and buying considerably more than she needed of other articles. As she was quitting the market on foot—for it had become disreputable in Richmond to ride in a carriage, and the ladies would not do it on any account—she was tapped on the shoulder by an officer who told her she was under arrest, for buying in market to sell again. As the lady was well known to prominent people she was speedily released, but she there after curbed her propensity to buy freely of cheap things. Buying to sell again had been forbidden under severe penalities—an absolutely necessary measure for the protection of the people against the rapacity of the hucksters, who, going early into the markets, would buy literally everything there and by agreement among themselves double or quadruple the already exorbitant rates.

It became necessary also to suppress the gambling houses in the interest of the half-starved people. At such a time, of course, gambling was a very common vice, and the gamblers made Richmond their headquarters. It was the custom of the proprietors of these establishments to set costly suppers in their parlors every night for the purpose of attracting visitors likely to become victims. For these suppers they must have the best of everything without stint, and their lavish rivalry in the poorly-stocked markets had the effect of advancing prices to a dangerous point. To suppress the gambling houses was the sole remedy, and it was only by uncommonly severe measures that the suppression could be accomplished. It was therefore enacted that any one found guilty of keeping a gambling house should be publicly whipped upon the bare back, and as the infliction of the penalty in one or two in stances effectually and permanently broke up the business of gambling, even in the disorganized and demoralized state in which society then was, it may be said with confidence that whipping is the one certain remedy for this evil. Whether it be not, in ordinary cases, worse than the evil which it cures, it is not our business just now to inquire.

—EGGLESTON, *A Rebel's Recollections*

XXII. 3

JEWS IN THE CONFEDERACY

As the war news worsened and the economy deteriorated, some Southerners took to scapegoating and finger-pointing. The South's Jewish minority was often subject to such criticisms. Jewish merchants were accused of being unprincipled speculators, and Jews were labeled as malingerers holding back the struggling nation. The distinguished rabbi Maximilian Michelbacher, of Richmond, Virginia, delivered the sermon below defending his people's conduct in the war.

Some of the most talented men in the Confederacy were Jews. Judah P. Benjamin served in President Davis's cabinet. He started in February, 1861 as the nation's first attorney general and ended his time in the administration in May 1865 after a distinguished tenure as secretary of state. Benjamin also served briefly as secretary of war. Davis called Benjamin "the most capable statesman I have ever known."

Many other Jews also served faithfully in the government and on the battlefield. The last order of the Confederate government was given to Major Raphael J. Moses, Commissary officer of the state of Georgia, to deliver $10,000 in bullion. Moses, a well-regarded Jewish businessman and Georgia state representative prior to secession, served in the Confederate army throughout the war and contributed much of his fortune to the cause. All three of his sons served in the military. One of them was killed at the Battle of Fair Oaks. To a critic, Moses once responded: "You do me honor. You call me a Jew."

Brethren of the House of Israel: It is due to you, to whom I always speak of your faults, without fear, favour or affection, to say: I have carefully investigated your conduct from the commencement of this war to the present time, and I am happy in coming to the unbiased conclusion, that you have fulfilled your duties as good citizens and as men, who love their country. It has been charged by both the ignorant and the evil-disposed against the people of our faith, that the Israelite does not fight in the battles of his country! All history attests the untruthfulness of this ungracious charge, generated in the cowardly hearts and born between the hypocritical lips of ungenerous and prejudiced foes. The Israelite has never failed to defend the soil of his birth, or the land of his adoption—the Emperors of France and Russia will bear evidence to the verity of this assertion. In respect to those Israelites, who are now in the army of the Confederate States, I will merely say, that their patriotism and valor have never been doubted by such men as have the magnanimous souls of Lee, Johnston, Jackson and others of like manhood. The recorded votes and acts of the Israelites of this Confederacy, amply prove their devotion to the support of its Government. They well understand their duties as citizens and soldiers, and the young men do not require the persuasion of conscription to convert them into soldiers, to defend, as they verily believe, the only free government in North America. Many of our young men have been crippled for life, or slain upon the field of battle, in the service of the

Confederate States, and there are several thousands yet coursing the campaigns of the war against those enemies of our Confederacy, who are as detestable to them, as were the Philistines to David and his countrymen.

The humanity and providence of the Israelite for the distressed families of the soldiers of our army, have allayed the pangs of poverty and brought comfort to households, wherein before were only seen hopelessness and misery. In this you have performed your duties as Israelites and as citizens—and, for this, may the God of our fathers shower upon you all the blessings which He confers upon His favorite children!

There is another cry heard, and it was even repeated in the Halls of Congress, that the Israelite is oppressing the people—that he is engaged in the great sin of speculating and extorting in the bread and meat of the land. To discover the character of this accusation, I have made due inquiry—the information I have acquired upon this head, from sources, that extend from the Potomac to the Rio Grande, plainly present the fact, that the Israelites are not speculators nor extortioners. As traders and as merchants, they buy merchandise and sell the same immediately; the merchandise is never put aside, or hoarded to enhance its value, by withdrawing it from the market. Flour, meal, wheat, corn, bacon, beef, coal and wood are hardly ever found in the mercantile magazines or storehouses of the Israelite—he buys some of these articles for his own consumption, but he buys none of them to sell again—he does not extort—it is obvious to the most obtuse mind that the high prices of the Israelite would drive all his customers in to the stores of his Christian neighbors; but is such the effect of the price of the Israelite's goods?

The peculiar characteristic of the Jewish merchant is seen in his undelayed, rapid and instant sales; his temperament does not allow him, by hoarding his goods, to risk time with his money, which, with him, is as restless as the waves of the sea that bears the ships that convey the manufactured goods of his customers. I thank God, that my investigation has proved to me that the cry against the Jew is a false one—this cry, though cunningly devised after the most approved model of villainy, will not subserve the base and unjust purpose of hindering the virtuous indignation of a suffering people, from facing the true path of the extortioner, and awarding to him, who deals in the miseries, life and blood of our fellow-citizens, that punishment, which the traitor to the happiness and liberties of his country deserves to have measured unto him.

—Rabbi Maximilian Michelbacher

XXII.4

Parthenia Hague Tells How Women Outwitted the Blockade

Probably not until 1863 was the blockade really effective, but even before that date the South began to feel the pinch for ordinary domestic necessities. Now the South was paying the price of neglecting to develop even local industries. Probably the best of all accounts of what life was like for a Southern family from day to day, is that by Parthenia Hague, a Georgia lady who went to live on an Alabama plantation during the war.

As no shoe-blacking or polish could be bought during the blockade, each family improvised its own blacking, which was soot and oil of some variety (either cottonseed, ground peas, or oil of compressed lard) mixed together. The shoes would be well painted with the mixture of soot and oil, with brushes made of the bristles of swine. Then a thin paste made of flour, bolted meal, or starch, was applied all over the blackened shoe with another brush, which paste, when dry, gave the shoe as bright and glossy an appearance as if "shined" by the best of bootblacks. Painters were very careful in killing their hogs to save a good supply of bristles, from which shapely brushes were manufactured.

The obtaining of salt became extremely difficult when the war had cut off our supply. This was true especially in regions remote from the sea-coast and border States, such as the interior of Alabama and Georgia. Here again we were obliged to have recourse to whatever expedient ingenuity suggested. All the brine left in troughs and barrels, where pork had been salted down, was carefully dipped up, boiled down, and converted into salt again. In some cases the salty soil under old smoke-houses was dug up and placed in hoppers, which resembled backwoods ash-hoppers, made from leaching ashes in the process of soap-manufacture. Water was then poured upon the soil, the brine which percolated through the hopper was boiled down to the proper point, poured into vessels, and set in the sun, which by evaporation completed the rude process. Though never of immaculate whiteness, the salt which resulted from these methods served well enough for all our purposes, and we accepted it without complaining.

Before the war there were in the South but few cotton mills. These were kept running night and day, as soon as the Confederate army was organized, and we were ourselves prevented by the blockade from purchasing clothing from the factories at the North, or clothing from France or England. The cotton which grew in the immediate vicinity of the mills kept them well supplied with raw material. Yet notwithstanding the great push of the cotton mills, they proved totally inadequate, after the war began, to our vast need for clothing of every kind. Every household now became a miniature factory in itself, with its cotton, cards, spinning-wheels, warping frames, looms, and so on. Wherever one went, the hum of the spinning wheel and the clang of the batten of the loom was borne on the ear.

Great trouble was experienced, in the beginning, to find dyes with which to color our stuffs; but in the course of time, both at the old mills and at smaller experimental factories, which were run entirely by hand, barks, leaves, roots, and berries were found containing coloring properties I was well acquainted with a gentleman in southwestern Georgia who owned a small cotton mill, and who, when he wanted coloring substances, used to send his wagons to the woods and freight them with a shrub known as myrtle, that grew teeming in low moist places near his mill. This myrtle yielded a nice gray for woolen goods.

That the slaves might be well clad, the owners kept, according to the number of slaves owned, a number of Negro women carding and spinning, and had looms running all the time. Now and then a planter would be so fortunate as to secure a bale or more of white sheeting and osnaburgs from the cotton mills, in exchange for farm products, which would be quite a lift, and give a little breathing-spell from the almost incessant whirr, hum, and clang of the spinning wheel and loom. . . .

I have often joined with neighbors, when school hours for the day were over, in gathering roots, barks, leaves, twigs, sumach berries, and walnuts, for the hulls, which dyed wool a beautiful dark brown. Such was the variety we had to choose from, to dye our cloth and thread. We used to pull our way through the deep tangled woods, by thickly shaded streams, through broad fields, and return laden with the riches of the Southern forest! Not infrequently clusters of grapes mingled with our freight of dyes. The pine-tree's roots furnished a beautiful dye, approximating very closely to garnet, which color I chose for the sheeting for my dress. A strong decoction of the roots of the pine-tree was used. Copperas of our own production was used as the mordant. A cask or some small vessel was set convenient to the dwelling-house and partly filled with water, in which a small quantity of salt and vinegar had been mingled; then pieces of rusty, useless iron, such as plows too much worn to be used again, rusty broken rails, old horse shoes, and bits of old chains were picked up and cast into the cask. The liquid copperas was always ready, and a very good substance we found it to fix colors in cloth or thread. The sheeting for the dress was folded smoothly and basted slightly so as to keep the folds in place. It was first thoroughly soaked in warm soapsuds, then dipped into the dye, and afterwards into a vessel containing liquid lye from wood-ashes; then it went again into the dye, then the lye, and

so on till the garnet color was the required shade. By varying the strength of the solution any shade desirable could be obtained. My garnet-colored dress of unbleached sheeting was often mistaken for worsted delaine. . . .

One of our most difficult tasks was to find a good substitute for coffee. This palatable drink, if not a real necessary of life, is almost indispensable to the enjoyment of a good meal, and some Southerners took it three times a day. Coffee soon rose to thirty dollars per pound; from that it went to sixty and seventy dollars per pound. (good workmen received thirty dollars per day; so it took two days' hard labor to buy one pound of coffee, and scarcely any could be had even at that fabulous price. Some imagined themselves much better in health for the absence of coffee, and wondered why they had ever used it at all, and declared it good for nothing any way; but "Sour grapes" would be the reply for such as they. Others saved a few handfuls of coffee, and used it on very important occasions, and then only as an extract, so to speak, for flavoring substitutes for coffee.

There were those who planted long rows of the okra plant on the borders of their cotton or corn fields, and cultivated this with the corn and cotton. The seeds of this, when mature and nicely browned, came nearer in flavor to the real coffee than any other substitute I now remember. Yam potatoes used to be peeled, sliced thin, cut into small squares, dried and then parched brown; they were thought to be next best to okra for coffee. Browned wheat, meal, and burnt corn made passable beverages; even meal-bran was browned and used for coffee if other substitutes were not obtainable.

We had several substitutes for tea which were equally as palatable, and, I fancy, more wholesome, than much that is now sold for tea. Prominent among these substitutes were raspberry leaves. Many during the blockade planted and cultivated the raspberry-vine all around their garden palings, as much for tea as the berries for jam or pies; these leaves were considered the best substitute for tea. The leaves of the blackberry bush, huckleberry leaves, and the-leaves of the holly-tree when dried in the shade, also made a palatable tea.

Persimmons dried served for dates.

Each household made its own starch, some of the bran of wheat flour. Green corn and sweet potatoes were grated in order to make starch. This process was very simple. The grated substance was placed to soak in a large tub of water; when it had passed through the process of fermentation and had risen to the surface, the grated matter was all skimmed off, the water holding the starch in solution was passed through a sieve, and then through a thin cloth to free al together from any foreign substance. A change of clear water twice a day for three or four days was made to more thoroughly bleach the starch. It would then be put on white cloth, placed on scaffolds in the yard, and left to drip and dry. Starch of wheat bran was made in the same manner. It was as white and fine as any ever bought.

A good makeshift had soon been devised for putty and cement, and the artlessness of it will perhaps cause a smile to flit across the face of glaziers. But no cement could be bought, and this was useful in many ways, as panes of glass had to be set in, or a break to be mended; the handle broken from a pitcher to be placed on anew, or repairing done to table ware. When it was necessary to repair any such breaks, a Spanish potato (none other of the species of that esculent root answered so well) was roasted in hot ashes, peeled while yet hot, immediately mashed very fine, and mixed with about a tablespoonful of flour; it was then, while warm, applied to whatever need there was. This paste, when it had became hardened, remained fixed and firm, and was as durable as putty.

In place of kerosene for lights, the oil of cotton seed and ground peas, together with the oil of compressed lard, was used, and served well the need of the times. For lights we had also to fall back on moulding candles, which had long years lain obsolete. When beeswax was plentiful it was mixed with tallow for moulding candles. Long rows of candles so moulded would be hung on the lower limbs of widespreading oaks, where, sheltered by the dense foliage from the direct rays of the sun, they would remain suspended day and night until they were bleached as white as the sperm candles we had been wont to buy, and almost as transparent as wax candles. When there was no oil for the lamps or tallow for moulding candles, which at times befell our households, mother-wit would suggest some expedient by which the intricate problem of light could be solved.

—HAGUE, A *Blockaded Family*

XXII.5

THE CONFEDERATES BURN THEIR COTTON

Two considerations persuaded the Confederacy to try to limit cotton production: the necessity of growing enough food for her needs, and the desire to create an artificial cotton scarcity for purposes of bargaining for foreign recognition The result of Confederate and state laws—the latter by all odds the most effective—and of invasion and the general derangement of war was a reduction in the cotton crop from over four million bales in 1861 to only three hundred thou sand bales in 1864. In addition to this reduction of planting, the Confederate Congress required owners to destroy all cotton that might fall into enemy hands, and it has been estimated that some two and one half million bales were destroyed by planters or by the Confederate armies. When Farragut forced the entrance to the Mississippi on April 24, 1862, the Confederates destroyed the cotton piled up in New Orleans to prevent it falling into Federal hands.

Sarah Dawson, whom we have met elsewhere, was the daughter of Judge Thomas Gibbes Morgan, whose home in Baton Rouge was sacked by the Federals in 1862. She later married Francis Warringtone Dawson, English journalist and littérateur, who ran the blockade to join the Confederacy, fought in the Army of Northern Virginia, and later edited the famous *Charleston News*. and *Courier.*

April 26, 1862.—We went this morning to see the cotton burning—a sight never before witnessed and probably never again to be seen. Wagons, drays— everything that can be driven or rolled—were loaded with the bales and taken a few squares back to burn on the commons. Negroes were running around, cutting them open, piling them up, and setting them afire. All were as busy as though their salvation depended on disappointing the Yankees. Later Charlie sent for us to come to the river and see him fire a flatboat loaded with the precious material for which the Yankees are risking their bodies and souls. Up and down the levee, as far as we could see, Negroes were rolling it down to the brink of the river where they would set the bales afire and push them in to float burning down the tide. Each sent up its wreath of smoke and looked like a tiny steamer puffing away. Only I doubt that from the source to the mouth of the river there are as many boats afloat on the Mississippi. The flatboat was piled with as many bales as it could hold without sinking. Most of them were cut open, while Negroes staved in the heads of barrels of alcohol, whisky, etc., and dashed bucketfuls over the cotton. Others built up little chimneys of pine every few feet, lined with pine knots and loose cotton, to burn more quickly. There, piled the length of the whole levee or burning in the river, lay the work of thousands of Negroes for more than a year past. It had come from every side. Men stood by who owned the cotton that was burning or waiting to burn. They either helped or looked on cheerfully. Charlie owned but sixteen bales—a matter of some fifteen hundred dollars, but he was the head man of the whole affair and burned his own as well as the property of others. A single barrel of whisky that was thrown on the cotton cost the man who gave it one hundred and twenty-five dollars. (It shows what a nation in earnest is capable of doing.) Only two men got on the flatboat with Charlie when it was ready. It was towed to the middle of the river, set afire in every place, and then they jumped into a little skiff fastened in front and rowed to land. The cotton floated down the Mississippi one sheet of living flame, even in the sunlight. It would have been grand at night. But then we will have fun watching it this evening anyway, for they cannot get through today, though no time is to be lost. Hundreds of bales remained untouched. An incredible amount of property has been destroyed today, but no one begrudges it.

Every grogshop has been emptied, and gutters and pavements are floating with liquors of all kinds. So that if the Yankees are fond of strong drink, they will fare ill.

—Dawson, A *Confederate Girl's Diary*

XXII.6

"The Yankees Are Coming"

It was the fate of the South to know invasion—and the ruth of war. Sometimes—as with Sheridan and Hunter in the Valley or Sherman in Georgia and the Carolinas—invasion meant pillaging and destruction; sometimes it was orderly enough. Occasionally, as in Mrs. Ward's account, it turned out to be merely the coming of Federal prisoners. We have met Mrs. Ward before; she was twenty-three when the events which she described took place; her description came in the form of testimony before the Congressional committee 20 years later. Of this testimony Margaret Mitchell wrote, "If I had had that book, I'm sure I would not have had to read hundreds of memoirs, letters and diaries to get the background of *Gone with the Wind* accurately."

In the fall of 1863 we were very much menaced by General Rosecrans' army up about Dalton and Resaca, and every little while we would have an alarm that a raid was coming. A raid was a very amusing thing, or rather, it is amusing to think of now. We would wake up out of our sleep and everybody would spring out of bed saying, "The Yankees are com ing; they are only 10 miles out of town; they are coming with a sword in one hand and a torch in the other." That was the watchword. Then we would all try to think what we had that was valuable, although at that time we didn't have much except the family silver and furniture, which were rapidly wearing out. The supply of bed linen was also getting small. The blankets had been all sent to the soldiers long before. Very few housekeepers had blankets as late as 1863. On these occasions the ladies would put on three or four dresses and tie around under the dresses everything that could be suspended and hidden in that way. Hams would be jerked out of the smoke-house, and holes would be dug and every thing thrown in pell mell. Then we would begin to imagine that because we knew where those things were, the first Yankee that appeared would know, too, and often we would go and take them all up from there and dig another hole and put them in that; so that our yards came to look like graveyards. It is very funny to think of now, but it wasn't funny then—to be flying around in the middle of the night that way. Then, to add to the confusion, the children would wake up and would stare around with a vacant look, and begin saying, "What is the matter? What is the matter?" And then we would tell them "The Yankees are coming.". . .

The ideas of the children about the Yankees was very funny. As soon as they heard the Yankees were coming they would jump up and get under the bed, or run out of the house. In fact they would have no idea of what they ought to do to preserve themselves. If you told them the house was on fire of course their first impulse would have been to get out of the house, but when you told them the Yankees were coming they didn't know what to do or which way to turn—whether to run out of the house or to get under the bed or go up the chimney.

I remember one night—all these things come up to me now so vividly—I remember just such a night as I have been describing, when all the children jumped up and got under the bed. We asked what was the matter. Well, "the Yankees were coming." There was one little girl who was terribly frightened. She had no idea whether the Yankees were men, or horses, or what kind of animals they were. She just knew that they were something dreadful. That business went on through the whole of that night; we would hear that the Yankees were six miles off; that they were two miles off, and every sound we heard, whether it was the baker's cart, or anything else, we would think it was the Yankees; that they were actually in town.

On these occasions, after we had secured the things, as we thought, there would be consultations as to which of the servants would be the most trustworthy to do the manual labor—which ones we could take into our confidence, for of course it was necessary to have a Negro man around to lift

things. We were obliged to take them into our confidence, and yet we mistrusted them on such occasions, because this was in 1863, and by that time there had been a great many stories told among us of the disloyalty of servants in such emergencies.

On the night I am now speaking of this excitement continued until morning came. Everybody had been up all night, and it would have been a relief to us to have known that the Yankees had come; but after awhile we ascertained that it was an unmistakable demonstration; that the Yankees were really down here about Gadsden, and that the report brought to Rome had come from a very reliable man, who had traveled all night to carry the news. The first alarm came from some body who had heard of the matter but was not able to report the entire truth. That night and the next morning all was suspense. . . .

Just as we were all expecting the Yankees to come in, and expecting that we were just literally going to be butchered—in fact I don't know what we did think—a courier came rushing into town with the news that Forrest had captured the Yankees and was bringing them in with him as captives. Then there was a reaction, and the excitement was worse than any camp-meeting you ever saw. Everybody was flying from one end of the town to the other. Suppers that were just ready to be cooked were never cooked or eaten; there was a general jollification. Everybody in town felt relieved from a terrible pressure. Forrest came into town and every lady insisted on going up and speaking to the general and shaking hands with him and his forces. My daughter Minnie was a baby at the time, and I took her with me and went up and spoke to him and he took her and kissed her. He told us that his prisoners were coming into town, and he wanted them to eat at once. Everybody went home and there was just a regular wholesale cooking of hams and shoulders and all sorts of provisions that we had, and everything was sent down to the respective camps. We were quite willing to feed the Yankees when they had no guns.

—Testimony of Mrs. MARY A. WARD

XXII.7

"THE LIVES WHICH WOMEN HAVE LEAD SINCE TROY FELL"

The Union had no such galaxy of woman diarists and memoir writers as the Confederacy—women like Mrs. Chesnut, Sarah Morgan, Judith McGuire, Parthenia Hague, Eliza Andrews, and others. To this brilliant group belongs Julia LeGrand. Her father had been a colonel in the War of 1812 and one of the lordly planters of Louisiana, and Julia grew up in the world of fashion and of culture. Impoverished by her father's death, and by the war, Miss LeGrand and her sister opened a girls' school in New Orleans, and were there when the Federals captured the city. Later they took refuge in Georgia and in Texas. Only fragments of the wartime diary have been preserved.

To Mrs. Shepard Brown.

New Orleans, Nov. 17th, 1862

Dear Mrs. B—:

I have nothing to say, and might not say it if I did have it, for you know there is a heaviness prevailing in this latitude, which is not favorable to expansion of idea. I only send a line to remind you that I live and wish you to remember me. A dull and heavy anxiety has settled upon us. We hear nothing to which we can cling with comfort. Those who come in say there is much joy beyond the lines, but no one can give the why and wherefore. In the meantime we are leading the lives which women have lead since Troy fell; wearing away time with memories, regrets and fears; alternating fits of suppression, with flights, imaginary, to the red fields where great principles are contended for, lost and won; while men, more privileged, are abroad and astir, making name and fortune and helping to make a nation.

There was a frolic on board the English ship a few nights since for the benefit, the *Delta* says, of Secession women. I did not go, though Miss Betty Callender offered her services in the way of invitation. I am told that the contraband "bonny blue flag" waved freely over seas of red wine and promontories of sugar-work. The ship represents secessiondom just now; it has not a stronghold in the city. Many a lady opened her vial of wrath, I suppose, for all were told that freedom of speech should be the order of the night. There was acting and dancing, and fish, flesh and fowl suffered in the name of our cause. Toasts were drunk to our great spirits to whom it seems the destiny of a nation is entrusted. How my heart warms to the weary, battle-stained heroes. I never fancied carpet knights even before the stern trial came.

I can't tell you what a life of suppression we lead. I feel it more because I know and feel all that is going on outside. I am like a pent-up volcano. I wish I had a field for my energies. I hate common life, a life of visiting, dressing and tattling, which seems to devolve on women, and now that there is better work to do, real tragedy, real romance and history weaving every day, I suffer, suffer, leading the life I do. . . .

Things go on just as they did. Daily life presents the same food for sorrowful reflection. Tiger, Jake and Emma hold their own within doors, and nothing has happened to prevent us from parading the streets without. A shrill horn breaks often upon my sad speculations. I rush out perhaps and some times find a train of striped and bestarred cavalry and some times only an orange cart. "What an age we live in?" says philosophy, and goes in again to repine and wonder. The Ad*vocate* was suppressed an hour or two ago, but the pliant Jacob made haste to smooth his phrases. A quarrel is reported between the French admiral and the General. There has been a great commotion about the money sent from the New Or leans bank. Lemore has gone to prison and some others. Where are our people? Can't you contrive to let me into the secret, if you have any? You can't read if I keep on, so good-bye with best wishes to all.

Ever your friend,

J.E. Legrand.

—ROWLAND AND CROXALL, eds.,
The Journal of Julia LeGrand

XXII.8

"They Must Reap the Whirlwind"

This brief excerpt from a letter of General Sherman's to his wife is a fitting commentary on the two preceding items. The "enmity of the women of the South" is a familiar theme in Civil War literature. Mrs. Chesnut herself wrote that "we hate our enemies and love our friends," and Stephen Vincent Benét, whose *John Brown's Body* is in some ways the most faithful of an interpretations of the war, has written of

> The terrible hate of women's ire
> The smoky, the long-consuming fire.*

To his wife.

Camp on Bear Creek, 20 Miles
N.W. of Vicksburg,

June 27, 1863

I doubt if history affords a parallel to the deep and bitter enmity of the women of the South. No one who sees them and hears them but must feel the intensity of their hate. Not a man is seen; nothing but women with houses plundered, fields open to the cattle and horses, pickets lounging on every porch, and desolation sown broadcast, servants all gone and women and children bred in luxury, beautiful and accomplished, begging with one breath for the soldiers' ration and in another praying that the Almighty or Joe Johnston will come and kill us, the despoilers of their homes and all that is sacred. Why cannot they look back to the day and hour when I, a stranger in Louisiana, begged and implored them to pause in their career, that secession was death, was everything fatal, and that their seizure of the public arsenals was an insult that the most abject nation must resent or pass down to future ages an object of pity and scorn? Vicksburg contains many of my old

pupils and friends; should it fall into our hands I will treat them with kindness, but they have sowed the wind and must reap the whirlwind. Until they lay down their arms and submit to the rightful authority of the government they must not appeal to me for mercy or favors.

—Howe, ed., *Home Letters of General Sherman*

XXII.9

"I Do Want to See You So Much"

Despite Sherman's political justifications for the harshness of his tactics, for those on the receiving end of his cannonades, the war was an intensely personal experience. With their husbands away, food scarce, and their hungry children potential victims of cannonades, it is little wonder that Sherman and his men felt the "enmity" of Southern women.

The following is a brief letter from ten-year-old Loulie Gilmer of Savannah, Georgia, to her father, Major Jeremy G. Gilmer early in the war. It was one of hundreds of thousands of letters illustrating how the stakes of war were much more personal for the men and women who lived it than the relatively sterile issues of states' rights and insults to national integrity. Major Gilmer was captured at Fort Donelson, escaped from prison, and returned to the Confederate army.

My Dear, Dear Father:

I do want to see you so much. I do miss you so much in the evening when I come in and no one is in, and I am so lonesome by myself and if you were here you would tell me stories and so I would not be so lonesome. . . . Write to me what your horse is named. . . . The Yankees have not got near the city yet. The other day some heavy firing was heard and it was them firing into one of our Boats. . . . Mother and Auntee had the headache the day before yesterday. . . .

I have no more to say. I am your loving child

—Loulie Gilmer

---

* From *John Brown's Body* in *The Selected Works of Stephen Vincent Benét*, published by Rinehart and Company, Inc. Copyright 1927, 1928 by Stephen Vincent Benét.

XXII.10

They are Intelligent on All Subjects but that of Negro Slavery, on This They Are Mad

Despite the demands of war, the South produced new textbooks for their children. This excerpt from *Geographical Reader of the Dixie Children*, written in 1863, offers a description of the United States and the Confederate version of the causes of the Civil War. Other texts incorporated the themes of the war. Math texts posed questions such as "If one Southerner can whip three Yankees, how many Southerners does it take to whip fifteen Yankees?"

The United States

1. This was once the most prosperous country in the world. Nearly a hundred years ago it belonged to England, but the English made such hard laws that the people said they would not obey them. After a long, bloody war of seven years, they gained their independence; and for many years were prosperous and happy.

2. In the mean time both English and American ships went to Africa and brought away many of those poor heathen negroes, and sold them for slaves. Some people said it was wrong and asked the King of England to stop it. He replied that "he knew it was wrong; but that slave trade brought much money into his treasury, and it should continue." But both countries afterwards did pass laws to stop this trade. In a few years, the Northern States finding their climate too cold for the negro to be profitable, sold them to the people living farther South. Then the Northern States passed laws to forbid any person owning slaves in their borders.

3. Then the northern people began to preach, to lecture, and to write about the sin of slavery. The money for which they sold their slaves, was now partly spent trying to persuade Southern States to sent their slaves back to Africa. And when the territories were settled they were not willing for any of them to become slaveholding. This would soon have made the North much stronger than the South; and many of the men said they would vote for a law to free all the negroes in the country. The Southern men tried to show them how unfair this would be, but they still kept on.

4. In the year 1860 the Abolitionists become strong enough to elect one of their own men for president. Abraham Lincoln was a weak man, and the South believed he would deprive them of their rights. So the Southern States seceded, and elected Jefferson Davis for their President. This so enraged President Lincoln that he declared war, and has exhausted nearly all the strength of the nation, in vain attempt to whip the South back into the Union. Thousands of lives have been lost, and the earth has been drenched with blood; but still Abraham is unable to conquer the "Rebels" as he calls the south. The South only asked to be let alone, and divide the public property equally. It would have been wise in the North to have said to her Southern sisters, "If you are not content to dwell with us longer, depart in peace. We will divide the inheritance with you, and may you be a great nation."

5. This country possesses many ships, has fine cities and towns, many railroads, steamboats, canals, manufacturers, etc. the people are ingenious, and enterprising, and are noted for their tact in "driving a bargain." They are refined, and intelligent on all subjects but that of negro slavery, on this they are mad.

6. The large lakes, the long rivers, the tall mountains, with the beautiful farms and pretty towns and villages, make this a very interesting country to travelers.

—*Geographical Reader of the Dixie Children*

XXII.II

RESISTANCE AT HOME

The deprivations of war exacted a profound toll on families in both the cities and the countryside. Although many were willing to tolerate inconveniences early in the war, growing disaffection with the Southern cause spurred resistance. Food riots were not uncommon in cities. Women who could not find enough food to feed their families took to the streets. John B. Jones, the Rebel war clerk quoted earlier in this chapter, recalls an 1863 food riot in Richmond.

In rural sections of the South, the conscription of white men into the army and impressment of slaves caused a wide range of problems and tensions. In large plantations, white women often feared that the departure of so many men made them vulnerable to slave violence and rebellions. Women living near New Bern, North Carolina, petitioned the governor to exempt the remaining men still at home from serving in the Army.

"We pray your Excellency to consider that in the absence of all protection the female portion of this community may be subjected to a system of outrage that may be justly denomenated the harrow of harrows more terrable to the contemplation of the virtuous maiden and matron than death," read the petition to Governor Zebulon Vance.

In other parts of the South, small farmers objected to policies that favored plantation counties. Forty-six men in Randolph County in eastern Alabama petitioned President Jefferson Davis to relieve the impoverished yeomen from government demands that were literally starving people to death. The dire circumstances faced in Randolph County are described in the petition below.

A. President Davis Quells a Food Riot in Richmond

April 2d, 1863. This morning early a few hundred women and boys met as by concert in the Capitol Square [Richmond], saying they were hungry, and must have food. The number continued to swell until there more than a thousand. But few men were among them, and these were mostly foreign residents with exemptions in their pockets. About 9:00 A.M. the mob emerged from the western gates of the square and proceeded down Ninth Street, passing the War Department and crossing Main Street, increasing in magnitude at every step, but preserving silence and (so far) good order. Not

knowing the meaning of such a procession, I asked a pale boy where they were going. A young woman, seemingly emaciated, but yet with a smile, answered that they were going to find something to eat. I could not for the life of me refrain from expressing the hope that they might be successful, and I remarked they were going in the right direction to find plenty in the hands of the extortioners. I did not follow to see what they did, but I learned an hour after that they marched through Cary Street and entered diverse stores of the speculators, which they proceeded to empty of their contents. They impressed all the carts and drays in the street, which were speedily laden with meal, flour, shoes, etc. I did not learn whither these were driven, but probably they were rescued from those in charge of them. Nevertheless, an immense amount of provisions and other articles were borne by the mob, which continued to increase in numbers. An eye-witness says he saw boy come out of a store with hat full money (notes), and I learned that when the mob turned up into Main Street, where all the shops were by this time closed, they broke in the plate-glass windows, demanding silks, jewelry, etc. here they were incited to pillage valuables, not necessary for subsistence, by the class of residents (aliens) exempted from military duty by Judge Campbell, Assistant Secretary of War, in contravention of Judge Meredith's decision. Thus the work of spoliation went on until the military appeared upon the scene, summoned by Governor Letcher, whose term of service is near its close. He had the Riot Act read (by the mayor) and then threatened to fire on the mob. He gave them five minutes' time to disperse in, threatening to use military force (the city battalion being present) if they did not comply with the demand. The timid women fell back, and a pause was put to the devastation, though but few believed he would venture to put his threat in execution. If he had done so, he would have been hung, no doubt.

About this time the President appeared and, ascending a dray, spoke to the people. He urged them to return to their homes so that the bayonets there menacing them might be sent against their common enemy. He told them that such acts would bring famine upon them in the only form which could not be provided against, as it would deter people from brining food to the city. He said he was willing to share his last loaf with the suffering people (his best horse had been stolen the night before), and he trusted we would all bear our privations with fortitude and continue united against the Northern invaders, who were the authors of all our sufferings. He seemed deeply moved, and indeed it was a frightful spectacle, and perhaps an ominous one, if the government does not remove some of the quartermasters who have contributed very much to bring about the evil of scarcity. I mean those who have allowed transportation to forestallers and extortioners.

General Elzey and General Winder waited upon the Secretary of War in the morning asking permission to call the troops from the camps near the city, to suppress the women and children by a summary process. But Mr. Seddon hesitated and then declined authorizing any such absurdity. He said it was a municipal or state duty, and therefore he would not take the responsibility of interfering in the matter. Even in the moment of aspen consternation, he will still be the politician.

I have not heard of any injuries sustained by the women and children. Nor have I heard how many stores the mob visited, and it must have been many.

All is quiet now (3 P.M.), and I understand the government is issuing rice to the people.

— J. B. Jones, *A Rebel War Clerk's Diary*

B. Deaths from Starvation Have Absolutely Occurred

Wesabulga Randolph Co Ala
May 6th 1864

To his Excellency Jefferson Davis
The undersigned citizens & Slaveholders of the county of Randolph & State of Alabama would respectfully represent to your Excellency That Col. Blount impressing agent of Slaves Stationed

at Mobile, Ala., has recently ordered an impressment of 33 1/3 per cent of the able bodied Slaves of this Count; when in adjoining counties where the Slave population is greater only from 5 to 10 per cent have been taken. This we think to be unjust, & *not* in accordance with the intentions of the act. We think that an uniform rate should be levied in the whole State; or so much of it as is now within our lines; So that the burden Should fall uniformly on all; but he appears to order an arbitrary number from each county without reference to the number of Slaves in the County. He thus levies a percentage which is uniform in the county, but does not bear any proportion to the levies in adjoining Counties—He also counts in all the women that are within the ages of 17 to 50 & takes one third of the total number of men between the ages of 17 to 50.

Randolph is a poor & mountainous County with the largest population of any in the State. There are only 300 negroes (women and men) within the prescribed ages in the county & he takes one Hundred. Seventy five per cent of the White Males are now in the Service; leaving the great majority of their wives & children to be Supported by the remainder. There are numbers of widows & orphans of the Soldiers who have perished by the casualties of war to be also Supported by public funds—

The County does not in ordinary times produce more than a Sufficiency of food for its population; last year there was a deficit of over 40,000 bushels; of corn about one half of which has been provided from the tax in Kind; the ballance has to be purchased in the Canebrake; transported a distance of 125 miles on R. R. & hauled thence in waggons from 30 to 50 mile to reach the various points of distribution in the county—

There are now on the rolls of the Probate court, 1,600 indigent families to be Supported; they average 5 to each family; making a grand total of 8,000 persons. Deaths from Starvation have absolutely occurred; notwithstanding the utmost efforts that we have been able to make; & now many of the women & children are seeking & feeding upon the bran from the mills.

Women riots have taken place in Several parts of the County in which Govt wheat & corn has been seized to prevent Starvation of themselves & families; Where it will end unless relief is afforded we cannot tell

We have entered into these details that your Excellency may See the deplorable condition of things in this County, & aid us if in your power & the exigencies of the Service permit—

To take the Negroes *now* from the fields when the crop is just planted & ready for cultivation would inevitably cause the loss of a portion of the crops So essential to feed the County we have appealed to Col. Blount asking that the impressment be delayed or abandoned; but without effect & we now appeal to your Excellency as our last resource under God to give us Such measure of assistance as you can. If you refuse us—we Submit & take our [chance]—do our duty & trust to Almighty Providence for the result. Under the circumstances we therefore pray your Excellency.

That Randolph County be exempt from the operations of the impressment act. If, however, the Case is so urgent & the hands are so essential to save Mobile; then we ask that the impressment be delayed until fall when the crops are gathered; In case neither of these prayers can be granted we pray that the rate be made uniform in the Whole State—& that *we* be not punished for our poverty—We would Humbly Suggest to your Excellency that there are large numbers of negroes about our towns & cities (used for the pleasure of their owners; or idling about; a curse to the community—consumers not producers) that we think might be exhausted before the agricultural labour of the county is interfered with.

Hoping that your Excellency may favourably consider our humble prayer—we remain as ever your Excellencies devoted Servants

—46 SIGNATURES OF RANDOLPH COUNTY CITIZENS

XXII.12

GEORGIA'S GOVERNOR LAMENTS DAVIS' DESPOTISM

If Lincoln had his Seymours and Vallandighams, Davis had men like Governor Brown and Governor Vance to contend with. There was, if anything, more discontent and positive disloyalty in the Confederacy than in the Union. Part of it was inspired by sincere State-rights sentiment, part by personal hostility to President Davis, part by dissatisfaction with the conduct of the war. State-righters like Stephens and Brown and Vance thought the tyranny of Richmond worse than that of Washington; they were particularly outraged by such things as conscription and the suspension of the writ of habeas corpus. Others were sure that Davis was a monster of wickedness and of incompetence, and exhausted their energies denouncing him and his administration.

The letter given here is from the egregious Governor Brown of Georgia, the most powerful of all the state governors, and one who by his policy of putting Georgia interests first effectively sabotaged the Confederacy.

Joseph E. Brown to Alexander H. Stephens (Private)

Canton [Georgia], Sept. 1st, 1862

Dear Sir: I have the pleasure to acknowledge the receipt of your letter of the 26th ult. and am gratified that you take the view which you have expressed about the action of Genl. Bragg in his declaration of martial law over Atlanta and his appoint[ment], as the newspapers say, of a civil governor with aids, etc.

I have viewed this proceeding as I have others of our military authorities of late with painful apprehensiveness for the future. It seems military men are assuming the whole powers of government to themselves and setting at defiance constitutions, laws, state rights, state sovereignty, and every other principle of civil liberty, and that our people engrossed in the struggle with the enemy are disposed to submit to these bold usurpations tending to military despotism without murmur, much less resistance. I should have called this proceeding into question before this time but I was hopeful from the indications which I had noted that Congress would take such action as would check these dangerous usurpations of power, and for the further reasons that I have already come almost into conflict with the Confederate authorities in vindication of what I have considered the rights of the State and people of Georgia, and I was fearful. as no other governor seems to raise these questions, that I might be considered by good and true men in and out of Congress too refractory for the times. I had therefore concluded to take no notice of this matter till the meeting of the legislature when I expect to ask the representatives of the people to define the bounds to which they desire the Governor to go in the defense of the rights and sovereignty of the state. I confess I have apprehensions that our present General Assembly does not properly reflect the sentiments of our people upon this great question, but if the Executive goes beyond the bounds where he is sustained by the representatives of the people he exposes himself to censure without the moral power to do service to the great principles involved. I fear we have much more to apprehend from military despotism than from subjugation by the enemy. I trust our generals will improve well their time while we have the advantage and the enemy are organizing another army. Hoping that your health is good and begging that you will write me when your important duties are not too pressing to permit it, I am very truly your friend.

—PHILLIPS, ed., *"The Correspondence of Robert Toombs, Alexander H. Stephens, and Howell Cobb"*

XXII.13

PEACE AT ANY PRICE

Jonathan Worth was an old-line Whig politician who fought nullification in the thirties and secession in 1861 but—like so many others—went with his state when the crisis materialized. During the war he was State Treasurer of North Carolina, in 1865 he was elected to the governorship, and re-elected again the following year.

Jonathan Worth to Jesse G. Henshaw
Raleigh Aug. 24, 1863

I hardly know whether I am in favor of the peace meetings or not. On the one hand, it is very certain that the President and his advisers will not make peace, if not forced into it by the masses and the privates in the army. Their cry echoed by almost every press is: "Independence, or the last man and the last dollar." The North will not make peace on the basis of Independence. The real question which nobody—not even Holden—will squarely present is, shall we fight on with certain desolation and impoverishment and probably ultimate defeat; or make peace on the basis of reconstruction? Nearly every public man—every journal, political and religious, and every politician, in the fervor of their patriotism, has vociferously declared in favor of "the last man and the last dollar" cry. These classes cannot be consistent unless they still cry war. Many believe the masses in their saner hours never approved the war and would rather compromise on the basis of the Constitution of the U.S. with such additional securities against any future rupture as could be agreed on. If there be any sense in peace meetings they mean reconstruction. They may rather do mischief if they are not so imposing as to force the administration to reconstruction. They will be impotent and mischievous if the army is still for war to the last man and the last dollar. I do not know the sentiments of the rank and file of the army.

I am for peace on almost any terms and fear we shall never have it until the Yankees dictate it. Upon the whole I would not go into a peace meeting now or advise others to go into one, particularly in Randolph—but I have no repugnance to them in other places and see no other chance to get to an early end of this wicked war, but by the action of the masses who have the fighting to do. If an open rupture occur between Gov. V[ance] and Mr. Holden, it will be ruinous to us. There ought to be none and I trust there will be none. There is no difference between them that justifies a breach. The Governor concedes the right of the people to hold meetings and express their wishes, but he deems such meetings inexpedient and tending to dissatisfaction and disorganization in the army and that no honorable peace can be made, after we cease to present a strong military front. The Gov. acts consistently and in the eminent difficult position he occupied, I doubt whether any pilot could manage the crippled ship in such a storm with more skill. Repress all expressions of dissatisfaction against him. He values the extravagant eulogiums of the fire-eaters at their worth. They are playing an adroit game. They would get up dissention between the Gov. and Holden and then break up the Conservative party and seize the helm of Government.

—HAMILTON, ed., *The Correspondence of Jonathan Worth*

— XXII.14 —

"The Man Who Held His Conscience Higher Than Their Praise"

Unionist sentiment was weaker in South Carolina than in any other Southern state and weaker, probably, in Charleston than in any other city. This epitaph on the Petigru monument in St. Michael's churchyard, Charleston, is included as evidence of the respect with which the South, even in wartime, respected honest difference of opinion. Member of a famous Charleston family, lawyer and public servant, James Petigru was probably the most distinguished of South Carolina Unionists. The toleration accorded him was a product in part of the sophistication of Charleston, in part of that class consciousness which accepted eccentricity in its aristocracy, in part of a respect for intellectual independence common in the Civil War generation than in our own.

JAMES LOUIS PETIGRU
Born at
Abbeville May 10th 1789
Died at Charleston March 9th 1863

JURIST. ORATOR. STATESMAN.
PATRIOT.

Future times will hardly know how great a life
This simple stone commemorates—
The tradition of his Eloquence, his
Wisdom and his Wit may fade:
But he lived for ends more durable than fame,
His Eloquence was the protection of the poor and
wronged;
His Learning illuminated the principles of Law—
In the admiration of his Peers,
In the respect of his People,
In the affection of his Family
His was the highest place;
The just meed
Of his kindness and forbearance
His dignity and simplicity
His brilliant genius and his unwearied industry
Unawed by Opinion,
Unseduced by Flattery,
Undismayed by Disaster,
He confronted Life with antique Courage
And Death with Christian Hope.

———

In the great Civil War
He withstood his People for his Country
But his People did homage to the Man
Who held his conscience higher than their praise
And his Country
Heaped her honors on the grave of the Patriot,
To whom living,
His own righteous self-respect sufficed
Alike for Motive and Reward.

———

"Nothing is here for tears, nothing to wail,
Or knock the breast; no weakness, no contempt,
Dispraise or blame; nothing but well and fair
And what may quiet us in a life so noble."

—CARSON, *Life and Letters of James Petigru*

XXIII

HOSPITALS, SURGEONS, AND NURSES

The story of Civil War medicine is only less depressing than the story of Civil War prisons; if the first is lighted by flashes of heroism, the second is ameliorated by generosity and self sacrifice on the part of doctors and nurses. As we have seen, one reason for the high mortality rate in prisons was the low state of medical and nursing services and the primitive standards of sanitation that obtained generally. This situation reflected in part conditions in civil life, in part the wholly inadequate preparation for war, in part the conditions of medicine and public health at mid-century.

At the outbreak of the war the United States Surgeon General's office consisted of a total of 115 surgeons; 24 of these resigned to form the nucleus of the Confederate medical services. Eventually both services were vastly—but quite inadequately—expanded. Nursing services, too, were primitive. The army still relied on male nurses, most of them quite untrained. At the outbreak of the war the famous humanitarian, Dorothea Dix, hurried to Washington to offer her services; she was appointed Superintendent of Women Nurses, but never allowed any real independence. Most of the nursing service on both sides was voluntary; the United States Sanitary Commission did invaluable work in nursing and relief both at the front and in hospitals behind the line. Hospitals were mostly hastily improvised and inadequate. It is sobering to read that inspection of hospitals in the Union Army at the mid-war period (November 1862 to March 1863) reported a total of 589 as good arid no less than 303 as bad or very bad, while inspections of medical officers from the beginning of the war to March 1863 found 2,727 good and 851 bad! It is to be remembered, too, when we read of the work of the surgeons and contemplate the mortality figures, that antiseptics were unknown, the relation of dirt to infection was generally not understood, anesthesia was just coming into general use, and drugs were inadequate.

It is not surprising in the light of all this that mortality from disease and wounds was far higher than from bullets, and that hospitalization was often regarded as equivalent to a death sentence. While no statistics are satisfactory and those for the Confederacy in a state of total confusion, it is a safe generalization that deaths from wounds were as numerous as deaths on the battlefield and that deaths from disease were more than twice both these combined. Perhaps the least unreliable statistics for the Union armies give 67,000 killed in action, 43,000 died of wounds, and 224,000 died of disease; an additional 24,000 are listed as dead from other causes—doubtless either wounds or disease. Confederate statistics indicate a comparable situation. Fortunately most of the soldiers were young—the largest single age group was eighteen—and from the country, and had therefore high powers of resistance and recuperation; otherwise the situation would have been even more appalling.

XXIII. I

GEORGE TOWNSEND DESCRIBES THE WOUNDED ON THE PENINSULA

George Alfred Townsend was only twenty when he began to report the Civil War for the *New York Herald,* but he quickly established himself as one of the most brilliant of an the many war correspondents. We have already read his account of Fitz John Porter's ascent in a balloon; we shall meet him again describing the Battle of Five Forks. Townsend followed McClellan's army up the Peninsula and through that campaign to its inglorious close. There are few more graphic accounts of wounds, disease and death than those from his gifted pen.

It was evening, as I hitched my horse to a stake near-by, and pressed up to the receptacle for the unfortunates. Sentries enclosed the pen, walking to-and-fro with loaded muskets; a throng of officers and soldiers had assembled to gratify their curiosity; and new detachments of captives came in hourly, encircled by sabremen, the Southerners being disarmed and on foot.

The scene within the area was ludicrously moving. It reminded me of the witch-scene in Macbeth, or pictures of brigands or Bohemian gypsies at rendezvous, not less than five hundred men, in motley, ragged costumes, with long hair, and lean, wild, haggard faces, were gathered in groups or in pairs, around some fagot-fires. In the glowing darkness their expressions were imperfectly visible; but I could see that most of them were weary, and hungry, and all were depressed and ashamed. Some were wrapped in blankets of rag-carpet, and others wore shoes of rough, untanned hide. Others were without either shoes or jackets, and their heads were bound with red handkerchiefs. Some appeared in red shirts; some in stiff beaver hats; some were attired in shreds and patches of cloth; and a few wore the soiled garments of citizen gentlemen; but the mass adhered to homespun suits of gray, or "butternut," and the coarse blue kersey common to slaves. In places I caught glimpses of red Zouave breeches and leggings; blue Federal caps, Federal buttons, or Federal blouses; these were the spoils of anterior battles, and had been stripped from the slain. Most of the captives were of the appearances denominated "scraggy" or "knotty." They were brown, brawny, and wiry, and their countenances were intense, fierce, and animal. They came from North Carolina, the poorest and least enterprising Southern State, and ignorance, with its attendant virtues, were the common facial manifestations. Some lay on the bare ground, fast asleep; others chatted nervously as if doubtful of their future treatment; a few were boisterous, and anxious to beg tobacco or coffee from idle Federals; the rest—and they comprehended the greater number—were silent, sullen, and vindictive. They met curiosity with scorn, and spite with imprecations.

A child—not more than four years of age, I think—sat sleeping in a corner upon an older comrade's lap. A gray bearded pard was staunching a gash in his cheek with the tail of his coat. A fine-looking young fellow sat with his face in his hands, as if h-is heart were far off, and he wished to shut out this bitter scene. In a corner, lying morosely apart, were a Major, three Captains, and three Lieutenants,—young athletic fellows, dressed in rich gray cassimere, trimmed with black, and wearing soft black hats adorned with black ostrich feather. Their spurs were strapped upon elegantly fitting boots, and they looked as far above the needy, seedy privates, as lords above their vassals. . . .

I rode across the fields to the Hogan, Curtis, and Gaines mansions; for some of the wounded had meantime been deposited in each of them. All the cow-houses, wagon-sheds, hay-barracks, hen-coops, Negro cabins, and barns were turned into hospitals. The floors were littered with "corn-shucks" and fodder; and the maimed, gashed, and dying lay confusedly together. A few slightly wounded, stood at windows, relating incidents of the battle; but at the doors sentries stood with crossed muskets, to keep out idlers and gossips. The mention of my vocation was an "open sesame," and I went unrestrained, into all the largest hospitals. In the first of these an amputation was being performed, and at the door lay a little heap of human fingers, feet, legs, and arms. I shall not soon forget the bare-armed surgeons, with bloody instruments, that leaned over the rigid and insensible figure, while the comrades of the subject looked horrifiedly at the scene.

The grating of the murderous saw drove me into the open air, but in the second hospital which I visited, a wounded man had just expired, and I encountered his body at the threshold. Within, the sickening smell of mortality was almost insupportable, but by degrees I became accustomed to it. The lanterns hanging around the room streamed fitfully upon the the red eyes, and half-naked figures. All were looking up, and saying, in pleading monotone: "Is that you, doctor?" Men with their arms in slings went restlessly up and down, smarting with fever. Those who were wounded in the lower extremities, body, or head, lay upon their backs, tossing even in sleep. They listened peevishly to the wind whistling through the chinks of the barn. They followed one with their rolling eyes. They turned away from the lantern, for it seemed to sear them. Soldiers sat by the severely wounded, laving their sores with water. In many wounds the balls still remained, and the discolored flesh was swollen unnaturally. There were some who had been shot in the bowels, and now and then they were frightfully convulsed, breaking into shrieks and shouts. Some of them iterated a single word, as, "doctor," or "help," or "God," or "oh!" commencing with a loud spasmodic cry, and continuing the same word till it died away in cadence. The act of calling seemed to lull the pain. Many were unconscious and lethargic, moving their fingers and lips mechanically, but never more to open their eyes upon the light; they were already going through the valley and the shadow.

I think, still, with a shudder, of the faces who were told mercifully that they could not live. The unutterable agony; the plea for somebody on whom to call; the longing eyes that poured out prayers; the looking on mortal as if its resources were infinite; the fearful looking to the immortal as if it were so far off, so implacable, that the dying appeal would be in vain; the open lips, through which one could almost look at the quaking heart below; the ghastliness of brow and tangled hair; the closing pangs; the awful *quietus*. I thought of Parrhasius, in the poem, as I looked at these things:—

"Gods!
Could I but paint a dying groan—"

And how the keen eye of West would have turned from the reeking cockpit of the *Victory,* or the tomb of the Dead Man Restored, to this old barn, peopled with horrors. I rambled in and out, learning to look at death, studying the manifestations of pain,—quivering and sickening at times, but plying my avocation, and jotting the names for my column of mortalities. . . .

Ambulances, it may be said, incidentally, are either two wheeled or four-wheeled. Two-wheeled ambulances are commonly called "hop, step, and jumps." They are so constructed that the forepart is either very high or very low, and may be both at intervals. The wounded occupants may be compelled to ride for hours in these carriages, with their heels elevated above their heads, and may finally be shaken out, or have their bones broken by the terrible jolting. The four-wheeled ambulances are built in shelves, or compartments, but the wounded are in danger of being smothered in them.

It was in one of these latter that I rode, sitting with the driver. We had four horses, but were thrice "swamped" on the road, and had to take out the wounded men once, till we could start the wheels. Two of these men were wounded in the face, one of them having his nose completely severed, and the other having a fragment of his jaw knocked out. A third had received a ball among the thews and muscles behind his knee, and his whole body appeared to be paralyzed. Two were wounded in the shoulders, and the sixth was shot in the breast, and was believed to be injured inwardly, as he spat blood, and suffered almost the pain of death.

The ride with these men, over twenty miles of hilly, woody country, was like one of Dante's excursions into the Shades. In the awful stillness of the dark pines, their screams frightened the hooting owls, and the whirring insects in the leaves and tree-tops quieted their songs. They heard the gurgle of the rills, and called aloud for water to quench their insatiate thirst. One of them sang a shrill, fierce, fiendish ballad, in an interval of relief, but plunged, at a sudden relapse, in prayers and curses. We heard them groaning to themselves, as we sat in front, and one man, it seemed, was quite out of his mind. These were the outward manifestations; but what chords trembled and smarted within, we could only guess. What regrets for good resolves unfulfilled, and remorse for years misspent, made hideous these sore and panting hearts? The moonlight pierced through the foliage of the wood, and streamed into our faces, like invitations to a better life. But the crippled and bleeding could not see or feel it,—buried in the shelves of the ambulance.

—Townsend, *Campaigns of a Non-Combatant*

XXIII.2

THE SANITARY COMMISSION
TO THE RESCUE

The United States Sanitary Commission, the leading private relief organization of the Civil War period, was created—against strong opposition in the army—in June 1861. A distinguished Unitarian divine, the Reverend Henry W. Bellows, was President; the famous landscape architect, Frederick Law Olmsted, was Secretary; and the Commission enlisted scores of physicians and literally hundreds of public-spirited men and women. Its object, wrote Mary Livermore, "was to do what the Government could not." The "could" here is, of course, relative; it was merely that governments had not yet conceived it their responsibility to take care of the health, comfort, and general welfare of soldiers.

The Commission did a little bit of everything. Its inspectors looked into the sanitary arrangements in camps—hence its name—and brought about reforms. It reviewed matters of diet, cooking, clothing; provided private aid to soldiers and to their dependents; took care of fugitives; collected and forwarded boxes of food to the soldiers—a combination, as we have said elsewhere, of YMCA, Red Cross, and USO—and helped out even with nursing and hospital care. At the time of the Peninsular campaign the Commission obtained some hospital transports for the wounded.

We give an account here of the use of these hospital transports. Katharine Wormeley, who tells the story, was one of the many women who worked heroically for the Sanitary Commission. Born in England, the daughter of an admiral, she later distinguished herself in philanthropy and literature. She is remembered today for her remarkable translations of Balzac and of other modern French writers.

"Wilson Small," 5 June, 1862

Dear Mother: I finished my last letter on the afternoon of the day when we took eighty men on the *Small*, and transferred them to the *Webster*.

We had just washed and dressed, and were writing letters when Captain Sawtelle came on board to say that several hundred wounded men were lying at the landing; that the *Daniel Webster No. 2* had been taken possession of by the medical officers, and was already half full of men, and that the surplus was being carried across her to the *Vanderbilt*; that the confusion was terrible; that there were no stores on board the *Daniel Webster*

No. 2 (she was being seized the moment she reached the landing on her return from Yorktown, without communicating with the Commission), nor were there any stores or preparations, not even mattresses, on board the *Vanderbilt*.

Of course the best in our power had to be done. Mrs. Griffin and I begged Mr. Olmsted not to refrain from send ing us, merely because we had been up all night. He said he wouldn't send us, but if we chose to offer our services to the United States surgeon, he thought it would be merciful. Our offer was seized. We went on board; and such a scene as we entered and lived in for two days I trust never to see again. Men in every condition of horror, shattered and shrieking, were being brought in on stretchers borne by "contrabands," who dumped them anywhere, banged the stretchers against pillars and posts, and walked over the men without compassion. There was no one to direct what ward or what bed they were to go into. Men shattered in the thigh, and even cases of amputation, were shovelled into top berths without thought or mercy. The men had mostly been without food for three days, but there was *nothing* on board either boat for them; and if there had been, the cooks were only engaged to cook for the ship, and not for the hospital.

We began to do what we could. The first thing wanted by wounded men is something to drink (with the sick, stimulants are the first thing). Fortunately we had plenty of lemons, ice, and sherry on board the *Small*, and these were available at once. Dr. Ware discovered a barrel of molasses, which, with vinegar, ice, and water, made a most refreshing drink. After that we gave them crackers and milk, or tea and bread. It was hopeless to try to get them into bed; indeed, there were no mattresses on the *Vanderbilt*. All we could do at first was to try to calm the confusion, to stop some agony, to revive the fainting lives, to snatch, if possible, from immediate death with food and stimulants. Imagine a great river or Sound steamer filled on every deck,—every berth and every square inch of room covered with wounded men; even the stairs and gangways and guards filled with those who are less badly wounded; and then imagine fifty well men, on every kind of errand, rushing to and fro over them, every touch bringing agony to the poor fellows, while stretcher after stretcher came along, hoping to find an empty place; and then imagine what it was to keep calm ourselves, and make sure that every man on both those boats was properly refreshed and fed. We got through about 1 A.M., Mrs. M. and Georgy having come off other duty and reenforced us.

We were sitting for a few moments, resting and talking it over, and bitterly asking why a Government so lavish and perfect in its other arrangements should leave its wounded almost literally to take care of themselves, when a message came that one hundred and fifty men were just arriving by the cars. It was raining in torrents, and both boats were full. We went on shore again: the same scene repeated. The wretched *Vanderbilt* was slipped out, the *Kennebec* brought up, and the hundred and fifty men carried across the *Daniel Webster No. 2* to her, with the exception of some fearfully wounded ones, who could not be touched in the darkness and rain, and were therefore made as comfortable as they could be in the cars. We gave refreshment and food to all, Miss Whetten and a detail of young men from the *Spaulding* coming up in time to assist, and the officers of the *Sebago*, who had seen how hard pressed we were in the afternoon, volunteering for the night-watch. Add to this sundry Members of Congress, who, if they talked much, at least worked well. One of them, the Hon. Moses F. Odell, proposed to Mr. Olmsted that on his return to Washington he should move that the thanks of Congress be returned to us! Mr. Olmsted, mindful of our feelings, promptly declined.

We went to bed at daylight with *breakfast* on our minds, and at six o'clock we were all on board the *Daniel Webster No. 2*, and the breakfast of six hundred men was got through with in good time. Captain Sawtelle kindly sent us a large wall-tent, twelve caldrons and camp-kettles, two cooks, and a detail of six men. The tent was put up at once, Dr. Ware giving to its preparation the only hour when

he might have rested during that long nightmare. We began to use it that (Tuesday) morning. It is filled with our stores; there we have cooked not only the sick-food, but *all* the food needed on the Government boats. It was hard to get it in sufficient quantity; but when everything else gave out, we broke up "hard-tack" into buckets full of hot milk and water a little sweetened,—"bread and milk" the men called it. Oh, that precious condensed milk, more precious to us at that moment than beef essence!

Tuesday was very much a repetition of Monday night. The men were cleared from the main-deck and gangways of the *Daniel Webster No. 2* onto the *Kennebec*. The feeding business was almost as hard to manage as before. But still it was done, and we got to bed at 1 A.M. Mrs. M. and I were to attend to the breakfast at 6 next morning. By some accident Mrs. M., who was ready quite as soon as I was, was carried off by the *Small*, which started suddenly to run down to the *Spaulding*. I had, therefore, to get the breakfast alone. I accomplished it, and then went ashore and fed some men who were just arriving in cars, and others who were in tents near the landing. The horrors of that morning are too great to speak of. The men in the cars were brought on board the *Daniel Webster No. 2* and laid about the vacant main-deck and guards and on the dock of a scow that lay alongside. I must not, I ought not to tell you of the horrors of that morning. One of the least was that I saw a "contraband" step on the amputated stump of a wretched man. I took him by the arm and walked him into the tent, where I ordered them to give him other work, and forbade that he should come upon the ships again. I felt white with anger, and dared not trust myself to speak to *him*. While those awful sights pass before me I have comparatively no feeling, except the anxiety to alleviate as much as possible. I do not suffer under the sights; but oh! the sounds, the screams of men. It is when I think of it afterwards that it is so dreadful. . . .

About nine hundred wounded remain to be brought down. Mr. Olmsted says *our* boats have transported one thousand seven hundred and fifty-six since Sunday; the Government and Pennsylvania boats together about three thousand. Mr. Clement Barclay was with us on Monday night on the *Vanderbilt. I* believe he went with her to Fortress Morroe. He was working hard, with the deepest interest and skill. I went with him to attend to a little "Secesh" boy, wounded in the thigh; also to a Southern colonel, a splendid-looking man, who died, saying to Mr. Barclay, with raised hand: "Write to my wife and tell her I die penitent for the part I have taken in this war." I try to be just and kind to the Southern men. One of our men stopped me, saying: *"He's* a rebel; give that to me." I said: "But a wounded man is our brother!" (rather an obvious sentiment, if there is anything in Christianity); and they both touched their caps. The Southerners are constantly expressing surprise at one thing or another, and they are shy, but not surly, at receiving kindness. Our men are a noble set of fellows, so cheerful, uncomplaining, and generous.

Remember that in all I have written, I have told you only about ourselves—the women. What the gentlemen have seen, those of our party, those of the *Spaulding* and of the other vessels, is beyond my power to relate. Some of them fainted from time to time.

Last night, shining over blood and agony, I saw a lunar rainbow; and in the afternoon a peculiarly beautiful effect of rainbow and stormy sunset,—it flashed upon my eyes as I passed an operating-table, and raised them to avoid seeing anything as I passed.

—WORMELEY, *The Other Side of War*

—— XXIII.3 ——

CLARA BARTON SURMOUNTS THE FAITHLESSNESS OF UNION OFFICERS

It was not only doctors and nurses who were, at times, incompetent but army officers as well. At least so Clara Barton often thought. She was a strong-minded woman, and a bit inclined to think the worst of her superiors and associates. When the war broke out Miss Barton was working-in the Patent Office in Washington. Deeply moved by the distress of the soldiers after First Bull Run she wrote a letter to the *Worcester* (Massachusetts) Spy asking for food, clothing, and bandages for the soldiers. Provisions poured in—and she had found her mission. Never formally associated either with the Sanitary Commission or, except for a brief interlude, with the army, she conducted something of a one-woman relief organization. She carried on her beneficent activities with the Army of the Potomac, the Army of the James, around Charles ton, and in and around Washington. After the war she was the moving spirit in the establishment of the American Red Cross, and for over twenty years its director.

This excerpt comes from her war diary.

No one has forgotten the heart-sickness which spread over the entire country as the busy wires flashed the dire tidings of the terrible destitution and suffering of the wounded of the Wilderness whom I attended as they lay in Fredericksburg. But you may never have known how many hundredfold of these ills were augmented by the conduct of improper, heartless, unfaithful officers in the immediate command of the city and upon whose actions and indecisions depended entirely the care, food, shelter, comfort, and lives of that whole city of wounded men. One of the highest officers there has since been convicted a traitor. And another, a little dapper captain quartered with the owners of one of the finest mansions in the town, boasted that he had changed his opinion since entering the city the day before; that it was in fact a pretty hard thing for refined people like the people of Fredericksburg to be compelled to open their homes and admit "these dirty, lousy, common soldiers," and that he was not going to compel it.

This I heard him say, and waited until I saw him make his words good, till I saw, crowded into one old sunken hotel, lying helpless upon its bare, wet, bloody floors, five hundred fainting men hold up their cold, bloodless, dingy hands, as I passed, and beg me in Heaven's name for a cracker to keep them from starving (and I had none); or to give them a cup that they might have something to drink water from, if they could get it (and I had no cup and could get none); till I saw two hundred six-mule army wagons in a line, ranged down the street to headquarters, and reaching so far out on the Wilderness road that I never found the end of it; every wagon crowded with wounded men, stopped, standing in the rain and mud, wrenched back and forth by the restless, hungry animals all night from four o'clock in the afternoon till eight next morning and how much longer I know not. The dark spot in the mud under many a wagon, told only too plainly where some poor fellow's life had dripped out in those dreadful hours.

I remembered one man who would set it right, if he knew it, who possessed the power and who would believe me if I told him I commanded immediate conveyance back to Belle Plain. With difficulty I obtained it, and four stout horses with a light army wagon took me ten miles at an unbroken gallop, through field and swamp and stumps and mud to Belle Plain and a steam tug at once to Washington. Landing at dusk I sent for Henry Wilson, chairman of the Military Committee of the Senate. A messenger brought him at eight, saddened and appalled like every other patriot in that fearful hour, at the weight of woe under which the Nation staggered, groaned, and wept.

He listened to the story of suffering and faithlessness, and hurried from my presence, with lips compressed and face like ashes. At ten he stood in the War Department. They could not credit his report. He must have been deceived by some frightened villain. No official report of unusual suffering had reached them. Nothing had been called for by the military authorities commanding Fredericksburg.

Mr. Wilson assured them that the officers in trust there were not to be relied upon. They were faithless, overcome by the blandishments of the wily inhabitants. Still the Department doubted. It was then that he proved that my confidence in his firmness was not misplaced, as, facing his doubters he replies: "One of two things will have to be done—either you will send some one to-night with the power to investigate and correct the abuses of our wounded men at Fredericksburg, or the Senate will send some one tomorrow."

This threat recalled their scattered senses.

At two o'clock in the morning the Quartermaster-General and staff galloped to the 6th Street wharf under the orders; at ten they were in Fredericksburg. At noon the wounded men were fed from the food of the city and the houses were opened to the "*dirty, lousy* soldiers" of the Union Army.

Both railroad and canal were opened. In three days I re turned with carloads of supplies.

No more jolting in army wagons! And every man who left Fredericksburg by boat or by car owes it to the firm decision of one man that his grating bones were not dragged ten miles across the country or left to bleach in the sands of that city.

—*The Diary of Clara Barton*

XXIII.4

SUSAN BLACKFORD NURSES THE WOUNDED AT LYNCHBURG

The South had no organization comparable to the Sanitary Commission, but a Women's Relief Society dedicated itself to collecting money to help sick and wounded soldiers, and thousands of Southern women volunteered for nursing duty. Mrs. Arthur Hopkins for example not only contributed some $200,000 to hospital work but went to the front and was wounded at Seven Pines; others, like Mrs. Ella Newsom and Miss Kate Cumming, worked indefatigably in the make shift hospitals of the Confederacy; Mrs. Phoebe Yates Pember—superintendent of a division of the vast Chimborazo Hospital in Richmond—was tireless in hospital and nursing home and even at the front.

Mrs. Blackford,* was a member of one of Virginia's first families, wife to the distinguished Charles Blackford, judge advocate under Longstreet.

May 7th [1864]. The wounded soldiers commenced arriving on Saturday, and just as soon as I heard of it, which was before breakfast, I went to see Mrs. Spence to know what I could do for them. She said the ladies had been so shamefully treated by the sur-

---

* Letter reprinted from *Letters from Lee's Army* by Susan Lee Blackford; copyright 1947 by Charles Scribner's Sons; used by permission of the publishers.

geons that she was afraid to take any move in the matter. I told her I would go and see Dr. Randolph and ask him if we could not do something. I went down and did so at once and asked him what we could do. He said we might do any thing we pleased in the way of attention to them; send or carry anything to them we wished and he would be glad of our help. As soon as I reported to Mrs. Spence what he said she started messengers in every direction to let it be known and I went to eleven places myself. We then determined to divide our pro visions into two divisions: the bread, meat, and coffee to be sent to the depot, the delicacies to the hospitals. The reception of wounded soldiers here has been most hospitable. You would not believe there were so many provisions in town as have been sent to them.

On Saturday evening I went up to Burton's factory, where most of the wounded were taken, and found the committee of ladies who had been selected, of whom I was one, just going in with the supper. I went in with them. We had bountiful supplies of soup, buttermilk, tea, coffee, and loaf bread, biscuits, crackers, and wafers. It did my heart good to see how the poor men enjoyed such things. I went around and talked to them all. One man had his arm taken off just below the elbow and he was also wounded through the body, and his drawers were saturated with blood. I fixed his pillow comfortably and stroked his poor swelled and burning arm. An other I found with his hand wounded and his nose bleeding. I poured water over his face and neck, and after the blood ceased to flow wiped his pale face and wounded hand which was black from blood and powder. They were very grateful and urged us to come and see them again.

On Sunday evening news came that six hundred more would arrive and Mrs. Spence sent me word to try and do something. The servants were away and I went into the kitchen and made four quarts of flour into biscuits and two gallons of coffee, and Mrs. Spence gave me as much more barley, so I made, bying them, a great deal of coffee. I am very tired.

May 12th. My writing desk has been open all day, yet I have just found time to write to you. Mrs. Spence came after me just as I was about to begin this morning and said she had just heard that the Taliaferro's factory was full of soldiers in a deplorable condition. I went down there with a bucket of rice milk, a basin, towel, soap, etc. to see what I could do. I found the house filled with, wounded men and not one thing provided for them. They were lying about the floor on a little straw. Some had been there since Tuesday and had not seen a surgeon. I washed and dressed the wounds of about fifty and poured water over the wounds of many more. The town is crowded with the poor creatures, and there is really no preparations for such a number. If it had not been for the ladies many of them would have starved to death. The poor creatures are very grateful, and it is a great pleasure to us to help them in any way. I have been hard at work ever since the wounded commenced coming. I went to the depot twice to see what I could do. I have had the cutting and distribution of twelve hundred yards of cotton cloth for bandages, and sent over three bushels of rolls of bandages, and as many more yesterday. I have never worked so hard in all my life and I would rather do that than anything else in the world. I hope no more wounded are sent here as I really do not think they could be sheltered. The doctors, of course, are doing much, and some are doing their full duty, but the majority are not. They have free access to the hospital stores and deem their own health demands that they drink up most the brandy and whiskey in stock, and, being fired up most the time, display a cruel and brutal indifference to the needs of the suffering which is a disgrace to their profession and to humanity.

—BLACKFORD, ed., *Letters from Lee's Army*

XXIII.5

CORNELIA HANCOCK NURSES SOLDIERS AND CONTRABANDS

Of the many nursing narratives this is probably the best. Cornelia Hancock was a young lady of twenty-three when she responded to the call of her brother-in-law, Dr. Henry Child of Philadelphia, to help out as a nurse. A New Jersey Quaker, she found in nursing her vocation; after the war she worked with Southern Negroes and among the Philadelphia poor.

Her letters, covering her nursing and hospital experience from Gettysburg to the Wilderness and beyond, are simple, vivid and sincere.

Gettysburg—July 8th, 1863

My Dear Sister

We have been two days on the field; go out about eight and come in about six—go in ambulances or army buggies. The surgeons of the Second Corps had one put at our disposal. I feel assured I shall never feel horrified at anything that may happen to me hereafter. There is a great want of surgeons here; there are hundreds of brave fellows, who have not had their wounds dressed since the battle. Brave is not the word; more, more Christian fortitude never was witnessed than they exhibit, always say—"Help my neighbor first he is worse." The Second Corps did the heaviest fighting, and, of course, all who were badly wounded, were in the thickest of the fight, and, therefore, we deal with the very best class of the men—that is the bravest. My na-me is particularly grateful to them because it is Hancock. General Hancock is very popular with his men. The reason why they suffer more in this battle is because our army is victorious and marching on after Lee, leaving the wounded for citizens and a very few surgeons. The citizens are stripped of everything they have, so you must see the exhausting state of affairs. The Second Army Corps alone had two thousand men wounded, this I had from the Surgeon's headquarters.

I cannot write more. There is no mail that comes in, we send letters out: I believe the Government has passession of the road. I hope you will write. It would be very pleasant to have letters to read in the evening, for I am so tired I cannot write them. Get the Penn Relief to send clothing here; there are many men without anything but a shirt lying in poor shelter tents, calling on God to take them from this world of suffering; in fact the air is rent with petitions to deliver them from their sufferings. . . .

I do not know when I shall go home—it will be according to how long this hospital stays here and whether another battle comes soon. I can go right in an ambulance without being any expense to myself. The Christian Committee support us and when they get tired the Sanitary is on hand. Uncle Sam is very rich, but very slow, and if it was not for the Sanitary, much suffering would ensue. We give the men toast and eggs for breakfast, beef tea at ten o'clock, ham and bread for dinner, and jelly and bread for supper. Dried rusk would be nice if they were only here. Old sheets we would give much for. Bandages are plenty but sheets very scarce. We have plenty of woolen blankets now, in fact the hospital is well supplied, but for about five days after the battle, the men had no blankets nor scarce any shelter.

It took nearly five days for some three hundred surgeons to perform the amputations that occurred here, during which time the rebels lay in a dying condition without their wounds being dressed or scarcely any food. If the rebels did not get severely punished for this battle, then I am no judge. We have but one rebel in our camp now; he says he never fired his gun if he could help it, and, therefore, we treat him first rate. One man died this morning. I fixed him up as nicely as the place will allow; he will be buried this afternoon. We are becoming somewhat civilized here now and the men are cared for well.

On reading the news of the copperhead performance, in a tent where eight men lay with nothing but stumps (they call a leg cut off above the knee a "stump") they said if they held on a little longer they would form a stump brigade and go and fight them. We have some plucky boys in the hospital, but they suffer awfully. One had his leg cut off yesterday, and some of the ladies, newcomers, were up to see him. I told them if they had seen as many as I had they would not go far to see the sight again. I could stand by and see a man's head taken off I believe—you get so used to it here. I should be perfectly contented if I could receive my letters. I have the cooking all on my mind pretty much. I have torn almost all my clothes off of me, and Uncle

Sam has given me a new suit. William says I am very popular here as I am such a contrast to some of the office-seeking women who swarm around hospitals. I am black as an Indian and dirty as a pig and as well as I ever was in my life—have a nice bunk and tent about twelve feet square. I have a bed that is made of four crotch sticks and some sticks laid across and pine boughs laid on that-with blankets on top. It is equal to any mattress ever made. The tent is open at night and sometimes I have laid in the damp all night long, and got up all right in the morning.

The suffering we get used to and the nurses and doctors, stewards, etc., are very jolly and sometimes we have a good time. It is very pleasant weather now. There is all in getting to do what you *want* to do and I am doing that. . . .

Pads are terribly needed here. Bandages and lint are plenty. I would like to see seven barrels of dried rusk here. I do not know the day o£ the week or anything else. Business is slackening a little though—order is beginning to reign in the hospital and soon things will be right. One poor fellow is hollering fearfully now while his wounds are being dressed.

There is no more impropriety in a *young* person being here provided they are sensible than a sexagenarian. Most polite and obliging are all the soldiers to me.

It is a very good place to meet celebrities; they come here from all parts of the United States to see their wounded. Senator Wilson, Mr. Washburn, and one of the Minnesota Senators have been here. I get beef tenderloin for dinner.— Ladies who work are favored but the dress-up palaverers are passed by on the other side. I tell you I have lost my memory almost entirely, but it is gradually returning. Dr. Child has done very good service here. All is well with me; we do not know much war news, but I know I am doing all I can, so I do not concern further. Kill the copperheads. Write everything, how ever trifling, it is all interest here.

From thy affectionate
C. Hancock

Contraband Hospital, Washington,
Nov. 15th, 1863

My dear Sister:

I shall depict our wants in true but ardent words, hoping to affect you to some action. Here are gathered the sick from the contraband camps in the northern part of Washington. If I were to describe this hospital it would not be believed. North of Washington, in an open, muddy mire, are gathered all the colored people who have been made free by the progress of our Army. Sickness is inevitable, and to meet it these rude hospitals, only rough wooden barracks, are in use—a place where there is so much to be done you need not remain idle. We average here one birth per day, and have no baby clothes except as we wrap them up in an old piece of muslin, *that* even being scarce. Now the Army is advancing it is not uncommon to see from 40 to 50 arrivals in one day. They go at first to the Camp but many of them being *sick* from exhaustion soon come to us. They have nothing that any one-in the North would call clothing. I always see them as soon as they arrive, as they come here to be vaccinated; about 25 a day are vaccinated.

This hospital is the reservoir for all cripples, diseased, aged, wounded, infirm, from whatsoever cause; all accidents happening to colored people in all employs around Washington are brought here. It is not uncommon for a colored driver to be pounded nearly to death by some of the white soldiers. We had a dreadful case of Hernia brought in today. A woman was brought here with three children by her side; said she had been on the road for some time; a more forlorn, wornout looking creature I never beheld. Her four eldest children are still in Slavery, her husband is dead. When I first saw her she laid on the floor, leaning against a bed, her children crying around her. One child died almost immediately, the other two are still sick. She seemed to need most, food and rest, and those two comforts we gave her, but clothes she still wants. I think the women are more trouble than the men. One of the white guards called to me today and asked me if I got any pay. I told him no. He said he was going to be paid soon and he would give me 5 dollars. I do not know what was running through his mind as he made no other remark. I ask for clothing for women and children, both boys and girls. Two little boys, one 3 years old, had his leg amputated above the knee the cause being his mother not being allowed to ride inside, became dizzy and had dropped him. The other had his leg broken from the same cause. This hospital consists of all the lame, halt, and blind escaped from slavery. We have a man and woman here without any feet, theirs being frozen so they had to be amputated. Almost all have scars of some description and many have very weak eyes.

There were two very fine looking slaves arrived here from Louisiana, one of them had his master's name branded on his forehead, and with him he brought all the instruments of torture that he wore at different times during 39 years of very hard slavery. I will try to send you a Photograph of him he wore an iron collar with 3 prongs standing up so he could not lay down his head; then a contrivance to render one leg entirely stiff and a chain clanking behind him with a bar weighing 50 lbs. This he wore and worked all the time hard.

At night they hung a little bell upon the prongs above his head so that if he hid in any bushes it would tinkle and te11 his whereabouts. The baton that was used to whip them he also had. It is so constructed that a little child could whip them till the blood streamed down their backs. This system of proceeding has been stopped in New Orleans and may God grant that it may cease all over this boasted free land, but you may readily imagine what development such a system of treatment would bring them to. With *this* class of beings, those who wish to do good to the contrabands must labor. Their standard of morality is very low.

—JAQUETTE, ed., *South after Gettysburg*

THE GHASTLY WORK OF THE FIELD SURGEONS

These two descriptions of the work of the surgeons could be matched in letter after letter, diary after diary, North and South. One Kentucky editor charged that the doctors had "slain more of our troops than all of Lincoln's minions," and a Richmond one characterized the Medical Department as "unfeeling, shameful and brutal." We must remember however that it is the exceptionally bad conduct that gets recorded; routine work is taken for granted. On the whole the surgeons and nurses did about as well as they could. Certainly many of those who worked all through the war, at great peril to themselves, were distinguished members of a distinguished profession.

The first of these critics, Samuel Nichols, was an Amherst College student who enlisted in the 37th Massachusetts Volunteers; served through the war; and later edited the *Pittsfield (Massachusetts) Sun*. The second is Augustus Brown, captain in the 4th New York Heavy Artillery.

A. The Heartlessness of the Surgeons

> Hd. Qtrs. 37th Regiment Mass. Vols.
> Camp near Stafford Court House
> Nov. 23rd 1862

My Dear Cousin Phebe:

As yet only four of our number have died and some six have been discharged, two of the latter of whom were officers. Lieut. Eli T. Blackmer, a son of the Blackmer that moved from Hodges Corner in Warren, is discharged and has gone to his home in Chicopee. His health is much impaired, and his discharge was merited. Everything here concerning sickness and its management seems so repulsive that the thought of being sick or of having one of your friends in the Hospital, is filled with gloom. I will relate an instance. It is probably an instance more censurable to those having charge than usually occurs; but if the whole history of this war were brought to light more such facts would be revealed, in my mind, than would be pleasing to men (no, brutes) whose duty it is to look after the physical health of the soldier.

In our regiment was a man, private of course, who came under my notice while we were at New Baltimore, a little over one week since. He was emaciated and almost spiritless. He, to be sure, was not as cleanly as he should have been; but I know that it requires much exertion where water is scarce (and it always is in the vicinity of an army like ours) to keep decent. He looked as though he had been sick for some time. He like many others had acquired a dislike to reporting him self to the surgeons, as they have an idea the surgeons are destitute of feeling and unjust. I will not say how far this feeling is just. He at length came with those of his company who reported sick that day to the Surgeon's office within a few steps of where I sleep. I stood at the mouth of my tent and saw and heard the treatment each patient received. This fellow was treated as the rest. He took his turn and came to the front of the Doctor's tent, and received the customary question, "What's the matter with you?" (pretty question for a doctor). "What are you here for? Let's see your tongue. Shall return you to duty."

He was returned to duty. He refused to do duty and as punishment was sentenced to stand on the barrel (a very severe punishment), and added to this, to hold a heavy stone in his hand, two hours on and two off. This was the Doctor's work and not the Colonel's. I admit that it was the Colonel's duty to stop an unjust punishment if he saw one being exacted, but he would probably refer the whole case to the Doctor. To continue my story: after this I watched that young man. All energy seemed absent from him, and he acted as if he was unable to stir. I went to him and advised him to go to the Surgeon again, knowing that by tiring out the M.D. he might receive attention. I could not induce him. I saw during my conversation that he was really sick; and I was anxious to find out what ailed him, knowing if I did, I could find him medicine. I went to another regiment to get a doctor with whom I was acquainted to come and see him; but the regiment had moved that morning, and so I let the matter go for the time being. Two morn-

ings after I saw him again at the Doctor's tent. With the usual flourishes he was reported for duty, and the next morning he was brought to the Hospital to die almost immediately. The same day he was buried with soldier's honors; and with the last volleys fired over his grave died all feelings of remissness or regret, if any such feelings were entertained.

—UNDERHILL, ed., *"Your Soldier Boy Samuel"*

B. The Horrors of the Wilderness

Tuesday, May 10th [1864]. Heavy cannonading from 8 A.M. to 1 P.M. The Pontoon train has been sent back to Fredericksburg, apparently to get it out of the way, and the army horses are put on half-rations, that is, five pounds of food. Ambulances and army wagons with two tiers of flooring, loaded with wounded and drawn by four and six mule teams, pass along the plank, or rather, corduroy road to Fredericksburg, the teamsters lashing their teams to keep up with the train, and the wounded screaming with pain as the wagons go jolting over the corduroy. Many of the wounds are full of maggots. I saw one man with an arm off at the shoulder, with maggots half an inch long crawling in the sloughing flesh, and several poor fellows were holding stumps of legs and arms straight up in the air so as to ease the pain the rough road and the heartless drivers subjected them to. These men had been suffering in temporary field hospitals, as no opportunity had been afforded to send them to the rear until we got within reach of the road running to Fredericksburg.

And this reminds me of a scene I witnessed a day or two since which seemed to me to cap the climax of the horrors of war. Passing along a little in the rear of the lines when a battle was raging in which my battalion was not engaged, I carne upon a field-hospital to which the stretcher-bearers were bringing the men wounded in the conflict. Under three large "tent flies," the center one the largest of all, stood three heavy wooden tables, around which were grouped a number of surgeons and their assistants, the former bareheaded and clad in long linen dusters reaching nearly to the ground, which were covered with blood from top to bottom and had the arms cut off or rolled to the shoulders. The stretcher-bearers deposited their ghastly freight side by side in a winrow on the ground in front of the table under the first tent fly. Here a number of assistants took charge of the poor fellows, and as some of them lifted a man on to the first table others moved up the winrow so that no time nor space should be lost. Then some of the surgeons administered as anaesthetic to the groaning and writhing patient, exposed his wound and passed him to the center table. There the surgeons who were operating made a hasty examination and determined what was to be done and did it, and more often than not, in a very few moments an arm or a leg or some other portion of the subject's anatomy was flung out upon a pile of similar fragments behind the hospital, which was then more than six feet wide and three feet high, and what remained of the man was passed on to the third table, where other surgeons finished the bandaging, resuscitated him and posted him off with others in an ambulance. Heaven forbid that I should ever again witness such a sight!

—Brown, *Diary of a Line Officer*

XXIII.7

Hospital Sketches

Civil War hospitals were not only remarkable for the horror of the injuries and the sheer number of men and boys who suffered, but also for the sadness of their individual stories. Louisa May Alcott spent three weeks working in a Washington, D. C., hospital before being struck down by typhoid. The future author of the classics *Little Women* (1868), *Little Men* (1871), and *Jo's Boys* (1886), Alcott wrote numerous letters about the experience.

Upon recovering from her illness, Alcott's letters were published. *Hospital Sketches* was enormously popular. Alcott's detailed descriptions of the stories behind the injured men touched readers. Although it was her first published work and later eclipsed by Alcott's more famous books, Alcott never put her brief stint in an army hospital completely behind her. "I never tire of thinking and talking about 'my boys,'" she said many years later.

The night whose events I have a fancy to record, opened with a little comedy, and closed with a great tragedy; for a virtuous and useful life untimely ended is always tragical to those who see not as God sees. My headquarters were beside the bed of a New Jersey boy, crazed by the horrors of that dreadful Saturday. A slight wound in the knee brought him there; but his mind had suffered more than his body; some sting of that delicate machine was over strained, and, for days, he had been reliving, in imagination, the scenes he could not forget, till his distress broke out in incoherent ravings, pitiful to hear. As I sat by him, endeavoring to soothe his poor distracted brain by the constant touch of wet hands over his hot forehead, he lay cheering his comrades on, hurrying them back, then counting them as they fell around him, often clutching my arm, to drag me from the vicinity of a bursting shell, or covering up his head to screen himself from a shower of shot; his face brilliant with fever; his eyes restless; his head never still; every muscle strained and rigid; while an incessant stream of defiant shouts, whispered warnings, and broken laments, poured from his lips with that forceful bewilderment which makes such wanderings so hard to overhear.

It was past eleven, and my patient was slowly wearying himself into fitful intervals of quietude, when, in one of these pauses, a curious sound arrested my attention. Looking over my shoulder, I saw a one-legged phantom hopping nimbly down the room, and, going to meet it, recognized a certaiun Pennsylvania gentleman, whose wound-fever had taken a turn for the worse, and, depriving him of the few wits a drunken campaign had left him, set him literally tripping on the light, fantastic to "toward home," as he blandly informed me, touching the military cap which formed a striking contrast to the severe simplicity of the rest of his decidedly undress uniform. When sane, the least movement produced a road of pain or a volley of oaths; but the departure of reason seemed to have wrought an agreeable change, both in the man and his manners; for, balancing himself on one leg, like a medieval stork, he plunged into an animated discussions of the war, the President, lager beer, and Enfield rifles, regardless of any suggestions of mine as to the propriety of returning to bed, lest he be court-martialed for desertion.

Anything more supremely ridiculous can hardly be imagined than this figure, scantily draped in white, its one foot covered with a big blue sock, a dingy cap set rakingly askew on its shaven head, and placid satisfaction beaming in its broad red face, as it flourished a mug in one hand, an old boot in the other, calling them canteen and knapsack, while it skipped and fluttered in the most unearthly fashion. What to do with the creature I don't know; Dan was absent, and if I went to find him, the perambulator might festoon himself out of the window, set his toga on fire, or do some of his neighbors a mischief. The attendant of the room was sleeping like a near relative of the celebrated Seven and nothing short of pins would rouse him; for he had been out that day, and whiskey asserted its supremacy in balmy whiffs. Still declining, in a fine flow of eloquence, the demented gentleman hopped on, blind and deaf to my graspings and entreaties; and I was about to slam the door in his face, and run for help, when a saner and second phantom, "all in white," came to the rescue, in the likeness of a big Prussian, who spoke no English, but divined the crisis, and put an end to it, by bundling the lively monoped into his bed, like a baby, with an authoritative command to "stay put," which received added weight from being delivered in an odd conglomeration of French and German, accompanied by warning wags of a head decorated with a yellow cotton night cap, rendered most imposing by a tassel like a bell-pull. Rather exhausted by his excursion, the member from Pennsylvania subsided; and, after an irrepressible laugh together, my Prussian ally and myself were returning to our places. . . .

"This is my first battle; do they think it's going to be my last?"

"I'm afraid they do, John."

It was the hardest question I had ever been called upon to answer, doubly hard with those clear eyes fixed on mine, forcing a truthful answer by their own truth. He seemed a little startled at first, pondered over the fateful fact a moment then shook his head, with a glance at the broad chest and muscular limbs stretched out before him:

"I'm not afraid, but it's difficult to believe all at once. I'm so strong it don't seem possible for such a little wound to kill me."

Merry Mercutio's dying words glanced through my memory as he spoke: "'Tis not so deep as a well, nor so wide as a church door, but 'tis enough." And John would have said the same could he have seen the ominous black holes between his shoulders, he never had; and, seeing the ghastly sights before him, could not believe his own wound more fatal than these, for all the suffering it caused him.

"Shall I write to your mother, now?" I asked, thinking that these sudden tidings might change all plans and purposes; but they did not; for the man received the order of the Divine Commander to march with the same unquestioning obedience with which the soldier had received that of the human one, doubtless remembering that the first led him to life, and the last to death.

"No, ma'am; to Laurie just the same; he'll break it to her best, and I'll add a line to her myself when you get done."

So I wrote the letter which he dictated, finding it better than any I had sent; for, though here and there a little ungrammatical or inelegant, each sentence came to me briefly worded, but most expressive; full of excellent counsel to the boy, tenderly bequething "mother and Lizzie" to his care, and bidding him good bye in words the sadder for their simplicity. He added a few lines, with steady hand, and, I sealed it, said, with a patient sort of sigh, "I hope the answer will come in time for me to see it"; then, turning away his face, laid the flowers against his lips, as if to hide some quiver of emotion at the thought of such a sudden sundering of all dear home ties.

These things had happened two days before; now John was dying, and the letter had not come. I had been summoned to many death beds in my life, but to none that made my heart ache as it did then, since my mother called me to watch the departure of a spirit akin to this in its gentleness and patient strength. As I went in, John stretched out both hands:

"I knew you'd come! I guess I'm moving on, ma'am."

He was; and so rapidly that, even while he spoke, over his face I saw the gray veil falling that no human hand can lift. I sat down by him, wiped the drops from his forehead, stirred the air about him with the slow wave of a fan, and waited to help him die. He stood in sore need of help—and I could do so little; for, as the doctor had foretold, the strong body rebelled against death, and fought every inch of the way, fording him to draw each breath with a spasm, and clench his hands with an imploring look, as if he asked, "How long must I endure this, and be still!" For hours he suffered dumbly, without a moment's respite, or a moment's murmuring; his limbs grew cold, his face damp, his lips white, and, again and again, he tore the covering off his breast, as if the lightest weight added to his agony; yet through it all, his eyes never lost their perfect serenity, and the man's soul seemed to sit therein, undaunted by the ills that vexed his flesh.

One by one, the men woke, and round the room appeared a circle of pale faces and watchful eyes, full of awe and pity; for, though a stranger, John was beloved by all. Each man had wondered at his patience, respected his piety, admired his fortitude, and now lamented his hard death; for the influence of an upright nature had made itself deeply felt, even in one little week. Presently, the Jonathan who so loved this comely David, came creeping from his bed for a last look and word. The kind soul was full of trouble, as the choke in his voice, the grasp of his hand, betrayed; but there were no tears, and the farewell of the friends was the more touching for its brevity.

"Old boy, how are you?" faltered the one.

"Most through, thank heaven!" whispered the other.

"Can I say or do anything for you anywheres?"

"Take my things home, and tell them that I did my best."

"I will! I will!"

"Good bye, Ned."

"Good bye, John, good bye!"

They kissed each other, tenderly as women, and so parted, for poor Ned could not stay to see his comrade die. For a little while, there was no sound in the room but the drip of water, from a stump or two, and John's distressful gasps, as he slowly breathed his life away. I thought him nearly gone, and had just laid down the fan, believing its help to be no longer needed, when suddenly he rose up in his bed, and cried out with a bitter cry that broke the silence, sharply startling every one with its agonized appeal:

"For God's sake, give me air!"

It was the only cry pain or death had wrung from him, the only boon he had asked; and none of us could grant it, for all the airs that blew were useless now. Dan flung up the window. The first red streak of dawn was warming the grey east, a herald of the coming sun; John saw it, and with the love of light which lingers in us to the end, seemed to read in it a sign of hope of help, for, over his whole face there broke that mysterious expression, brighter than any smile, which often comes to eyes that look their last. He laid himself gently down; and, stretching out his strong right arm, as if to grasp and bring the blessed air to his lips in a fuller flow, lapsed into a merciful unconsciousness, which assured us that for him suffering was forever past. He died then; for, though the heavy breaths still tore their way up for a little longer, they were but the waves of an ebbing tide that beat unfelt against the wreck, which an immortal voyager had deserted with a smile. He never spoke again, but to the end held my hand close, so close that when he was asleep at last, I could not draw it away. Dan helped me, warning me as he did so that it was unsafe for dead and living flesh to lie so long together; but though my hand was strangely cold and stiff, and four white marks remained across its back, even when warmth and color had returned elsewhere, I could not but be glad that, through its touch, the presence of human sympathy, perhaps, had lightened that hard hour.

When they made him ready for the grave, John lay in state for half an hour, a thing which seldom happened in that busy place; but a universal sentiment of reverence and affection seemed to fill the hearts of all who had known or heard of him; and when the rumor of his death went through the house, always astir, many came to see him, and I felt a tender sort of pride in my lost patient; for he looked a most heroic figure, lying there stately and still as the statue of some young knight asleep upon his tomb. The lovely expression which so often beautifies dead faces, soon replaced the marks of pain, and I longed for those who loved him best to see him when half an hour's acquaintance with Death had made them friends. As we stood looking at him, the ward master handed me a letter, saying it had been forgotten the night before. It was John's letter, come just an hour too late to gladden the eyes that had longed and looked for it so eagerly: yet he had it; for, after I had cut some brown locks for his mother, and taken off the ring to send her, telling how well the talisman had done its work, I kissed this good son for her sake, and laid the letter in his hand, still folded as when I drew my own away, feeling that its place was there, and making myself happy with the thought, that, even in his solitary place in the "Government Lot," he would not be without some token of love which makes life beautiful and outlives death. Then I left him, glad to have known so genuine a man, and carrying with me an enduring memory of the brave Virginia blacksmith, as he lay serenely waiting for the dawn of that long day which knows no night.

—Louisa May Alcott, *Hospital Sketches*

The Regimental Hospital

Although Charles Johnson wrote this many years after the war, it is one of the best of the comparatively few accounts of military field hospitals. Johnson had enlisted as a boy of eighteen, and was assigned to hospital duty in the West; he was with Grant in the siege of Vicksburg and later took part in the expedition into the Bayou Teche country. His account goes far to explain the failure of medical services in the war and to place responsibility not on the medical officers but on the state of medical science at the time.

In the field the Regimental Hospital department was allowed two small tents for the officers, medicines, etc., another small tent for the kitchen department and supplies, and a larger one for the sick. This last, known as the hospital tent, was about fourteen feet square and was capable of containing eight cots with as many patients.

In the field we almost never had sheets and white pillow cases, but made use of army blankets that were made of the coarsest, roughest fiber imaginable. In warm weather the walls of the tent were raised, which made it much more pleasant for the occupants.

However, the policy that obtained was to send those who were not likely to recover quickly to the base hospitals, though this was not always to the patient's best interests, for these larger hospitals were oftentimes centers of infection of one kind or another, especially of hospital gangrene, which seldom attacked the wounded in the field.

During a campaign our stock of medicines was necessarily limited to standard remedies, among which could be named opium, morphine, Dover's powder, quinine, rhubarb, Rochelle salts, castor oil, sugar of lead, tannin, sulphate of copper, sulphate of zinc, camphor, tincture of opium, tincture of iron, tincture opii, camphorata, syrup of squills, simple syrup, alcohol, whiskey, brandy, port wine, sherry wine, etc. Upon going into camp, where we were likely to remain a few days, these articles were unpacked and put on temporary shelves made from box-lids; and, on the other hand, when marching orders came, the medicines were again packed in boxes, the bottles protected from breaking by old papers, etc.

Practically all the medicines were administered in powder form or in the liquid state. Tablets had not yet come into use, and pills were very far from being as plentiful as they are today. The result was that most powders were stirred in water and swallowed. In the case of such medicine as quinine, Dover's powder, tannin, etc., the dose, thus prepared, was a bitter one. The bromides, sulfonal, trional and similar soporifices and sedatives, had not come in use, and asafetida, valerian and opium and its derivatives were about all the Civil War surgeon had to relieve nervousness and induce sleep.

Among the surgical supplies were chloroform, ether, brandy, aromatic spirits of ammonia, bandages, adhesive plaster, needles, silk thread for ligatures, etc. There were, also, amputating cases well supplied with catlins, artery forceps, bone forceps, scalpels, scissors, bullet probes, a tourniquet, etc. But while all the instruments were washed in water and wiped dry to keep from rusting, such an idea as making them aseptic never entered the head of the most advanced surgeon.

There was an emergency case, about the size of a soldier's knapsack, and, indeed, intended to be carried on an attendant's back like a knapsack. In this emergency case were bandages, adhesive plaster, needles, artery forceps, scalpels, spirits of ammonia, brandy, chloroform, ether, etc. This emergency case, or hospital knapsack, was always taken with the regiment when the firing-line was about to be approached, and where the First Assistant Surgeon was in charge and was ready to render first aid to any who might be wounded.

This first aid, however, never went further than staunching bleeding vessels and applying temporary dressings. Thus attended to, the wounded were taken to an ambulance, and in this conveyed to the field hospital in the rear, generally out of musket range, but almost never beyond the reach of shells and cannon balls.

Arrived at the larger field hospital the patient was cared for by the surgeons and male nurses. The wounds were examined and dressed, but never antiseptically, for no one knew the importance of antisepsis or how to put it in practise; consequently, every wound suppurated, and so-called *laudable pus* was welcomed by those in charge as an indication that the patient had reached one of the mile-posts that had to be passed on his road to recovery. Careful handwashing and nail scrubbing was never practised before operations or in dressing recent wounds. And yet, for the most part, the wounds in the end healed satisfactorily. The fact that those receiving them were, in the great majority of cases, vigorous young men had much to do with the good results. Here it may be proper to say that in the Civil War by far the largest proportion of wounds were made with bullets from what were called minie balls. There were fired, in most instances, from single-shooters and muzzle-loaders, such as the Springfield rifled musket, the Enfield rifled musket, the Austrian rifled musket, etc. These bullets weighed an ounce or more, and the guns from which they were fired would kill a man nearly a mile away, and that they produced large, ugly wounds goes without saying.

When a minie ball struck a bone it almost never failed to fracture and shatter the contiguous bony structure, and it was rarely that only a round perforation, the size of the bullet, resulted. When a joint was the part the bullet struck, the results were especially serious in Civil War days. Of course, the same was true of wounds of the abdomen and head, though to a much greater degree. Indeed, recovery from wounds of the abdomen and brain almost never occurred. One of the prime objects of the Civil War surgeon was to remove the missile, and, in doing this, he practically never failed to infect the part with his dirty hands and instrument.

When Captain William M. Colby of my company was brought from the firing-line to our Division Hospital he was in a comatose state from a bullet that had penetrated his brain through the upper portion of the occipital bone. The first thing our surgeon did was to run his index finger its full length into the wound; and this without even ordinary washing. Next he introduced a dirty bullet probe. The patient died a day or two later. . . . These facts are narrated to show the frightful handicap Civil War surgery was under from a lack of knowledge of asepsis and antisepsis; and it is needless to say that no reflection is intended to be made on our surgeon, for he was making use of the very best lights of his day, dangerous as some of these were. . . .

I think wounds from bullets were five times as frequent as those from all other sources. Shell wounds were next in frequency, and then came those from grape and canister. I never saw a wound from a bayonet thrust, and but one made by a sword in the hands of an enemy. In another chapter a reference is made to a man who received a deep wound in the upper part of his thigh, which, after some days, proved fatal. Not long after the wound was received the parts began to assume a greenish tinge and this became of a deeper hue, and when after death the parts were cut down upon, a copper tap from an exploding shell was found to be the ugly missile which had inflicted the injury that, in the end, proved fatal.

Where so many men are grouped together accidents of greater or less gravity are liable to occur. On the whole, how ever, our regiment was fortunate. We lost two or three by drowning and one by a steamboat explosion . . . , and I can recall but three who received accidental bullet wounds. One of these was a pistol shot of small caliber . . . ,

and the other was from one of the Springfield guns that was sup posed not to be loaded. Looking back, I can but regard our record in this direction as especially fortunate, when the handling of so many loaded guns through so long a period is taken into account.

The only light vehicle in the regiment was our hospital ambulance, . . . a four-wheeled vehicle with bed on springs and covered with strong ducking. The rear end-gate opened with hinges at its lower part for the convenience of putting in and taking out very sick or severely injured patients. The driver of our hospital ambulance was a soldier by the name of Throgmorton, who knew his business, and attended to it. He was an expert horseman, and kept the pair of bays under his care well-groomed and properly attended to in every way. They were, to a degree, spirited, and when the occasion called for it, were good steppers. Besides serving its purpose in conveying sick and wounded, our ambulance proved useful as a sort of family carriage, upon several occasions taking *certain* of us *well ones* "here-and-yon."

For service about the hospital men were detailed from the regiment to serve in the several capacities of nurses, cooks, and ambulance drivers, etc. Service of this kind was known as "special duty," and not a few came to have no little aptness in their new duties. Especially was this true of the men who cared for the sick, some of whom developed quite a little insight into disease, and were frequently able to make tolerable diagnoses and prognoses.

—JOHNSON, *Muskets and Medicine*

XXIV

THE AFRICAN-AMERICAN EXPERIENCE

The efforts that African Americans undertook on their own behalf throughout the Civil War played a crucial role in shaping their destiny during and after the war. Emancipation was not simply a granting of freedom from the top down. It was also a grassroots issue slaves helped push to the forefront through their own actions. By fleeing their masters for the safety of the Union lines, runaway slaves compelled the North to confront the issue of emancipation. The Northern army did not know what to do with these fugitive slaves. If slaves were not emancipated, they should be returned to their owners. But the North was at war with their owners. Something had to be done with the runaway slaves, and as events unfolded, military necessity forced the North to consider emancipation. The granting of freedom not only stripped the South of the manpower slaves provided, it also bolstered the Union's might as slaves flocked to assist Northern armies.

Runaway slaves and freedmen joined the army to serve as soldiers. The impact went beyond the battlefield, although their conduct in combat greatly aided the war effort. Fighting would give black men the right to citizenship. "Once let the black man get upon his person the brass letters, 'U.S'," Frederick Douglass said, "let him get an eagle on his buttons and a musket on his shoulder and bullets in his pocket, and there is no power on earth which can deny that he has earned the right to citizenship in the United States."

As black soldiers distinguished themselves repeatedly in battle, it led to greater recognition of their rights as citizens and a bolstered sense of entitlement on the part of blacks themselves. No longer content to sit idle while others debated their fate, they stood and demanded the rights of citizenship. Their combat experience led directly to winning the right to vote after the war. New leaders emerged from the military ranks. War experience provided a previously unknown sense of confidence and pride in having helpd to forge the nation's history.

But the experience of freedom was not a universally beneficial one. In many ways, the Civil War was both the best of times and the worst of times for African Americans. Weighing against the opportunities of freedom were the risks of dislocation in a war in which neither side acknowledged the rights of blacks.

The Confederacy vowed to treat captured black prisoners of war as escaped slaves. Many were sold back into slavery. In some instances, captured black soldiers were executed by Confederate troops, as after the Confederate assault on Fort Pillow in April 1864, when General Nathan Bedford Forrest's men massacred scores of black soldiers. And white slave owners often retaliated against the families of slaves who ran away to join the Union army.

At best, the North's treatment of blacks was heavily laced by racism; at worst, its treatment of them was criminal. Black soldiers received less pay than white soldiers. They were often given the more tedious and dangerous assignments, as their higher casualty rates reflected. Prior to proving themselves in combat, they were the objects of widespread derision. Even after demonstrating bravery on the field, blacks were still often subject to abusive treatment by corrupt, racist officers. The slaves' joy of liberation at the hands of the Union Army was often dashed by the robbery of their food and property by the same invading soldiers.

Lincoln and others tried to convince blacks that the best course for them would be to colonize foreign lands, a venture the government was willing to help finance. A handful of African Americans acquiesced to this proposal, but most blacks wanted to stay in the United States. They were keen to become full-fledged American citizens. The actions they had taken during the Civil War, in the face of tremendous peril, gave them that opportunity.

XXIV.I

"You Debauched a Young Negro Girl"

Even the most benign slave-master relationships were deeply ambiguous. The following document is a letter from the Reverend Doctor Charles Colcock Jones, owner of Montevideo, one of the great plantations of Georgia. Jones accused a fellow minister, the Reverend William Slates Lee, of impregnating a slave. As the Charleston diarist Mary Chesnut observed, one of the impacts of slavery was to give white men almost unrestricted sexual access to black women. But Jones was very protective of his slaves, concerned about their welfare and morals. Nevertheless, the dynamics of Southern slave society prevented the slave from speaking for herself. Lee denied Jones's charge, though he had previously been accused of fathering another child with a slave woman. In that instance he also denied the accusation and suggested instead that the woman be punished, which she was.

August 26, 1861

. . . You were right under my roof but a short time before you debauched a young Negro girl—a seamstress, and one of our chambermaids. And you continued your base connections with this Negro woman week after week until you took your final leave! Of the hundred men of all classes and conditions and professions—men of church and men of the world, married and unmarried—who have been guests in my house for days, weeks, months, and some for years, you, sir, are the only man who has ever dared to offer to me personally and to my family and to my neighbors so vile and so infamous an insult. You are the only man who has ever dared to debauch my family servants—it being the only instance that has occurred—and to defile my dwelling with your adulterous and obscene pollutions. Had you been detected, I should have driven you instantly out of the house and off the premises, with all the accompanying disgrace which you merited; and I regret that the law affords me no redress under so serious an indignity and injury.

The proof of your criminality is of so clear a character as to remove all doubts. There is the free, unconstrained confession of the Negro woman herself in full detail; there is the correspondence between the time of your connection with her and the birth of the child—a mulatto, now some time born; and there is the resemblance to you beyond mistake. In this last proof I do not rely upon my own convictions. I have submitted the child to the inspection of three gentlemen in the county who know you well personally and are familiarly acquainted with your countenance and physiognomy, and they without hesitation declare its resemblance to you to be as striking as possible. And all who have seen it are of the same opinion. The evidence is amply sufficient to warrant the submission of the case to the session of the Columbus church for action.

And now, sir, what are your former Christian friends to think of you? You have sinned under the most forbidding and aggravating circumstances, and it is difficult to conceive of a more degrading and hypocritical course of wickedness and folly, or one which argues a greater destitution of principle or more callousness of conscience! I never have been more deceived in a man in all my life. How have you wounded the Saviour, and brought disgrace upon religion, and given occasion for the ungodly to triumph! What an injury you have done to the soul of the poor Negro! What disgrace and ruin of character have you brought on yourself! I pity you, and try to pray for your redemption. You know well what your duty is toward God and man, and I hope you may find grace to perform it.

I voluntarily offered you my name on your school circular. I request you take it off. You have betrayed my confidence and injured me grievously, and I cannot look upon you as I once did nor hold any further intercourse with you.

—The Reverend Doctor Charles Colcock Jones

XXIV.2

No Choice But Escape

Although the institution of slavery contributed to Southern secession, the slaves themselves largely played a passive role in the raging debate that led up to the Civil War. There was little they could do. Literally under the whip of their white masters, they had no influence over the course of their own lives. Escape was an almost futile gesture, as flight offered little sanctuary. The Fugitive Slave Law, requiring that runaway slaves be returned to their owners, had removed the promise of freedom that the North once held..

When Union armies entered the South, however, running away became a more realistic option. Many slaves took that chance, which was a perilous choice—as the documents below reflect. The flight of slaves into Union lines would have powerful consequences.

A. "The Alligators Preferred Dog Flesh to Personal Flesh"

I was born in New Orleans; I am 23 years of age; I was raised by Arthur Thiboux of New Orleans; I am by trade a cooper; I was treated pretty well at home; in 1855 master sold my mother, and in 1861 he sold me to S. Contrell of St. James Parish for $2,400; here I worked by task at my trade; one morning the bell was rung for us to go to work so early that I could not see, and I lay still, because I was working by task; for this the overseer was going to have me whipped, and I ran away to the woods, where I remained for a year and a half; I had to steal my food; took turkeys, chickens and pigs; before I left our number had increased to thirty, of whom ten were women; we were four miles in the rear of a plantation house; sometimes we would rope beef cattle and drag them out to our hiding place; we obtained matches from our friends on the plantation; we slept on logs and burned cypress leaves to make a smoke and keep away mosquitoes; Eugene Jardeau, mast[er] of hounds, hunted for us for three months; often those at work would betray those in the swamp, for fear of being implicated in their escape; we furnished meat to our fellow-servants in the field, who would return corn meal; one day twenty hounds came after me; I called the

party to my assistance and we killed eight of the bloodhounds; then we all jumped into Bayoue Faupron; the dogs followed us and the alligators caught six of them; "the alligators preferred dog flesh to personal flesh;" we escaped and came to Camp Parapet, where I was first employed in the Commissary's office, then as a servant to Col. Hanks; then I joined his regiment.

—Octave Johnson, Corporal Co. C, 15th Regt. Corps d'Afrique

B. Confederate Officer Tracks Down Runaway Slaves

Christal river Flor[ida]. September 8th 1863

In my report to you of the 1st inst I stated that I had succeeded in capturing the boat and had the negroes cut off so as there would not be much doubt in my getting the negroes . . . raid on Mr. King's plantations. on the morning of the second day I took their trail from where I fired on them the evening previous. they led off towards the mouth of Withlacoochee River, edgeing the Coast as near as they could for tide creeks &c. about 4 ock in the evening we discovered one in a cedar tree looking out, on an Island they discovered us about the same time, we being in the open marsh. here they seem to have separated only two being together. after chasing them about two miles through the saw Grass we came up in gun shot of them. we began to fire at them, and they returned the fire very cool and deliberately but we soon got in close range of them and killed them. one of these negroes was recognized by some of my men as belonging to Mr. Everett, who lives near hear, which ran away from him about nine months ago. he was styled Captain of the party, as I learned from the negroes recaptured of Mr. Kings. myself and men being completely tired down for the want of water, we had to go back and camp until next morning when we took the trail and followed on the third day. about the same time in the evening of the third day, we came up with two more, and after a Similar chase of the second day, we succeeded in Killing both of them. from here I never could strike the trail of any more of them, but I am under the impression that we killed or wounded the other three the first day. I could not get any information from either of the four that was killed, as they were all dead.

The only information that I have been able to get is from an old negro man of Mr Kings who ran away from them the first day and came back home. he says that [they left] Sea Horse Key at the same time [that] boat did destined for Homasassa, but as yet they have not reached there. he also states that a Gun-boat had gone up the Suwanee River and as soon as it returned it was to come up the river.

Night before last my picket Guard heard several guns down the River in the direction of shell Island. it may be them, but I think if they go up either River their destiny will be as these has been. I am Captain Very Respectfully Your obt Sevt

—SAMUEL E. HOPE

XXIV.3

THE PROCLAMATION AND THE NEGRO ARMY

The issuing of the Emancipation Proclamation in the fall of 1862 provided for the receiving of freed slaves into the army as soldiers. Although the contribution of African-American soldiers proved to be critical to the outcome of the war, there was at the outset strong resistance from the North to let blacks bear arms. Abolitionists argued African-American soldiers had fought alongside whites during the American Revolution. Though a congressional act in 1792 later banned blacks from the army, many blacks served under Andrew Jackson during the War of 1812.

"Mark here our nation's degeneracy," Frederick Douglass roared in a February 1862 speech. "Colored men were good enough to fight under Washington. They are not good enough to fight under McClellan. They were good enough to fight under Andrew Jackson. They are not good enough to fight under General Halleck. They were good enough to help win American independence but they are not good enough to help preserve that independence against treason and rebellion. They were good enough to defend New Orleans but not good enough to defend our beleaguered Capital."

One reason for Lincoln's hesitancy was his concern about how the border states would react. Until the Emancipation Proclamation, the war had been to preserve the Union; freeing slaves was not a goal of the war. Lincoln feared that emancipat-

ing the slaves would encourage some states that had not left the Union to join the Confederacy. "To arm the negro would put 50,000 bayonets that are for us, against us," Lincoln said.

Racist doubts about the black man's ability to fight cast a shadow over the debate, as well. Northerners shared many of the beliefs of Southern slave owners regarding blacks. They questioned whether blacks could bear the burdens of war and doubted their courage in battle. Finally, there was concern that blacks in combat would lead to excessive violence on both sides. Black soldiers might seize the opportunity of battle to wreak revenge on white slave owners, and Southern white soldiers might violate the conventions of war when confronted with armed black men.

Nonetheless, Northern blacks and abolitionists pressed the issue. With the Emancipation Proclamation, blacks clamored to join the army and help liberate slaves—many of whom were their wives, children, friends, and family—from white ownership. Douglass, one of the most powerful voices for calling blacks into the service, delivered the following speech in New York City in February 1863. Soon afterward, two of his sons would join the Union army and survive the legendary assault on Ft. Wagner.

. . . Born and raised as a slave, as I was, and wearing on my back the marks of the slavedriver's lash, as I do, it is natural that I should value the Emancipation Proclamation for what it is destined to do for the slaves. I do value it for that. It is a mighty event for the bondman, but it is a still mightier event for the nation at large, and mighty as it is for both, the slave and the nation, it is still mightier when viewed in its relation to the cause of truth and justice throughout the world. It is in this last character that I prefer to consider it. . . .

It is again objected to this Proclamation that it is only an ink and paper proclamation. I admit. The objector might go a step further, and assert that there was a time when this Proclamation was only a thought, a sentiment, an idea—a hope of some radical Abolitionist—for such it truly was. But what of it? The world has never advanced a single inch in the right direction, when the movement could not be traced to some such small beginning. The bill abolishing Slavery, and giving freedom to eight hundred thousand people in the West Indies, was a paper bill. The act of Catholic Emancipation was a paper act; and so was the bill repealing the Corn Laws. Greater than all, our own Declaration of Independence was at one time but ink and paper. The freedom of the American colonies dates from one particular battle during the war. No man can tell upon what particular day we won our national independence. But the birth of our freedom is fixed on the day of the going forth of the Declaration of Independence. In like manner aftercoming generations will celebrate the first of January as the day which brought liberty and manhood to the American slaves. How shall this be done? I answer: That the paper Proclamation must now be made iron, lead and fire, by the prompt employment of the negro's arm in this contest. I hold that the Proclamation, good as it is, will be worthless—a miserable mockery—unless the nation shall so far conquer its prejudice as to welcome into the army full-grown black men to help fight the battles of the Republic. . . .

Do you ask me whether black men will freely enlist in the service of the country? I tell you that that depends upon the white men of the country. The Government must assure them of protection as soldiers, and give them a fair chance of winning distinction and glory in common with other soldiers. They must not be made the mere hewers of wood and drawers of water for the army. When a man leaves home, family, and security, to risk his limbs and life in the field of battle, for God's sake let him have all the honor which he may achieve, let his color be what it may. If, by the fortunes of war he is flung into the hands of the Rebels, let him be assured that the loyal Government will not desert him, but will hold the Confederate Government strictly responsible, as much for a black as for a white soldier. Give us fair play, and open here your recruiting offices, and their doors shall be crowded with black recruits to fight battles of the country. Do your part, my white fellow-countrymen, and we will do ours. . . . The colored man only waits for honorable admission into the service of the country. They know that who would be free, themselves must strike the blow, and they long for the opportunity to strike that blow. . . .

I know the colored men of the North; I know the colored men of the South. They are ready to rally under the stars and stripes at the first tap of the drum. Give them a chance; stop calling them "niggers," and call them soldiers. Give them a chance to seek the bubble reputation at the cannon's mouth. Stop telling them they can't fight, and tell them they can fight and shall fight, and they will fight, and fight with vengeance. Give them a chance. . . .

—Frederick Douglass

XXIV.4

Black Soldiers Serve Bravely

When Lincoln finally allowed African Americans to enlist in the army, black soldiers were eager to refute charges that they would not fight. At first, black soldiers were used solely in supporting roles and were kept out of combat. White commanders feared that if black units bolted, it might endanger other soldiers. But in the late spring and summer of 1863, African-American soldiers proved their doubters wrong in three bloody battles. On June 7, 1,500 Confederate soldiers attacked a smaller force of black and white federal troops at Milliken's Bend, Louisiana. The assault was repulsed in bitter hand-to-hand combat. "The bravery of the blacks at Milliken's Bend completely revolutionized the sentiment of the army with regard to the employment of Negro troops," one Union officer wrote. "I heard prominent officers who formerly had sneered . . . at the idea of Negroes fighting, express themselves after that, as heartily in favor of it."

Six weeks later, Colonel Robert Gould Shaw and his fellow white officers led their black troops of the 54th Massachusetts Volunteer Regiment in the doomed assault of Fort Wagner, South Carolina. All the officers save one were killed or wounded, and half the soldiers were killed, wounded, or captured. News accounts of the soldiers' bravery helped change public sentiment, sealing the government's commitment to enlisting black soldiers.

The first test of black soldiers' conduct in the face of enemy fire, however, took place at the siege of Port Hudson in May. A Union officer describes their bravery in a letter to the chief recruiter of black troops in southern Louisiana. Nothing changed white soldiers' prejudices against blacks as quickly as the experience of fighting alongside them. As General James S. Brisbin's report in 1864 shows, it was an experience repeated time after time throughout the war.

All told, 185,000 African Americans served in the Union army. About 35,000 came from the free states, 42,000 from the border states, and the rest were escaped slaves from the South. By the end of the war, Congress awarded 20 Medals of Honor to black soldiers. Blacks represented about one percent of the population of the North, but constituted almost 10 percent of the Union army. Casualty rates were much higher for black soldiers. More than 36,000 soldiers were killed or died from disease.

A. "Unequaled Coolness and Bravery"

Baton Rouge May 29th/1863

General.

[F]eeling deeply interested in the cause which you have espoused, I take the liberty to transmit the following, concerning the colored Troops engaged in the recent battles at Port Hudson.

I arrived here the evening of the 26th Inst, was mustered and reported to Maj. Tucker for duty—

During the night I heard heavy cannonadeing at Port Hudson. Early next morning I obtained permission and went to the front. But was so much detained, I did not reach our lines until the fighting for the day had nearly ceased—There being no renewal of the engagement the following day—I engaged in removing and administering to the wounded, gathering meantime as much information as possible concerning the battle and the conduct of our Troops. My anxiety was to learn all I could concerning the Bravery of the Colored Reg. engaged, for their good conduct and bravery would add to your undertakings and make more popular the movement. Not that I am afraid to meet unpopular doctrines, for I am not. But that we may show our full strength. The cause should be one of general sanction.

I have ever believed, from my idea of those traits of character which I deem necessary to make a good soldier, together with their history, that in them we should find those characteristics necessary, for an effective army. And I rejoice to learn, in the late engagements the fact is established beyond a doubt.

The following is (in substance) a statement personally made to me, by 1st Lt. Co. F. 1st R[egi-

ment]. La. Native Guard who was wounded during the engagement.

"We went into action about 6 A.M. and was under fire most of the time until sunset.

The very first thing after forming line of battle we were ordered to charge—My Co. was apparently brave. Yet they are mostly contrabands, and I must say I entertained some fears as to their pluck. But I have now none—The moment the order was given, they entered upon its execution. Valiantly did the heroic descendants of Africa move forward cool as if Marshaled for dress parade, under a most murderous fire from the enemies guns, until we reached the main ditch which surrounds the Fort. Finding it impassible we retreated under orders to the woods and deployed as skirmishers—In the charge we lost our Capt. and Colored sergeant, the latter fell wrapped in the flag he had so gallantly borne—Alone we held our position until 12 o'clock when we were relieved.

At two o'clock P.M. we were again ordered to the front where we made two separate charges each in the face of a heavy fire from the enemies Battery of seven guns—whose destructive fire would have confuse[d] and almost disorganized the bravest troops. But these men did not swerve, or show cowardice. I have been in several engagements, and I never before beheld such coolness and darring—

Their gallantry entitles them to a special praise. And I already observe, the sneers of others are being tempered into eulogy—"

It is pleasant to learn these things, and it must be indeed gratifying to the General to know that his army will be composed of men of almost unequaled coolness & bravery—

The men of our Reg. are very ready in learning the drills, and the officers have every confidence in their becoming excellent soldiers. . . .

—Elias D. Strunke

B. Silencing the "Jeers and Taunts"

Lexington Ky oct 20/64

General

I have the honor to forward herewith a report of the operations of a detachment of the 5th U.S.

Colored Cavalry during the late operations in Western Virginia against the Salt Works.

After the main body of the forces had moved, Gen'l Burbridge Comdg District was informed I had some mounted recruits belonging to the 5th U.S. Colored Cavalry, then organizing at Camp Nelson and he at once directed me to send them forward.

They were mounted on horses that had been only partly recruited and that had been drawn with the intention of using them only for the purpose of drilling. Six hundred of the best horses were picked out, mounted and Col Jas. F. Wade 6th. U.S.C. Cav'y was ordered to take command of the Detachment.

The Detachment came up with the main body at Prestonburg Ky and was assigned to the Brigade Commanded by Colonel R. W. Ratliff 12th O[hio]. V. Cav.

On the march the Colored Soldiers as well as their white Officers were made the subject of much ridicule and many insulting remarks by the White Troops and in some instances petty outrages such as the pulling off the Caps of Colored Soldiers, stealing their horses etc. was practiced by the White Soldiers. These insults as well as the jeers and taunts that they would not fight were borne by the Colored Soldiers patiently or punished with dignity by their Officers but in no instance did I hear Colored soldiers make any reply to insulting language used toward [them] by the White Troops.

On the 2d of October the forces reached the vicinity of the Salt Works and finding the enemy in force preparations were made for battle. Col Ratliffs Brigade was assigned to the left of the line and the Brigade dismounted was disposed as follows. 5th U.S.C. Cav. On the left. 12th [Ohio]. V.C. in the centre and the 11th Mich. Cav. On the right. The point to be attacked was the side of a high mountain, the Rebels being posted about half way up behind rifle pits made of logs and stones to the height of three feet. All being in readiness the Brigade moved to the attack. The Rebels opened upon them a terrible fire but the line pressed steadily forward up the steep side of the mountain until they found themselves within fifty yards of the Enemy. Here co. Wade ordered his force to charge and the Negroes rushed upon the works with a yell and after a desperate struggle carried the entire line killing and wounding a large number of the enemy and capturing some prisoners. There were four hundred black soldiers engaged in the battle, one hundred having been left behind sick and with broken down horses on the march, and one hundred having been left in the Valley to hold horses. Out of the four hundred engaged, one hundred and fourteen men and four officers fell killed or wounded. Of this fight I can only say that men could not have behaved more bravely. I have seen white troops fight in twenty-seven battles and I never saw any fight better. At dusk the Colored Troops were withdrawn from the enemies works, which they had held for over two hours, with scarcely a round of ammunition in their Cartridge Boxes.

On the return of the forces those who had scoffed at the Colored Troops on the march out were silent.

Nearly all the wounded were brought off though we had not an Ambulance in the command. The negro soldiers preferred present suffering to being murdered at the hands of the cruel enemy. I saw one man riding with his arm off another shot through the lungs and another shot through both hips.

Such of the Colored Soldiers as fell into the hands of the Enemy during the battle were brutally murdered. The negroes did not retaliate but treated the Rebel wounded with great kindness, carrying them water in their canteens and doing all they could to alleviate the sufferings of those whom the fortunes of war had placed in their hands.

Col. Wade handled his command with skill and bravery and good judgment, evincing his capacity to command a much larger force.
I am General Very Respectfully Your Obedt. Servant

—JAMES S. BRISBIN

XXIV.5

THOMAS WENTWORTH HIGGINSON CELEBRATES LIFE IN A BLACK REGIMENT

Colonel Higginson is one of the romantic figures of the war. A Massachusetts aristocrat, he had early thrown in his lot with the poor and the oppressed, had championed such causes as abolition and woman's rights, taken part in the attempted rescue of Anthony Burns, and gone to Kansas for the Emigrant Aid Society. A Unitarian clergyman in Worcester at the outbreak of the war, he had raised and drilled a company when he was offered the colonelcy of the first colored regiment—the famous 1st South Carolina. He joined his regiment at Beaufort, sailed with it to Florida, where he raided up the St. John's River and temporarily occupied Jacksonville. Bad health and a wound forced Higginson to resign his commission in '64 and return to the North.

After the war he had a long and distinguished career in literature, writing novels, short stories, critical essays, biographies of notable literary figures, and some charming reminiscences, *Cheerful Yesterdays*. It is no exaggeration to say that the best of all his many literary productions is this classic *Army Life in a Black Regiment*.

Camp Saxton, near Beaufort, S.C.,
November 27, 1862

Thanksgiving-Day; it is the first moment I have had for writing during these three days, which have installed me into a new mode of life so thoroughly that they seem three years. Scarcely pausing in New York or in Beaufort, there seems to have been for me but one step from the camp of a Massachusetts regiment to this, and that step over leagues of waves.

It is a holiday wherever General Saxton's proclamation reaches. The chilly sunshine and the pale blue river seem like New England, but those alone. The air is full of noisy drumming, and of gunshots; for the prize-shooting is our great celebration of the day, and the drumming is chronic. My young barbarians are all at play. I look out from the broken windows of this forlorn plantation house, through avenues of great live-oaks, with their hard, shining leaves, and their branches hung with a uni-

versal drapery of soft, long moss, like fringe-trees struck with grayness. Below, the sandy soil, scantly covered with coarse grass, bristles with sharp palmettos and aloes; all the vegetation is stiff, shining, semi tropical, with nothing soft or delicate in its texture. Numerous plantation-buildings totter around, all slovenly and unattractive, while the interspaces are filled with all manner of wreck and refuse, pigs, fowls, dogs, and omnipresent Ethiopian infancy. All this is the universal Southern panorama; but five minutes' walk beyond the hovels and the live-oaks will bring one to something so unSouthern that the whole Southern coast at this moment trembles at the suggestion of such a thing,—the camp of a regiment of freed slaves.

One adapts one's self so readily to new surroundings that already the full zest of the novelty seems passing away from my perceptions, and I write these lines in an eager effort to retain all I can. Already I am growing used to the experience, at first so novel, of living among five hundred men, and scarce a white face to be seen,—of seeing them go through all their daily processes, eating, frolicking, talking, just as if they were white. Each day at dress-parade I stand with the customary folding of the arms before a regimental line of countenances so black that I can hardly tell whether the men stand steadily or not; black is every hand which moves in ready cadences as I vociferate, "Battalion! Shoulder arms!" nor is it till the line of white officers moves forward, as parade is dismissed, that I am reminded that my own face is not the color of coal…

It needs but a few days to show the absurdity of distrusting the military availability of these people. They have quite as much average comprehension as whites of the need of the thing, as much courage (I doubt not), as much previous knowledge of the gun, and, above all, a readiness of ear and of imitation, which, for purposes of drill, counterbalances any defect of mental training. To learn the drill, one does not want a set of college professors; one wants a squad of eager, active, pliant school-boys; and the more childlike these pupils are the better. There is no trouble about the drill; they will surpass whites in that. As to camp-life, they have little to sacrifice; they are better fed, housed, and clothed than ever in their lives before, and they appear to have few inconvenient vices. They are simple, docile, and affectionate almost to the point of absurdity. The same men who stood fire in open field with perfect coolness, on the late expedition, have come to me blubbering in the most irresistibly ludicrous manner on being transferred from one company in the regiment to another.

In noticing the squad-drills I perceive that the men learn less laboriously than whites that "double, double, toil and trouble," which is the elementary vexation of the drill-master,—that they more rarely mistake their left for their right,—and are more grave and sedate while under instruction. The extremes of jollity and sobriety, being greater with them, are less liable to be intermingled; these companies can be driven with a looser rein than my former one, for they restrain themselves; but the moment they are dismissed from drill every tongue is relaxed and every ivory tooth visible. This morning I wandered about where the different companies were target-shooting, and their glee was contagious. Such exulting shouts of "Ki! ole man," when some steady old turkey-shooter brought his gun down for an instant's aim, and then unerringly hit the mark; and then, when some unwary youth fired his piece into the ground at half-cock, such infinite guffawing and delight, such rolling over and over on the grass, such dances of ecstasy, as made the "Ethiopian minstrelsy" of the stage appear a feeble imitation.

December 3, 1862—7 P.M.

What a life is this I lead! It is a dark, mild, drizzling evening, and as the foggy air breeds sand-flies, so it calls out melodies and strange antics from this mysterious race of grown-up children with whom my lot is cast. All over the camp the lights glimmer in the tents, and as I sit at my desk in the open doorway, there come mingled sounds of stir and glee. Boys laugh and shout,—a feeble flute stirs somewhere in some tent, not an officer's—a drum throbs far away

in another,—wild kildeer-plover flit and wail above us, like the haunting souls of dead slave-masters,—and from a neighboring cook-fire comes the monotonous sound of that strange festival, half pow-wow, half prayer-meeting, which they know only as a "shout." These fires are usually enclosed in a little booth, made neatly of palm-leaves and covered in at top, a regular native African hut, in short, such as is pictured in books, and such as I once got up from dried palm leaves for a fair at home.

This hut is now crammed with men, singing at the top of their voices, in one of their quaint, monotonous, endless, Negro-Methodist chants, with obscure syllables recurring constantly, and slight variations interwoven, all accompanied with a regular drumming of the feet and clapping of the hands, like castanets. Then the excitement spreads: inside and outside the enclosure men begin to quiver and dance, others join, a circle forms; some "heel and toe" tumultuously, others merely tremble and stagger on, others stoop and rise, others whirl, others caper sideways, all keep steadily circling like dervishes; spectators applaud special strokes of skill; my approach only enlivens the scene; the circle enlarges, louder grows the singing, rousing shouts of encouragement come in, half bacchanalian, half devout, "Wake 'em, brudder!" "Stan' up to 'em, brudder!"—and still the ceaseless drumming and clapping, in perfect cadence, goes steadily on. Suddenly there comes a sort of snap, and the spell breaks, amid general singing and laughter. And this not rarely and occasionally, but night after night, while in other parts of the camp the soberest prayers and exhortations are proceeding sedately.

A simple and lovable people, whose graces seem to come by nature, and whose vices by training. Some of the best superintendents confirm the first tales of innocence, and Dr. Zachos told me last night that on his plantation, a sequestered one, "they had absolutely no vices." Nor have these men of mine yet shown any worth mentioning; since I took command I have heard of no man intoxicated, and there has been but one small quarrel. I suppose that scarcely a white regiment in the army shows so little swearing. . . . If camp regulations are violated, it seems to be usually through heedlessness. They love passionately three things besides their spiritual incantations; namely, sugar, home, and tobacco. This last affection brings tears to their eyes, almost, when they speak of their urgent need of pay; they speak of their last-remembered quid as if it were some deceased relative, too early lost, and to be mourned forever. As for sugar, no white man can drink coffee after they have sweetened it to their liking.

I see that the pride which military life creates may cause the plantation trickeries to diminish. For instance, these men make the most admirable sentinels. It is far harder to pass the camp lines at night than in the camp from which I came; and I have seen none of that disposition to connive at the offences of members of one's own company which is so troublesome among white soldiers. Nor are they lazy, either about work or drill; in all respects they seem better material for soldiers than I had dared to hope.

December 5, 1862

This evening, after working themselves up to the highest pitch, a party suddenly rushed off, got a barrel, and mounted some man upon it, who said, "Gib anoder song, boys, and I'se gib you a speech." After some hesitation and sundry shouts of "Rise de sing, somebody," and "Stan' up for Jesus, brudder," irreverently put in by the juveniles, they got upon the John Brown song, always a favorite, adding a jubilant verse which I had never before heard,— "We'll beat Beauregard on de clare battle-field." Then came the promised speech, and then no less than seven other speeches by as many men, on a variety of barrels, each orator being affectionately tugged to the pedestal and set on end by his special constituency. Every speech was good, without exception; with the queerest oddities of phrase and pronunciation, there was an invariable enthusiasm, a pungency of statement, and an understanding of the points at issue, which made them all rather thrilling. . . .

The most eloquent, perhaps, was Corporal Prince Lambkin, just arrived from Fernandina, who evidently had a previous reputation among them. His historical references were very interesting. He reminded them that he had predicted this war ever since Fremont's time, to which some of the crowd assented; he gave a very intelligent account of that Presidential campaign, and then described most impressively the secret anxiety of the slaves in Florida to know all about President Lincoln's election, and told how they all refused to work on the fourth of March, expecting their freedom to date from that day. He finally brought out one of the few really impressive appeals for the American flag that I have ever heard.

January 1, 1863 (evening)

A happy New Year to civilized people,—mere white folks. Our festival has come and gone, with perfect success, and our good General has been altogether satisfied. Last night the great fires were kept smouldering in the pit, and the beeves were cooked more or less, chiefly more,—during which time they had to be carefully watched, and the great spits turned by main force. Happy were the merry fellows who were permitted to sit up all night, and watch the glimmering flames that threw a thousand fantastic shadows among the great gnarled oaks. And such a chattering as I was sure to hear whenever I awoke that nightl

My first greeting to-day was from one of the most stylish sergeants, who approached me with the following little speech, evidently the result of some elaboration:—

"I tink myself happy, dis New Year's Day, for salute my own Cunnel. Dis day las' year I was servant to a Cunnel ob Secesh; but now I hab de privilege for salute my own Cunnel."

That officer, with the utmost sincerity, reciprocated the sentiment.

About ten o'clock the people began to collect by land, and also by water,—in steamers sent by General Saxton for the purpose; and from that time all the avenues of approach were thronged. The multitude were chiefly colored women, with gay handkerchiefs on their heads, and a sprinkling of men, with that peculiarly respectable look which these people always have on Sundays and holidays. There were many white visitors also,—ladies on horseback, and in carriages, superintendents and teachers, officers, and cavalry-men. Our companies were marched to the neighborhood of the platform, and allowed to sit or stand, as at the Sunday services; the platform was occupied by ladies and dignitaries, and by the band of the Eighth Maine, which kindly volunteered for the occasion; the colored people filled up all the vacant openings in the beautiful grove around, and there was a cordon of mounted visitors beyond. Above, the great live oak branches and their trailing moss; beyond the people, a glimpse of the blue river.

The services began at halfpast eleven o'clock, with prayer by our chaplain, Mr. Fowler, who is always, on such occasions, simple, reverential, and impressive. Then the President's Proclamation was read by Dr. W. H. Brisbane, a thing infinitely appropriate; a South Carolinian addressing South Carolinians; for he was reared among these very islands, and here long since emancipated his own slaves. Then the colors were presented to us by the Rev. Mr. French, a chaplain who brought them from the donors in New York. All this was according to the programme. Then followed an incident so simple, so touching, so utterly unexpected and startling, that I can scarcely believe it on recalling, though it gave the key-note to the whole day. The very moment the speaker had ceased, and just as I took and waved the flag, which now for the first time meant anything to these poor people, there suddenly arose, close beside the platform, a strong male voice (but rather cracked and elderly), into which two women's voices instantly blended, singing, as if by an impulse that could no more be repressed than the morning note of the song-sparrow.—

"My Country, 'tis of thee,
Sweet land of liberty,
Of thee I sing!"

People looked at each other, and then at us on the plat form, to see whence came this interruption, not set down in the bills. Firmly and irrepressibly the quavering voices sang on, verse after verse; others of the colored people joined in; some whites on the platform began, but I motioned them to silence. I never saw anything so electric; it made all other words cheap; it seemed the choked voice of a race at last unloosed. Nothing could be more wonderfully unconscious; art could not have dreamed of a tribute to the day of jubilee that should be so affecting; history will not believe it; and when I came to speak of it, after it was ended, tears were everywhere. If you could have heard how quaint and innocent it was! Old Tiff and his children might have sung it; and close before me was a little slave-boy, almost white, who seemed to belong to the party, and even he must join in. Just think of it!—the first day they had ever had a country, the first flag they had ever seen which promised anything to their people, and here, while mere spectators stood in silence, waiting for my stupid words, these simple souls burst out in their lay, as if they were by their own hearths at home! When they stopped, there was nothing to do for it but to speak, and I went on; but the life of the whole day was in those unknown people's song.

—HIGGINSON, *Army Life in a Black Regiment*

XXIV.6

STANDING UP FOR THE RIGHTS OF BLACK SOLDIERS

Despite the success of black soldiers in the Union army, they still faced tremendous discrimination. Black regiments were commanded by white officers. Black soldiers were disciplined much more severely than white soldiers. Black military units were frequently given the least desirable assignments. One reason why African Americans suffered a higher casualty rate than whites was because they were often sent to fight in swamps and tropical conditions under the mistaken belief they would be less susceptible to diseases there. Often white doctors were reluctant to treat black soldiers.

But the experience of battle emboldened African Americans. They would no longer simply submit to lesser treatment.

One of the most galling inequities was the pay differential between black and white soldiers. Whites received thirteen dollars a month plus a clothing allowance, while black soldiers only earned ten dollars. Corporal James Henry Gooding, of New Bedford, Massachusetts, served with the 54th Massachusetts Regiment. A free black man prior to the war, he wrote a column for his hometown newspaper, *The New Bedford Mercury*, throughout his time of service. After the Battle of Fort Wagner, he wrote a letter to Abraham Lincoln asking that he and his fellow black soldiers receive equal pay. Five months later, Gooding was killed in action at the Battle of Olustee Station in Florida. Captain James W. Grace wrote a letter to *The New Bedford Mercury* informing Gooding's editors of his death, and of the resolution on the issue of pay for black soldiers.

Similarly, Hannah Johnson wrote Abraham Lincoln from Buffalo, New York, demanding that her son and his fellow black soldiers be given equal treatment, and imploring the president to insist that captured black soldiers be treated as prisoners of war and not runaway slaves. Unknown to Johnson, Lincoln had already pledged to retaliate against Confederate prisoners for the mistreatment of black prisoners of war. In other instances, black soldiers were simply taken advantage of by unscrupulous white officers, as reflected in the petition written by soldiers at the end of the war.

A. "Are We Soldiers, or Are We Labourors?"

Camp of the 54th Massachusetts colored regt.,
Morris Island.
Dept. Of the South. Sept. 28th, 1863.

Your Excellency, Abraham Lincoln:

Your Excellency will pardon the presumption of an humble individual like myself, in addressing you, but the earnest Solicitation of my comrades in Arms beside the genuine interest felt by myself in the matter is my excuse, for placing before the Executive head of the Nation our Common Grievance.

On the 6th day of the last Month, the Paymaster of the department informed us, that if we would decide to receive the sum of $10 per month, he would come and pay us that sum, but that, on the sitting of Congress, the Regt., would, in his opinion, be allowed the other three. He did not give us any guarantee that this would be, as he hoped; certainly he had no authority for making any such guarantee, and we cannot suppose him acting in any way interested.

Now the main question is, Are we Soldiers, or are we Labourers? We are fully armed and equipped, have done all the various Duties pertaining to a Soldier's life, have conducted ourselves to the complete satisfaction of General Officers, who were, if any[thing], prejudiced against us, but who now accord us all the encouragement and honour due us; have shared the perils and Labour of Reducing the first stronghold that flaunted a Traitor Flag; and more, Mr. President. Today the Anglo-Saxon Mother, Wife, or Sister are not alone in tears for departed Sons, Husbands and Brothers. The patient, trusting Descendants of Africa's Clime have dyed the ground with blood, in defense of the Union, and Democracy. Men, too, your Excellency, who know in a measure the cruelties of the Iron heel of oppression, which in years gone by, the very Power their blood is now being spilled to maintain, ever ground them to the dust.

But When the war trumpet sounded o'er the land, when men knew not the Friend from the Traitor, the Black man laid his life at the Altar of the Nation,—and he was refused. When the arms of the Union were beaten, in the first year of the War, and the Executive called [for] more food for its ravaging maw, again the black man begged the privilege of aiding his country in her need, to be again refused.

And now he is in the War, and how has he conducted himself? Let their dusky forms rise up, out [of] the mires of James Island, and give the answer. Let the rich mould around Wagner's parapets be upturned, and there will be found an Eloquent answer. Obedient and patient and Solid as a wall are they. All we lack is a paler hue and a better acquaintance with the Alphabet.

Now your Excellency, we have done a Soldier's Duty. Why Can't we have a Solider's pay? You caution the Rebel Chieftain, that the United States knows no distinction in her Soldiers. She insists on having all her Soldiers of whatever creed or Color, to be treated according to the usages of War. Now if the United States exacts uniformity of treatment of her Soldiers from the Insurgents, would it not be well and consistent to set the example herself by paying all her Soldiers alike?

We of this Regt. were not enlisted under any "contraband" act. But we do not wish to be understood as rating our Service of more Value to the Government than the service of the ex-slave. Their Service is undoubtedly worth much to the Nation, but Congress made express provision touching their case, as slaves freed by military necessity, and assuming the Government to be their temporary Guardian. Not so with us. Freemen by birth and consequently having the advantage of thinking and acting for ourselves so far as the laws would allow us, we do not consider ourselves fit subject for the Contraband act.

We appeal to you, Sir, as the Executive of the Nation, to have us justly Dealt with. The Regt. do pray that they be assured their service will be fairly appreciated by paying them as American Soldiers, not as menial hirelings. Black men, you may well know, are poor; three dollars per month for a year will supply their needy Wives and little ones with fuel. If you, as Chief magistrate of the Nation, will assure us of our whole pay, we are content. Our Patriotism, our enthusiasm will have a new impetus, to exert our energy more and more to aid our Country. Not that our hearts ever flagged in Devotion, spite the evident apathy displayed in our behalf, but We feel as though our Country spurned us, now that we are sworn to serve her. Please give this a moment's at'ention.

—James Henry Gooding

Jacksonville, Fla., Feb. 25, 1864

Messrs. Editors:

I am pained to inform you that Corporal James H. Gooding was killed in battle on the 20th inst. at Olustee Station. He was one of the Color Corporals and was with the colors at the time. So great was the rout of our troops that we left nearly all our dead and wounded on the field. The fight lasted four hours. We were badly beaten that night, and the next day we kept falling back, until we reached Jacksonville. The fifty-fourth did honor to themselves and our city. All concede that no regiment fought like it.

James H. Buchanan, of New Bedford, was killed; and Sergeant Wharton A. Williams, also of our city, was wounded in the hand. Many others of Co. C were wounded, but none of them from our city.

The regiment is pleased to learn that the bill to pay them $13 per month passed.

The total loss of the regiment, I am unable to give you at this time. All we want now is more troops; with them we would go forward again and drive the rebels from the State.

Your friend

—James W. Grace

B. Hannah Johnson to Abraham Lincoln

Buffalo July 31 1863

Excellent Sir

My good friend says I must write to you and she will send it My son went in the 54th regiment. I am a colored woman and my son was strong and able as any to fight for his country and the colored people have as much to fight for as any. My father was a Slave and escaped from Louisiana before I was born morn forty years agone I have but poor education but I never went to schol, but I know just as well as any what is right between man and man. Now I know it is right that a colored man should go and fight for his country, and so ought a white man. I know that a colored man ought to run no greater risques than a white, his pay is no greater his obligation to fight is the same. So why should not our enemies be compelled to treat him the same, Made to do it.

My son fought at Fort Wagoner but thank God he was not taken prisoner, as many were I thought of this thing before I let my boy go but then they said Mr. Lincoln will never let them sell our coulored soldiers for slave, if they do he will get them back quck he will rettallyate and stop it. Now Mr. Lincoln dont you think you oght to stop this thing and make them do the same by the colored man they have lived in idleness all their lives on stolen labor and made savages of the colored people, but they now are so furious because they are proving themselves to be men, such as have come away and got some edication. It must not be so. You must put the rebels back to work in State prisons to making shoes and things, if they sell our colored soldiers, till they let them all go. And give their wounded the same treatment. It would seem cruel, but their no other way, and a just man must do hard things sometimes, that shew him to be a great man. They tell me some do you will take back the Proclamation, don't do it. When you are dead and in Heaven, in a thousand years that action of yours will make the Angels sing your praises I know it. Ought one man to own another, law for or not, who made the law, surely the poor slave did not. So it is wicked, and a horrible Outrage, there is no sense in it, because a man has lived by robbing all his life and his father before him, should he complain because the stolen things are found on him are taken. Robbing the colored people of their labor is but a small part of the robbery their souls are almost taken, they are made bruits of often. You know all about this

Will you see that the colored men fighting now, are fairly treated. You ought to do this, and do it at once, Not let the thing run along meet it quickly and manfully, and stop this, mean cowardly cruelty. We poor oppressed ones, appeal to you, and ask fair play.

Yours for Christs sake

—HANNAH JOHNSON.

C. Black Regiment Petitions Government for Redress

Genl:

We the soldiers of the 36 U.S. Col[ored] Regt Humbly petition to you to alter the Affairs at Roanoke Island. We have served in the US Army faithfully and don our duty to our Country, for which we thank God (that we had the opportunity) but at the same time our family's are suffering at Roanoke Island N.C.

1 When we were enlisted in the service we were prommised that our wifes and family's should receive rations from goverment. The rations for our wifes and family's have been (and are now cut down) to one half the regular ration. Consequently three or four days out of every ten days, they have nothing to eat. at the same time our ration's are

stolen from the ration house by Mr Streeter the Asst Supt at the Island (and others) and sold while our family's are suffering from some thing to eat.

2nd Mr. Steeter the Asst Supt of Negroe aff's at Roanoke Island is a througher [Copperhead] a man who says that he is no part of a Abolitionist. takes no care of the colored people and has no Simpathy with the colored people. A man who kicks our wives and children out of the ration house or commissary, he takes no notice of their actual suffering and sells the rations and allows it to be sold, and our family's suffer for something to eat.

3rd Captn James the Suptn in Charge has been told of these facts and has taken no notice of them. so has Coln Lahaman the Commander in Charge of Roanoke, but no notice is taken of it, because it comes from Contrabands or Freedmen the cause of much suffering is that Captn James has not paid the Colored people for their work for near a year and at the same time cuts the ration's off to one half so the people have neither provisions or money to buy it with. There are men on the Island that have been wounded at Dutch Gap Canal, working there, and some discharged soldiers, men that were wounded in the service of the U.S. Army, and returned home to Roanoke that Cannot get any rations and are not able to work, some soldiers are sick in Hospitals that have never been paid a cent and their familys are suffering and their children going crying without anything to eat.

4th our familys have no protection the white soldiers break into our houses act as they please stell our chickens rob our gardens and if any one defends their-Selves against them they are taken to the gard house for it. so our familys have no protection when Mr Streeter is here to protect them and will not do it.

5th Genl we the soldiers of the 36 U.S. Co Troops having familys at Roanoke Island humbly petition you to favor us by removeing Mr Street the present Asst Supt at roanoke Island under Capt James.

Genl perhaps you think the Statements against Mr. Street too strong, but we can prove them.

Genl order Chaplain Green to Washington to report the true state of things at Roanoke Island. Chaplain green is an asst Supt at Roanoke Island, with Mr. Holland Streeter and he can prove the facts. and there are plenty of white men here that can prove them also, and many more thing's not mentioned Signed on behalf of humanity

—RICHARD ETHEREDGE AND WM. BENSON

XXIV·7

HARDSHIPS OF AN UNEQUAL FREEDOM

Freedom was not a panacea. Economically dependent upon whites, and with no legal rights, blacks were frequently at the mercy of abusive whites from both the North and the South. In the worst instances they were robbed, beaten, raped, even killed at the hands of their supposed liberators. The two letters that follow were written by white Union officers petitioning authorities on behalf of abused blacks.

A. Contrabands Experience Hardships

Helena Arkansas Dec 29th 1862

General

The undersigned Chaplains and Surgeons of the army of the Eastern district of Arkansas would respectfully call your attention to the Statements & Suggestions following

The Contrabands within our lines are experiencing hardships oppression & neglect the removal of which calls loudly for the intervention of authority. We daily see & deplore the evil and leave it to your wisdom to devise a remedy. In a great degree the contrabands are left entirely to the mercy and rapacity of the unprincipled part of our army (excepting only the limited jurisdiction of cat. Richmond) with no person clothed with Specific authority to look after & protect them. Among their list of grievances we mention these:

Some who have been paid by individuals for cotton or for labor have been waylaid by soldiers, robbed, and in several instances fired upon, as well as robbed, and in no case that we can now recal have the plunderers been brought to justice—

The wives of some have been molested by soldiers to gratify their licentious lust, and their husbands murdered in endeavoring to defend them, and yet the guilty parties, though known, were not arrested. Some who have wives and families are required to work in the Fortifications, or to unload Government Stores, and receive only their meals at the Public table, while their families, whatever provision intended for them, are, as a matter of fact, left in helpless & starving condition.

Many of the contrabands have been employed, & received in numerous instances, from officers & privates, only counterfeit money or nothing at all for their services. One man was employed as a teamster by the Government & he died in the service (the government indebted to him nearly fifty dollars) leaving an orphan child eight years old, & there is no apparent provision made to draw the money, or to care for the orphan child. The negro hospital here has become notorious for filth, neglect, mortality & brutal whipping, so that the contrabands have lost all hope of kind treatment there, & would almost as soon go to their graves as to their hospital. These grievances reported to us by persons in whom we have confidence, & some of which we know to be true, are but a few of the many wrongs of which they complain—for the sake of humanity, for the sake of christianity, for the good name of our army, for the honor of our country, cannot something be done to prevent this oppression & to stop its demoralizing influences upon the Soldiers themselves? Some have suggested that the matter be laid before the [War] Department at Washington, in the hope that they will clothe an agent with authority, to register all the names of the contrabands, who will have a benevolent regard for their welfare, though whom all details of fatigue & working parties shall be made though whom rations may be drawn & money paid, & who shall be empowered to organize schools, & to make all needfull Regulations for the comfort and improvement of the condition of the contrabands; whose accounts shall be open at all times for inspection, and who shall make stated reports to the Department—All which is respectfully submitted

—Committee, Samuel Sawyer, Pearl P. Ingall, J. G. Forman

B. "A Sense of Disgust Must be Awakened"

Fort Leavenworth, Mar. 13, 1864

General

A negro "Sam Marshall" who resides in Leavenworth, reports to me that yesterday he went over to Platte City Missouri, to get his children, who he was told would be allowed to come away free. The children were at a Mr Greens. Sam went in day light, with a team, driven by a white man, and made no demonstration of insolance or disrespect to any body. He was arrested by the Military, Commanded by one Captain David Johnson of the Mo Militia, who talked to him about the impropriety of his conduct. The Sheriff one Jesse Morris also lectured him, and told him the Captain would send a guard to take him away, as it was a wonder he was not killed. About a dozen of the soldiers did escort him about half a mile out of Platte City, where they tied him to a tree, and stripping him to the waste lacerated his back with a cow skin the marks of which Sam will carry to his grave. They told him they were "introducing him to the Pawpaw Militia" and that if Col Jennison would come to Platte City, they would treat him in the same way.

The Militia were dressed in Federal uniform, and armed with revolvers

Two of them Sam knew. They are young— "Chinn", and a young "Cockeril".

Sam is a quiet well behaved negro, whose tears and sorely lacerated back, seem to attest the truth of his statement.

The white man that drove the wagon, was arrested, but had sufficient influence (as formerly a citizen of the County) to get off without being harmed.

I call your attention to the use made of Federal troops, or troops clothed, fed, and foraged if not paid by the Federal Government.

I most respectfully suggest General, that on both sides, it is far better that troops unconnected with old border difficulties, and negro katching and negro whipping, should be substituted by such miserable wretches as those who disgrace their uniforms, and humanity, by acts of cruelty and baseness.

I hope General you will not suppose I hold you accountable for such transactions in a Command to which you have so recently been assigned; but I know a Sense of duty and disgust must be awakened by any loyal citizen acquainted with such brutality, and I report Such matters to you, for early correction.

They called "Sam" a Jayhawker, and pretended that he had run off horses; but all this was no doubt a mere subterfuge; as probably the only real offense "Sam" has been guilty of, was to run himself off, with a son who has entered the Federal Army.

Platte City, is only about 6 miles from my lines and Such treatment of men from here going into that place, is well Calculated to induce fierce resentments from this Side, which of course I shall restrain; Conscious of your own desire to correct such outrages. I remain General Very Respectfully Yours

—S. R. Curtis

XXIV.8

The Fate of the Black Soldier—And Those Left Behind

The emotional highs and lows experienced by runaway slaves entering the Union army are almost impossible for the contemporary reader to imagine—from the hopes of what freedom might bring, to anxiety over the uncertainty of what harm may come to those left behind. The three documents that follow offer anecdotal hints of their experience.

Spotswood Rice was a Union soldier in Missouri. In the fall of 1864 his military unit was about to invade the area where he formerly lived as a slave and where his family and master remained. Unable to contain his emotions, Rice wrote one letter to his children exulting in being able to help bring them freedom, and a second letter to his former master seething with vengeance.

Martha Glover wrote to her soldier-husband, a former slave, about the troubles that had befallen her and her family in Missouri since his departure. Like many slave owners, Glover's master grew increasingly bitter as his slaves fled and took it out on those who remained. Shortly after writing this letter, Glover's master tried unsuccessfully to take her and three of her children to Kentucky to avoid having them emancipated.

Despite the indignities and atrocities committed by Confederate soldiers and white masters, former slaves rarely acted out their vengeance through violence. One unusual instance of blacks realizing revenge on former owners comes from a description by a white abolitionist officer, General Edward A. Wild, who seized a prominent slave owner. He seems almost disappointed in the lack of enthusiasm by the former slaves to apply the lash against their former owner. Wild was court-martialed for his action.

A. "The Whole Government Gives Cheer to Me"

[Benton Barracks Hospital, St. Louis, Mo., September 3, 1864]

My Children

I take my pen in hand to rite you A few lines to let you know that I have not forgot you and that I want to see you as bad as ever now my Dear Children I want you to be contented with whatever may be your lots be assured that I will have you if it cost me my life on the 28th of the mounth, 8 hundred White and 8 hundred black solders expects to start up the rivore to Glasgow and above there thats to be jeneraled by a jeneral that will give me both of you when they Come I expect to be with, them and expect to get you both in return. Dont be uneasy children I expect to have you. If Diggs dont give up this Government will and I feel confident that I will get you Your Miss Kaitty said that I tried to steal you But I'll let her know that god never intended for man to steal his own flesh and blood. If I had no confidence in God I could have confidence in her. But as it is If I ever had any Confidence in her I have none now and never expect to have And I want her to remember if she meets me with ten thousand soldiers she [will] meet her enemy I once [thought] that I had some respect for them but new my respects is worn out and have no sympathy for Slaveholders. And as for her cristianitty I expect the Devil has Such in hell You tell her from me that She is the first Christian that I ever hard say that man could Steal his own child especially out of human bondage

You can tell her that She can hold to you as long as she can I never would expect to ask her again to let you come to me because I know that the devil has got her hot set againsts that that is write now my Dear children I am a going to close my letter to you Give my love to all enquiring friends tell them all that we are well and want to see them very much and Corra and Mary receive the greater part of it you sefves and dont think hard of us not sending you any thing I you father have a plenty for you when I see you Spott & Noah sends their love to both of you Oh! My Dear children how I do want to see you.

—Spotswood Rice

I received a letter from Caroline telling me that you say I tried to steal to plunder my child away from you now I want you to understand that mary is my Child and she is a God given rite of my own and you may hold on to hear as long as you can but I want you to remember this one thing that the longer you keep my Child from me the longer you will have to burn in hell and the qwicer youll get their for we are now makeing up a bout one thoughsand blacke troops to Come up tharough and want to come through Glasgow and when we come wo be to Copperhood rabbels and to the Slaveholding rebbels for we dont expect to leave them there root neor branch but we thinke how ever that we that have Children in the hands of you devels we will trie your [virtues] the day that we enter Glasgow I want you to understand ktty diggs that where ever you and I meets we are enmays to each orthere I offered once to pay you forty dollars for my own Child but I am glad now that you did not accept it Just hold on now as long as you can and the worse it will be for you you never in your life befor I came down hear did you give Children any thing not eny thing whatever not even a dollers worth of expencs now you call my children your pro[per]ty not so with me my Children is my own and I expect to get them and when I get ready to come after mary I will have bout a powrer and autherity to bring hear away and to exacute vengencens on them that holds my Child you will then know how to talke to me I will assure you that and you will know how to talk rite too I want you now to just hold on to hear if you want to iff your conchosence tells thats the road go that road and what it will brig you to kittey diggs I have no fears about getting mary out of your hands this whole Government gives chear to me and you cannot help your self

—Spotswood Rice

B. "I Am in Too Much Trouble"

Mexico Mo Dec 30th 1863

My Dear Husband

I have received your last kind letter a few days ago and was much please to hear from you once more. It seems like a long time since you left me. I have had nothing but trouble since you left. You recollect what I told you how they would do after you was gone. they abuse me because you went & say they will not take care of our children & do nothing but quarrel with me all the time and beat me scandalously the day before yester-day—Oh I never thought you would give me so much trouble as I have got to bear now. You ought not to left me in the fix I am in & all these little helpless children to take care of. I was invited to a party to night but I could not go I am in too much trouble to want to go to parties. the children talk about you all the time. I wish you could get a fur-lough & come to see us once more. We want to see you worse than we ever did before. Remember all I told you about how they would me after you left—for they do worse than they ever did & I do not know what will become of me & my poor lit-tle children. Oh I wish you had staid with me & not gone till I could go with for I do nothing but grieve all the time about you. write & tell me

when you are coming.

Tell Isaac that his mother come & got his clothes she was so sorry he went. You need not tell me to beg any more married men to go. I see too much trouble to try to get any more into trouble too—Write to me & do not forget me & my children—farewell my dear husband from your wife

—Martha Glover

C. "I Wish That His Back Had Been as Deeply Scarred"

Wilson's Wharf, James River

May 12th [18]64

Sir—

On Tuesday May 10th William H. Clopton, was brought in by the Pickets. He had been active-ly disloyal so that I held him as Prisoner of War, and have sent him as such to Fortress Monroe. He has acquired a notoriety as the most cruel Slave Master in this region, but in my presence he put on the character of a Snivelling Saint. I found half a dozen *women* among our refugees, whome he had often whipped unmercifully, even baring their whole persons for the purpose in presence of Whites and Blacks. I laid him bare and putting the whip into the hands of the Women, three of Whom took turns in settling some old scores on their masters back. A black Man, whom he had abused finished the administration of Poetical jus-tice, and even in this scene the superior humanity of the Blacks over their white master was manifest in their moderation and backwardness. I wish that his back had been as deeply scarred as those of the women, but I abstained and left it to them—I wish it to be distinctly understood by Brig. Genl. Hinks that I shall do the same thing again under similar circumstances. I forgot to state that this Clopton is a high minded Virginia Gentleman, living for many years next door to the late John Tyler, ExPresident of the U.S. and then and still intimate with his family.

—General Edward A. Wild

XXIV.9

"IF WE ARE REGARDED AS EVIL HERE"

In April 1862, Lincoln signed a new law freeing slaves in Washington, D. C. The law designated $100,000 "to aid in the colonization and settlement" of freed African Americans to "Hayti, Liberia, or any such country beyond the limits of the United States." No clear plan had emerged over what to do with emancipated slaves. Lincoln and the vast majority of whites did not view African Americans as equals and were at a loss over what role freed slaves would play in society.

Many African Americans were keenly aware of this problem. Several schemes emerged to create new colonies abroad. Hundreds emigrated to Haiti after the war broke out. In April 1862 40 of the leading African-American citizens in Washington, D.C., wrote the following petition to Congress seeking financial assistance to colonize land in Central America. Three months later, the Second Confiscation Act appropriated another $600,000 for colonization, an option that Lincoln actively sought as a way to avoid race violence.

To the Honorable the Senate and House of Representatives of the United States of America, in Congress assembled:

The undersigned, for themselves, their relatives, and friends, whom they represent; desire, by this memorial, most respectfully to show to the Congress and people of this great country—of which, too, they are natives, but humbly born—that they appreciate, to the fullest extent, the humane actions which are now inaugurated to give freedom to their so long oppressed colored race; but they believe that this freedom will result injuriously, unless there shall be opened to the colored people a region, to which they may immigrate—a country which is suited to their organization, and in which they may seek and secure, by their own industry, that mental and physical development which will allow them an honorable position in the families of God's great world.

That there is ignorance in the mass of the colored race, is not to be denied: this is caused by the peculiar condition in which they have been raised—without the advantages of general educa-

tion so wisely and freely accorded to the white citizens. But there are those amongst them who have secured the blessings of knowledge, and who are capable of informing their brethren of what is for their ultimate good, as the leaders of the Pilgrim Fathers informed those who came with them to plant civil and religious liberty upon this continent.

To these we are indebted for the knowledge that Liberia is too distant from the land of our birth, and that however kindly and wisely the original plans of colonization may have been laid for that country, neither those plans, nor that region, are suited to our present condition, and that it will be impossible for us ever to move there in sufficient numbers to secure for us the full liberties of the human race, the elements of which we have learned here.

From there, too, we have learned the deep degradation and wretchedness in which our relatives were sunk, who were induced by heartless speculators to immigrate to Hayti. Slavery, if it must be borne, is more endurable under a race we have long been taught to look up to and regard as superior, than under one originated in Africa, degraded by abject slavery under Spanish and French greed, and still further brutalized by unrestrained and licentious liberty, such as exists with those who hold the power to control the poor immigrant in Hayti, or either of the Afro-West India Islands.

Of our own will, we cannot go either to Liberia or these islands. We have, in the United States, been taught to venerate virtue, to strive to attain it, and we can, with humble pride, point to as wide spread examples of the benefit of these teachings, as can any similar number of men, with no greater advantages than ourselves. Therefore we wish to shun those countries where the opposite of virtue rules, where vice reigns supreme, where our very blood would be required if we opposed its indulgence.

Though colored, and debarred from rights of citizenship, our hearts none the less, cling to the land of our birth. We do not wish to be driven beyond the Ocean, where old hands of kindness cannot reach us, where we cannot hear from those with whom we have grown up, with all the fond remembrances of childhood.

We now number as many souls as won the freedom of your sires from British rule. We may not now be as capable to govern ourselves as they were, but we will, with your aid, be as zealous, and with God's blessing, we will be as successful.

There is a land—part of this your own continent—to which we wish to go. It is that portion generally called Central America. There are land there without inhabitants, yet bearing spontaneously all that is suited to our race.

Aid us to get there—protect us for a short while, and we will prove ourselves worthy and grateful. The labor, which, in servitude, has raised cotton, sugar, and tobacco, will do the same, not in the blood of bondage, but in the free spirit of liberty, and with the exultant knowledge, that it is to be part of your commerce, and to be given in exchange for the productions of our old native land.

If we are regarded as an evil here, (and we may become so by our competing with your white labor while here for the necessities of existence,) send us where, instead of being an evil, we may be made a blessing, by increasing the value of that white labor, while at the same time we offer it greater comforts in reducing the costs in producing, by our own labor, those articles in abundance which all require for health and sustenance.

Do not, we beseech you, recognize and build up foreign nations of the black race, who have no sympathy or thought or language with that race which has grown up with you, and who only seek by such recognition, shaped as it is, by European diplomacy, to sow discord and trouble with us here, that you and ourselves may be involved in a common ruin.

Send us—our prayer is, send us—to that country we have indicated, that we may not be wholly excluded from you, that we may aid in bringing to

you that great commerce of the Pacific, which will still further increase the wealth and power of your country: and your petitioners will ever pray.

—THE REVEREND HENRY M. TURNER

XXIV.10

"A GREAT DESIRE FOR KNOWLEDGE"

Slaves craved education. They saw it as one of the most important paths to citizenship. Frederick Douglass recalled that it was after learning to read that he first began to think about securing his own freedom. Slave owners understood this and made it illegal to teach slaves how to read. As a result, more than 90 percent of African Americans were illiterate when the Civil War started.

As slaves became free, they sought teachers. Northern Republicans helped found schools and fund missionary teachers to assist emancipated slaves. There was an explosion of new schools throughout the South. Some of the most important all-black colleges—Fisk, Howard and the Hampton Institute—were all founded shortly after the Civil War.

Charlotte Forten, a young black Massachusetts schoolteacher, was one of the first teachers to go to the South and educate freed slaves. Forten sailed to the occupied South Carolina islands in 1862. She came from a distinguished Philadelphia family and was determined to make a difference on behalf of former slaves. In 1864, she wrote an article for Atlantic Monthly magazine about her experiences in South Carolina, hoping to show that emancipated slaves were capable of improving their lot. That spirit influenced much of the sentiment behind the post-Civil War Reconstruction policies.

May/June 1864

It was on the afternoon of a warm, murky day late in October that our steamer, the *United States*, touched the landing at Hilton Head. A motley assemblage had collected on the wharf, officers, soldiers, and "contrabands" of every size and hue: black was, however, the prevailing color. The first view of Hilton Head is desolate enough, a long low, sandy point, stretching out into the sea, with no visible dwellings upon it, except the rows of small white-roofed houses which have lately been built for the freed people.

From Hilton Head to Beaufort the same long, low line of sandy coast, bordered by trees; formidable gunboats in the distance, and the gray ruins of an old fort, said to have been built by the Huguenots more than two hundreds years ago. . . . A large building which was once the Public Library is now a shelter for freed people from Fernandia. Did the Rebels know it, they would doubtless upturn their aristocratic noses, and exclaim in disgust, "To what base uses," etc. We confess that it was highly satisfactory to us to see how the tables are turned, now that the "whirlgig of time has brought about its revenge.". . . There were indications that already Northern improvements had reached this Southern town. Among them was a wharf, a convenience that one wonders how the Southerners could have so long existed without. The more we know of their mode of life, the more we are inclined to marvel at its utter shiftlessness.

Little colored children of every hue were playing about the streets, looking as merry and happy as children ought to look, now that the evil shadow of Slavery no longer hangs over them. Some of the officers we met did not impress us favorably. They talked flippantly, and sneeringly at the negroes, whom they found we had come down to teach, using an epithet more offensive than gentlemanly. . .
.

The next morning L. and I were awakened by the cheerful voices of men and women, children and chickens, in the yard below. We ran to the window, and looked out. Women in bright-colored handkerchiefs, some carrying pails on their heads, were crossing the yard, busy with their morning work; children were playing and tumbling around them. On every face there was a look of serenity and cheerfulness. My heart gave a great throb of happiness as I looked at them and thought, "They are free! So long down-trodden, so long crushed to the earth, but now in their old homes, forever free!" And I thanked God that I had lived to see this day.

The first day of school was rather trying. Most of my children were very small, and consequently restless. Some were too young to learn the alphabet. These little ones were brought to school because the older children—in whose care their parents leave them while at work—could not come without them. We were therefore willing to have them come, although they seemed to have discovered the secret of perpetual motion, and tried one's patience sadly. But after some days of positive, though not severe treatment, order was brought out of chaos, and I found but little difficulty in managing and quieting the tiniest and most restless spirits. I never before saw children so eager to learn, although I had had several years' experience in New England schools. Coming to school is a constant delight and recreation to them. They come here as other children go to play. The older ones, during the summer, work in the fields from early morning until eleven or twelve o'clock, and then come into school, after their hard toil in the hot sun, as bright and as anxious to learn as ever. . .

It is wonderful how a people who have been so long crushed to the earth, so imbruted as these have been, and they are said to be among the most degraded negroes of the South, can have so great a desire for knowledge, and such a capability for attaining it. One cannot believe that the haughty Anglo-Saxon race, after centuries of such an experience as these people have had, would they themselves use every means in their power to crush and degrade them, denying them every right and privilege, closing against them every avenue of elevation and improvement. Were they, under such circumstances, intellectual and refined, they would certainly be vastly superior to any other race that ever existed. . . .

—Charlotte Forten

XXIV.11

Tennessee Petition

When the Civil War ended, African Americans were in a very different place than when the war started. Having proved themselves in the battlefield, they could assert themselves in public affairs. Now, for the first time, a significant number of African Americans could demand a seat at the table of political decision-making.

In January 1865, black Tennesseans petitioned a convention of white Unionists that was considering the reorganization of the state government. Emphasizing the role blacks had played in fighting the war, the petitioners sought the rights of full citizenship. They wanted not only the abolition of slavery, but also the right for blacks to vote and equal rights in court. The convention voted to abolish slavery, but took no action on black suffrage or the right of black Tennesseans to testify in court. These were issues to be addressed in a national debate during Reconstruction.

We the undersigned petitioners, American citizens of African descents, natives and residents of Tennessee, and devoted friends of the great National cause, do most respectfully ask a patient hearing of your honorable body in regard to matters deeply affecting the future condition of our unfortunate and long-suffering race.

First of all, however, we would say that words are too weak to tell how profoundly grateful we are to the Federal government for the good work of freedom which it is gradually carrying forward; and for the Emancipation Proclamation which has set free all the slaves in some of the rebellious States, as well as many of the slaves in Tennessee.

After two hundred years of bondage and suffering a returning sense of justice has awakened the great body of American people to make amends for the unprovoked wrongs committed against us for over two hundred years.

Your petitioners would ask you to complete the work begun by the nation at large, and abolish the last vestige of slavery by the express words of your organic law.

Many masters in Tennessee whose slaves have left them, will certainly make every effort to bring them back to bondage after the reorganization of the State government, unless slavery be expressly abolished by the Constitution.

We hold that freedom is the natural right of all men, which they themselves have no more right to give or barter away, than they have to sell their honor, their wives, or their children.

We claim to be men belonging to the great human family, descended from one great God, who is the common Father of all, and who bestowed on all races and tribes the priceless right of freedom. Of this right, for no offence of ours, we have long been cruelly deprived, and the common voice of the wise and good of all countries, has remonstrated against our enslavement, as one of the greatest crimes in all history.,

We claim freedom, as our natural right, and ask that in harmony and co-operation with the nation at large, you should cut up by the roots the system of slavery, which is not only a wrong to us, but the source of all the evil which at present afflicts the State. For slavery, corrupt itself, corrupted nearly all, also, around it, so that it has influenced nearly all the slave States to rebel against the Federal Government, in order to set up a government of pirates under which slavery might be perpetrated.

In the contest between the nation and slavery, our unfortunate people have sided, by instinct, with the former. We have little fortune to devote to the national cause, for a hard fate has hitherto forced us to live in poverty, but we do devote to its success, our hopes, our toils, our whole heart, our sacred honor, and our lives. We will work, pray, live, and if need be, die for the Union, as cheerfully as ever a white patriot died for his country. The color of our skin does not lesson in the least degree, our love either for God or for the land of our birth.

We are proud to point your honorable body to the fact, that so far as our knowledge extends, not a negro traitor has made his appearance since the beginning of this wicked rebellion.

Whether freeman or slaves the colored race in this country have always looked upon the United States as the Promised Land of Universal freedom, and no earthly temptation has been strong enough to induce us to rebel against it. We love the Union by an instinct which is stronger than any argument or appeal which can be used against it. It is the attachment of a child to its parent.

Devoted as we are to the principles of justice, of love to all men, and of equal rights on which our Government is based, and which make it the hope of the world. We know the burdens of citizenship, and are ready to bear them. We know the duties of the good citizen, and are ready to perform them cheerfully, and would ask to be put in a position in which we can discharge them more effectually. We do not ask for the privilege of citizenship, wishing to shun the obligations imposed by it.

Near 200,000 of our brethren are to-day performing military duty in the ranks of the Union army. Thousands of them have already died in battle, or perished by a cruel martyrdom for the sake of the Union, and we are ready and willing to sacrifice more. But what higher order of citizen is there than the soldier? Or who has a greater trust confided to his hands? If we are called on to do military duty against the rebel armies in the field, why should we be denied the privilege of voting against rebel citizens at the ballot-box? The latter is as necessary to save the Government as the former.

The colored man will vote by instinct with the Union party, just as uniformly as he fights with the Union army.

This is not a new question in Tennessee. From 1796 to 1835, a period of thirty-nine years, free colored men voted at all her elections without question. Her leading politicians and statesmen asked for and obtained the suffrages of colored voters, and were not ashamed of it. Such men as Andrew Jackson, President of the United States, Hon. Felix Grundy, John Bell, Hon. Hugh L. White, Cave Johnson, and Ephraim H. Foster; members of the United States Senate and of the Cabinet, Gen. William Carroll, Samuel Houston, Aaron V. Brown, and, in fact, all the politicians and candidates of all parties in Tennessee solicited colored free men for their votes at every election.

Nor was Tennessee alone in this respect, for the same privileges was granted to colored free men in North Carolina, to-day the most loyal of all the rebellious States, without ever producing any evil consequences.

If colored men have been faithful and true to the Government of the United States in spite of the Fugitive Slave Law, and the cruel policy often pursued toward them, will they not be more devoted to it now than ever, since it has granted them that liberty which they desired above all things? Surely, if colored men voted without harm to the State, while their brethren were in bondage, they will be much more devoted and watchful over her interests when elevated to the rank of freemen and voters. If they are good law-abiding citizens, praying for its prosperity, rejoicing in its progress, paying its taxes, fighting its battles, making its farms, mines, work-shops and commerce more productive, why deny them the right to have a voice in the election of its rulers?

This is a democracy—a government of the people. It should aim to make every man, without regard to the color of his skin, the amount of his wealth, or the character of his religious faith, feel personally interested in its welfare. Every man who lives under the Government should feel that it is his property, his treasure, the bulwark and defence of himself and his family, his pearl of great price, which he must preserve, protect, and defend faithfully at all times, on all occasions, in every possible manner.

This is not a Democratic Government if a numerous, law-abiding, industrious, and useful class of citizens, born and bred on the soil, are to be treated as aliens and enemies, as an inferior degraded class, who must have no voice in the government which they support, protect and defend, with all their heart, soul, mind, and body, both in peace and war.

This Government is based on the teachings of the Bible, which prescribes the same rules of action for all members of the human family, whether their complexion be white, yellow, red, or black. God no where in his revealed word, makes an invidious and degrading distinction against his children, because of their color. And happy is that nation which makes the Bible its rule of action, and obeys principle, not prejudice.

Let no man oppose this doctrine because it is opposed to his old prejudices. The nation is fighting for its life, and cannot afford to be controlled by prejudice. Had prejudice prevailed instead of principle, not a single colored soldier would have been in the Union army to-day. But principle and justice triumphed, and now near 200,000 colored patriots stand under the folds of the national flag, and brave their breasts to the bullets of the rebels. As we are in the battlefield, so we swear before heaven, by all that is dear to men, to be at the ballot-box faithful and true to the Union.

The possibility that the negro suffrage proposition may shock popular prejudice at first sight, is not a conclusive argument against its wisdom and policy. No proposition ever met with more furious or general opposition than the one to enlist colored soldiers in the United States army. The opponents of the measure exclaimed on all hands that the negro was a coward; that he would not fight; that one white man, with a whip in his hand could put to flight a regiment of them; that the experiment would end in the utter rout and ruin of the Federal army. Yet the colored man has fought so well, on almost every occasion, that the rebel government is prevented, only by its fears and distrust of being able to force him to fight for slavery as well as he fights against it, from putting half a million of negroes into its ranks.

The Government has asked the colored man to fight for its preservation and gladly has he done it. It can afford to trust him with a vote as safely as it trusted him with a bayonet.

How boundless would be the love of the colored citizen, how intense and passionate his zeal and devotion to the government, how enthusiastic and how lasting would be his gratitude, if his white brethren were to take him by the hand and say, "You have been ever loyal to our government; henceforward be voters." Again, the granting of this privilege would stimulate the colored man to greater exertion to make himself an intelligent, respected, useful citizen. His price of character would be appealed to this way most successfully; he

would send his children to school, that they might become educated and intelligent members of society. It used to be thought that ignorant negroes were the most valuable, but this belief probably originated from the fact that it is almost impossible to retain an educated, intelligent man in bondage. Certainly, if the free colored man be educated, and his morals enlightened and improved, he will be a far better member of society, and less liable to transgress its laws. It is the brutal, degraded, ignorant man who is usually the criminal.

One other matter we would urge on your honorable body. At present we can only have partial protection from the courts. The testimony of twenty of the most intelligent, honorable, colored loyalists cannot convict a white traitor of treasonable action. A white rebel might sell powder and lead to a rebel soldier in the presence of twenty colored soldiers, and yet their evidence would be worthless so far as the courts are concerned, and the rebel would escape. A colored man may have served for years faithfully in the army, and yet his testimony in court would be rejected, while that of a white man who had served in the rebel army would be received.

If this order of things continue, our people are destined to a malignant persecution at the hands of rebels and their former rebellious masters, whose hatred they may have incurred, without precedent even in the South. Every rebel soldier or citizen whose arrest in the perpetration of crime they may have effected, every white traitor whom they may have brought to justice, will torment and persecute them and set justice at defiance, because the courts will not receive negro testimony, which will generally be the only possible testimony in such cases. A rebel may murder his former slave and defy justice, because he committed the deed in the presence of half a dozen respectable colored citizens. He may have the dwelling of his former slave burned over his head, and turn his wife and children out of doors, and defy the law, for no colored man can appear against him. Is this the fruit of freedom, and the reward of our services in the field? Was it for this that colored soldiers fell by hundreds before Nashville, fighting under the flag of the Union? Is it for this that we have guided Union officers and soldiers, when escaping from the cruel and deadly prisons of the South through forests and swamps, at the risk of our own lives, for we knew that to us detection would be death? Is it for this that we have concealed multitudes of Union refugees in caves and cane-brakes, when flying from the conscription officers and tracked by bloodhounds, and divided with them our last morsal of food? Will you declare in your revised constitution that a pardoned traitor may appear in court and his testimony be heard, but that no colored loyalist shall be believed even upon oath? If this should be so, then will our last state be worse than our first, and we can look for no relief on this side of the grave. Has not the colored man fought, bled and died for the Union, under a thousand great disadvantages and discouragements? Has his fidelity ever had a shadow of suspicion cast upon it, in any matter of responsibility confided to his hands?

There have been white traitors in multitudes in Tennessee, but where, we ask, is the black traitor? Can you forget how the colored man has fought at Fort Morgan, at Milliken's Bend, at Fort Pillow, before Petersburg, and your own city of Nashville?

When has the colored citizen, in this rebellion been tried and found wanting?
In conclusion, we would point to the fact that the States where the largest measure of justice and civil rights has been granted to the colored man, both as to suffrage and his oath in court, are among the most rich, intelligent, enlightened and prosperous. Massachusetts, illustrious for her statesmen and her commercial and manufacturing enterprises and

thrift, whose noble liberality has relieved so many loyal citizens to vote, and is ever jealous of their rights. She has never had reason to repent the day when she gave them the right of voting.

Had the southern states followed her example the present rebellion never would have desolated their borders.

Several other Northern States permit negro suffrage, nor have bad effects ever resulted from it. It may be safely affirmed that Tennessee was quite as safe and prosperous during the 39 years while she allowed negro suffrage, as she has been since she abolished it.

In this great and fearful struggle of the nation with a wicked rebellion, we are anxious to perform the full measure of our duty both as citizens and soldiers to the Union cause we consecrate ourselves, and our families, with all that we have on earth. Our souls burn with love for the great government of freedom and equal rights. Our white brethren have no cause for distrust as regards our fidelity, for neither death nor life, nor angels, nor principalities, nor powers, nor things present, nor things to come, nor height, nor depth, nor any other creature, shall be able to separate us from the love of the union.

Praying that the great God, who is the common Father of us all, by whose help the land must be delivered from present evil, and before whom we must all stand at last to be judged by the rule of eternal justice, and not by passion and prejudice, may enlighten your minds and enable you to act with wisdom, justice, and magnaminity, we remain your faithful friends in all the perils and dangers which threaten our beloved country.

—[59 SIGNATURES] AND MANY OTHER COLORED CITIZENS OF NASHVILLE

XXV

A WAR FOR
EMANCIPATION

The Civil War began as a war to preserve the Union, but it ended as a war to abolish slavery. Slavery was a cause of the war, but it would be too much to say that the Union went to battle to liberate the slaves. The Northern abolitionists believed fervently that the war should be over slavery. Southerners claimed to fight for the preservation of slavery. But for Abraham Lincoln, slavery was a secondary issue. He set aside his moral opposition to slavery to execute his constitutional duty to keep the nation united.

"My paramount object in this struggle is to save the Union, and is not either to save or destroy Slavery," Lincoln wrote in a famous open letter to Horace Greeley. "If I could save the Union without freeing any slave, I would do it; and if I could save it by freeing all the slaves, I would do it; and if I could do it by freeing some and leaving others alone, I would also do that."

Lincoln opposed turning the war into a revolutionary struggle. He did not want to reconfigure Southern slave society into the shape of Northern free-labor society. Because Lincoln never acknowledged the constitutional legitimacy of the Confederacy, he initially preserved the Confederates' rights to protection of personal property, which included slaves.

As Commander in Chief, Lincoln had to keep the northern states united in the war effort. Four slaveholding states—Missouri, Maryland, Kentucky and Delaware—remained loyal to the Union. If the war had become a conflict over emancipation, these states would almost certainly have joined the South. "I want to have God on my side," Lincoln said, "but I must have Kentucky." When the war first broke out, Lincoln required military units to return escaped slaves back to their masters, even if they were rebel owners. Military commanders who attempted to free slaves were often replaced.

But as the war unfolded, the issue of emancipation kept getting pushed to the forefront. Republicans, who controlled Congress now that the southern Democrats had left, passed legislation freeing slaves in Washington, D.C., and the federal territories. Abolitionists raged against the administration for its hesitancy in liberating slaves. Diplomats believed that the transformation of the war into a conflict over slavery and freedom would prevent the English from becoming a military ally of the South.

Slaves themselves forced Lincoln and the North to confront the issue by seeking safety in Union lines and offering to assist troops in the war effort. By making the issue of slavery a war measure to weaken the South's ability to wage war and strengthen the North's, blacks compelled Lincoln to adopt emancipation. Lincoln took a hesitating, labored path to this conclusion.

The First Confiscation Act in 1861 authorized the military to seize property (including slaves) used in the military support of the war. In July 1862, the Second Confiscation Act deemed all slaves that came into the Union lines captives of war, whether or not they had been used to assist the Confederate army. One month later, Lincoln authorized the arming of 5,000 black soldiers in South Carolina. In the meantime, Lincoln implored the reluctant border states to allow for the gradual emancipation of slavery. It was becoming increasingly clear that slavery could not last in a war between North and South.

That same summer Lincoln concluded that emancipating the slaves of the rebellious South was the best and fastest way to win the war. He wanted to issue an emancipation proclamation on the heels of a military victory in order to give it teeth. The Battle of Antietam in September 1862 presented that opportunity.

The proclamation itself does not wax poetic on the issue of slavery, but is rather written as the martial document it was intended to be. To Lincoln, freeing the slaves was a war measure. But it unleashed a new type of war. The Civil War became an ideological war. Northern troops were now more than preservers of the union. They had become liberators.

---— **XXV.1** ———

Slavery, the Cornerstone of the Confederacy

Prior to secession, Alexander Stephens of Georgia had been both a Unionist and a Southern patriot. Abraham Lincoln wrote to Stephens shortly after his election that there was no cause to fear "that a Republican administration would directly, or indirectly, interfere with their slaves or with them about their slaves."

Stephens had opposed immediate secession as a delegate to the Georgia secession convention. But he also declared that if the state seceded, he would go with Georgia. The Montgomery Convention named Stephens Vice-President of the Confederacy—a position for which he proved singularly unfitted. During the war, Stephens was a leader of the moderates and an early advocate of peace, although by the end of the war he acknowledged there was no room for compromise between North and South.

The "Cornerstone Speech," Stephens's most important political statement, was delivered in Savannah, Georgia, on March 21, 1861, shortly after the organization of the Confederacy. Like many of the declarations and resolutions of the Southerners, it emphasized slavery as the fundamental cause of the war and as a founding principle of the Confederacy.

. . . The new Constitution has put at rest forever the agitating questions relating to our peculiar institutions—African slavery as it exists among us—the proper status of the negro in our form of civilization. This was the immediate cause of the late rupture and present revolution. Jefferson, in his forecast, had anticipated this, as the "rock upon which the old Union would split." He was right. What was conjecture with him, is now a realized fact. But whether he fully comprehended the great truth upon which that rock stood and stands, may be doubted. The prevailing ideas entertained by him and most of the leading statesmen at the time of the formation of the old Constitution were, that the enslavement of the African was in violation of the laws of nature; that it was wrong in principle, socially, morally and politically. It was an evil they knew not well how to deal with; but the general opinion of the men of that day was that, somehow or other, in the order of Providence, the institution would be evanescent and pass away. This idea,

though not incorporated in the Constitution, was the prevailing idea at the time. The Constitution, it is true, secured every essential guarantee to the institution while it should last, and hence no argument can be justly used against the constitutional guarantees thus secured, because of the common sentiment of the day. Those ideas, however, were fundamentally wrong. They vested upon the assumption of the equality of races. This was an error. It was a sandy foundation, and the idea of a Government built upon it—when the "storm came and the wind blew, it fell."

Our new Government is founded upon exactly the opposite ideas; its foundations are laid, its cornerstone rests, upon the great truth that the negro is not equal to the white man; that slavery, subordination to the superior race, is his natural and moral condition. This, our new Government, is the first, in the history of the world, based upon this great physical, philosophical, and moral truth. . . .

As I have stated, the truth of this principle may be slow in development, as all truths are, and ever have been, in the various branches of science. It was so with the principles announced by Galileo—it was so with Adam Smith and his principles of political economy. It was so with Harvey, and his theory of the circulation of the blood. It is stated that not a single one of the medical profession, living at the time of the announcement of the truths made by him, admitted them. Now, they are universally acknowledged. May we not therefore look with confidence to the ultimate universal acknowledgment of the truths upon which our system rests? It is the first Government ever instituted upon principles in strict conformity to nature, and the ordination of Providence, in furnishing the materials of human society. Many Governments have been founded upon the principles of certain classes; but the classes thus enslaved, were of the same race, and in violation of the laws of nature. Our system commits no such violation of nature's laws. The negro by nature, or by the curse against Canaan, is fitted for that condition which he occupies in our system. The architect, in the construction of buildings, lays the foundation with the proper material—the granite—then comes the brick or the marble. The substratum of our society is made of the material fitted by nature for it, and by experience we know that it is the best, not only for the superior but for the inferior race, that it should be so. It is, indeed, in conformity with the Creator. It is not for us to inquire into the wisdom of His ordinances or to question them. For His own purposes He has made one race to differ from another, as He has made "one star to differ from another in glory."

The great objects of humanity are best attained, when conformed to his laws and degrees, in the formation of Governments as well as in all things else. Our Confederacy is founded upon principles in strict conformity with these laws. This stone which was rejected by the first builders "is become the chief stone of the corner" in our new edifice. . . .

—Alexander Stephens

XXV.2

"This Imbecile Pro-slavery Government Does Try Me So"

Lincoln's insistence at the outset of the war that the conflict was not, and would not be, about eradication of slavery enraged abolitionists. Abolitionists viewed the Civil War as an opportunity to transform Southern society. Instead of being a war to restore the nation, they saw it as a second revolution to eradicate slavery. "The war now being waged in this land is a war for and against slavery," the former slave Frederick Douglass said, "and it can never be effectively put down until one or the other is completely destroyed."

Lydia Maria Child was one of the best-known female abolitionists of that day. She had gained fame as author of the best-selling books *Hobomok* (1824) and *The Frugal Housewife* (1829), but her strident support of the antislavery movement damaged her national standing. Nevertheless, she edited an abolitionist newspaper and corresponded with John Brown. As these excerpts from letters to her friend Lucy Searle demonstrate, Child did not abide Lincoln's policy on slavery, even if his position had driven the South to secede.

Toward the end of the war Child published *The Freedmen's Book*, a collection of biographies of African Americans, political speeches by Republicans, stories, hymns, poems and practical advice. Although some of Child's writings come across as jarring and patronizing to readers today, they did contribute to the development of a distinct African-American heritage.

June 9, 1861

. . . The fact is I identify myself so completely with the slaves, that I am kept in alternating states of anxiety and wrath, concerning the rendition by officers of the U.S. If I wake up in the middle of the night, it is the first thing I think of. I long to get at the poor creatures, to tell them to run away to Canada or Hayti, and not trust to the promises of the U.S. always perfidious and cruel to the colored man.

I am waiting with great anxiety to see what will be the results of this war; for if things are patched up on the old foundation, I will quit the country, and lay my bones on a foreign soil; *any* soil not cursed by a Fugitive Slave Law. Under that law I will not live.

It is a beautiful peaceful Sabbath. Cloud-shadows are flitting over the broad green meadows, in front of my window; and all is so still that one might "hear the grass grow," if the ear were fine enough. It seems difficult to realize the fierce passions that are raging a few hundred miles from us. You will think it strange and perhaps wrong, that I do not wish them to be less fierce, at present. I want the "irrepressible conflict" to intensify to a focus that will kindle a fire powerful enough to sweep over and effectually destroy the *cause* of the conflict. This does not arise from partisan feelings on my part, from any hatred to slave-holders, or any want of love for my country; but because it is my deliberate and firm conviction that in no other way can our free institutions be saved. It will be better for *all* parties to have the question completely settled now; and it does seem as if Divine Providence were wonderously over-ruling things for that result.

October 11, 1861

. . . I did not mean to talk so much about public affairs; but this imbecile, pro-slavery government does try me so, that it seems as if I must shoot somebody. Willis is out again with a florid description of Mrs. Lincoln's autumn bonnet called "The Princess." Rose-colored velvet, with guipine medallions, trimmed with black thread lace, put on full, and this again trimmed on the edge with a deeper fringe of minute black marabout and ostrich feather. &c &c. . .

So this is what the people are taxed for! To deck out this vulgar doll with foreign frippery! And oppressed millions must groan on, lest her "noble native State" should take offence, if Government made us the beneficient power God has so miraculously placed in its hand. To see these things, and have no power to change them, to see the glorious opportunity so near, yet slipping away, leaving the nation to sink deeper and deeper into the abyss of degradation—this is really the torment of Tantalus.

—LYDIA MARIA CHILD

XXV.3

THE PROBLEM OF CONTRABANDS

The problem of the refugee slaves was one of the most difficult which the federal government had to face. Taking advantage of the dislocations of war, many slaves bolted from their owners and fled into Union lines. Military commanders were often at a loss over what to do with them. Standing orders at the outset of the war were for runaway slaves to be returned to their masters. But this often placed Union officers in the awkward position of assisting the Confederate army.

General Benjamin Butler, commanding at Fortress Monroe, took matters into his own hands when runaway slaves, who had been working on Confederate fortifications, sought freedom and safety with his army. Refusing to return the slaves to enemy soldiers, Butler declared the runaway slaves "contraband of war." The term "contraband" for runaway slaves in Union lines stuck.

Butler, who opposed slavery, argued that if slaves were property, then the government had the right to confiscate slaves when they were being used in the military support of the rebellion. This policy was formally adopted by Congress with the First Confiscation Act and was signed by Lincoln.

The measure was limited to the military use of slaves and it did not emancipate them.. In fact, Lincoln reversed attempts by military commanders who tried to proclaim slaves free. John

Charles Frémont, commander of the Department of the West, declared martial law in Missouri and issued the proclamation of August 30 confiscating rebel property and emancipating their slaves. Although abolitionists cheered Frémont, Lincoln countermanded his declaration.

A. General Butler's "Contrabands"

Headquarters Department of Virginia,
Fortress Monroe, July 30, 1861

Hon. Simon Cameron, Secretary of War:

Sir: . . . In the village of Hampton there were a large number of negroes, composed in a great measure of women and children of the men who had fled thither within my lines for protection, who had escaped from marauding parties of rebels who had been gathering up able-bodied blacks to aid them in constructing their batteries on the James and York Rivers. I have employed the men in Hampton in throwing up intrenchments, and they were working zealously and efficiently at that duty, saving our soldiers from that labor under the gleam of the mid-day sun. The women were earning substantially their own subsistence in washing, marketing, and taking care of the clothes of the soldiers, and rations were being served out to the men who worked for the support of the children. But by the evacuation of Hampton, rendered necessary by the withdrawal of troops, leaving me scarcely 5,000 men outside the Fort, including the force at Newport News, all these black people were obliged to break up their homes at Hampton, fleeing across the creek within my lines for protection and support. Indeed, it was a most distressing sight to see these poor creatures, who had trusted to the protection of the arms of the United States, and who aided the troops of the United States in their enterprise, to be thus obliged to flee from their homes, and the homes of their masters who had deserted them, and become fugitives from fear of the return of the rebel soldiery, who had threatened to shoot the men who had wrought for us, and to carry off the women who had served us, to a worse than Egyptian bondage. I have, therefore, now within the Peninsula, this side of Hampton Creek, 900 negroes, 300 of whom are able-bodied men, 30 of whom are substantially past hard labor, 175 women, 225 children under the age of 10 years, and 170 between 10 and 18 years, and more coming in. The questions which this state of facts presents are very embarrassing.

First, What shall be done with them? And, *Second*, What is their state and condition?

Upon these questions I desire the instructions of the Department.

The first question, however, may perhaps be answered by considering the last. Are these men, women, and children, slaves? Are they free? Is their condition that of men, women, and children, or of property, or is it a mixed relation? What their *status* was under the Constitution and the laws, we all know. What has been the effect of rebellion and a state of war upon that *status*? When I adopted the theory of treating the able-bodied negro fit to work in the trenches as property liable to be used in aid of rebellion, and so contraband of war, that condition of things was in so far met, as I then and still believe, on a legal and constitutional basis. But now a new series of questions arises. Passing by women, the children, certainly cannot be treated on that basis; if property, they must be considered an incumbrance rather than an auxiliary of an army, and, of course, in no possible legal relation could be treated as contraband. Are they property? If they were so, they have been left by their masters and owners, deserted, thrown away, abandoned, like the wrecked vessel upon the ocean. Their former possessors and owners have causelessly, traitorously, rebelliously, and, to carry out the figure, practically abandoned them to be swallowed up by the winter storm of starvation. If property, do they not become the property of the salvors? But we, their salvors, do not need and will not hold such property, and will assume no such ownership: has not, therefore, all proprietary relation ceased? Have they not become, thereupon, men, women, and children? No longer under ownership of any kind, the fearful relics of fugitive master, have they not by their masters' acts, and the state of war, assumed the condition, which we hold to be the normal

one, of those made in God's image? Is not every constitutional, legal, and moral requirement, as well to the runaway master as their relinquished slaves, thus answered? I confess that my own mind is compelled by this reasoning to look upon them as men and women. If not free born, yet free, manumitted, sent forth from the hand that held them never to be reclaimed. . . .

In a loyal State I would put down a servile insurrection. In a state of rebellion I would confiscate that which was used to oppose my arms, and take all that property, which constituted the wealth of that State and furnished the means by which the war is prosecuted, beside being the cause of the war; and if, in so doing, it should be objected that human beings were brought to the free enjoyment of life, liberty, and the pursuit of happiness, such objection might not require much consideration.

Pardon me for addressing the Secretary of War directly upon this question, as it involves some political considerations as well as propriety of military action. I am, sir, your obedient servant,

—BENJAMIN F. BUTLER

B. Frémont's Proclamation on Slaves

Head-quarters Western Department

St. Louis, Aug. 30, 1861.

Circumstances in my judgment are of sufficient urgency to render it necessary that the commanding General of this department should assume the administrative powers of the State. Its disorganized condition, helplessness of civil authority and the total insecurity of life, and devastation of property by bands of murderers and marauders, who infest nearly every county in the States, and avail themselves of public misfortunes, in the vicinity of a hostile force, to gratify private and neighborhood vengeance, and who find an enemy wherever they find plunder, finally demand the severest measures to repress the daily increasing crimes and outrages, which are driving off the inhabitants and ruining the State.

In this condition, the public safety and success of our arms require unity of purpose, without let or hindrance to the prompt administration of affairs. In order, therefore, to suppress disorders, maintain the public peace, and give security to the persons and property of loyal citizens, I do hereby extend and declare established martial law throughout the state of Missouri. The lines of the army occupation in this State are for the present declared to extend from Leavenworth, by way of posts of Jefferson City, Rolla, and Ironton, to Cape Girardeau on the Mississippi River. All persons who shall be taken with arms in their hands within these lines shall be tried by court-martial and if found guilty, will be shot. Real and personal property of those who shall take up arms against the United States, or who shall be directly proven to have taken an active part with their enemies in the field, is declared confiscated to public use, and their slaves, if any they have, are hereby declared free men.

All persons who shall be proven to have destroyed, after the publication of this order, railroad tracks, bridges, or telegraph lines, shall suffer the extreme penalty of the law. All persons engaged in treasonable correspondence, in giving or procuring aid to the enemy, in fermenting turmoil, and disturbing public tranquility, by creating or circulating false reports, or incendiary documents, are warned that they are exposing themselves.

All persons who have been led away from allegiance, are required to return to their homes forthwith. Any such absence without sufficient cause, will be held to the presumptive evidence against them. The object of this declaration is to place in the hands of military authorities power to give instantaneous effect to the existing laws, and supply such deficiencies as the conditions of the war demand; but it is not intended to suspend the ordinary tribunals of the country, where law will be administered by civil officers in the usual manner, and with their customary authority, while the same can be peaceably administered.

The commanding General will labor vigilantly for the public welfare, and, by his efforts for their safety, hopes to obtain not only acquiescence, but the active support of the people of the country.

J.C. FRÉMONT,
Major-General Commanding

XXV.4

MESSAGES TO CONGRESS ON COMPENSATED EMANCIPATION

Although Lincoln's initial goal was not to free slaves, but preserve the Union, it became clear with time that at least some slaves would become free. From the beginning to the end of the Civil War, Lincoln hoped that emancipation could be carried through without violence and with the cooperation of the slave states that had not seceded from the Union. The proposal he turned to again and again was compensated emancipation.

He first recommended a "gradual" emancipation in December 1861, but with no success. In a message to Congress on March 6, 1862, he repeated the suggestion and followed up with a direct appeal to congressmen from the border states, who rejected it as too extreme a measure. Abolitionists despised Lincoln's gradualist approach. "The President does not have a drop of anti-slavery blood in his veins," William Lloyd Garrison proclaimed.

Nevertheless, Lincoln made another appeal to border-state congressmen in July. Moving deliberately and cautiously, Lincoln implored the congressmen to agree to a gradual emancipation. "You cannot be blind to the signs of the times," he said. But they once again rejected the proposal.

Lincoln's annual message of December 1, 1862, (given after the Emancipation Proclamation, but one month before the declaration went into effect) contained a specific plan for compensated emancipation and concluded with a moving appeal for support.

A. The Gradual Abolishment of Slavery

March 6, 1862

Fellow-Citizens of the Senate and House of Representatives: I recommend the adoption of a joint resolution by your honorable bodies which shall be substantially as follows:

"Resolved, That the United States ought to co-operate with any State which may adopt gradual abolishment of slavery, giving to such State pecuniary aid, to be used by such State, in its discretion, to compensate for the inconveniences, public and private, produced by such change of system."

If the proposition contained in the resolution does not meet the approval of Congress and the country, there is the end; but if it does command such approval, I deem it of importance that the States and people immediately interested should be at once distinctly notified of the fact, so that they may begin to consider whether to accept or reject it. The Federal Government would find its highest interest in such a measure, as one of the most efficient means of self-preservation. The leaders of the existing insurrection entertain the hope that this government will ultimately be forced to acknowledge the independence of some part of the disaffected region, and that all the slave States north of such part will then say, "The Union for which we have struggled being already gone, we now choose to go with the Southern section." To deprive them of this hope substantially ends the rebellion, and the initiation of emancipation completely deprives them of it as to all the States initiating it. The point is not that all the States tolerating slavery would very soon, if at all, initiate emancipation; but that, while the offer is equally made to all, the more northern shall by such initiation make it certain to the more southern that in no event will the former ever join the latter in their proposed confederacy. I say "initiation" because, in my judgment, gradual and not sudden emancipation is better for all. In the mere financial or pecuniary view, any member of Congress with the census tables and treasury reports before him can readily see for himself how very soon the current expenditures of this war would purchase, at fair valuation, all the slave in any named State. Such a proposition on the part of the general Government sets up no claim of a right by Federal authority to interfere with slavery within State limits, referring, as it does, the absolute control of the subject in each case to the State and its people immediately interested. It is proposed as a matter of perfectly free choice with them. . . .

The proposition now made (though an offer only), I hope it may be esteemed no offense to ask whether the pecuniary consideration tendered would not be of no more value to the States and private persons concerned than are the institution and property in it in the present aspect of affairs.

While it is true that the adoption of the proposed resolution would be merely initiatory, and not within itself a practical measure, it is recommended in the hopes that it would soon lead to important practical results. In full view of my great responsibility to my God and to my country, I earnestly beg the attention of Congress and the people to the subject.

—ABRAHAM LINCOLN

B. "We Cannot Escape History"

Message to Congress, December 1 1862

. . . Our strife pertains to ourselves—to the passing generations of men—and it can without convulsion be hushed forever with the passing of one generation.

In this view I recommend the adoption of the following resolution and articles amendatory to the Constitution of the United States:

Resolved by the Senate and House of Representatives of the United States of America, in Congress assembled, (two-thirds of both Houses concurring), that the following articles be proposed to the Legislatures (or conventions) of the several States as amendments to the Constitution of the United States, all or any of which articles, when ratified by three-fourths of the said Legislatures (or conventions), to be valid as part or parts of the said Constitution, viz:

Art.—. Every State wherein slavery now exists which shall abolish the same therein at any time or times before the 1st day of January, A.D. 1900, shall receive compensation from the United States as follows,. . .

Art.—. All slaves who shall have enjoyed actual freedom by the chances of the war at any time before the end of the rebellion shall be forever free; but all owners of such who shall not have been disloyal shall be compensated for them at the same rates as is provided for States adopting abolishment of slavery, but in such way that no slave shall be twice accounted for.

Art.—. Congress may appropriate money and otherwise provide for colonizing free colored persons with their own consent at any place or places without the United States.

I beg indulgence to discuss these proposed articles at some length. Without slavery the rebellion could never have existed; without slavery it could not continue.

Among the friends of the Union there is great diversity of sentiment and of policy in regard to slavery and the African race amongst us. Some would perpetuate slavery; some would abolish it gradually and with compensation; some would remove the freed people from us, and some would retain them with us; and there are yet other minor diversities. Because of these diversities we waste much strength in struggles among ourselves. By mutual concession we should harmonize and act together. This would be compromise, but it would be compromise among the friends and not with the enemies of the Union. These articles are intended to embody a plan of such mutual concessions. If the plan shall be adopted, it is assumed that emancipation will follow, at least in several of the States.

As to the first article, the main points are, first, the emancipation, secondly, the length of time for consumating it (thirty-seven years); and, thirdly, the compensation.

The emancipation will be unsatisfactory to the advocates of perpetual slavery, but the length of time should greatly mitigate their dissatisfaction. The time spares both races from the evils of sudden derangement—in fact, from the necessity of any derangement—while most of those whose habitual course of thought will be disturbed by the measure will have passed away before its consumation. They will never see it. Another class will hail the prospect of emancipation, but will deprecate the length of time. They will feel that it gives too little to the now living slaves. But it really gives them

much. It saves them from the vagrant destitution which must largely attend immediate emancipation in localities where their numbers are very great, and it gives the inspiring assurance that their posterity shall be free forever. The plan leaves each State choosing to act under it to abolish slavery now or at the end of the century, or at any intermediate time, or by degrees extending over the whole or any part of the period, and it obliges no two States to proceed alike. It also provides for compensation, and generally the mode of making it. This, it would seem, must further mitigate the dissatisfaction of those who favor perpetual slavery, and especially of those who are to receive the compensation. . . .

And if with less money, or money more easily paid, we can preserve the benefits of the Union by this means than we can by the war alone, is it not also economical to do it? Let us consider it, then. Let us ascertain the sum we have expended in the war since compensated emancipation was proposed last March, and consider whether if that measure had been promptly accepted by even some of the slave States the same sum would not have done more to close the war than has been otherwise done. If so, the measure would save money, and in that view would be a prudent and economical measure. . . . The aggregate sum necessary for compensated emancipation of course would be large. But it would require no ready cash, nor the bonds even any faster than the emancipation progresses. This might not, and probably would not, close before the end of thirty-seven years. At that time we shall probably have a hundred millions of people to share the burden, instead of thirty-one millions as now. . . .

The proposed emancipation would shorten the war, perpetuate the peace, insure this increase of population, and proportionately the wealth of the country. With these we should pay all the emancipation would cost, together with our other debt, easier than we should pay our other debt without it. . . .

The third article relates to the future of the freed people. It does not oblige, but merely authorizes Congress to aid in colonizing such as may consent. This ought not to be regarded as objectionable on the one hand or on the other, insomuch as it comes to nothing unless by the mutual consent of the people to be deported and the American voters through their representatives in Congress. . . .

The plan consisting of these articles is recommended, not but that a restoration of the national authority would be accepted without its adoption.

Nor will the war nor proceedings under the proclamation of September 22, 1862, be stayed because of the recommendation of this plan. Its timely adoption, I doubt not, would bring restoration, and thereby stay both.

And notwithstanding this plan, the recommendation that Congress provide by law for compensating any State which may adopt emancipation before this plan shall have been acted upon is hereby earnestly renewed. Such would be only an advance part of the plan, and the same arguments apply to both.

This plan is recommended as a means, not in exclusion of, but additional to, all others for restoring and preserving the national authority throughout the Union. The subject is presented exclusively in its economical aspect. The plan would, I am confident, secure peace more speedily and maintain it more permanently than can be done by force alone, while all it would cost, considering amounts and manner of payment and times of payment, would be easier paid than will be the additional cost of the war if we rely solely upon force. It is much, very much, that it would cost no blood at all.

The plan is proposed as permanent constitutional law. It cannot become such without concurrence of, first, two thirds of Congress, and afterwards three fourths of the States. The requisite three fourths of the States will necessarily include seven of the slave States. Their concurrence, if obtained, will give assurance of their severally adopting emancipation at no very distant day upon the new constitutional terms. This assurance would end the struggle now and save the Union forever. . . .

Fellow-citizens, we can not escape history. We of this Congress and this administration will be remembered in spite of ourselves. No personal significance or insignificance can spare one or another of us. The fiery trial through which we pass will light us down in honor or dishonor to the latest generation. We say we are for the Union. The world will not forget that we say this. We know how to save the union. The world knows we do know how to save it. We, even we here, hold the power and bear the responsibility. In giving freedom to the slave we assure freedom to the free—honorable alike in what we give and what we preserve. We shall nobly save or meanly lose the last, best hope of earth. Other means may succeed; this could not fail. The way is plain, peaceful, generous, just—a way which if followed the world will forever applaud and God must forever bless.

—ABRAHAM LINCOLN

—— XXV.5 ——

"MY PARAMOUNT OBJECT IS TO SAVE THE UNION"

Horace Greeley was the powerful, if erratic, editor of the New York Tribune, the largest and most influential newspaper in the United States, with a circulation that reached almost 300,000. Although Greeley opposed slavery, he had urged letting the "erring sisters go in peace" at the beginning of the secessionist movement.

By the summer of 1862, however, Greeley was fully allied with the leading abolitionists. In a famous open letter to the President, Greeley demanded that the conflict become a war for emancipation. Greeley called his letter of August 19 "The Prayer of Twenty Millions," though it certainly did not speak for that number of Northerners, many of whom opposed the freeing of slaves.

Greeley's appeal spoke not just of the moral obligation to free slaves, but also the military necessity of doing so. This was a theme that the abolitionists pounded throughout the war. Emancipation, Greeley and others argued, was a military measure that would allow African Americans to aid the North in the execution of the war. It would also eliminate the central difference between North and South that caused the war.

Lincoln's reply clearly states his view that the war was about the preservation of the Union, and not the freeing of slaves. What Lincoln does not say in his answer to Greeley was that he had already decided on the last of the three options he cites—to free some slaves, but not others—by issuing the Emancipation Proclamation. Lincoln agreed with Greeley that the slaves of the Confederacy needed to be freed. Liberating them would prevent the South from using these slaves as a part of the Confederate war machine, and allow them to contribute to the Union's. But Lincoln viewed this strategy as a means to preserve the Union, not as a goal in itself of the war. For this reason, and because he did not want to punish pro-Unionist slave owners by confiscating their slaves, for fear it would encourage more states to secede from the Union, Lincoln continued to urge for compromise through gradual compensated emancipation of the border states, whereby Union slaveowners would be financially reimbursed for the slaves they set free.

A. "The Prayer of Twenty Millions"

August 19, 1862

Dear Sir: . . . We complain that the Union cause has suffered, and is now suffering immensely, from mistaken deference to rebel Slavery. Had you, sir, in your Inaugural Address, unmistakably given notice that, in case the rebellion already commenced, were persisted in, and your efforts to preserve the Union and enforce the laws should be resisted by armed force, you *would recognize no loyal person as rightfully held in Slavery by a traitor*, we believe the rebellion would therein have received a staggering if not fatal blow. . . .

On the face of this wide earth, Mr. President, there is not one disinterested, determined, intelligent champion of the Union cause who does not feel that all attempts to put down the rebellion and at the same time uphold its inciting cause are preposterous and futile—that the rebellion, if crushed out to-morrow, would be renewed within a year if Slavery were left in full vigor—that army officers who remain to this day devoted to Slavery can at best be but half-way loyal to the Union—and that every hour of deference to Slavery is an hour of added and deepened peril to the Union. I appeal to the testimony of your ambassadors in Europe. It is freely at your service, not at mine. Ask them to tell you candidly whether the seeming subserviency of your policy to the slave holding, slavery-upholding interest, is not the perplexity, the despair of states-

men of all parties, and be admonished by the general answer!

I close as I began with the statement that what an immense majority of the loyal millions of your countrymen require of you is a frank, declared, unqualified, ungrudging execution of the laws of the land, more especially of the Confiscation Act. That act gives freedom to the slaves of rebels coming within our lines, or whom those lines may at any time inclose—we ask you to render it due obedience by publicly requiring all your subordinates to recognize and obey it. The rebels are everywhere using the late anti-Negro riots in the North, as they have long used your officers' treatment of Negroes in the South, to convince the slaves that they have nothing to hope from a Union success—that we mean in that case to sell them into a bitter bondage to defray the cost of the war. Let them impress this as a truth on the great mass of their ignorant and credulous bondmen, and the Union will never be restored—never. We cannot conquer ten millions of people united in solid phalanx against us, powerfully aided by Northern sympathizers and European allies. We must have scouts, guides, spies, cooks, teamsters, diggers, and choppers from the blacks of the South, whether we allow them to fight for us or not, or we shall be baffled and repelled. As one of the millions who would gladly have avoided this struggle at any sacrifice but that of principle and honor, but who now feel that the triumph of the Union is indispensable not only to the existence of our country but to the well-being of mankind, I entreat you to render a hearty and unequivocal obedience to the law of the land.

Yours,

Horace Greeley.

—MOORE, ed., *The Rebellion Record*

B. "I Would Save the Union"

Executive Mansion, Washington, August 22, 1862

Hon. Horace Greeley:

DEAR SIR: I have just read yours of the nineteenth, ad dressed to myself through the New-York

Tribune. If there be in it any statements or assumptions of fact which I may know to be erroneous, I do not now and here controvert them. If there be in it any inferences which I may believe to be falsely drawn, I do not now and here argue against them. If there be perceptible in it an impatient and dictatorial tone, I waive it in deference to an old friend, whose heart I have always supposed to be right.

As to the policy I "seem to be pursuing," as you say, I have not meant to leave any one in doubt.

I would save the Union. I would save it the shortest way under the Constitution. The sooner the National authority can be restored, the nearer the Union will be "the Union as it was." If there be those who would not save the Union unless they could at the same time *save* Slavery, I do not agree with them. If there be those who would not save the Union unless they could at the same time *destroy* Slavery, I do not agree with them. My paramount object in this struggle *is* to save the Union, and is *not* either to save or destroy Slavery. If I could save the Union without freeing *any* slave, I would do it; and if I could save it by freeing *all* the slaves, I would do it; and if I could do it by freeing some and leaving others alone, I would also do that. What I do about Slavery and the colored race, I do because I believe it helps to save this Union; and what I forbear, I forbear because I do *not* believe it would help to save the Union. I shall do *less* whenever I shall believe what I am doing hurts the cause, and I shall do *more* whenever I shall believe doing more will help the cause. I shall try to correct errors when shown to be errors; and I shall adopt new views so fast as they shall appear to be true views. I have here stated my purpose according to my view of *official* duty, and I intend no modification of my oft-expressed *personal* wish that all men, everywhere, could be free.

Yours,

A. Lincoln.

—Moore, ed., *The Rebellion Record*

XXV. A War for Emancipation

Lincoln Becomes the Great Emancipator

Lincoln had read to his Cabinet on July 22, 1862, a preliminary draft of an emancipation proclamation. The Cabinet had been divided, from the start of the war, on the advisability of pronouncing officially in favor of emancipation. Yet public opinion in the North was becoming increasingly insistent on some declaration of the administration's policy. The danger of foreign intervention provided a persuasive argument for rallying English support to the North by making the war openly one of freedom.

It did not, however, seem wise to announce an emancipation policy as long as Union armies were unsuccessful. Seward remarked that that would be interpreted as "our last shriek, on the retreat." Lincoln resolved to issue the proclamation as soon as the Union had won a military victory. Union forces prevailed at Antietam on September 17, 1862, and five days later, Lincoln presented the Cabinet with his decision. The preliminary proclamation was followed by a formal proclamation on January 1, 1863.

What follows is Secretary Chase's account of the famous Cabinet meeting, and the official proclamation.

A. Secretary Chase Recalls a Famous Cabinet Meeting

September 22, 1862.—To department about nine. State Department messenger came with notices to heads of departments to meet at twelve. Received sundry callers. Went to the White House. All the members of the cabinet were in attendance. There was some general talk, and the President mentioned that Artemus Ward had sent him his book. Pro posed to read a chapter which he thought very funny. Read it and seemed to enjoy it very much; the heads also (except Stanton). The chapter was "High-Handed Outrage at Utica."

The President then took a graver tone and said: "Gentlemen, I have, as you are aware, thought a great deal about the relation of this war to slavery, and you all remember that, several weeks ago, I read to you an order I had prepared upon the subject, which, on account of objections made by some of you, was not issued. Ever since then my mind has been much occupied with this subject, and I have thought all along that the time for acting on it might probably come. I think the time has come now. I wish it was a better time. I wish that we were in a better condition. The action of the army against the rebels has not been quite what I should have liked best. But they have been driven out of Maryland, and Pennsylvania is no longer in danger of invasion. When the rebel army was at Frederick I determined, as soon as it should be driven out of Maryland, to issue a proclamation of emancipation such as I thought most likely to be useful. I said nothing to any one, but I made a promise to myself and (hesitating a little) to my Maker. The rebel army is now driven out, and I am going to fulfill that promise. I have got you together to hear what I have written down. I do not wish your advice about the main matter, for that I have determined for myself. This I say without intending anything but respect for any one of you. But I already know the views of each on this question. They have been heretofore expressed, and I have considered them as thoroughly and carefully as I can. What I have written is that which my reflections have determined me to say. If there is anything in the expressions I use or in any minor matter which any one of you thinks had best be changed, I shall be glad to receive your suggestions. One other observation I will make. I know very well that many others might, in this matter as in others, do better than I can; and if I was satisfied that the public confidence was more fully possessed by any one of them than by me, and knew of any constitutional way in which he could be put 'in my place, he should have it. I would gladly yield it to him. But though I believe that I have not so much of the confidence of the people as I had some time since, I do not know that, all things considered, any other person has more; and however this may be, there is no way in which I can have any other man put where I am. I am here. I must do the best I can and bear the responsibility of taking the course which I feel I ought to take."

The President then proceeded to read his Emancipation Proclamation, making remarks on the several parts as he went on, and showing that he had fully considered the subject in all the lights under which it had been presented to him.

After he had closed, Governor Seward said: "The general question having been decided, nothing can be said further about that. Would it not, however, make the proclamation more clear and decided to leave out all reference to the act being sustained during the incumbency of the present President; and not merely say that the Government 'recognizes' but that it will maintain the freedom it proclaims?"

I followed, saying: "What you have said, Mr. President, fully satisfies me that you have given to every proposition which has been made a kind and candid consideration. And you have now expressed the conclusion to which you have arrived clearly and distinctly. This it was your right and, under your oath of office, your duty to do. The proclamation does not, indeed, mark out the course I would myself prefer; but I am ready to take it just as it is written and to stand by 'it with all my heart. I think, however, the suggestions of Governor Seward very judicious, and shall be glad to have them adopted."

The President then asked us severally our opinions as to the modifications proposed, saying that he did not care much about the phrases he had used. Every one favored the modification, and it was adopted. Governor Seward then proposed that in the passage relating to colonization some language should be introduced to show that the colonization proposed was to be only with the consent of the colonists and the consent of the states in which the colonies might be at tempted. This, too, was agreed to; and no other modification was proposed. Mr. Blair then said that the question having been decided, he would make no objection to issuing the proclamation; but he would ask to have his paper, presented some days since, against the policy, filed with the proclamation. The President consented to this readily. And then Mr. Blair went on to say that he was afraid of the influence of the proclamation on the border states and on the army and stated at some length the grounds of his apprehensions. He disclaimed most expressly, however, all objections to emancipation *per se*, saying he had always been personally in favor of it—always ready for immediate emancipation in the midst of slave states, rather than submit to the perpetuation of the system.

—"Diary of S. P. Chase"

B. "Forever Free"

Whereas on the 22d day of September, A.D. 1862, a proclamation was issued by the President of the United States, containing, among other things, the following, to wit:

"That on the 1st day of January, A.D. 1863, all persons held as slaves within any state or designated part of a state the people whereof shall then be in rebellion against the United States shall be then, thenceforward, and forever free; and the executive government of the United States, including the military and naval authority thereof, will recognize and maintain the freedom of such persons and will do no act or acts to repress such persons, or any of them, in any efforts they may make for their actual freedom.

"That the executive will on the 1st day of January afore said, by proclamation, designate the states and parts of states, if any, in which the people thereof, respectively, shall then be in rebellion against the United States; and the fact that any state or the people thereof shall on that day be in good faith represented in the Congress of the United States by members chosen thereto at elections wherein a majority of the qualified voters of such states shall have participated shall, in the absence of strong countervailing testimony, be deemed conclusive evidence that such state and the people thereof are not then in rebellion against the United States."

Now, therefore, I, Abraham Lincoln, . . . do, on this 1st day of January, A.D. 1863, . . . order and designate . . . the states and parts of states wherein the people thereof, respectively, are this day in rebellion against the United States. . . .

And by virtue of the power and for the purpose aforesaid, I do order and declare that all persons held as slaves within said designated states and parts of states are, and henceforward shall be, free; and that the executive government of the United States, including the military and naval authorities thereof, will recognize and maintain the freedom of said persons.

And I hereby enjoin upon the people so declared to be free to abstain from all violence, unless in necessary self-defense; and I recommend to them that, in all cases when allowed, they labor faithfully for reasonable wages.

And I further declare and make known that such persons of suitable condition will be received into the armed service of the United States to garrison forts, positions, stations, and other places, and to man vessels of all sorts in said service.

And upon this act, sincerely believed to be an act of justice, warranted by the Constitution upon military necessity, I invoke the considerate judgment of mankind and the gracious favor of Almighty God.

—LINCOLN, "The Emancipation Proclamation"

XXV.7

REACTIONS TO THE EMANCIPATION PROCLAMATION

Technically, the Emancipation Proclamation did not free a single slave upon its pronouncement. It only affected regions of the country not already under federal authority. The 500,000 slaves in the border states and in occupied territories remained in bondage. The 3.5 million slaves in the unconquered bulk of the Confederacy were beyond federal control, at least for the moment. But the Emancipation Proclamation transformed the purpose of the war. The Union army became an army of liberation.

Abolitionists rejoiced. In November, two months before the proclamation formally went into effect, Ralph Waldo Emerson urged: "Do not let the dying die. Hold them back into this world until you have charged their ear and their heart with this message announcing the amelioration of this planet." Lincoln's past hesitancy—formerly cursed and disparaged—was forgiven. "Forget all that we thought shortcomings, every mistake, every delay," Emerson wrote. "In the extreme embarrassments of his part, call these endurance, wisdom, magnanimity, illuminated, as they now are, by this dazzling success."

But not all Northerners were pleased by the proclamation. Many were outraged, especially in the border states and west. In the elections of 1862 later that fall, the Peace Democrats won 32 seats in the House of Representatives and gained control of several state legislatures, in part because of opposition to the proclamation. Some states issued formal declarations against the war, citing the emancipation of slaves as an illegitimate war aim.

In places such as Kentucky, the impact was very complex. Many Union soldiers who had not had contact with slaves prior to the war were suddenly confronted with the face of slavery, and they did not like what they saw. The Emancipation Proclamation emboldened them to protect runaway slaves, even ones that came from loyal Kentucky families. "Under the President's proclamation of Sept. 22nd, I cannot conscientiously force my boys to become the slavehounds of Kentuckians & I am determined I will not," Colonel Smith D. Atkins wrote to a friend in Chicago. "Doubtless before you get this I will [be] under arrest, & undergoing Court Martial."

But loyal soldiers and families who owned slaves were not willing to support a war of emancipation. Colonel Marcellus Mundy, who commanded a Kentucky regiment and was a slaveholder, believed the Union army had become "a mere negro freeing machine." He wrote Lincoln directly to object to the Emancipation Proclamation.

Reaction in the South was muted. Although the document all but eliminated any hope that a European nation would come to the South's aid, politicians and commentators tried to downplay the impact of the Emancipation Proclamation, describing it as a desperate act. President Davis said it was "the fullest vindication of the wisdom of secession," noting that Lincoln's act was proof of the Southern contention that Lincoln's aim all along was to free the slaves.

The following documents reflect some of the diverse reactions to Lincoln's proclamation.

A. The Day of Jubilee Comes

An Address Delivered in Rochester, New York, December 28, 1862

This is scarcely a day for prose. It is a day for poetry and song, a new song. These cloudless skies, this balmy air, this brilliant sunshine, (making December as pleasant as May) are in harmony with the glorious morning of liberty about to dawn upon us. Out of a full heart and with sacred emotion, I congratulate you my friends, and fellow citizens, on the high and hopeful condition, of the cause of human freedom and the cause of our common country, for these two causes are now one and inseparable and must stand or fall together. We stand to-day in the presence of a glorious prospect. This sacred Sunday in all the likelihoods of the case, is the last which will witness the existence of legal slavery in all the Rebel slaveholding States of America. Henceforth and forever, slavery in those States is to be recognized, by all the departments [of] the American Government, under its appropriate character, as an unmitigated robber and pirate, branded as the sum of all villainy, an outlaw having no rights which any man white or colored is bound to respect. It is difficult for us who have toiled so long and hard to believe that this event, so stupendous, so far reaching and glorious is even now at the door. It surpasses our most enthusiastic hopes that we live at such a time and are likely to witness the downfall, at least the legal downfall of slavery in America. It is a moment for joy, thanksgiving and Praise. . . .

Slavery has existed in this country too long and has stamped its character too deeply and indelibly, to be blotted out in a day or a year, or even in a generation. The slave will yet remain in some sense a slave, long after the chains are taken from his limbs, and the master will retain much of the pride, the arrogance, imperiousness and conscious superiority, and love of power, acquired by his former relation of master. Time, necessity, education, will be required to bring all classes into harmonious and natural relations. . . .

Laws and the sword can and will, in the end abolish slavery. But law and the sword cannot abolish the malignant slaveholding sentiment which has kept the slave system alive in this country during two centuries. Pride of race, prejudice against color, will raise their hateful clamor for oppression of the negro as heretofore. The slave having ceased to be the abject slave of a single master, his enemies will endeavor to make him the slave of society at large. . . . [T]he friends of freedom, the men and women of the land who regard slavery as a crime and the slave as a man will still be needed even after slavery is abolished.

—FREDERICK DOUGLASS

B. Illinois State Legislature Opposes Emancipation Proclamation

January 7, 1863

Resolved: that the emancipation proclamation of the President of the United States is as unwarrantable in military as in civil law; a gigantic usurpation, at once converting the war, professedly commenced by the administration for the vindication of the authority of the constitution, into the crusade for the sudden, unconditional and violent liberation of 3,000,000 negro slaves; a result which would not only be a total subversion of the Federal Union but a revolution in the social organization of the Southern States, the immediate and remote, the present and far-reaching consequences of which to both races cannot be contemplated without the most dismal foreboding of horror and dismay. The proclamation invites servile insurrection as an element in this emancipation crusade—a means of warfare, the inhumanity and diabolism of which are without example in civilized warfare, and which we denounce, and which the civilized world will denounce, as an uneffaceable disgrace to the American people.

—ILLINOIS STATE LEGISLATURE

C. Kentucky Union Officer Objects to Emancipation

Louisville, Nov 27th 1862

Mr President.

I deem it my privilege as a Citizen to make the following Complaint directly to you. While I have been absent from my home serving our Country in the field to the utmost of my humble ability, I have not only suffered large pecuniary loss from rebel depradations but worse still, federal officers, particularly those of the 18th Michigan Infantry Volunteers have taken within their lines and hold the negroes of my loyal neighbours and myself. That regiment has now not less than twenty five negroes in Camp at Lexington Ky, who belong to loyal union men who have been masters for loyalty's sake, and among the rest one of mine. I called upon the officer Commanding

the regiment and mildly remonstrated against this injustice, particularly to myself, and requested him to have my negro turned out of his line, which he flatly refused to do, justifying his detention by virtue of Your proclamation and the new article of war. My father-in-law, Col E. N. Offutt had in the mean time, during my absence, as the best means of recovering my slave which they refused him permission to take, issued a writ of repleving for the negro which was duly served by the Sheriff of Fayette County—but was disobeyed by the officer and the civil authorities defied. Another fact I should mention in this Connection, which is, that our negroes are being taught by the abolition officers from Michigan and other northern states now serving in Kentucky, that on the first day of January next, they are all to be free, and will have a right even to kill their masters who may attempt to restrain them, which has aroused a lively apprehension in the minds of Citizens in Central Kentucky of a servile insurrection at that time unless prevented by such orders as will check the evil—This is neither slander upon those officers or idle rumor; but a fact for which I and hundreds of citizens can vouch. Mr President I deem it unnecessary to resort to argument to show to you the magnitude of the injustice in this case to me—When I became a soldier I sacrificed a large and lucrative practice as an attorney in Philadelphia and placed my property in this state at the mercy of our enemies—who have revenged themselves largely upon me—and now my utter ruin is to be Completed by our own officers to promote a fanatical partizan theory—which not only ignores gratitude as a principle; but does me and many loyal men of my state bold wrong for a supposed benefit of another race. Mr President is this right and will you sanction it? While in opinion I must dissent from your policy of freeing the slaves of rebels, which would result in great wrong to loyal slave owners, as well as to all loyal men burthened with this immense war debt—I approve of the Confiscation of the slaves and all property of rebels to weaken the resources of our enemy and relieve the tax burthen of our friends. Being a soldier whether palatable or impalatable, I am always ready to execute the orders of the President as my Commander in Chief; but Mr President were I Commander in Chief I would never trample upon the Constitutional rights of a loyal people in a loyal state whereby our friends would be estranged and our enemies advantaged I need not reassure you sir of my abiding faith in your goodness, integrity of purpose and sense of justice of which this appeal is the evidence. I have the Honor to be Your Ob Sert.

—Colonel Marcellus Mundy

D. Jefferson Davis Replies to the Emancipation Proclamation

. . . The public journals of the North have been received, containing a proclamation, dated on the 1st day of the present month, signed by the President of the United States, in which he orders and declares all slaves within ten of the States of the Confederacy to be free, except such as are found within certain districts now occupied in part by the armed forces of the enemy. We may well leave it to the instincts of that common humanity which a beneficent Creator has implanted in the breasts of our fellowmen of all countries to pass judgment on a measure by which several millions of human beings of an inferior race, peaceful and contented laborers in their sphere, are doomed to extermination, while at the same time they are encouraged to a general assassination of their master by the insidious recommendation "to abstain from violence unless in necessary self-defense." Our own detestation of those who have attempted the most execrable measure recorded in the history of guilty man is tempered by profound contempt for the impotent rage which it discloses. So far as regards the action of this Government on such criminals as may attempt its execution, I confine myself to informing you that I shall, unless in your wisdom you deem some other course more expedient, deliver to the several State authorities all commissioned officers of the united States that may hereafter be captured by our forces in any of the

States embraced in the proclamation, that they may be dealt with in accordance with the laws of those States providing for the punishment of criminals engaged in exciting servile insurrection. The enlisted soldiers I shall continue to treat as unwilling instruments in the commission of these crimes, and shall direct their discharge and return to their homes on the proper and usual parole.

In its political aspect this measure possesses great significance, and to it in this light I invite your attention. It affords to our whole people the complete and crowning proof of the true nature of the designs of the party which elevated to power the present occupant of the Presidential chair at Washington and which sought to conceal its purpose by every variety of artful device and by the perfidious use of the most solemn and repeated pledges on every possible occasion. . . .

The people of this Confederacy, then, cannot fail to receive this proclamation as the fullest vindication of their own sagacity in foreseeing the uses to which the dominant party in the United States intended from the beginning to apply their power, nor can they cease to remember with devout thankfulness that it is to their own vigilance in resisting the first stealthy progress of approaching despotism that they owe their escape from consequences now apparent to the most skeptical. This proclamation will have another salutary effect in calming the fears of those who have constantly evinced the apprehension that this war might end by some reconstruction of the old Union or some renewal of close political relations with the United States. These fears have never been shared by me, nor have I ever been able to perceive on what basis they could rest. But the proclamation affords the fullest guarantee of the impossibility of such a result; it has established a state of things which can lead to but one of three possible consequences— the extermination of the slaves, the exile of the whole white population from the Confederacy, or absolute and total separation of these States from the United States. . . .

—Jefferson Davis, January 12, 1863

E. A Note on the Emancipation Proclamation

Lincoln seems to be in a state of desperation. He has issued a proclamation, declaring all negroes belonging to rebels as free. As his armies have freed the negroes wherever they have been, this proclamation does not at all alter the character of the war. He has issued another, in which he proclaims martial law all over the United States. As he has no authority in the Southern States, of course it is altogether inoperative there. But it does operate in the Yankee States, and was no doubt designed for them. The Democratic party has of late begun to show itself very formidable in those States, and there was fair prospect of their beating the Abolitionists proper, at the next elections. This proclamation is intended to keep them quiet, or to dispose of them in the most summary manner, if they should succeed in their ticket. Opposition is not tolerated north of the Potomac, and any man who attempts it will be dealt with as a traitor. The government there is a military despotism, as absolute as that of Russia. The old Constitution of the United States has sunk into absolute contempt. Those who express a wish to see it respected, are forthwith clapped into jail on a charge of treason.

—*The Southern Illustrated News*

XXV.8

A WAR FOR LIBERTY

David Hunter, an abolitionist Union general, had helped push the issue of emancipating slaves and arming black soldiers. He embraced the war as a chance to revolutionize society. The Emancipation Proclamation, combined with Lincoln's decision to allow African Americans to serve in the military, enabled abolitionist officers to realize that goal.

Hunter wrote a letter to Jefferson Davis, with whom he had once been friendly, in the spring of 1863. The letter brims with bitterness and outrage. Furious that Confederate troops are murdering black soldiers and sending others back into slavery, Hunter vows retribution against Confederate officers. The letter reflects how the Emancipation Proclamation helped both raise

the stakes of the Civil War and changed its context into a conflict of different interpretations over the nature of liberty. It was now a full-fledged war between cultures fundamentally opposed, and there was no turning back.

Hilton Head, Port Royal, S.C.,
April 23rd 1863.

The United States flag must protect all its defenders, white, black or yellow. Several negroes in the employ of the government, in the Western Department, have been cruelly murdered by your authorities, and others sold into slavery. Every outrage of this kind against the laws of war and humanity, which may take place in this Department, shall be followed by the immediate execution of the Rebel of highest rank in my possession; man for man, these executions will certainly take place, for every one murdered, or sold into a slavery worse than death. On your authorities will rest the responsibility of having inaugurated this barbarous policy, and you will be held responsible, in this world and in the world to come, for all blood thus shed.

In the month of August last you declared all those engaged in arming the negroes to fight for their country, to be felons, and directed the immediate execution of all such, as should be captured. I have given you long enough to reflect on your folly. I now give you notice, that unless this order is immediately revoked, I will at once cause the execution of every rebel officer, and every rebel slaveholder in my possession. This sad state of things may be kindly ordered by an all wise providence, to induce the good people of the North to act earnestly, and to realize that they are at war. Thousands of lives may thus be saved.

The poor negro is fighting for liberty in its truest sense; and Mr. Jefferson has beautifully said,—"in such a war, there is no attribute of the Almighty, which will induce him to fight on the side of the oppressor."

You say you are fighting for liberty. Yes you are fighting for liberty: liberty to keep four millions of your fellow-beings in ignorance and degradation;— liberty to separate parents and children, husband

and wife, brother and sister;—liberty to steal the products of their labor, exacted with many a cruel lash and bitter tear;—liberty to seduce their wives and daughters, and to sell your own children into bondage;—liberty to kill these children with impunity, when the murder cannot be proven by one of pure white blood. This is the kind of liberty—the liberty to do wrong—which Satan, Chief of fallen Angels, was contending for when he was cast into Hell. I have the honor to be, very respectuflly, Your mo. ob. ser.

—David Hunter

XXV.9

ARMING SLAVES FOR THE CONFEDERATE ARMY

By the end of the war, even the South looked to emancipation as a source of military strength. Confederate soldiers had faced black soldiers in combat and experienced firsthand their effectiveness. Confederate military leaders increasingly looked to arming slaves as a way to bolster the number of soldiers in their shrinking armies.

President Davis proposed enlisting slaves as soldiers in November 1864. Many people suggested granting slaves their freedom as an inducement for serving in the army. There was intense opposition, particularly from the planter class. "If slaves would make good soldiers, our whole theory of slavery is wrong," one planter said. But in February 1865, Robert E. Lee endorsed the proposal and encouraged soldiers to voice their opinions and state their willingness to fight alongside former slaves.

The 18th Virginia Infantry Regiment voted on the issue. Out of 325 officers and common soldiers, only 14 opposed the measure. The regiment issued the resolution below. The Confederate Congress voted on March 13th to allow owners to volunteer their slaves for military service. The decision came too late to impact the course of the war, but it confirmed that slavery's twilight was at hand.

Headquarters 18th Virginia Infantry
Feb 20th 1865

Resolved 1st That the 18th Virginia Infantry, reposing the most implicit, & unlimited confidence in the wisdom, skill & patriotism of our beloved General in Chief [Robert E. Lee], will cheerfully acquiesce in the arming of any portion of our slaves for the defence of our Common Country whenever in his opinion this grave action on the part of Congress becomes necessary in order to successfully resist the further progress of a devastating & remorseless foe—provided that such armed slaves shall form a separate & distinct Corps, & shall not be incorporated with our skeleton Regts—

Resolved 2nd That believing that freedom is not a boon to the negroe we are in favor of offereing freedom to those only who elect it—

—18th Virginia Infantry Regiment

XXV.10

"ABOLITIONISTS WERE THE ONLY TRAITORS"

By the end of the Civil War, slavery was doomed. In February 1865, Congress approved the 13th Amendment abolishing slavery. It seemed only a matter of time before the required number of states ratified the measure.

Nonetheless, bitter resistance to emancipation lingered, and not just in the South. Congressional approval of the amendment passed by only two votes. The well-known actor and Southern sympathizer John Wilkes Booth viewed the liberation of slaves as a destruction of society. He wrote the letter below to the *Philadelphia Inquirer* in 1864, wherein he expressed his violent racist views. The letter was published on April 19, 1865, four days after Booth assassinated Lincoln.

In the South, many slave owners refused to acknowledge the emancipation of their slaves. In an attempt to avoid the Northern armies, some sent their slaves to Texas. When the Union army arrived in Texas in June 1865 to enforce the emancipation, some owners preferred to murder their slaves rather than permit them to become free, as the reported testimony from an anonymous slave attests.

A. "The Country was Formed for the White, Not for the Black Man"
The country was formed for the white, not for the black man. And looking upon African slavery from

the same standpoint held by the noble framers of our Constitution. I, for one, have ever considered it one of the greatest blessings (both for themselves and us) that God ever bestowed upon a favored nation. Witness heretofore our wealth and power: witness their elevation and enlightenment above their race elsewhere. I have lived among it most of my life, and I have seen less harsh treatment from master to man than I have beheld in the North from father to son. Yet, heaven knows, no one would be willing to do more for the Negro race than I, could I but see the way to still better their condition.

But Lincoln's policy is only preparing a way for their total annihilation. The South are not, nor have they been fighting for the continuation of slavery. The first battle of Bull Run did away with that idea. Their causes of war have been as noble and greater [by] far than those that urged our fathers on. Even should we allow they were wrong at the beginning of this contest, cruelty and injustice have made the wrong become the right, and they stand now (before the wonder and admiration of the world) as a noble band of patriotic heroes. Hereafter, reading of their deeds, Thermopylæ will be forgotten.

When I aided in the capture and execution of John Brown (who was a murderer on our Western border and who was fairly tried and convicted before an impartial judge and jury, of treason, and who, by the way, has since been made a god) I was proud of my little share in the transaction, for I deemed it my duty that it was helping our common country to perform an act of justice. But what was a crime in poor John Brown is considered (by themselves) as the greatest and only virtue of the whole Republican party. Strange transmigration. Vice so becomes a virtue, simply because more indulged in. I thought then as now that the Abolitionists were the only traitors in the land and that the entire party deserved the fate of poor John Brown, not because they wish to abolish slavery, but on account of the means they have ever used to effect that abolition. If Brown were living I doubt

whether he himself would set slavery against the Union. Most or many in the North do, and openly curse the Union, if the South are to return and retain a single right guaranteed to them by every tie which we once revered as sacred.

I have also studied hard to know upon what grounds the right of a state to secede has been denied, when our very name United States, and the Declaration of Independence both provide for secession.

But there is no time for words. I write in haste. I know how foolish I shall be deemed for taking such a step as this . . .

—John Wilkes Booth

B. Emancipation Arrives in Texas

I heard about freedom in September and they were picking cotton and a white man rode up to a master's house on a big, white horse and the houseboy told master a man wanted to see him and he hollered, "Light, stranger." It was a government man and he had the big book and a bunch of papers and said why hadn't master turned the n—s loose. Master said he was trying to get the crop out and he told master to have the slaves in. Uncle Sam blew the cow horn that they used to call to eat and all the n—s came running, because that horn meant, "Come to the big house, quick." The man read the paper telling us we were free, but master made us work several months after that. He said we would get 20 acres of land and a mule but we didn't get it.

Lots of n—s were killed after freedom, because the slaves in Harrison County were turned loose right at freedom and those in Rusk county weren't. but they heard about it and ran away to freedom in Harrison County and their owners had them bushwhacked, then shot down. You could see lots of n—s hanging from trees in Sabine bottom right after freedom, because they caught them swimming across Sabine River and shot them. There sure are going to be lots of crying souls crying against them in judgment!

—Anonymous

"The Work of the Abolitionists Is Not Done"

Legal emancipation alone was not enough to ensure the freedom of African Americans. As the prior commentary shows, too many other obstructions lay in the way of liberty. Blacks may have been free, but they had no political authority, no legal standing in courts and remained economically dependent upon whites.

In early 1865, the Anti-Slavery Society met to consider disbanding. On the face of it, the organization's job was done. Slavery would soon be officially abolished. Frederick Douglass urged the organization on May 10 to continue its fight for emancipation. Douglass, who had experienced slavery in the South and intense bigotry in the North, knew that the battle for true freedom for blacks in the United States had only achieved a partial victory.

I do not whish to appear here in any fault-finding spirit, or as an impugner of the motives of those who believe that the time has come for this Society to disband. I am conscious of no suspicion of the purity and excellence of the motives that animate the President of this Society, and other gentlemen who are in favor of its disbandment. I take this ground; whether this Constitutional Amendment [the thirteenth] is law or not, whether it has been ratified by a sufficient number of states to make it law or not. I hold that the work of Abolitionists is not done. Even if every State in the Union had ratified that Amendment, while the black man is confronted in the legislation of the South by the word "white," our work as Abolitionists, as I conceive it, is not done. I took the ground, last night, that the South, by unfriendly legislation, could make our liberty, under that provision, a delusion, a mockery, and a snare, and I hold that ground now. What advantage is a provision like this Amendment to the black man, if the Legislature of any State can to-morrow declare that no black man's testimony shall be received in a court of law? Where are we then? Any wretch may enter the house of a black man, and commit any violence he pleases; if he happens to do it only in the presence of black per-

sons, he goes unwhipt of justice. And don't tell me that those people down there have become so just and honest all at once that they will not pass laws denying to black men the right to testify against white men in the courts of law. Why, our Northern States have done it. Illinois, Indiana and Ohio have done it. Here, in the midst of institutions that have gone forth from old Plymouth Rock, the black man has been excluded from testifying in the courts of law; and if the Legislature of Every Southern State to-morrow pass a law, declaring that no Negro shall testify in any courts of law, they will not violate that provision of the Constitution. Such laws exist now at the South, and they might exist under this provision of the Constitution, that there shall be neither slavery nor involuntary servitude in any State of the Union. . . .

Slavery is not abolished until the black man has the ballot. While the legislatures of the South retain the right to pass laws making any discrimination between black and white, slavery still lives there. As Edmund Quincy once said, "While the word 'white' is on the statute-book of Massachusetts, Massachusetts is a slave state. While a slave can be taken from old Massachusetts, Massachusetts is a slave State." That is what I heard Edmund Quincy say twenty-three or twenty-four years ago. I never forgot such a thing. Now, while the black man can be denied a vote, while the Legislatures of the South can take from him the right to keep and bear arms, as they can—they would not allow a Negro to walk with a cane where I came from, they would not allow five of them to assemble together—the work of the Abolitionists is not finished. Notwithstanding the provision in the Constitution of the United States, that the right to keep and bear arms shall not be abridged, the black man has never had the right either to keep and bear arms; and the Legislatures of the States will still have the power to forbid it, under this Amendment. They can carry on a system of unfriendly legislation, and will they not do it? Have they not got prejudice there to do it with? Think you, that because they are for the moment in the talons and beak of our glorious eagle, instead of the slave being there, as formerly, that they are converted? I hear of the loyalty at Wilmington, the loyalty at South Carolina—what is it worth?

[From the audience: "Not a straw."]

Not a straw. I thank my friend for admitting it. They are loyal while they see 200,000 sable soldiers, with glistening bayonets, walking in their midst. But let the civil power of the South be restored, and the old prejudices and hostility to the Negro will revive. Aye, the very fact that the Negro has been used to defeat this rebellion and strike down the standards of the Confederacy will be a stimulus to all their hatred, to all their malice, and lead them to legislate with greater stringency towards this class than ever before. The American people are bound—bound by their sense of honor (I hope by their sense of honor, at least by just a sense of honor), to extend the franchise to the Negro; and I was going to say, that the Abolitionists of the American Anti-Slavery Society were bound to "stand still, and see the salvation of God," until that work is done. Where shall the black man look for support, my friends, if the American Anti-Slavery Society fails him? From whence shall we expect a certain sound from the trumpet of freedom, when the old pioneer, when this Society that has survived mobs, and martyr-

dom, and the combined efforts of priest-craft and state-craft to suppress it, shall all at once subside, on the mere intimation that the Constitution has been amended, so that neither slavery nor involuntary servitude shall hereafter be allowed in this land? What did the slaveholders of Richmond say to those who objected to arming the Negro, on the ground that it would make him a freeman? Why, they said, "the argument is absurd. We may make these Negroes fight for us; but while we retain the political power of the South, we can keep them in their subordinate positions." That was the argument; and they were right. They might have employed the Negro to fight for them, and while they retained in their hands power to exclude him from political rights, they could have reduced him to a condition similar to slavery. They would not call it slavery, but some other name. Slavery has been fruitful in giving itself names. It has been called "the peculiar institution," "the social system," and the "impediment," as it was called by the General conference of the Methodist Episcopal Church. It has been called by a great many names, and it will call itself by yet another name; and you and I and all of us had better wait and see what new form this old monster will assume, in what new skin this old snake will come forth.

—Frederick Douglass

XXVI

THE COAST AND INLAND WATERS

Sea power played a decisive role in the Civil War. It was the blockade, as much as any other single factor, that assured Union victory; had the Confederacy been able to break the blockade, or to persuade European nations to do so, she could probably have held out indefinitely. Almost equally important was Federal control of the major ports along the Atlantic and the Gulf coasts and of the river systems that led deep into the heart of the Confederacy. This control of coast and inland waters not only enabled the Union to supply its own forces and to move along interior lines of communication, but cut o• the flow of supplies from one part of the Confederacy to another and broke Confederate lines of communication.

In the nature of the case naval supremacy rested, from the beginning, with the Union. It was possible, after a fashion, to improvise an army, and certainly to improvise a defense; it was not possible to improvise a navy, though here the Confederacy almost did the impossible. Although the Union Navy numbered less than 40 effective vessels at the beginning of the war, it was rapidly built up to really effective strength. The Confederacy had nothing to start with—only two navy yards, no merchant marine, no seafaring population on which to draw. It was something of a miracle that the Confederacy did as well as it did on water.

The war found the Union Navy as unprepared as the army. The total number of vessels on the navy list was about 90; of these 50 were obsolete sailing ships. Most of the 40 steamers comprising the fleet were scattered around the globe; only 12 were actually available in the Home Squadron. Naval personnel was equally inadequate. Of the almost 1,500 officers, over 300 had resigned at the beginning of the war, and there were less than 7,500 seamen to man the fleet. Yet this fleet was expected to blockade over 3,000 miles of coast and co operate with the army in attacks on coastal ports and along the inland rivers.

The Confederacy was in an even worse situation. It had no navy, and no naval personnel except such as had resigned from the Union Navy at the outbreak-of the war. Both its navy yards fell to the Union before the end of the war. Yet some how it managed to create a navy. It captured some ships, built others, raised several that had been sunk at Norfolk, converted a few merchant ships into warships, fitted out privateers, bought and built vessels abroad. At the same time it greatly strengthened its harbor defenses: Fort Fisher did not fall until January 1865; Charleston resisted every assault by sea.

The United States Navy faced a twofold task. First it had to enforce the blockade. This actually proved less difficult than had been anticipated, for there were comparatively few ports which combined adequate harbors, harbor defenses, and connections with the interior. The most important were Norfolk (lames River), Roanoke Island, New Bern (Neuse River), Beaufort, Wilmington (Cape Fear River), Charleston, Beaufort (South Carolina), Savannah, and, on the Gulf, Pensacola, Mobile, New Orleans, and Galveston. Obviously it was easier to capture these ports, once and for an than to blockade them throughout the war, and it was to this task of reducing coastal forts and capturing ports that the Federal Army-Navy team first addressed itself.

One after another the ports fell: first Hilton Head, Port Royal, and Beaufort (South Carolina); then Roanoke Island, controlling Albemarle Sound; then—after the Monitor had forced the Merrimac to withdraw—Norfolk at the mouth of the lames; and then lames Island, outside Charleston. The great prize was, however, New Orleans, greatest city in the Confederacy and key to the Gulf and the Mississippi. After that the Confederacy had only a few good ports to which the swift blockade-runners could sail: Charleston, Wilmington, Mobile, and Galveston. It took longer to capture these, and Charleston was never captured from the sea, but it is no exaggeration to say that by the end of 1862 the Confederacy was pretty well bottled up.

Even more arduous was the task of clearing the Mississippi and co-operating with the army in warfare along its tributaries—

the Tennessee, the Cumberland, the Arkansas, and the Red—which Federal strategy imposed upon the navy. For most of the victories in the West the army got the credit, yet without the navy the story of Fort Donelson, Shiloh, New Madrid, Vicksburg, Port Hudson, and even the Red River campaign would have been very different.

What we have here is amphibious warfare, and the problem of allocating its history to the services is a perplexing one. Certainly it does some violence to history to place the attack on Battery Wagner, for example, in a chapter devoted to the navy, or to separate the naval and the military history of the Vicksburg campaign. To break up this story, however, inserting its various segments into the history of military campaigns, would be to lose sight of the remarkable achievement of the Union Navy—and the interesting achievement of the Confederate Navy, in the war; and that would be a pity.

XXVI. 1

THE MERRIMAC AND THE MONITOR

This is one of the half-dozen most famous engagements in American history. If it did not revolutionize naval warfare, as is often erroneously asserted, it did dramatize the advent of the revolution that had taken place—the substitution of iron or steel for oak.

When the Federals abandoned Norfolk they fired and sank a number of their ships there; among them was the 350 ton frigate, *Merrimac*. The Confederates raised this ship and converted her into an ironclad—renaming her, but in vain, the *Virginia*. Alarmed by rumors of progress on the *Merrimac*, the Navy Department asked for bids for the building of armored vessels. The well-known naval engineer, John Ericsson, who had been born in Sweden, was among those who submitted plans. These were accepted, and Ericsson began building his armored ship in October 1861. It was launched at the end of January, ready for sea on February 19, and sailed from New York March 6, under the command of Lieutenant John L. Worden. It arrived off Hampton Roads just in the nick of time—or perhaps a bit too late. For on March 8 the Merrimac had come out and attacked the Union fleet off Fortress Monroe.

We give here the account of the terrible destruction wrought by the Merrimac on the eighth and of the tremendous duel between the two ironclads the following day. Our first historian is Captain Van Brunt of the *Minnesota*; our second the intrepid Lieutenant S. Dana Greene, who succeeded the blinded Worden in command of the *Monitor*.

A. The *Minnesota* Fights for Her Life in Hampton Roads

United States Steamer Minnesota,
March 10, 1862

SIR: On Saturday, the eighth instant, at forty-five minutes after twelve o'clock P.M. , three small steamers, in appearance, were discovered rounding Sewall's Point, and as soon as they came into full broadside view, I was convinced that one was the iron-plated steam-battery *Merrimac*, from the large size of her smoke-pipe. They were heading for Newport News, and I, in obedience to a signal from the senior officer present, Capt. John Marston, immediately called all hands, slipped my cables, and got under way for that point, to engage her. While rapidly passing Sewall's Point, the rebels there opened fire upon us from a rifle-battery, one shot from which going through and crippling my main-mast. I returned the fire with my broadside-guns and forecastle-pivot. We ran without further difficulty within about one and a half miles of Newport News, and there, unfortunately, grounded. The tide was running ebb, and although in the channel there was not sufficient water for this ship, which draws twenty-three feet, I knew the bottom was soft and lumpy, and endeavored to force the ship over, but found it impossible so to do. At this time it was reported to me that the *Merrimac* had passed the frigate *Congress* and run into the sloop-of-war *Cumberland*, and in fifteen minutes after, I saw the latter going down by the head. The *Merrimac* then hauled off, taking a position, and about half-past two o'clock P.M. , engaged the *Congress*, throwing shot and shell into her with terrific effect, while the shot from the *Congress* glanced from her iron-plated sloping sides, without doing any apparent injury. At half-past three o'clock P.M. , the *Congress* was compelled to haul down her colors. Of the extent of her loss and injury, you will be in formed from the official report of her commander.

At four o'clock P.M. , *the Merrimac, Jamestown* and *Patrick Henry*, bore down upon my vessel. Very fortunately, the iron battery drew too much water to come within a mile of us. She took a position on my starboard bow, but did not fire with accuracy, and only one shot passed through the ship's bow. The other two steamers took their position on my port bow and stern, and their fire did most damage in killing and wounding men, inasmuch as they fired with rifled guns; but with the heavy gun that I-could bring to bear upon them, I drove them off, one of them apparently in a-crippled state. I fired upon the *Merrimac* with my ten-inch pivot-gun, without any apparent effect, and at seven o'clock P.M. , she too hauled off, and all three vessels steamed toward Norfolk.

The tremendous firing of my broadside guns had crowded me further upon the mud-bank, into which the ship seemed to have made herself a cradle. From ten P.M. , when the tide commenced to run flood, until four A.M. , I had all hands at work, with steamtugs and hawsers, endeavoring to haul the ship off the bank; but without avail, and as the tide had then fallen considerably, I suspended further proceedings at that time.

At two A.M. the iron battery *Monitor,* Com. John L. Worden, which had arrived the previous evening at Hampton Roads, came alongside and reported for duty, and then all on board felt that we had a friend that would stand by us in our hour of trial.

At six A.M. the enemy again appeared, coming down from Craney Island, and I beat to quarters; but they ran past my ship, and were heading for Fortress Monroe, and the retreat was beaten, to allow my men to get something to eat. The *Merrimac* ran down near the Rip Raps, and then turned into the channel through which I had come. Again all hands were called to quarters, and opened upon her with my stern-guns, and made signal to the *Monitor* to attack the enemy. She immediately ran down in my wake, right within the range of the *Merrimac,* completely covering my ship, as far as possible with her diminutive dimensions, and, much to my astonishment, laid herself right alongside of the *Merrimac,* and the contrast was that of a pigmy to a giant. Gun after gun was fired by the *Monitor,* which was returned with whole broad sides from the rebels, with no more effect, apparently, than so many pebble-stones

thrown by a child. After a while they commenced manaeuvering, and we could see the little battery point her bow for the rebel's, with the intention, as I thought, of sending a shot through her bow-porthole; then she would shoot by her, and rake her through her stern. In the mean time the rebels were pouring broadside after broadside, but almost all her shot flew over the little submerged propeller; and when they struck the bomb-proof tower, the shot glanced off without producing any effect, clearly establishing the fact that wooden vessels cannot contend successfully with iron clad ones, for never before was anything like it dreamed of by the greatest enthusiast in maritime warfare.

The *Merrimac,* finding that she could make nothing of the *Monitor,* turned her attention once more to me in the morning. She had put one eleven-inch shot under my counter, near the water-line, and now, on her second approach, I opened upon her with all my broadside-guns and ten-inch pivot—a broadside which would have blown out of water any timber-built ship in the world. She returned my fire with her rifled bow-gun, with a shell which passed through the chief engineer's state-room, through the engineer's mess-room amid ships, and burst in the boatswain's room, tearing four rooms all into one, in its passage exploding two charges of powder, which set the ship on fire, but it was promptly extinguished by a party headed by my first lieutenant. Her second went through the boiler of the tugboat *Dragon,* exploding it, and causing more consternation on board my ship for the moment, until the matter was explained. This time I had concentrated upon her an incessant fire from my gun-deck, spar-deck and forecastle pivot-guns, and was informed by my marine officer, who was stationed on the poop, that at least fifty solid shot struck her on her slanting side, without producing any apparent effect. By the time she had fired her third shell, the little *Monitor* had come down upon her, placing herself between us, and compelled her to change her position, in doing which she grounded, and again I poured into her all the guns which could be brought to bear upon her.

As soon as she got off, she stood down the bay, the little battery chasing her with all speed, when suddenly the *Merrimac* turned around, and ran full speed into her antagonist. For a moment I was anxious, but instantly I saw a shot plunge into the iron roof of the *Merrimac,* which surely must have dam aged her, for some time after the rebels concentrated their whole battery upon the tower and pilothouse of the *Monitor,* and soon after the latter stood down for Fortress Monroe, and we thought it probable she had exhausted her supply of ammunition, or sustained some injury. Soon after the *Merrimac* and the two other steamers headed for my ship, and I then felt to the fullest extent my condition. I was hard and immovable aground, and they could take position under my stern and rake me. I had expended most of my solid shot, and my ship was badly crippled, and my officers and men were worn out with fatigue; but even in this extreme dilemma I determined never to give up the ship to the rebels, and after consulting my officers, I ordered every preparation to be made to destroy the ship, after all hope was gone to save her. On ascending the poopdeck, I observed that the enemy's vessels had changed their course, and were heading for Craney Island; then I determined to lighten the ship by throwing over board my eight-inch guns, hoisting out provisions, starting water, etc.

At two P.M. I proceeded to make another attempt to save the ship, by the use of a number of powerful tugs and the steamer *S. R. Spaulding* . . . and succeeded in dragging her half a mile distant, and then she was again immovable, the tide having fallen. At two A.M. this morning I succeeded in getting the ship once more afloat, and am now at anchor opposite Fortress Monroe.

It gives me great pleasure to say that, during the whole of these trying scenes, the officers and men conducted themselves with great courage and coolness.

I have the honor to be your very obedient servant,

G. J. Van Brunt,

Captain U. S. N., Commanding Frigate *Minnesota.*

Hon. Gideon Welles,

Secretary of the Navy, Washington, D. C.

—"Report of Captain Van Brunt"

B. The *Monitor* Repels the *Merrimac*

U.S. Steamer *Monitor,* Hampton Roads, Va.—At 4 P.M. [March 8, 1862] we passed Cape Henry and heard heavy firing in the direction of Fortress Monroe. As we approached, it increased, and we immediately cleared ship for action. When about halfway between Fortress Monroe and Cape Henry we spoke the pilot boat. He told us the *Cumberlend* was sunk and the *Congress* was on fire and had surrendered to the *Merrimac.* We could not credit it at first, but as we approached Hampton Roads, we could see the fine old *Congress* burning brightly; and we knew it must be true. Sad indeed did we feel to think those two fine old vessels had gone to their last homes with so many of their brave crews. Our hearts were very full, and we vowed vengeance on the *Merrimac* if it should be our lot to fall in with her. At 9 P.M. we anchored near the frigate *Roanoke,* the flagship, Captain Marston. Captain Worden immediately went on board and received orders to proceed to Newport News and protect the *Minnesota* (then aground) from the *Merrimac.*

We got under way and arrived at the *Minnesota* at 11 P.M. I went on board in our cutter and asked the captain what his prospects were of getting off. He said he should try to get afloat at 2 A.M. , when it was high water. I asked him if we could render him any assistance, to which he replied, "No!" I then told him we should do all in our power to protect him from the *Merrimac.* He thanked me kindly and wished us success. Just as I arrived back to the *Monitor* the *Congress* blew up, and certainly a grander sight was never seen; but it went straight to the marrow of our bones. Not a word was said, but deeply did each man think and wish we were by the side of the *Merrimac.* At 1 A.M. we anchored near the *Minnesota.* The captain and myself remained on deck, waiting for the appearance of the *Merrimac.* At 3 A.M. we thought the *Minnesota* was afloat and coming down on us; so we got under way as soon as possible and stood out of the channel. After backing and filling about for an hour, we found we were mistaken and anchored again. At daylight we discovered the *Merrimac* at anchor with several vessels under Sewall's Point. We immediately made every preparation for battle. At 8 A.M. on Sunday the *Merrimac* got under way, accompanied by several steamers, and started direct for the *Minnesota*. When a mile distant she fired two guns at her. By this time our anchor was up, the men at quarters, the guns loaded, and everything ready for action. As the *Merrimac* came close, the captain passed the word to commence firing. I triced up the port, ran out the gun, and fired the *first* gun, and thus commenced the great battle between the *Monitor* and the *Merrimac*.

Now mark the condition our men and officers were in. Since Friday morning, forty-eight hours, they had had no rest and very little food, as we could not conveniently cook. They had been hard at work all night, and nothing to eat for breakfast except hard bread, and were thoroughly worn out. As for myself, I had not slept a wink for fifty-one hours and had been on my feet almost constantly.

But after the first gun was fired we forgot all fatigues, hard work, and everything else and fought as hard as men ever fought. We loaded and fired as fast as we could. I pointed and fired the guns myself. Every shot I would ask the captain the effect, and the majority of them were encouraging. The captain was in the pilothouse, directing the movements of the vessel; Acting Master Stodder was stationed at the wheel which turns the tower but, as he could not manage it, was relieved by Steiners. The speaking trumpet from the tower to the pilothouse was broken; so we passed the word from the captain to myself on the berth deck by Paymaster Keeler and Captain's Clerk Toffey.

Five times during the engagement we touched each other, and each time I fired a gun at her, and I will vouch the hundred and sixty-eight pounds penetrated her sides. Once she tried to run us down with her iron prow but did no damage whatever. After fighting for two hours we hauled off for half

an hour to hoist shot in the tower. At it we went again as hard as we could, the shot, shell, grape, canister, musket, and rifle balls flying in every direction but doing no damage. Our tower was struck several times, and though the noise was pretty loud it did not affect us any. Stodder and one of the men were carelessly leaning against the tower when a shot struck it exactly opposite them and disabled them for an hour or two.

At about 11:30 A.M. the captain sent for me. I went for ward, and there stood as noble a man as lives, at the foot of the ladder to the pilothouse, his face perfectly black with powder and iron, and apparently perfectly blind. I asked him what was the matter. He said a shot had struck the pilothouse exactly opposite his eyes and blinded him, and he thought the pilothouse was damaged. He told me to take charge of the ship and use my own discretion. I led him to his room, laid him on the sofa, and then took his position. On examining the pilothouse I found the iron hatch on top, on the forward side, was completely cracked through.

We still continued firing, the tower being under the direction of Steiners. We were between two fires, the *Minnesota* on one side and the *Merrimac* on the other. The latter was retreating to Sewall's Point, and the *Minnesota* had struck us twice on the tower. I knew if another shot should strike our pilothouse in the same place, our steering apparatus would be disabled, and we should be at the mercy of the batteries on Sewall's Point. We had *strict* orders to act on the defensive and protect the *Minnesota*. We had evidently finished the *Merrimac* as far as the *Minnesota* was concerned. Our pilothouse was damaged, and we had orders *not* to follow the *Merrimac up*; therefore, after the *Merrimac* had re treated. I went to the *Minnesota* and remained by her until she was afloat. General Wool and Secretary Fox both com mended me for acting as I did and said it was the strict military plan to follow. This is the reason we did not sink the *Merrimac*, and every one here capable of judging says we acted perfectly right.

—Post, ed., *Soldiers' Letters from Camp,*
Battle-field and Prison

XXVI.2

Commodore Farragut Captures New Orleans

From the beginning of the war the government had appreciated the paramount importance of capturing New Orleans and sealing up the Mississippi from blockade-runners. New Orleans was, however, a very tough nut to crack. Well up from the mouth of the river, it was defended by formidable forts, and across the river the Confederates had built a powerful boom consisting of chains, hulks of ships, and other obstacles.

In December 1861 the President selected David G. Farragut to command the West Gulf Blockading Squadron and directed him "to proceed up the Mississippi River and reduce the defenses which guard the approaches to New Orleans, when you will appear off that city and take possession of it." Farragut was, at the time, sixty years old, and a veteran with 49 years of service at sea; his career, so far, had been exemplary rather than brilliant.

On February 2 Farragut sailed from Hampton Roads with 17 wooden vessels and a mortar flotilla of 20 schooners under the command of David D. Porter. On April 18, 1862, he began the bombardment of Forts Jackson and St. Philip, but was unable to make any impression on them. He then decided to run the forts, smash the boom, and sail up to New Orleans—an audacious feat which he carried through with spectacular success.

The story is told here by the New Hampshire lieutenant, George H. Perkins, of the gunboat Cayuga; Perkins later commanded the monitor Chickasaw at Mobile Bay and retired from the navy with the rank of captain in 1881.

New Orleans, April 27, 1862

We arrived here two days ago, after what was "the most desperate fight and greatest naval achievement on record," so every one says. Wednesday night, April 23, we were ordered to lead the way, and be ready to run by the forts at two o'clock in the morning; and at two o'clock precisely the signal was made from the *Hartford* to "get underweigh."

Captain Harrison paid me the compliment of letting me pilot the vessel, and though it was a starlight night we were not discovered until we were well under the forts; then they opened a tremendous fire on us. I was very anxious, for the steering of the vessel being under my charge gave me really the whole management of her. The *Cayuga* received the first fire, and the air was filled with shells and explosions which almost blinded me as I stood on the forecastle trying to see my way, for I had never been up the river before. I soon saw that the guns of the forts were all aimed for the mid stream, so I steered close under the walls of Fort St. Philip, and although our masts and rigging got badly shot through, our hull was but little damaged.

After passing the last battery and thinking we were clear, I looked back for some of our vessels, and my heart jumped up into my mouth, when I found I could not see a *single one*. I thought they all must have been sunk by the forts. Then looking ahead I saw eleven of the enemy's gunboats coming down upon us, and it seemed as if we were "*gone*" sure. Three of these made a dash to board us, but a heavy charge from our eleven-inch gun settled the *Gov. Moore*, which was one of them. A ram, the *Manasses*, in attempting to butt us, just missed our stern, and we soon settled the third fellow's "hash." Just then some of our gunboats, which had passed the forts, came up, and then all sorts of things happened. There was the wildest excitement all round. The *Varuna* fired a broadside into us, instead of the enemy. Another of our gun boats attacked one of the *Cayuga's* prizes,—I shouted out, "Don't fire into that ship, she has surrendered!" Three of the enemy's ships had surrendered to us before any of our vessels appeared, but when they did come up we all pitched in, and settled the eleven rebel vessels, in about twenty minutes. Our short fight with the *Gov. Moore*—it used to be the *Morgan*—was very exciting. We were alongside of each other, and had both fired our guns, and it all depended on which should get reloaded first. The large forward gun on the Gov. *Moore* was a ten-inch shell, ours an eleven-inch, and we were so near, they were almost muzzle to muzzle.

Ours was fired first, and Beverly Kennon, the Captain of the *Gov. Moore*, *is* now a prisoner on board the *Cayuga*. He tells me our shot was the one that ruined him,—disabled his vessel, capsized his gun, and killed thirteen of the gun's crew. Beverly Kennon used to be an officer in our navy.

The *Cayuga* still led the way up the river, and at daylight we discovered a regiment of infantry encamped on shore. As we were very close in, I shouted to them to come on board and deliver up their arms, or we would blow them all to pieces. It seemed rather odd for a regiment on shore to be surrendering to a ship! They hauled down their colors, and the Colonel and command came on board and gave themselves up as prisoners of war. The regiment was called the Chalmette Regiment, and has been quite a famous one. The officers were released on parole and allowed them to retain their side-arms, all except one Captain, who I discovered was from New Hampshire. His name is Hickery, and he came from Portsmouth. I took his sword away from him and have kept it.

The next thing that happened was the sinking of the *Varuna*, which had been disabled by one of the enemy's vessels running into her. Soon after this the Commodore came up in the *Hartford* and ordered us all to anchor and take a little rest before attacking New Orleans, which was now within twenty miles.

By this time our ship had received forty-two shots in masts and hull, and six of our men had been wounded; one of the boys had to have one of his legs cut off. All this time, night and day, fire-rafts and ships loaded with burning cotton had been coming down the river and surrounded us everywhere. Besides these, the bombardment was continuous and perfectly awful. I do npt believe there ever was anything like it before, and I never expect to see such a sight again. The river and shore were one blaze, and the sounds and explosions were terrific. Nothing I could say would give you any idea of these last twenty-four hours!

The next morning, April 25, we all got underweigh again, the *Cayuga* still leading, and at about nine o'clock New Orleans hove in sight. We called all hands and gave three cheers and a tiger!

There were two more fortifications still between us and New Orleans, called the Chalmette Batteries, but Captain Bailey thought they could not be of much account, and that we had-best push on. When we arrived in sight of these batteries, no flag floated over them, and there was not a man to be seen—nothing but the guns, which seemed abandoned. In fact, though, there were a lot of treacherous rascals concealed in these batteries, and when we had come close enough to make them feel sure they could sink us, they opened a heavy fire. We gave them back as well as we could, but they were too much for one gunboat; so, after getting hit fourteen times, and the shot and shell striking all about us, we decided not to advance any further until some of the ships came up. Soon we had the *Hartford* on one side and the *Pensacola* on the other, and then the rebel battery was silenced very quick.

After this, there were no further obstacles between us and the city, and the fleet were soon anchored before it. The Commodore ordered Captain Bailey to go on shore, and demand its surrender, and he asked me to go with him. We took just a boat and a boat's crew, with a flag of truce, and started off. When we reached the wharf there were no officials to be seen; no one received us, although the whole city was watching our movements, and the levee was crowded in spite of a heavy rain-storm. Among the crowd were many women and children, and the women were shaking rebel flags, and being rude and noisy.

They were all shouting and hooting as we stepped on shore, but at last a man, who, I think, was a German, offered to show us the way to the councilroom, where we should find the mayor of the city.

As we advanced, the mob followed us in a very excited state. They gave three cheers for Jeff Davis and Beauregard, and three groans for Lincoln. Then they began to throw things at us, and shout, "Hang them!" "Hang them!" We both thought we were in a *bad fix*, but there was nothing for us to do, but just go on.

We reached the city hall, though, in safety, and there we found the mayor and council. They seemed in a very solemn state of mind, though I must say, from what they said, they did not impress me as having much *mind* about anything, and certainly not much sense. The mayor said *he* had nothing to do with the city, as it was under martial law, and we were obliged to wait till General Lovell could arrive.

In about half an hour this gentleman appeared. He was very pompous in his manner and silly and wiry in his remarks. He had about fifteen thousand troops under his command, and said he would "never surrender," but would withdraw his troops from the city as soon as possible, when the city would fall into the hands of the mayor and he could do as he pleased with it.

The mob outside had by this time become perfectly infuriated. They kicked at the doors and swore they would have us out and hang us! Of course Captain Bailey and I *felt perfectly at our ease an this while!* Indeed, every person about us, who had any sense of responsibility, was frightened for our safety. As soon as the mob found out that General Lovell was not going to surrender, they swore they would have us out anyway; but Pierre Soule and some others went out and made speeches to them, and kept them on one side of the building, while we went out the other, and were driven to the wharf in a close carriage. Finally we got on board ship all right; but of all the blackguarding I ever heard in my life that mob gave us the worst.

—BELKNAP, ed., *Letters of Capt. Geo. Hamilton Perkins*

XXVI.3

NEW ORLEANS FALLS TO THE YANKEES

Farragut's fleet appeared before New Orleans about noon of April 25. The Confederate General Lovell had already fled, the coal, cotton, and ships at the levee were ablaze, the city in a state of excitement bordering on frenzy. On the afternoon of the twenty-fifth the city surrendered; on May 1 General Benjamin Butler arrived and the control of the city was turned over to the army.

Butler's rule in New Orleans was highhanded, and possibly corrupt; it is still an article of faith throughout the South that Butler stole all the silver spoons in the city! The insults which Union soldiers suffered from the men and women of New Orleans impelled Butler to issue his notorious Order No. 28.

Although there appeared to be justification for this order, it excited dismay in the North and indignation abroad. Palmerston, who made it the occasion for an unofficial protest, had to be put in his place by Minister Adams.

We give here Julia LeGrand's account of the surrender of New Orleans; General Butlei's Order; Palmerston's protest against the Order; and Secretary Moran's account of the exchange between Palmerston and Adams.

A. Julia LeGrand Describes the Surrender of New Orleans

Behold, what has now come to the. city! Never can I forget the day that the alarm bell rang. I never felt so hopeless and forsaken. The wretched generals, left here with our troops, ran away and left them. Lovell knew not what to do; some say he was intoxicated, some say frightened. Of course the greatest confusion prevailed, and every hour, indeed almost every moment, brought its dreadful rumor. After it was known that the gunboats had actually passed, the whole city, both camp and street, was a scene of wild confusion. *The Women only* did not seem afraid. They were all in favor of resistance, *no matter how hopeless* that resistance might be.

The second day matters wore a more favorable aspect, and the Mayor and the City Council assumed a dignified position toward the enemy. Flag Officer Farragut demanded the unconditional surrender of the town. He was told that as brute force, and brute force only, gave him the power that he might come and take it. He then demanded that we, with our own hands, pull down the flag of Louisiana. This I am happy to say, was refused. Four days we waited, expecting to be shelled, but he concluded to waive the point; so he marched in his marines with two cannons and our flag was taken down and the old stars and stripes lifted in a dead silence. We made a great mistake here; we should have shot the man that brought down the flag, and as long as there was a house-top in the city left, it should have been hoisted. The French and English lay in the Gulf and a French frigate came up the river to protect French subjects.

Farragut allowed the women and children but forty-eight hours to leave the city, but the foreign consuls demanded a much longer time to move the people of their respective nations. If we had been staunch and dared them to shell, the Confederacy would have been saved. The brutal threat would never have been carried out, for England and France would never have allowed it. The delay would have enabled us to finish our boat, and besides a resistance would have showed the enemy and foreign nations, too, what stuff we were made of and how very much we were in earnest.

I never wished anything so much in my life as for resistance here. I felt no fear—only excitement. The ladies of the town signed a paper, praying that it should never be given up. We went down to put our names on the list, and met the marines marching up to the City Hall with their cannon in front of them. The blood boiled in my veins—I felt no fear—only anger. I forgot myself and called out several times: "Gentle men, don't let the State Flag come down," and, "Oh, how can you men stand it?" Mrs. Norton was afraid of me, I believe, for she hurried me off.

I have forgotten to mention—at first, the Germans at the fort mutinied and turned their guns on their officers. In the first place, several gunboats had passed the fort at night because a traitor had failed to give the signal. He was tried and shot, and Duncan telegraphed to the city that no more should pass—then came a report that the Yankee vessels were out of powder and coal and they could not get back to their transports which they had expected to follow them. We were quite jubilant at the idea of keeping them in a sort of imprisonment, and this we could have done but for the German mutineers. The wives of these men were allowed to visit the fort, and they represented the uselessness of the struggle, because the city had already surrendered. They were told, too, that Duncan intended to blow up the fort over their heads rather than surrender. So they spiked their cannon and threatened the lives of their officers and then the Yankee fleet poured up.

These people have complimented us highly. To quell a small "rebellion," they have made preparations enough to conquer a world. This is a most cowardly struggle these people can do nothing without gunboats. Beauregard in Tennessee can get

no battle from them where they are protected by these huge block steamers. These passive instruments do their fighting for them. It is at best a dastardly way to fight. We should have had gunboats if the Government had been efficient, wise or earnest. We have lost our city, the key to this great valley, and my opinion is that we will never, never get it more, except by treaty.

—ROWLAND AND CROXALL, eds., *The Journal of Julia LeGrand*

B. General Butler Outrages the Moral Sentiment of the World

Order No. 28

Headquarters, Department of Gulf
New-Orleans, May 15 [1862]

As officers and soldiers of the United States have been subject to repeated insults from women calling themselves ladies, of New-Orleans, in return for the most scrupulous non-interference and courtesy on our part, it is ordered here after, when any female shall by mere gesture or movement insult, or show contempt for any officers or soldiers of the United States, she shall be regarded and held liable to be treated as a woman about town plying her avocation.

By command of Major-Gen. Butler
Geo. C. Strong, A. A. G.

—MOORE, ed., *The Rebellion Record*

C. Palmerston Protests Butler's Proclamation

Brocket, 11 June, 1862

Confidential.

My Dear Sir,—I cannot refrain from taking the liberty of saying to you that it is difficult if not impossible to express adequately the disgust which must be excited in the mind of every honorable man by the general order of General Butler given in the inclosed extract from yesterday's *Times*. Even when a town is taken by assault it is the practice of the Commander of the conquering army to protect to his utmost the inhabitants and especially the female part of them, and I will venture to say that no example can be found in the history of civilized nations till the publication of this order, of a general guilty in cold blood of so infamous an act as deliberately to hand over the female inhabitants of a conquered city to the unbridled license of an unrestrained soldiery.

If the Federal Government chuses to be served by men capable of such revolting outrages, they must submit to abide by the deserved opinion which mankind will form of their conduct. My dear Sir, Yours faithfully,

Palmerston

—*Proceedings of the Massachusetts Historical Society*

D. "A More Impudent Proceeding Cannot Be Discovered"

Wednesday, June 25, 1862. A serious correspondence has just taken place between Lord Palmerston and Mr. Adams which is destined to become historical. His Lordship with that impudence that only an Englishman can be guilty of wrote a private and confidential note to Mr. Adams on the 11th Inst., about Gen'l Butler's late order at New Orleans in which he said he could not "express adequately the disgust which must be excited in the mind of every honorable man" at that regulation "of a General guilty of so infamous an act as to deliberately hand over the female inhabitants of a conquered city to the unbridled license of an unrestrained soldiery."

Mr. Adams replied on the 12th refusing to recognise the note, unless he was assured it was official, and expressing surprise at such an unusual proceeding on the part of the Prime Minister, instead of the Minister of Foreign Affairs,—with whom Foreign Ministers carry on their correspondence on matters connected with the duties of their Mission.

To this Ld. Palmerston rejoined on the 15th by saying his note was official.

In the interview Mr. Adams saw Lord Russell and stated the case to him. He was much offended, & said Ld. Palmerston had exceeded the bounds of good behavior—a thing he had often done of late, and had no business to write such a note.

Mr. Adams renewed the subject on the 16th and after commenting on the nature of his Lordship's letter, said that "the Government he represented would visit with just indignation upon its servants abroad their tame submission to receive under the seal of privacy any indignity which it might be the disposition of the servants of any sovereign however exalted, to offer to it in that form."

Palmerston with his usual insolence answered this in a sophistical strain on the 19th, & on the 20th Mr. Adams closed the affair by a note in which he said he would decline while here to receive such communications from him. This severe reprimand had its intended effect, and his Lordship has remained silent under it.

The incident placed Mr. Adams in a very critical position, and for a few days we considered things so serious as to strongly anticipate a sudden rupture of all intercourse. Fortunately, Mr. Adams' decision saved such a result.

A more impudent proceeding than that of Palmerston in this case cannot be discovered in the whole range of political life. Knowing the brutality of his own officers and soldiers he readily imagined ours of the same stamp, and insolently presumed to lecture Mr. Adams on a thing which was not his business. His ill-manners were properly rebuked. American soldiers, he will find out, are not beasts, altho' English soldiers are; and he will also learn that it is only a debased mind that would construe Gen'l Butler's order as he has done. He has defined it according to English practice. That is all.

This proceeding of Lord Palmerston is one of the most remarkable, and probably without a parallel in Diplomatic history. Mr. Adams was placed in a most awkward predicament & managed the affair with great skill. When the story shall be made public, it will create astonishment in certain quarters. Had not Palmerston taken the course he did, it was Mr. Adams' intention to have published the correspondence privately and sent it to his colleagues so that they might know what they might at some time or other expect from his Lordship should he remain in office.

—WALLACE AND GILLESPE, eds., *The Journal of Benjamin Moran*

XXVI.4

ELLET'S STEAM RAMS SMASH THE CONFEDERATE FLEET AT MEMPHIS

At the beginning of the war Commander John Rodgers was instructed to prepare a naval force for the Mississippi. He bought three river steamers, authorized J. B. Eads of St. Louis to build seven gunboats, built a fleet of mortar boats, and prepared to co-operate with the army in its advance into the South. In January 1862 he was succeeded in command by Flag Officer Andrew Foote, who took part in the Fort Donelson expedition, and after the reduction of that fort preached in Cairo on the text "Ye believe in God; believe also in me." Foote's river fleet ran the batteries of Island No. 10 and helped reduce that island and New Madrid. Foote was disabled in action, and command of the river fleet was turned over to Captain Charles H. Davis.

Meantime an army engineer, Colonel Charles Ellet, had been authorized by the War Department to build a fleet of rams for service on the Mississippi. Two of these, the Queen of the West and the Monarch, participated in the attack on the Confederate River Defense Fleet at Memphis, on lune 6. Ellet himself was mortally wounded in action.

The story of the battle is told by Colonel Ellet's brother, Alfred W. Ellet, who succeeded to the command of the rams.

Upon the startling verification of his neglected admonitions afforded by the *Merrimac*, Mr. Ellet was called to the War Department, and, after a short conference with Secretary Stanton, was given authority to purchase, refit, man, and command, with the rank of colonel, any number of vessels deemed, in his judgment, necessary to meet and defeat the fleet of iron-clad rams then known to be in process of construction on the lower Mississippi River.

Never was work more promptly or more effectually performed. Colonel Ellet purchased a number of steamboats at different points on the Ohio River, the best he could find in the short time at his disposal. He took some old and nearly worn-out boats, strengthened their hulls and bows with heavy timbers, raised bulkheads of timber around the boilers, and started them down the river to Cairo as fast as they could be got off the ways. They were the *Dick*

Fulton, Lancaster, Lioness, Mingo, Monarch, Queen of the West, Samson, Switzerland, and *T. D. Horner.*

While the work was progressing, and before any one of the rams was nearly completed, information was received that the Confederate fleet had come out from under the batteries of Fort Pillow, had attacked our fleet of gun-boats lying near Craighead's Point, and had disabled two of them. Colonel Ellet received most urgent telegrams from the Secretary of War to hurry the rams forward at the earliest possible movement. In consequence of these demands, five of them were immediately dispatched down the river under my command, work upon them being continued as they proceeded and for several days after their arrival at Fort Pillow. The other rams followed, and about the 25th of May Colonel Ellet joined the fleet on board the *Switzerland*, and the ram-fleet was now ready for action.

Colonel Ellet at once conferred with Flag-Officer Charles H. Davis on the propriety of passing Fort Pillow, and engaging the enemy's fleet wherever found. Flag-Offlcer Davis did not approve the plan suggested, but offered no objection to Colonel Ellet's trying the experiment. Accordingly, immediate preparations were begun for running the batteries with the entire ram-fleet.

During this period of preparation, constant watch was kept upon the fort and the enemy's fleet. On the night of the 4th of June [1862] I crossed the timber point in front of the fort, and reported to the colonel commanding my conviction that the fort was being evacuated. About 2 o'clock in the morning I obtained permission, with many words of caution from Colonel Ellet, to run down opposite the fort in a yawl and, after lying off in order to become assured that the place was abandoned, to land, with the assurance that the rams would follow in case my yawl did not return before daylight. I landed with my little band, only to find the fort entirely deserted; and after planting the National colors upon the ruins of one of the magazines, we sat down to wait for the coming of daylight and the rams. They came, followed by the entire fleet, and after a short stop all proceeded down the river, the rams taking the lead, to Fort Randolph, where they delayed long enough to plant the National flag and to examine the abandoned fortifications, the gunboats at this point taking the advance.

After leaving Fort Randolph the ram-fleet proceeded with out incident to within about twenty-five miles of Memphis, where they all rounded to and tied up for the night, with orders of sailing issued to each commander; instructions to be ready to round out at the signal from the flag-ship, and that "each boat should go into the anticipated fight in the same order they maintained in sailing." At the first dawn of day (June 6th) the fleet moved down the river, and at sunrise the flag ship rounded the bend at "Paddy's Hen and Chickens," and immediately after came in sight of the Federal gunboats anchored in line across the river, about a mile above Memphis. Colonel Ellet promptly signaled his vessels to tie up on the Arkansas shore, in the order of their sailing, as he desired to confer with Flag-Officer Davis before passing further.

The *Queen of the West* came to first, followed by the *Monarch* and other rams in regular succession. The *Queen of the West* had made the-land, and passed out line to make fast; the *Monarch* was closing in just above, but had not yet touched the shore. At this moment, and as the full orb of the sun rose above the horizon, the report of a gun was heard from around the point and down the river. It was the first gun from the Confederate River Defense Fleet moving to attack w. Colonel Ellet was standing on the hurricane-deck of the *Queen of the West*. He immediately sprang forward, and, waving his hat to attract my attention, called out: "It is a gun from the enemy Round out and follow me! Now is our chancel" With out a moment's delay, the *Queen* moved out gracefully, and the *Monarch* followed. By this time our gun-boats had opened their batteries, and the reports of guns on both sides were heavy and rapid.

The morning was beautifully clear and perfectly still; a heavy wall of smoke was formed across the river, so that the position of our gun-boats could only be seen by the flashes of their guns. The *Queen* plunged forward, under a full head of

steam, right into this wall of smoke and was lost sight of, her position being known only by her tall pipes which reached above the smoke. The *Monarch,* following, was greeted, while passing the gun-boats, with wild huzzas from our gallant tars. When freed from the smoke, those of who were on the *Monarch* could see Colonel Ellet's tall and commanding form still standing on the hurricane-deck, waving his hat to show me which one of the enemy's vessels he desired the *Monarch* to attack,—namely, the *General Price,* which was on the right wing of their advancing line. For himself he selected the *General Lovell* and directed the *Queen* straight for her, she being about the middle of the enemy's advancing line.

The two vessels came toward each other in most gallant style, head to head, prow to prow; and had they met in that way, it is most likely that both vessels would have gone down. But at the critical moment the *General Lovell* began to turn; and that moment sealed her fate. The *Queen* came on and plunged straight into the *Lovell's* exposed broad side; the vessel was cut almost in two and disappeared under the dark waters in less time than it takes to tell the story. The *Monarch* next struck the *General Price* a glancing blow which cut her starboard wheel clea4 off, and completely disabled her from further participation in the fight.

As soon as the *Queen* was freed from the wreck of the sinking *Lovell,* and before she could recover headway, she was attacked on both sides-by the enemy's vessels, the *Beauregard* on one side and the *Sumter* on the other. In the melee one of the wheels of the *Queen* was disabled so that she could not use it, and Colonel Ellet, while still standing on the hurricane-deck to view the effects of the encounter with the *General Lovell,* received a pistol-ball in his knee, and, lying prone on the deck, gave orders for the *Queen* to be run on her one remaining wheel to the Arkansas shore, whither she was soon followed by the *General Price* in a sinking condition. Colonel Ellet sent an officer and squad of men to meet the *General Price* upon her making the shore, and received her entire crew as prisoners of war. By this time consternation had seized upon the enemy's fleet, and all had turned to escape. The fight had drifted down the river, below the city.

The *Monarch*, as soon as she could recover headway after her conflict with the *General Price*, drove down upon the *Beauregard*, which vessel, after her encounter with the *Queen of the West*, was endeavoring to escape. She was thwarted by the *Monarch* coming down upon her with a well-directed blow which crushed in her side and completely disabled her from further hope of escape. Men on the deck waved a white flag in token of surrender, and the *Monarch* passed on down to intercept the *Little Rebel*, the enemy's flag-ship. She had received some injury from our gun-boats' fire, and was making for the Arkansas shore, which she reached at the moment when the *Monarch*, with very slight headway, pushed her hard and fast aground; her crew sprang upon shore and ran into the thick woods, making their escape. Leaving the *Little Rebel* fast aground, the *Monarch* turned her attention to the sinking *Beauregard*, taking the vessel in tow, and making prisoners of her crew. The *Beauregard* was towed by the *Monarch* to the bar, where she sank to her boiler-deck and finally became a total loss.

The others of the enemy's fleet were run ashore and fired by the crews before they escaped into the adjoining Arkansas swamps. The *Jeff. Thompson* burned and blew up with a tremendous report; the *General Bragg* was secured by our gun-boats before the fire gained headway, and was saved. The *Van Dorn* alone made her escape, and was afterward burned by the enemy at Liverpool Landing, upon the ap proach of two of our rams in Yazoo River, in order to prevent her from falling into our hands. Two other rebel boats were burned at the same time,—the *Polk* and the *Livingston*. . . .

Colonel Ellet did not rely on heavy ordnance, and did not recommend arming his rams. At the battle of Memphis there were no firearms on board the ram-fleet except a few short carbines and some pocket-revolvers; his reliance was upon the prow of his vessel. He desired, as far as possible, to protect the vulnerable parts of his ship, the boilers and engines, and with simply enough men as crew to handle the boat with certainty and dispatch, to run the gauntlet of any fire that could be precipitated upon him, and drive his ram deep into his unwieldy adversary. At the battle of Memphis the enemy concentrated their fire upon the *Queen of the West* and the *Monarch*, but their missiles passed harmlessly by. Not a splinter was raised off either of the rams, and not a man sustained the slightest injury except Colonel Ellet, whose fatal wound was received from a pistol-ball.

The battle of Memphis was, in many respects, one of the most remarkable naval victories on record. For two unarmed, frail, wooden river steamboats, with barely men enough on board to handle the machinery and keep the furnace-fires burning, to rush to the front, between two hostile fleets, and *into* the enemy's advancing line of eight iron-clad, heavily armed, and fully manned steam-rams, sinking one, disabling and capturing three, and carrying consternation to the others, was a sight never before witnessed.

The River Defense Fleet was composed of strong, well-built ocean steamers, well strengthened and protected with railroad iron so as to be almost invulnerable to shat when advancing. The intention was apparent to repeat at Memphis the tactics which had proved so successful at Fort Pillow,—to ram the Union gun-boats at anchor; and had the rams *Queen of the West* and *Monarch* got run through the line of gun-boats and attacked the Defense fleet as it approached, sinking, disabling, and scattering its vessels, and thus removing the fight half a mile below, the result of the affair might have been very different. The Defense Fleet was advancing upstream, thus exposing the strongest and best-protected portions of each vessel; the gun-boats, relying upon their guns, were at anchor, with their sterns, their most vulnerable part, pointing down-stream and consequently exposed to the tremendous attack of the enemy. Had the Confederate commanders trusted only to the strength of their vessels, ceased firing, and with every pound of steam on plunged at full speed into our anchored gun-boat fleet, who could doubt what the result would have been?

—ELLET, "Ellet and His Steam Rams at Memphis"

XXVI.5

ATTACK AND REPULSE AT BATTERY WAGNER

Throughout the war the Federals tried to capture Charleston; not until Sherman's march through South Carolina forced its evacuation did they succeed. The first major effort came in June 1862, when General Hunter landed on Iames Island but failed to take the fort of Secessionville (June 16). The second came on April 7, 1863, when an attempt by the Iron sides and eight monitors to break through the harbor defenses and bombard the city was repulsed with heavy loss. The third, and most substantial, was the occupation of Morris Island in the summer of 1863, and the series of land and sea assaults on Battery Wagner that finally forced its surrender.

Early in July General Gillmore, Commander of the Department of the South, landed on the southern end of Morris Island, carried the Confederate lines by assault, and advanced on Fort (or Battery) Wagner, at the northern tip of the island and only a mile from Fort Sumter. Instead of attacking at once Gillmore waited until the following day; by that time the Confederates were ready for him, and repulsed the assault. The second attack came on July 18. The advance was led by Colonel Shaw of the famous 54th Massachusetts (Colored) Regiment; supporting him were Colonel Barton's 3rd New Hampshire, Colonel Putnam's 7th New Hampshire, Colonel Jackson's 76th Pennsylvania, Colonel Commager's 67th Ohio, and others. The attack was almost—but not quite successful. After its failure the navy took over. In early September there was a 42-hour bombardment which eventually forced the Confederates to evacuate. Yet Charleston was still impregnable.

We give here the *New York Tribune* account of the assault of July 18.

Morris Island, S. C., July 19, 1863

Again Fort Wagner has been assaulted and again we have been repulsed, and with, I regret to say, a much more formidable loss in killed, wounded, and missing than in the first attempt. . . .

In the assault of the eleventh instant, but one brigade, and that a very small one, under the command of General Strong, were engaged; in that of last evening a whole division, consisting of three full brigades, were drawn out in line to take part in the action, but on account of some misunderstanding of orders, but two actually participated in the fight. . . .

General Gillmore designed to commence the bombardment of the Fort at daylight yesterday morning, but on account of a terrific thunderstorm, which commenced early in the evening and continued until morning, delaying the work of the engineers and dampening the ammunition, the action did not open until half-past twelve. At that hour Admiral Dahlgren signalled that he was ready, and in a few moments the *Montauk,* (his flag-ship,) the *Ironsides,* the *Catskill,* the *Nantucket,* the *Weehawken,* and the *Patapsco* moved into line in the order in which I have named them, and commenced hurling their heaviest shot and shell around, upon, and within the Fort, and, with intervals of but a very few minutes, continued this terrible fire until one hour after the sun had gone down. During all the afternoon the iron fleet lay about one mile off from the Port, but just at the close of the engagement, and but a few moments before the first assault was made by General Strong, the Admiral ran the *Montauk* directly under the guns of Fort Wagner, and, within two hundred and eighty yards, fired round after round from his fifteen-inch gun, send ing, as every shot struck, vast clouds of sand, mud, and timber high up into the air, making one huge sand-heap of that portion of the Fort facing the sea, and dismounting two of the heaviest guns. . . .

The firing was almost entirely from our own side. With the most powerful glass, but very few men could be seen in the Fort. At half-past two, a shot from one of our guns on the left cut the halyards on the flag-staff and brought the rebel flag fluttering to the ground.

In a moment, almost before we had begun to ask ourselves whether they had really lowered their flag, and were upon the point of surrendering or not, the old red battle-flag, which the army of the Potomac has so often had defiantly shaken in its face, was run up about ten feet above the parapet, a little cluster of men rallied around it, cheered, waved their hats, and then disappeared, and were not again seen during the day. Fort Sumter, the moment the rebel flag came to the ground, sent a

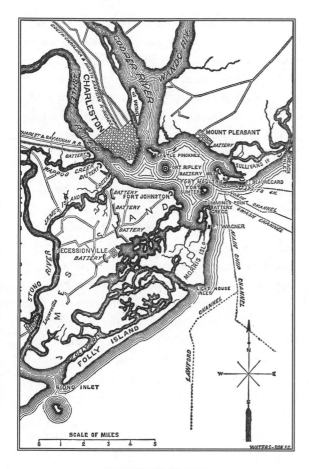

CHARLESTON HARBOR

command. "We must storm the Fort to-night and carry it at the point of the bayonet!"

In a few moments signals are made from the top of the look-out, and soon generals and colonels commanding divisions and brigades were seen galloping to the headquarters of the Commanding General. . . . Officers shout, bugles sound, the word of command is given, and soon the soldiers around, upon, and under the sand-hills of Morris Island spring from their hiding-places, fall into line, march to the beach, are organized into new brigades, and in solid column stand ready to move to the deadly assault.

Not in widely extended battle-line, with cavalry and artillery at supporting distances, but in solid regimental column, on the hard ocean beach, for half a mile before reaching the Fort, in plain view of the enemy, did these three brigades move to their appointed work.

General Strong, who has so frequently since his arrival in this department braved death in its many forms of attack, was assigned to the command of the First brigade. Colonel Putnam of the Seventh New-Hampshire . . . took command of the Second, and General Stevenson the Third, constituting the reserve. The Fifty-fourth Massachusetts, (colored regiment,) Colonel Shaw, was the advanced regiment in the First brigade, and the Second South-Carolina, (Negro,) Colonel Montgomery, was the last regiment of the reserve. . . .

Just as darkness began to close in upon the scene of the afternoon and the evening, General Strong rode to the front and ordered his brigade . . . to advance to the assault. At the instant, the line was seen slowly advancing in the dusk toward the Fort, and before a double-quick had been ordered, a tremendous fire from the barbette guns on Fort Sumter, from the batteries on Cumrning's Point, and from all the guns on Fort Wagner, opened upon it. The guns from Wagner swept the beach, and those from Sumter and Cumming's Point enfiladed it on the left. In the midst of this terrible shower of shot and shell they pushed their way, reached the Fort, portions of the Fifty-fourth

shot over our heads to assure us that it had been lowered by accident and not by design. In this shot she also desired us to distinctly understand that before Fort Wagner surrendered, she herself would have to be consulted. With the exception of this little episode, almost profound silence, so far as the rebel garrison themselves could maintain it, prevailed within the Fort. . . .

For eight hours the monitors and the *Ironsides* have kept up a continuous fire, and Fort Wagner has not yet surrendered. For eight hours fifty-four guns from the land-batteries have hurled their shot and shell within her walls, and still she flaunts the red battle-flag in our face.

"Something must be done, and that, too, quickly, or in a few days we shall have the whole army in Virginia upon us," said an officer high in

Massachusetts, the Sixth Connecticut, and the Forty-eighth New-York dashed through the ditches, gained the parapet, and engaged in a hand-to-hand fight with the enemy, and for nearly half an hour held their ground, and did not fall back until nearly every commissioned officer was shot down. . . .

When the brigade made the assault General Strong gallantly rode at its head. When it fell back, broken, torn, and bleeding, Major Plimpton of the Third New-Hampshire was the highest commissioned officer to command it. General Strong, Colonel Shaw, Colonel Chatfield, Colonel Barton, Colonel Green, Colonel Jackson, all had fallen; and the list I send you will tell how many other brave officers fell with them. . . . It must be remembered, too, that this assault was made in the night—a very dark night even the light of the stars was obscured by the blackness of a heavy thunderstorm, and the enemy could be distinguished from our own men only by the light of bursting shell and the flash of the howitzer and the musket. The Fifty-fourth Massachusetts, (Negro,) whom copperhead officers would have called cowardly if they had stormed and carried the gates of hell, went boldly into battle, for the second time, commanded by their brave Colonel, but came out of it led by no higher officer than the boy, Lieuten ant Higginson.

The First brigade, under the lead of General Strong, failed to take the Fort. It was now the turn of Colonel Putnam, commanding the Second brigade, composed of the Seventh New-Hampshire, the Sixty-second Ohio, Colonel Vorhees, the Sixty-seventh Ohio, Colonel Commager, and the One Hundredth New-York, Colonel Dandy, to make the attempt. But alas! the task was too much for him. Through the same terrible fire he led his men to, over, and into the Fort, and for an hour held one half of it, fighting every moment of that time with the utmost desperation, and, as with the First brigade, it was not until he himself fell killed, and nearly all his officers wounded, and no reenforcements arriving, that his men fell back, and the rebel shout and cheer of victory was heard above the roar of Sumter and the guns from Cumming's Point. . . .

Without a doubt, many of our men fell from our OWD Sre. The darkness was so intense, the roar of artillery so loud, the flight of grape and canister shot so rapid and destructive, that it was absolutely impossible to preserve order in the ranks of individual companies, to say nothing of the regiments.

More than half the time we were in the Fort, the fight was simply a hand-to-hand one, as the wounds received by many clearly indicate. Some have sword-thrusts, some are hacked on the head, some are stabbed with bayonets, and a few were knocked down with the butt-end of muskets, but re covered in time to get away with swollen heads. There was terrible fighting to get into the Fort, and terrible fighting to get out of it. The cowardly stood no better chance for their lives than the fearless. Even if they surrendered, the shell of Sumter were thickly falling around them in the darkness, and, as prisoners, they could not be safe, until victory, decisive and unquestioned, rested with one or the other belligerent.

The battle is over; it is midnight; the ocean beach is crowded with the dead, the dying, and the wounded. It is with difficulty you can urge your horse through to Lighthouse Inlet. Faint lights are glimmering in the sandholes and rifle pits to the right, as you pass down the beach. In these holes many a poor wounded and bleeding soldier has lain down to his last sleep. Friends are bending over them to staunch their wounds, or bind up their shattered limbs, but the deathly glare from sunken eyes tells that their kind services are all in vain.

—"The Attack on Fort Wagner, *New York Tribune* Account"

— XXVI.6 —

Farragut Damns the Torpedoes at Mobile Bay

With the fall of New Orleans and the conquest of much of the Tennessee-Mississippi area by Federal arms, Mobile Bay assumed a position of primary importance to Confederate economy. Farragut had wanted to attack Mobile early in 1863, but had been held to Mississippi River duty by the demands of the Vicksburg and Port Hudson campaigns. After the successful reduction of Port Hudson he sailed for New York for a rest; then in January 1864 he was ordered back to the Gulf and authorized to reduce Mobile. This task required the support of land forces, and not until August 1864 were these available. Early on the morning of August 5 Farragut gave the signal for the attack, and his flotilla steamed up the broad bay, the Brooklyn in the lead.

John Kinney, who tells the story of that famous day, was lieutenant and signal officer on the flagship *Hartford*.

Except for what Farragut had already accomplished on the Mississippi, it would have been considered a foolhardy experiment for wooden vessels to attempt to pass so close to one of the strongest forts on the coast, but when to the forts were added the knowledge of the strength of the ram and the supposed deadly character of the torpedoes, it may be imagined that the coming event impressed the person taking his first glimpse of naval warfare as decidedly hazardous and unpleasant. So daring an attempt was never made in any country but ours, and was never successfully made by any commander except Farragut, who, in this, as in his previous exploits in passing the forts of the Mississippi, proved him self one of the greatest naval commanders the world has ever seen. . . .

After the reconnoissance the final council of war was held on board the *Hartford*, when the positions of the various vessels were assigned, and the order of the line was arranged. Unfortunately Captain (now Rear-Admiral) Thornton A. Jenkins was absent, his vessel, the *Richmond*, having been unavoidably delayed at Pensacola, whither she had gone for coal and to escort the monitor *Tecumseh*. Had he been present he certainly would have been selected to take the lead, in which event the perilous halt of the next day would not have occurred. Much against his own wish Admiral Farragut yielded to the unanimous advice of his captains and gave up his original determination of placing his flagship in the advance, and, in the uncertainty as to the arrival of the *Richmond*, assigned the *Brooklyn*, Captain Alden, to that position. . . .

It was the admiral's desire and intention to get underway by daylight, to take advantage of the inflowing tide; but a dense fog came on after midnight and delayed the work of forming the line.

It was a weird sight as the big ships "balanced to partners," the dim outlines slowly emerging like phantoms in the fog. The vessels were lashed together in pairs, fastened side by side by huge cables. All the vessels had been stripped for the fight, the top-hamper being left at Pensacola, and the starboard boats being either left behind or towed on the port side. The admiral's steam-launch, the *Lovall*, named after his son, steamed alongside the flag-ship on the port side.

It was a quarter of six o'clock before the fleet was in motion. Meantime a light breeze had scattered the fog and left a clear, sunny August day. The line moved slowly, and it was an hour after starting before the opening gun was fired. This was a 15-inch shell from the *Tecumseh*, and it exploded over Fort Morgan. Half an hour afterward the fleet came within range and the firing from the starboard vessels became general, the fort and the Confederate fleet replying. The fleet took position across the entrance to the bay and raked the advance vessels fore and aft, doing great damage, to which it was for a time impossible to make effective reply. Gradually the fleet came into close quarters with Fort Morgan, and the firing on both sides became terrific. The wooden vessels moved more rapidly than the monitors, and as the *Brooklyn* came opposite the fort, and approached the torpedo line, she came nearly alongside the armored monitor. To have kept on would have been to take the lead, with the ram *Tennessee* approaching and with the unknown danger of the torpedoes underneath. At this critical moment the *Brooklyn* halted and began backing and signaling with the army signals. The *Hartford* was immediately behind and the following vessels were in close proximity, and the sudden stopping of the *Brooklyn* threatened to bring the whole fleet into collision, while the strong in flowing tide was likely to carry some of the vessels to the shore under the guns of the fort. . . .

Nearly every man had his watch in his hand awaiting the first shot. To us, ignorant of everything going on above, every minute seemed an hour, and there was a feeling of great relief when the boom of the *Tecumseh's* first gun was heard. Presently one or two of our forward guns opened, and we could hear the distant sound of the guns of the fort in reply. Soon the cannon-balls began to crash through the deck above us, and then the thunder of our whole broad side of nine Dahlgren guns kept the vessel in a quiver. But as yet no wounded were sent down, and we knew we were still at comparatively long range. In the intense excitement of the occasion it seemed that hours had passed, but it was just twenty minutes from the time we went below, when an officer shouted down the hatchway: "Send up an army signal officer immediately; the *Brooklyn is* signaling."

In a moment the writer was on deck, where he found the situation as already described. Running on to the forecastle, he hastily took the *Brooklyn's* message, which imparted the unnecessary information, "The monitors are right ahead; we cannot go on without passing them."

The reply was sent at once from the admiral, "Order the monitors ahead and go on."

But still the *Brooklyn* halted, while, to add to the horror of the situation, the monitor *Tecumseh*, a few hundred yards in the advance, suddenly careened to one side and almost instantly sank to the bottom, carrying with her Captain Tunis A. M. Craven and the greater part of his crew, numbering in all 114 officers and men. . . . Meantime the *Brooklyn* failed to go ahead, and the whole fleet became a stationary point-blank target for the guns of Fort Morgan and of the rebel vessels. It was during these few perilous moments that the most fatal work of the day was done to the fleet.

Owing to the *Hartford's* position, only her few bow guns could be used, while a deadly rain of shot and shell was falling on her, and her men were being cut down by scores, unable to make reply. The sight on deck was sickening beyond the power of words to portray. Shot after shot came through the side, mowing down the men, deluging the decks with blood, and scattering mangled fragments of humanity so thickly that it was difficult to stand on the deck, so slippery was it. The old expressions of the "scuppers running blood," "the slippery deck," etc., give but the faintest idea of the spectacle on the *Hartford.* the bodies of the dead were placed in a long row on the port side, while the wounded were sent below until the surgeons' quarters would hold no more. A solid shot coming through the bow struck a gunner on the neck, completely severing head from body. One poor fellow lost both legs by a cannon-ball; as he fell he threw up both arms, just in time to have them also carried away by another shot. At one gun, all the crew on one side were swept down by a shot which came crashing through the bulwarks. A shell burst between the two forward guns in charge of Lieutenant Tyson, killing and wounding fifteen men. The mast upon which the writer was perched was twice struck, once slightly, and again just below the foretop by a heavy shell, from a rifle on the Confederate gun-boat *Selma.* . . . Looking out over the water, it was easy to trace the course of every shot, both from the guns of the *Hartford* and from the Confederate fleet.

Another signal message from the *Brooklyn* told of the sinking of the *Tecumseh,* a fact known already, and another order to "go on" was given and was not obeyed.

Soon after the fight began, Admiral Farragut, finding that the low-hanging smoke from the guns interfered with his view from the deck, went up the rigging of the mainmast as far as the futtock-shrouds, immediately below the maintop. The pilot, Martin Freeman, was in the top directly overhead, and the fleet-captain was on the deck below. Seeing the admiral in this exposed position, where, if wounded, he would be killed by falling to the deck, Fleet-Captain Drayton ordered Knowles, the signal-quartermaster, to fasten a rope around him so that he would be prevented from falling.

Finding that the *Brooklyn* failed to obey his orders, the admiral hurriedly inquired of the pilot if there was sufficient depth of water for the *Hartford* to pass to the left of the *Brooklyn*. Receiving an affirmative reply, he said: "I will take the lead," and immediately ordered the *Hartford* ahead at full speed. As he passed the *Brooklyn* a voice warned him of the torpedoes, to which he returned the contemptuous answer, "Damn the torpedoes." This is the current story, and may have some basis of truth. But as a matter of fact, there was never a moment when the din of the battle would not have drowned any attempt at conversation between the two ships, and while it is quite probable that the admiral made the remark it is doubtful if he shouted it to the *Brooklyn*.

Then was witnessed the remarkable sight of the *Hartford* and her consort, the *Metacomet*, passing over the dreaded torpedo ground and rushing ahead far in advance of the rest of the fleet, the extrication of which from the confusion caused by the *Brooklyn's* halt required many minutes of valuable time. The *Hartford* was now moving over what is called the "middle ground," with shallow water on either side, so that it was impossible to move except as the channel permitted. Taking advantage of the situation, the Confederate gun-boat *Selma* kept directly in front of the flagship and raked her fore and aft, doing more damage in reality than all the rest of the enemy's fleet. The other gun-boats, the *Gaines* and the *Morgan*, were in shallow water on our starboard bow, but they received more damage from the *Hartford's* broadsides than they were able to inflict. Meanwhile the ram *Tennessee*, which up to this time had contented herself with simply firing at the approaching fleet, started for the *Hartford*, apparently with the intention of striking her amidships. She came on perhaps for half a mile, never approaching nearer than a hundred yards, and then suddenly turned and made for the fleet, which, still in front of the fort, was gradually getting straightened out and following the *Hartford*. This change of course on the part of the ram has always been a mystery. The captain of the ram, in papers published since the war, denies that any such move was made, but it was witnessed by the entire fleet, and is mentioned by both Admiral Farragut and Fleet-Captain Drayton in their official reports.

The *Hartford* had now run a mile inside the bay, and was suffering chiefly from the raking fire of the *Selma*, which was unquestionably managed more skillfully than any other Confederate vessel. Captain (now Admiral) Jouett, commanding the *Hartford's* escort, the *Metacomet*, repeatedly asked permission of the admiral to cut loose and take care of the *Selma*, and finally, at five minutes past eight, consent was given. In an instant the cables binding the two vessels were cut, and the *Metacomet*, the fastest vessel in the fleet, bounded ahead. The *Selma* was no match for her, and, recognizing her danger, endeavored to retreat up the bay. But she was speedily overhauled, and when a shot had wounded her captain and killed her first lieutenant she surrendered. Before this the *Gaines* had been crippled by the splendid marksmanship of the *Hartford's* gunners, and had run aground under the guns of the fort, where she was shortly afterward set on fire, the crew escaping to the shore. The gunboat *Morgan*, after grounding for a few moments on the shoals to the east of Navy Cove, retreated to the shallow water near the fort, whence she escaped the following night to Mobile. The *Hartford*, having reached the deep water of the bay, about three miles north of Dauphine Island, came to anchor.

Let us now return to the other vessels of the fleet, which we left massed in front of Fort Morgan by the remarkable action of the *Brooklyn* in stopping and refusing to move ahead. When the ram *Tennessee* turned away from the *Hartford*, as narrated, she made for the fleet, and in their crowded and confused condition it seemed to be a matter of no difficulty to pick out whatever victims the Confederate commander (Admiral Franklin Buchanan) might desire, as he had done in 1861 when commanding the *Merrimac* in Hampton Roads. Before he could reach them the line had been straightened, and the leading vessels had passed the fort. . . .

Whatever damage was done by the *Tennessee* to the fleet in passing the fort was by the occasional discharge *of* her guns. She failed to strike a single one of the Union vessels, but was herself run into by the *Monongahela*, Captain Strong, at full speed. . . . The *Monongahela* was no match for the *Tennessee*, but she had been strengthened by an artificial iron prow, and being one of the fastest—or rather, *least slow*—of the fleet, was expected to act as a ram if opportunity offered. Captain Strong waited for no orders, but seeing the huge ram coming for the fleet left his place in the line and attacked her. .. .

At last all the fleet passed the fort, and while the ram ran under its guns the vessels made their way to the *Hartford* and dropped their anchors, except the *Metacomet*, *Port Royal*, *Kennebec*, and *Itasca*. After the forts were passed, the three last named had cut loose from their escorts and gone to aid the *Metacomet* in her struggle with the *Selma* and *Morgan* . . .

The *Tennessee*, after remaining near Fort Morgan while the fleet had made its way four miles above to its anchorage,—certainly as much as half an hour,—had suddenly decided to settle at once the question of the control of the bay. Single handed she came on to meet the whole fleet, consisting now of ten wooden vessels and the three monitors. At that time the *Tennessee* was believed to be the strongest vessel afloat, and the safety with which she carried her crew during the battle proved that she was virtually invulnerable. Fortunately for the Union fleet she was weakly handled, and at the end fell a victim to a stupendous blunder in her construction—the failure to protect her rudder-chains.

The spectacle afforded the Confederate soldiers, who crowded the ramparts of the two forts,—the fleet now being out of range,—was such as has very rarely been furnished in the history of the world. To the looker-on it seemed as if the fleet was at the mercy of the ram, for the monitors, which were expected to be the chief defense, were so destitute of speed and so difficult to manoeuvre that it

seemed an easy task for the *Tennessee* to avoid them and sink the wooden vessels in detail.

Because of the slowness of the monitors, Admiral Farragut selected the fastest of the wooden vessels to begin the attack. While the navy signals for a general attack of the enemy were being prepared, the *Monongahela* (Captain Strong) and the *Lackawanna* (Captain Marchand) were ordered by the more rapid signal system of the army to "run down the ram," the order being immediately repeated to the monitors.

The *Monongahela*, with her prow already somewhat weakened by the previous attempt to ram, at once took the lead, as she had not yet come to anchor. The ram from the first headed for the *Hartford*, and paid no attention to her assailants, except with her guns. The *Monongahela*, going at full speed, struck the *Tennessee* amidships—a blow that would have sunk almost any vessel of the Union navy, but which inflicted not the slightest damage on the solid iron hull of the ram. (After the surrender it was almost impossible to tell where the attacking vessel had struck.) Her own iron prow and cutwater were carried away, and she was otherwise badly damaged about the stem by the collision.

The *Lackawanna* was close behind and delivered a similar blow with her wooden bow, simply causing the ram to lurch slightly to one side. As the vessels separated the *Lackawanna* swung alongside the ram, which sent two shots through her and kept on her course for the *Hartford*, which was now the next vessel in the attack. The two flag-ships approached each other, bow to bow, iron against oak. It was impossible for the *Hartford*, with her lack of speed, to circle around and strike the ram on the side; her only safety was in keeping pointed directly for the bow of her assailant. The other vessels of the fleet were unable to do anything for the defense of the admiral except to train their guns on the ram, on which as yet they had not the slightest effect.

It was a thrilling moment for the fleet, for it was evident that if the ram could strike the

Hartford the latter must sink. But for the two vessels to strike fairly, bows on, would probably have involved the destruction of both, for the ram must have penetrated so far into the wooden ship that as the *Hartford* filled and sank she would have carried the ram under water. Whether for this reason or for some other, as the two vessels came together the *Tennessee* slightly changed her course, the port bow of the *Hartford* met the port bow of the ram, and the ships grated against each other as they passed. The *Hartford* poured her whole port broadside against the ram, but the solid shot merely dented the side and bounded into the air. The ram tried to return the salute, but owing to defective primers only one gun was discharged. This sent a shell through the berth-deck, killing five men and wounding eight. The muzzle of the gun was so close to the *Hartford* that the powder blackened her side.

The admiral stood on the quarter-deck when the vessels came together, and as he saw the result he jumped on to the port-quarter rail, holding to the mizzen-rigging, a position from which he might have jumped to the deck of the ram as she passed. Seeing him in this position, and fearing for his safety, Flag-Lieutenant Watson slipped a rope around him and 8ecured it to the rigging, so that during the fight the admiral was twice "lashed to the rigging," each time by devoted officers who knew better than to consult him before acting. Fleet-Captain Drayton had hurried to the bow of the *Hartford* as the collision was seen to be inevitable, and expressed keen satisfaction when the ram avoided a direct blow.

The *Tennessee* now became the target for the whole fleet, all the vessels of which were making toward her, pounding her with shot, and trying to run her down. As the *Hartford* turned to make for her again, we ran in front of the *Lackawanna*, which had a1ready turned and was moving under full headway with the same object. She struck us on our starboard side, amidships, crushing halfway through, knocking two port-holes into one, upsetting one of the Dahlgren guns, and creating general consternation. For a time it was thought that we

must sink, and the cry rang out over the deck: "Save the admiral! Save the admiral!" The port boats were ordered lowered, and in their haste some of the sailors cut the "falls," and two of the cutters dropped into the water wrong side up, and floated astern. But the admiral sprang into the starboard mizzen-rigging, looked over the side of the ship, and, finding there were still a few inches to spare above the water's edge, instantly ordered the ship ahead again at full speed, after the ram.

The unfortunate *Lackawanna*, which had struck the ram a second blow, was making for her once more, and, singularly enough, again came up on our starboard side, and another collision seemed imminent. And now the admiral became a trifle excited. He had no idea of whipping the rebels to be him self sunk by a friend, nor did he realize at the moment that the *Hartford* was as much to blame as the *Lackawanna*. Turning to the writer he inquired. "Can you say 'For God's sake' by signal?"

"Yes, sir," was the reply.

"Then say to the *Lackawanna*, 'For God's sake get out of our way and anchor!' "

In my haste to send the message, I brought the end of my signal flag-staff down with considerable violence upon the head of the admiral, who was standing nearer than I thought, causing him to wince perceptibly. It was a hasty message, for the fault was equally divided, each ship being too eager to reach the enemy, and it turned out all right, by a fortunate accident, that Captain Marchand never received it. The army signal officer on the *Lackawanna*, Lieutenant Myron Adams (now pastor of Plymouth Congregational Church in Rochester, N.Y.) had taken his station in the foretop, and just as he received the first five words, "For God's sake get out"—the wind flirted the large United States flag at the mast head around him, so that he was unable to read the conclusion of the message.

The remainder of the story is soon told. As the *Tennessee* left the *Hartford* she became the target of the entire fleet, and at last the concentration of solid shot from so many guns began to tell. The flag-staff was shot away, the smoke-stack was riddled with holes, and finally disappeared. The monitor *Chickasaw*, Lieutenant-Commander Perkins, succeeded in coming up astern and began pounding away with 11-inch solid shot, and one shot from a 15-inch gun of the *Manhattan* crushed into the side sufficiently to prove that a few more such shots would have made the casemate untenable. Finally, one of the *Chickasaw's* shots cut the rudder-chain of the ram and she would no longer mind her helm. At this time, as Admiral Farragut says in his report, "she was sore beset. The *Chickasaw* was pounding away at her stern, the *Ossipee* was approaching her at full speed, and the *Monongahela*, *Lackawanna*, and this ship were bearing down upon her, determined upon her destruction." From the time the *Nartford* struck her she did not fire a gun. Finally the Confederate admiral, Buchanan, was severely wounded by an iron splinter or a piece of shell, and just as the *Ossipee* was about to strike her the *Tennessee* displayed a white flag, hoisted on an improvised staff through the grating over her deck. The *Ossipee* (Captain Le Roy) reversed her engine, but was so near that a harmless collision was inevitable.

Suddenly the terrific cannonading ceased, and from every ship rang out cheer after cheer, as the weary men realized that at last the ram was conquered and the day won.

—KINNEY, "Farragut at Mobile Bay"

------------ XXVI.7 ------------

LIEUTENANT CUSHING
TORPEDOES THE
ALBEMARLE

In a war memorable for many deeds of daring, there were few more spectacular than the destruction of the Confederate ram Albemarle by young Lieutenant William B. Cushing. A "bilged" midshipman, Cushing had managed to get into the navy as master's mate, then proceeded to distinguish himself by one heroic deed after another. He captured numerous prizes, destroyed saltworks along the Atlantic coast, captured enemy officers and couriers, and in the fall of 1864 conceived and carried through the plan to torpedo the *Albemarle*. This formidable vessel, which had already destroyed several Federal ships, was then lying at Plymouth, North Carolina, some eight miles up the Roanoke River.

Cushing himself tells us how he attacked and sank her. For this act, of which the captain of the Albemarle said, "a more gallant thing was not done during the war," Cushing was made lieutenant commander, at twenty-two, and given a formal vote of thanks by Congress.

Finding some boats building for picket duty, I selected two, and proceeded to fit them out. They were open launches, about thirty feet in length, with small engines, and propelled by a screw. A 12-pounder howitzer was fitted to the bow of each, and a boom was rigged out, some fourteen feet in length, swinging by a goose-neck hinge to the bluff of the bow. A topping lift, carried to a stanchion inboard, raised or lowered it, and the torpedo was fitted into an iron slide at-the end. This was intended to be detached from the boom by means of a heel-jigger leading inboard, and to be exploded by another line, connecting with a pin, which held a grape shot over a nipple and cap. The torpedo was the invention of Engineer Lay of the navy, and was introduced by Chief-Engineer Wood. Everything being completed, we started to the south ward, taking the boats through the canals to Chesapeake Bay. My best boat having been lost in going down to Norfolk, I proceeded with the other through the Chesapeake and Albemarle canal. Half-way through, the canal was filled up, but finding a small creek that emptied into it below the obstruction, I endeavored to feel my way through. Encountering a mill-dam, we waited for high water, and ran the launch over it; below she grounded, but I got a flat-boat, and, taking out gun and coal, succeeded in two days in getting her through. Passing with but seven men through the canal, where for thirty miles there was no guard or Union inhabitant, I reached the sound, and ran before a gale of wind to Roanoke Island.

In the middle of the night I steamed off into the darkness, and in the morning was out of sight. Fifty miles up the sound I found the fleet anchored off the mouth of the river, and awaiting the ram's appearance. Here, for the first time, I disclosed to my officers and men our object, and told them that they were at liberty to go-or not, as they pleased. These, seven in number, all volunteered. One of them, Mr. Howarth of the *Monticello*, had been with me repeatedly in expeditions of peril.

The Roanoke River is a stream averaging 150 yards in width, and quite deep. Eight miles from the mouth was the town of Plymouth, where the ram was moored. Several thousand soldiers occupied town and forts, and held both banks of the stream. A mile below the ram was the wreck of the *Southfield*, with hurricane deck above water, and on this a guard was stationed. Thus it seemed impossible to surprise them, or to attack with hope of success.

Impossibilities are for the timid: we determined to overcome all obstacles. On the night of the 27th of October we entered the river, taking in tow a small cutter with a few men, whose duty was to dash aboard the wreck of the *Southfield* at the first hail, and prevent a rocket from being ignited.

We passed within thirty feet of the pickets without discovery, and neared the vessel. I now thought that it might be better to board her, and "take her alive," having in the two boats twenty men well armed with revolvers, cutlasses, and hand-grenades. To be sure, there were ten times our number on the ship and thousands near by; but a surprise is everything, and I thought if her fasts were cut at the instant of boarding, we might overcome those on board, take her into the stream, and use her iron sides to protect us afterward from the forts. Knowing the town, I concluded to land at the lower wharf, creep around, and suddenly dash aboard from the bank; but just as I was sheering in close to the wharf, a hail came, sharp and quick, from the ironclad, and in an instant was repeated. I at once directed the cutter to cast off, and go down-to capture the guard left in our rear, and, ordering all steam, went at the dark mountain of iron in front of us. A heavy fire was at once opened upon us, not only from the ship, but from men stationed on the shore. This did not disable us, and

we neared them rapidly. A large fire now blazed upon the bank, and by its light I discovered the unfortunate fact that there was a circle of logs around the *Albemarle*, boomed well out from her side, with the very intention of preventing the action of torpedoes. To examine them more closely, I ran alongside until amidships, received the enemy's fire, and sheered off for the purpose of turning, a hundred yards away, and going at the booms squarely, at right angles, trusting to their having been long enough in the water to have become slimy—in which case my boat, under full headway, would bump up against them and slip over into the pen with the ram. This was my only chance of success, and once over the obstruction my boat would never get out again. As I turned, the whole back of my coat was torn out by buckshot, and the sole of my shoe was carried away. The fire was very severe.

In a lull of the firing, the captain hailed us, again demanding what boat it was. All my men gave comical answers, and mine was a dose of canister from the howitzer. In an other instant we had struck the logs and were over, with headway nearly gone, slowly forging up under the enemy's quarterport. Ten feet from us the muzzle of a rifle gun looked into our faces, and every word of command on board was distinctly heard.

My clothing was perforated with bullets as I stood in the bow, the heeljigger in my right hand and the exploding-line in the left. We were near enough then, and I ordered the boom lowered until the forward motion of the launch carried the torpedo under the ram's overhang. A strong pull of the detaching-line, a moment's waiting for the torpedo to rise under the hull, and I hauled in the left hand, just cut by a bullet.

The explosion took place at the same instant that 100 pounds of grape, at 10 feet range, crashed among us, and the dense mass of water thrown out by the torpedo came down with choking weight upon us.

—CUSHING, "The Destruction of the 'Albemarle'"

XXVI.8

THE CONFEDERATES REPULSE AN ATTACK ON FORT FISHER

With the fan of Mobile and the effective bottling up of Charleston, Wilmington, on the Cape Fear River, was the only major port still in Confederate hands, and all through 1864 it was the chief haven of blockade-runners. With the advance of Sherman northward through the Carolinas it became important to capture the Cape Fear entrance and Wilmington in order to afford a supply base for the Union armies. The mouth of the Cape Fear was controlled by Fort Fisher, whose ramparts faced both the land and the sea. The first attack on Fort Fisher came on December 24, 1864, from a fleet of 60 vessels under Admiral Porter.

The attack, as the Confederate commander, Colonel William Lamb, here tells us, was a failure. Yet the Confederate defense, too, was something of a failure. While the defenders of the fort acquitted themselves gloriously, General Bragg with 3,500 men at near-by Wilmington made no move to strike at the troops that General Butler had landed for the attack but allowed them to get off unmolested.

Saturday, December 24, was one of those perfect winter days that are occasionally experienced in the latitude of the Cape Fear. The gale which had backed around from the north east to the southwest had subsided the day before, and was followed by a dead calm. The air was balmy for winter, and the sun shone with almost Indian summer warmth, and the deep blue sea was calm as a lake, and broke lazily on the bar and beach.

A grander sight than the approach of Porter's formidable armada towards the fort was never witnessed on our coast. With the rising sun out of old ocean, there came upon the horizon, one after another, the vessels of the fleet, the grand frigates leading the van, followed by the ironclads,—more than fifty men-of-war, heading for the Confederate strong hold. At nine o'clock the men were beat to quarters, and silently the detachments stood by their guns. On the vessels came, growing larger and more imposing as the distance lessened between them and the resolute men who had rallied to defend their

homes. The *Minnesota, Colorado,* and *Wabash,* came grandly on, floating fortresses, each mounting more guns than all the batteries on the land, and the two first, combined, carrying more shot and shell than all the magazines in the fort contained. From the left salient to the mound Fort Fisher had 44 heavy guns, and not over 3600 shot and shell, exclusive of grape and shrapnel. The Armstrong gun had only one dozen rounds of fixed ammunition, and no other projectile could be used in its delicate grooves. The order was given to fire no shot until the Columbiad at headquarters fired, and then each gun that bore on a vessel could be fired every thirty minutes, and not oftener except by special order; unless an attempt was made to cross the bar, when every gun bearing on it should be fired as rapidly as accuracy would permit, the smooth bores at ricochet.

Before coming within range, the wooden ships slowed down-and the great *Ironsides* and three monitors slowly forged ahead, coming within less than a mile of the northeast salient, the other ships taking position to the right and left, the line extending more than a mile. As the *Ironsides* took her position she ran out her starboard guns, a flash was seen from the forward one, then a puff of white smoke, a deep boom was heard and over our heads came an 11-inch shell, which I saw distinctly in its passage across our flag-staff, past which it exploded harmlessly with a sharp report. . . .

This was the commencement of the most terrific bombardment from the fleet which war had ever witnessed. Ship after ship discharged its broadsides, every description of deadly missile, from a 3-inch rifle-bolt to a 15-inch shell flying widely into and over the fort until the garrison flag-staff was shattered. Most of the firing seemed directed towards it, and as it stood in the centre of the parade, all these bolts fell harmless as to human life, many of the shells, especially the rifle-shots, going over the fort and into the river in the rear. The dead calm which prevailed in nature caused the smoke to hang around the hulls of the vessels, so enveloping them as to prevent the effect of the shots our gunners were allowed to fire from being seen. It was two hours after the bombardment commenced before the flag was shot away, and in that time, although thousands of shot and shell were hurled at us, I had heard of no casualty in the works. For those two hours I had remained on the parapet of the sea face watching intently for any effort to cross the bar, and in all that time only one shell had exploded near enough to endanger my life. In the rear of the flag-staff the wooden quarters of the garrison were situated, and these were soon set on fire by the bursting shells and more than half of them were consumed. The day being balmy, most of the men had left their overcoats and blankets in their bunks and these were consumed. There was quite a quantity of naval stores,—tar and pitch near these quarters,—and they took fire and made an imposing bonfire in sympathy with the occasion.

As soon as the garrison flag was shot away, finding the staff so split and shivered that it could not be raised, I sent word to Captain Munn to raise the flag on the mound. It seems the halyards had gotten unreeved and it was necessary to climb the staff to fasten the flag. Private Christopher C. Bland volunteered for the service, and climbed the staff under heavy fire and secured the battle-flag to the masthead. At once a terrific fire was poured on the mound and the lower end of the flag having been cut loose, again that heroic soldier repeated the daring act amid the cheers of the garrison, and securely fastened the flag where it floated in triumph, although torn and rent by fragments of shell, until the victory was won. While this was being done I went to the left salient and planted a company battle-flag on the extreme left. My two hours' experience had taught me that the fleet would concentrate a heavy fire on it, and I wanted to put it where it would do the most good by causing the least harm. For five hours this tremendous hail of shot and shell was poured upon the devoted works, but with little effect. At 5:30 P.M the fleet withdrew. . . .

In the first day's fight I had about one half of the quarters burned, three gun carriages disabled, a light artillery caisson exploded, large quantities of

the earthworks torn and ploughed up, with some revetments broken and splintered, but not a single bomb proof or magazine injured. Only twenty-three men wounded, one mortally, three seriously and nineteen slightly.

Never, since the invention of gunpowder, was there so much harmlessly expended, as in the first day's attack on Fort Fisher. All was quiet during the night, but next morning, Christmas Day, at about ten o'clock, the great fleet again moved in towards the fort, being reenforced by another monitor and some additional wooden ships of war. At half past ten the *Ironsides* opened and the fleet commenced an incessant bombardment, if possible, more noisy and furious than that of the preceding day. At about two o'clock several of the frigates came up to the bar and lowered boats, apparently to sound the entrance, but a heavy fire was immediately directed against them and they were promptly driven out. At half-past three a very gallant attempt was made by a number of barges to sound the Carolina shoals, south of the mound. A few shots from Battery Buchanan, the naval battery in my command, first cut the flag from a barge and then cut the barge in two, causing the remainder, after rescuing their comrades, to retreat rapidly.

My two 7-inch Brooke rifles both exploded in the after noon of this day. Being manned by a detachment of sailors and situated opposite to the bar I had given the officer in charge discretion to fire upon the vessels which had approached the bar, and his fire had been more rapid than from any other guns, and with this disastrous result, the explosion wounding a number of men.

Strange as it may appear, no attempt to pass the fort was made by any of the fleet, and none except the armored vessels came within a mile of the heaviest guns. Whether the smoke obscured the fort or the gunners were untrained, it is hard to account for the wild firing of these two days. If they had tried to miss the guns on the sea face they could not have succeeded better, no gun or carriage on that face being injured by the fire of the fleet; the only two guns disabled were the two Brooke rifles, which exploded. All the disabled guns were on the land face, which was enfiladed by the fleet as well as subjected to the direct fire of the armored ships, which came within half a mile of the fort. With the exception of the Brooke Battery, and some special firing on vessels, the firing of the fort was slower and more deliberate than on the previous day, only 600 shot and shell being expended. The temptation to concentrate the whole of the available fire of the fort on a single frigate and drive her out or destroy her was very great, as I found the garrison were disappointed at having no trophy for the first day's engagement, but I had a limited supply of ammunition, and did not know when it could be replenished. Already on the first day I had expended nearly one sixth of my supply in merely keeping the men in heart by an occasional shot. I could easily have fired every shot and shell away the first day. Admiral Porter expended nearly all of his ammunition in the two days' bombardment. The *Minnesota* fired 1982 shots and the *Colorado* 1569 shots, a total of these two frigates of 3551, about as many as we had in all the batteries of Fort Fisher. On both days I fired the last gun to let our naval visitors know that we had another shot in the locker. In the bombardment the second day, most of the remaining quarters were destroyed, more of the earthworks' were displaced, but none seriously damaged, and five guns were disabled by the enemy. The greatest penetration noticed (from 15-inch shell) was five feet perpendicularly.

During the day a large fleet of transports were seen up the beach, and the Federals landed a large force at Battery Anderson, three miles from the fort. At 4:30 P.M. sharpshooters were seen on our left flank and they fired upon our gunners from the old quarters across the causeway, and killed a young courier, who had been, without my knowledge, sent out of the fort, capturing his horse. I had two pieces of artillery run-out of the sallyport, and a few discharges of canister stopped the annoyance. At this time, on the 25th, my effective force had been increased to 921 regulars and 450 Junior Reserves, total 1371. At 5:30 P.M. a most furious enfilading fire against the land face and palisade line commenced, certainly never surpassed in warfare, 130 shot and shell per minute, more than two every second. I ordered my men to protect themselves behind the traverses, and removed all extra men from the chambers, with the order the moment the firing stopped, to rally to the ramparts without further orders.

As soon as this fire commenced, I saw a heavy line of skirmishers advancing on our works. Just as the naval fire ceased, the guns were manned and opened with grape and canister, and as it was becoming too dark to see the advance from the ramparts, I threw 800 men and boys behind the palisades, which had been scarcely injured. I never shall for get the gallant youths whom I rallied that night to meet the enemy. I had ordered all to man the parapets as soon as the naval fire ceased, as I supposed it would be followed by an assault. I thought the Junior Reserves were coming up too slowly and I called out rather impatiently, "Don't be cowards, boys," when one manly little officer rushed over the work followed by his companions, shouting, "We are no cowards, colonel," and manned the palisades. I ordered them not to fire until the enemy were within a few feet of the palisades, but the whistle of bullets from Butler's skirmish line so excited them that in spite of my orders they kept up a fusilade until the Federals retired.

I was determined to meet the enemy at the palisade, feeling confident the few who reached it would be easily captured or repulsed. I had the land guns, heavy and light, manned, with orders to fire grape and canister whenever they saw an advance in force, and the operators stood ready, upon my order, to explode some of the sub-terra torpedoes. I stood upon the parapet to the left of the centre sallyport, after giving directions in person to the officers on the land front. The fleet had ceased except an occasional shell from the ironclads down this face. The Federal sharpshooters were firing wildly in the darkness at our ramparts, but the bullets which were few and far between, went harmlessly over our heads. My plan was to open with grape and canister on the assaulting column, and when its front reached the palisade, to open the infantry fire and explode a line of torpedoes in their rear to stop the reenforcing line. I am confident this would have resulted in a repulse of the main body and the capture of the first line. But Butler, with wise discretion, determined not to assault. There were not enough Federal troops landed to have stormed our palisade that Christmas night. If the assaulting column could have reached the comparatively uninjured palisades through the fire of canister and grape, the explosion and infantry fire would have resulted in their capture or destruction.

My only uneasiness was from a boat attack in the rear between the Mound and Battery Buchanan, where a thousand sailors and marines could have landed with little opposition at that time and attacked us in the rear. About 3 A.M. it was reported that such an advance was being made and I sent Major Reilly with two companies to repulse them, following shortly after in person with a third company to reenforce him. A heavy wind and rain storm had arisen at midnight, and if such a movement was contemplated, it was abandoned.

Two prisoners from the.l42nd New York were captured in our front at night, and next morning a number of new graves were found. Our casualties for the second day were: killed, 3; wounded, mortally, 2; severely, 7; slightly, 26. Total for the two days, 3 killed and 61 wounded.

—LAMB, "The Defence of Fort Fisher"

XXVI.9

"IT BEAT ANYTHING IN HISTORY"

General Lee had informed the defenders of Fort Fisher that they must hold it at all costs; otherwise he could not continue to subsist his army. For the same reason Grant was determined to reduce it. The repulse of December 24, there fore, was not accepted as final, and preparations were made for e-renewal of the attack on a grander scale. On the morning of January 13,

1865, "the most formidable armada the world had ever known"—the words are those of Colonel Lamb—sailed over the horizon, 60 men-of-war under Admiral Porter and transports carrying 8500 troops under General Terry. To beat off this force Colonel Lamb had some 1,900 men, 44 guns, and inadequate ammunition; that evil genius of the Confederacy, Braxton Bragg, kept his army of 3,500 men safely at Wilmington. The bombardment opened on the thirteenth, and continued without pause through the fourteenth. On the fifteenth an assaulting column attacked the fort from the river shore, and overwhelmed its gallant defenders. Thus fell the last available Confederate port.

Our narrator is again the "boy cannoneer," Augustus Buell.

I wouldn't have missed seeing that bombardment of Port Fisher for 10 years of my life. It beat anything in history for weight of ordnance used even greater than the bombardment of the Sebastopol forts by the English and French fleets, because the guns we used were so much heavier. I cannot describe the discharges of those 13 and 15-inch Rod man guns of the monitors, or the explosion of their great shells in the air over the fort or among its traverses. To me it seemed like firing meteors out of volcanoes. I had hitherto thought that the long percussion shell bolt of a four-and-a half-inch Rodman siege gun, which I had "gunned" a couple of times in cannonades in the redan in the early part of the great siege was a big thing, but now I hauled down my colors. I would watch the turrets of the monitors through my glass. They would turn their iron backs on the enemy to load, and I could distinctly see the big rammer staves come out of the ports. Then they would wheel round on a line with the fort, there would be two puffs of blue smoke about the size of a thunder cloud in June, and then I could see the big shell make a black streak through the air with a tail of white smoke behind it—and then would come over the water, not the quick bark of a field gun, but a slow, quivering, overpowering roar like an earthquake, and then, away among the Rebel traverses, there would be another huge ball-of mingled smoke and flame as big as a meeting house. . . .

Imagine a cold, bright day in the middle of January; a low, sandy coastline, with a dull surf combing up on the beach; a tremendous fort of the most elaborate construction, with ramparts in some places 30 feet high; huge bastions every little way; deep-throated embrasures from which frowned the muzzles of seven, eight and 10-inch Armstrong and Brooke rifled cannon and Columbiads; and the doomed flag of the gallant Confederacy floating defiantly from its tall staff!

Look, then, seaward, and see 60 steam men-of-war formed in a great arc of a circle, all steaming slowly to their anchors and rolling great volumes of smoke from their fun nels. Inside of this outer arc five or six of those low, black, sullen monitors "in line abreast," as the sailors called it, slowly and steadily creeping toward the fort, no visible sign of life about them, except now and then you could see an officer's head come up over the breastwork or barbet on top of the turret.

The sullen monitors never said a word till their noses touched the beach, which was as close as they could get to their antagonist, and then—well, the like of it was never seen. Prom where our transport was anchored it looked as if the *Canonicus*, which was considerably nearer to the fort than any other ship, must be within 400 yards of the north east main bastion. I kept my glass trained on her all the time. I could see the fire fly from her iron turret, deck and sides when the big bolts from the Rebel guns struck her. It did not seem possible that anything made by human hands could stand it. At this moment the three single-turreted monitors *Canonicus*, *Saugus* and *Mahopac*—were in a bunch together, the *Canonicus* in the center and ahead, not 1,200 feet from the great bastion! On one flank, a little farther from the fort, was the double-turreted *Monadnock*, and on the other, still farther out, was a great, enormous mass of iron, flame and smoke, which the old Quartermaster told us was the famous *New Ironsides*, of which we had read so much in the stories of Fort Sumter. The *Ironsides* was a "broadsider," and she had 11-inch guns, of which she carried eight or nine on each side. As her guns were lighter than those of the monitors and mounted in the ordinary way, she could fire

much faster than they could, and so she was pretty much a solid mass of flame all the time.

The bombardment lasted from 10 A.M. till past 2 in the afternoon. Meantime quite a force of sailors and marines had been landed below the fort, but they were not at first in sight from our anchorage. By 2 o'clock the fire from the heavy guns of the fort had ceased. Many of them were dismounted, and the shells from the fleet had driven the Confederate Cannoneers to take shelter in their bombproofs. The fleet now suddenly ceased firing and began to blow their steam whistles, which made a din almost equal to the cannonade. This was the signal for assault. At this time the infantry nearest the river had gotten up within 80 or 100 yards of the fort, and in order to get a clear view of the assault the sailors on the transport began to mount into the rigging. "Old Sig" took his station in the maintop, together with First Officer Hanscomb, and by permission of this officer I climbed up too. The ship was rolling considerably, which made the maintop a ticklish place for a landsman. . . .

The right of the line of men-of-war was now hauled in or shortened, the vessels of the right division falling into a second line astern of the center division. Probably 15 minutes elapsed between the blowing of the whistles and the grand advance of the infantry against the north face of the fort. They did not encounter so heavy a fire of musketry at first as I expected to see, but the sailors and marines who were assaulting the sea face got cold lead in big doses. From where we were it looked as if the enemy was concentrating his whole defense on the sea face. In less time than it takes to write it the infantry had mounted the parapet nearest the river and jumped down into the works. We, of course, supposed that this would finish the business, and momentarily expected the tokens of surrender. But we little understood the nature of the fort. It was so traversed and retrenched on the inside that it really amounted to a line of small re doubts inside of one large fortress, and the continuous angry crackle of musketry, with dense volumes of smoke rolling up from the inside, told that the garrison was defending every inch of the works with desperate resolution. At the time this looked like useless slaughter, though in the light of subsequent history it appears that the gallant garrison was holding out in the vain hope that Hoke's column from Wilmington would make a diversion in their favor; though they must have had a queer idea of what would have been involved in an attempt to advance infantry over that narrow sandspit, swept as it was from sea to river by the guns of 60 men-of-war!

However, the struggle inside the great fort went on until it assumed the proportions of a regular battle, lasting until after dark. The monitors kept throwing a shell now and then, but it was dangerous business as our troops had cleaned out about half the enemy's traverses and they were slowly working their way through the others. Darkness did not end the com bat, but the fitful flashes kept lighting up the crest of the long sand parapet and revealing the outlines of the traverses and retrenchments inside. The monitors and *New Ironsides* also opened again with shell against the south end of the sea face, from which our sailors and marines had been repulsed, and for half or three-quarters of an hour the sight was indescribably grand. But about this time the wind lulled, so that the smoke did not drift away, and the fort and the monitors lay enveloped in a huge pall, which, added to the gloom of the night, gave a weird effect to the flashes of the 15-inch guns and the blaze of bursting shells. This lasted till about 9 o'clock at night, when the musketry ceased inside the fort, and soon after the ships began signaling with different-colored rockets, which made another beautiful spectacle. There was not much sleep that night. Shortly after the fort surrendered—say about 11 o'clock.

—BUELL, *"The Cannoneer'*

———————— X X V I I ————————

T H E B L O C K A D E A N D
T H E C R U I S E R S

We are not wholly unfamiliar with the subject of this chapter. Our review of fighting along the coast and inland waters introduced us to the blockade, and our survey of British American relations to the delicate problem of the Confederate cruisers. We record here something of the story of the blockade itself—as distinct from the attack on coastal ports—of blockade-running, and of Confederate warfare on Union shipping on the high seas.

Lincoln had formally blockaded the whole coast of the Confederacy from the Chesapeake Bay to the Rio Grande by two proclamations of April 1861. We need not rehearse here the vexatious issue of the legality of his proclamations either in American constitutional law or in international law. Suffice it to say that the constitutionality of the blockade was sustained in the Prize Cases, and that foreign governments respected the blockade. More relevant is the question of the effectiveness of the blockade itself. And that is a very difficult question to answer.

To bottle up a dozen major ports and almost 200 minor ports and inlets the Union had, at the outbreak of the war, less than 20 vessels. By 1865 this number had been increased to over 600— and its task correspondingly diminished by the capture of all major ports. The Confederacy, of course, began at once to evade the blockade, and to persuade other nations to co-operate in this, or to break it by intervention. It had no navy with which to challenge Union control of the seas and coastal waters; the cruisers it built abroad were designed rather to prey on Union commerce than to attack Union men-of-war. Four categories of ships engaged in blockade running: those owned by the Confederate government; those owned by state governments; those owned by private individuals or groups of speculators; and foreign ships. Of these the third and fourth categories were the most important, though government-owned blockade-runners gave a good account of themselves. It has been estimated that altogether some 600 ships were engaged, at one time or another, in the lucrative and exciting business of blockade-running, but this estimate is palpably too low;

that there were, altogether, some 8,000 violations of the blockade; and that blockade-runners brought in altogether over 600,000 small arms, 550,000 pairs of shoes, and large quantities of meat, coffee, saltpeter, lead, and other items. At the same time substantial quantities of supplies were brought in from Mexico, across the Rio Grande, and there was at all times a lively trade with the North: General Sherman said that Cincinnati furnished more goods to the Confederacy than Charleston!

All this would indicate that the blockade was but loosely enforced, and it cannot be denied that it was pretty ineffective in 1861 and even in 1862. Thereafter, however—what with the fall of New Orleans and of Fort Royal and the sealing off of other harbors—it became increasingly effective, and the South felt the pinch seriously. It is estimated that the chances of capture were one in ten in 1861, but one in three by 1864, and with the capture of Wilmington in January 1865 blockade-running practically ceased.

What all this adds up to is that the blockade was a decisive factor in Union victory. We cannot say that without it the Confederacy would have won, but it is clear that without it the war would have been greatly prolonged and might have ended in a stalemate. Yet it must be kept in mind that Confederate susceptibility to the blockade was enhanced by several factors, and that the blockade need not have been as injurious as it actually was. First, the Confederacy was unprepared to take advantage of the feebleness of the blockade in 1861; as the Confederates did not anticipate a long war there was no long-range buying program. Second, the blockade sent prices skyrocketing, and the Confederacy was unable to buy all that it might have obtained had it taxed more successfully or controlled prices or raised money abroad. Third, blockade-running was largely a private enterprise, and shipowners imported luxuries rather than war essentials; not until 1864 did the government assume control over it, requiring that every blockade-runner have a permit and allot at least one half of its cargo space to military essentials. Fourth, imports through Mexico and Texas were large—Galveston, for example, remained in Confederate hands—but the Federal victories on the Mississippi nullified this immense advantage.

Lacking a navy, the Confederacy early authorized letters of marque and set about outfitting privateers. Privateering had been outlawed by the Declaration of Paris, of 1856, but the United States was not a signatory to this declaration, and the Confederacy could thus claim some legal right to ignore it. There were perhaps a dozen privateers, and altogether they captured or destroyed 60 Union vessels. Far more important, for offensive purposes, were the cruisers, or commerce destroyers. As we have already seen the Confederate government sent Captain James Bulloch to Britain, at the outbreak of the war, to arrange for the purchase or construction of cruisers and rams. This service he performed with brilliant success. Altogether the Confederacy acquired 18 cruisers, of which the *Alabama*, the *Florida*, the *Shenandoah*, the *Georgia*, the *Sumter*, and the *Tallahassee* were most effective. The results of the depredations of these commerce destroyers upon the American merchant marine were disastrous; not for two generations did the American fleet regain its place on the high seas, and as late as 1910 American-flag merchant ships totaled only one third the tonnage of 1860.

We have given in this chapter something of the story of the blockade and the blockade-runners; a glimpse of privateerings; and an account of war on the high seas.

XXVII. I

THE UNITED STATES NAVY BLOCKADES THE CONFEDERACY

This general account of the Union blockade is self-explanatory. It is, however, worth underlining one point that our author makes: that the blockade of the Confederacy was "an undertaking without precedent in history." The British blockade of the continent during the Napoleonic Wars had been largely a paper affair and had not presented a task comparable to that which confronted the Navy Department in 1861. It is appropriate to recall, too, what Wait takes for granted, that Gideon Welles was one of the ablest of American Secretaries of the Navy, and that the Navy Department was, throughout the war, well run.

Horatio Wait was a paymaster in the United States Navy.

At the beginning of the war in 1861, a perplexing question arose as to whether it would be best for the government to declare all the Southern ports of entry to be closed, or to proclaim a blockade. . . .

The urgency of the case caused President Lincoln to act promptly. On April 19, 1861, six days after the surrender of Fort Sumter, he issued a proclamation declaring a blockade of the entire coast of the Confederacy, from South Carolina to Texas; and on April 27 extended it to cover Virginia and North Carolina, making a coast-line of over three thousand miles to be blockaded, greater in extent than the Atlantic coast of Europe—an undertaking without precedent in history. . . .

When Mr. Lincoln issued this proclamation we had only forty-two ships in commission in our navy. Most of them were absent on foreign stations, and only one efficient warship, the *Brooklyn*, was available for immediate service. The days of paper blockades had long since passed away. The universally recognized rule of international law on this subject was that "blockades, to be binding, must be effectual. There must be a squadron lying off the harbor to be blockaded, and it must be strong enough to constitute an actual blockade of the port. The neutral must have had due notice of its existence, and to affect a neutral vessel she must have been guilty of an act of violation, by passing, or attempting to pass, in or out of the port, with a cargo laden after the commencement of the blockade. The neutral must be ready to prove himself that which he professes to be; therefore he is subject to the right of visitation and search."

A more serious difficulty now presented itself. How was it possible to undertake such a blockade as this, along such a vast extent of coast, when so few ships of any kind were available, without its being open to the charge of being a mere paper blockade? In the early part of the century European powers had attempted to enforce paper blockades, but the same nations were now the first to make merry over the subject of our paper blockade. Some of the most prominent European statesmen publicly declared it a "material impossibility to enforce it." To avoid any chance of technical complications, a special notice was given by our vessels at the entrance of each port actually closed by them, in addition to the general diplomatic notice, so that for a time one warning was allowed every ship

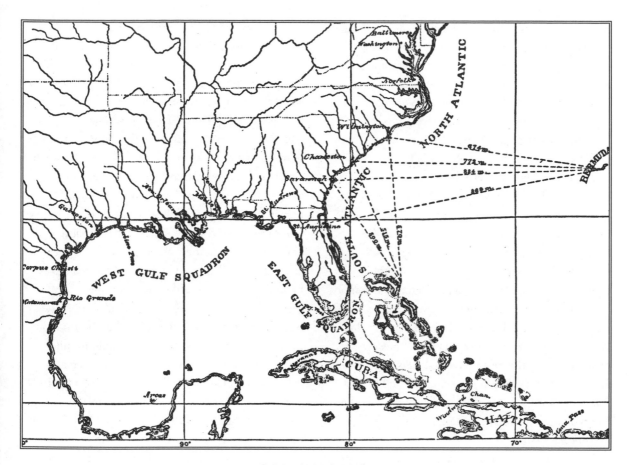

THE BLOCKADED COAST

touching at a blockaded port before she was liable to capture. Thus each port was brought under the full operation of the proclamation only when it was actually blockaded by one or more armed vessels.

By degrees, as the blockading force was increased, and the blockade became more extended and stringent, it was assumed that the general notice rendered the special notice unnecessary; it was finally discontinued entirely, and capture took place without warning. The magnitude of the task of establishing and maintaining the blockade was not realized by the people generally, public attention being absorbed by the raising of many large armies from the body of the people.

When the Secretary of the Navy asked the principal shipping merchants and shipowners of New York to aid him in procuring vessels for the blockade, it is related that their committees decid-

ed that thirty sailing-ships would be needed. As it took over six hundred ships, mostly steamers, to do the work, it is manifest that they had a very faint conception of what was to be done. There were twenty-eight old ships of war lying dismantled at the various navy-yards. Those that were worth repairing were fitted for sea as rapidly as possible. All the available merchant vessels that could be made to carry a battery, including tugs and old New York ferry boats, were purchased and converted into fighting ships as hastily as the limited facilities of the Northern ports would permit. The scanty resources of the navy-yards were inadequate. All the private ship-yards were crowded with work. There were not enough skilled workmen to meet this sudden demand, and the naval officers found it necessary personally to direct the unskilled artisans, or to assist with their own hands in fitting these nondescript vessels for the mounting and working of heavy guns. As fast as the vessels could be purchased, altered, and equipped, they were stationed along the coast or sent to sea. Many such vessels, by the tact and skill of the officers in charge of them, were made to do good service. One of the most important prizes captured, the steamer *Circassian*, was taken near the harbor of Havana by one of the old Fulton Perry boats.

The lack of men was as great an embarrassment as the want of vessels. Three hundred and twenty-two officers of the old navy joined the insurgent forces, many of them-having already distinguished themselves in service. One of these, Commander John M. Brooke, rendered very important services to the Southerners by converting the ten-inch columbiads captured by them into rifled guns. They proved to be very effective pieces, and were said to be the best converted guns ever made. He also aided in devising the simplest and best of the many kinds of torpedoes and fuses used by the Confederates, as well as in designing the ram *Merrimac*.

The total number of seamen at all the Northern naval stations available for immediate detail amounted to only two hundred and seven; and it must be remembered that it was as important that they should be trained to handle heavy guns at sea as that they should be good seamen. The true sailor will soon make himself efficient on board any ship, as far as the handling of the vessel is concerned; but in the effective use of the battery only the trained man-o'-war's-man can safely be relied upon; and there are many other minor matters, such as the division of duties, the exercise at quarters and in boats, forming essential features of the system on a man-o' war, that are unknown outside the naval service. Officers and men from the merchant service freely offered themselves. Gunnery schools were established at the naval stations for their instruction. As fast as the volunteers could be given an elementary training in the handling of heavy guns, they were sent to sea. This was continued for three years, by which time we had six hundred and fifty vessels and over fifty thousand men afloat.

The service to be performed by this hastily improvised force was as unique as the fleet itself. The entire outer coast-line of the Confederacy was 3549 miles in extent, with several large seaports. To guard the ordinary entrances to these ports was comparatively a simple task. There was, however, a greater difficulty to be met; for the outer coast line is only the exterior edge of a series of islands between which and the mainland there is an elaborate network of navigable sounds and passages, having numerous inlets communicating with the sea. These inlets were frequently changing under the influence of the great storms; new channels would be opened and old ones filled up. As soon as we closed a port, by stationing vessels at the main entrance thereto, the blockade-runners would slip in at some of the numerous remote inlets, reaching their destination by the inside pas sages; so that blockade-running flourished until we were able to procure as many blockaders as there were channels and inlets to be guarded. The extreme diversity of the services required of these blockading vessels made it difficult to obtain ships that could meet the varying necessities. They must be heavy enough to contend with the enemy's rams, or they would be driven away from the principal ports. They must be light enough to chase and capture the swift blockade-runners. They must be deep enough in the water to ride out in safety the violent winter gales, and they must-be of such light draft as to be able to go near enough to the shallow inlets to blockade them efficiently.

The blockading fleets of all the important harbors were composed of several very heavy ships, with a few vessels of the lighter class; the rest of the fleet represented some of the other classes needed. But it was impossible to do this along the entire coast, and it sometimes happened that the Confederate ironclads perversely attacked the lighter vessels, as in the case of the rams at Charleston selecting for their victims the *Mercedita* and the *Keystone State*, instead of the heavier ships; while, on the other hand, the swift blockade runners disclosed themselves most frequently to the ponderous and slow-moving ships that were least able to catch them. . . .

Many of the islands controlled by foreign governments, and lying conveniently near our coast, had good harbors that afforded admirable places of rendezvous for the blockade runners, where they could safely refit, and remain unmolested until a favorable time came for them to slip out and make a quick run over to the forbidden port; and if unsuccessful in their illicit attempt, they could return as quickly to the protection of the neutral port. As soon as the attention of the naval authorities was drawn to the port of Nassau as a place likely to become the main depot of the contraband trade, Lieutenant-Commander Temple was sent over there privately, in the guise of a civilian, to ascertain the attitude of the officials, the state of public sentiment, and to obtain all the information possible as to the prospects of the blockade running business. While there he managed to be present at a dinner attended by the local diplomats. There were many indications that the feeling of hostility to the United States was very general. When the old French consul was called upon to express his views, he jumped up, overflowing with an intense desire to express himself in a vigorous manner; but in spite of his profound emotions, all he could manage to utter was: "Ze American people zey sink zey are somewhat, but zey cannot!" This terse presentation of his views was received with such uproarious applause that Temple was no longer in doubt as to which way the wind blew in that place. . . .

Supplies were brought to the South from various sources, but principally from European ports. At the beginning of the war the blockade-running was carried on from Chesapeake Bay to the mouth of the Rio Grande, by vessels of all sorts, sizes, and nationalities. The steamers formerly engaged in the coasting-trade, that had been interrupted in their regular business by the war, were at first the most successful. The small sailing-vessels did well for some time before the blockade became vigorous; but as the number of our war ships increased, the earlier groups of blockade-runners were either captured, destroyed, or drawn off. This diminished the volume of supplies to the Confederates just at the time when the demand was greatly increased by the emergencies of warfare, causing general distress and embarrassment in the Confederacy. Prices reached an unprecedented height. Cotton was as low as eight cents a pound in the Confederacy, as high as sixty cents a pound in England, and over one dollar a pound in New York. The moment this state of affairs became known, the science, ingenuity, and mechanical skill of the British seemed to be directed to the business of violating our blockade. Stock companies were formed, by whom the swiftest steamers in the European merchant service were quickly freighted with the supplies that would bring the highest prices in the Confederacy. Officers of rank in the royal navy, under assumed names; officers of the Confederate navy, who had but just resigned from the United States navy; and adventurous spirits from all quarters, flocked to this new and profitable, though hazardous, occupation. The Confederate government also embarked in the business, procuring swift steamers from English builders, officered with Confederate naval officers, and sailing under the British ensign. They also shipped merchandise in other vessels on government account. . . .

When the blockade-running was at its height, in 1863, a Confederate officer stated that the arrivals and departures were equal to one steamer a day, taking all of the Confederate ports together. Prior to this no such attempts had ever been made to violate a blockade. The industrial necessities of the principal maritime nations stimulated them to unusual efforts, in return for which they looked forward to a rich harvest. The British especially had abundant capital, the finest and swiftest ships ever built, manned by the most energetic seamen. They felt confident that they could monopolize the Southern cotton and the markets of the Confederacy; but when it was found that neither swift steamers, skilled officers, nor desperate efforts could give security to their best investments of capital, and that the perils to their beautiful vessels and precious cargoes increased as fast as their efforts to surmount them, ultimately becoming even greater in proportion than the enormous gains of the traffic when successful, they were at last driven off from our coast entirely, and kept at bay, though armed and supported by the greatest of foreign powers. They finally gave up the business, admitting that the blockade was a success. A Confederate officer stated that when Port Fisher fell their last port was gone, and blockade-running was at an end.

This signal defeat of that extraordinary development of our Civil War has been spoken of as one of the great moral lessons of our struggle. After the war British officers frankly stated to our naval officers that they considered the blockade and its enforcement the great fact of the war. This was the first time in the history of naval warfare that a steam navy had been kept at sea for so long a period. The Confederates menaced the blockading fleets with nine ironclads which would have been a match for any ironclads in the French or English navy afloat at that time; therefore it becomes manifest that a fleet which could hold in check ironclads, as well as shut out blockade-runners that were the swiftest steamers built at that time, must have combined speed and power to an extent never before displayed in naval warfare. . . .

During the war our navy captured or destroyed 1504 blockade-runners, besides causing many valuable cargoes to be thrown overboard by the long-continued and close pursuit of fugitives, who escaped capture by resorting to this expedient to lighten the vessels. A Confederate officer stated that all the approaches to Wilmington harbor were as thickly paved with valuable merchandise as a certain place is said to be with "good intentions." This assertion would apply to some other harbors.

The value of prizes captured was $31,000,000. The most valuable prize taken was the English steamer *Memphis*, which brought $510,000. She was captured early in the war by the steamer *Magnolia*. The captor was herself a prize-vessel that had been bought by our government and fitted out as a gun boat. The least valuable was a sloop captured by the gunboat *Tahoma*, called the *Alligator*, which brought $50. Many of the most important prizes were taken by mere chance, or when least

expected; while many a long and hard chase resulted in the overhauling of an empty vessel, the cargo having been thrown overboard in the efforts to escape.

Before the refinements of the blockade-running system began, the men-o'-war as well as the contraband vessels were all painted the conventional black; but as black objects are readily seen on the water at night, the blockade-runners were soon painted various neutral tints. Our naval authorities at once caused experiments to be made with boats painted different colors. The tint that was least conspicuous under the greatest varieties of conditions was selected, and called "Union color." It was a bluish gray; and a formula for its preparation, together with the necessary materials, was at once distributed among the blockading fleets. It was very difficult to see a vessel of this color.

—Wait, "The Blockade of the Confederacy"

XXVII.2

The *Robert E. Lee* Runs the Blockade

The *Robert E. Lee* was one of the most famous of an the blockade-runners. A Clyde-built iron steamer she was reputed to be the fastest afloat. Unlike most of the blockade runners, she was owned by the Confederate government. Altogether the Lee ran the blockade 21 times—mostly out of Wilmington—before she was finally captured.

John Wilkinson, who here tells his own story, was one of more than 300 naval officers who resigned, in 1861, to go with the Confederacy. He first saw duty on a shore battery in Virginia; then fought at the Battle of New Orleans, where he was captured. After his exchange he went to England, bought the ship which he christened *Robert E. Lee,* and earned a reputation as the boldest of blockade-runners. In 1864 he was engaged in the attempt to capture Johnson's Island in Lake Erie; later he commanded the blockade-runner *Chickamauga.*

The *Lee* continued to make her regular trips either to Nassau or Bermuda, as circumstances required, during the summer of 1863; carrying abroad cotton and naval stores, and bringing in "hardware," as munitions of war were then invoiced. Usually the time selected for sailing was during the "dark of the moon," but upon one occasion, a new pilot had been detailed for duty on board, who failed in many efforts to get the ship over the "rip," a shifting sand bar a mile or more inside the true bar. More than a week of valuable time had thus been lost, but the exigencies of the army being at that time more than usually urgent, I determined to run what appeared to be a very great risk.

The tide serving at ten o'clock, we succeeded in crossing the rip at that hour, and as we passed over New Inlet bar, the moon rose in a cloudless sky. It was a calm night too, and the regular beat of our paddles through the smooth water sounded to our ears ominously loud. As we closely skirted the shore, the blockading vessels were plainly visible to us, some at anchor, some under way; and some of them so near to us that we saw, or fancied we saw, with our night glasses, the men on watch on their forecastles; but as we were inside of them all, and invisible against the background of the land, we passed beyond them undiscovered. The roar of the surf breaking upon the beach, prevented the noise of our paddles from being heard. The *Lee's* head was not pointed seaward, however, until we had run ten or twelve miles along the land so close to the breakers that we could almost have tossed a biscuit into them, and no vessel was to be seen in any direction.

Discovery of us by the fleet would probably have been fatal to us, but the risk was not really so great as it appeared; for, as I had been informed by a blockade-runner who had been once captured and released, being a British subject, the vigilance on board the blockading fleet was much relaxed during the moonlit nights. The vessels were sent to Beaufort to coal at these times. My informant was an officer of the British Navy, and was the guest, for a few days after his capture, of Captain Patterson then commanding the blockading fleet off the Cape Fear. Speaking of the arduous service, P. remarked to him, that he never undressed nor retired to bed, during the dark nights; but could enjoy those luxuries when the moon was shining. On this hint I acted.

It was about this time that I adopted an expedient which proved of great service on several occasions. A blockade runner did not often pass through the fleet without receiving one or more shots, but these were always preceded by the flash of a calcium light, or by a blue light; and immediately followed by two rockets thrown in the direction of the blockade-runner. The signals were probably concerted each day for the ensuing night, as they appeared to be constantly changed; but the rockets were invariably sent up. I ordered a lot of rockets from New York. Whenever all hands were called to run through the fleet, an officer was stationed along side of me on the bridge with the rockets. One or two minutes after our immediate pursuer had sent his rockets, I would direct ours to be discharged at a right angle to our course. The whole fleet would be misled, for even if the vessel which had discovered us were not deceived, the rest of the fleet would be baffled. . . .

We were ready to sail for Nassau on the 15th of August, 1863, and had on board, as usual, several passengers. . . .

We passed safely through the blockading fleet off the New Inlet Bar, receiving no damage from the few shots fired at us, and gained an offing from the coast of thirty miles by day light. By this time our supply of English coal had been exhausted, and we were obliged to commence upon North Carolina coal of very inferior quality, and which smoked terribly. We commenced on this fuel a little after daylight. Very soon afterwards the vigilant look-out at the mast head called out "Sail ho!" and in reply to the "where away" from the deck, sang out "Right astern, sir, and in chase."

The morning was very clear. Going to the mast-head I could just discern the royal of the chaser; and before I left there, say in half an hour, her top-gallant sail showed above the horizon. By this time the sun had risen in a cloudless sky. It was evident our pursuer would be alongside of us by midday at the rate we were then going. The first orders given were to throw overboard the deck-load of cotton and to make more steam. The latter proved to be more easily given than executed; the chief engineer reporting that it was impossible to make steam with the wretched stuff filled with slate and dirt. A moderate breeze from the north and east had been blowing ever since daylight and every stitch of canvas on board the square-rigged steamer in our wake was drawing.

We were steering east by south, and it was clear that the chaser's advantages could only be neutralized either by bringing the *Lee* gradually head to wind or edging away to bring the wind aft. The former course would be running toward the land, besides incurring the additional risk of being intercepted and captured by some of the inshore cruisers. I began to edge away, therefore, and in two or three hours enjoyed the satisfaction of seeing our-pursuer clew up and furl his sails. The breeze was still blowing as fresh as in the morning, but we were now running directly away from it, and the cruiser was going literally as fast as the wind, causing the sails to be rather a hindrance than a help. But she was still gaining on us.

A happy inspiration occurred to me when the case seemed hopeless. Sending for the chief engineer I said "Mr. S., let us try cotton, saturated with spirits of turpentine." There were on board, as part of the deck load, thirty or forty barrels of "spirits." In a very few moments, a bale of cotton was ripped open, a barrel tapped, and buckets full of the saturated material passed down into the fire-room. The result exceeded our expectations. The chief engineer, an excitable little Frenchman from Charleston, very soon made his appearance on the bridge, his eyes sparkling with triumph, and reported a full head of steam. Curious to see the effect upon our speed, I directed him to wait until the log was hove. I threw it myself, nine and a half knots. "Let her go now sir!" I said. Five minutes afterwards, I hove the log again, *thirteen and a quarter.* We now began to hold our own, and even to gain a little upon the chaser; but she was fearfully near, and I began to have visions of another residence at Fort Warren, as I saw the "big bone in the mouth" of our pertinacious friend, for she was near enough us at one time for us to see distinctly the white curl of foam under her bows, called by that name among seamen. I wonder if they could

have screwed another turn of speed out of her if they had known that the *Lee* had on board, in addition to her cargo of cotton, a large amount of gold shipped by the Confederate Government?

There continued to be a very slight change in our relative positions till about six o'clock in the afternoon, when the chief engineer again made his appearance, with a very ominous expression of countenance. He came to report that the burnt cotton had choked the flues, and that the steam was running down. "Only keep her going till dark, sir," I replied, "and we will give our pursuer the slip yet." A heavy bank was lying along the horizon to the south and east; and I saw a possible means of escape.

At sunset the chaser was about four miles astern and gaining upon us. Calling two of my most reliable officers, I stationed one of them on each wheel-house, with glasses, directing them to let me know the instant they lost sight of the chaser in the growing darkness. At the same time, I ordered the chief engineer to make as black a smoke as possible, and to be in readiness to cut off the smoke by closing the dampers instantly, when ordered. The twilight was soon succeeded by darkness. Both of the officers on the wheel house called out at the same moment, "We have lost sight of her," while a dense column of smoke was streaming far in our wake. "Close the dampers," I called out through the speaking tube, and at the same moment ordered the helm "hard a starboard." Our course was altered eight points, at a right angle to the previous one. I remained on deck an hour, and then retired to my state-room with a comfortable sense of security.

—WILKINSON, *The Narrative of a Blockade-Runner*

XXVII.3

THE *ROB ROY* RUNS THE BLOCKADE OUT OF HAVANA

Cuba, the Bahamas, and Bermuda were the most important islands from which the blockade-runners operated. The chief ports here—especially Havana and Nassau—were friendly, transshipment to vessels bound for the British Islands convenient, and the run either to the Atlantic ports of Savannah, Charleston, and Wilmington, or to such Gulf ports as Galveston, relatively easy. The risks, to be sure, were great—but so were the profits. A captain received—so Thomas Scharf of the Confederate Navy tells us—$5,000 a month, and officers and seamen in proportion. Two successful trips usually paid the cost of the vessel; after that everything was profit, and some blockade runners made 30 or. 40 trips before capture.

William Watson, who here tells of blockade-running into Galveston, is our old friend from the campaigns in Arkansas—a Scotsman who enlisted in the Confederate Army and, after capture and exchange, went into blockade-running. He appears to be the only chronicler who has left us narratives of both land and sea campaigns.

It was already into the month of April [1864], and it was a very bad time to make a trip, owing to the lengthened days and the prevailing calms. There would be no chance of good steady winds before September, and there would be on the Texas coast about three hours more daylight each day than in winter, and the danger of capture would be very great.

On the other hand, I opined that to lay here (Havana) heavy loss was certain. The vessel not being coppered, the sea-worms would penetrate her bottom, unless often docked and painted; expenses were high, and it was almost impossible to avoid being victimized by the numerous harpies who regarded blockade runners as a legitimate prey to pick at; and I felt that if I was to lose what little I had, I would rather lose it under the guns of an honest cruiser, than have it wheedled away from me by the flattery of pretended friends; so I determined to venture a trip if I could make arrangements to do so.

The vessel was taken to the ship-yard and put on the slip dock to be thoroughly examined, caulked, and otherwise put in the best sailing trim preparative for another voyage.

As I have already said, specie money was not to be had in the Confederate States and it was not to the interest of the blockade runners to run a heavy risk on the inward trip, by taking in a valuable cargo, and many had run in with light cargoes, knowing that they could always obtain a cargo of cotton cheap, or a freight outward at very high rates.

This, however, had now been stopped by the Confederate authorities, and stringent rules had been enforced whereby all vessels entering a Confederate port must take in a full and valuable cargo.

To obtain this cargo was what I desired either as freight or on the vessel's account, and as a large part of the money we had left would be expended in the repairs of the vessel, it would be necessary— if we could not get a freight—to get some one to take a share in the adventure, and as there were so many merchants and speculators who sympathized excessively with the Confederate States and took great interest in furnishing them with supplies, I thought there would be no difficulty in making an engagement.

Applying to several of them, I found their terms to be all about the same; which was, that they were exceedingly wishful to sell me goods for a cargo, but none willing to take a share in the adventure or run any risk. . . .

I may here say that up to this time blockade running by steamers had been confined almost entirely to the Atlantic ports, while nearly the whole trade into the Gulf States had been done by sailing craft, mostly light-draught schooners. When Charleston and the other ports on the Atlantic were captured, or so closely invested that entrance to them was almost impossible, many of those steamers came to Havana to try what could be done between that port and the Gulf States, and the basis for blockade running was transferred from Nassau to Havana.

Steamers, however, were not much in favour at Havana for blockade-running purposes, and it was considered by some that their utility for this trade was more ideal than real, but of this I will speak hereafter.

Havana having now become the principal centre for blockade running, a crowd of speculators soon found their way to the place, who bought up the goods in the limited market, and ran them up to a high figure to sell to blockade runners, representing them, of course, as consignments recently got out from Europe specially selected for the

Confederate market. And while trumpeting their zeal for the Confederate cause, they took special care to pocket large profits without running any risk. While to those who actually ran the blockade and incurred the risk and danger, but little accrued.
. . .

About the same time my old friend Mr. R. M came to the yard and took a look at the *Rob Roy* as she lay on the ways.

He asked me if I had made any arrangements for a trip yet. I said I had not. He said I might come and see him the following day, and he would make me an offer.

On the following day I called upon him. He asked what value I now placed upon the vessel. I said 5,000 dollars when repaired and fitted out ready for sea.

He then said that his offer was that he would furnish a cargo equal in value to that amount, which cargo he would guarantee would satisfy the requirements of the Confederate Government as to inward cargo, and purchase much more cotton than the vessel could carry out, and the surplus would be invested in cotton bonds, which were still worth something in Havana. He would then become owner of half of the vessel, and I would be owner of half of the cargo. We would then be equal partners in the vessel and cargo, each paying his half of the disbursements, out of which he would allow me for my services as captain 500 dollars, to be paid in advance before sailing, and 7 dollars for every bale of cotton when landed in a neutral port.

The cargo which he had to put on board consisted chiefly of arms, which the Confederate Government in Texas stood much in want of at that time.

This offer I accepted, and I asked him to make a memorandum of it in writing, which he did, and handed it to me.

I then got a list of the cargo he proposed to furnish. It consisted of 200 Enfield rifles with bayonets and accoutrements, 400 Belgium muskets with bayonets, 400 cavalry swords, six cases of saddlery and accoutrements, twenty five boxes of ammunition, a large box of cavalry currycombs and horse

brushes, and several bales and cases of blankets, clothing, boots and shoes, hardware, and other goods. Besides this it was good policy to have a good supply of some things which were much esteemed by the Southern people, but which the blockade had cut off and made extremely rare, and in some parts almost unknown, such as tea, coffee, cheese, spices, etc., also thread, needles, and such furnishings. Brandies and wines as well as all spirituous liquors were for bidden to be taken in, but they were received with great thankfulness if given as donations for the use of the hospitals. All these might be entered as ship stores.

This cargo, although valuable, was far from filling up the hold of the schooner, and as I knew that a good inward cargo had great weight with the authorities in the Confederacy, I sent word to Mr. Helm, the Confederate States Consul, that I would sail in a few days for Texas, and I would take free of freight any goods which he might wish to send in.

I received a reply thanking me for the offer, and saying that he would send by my vessel 400 guns. He also said that he had some important despatches to send to General Magruder, which he would confide to my care. . . .

I was now thinking over what port I would try to enter. I was a little sick with the Brazos River on account of the troubles I had had there on last trip, and the entrance to it now was generally blockaded, and it would be impossible to enter during the day, and the bar was dangerous to enter at night without a pilot.

Captain Dave had determined to make for St. Louis Pass at the west end of Galveston Island. . . .

It was impossible, however, for the *Rob Roy* to enter there, and on the advice of Captain M. I determined to shape for Galveston, and take my chance of getting past the fleet.

Captain M. was well acquainted with all the shallow en trances to Galveston Bay, and he gave me some information as to how a light draught vessel like the *Rob Roy* might enter from the eastward or windward side. . . .

We were now all ready to sail, and I only waited for a favourable opportunity.

There were two Federal gunboats which lay between us and the Moro Castle, and which we should have to pass on the way out to sea, and I was pretty certain that they knew we had a cargo of arms on board, but they were to a considerable extent powerless, and we were cleared for Belize, Honduras.

As no vessels were allowed to leave or enter Havana harbour between sunset and sunrise, the best time to leave was just about sunset, so that if any cruisers were lying in the offing we could come to, under the guns of the Moro, until it got quite dark, and then put to sea.

Captain Dave had determined to sail at the same time that we sailed, and as I had been laughing at his vessel, he wished to bet with me a case of brandy that he would arrive in Texas before me if not captured. I did not, however, take the bet, as I intended to creep along cautiously.

I was now well manned and prepared, and my policy was—when it became calm to take down all sail, and make the vessel as inconspicuous as possible; keep a sharp look-out from the mast-head, and if anything appeared on the horizon to get out the sweeps and pull away in the opposite direction before we were observed.

Everything being now ready we got what we called the mail on board. This consisted of letters for people in Texas and other parts of the Confederate States, west of the Mississippi River from all parts of the world. . . .

We now awaited a favourable wind, and were wishful to get away, as Havana is a very bad place for a vessel's bottom fouling, and every day we lay was injuring the sailing qualities of the vessel. . . .

At last a steady breeze sprang up from the south, which freshened towards the afternoon, and we stood down the bay just before sunset.

We passed the two Federal cruisers as they lay at anchor. We saw the officers scrutinizing us with their glasses, but as neither of the vessels had steam up, it was impossible that they could follow us that night.

—WATSON, *The Adventures of a Blockade Runner*

XXVII.4

BLOCKADE-RUNNERS SUPPLY CHARLESTON

Here is a short account of what blockade-running meant to a city. Charleston was pretty well bottled up, from early in the war; yet swift blockade-runners managed to get past the Federal ships and keep the city supplied with necessities—and with luxuries. This account describes the situation in 1864.

During those long wearisome days and weeks when the city was under fire almost the only event of joy which would occur would be the arrival of some one of these blockade runners. The business was finally reduced to a science. Even in the darkest night the cunning craft would work their way in or out through the tortuous channels of the harbor. When outward-bound the captain generally went down to Sullivan's Island upon the evening of sailing to learn the disposition of the Union fleet and plan the course of his exit. Lights also were always prearranged along the shores of the island, or suspended from boats in the harbor, in order to indicate the channel.

The most dangerous point, and that which demanded the exercise of the greatest skill to avoid, was a narrow tongue of land which ran out from Sullivan's Island just opposite Sumter, and which was known as the Breakwater Jetty. Here the channel is not only very narrow but takes a sudden turn, and it was in making this turn that the vessel was in danger of getting aground. The Union artillerists after a while learned many of the cunning arts of the blockade-runner, and when ever they saw a light from the opposite shore of Morris Island, which they supposed was intended for the guidance of a vessel, they would immediately open fire. They had a way too of sending out picket-boats which would quietly allow the vessel to pass till it had rounded the jetty and return became impossible, and then by means of rockets would signalize the fleet outside.

The chase of a blockade-runner was the most exciting thing imaginable. Like a hunted deer it would speed through the water, its fierce avenger after it, every beam from stem to stern quivering through the violent pulsations of its great iron heart, and the dash of the paddles as in their lightning like revolutions they would strike the water. Sometimes not only was one half of the cargo thrown overboard, but every combustible thing that could be laid hold of crowded into the furnaces to increase the steam. Some of these blockade runners were very successful. I knew of one which had run the gauntlet no less than nineteen times, and had consequently proved a mine of wealth to its owners. When a vessel had once run the blockade it was considered to have paid for itself, and every subsequent trip was consequently clear gain. The captain generally cleared on each round trip ten thousand dollars in gold, and the pilot and mate in proportion.

To be at all connected with or interested in a blockade runner was in those days esteemed in Charleston a signal piece of good fortune. It insured at least a partial supply of the comforts and luxuries of life; for the ladies an occasional new silk dress, the envy and admiration of the streets; for the gentlemen a good supply of Bourbon—a box or two of cigars, or a larder filled with Stilton cheese or West India fruits. By-and-by came an edict from Richmond forbidding the importation of luxuries of this kind, and restricting the cargo of a vessel entirely to those articles which the country needed in its military operations, or which contributed to the supply of the actual necessities of the people. One half of the cargo of the vessel going out was also required to be devoted to government account, and one half of the cargo of the vessel coming in. This, of course, greatly curtailed the profits of the owners, but still immense fortunes continued to be made on both sides of the water.

—Peck, "Four Years Under Fire at Charleston"

XXVII.5

Confederate Privateers Harry Northern Merchantmen

The Confederacy early had recourse to letters of marque, and altogether William M. Robinson, foremost authority on Confederate privateering, lists some 64 privateers of various boats, and others. These did considerable damage to Union shipping during the first year of the war, but with the rapid growth of the United States Navy and the successful establishment of the blockade, the privateer became ineffective. Privateering had been outlawed by the Declaration of Paris, but the United States was not a signatory to this Declaration and therefore in no position to protest Confederate privateering. Yet at first Federal authorities tried to treat captured privateersmen as pirates, and there was a notable trial of the crew of the *Jeff Davis* for piracy. The Confederacy quickly put a stop to that policy by the threat of retaliation.

We give here two brief excerpts illuminating the story of privateering. The first introduces us to the Ivy, one of the earliest and most successful of the privateers, later taken into the Confederate Navy. The second is the story of the capture of the *John Welsh* by the famous *Jefferson Davis,* and is told by the master of the *John Welsh*, Captain Fitfield.

A. The *Ivy* Prowls Outside New Orleans

Last Friday I left New Orleans for this place and boat for a little privateering—to assist in annoying the enemy's commerce; but the enemy's commerce has ceased almost to spread its wings in this latitude. On board the Ivy are guns and men enough to accomplish great destruction, were we called on to open with our cannon. Our human fighting material is constituted of good bone, sinew and pluck, and some of the crew having entered the privateer service with only one intent—commendable revenge on the North.

Today we succeeded in sighting a vessel of the largest dimensions, and full rigged, which proved to be the *Sarah E. Pettigrew*, which, to our sorrow, was without a cargo, there being in her hold only two or three thousand sacks of salt, from Liverpool. We soon had a prize crew on her broad decks, greatly to the muddled surprise of her officers and crew. After the formality of taking possession, your correspondent being among the boarders—we do not pay weekly—I overhauled the flag-bag, and soon had bunting in plenty for a pretty Southern Confederacy flag, which was immediately set afloat to flutter defiance to all who don't like us. The Ivy's capacity enables her to do her own towing, and after she had cruised around in the Gulf two or three hours to overhaul other sails, she returned to us and we turned our prows toward Pass a L'Outre, near where the *Pettigrew* now lies, awaiting to be towed to your city. The privateer *Calhoun* gave chase for the same vessel, but the *Ivy* was too fast for her.

We lie in or near the river every night, but start out soon after midnight, and keep a sharp lookout for any speck on the horizon, and when the cry of "sail-ho!" is heard the Ivy's "tendrils" don revolvers, swords, knives and rifles with great excitement and good nature. We have exceedingly good times and "duff" but I fear all will be closed with the appearance of the blockading force.

—Letter by M. REPARD in *Daily Delta*

B. The *Jefferson Davis* Takes a Prize off Delaware

At 8:30 the privateer tacked and stood N. W., at the same time setting a French ensign, and from the fact of her having French-cut hempen sails we supposed she was a French merchant brig. In answer to her colors we set the Stars and Stripes, and thought no more of the stranger. At 9 o'clock, to our surprise, she fired a shot across our bows, when we took in the studding sails and hove the *John Welsh* to. We then supposed her to be a French man-of-war brig; but her ports were closed and the guns covered up, while but few men were to be seen on her decks.

She came within musket shot of us, and lowered a boat which was manned by expert seamen and contained Lieutenant Postell, late of the United States Navy. Just before the boat came alongside the French flag was hauled down and the Confederate flag run up. In about two minutes afterwards the armed crew was on our deck. After inquiring after my health, Lieutenant Postell

desired me to show him the brig's papers. I invited him into the cabin, and after showing them, I stated the cargo was Spanish property. Said he, "You are our prize, and the Spaniards had no business to ship their cargoes in American bottoms." He then came on deck and ordered four of my men to go in the privateer's boat, and told the remainder of the crew to pack up their things and stand by to do as ordered. They immediately set to work and broke out the ship's stores and took about eight months' provisions on board of the privateer, leaving only enough to take the prize-crew back with the vessel. This occupied about five hours.

I was transferred with the remainder of my crew on board of the privateer, and they took my boat and sent theirs on board of the *John Welsh*, as mine was the best. A prize-crew corresponding in appearance and number was then put on board in charge of Prize-Master Stevens, and she was ordered to go South but I was not allowed to know of her destination. I think they will palm themselves off as the genuine crew if they fall in with the Federal cruisers. After the work of transferring the stores had been completed, Capt. Coxetter mustered all hands aft and said to them, "Boys, if you molest the crew of that brig or their things to the value of a rope yarn, I will punish you to the utmost of my power. Do you understand? Now go forward." Turning to his officers he said, "Gentlemen, I desire that you do everything in your power to make the stay of these gentlemen as agreeable as possible." He then invited me to dine with him in his cabin while my mate was taken into the officer's mess.

—CAPTAIN FITFIELD, in the *Charleston Mercury*

——— XXVII.6 ———

THE GEORGIA FIRES THE BOLD HUNTER

The *Georgia* was one of the most successful of the commerce destroyers purchased or built in England. A swift and powerful ship of 600 tons, she was purchased by Commodore Matthew F. Maury, at Dumbarton, Scotland; obtained her guns and ordnance from the *Alar*, off the French coast, and embarked upon a brief but highly successful career as commerce destroyer. Altogether she captured and destroyed at least nine American ships.

Here is James Morgan's account of the burning of one of them, the misnamed *Bold Hunter*. Morgan was a midshipman on the Georgia; later he served in the Egyptian Army, engaged in journalism in South Carolina, went to Australia as consul general and helped build the Statue of Liberty.

On October 9, 1863, in a light breeze and after a lively chase we brought to, with our guns, the splendid American full rigged ship *Bold Hunter*, of Boston, from Dundee, bound to Calcutta with a heavy cargo of coal. We hove to leeward of her and brought her captain and crew over to our ship, where as usual the crew were placed in irons and below decks. Being short of coal and provsions we proceeded to supply our wants from the prize. This was easy so far as the pro visions were concerned, but when it came to carrying the coal from one ship to the other in our small boats, in some thing of a seaway, that was another matter. After half a dozen trips one of our boats came very near being swamped, and the wind and sea rapidly rising, we give it up as a bad job. This was about two bells (1 P.M.) in the afternoon watch. We signalled our prize-master to set fire to the *Bold Hunter* and also to come aboard the *Georgia* at once, which he did.

We had hardly finished hoisting our boats to the davits when a great cloud of smoke burst from the hatches of the *Bold Hunter*, coming from the thousands of tons of burning coal in her hold. The wind had by this time increased to a gale and the sea was running very high. As before mentioned, the wind was very light when we captured the ship and she had hove to with all sail set, even to her royals. The flames leaped from her deck to her tarry rigging and raced up the shrouds and backstays and burned away her braces—her yards swung around, her sails filled, and the floating inferno, like a mad bull, bore down on us at full speed, rushing through the water as though she was bent on having her revenge.

To avoid a collision, the order was given on the *Georgia* to go ahead at full speed. The gong in the engine-room sounded, the engine turned the

screw, and the screw began to churn the water under our counter. The engine made two or three revolutions—then there was a crash—followed by yells as the engineers and oilers rushed on to the deck accompanied by a shower of lignum-vitae cogs and broken glass from the engine-room windows. The order to make sail was instantly given, but before the gaskets which confined the furled sails to the yardarms could be cast off, the burning ship was upon us.

She had come for us with such directness that one could easily have imagined that she was being steered by some demon who had come out of the inferno which was raging in her hold. We stood with bated breath awaiting the catastrophe which seemingly was about to overtake us. The *Bold Hunter* was rated at over three thousand tons, and had inside her a burning cargo of coal of even greater weight—the *Georgia* was scarcely one-sixth her size. Onward rushed the blazing ship, presenting an awesome spectacle, with the flames leaping about her sails and rigging, while a huge mass of black smoke rolled out of her hatches. High above our heads her long, flying jib-boom passed over our poop deck as she arose on a great wave and came down on our quarter, her cutwater cleaving through the *Georgia's* fragile plates as cleanly as though they had been made out of cheese. The force of the impact pushed the *Georgia* ahead, and for a moment we congratulated ourselves that we had escaped from the fiery demon whose breath was scorching us.

But the *Bold Hunter* was not yet satisfied with the injuries she had inflicted. Recovering from the recoil she again gathered way and struck us near the place she had previously damaged, but fortunately this was a glancing blow which had the effect only of wrenching off our port quarter davits and reducing the boat which was slung to them to kindling wood.

Not yet satisfied, the apparently infuriated inanimate object made a third attempt to destroy the *Georgia*, this time, fortunately, missing her mark and passing a few yards to leeward of us. Her sails having burned, she soon lost headway and helplessly lay wallowing in the trough of the sea while the fire ate through her sides, and her tall masts, one after the other, fell with a great splash into the sea. Before she went down surrounded by a cloud of steam, we had a good view through the great holes burned in her sides of the fire raging inside her. I imagine it was a very realistic imitation of what hell looks like when the forced draughts are turned on in honour of the arrival of a distinguished sinner.

—MORGAN, *Recollections of a Rebel Reefer*

XXVII. 7

THE *KEARSARGE* SINKS THE ALABAMA OFF CHERBOURG

With the possible exception of the duel between the *Monitor* and the *Merrimac,* the fight between the *Kearsarge* and the *Alabama* is the most famous naval battle of the Civil War. The *Alabama* was the most notorious of the cruisers that James Bulloch had had built at Liverpool for the Confederacy.

Captained by the brilliant Raphael Semmes and outfitted at the Azores, in midsummer 1862, she embarked on a career of destruction unparalleled in modern naval annals. Within two years Semmes captured or destroyed over 80 merchant men and one warship. In June 1864 his battered ship put in at the harbor of Cherbourg for repairs. There the U. S. S. *Kearsarge,* commanded by Captain John A. Winslow, caught up with her. Semmes accepted the challenge and steamed out to battle and destruction.

After the battle Semmes, now a rear admiral, returned to Richmond to take command of the James River Squadron. With the end of the war he served as professor of moral philosophy at Louisiana State University; then engaged in journalism and law. Commodore Winslow, whose career before this battle had been unspectacular, later commanded the Gulf Squadron.

The story of the famous battle is told here by John Kell, executive officer of the *Alabama.*

Soon after our arrival at Cherbourg an officer was sent on shore to ask permission of the port admiral to land our prisoners of the two captured ships. This being obtained without trouble or delay, Captain Semmes went on shore to see-to the docking of the ship for repairs. Cherbourg being a naval station and the dock belonging to the government, permission had to be obtained of the emperor before we could do anything. The port admiral told

us "we had better have gone into Havre, as the government might not give permission for repairs to a belligerent ship." The emperor was absent from Paris at some watering place on the coast, and would not return for some days.

Here was an impediment to our plans which gave us time for thought, and the result of such thought was the unfortunate combat between the *Alabama* and the *Kearsarge.* The latter ship was lying at Flushing when we entered Cherbourg. Two or three days after our arrival she steamed into the harbor, sent a boat on shore to communicate, steamed outside and stationed off the breakwater. While Captain Semmes had not singled her out as an antagonist, and would never have done so had he known her to be chain, clad (an armored ship), he had about made up his mind that he would cease fleeing before the foe, and meet an equal in battle when the opportunity presented itself. Our cause was weakening daily, and our ship so disabled it really seemed to us our work was almost done! We might end her career gloriously by being victorious in battle, and defeat against an equal foe we would never have allowed ourselves to anticipate.

As soon as the *Kearsarge* came into the harbor Captain Semmes sent for me to come to his cabin, and abruptly said to me: "Kell, I am going out to fight the *Kearsarge.* What do you think of it?" We then quietly talked it all over. We discussed the batteries, especially the *Kearsarge's* advantage in 11-inch guns. I reminded him of our defective powder, how our long cruise had deteriorated everything, as proven in our target-practice off the coast of Brazil on the Ship *Rockingham,* when certainly every third shot was a failure even to explode. I saw his mind was fully made up, so I simply stated these facts for myself. I had always felt ready for a fight, and I also knew that the brave young officers of the ship would not object, and the men would be not only willing, but anxious, to meet the enemy! To all outward seeming the disparity was not great between the two ships, barring the unknown (because concealed) chain armor.

The *Kearsarge* communicated with the authorities to re quest that our prisoners be turned over to them. Captain Semmes made an objection to her increasing her crew. He addressed our agent, Mr. Bonfils, a communication requesting him to inform Captain Winslow, through the United States Consul, that "if he would wait until the *Alabama* could coal ship he would give him battle." We began to coal and at the same to make preparation for battle. We overhauled the magazine and shell rooms, gun equipments, etc.

The *Kearsarge* was really in the fullest sense of the word a man-of-war, stanch and well built; the *Alabama* was made for flight and speed and was much more lightly constructed than her chosen antagonist. The *Alabama* had one more gun, but the *Kearsarge* carried more metal at a broadside. The seven guns of the *Kearsarge* were two 11-inch Dahlgrens, four 32-pounders, and one rifled 28-pounder. The *Alabama's* eight guns were six 32-pounders, one 8-inch and one rifled 100-pounder. The crew of the *Alabama* all told was 149 men, while that of the *Kearsarge* was 162 men.

By Saturday night, June 18th, our preparations were completed. Captain Semmes notified the admiral of the port that he would be ready to go out and meet the *Kearsarge* the following morning. Early Sunday morning the admiral sent an officer to say to us that "the ironclad Frigate *Couronne* would accompany us to protect the neutrality of French waters." . . .

Between 9 and 10 o'clock, June 19th, everything being in readiness, we got under way and proceeded to sea. We took the western entrance of the harbor. The *Couronne* accompanied us, also some French pilot-boats and an English steam yacht, the *Deerhound*, owned by a rich Englishman (as we afterward learned), who with his wife and children, was enjoying life and leisure in his pleasure yacht. The walls and fortifications of the harbor, the heights above the town, the buildings, everything that looked seaward, was crowded with people. About seven miles from the land the *Kearsarge* was quietly awaiting our arrival.

Officers in uniforms, men at their best, Captain Semmes ordered them sent aft, and mounting a gun-carriage made them a brief address:

"Officers and seamen of the *Alabama:* You have at length another opportunity to meet the enemy, the first that has presented to you since you sank the *Hatteras.* In the mean time you have been all over the world, and it is not too much to say that you have destroyed and driven for protection under neutral flags one-half of the enemy's commerce, which at the beginning of the war covered every sea. This is an achievement of which you may well be proud, and a grateful country will not be unmindful of it. The name of your ship has become a household word wherever civilization extends. Shall that name be tarnished by defeat? [An outburst of Never! Never!] The thing is impossible. Remember that you are in the English Channel, the theatre of so much of the naval glory of our race. The eyes of all Europe are at this moment upon you! The flag that floats over you is that of a young Republic that bids defiance to her enemies, whenever and wherever found! Show the world that you know how to uphold it. Go to your quarters!"

We now prepared our guns to engage the enemy on our starboard side. When within a mile and a-quarter he wheeled, presenting his starboard battery to us. We opened on him with solid shot, to which he soon replied, and the action became active. To keep our respective broadsides bearing we were obliged to fight in a circle around a common center, preserving a distance of three quarters of a mile. When with in distance of shell range we opened on him with shell. The spanker gaff was shot away and our ensign came down. We replaced it immediately at the mizzen masthead.

The firing now became very hot and heavy. Captain Semmes, who was watching the battle from the horse block, called out to me, "Mr. Kell, our shell strike the enemy's side, doing little damage, and fall off in the water; try solid shot." From this time we alternated shot and shell.

The battle lasted an hour and ten minutes. Captain Semmes said to me at this time (seeing the great apertures made in the side of the ship from their 11-inch shell, and the water rushing in rapidly), "Mr. Kell, as soon as our head points to the

French coast in our circuit of action, shift your guns to port and make all sail for the coast." This evolution was performed; righting the helm, hauling aft the fore-trysail sheet, and pivoting to port, the action continuing all the time without cessation,—but it was useless, nothing could avail us.

Before doing this, and pivoting the gun, it became necessary to clear the deck of parts of the dead bodies that had been torn to pieces by the 11-inch shells of the enemy. The captain of our 8-inch gun and most of the gun's crew were killed. It became necessary to take the crew from young Anderson's gun to make up the vacancies, which I did, and placed him in command. Though a mere youth, he managed it like an old veteran.

Going to the hatchway, I called out to Brooks (one of our efficient engineers) to give the ship more steam, or we would be whipped.

He replied she "had every inch of steam that was safe to carry without being blown up!"

Young Matt O'Brien, assistant engineer, called out, "Let her have the steam; we had better blow her to hell than to let the Yankees whip us!"

The chief engineer now came on deck and reported "the furnace fires put out," whereupon Captain Semmes ordered me to go below and "see how long the ship could float."

I did so, and returning said, "Perhaps ten minutes."

"Then, sir," said Captain Semmes, "cease firing, shorten sail, and haul down the colors. It will never do in this nineteenth century for us to go down and the decks covered with our gallant wounded."

This order was promptly executed, after which the *Kearsarge* deliberately fired into us five shots! In Captain Winslow's report to the Secretary of the Navy he admits this, saying, "Uncertain whether Captain Semmes was not making some ruse, the *Kearsarge* was stopped."

Was this a time,—when disaster, defeat and death looked us in the face,—for a ship to use a ruse, a Yankee trick? I ordered the men to "stand to their quarters," and they did it heroically; not even flinching, they stood every man to his post. As soon as we got the first of these shot I told the quartermaster to show the white flag from the stern. It was done. Captain Semmes said to me, "Dispatch an officer to the *Kearsarge* and ask that they send boats to save our wounded—ours are disabled." Our little dingey was not injured, so I sent Master's Mate Pulham with the request. No boats coming, I had one of our quarter boats (the least damaged one) lowered and had the wounded put in her. Dr. Galt came on deck at this time, and was put in charge of her, with orders to take the wounded to the *Kearsarge*. They shoved off in time to save the wounded.

When I went below to inspect the sight was appalling! Assistant Surgeon Llewellyn was at his post, but the table and the patient on it had been swept away from him by an 11-inch shell, which made an aperture that was fast filling with water. This was the last time I saw Dr. Llewellyn in life. As I passed the deck to go down below the stalwart seaman with death's signet on his brow called to me. For an instant I stood beside him. He caught my hand and kissed it with such reverence and loyalty,—the look, the act, it lingers in my memory still! I reached the deck and gave the order for "every man to save himself, to jump overboard with a spar, an oar, or a grating, and get out of the vortex of the sinking ship."

As soon as all were overboard but Captain Semmes and I, his steward, Bartelli, and two of the men—the sailmaker, Alcott, and Michael Mars—we began to strip off all superfluous clothing for our battle with the waves for our lives. Poor, faithful-hearted Bartelli, we did not know he could not swim, or he might have been sent to shore he was drowned. The men disrobed us, I to my shirt and drawers, but Captain Semmes kept on his heavy pants and vest. We together gave our swords to the briny deep and the ship we loved so well! The sad farewell look at the ship would have wrung the stoutest heart! The dead were lying on her decks, the surging, roaring waters rising through the death-wound in her side. The ship agonizing like a living thing and going down in her brave beauty, settling lower and lower, she sank fathoms deep— lost to all save love, and fame, and memory! . . .

The next thing that I remember, a voice called out, "Here's our first lieutenant," and I was pulled into a boat, in the stern sheets of which lay Captain Semmes as if dead. He had received a slight wound in his hand, which with the struggle in the water had exhausted his strength, long worn by sleeplessness, anxiety and fatigue. There were several of our crew in the boat. In a few moments we were alongside a steam yacht, which received us on her deck, and we learned it was the *Deerhound*, owned by an English gentleman, Mr. John Lancaster, who used it for the pleasure of himself and family, who were with him at this time, his sons having preferred going out with him to witness the fight to going to church with their mother, as he afterwards told us.

In looking about us I saw two French pilot boats rescuing the' crew, and finally two boats from the *Kearsarge*. I was much surprised to find Mr. Fulham on the *Deerhound*, as I had dispatched him in the little dingey to ask the *Kearsarge* for boats to save our wounded. Mr. Fulham told me that "our shot had torn the casing from the chain armor of the *Kearsarge*, indenting the chain in many places." This now explained Captain Semmes' observation to me during the battle—"our shell strike the enemy's side and fall into the water." Had we been in possession of this knowledge the unequal battle

between the *Alabama* and the *Kearsarge* would never have been fought, and the gallant little *Alabama* have been lost by an error. She fought valiantly as long as there was a plank to stand upon.

History has failed to explain, unless there were secret orders forbidding it, why the *Kearsarge* did not steam into the midst of the fallen foe and generously save life! The *Kearsarge* fought the battle beautifully, but she tarnished her glory when she fired on a fallen foe and made no immediate effort to save brave living men from watery graves! Both heroic commanders are now gone—before the great tribunal where "the deeds done in the body" are to be accounted for but history is history and truth is truth!

Mr. Lancaster came to Captain Semmes and said: "I think every man is saved, where shall I land you?"

He replied, "I am under English colors; the sooner you land me on English soil the better."

The little yacht, under a press of steam, moved away for Southampton. Our loss was nine killed, twenty-one wounded and ten drowned. That afternoon, the 19th of June, we were landed in Southampton and received with every demonstration of kindness and sympathy.

—KELL, *Recollections of a Naval Life*

XXVIII

CHICKAMAUGA AND CHATTANOOGA

With the fall of Vicksburg and Port Hudson the whole central Mississippi Valley fell under Union control and the fighting shifted to the margins—to Arkansas and the Red River in the West, to eastern Tennessee on the East. After Stones River Bragg had retired to Tullahoma while Rosecrans made his headquarters at Murfreesboro. Not until after Vicksburg did Rosecrans feel justified in advancing on Chattanooga. Under his command was an army of some 60,000, divided into three corps under Thomas, McCook and Cnttenden, and a reserve corps under Granger. General Braxton Bragg commanded some 40,000 Confederates—over 10,000 of them cavalry and reinforcements were soon on their way from the Army of Northern Virginia.

Again a word about geography is necessary. There was no more formidable theater of operations in the Civil War than that around Chattanooga. Chattanooga was the gateway to the East; it stood on a great bend of the Tennessee River, and on it converged the Memphis & Charleston and the Nashville & Chattanooga railroads. If the Confederates could hold it they would be able to use it as a base for offensive operations in Tennessee and Kentucky; if the Federals took it they could advance from it into Georgia. The Federals enjoyed numerical superiority, but-the Confederates were favored by terrain. Between Chattanooga and Murfreesboro lay the great Cumberland plateau, a rugged mountainous area, heavily wooded and crisscrossed with streams and ravines. Chattanooga itself lay on the eastern side of a sharp bend of the Tennessee which then swerved north again and flowed in a great bend toward the southwest. This great bend was dominated by Raccoon Mountain, while immediately to the south of the city itself lay the long Lookout Mountain and to the east and south the Missionary Ridge. Southward toward Ringgold and Dalton stretched a series of heavily wooded hills and valleys cut by gorges and ravines.

Rosecrans decided to cross the Tennessee below Chattanooga. As he advanced Bragg drew back into Chattanooga. By the end of August the so-called Tullahoma campaign—a wholly bloodless one—was over, and by September 4 the Federals were across the Tennessee and below Chattanooga. If Rosecrans succeeded in cutting Bragg's communications to Atlanta, Bragg would be lost, so on September 9 he evacuated Chattanooga and retired southeastward to Chickamauga Creek. Rosecrans advanced on him in three columns, each separated from the other by mountain ridges and the two flanks some 40 miles apart. This was the moment for Bragg to strike. With that fatuousness which characterized all of his military operations, he failed to do so. He was waiting for Longstreet's division, which—because Burnside had moved into Knoxville—had to go the long way around through Augusta and Atlanta. Thus the golden opportunity to smash the Army of the Cumberland passed. Between September 13 and 17 Rosecrans succeeded in concentrating his scattered forces west of Chickamauga Creek.

Since—by waiting for Longstreet—Bragg had thrown away the chance to destroy Rosecrans' army piecemeal, he should have waited until both of Longstreet's divisions arrived, and then assumed the defensive. Instead he brought on battle when only half of the reinforcements had come up. There was some preliminary fighting on September 18. On the nineteenth-twentieth came the battle itself. It was, as our accounts tell us, a Confederate victory, but a curiously inconclusive one. Bragg drove in the Union right and sent it hurtling back to Rossville; he attacked the Union left and curled it up on the center. But at the center stood Thomas, who here earned his name, the Rock of Chickamauga, and when Thomas' situation was most desperate Granger came to his rescue. The Union army was beaten, but not destroyed. It retired to Chattanooga—its original objective— and Bragg invested the city.

Now, for the first time in the war, a large Federal army was besieged. Could Bragg starve it into surrender? Again we must have recourse to our maps. Railroad communications with Chattanooga from the north and the west ran through the town of Bridgeport, on the Tennessee. But Confederate batteries on Raccoon Mountain dominated Bridgeport, and Confederate guns and sharpshooters controlled the winding Tennessee. The only supply route was down the Sequatchie Valley and across the rugged Walden's Ridge; this route was raided by Wheeler and churned into mud by the autumn rains. By the end of October the situation of Rosecrans' army was critical.

Washington had already taken alarm. Rosecrans was removed and General Thomas put in temporary command. Burnside was ordered to go to his support; Grant was instructed to hurry up reinforcements; Hooker was started, with two divisions, from Virginia. During October and November Grant and Hooker converged on the Chattanooga region. Meantime Bragg did nothing effective; instead he detached Longstreet for an attack on Knoxville. By the end of October Hooker had opened the "cracker line" to Chattanooga and Thomas' army was saved. Then Grant assumed the offensive. He sent Sherman on a wide swing from Brown's Ford to the northern end of Missionary Ridge. On the twenty-fourth Hooker carried Lookout Mountain. The next day Sherman and Thomas assaulted the Confederates all along Missionary Ridge, drove them from their entrenchments, and sent them flying toward Dalton. It was one of the most spectacular victories of the war. It was also one of the most consequential. For now the Confederacy had been squeezed into the Atlantic coastal states. And with Burnside at Knoxville and Grant and Sherman at Chattanooga the way was open into Georgia and the Carolinas.

XXVIII.1

THE FEDERALS OPPOSE HOOD WITH DESPERATION

By September 18 Bragg had most of his army west of the Chickamauga; that day Hood arrived with three brigades. There was sharp fighting on the flanks on the eighteenth but the main attack came on the nineteenth. Thomas brought on the battle that day by attacking Forrest's dismounted cavalry men, on the Confederate right. Soon the engagement was general. Hood struck with fury at the Union center, and pushed it back across the Lafayette road. Negley's division counterattacked and restored the Federal position, and night fell without decisive fighting.

Captain James R. Carnahan of the 86th Indiana Volunteers here tells us how his men fought with desperation to hold Hood's assault.

Noonday has passed, when suddenly from out the woods to our front and left onto the open field, dashes an officer, his horse urged to its greatest speed toward our command. The men see him coming, and in an instant they are aroused to the greatest interest. "There come orders," are the words that pass from lip to lip along that line. . . . He reaches our line, and is met by our brigade commander, Colonel Geo. F. Dick, as anxious to receive the orders as he is to give them. The command comes in quick, sharp words: "The general presents his compliments, and directs that you move your brigade at once to the support of General Beard [Baird]. Take the road moving by the flank in 'double quick' to the left and into the woods, and go into line on the left of General Beatty's brigade. I am to direct you. Our men are hard pressed." The last sentence was all that was said in words as to the condition of our troops, but it told that we had read aright before he had spoken.

Scarce had the order been delivered when the command to "take arms" is heard along the line, and to drivers and cannoneers to mount. It scarcely took the time required to tell it for our brigade to get in motion, moving off the field, the artillery taking the wagon road, the infantry alongside. It was a grand scene as we moved quickly into place, closing up the column, and waiting but a moment for the command. The guns are at a right shoulder, and all have grown eager for the order—"Forward." The bugle sounds the first note of the command. Now, look along that column; the men are leaning forward for the start; you see the drivers on the artillery teams tighten the rein in the left hand, and, with the whip in the uplifted right arm, rise in their stirrups; and, as the last note of the bugle is sounded, the crack of the whips of thirty-six drivers over the backs of as many horses, and the stroke of the spurs, sends that battery of six guns and its caissons rattling and bounding over that road, while the infantry alongside are straining every nerve as they hasten to the relief of the comrades so hard pressed.

The spirits of the men grow higher and higher with each moment of the advance. The rattling of the artillery and the hoof-beats of the horses add to the excitement of the onward rush, infantry and artillery thus side by side, vieing each with the other which shall best do his part. Now, as we come nearer, the storm of the battle seems to grow greater and greater. On and yet on we press, until, reaching the designated point, the artillery is turned off to the left, on to a ridge, and go into position along its crest, while the lines of the infantry are being formed to the right of the road over which we have just been hurrying.

Our lines are scarcely formed, and the command to move forward given, when the lines which are in advance of us are broken by a terrific charge of the enemy, and are driven back in confusion onto our line friend and foe so inter mingled that we can not fire a shot without inflicting as much injury on our men as upon the enemy.

Our artillery, on the crest of the ridge back of us, have unlimbered and gone into action, and their shells are now flying over our heads in the woods, where the enemy's lines had been. Confusion seems to have taken possession of our lines, and, to add to it, the lines of our right have been broken and the enemy are sweeping past our flank. The order is given to fall back on line with the artillery. Out of the wood, under the fire of our cannon, the men hasten. Now on the crest of that ridge, without works of any kind to shelter them, our troops are again hastily formed, and none too soon. Down the gentle slope of that ridge, and away to our right and left and front stretches an open field, without tree or shrub to break the force of the balls. In our front, and at the edge of the field, two hundred yards away, runs the road parallel with our lines; beyond the road the heavy timber where the Confederate lines are formed, and well protected in their preparations for their charge.

Scarce had our lines been formed, when the sharp crack of the rifles along our front, and the whistling of the balls over our heads, give us warning that the advance of the enemy has begun, and in an instant the shots of the skirmishers are drowned by the shout that goes up from the charging column as it starts down in the woods. Our

men are ready. The Seventh Indiana Battery—six guns—is on the right of my regiment; Battery M, Fourth United States Artillery, is on our left. The gunners and every man of those two batteries are at their posts of duty, the tightly drawn lines in their faces showing their purpose there to stand for duty or die. Officers pass the familiar command of caution along the line—"Steady, men, steady." The shout of the charging foe comes rapidly on; now they burst out of the woods and onto the road. As if touched by an electric cord, so quick and so in unison was it, the rifles leap to the shoulder along the ridge where waves the stars and stripes.

Now the enemy are in plain view along the road covering our entire front; you can see them, as with cap visors drawn well down over their eyes, the gun at the charge, with short, shrill shouts they come, and we see the colors of Longstreet's corps, flushed with victory, confronting us. Our men recognize the gallantry of their foe, and their pride is touched as well. All this is but the work of an instant, when, just as that long line of gray has crossed the road, quick and sharp rings out along our line the command, "Ready," "Fire!" It seems to come to infantry and artillery at the same instant, and out from the rifles of the men and the mouths of those cannons leap the death-dealing bullet and canister; again and again, with almost lightning rapidity, they pour in their deadly, merciless fire, until along that entire ridge it had become almost one continuous volley. Now that corps that had known little of defeat begins to waver; their men had fallen thick and fast about them. Again and yet again the volleys are poured into them, and the artillery on our right and left have not ceased their deadly work. No troops can long withstand such fire; their lines waver; another volley, and they are broken, and now fall back in confusion. The charge was not long in point of time, but was terrible in its results to the foe.

Along the entire line to our right and left we can hear the battle raging with increased fury. We are now on the defensive; and all can judge that the lull in our front is only the stillness that forbodes the more terrible storm that is to come. A few logs and rails are hastily gathered together to form a slight breastwork. Soon the scattering shots that began to fall about us gave us warning that our foe was again moving on us. Again we are ready, now laying behind our hastily prepared works. Again we hear the shout, as on they come with more determination-than before. But with even greater courage do our men determine to hold their lines. The artillery is double shotted with canister. Again the command, "Fire!" and hotter, fiercer than before the battle rages along our front. Shout is answered with shout, shot by shots tenfold, until again our assailants break before our fire and are again forced back.

But why repeat further the story of that Saturday after noon. Again and again were those charges repeated along our line, only to be hurled back—broken and shattered. It did seem as though our men were more than human. The artillerymen worked as never before. Their guns—double shotted—had scarce delivered their charges, and, before the gun could complete its recoil, was caught by strong arms, made doubly strong in that fever-heat of battle; was again in position, again double shotted, and again fired into the face of the foe. The arms bared, the veins standing out in great strong lines, the hat or cap gone from the head, the eye starting almost from the socket, the teeth set, the face beaded with perspiration, balls falling all about them, those men of the Seventh Indiana Battery and Battery M seemed to be supernaturally endowed with strength.

Their comrades of the infantry vied with them in acts of heroism, and daring, and endurance. They shouted defiance at the foe with every shot; with face and hands begrimed in the smoke and dust and heat of the battle; with comrades falling about them, the survivors thought only of vengeance. All the horses on two of the guns of the Seventh Indiana Battery are shot down; another charge is beginning; those two guns might be lost; they must be gotten back. Quick as thought, a company of infantry spring to the guns, one hand holding the rifle, the other on the cannon, and, with the shot falling thick and

fast in and about them, drag the guns over the brow of the ridge and down into the woods, just in the rear of our lines, and hasten back again to take their places in line, ready to meet the on-coming charge. An artilleryman is shot down; a man from the infantry takes his place and obeys orders as best he can. When the charge begins our men are lying down. Now, in the midst of it, so great has become the excitement, so intense the anxiety, all fear and prudence vanishes, and the men leap to their feet, and fire and load, and fire and load, in the wildest frenzy of desperation. They have lost all ideas of danger or the strength of the assailants. It was this absolute *desperation* of our men that held our lines.

—Carnahan, "Personal Recollections of Chickamauga"

XXVIII.2

Thomas Stands Like a Rock at Chickamauga

During the night of the nineteenth Longstreet came up with two more brigades, and Bragg prepared to renew the battle by a series of attacks on the attenuated Union line. from north to south. The crisis came in the afternoon of the twentieth. Fierce Confederate attacks upon the Union left led Rosecrans to weaken his right. Through some misunderstanding General Wood withdrew his division, near the center, and into the gap thus created Longstreet hurled his fresh brigades like a thunderbolt. The whole Union line cracked and broke; the right crumbled and retreated toward Rossville; the left was in desperate danger. It was then that Thomas earned for himself the title "Rock of Chickamauga"—Thomas who during the whole war never left the battle field and never lost an engagement. It was Stones River over again, but without the artillery, without even ammunition, for at one time Thomas was forced to rely on the bayonet to hurl back the Confederate attacks. lust as the situation appeared most desperate Gordon Granger came pounding up with his reserve division and saved the day.

The story of the break-through is told here by a Confederate general, and the story of Thomas stand by a brigadier attached to Rosecrans' staff. D. H. Hill was one of Lee's greatest lieutenants and needs neither introduction nor celebration. Thruston was a brigadier general in the Army of the Cumberland.

A. Longstreet Breaks the Federal Line

The heavy pressure on Thomas caused Rosecrans to support him by sending the divisions of Negley and Van Cleve and Brannan's reserve brigade. In the course of these changes, an order to Wood, which Rosecrans claims was misinterpreted, led to a gap being left into which Longstreet stepped with the eight brigades which he had arranged in three lines to constitute his grand column of attack. Davis's two brigades, one of Van Cleve's, and Sheridan's entire division were caught in front and flank and driven from the field. Disregarding the order of the day, Longstreet now gave the order to wheel to the right instead of the left, and thus take in reverse the strong position of the enemy. Five of McCook's brigades were speedily driven off the field. He estimates the loss at forty per cent. Certainly that flank march was a bloody one. I have never seen the Federal dead lie so thickly on the ground, save in front of the sunken wall at Fredericksburg.

But that indomitable Virginia soldier, George H. Thomas, was there and was destined to save the Union army from total rout and ruin, by confronting with invincible pluck the forces of his friend and captain in the Mexican war. Thomas had ridden to his right to hurry up reenforcements, when he discovered a line advancing, which he thought at first was the expected succor from Sheridan, but he soon heard that it was a rebel column marching upon him. He chose a strong position on a spur of Missionary Ridge, running east and west, placed upon it Brannan's division with portions of two brigades of Negley's; Wood's division (Crittenden's) was placed on Brannan's left. These troops, with such as could be rallied from the two broken corps, were all he had to confront the forces of Longstreet, until Steedman's division of Granger's corps came to his relief about 3 P.M. Well and nobly did Thomas and his gallant troops hold their own against foes flushed with past victory and confident of future success. His new line was nearly at right angles with the line of log-works on the west side of the Rossville road, his right being an almost impregnable wall-like hill, his left nearly an inclosed fortification. Our only hope of success was to get in his rear by moving far to our right, which overlapped the Federal left, Bushrod Johnson's three brigades in Longstreet's center were the first to fill the gap left by Wood's withdrawal from the Federal right; but the other five brigades under Hindman and Kershaw moved promptly into line as soon as space could be found for them, wheeled to the right, and engaged in the murderous flank attack. On they rushed, shouting, yelling, running over batteries, capturing trains, taking prisoners, seizing the headquarters of the Federal commander, at the Widow Glenn's, until they found themselves facing the new Federal line on Snodgrass Hill. Hindman had advanced a little later than the center, and had met great and immediate success. The brigades of Deas and Manigault charged the breast works at double-quick, rushed over them, drove Laiboldt's Federal brigade of Sheridan's division off the field down the Rossville road; then General Patton Anderson's brigade of Hindman, having come into line, attacked and beat back the forces of Davis, Sheridan, and Wilder in their front, killed the hero and poet General Lytle, took 1100 prisoners, 27 pieces of artillery, commissary and ordnance trains, etc. Finding no more resistance on his front and left, Hindman wheeled to the right to assist the forces of the center. The divisions of Stewart, Hood, Bushrod Johnson, and Hindman came together in front of the new stronghold of the Federals.

It was now 2:30 P.M Longstreet with his staff, was lunching on sweet-potatoes. A message came just then that the commanding general wished to see him. He found Bragg in rear of his lines, told him of the steady and satisfactory progress of the battle, that sixty pieces of artillery had been reported captured (though probably the number was over-estimated), that many prisoners and stores had been taken, and that all was going well. He then asked for additional troops to hold the ground gained, while he pursued the two broken corps down the Dry Valley road and cut off the retreat of Thomas. Bragg replied that there was no more fight in the troops of Polk's wing, that he could give Longstreet no reenforcements. . . .

Some of the severest fighting had yet to be done. . . . Hindman and Bushrod Johnson organized a column of attack upon the front and rear of the stronghold of Thomas. . . . It began at 3:30 P.M. A terrific contest ensued. The bayonet was used, and men were killed and wounded with clubbed muskets. A little after 4, the enemy was reenforced, and advanced, but was repulsed by Anderson and Kershaw.

—HILL, "Chickamauga—The Great Battle of the West"

B. Thomas Holds the Horseshoe Ridge

The furious initial attack on the Federal left, on the morning of the 20th, although repulsed, unfortunately led to changes in Rosecrans's army materially affecting the results of the general conflict. Thomas, discovering his position turned and his front assaulted, hurried messengers to Rose crans for assistance. Two aides, in rapid succession, called for reenforcements. All was still on the Federal right. The fight was raging with grand fury on the left.

Rosecrans felt that his apprehensions of the morning were to be realized. The Confederates were doubtless massing on his left. They had reached the much-coveted Chattanooga road. McCook was at once notified that Thomas was heavily pressed, that the left must be held at all hazards, and that he must be ready to reenforce Thomas at a moment's warning. Five minutes later came the order to hurry Sheridan's two brigades to the left. Negley's troops, replaced by Wood, had started. Van Cleve, with two brigades, was also sent to aid Thomas. McCook was now left with one of Sheridan's brigades and two of Jefferson C. Davis's, all depleted by Saturday's losses. They were unable to form a connected front, but joined Wood on their left. Captain Kellogg, of Thomas's staff, hurrying along the line with orders, unfortunately re ported ta Rosecrans that he had noticed "Brannan was out of line, and Reynolds's right exposed."

Turning to an aide Rosecrans directed him to order Wood "to close up on Reynolds as fast as possible and support him." In fact, Reynolds was *not*

needing help, and Brannan was in position on his right, but slightly in rear. Wood, whose left connected with Brannan's right, passed to the rear of Brannan to reach Reynolds's position; thus a wide gap was left in the Union line. McCook had already called up Wilder to strengthen his front, and sent for the main cavalry to protect the right. The right had unexpectedly become, as it were, the *rear* of the army.

Unhappily for the National army, Bragg was *not* now massing his forces on our left. He had just been defeated and repulsed there. Bragg's main plan had failed; but in the quiet forest, within almost a stone's-throw of our right, and in the still overclouding mist, were Longstreet and Buckner, with the left wing of the Confederate army massed in battle array, impatiently awaiting the signal for attack.

Longstreet's troops were placed in column of brigades at half distance,—a masterpiece of tactics. Hood, a soldier full of energy and dash, was to lead the column, his own division being massed five brigades deep, with the brigades of Kershaw and Humphreys as additional supports.

The order to advance came at last. The deep Confederate lines suddenly appeared. The woods in our front seemed alive. On they came like an angry flood. They struck McCook's three remaining brigades, the remnants of the Federal right. Under the daring personal exertions of McCook and Davis, they made a gallant but vain resistance. The massed lines of the enemy swarmed around their flanks. Pouring through the opening made by Wood's withdrawal, they struck his last brigade as it was leaving the line. It was slammed back like a door, and shattered. Brannan, on Wood's left, was struck in front and flank. His right was flung back; his left stood fast. Sheridan, hastening to the left with two brigades, was called back, and rushed to the rescue. His little force stayed the storm for a time. Wave after wave of Confederates came on, resistance only increased the multitude. Brannan's artillery, attacked in flank, rushed to the rear for clearer ground, and, with the Confederates at their heels, suddenly plunged into Van Cleve marching to the aid of Thomas. Disorder ensued; effective resistance was lost. The Reserve Artillery of the center, well posted in rear, unable to manoeuvre in the undergrowth, hedged around by infantry a half hour before, was now without immediate support. The sudden rush of Longstreet's compact column through the forest had foiled all plans. The astonished artillerists were swept from their guns. General Negley, with one of his brigades isolated in rear, shared the general fate of the right.

When Longstreet struck the right, Rosecrans was near McCook and Crittenden. Seeing our line swept back, he hurried to Sheridan's force for aid. With staff and escort he recklessly strove to stem the tide. They attempted to pass to the left through a storm of canister and musketry, but were driven back.

All became confusion. No order could be heard above the tempest of battle. With a wild yell the Confederates swept on far to their left. They seemed everywhere victorious. Rosecrans was borne back in the retreat. Fugitives, wounded, caissons, escort, ambulances, thronged the narrow pathways. He concluded that our whole line had given way, that the day was lost, that the next stand must be made at Chattanooga. McCook and Crittenden, caught in the same tide of retreat, seeing only rout everywhere, shared the opinion of Rosecrans, and reported to him for instructions and cooperation.

Briefly, this is the story of the disaster on our right at Chickamauga: We were overwhelmed by numbers; we were beaten in detail. Thirty minutes earlier Longstreet would have met well-organized resistance. Thirty minutes later our marching division could have formed beyond his column of attack. . . .

The sound of battle had lulled. No Union force was in sight. A Confederate line nearby was advancing against the position. Harrison, dismounting his men, dashed at the enemy in a most effective charge. Wilder, coming up on our right, also attacked. Wilder had two regiments armed with the same repeating-rifles. They did splendid work. Longstreet told Wilder after the war that the steady and continued racket of these guns led him

to think an army corps had attacked his left flank. Bragg, cautious by nature, hesitated. By the time he was ready to turn Longstreet's force against Thomas, valuable time had elapsed.

Brannan, partly knocked out of line, had gathered his division on a hill at right angles to his former position, and a half mile in rear of Reynolds. General Wood came up with Harker's brigade and part of George P. Buell's, and posted them near Brannan's left. Some of Van Cleve's troops joined them, and fragments of Negley's.

General Thomas, ignorant of these movements and of the disaster to the right of the Union army, had again been attacked by Breckinridge and Forrest. They were again in Baird's rear with increased force. Thomas's reserve brigades, Willich, Grose, and Van Derveer, hurried to meet the attack. After a fierce struggle the Confederates were beaten back. Thomas, expecting the promised assistance of Sheridan, had sent Captain Kellogg to guide him to the left. Kellogg, hurrying back, reported that he had been fired on by a line of Confederates advancing in the woods in rear of Reynolds, who held the center of our general line.

The men in gray were coming on the right instead of Sheridan! Wood and Harker hoped the force advancing in the woods on their new front was a friendly one. The National flag was waved; a storm of bullets was the response. It was Stewart and Bate coming with their Tennesseeans. They had finally forced their way across the ragged edge of the Federal right, and were following Hood. Fortunately Thomas had just repulsed Breckinridge's attack on his left, and Stanley, Beatty, and Van Derveer had double quicked across the "horseshoe" to our new right. They did not come a moment too soon. The improvised line of Federals thus hastily formed on "Battery Hill" now successfully withstood the assault of the enemy. The Union line held the crest. Longstreet was stayed at last. Gathering new forces, he soon sent a flanking column around our right. We could not extend our line to meet this attack. They had reached the summit, and were coming around still farther on through a protected ravine. For a time the fate of the Union army hung in the balance. All seemed lost, when unexpected help came from Gordon Granger and the right was saved.

—THRUSTON, "The Crisis at Chickamauga"

XXVIII.2

CHATTANOOGA UNDER SIEGE

After Chickamauga the Federals retired into Chattanooga; thus the army that had set out to capture the city ended by being caught in its own net. So serious was the situation that Grant himself came on to take charge of its relief. The immediate task was for Hooker to move into the area en closed by the great bend of the Tennessee, between Bridge port and Chattanooga; the second for Thomas to get control of Brown's Ferry. Then the two could link up. Nad Bragg been on the alert neither of these movements could have succeeded, for Raccoon Mountain and Lookout Mountain commanded both approaches. Bragg however er failed to build up adequate strength in this region south and west of Chattanooga. On October 26 Hooker crossed the Tennessee at Bridgeport and moved overland toward Brown's Ferry, and some of Thomas' forces captured Brown's Ferry and the heights above it.

The war correspondent, W. F. G. Shanks, who was with the Army of the Cumberland, here tells what life was like during the siege and how the siege was raised by opening the "cracker line."

The siege of Chattanooga was the only one which any one of the Union armies suffered or sustained. It is a singular fact, worthy of mention just here, that the troops of the Union never abandoned a siege once begun, nor surrendered a position regularly invested, and were compelled to surrender all those fortresses in which they were besieged. The Union armies invested and finally captured Yorktown, Fort Donelson, Corinth, Vicksburg, Island No. 10, Port Hudson, Peters burg, Atlanta, Mobile, Savannah, Charleston, Fort Fisher, Wilmington, and many other points of lesser importance and held by mere detachments, not, like those mentioned, garrisoned by entire armies. The rebels besieged Nashville, Knoxville, Chattanooga, and other minor positions held by fragments of armies and failed in all. They came nearest to success at Chattanooga. . . .

If there was little of beauty or elegance in the place when our troops retreated into it from Chickamauga, there was a great deal less a fortnight subsequently. Like many another Southern town Chattanooga grew suddenly old; one might say it turned gray during the brief but dark night of the siege. General Saint Clair Morton, the chief of Rosecrans's engineers, had no mercy; he had no idea of economy either. As one of his fellow-officers once said of him, "if Morton needed a certain quantity of earth for a fort, the fact that it was a gold mine would make no difference to him; he would only say, 'Gold dust will resist artillery—it will do.' " So laying out his line of works Morton budged from his course not an inch to spare the town. Residences were turned into block-houses; black bastions sprang up in former vine yards; rifle-pits were run through the grave-yards; and soon a long line of works stretched from the river above to the river below the city, bending crescentlike around it, as if it were a huge bow of iron, and rendering it impregnable. For a fortnight the whole army worked on the fortifications, and it became literally a walled city.

Not alone from the fact that it was shut in by the mud walls of these impregnable fortifications was the town an intrenched camp, and the engineers alone did not despoil Chattanooga of its small modicum of beauty. The winter quarters of the troops, composed of small dog-kennel-shaped huts, built of boards and roofed over with the shelter-tents with which the soldiers were provided, were scattered all over the town in valley and on hill-side, and it was not difficult to imagine it again the little Indian town of huts and wigwams which Hanging Bird had described. The camps of soldiers were not cantonments in the proper sense of the term. The immediate presence and threatening proximity of the enemy rendered it necessary to safety and discipline that the troops should encamp in the regular order of regiments and brigades, so as to be prepared to form at the sound of alarm, ready to repulse or to make an attack. Instead, there fore, of camping indiscriminately in houses as they stood, the men tore down the houses and fences, and of the frame work built their

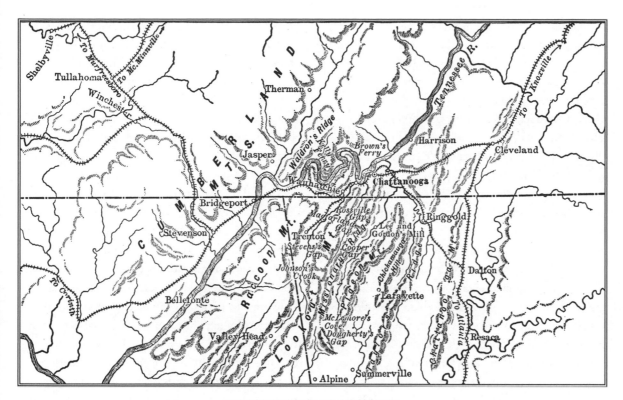

CHATTANOOGA AND ITS APPROACHES

huts, and of the bricks their chimneys and fire-places.

The veteran soldier is very ingenious, and makes himself happy on very little; and the quarters of those at Chattanooga during the siege possessed all the "modern improvements." They had curious modes of making themselves comfortable. The rebels used to call our men, when working on forts, rifle-pits, etc., "beavers in blue." The veteran was a regular beaver when building his house. He would buy, beg, or steal from the quarter-master (a species of theft recognized by the camp code of morals as entirely justifiable) the only tool he needed, an axe. With this he would cut, hew, dig, drive—any thing you like, in fact. With his axe he would cut the logs for his cabin—miniature logs, two inches in diameter—trim them to the proper length, and drive the necessary piles. With his axe he would cut the brushwood or the ever green, and thatch his roof or cover it with his shelter-tent. With his axe he would dig a mud-hole in which to make his plaster for filling the crevices of the logs, and thus shut out the cold. Doors, chimneys, benches, chairs,

tables, all the furniture of his commodious house, he would make with the same instrument.

When all was finished he would sit down to enjoy himself, sleeping on good clean straw, dining off a wooden table, drinking from glassware made from the empty ale or porter bottles from the suttler's tent, combing his whiskers before a framed looking-glass on a pine-board mantel-shelf, and looking with the air and contentedness of a millionaire on the camped world around him. These huts of the veterans were not perhaps so large and picturesque as the wigwams of the Cherokees. They really resembled more in size and appearance the huts of the beaver or prairie-dogs, and this comparison did not seem so foreign or forced as it may appear to the reader when, on the occasional bright days of the bleak siege, the gallant "war dogs" were to be seen issuing forth to bay a deep-mouthed welcome to the enterprising news-boy or faithful postman, who had run the gauntlet of rebel sharpshooters or the embargo of mud to furnish the news from home.

Life in Chattanooga during the two months of the siege was dreary enough. There was no fighting to do; the enemy daily threw a few shells from the top of Lookout Mountain into our camps, but they were too wise to attack with infantry the works which soon encircled the city. Bragg preferred to rely for the final reduction of the garrison upon his ally Famine, and a very formidable antagonist did our men find him in the end. Bragg held the railroad line from Bridgeport to Chattanooga, thereby preventing its use by Rosecrans as a line of supplies, and compelling him to haul his pro visions in wagon trains from Stevenson across the Cumber land Mountains. Every exertion of the quarter-masters failed to fully supply the army by this route, the only practicable one while the siege lasted. The animals of the army were overworked and ill-fed, and thousands died from exhaustion. It was almost impossible to obtain forage for those in Chattanooga, and the quarter-masters reported that ten thousand horses and mules died of actual starvation during the siege. Thousands were turned loose in the mountains and perished. I passed over the route from Chattanooga to Stevenson during the siege, and was never out of sight of these dead or dying "heroes whose names were never mentioned." They would frequently gather in groups around a small pool at which they could quench the thirst that consumed them, and lie down to die. Finding it impossible to obtain forage for an animal which I had in Chattanooga, and which had been latterly subsisting on the pine-board fence to which his halter was attached, I turned the poor animal loose to graze near a small stream in the town. He was too exhausted to stray away from it; lying down he picked the few blades of grass within his reach, stretched his neck to the pool for the few drops of water which it gave, and at length gave up the ghost.

The other heroes in the beleaguered town hardly suffered less. Famine became a familiar fiend; they laughed in his face, as crowds will laugh in the face of great dangers and disasters, but it was a very forced laugh. The trains of supplies for the army were frequently twenty days on the route from Stevenson, only sixty miles distant, and as the

trains were not numerous naturally the supplies in the town did not increase. And many of these trains frequently came in *empty*. They could not carry full loads across the mountains with skeletons for horses; each train had to be guarded, and the guards had to be supplied from the train whose safety they secured. Most of these guards were men from the besieged city, they had been on quarter rations of fat bacon and mouldy hard bread for weeks, and they did not lose the opportunity to satisfy the cravings of their appetites when guarding the trains. It was all nonsense for quarter-masters in charge to tell them they ought to remember their starving comrades in the besieged city, to appeal to their patriotism, and to talk about discipline; if there are any, periods when discipline, patriotism, and sympathy are entirely sunk in a soldier's breast they are when he is thoroughly demoralized by defeat or reckless from hunger. So it frequently happened that the guards of a train eat it *in transitu*. After the third week of the siege the men were put on quarter rations, and only two or three articles were supplied in this meagre quantity. The only meat to be had was bacon, "side bacon" or "middling," I think it is called, and a slice about the size of the three larger fingers of a man's hand, sandwiched between the two halves of a "Lincoln Platform," as the four inches square cake of "hard bread" was called, and washed down by a pint of coffee, served for a meal.

Men can not dig fortifications and fight very long on such rations; and the whole army was half famished. I have often seen hundreds of soldiers following behind the wagon trains which had just arrived, picking out of the mud the crumbs of bread, coffee, rice, etc., which were wasted from the boxes and sacks by the rattling of the wagons over the stones. Nothing was wasted in those days, and though the inspectors would frequently condemn whole wagon loads of provisions as spoiled by exposure during the trip, and order the contents to be thrown away, the soldiers or citizens always found some use for it.

The hundreds of citizens who were confined in the town at the same time suffered even more than the men. They were forced to huddle together in the centre of the town as best they could, and many of the houses occupied by them during the siege surpassed in filth, point of numbers of occupants, and general destitution, the worst tenement-house in New York city. . . .

The siege which was thus conducted was raised by strategy—the strategy of the same man who had captured the city, though he did not execute the movements. The enemy which was in reality investing the town was Famine: the way to defeat him was to find a shorter line of supplies by which the besieged army might be fed. A close study of the map had shown to Rosecrans that if Bragg could be driven from a small peninsula of land near Chattanooga, and on the south side of the Tennessee River, a very short route could be opened by the river to Bridgeport, and that by means of a couple of boats which the soldiers had built the army could be fed. Hooker's corps from the Army of the Potomac had arrived at Bridgeport on Oct. 20, and with this force the peninsula could be seized. But before he could get ready for the movement Rosecrans was relieved of the command, and General Thomas assumed control, with General Grant in chief command. In the mean time the troops in Chattanooga. were on the eve of starvation. "We are issuing," said General Gordon Granger, "quarter rations for breakfast only." But Thomas, on assuming command, and being urged by Grant to hold on to the strong-hold at all hazards, had telegraphed in reply, "I will hold the town until we starve;" and the men cheerfully agreed to starve a while longer.

On the arrival of General Grant the movements which Rosecrans had planned were begun. Two columns to seize the peninsula started simultaneously—the one from Bridgeport under General Hooker, the other from Chattanooga under General W. F. Smith. Hooker moved overland along the railroad and seized upon Wauhatchie and three small hills near the mouth of Lookout Creek. Smith, with his command in pontoon boats, on the night of October 26, 1863, dropped down the Tennessee River, running past the rebel batteries to Brown's Ferry, where a prominent and commanding peak of hills on the peninsula was seized, and the boats were soon transformed into a pontoon bridge across the river at that point. General Hooker's position, which was only won after two very desperate engagements, one of which was fought at midnight, covered a road to Kelley's Ferry, a landing place on the west side of the all-important peninsula, and the result of the whole operation was that a short and good road, only seven miles in length, was obtained from Chattanooga by way of Brown's Ferry to Kelley's Ferry; at which latter place the steamboats built by the troops landed supplies from Bridgeport. Supplies by this route could be very easily carried through in a day, and the army was very soon on full rations again.

—Shanks, "Chattanooga, and How We Held It"

XXVIII.4

HOOKER WINS THE "BATTLE ABOVE THE CLOUDS"

As soon as the peril of the Federal position at Chattanooga was clear, Halleck ordered General Hooker to proceed west with two corps of the Army of the Potomac. Hooker arrived at Bridgeport early in October and, as we have seen, crossed the river into the Raccoon Mountain region on October 26. After he had cleared this area of Confederates, his next task was to seize control of Lookout Mountain, lying directly south of Chattanooga. Early on the morning of November 24 his forces, 10,000 strong, began their attack. Bragg,-with characteristic imbecility, had less than 2,000 men posted here; these put up a stiff resistance but were overwhelmed.

The story of the "Battle above the Clouds" is told by Major Joseph Fullerton of the Army of the Cumberland.

The morning of November 24th opened with a cold, drizzling rain. Thick clouds of mist were settling on Lookout Mountain. At daybreak Geary's division, and Whitaker's brigade of Cruft's division, marched up to Wauhatchie, the nearest point at which Lookout Creek, swelled by recent rains, could be forded, and at 8 o'clock they crossed. The heavy clouds of mist reaching down the mountain-side hid the movement from the enemy, who was expecting and was well prepared to resist a crossing at the Chattanooga road below. As soon as this movement was discovered, the enemy withdrew his troops from the summit of the mountain, changed front, and formed a new line to meet our advance, his left resting at the palisade, and his right at the heavy works in the valley, where the road crossed the creek. Having crossed at Wauhatchie, Whitaker's brigade, being in the advance, drove back the enemy's pickets, and quickly ascended the mountain till it reached the foot of the palisade. Here, firmly attaching its right, the brigade faced left in front, with its left joined to Geary's division. Geary now moved along the side of the mountain, and through the valley, thus covering the crossing of the rest of Hooker's command. In the meantime Grose's brigade was engaging the enemy at the lower road crossing, and Woods' brigade of Osterhaus's division was building a bridge rather more than half a mile farther up the creek. Geary, moving down the valley, reached this point at 11 o'clock, just after the bridge was finished, and as Osterhaus's division and Grose's brigade were crossing.

Hooker's command, now united in the enemy's field, was ready to advance and sweep around the mountain. His line, hanging at the base of the palisades like a great pendulum, reached down the side of the mountain to the valley, where the force that had just crossed the creek was attached as its weight. Now, as, at the command of Hooker, it swung forward in its upward movement, the artillery of the Army of the Cumberland, on Moccasin Point, opened fire, throwing a stream of shot and shell into the enemy's rifle-pits at the foot of the mountain, and into the works thickly planted on the "White House" plateau. At the same time the guns planted by Hooker on the west side of the creek opened on the works which covered the enemy's right. Then followed a gallant assault by Osterhaus and Grose. After fighting for nearly two hours, step by step up the steep mountain-side, over and through deep gullies and ravines, over great rocks and fallen trees, the earthworks on the plateau were assaulted and carried, and the enemy was driven out and forced to fall back. He did so

slowly and reluctantly, taking advantage of the rough ground to continue the fight.

It was now 2 o'clock. A halt all along the line was ordered by General Hooker, as the clouds had grown so thick that further advance was impracticable, and as his ammunition was almost exhausted and more could not well be brought up the mountain. But all the enemy's works had been taken. Hooker had carried the mountain on the east side, had opened communication with Chattanooga, and he commanded the enemy's line of defensive works in Chattanooga Valley.

At 2 o'clock Hooker reported to General Thomas and informed him that he was out of ammunition. Thomas at once sent Carlin's brigade from the valley, each soldier taking with him all the small ammunition he could carry. At S o'clock Carlin was on the mountain, and Hooker's skirmishers were quickly supplied with the means of carrying on their work.

In the morning it had not been known in Chattanooga, in Sherman's army, or in Bragg's camp, that a battle was to be fought. . . . Soon after breakfast, Sherman's men at the other end of the line, intent on the north end of Missionary Ridge, and Thomas's men in the center, fretting to be let loose from their intrenchments, were startled by the sound of artillery and musketry firing in Lookout Valley. Surprise possessed the thousands who turned their anxious eyes toward the mountain. The hours slowly wore away; the roar of battle increased, as it came rolling around the point of the mountain, and the anxiety grew. A battle was being fought just before and above them. They could hear, but could not see how it was going Finally, the wind, tossing about the clouds and mist, made a rift that for a few minutes opened a view of White House plateau. The enemy was seen to be in flight, and Hooker's men were in pursuit! Then went up a mighty cheer from the thirty thousand in the valley that was heard above the battle by their comrades on the mountain.

As the sun went down the clouds rolled away, and the night came on clear and cool. A grand sight was old Look out that night. Not two miles apart were the parallel camp fires of the two armies, extending from the summit of the mountain to its base, looking like streams of burning lava, while in between, the flashes from the skirmishers' muskets glowed like giant fire-flies.

—Fullerton, "The Army of the Cumberland at Chattanooga"

XXVIII.5

The Army of the Cumberland Carries Missionary Ridge

Grant's plan was strategically simple but tactically complex. His purpose was to assault Bragg all along the line, drive him from his entrenchments, and, if possible, cut off his retreat and destroy him. To achieve this he planned a three-pronged operation. Sherman was to cross the Tennessee on pontoons, march up the tongue of land in front of Chattanooga, cross over to the east, and attack Bragg at the northern tip of Missionary Ridge. Once this attack was under way Thomas was to launch an attack on the center. If and when these had succeeded Hooker was to strike from the south. The attack jumped o• at dawn of November 25, and all went as planned except that Sherman was held and thrown back while Thomas' supporting attack achieved victory.

What Pickett's charge is to the Confederacy, Thomas' attack of November 25 on Missionary Ridge is to the North, one of those moments of gallantry that seem suspended in time and are ever present and ever real. The Confederates had constructed three rows of entrenchments on rugged boulder-strewed Missionary Ridge. When Grant saw that Sherman was in trouble he asked Thomas to create a diversion by carrying the first line of entrenchments; Thomas' men carried them, and kept going to the top.

Here are two accounts of this great dramatic event. The first is by William Morgan, a lieutenant in the 23rd Kentucky Infantry, part of Hazen's brigade. The second comes from our old acquaintance, Major Connolly of the 123rd Illinois Volunteers.

A. "First One Flag, Then Another, Leads"

From the position occupied by my regiment, Orchard Knob was in view and all eyes were leveled in that direction. Suddenly a commotion was discernible on Orchard Knob. Officers were seen mounting their horses and riding towards the sever-

al commands. Then every man in the line knew the crucial hour had come. Intense excitement seemed to stir every soldier and officer. Excitement is followed by nervous impatience.

Time moves slowly. Here and there a soldier readjusts his accouterments or relaces his shoes. All know that many will never reach the enemy's works, yet not a countenance shows fear. The delay is becoming unbearable.

At last the first boom of the signal is heard. Men fall in and dress without command. Another gun, and nervous fingers play with gunlocks. Another and another, and each man looks into the eyes of his comrade to ascertain if he can be relied upon. The examination must have been satisfactory, for, just as the report of the fifth gun breaks upon their ears, the line is moving without a word of command from anyone, and when the sixth gun is fired the troops are well on the way, with colors unfurled and guns at "right shoulder shift." All sensations have now given way to enthusiasm. It is a sight never to be forgotten. Fifteen to twenty thousand men in well-aligned formation, with colors waving in the breeze, almost shaking the earth with cadenced tread, involuntarily move to battle.

The troops have scarcely left the rifle-pits when the guns upon the ridge open upon them. Our heavy guns in Fort Wood and the field batteries vigorously respond. We see the enemy in the rifle-pits, at the base of the ridge, looking over the works, with guns in hand, prepared to deliver fire. Why do they hesitate? We are in range. They are evidently waiting so that every shot will tell. From the enemy's lower lines now comes a storm of bullets and the air is filled with every sound of battle. The noise is terrible. Our artillery is exploding shells along the top of the ridge, and a caisson is seen to burst off to the right.

Now all feeling seems to have changed to one of determination. A terrific cheer rolls along the line. Not a rifle has yet been fired by the assaulting column. The quick step has been changed to the "double quick." Another cheer, and the enemy's first line of work at the base of the ridge is ours, together with many of his troops. Shelter is sought on the re verse side of the enemy's works, but the fire from the hilltop makes protection impossible.

Over fifty cannon, supported by veterans of many battle fields, covered by well-built fortifications, are sending down a rain of shell, shrapnel, and rifle-bullets. The bursting projectiles seem to compress the air and one's head feels as if bound with iron bands. Unable to return the enemy's fire, the delay drives the men to desperation. To remain is to be annihilated; to retreat is as dangerous as to advance. Here and there a man leaps the works and starts towards the hill top; small squads follow. Then someone gave the command, "Forward!" after a number of men began to advance. Officers catch the inspiration. The mounted officers dismount and stone their horses to the rear. The cry, "Forward!" is repeated along the line, and the apparent impossibility is under taken. . . .

But little regard to formation was observed. Each battalion assumed a triangular shape, the colors at the apex surrounded by the strongest men, the flanks trailing to the rear.

First one flag passes all others and then another leads. One stand of colors, on our left, is particularly noticeable. The bearer is far ahead of his regiment and advances so rapidly that he draws the enemy's concentrated fire. Then another color-bearer dashes ahead of the line and falls. A comrade grasps the flag almost before it reaches the ground. He, too, falls. Then another picks it up, smeared with his comrade's blood, waves it defiantly, and, as if bearing a charmed life, he advances steadily towards the top. Up, up he goes, his hat pulled over his eyes, his head bent forward as if facing a storm of rain and wind. The bullets whistle about him, splintering the staff. Onward he goes, followed by the admiring cheers of his comrades, who press close behind.

As far advanced as any, Hazen's brigade struggles slowly upward. Willich's brigade on Hazen's left was somewhat in advance, but his left has met a resistance it cannot apparently overcome. On the right, Sheridan's left is considerably in the rear. This is the result of someone recalling it after it had advanced about one-fourth the way up the ridge, but before it had retreated very far the order was countermanded, and now it is forging to the front. The advance of Hazen's brigade is approaching the Rebel works. The enemy is sweeping the face of the hill with a rain of bullets, and his artillery fire crashes along the hillside from vantage-point on both flanks, killing and maiming with all the destruction of double shotted guns. The men push upward.

Colonel Langdon, who has held his place close to the colors of his consolidated battalion, has reached a sheltered place about twenty yards from the top. Halting the colors there until he had collected about 200 men, he ordered them to fix bayonets. It is hard to tell now whose command is the most advanced. All are losing men rapidly; but not a man lags. Turchin, away to the left, closes with the enemy. His advance has evidently been stopped. Colonel Langdon rises to his feet and is shot, but before he falls he gives the command, "Porward!" The men leap forward, fire into the faces of the enemy, and the colors of the 1st Ohio and 23d Kentucky, fifty minutes after the firing of the signal-guns are planted on the works, quickly followed by the entire brigade. Of the eight corporals composing the color guard of the consolidated battalion, all fell on the hillside, and of the two sergeants who started with the colors, one is dead and the other wounded. Willich's brigade, having overcome all resistance, is over the works and his troops with a portion of Hazen's are moving along the ridge to the left. Hazen personally directs his troops along the ridge to the right, two guns taken are turned upon the enemy on our right, and discharged by firing muskets over the vent until primers could be procured.

Hooker, all this time, has been closing in on the enemy's extreme left and rear. Thus attacked on the flank, with its center pierced, a panic pervades the enemy's line, and gives Sheridan, who has had one of the steepest and highest points to climb, his opportunity, of which he promptly takes advantage. At every point now the enemy's lines begin to melt away except near Bragg's headquarters, in front of Sheridan's center. Suddenly they too give up the fight, abandon their works, and roll down the eastern slope, followed by Sheridan's division. Now cheer upon cheer greets "Old Glory" as it dots the ridge at every point and waves in triumph in the bright rays of the western sun, and the campaign, begun by the Army of the Cumberland three months before, is ended.

The loss in Hazen's brigade was 530 killed and wounded, more than one-half the loss of the entire division. It captured, during this battle, about 400 prisoners, large quantities of small-arms, sixteen to eighteen pieces of artillery, and two stands of colors, and was the first to plant its colors on the ridge.

—Morgan, "Hazen's Brigade at
Missionary Ridge"

B. "Amid the Din of Battle 'Chickamauga' Could be Heard"

Chattanooga, Dec. 7,1863

Dear wife: . . . On Monday, Nov. 23rd our Division was ordered to move out just in front of the fortifications. We did so, and the rebels, as they looked down on us from Look out Mountain and Mission Ridge, no doubt thought we had come out for a review. But Sheridan's Division followed us out and formed in line with us. Wonder what the rebels thought then? "Oh, a Yankee review; we'll have some fun shelling them directly." But out came Wood's Division, then Cruft's Division, then Johnson's Division, then Howard's entire Corps of "Potomacs." "What can those Yankee fools mean," Bragg must have thought, as he sat at the door of his tent on Mission Ridge and watched the long lines of blue coats and glistening guns marching around in the valley be low him, almost within gun shot of his pickets, and yet not a gun fired. All was peace in Chattanooga valley that day.

The sun shone brightly, the bands played stirring airs; tattered banners that had waved on battle fields from the Potomac to the Mississippi streamed out gaily, as if proud of the battle scars they wore. Generals Grant and Hooker, and Sherman and Thomas and Logan and Reynolds and Sheridan and scores of others, with their staffs, galloped along the lines, and the scene that spread out around me like a vast panorama of war filled my heart with pride that

I was a soldier and member of that great army. But what did it all mean? Bragg, from his mountain eyrie, could see what we were doing just as well as Grant who was riding around amongst us. The rebels thought they had us hemmed in so that we dared not move, and so near starved that we could not move. Two o'clock came, and all was yet quiet and peaceful, gay as a holiday review; we could see crowds of rebels watching us from Mission Ridge and Lookout Mountain, but three o'clock came, and a solitary shot away over on our left, among Wood's men, made every fellow think: "Hark"! A few moments and another shot, then a rat-tat-tat-tat made almost every one remark: "Skirmishing going on over there." Wood's line moved forward, a few volleys, still Wood's line moved forward, and Sheridan's started forward, heavy work for a few minutes then all was quiet; two important hills were gained; cheer after cheer rang out in the valley and echoed and reverberated through the gorges of Lookout and Mission Ridge; still it was only S o'clock Monday afternoon. The bands commenced playing and the valley was again peaceful, but we all knew there was "something up," and Bragg must have thought so too. We lay there all night, sleeping on our arms.

Tuesday morning, Nov. 24th, broke bright and beautiful; the sun rose clear; but for whom was it a "sun of Austerlitz"? Grant or Bragg? We talked of Austerlitz and Waterloo at headquarters that morning. During the night the moon was almost totally eclipsed. We talked of that also. It was considered a bad omen among the ancients, on the eve of battle; we concluded also that it was ominous of defeat, but not for us; we concluded that it meant Bragg because he was perched on the mountain top, nearest the moon. Daylight revealed the hills which Wood and Sheridan had won the day before, bristling with cannon of sufficient calibre to reach Bragg's eyrie on Mission Ridge. About 9 o'clock in the morning some 30 heavy guns opened on Mission Ridge. It appeared then that we were to advance right down the valley and attack the rebel centre, but, hark! Away off on our right—3 miles away, on the opposite side of Lookout—we hear firing. What can that mean? Suddenly the cannon, with which we have been pounding away at Mission Ridge, are silent, and all eyes are turned westward toward Lookout Mountain. The sounds of battle increase there but it is on the other side of the mountain from us and we can see nothing, but the word passes around: "Hooker is storming Lookout"! My heart grows faint. Poor Hooker, with his Potomac boys arc to be the forlorn hope! What? Storm that mountain peak 2400 feet high, so steep that a squirrel could scarcely climb it, and bristling all over with rebels, bayonets and cannon? Poor boys! far from your quiet New England homes, you have come a long way only to meet defeat or that mountain peak, and find your graves on its rugged sides! Lookout Mountain will only hereafter be known as a monument to a whole Corps of gallant New Englanders who died there for their country! But hold! Some one exclaims: "The firing comes nearer, our boys are getting up"! All eyes are turned toward the Mountain, and the stillness of death reigns among us in the valley, as we listen to the sounds of battle on the other side of the Mountain while all was quiet as a Puritan sabbath on our side of it. How hope and despair alternated in our breasts! How we prayed for their success and longed to assist them, can only be known by those of us who. ill that valley, stood watching that afternoon and listening to the swelling diapason of their battle. But the firing actually did grow nearer, manifestly our men were driving them; Oh! now if they only can continue it, but we fear they cannot! I have a long telescope with which I can distinctly see everything on our side of the mountain. I scan the mountain with it closely and continuously, but not a soul can I see. After hours of anxious suspense I see a single rebel winding his way back from the firing and around to our side of the mountain.

I announce to the crowd of Generals standing around: "There goes a straggler"! and in an instant everybody's glass is to his eye, but no more stragglers are seen, still the battle rages, and the little gleam of hope, that solitary straggler raised in our breasts, dies out. Minutes drag like hours, the suspense is awful, but look! look! Here comes a crowd of stragglers! here they come by hundreds, yes by thou-

sands! The mountain is covered with them! They are broken, running! There comes our flag around the point of the mountain! There comes one of our regiments on the double quick! Oh! such a cheer as then went up in the valley! Manly cheeks were wet with tears of joy, our bands played "Hail to the Chief," and 50 brazen throated cannon, in the very wanton ness of joy, thundered out from the fortifications of Chattanooga, a salute to the old flag which was then on the mountain top. The work was done. Lookout was ours, never again to be used as a perch by rebel vultures. Didn't we of the old Army of the Cumberland feel proud though? It was one of the regiments that fought at Chickamauga that carried that first flag to the mountain top. It was a brigade of the old Chickamauga army that led the storming party up the mountain. A straggling skirmish fire was kept up along our (the Eastern) side of the mountain, which we could trace by the flashes of the guns, until 11 o'clock at night, but then all became quiet, and again we passed the night in line of battle, sleeping on our arms.

Bragg, no doubt, thought Hooker would continue to press forward across the valley from Lookout and attack his left on Mission Ridge in the morning, so he prepared for that during the night, by moving troops from his right to his left, to meet the anticipated attack of the morning, but Sherman, with his Vicksburg veterans, had all this time been lying concealed behind the hills on the North side of the Tennessee river, just North of the northern end of Mission Ridge, where Bragg's right was, awaiting the proper moment to commence his part of the stupendous plan. The time was now come.

Lookout was ours; now for Mission Ridge! Before daylight of Wednesday Nov. 25th, Sherman had his pontoons across the river, about 3 miles north of Chattanooga, and under cover of a dense fog, crossed his whole Corps and took possession of the northern extremity of Mission Ridge, finding nothing there but a few pickets, and there he fell to work fortifying. By this time Bragg saw his mistake. The attack of Wednesday was to be on his right, at the North end of Mission Ridge, instead of his left at the South end of the Ridge, so he hurriedly countermarched his troops back from his left to his right. When the fog rose, about ten o'clock in the morning, Sherman attempted to carry the summit of the Ridge but was repulsed; again he tried it but was again re pulsed, still again he tried it and was repulsed. This time the fighting was all to the left of where we were instead of to the right, as it had been the day before. Sherman, after terrible fighting, had been repulsed in three successive efforts to crush the enemy's right on the top of the Ridge, and an order came for our Division to move up the river to his support. We started. The enemy could see us from the top of the Ridge, and quickly understood (or thought they did) our design, so they commenced shelling us, as our long line of 20 regiments filed along, but we moved along until we came to where a thin strip of woodland intervened between us and the Ridge. Sheridan's Division followed us and did the same. The enemy supposed of course that we were moving on up the river to the support of Sherman, but we were not; we halted and formed line of battle in that strip of woodland, facing Mission Ridge.

This, I confess, staggered me; I couldn't understand it; it looked as though we were going to assault the Ridge, and try to carry it by storm, lined and ribbed as it was with rifle pits, and its topmost verge crowded with rebel lines, and at least 40 cannon in our immediate front frowning down on us; we never could live a moment in the open spaces of 600 yards between the strip of woods in which we were formed, and the line of rifle pits at the base of the mountain, exposed as we would be to the fire of the 40 cannon massed, and from five to eight hundred feet immediately above us, also to the infantry fire from the rifle pits. I rode down along the line of our Division, and there I found Woods Division formed on our right and facing the Ridge just as we were; I rode on and came to Sheridan's Division formed on Woods right and facing the same. Here was a line of veteran troops nearly two miles long, all facing Mission Ridge, and out of sight of the enemy. The purpose at once became plain to me, and I hurried back to my own Division, and on asking Gen. he replied: "When 6 guns are fired in quick succession from Fort Wood, the line advances to storm the heights and carry the Ridge if possible. Take that order to Col.——" (commanding the third brigade of our Division) "and tell him to move forward rapidly when he hears the signal." I communicated the order at once and that was the last I saw of the brigade commander, for he was killed just as he reached the summit of the Ridge.

A few moments elapse, it is about half past three o'clock P.M. , when suddenly, 6 guns are rapidly fired from Fort Wood. "Forward"! rings out along that long line of men, and for ward they go, through the strip of woods, we reach the open space, say 600 yards, between the edge of the woods and the rifle pits at the foot of the Ridge. "Charge"! is shouted wildly from hundreds of throats, and with a yell such as that valley never heard before, the three Divisions (60 regiments) rushed forward; the rebels are silent a moment, but then the batteries on top of the Ridge, open all at once, and the very heavens above us seemed to be rent asunder; shells go screaming over our heads, bursting above and behind us, but they hurt no body and the men don't notice them; about midway of the open space a shell bursts directly over my head, and so near as to make my horse frantic and almost unmanageable; he plunges and bursts breast strap and girth and off I tumble with the saddle between my legs. My orderly catches my horse at once, throws the blanket and saddle on him, gives me a "leg lift" and I am mounted again, without girth, but I hold on with my knees and catch up with our madcaps at the first rifle pits, over these we go to the second line of pits, over these we go, some of the rebels lying down to be run over, others scrambling up the hill which is becoming too steep for horses, and the General and staff are forced to aban don the direct ascent at about the second line of rifle pits; the long line of men reach the steepest part of the mountain, and they must crawl up the best way they can 150 feet more before they reach the summit, and when they do reach it, can they hold it? The rebels are there in thousands, behind breastworks, ready to hurl our brave boys back as they reach their works.

One flag bearer, on hands and knees, is seen away in advance of the whole line; he crawls and climbs toward a rebel flag he sees waving above him, he gets within a few feet of it and hides behind a fallen log while he waves his flag defiantly until it almost touches the rebel flag; his regiment follows him as fast as it can; in a few moments another flag bearer gets just as near the summit at another point, and his regiment soon gets to him, but these two regiments dare not go the next twenty feet or they would be annihilated, so they crouch there and are safe from the rebels above them, who would have to rise up, to fire down at them, and so expose themselves to the fire of our fellows who are climbing up the mountain.

The suspense is greater, if possible, than that with which we viewed the storming of Lookout. If we can gain that Ridge; if we can scale those breastworks, the rebel army is routed, everything is lost for them, but if we cannot scale the works few of us will get down this mountain side and back to the shelter of the woods. But a third flag and regiment reaches the other two; all eyes are turned there; the men away above us look like great ants crawling up, crouching on the outside of the rebel breastworks. One of our flags seems to be moving; look! look! look! Up! Up! Up! it goes and is planted on the rebel works; in a twinkling the crouching soldiers are up and over the works; apparently quicker than I can write it the 3 flags and 3 regiments are up, the close fighting is terrific; other flags go up and over at different points along the mountain top—the batteries have ceased, for friend and foe are mixed in a surging mass; in a few moments the flags of 60 Yankee regiments float along Mission Ridge from one end to the other, the enemy are plunging down the Eastern slope of the Ridge and our men in hot pursuit, but darkness comes too soon and the pursuit must cease; we go back to the summit of the Ridge and there behold our trophies—dead and wounded rebels under our feet by hundreds, cannon by scores scattered up and down the Ridge with yelling soldiers astraddle them, rebel flags lying around in profusion, and soldiers and officers completely and frantic ally drunk

with excitement. Four hours more of daylight, after we gained that Ridge would not have left two whole pieces of Bragg's army together.

Our men, stirred by the same memories, shouted "Chickamauga"! as they scaled the works at the summit, and amid the din of battle the cry "Chickamauga"! "Chickamauga"! could be heard. That is not *fancy* it is *fact*. Indeed the plain unvarnished facts of the storming of Mission Ridge are more like romance to me now than any I have ever read in Dumas, Scott or Cooper. On that night I lay down upon the ground without blankets and slept soundly, without inquiring whether my neighbors were dead or alive, but, on waking found I was sleeping among bunches of dead rebels and Federals, and within a few rods of where Bragg slept the night before, if he slept at all.

—"Major Connolly's Letters to His Wife"

XXVIII.6

"THE DISASTER ADMITS OF NO PALLIATION"

Poor Braxton Bragg! He had come out of the Mexican War with a great reputation, he had won Jefferson Davis' admiration and confidence, as early as February 1861 he had been commissioned brigadier general in the new Confederate Army. But he was sti•-necked, arrogant, and quarrelsome, unpopular alike with officers and with rank and file. Victories might have made these traits bearable, but Bragg could not win victories or—if he did, as at Chickamauga—could not exploit them. After Chattanooga he asked to be relieved of his command; Davis brought him back to Richmond as military advisor.

Headquarters Army of Tennessee
Dalton, Ga., December 1, 1863

His Excellency, JEFFERSON DAVIS,
President Confederate States, Richmond:

Mr. President: I send by Lieutenant Colonel Urquhart a plain, unvarnished report of the operations at Chattanooga, resulting in my shameful discomfiture. The disaster admits of no palliation, and is justly disparaging to me as a commander. I trust, however, you may find upon full investigation that the fault is not entirely mine. Colonel Urquhart will inform you on any point not fully explained in the report. I fear we both erred in the conclusion for me to retain command here after the clamor raised against me. The warfare has been carried on successfully, and the fruits are bitter. You must make other changes here, or our success is hopeless. Breckinridge was totally unfit for any duty from the 23rd to the 27th—during all our trials—from drunkenness. The same cause prevented our complete triumph at Murfreesborough. I can bear to be sacrificed myself, but not to see my country and my friends ruined by the vices of a few profligate men who happen to have an undue popularity. General Hardee will assure you that Cheatham is equally dangerous.

May I hope, as a personal favor, that you will allow my friend Colonel Urquhart to continue with me as a part of my personal staff? He has never acted in any other capacity, and is almost a necessity in enabling me to bring up my records. I shall ever be ready to do all in my power for our common cause, but feel that some little rest will render me more efficient than I am now.

Most respectfully and truly, yours,
Braxton Bragg,
General, &c.

—*War of the Rebellion. . . Official Records*

XXVIII.7

BURNSIDE HOLDS OUT AT KNOXVILLE

Everywhere in the West that fall and winter of 1863 saw Confederate fortunes wane. While Rosecrans was organizing his army for the Tullahoma campaign, Burnside led the Army of the Ohio into East Tennessee. The purpose of his campaign was both military and political: to cut the railroad connection between Tennessee and Virginia, and to rescue the loyal Unionists of the mountainous region of eastern Tennessee. Bragg promptly sent a corps, under General Buckner, to contest this area with him, and later sent re inforcements under Longstreet. Burnside withdrew into the fortifications of Knoxville and there awaited attack.

Whet happened is here told by Major Burrage of the 35th Massachusetts Volunteers. Henry S. Burrage was a student at the Newton Theological Seminary when the war broke out. He enlisted as a private and rose to a majority; he fought in Tennessee, was wounded at Cold Harbor, and captured at Petersburg. After the war he had a long and distinguished career as clergyrnan and historian.

On November 13, Burnside received information that Long street had reached the Tennessee River at Hough's Ferry, a few miles below Loudon; and at once informing General Grant, he advised a concentration of his forces in East Tennessee for the purpose of giving battle, but expressed the opinion that the concentration should be neither in the neighborhood of Loudon nor at Kingston, but at Knoxville; thus drawing the enemy further away from Bragg, so far in fact that in case Bragg should order Longstreet to return because his assistance was needed at Chattanooga, he could not be recalled in season to render it. To this General Grant made reply: "It is of the most vital importance that East Tennessee should be held. Take immediate steps to that end. Evacuate Kingston if you think best."

Thrown thus upon his own resources, General Burnside's plan plainly was this—to draw Longstreet up the valley, checking his advance as much as possible and making Knoxville as secure as the circumstances would admit, until Grant, having grappled with Bragg at Chattanooga, should be able to send reenforcements compelling Longstreet to with draw. . . .

At the time of the arrival of the troops on the morning of November 17, Knoxville was by no means in a defensible condition. The bastion-work occupied by Benjamin's and Buckley's batteries was not only unfinished, but was little more than begun. It required the labor of two hundred Negroes four hours to clear a place for the guns. There was also a fort in process of construction on Temperarice Hill. But the work all along the line was now hurried forward with eagerness and even enthusiasm. As fast as the troops were placed in position, they commenced the construction of rifle pits in their front, but with only a meagre supply of either spades or shovels. Though wearied by three days of marching and fighting, the troops gave themselves to the work with the energy of fresh men. As helpers, both citizens and contra bands were pressed into the service. Many of the former were loyal to the Union cause and devoted themselves to their tasks with a zeal that evinced the interest they felt in making good the defence of the town; but some of them were bitter rebels, and, as Captain Poe well remarked, "worked with a very poor grace, which blistered hands did not tend to improve." The contrabands engaged in the work with that heartiness which throughout the war characterized their labors for the Union cause. . . .

Longstreet did not leave Campbell's Station until the morning of November 17. McLaws' division led the column, and reached the vicinity of Knoxville about noon. General Burn side had ordered General Shackelford-to dismount his cavalry command under General Sanders and take position on the Kingston Road a mile or more in front of the Union line of defence on that side of Knoxville. This he did, and during the forenoon of the 17th General Sanders strengthened his position in all possible ways, so that when McLaws approached, he found Sanders' little force blocking his further progress. "Part of our line," says Longstreet, "drove up in fine style and was measurably successful, but other parts, smarting under the stiff musket-fire, hesitated and lay down under such slight shelter as they could find, but close under fire,—so close that to remain inactive would endanger repulse." With such stubbornness did General Sanders contest the approach of McLaws that the latter was compelled at length to bring up his artillery; and only by the combined assault of infantry and artillery was Sanders dislodged from his position. After his men fell back, the enemy pressed forward and established lines within rifle range of our own. McLaws' division formed the Confederate right, his right extending to the river. When Jenkins came up late in the afternoon, he continued the line from McLaws' left and extending to the Tazewell Road; while Hart's and Wheeler's cavalry continued the Confederate line to the Holston River. . . .

Meanwhile Burnside's men were devoting themselves with all diligence to the labor of strengthening and completing their works around the town. For the most part, in campaigns hitherto, they had been the attacking party. So it had been at Fredericksburg, where the Ninth Corps had last faced Longstreet. Here, they were behind defensive works, and it was evident that they regarded the more advantageous position with contentment and even satisfaction. When the main line had been made reasonably secure, the usual devices in the way of obstruction received attention, such as the construction of abatis, chevaux-de-frise, to which were added wire entanglements extending from the stumps of trees, especially in front of Fort Sanders. Along a portion of the line another obstacle was formed by erecting dams on First and Second creeks, and throwing back the water. The whole constituted a series of obstructions which could not be passed in the face of a heavy fire without great difficulty and a fearful loss of life. On November 21, General Burnside telegraphed to General Grant: "We have a reasonable supply of ammunition, and the command is in good spirits. The officers and men have been indefatigable in their labors to make this place impregnable."

But the question of food-supplies was a serious one. When the siege commenced, there was in the commissary department at Knoxville little more than a day's ration for the whole of Burnside's force. Should the enemy gain possession of the south bank of the Holston, the means of subsistence for the troops at Knoxville would be cut off. Thus far Long street's attempts to close this part of East Tennessee to the Union forces had failed, and the whole country from the French Board to the Holston was open to our foraging parties. . . .

At length, foiled in these attempts to seize the south bank of the Holston, Longstreet commenced the construction of a raft at Boyd's Ferry, about six miles above Knoxville. Float ing this down the swift current of the river, he hoped to carry away Burnside's pontoon-bridge and thus break his communication with the country from which he was obtaining his subsistence supplies. To thwart this plan, Captain Poe commenced the construction of a boom one thousand feet in length, composed of 'iron bars borne up by wooden floats. This was stretched across the river above the bridge. After wards a boom of logs, fastened end to end by chains, was constructed further up the river. This boom was fifteen hundred feet in length. . . .

November 23, in the evening, there was a Confederate attack on the Union pickets in front of the left of the Second Division, Ninth Corps. In falling back, the pickets fired the buildings on the abandoned ground to prevent their use by the enemy's sharpshooters. Among the buildings destroyed were the arsenal and the machine-shops near the railway station. The light of the blazing buildings illuminated the town. On the following day, November 24, the Twenty-first Massachusetts and Forty-eighth Pennsylvania, under the command of Lieutenant-Colonel Hawkes of the Twenty-first, charging the Confederate line at this point, drove it back and reoccupied the abandoned position. Early in the morning of the same day also, an attack was made by the Second Michigan—numbering one hundred and ninety-seven men—on the advanced parallel which the enemy had so constructed as to envelop the northwest bastion of Fort Sanders. The works were gallantly carried, but before the supporting columns could come up, the men of the Second Michigan were repulsed by Confederate reenforcements. The Union loss, amounting to sixty-seven, included Major Byington, commanding the Second Michigan, who was left on the field mortally wounded. In anticipation of an attack that night at some point on the Union intrenchments, orders were issued that neither offlcers nor men, on either the outer or inner lines, should sleep. . . .

November 27 all was quiet along the lines until evening, when cheers and the strains of band-music enlivened the enemy's camps. Had reenforcements arrived, or had Grant met with reverses at Chattanooga? . . . Colonel Giltner, with his cavalry from Virginia, had reported, the first of approaching additions to Longstreet's command. As yet no word had come from Bragg to Longstreet, though there were rumors that a battle had been fought at Chattanooga. The brigades of Johnson were not yet up, and the artillery and infantry coming from Virginia were a five or six days' march away; but

General Leadbetter was impatient, and an order was given by Longstreet for an assault on Fort Sanders on November 28. The weather on that day, however, proved unfavorable.

Within the Union lines it was believed that the crisis of the siege was approaching. . . . On the night of the 27th, on our left we could hear chopping across the Holston on the knob which a few days before, as Longstreet tells us, had been selected as commanding the fort and the line from the fort to the river. His men were now clearing away the trees in front of the earthwork they had constructed at that point. Would they attack at daybreak? So we thought, connecting the chopping sounds with the sound of cheering and of music in the earlier part of the night; but the morning opened as quietly as any of its predecessors. Late in the afternoon the enemy seemed to be placing troops in position in front of our lines covering Fort Sanders; and our men stood in the trenches awaiting an attack. The day passed, however, with out further demonstrations.

The regiment with which I was connected was in the line between Fort Sanders and the river, and opposite the Powell house. About eleven o'clock in the evening there was a sound of heavy musketry on our right. It was a dark, cloudy night; and at the distance of only a few feet it was impossible to distinguish any object. The firing soon ceased, with the exception of an occasional shot on the picket-line. An attack had evidently been made at some point, but precisely where, or with what success, was as yet unknown. Reports soon came in. The enemy first had driven in the pickets in front of Fort Sanders, and then had attacked our line still further to the left, which also was obliged to fall back. Later we learned that the enemy had advanced along the whole line and established themselves as near as possible to our works.

It was now evident that Longstreet intended to make an attack at some point in our intrenched position. But where7 All the remainder of that long, cold night—our men were without overcoats largely—we stood in the trenches pondering that question. Might not this demonstration in front of Fort Sanders be only a feint designed to draw our attention from other parts of the line where the principal blow was to be struck? So some thought. Gradually the night wore away.

In the morning, a little after six o'clock, but while it was still dark, the enemy opened a furious fire of artillery. This was directed mostly against Fort Sanders; but several shells struck the Powell house in rear of Battery Noble. Roemer immediately responded from College Hill, but Benjamin and Buckley in Fort Sanders reserved their fire. In about twenty minutes the enemy's fire slackened, and in its place rose the well-known rebel yell in front of the fort. Then followed the rattle of musketry, the roar of cannon, and the bursting of shells. The yells died away, and then rose again. Now the roar of musketry and artillery was redoubled. It was a moment of the deepest anxiety along our brigade front and to the right of the fort. Our straining eyes were fixed upon the latter's dim outlines. The enemy had reached the ditch and were now endeavoring to scale the parapet. Whose will be the victory—oh whose? The yells again died away, and then followed three loud Union cheers from our men in the fort—"Hurrah! hurrah! hurrah!" How those cheers thrilled as we stood almost breathless in the trenches! They told us in language that could not be misunderstood that Longstreet had been repulsed and that the victory was ours. Peering through the morning mist toward the fort only a short distance away—a glorious sight—we saw that our flag was still there! . . .

The assault was made by three of McLaws' brigades,—Wofford's, Humphreys', and Bryan's,—with h'is fourth bri gade in reserve. . . . In support were the two brigades of Buckner's division commanded by General B. R. Johnson,—they had arrived the day before,—and General Jenkins was ordered to advance his three bAgades in echelon on the left of McLaws. The brigades were formed for attack in columns of regiments, and were directed to move with fixed bayonets and without firing.

When the artillery fire slackened on that cold gray morning the order for the charge was given.

The salient of the northwest bastion of Fort Sanders was the point of attack. McLaws' columns were much broken in passing the abatis. But the wire entanglements proved a greater obstacle. Whole companies were prostrated. Benjamin now opened his triple shotted guns. Nevertheless the weight of the attacking force carried the men forward, and in about two minutes from the time the charge was commenced they had reached the ditch around the fort, and were endeavoring to scale the parapet. The guns, which had been trained to sweep the ditch, now opened a most destructive fire. Lieutenant Benjamin also took shells in his hands and lighting the fuse tossed them over the parapet into the crowded ditch "It stilled them down," he said.

One of the Confederate reserve brigades, with added yells, now came up in support, and in the crowded ditch the slaughter was renewed. With desperate valor some of the men in the ditch endeavored to scale the parapet and even planted their flags upon it, but were swept off by the muskets of the Seventy-ninth New York (Highlanders) and of the Twenty-ninth Massachusetts. At length, satisfied of the hopelessness of their task, the survivors in the ditch surrendered. They represented eleven regiments and numbered nearly three hundred. Among them were seventeen commissioned officers. Over two hundred dead and wounded, including three colonels, lay in the ditch alone. . . . Our loss in the fort was eight men killed and five wounded, a total of thirteen.

To us of the Ninth Corps, as well as to Longstreet's men, this assault on Fort Sanders was Fredericksburg reversed. There, we were the attacking party. Now, we were behind a fortified line with artillery well placed, and we had an object lesson as to the great advantage one has in a good position, strongly defended, over one who is in the attacking force. . . . .

Never was a victory more complete and achieved at so slight a cost.

—Burrage, "Burnside's East Tennessee Campaign"

XXIX

ATLANTA AND THE MARCH TO THE SEA

With Chattanooga in Federal hands and the Confederates in retreat, the way was open to the east, and to the inauguration of that giant pincers movement that in the end strangled the Confederacy. The Mississippi was under Federal control; in all the vast area between that river and the Appalachians only Alabama and part of Mississippi was still held by the Confederates. What Grant—now general of all the Union armies planned for the spring of 1864 was a knockout blow: Meade to strike southward toward Richmond, Butler to move up from the James River, Sigel to advance from western Virginia, Sherman to capture Atlanta and "get into the interior of the enemy's country . . . inflicting all the damage you can against their war resources."

Sherman's march from Atlanta to the sea is probably the best known of all Civil War campaigns—and it scarcely rose to the dignity of a campaign. It was more nearly a glorified picnic, for Hardee, who took over the scattered forces left in Georgia, was unable to offer any effective opposition. But the campaign from Chattanooga to Atlanta was a different matter. It is just 100 miles between these two cities, a rugged mountainous country, crisscrossed by rivers and valleys—poor country in which to subsist a large army. And confronting Sherman was now Joseph E. Johnston, one of the most resourceful of all Confederate commanders, and a master of Fabian tactics.

After the debacle at Chattanooga Bragg had withdrawn to Dalton. There he was supplanted by Johnston, who r organized the stricken army, brought its strength up to about 60,000, and infused it with a new fighting spirit. Sherman, placed in command of the Grand Army of the West by Grant, reorganized his forces into three unequal armies, commanded by Thomas, Schofield, and McPherson. There was plenty of time for this reorganization: winter had set in, the roads were churned into mud, and not until April was Sherman ready to resume the offensive.

His advance was co-ordinated with Grant's offensive in the Wilderness, and jumped off on May 7. From Dalton to Atlanta is about 85 miles. It took Sherman two months to make that distance, and another two months to take Atlanta. If this seems like a long time it should be remembered that Grant enjoyed greater numerical superiority than Sherman, fought in less difficult country and closer to his bases, and found himself at the end of four months as far from Richmond as ever.

All the way from Dalton to Atlanta it was parry and thrust. Johnston would get astride the railroad, or a valley; Sherman would slide around his flank; threatened from the rear, Johnston would retire. Twice Sherman brought Johnston to battle, but both times on Johnston's terms, and both times was repulsed. Johnston was no Lee but he was the best retreater in either army. In the end the government, and public opinion, took alarm. Was Johnston going to give up Atlanta without a fight? So Davis feared, Davis who had never fully trusted him. Finally Johnston was removed from command and General Hood put in his place. A superb fighter, never happy except in battle, bearing his stump of a leg like a badge of honor, Hood was as impetuous as he was brave. He was expected to take the offensive, and he did. The results were disastrous. On September 1 Hood evacuated Atlanta. It was the first great Union victory of the year, and one that had important effects on the election that November.

What next? Where was Sherman to go? His communications were now stretched to the breaking point; Wheeler and Forrest operated in his rear. What he did was to get Grant's consent to abandon his communications and advance eastward into the heart of Georgia.

But meantime what of Hood? That general was no longer strong enough to oppose Sherman's mighty army. He decided, instead, to move westward and thus force Sherman either to return or lose Tennessee. His mind was bemused with even more ambitious plans. If Sherman marched eastward he would swing into Tennessee, reconquer Kentucky, and advance to the rescue of Lee!

But the day for all that was past. Sherman dispatched Thomas and Schofield back to Tennessee with forces which eventually, aggregated about 50,000. And in due course of time, as we shall see, Thomas took care of Hood.

Meantime Sherman was marching to the sea. Never was such a march! If to Sherman's soldiers it was a picnic, to the Negroes it was the "day of Jubilo." But to the South it was such devastation and ruin as had never before been known in American warfare. Sherman cut through Georgia like a giant scythe, leaving a swath of ruined towns and plantations and railroads and bridges 60 miles wide. On December 10 he reached Savannah. He captured the city; swung north through South Carolina; burned Columbia; and continued on to the end.

XXIX. I

GENERAL SHERMAN TAKES COMMAND

When Grant went to Washington to assume command of all the Union armies, he appointed Sherman to the command of the armies in the West. Though something was to be said for appointing Thomas to this position, Sherman's claims were strong. It was not only that he had had a long and brilliant military career, but that, however unlike in character and temperament, he and Grant understood each other perfectly and worked together like a well-trained team. Indeed the great strategic plan for the destruction of the Confederacy, elaborated in the spring of 1864, was in all probability as much Sherman's as Grant's. After the war Sherman succeeded to Grant's position as commanding general of an the armies of the United States.

John Chipman Gray, who gives us here a perspicacious picture of General Sherman, was barely out of the Harvard Law School when he was commissioned lieutenant in the 41st Massachusetts Volunteers. He served in the Peninsular campaign, and was then appointed judge advocate with the rank of major. He was later Story Professor of Law at the Harvard Law School and a lifelong student of the Civil War.

General Sherman is the most American looking man I ever saw, tall and lank, not very erect, with hair like a thatch, which he rubs up with his hands, a rusty beard trimmed close, a wrinkled face, sharp, prominent red nose, small, bright eyes, coarse red hands; black felt hat slouched over the eyes (he says when he wears anything else the soldiers cry out, as he rides along, "Hallo, the old man has got a new hat"), dirty dickey with the points wilted down, black, old-fashioned stock, brown field officer's coat with high collar and no shoulder-straps, muddy trowsers and one spur. He carries his hands in his pockets, is very awkward in his gait and motion, talks continually and with immense rapidity, and might sit to *Punch* for the portrait of an ideal Yankee. He was of course in the highest spirits and talked with an openness which was too natural not to be something more than apparent. In striving to recall his talk, I find it impossible to recall his language or indeed what he talked about, indeed it would be easier to say what he did not talk about than what he did. I never passed a more amusing or instructive day, but at his departure I felt it a relief and experienced almost an exhaustion after the excitement of his vigorous presence.

He has Savannah securely invested, his left rests securely on the Savannah River, his right at Fort McAllister, his line is within the 3 mile post from the city; he intends to throw a division across the Savannah to prevent the escape of Hardie [sic] from the city, and says he shall take his own time about reducing the city, unless he is hurried by despatches from General Grant; he has 60,000 men with him and only wishes there were more men in Savannah; he says the city is his sure game and stretches out his arm and claws his bony fingers in the air to illustrate how he has his grip on it. There is a "whip the creation" and an almost boastful confidence in himself which in an untried man would be very disgusting, but in him is intensely comic. I wish you could see him, he is a man after your own heart, like Grant he smokes constantly, and producing 6 cigars from his pocket said they were his daily allowance, but judging at the rate he travelled through them while he was on our boat, he must often exceed it. He scouted the idea of his going on ships and said he would rather march to Richmond than go there by water; he said he expected to turn North toward the latter end of December, at the same time the sun did, and that if he went through South Carolina, as he in all probability should, that his march through that state would be one of the most horrible things in the history of the world, that the devil himself could not restrain his men in that state; and I do not think that he (that is Sherman, not the devil) would try to restrain them much. He evidently purposes to make the South feel the horrors of war as much as he legitimately can, and if the men trespass beyond the strict limits of his orders he does not inquire into their cases too curiously. He told with evident delight how on his march he could look 40 miles in each direction and see the smoke rolling up as from one great bonfire.

—Letter of JOHN CHIPMAN GRAY to John Ropes, December 14, 1864

XXIX.2

SHERMAN MARCHES FROM CHATTANOOGA TO ATLANTA

We begin our account of the Atlanta campaign with a general survey by its chief architect, then turn to some of its more striking episodes. There is no better account of the first phase of the campaign than that by Sherman himself. Different as Sherman was from Grant, his *Memoirs* have much the same qualities as those of Grant—simplicity, lucidity, and objectivity. Sherman is concerned to make clear, here, that the campaign for Atlanta was a very tough affair. He was fighting in difficult terrain, with long lines of communications, and against an able and resourceful opponent.

I now turn with a feeling of extreme delicacy to the conduct of that other campaign from Chattanooga to Atlanta, Savannah, and Raleigh, which with liberal discretion was committed to me by General Grant in his minute instructions of April 4th and April l9th, 1864. To all military students these letters must be familiar, because they have been published again and again, and there never was and never can be raised a question of rivalry or claim between us as to the relative merits of the manner in which we played our respective parts. We were as brothers—I the older man in years, he the higher in rank. We both believed in our heart of hearts that the success of the Union cause was not only

necessary to the then generation of Americans, but to all future generations. We both professed to be gentlemen and professional soldiers, educated in the science of war by our generous Government for the very occasion which had arisen. Neither of us by nature was a combative-man; but with honest hearts and a clear purpose to do what man could we embarked on that campaign, which I believe, in its strategy, in its logistics, in its grand and minor tactics, has added new luster to the old science of war. Both of us had at our front generals to whom in early life we had been taught to look up,—educated and experienced soldiers like ourselves, not likely to make any mistakes, and each of whom had as strong an army as could be collected from the mass of the Southern people,—of the same blood as ourselves, brave, confident, and well equipped; in addition to which they had the most decided advantage of operating in their own difficult country of mountain, forest, ravine, and river, affording admirable opportunities for defense, besides the other equally important advantage that we had to invade the country of our unqualified enemy and expose our long lines of supply to the guerrillas of an "exasperated people." Again, as we advanced we had to leave guards to bridges, stations, and intermediate depots, diminishing the fighting force, while our enemy gained strength by picking up his detachments as he fell back, and had railroads to bring supplies and reenforcements from his rear. I instance these facts to offset the common assertion that we of the North won the war by brute force, and not by courage and skill.

On the historic 4th day of May, 1864, the Confederate army at my front lay at Dalton, Georgia, composed, according to the best authority, of about 45,000 men, commanded by Joseph E. Johnston, who was equal in all the elements of generalship to Lee, and who was under instructions from the war powers in Richmond to assume the offensive-north ward as far as Nashville. But he soon discovered that he would have to conduct a defensive campaign. Coincident with the movement of the Army of the Potomac, as announced by telegraph, I advanced from our base at

Chattanooga with the Army of the Ohio, 13,559 men; the Army of the Cumberland, 60,773, and the Army of the Tennessee, 24,465—grand total, 98,797 men and 254 guns.

I had no purpose to attack Johnston's position at Dalton in front, but marched from Chattanooga to feign at his front and to make a lodgment in Resaca, eighteen miles to his rear, on "his line of communication and supply." The movement was partly, not wholly, successful but it compelled Johnston to let go Dalton and fight us at Resaca where, May 13th 16th, our loss was 2747 and his 2800. I fought offensively and defensively, aided by earth parapets. He then fell back to Calhoun, Adairsville, and Cassville, where he halted for the battle of the campaign; but, for reasons given in his memoirs, he continued his retreat behind the next spur of mountains to Allatoona.

Pausing for a few days to repair the railroad without at tempting Allatoona, of which I had personal knowledge acquired in 1844, I resolved to push on toward Atlanta by way of Dallas; Johnston quickly detected this, and forced me to fight him, May 25th-28th, at New Hope Church, four miles north of Dallas, with losses of 3000 to the Confederates and 2400 to us. The country was almost in a state of nature—with few or no roads, nothing that a European could understand; yet the bullet killed its victim there as surely as at Sevastopol.

Johnston had meantime picked up his detachments, and had received reenforcements from his rear which raised his aggregate strength to 62,000 men, and warranted him in claiming that he was purposely drawing us far from our base, and that when the right moment should come he would turn on us and destroy us. We were equally confident, and not the least alarmed. He then fell back to his position at Marietta, with Brush Mountain on his right, Kenesaw his center, and Lost Mountain his left. His line of ten miles was too long for his numbers, and he soon let go his flanks and concentrated on Kenesaw. We closed down in battle array, repaired the railroad up to our very camps, and then prepared for the contest. Not a day, not an

hour, not a minute was there a cessation of fire. Our skirmishers were in absolute contact, the lines of battle and the batteries but little in rear of the skirmishers; and thus matters continued until June 27th, when I ordered a general assault, with the full cooperation of my great lieutenants, Thomas, McPherson, and Schofield, as good and true men as ever lived or died for their country's cause; but we failed, losing 3000 men, to the Confederate loss of 630. Still, the result was that within three days Johnston abandoned the strongest possible position and was in full retreat for the Chattahoochee River. We were on his heels; skirmished with his rear at Smyrna Church on the 4th day of July, and saw him fairly across the Chattahoochee on the 10th, covered and protected by the best line of field intrenchments I have ever seen, prepared long in advance. No officer or soldier who ever served under me will question the generalship of Joseph E. Johnston. His retreats were timely, in good order, and he left nothing behind. We had advanced into the enemy's country 120 miles, with a single track railroad, which had to bring clothing, food, ammunition, everything requisite for 100,000 men and 23,000 animals. The city of Atlanta, the gate city opening the interior of the important State of Georgia, was in sight; its protecting army was shaken but not defeated, and onward we had to go,—illustrating the principle that "an army once on the offensive must maintain the offensive."

We feigned to the right, but crossed the Chattahoochee by the left, and soon confronted our enemy behind his first line of intrenchments at Peach Tree Creek, prepared in advance for this very occasion. At this critical moment the Confederate Government rendered us most valuable service. Being dissatisfied with the Fabian policy of General Johnston, it relieved him, and General Hood was substituted to command the Confederate army [July 18th]. Hood was known to us to be a "fighter," a graduate of West Point of the class of 1853, No. 44, of which class two of my army commanders, McPherson and Schofield, were No. 1 and No. 7. The character of a leader is a large factor in the game of war, and I confess I was

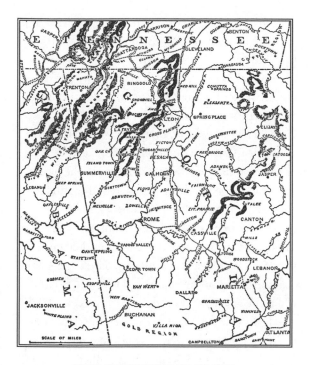

FROM CHATTANOOGA TO ATLANTA

pleased at this change, of which I had early notice. I knew that I had an army superior in numbers and *morale* to that of my antagonist; but being so far from my base, and operating in a country devoid of food and forage, I was dependent for supplies on a poorly constructed railroad back to Louisville, five hundred miles. I was willing to meet the enemy in the open country, but not behind well-constructed parapets.

Promptly, as expected, General Hood sallied from his Peach Tree line on the 20th of July, about midday, striking the Twentieth Corps (Hooker), which had just crossed-Peach Tree Creek by improvised bridges. The troops became com mingled and fought hand to hand desperately for about four hours, when the Confederates were driven back within their lines, leaving behind their dead and wounded. These amounted to 4796 men, to our loss of 1710. We followed up, and Hood fell back to the main lines of the city of Atlanta. We closed in, when again Hood, holding these lines with about one-half his force, with the other half made a wide circuit by night, under cover of the woods, and on the 22d of July enveloped our left flank "in air," a

movement that led to the hardest battle of the campaign. He encountered the Army of the Tennessee,—skilled veterans who were always ready to fight, were not alarmed by flank or rear attacks, and met their assailants with heroic valor. The battle raged from noon to night, when the Confederates, baffled and defeated, fell back within the intrenchments of Atlanta. Their losses are re ported 8499 to ours of 3641; but among these was McPherson, the commander of the Army of the Tennessee. Whilst this battle was in progress, Schofield at the center and Thomas on the right made efforts to break through the intrenchments at their fronts, but found them too strong to assault.

The Army of the Tennessee was then shifted, under its new commander (Howard), from the extreme left to the extreme right, to reach, if possible, the railroad by which Hood drew his supplies, when, on the 28th of July, he repeated his tactics of the 22d, sustaining an overwhelming defeat, losing 4623 men to our 700. These three sallies convinced him that his predecessor, General Johnston, had not erred in standing on the defensive. Thereafter the Confederate army in Atlanta clung to its parapets.

—SHERMAN, "The Grand Strategy of the War of the Rebellion"

XXIX.3

JOHNSTON HALTS SHERMAN AT NEW HOPE CHURCH

Only rarely, and then when he thought his position peculiarly favorable, could Johnston afford the offensive. New Hope Church (May 25-28) was one of those occasions. Here—a few miles north of Dalton—Sherman tried to pass around Johnston's right. Johnston succeeded in stopping this, but at a cost of almost 3,000 men; nothing daunted, Sherman then slid off on Johnston's left and continued his advance.

Here Johnston himself describes the engagement at New Hope Church.

In the mean time Jackson had given information of General Sherman's march toward the bridges near

Stilesboro', and of the crossing of the leading Federal troops there on the 23d [May]. In consequence of this intelligence, Lieutenant General Hardee was ordered to march that afternoon, by New Hope Church, to the road leading from Stilesboro', through Dallas, to Atlanta; and Lieutenant-General Polk to move to the same road, by a route farther to the left. Lieutenant-General Hood was instructed to follow Hardee on the 24th. . . . On the 25th the latter reached New Hope Church, early in the day. Intelligence was received from General Jackson's troops soon after, that the Federal army was near—its right at Dallas, and its line extending toward Alatoona.

Lieutenant-General Hood was immediately instructed to form his corps parallel with the road by which he had marched, and west of it, with the centre opposite to the church; Lieutenant-General Polk to place his in line with it, on the left, and Lieutenant-General Hardee to occupy a ridge extending from the ground allotted to Polk's corps, across the road leading from Dallas toward Atlanta—his left division, Bate's, holding that road.

As soon as his troops were in position, Lieutenant-General Hood, to "develop the enemy," sent forward Colonel Bush Jones, with his regiment and Austin's sharpshooters, in all about three hundred men. After advancing about a mile, this detachment encountered Hooker's corps. Having the written order of his corps commander to hold his ground after meeting the enemy, Colonel Jones resisted resolutely the attack of the overwhelming Federal forces. But, after a gallant fight he was, of course, driven back to his division—Stewart's.

An hour and a half before sunset, a brisk cannonade was opened upon Hood's centre division, Stewart's, opposite to New Hope Church. Major-General Stewart regarding this as the harbinger of assault, leaped upon his horse and rode along his line, to instruct the officers and encourage the men. He soon found the latter to be superfluous, from the confident tone in which he was addressed by his soldiers, and urged by them to lay aside all anxiety, and trust, for success, to their courage. Such pledges were well redeemed. The enemy soon

appeared—Hooker's corps—in so deep order that it presented a front equal only to that of Stewart's first line—three brigades. After opening their fire, the Federal troops ap proached gradually but resolutely, under the fire of three brigades and sixteen field-pieces, until within fifty paces of the Confederate line. Here, however, they were compelled first to pause, and then to fall back, by the obstinate resistance they encountered. They were led forward again, advancing as resolutely, and approaching as near to the Confederate line as before, but were a second time repulsed by the firmness of their opponents, and their deliberate fire of canister-shot and musketry. The engagement was continued in this manner almost two hours, when the assailants drew off.

In this action a few of the men of Clayton's and Baker's brigades were partially sheltered by a hasty arrangement of some fallen timber which they found near their line. The other brigade engaged, Stovall's, had no such protection. Nothing entitled to the term "breastworks" had been constructed by the division. . . .

The Federal troops extended their intrenched line so rap idly to their left, that it was found necessary in the morning of the 27th to transfer Cleburne's division of Hardee's corps to our right, where it was formed on the prolongation of Polk's line. Kelly's cavalry, composed of Allen's and Hannon's Alabama brigades, together less than a thousand men, occupied the interval, of half a mile, between Cleburne's right and Little Pumpkin-Vine Creek. Martin's division (cavalry) guarded the road from Burnt Hickory to Marietta, two miles farther to the right; and Humes's the interval between Kelly's and Martin's divisions.

Between five and six o'clock in the afternoon, Kelly's skirmishers were driven in by a body of Federal cavalry, whose advance was supported by the Fourth Corps. This advance was retarded by the resistance of Kelly's troops fighting on foot behind unconnected little heaps of loose stones. As soon as the noise of this contest revealed to Major-General Cleburne the manoeuvre to turn his right, he brought the right brigade of his second line,

Granberry's, to Kelly's support, by forming it on the right of his first line; when the thin line of dismounted cavalry, that had been bravely resisting masses of infantry gave place to the Texan brigade.

The Fourth Corps came on in deep order, and assailed the Texans with great vigor, receiving their close and accurate fire with the fortitude always exhibited by General Sherman's troops in the actions of this campaign. They had also to endure the fire of Govan's right, including two pieces of artillery, on their right flank. At the same time, Kelly's and a part of Humes's troops, directed by General Wheeler, met the Federal left, which was following the movement of the main body, and drove back the leading brigade, taking thirty or forty prisoners. The united force continued to press forward, however, but so much delayed by the resistance of Wheeler's troops as to give time for the arrival, on that part of the field, of the Eighth and Ninth Arkansas regiments under Colonel Bancum, detached by General Govan to the assistance of the cavalry. This little body met the foremost of the Federal troops as they were reaching the prolongation of Granberry's line, and, charging gallantly, drove them back, and preserved the Texans from an attack in flank which must have been fatal. Before the Federal left could gather to overwhelm Bancum and his two regiments, Lowry's brigade, hurried by General Cleburne from its position as left of his second line, came to join them, and the two, formed abreast of Granberry's brigade, stopped the advance of the enemy's left, and successfully resisted its subsequent attacks.

The contest of the main body of the Fourth Corps with Granberry's brigade was a very fierce one. The Federal troops approached within a few yards of the Confederates, but at last were forced to give way by their storm of well-directed bullets, and fell back to the shelter of a hollow near and behind them. They left hundreds of corpses within twenty paces of the Confederate line.

When the United States troops paused in their advance, within fifteen paces of the Texan front rank, one of their color-bearers planted his colors eight or ten feet in front of his regiment, and was instantly shot dead; a soldier sprang forward to his place, and fell also, as he grasped the color staff; a second and third followed successively, and each received death as speedily as his predecessors; a fourth, however, seized and bore back the object of soldierly devotion.

About ten o'clock at night, Granberry ascertained that many of the Federal troops were still in the hollow immediately before him, and charged and drove them from it, taking two hundred and thirty-two prisoners, seventy-two of whom were severely wounded.

—Johnston, *Narrative of Military Operations*

XXIX.4

Joe Johnston Gives Way to Hood

It was a fortunate day for Sherman when President Davis removed Johnston from command and appointed Hood to his place. Confronted by heavy numerical superiority Johnston had no alternative but to retreat; that he conducted his retreat in a masterly fashion is now generally admitted. Davis, however, had never fully trusted Johnston: the distrust probably dated from Johnston's protest, in 1861, against an appointment which made him only fourth in rank in the Confederate Army. Davis' suspicion of Johnston was deepened when Johnston failed either to rescue Pemberton or to strike the Federal army during the Vicksburg campaign. Johnston's appointment to Bragg's command, in December 1863, was welcomed by the officers and men of the Army of Tennessee; his dismissal was generally regarded as a calamity. When Lee was made commander in chief of Confederate armies, in February 1865, he promptly reappointed Johnston to command of what was left of his army.

We have here Davis' explanation of his dismissal of Johston, and Johnston's defense of his strategy.

A. President Davis Removes General Johnston before Atlanta

When it became known that the Army of Tennessee had been successively driven from one strong position to another, until finally it had reached the earthworks constructed for the exterior defense of Atlanta, the popular disappointment was extreme. The possible fall of the "Gate City," with its important railroad communication, vast stores, factories for the manufacture of all sorts of military supplies, rolling-mill and foundries, was now contemplated for the first time at its full value, and produced intense anxiety far and wide. From many quarters, including such as had most urged his assignment, came delegations, petitions, and letters, urging me to remove General Johnston from the command of the army, and assign that important trust to some officer who would resolutely hold and defend Atlanta.

While sharing in the keen sense of disappointment at the failure of the campaign which pervaded the whole country, I was perhaps more apprehensive than others of the disasters likely to result from it, because I was in a position to estimate more accurately their probable extent. On the railroads threatened with destruction, the armies then fighting the main battles of the war in Virginia had for some time to a great degree depended for indispensable supplies, yet I did not respond to the wishes of those who came in hottest haste for the removal of General Johnston; for here again, more fully than many others, I realized how serious it was to change commanders in the presence of the enemy. This clamor for his removal commenced immediately after it became known that the army had fallen back from Dalton, and it gathered volume with each remove toward Atlanta. Still I resisted the steadily increasing pressure which was brought to bear to induce me to revoke his assignment, and only issued the order relieving him from command when I became satisfied that his declared purpose to occupy the works at Atlanta with militia levies and withdraw his army into the open country for freer operations, would inevitably result in the loss of that important point, and where the retreat would cease could not be foretold. If the Army of Tennessee was found to be unable to hold positions of great strength like those at Dalton, Reseca, Etowah, Kenesaw, and on the Chattahoochee, I could not reasonably hope that it would be more successful in the plains below Atlanta, where it would find neither natural nor artificial advantages of position. As soon as the Secretary of War

showed me the answer which he had just received in reply to his telegram to General Johnston, requesting positive 'in formation as to the General's plans and purposes, I gave my permission to issue the order relieving General Johnston and directing him to turn over to General Hood the command of the Army of Tennessee. I was so fully aware of the danger of changing commanders of an army while actively engaged with the enemy, that I only overcame the objection in view of an emergency, and in the hope that the impending danger of the loss of Atlanta might be averted.

—DAVIS, *Rise and Fall of the Confederate Government*

B. General Johnston Justifies Himself

Macon, Ga., September 1st, 1864

My Dear Maury:

I have been intending ever since my arrival at this place to pay a part of the epistolary debt I owe you. But you know how lazy it makes one to have nothing to do, and so with the hot weather we have been enduring here, I have absolutely devoted myself to idleness. I have been disposed to write more particularly of what concerns myself—to explain to you, as far as practicable, the operations for which I was laid on the shelf, for you are one of the last whose unfavorable opinion I would be willing to incur.

You know that the army I commanded was that which, under General Bragg, was routed at Missionary Ridge. Sherman's army was that which routed it, reinforced by the Sixteenth and Twenty-third Corps. I am censured for not taking the offensive at Dalton—where the enemy, if beaten, had a secure refuge behind the fortified gap at Ringgold, or in the fortress of Chattanooga, and where the odds against us were almost ten to four. At Resaca he received five brigades, near Kingston three, and about 3500 cavalry; at New Hope Church one; in all about 14,000 infantry and artillery. The enemy received the Seventeenth Corps and a number of garrisons and bridge guards from Tennessee and Kentucky that had been relieved by "hundred-day men."

I am blamed for not fighting. Operations commenced about the 6th of May; I was relieved on the 18th of July. In that time we fought daily, always under circumstances so favorable to us as to make it certain that the sum of the enemy's losses was five times ours, which was 10,000 men. Northern papers represented theirs up to about the end of June at 45,000. Sherman's progress was at the rate of a mile and a quarter a day. Had this style of fighting been allowed to continue, is it not clear that we would soon have been able to give battle with abundant chances of victory, and that the enemy, beaten on this side of the Chattahoochee, would have been destroyed? It is certain that Sherman's army was stronger, compared with that of Tennessee, than Grant's, compared with that of Northern Virginia. General Bragg asserts that Sherman's army was stronger than Grant's. It is well known that the army of Virginia was much superior to that of Tennessee.

Why, then, should I be condemned for the defensive while General Lee was adding to his great fame by the same course? General Bragg seems to have earned at Missionary Ridge his present high position. People report at Columbus and Montgomery that General Bragg said that my losses had been frightful; that I had disregarded the wishes and instructions of the President; that he had in vain implored me to change my course, by which I suppose is meant assume the offensive.

As these things are utterly untrue, it is not to be supposed that they were said by General Bragg. The President gave me no instructions and expressed no wishes except just before we reached the Chattahoochee, warning me not to fight with the river behind us and against crossing it, and previously he urged me not to allow Sherman to detach to Grant's aid. General Bragg passed some ten hours with me just before I was relieved, and gave me the impression that his visit to the army was casual, he being on his way further west to endeavor to get us reinforcements from Kirby Smith and Lee. I thought him satisfied with the state of things, but not so with that in Virginia. He assured me that he had always maintained in

Richmond that Sherman's army was stronger than Grant's. He said nothing of the intention to relieve me, but talked with General Hood on the subject, as I learned after my removal. It is clear that his expedition had no other object than my removal and the giving proper direction to public opinion on the subject. He could have had no other object in going to Montgomery. A man of honor in his place would have communicated with me as well as with Hood on the subject. Being expected to assume the offensive, he attacked on the 20th, 22d, and 28th of July, disastrously, losing more men than I had done in seventy-two days. Since then his defensive has been at least as quiet as mine was.

Very truly yours,
J. E. Johnston
Major-General Maury
——Maury, *Recollections of a Virginian*

XXIX.5

Hardee Wins and Loses the Battle of Atlanta

Atlanta proved a hard nut to crack. Hood had been appointed because he was an aggressive fighter, and he promptly took the offensive. On July 20 he struck Thomas at Peachtree Creek, but was repulsed with heavy losses. Nothing daunted he tried again two days later, this time assaulting the left of the Union line, at Decatur (the Battle of Atlanta).

After Peachtree Creek Sherman sent McPherson eastward toward Decatur to cut off Hood's communications with the east and north. Hood withdrew into the defenses of Atlanta; supposing him in retreat McPherson set out "in pursuit." By a night march Hood—with Wheeler's cavalry—caught McPherson unprepared and assaulted him flank and rear. For a time disaster threatened. McPherson was killed; his army all but routed. But the Federals rallied and in the end inflicted a heavy defeat on their attackers. Confederate losses were between 7,000 and 8,000; Union less than 4,000.

Richard Tuthill, who here tells the story, was an officer of the 1st Michigan Light Artillery.

Hardee had struck us "endways," and his men could be plainly seen occupying the works from which ours had just been driven. The battery of regulars, near the end of our line, had been captured; and Lieutenant Justin of our battery had only been able to save his guns by the exercise of great coolness and quickness of movement. No sooner had the regulars been captured than we heard the booming of their guns, and saw their shot ploughing through our line in direct enfilade.

Some one may then have ordered a change of position. I have heard it said that such an order was given. At the same time, I beg leave respectfully to doubt it. The truth is that there was no time to give orders, and I saw neither general nor staff officer there to give them. All I know is, that we limbered up our guns, and sullenly—for we were much inclined to stay where we were—moved back. Our boys loved their black steel guns, and could not endure the thought of losing one of them. The Third Ohio Battery, in our division, had twenty-pounder Parrotts,—too heavy for field service,—and had to leave at least one of them behind, though it was afterward retaken. At least twice, as we were falling back a distance of not more than two or three hundred yards, as it seems to me, we unlimbered our guns and fired at the enemy. Then the infantry would move away from us, and we would limber up and fall back a little farther, to keep on a line with them.

It is hard now to recall the sensations of twenty-five years ago, but I never can forget thinking, "Can it be possible that the Third Division, victor in a hundred battles, has at last met defeat? Is it going to leave the field while as yet few have been killed or wounded? Better, ten thousand times better, that the entire division die fighting, than to have word sent back home that without serious losses in killed and wounded, it gave up the field." "It is better, sir," said Sir Colin Campbell, "that every man of her Majesty's Guards should lie dead upon the field than that they should now turn their backs upon the enemy." Such I know were my thoughts, and such I soon, from their action, learned was the thought of that glorious and never-conquered phalanx; for in their action their country and history can read their stern, brave thoughts and high determination.

Seeing then, for the first time since the fight began, our Chief of Artillery, Captain Williams,—as nonchalant a man as I ever saw in a place of great danger,—I rode to his side and said to him, "For God's sake, Captain, let us stop falling back and fight!" By that time we had reached a position about on a line drawn at right angles to the line occupied by us when the attack was first made, running toward the east from the top of Leggett's Hill.

Captain Williams replied to my remark, "All right! stop where you are!"

It was just the place to form a line of battle. Some general officer may have given an order to stop there. My own belief always has been that the boys did it of their own accord. They had been in so many fights that they did not need a general to tell them where and when to stop running and begin shooting.

Some distance to the rear of us was a rail fence. Consternation, I have been told, fell upon General Sherman, as with his glass he saw half of Leggett's division drop their guns and run to the rear. But when he saw them stop at the rail fence, and each man of them pick up two, three, and even four rails, and run back, carrying them to the place where they had left their guns, he understood what it meant, and smiled grimly. The operation was repeated; the rails were placed lengthways along their front; with bayonets, knives, and the tin plates taken from their haversacks, the earth was dug up and the rails covered, until, in less time, as it appeared to me, than it was possible to have done the same work with pick and shovel, a very fair protection for men lying on their bellies was made.

In front of us lay an open field, containing, I should think, not more than twenty acres. Beyond this were woods. Pat Cleburne's Texans,—whom Force's brigade had driven from this selfsame hillside the day before,—desperate and mad, were to make an attempt to wipe out the disgrace of their former defeat. Their line well formed, they emerged from their concealment in the woods, and yelling as only the steer drivers of Texas could yell, charged upon our division. On the top of the hill, in the apex of the angle of the line of works facing Atlanta and our new line, was a four-gun battery of twenty-four-pounder howitzers, commanded by its boy captain, Cooper. This was Battery D, of the First Illinois Artillery, better known as "McAllister's Battery." Our six guns were also near this point, and distributed along the line for a short distance to the east of it. On came the Texans; but they were met by a continuous volley of musketry and shrapnel, shell and canister from our six-rifled Rodmans and Cooper's howitzers. It seemed as if no man of all the host who were attacking us could escape alive; and yet, still yelling, they persisted in their desperate undertaking. Their line was reformed, and again and again they attempted the impossible,—to drive the Third Division from the line it had decided to hold.

Many of the enemy reached our line; some got across it; many were bayonetted, many killed with clubbed muskets; hand-to-hand conflicts were frequent. But not one inch did the Third Division give way. The boys obeyed Logan's well remembered command to them at Champion Hill,— "Give them the cold steel! give them hell!"

The smell of powder was everywhere; the smoke from the guns was so dense that though a July sun was shining, there was the appearance of a dense fog. Only as the breath of a passing breeze blew the smoke away could the movements of the enemy be discerned clearly; but his unearthly *yell* could be heard above the sound of muskets and cannon. The day being very warm, men and line officers were for the most part without other clothing than hats and shoes, woollen shirts and trousers. I had left my coat and all my traps, including my letters, at the spot where I had suspended my letter-writing, and never again recovered them.

The exact sequence of events that afternoon I cannot give; nor do I believe any man can, or ever could, do so. Some time during the fight, firing was heard from the direction of Atlanta. General Cheatham's corps—as we now know—made fierce attack upon the Seventeenth and Fifteenth corps

from our west front. The smoke was so dense that the men could not at first see whence this attack came. It was remarked that our own men farther to the right, thinking the enemy had taken the position on the hill, were firing upon us. General Force called for a flag. Some frightened young officer, thinking it time to give up when we were being attacked at the same moment from all sides, and that what Force wanted was a flag of truce, ran hither and thither to get a white handkerchief, or skirt, or anything that would answer the purpose. The talk among our boys was that that quiet Christian gentleman—now Judge Force of the Law Court of Cincinnati—was then betrayed into saying, "Damn you, sir! I don't want a flag of *truce; I* want the American flag!" If he did say it, we are sure that as in Uncle Tobey's case, "The accusing spirit which flew up to Heaven's chancery with the oath blushed as he gave it in; and the recording angel, as he wrote it down, dropped a tear upon the word and blotted it out forever."

A flag was soon obtained and planted upon the highest point in our earthworks, and there it remained. General Force him self was struck down by a minie-ball, which entered just at the lower outer corner of the eye, passed through his head, and came out near the base of the brain. The blood gushed from his eyes, nose, and mouth; but he uttered no moan, nor a word of complaint. The bones of his mouth were shattered, and he could not, in fact, speak. But from his eyes flashed a spirit unconquered and unconquerable,—the spirit of a soldier *sans peur et sans reproche*.

The attack made by Cheatham's corps from Atlanta was repulsed bloodily by Frank Blair's heroic men. But beyond the bushy ravine of which I have spoken as separating the Fifteenth Corps, where its line had been weakened by sending troops to strengthen our line fronting to the south, Cheatham had succeeded in breaking through, and was rushing in and forming in line of battle in the works from which our men had been driven. Some one asked that a part of our battery be at once sent to the ravine to shell this forming line. There was at that time comparative quiet in our immediate front, and my section of the battery hurried to the point indicated. The Confederates were there in plain sight. De Gress' battery of four twenty-pounder Parrotts had been captured, all of its horses killed, and its guns turned upon us. Taking a position on the edge of the ravine, the boys of my section poured into the forming line of the enemy an enfilading fire of short-range canister—"canned hell-fire," as they used to call it—that no living thing could withstand.

—TUTHILL, "An Artilleryman's Recollection of the Battle of Atlanta"

XXIX.6

"YOU MIGHT AS WELL APPEAL AGAINST THE THUNDER-STORM"

Even after Peachtree Creek and the Battle of Atlanta, Hood was able to put up a stiff fight for Atlanta. Sherman fell back on his now familiar tactics of flanking the Confederates, trying to cut their supply lines to the south and the east. Late July and early August witnessed a number of stiff cavalry engagements, as Hood tried to break up these extensive flanking movements. Convinced, finally, that Hood could not be defeated by these tactics, Sherman settled down to investing Atlanta. On August 25 he put his whole army in motion to encircle the city. With his communications cut, Hood evacuated Atlanta and moved south and west, and on September 1 Sherman wired Lincoln "Atlanta is ours, and fairly won." Already the bombardment of Atlanta had started numerous fires; when Sherman was ready to leave it for further campaigning, he ordered it destroyed. This required the evacuation of its inhabitants. Southerners looked on this as inhuman; Sherman thought it a necessary military measure, and the evacuation warning a gesture of courtesy.

What is most interesting about this letter, explaining the necessity of evacuation, is that it gives Sherman's theory of war. That Sherman inflicted heavier damage on the South than any other Union general is doubtless true; it is equally true that no other Union general was so sympathetic to the South or understood it so well.

Headquarters Military Division of the Mississippi in the Field,
Atlanta, Georgia, September 12, 1864
James M. Calhoun, Mayor, E.E. Rawson and S.C. Wells, representing City Council of Atlanta.

Gentlemen: I have your letter of the 11th, in the nature of a petition to revoke my orders removing all the inhabitants from Atlanta. I have read it carefully, and give full credit to your statements of the distress that will be occasioned, and yet shall not revoke my orders, because they were not designed to meet the humanities of the case, but to prepare for the future struggles in which millions of good people out side of Atlanta have a deep interest. We must have peace, not only at Atlanta, but in all America. To secure this, we must stop the war that now desolates our once happy and favored country. To stop war, we must defeat the rebel armies which are arrayed against the laws and Constitution that all must respect and obey. To defeat those armies, we must prepare the way to reach them in their recesses, provided with the arms and instruments which enable us to accomplish our purpose. Now, I know the vindictive nature of our enemy, that we may have many years of military operations from this quarter; and, therefore, deem it wise and prudent to prepare in time. The use of Atlanta for warlike purposes is inconsistent with its character as a home for families. There will be no manufactures, commerce, or agriculture here, for the maintenance of families, and sooner or later want will compel the inhabitants to go. Why not go now, when all the arrangements are completed for the transfer, instead of waiting till the plunging shot of contending armies will renew the scenes of the past month? Of course, I do not apprehend any such thing at this moment, but you do not suppose this army will be here until the war is over. I cannot discuss this subject with you fairly, because I cannot impart to you what we propose to do, but I assert that our military plans make it necessary for the inhabitants to go away, and I can only renew my offer of services to make their exodus in any direction as easy and comfortable as possible.

You cannot qualify war in harsher terms than I will. War is cruelty, and you cannot refine it; and those who brought war into our country deserve all the curses and maledictions a people can pour out. I know I had no hand in making this war, and I know I will make more sacrifices to-day than any of you to secure peace. But you cannot have peace and a division of our country. If the United States submits to a division now, it will not stop, but will go on until we reap the fate of Mexico, which is eternal war. The United States does and must assert its authority, wherever it once had power; for, *if* it relaxes one bit to pressure, it is gone, and I believe that such is the national feeling. This feeling assumes various shapes, but always comes back to that of Union. Once admit the Union, once more acknowledge the authority *of* the national Government, and, instead of devoting your houses and streets and roads to the dread uses of war, I and this army become at once your protectors and supporters, shielding you from danger, let it come from what quarter it may. I know that a few individuals cannot resist a torrent *of* error and passion, such as swept the South into rebellion, but you can point out, so that we may know those who desire a government, and those who insist on war and its desolation.

You might as well appeal against the thunderstorm as against these terrible hardships of war. They are inevitable, and the only way the people of Atlanta can hope once more to live in peace and quiet at home, is to stop the war, which can only be done by admitting that it began in error and is perpetuated in pride.

We don't want your Negroes, or your horses, or your houses, or your lands, or any thing you have, but we do want and will have a just obedience to the laws of the United States. That we will have, and if it involves the destruction of your improvements, we cannot help it.

You have heretofore read public sentiment in your news papers, that live by falsehood and excitement; and the quicker you seek for truth in other quarters, the better. I repeat then that, by the original compact of government, the United States had certain rights in Georgia, which have never been relinquished and never will be; that the South began war by seizing forts, arsenals, mints, custom-houses, etc., etc., long before Mr. Lincoln was

installed, and before the South had one jot or tittle of provocation. I myself have seen in Missouri, Kentucky, Tennessee, and Mississippi, hundreds and thousands of women and children fleeing from your armies and desperadoes, hungry and with bleeding feet. In Memphis, Vicksburg, and Mississippi, we fed thousands upon thousands of the families of rebel soldiers left on our hands, and whom we could not see starve. Now that war comes home to you, you feel very different. You deprecate its horrors, but did not feel them when you sent car-loads of soldiers and ammunition, and moulded shells and shot, to carry war into Kentucky and Tennessee, to desolate the homes of hundreds and thou sands of good people who only asked to live in peace at their old homes, and under the Government of their inheritance. But these comparisons are idle. I want peace, and believe it can only be reached through union and war, and I will ever conduct war with a view to perfect an early success.

But, my dear sirs, when peace does come, you may call on me for anything. Then will I share with you the last cracker, and watch with you to shield your homes and families against danger from every quarter.

Now you must go, and take with you the old and feeble, feed and nurse them, and build for them, in more quiet places, proper habitations to shield them against the weather until the mad passions of men cool down, and allow the Union and peace once more to settle over your old homes at Atlanta. Yours in haste,

W.T. SHERMAN, *Major-General commanding*
—*Memoirs of General William T. Sherman*

XXIX.7

CHILD'S DIARY OF ATLANTA SIEGE

Ten-year-old Carrie Berry kept a diary during the siege of Atlanta and its occupation. She describes the view from behind the ramparts of Atlanta as she, her pregnant mother, sister, and father coped with the bombardment, occupation and burning of the city. She was forced to live in her family cellar, witnessed a cannon shell land in her garden, and helped her mother tend to a newborn sister. For five months, the Berry family feared for its lives and safety.

The ambiguities of war struck home, as well as the terrors. Berry writes that many of the Yankee soldiers behaved well and, in one case, she would miss a kindly sergeant. Other Yankees, however, burned the houses of neighbors. The Berry family was one of only about 50 families who remained in Atlanta through the entire occupation.

August 4. The shells have been flying all day and we have stayed in the cellar. Mama put me [to work] on some stockings this morning and I will try to finish them before school commences.

August 5. I knit all the morning. In the evening we had to run to Auntie's to get in the cellar. We did not feel safe in our cellar, they fell so thick and fast.

August 6. We have been in the cellar all day. . . .

August 9. We have had to stay in the cellar all day the shells have been falling so thick around the house. Two have fallen in the garden, but none of us were hurt. . . .

August 11. Mama has ben very buisy to day and I have been trying to help her all I could. We had to go to the cellar often out of the shells. How I wish the federals would quit shelling us so we could get out and get some fresh air.

August 14. We had shells in abundance last night. We expected every one would come through and hurt some of us but to our joy nothing on the lot was hurt. . . . I dislike to stay in the cellar so close but our soldiers have to stay in ditches. . . .

August 18. When I woke up this morning, I thought the whole town would be torn up. The cannons were so near and so loud but we soon found out that it was our guns so we have been very well content all day.

August 22. I got up this morning and helped Mama pack up to move. We were glad to get out of our small cellar. We have a nice large cellar here where we can run as much as we please and enjoy it. Mama says that we make so much noise that she can't here the shells.

August 23. We feel very comfortable since we have moved but Mama is fretted to death all the time for fear of fire. There is a fire in town nearly every day. I get so tired of being housed up all the time. The shells get worse and worse every day. O that something would stop them! . . .

September 1. Directly after dinner Cousin Emma came down and told us that Atlanta would be evacuated this evening and we might look for the Federals in the morning. It was not long till the hole town found it out and such excitement there was.

September 2. Every one has been trying to get all they could before the Federals come in the morning. They have been running with sagues of meat, salt and tobacco. They did act rediculous breaking open stores and robbing them. About twelve o'clock there were a few Federals came . . . In about an hour the cavalry came. . . . We were all frightened. We were afraid they were going to treat us badly. It was not long till the Infantry came in. They were orderly and behaved very well. I think I shall like the Yankees very well. . . .

September 10. Every one I see seems sad. The citizens all think it is the most cruel thing to drive us from our home, but I think it would be so funny to move. Mama seems so troubled and she can't do any thing. Papa says he don't know where on earth to go.

September 14. Papa got into business today and the rest of us went to work in earnest thinking that we will get to stay. I hope that we will. . . . Mama dislikes to move so much. . . .

October 23. Mama and Papa took a walk this evening and they say that they never saw a place torn up like Atlanta is. Half the houses are torn down. . . .

October 30. They [the Union troops] are ready to move and it looks like every body is going to leave from here the way the soldiers are moving about. Our sargent left us this morning. We all were sorry to part with him. He has been a very good friend to us. . . .

November 12. We were fritened almost to death last night. Some mean soldiers set several houses on fire in different parts of the town. I could not go to sleep for fear that they would set our house on fire. We all dred the next few days to come for they said that they would set the last house on fire if they had to leave this place.

November 13. The federal soldiers have been coming to day and burning houses and I have ben looking at them come in nearly all day.

November 14. They came burning Atlanta to day. We all dread it because they say they will burn the last house before they stop. We will dread it.

November 15. This has been a dreadful day. Things have been burning all around us. We dread tonight because we do not know what moment they will set our house on fire.

November 16. Oh what a night we had. They came burning the store house and about night it looked like the whole town was on fire. We all set up all night. If we had not sat up our house would have been burnt up for the fire was very near the soldiers were going around setting houses on fire where they were not watched. They behaved very badly. They all left town about one o'-clock this evening and we were glad when they left for no body knows what we have suffered since they came in. . . .

November 18. We children have been plundering about to-day seeing what we could find. . . .

November 19. Mama and me have been ironing to-day. We have begun to feel at home but it doesn't look like Atlanta. The citizens all met at the City Hall. There are eighty men in town. . . .

December 7. I had a little sister this morning at eight o'-clock. Mama gave her to me. I think it's very pretty. . . .

December 20. I have been buisy making presents all day. I went down to Mrs. Lesters to make Mamas. . . . I think it is so pretty. I fear we will not get through with our presents. Christmas is getting so near.

December 22. We went to get our Christmas tree this evening. It was very cold but we did not feel it we were so excited about it.

December 24. I have been buisy to day making cakes to trim the tree. . . . I have it all ready trimed

and we are all going to night to see it. I think it looks very pretty. We will be sorry when it is all over.

December 25. We all went down to-night to see the tree and how pretty it looked. The room was full of ladies and children and Cap. Gave us music on the piano and tried all he could to make us enjoy ourselves and we did have a merry time . . .

January 2. Ella, me and Buddie are studying arithmetic, spelling, reading and geography. We are all trying to see which will learn the most. . . . We have to study very hard and we don't get time to do much of anything but we have been playing long enough to spend time on our books. . . .

January 15. We are all so glad that we could have church once more this evening and went out to the cemetery.

January 16. We started to school irly this morning and had perfect lessons all day. I missed one wird and that was in spelling.

—CARRIE BERRY

XXIX.8

SHERMAN MARCHES FROM ATLANTA TO THE SEA

Sherman's great decision was to break his own line of communications, and live off the country. Dispatching Schofield to Knoxville and Thomas to Nashville, to take care of Hood, he set out with what was left of his army, some 62,000 men, into the heart of the Confederacy.

Once again he is the best historian of his own achievements.

About 7 A.M. of November 16th [1864] we rode out of Atlanta by the Decatur road, filled by the marching troops and wagons of the Fourteenth Corps; and reaching the hill, just outside of the old rebel works, we naturally paused to look back upon the scenes of our past battles. We stood upon the very ground whereon was fought the bloody battle of July 22d and could see the copse of wood where McPherson fell. Behind us lay Atlanta, smoldering and in ruins, the black smoke rising high in air and hanging like a pall over the ruined city. Away off in the distance, on the McDonough road, was the rear of Howard's column, the gun barrels glistening in the sun, the white-topped-wagons stretching away to the south, and right before us the Fourteenth Corps, marching steadily and rapidly with a cheery look and swinging pace that made light of the thousand miles that lay between us and Richmond. Some band by accident struck up the anthem of "John Brown's soul goes marching on"; the men caught up the strain, and never before or since have I heard the chorus of "Glory, glory, hallelujah!" done with more spirit or in better harmony of time and place.

Then we turned our horses' heads to the east; Atlanta was soon lost behind the screen of trees and became a thing of the past. Around it clings many a thought of desperate battle, of hope and fear, that now seem like the memory of a dream; and I have never seen the place since. The day was extremely beautiful, clear sunlight, with bracing air, and an unusual feeling of exhilaration seemed to pervade all minds—a feeling of something to come, vague and undefined, still full of venture and intense interest. Even the common soldiers caught the inspiration, and many a group called out to me as I worked my way past them, "Uncle Billy, I guess Grant is waiting for us at Richmond!" Indeed, the general sentiment was that we were marching for Richmond and that there we should end the war, but how and when they seemed to care not; nor did they measure the distance or count the cost in life or bother their brains about the great rivers to be crossed and the food, required for man and beast, that had to be gathered by the way. There was a devil may-care feeling pervading officers and men that made me feel the full load of responsibility, for success would be accepted as a matter of course, whereas should we fail, this march would be adjudged the wild adventure of a crazy fool. I had no purpose to march direct for Richmond by way of Augusta and Charlotte but always designed to reach the sea coast first at Savannah or Port Royal, South Carolina, and even kept in mind the alternative of Pensacola.

The first night out we camped by the roadside near Lithonia. Stone Mountain, a mass of granite, was in-plain view, cut out in clear outline against the blue sky; the whole horizon was lurid with the bonfires of rail ties, and groups of men all night were carrying the heated rails to the nearest trees and bending them around the trunks. Colonel Poe had provided tools for ripping up the rails and twisting them when hot, but the best and easiest way is . . . heating the middle of the iron rails on bonfires made of the crossties and then winding them around a telegraph pole or the trunk of some convenient sapling. I attached much importance to this destruction of the railroad, gave it my personal attention, and made reiterated orders to others on the subject.

The next day we passed through the handsome town of Covington, the soldiers closing-up their ranks, the color-bearers unfurling their flags, and the band striking up patriotic airs. The white people came out of their houses to behold the sight, spite of their deep hatred of the invaders, and the Negroes were simply frantic with joy. Whenever they heard my name, they clustered about my horse, shouted and prayed in their peculiar style, which had a natural eloquence that would have moved a stone. I have witnessed hundreds, if not thousands, of such scenes and can now see a poor girl, in the very ecstasy of the Methodist "shout," hugging the banner of one of the regiments and jumping up to the "feet of Jesus."

I remember, when riding around by a bystreet in Covington to avoid the crowd that followed the marching column, that some one brought me an invitation to dine with a sister of Samuel Anderson, who was a cadet at West Point with me; but the messenger reached me after we had passed the main part of the town. I asked to be excused and rode on to a place designated for camp, at the crossing of the Ulcofauhachee River, about four miles to the east of the town. Here we made our bivouac, and I walked up to a plantation house close by, where were assembled many Negroes, among them an old gray-haired man, of as fine a head as I ever saw. I asked him if he understood about the war and its progress. He said he did; that he had been looking for the "angel of the Lord" ever since he was knee-high, and though we professed to be fighting for the Union, he supposed that slavery was the cause and that our success was to be his freedom. I asked him if all the Negro slaves comprehended this fact, and he said they surely did. I then explained to him that we wanted the slaves to remain where they were and not to load us down with useless mouths, which would eat up the food needed for our fighting men, that our success was their assured freedom, that we could receive a few of their young, hearty men as pioneers, but that if they followed us in swarms of old and young, feeble and helpless, it would simply load us down and cripple us in our great task. I think Major Henry Hitchcock was with me on that occasion and made a note of the conversation, and I believe that old man spread this message to the slaves, which was carried from mouth to mouth to the very end of our journey, and that it in part saved us from the great danger we incurred of swelling our numbers so that famine would have attended our progress.

It was at this very plantation that a soldier passed me with a ham on his musket, a jug of sorghum molasses under his arm, and a big piece of honey in his hand, from which he was eating, and catching my eye, he remarked *sotto voce* and carelessly to a comrade, "Forage liberally on the country," quoting from my general orders. On this occasion, as on many others that fell under my personal observation, I reproved the man, explained that foraging must be limited to the regular parties properly detailed and that al! provisions thus obtained must be delivered to the regular commissaries to be fairly distributed to the men who kept their ranks.

From Covington the Fourteenth Corps [Davis'], with which I was traveling, turned to the right for Milledgeville via Shady Dale. General Slocum was ahead at Madison with the Twentieth Corps, having torn up the railroad as far as that place, and thence had sent Geary's division on to the Oconee to burn the bridges across that stream when this corps turned south by Eatonton for Milledgeville, the common objective for the first stage of the march. We found abundance of corn, molasses, meal, bacon, and sweet potatoes. We also took a good many cows and oxen and a large number of mules. In all these the country was quite rich, never before having been visited by a hostile army; the recent crop had been excellent, had been just gathered and laid by for the winter. As a rule, we destroyed none but kept our wagons full and fed our teams bountifully.

The skill and success of the men in collecting forage was one of the features of this march. Each brigade commander had authority to detail a company of foragers, usually about fifty men, with one or two commissioned officers selected for their boldness and enterprise. This party would be dispatched before daylight with a knowledge of the intended day's march and camp, would proceed on foot five or six miles from the route traveled by their brigade, and then visit every plantation and farm within range. They would usually procure a wagon or family carriage, load it with bacon, cornmeal, turkeys, chickens, ducks, and everything that could be used as food or forage, and would then regain the main road, usually in advance of their train. When this came up, they would deliver to the brigade commissary the supplies thus gathered by the way. Often would I pass these foraging parties at the road side, waiting for their wagons to come up, and was amused at their strange collections—mules, horses, even cattle, packed with old saddles and loaded with hams, bacon, bags of corn meal, and poultry of every character and description. Although this foraging was attended with great danger and hard work, there seemed to be a charm about it that attracted the soldiers, and it was a privilege to be detailed on such a party. Daily they returned mounted on all sorts of beasts which were at once taken from them and appropriated to the general use, but the next day they would start out again on foot, only to repeat the experience of the day before. No doubt, many acts of pillage, robbery, and violence were committed by these parties of foragers, usually called bummers; for I have since heard of jewelry taken from women and the plunder of articles that never reached the commissary; but these acts were exceptional and incidental. I never heard of any cases of murder or rape, and no army could have carried along sufficient food and forage for a march of three hundred miles, so that foraging in some shape was necessary. The country was sparsely settled, with no magistrates or civil authorities who could respond to requisitions, as is done in all the wars of Europe, so that this system of foraging was simply indispensable to our success. By it our men were well supplied with all the essentials of life and health, while the wagons retained enough in case of unexpected delay, and our animals were well fed. Indeed, when we reached Savannah, the trains were pronounced by experts to be the finest in flesh and appearance ever seen with any army.

—*Memoirs of General William T. Sherman*

XXIX.9

Sherman's "Bummers"

The origin of the term "bummer" is a bit obscure; it was with Sherman's March to the Sea that it came into general usage. A bummer, wrote Major Nichols, "is a raider on his own account, a man who temporarily deserts his place in the ranks and starts out upon an independent foraging expedition." The term actually had more general application; cooks, orderlies, servants, were all called bummers, whether they de served the name or not.

Here are two descriptions of this peculiar appendage to the Grand Army that marched from Atlanta to the sea. The first is by Captain Henry Dwight of the 20th Ohio Infantry, and an aide to General Force; the second by Daniel Oakey, a captain in the 2nd Massachusetts Volunteers.

A. A Good Word for the Bummers

Besides the fighting population of our camps there is a population constitutionally opposed to warfare—cooks, ambulance nurses, stretcher-bearers, shirks, and sometimes surgeons, who all come under the class technically called *bummers*. These

are treated by the fighting men with a sort of cool contempt, no matter whether necessity or inclination keeps them to the rear, and they have a hard time. Frequently the rear of the army is a much more dangerous locality than the front line, for the missiles passing over the front line must fall somewhere, and often demoralize whole hosts of "bummers," who build miniature fortifications to live in, and collect together in crowds; for misery loves company. Any favorable ravine thus peopled immediately becomes denominated "Bummer's Roost." Here they spend their days in cooking for their nurses, if they are cooks, or attending to their own business, if their object be to escape duty and danger. Among them originate all sorts of marvelous reports of immense success or terrible disaster. They always know just what General Sherman said about the situation at any given time; and from them start many of the wild stories which penetrate the columns of our best papers.

To watch these cooks, freighted with the precious coffee for the men in the trenches, as they go out to the front three times a day, is amusing. From continually dodging the passing shells or stray bullets their forms become bent and stooping. As they approach the line, the men in the trenches commence shouting, "Hey, bummer! Run quick, bummer!" "A man was killed just there, bummer!" With such encouragements the coffee at last reaches its destination. and being distributed among the eager men the bummer is soon at liberty to hurry back to the "Roost."

—Dwight, "How We Fight at Atlanta"

B. "We Were Proud of our Foragers"

At length, when we left Savannah and launched cheerily into the untrodden land of South Carolina, the foragers began to assume their wonted spirit. We were proud of our foragers. They constituted a picked force from each regiment, under an officer selected for' the command, and were remarkable for intelligence, spirit, and daring. Before daylight, mounted on horses captured on the plantations, they were In the saddle and away, covering the country sometimes seven miles in advance. Although I have said "in the saddle," many a forager had nothing better than a bit of carpet and a rope halter; yet this simplicity of equipment did not abate his power of carrying off hams and sweet-potatoes in the face of the enemy. The foragers were also important as a sort of advance guard, for they formed virtually a curtain of mounted infantry screening us from the inquisitive eyes of parties of Wheeler's cavalry, with whom they did not hesitate to engage when it was a question of a rich plantation.

When compelled to retire, they resorted to all the tricks of infantry skirmishers, and summoned reënforcements of foragers from other regiments to help drive the "Johnnies" out. When success crowned their efforts, the plantation was promptly stripped of live stock and eatables. The natives were accustomed to bury provisions, for they feared their own soldiers quite as much as they feared ours. These subterranean stores were readily discovered by the practiced "Yankee" eye. The appearance of the ground and a little probing with a ramrod or a bayonet soon decided whether to dig. Teams were improvised; carts and vehicles of all sorts were pressed into the service and loaded with provisions. If any antiquated militia uniforms were discovered, they were promptly donned, and a comical procession escorted the valuable train of booty to the point where the brigade was expected to bivouac for the night. The regimentals of the past, even to those of revolutionary times, were often conspicuous.

On an occasion when our brigade had the advance, several parties of foragers, consolidating themselves, captured a town from the enemy's cavalry, and occupied the neighboring plantations. Before the arrival of the main column hostilities had ceased; order had been restored, and mock arrangements were made to receive the army. Our regiment in the advance was confronted by a picket dressed in continental uniform, who waved his plumed hat in response to the gibes of the men, and galloped away on his bareback mule to apprise his comrades of our approach. We marched into the town and rested on each side of the main street. Presently a forager, in ancient militia uniform indicating high rank, debouched from a side street to do the honors of the occasion. He was mounted on a raw-boned horse with a bit of carpet for a saddle. His old plumed chapeau in hand, he rode with gracious dignity through the street, as if reviewing the brigade. After him came a family carriage laden with hams, sweet potatoes, and other provisions, and drawn by two horses, a mule, and a cow, the two latter ridden by postitions.

At Fayetteville, North Carolina, the foragers as usual had been over the ground several hours before the heads of column arrived, and the party from my regiment had found a broken-down gristmill. Their commander, Captain Parker, an officer of great spirit and efficiency, and an expert machinist, had the old wheel hoisted into its place and put the mill in working order. Several parties from other regiments had been admitted as working members, and teams of all sorts were busy collecting and bringing in corn and carrying away meal for distribution. This bit of enterprise was so pleasing to the troops that plenty of volunteers were ready to relieve the different gangs, and the demand was so great as to keep the mill at work all night by the light of pine knot fires and torches.

—OAKEY, "Marching Through Georgia and the Carolinas"

XXIX.10

"THE HEAVENS WERE LIT UP WITH FLAMES FROM BURNING BUILDINGS"

Here is how the March to the Sea affected its victims. Dolly Lunt was a Maine girl, distantly related to Charles Sumner, who before the war went to Covington, Georgia, to teach school, and there married a planter, Thomas Burge. At the time Sherman's army swept through Georgia she was a widow, still managing the plantation. Her short but moving diary has been rescued from oblivion by Julian Street.

November 19, 1864

Slept in my clothes last night, as I heard that the Yankees went to neighbor Montgomery's on Thursday night at one o'clock, searched his house, drank his wine, and took his money and valuables. As we were not disturbed, I walked after breakfast, with Sadai, up to Mr. Joe Perry's, my nearest neighbor, where the Yankees were yesterday. Saw Mrs. Laura [Perry] in the road surrounded by her children, seeming to be looking for some one. She said she was looking for her husband, that old Mrs. Perry had just sent her word that the Yankees went to James Perry's the night before, plundered his house, and drove off all his stock, and that she must drive hers into the old fields. Before we were done talking, up came Joe and Jim Perry from their hidingplace. Jim was very much excited. Happening to turn and look behind, as we stood there, I saw some blue-coats coming down the hill. Jim immediately raised his gun, swearing he would kill them any how.

"No, don't!" said I, and ran home as fast as I could, with Sadai.

I could hear them cry, "Halt! Halt!" and their guns went off in quick succession. Oh God, the time of trial has come!

A man passed on his way to Covington. I halloed to him, asking him if he did not know the Yankees were coming.

"No—are they?"

"Yes," said I; "they are not three hundred yards from here."

"Sure enough," said he. "Well, I'll not go. I don't want them to get my horse." And although within hearing of their guns, he would stop and look for them. Blissful ignorance! Not knowing, not hearing, he has not suffered the suspense, the fear, that I have for the past forty-eight hours. I walked to the gate. There they came filing up.

I hastened back to my frightened servants and told them that they had better hide, and then went back to the gate to claim protection and a guard. But like demons they rush in! My yards are full. To my smoke-house, my dairy, pantry, kitchen, and cellar, like famished wolves they come, breaking locks and whatever is in their way. The thousand pounds of meat in my smoke-house is gone in a twinkling, my flour, my meat, my lard, butter, eggs, pickles of various kinds—both in vinegar and brine——wine, jars, and jugs are all gone. My eighteen fat turkeys, my hens, chickens, and fowls, my young pigs, are shot down in my yard and hunted as if they were rebels themselves. Utterly powerless I ran out and appealed to the guard.

"I cannot help you, Madam, it is orders."

As I stood there, from my lot I saw driven, first, old Dutch, my dear old buggy horse, who has carried my beloved husband so many miles, and who would so quietly wait at the block for him to mount and dismount, and who at last drew him to his grave; then came old Mary, my brood mare, who for years had been too old and stiff for work, with her three year-old colt, my two-year-old mule, and her last little baby colt. There they go! There go my mules, my sheep, and, worse than all, my boys [slaves]!

Alas! little did I think while trying to save my house from plunder and fire that they were forcing my boys from home at the point of the bayonet. One, Newton, jumped into bed in his cabin, and declared himself sick. Another crawled under the floor,—a lame boy he was,—but they pulled him out, placed him on a horse, and drove him off. Mid, poor Mid! The last I saw of him, a man had him going around the garden, looking, as I thought, for my sheep, as he was my shepherd. Jack came crying to me, the big tears coursing down his cheeks, saying they were making him go. I said:

"Stay in my room."

But a man followed in cursing him and threatening to shoot him if he did not go; so poor Jack had to yield. . . .

My poor boys! My poor boys! What unknown trials are before you! How you have clung to your mistress and assisted her in every way you knew. . .

Their cabins are rifled of every valuable, the soldiers swearing that their Sunday clothes were the white people's, and that they never had money to get such things as they had. Poor Frank's chest was broken open, his money and tobacco taken. He had always been a money-making and saving boy; not infrequently has his crop brought him five hundred dollars and more. All of his clothes and Rachel's clothes, which dear Lou gave her before her death and which she had packed away, were stolen from her. Ovens, skillets, coffee-mills, of which we had three, coffee-pots—not one have I left. Sifters all gone!

Seeing that the soldiers could not be restrained, the guard ordered me to have their remaining possessions brought into my house, which I did, and they all, poor things, huddled together in my room, fearing every movement that the house would be burned.

A Captain Webber from Illinois came into my house. Of him I claimed protection from the vandals who were forcing themselves into my room. . .

He felt for me, and I give him and several others the character of gentlemen. I don't believe they would have molested women and children had they had their own way. He seemed surprised that I had not laid away in my house, flour and other provisions. I did not suppose I could secure them there, more than where I usually kept them, for in last summer's raid houses were thoroughly searched. In parting with him, I parted as with a friend.

Sherman himself and a greater portion of his army passed my house that day. All day, as the sad moments rolled on, were they passing not only in front of my house, but from behind; they tore down my garden palings, made a road through my back-yard and lot field, driving their stock and riding through, tearing down my fences and desolating my home—wantonly doing it when there was no necessity for it.

Such a day, if I live to the age of Methuselah, may God spare me from ever seeing again!

As night drew its sable curtains around us, the heavens from every point were lit up with flames from burning buildings. Dinnerless and supperless as we were, it was nothing in comparison with the fear of being driven out homeless to the dreary woods.

Nothing to eat! I could give my guard no supper, so he left us. I appealed to another, asking him if he had wife, mother, or sister, and how he should feel were they in my situation. A colonel from Vermont left me two men, but they were Dutch, and I could not understand one word they said.

My Heavenly Father alone saved me from the destructive fire. My carriage-house had in it eight bales of cotton, with my carriage, buggy, and harness. On top of the cotton were some carded cotton rolls, a hundred pounds or more. These were thrown out of the blanket in which they were, and a large twist of the rolls taken and set on fire, and thrown into the boat of my carriage, which was close up to the cotton bales. Thanks to my God, the cotton only burned over, and then went out. Shall I ever forget the deliverance? . . .

The two guards came into my room and laid themselves by my fire for the night. I could not close my eyes, but kept walking to and fro, watching the fires in the distance and dreading the approaching day, which, I feared, as they had not all passed, would be but a continuation of horrors.

—Lunt, A *Woman's Wartime Journal*

XXIX.11

Eliza Andrews Comes Home Through the Burnt Country

This is what Georgia looked like after the Yankees were through with it, as seen by a Georgia girl, Eliza Andrews. *The War-Time Diary of a Georgia Girl,* from which this brief excerpt is taken, is one of the best of all Confederate diaries.

December 24, 1864.—About three miles from Sparta we struck the "burnt country," as it is well named by the natives, and then I could better understand the wrath and desperation of these poor people. I almost felt as if I should like to hang a Yankee myself. There was hardly a fence left standing all the way from Sparta to Gordon. The fields were trampled down and the road was lined with carcasses of horses, hogs, and cattle that the invaders, unable either to consume or to carry away with them, had wantonly shot down, to starve out the people and prevent them from making their crops. The stench in some places was unbearable; every few hundred yards we had to hold our noses or stop them with the cologne Mrs. Elzey had given us, and it proved a great boon. The dwellings that were standing all showed signs of pillage, and on every plantation we saw the charred remains of the ginhouse and packing screw, while here and there lone chimney stacks, "Sherman's sentinels," told of homes laid in ashes. The infamous wretches! I couldn't wonder now that these poor people should want to put a rope round the neck of every red-handed "devil of them" they could lay their hands on. Hayricks and fodder stacks were demolished, corncribs were empty, and every bale of cotton that could be found was burnt by the savages. I saw no grain of any sort except little patches they had spilled when feeding their horses and which there was not even a chicken left in the country to eat. A bag of oats might have lain anywhere along the road without danger from the beasts of the field, though I cannot say it would have been safe from the assaults of hungry man.

Crowds of soldiers were tramping over the road in both directions;' it was like traveling through the streets of a populous town all day. They were mostly on foot, and I saw numbers seated on the roadside greedily eating raw turnips, meat skins, parched corn—anything they could find, even picking up the loose grains that Sherman's horses had left. I felt tempted to stop and empty the contents of our provision baskets into their laps, but the dreadful accounts that were given of the state of the country before us made prudence get the better of our generosity.

Before crossing the Oconee at Milledgeville we ascended an immense hill, from which there was a fine view of the town, with Governor Brown's fortifications in the foreground and the river rolling at our feet. The Yankees had burnt the bridge; so we had to cross on a ferry. There

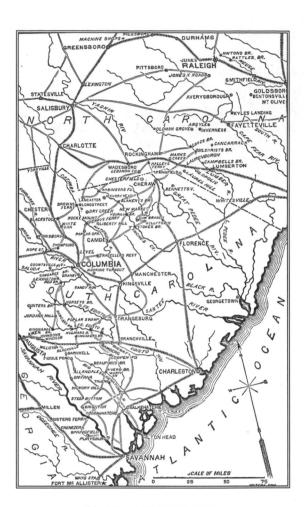

SAVANNAH TO BENTONVILLE

was a long train of vehicles ahead of us, and it was nearly an hour before our turn came; so we had ample time to look about us. On our left was a field where thirty thousand Yankees had camped hardly three weeks before. It was strewn with the debris they had left behind, and the poor people of the neighbor hood were wandering over it, seeking for anything they could find to eat, even picking up grains of corn that were scattered around where the Yankees had fed their horses. We were told that a great many valuables were found there at first, plunder that the invaders had left behind, but the place had been picked over so often by this time that little now remained except tufts of loose cotton, piles of half-rotted grain, and the carcasses of slaughtered animals, which raised a horrible stench. Some men were plowing in one part of the field, making ready for next year's crop.

—ANDREWS, *The War-Time Journal of a Georgia Girl*

XXIX.12

THE BURNING OF COLUMBIA

Sherman reached Columbia, capital of South Carolina, or? February 17. That night the city burned. Whether "Sherman burned Columbia" or not is still hotly debated. Sherman himself denied responsibility for the conflagration, but he did say that "having utterly ruined Columbia, the right wing began its march northward." Perhaps the fire was started by accident; perhaps by the Confederates burning their cotton; perhaps by Negroes; perhaps by soldiers out of control.

We have here two accounts of the tragedy. The first comes from George Nichols, whose *Story of the Great March* was the most widely read of contemporary Civil War narratives; the second from Henry Hitchcock, whom we have already met.

A. "A Scene of Shameful Confusion"

Columbia, February 17th [1865]—It is with a feeling of proud exultation that I write the date of Columbia. We have conquered and occupy the capital of the haughty state that instigated and forced forward the treason which has brought on this desolating war. The city which was to have been the capital of the Confederacy if Lee and the Rebel hosts had been driven from Richmond is now overrun by Northern soldiers. The beautiful capitol building bears the marks of Yankee shot and shell, and the old flag which the Rebels insulted at Sumter now floats freely in the air from the house tops of the central city of South Carolina. . . .

General Sherman and General Howard were the first to cross the bridge, and entered the city, followed by their staffs. A scene of shameful confusion met their eyes. On every side were evidences of disorder; bales of cotton scattered here and there; articles of household furniture and merchandise of every description cast pell-mell 'in every direction by the frightened inhabitants, who had escaped from a city which they supposed was doomed to destruction. . . .

The three or four days' notice of our approach enabled the government officials to remove most of the material be longing to the branch of the Treasury Department which was located at this point; yet large quantities of paper for printing Confederate notes and bonds, with type, printing-presses, etc., has fallen into our hands. This loss is irreparable to the Rebel government.

The arsenal was found well stocked with shot, shell, fixed ammunition, powder, Enfield rifles, carbines, and other material of war. A full battery of four rifled English Blakely guns, which were in a battery commanding the bridge, was also taken, with caissons and other material. Connected with the arsenal are shops full of costly machinery for the manufacture of arms and ammunition, with founderies for all sorts of castings. A little way down the river there is a large powder-mill. All of this will be thoroughly destroyed. . . .

The store-houses are filled with all sorts of supplies—flour, meal, bacon, corn, harness, hardware, etc.—while cotton is found in every direction. As there is no treasury agent of our government to appropriate this costly material for somebody's benefit, I doubt if a very correct record of the quantity will be made before it is burned. . . .

I began to-day's record early in the evening, and while writing I noticed an unusual glare in the sky, and heard a sound of running to and fro in the streets, with the loud talk of servants that the horses must be removed to a safer place. Running out, I found, to my surprise and real sorrow, that the central part of the city, including the main business street, was in flames, while the wind, which had been blowing a hurricane all day, was driving the sparks and cinders in heavy masses over the eastern portion of the city, where the finest residences are situated. These buildings, all wooden, were instantly ignited by the flying sparks. In half an hour the conflagration was raging in every direction, and but for a providential change of the wind to the south and west, the whole city would in a few hours have been laid in ashes.

As it is, several hundred buildings, including the old State House, one or two churches, most of the carved work stored in the sheds round about the new capitol, and a large number of public store-houses, have been destroyed. In some of the public buildings the Rebels had stored shot, shell, and other ammunition, and when the flames reached these magazines we had the Atlanta experience over again—the smothered boom, the huge columns of fire shooting heavenward, the red-hot iron flying here and there. But there was one feature, pitiable indeed, which we did not find at Atlanta. Groups of men, women, and children were gathered in the streets and squares, huddled together over a trunk, a mat tress, or a bundle of clothes. Our soldiers were at work with a will, removing household goods from the dwellings which were in the track of the flames, and here and there extinguishing the fire when there was hope of saving a building. General Sherman and his officers worked with their own hands until long after midnight, trying to save life and property. The house taken for headquarters is now filled with old men, women, and children who have been driven from their homes by a more pitiless enemy than the detested "Yankees."

Various causes are assigned to explain the origin of the fire. I am quite sure that it originated in sparks flying from the hundreds of bales of cotton which the Rebels had placed along the middle of the main street, and fired as they left the city. Fire from a tightly-compressed bale of cotton is unlike that of a more open material, which burns itself out. The fire lies smouldering in a bale of cotton long after it appears to be extinguished; and in this instance, when our soldiers supposed they had extinguished the fire, it suddenly broke out again with the most disastrous effect.

There were fires, however, which must have been started independent of the above-named cause. The source of these is ascribed to the desire for revenge from some two hundred of our prisoners, who had escaped from the cars as they were being conveyed from this city to Charlotte, and, with the memories of long sufferings in the miserable pens I visited yesterday on the other side of

the river, sought this means of retaliation. Again, it is said that the soldiers who first entered the town, intoxicated with success and a liberal supply of bad liquor, which was freely distributed among them by designing citizens, in an insanity of exhilaration set fire to unoccupied houses.

Whatever may have been the cause of the disaster, the direful result is deprecated by General Sherman most emphatically; for however heinous the crimes of this people against our common country, we do not war against women and children and helpless persons.

—Nichols, *The Story of the Great March*

B. Major Hitchcock Explains the Burning of Columbia

Fayetteville, North Carolina, Sunday, March 12, 186S

One word about Columbia. It was not burned by orders, but expressly against orders and in spite of the utmost effort on our part to save it. Everything seemed to conspire for its destruction. The streets were full of loose cotton, brought out and set on fire *by the rebels* before they left,—I saw it when we rode into town. A gale of wind was blowing all that day and that night, and the branches of the trees were white with cotton tufts blown about everywhere. The citizens themselves—like idiots, madmen,—brought out large quantities of liquor as soon as our troops entered and distributed it freely among them, even to the guards which Gen. Howard had immediately placed all over the city as soon as we came in. This fact is unquestionable, and was one chief cause of what followed. Here in Fayetteville a lady has told Gen. Sherman that Gen. Joe Johnson told her, yesterday morning, that the burning of Columbia was caused by liquor which the people there gave our soldiers. Besides there were 200 or 300 of "our prisoners" who had escaped from rebel hands before, and when we reached Columbia burning to revenge themselves for the cruel treatment they had received; and our own men were fully aware of the claims of Columbia to eminence as the "cradle of secession." In that same town, in 1861, a woman, a school-teacher from New England, was *tarred and feathered* and sent North "for abolition sentiments."

The result of all this was that partly by accident, from the burning cotton, partly by design by our escaped prisoners, and by our drunken men, fire was started in several places,—and once started, with the furious wind blowing, it was simply impossible to put it out. *Nothing was left undone,—* I speak advisedly—to prevent and stop it; Gen. Howard, Sherman, and other Generals and their staffs, and many other officers and hundreds of men were up and at work nearly all night, trying to do it, but in vain. The guard was changed—*three times* as many men were on guard as were ever on guard at any one time in Savannah where perfect order was preserved; our own officers shot our men down like dogs wherever they were found riotous or drunk—in short no effort was spared to stop it; and but for the liquor it might perhaps have been stopped. This is the truth; and Wade Hampton's letter to Sherman—it will be in the New York Herald if not already published North—charging him with sundry crimes at Columbia is a tissue of lies.

—Hitchcock, "Letters and Diaries"

XXIX.13

General Sherman Thinks His Name May Live

We have already read Sherman's statement to the Mayor of Atlanta on the iron necessities of war. Here is an explanation*—and a prophecy—directed to his wife. On the death of his father, Sherman had been practically adopted by Senator Ewing of Ohio. In 1850 he married Ewing's daughter, Ellen. His war letters to his wife are among the most revealing and touching of Civil War letters.

---

* Reprinted from *Home Letters of General Sherman* edited by M. A. De Wolfe Howe, copyright 1909 by Charles Scribner's Sons, 1937 by M. A. De Wolfe Howe; used by permission of the publishers.

Savannah, January 5, 1865

John writes that I am in everybody's mouth and that even he is known as my brother, and that all the Shermans are now feted as relatives of me. Surely you and the children will not be overlooked by those who profess to honor me. I do think that in the several grand epochs of this war, my name will have a prominent part, and not least among them will be the determination I took at Atlanta to destroy that place, and march on this city, whilst Thomas, my lieutenant, should dispose of Hood. The idea, the execution and strategy are all good, and will in time be understood. I don't know that you comprehend the magnitude of the thing, but you can see the importance attached to it in England where the critics stand ready to turn against any American general who makes a mistake or fails in its execution. In my case they had time to commit themselves to the conclusion that if I succeeded I would be a great general, but if I failed I would be set down a fool. My success is already assured, so that I will be found to sustain the title. I am told that were I to go north I would be feted and petted, but as I have no 'intention of going, you must sustain the honors of the family. I know exactly what amount of merit attaches to my own conduct, and what will survive the clamor of time. The quiet preparation I made before the Atlanta Campaign, the rapid movement on Resaca, the crossing the Chattahoochee without loss in the face of a skillful general with a good army, the movement on Jonesboro, whereby Atlanta fell, and the resolution I made to divide my army, with one part to take Savannah and the other to meet Hood in Tennessee are all clearly mine, and will survive us both in history. I don't know that you can understand the merit of the latter, but it will stamp me in years to come, and will be more appreciated in Europe than in America. I warrant your father will find parallel in the history of the Greeks and Persians, but none on our continent. For his sake I am glad of the success that has attended me, and I know he will feel more pride in my success than you or I do. Oh that Willy were living! how his eyes would brighten and his bosom swell with honest pride if he could hear and understand these things. . . .

You will doubtless read all the details of our march and stay in Savannah in the papers, whose spies infest our camps, spite of all I can do, but I could tell you thousands of little incidents which would more interest you. The women here are, as at Memphis, disposed to usurp my time more from curiosity than business. They have been told of my burning and killing until they expected the veriest monster, but their eyes were opened when Hardee, G. W. Smith and McLaws, the three chief officers of the Rebel army, fled across the Savannah river consigning their families to my special care. There are some very elegant people here, whom I knew in better days and who do not seem ashamed to call on the 'Vandal Chief.' They regard us just as the Romans did the Goths and the parallel is not unjust. Many of my stalwart men with red beards and huge frames look like giants, and it is wonderful how smoothly all things move, for they all seem to feel implicit faith in me not because I am strong or bold, but because they think I know everything. It seems impossible for us to go anywhere without being where I have been before. My former life from 1840 to 1846 seems providential and every bit of knowledge then acquired is re turned, tenfold. Should it so happen that I should approach Charleston on that very ground where I used to hunt with Jim Poyas, and Mr. Quash, and ride by moonlight to save day time, it would be even more strange than here where I was only a visitor.

—Howe, ed., *Home Letters of General Sherman*

XXX

THE WILDERNESS

In February 1864 U. S. Grant was made lieutenant general and placed in command of all the armies of the United States. For the first time it was possible to organize a unified plan of operations against the Confederacy, and this Grant promptly proceeded to do. Grant might have stayed in Washington to supervise all the complex operations which his plan involved; he preferred to accompany Meade in the crucial campaign against Lee. Thus at last these two great military chieftains were to meet in battle, a battle which ended with Lee's surrender at Appomattox just a year later. In the campaigns of 1864-65 Grant enjoyed most of the advantages. He had a numerical superiority of about two to one, and no difficulty in getting reinforcements when needed. He could count on simultaneous attacks from other quarters which would drain the Confederacy of manpower, war materiel, and—in the end—the will to resist. If he did not enjoy interior lines of communication he did have command of the seas and the assistance of the navy. His armies were well fed, well clothed, and well equipped, and never lacked for munitions. As he took, and held, the offensive, he had the initiative. Lee had only the advantage of geography, and of his own military genius. The terrain over which the armies fought was well adapted to defensive operations; Lee knew it intimately; he could draw on some help from Richmond and from Beauregard on the James. But by 1864 death, disease, and desertion had reduced the Army of Northern Virginia to a point well below its strength of earlier years, and the blockade and the capture of Confederate arsenals had reduced its fighting strength. Its soldiers were hungry, ill-clad, ill-shod, and battle weary; they knew that they could not count on reinforcement or replacement, and they knew, too, that things were going badly almost everywhere else in the Confederacy. That for a year they held off Grant's mighty hosts is a tribute to their fortitude, their fighting qualities, and their devotion to their heroic leader.

The strategy of Grant's campaign against Lee is simple enough. His objective was not so much Richmond as Lee's army; his policy to hammer away at it until it was decimated. Lee's task was to keep Grant away from Richmond and to inflict such losses upon him that he would abandon the offensive or that the North would despair of victory and turn Lincoln out at the fall elections. With almost anyone else Lee's strategy might have worked, but in Grant he had an opponent who never knew when he was licked.

The Wilderness campaign was really one prolonged battle, from May 4, when Grant crossed the Rapidan, to June 14, when he crossed the James. The details of this battle are confusing but the general pattern is clear. To get to Richmond Grant had to whip Lee's army, or destroy it; Lee's job was to tangle him up in the Wilderness and destroy him. Imagine a diagonal line of about sixty miles, stretching roughly south easterly from Germanna Ford on the Rapidan to Cold Harbor, just ten miles east of Richmond. Grant smashed at Lee's line, was held and thrust back, and then slid down the diagonal with Lee racing on a parallel line to stop him. Attack, repulse. slide, attack, repulse, slide—that is the tactical story of the Battle of the Wilderness, Spotsylvania, Hanover Court House, and Cold Harbor. No single battle in this campaign reached the dimensions of Gettysburg or Shiloh, but collectively they constituted the most costly campaign of the war and they embraced, too, the hottest fighting of the war. Grant's losses in the Wilderness campaign came to about 55,000; Lee's are unknown, but were probably about half that number.

Who won the Battle of the Wilderness? That is hard to say. On the face of it the victory was Lee's. He had prevented Grant from breaking his lines, had saved Richmond, had forced Grant to abandon the campaign of the direct attack from the north and fall back on siege, and had inflicted on Grant losses almost as large as the whole of Lee's own army. Yet Grant had largely achieved his own primary objective. He had so punished Lee that the Army of Northern Virginia never really recovered. He had thus prepared the way for the subsequent attack on Richmond from the south. And he ended his campaign with more men in his army than he had when he crossed the Rapidan.

XXX.I

U.S. GRANT PLANS HIS SPRING CAMPAIGN

Here is Grant's own statement of the grand strategy which he formulated for the spring of 1864; it has all his characteristic sparseness of phrase and his objectivity.

The Union armies were now divided into nineteen departments, though four of them in the West had been concentrated into a single military division. The Army of the Potomac was a separate command, and had no territorial limits. There were thus seventeen distinct commanders. Before this time these various armies had acted separately and independently of each other, giving the enemy an opportunity, often, of depleting one command, not pressed, to reenforce another more actively engaged. I determined to stop this. To this end I regarded the Army of the Potomac as the center, and all west to Memphis, along the line described as our position at the time, and north of it, the right wing; the Army of the James, under General Butler, as the left wing, and all the troops south as a force in rear of the enemy. Some of these last were occupying positions from which they could not render-service proportionate to their numerical strength. All such were depleted to the minimum necessary to hold their positions as a guard against blockade-runners; when they could not do this, their positions were abandoned altogether. In this way ten thousand men were added to the Army of the James from South Carolina alone, with General Gillmore in command. It was not contemplated that Gillmore should leave his department; but as most of his troops were taken, presumably for active service, he asked to accompany them, and

was permitted to do so. Officers and soldiers on furlough, of whom there were many thousands, were ordered to their proper commands; concentration was the order of the day, and the problem was to accomplish it in time to advance at the earliest moment the roads would permit.

As a reënforcement to the Army of the Potomac, or to act in support of it, the Ninth Army Corps, over twenty thousand strong, under General Burnside, had been rendezvoused at Annapolis, Maryland. This was an admirable position for such a reenforcement. The corps could be brought at the last moment as a reenforcement to the Army of the Potomac, or it could be thrown on the sea-coast, south of Norfolk, to operate against Richmond from that direction. In fact, up to the last moment Burnside and the War Department both thought the Ninth Corps was intended for such an expedition.

My general plan now was to concentrate all the force possible against the Confederate armies in the field. There were but two such, as we have seen, east of the Mississippi River and facing north: the Army of Northern Virginia, General Robert E. Lee commanding, was on the south bank of the Rapidan, confronting the Army of the Potomac; the second, under General Joseph L. Johnston, was at Dalton, Georgia, opposed to Sherman, who was still at Chattanooga. Besides these main armies, the Confederates had to guard the Shenandoah Valley—a great storehouse to feed their armies from—and their line of communications from Richmond to Tennessee. Forrest, a brave and intrepid cavalry general, was in the West, with a large force, making a larger command necessary to hold what we had gained in middle and west Tennessee. We could not abandon any territory north of the line held by the enemy, because it would lay the Northern States open to invasion. But as the Army of the Potomac was the principal garrison for the protection of Washington, even while it was moving on to Lee, so all the forces to the West, and the Army of the James, guarded their special trusts when advancing from them as well as when remaining at them—better, indeed, for they forced the enemy to guard his own lines and resources, at a greater distance from ours and with a greater force, since small expeditions could not so well be sent out to destroy a bridge or tear up a few miles of railroad track, burn a storehouse, or inflict other little annoyances. Accordingly I arranged for a simultaneous movement all along the line.

Sherman was to move from Chattanooga, Johnston's army and Atlanta being his objective points. General George Crook, commanding in West Virginia, was to move from the mouth of the Gauley River with a cavalry force and some artillery, the Virginia and Tennessee railroad to be his objective. Either the enemy would have to keep a large force to protect their communications or see them destroyed, and a large amount of forage and provisions, which they so much needed, would fall into our hands. Sigel, who was in command in the valley of Virginia, was to advance up the valley, covering the North from an invasion through that channel as well while advancing as by remaining near Harper's Perry. Every mile he advanced also gave up possession of stores on which Lee relied. Butler was to advance by the James River, having Richmond and Petersburg as his objective. Before the advance commenced I visited Butler at Fort Monroe. This was the first time I had ever met him. Before giving him any order as to the part he was to play in the approaching campaign I invited his views. They were very much such as I intended to direct, and as I did direct, in writing, before leaving. . . .

Banks in the Department of the Gulf was ordered to assemble all his troops at New Orleans in time to join in the general move, Mobile to be his objective.

—Personal Memoirs of U. S. Grant

XXX.2

Colonel Porter Draws a Portrait of General Grant

This portrait of Grant is, as might be expected, a friendly one. Horace Porter left Harvard to enter West Point, and graduated

third in rank in the class of 1860. He was appointed chief ordnance officer of the Army of the Potomac and then to the same position in the Army of the Cumberland, where he first made Grant's acquaintance. In November 1863 he was recalled for duty in Washington, and in April 1864 appointed aide-de-camp to Grant. He was at Grant's side all through the Wilderness and Petersburg campaigns, and his book, *Campaigning with Grant,* is perhaps the best description of that chapter of Grant's military career. After the war Porter had a long and distinguished career in business and public affairs. He was vice-president of the Pullman Company, Ambassador to France, American delegate to the Hague Tribunal, and active in Republican politics and in social life.

A description of General Grant's personal appearance at this important period of his career may not be out of place here, particularly as up to that time the public had received such erroneous impressions of him. There were then few correct portraits of him in circulation. Some of the earliest pictures purporting to be photographs of him had been manufactured when he was at the distant front, never stopping in one place long enough to be "focused." Nothing daunted, the practisers of that art which is the chief solace of the vain had photographed a burly beef-contractor, and spread the pictures broadcast as representing the determined, but rather robust, features of the coming hero, and it was some time before the real photographs which followed were believed to be genuine. False impressions of him were derived, too, from the fact that he had come forth from a country leather store, and was famous chiefly for striking sledge-hammer blows in the field, and conducting relentless pursuits of his foes through the swamps of the Southwest. He was pictured in the popular mind as striding about in the most approved swash-buckler style of melodrama.

Many of us were not a little surprised to find in him a man of slim figure, slightly stooped, five feet eight inches in height, weighing only a hundred and thirty-five pounds, and of a modesty of mien and gentleness of manner which seemed to fit him more for the court than for the camp. His eyes were dark-gray, and were the most expressive of his features. Like nearly all men who speak little, he was a good listener; but his face gave little indication of his thoughts, and it was the expression of his eyes which furnished about the only response to the speaker who conversed with him. When he was about to say anything amusing, there was always a perceptible twinkle in his eyes before he began to speak, and he often laughed heartily at a witty remark or a humorous incident.

His mouth, like Washington's, was of the letter-box shape, the contract of the lips forming a nearly horizontal line. This feature was of a pattern in striking contrast with that of Napoleon, who had a bow mouth, which looked as if it had been modeled after a front view of his cocked hat. The firmness with which the general's square-shaped jaws were set when his features were in repose was highly expressive of his force of character and the strength of his will-power. His hair and beard were of a chestnut-brown color. The-beard was worn full, no part of the face being shaved, but, like the hair, was always kept closely and nearly trimmed. Like Cromwell, Lincoln, and several other great men in history, he had a wart on his cheek. In his case it was small, and located on the right side just above the line of the beard.

His face was not perfectly symmetrical, the left eye being a very little lower than the right. His brow was high, broad, and rather square, and was creased with several horizontal wrinkles, which helped to emphasize the serious and somewhat careworn look which was never absent from his countenance. This expression, however, was in no wise an indication of his nature, which was always buoyant, cheerful, and hopeful. His voice was exceedingly musical, and one of the clearest in sound and most distinct in utterance that I have ever heard. It had a singular power of penetration, and sentences spoken by him in an ordinary tone in camp could be heard at a distance which was surprising.

His gait in walking might have been called decidedly unmilitary. He never carried his body erect, and having no ear for music or rhythm, he never kept step to the airs played by the bands, no matter how vigorously the bass drums emphasized the accent. When walking in company there was no attempt to keep step with others. In conversing he usually employed only two gestures; one was the stroking of his chin beard with his left hand; the other was the raising and lowering of his right hand, and resting it at intervals upon his knee or a table, the hand being held with the fingers close together and the knuckles bent, so that the back of the hand and fingers formed a right angle. When not pressed by any matter of importance he was often slow in his movements, but when roused to activity he was quick in every motion, and worked with marvelous rapidity.

He was civil to all who came in contact with him, and never attempted to snub any one, or treat anybody with less consideration on account of his inferiority in rank. With him there was none of the puppyism so often bred by power, and none of the dogmatism which Samuel Johnson characterized as puppyism grown to maturity. . . .

Throughout this memorable year (1864-5), the most important as well as the most harassing of his entire military career, General Grant never in any instance failed to manifest those traits which were the true elements of his greatness. He was always calm amid excitement, and patient under trials. He looked neither to the past with regret nor to the future with apprehension. When he could not control he endured, and in every great crisis he could "convince when others could not advise." His calmness of demeanor and unruffled temper were often a marvel even to those most familiar with him. In the midst of the most-exciting scenes he rarely raised his voice above its ordinary pitch or manifested the least irritability. Whether encountered at noonday or awakened from sleep at midnight, his manner was always the same; whether receiving the report of an army commander or of a private soldier serving as a courier or a scout, he listened with equal deference and eave it the same strict attention. He could not only discipline others, but he could discipline himself. If he had lived in ancient days he might, in his wrath, have broken the two tables of stone: he never would have broken the laws which were written on them. The only manifestation of anger he had indulged in during the campaign was upon the occasion . . . when he found a teamster beating his horses near the Totopotomoy.

He never criticized an officer harshly in the presence of others. If fault had to be found with him, it was never made an occasion to humiliate him or wound his feelings. The only pointed reprimand he ever administered was in the instance mentioned in the battle of the Wilderness, when an officer left his troops and came to him to magnify the dangers which were to be feared from Lee's methods of warfare. The fact that he never "nagged" his officers, but treated them all with consideration, led them to communicate with him freely and intimately; and he thus gained much information which other wise he might not have received. To have a well-disciplined command he did not deem it necessary to have an unhappy army. His ideas of discipline did not accord with those of the Russian officer who, one night in the Moscow campaign, reprimanded a soldier for putting a ball of snow under his head for a pillow, for the reason that indulgence in such uncalled-for luxuries would destroy the high character of the army.

It was an interesting study in human nature to watch the general's actions in camp. He would sit for hours in front of his tent, or just inside of it looking out, smoking a cigar very slowly, seldom with a paper or a map in his hands, and looking like the laziest man in camp. But at such periods his mind was working more actively than that of any one in the army. He talked less and thought more than any one in the service. He studiously avoided performing any duty which some one else could do as well or better than he, and in this respect demonstrated his rare powers of administration and executive methods. He was one of the few men holding high position who did not waste valuable hours by giving his personal attention to petty details. He never consumed his time in reading over court-martial proceedings, or figuring up the

items of supplies on hand, or writing unnecessary letters or communications. He held subordinates to a strict accountability in the performance of such duties, and kept his own time for thought. It was this quiet but intense thinking, and the well-matured ideas which resulted from it, that led to the prompt and vigorous action which was constantly witnessed during this year, so pregnant with events.

—PORTER, *Campaigning with Grant*

XXX.3

PRIVATE GOSS DESCRIBES THE BATTLE OF THE WILDERNESS

Though the entire campaign from early May to mid-June is generally described as the Wilderness, it is the fighting of May 5 and 6 that is called the Battle of the Wilderness. As was so often the case in the war, neither commander wanted to bring on a general engagement that day. Grant much preferred to get out of the Wilderness, if he could, and in any event he had not yet brought Burnside up to his army; Lee was waiting for Longstreet, who, starting on the fourth, made a spectacular march of 35 miles in one day. Warren's corps, however, ran into Ewell at the Old Wilderness Tavern, and the two tangled up. Then Heth's division, of A. P. Hill's corps, advancing up the Orange Plank Road, ran into Getty, of Hancock's corps. The fighting that day was fierce but inconclusive, and it was renewed the next day on a larger scale.

Warren Goss, who here tells the story of the fighting on the fifth and the sixth, we have met before.

Leading our right column on the morning of the 5th [May, 1864], Warren's corps resumed its prescribed march towards Parker's Store, which is on the Orange plank road. . . . Early in the morning, Ewell began his march on the same road by which Griffin was advancing. They met. The Union skirmishers were driven in. The intelligence of the meeting was conveyed to Grant, and orders suspending the movements prescribed to the different corps were at once given.

Grant and Meade both arrived at the Wilderness Tavern shortly after the initial encounter. Meade was heard to say: "They have left a division here to fool us while they concentrate and prepare a position towards the North Anna, and what I want is to prevent those fellows getting back to Mine Run." Grant, with this misconception, at once ordered an attack to brush away or capture this obtruding force.

The attack was opened by Griffin's division, which at first swept everything in its front. It had simply encountered the van of Ewell's column. . . . The disordered van of Ewell's column re-formed on a wooded hill, and resumed at once the offensive. It so happened that the right of Warren's Corps was at this time uncovered. Wright's division of the Sixth Corps, which should have covered this flank, had not come up, owing to the dense underbrush through which it was compelled to move. On this exposed flank Ewell directed his attack. On Griffin's left was Wadsworth's division. This advanced, but while beating through the dense undergrowth encountered a terrible fire from an unseen enemy. It illustrates the difficulty that beset troops operating in this tangled region, that there being no other guides, their directions were given them by the points of the compass. The orders were to advance due west. For some unknown reason Wadsworth advanced northwest, and this brought the fire of the enemy on his flank. Under this terrible flank fire the division broke in disorder. The best way to retreat was for each man to get to the rear, and not stand on the order of his going. The division of Wadsworth finally reformed in the rear and did good service during the fight which followed. . . .

In this abrupt encounter began the battle of the Wilderness. The opening was not auspicious. Warren had lost three thousand men. The enemy was in force 'in our front. . . .

The encounter . . . awakened Grant to the fact that the Army of Northern Virginia was in his front. He countermanded the previously ordered marches, and at once accepted Lee's challenge to battle. Here in the gloomy forest, with dogged resolution, he prepared to grapple with the enemy in this blind wrestle to the death. He at once recalled Hancock's corps from its march to Shady Grove Church. Our corps had advanced about ten miles when the order reached us, and at eleven o'clock we began our return march up the Brock road. . . .

Getty had already begun the fight before our arrival. Cheers went up from our sweat-begrimed, dusty veterans, as they came up at about three o'clock and formed 'in double line of battle in front of the Brock road. The road was very narrow, and densely wooded on both sides. Here we began to construct rifle-pits, by piling up logs and throwing up the soil against them. For this purpose men used their tin drinking-cups, bayonets, and caseknives, as well as the few shovels and picks which accompanied each division on pack-mules. We had not completed our rifle-pits when an order came to move on the enemy.

The scene of savage fighting with the ambushed enemy, which followed, defies description. No one could see the fight fifty feet from him. The roll and crackle of the musketry was something terrible, even to the veterans of many battles. The lines were very near each other, and from the dense underbrush and the tops of the trees came puffs of smoke, the "ping" of the bullets, and the yell of the enemy. It was a blind and bloody hunt to the death, in bewildering thickets, rather than a battle.

Amid the tangled, darkened woods, the "ping! ping! ping!" the "pop! pop! pop!" of the rifles, and the long roll and roar of musketry blending on our right and left, were terrible. In advancing it was next to impossible to preserve a distinct line, and we were constantly broken into small groups. The underbrush and briars scratched our faces, tore our clothing, and tripped our feet from under us, constantly.

On our left, a few pieces of artillery, stationed on cleared high ground, beat time to the steady roar of musketry. On the Orange plank road, Rickett's battery, or Kirby's, familiar to us in so many battles, was at work with its usual vigor, adding to the uproar.

"We are playing right into these devils' hands! Bushwhacking is the game! There ain't a tree in our front, twenty feet high, but there is a reb up that tree!" said Wad Rider. Two, three, and four times we rushed upon the enemy, but were met by a murderous fire and with heavy loss from concealed enemies. As often as we rushed forward we were compelled to get back. . . .

The uproar of battle continued through the twilight hours. It was eight o'clock before the deadly crackle of musketry died gradually away, and the sad shadows of night, like a pall, fell over the dead in these ensanguined thickets. The groans and cries for water or for help from the wounded gave place to the sounds of the conflict. . . . Thus ended the first day's fighting of the Army of the Potomac under Grant.

Our lines now faced westward. Burnside's corps had arrived early in the morning, and the formation was north and south in the following order: Sedgwick on the right, then Warren's, Burnside's and Hancock's corps, in the order named. The orders given for the battle were very simple. They were these: "Attack along the entire line at five o'clock."

There was no opportunity for grand maneuvers on this difficult field. It so happened that the commanders of both armies had aggressively determined to assume the offensive early on the morning of the 6th. The plan of the Confederate commander was to overwhelm our left and compel us to retreat to the Rapidan. Longstreet had, however, not yet arrived to participate in the fight, and Lee could not deliver his decisive blow until he came up. Pending his arrival he determined to call our attention from our left by a movement against our right. It thus fell out that Lee began his movement before the hour of attack designated by Grant.

Before five o'clock the roar of musketry on our right told that Sedgwick was attacked by the enemy. Then Hancock and Warren joined in the attack, and the whole line was engaged. . . . The enemy were at once attacked with such vigor that their lines were broken at all points, and they were driven confusedly through the woods. Their dead

and wounded lay thick in the jungle of scrub-oaks, pines, and underbrush, through which we rushed upon them. Squads of prisoners constantly going to the rear exchanged rough but good natured salutations with our men. . . .

By six o'clock the rebel lines had been driven a mile and a half and were broken and disordered. The advance of our corps through swamps and tangled thickets, in this hot en counter, had broken our own lines. A proper formation of the ranks, or any control by the officers in command, in this tangled region, seemed impossible. In this disorganized condition a portion of our lines, under Birney, was brought to a stand by the firm resistance of the enemy. It had encountered the van of Longstreet's corps hastening to the fight. A halt was ordered, and the lines which had become irregular, and the brigades and regiments confusedly mixed, were reorganized.

Longstreet had, meanwhile, begun to form on the plank road, and when a further advance was attempted by the Union lines, they met this new force, and the fighting became fierce and bloody. Hancock had promptly informed Meade of the presence of some of Longstreet's men on his front. Neither was aware that he had met the entire force of that general. Intelligence had been gathered from prisoners the night previous, which led to the inference that he was moving to attack the Union left. Expecting him in this direction proved to be a great hindrance to Hancock. It was for this that he had allowed his left, under Gibbon, to remain on the Brock road. . . .

At eleven o'clock the firing died away. Burnside though constantly ordered, had not attacked. Longstreet, mean while, was preparing for a decisive onslaught on our front. His first blow fell on Frank's brigade of Hancock's command, which was soon swept away by the whirlwind of attack, then struck Mott's division and scattered it like leaves before the wind. Hancock answered to this by attempting to swing back his left to the plank road, and unite with his right, which was still holding its advance position.

On the right of Hancock, Wadsworth's division fought with heroic firmness. It charged the enemy several times, but was finally driven back in disorder. In this encounter General Wadsworth, while in the rear and centre of his lines cheering his men, fell mortally wounded. In the confusion which followed he was abandoned to the enemy, and died next day within their lines.

It was impossible to maneuver on account of the obstructive undergrowth, where no one could see a hundred paces in any direction. The roar of musketry alone disclosed the position of the foe, and the movements were generally learned only by actual collisions. Under these circumstances, general officers could hold but little control of their lines.

The troops fell back, in the confusion caused by the difficult field on which they fought, and re-formed in two lines behind their old intrenchments on the Brock road. Before this the tempest of the attack had ceased as suddenly as it began.

Longstreet, at the head of the assaulting column, was desperately wounded. He had, by mistake, been fired on by his own men when the tempest was at its height. This caused the halt in the attack. Lee now took command of this part of the line in person, and cautiously postponed further battle until more perfect dispositions of his troops were made. This lull in the storm lasted until four o'clock. The attack was then resumed. Then the Confederate columns came dashing on through the undergrowth until within a hundred yards of our lines. Here they halted and opened fire. Protected by their breastworks, for a time our men received but little harm. . . .

Flames sprang up in the woods in our front, where the fight of the morning had taken place. With crackling roar, like an army of fire, it came down upon the Union line. The wind drove the blinding smoke and suffocating heat into our faces. This, added to the oppressive beat of the weather, was almost unendurable. It soon became terrible. The line of fire, with resistless march, swept the thickets before its advance, then reaching out its tongue of flame, ignited the breastworks com posed of resinous logs, which soon roared and crackled along their entire length. The men fought the enemy and the flames at the same time. Their hair and beards were singed and their faces blistered.

At last, blinded by the smoke and suffocated by the hot breath of the flames, with the whole length of their intrenchments a crackling mass of fire, they gave way and fell back to the second line of log intrenchments. With a shout the rebel column approached the road and attempted to seize the abandoned position. The impartial flames in turn drove them back.

The fire soon consumed the logs? and the rebels planted their colors there.

The fire swept on and reached our second line of intrenchments. This, like the first, was soon consumed. The men formed at some places eight and ten ranks deep, the rear men loading the muskets for the front ranks, and thus undauntedly kept up the fight while the logs in front of them were in flames. Finally blistered, blinded, and suffocating, they gave way. The enemy yelled with exultation. They rushed forward and attempted to place their colors on this line of our defense. Their triumph was brief, for the last line of log defences was soon consumed like the first. Then, with a shout resembling the rebel yell, our men charged the enemy, and swept them back from the field. At sunset our pickets were advanced half a mile without opposition.

During the conflict our men had exhausted their ammunition and had been obliged to gather cartridges from the dead and wounded. Their rifles, in many instances, became so hot by constant firing, that they were unable to hold them in their hands. The fire was the most terrible enemy our men met that day, and few survivors will forget this attack of the flames on their lines. . . .

After sundown the Confederates made an attack on the right of Burnside's corps, creating considerable confusion. The night prevented them from following up their success. Thus ended this terrible battle, the full details of which were hid in the-tangled woods and darkling forests, where its mysteries will never be disclosed.

—Goss, *Recollections of a Private*

XXX.4

"Texans Always Move Them"

The battle of the sixth was a near disaster for Lee. Early in the morning the Federals renewed the attack, Sedgwick and Warren smashing at Ewell but making no headway against his breastworks. Meantime the fighting shifted to the Union right, where Hancock was trying to break through Hill's Corps. At midafternoon Wadsworth's division rolled up Hill's right flank while Birney's division struck on the left; the Confederate line broke and the victorious Federals poured through. But Longstreet's veterans were already coming up, Gregg's Texans in the van. Lee rallied them, and they dashed in and saved the day for the Confederacy. This is the first of the "Lee to the Rear" episodes. The author of this stirring account is unknown.

As we stood upon this hill, Lee excited and in close consultation with Longstreet—our batteries thundering into the Wilderness below, the roar of musketry from the under growth below—our men retreating in a disorganized mass, and the Yankees pressing on and within musket shot, almost, of the hill upon which stood our idolized chief, indeed was an exciting time, and the emergency called for *immediate* and *determined* action upon the part of the Confederate General. Lee was equal to the hour. Action must *not* be delayed, for in less than five minutes the enemy would be upon the hill. Longstreet's corps as it then stood in one mingled mass upon the plank road, could not be thrown in, and time must be allowed for it to reform, and place itself in line of battle. The cannon thundered, musketry rolled, stragglers were fleeing, couriers riding here and there in post-haste, minnies began to sing, the dying and wounded were jolted by the flying ambulances, and filling the road-side, adding to the excitement the terror of death. The "Texas brigade," was in front of Fields' division—while "Humphrey's brigade" of Mississippians led the van of Kershaw's division.

The consultation ended. Gen. Gregg and Gen. Humphrey were ordered to form their brigades in line of battle, which was quickly done, and we found ourselves near the brow of the hill, Gregg on the left—Humphrey on the right.

"Gen. Gregg prepare to move," was the order from Gen. L.

About this time, Gen. Lee, with his staff, rode up to Gen. Gregg—"General what brigade is this?" said Lee.

"The Texas brigade," was General G's. reply.

"I am glad to see it," said Lee. "When you go in there, I wish you to give those men the cold steel—they will stand and fire all day, and never move unless you charge them."

"That is my experience," replied the brave Gregg.

By this time an aid from General Longstreet rode up and repeated the order, "advance your command, Gen. Gregg." And now comes the point upon which the interest of this "o'er true tale" hangs. *"Attention Texas Brigade"* was rung upon the morning air, by Gen. Gregg, *"the eyes of General Lee are upon you, forward, march."* Scarce had we moved a step, when Gen. Lee, in front of the whole command, raised himself in his stirrups, uncovered his grey hairs, and with an earnest, yet anxious voice, exclaimed above the din and confusion of the hour, *"Texans always move them."*

Reader, for near four years I followed the fortunes of the Virginia army, heard, saw and experienced much that saddened the heart or appealed in one form or another to human passions, but never before in my lifetime or since, did I ever witness such a scene as was enacted when Lee pronounced these words, with the appealing look that he gave. A yell rent the air that must have been heard for miles around, and but few eyes in that old brigade of veterans and heroes of many a bloody field was undimmed by honest, heartfelt tears. Leonard Gee, a courier to Gen. Gregg, and riding by my side, with tears coursing down his cheeks and yells issuing from his throat exclaimed, "I would charge hell itself for that old man." It was not what Gen. Lee said that so infused and excited the men, as his tone and look, which each one of us knew were born of the dangers of the hour.

With yell after yell we moved forward, passed the brow of the hill, and moved down the declivity towards the undergrowth—a distance in all not exceeding 200 yards. After moving over half the ground we all saw that Gen. Lee was following us into battle—care and anxiety upon his countenance—refusing to come back at the request and advice of his staff. If I recollect correctly, the brigade halted when they discovered Gen. Lee's intention, and all eyes were turned upon him. Five and six of his staff would gather around him, seize him, his arms, his horse's reins, but he shook them off and moved forward. Thus did he continue until just before we reached the undergrowth, not, however, until the balls began to fill and whistle through the air. Seeing that we would do all that men could do to retrieve the misfortunes of the hour, accepting the advice of this staff, and hearkening to the protest of his advancing soldiers, he at last turned round and rode back to a position on the hill.

We reached the undergrowth—entered it with a yell, and in less than 100 yards came face to face with the advancing, triumphant, and sanguine foe—confronted only by a few brave souls who could only fire and yield their ground. The enemy were at least five or six to one of us, and death seemed to be our portion. With only 15 or 20 paces separating us, the contest waxed hot and deadlier. We gave a cheer and tried a charge, but with our handful of men our only success was to rush up to them, shoot them down, and shove them back some 10 or 15 yards. For 25 minutes we held them steady—not a foot did they advance, and at the expiration of that time more than half of our brave fellows lay around us dead, dying and wounded, and the few survivors could stand it no longer. By order of Gen. Gregg, whose manly form was seen wherever danger gloried most—I bore the order to the 5th and 1st Texas, to fall back in order.

After retreating some 50 yards, a most deafening yell was borne upon the breeze, and ere we were prepared to realize its cause, Gen. Longstreet's corps came sweeping by us, reformed, and reinforced by Gen. Anderson's division, and with a valor that stands unrivaled swept everything before

them for three long miles—driving, in that long charge, the yankees from four different lines of breastworks that they had thrown up in their rear. The "Battle of the Wilderness" was won—all other fighting by the enemy that day and next was to prevent defeat from terminating in destruction. . . .

The "Texas Brigade" entered the fight 673 strong. We lost in killed and wounded over 450.— Did we or did we not do all that men could? Gen. Gregg entered the fight with at least 12 commissioned and non-commissioned on his staff. Of these, several were killed, some wounded, and only two horses untouched. Gen. G's. horse was pierced by 5 balls—each creating a mortal wound—though he rode him until we fell back—sent him to the rear where he died.

—R.C. in *The Land We Love*

XXX.5

"Their Dead and Dying Piled Higher than the Works"

On the night of May 6, Grant gave up the attempt to smash his way through Lee, and started the first of his sliding movements southward. From the seventh to the tenth he moved his great army down the Germanna Plank Road and the Brock Road toward Spotsylvania Court House. Lee anticipated his move, as he anticipated all of Grant's moves during the campaign, and had his army behind breastworks before Grant reached his objective.

By May 10 the two armies were in position, around Spotsylvania Court House, the Confederate line extending along some convenient heights in a great arc northward to the McCool house—later to be famous—and then swinging back again and stretching over two miles westward, the Union forces concentrated on either side of the angle of the Confederate line. Early on the morning of the tenth Hancock, on the Union right, threw one division across the little Po River, where it was savagely attacked by Hill and forced back. The real battle did not begin, however, until midafternoon, when Generals Warren and Wright of Hancock's corps led off with a heavy assault on the Confederate left. A little later General Upton attacked the apex of the Confederate angle, penetrated it, and threatened to take the whole Confederate line from the rear.

Once again Lee came up to rally his broken troops; once again he was prepared to lead the charge in person. This time it was Gordon and his Georgians who came to the rescue. This is the second of the "Lee to the Rear" episodes. That night the Federals drew back, and both sides licked their wounds.

Now it is our old friend Robert Stiles who tells the story.

The 10th of May, '64, was pre-eminently a day of battle with the Army of Northern Virginia. I know, of course, that the 12th is commonly regarded as the pivotal day, the great day, and the Bloody Angle as the pivotal place, the great place, of the Spottsylvania fights, and that for an hour or so along the sides and base of that angle the musketry fire is said to have been heavier than it ever was at any other place in all the world, or for any other hour in all the tide of time. But for frequency and pertinacity of attack and repetition and constancy of repulse, I question if the left of General Lee's line on the 10th of May, 1864, has ever been surpassed. I cannot pretend to identify the separate attacks or to distinguish between them, but should think there must have been at least a dozen of them. One marked feature was that, while fresh troops poured' to almost every charge, the same muskets in the hands of the same men met the first attack in the morning and the last at night; and so it was that the men, who in the early morning were so full of fight and fun that they leaped upon the breastworks and shouted to the retiring Federals to come a little closer the next time, as they did not care to go so far after the clothes and shoes and muskets, were so weary and worn and heavy at night that they could scarcely be roused to meet the charging enemy.

The troops supporting the two Napoleon guns of the Howitzers were, as I remember, the Seventh (or Eighth) Georgia and the First Texas. Toward the close of the day everything seemed to have quieted down, in a sort of implied truce There was absolutely no fire, either of musketry or cannon. Our weary, hungry infantry stacked arms and were cooking their mean and meager little rations. Some one rose up and, looking over the works—it was shading down a little toward the dark—cried out: "Hello! What's this? Why, here come our men on a run, from—no, by Heavens! it's the Yankees!" and before any one could realize the situation or even

start toward the stacked muskets the Federal column broke over the little work between our troops and their arms, bayonetted or shot two or three who were asleep before they could even awake, and dashed upon the men crouched over their low fires—with cooking utensils instead of weapons in their hands. Of course they ran. What else could they do?

The Howitzers—only the left, or Napoleon section, was there—sprang to their guns, swinging them around to bear inside our lines, double-shotted them with canister and fairly spouted it into the Federals, whose formation had been broken in the rush and the plunge over the works and who seemed to be somewhat massed and huddled and hesitating, but only a few rods away. Quicker almost than I can tell it our infantry supports, than whom there were not two better regiments in the army, had rallied and gotten to their arms, and then they opened out into a V-shape and fairly tore the head of the Federal column to pieces. In an incredibly short time those who were able to do so turned to fly and our infantry were following them over the intrenchments; but it is doubtful whether this would have been the result had it not been for the prompt and gallant action of the artillery. . . .

When it became evident that the attack had failed, I suggested to the chaplain—who happened to be with the Howitzer guns, perhaps for that sundown prayer meeting which Willy Dame mentioned—that there might be some demand for his ministrations where the enemy had broken over; so we walked up there and found their dead and dying piled higher than the works themselves. It was almost dark, but as we drew near we saw a wounded Federal soldier clutch the pantaloons of Captain Hunter, who at that moment was passing by, frying pan in hand, and heard him ask with intense eagerness: "Can you pray, sir? Can you pray?"

The old captain looked down at him with a peculiar expression, and pulled away, saying, "No; my friend, I don't wish you any harm now, but praying's not exactly my trade."

—STILES, *Four Years Under Marse Robert*

XXX.6

SPOTSYLVANIA AND THE
BLOODY ANGLE

The heaviest fighting of the Wilderness campaign came on May 12, when Grant came within a hairbreadth of winning the campaign and perhaps the war. The Confederates should have learned from the experience of the tenth that their salient around the McCool house was peculiarly vulnerable, but—probably because the high ground appeared to offer advantages—they failed to straighten their lines Not only this but they withdrew their artillery from the apex of this salient, an almost fatal move. At dawn on the twelfth Hancock's division launched a large-scale attack on the salient, the brigades marching twenty deep. Within an hour they had breached the Confederate line, and as Hancock hurried up reinforcements, atorrent of blue poured through the break. Yet once again, as we shall see, Lee managed to plug up the gap and save the day.

Here is the story of the fighting of the twelfth as seen from Grant's headquarters; it is told by Horace Porter, whose description of Grant we have already read.

I had been out all night looking after the movements of the troops which were to form the assaulting columns. After they had all been placed in position I started for headquarters, in obedience to instructions, to report the situation to the general in-chief. . . . By feeling the way for some hours I reached headquarters about daylight the next morning, May 12.

When I arrived the general was up and sitting wrapped in his overcoat close to a camp-fire which was struggling heroically to sustain its life against the assaults of wind and rain. It had been decided to move headquarters a little nearer to the center of the lines, and most of the, camp equipage had been packed up ready to start. The general seemed in excellent spirits, and was even inclined to be jocose. He said to me: "We have just had our coffee, and you will find some left for you", and then, taking a critical look at my drenched and bespattered clothes and famished appearance, added, "But perhaps you are not hungry." To disabuse the chief's mind on this score, I sent for a cup of coffee, and drank it with the relish of a shipwrecked mariner,

while I related the incidents of the embarrassments encountered in Hancock's movement, and the position he had taken up. Before I had quite finished making my report the stillness was suddenly broken by artillery-firing, which came from the direction of Burnside's position. A few minutes after came the sound of cheers and the rattle of musketry from Hancock's front, telling that the main assault upon the "angle" had begun. No one could see a hundred yards from our position on account of the dense woods, and reports from the front were eagerly awaited.

It was nearly an hour before anything definite was received, but at 5:30 an officer came galloping through the woods with a report from Hancock saying he had captured the first line of the enemy's works. This officer was closely followed by another, who reported that many prisoners had been taken. Fifteen minutes later came the announcement that Hancock had captured two general officers. General Grant sent Burnside this news with a message saying, "Push on with all vigor." Wright's corps was now ordered to attack on the right of Hancock. Before six o'clock a message from Hancock's head quarters reported the capture of two thousand prisoners, and a quarter of an hour later Burnside sent word that he had driven the enemy back two miles and a half in his front. Hancock called for reinforcements, but Grant had anticipated him and had already ordered troops to his support. The scene at headquarters was now exciting in the extreme. As aides galloped up one after the other in quick succession with stirring bulletins, all bearing the glad tidings of overwhelming success, the group of staff-officers standing about the camp fire interrupted their active work of receiving, receipting for, and answering despatches by shouts and cheers which made the forest ring.

General Grant sat unmoved upon his camp-chair, giving his constant thoughts to devising methods for making the victory complete. At times the smoke from the struggling camp-fire would for a moment blind him, and occasionally a gust of wind would blow the cape of his greatcoat over his face, and cut off his voice in the middle of a sentence. Only once during the scene he rose from his seat and paced up and down for about ten minutes. He made very few comments upon the stirring events which were crowding so closely upon one another until the reports came in regarding the prisoners. When the large numbers captured were announced, he said, with the first trace of animation he had shown: "That's the kind of news I like to hear. I had hoped that a bold dash at daylight would secure a large number of prisoners. Hancock is doing well."

This remark was eminently characteristic of the Union commander. His extreme fondness for taking prisoners was manifested in every battle he fought. When word was brought to him of a success on any part of the line, his first and most eager question was always, "Have any prisoners been taken?" The love for capturing prisoners amounted to a passion with him. It did not seem to arise from the fact that they added so largely to the trophies of battle, and was no doubt chiefly due to his tenderness of heart, which prompted him to feel that it was always more humane to reduce the enemy's strength by captures than by slaughter. His desire in this respect was amply gratified, for during the war it fell to his lot to capture a larger number of prisoners than any general of modern times.

Meade had come over to Grant's headquarters early, and while they were engaged in discussing the situation, about 6:30 A.M, a horseman rode up wearing the uniform of a Confederate general. Halting near the camp-fire, he dismounted and walked forward, saluting the group of Union officers as he approached. His clothing was covered with mud, and a hole had been torn in the crown of his felt hat, through which a tuft of hair protruded, looking like a Sioux chief's warlock. Meade looked at him attentively for a moment, and then stepped up to him, grasped him cordially by the hand, and cried, "Why, how do you do, general?" and then turned to his general-in-chief and said, "General Grant, this is General Johnson—Edward Johnson."

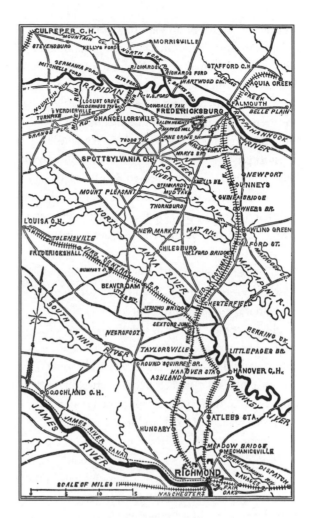

THE WILDERNESS

General Grant shook hands warmly with the distinguished prisoner, and exclaimed, "How do you do? It is a long time since we last met."

"Yes," replied Johnson; "it is a great many years, and I had not expected to meet you under such circumstances."

"It is one of the many sad fortunes of war," answered General Grant, who offered the captured officer a cigar, and then picked up a camp-chair, placed it with his own hands near the fire, and added, "Be seated, and we will do all in our power to make you as comfortable as possible." . . .

While Generals Grant and Meade were talking with General Johnson by the camp-fire, a despatch came in from Hancock, saying, "I have finished up Johnson, and am now going to Early." General Grant passed this despatch around, but did not read it aloud, as usual, out of consideration for Johnson's feelings. Soon after came another report that Hancock had taken three thousand prisoners, then another that he had turned his captured guns upon the enemy and made a whole division prisoners, including the famous Stonewall Brigade. Burnside now reported that his right had lost its connection with Hancock's corps. General Grant sent him a brief, characteristic note in reply, saying, "Push the enemy with all your might; that's the way to connect." . . .

The battle near the "angle" was probably the most desperate engagement in the history of modern warfare, and presented features which were absolutely appalling. It was chiefly a savage hand-to-hand fight across the breastworks. Rank after rank was riddled by shot and shell and bayonet thrusts, and finally sank, a mass of torn and mutilated corpses; then fresh troops rushed madly forward to replace the dead, and so the murderous work went on. Guns were run up close to the parapet, and double charges of canister played their part in the bloody work. The fence-rails and logs in the breastworks were shattered into splinters, and trees over a foot and a half in diameter were cut completely in two by the incessant musketry fire. A section of the trunk of a stout oak-tree thus severed was afterward sent to Washington, here it is still on exhibition at the National Museum. We had not only shot down an army, but also a forest.

The opposing flags were in places thrust against each other, and muskets were fired with muzzle against muzzle. Skulls were crushed with clubbed muskets, and men stabbed to death with swords and bayonets thrust between the logs in the parapet which separated the combatants. Wild cheers, savage yells, and frantic shrieks rose above the sighing of the wind and the pattering of the rain, and formed a demoniacal accompaniment to the booming of the guns as they hurled their missiles of death into the contending ranks. Even the darkness of night and the pitiless storm failed to stop the fierce contest, and the deadly strife did not cease till after midnight. Our troops had been under fire for twenty hours, but they still held the position which they had so dearly purchased.

My duties carried me again to the spot the next day, and the appalling sight presented was harrowing in the extreme. Our own killed were scattered over a large space near the "angle," while in front of the captured breastworks the enemy's dead, vastly more numerous than our own, were piled upon each other in some places four layers deep, exhibiting every ghastly phase of mutilation. Below the mass of fast decaying corpses, the convulsive twitching of limbs and the writhing of bodies showed that there were wounded men still alive and struggling to extricate themselves from their horrid entombment. Every relief possible was afforded, but in too many cases it came too late. The place was well named the "Bloody Angle."

—PORTER, *Campaigning with Grant*

XXX.7

"THESE MEN HAVE NEVER FAILED YOU ON ANY FIELD"

Perhaps only once before in the history of the war had the situation been so critical to the Confederacy as it was on the morning of May 12, when the Confederate line broke: that was at Antietam. The Federal advance had not only broken through, it had enveloped General Johnson and taken him and 4,000 men prisoners. Lee tried to rally the fleeing soldiers. "Hold on!" he cried. "We are going to form a new line." But most of the men were panic-stricken, and ran to the rear. Already General Gordon had started his men forward to plug the gap—or at least hold the line. Meeting General Lee Gordon found that Lee was prepared to lead the counterattack himself.

But let Gordon tell the story—the third and the best authenticated of the "Lee to the Rear" episodes.

During the night Hancock had massed a large portion of General Grant's army in front of that salient, and so near to it that, with a quick rush, his column had gone over the breast works, capturing General Edward Johnson and General

George Steuart and the great body of their men before these alert officers or their trained soldiers were aware of the movement. The surprise was complete and the assault practically unresisted. In all its details—its planning, its execution, and its fearful import to Lee's army—this charge of Hancock was one of that great soldier's most brilliant achievements.

Meantime my command was rapidly moving by the flank through, the woods and underbrush toward the captured salient. The mist and fog were so heavy that it was impossible to see farther than a few rods. Throwing out in front a small force to apprise us of our-near approach to the enemy, I rode at the head of the main column, and by my side rode General Robert Johnson, who commanded a brigade of North Carolinians. So rapidly and silently had the enemy moved inside of our works—indeed, so much longer time had he been on the inside than the reports indicated—that before we had moved one half the distance to the salient the head of column butted squarely against Hancock's line of battle. The men who had been placed in our front to give warning were against that battle line before they knew it. They were shot down or made prisoners. The sudden and unexpected blaze from Hancock's rifles made the dark woodland strangely lurid. General Johnson, who rode immediately at my side, was shot from his horse, severely but not, as I supposed, fatally wounded in the head. His brigade was thrown inevitably into great confusion, but did not break to the rear. As quickly as possible, I had the next ranking officer in that brigade notified of General Johnson's fall and directed him at once to assume command. He proved equal to the emergency. With great coolness and courage he promptly executed my orders.

The Federals were still advancing, and every movement of the North Carolina-brigade had to be made under heavy fire. The officer in charge was directed to hastily withdraw his brigade a short distance, to change front so as to face Hancock's lines, and to deploy his whole force in close order as skirmishers, so as to stretch, if possible, across the entire front of Hancock. This done, he was ordered to charge with his line of skirmishers the solid battle lines before him. His looks indicated some amazement at the purpose to make an attack which appeared so utterly hopeless, and which would have been the very essence of rashness but for the extremity of the situation. He was, however, full of the fire of battle and too good a soldier not to yield prompt and cheerful obedience. That order was given in the hope and belief that in the fog and mists which concealed our numbers the sheer audacity of the movement would confuse and check the Union advance long enough for me to change front and form line of battle with the other brigades. The result was not disappointing except in the fact that Johnson's brigade, even when so deployed, was still too short to reach across Hancock's entire front. This fact was soon developed: not by sight, but by the direction from which the Union bullets began to come.

When the daring charge of the North Carolina brigade had temporarily checked that portion of the Federal forces struck by it and while my brigades in the rear were being placed in position, I rode with Thomas G. Jones, the youngest member of my staff, into the intervening woods, in order, if possible, to locate Hancock more definitely. Sitting on my horse near the line of the North Carolina brigade, I was endeavoring to get a view of the Union lines, through the woods and through the gradually lifting mists. It was impossible, however, to see those lines; but, as stated, the direction from which they sent their bullets soon informed us that they were still moving and had already gone beyond our right. One of those bullets passed through my coat from side to side, just grazing my back.

Jones, who was close to me, and sitting on his horse in a not very erect posture, anxiously inquired: "General, didn't that ball hit you?"

"No," I said; "but suppose my back had been in a bow like yours? Don't you see that the bullet would have gone straight through my spine? Sit up or you'll be killed."

The sudden jerk with which he straightened himself, and the duration of the impression made, showed that this ocular demonstration of the necessity for a soldier to sit up right on his horse had been more effective than all the ordinary lessons that could have been given. It is but simple justice to say of this immature boy that even then his courage, his coolness in the presence of danger, and his strong moral and mental characteristics gave promise of his brilliant future.

The bullets from Hancock's rifles furnished the information which I was seeking as to the progress he had made within and along our earthworks. I then took advantage of this brief check given to the Union advance, and placed my troops in line for a countercharge, upon the success or failure of which the fate of the Confederate army seemed to hang. General Lee evidently thought so. His army had been cut in twain by Hancock's brilliant *coup de main*. Through that wide breach in the Confederate lines, which was becoming wider with every step, the Union forces were rushing like a swollen torrent through a broken mill-dam. General Lee knew, as did every one else who realized the momentous import of the situation, that the bulk of the Confederate army was in such imminent peril that nothing could rescue it except a counter movement, quick, impetuous, and decisive. Lee resolved to save it, and, if need be, to save it at the sacrifice of his own life. With perfect self-poise, he rode to the margin of that breach, and appeared upon the scene just as I had completed the alignment of my troops and was in the act of moving in that crucial countercharge upon which so much depended.

As he rode majestically in front of my line of battle, with uncovered head and mounted on Old Traveller, Lee looked a very god of war. Calmly and grandly, he rode to a point near the centre of my line and turned his horse's head to the front, evidently resolved to lead in person the desperate charge and drive Hancock back or perish in the effort. I knew what he meant; and although the passing moments were of price less value, I

resolved to arrest him in his effort, and thus save to the Confederacy the life of its great leader. I was at the centre of that line when General Lee rode to it. With uncovered head, he turned his face toward Hancock's advancing column.

Instantly I spurred my horse across Old Traveller's front, and grasping his bridle in my hand, I checked him. Then, in a voice which I hoped might reach the ears of my men and command their attention, I called out, "General Lee, you shall not lead my men in a charge. No man can do that, sir. Another is here for that purpose. These men behind you are Georgians, Virginians, and Carolinians. They have never failed you on any field. They will not fail you here. Will you, boys?" The response came like a mighty anthem that must have stirred his emotions as no other music could have done. Although the answer to those three words, "Will you, boys?" came in the monosyllables, "No, no, no; we'll not fail him," yet they were doubtless to him more eloquent because of their simplicity and momentous meaning.

But his great heart was destined to be quickly cheered by a still sublimer testimony of their deathless devotion. As this first thrilling response died away, I uttered the words for which they were now fully prepared. I shouted to General Lee, "You must go to rear." The echo, "General Lee to the rear, General Lee to the rear!" rolled back with tremendous emphasis from the throats of my men, and they gathered around him, turned his horse in the opposite direction, some clutching his bridle, some his stirrups, while others pressed close to Old Traveller's hips, ready to shove him by main force to the rear. I verily believe that, had it been necessary or possible, they would have carried on their shoulders both horse and rider to a place of safety. . . .

I turned to my men as Lee was forced to the rear, and reminding them of their pledges to him, and of the fact that the eyes of their great leader were still upon them, I ordered, "Forward!" With the fury of a cyclone, and almost with its resistless power, they rushed upon Hancock's advancing column. With their first terrific onset, the impetuosity of which was indescribable, his leading lines were shivered and hurled back upon their stalwart supports. In the inextricable confusion that followed, and before Hancock's lines could be reformed, every officer on horseback in my division, the brigade and regimental commanders, and my own superb staff, were riding among the troops, shouting in unison: "Forward, men, forward!"

But the brave line officers on foot and the enthused privates needed no additional spur to their already rapt spirits. Onward they swept, pouring their rapid volleys into Hancock's confused ranks, and swelling the deafening din of battle with their piercing shouts. Like the debris in the track of a storm, the dead and dying of both armies were left in the wake of this Confederate charge. In the meantime the magnificent troops of Ramseur and Rodes were rushing upon Hancock's dissolving corps from another point, and Long's artillery and other batteries were pouring a deadly fire into the broken Federal ranks. Hancock was repulsed and driven out. Every foot of the lost salient and earthworks was retaken, except that small stretch which the Confederate line was too short to cover.

—GORDON, *Reminiscences of the Civil War*

XXX.8

GRANT HURLS HIS MEN TO DEATH AT COLD HARBOR

Lee had saved himself by the narrowest of margins at Spotsylvania, but the Federals, too, took heavy punishment. Once more Grant pulled off on one of his sliding movements to the south. This time he headed for Hanover Junction. Lee hurried along parallel with him, and by May 23 had taken position along the North Anna. Grant maneuvered for an at tack but found Lee's defenses formidable, and decided to move on. His objective this time was Hanover Town, not far from Richmond. Lee took position on the south bank of the Totopotomy, a branch of the Pamunkey, and not far from Mechanicsville, where he had first

met and defeated a Federal army. Then on June I the two armies shifted their positions to Cold Harbor, on the north side of the Chickahominy. On June 3 Grant decided on a head-on assault. It was probably the greatest mistake of his military career. Within a few hours he had lost about 10,000 men.

We have met Colonel William Oates before, notably at Gettysburg.

On the 2nd of June [1864] Law was ordered farther down our entrenched line, with his own and Anderson's Georgia brigade, to Cold Harbor, or near it for the purpose of re taking about 300 yards of badly constructed Confederate trenches which the enemy had succeeded in capturing on General Hoke's left. . . .

None of us had slept any. The men worked all night and by day had an excellent line of defensive works completed. When day came details were sent to the rear to fill the canteens at a bold spring of pure water. They had returned, and, just before I could see the sun, I heard a volley in the woods, saw the major running up the ravine in the direction of Anderson's brigade, which lay to the right o£ Law's, and the skirmishers running in, pursued by a column of the enemy ten lines deep, with arms at a trail, and yelling "Huzzah! huzzah!" I ordered my men to take arms and fix bayonets. Just then I remembered that not a gun in the regiment was loaded. I ordered the men to load and the officers each to take an ax and stand to the works. I was apprehensive that the enemy would be on our works before the men could load.

As Capt. Noah B. Feagin and his skirmishers crawled over the works I thought of my piece of artillery. I called out: "Sergeant, give them double charges of canister; fire, men; fire!" the order was obeyed with alacrity. The enemy were within thirty steps. They halted and began to dodge, lie down, and recoil. The fire was terrific from my regiment, the Fourth Alabama on my immediate right, and the Thirteenth Mississippi on my left, while the piece of artillery was fired more rapidly and better handled than I ever saw one before or since. The blaze of fire from it at each shot went right into the ranks of our assailants and made frightful gaps through the dense mass of men. They endured it but for one or two minutes, when they retreated, leaving the ground covered with their dead and dying. There were 3 men in my regiment killed, 5 wounded. My piece of artillery kept up a lively fire on the enemy where they halted in the woods, with shrapnel shell.

After the lapse of about forty minutes another charge was made by the Twenty-third and Twenty-fifth Massachusetts regiments, in a column by divisions, thus presenting a front of two companies only. Bryan's Georgia brigade came up from the rear and lay down behind Law's. The charging column, which aimed to strike the Fourth Alabama, received the most destructive fire I ever saw. They were subjected to a front and flank fire from the infantry, at short range, while my piece of artillery poured double charges of canister into them. The Georgians loaded for the Alabamians to fire. I could see the dust fog out of a man's clothing in two or three places at once where as many balls would strike him at the same moment. In two minutes not a man of them was standing. All who were not shot down had lain down for protection. One little fellow raised his head to look, and I ordered him to come in. He came on a run, the Yankees over in the woods firing at him every step of the way, and as he climbed over our works one shot took effect in one of his legs. They evidently took him to be a deserter. I learned from him that there were many more out there who were not wounded. This I communicated to Colonel Perry, who was again in command, General Law having been wounded in the head during the first assault; and thereupon Perry sent a company down a ravine on our right to capture them; they soon brought the colonel who led the charge, and about one hundred other prisoners. The colonel was a brave man. He

said he had been in many places, but that was the worst.

This closed their efforts against us on this field for the remainder of that day. The following night they constructed works along the edge of the woods and sharpshooting became incessant. The next day a white flag was displayed and firing was suspended. A Union officer came half-way and met a Confederate staff officer, with a request from Major-General Augur for an armistice for six hours with permission to bury the dead. It was sent to General Lee, who returned it, saying that he did not know General Augur as commander of the Army of the Potomac.

Sharp-shooting was resumed. The stench from the dead between our lines and theirs was sickening. It was so nauseating that it was almost unendurable; but we had the advantage, as the wind carried it away from us to them. The dead covered more than five acres of ground about as thickly as they could be laid. A half hour elapsed, when another white flag was displayed and another request came for an armistice for six hours, with permission to bury the dead in front of our lines, signed this time by General Grant. Lee acceded to the request and hostilities ceased for the six hours. They sent a heavy detail upon the field, and when the time expired they had to get it extended in order to finish burying, although they worked rapidly the whole time. I have no means of knowing the exact number of bodies buried, but from appearances there could not have been less than five or six hundred, and may have been a much greater number. They belonged to Baldy Smith's corps.

—OATES, *The War Between the Union and the Confederacy*

XXXI

THE SIEGE
OF PETERSBURG

The Wilderness campaign had decimated Lee's army, but it had not destroyed it, nor had it captured Richmond. What was Grant to do? If he could not take Richmond from the north or the east, he might take it from the south; if he could not destroy Lee's army in battle, he might wear it down by siege. His next move was, therefore, logical enough. Under the protection of his gunboats he threw his army across the James and struck at Richmond from the south. Petersburg was the key to Richmond, and to the whole of eastern Virginia. Through it ran a whole network of railroads connecting with the south and west: the Petersburg & Norfolk, the Weldon, and the Southside. If Grant could cut across these, he would break Richmond's connection with the rest of the Confederacy except for the Richmond & Danville Railroad to the west. And not only would he isolate Richmond; even more important he could cut Lee's army off from its supplies.

Grant began to ferry his army across the James on June 12; by midnight of the sixteenth the movement was completed. Lee, who had anticipated this movement, was in a dilemma. If he hurried his own army across the James Grant might arrest his movement and assault Richmond with half of his force on the north, the rest on the south; either part would equal the whole of Lee's army. Lee had therefore to move with utmost caution, relying on Beauregard to hold Petersburg as long as possible and feeding him reinforcements as fast as safety permitted. Grant's movement was undoubtedly brilliantly conceived and executed but it should be remembered that it failed of its immediate objective; it neither broke the Confederate lines nor captured Petersburg.

It is often said that Grant's strategy was fundamentally that of McClellan, in 1862, and that Grant's eventual success is a vindication of McClellan. There is neither evidence nor logic to support this. McClellan at no time proposed to attack Richmond from south of the James nor did he, apparently, appreciate the importance of Petersburg as the railway focus of eastern Virginia.

Even before Grant crossed the James he ordered attacks on Richmond from Bermuda Hundred and on Petersburg; neither of these succeeded. Another opportunity to capture Petersburg presented itself on June 15 when W. F. Smith's corps was available for reinforcement of the attack. Once again the opportunity was fumbled. By the sixteenth Beauregard was strong enough to resist attack, and after some in effectual fighting Grant settled down to besiege Petersburg. His strategy was elementary but sound. With a numerical superiority of two to one, he continued to push his lines ever farther to the west, thus forcing Lee to extend his lines in turn. Eventually Lee was holding 35 miles of defensive works; with his lines stretched thin they were bound to snap somewhere, sooner or later. Because Lee showed the same superb generalship that he had showed in the Wilderness, they did not snap until the following spring, and then it was Sheridan, coming on from the Valley, who broke them.

The siege of Petersburg was the most prolonged of the war—a nine-months affair. It was punctuated by a series of battles, chiefly for the railroads leading to the south and west, and by minor diversionary battles north of the James. While no one of these battles was a major affair, all of them wore down Lee's forces by attrition. At the same time Lee's army was being reduced by sickness and desertion. That Lee was able to sustain this nine-months siege is another tribute to his resourcefulness and fortitude.

XXXI.I

GRAND'S ARMY CROSSES THE JAMES

Here, in the restrained language characteristic of official re ports, is Grant's own summary account of the crossing of the James, one of the notable operations of the war. For many years historians assumed that Lee was completely deceived by this movement; Douglas S. Freeman has clearly established that Lee anticipated it, prepared for it, and met it as best he could with his inadequate forces. Part of Grant's army was ferried across by ships; part of it crossed on a 2,000-foot pontoon bridge at Wilcox's landing.

From the proximity of the enemy to his defenses around Richmond it was impossible by any flank movement to inter pose between him and the city. I was still in a condition to either move by his left flank and invest Richmond from the north side or continue my move by his right flank to the south side of the James. While the former might have been better as a covering for Washington, yet a full survey of all the ground satisfied me that it would be impracticable to hold a line north and east of Richmond that would protect the Fredericksburg railroad—a long, vulnerable line which would exhaust much of our strength to guard, and that would have to be protected to supply the army, and would leave open to the enemy all his lines of communication on the south side of the James. My idea, from the start, had been to beat Lee's army north of Richmond if possible; then, after destroying his lines of communication north of the James River, to transfer the army to the south side and besiege Lee in Richmond or follow him south if he should retreat. After the battle of the Wilderness it was evident that the enemy deemed it of the first importance to run no risks with the army he then had. He acted purely on the defense behind breastworks, or. feebly on the offensive immediately in front of them, and where in case of repulse he could easily retire be hind them. Without a greater sacrifice of life than I was willing to make, all could not be accomplished that I had designed north of Richmond. I therefore determined to continue to

hold substantially the ground we then occupied, taking advantage of any favorable circumstances that might present themselves, until the cavalry could be sent to Charlottesville and Gordonsville to effectually break up the rail road connection between Richmond and the Shenandoah Valley and Lynchburg; and when the cavalry got well off to move the army to the south side of the James River, by the enemy's right flank, where I felt I could cut off all his sources of supply except by the canal. . . .

The Second Corps commenced crossing the James River on the morning of the 14th by ferryboats at Wilcox's Landing. The laying of the pontoon bridge was completed about midnight of the 14th, and the crossing of the balance of the army was rapidly pushed forward by both bridge and ferry. After the crossing had commenced, I proceeded by a steamer to Bermuda Hundred to give the necessary orders for the immediate capture of Petersburg. The instructions to General Butler were verbal, and were for him to send General Smith immediately, that night, with all the troops he could give him without sacrificing the position he then held. I told him that I would return at once to the Army of the Potomac, hasten its crossing, and throw it forward to Petersburg by divisions as rapidly as it could be done; that we could re-enforce our armies more rapidly there than the enemy could bring troops against us. General Smith got off as directed, and confronted the enemy's pickets near Petersburg before daylight next morning, but, for some reason that I have never been able to satisfactorily understand, did not get ready to assault his main lines until near sundown. Then, with a part of his command only, he made the assault, and carried the lines northeast of Petersburg from the Appomattox River, for a distance of over 2l/2 miles, capturing fifteen pieces of artillery and 300 prisoners. This was about 7 P.M. Between the line thus captured and Petersburg there were no other works, and there was no evidence that the enemy had re-enforced Petersburg with a single brigade from any source. The night was clear, the moon shining brightly, and favorable to further operations. General Hancock, with two divisions of the Second Corps, reached General Smith just after

dark, and offered the service of these troops as he (Smith) might wish, waiving rank to the named commander, who he naturally supposed knew best the position of affairs and what to do with the troops. But instead of taking these troops, and pushing at once into Petersburg, he requested General Hancock to relieve a part of his line in the captured works, which was done before midnight. By the time I arrived the next morning the enemy was in force.
—"Grant's Report covering operations of all armies of the U.S. from March, 1864 to May, 1865"

XXXI.2

BEAUREGARD HOLDS THE LINES AT PETERSBURG

Grant's advance was across the James on June 14, and he ordered an attack on the feebly held Petersburg lines on the fifteenth. For this attack Smith had available some 16,000 men; Beauregard could muster no more than some 3,000. But Smith wasted the day, and before he could be joined by Hancock's corps, which had crossed the river on the fifteenth, Beauregard had rounded up enough reinforcements to hold his lines. On the sixteenth the fighting was renewed but by that time Beauregard had some 14,000 men available for defense. A series of powerful assaults by the Federals took some of the outer lines, and several of the redoubts, but the Con federates held firm on the inner lines, and by the eighteenth Lee had sent across sufficient reinforcements to make Petersburg safe. The fighting from the fifteenth to the eighteenth cost the Federals almost 10,000 in killed, wounded, and missing; there are no figures for Confederate losses, but they were less than half the Federal.

Beauregard himself tells the story of the defense of Petersburg.

The movement of the Army of the Potomac to the south side of the James began on the evening of the 12th of June, and Smith's corps was at Bermuda Hundred in the early afternoon of the 14th. From Point of Rocks it crossed the river that night and was pushed forward without delay against Petersburg. Kautz's cavalry and Hinks's command of colored troops had been added to it.

It was with a view to thwart General Grant in the execution of such a plan that I proposed to the War Department [June 9th] the adoption—should the emergency justify it, and I thought it did—of the bold and, to me, safer plan of concentrating all the forces we could readily dispose of to give battle to Grant, and thus decide at once the fate of Richmond and of the cause we were fighting for, while we still possessed a comparatively compact, well-disciplined, and enthusiastic army in the field.

From Swift Creek, early on June 14th, I telegraphed to General Bragg: "Movement of Grant's across Chickahominy and increase of Butler's force render my position here critical. With my present forces I cannot answer for consequences. Cannot my troops sent to General Lee be returned at once? . . . " No answer came. Late in the evening of the same day, having further reason to believe that one corps at least of General Grant's army was already within Butler's lines, I telegraphed to General Lee: "A deserter from the enemy reports that Butler has been reenforced by the Eighteenth and a part of the Tenth Army Corps." To this dispatch, likewise, there came no response. But, as prompt and energetic action became more and more imperative, and as I could no longer doubt the presence of Smith's corps with Butler's forces, I sent one of my aides, Colonel Samuel B. Paul, to General Lee with instructions to explain to him the exact situation. General Lee's answer to Colonel Paul was not encouraging. He said that I must be in error in believing the enemy had thrown a large force on the south side of the James; that the troops referred to by me could be but a few of Smith's corps going back to Butler's lines. Strange to say, at the very time General Lee was thus expressing himself to Colonel Paul, the whole of Smith's corps was actually assaulting the Petersburg lines. But General Lee finally said that he had already issued orders for the return of Hoke's division; that he would do all he could to aid me, and even come him self should the necessity arise.

The Confederate forces opposed to Smith's corps on the 15th of June consisted of . . . a real effective for duty of 2200 only. These troops occupied the Petersburg line on the left from Battery

No. 1 to what was called Butterworth's Bridge, toward the right, and had to be so stationed as to allow but one man for every 1/2 yards. From that bridge to the Appomattox—a distance of fully 1/2 miles—the line was defenseless.

Early in the morning—at about 7 o'clock—General Dearing, on the Broadway and City Point roads, reported his regiment engaged with a large force of the enemy. The stand made by our handful of cavalry, near their breastworks, was most creditable to themselves and to their gallant commander, and the enemy's ranks, at that point, were much thinned by the accurate firing of the battery under Graham. But the weight of numbers soon produced its almost inevitable result, and, in spite of the desperate efforts of our men, the cavalry breastworks were flanked and finally abandoned by us, with the loss of one howitzer. Still, Dearing's encounter with the enemy, at that moment and on that part of the field, was of incalculable advantage to the defenders of our line, inasmuch as it afforded time for additional preparation and the distribution of new orders by Wise.

At 10 o'clock A.M. the skirmishing had assumed very alarming proportions. To the urgent demands of General Wise for reenforcements, I was enabled at last to answer that part of Hoke's division was on the way from Drewry's Bluff and would be in time to save the day, if our men could stand their or deal, hard as it was, a little while longer. Then all along the line, from one end to the other, the order was given "to hold on at all hazards!" It was obeyed with the resolute fortitude of veterans, though many of the troops thus engaged, with such odds against them, had hardly been under fire before. At 12 P.M., and as late as 2 P.M., our center was vigorously pressed, as though the Norfolk and Petersburg Railroad were the immediate object of the onset. General Wise now closed the line from his right to strengthen Colonel J. T. Goode and, with him, the 34th Virginia; while, at the same time and with equal perspicacity, he hurried Wood's battalion toward the left in support of Colonel P. R. Page and his command.

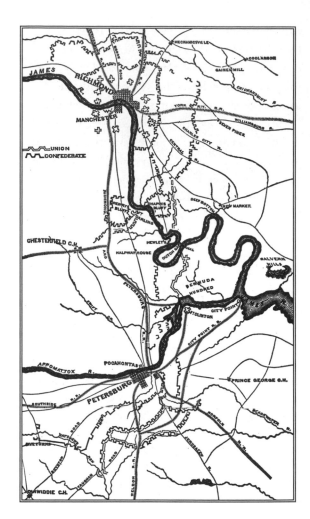

DEFENSES OF RICHMOND AND PETERSBURG

The enemy, continuing to mass his columns toward the center of our line, pressed it more and more and concentrated his heaviest assaults upon Batteries Nos. 5, 6, and 7. Thinned out and exhausted as they were, General Wise's heroic forces resisted still, with such unflinching stubbornness as to equal the veterans of the Army of Northern Virginia. I was then on the field and only left it when darkness set in. Shortly after 7 P.M. the enemy entered a ravine between Batteries 6 and 7, and succeeded in flanking Battery No. 5.

But just then very opportunely appeared, advancing at double-quick, Hagood's gallant South Carolina brigade, followed soon afterward by Colquitt's, Clingman's, and, in fact, by the whole of

Hoke's division. They were shown their positions, on a new line selected at that very time by my orders, a short distance in the rear of the captured works, and were kept busy the greatest part, of the night throwing up a small epaulement for their additional protection.

Strange to say, General Smith contented himself with breaking into our lines, and attempted nothing further that night. All the more strange was this inaction on his part, since General Hancock, with his strong and well-equipped Second Army Corps, had also been hurried to Petersburg, and was actually there, or in the immediate vicinity of the town, on the evening of the 15th. He had informed General Smith of the arrival of his command and of the readiness of two of his divisions—Birney's and Gibbon's—to give him whatever assistance he might require. Petersburg at that hour was clearly at the mercy of the Federal commander, who had all but captured it, and only failed of final success because he could not realize the fact of the unparalleled disparity between the two contending forces. Although the result of the fighting of the 15th had demonstrated that 2200 Confederates successfully withheld nearly a whole day the repeated assaults of at least 18,000 Federals, it followed, none the less, that Hancock's corps, being now in our front, with fully 28,000 men,—which raised the enemy's force against Petersburg to a grand total of 46,000,—our chance of resistance, the next morning and in the course of the next day, even after the advent of Hoke's division, was by far too uncertain to be counted on, unless strong additional-reenforcements could reach us in time. . . .

General Hancock, the ranking Federal officer present, had been instructed by General Meade not to begin operations before the arrival of Burnside's command. Hence the tardiness of the enemy's attack, which was not made till after 5 o'clock P.M., though Burnside had reached Petersburg, ac cording to his own report, at 10 o'clock A.M. [June 16].

The engagement lasted fully three hours, much vigor being displayed by the Federals, while the Confederates confronted them with fortitude, knowing that they were fighting against overwhelming odds, constantly increasing. Birney's division of Hancock's corps finally broke into part of our line and effected a lodgment. The contest, with varying results, was carried on until after nightfall, with advantage to us on the left and some serious loss on the right. It then slackened and gradually came to an end. In the meantime Warren's corps, the Fifth, had also come up, but too late to take a part in the action of the day. Its presence before our lines swelled the enemy's aggregate to about 90,000, against which stood a barrier of not even 10,000 exhausted, half-starved men, who had gone through two days of constant hard fighting and many s1eepless nights in the trenches.

Hostilities began early on the 17th. . . . The firing lasted, on the 17th, until a little after 11 o'clock P.M. Just before that time I had ordered all the campfires to be brightly lighted, with sentinels well thrown forward and as near as possible. to the enemy's. Then, at about 12:30 A.M., on the 18th, began the retrograde movement, which, notwithstanding the exhaustion of our troops and their sore disappointment at receiving no further reënforcements, was safely and silently executed, with uncommonly good order and precision, though the greatest caution had to be used in order to retire unnoticed from so close a contact with so strong an adversary.

The digging of trenches was begun by the men as soon as they reached their new position. Axes, as well as spades, bayonets and knives, as well as axes,—in fact, every utensil that could be found,— were used. And when all was over, or nearly so, with much anxiety still, but with comparative relief, nevertheless, I hurried off this telegram to General Lee [18th, 12:40 A.M.]: "All quiet at present. I expect renewal of attack in morning. My troops are becoming much exhausted. With out immediate and strong reenforcements, results may be unfavorable. Prisoners report Grant on the field with his whole army." . . .

The evening of the 18th was quiet. There was no further attempt on the part of General Meade to assault our lines. He was "satisfied," as he said in his report, that there was "nothing more to be gained by direct attacks." The spade took the place of the musket, and the regular siege was begun. It was only raised April 2, 1865.

—BEAUREGARD, "Four Days of Battle at Petersburg"

XXXI.3

"A HURRICANE OF SHOT AND SHELL"

On the night of June 17 Meade issued orders for a general assault of the Confederate lines. These assaults did not get under way early in the morning, as planned, and before they did Beauregard had been strongly reinforced by Anderson's corps and by part of Hill's corps. The Federals hurled them selves desperately against the Confederate lines, but were unable to dent them.

Here is an account of the fighting by Captain Augustus Brown of the 4th New York Artillery.

June 18 [1864]—About nine o'clock orders came to continue the charge. From the fence . . . the ground, covered with some sort of growing grain, sloped gently down for a hundred yards to a narrow belt of trees in which was the dry bed of a little stream, and beyond this belt the grade ascended gradually for some five hundred yards to the rebel works on the brow of the hill, the intervening field being covered with a luxuriant growth of corn about three feet high. Captain Vanderwiel was assigned to command a picket line which was to precede us, and the advance from this point was to be made in two lines of battle, our five companies forming part of the front line. I saw no second line of battle upon our part of the field during the earlier part of the charge, and I certainly was not informed of any in advance. The enemy had posted two pieces of artillery, perhaps more, in what appeared to be angles of its new works, and our battalion very nearly covered the front between these guns.

To those of us who had anxiously watched all the morning the preparations for our reception, and had seen some of the guns moved into position and the troops deployed behind the breastworks, it seemed perfectly evident that the charge would now prove a disastrous failure, but when the order was given, though we felt we were going to almost certain death, these five companies of artillerymen, always accustomed to obey orders, scaled the fence with a cheer, the enemy commencing to fire the moment we left the road. Reaching the belt of timber, we found the picket line halted and firing from behind trees, but the main line pushed on and out into the open cornfield.

One of my men, a good man, too, but for the moment forgetful that the question was not for him or me to decide, stopped behind a tree, and when ordered forward began to argue that we never could carry that breastwork, a proposition in which I heartily concurred, but it being no time or place for the interchange of our views I leveled my revolver at his head and he broke cover instantly. Another of my men had his musket struck by a ball and bent double like a hairpin, but straightening out his arm, which was nearly paralyzed for an instant, he picked up another musket and went on, keeping place in the line. Just at that moment Major Williams received a rifle ball in the shoulder, and falling near me, though I was not the ranking Captain on the field, directed me to assume command of the battalion, and I turned my own company over to Lieutenant Edmonston.

On assuming command, I noticed that the men in the company on the right of my own, whose Captain had allowed them a ration of whiskey just before we started, were dropping into a little ditch just outside of the line of trees, and that the Captain, who was as brave a man as ever lived, but was rather noted for his varied and vigorous vocabulary, was passing up and down the ditch poking them with his sword and with tears streaming down his face, but without an oath, was begging them to get out and keep in line and not disgrace themselves and him. Thinking to shame his men by letting them know that I, the Captain of a rival company, saw them skulking, I shouted to him to get his men out of the ditch and press forward.

I shall never forget the hurricane of shot and shell which struck us as we emerged from the belt of trees. The sound of the whizzing bullets and exploding shells, blending in awful volume, seemed like the terrific hissing of some gigantic furnace. Men, torn and bleeding, fell headlong from the ranks as the murderous hail swept through the line. A splash of blood from a man hit in the cheek struck me in the face. The shrieks of the wounded mingled with the shouts of defiance which greeted us as we neared the rebel works, and every frightful and sickening incident conspired to paint a scene which no one who survived that day will care again to witness.

This part of the charge was made across a portion of an old race course, and the belt of trees which bordered the track at that point and in which lay the dry bed of the little stream, formed a sort of arc with the ends projected toward the enemy, and as the flanks of the battalion came out in full view, and we were within about one hundred and fifty yards of the rebel line, I was astonished to see that there were no troops on either side of us, and looking back, I discovered that my five companies were the only troops of all the charging lines which were in sight, that had obeyed the order and advanced from the sunken road. Then for the first time I understood the fierceness of the fire to which we were being subjected; saw that we were receiving not only the fire from the works in our front, to which we were entitled, but a cross fire from troops and artillery on the right and left of our front which would have been directed toward other parts of the charging lines if we had been supported, and realized that with this little handful of men, being then so rapidly decimated, it was worse than useless to continue the attack. Accordingly I halted the line and gave the order to lie down, the corn being high enough to furnish some little concealment. A general break to the rear would have cost as many lives as the double quick to the front had done, so I instantly followed my first order with another to the effect that each man should get to the rear as best he could.

When we left the sunken road the Colonel of a regiment on our left whose men, like most of our infantry after six weeks of that sort of strategy, tired of charging a breastwork three times and then going around it, had flatly refused to follow him, joined us with his color-guard and gallantly accompanied us as far as we went, and there planted his flags in the soft earth. He must have discovered the futility of a further advance about the time that I did, for just as I ordered the men down he ordered a retreat, though we were not under his command, and under the combined orders the men at once disappeared in the corn. My orders were intended to embrace the officers of the battalion as well as the men but they were not so understood, and after the men were out of sight there stood the line officers, still targets for the enemy, calmly facing him and awaiting further orders. I shall never forget my thrill of admiration for those brave men as I glanced for an instant up and down the line, but it was no time for a dress parade and I immediately ordered them down and laid down myself.

The sun was blazing straight down upon us and the surface of the ground was very hot, and added to these discomforts, the enemy was firing into the corn in the hope of hitting some of us, which no doubt was done. Although by no means over charged with physical courage . . . I was not, up to this point, conscious of the slightest apprehension for my own personal safety, my intense anxiety for my men and my fixed determination to go over that breastwork at all hazards having probably banished all other considerations from my mind, but as I lay there broiling in the sun, normal conditions began to return, and it occurred to me that some stray bullet might possibly search me out, and, what seemed even worse,—for there is no measuring the limits and effect of personal vanity,—the reflection forced itself upon me that the rebels, and perhaps some of our own men at the rear, had seen the leader of that charge, an acting Major at least, actually hide in the corn.

That last idea settled it, and reflecting that if I should go directly to the rear I would be an easier mark than if I should go across the fire, and that a wound in the back was not considered ornamental for a soldier, I arose and deliberately walked diagonally to the rear until I came to the continuation of the ditch or runway up which, at its distant lower end, we had filed the night before to build a rifle pit, and dropping into that, worked my way down to the piece of race track just outside of the belt of trees, and crossing that reached our works in safety. Why I was not struck while making that trip is more than I can tell . . . and, as giving some idea of the severity of the fire we faced that day,-I may mention that on returning to our lines I counted twenty-four shot and shell marks on the side towards the enemy of a little pine tree not more than eight inches through at the butt, and that the battalion lost, according to the company reports, one hundred and fifteen killed and wounded in this charge.

—BROWN, *The Diary of a Line Officer*

--- XXXI.4 ---

THE MINE AND THE BATTLE OF THE CRATER

With the failure of the assaults on the eighteenth, Grant settled down to invest Petersburg, meantime extending his lines as far to the left as he could. During the rest of June, and July, the two armies stood in their entrenchments, sniping at each other and wilting in the broiling sun. So formidable were Confederate defenses that a break-through seemed impossible. In this juncture Colonel Pleasants of the 48th Pennsylvania—a miners' regiment—proposed tunneling under the Confederate lines and breaching them by exploding a mine. The proposal was accepted, responsibility for laying the mine assigned to Colonel Pleasants' division and for breaking through the Confederate lines after the explosion to General Burnside's IX Corps. The mine was exploded at 5:00 a.m. on June 30; Union artillery opened all along the line; General Ledlie's 1st Division, minus its general, surged into the crater—and stopped.

The details of the operation are somewhat confused, but the outcome is clear enough. The attack—well planned as it was—failed. Federal casualties were over 4,000, Confederate around 1,000. General Ledlie resigned; charges were preferred against Burnside, who shortly resigned. Ferrero, whose colored division had borne the brunt of the fighting, was transferred to a post of less responsibility.

John Wise, son of Virginia's Governor Henry S. Wise, was a student at the Virginia Military Institute when he fought in the Battle of New Market; after that engagement—whose history we will read in our next chapter—he came east to fight for the defense of Petersburg. After the war he went into politics, joined the Republican party, and became a cog in the Mahone political machine.

In the whole history of war, no enterprise so auspiciously begun ever resulted in a conclusion more lame and impotent. The Union troops designated for the assault, instead of drawing inspiration from the sight of the breach they had effected, actually appeared to recoil from the havoc. For some time no demonstration followed the explosion; when they finally advanced, it was not with the eagerness of grenadiers or guards men, but with rushes and pauses of uncertainty; and when they reached our lines, instead of treating the opening as a mere passageway to their objective point beyond, they halted, peeped, and gaped into the pit, and then, with the stupidity of sheep, *followed their bell-wethers into the crater itself*, where, huddled together, all semblance of organization vanished, and company, regimental, and brigade commanders lost all power to recognize, much less control, their respective troops. Meade, from his position a mile away, was demanding of Burnside why he did not advance beyond the crater to the Blandford cemetery. Burnside, safely in the Union lines, and separated from his assaulting columns, was replying that difficulties existed,—difficulties which he could not specify, for the double reason that he did not know what they were, and that they did not in fact exist. . . .

From our ten-inch and eight-inch mortars in the rear of the line, a most accurate fire was opened upon the troops in the breach; and our batteries to north and south began to pour a deadly storm of shell and canister upon their crowded masses. The situation looked desperate for us, nevertheless, for it was all our infantry could do to hold their lines, and not a man could be spared to meet an advance upon Blandford cemetery heights, which lay before the Union troops. At this juncture, heroic John Haskell, of South Carolina, came dashing up the plank road with two light batteries, and from a position near the cemetery began the most effective work of the day.

Exposed to the batteries and sharpshooters of the enemy, he and his men gave little heed to danger. Haskell, in his impetuous and ubiquitous gallantry, dashed and flashed about: first here, next there, like Ariel on the sinking ship. Now he darted into the covered way to seek Elliott, and implore an infantry support for his exposed guns; Elliott, responding to his appeal, was severely wounded as he attempted with a brave handful of his Carolinians to cover Haskell's position; now Haskell cheered Lampkin, who had already opened with his eight-inch mortars; now he hurried back to Flanner, where he had left him and found him under a fire so hot that in mercy he resolved to retire all his guns but six, and call for volunteers to man them, but that was not the temper of Lee's army: every gun detachment volunteered to remain. Hurrying to the right again, he found but one group of cowards in his whole command, and these he replaced by Hampton Gibbs, and Captain Sam Preston of our brigade, whose conspicuous bravery more than atoned for the first defection; both fell desperately wounded, and were replaced by peerless Hampden Chamberlayne, who left the hospital to hurry to the fight, and won promotion by the brilliancy of his behavior. .

It was fully six o'clock before General Lee heard the news, from Colonel Paul, of Beauregard's staff! Colonel Paul lived in Petersburg, and, being at home that night and learning of the disaster, galloped out and informed General Lee as he was sitting down to his breakfast. Before Lee even knew of the occurrence, General Meade had had time to converse with prisoners captured at the crater, and to advise Burnside that Blandford cemetery was unprotected; that none of our troops had returned from the James; that his chance was now; and to implore him to move forward at all hazards, lose no time in making formations, and rush for the crest.

General Lee immediately sent Colonel Venable, of his staff, direct to Mahone, with instructions to come with two brigades of his division to Blandford cemetery to support the artillery. The urgency was so great that he did not transmit the order through General Hill, the corps commander. . . .

Meanwhile, Venable had communicated with Mahone, and Mahone, always cunning, had retired his two brigades from the lines so quietly that General Warren, opposite to him, re ported that no troops had been withdrawn from his front. The Virginia and Georgia brigades of Mahone's division were the troops selected. The message to Mahone was to send them, but he insisted that he should go with them. They passed rapidly by way of a ravine from Mahone's position on the lines covering the Jerusalem plank road to a point in rear of the crater. The Virginia brigade, commanded by Weisiger, led. It was now eight o'clock. One cannot but think of what might have happened during all this time, if Burnside had acted upon Meade's urgent appeals.

The appearance of this infantry was balm and solace to the artillery blazing away upon the crest just above them. For hours they had been fighting there, almost decimated by the artillery concentrated upon them, and the distant firing of sharpshooters. They could not have withstood even a feeble assault of infantry, and had expected it during every minute they had been engaged: the coming of Mahone was their deliverance. With but an instant's pause in the ravine to strip for battle, Mahone's division, headed by their gallant little general, clambered up the slope, crossed the Jerusalem road, and passed in single file at double-quick into a covered way. There was no cheering, and no gaudy flaunting of uniforms or standards; with them, war's work had become too grim and too real for all that. In weather-worn and ragged clothes, with hats whose brims could shade their eyes for deadly aim, with bodies hardened down by march and exposure to race-horse lines, they came, not with the look or feelings of mercenaries, but like anxious, earnest men whose souls were in their work, who knew what the crisis was, and who were anxious to perform the task which that crisis demanded. Agile as cats, they sprang across the road and entered the covered way; as they skipped by, many a fellow kissed his hand to the artillerymen to right and left, or strained on tiptoe to catch sight of the ground in front, before entering the sheltered passage. For the first time during the day, a line of infantry was between our guns and the enemy; and the boys at the guns, knowing what reliance could be placed upon Mahone's veterans, took new heart and new courage, and pounded away with redoubled energy.

Venable parted with Mahone at the mouth of the covered way, and, seeking General Lee, informed him that Mahone was up, and proposed to lead his two brigades in person. The general expressed his gratification, and gave a sigh of relief. . . . The ground from the crater sloped to the north and west into a little ravine, into which the covered way, by which Mahone had entered, debouched; in this hollow Mahone formed his troops for battle, the Virginia brigade on the left.

Springing quickly from the covered way, the eight hundred Virginians lay flat upon the ground. The Georgians were forming on their right. Before the Georgians could come into position, the enemy, occupying our gorge line, succeeded in forming an attacking column, and advanced to the assault. Weisiger, commanding the Virginians, was a grim, determined man. Our boys were lying down within one hundred and sixty yards of the works, and saw within them a vast throng of Union troops, and counted eleven Union flags. A gallant Union officer, seizing a stand of Union colors, leaped upon their breastworks and called upon his men to charge. Fully realizing the paucity of his own numbers, and the danger of being overwhelmed by the mass of the enemy if they poured down upon him, Weisiger determined to anticipate the threatened movement by charging. Cautioning his men to reserve their fire, he ordered them forward. Those who saw this assault pronounce it to have been, in many respects, the most remarkable which they ever witnessed. At the command "Forward!" the men sprang to their feet; advanced at a run in perfect alignment; absolutely refrained from firing until within a few feet of the enemy; then, with their

guns almost upon the bodies of their foes, delivered a deadly fire, and, rushing upon them with bayonets and clubbed muskets, drove them pell-mell back into the intrenchments which they had just left.

General Lee, when advised of this brilliant assault, remarked, "That must have been Mahone's old brigade." When news came confirming it, he again said, "I thought so." . . .

In the position gained by Mahone's old brigade, nothing intervened between them and the enemy but the pile of breast works,—they on the outside, the enemy within the crater and gorge line. The fighting by which they established themselves was desperate and hand-to-hand.

Superb Haskell once more came to their rescue: he moved up his little Eprouvette mortars almost to our lines, and, cutting down his charge of powder to an ounce and half, so that his shell scarcely mounted fifty feet, threw a continuous hail of small shell into the pit, over the heads of our men. Our fellows seized the muskets abandoned by the retreating enemy, and threw them like pitchforks into the huddled troops over the ramparts. Screams, groans, and explosions throwing up human limbs made it a scene of awful carnage. Yet the artillery of the enemy searched every spot, and they still had a formidable force of fighting men.

The Georgia brigade, charging a little after Weisiger's, was decimated and repulsed. Our own brigade, which was engaged from first to last and never yielded a foot of ground, lost heavily, and Mahone's brigade, the "immortals" of that day, was almost annihilated. About one o'clock, the Alabama brigade of Mahone's division, under Saunders, arrived upon the scene, formed and charged, and the white flag went up from the crater. Out of it into our lines filed as prisoners eleven hundred and one Union troops, including two brigade commanders, and we captured twenty-one standards and several thousand of small arms. Over a thousand of the enemy's dead were in and about the breach, and his losses exceeded five thousand effective troops, while our lines were reestablished just where they were when the battle began.

—WISE, *The End of an Era*

XXXI.5

LEE STOPS HANCOCK AT THE GATES OF RICHMOND

Sheridan's offensive in the Valley forced Lee, early in August, to send reinforcements to that threatened area. To prevent the detachment of further reinforcements Grant sent Hancock's corps north of the James to make demonstrations against Richmond and, if possible, capture Chapin's Bluff, on the James River. It was expected that this attack would take Lee by surprise, but surprise was not achieved. Yet the threat to Richmond was a serious one. During the fighting of August 16 two Confederate brigades broke and fled; "not only the day but Richmond seemed to be gone," wrote General C. W. Field.

The confused fighting from August 14 to 18 is here described by Richard Corbin, who had run the blockade in order to serve in the Confederate Army.

Headquarters, Field's Division, Petersburg, Va., August 26, 1864.—My dear mother: Some three weeks have flown by since I wrote to you from the north side of the James River, wither this division had been sent at the time of Grant's grand subterranean operation before Petersburg, the strategy of which was characterized by the fiendish ingenuity of Yankee warfare. . . . As I told you from my headquarters near Chapin's Bluff, we fully expected to pitch into the Yankees immediately on arriving on the north side of the river; but when our division had got into position the enemy had disappeared from our front. As far as the fighting was concerned, we had a little respite, but the staff did not profit much by it, for General Field having been placed ad interim in command of that division of the Richmond defenses, our duties became very onerous; but we were to a certain extent compensated by the importance it gave us, for we literally became monarchs of all we surveyed.

This comparative repose was, however, of short duration. Our scouts, a few days after, brought us the intelligence that the enemy had thrown a pontoon bridge across the river and that a large force was moving across it. We had but few troops with us, but preparations were made for a resolute defense of the line committed to our care. On

Sunday they drove our skirmishers in, and in the afternoon they attempted to carry a portion of our intrenchments. For that purpose they hurled against us two divisions of their Second Corps, which rushed toward our position with yells, banners flying and bands playing. When they advanced to within about seven hundred yards of our line two twelve-pounders loaded with canister blazed away at them. Our artillery is not considered by any means the most efficient branch of our service and of late has been rather sneered at in this army, but on this occasion it did terrible execution. The Yanks advanced in four lines of battle, and a magnificent spectacle it was to witness that mighty host bearing down upon our thinly manned breastworks. Notwithstanding my emotion, I could not refrain from admiring the sight. Our fire made wide breaches in their ranks, and after the third discharge the whole line wavered and fluttered like a flag in the wind; another shell exploding in their midst, they broke and fled in every direction without retaining a shadow of their former organization. In their frantic haste to get out of range of our murderous shots they threw away guns, equipment, and all their warlike paraphernalia. Deserters told us that they lost very heavily in that abortive charge. They again renewed the attack, but with less vigor, on our left, and were driven back with great loss by our dismounted cavalry. This was the last of that day's fighting—with the shades of night there came a cessation of hostilities.

In the morning of Tuesday the Yankees attacked us in heavy force, but we repulsed them very handsomely. Finding that these repeated assaults on that part of the line did not pay, General Hancock felt for a more vulnerable point, which he discovered on our left. After riding about ever since dawn, the general and his staff halted in a field in the rear of Wright's brigade of A. P. Hill's corps. The day was a sultry one, and the heat, superadded to other exertions, made us so weary that we got off our horses and lay down for a few moments on the grass. We had not been there many seconds when we were aroused by a terrific cannonade followed by heavy volleys of musketry.

We mounted horses in a trice; presently squads of frightened men came from the front in anything but a leisurely manner. They informed us that the whole Yankee army had charged them and that they had been obliged to give way. The firing increased; the air was alive with Minie balls; the ground was torn up by shells and cannonballs, and in a few minutes the whole of Wright's brigade was stampeding toward us. We strove to rally them by entreaties and by menaces, and with pistols drawn we threatened to shoot them if they did not go back, but it was of no avail; you might as well try to argue with a flock of affrighted sheep as with a crowd of panic-stricken soldiers.

Up to this time we cannot account for this stampede. The attack, it was true, was sudden and unexpected and the force of the enemy enormous; but the men who were now flying before the Yankees had always beaten them and had invariably borne themselves on every battlefield with distinguished bravery. We are therefore much puzzled to find out what caused them to disgrace the name of their brigade in that manner. . . .

The General, finding that nothing can be got out of these men, decided to fall back, for the Federals were swooping down upon us in overwhelming numbers; it seemed as though forty thousand men would be an underestimate of the force. I was sent by him for reinforcements. I had orders to bring up without delay two brigades of our own division, viz. Laws's Alabama and Binning's Georgians. They came up at a double-quick amid a very galling fire; they were formed right under the guns of the enemy, and then they rushed in with a deafening war-whoop. It was really splendid to witness the dash of these gallant fellows. I was so carried away with enthusiasm that I cantered alongside of them, but, alas! I did not accompany them during the whole of their triumphant advance, for my faithful charger, poor Palmetto, fell under me, pierced in the left hip by a Minie ball. I was a little stunned by the fall, and when I managed to extricate myself from under him our brave boys had beaten back the foe and recaptured the position which they had taken from us.

On the whole, notwithstanding the misbehavior of that brigade of Hill's corps, our achievement was a very brilliant one; for with a handful of men, say seven thousand at the outside, we drove back three of the enemy's largest corps; and as usual our division won for itself and its commander golden opinions. General Lee, toward the close of the fight, rode up and congratulated the general on the able manner in which he had handled his troops. At one time it was touch and go, and it required great coolness and skill on the part of our general to parry the attempts of the Yankees to turn our flanks; had they succeeded in accomplishing that, the consequences might have been very serious. The reverse was a very heavy one to the enemy; by sending over the best troops they evidently counted on a success. We had several small artillery and picket engagements during the rest of the week, but finally they sloped off without trumpet or drum, and on Sunday morning Hancock and Company had vamosed. Desertions from the Yankee army have been so frequent during this campaign that General Lee has desired to encourage them by circulating throughout Grant's army a paper in which kind treatment and protection is promised to those soldiers who come over to us voluntarily. This has produced the desired effect, for deserters flock into our lines at a monstrous rate, and the cry is "still they come."

—[CORBIN], "Letters of a Confederate Officer"

XXXI.6

THE IRON LINES OF PETERSBURG

Direct assault on the Confederates lines was out of the question; the mine had proved a ghastly failure; attacks north of the James were abortive. Grant fell back on traditional siege operations, meantime striking constantly at the Weldon and the Southside railroads, and persistently pushing his lines westward. Lee's army was stretched to the breaking point; his soldiers were tired, hungry, and dispirited; and he lost as many men by desertion as he gained by recruits and levies.

Here are three letters from a North Carolina soldier who fought through the winter in the iron lines of Petersburg.

Luther Rice Mills to John Mills

Trenches Near Crater, Petersburg, Va.
Nov. 26th [1864]

Brother John:

In my short note to you about a week ago I was unable to give you any of the army news &c. for that can only be gathered by observation. We have just passed through a spell of very hard weather. The suffering in the Trenches was much greater than it should have been. Many of the men were entirely destitute of blankets and overcoats and it was really distressing to see them shivering over a little fire made of green pine wood. Duty too is quite heavy. The men have twelve hours of Picket and twelve of Camp Guard every thirty-six hours. The effect that one cold wet night has upon the boys is a little remarkable. They are generally for *peace on any terms* toward the close of a cold wet night but after the sun is up and they get warm they are in their usual spirits. I have never seen our army so *completely whipped.* The men do not seem to fear the winter Campaign so much as they do the coming of spring. . . . I hardly know what to think of our prospect for next spring. Some men desert from our Brigade nearly every day or two, yet I believe there will be a great many more next spring. Our army however is quite large—perhaps as large as it was last spring. . . . There is a rumor in our camp that our Division will go to Georgia. This I think extremely doubtful. One good decisive victory in the valley or Georgia would do a great deal towards cheering our men up. We have been supplied within the last few days with shoes and blankets and it is to be hoped that our men will do better. We have to carry some men to hospital for frostbites &c. Some have come in off picket crying from cold like children. In fact I have seen men in the trenches with no shoes at all. I saw Capt. John Williams a few days ago but have not been able to see Baldy yet. We are still near the old mine. I suppose that I am now within fifty yards of the spot where I was wounded. I am doing very well. My shoulder does not worry me much.

Please write soon and give me all the news.
Yours truly
L. R. Mills

Trenches Near Crater, Petersburg Va.
Jany. 3rd, 1865

Brother John:

We are still at our old position—Right of the Brigade extending just beyond Rive's Salient and Left resting near the Blowup. There is a rumor afloat that we will be relieved some time this month and sent to the rear to rest &c. Everything seems to indicate that we are fixed up here for the winter. Our Division holds the hottest part of the entire lines. The front of Wilcox's Division immediately on our right the enemy can not be seen from the main lines. Here our Picket lines are from 50 to 200 yards from the enemy and a man dares not show his head. We have the biggest rows here some days you ever heard of. The batteries in the rear lines and the enemy's battries get to shelling occasionally and shells fly by as thick as bats in a summer night. After a row last week some men picked up at least 500 pounds of fragments of shells within a hundred yards of my tent. It was an amusing sight to hear our boys taunting and inviting Grant's army to fight with us while they were firing salutes and rejoicing over Sherman's great victory in Georgia. Our men need a good Victory badly. It would do us a great deal of good for Grant to charge our lines. I believe every man would hail such an attack with joy. We are preparing to put out two more lines of Chevaux de Frise. The spirit of our men is improving slowly. A good many are deserting to the enemy—more than come to us. Two men of my company deserted to the enemy last Christmas night. One was a substitute from Georgetown and the other from near Wheeling. We get pit coal now instead of green pine. I guess we will be a little better now. If I could get a good big cat I could do a great deal better. We have rats and mice and something else in abundance. We can say with old Burns

"Ha! Where ye gaun ye crawlie ferties &c."

I saw a man catch a large rat and eat it about a week ago. What is it that a dirty soldier won't do? The Richmond Examiner says "Coming events cast their shadows before them" but I have not seen the shadow of that big New Year's Dinner yet. Perhaps it is not a coming event. . . . One of the men lamenting his own hard luck and Younger's good luck said five balls have struck me this campaign and the one that would have given me a furlough "I cotch in a blanket." I am in good health and doing well.

Yours truly
L. R. Mills

Trenches Near Crater, March 2, 1865
Brother John:

Something is about to happen. I know not what. Nearly every one who will express an opinion says Gen'l Lee is about to evacuate Petersburg. The authorities are having all the cotton, tobacco &c. moved out of the place as rapidly as possible. This was commenced about the 22nd of February. Two thirds of the Artillery of our Division has been moved out. The Reserved Ordnance Train has been loaded up and is ready to move at any time. I think Gen'l Lee expects a hard fight on the right and has ordered all this simply as a precautionary measure. Since my visit to the right I have changed my opinion about the necessity for the evacuation of Petersburg. If it is evacuated Johnson's Division will be in a bad situation for getting out. Unless we are so fortunate as to give the Yankees the slip many of us will be captured. I would regret very much to have to give up the old place. The soiled and tattered Colors borne by our skeleton Regiments is sacred and dear to the hearts of every man. No one would exchange it for a new flag. So it is with us. I go down the lines, I see the marks of shot and shell, I see where fell my comrades, the Crater, the grave of fifteen hundred Yankees, when I go to the rear I see little mounds of dirt some with headboards, some with none, some with shoes protruding, some with a small pile of bones on one side near the end showing where a hand was left uncovered, in fact everything near shows desperate fighting. And here I would rather "fight it out." If Petersburg and Richmond is evacuated—from what I have seen & heard in the army—our cause will be hopeless. It is useless to conceal the truth any longer. Many of our people at home have become so demoralized that they write to their husbands, sons and brothers that desertion *now is* not *dishonorable*. It would be impossible to keep the army from straggling to a ruinous extent if we evacuate. I have just received an order from Wise to carry out on picket tonight a rifle and ten rounds of Cartridges to shoot men when they desert. The men seem to think desertion no crime & hence never shoot a deserter when he goes over—they always shoot but never hit. I am glad to say that we have not had but four desertions from our Reg't to the enemy. . . . I send you this morning "Five Months in a Yankee prison" by a Petersburg Militiaman.

Write soon.
Yours truly
L. R. Mills
—Harmon, ed., "Letters of Luther Rice Mills"

XXXII

THE VALLEY
IN 1864

The Valley campaigns of 1864 are among the most interesting in the history of the war. There was no Stonewall Jackson to give them glamour, to be sure, but Jube Early and Phil Sheridan were not bad substitutes. Heretofore the Valley had been, chiefly, the theater for Confederate offensives; this, to some extent, it remained, but the more important offensive operations of 1864 were Federal. The final campaign of 1864 was, too, one of the most decisive of the war, for it deprived Lee's army of its major source of supply and cut it off from the west.

Grant's grand strategy, it will be remembered, called for advances up the Valley by General Sigel and from the west by Generals Averell and Crook to mesh with the major attacks by Meade and Butler. These Valley offensives got under way on time, but accomplished little; not until Sheridan took command was Grant's strategic plan vindicated.

At the end of April Averell and Crook, then along the Kanawha in western Virginia, advanced toward Lynchburg with a view to cutting the important Virginia & Tennessee Railroad. General John Morgan met them and, in a smart action, drove them back to their bases. Meantime Sigel had advanced cautiously up the Valley toward New Market. There, on May 15, he was met by Breckinridge, defeated, and hurled back. General Hunter—next to Butler the most detested of Union commanders—supplanted him and embarked on a program of systematic devastation of the Valley. His military objective was Staunton and the Virginia Central Railroad. Early in June he reached Staunton and then advanced on the town of Lexington, home of Virginia Military Institute, which he put to flames, and of Washington College, which he gutted. Lee hurried Early to the Valley to deal with this menace to his communications; Hunter retreated into western Virginia; and the Confederates were once more in undisputed control of the Valley.

Early seized the opportunity to relieve pressure on Petersburg by striking across the Potomac and at Washington. Swift marches brought him to the outskirts of Washington by July 10; as Federal forces concentrated against him he withdrew to home ground. The bold stroke had achieved its immediate objective; Grant sent large reinforcements to the Valley and appointed Sheridan to temporary command of the whole theater of operations. In two months Sheridan made a national reputation. With a numerical superiority of at least two to one, he was able to seize and hold the offensive. First he struck Early along the Opequon; then at Winchester. These two battles all but destroyed the Confederate forces in the Valley.

Once again Lee was forced to send reinforcements, and once again the intrepid Early took the offensive, scoring what at first seemed a spectacular victory at Cedar Creek. This victory Sheridan turned into defeat. After that there was nothing to stop the deliberate and calculated destruction that Grant ordered and Sheridan willingly executed. By winter the Valley, scene of so many Confederate victories, was firmly in Union hands. And it was from the Valley that Sheridan finally rode down to the triumph of Five Forks.

XXXII. I

V.M.I. BOYS FIGHT AT
NEW MARKET

On April 30 General Franz Sigel, in command of the Department of West Virginia, started up the Valley toward Strasburg. Meeting no opposition he pressed on toward New Market. Breckinridge was already on his way to meet him, with a miscellaneous force including the Cadet Corps from the Virginia Military Institute—Stonewall Jackson's school—at Lexington.

John Wise, then a cadet of seventeen, here tells the story of the dash from Lexington to New Market and of "the most glorious day" of his life. The battle was a minor one, but had far-reaching consequences, for it enabled the Confederates to hold the Valley long enough to gather the harvest, so essential to Lee's hungry army.

On the 10th of May, 1864, the Cadet Corps was the very pink of drill and discipline, and mustered 350 strong. The plebes of the last fall had passed through squad and company drill, and the battalion was now proficient in the most intricate manceuvre. The broad parade ground lay spread out like a green carpet. The far-off ranges of the Blue Ridge seemed nearer in the clear light of spring. The old guard tree, once more luxuriantly green, sheltered its watching groups of admiring girls and prattling children. . . .

Suddenly the barracks reverberated with the throbbing of drums; we awoke and recognized the long roll. Lights were up; the stoops resounded with the rush of footsteps seeking place in the ranks; the adjutant, by lantern-light, read our orders amid breathless silence. They told us that the enemy was in the valley, that Breckinridge needed help, and that we were ordered to march for Staunton at daybreak—a battalion of infantry and a section of artillery—with three days' rations. Not a sound was uttered, not a man moved from the military posture of "parade rest." Our beating hearts told us that our hour had come at last.

"Parade's dismissed," piped the adjutant. Then came a wild halloo, as company after company broke ranks. Again in fancy I see the excited rush of that gay throng, eager as greyhounds in the leash, hurrying back and forth, preparing for the start, forgetful that it would be six hours before they should march.

Daybreak found us on the Staunton pike after a sleepless night and a breakfast by candle-light. . . And now, fairly started upon our journey, we were plodding on right merrily, our gallant little battery rumbling behind.

At midday on the 12th of May we marched into Staunton to the tune of "The girl I left behind me." We were not quite as fresh or as neat as at the outset, but still game and saucy. . . .

Breckinridge's army, which had hurried up from southwestern Virginia to meet Sigel, soon filled the town and suburbs. Now and then a bespattered trooper came up wearily from Woodstock or Harrisonburg to report the steady advance of Sigel with an army thrice the size of our own. Ever and anon the serious shook their heads and predicted hot work in store for us. Even in the hour of levity the shadow of impending bloodshed hung over all but the cadet. At evening parade the command came to move down the valley.

Morning found us promptly on the march. A few lame ducks had succumbed and were left behind, but the body of the corps were still elated and eager, although rain had aver taken us. The first day's march brought us to Harrisonburg; the second to Lacy's Springs, within ten miles of New Market. On this day evidences of the enemy's approach thickened on every hand. At short intervals upon the pike, the great artery of travel in the valley, carriages and vehicles of all sorts filled the way, laden with people and their household effects, fleeing from the hostile advance. Now and then a haggard trooper, dispirited by long skirmishing against overwhelming force, would gloomily suggest the power and numbers of the enemy. Towards nightfall, in a little grove by a church, we came upon a squad of Federal prisoners, the first that many of us had ever seen. It was a stolid lot of Germans, who eyed us with curious inquiry as we passed. Laughter and badinage had somewhat subsided when we pitched camp that night in sight of our picket-fires twinkling in the gloaming but a few miles below us down the valley. We learned, beyond doubt, that Franz Sigel and his army were sleeping within ten miles of the spot on which we rested. . . .

The day, breaking gray and gloomy, found us plodding on ward in the mud. The exceedingly sober cast of our reflections was relieved by the light-heartedness of the veterans. Wharton's brigade, with smiling "Old Gabe" at their head, cheered us heartily as we came up to the spot where they were cooking breakfast by the road-side. Many were the good-natured gibes with which they restored our confidence. The old soldiers were as merry, nonchalant, and indifferent to the coming fight as if it was a daily occupation. . . .

The mile-posts on the pike scored four miles, three miles, two miles, one mile to New Market. Then the mounted skirmishers crowded past us hurrying to the front. Cheering began in our rear and was caught up by the troops along the line of march. We learned its import as Breckinridge and his staff approached, and we joined in the huzza as that soldierly man, mounted magnificently, dashed past us, uncovered, bowing, and riding like the Cid. Along the crest of the elevation in our front we beheld our line of mounted pickets and the smoldering fires of their night's bivouac. We halted with the realization that one turn in the road would bring us in full view of the enemy's position. Echols's and Wharton's brigades hurried past us. There was not so much banter then. "Forward!" was the word once more, and New Market appeared in sight.

The turn of the road displayed the whole position. A bold range of hills parallel with the mountains divides the Shenandoah Valley into two smaller valleys, and in the eastern-most of these lies New Market. . . .

Orchards skirt the village in these meadows between our position and the town, and they are filled with the enemy's skirmishers. A heavy stone fence and a deep lane run west ward from the town and parallel with our line of battle. Here the enemy's infantry was posted to receive our left flank, and behind it his artillery was posted on a slope, the ground rising gradually until, a short distance beyond the town, to the left of the pike, it spreads out in an elevated plateau. The hillsides from this plateau to the pike are gradual and broken by several gullies heavily wooded by scrub-cedar.

It was Sunday morning, and 11 o'clock. In a picturesque little churchyard, right under the shad-ow of the village spire and among the white tombstones, a six-gun battery was posted in rear of the infantry line of the enemy. The moment we debouched it opened upon us.

Away off to the right, in the Luray Gap of the Massanutten range, our signal corps was telegraphing the position and numbers of the enemy. Our cavalry was moving at a gallop to the cover of the creek to attempt to flank the town. Echols's brigade was moving from the pike at a double quick by the right flank and went into line of battle across the meadow, its left resting on the pike. Simultaneously his skirmishers were thrown forward at a run and engaged the enemy. Out of the orchards and out on the meadows arose puff after puff of blue smoke as our sharpshooters advanced, the "pop,' pop" of their rifles ringing forth excitingly. Thundering down the pike came McLaughlin with his artillery, and wheeling out into the meadows he swung into battery action left, and let fly with all his guns. The cadet section of artillery pressing a little farther forward wheeled to the left, toiled up the slope, and with a plunging fire replied to the Federal battery in the graveyard. At the first discharge of our guns a beautiful wreath of smoke shot upward and hovered over them.

The little town, which a moment before had seemed to sleep so peacefully upon that Sabbath morn, was now wreathed in battle-smoke and swarming with troops hurrying to their positions. We had their range beautifully, and every shell, striking some obstruction, exploded in the streets. Every man of our army was in sight. Every position of the enemy was plainly visible. . . .

My orders were to remain with the wagons at the bend in the pike, unless our forces were driven back; in which case we were to retire to a point of safety. When it became evident that a battle was imminent, a single thought took possession of me, and that was, that I would never be able to look my father in the face again if I sat on a baggage-wagon while my command was in its first, perhaps its only, engagement. He was a grim old fighter, at that moment commanding at Petersburg. . . . If, now that I had the opportunity, I should fail to take part in the fight I knew what was in store for me. Napoleon in Egypt pointed to the Pyramids and told his soldiers that from their heights forty centuries looked down upon them. My oration, delivered from the baggage-wagon, was not so elevated in tone, but equally emphatic. It ran about this wise:

"Boys, the enemy is in our front. Our command is about to go into action. I like fighting no better than anybody else. But I have an enemy in my rear as dreadful as any before us. If I return home and tell my father that I was on the baggage guard when my comrades were fighting I know my fate. He will kill me with worse than bullets—ridicule. I shall join the command forthwith. Any one who chooses to remain may do so."

All the guard followed. The wagon was left in charge of the black driver. Of the four who thus went, one was killed and two were wounded.

We rejoined the battalion as it marched by the left flank from the pike. Moving at double-quick we were in an instant in line of battle, our right near the turnpike. Rising ground in our immediate front concealed us from the enemy. The command was given to strip for action. Knapsacks, blankets, everything but guns, canteens, and cartridge-boxes, were thrown down upon the ground. Our boys were silent then. Every lip was tightly drawn, every cheek was pale; but not with fear. With a peculiar nervous jerk we pulled our cartridge-boxes round to the front and tightened our belts. Whistling rifled-shell screamed over us as, tipping the hill crest in our own front, they bounded over our heads. Across the pike to our right Patton's brigade was lying down, abreast of us.

"At-ten-tion-n-n! Battalion Forward! Guide—Center-r-rr!" shouted Ship, and off we started. At that moment, from the left of the line, sprang Sergeant-Major Woodbridge, and posted himself forty paces in front of the colors as directing guide. Brave Evans, standing over six feet two, unfurled our colors that for days had hung limp and bedraggled about the staff, and every cadet in the

Institute leaped forward, dressing to the ensign, elate and thrilling with the consciousness that *"This is war!"* We reached the hill-crest in our front, where we were abreast of our smoking battery and in full sight and range of the enemy. We were pressing towards him at "arms port" with the light tripping gait of the French infantry. The enemy had obtained our range, and began to drop his shell under our noses along the slope. Echols's brigade rose up and were charging on our right with the rebel yell. . . .

Down the green slope we went, answering the wild cry of our comrades as their musketry rattled out its opening volleys. In another moment we should expect a pelting rain of lead from the blue line crouching behind the stone wall at the lane. Then came a sound more stunning than thunder, that burst directly in my face; lightnings leaped; fire flashed; the earth rocked; the sky whirled round, and I stumbled. My gun pitched forward, and I fell upon my knees. Sergeant Cabell looked back at me sternly, pityingly, and called out, "Close up, men," as he passed on.

I knew no more. When consciousness returned it was raining in torrents. I was lying on the ground, which all about was torn and plowed with shell which were still screeching in the air and bounding on the earth. . . .

From this time forth I may speak of the gallant behavior of the cadets without the imputation of vanity, for I was no longer a participant in their glory. . . .

Bloody work had been done. The space between the enemy's old and new positions was dotted with their dead and wounded—shot as they fled across the open field. But this same exposed ground now lay before, and must be crossed by our own men, under a galling fire from a strong and protected position. The distance was not three hundred yards, but the ground to be traversed was a level green field of young wheat. Again the advance was ordered. Our men responded with a cheer. Poor fellows! they had already been put upon their mettle in two assaults. Exhausted, wet to the skin, muddied to their eyebrows with the stiff clay through which they had pulled,—some of them actually shoeless after their struggle across the plowed ground,—they nevertheless advanced with great grit and eagerness; for the shouting on their right meant victory.

But the foe in our front was far from conquered. As our fellows came on with a dash the enemy stood his ground most courageously. That battery, now charged with canister and shrapnel, opened upon the cadets with a murderous hail the moment they uncovered. The infantry lying behind fence-rails piled upon the ground, poured in a steady, deadly fire. . . .

The men were falling right and left. The veterans on the right of the cadets seemed to waver. Ship, our commandant, fell wounded. For the first time the cadets seemed irresolute. Some one cried out, "Lie down," and all obeyed, firing from the knee—all but Evans, the ensign, who was standing bolt upright. Poor Stanard's limbs were torn asunder and he lay there bleeding to death. Some one cried out, "Fell back, and rally on Edgar's battalion." Several boys moved as if to obey; but Pizzini, orderly of "B" company, with his Italian blood at the boiling-point, cocked his gun and swore he would shoot the first man who ran. Preston, brave and inspiring, with a smile lay down upon his only arm, remarking that he would at least save that. Collona, captain of "D," was speaking words of encouragement and bidding the boys shoot close. The boys were being decimated; manifestly they must charge or retire; and charge it was.

For at that moment, Henry A. Wise, our first captain, be loved of every boy in the command, sprung to his feet, shouted the charge, and led the Cadet Corps forward to the guns. The guns of the battery were served superbly; the musketry fairly rolled. The cadets reached the firm greensward of the farm yard in which the battery was planted. The Federal infantry began to break and run behind the buildings. Before the order to "Limber up" could be obeyed our boys disabled the trails and were close upon the guns; the gunners dropped

their sponges and sought safety in flight. Lieutenant Hanna hammered a burly gunner over the head with his cadet sword. Winder Garrett outran another and attacked him with his bayonet. The boys leaped on the guns, and the battery was theirs; while Evans was wildly waving the cadet colors from the top of a caisson. . . .

We had won a victory,—not a Manassas . . . but, for all that, a right comforting bit of news went up the pike that night to General Lee; for from where he lay, locked in the death grapple with Grant in the Wilderness, his thoughts were, doubtless, ever turning wearily and anxiously towards this flank movement in the valley.

—WISE, "The West Point of the Confederacy"

XXXII.2

GENERAL HUNTER DEVASTATES THE VALLEY

After New Market Sigel wired that his "retrograde" movement was carried out in good order; Halleck telegraphed in disgust to Grant, "Sigel is in full retreat on Strasburg. He will do nothing but run; never did anything else." He was relieved from command, and David Hunter appointed to his place.

No other Union general, except Butler, was so cordially detested by the South; few did so much to earn that detestation. A veteran of the Mexican War Hunter had replaced Fremont in Missouri, and been replaced, in turn, himself. He had commanded the Department of the South and issued a proclamation freeing the slaves within his lines which Lincoln was forced to repudiate. When he raised a Negro regiment the Confederate Congress proclaimed him a felon and ordered his execution if captured. Perhaps it was no wonder that he was bitter toward the South! When he replaced Sigel he embarked on a plan of systematic destruction of the Valley—a plan which Sheridan was to complete. The destruction itself was justified by those same military considerations that con trolled Sherman in Georgia; what embittered Southerners was the animosity which appeared to inspire Hunter and the extent to which he exposed women and children to danger.

General John Imboden, who here describes Hunter's depredations, was a veteran of Jackson's Valley campaign, had covered the retreat at Gettysburg, and was now once more back in his familiar Valley.

From Brownsburg General Hunter proceeded to Lexington.

. . . At Lexington he enlarged upon the burning operations begun at Staunton. On his way, and in the surrounding country, he burnt mills, furnaces, storehouses, granaries, and all farming utensils he could find, beside a great amount of fencing, and a large quantity of grain. In the town he burnt the Virginia Military Institute, and all the professors' houses except the superintendent's (General Smith's), where he had his headquarters, and found a portion of the family too sick to be removed. He had the combustibles collected to burn Washington College, the recipient of the benefactions of the Father of his Country by his will; but, yielding to the appeals of the trustees and citizens, spared the building, but destroyed the philosophical and chemical apparatus, libraries and furniture. He burned the mills and some private stores in the lower part of the town.

Captain Towns, an officer in General Hunter's army, took supper with the family of Governor John Letcher. Mrs. Letcher having heard threats that her house would be burned, spoke of it to Captain Towns, who said it could not be possible, and remarked that he would go at once to headquarters and let her know. He went, returned in a half hour, and told her that he was directed by General Hunter to assure her that the house would not be destroyed, and she might, therefore, rest easy. After this, she dismissed her fears, not believing it possible that a man occupying Hunter's position would be guilty of wilful and deliberate falsehood to a lady. It, however, turned out otherwise, for the next morning, at half-past eight o'clock, his assistant provost marshal, accompanied by a portion of his guard, rode up to the door, and Captain Berry dismounted, rang the door-bell, called for Mrs. Letcher, and informed her that General Hunter had ordered him to burn the house. She replied: "There must be some mistake," and requested to see the order. He said it was verbal. She asked if its execution could not be delayed till she could see Hunter?

He replied: "The order is peremptory, and you have five minutes to leave the house."

Mrs. Letcher then asked if she could be allowed to remove her mother's, her sister's, her own and her children's clothing. This request being refused, she left the house. In a very short time they poured camphene on the parlor floor and ignited it with a match. In the meantime Miss Lizzie Letcher was trying to remove some articles of clothing from the other end of the house, and Berry, finding these in her arms, set fire to them. The wardrobe and bureaus were then fired, and soon the house was enveloped in flames.

Governor Letcher's mother, then seventy-eight years old, lived on the adjoining lot. They fired her stable, within forty feet of the dwelling, evidently to burn it, too; but, owing to the active exertions of Captain Towns, who made his men carry water, the house was saved. While Hunter was in Lexington, Captain Mathew X. White, residing near the town, was arrested, taken about two miles, and, without trial, was shot, on the allegation that he was a bushwhacker. During the first year of the war he commanded the Rockbridge Cavalry, and was a young gentleman of generous impulses and good character. The total destruction of private property in Rockbridge county, by Hunter, was estimated and published in the local papers at the time as over $2,000,000. The burning of the Institute was a public calamity, as it was an educational establishment of great value.

From Lexington he proceeded to Buchanan, in Bottetourt county, and camped on the magnificent estate of Colonel John T. Anderson, an elder brother of General Joseph R. Anderson, of the Tredegar Works, at Richmond. Colonel Anderson's estate, on the banks of the Upper James, and his mansion, were baronial in character. The house crowned a high, wooded hill, was very large, and furnished in a style to dispense that lavish hospitality which was the pride of so many of the old time Virginians. It was the seat of luxury and refinement, and in all respects a place to make the owner contented with his lot in this world. Colonel Anderson was old—

his head as white as snow—and his wife but a few years his junior. He was in no office, and too old to fight—hence was living on his fine estate strictly the life of a private gentleman. He had often, in years gone by, filled prominent representative positions from his county. There was no military or public object on God's earth to be gained by ruining such a man. Yet Hunter, after destroying all that could be destroyed on the plantation when he left it, ordered the grand old mansion, with all its contents, to be laid in ashes.

From Buchanan he proceeded toward Lynchburg, by way of the Peaks of Otter; but on arriving within four miles of the city, where a sharp skirmish occurred between General Crook's command and three brigades under my command, at a place called the Quaker Meeting-House, he ascertained that General Early was in town with Stonewall Jackson's old corps. This was enough for him. That night he began a rapid retreat to ward Salem, leaving his cavalry to make demonstrations on Early's lines long enough to give him a good day's start. . . .

I shall conclude this already long narrative by citing a few more instances of Hunter's incendiarism in the Lower Valley. It seems that, smarting under the miserable failure of his grand raid on Lynchburg, where, during a march of over two hundred miles, the largest force he encountered was under Jones at Piedmont, and he routed that, thus leaving the way open to reach Lynchburg within three days, destroy the stores there and go out through West Virginia unmolested, he had failed to do anything but inflict injury on private citizens, and he came back to the Potomac more implacable than when he left it a month before.

His first victim was the Hon. Andrew Hunter, of Charlestown, Jefferson county, his own first cousin, and named after the General's father. Mr. Hunter is a lawyer of great eminence, and a man of deservedly large influence in his county and the State. His home, eight miles from Harper's Ferry, in the suburbs of Charlestown, was the most costly and elegant in the place, and his family as refined and cultivated as any in the State. His offense, in General Hunter's eyes, was that he had gone politically with his State, and was in full sympathy with the Confederate cause. The General sent a squadron of cavalry out from Harper's Ferry, took Mr. Hunter prisoner, and held him a month in the common guard-house of his soldiers, without alleging any offense against him not common to nearly all the people of Virginia, and finally discharged him without trial or explanation, after heaping these indignities on him. Mr. Hunter was an old man, and suffered severely from confinement and exposure. While he was thus a prisoner, General Hunter ordered his elegant mansion to be burned to the ground, with all its contents, not even permitting Mrs. Hunter and her daughter to save their clothes and family pictures from the flames; and, to add to the desolation, camped his cavalry within the inclosure of the beautiful grounds, of several acres, surrounding the residence, till the horses had destroyed them.

—IMBODEN, "Fire, Sword, and the Halter"

XXXII.3

GENERAL RAMSEUR FIGHTS AND DIES FOR HIS COUNTRY

There was no more gallant figure in the Confederate Army than young Stephen Dodson Ramseur of North Carolina. After graduating from West Point in 1860 he resigned a commission in the U. S. Army to go with his state the following year. His military career was meteoric: within a year he had been promoted from lieutenant to brigadier general. He fought with distinction during the Seven Days; was wounded at Malvern Hill; fought and was wounded again at Chancellorsville; recovered and fought at Gettysburg and in the Wilderness. He led the counterattack that threw Hancock back at the Bloody Angle, and there was wounded a third time. Promoted to major general, at twenty-seven, he joined Early in the Valley campaign and fought with his customary courage at Winchester and Cedar Creek.

In October 1863 Ramseur had married Ellen Richmond, and his letters to his beloved wife give a running account of the war. Those we print here describe the fighting in the Valley campaign. The day before Cedar Creek Ramseur heard that his baby had been born, and he went into battle wearing a white rose in honor of the daughter he was never to see. He was mortally wounded trying to stem Sheridan's counterattack at Cedar Creek and died the following day. "He was," wrote General Early, "a most gallant and energetic officer whom no disaster appalled, but his courage and energy seemed to gain new strength in the midst of confusion and disorder."

Staunton—Va—June 27th—1864

Have time for only a line—to tell you I am well. We have had hardest march of the war. Couldn't catch Hunter—but we hope yet to strike the Enemy a heavy blow. Do not be uneasy if you fail to hear from us. We are going still further & all communications will be cut. We hope to relieve Richmond & make Yankeedom smart. I may be pardoned for saying to you that I am making a reputation as a Maj. Genl. The greatest hardship is being separated from you.

H'dqr'ts Early's Div—July 23rd—1864

Again we have passed thro the ordeal of battle. Caleb [Genl Rs brother in law & aide de camp] & I are both safe wonderful to say. I am greatly mortified at result of battle. My men behaved shamefully. They ran from the enemy. And for the first time in my life, I am deeply mortified at the conduct of troops under my command. Had these men behaved like *my old Brigade* would have done under similar circumstances, a disgraceful retreat would have been a brilliant victory. Caleb & I are both safe wonderful to say. Do not mention to anyone the bad conduct of my troops.

Camp near Bunker Hill. Aug 28th—1864

Last night I rec'd two letters from you. Do you know how precious they are, & how much good they did me? After a long march & a sharp skirmish I had gone to bed, & was thinking of you only, when they were brought to me. I am so glad that you continue cheerful & hopeful through these terrible days. Courage my little wife maybe I will be per mitted to come & see you before long. . . . Do you know that I am beginning to believe that we may very soon have peace! Everybody seems to think that the peace party will carry the election in the north. Oh

may these expectations be realized & soon may this terrible war that separates us cease. It is such a happiness to be able to write to you often—wish I had time to write more fully & more often. Is there anything you want that I can get for you. I have a bottle of fine *Old French* brandy I'll send you by first opportunity, also some money I am anxious to send you by first safe messenger.

Camp near Bunker Hill—Aug 29th—1864

This morning, much to my surprise, we are quiet—how long we will remain so is very doubtful. In fact, I have every thing now ready to move. Thus, you see, our life is one of constant action—marching & counter-marching—manoeuvering & sometimes a little fighting. So far we have been very successful. God grant that we may continue to strike telling blows for our bleeding country. I am growing more hopeful about the ending of the War. Every man whose opinion I have asked & who has had an opportunity of learning the feeling of the Yankee people & soldiery, assures me that the north is tired of war & will elect an out & out, unconditional peace man at the Presidential election next November. I trust these opinions may be verified. For myself I think now, as I did several months ago, that everything depends upon the result of operations at Richmond & Atlanta. If we are enabled to baffle all of Grant's movements & to drive back Sherman, it does seem to me that the Yankee nation will be forced to conclude that the task of subjugating the South is more than they can accomplish. At all events we have reason for great thankfulness to the Giver of all Good for his wonderful mercy & care so continually shown toward us during this tremendous campaign. . . . Could we be permitted to see each other for even a short while how we would be encouraged & strengthened. But duty separates us—let us bear it all bravely—& the time will soon come let us hope when we will receive our rich reward—Reunion in peace, independence & happiness!

Nothing new here. Will write as often as I can do not be uneasy if you do not hear regularly. Army movements & irregular mail facilities may prevent.

Camp near Winchester, Sept 6th—1864

This is certainly a time to try our souls! We see in Yankee papers that Sherman has defeated Hood & captured Atlanta. We do not wish to believe this, but are compelled to be apprehensive & anxious. Our hopes for Peace depend upon the success of our armies in the field. Even tho Sherman takes Atlanta, provided he does not destroy nor disorganize Hood's army it will still be alright as long as Gen'l Lee (God bless our old Hero!) & his glorious army continue to baffle the tremendous efforts made to capture Richmond & over run Virginia—so let us be hopeful. Our own accounts may put a different face upon northern news. You will know before this reaches you that McClellan & Pendleton are the nominees of the Chicago Convention. Their Platform is ingeniously contrived to mean either war or peace—so as to catch all of the opponents of the Lincoln administration—& to be governed by events between now & the election. If our armies can hold their own, suffer no crushing disaster before the next election. We may reasonably expect a termination of this war. Let us therefore devote all of our energies to the defense of our country—& persevere in Prayer to the Ruler of Nations. What is the news at home? I am sending you a recpt for apple butter—& as it requires no *store* things—except a few spices, it is one kind of *preserves* we can have! If our army moves forward again, I will get you a circular cloak (forget the technical name) they are "all the rage" now. If we go back up the valley as far as Strasburg soon—(as I think we will before long) & everything promises well; I intend to ask for a furlough to come to see you—dont know tho how things will be. I predict orders for a move before long. . . . We cannot use Confederate money in Maryland—& we have to give six dollars Confed. for *one* Greenback.

Camp near Winchester, Sept. 11th '64

Our campaign, tho a very active & arduous one, I think has been far more free from vexations & trials, upon our patience & endurance than the campaign around Richmond would have been. We have enjoyed a great variety of scenes—have trav-elled over & sojourned in the most beautiful part of the valley of Va have had pure water, a few vegetables & plenty of fresh meat. Altogether we consider our selves very fortunate thus far. If we have an active winter campaign, we will not fare so well—tho it will be far more comfortable to campaign there this winter, than to remain in the trenches at Richmond & Petersburg. One great advantage I would have there however, that is I would be so much nearer you. I wish you could see this magnificent Valley—at this beautiful season of the year. Although plantations are ruined—& the blackened remains of once splendid mansions are to be seen on all sides yet nature is triumphant—magnificent meadows, beautiful forests & broad undulating fields rich in grass & clover! Truly it does seem sacreligious to despoil such an Eden! by the ravages of War.

I thank God that my loved ones have not yet known the terror & wretchedness caused by the presence of our mean cowardly foes, Foes who respect not helpless Age nor tender women. Surely a just God will visit upon such a nation the just indignation of His wrath! The Yankees tis true have Atlanta, Yankee like are making a tremendous glorification over it. But Hoods Army is intact. Sherman is far away from the base of his supplies & it does seem to me that if our army is *at all energetic* his position is obliged to be a very dangerous one to him. I still hope for good news from Ga. At Richmond all efforts of Grants powerful army have heretofore been baffled—by our noble General & his gallant troops. In the "Valley District" we have forced Lincoln to send a heavy force to check our *perigrinations*. We have at least 45,000 or 50,000 men opposed to us. We have offered them battle several times on a fair field. Every offer has been declined. The Yankees hurrying behind their breast works whenever we advance. We are thus accomplishing much good by neutralizing (holding in check) this large force. We are gathering all of the wheat in this wonderfully productive valley enough to supply ourselves & to send large supplies to Gen'l Lee's Army. We have also sent Gen'l Lee several hundred fine beef cattle &c. At this time the

Yankees hold less of the territory of this old Commonwealth than at any time since 1862. We learn from gentlemen recently from the North that the Peace party is growing rapidly—that McClellan will be elected & that his election will bring peace, *provided always* that we continue *to hold our own* against the Yankee Armies.

Camp near Winchester, Sept 14th—'64

I wish you could take a peep at my H'dquarters. You would observe two small tents rather the worse for wear, several wagons with their shivering mules—but the interesting & attractive feature would be a flock of ducks & chickens taking shelter under the wagons. We are really growing fat up here, with Yankee money we can buy almost anything for the table except sugar & coffee. . . . We have had no news from Richmond & the West for several days. I do hope that we may be enabled to continue to baffle Grant, & to drive back Sherman. I think everything depends upon this Fall campaign. If we whip the Yankees everywhere, or even, if we can man age to prevent their gaining any important success I surely believe that the Peace party will have grown sufficiently strong to compel a cessation of hostilities. Whatever course the North follows, *our duty is very plain*. We must fight this fight out—there must be no turning back now—too much precious blood has been shed for the maintainance of our rights! Too great a gulf has opened up between us & our foes! to allow even the thought of re-union to be entertained. No, we can & must bear & suffer all things rather than to give up to Yankees & mercenaries our glorious Birthright. If I can know you are well & hopeful & cheerful I can bear most anything—tho the separation is cruel, when I know how you need me. . . . I need some socks like those you knit for me last winter—would you like to knit me some more?

Camp near Waynesboro—Va.
Sept 30th—1864

I have been too busy & too much mortified to write to you for several days. At Winchester after

hard fighting, we had prevailed against the largely superior forces in our front & on our right, when the enemy's Cavalry in heavy force broke our Cavalry on the left & created a terrible disorder throughout our lines. We lost my friend Gen'l Rodes. We then fell back to Strasburg (or Fishers Hill). Here the enemy concentrated heavily on our weak point (guarded by our Cavalry) drove everything before them there, & then poured in on our left & rear. I am sorry to say that our men were very much stampeded & did not keep cool nor fight as well as they have here-to-fore done. We then retreated to Port Republic & from there to this point, 12 miles from Staunton. I am daily expecting Gen'l Early to advance. I believe if we could get enough Cavalry to even hold the Yankee Cavalry in check, that our Infantry can drive back Sheridans forces. I cannot tell you . . . how much I have thought of you during this past week. I do hope you have not given up your bright hopeful spirits. Anybody can be hopeful when everything is prosperous. *Adversity calls forth the nobler qualities of our natures*. Continue my beloved to be brave—nothing but Gods mercy has spared our lives. Cease not to pray for us & our Cause. . .

I still feel confident of the final triumph of our Cause. It may be a long & weary time, but above all things let us never despair of the establishment of our independence. We must steel ourselves for great trials & sacrifice—& have brave hearts for any fate. . . .

I would give *anything* to be with you, but these recent battles & defeats will make it almost impossible for me to leave this army now.

Camp near Staunton Va Oct. 2nd '64

This is a very lovely quiet Sabbath day. . . I hope that you have not allowed the bad news from the Army of the Valley District to discourage you. We must bear up bravely in the midst of disaster nor can we always hope to be successful. We must be prepared for any event, with brave hearts for any fate. . . . I hope in a few days we will be enabled to go after the Yankees & drive them down the Valley. At present we are all anxiety to hear from

Richmond. We hear all sorts of rumors. I hope and pray Gen'l Lee may be enabled to overcome & drive Grant from before Richmond. Our disaster in the Valley with Hood's at Atlanta make me feel now the War Party will prevail at the North. But tho peace may be a long way off—I feel that surely Justice & Right must finally triumph. We must nerve ourselves to greater exertions & prepare to endure greater privations & hardships—do our duty bravely, hoping for a happy ending of all of our troubles. Surely all true Southrons would prefer anything to submission. How I long for you to be well & happy! May we learn wisdom from our trials. Our movements may prevent my writing frequently now.

Camp near Staunton—Oct 5th '64

After the death of Gen'l Rodes I was assigned the command of his Division. This of course is very pleasing to me. Address y'r letters now "Army of the Valley"—& they will reach me sooner than old address. We have been very quiet for several days, but I expect active service before the month is out. We are very anxious about Richmond. The Yankees are said to be sending a force toward Orange Court House. They seem to stick to McClellan's plan of approaching Richmond from three directions. Everything calls for all the bravery we possess every effort in our power to meet & hurl back our foes— while we fight battles our beloved Wives, Sisters & Mothers must be constant & earnest in prayer that we may have strength courage & wisdom to overcome & drive back our powerful & cruel enemies. These are times calling for great sacrifices. We must bear separation, hardship & danger for the sake of our Country. We must dare & do in the Cause of liberty. We must never yield an inch, nor relax any effort in the defence of our home or the establishment *of* our nationality. We will do our duty leaving the result to God.

Camp near New Market—Oct 10th '64

I can't help feeling the most intense anxiety & solicitude on your behalf—since our disaster in the Valley, my prospect for a furlough is greatly dimin-

ished. I think my duty is plain. I ought not to leave now, even if I could do so—so my Beloved —you must be brave & cheerful without me for awhile—to be separated from you is the hardest trial of my life. . . .

Father writes me that tho discouraged by our late disasters—he is still hopeful as to the final result. I agree with you about your remarks about the "Croakers." I must confess I would be willing to take a musket & fight to the bitter end rather than submit to these miserable Yankees. I feel that they have put themselves beyond the pale of civilization by the course they have pursued in this campaign. This beautiful & fertile valley has been totally destroyed. Sheridan had some of the houses, *all* of the mills & barns, every straw & wheat stack burned. This valley is one great desert. I do not see how these people are to live. We have to haul our supplies from far up the valley. It is rumored that the Yankees are rebuilding the Manassas Gap R. R. If this is true, Sheridan will not give up his hold on the valley, & we will probably remain here for the winter—unless Gen'l Lee becomes so hard pressed that we will have to go to him. My hope now is from Hood. I do hope he may be able to overwhelm Sherman & send reinforcements to our great General Lee. The last private advices I had from Ga. were encouraging. Time is an important element. I believe that Hood can whip Sherman, & I trust he will do it quickly. I have not written you as often recently—because I have been either so constantly occupied or (I must acknowledge it) so much mortified at the recent disasters to our army of the valley that I could not write with any pleasure. There is nothing new to write about right now.

Camp near Strasburg—Va. Oct 17th—1864

My own Darling Wife—

I rec'd late last night through the Signal Corps, the telegram [announcing the birth of his baby]. It has relieved me of the greatest anxiety of my life. I hope that my darling precious wife & our darling babe too are well. . . . I cannot express my feelings. . . . I dont know how I can bear the separation from you much longer. . . . I must see you & be with you & our little Darling & The telegram did not state whether we have a son or a daughter! . . .

Tell Sister Mary for *pity's* sake if not for love's sake to write me a long letter about my little wife & baby! May God bless my Darlings & me, & soon reunite us in happiness & peace—a joyful family. Goodbye, sweetest With love inexpressible Yr devoted Husband

—RAMSEUR, Letters to his fiancée and wife

XXXII.4

EARLY SURPRISES THE FEDERALS AT CEDAR CREEK

After the defeats at Opequon and Strasburg Early* slender force was shattered, and Sheridan was master of the Valley. Early retired to Port Republic, where he awaited Kershaw's brigade, which Lee was hurrying to him, as well as Rosser's cavalry. With these reinforcements the ever-sanguine Early resumed the offensive, and Sheridan withdrew beyond New Market, taking up a position along Cedar Creek, north of Strasburg. At this juncture Sheridan was called to Washington to confer with Halleck; while at Winchester he heard that Early had surprised his army at Cedar Creek and inflicted a heavy defeat upon it.

Early had indeed. On October 13 he had begun his advance northward, taking up a position at Fisher's Hill, just south of Strasburg. From the summit of this hill he could see the whole Federal camp spread out along Cedar Creek. On the nineteenth Early directed Ramseur, Gordon, and Pegram to cross the Shenandoah and attack the Federals on the flank. The attack achieved complete surprise and complete initial success; had it not been for the heroic stand of Getty's division the Union defeat might have turned into a rout.

We give here Captain Howard's account of the morning surprise.

I was wakened at the first signs of day [October 19, 1864] by a terrific clap of thunder, and sprang into a sitting position and listened. The thunder was the tremendous volley that the enemy was pouring into Crook's devoted camp. The thought went through my mind like lightning that in some way the enemy had run against General Crook's corps and were get

ting punished for their temerity. It never occurred to me at the instant that it was possible the boot was on the other foot. I listened for the yell of our men, but, alas, it never came; instead, the Yi Yi Yi! of the Confederates, and horror of horrors,—it seemed to me as if our whole left were enveloped, enfolded, by this cry. It was like the howls of the wolves around a wagon train in the early days on the great prairies. This had taken but a moment. The camp was awake. The men sprang into line with the celerity of veterans. It was apparent to everyone from the heavy firing and the yells on our left that a great calamity impended if it had not already become a fact.

General Emory rode down in person, ordering the brigade to cross the pike, to throw a skirmish line into the timber in Crook's direction, until it met the enemy, and then to hold on as long as possible.

Away we went on a double quick through the darkness, the eastern sky at this moment showing the faint gray tinge of dawn. As we rushed along, the infernal torch on Massanutton, dire omen of impending disaster, still flashed against the southern sky. The moment the timber was reached the column came into line on the run, and skirmishers pushed rapidly forward, followed by the main body. Here we met the gallant fellows from Crook's camp who had been as sailed while lying asleep and who had done the only possible thing under the circumstances,—run for their lives. They did not seem excited, only stolidly, doggedly determined to go to the rear. Many of them were only partly dressed, some wearing only underclothing, but they generally carried their muskets. An officer wearing his cap and carrying his naked sword was attired in a shirt, drawers and shoes. The flash of a musket showed him to be a man of forty with full beard, and I think I should recognize his face to-day. They passed around us, through our ranks, and almost over us, insistent, determined. They heeded none of our cries to "Turn back!" "Make a stand!" but streamed to the rear. We had little time to argue with them.

The skirmish line had not advanced a hundred yards when it ran in the darkness plump into a body of the enemy; in an instant the timber was in a blaze of light from the musketry, and we were in the midst of one of the most fearful struggles of the war. The enemy were upon us in overwhelming numbers, flushed with victory and with the capture of Crook's camps. We were a little brigade of four regiments consisting of the 12th Connecticut, 160th New York, 47th Pennsylvania and the 8th Vermont. The first two and the 8th Vermont had been brigaded together back in the Louisiana days when Godfrey Weitzel commanded us, and in many a bloody fight had we fought together. It was literally true that we had never been beaten on any field, but we were to have a new experience.

We were commanded by Colonel Stephen Thomas of the 8th Vermont, . . . the bravest man I have ever known. What Sheridan was to the army under him, Colonel Thomas was to his regiment. Many had been the critical moments in our history when his level head and iron nerve had been our salvation. More than once in the very pinch of a fight, when it seemed as if one straw more would ruin us, had we seen him on his big bay shouting in a voice which rang over the tumult of battle, "Steady, men! Old Vermont is looking at you to-day!" We had never needed him so much as now.

The 8th Vermont was on the left of our line, the most exposed position. We were hotly pressed on our front and left. The timber was ablaze with musketry and the air was filled with the yells of our confident foes. They flung themselves upon us in a mass and for a moment the struggle was hand to hand. Then came the cry "The Colors! The Colors! They've got the Colors!?' and with one impulse, as if one mind had moved it, the regiment flung itself into the boiling caldron where the fight for the colors was seething and dragged them out. . . . Again and again the enemy flung many times our number against us, only to be forced back and gather for a fresh trial.

Men fought hand to hand; skulls were crushed with clubbed muskets; bayonets dripped with blood. Men actually clenched and rolled upon the ground in the desperate frenzy of the contest for the flags.

Three color bearers were killed, and with one exception every member of the color-guard was killed or wounded. There was not much attempt at order. Not many orders were given. The men realized that they were in a terrible mess and fought like tigers. Stephen Thomas, "Colonel commanding" as we loved to call him, was a very present help in trouble. He raged like a lion and was everywhere present to encourage and hold fast the line. Of course only one result was possible. The time came when valor and devotion proved vain. In a moment, without warning, and as if by common consent we were being swept back, every man for himself and the enemy on every hand. I had received two severe wounds, and though not wholly disabled, was unable to make anything like good time, and I looked with envy on Captain Ford who was just in advance of me running like a buck. In an instant he went down all in a heap, but was up and off again in a second. My mental comment was, "What a lummux to fall down in such a scrape as this!" It never once entered my mind that he had been hit by one of the bullets of which the air was full. Later in the day I saw him at the hospital, and expressed my disapproval of his clumsiness under such circumstances, to which he replied, "I guess you would fall down if you were shot through both legs." . . .

Private Robert Sturgeon of my own company was a few yards in advance of me on my right, and I need not say was making good time In an instant a tall bearded fellow in gray bounded out of the mist which overhung the field where day light was just gaining the supremacy and ordered him to halt. They were not twenty feet apart. Sturgeon's gun was empty and his bayonet lost. He cast a startled glance over his shoulder and ran at the top of his speed. The Confederate's long legs took tremendous strides,—he sprang forward with a rush and gave a vicious lunge with his bayonet. Sturgeon swerved at the moment, but the steel caught him under the left arm, and passed through the cape of his overcoat, through the overcoat itself, through blouse and flannel shirt, between shirt and skin. It left a vivid mark along his side where the cold steel raked, but did not pierce the skin. Sturgeon stopped and threw up his hands dropping his gun. The stalwart in gray was reaching out as if to take him by the collar, when presto! one in blue, pausing in his hot haste for scarcely one second placed the muzzle of his gun hardly a foot from the Confederate's head, fired, blowing the head to fragments, and without a word was gone. Sturgeon, like a good soldier, picked up his gun and ran like a deer.

Farther back Colonel Thomas had chosen a point where he was rallying the men and making some progress toward a line; still further a skirmish line was stretched across the country to stop and collect those who were still able for duty. Challenged here, I pointed to the blood in my shoe and running down my sleeve, and passed on; passed on with greater grief and despair weighing me down than I had ever before in my life felt.

Our campaign, as I have said, had been a great success. The Shenandoah Valley, the great artery of supply, the granary of the rebellion, had the night before seemed firmly and forever in our grasp, and now before the next sunrise, I had seen it taken away from us with the fierce ruthlessness of a hurricane. There was no question about it in my mind. Harper's Ferry was the only point where the shattered army could stand. I had seen the collapse of the Eighth Corps. I had seen our whole left swept away, our camps captured, our artillery taken, our whole army forced our of its works, forced to change its line from front to left, forced far back from its proper position,—sullenly on the defensive, dangerous, but clearly out-matched. The enemy was pressing his victorious columns forward. It would be impossible to withstand him. I pictured the defense we would make of the heights of Harper's Ferry, of the weary months, perhaps years, it would take to retrieve what we had lost, and my heart beat with great throbs of grief as I dragged myself painfully to the rear. General Sheridan I well knew, was absent. . . . Unreasonably I attributed the whole disaster to General Sheridan's absence. Had he been there it

could never have happened, and thereby I did injustice to the gallant Wright in command.

Pressing back to get out of danger I threw myself exhausted upon the-ground a short distance south of Newtown. The country was full of men, all, it seemed to me, going to the rear; wounded men by themselves; wounded men helped by others; wounded-men being carried; men strong and unhurt. Their faces were sullen, despairing, and they were turned to the north. Many halted and rested; some went to sleep, for the exhaustion of a week had been crowded into two hours. Our brigade in its struggle beyond the pike had lost more than one-third of its numbers, and the 8th Vermont, holding the left and most exposed position, had lost more than two-thirds of all the men engaged, and of the six teen officers who gathered about our camp-fire the evening before, thirteen had been killed and wounded on this horrible hill of sacrifice.

—Howard, "The Morning Surprise at Cedar Creek"

XXXII.5

Sheridan Rides Down the Valley Pike to Victory and Fame

The resolute stand by Getty, the confusion in Confederate ranks, and the strong defensive position to which the Federals retired, all persuaded Early to halt his own attack midway. Meantime Sheridan was riding down the Newtown and the Valley Pike from Winchester. By the time he arrived at the battlefield the Federals had steadied and were prepared to repulse Early. Sheridan speedily organized a counterattack which jumped off in midafternoon and was completely successful. Everywhere the Confederate line gave way. "They would not listen to entreaties, threats or appeals of any kind," Early reported "A terror of the enemy's cavalry had seized them and there was no holding them." It was the end of Early—and the beginning of a legend.Here Sheridan tells his own story.

Toward 6 o'clock the morning of the 19th [October], the officer on picket duty at Winchester came to my room, I being yet in bed, and reported artillery firing from the direction of Cedar Creek. I asked him if the firing was continuous or only desultory, to which he replied that it was not a sustained fire, but rather irregular and fitful. I remarked: "It's all right; Grover has gone out this morning to make a reconnoisance, and he is merely feeling the enemy." I tried to go to sleep again, but grew so restless that I could not, and soon got up and dressed myself. A little later the picket officer came back and reported that the firing, which could be distinctly heard from his line on the heights outside of Winchester, was still going on. I asked him if it sounded like a battle, and as he again said that it did not, I still inferred that the cannonading was caused by Grover's division banging away at the enemy simply to find out what he was up to. However, I went downstairs and requested that breakfast be hurried up, and at the same time ordered the horses to be saddled and in readiness, for I concluded to go to the front before any further examinations were made in regard to the defensive line.

We mounted our horses between half-past 8 and 9, and as we were proceeding up the street which leads directly through Winchester, from the Logan residence, where Edwards was quartered, to the Valley pike, I noticed that there were many women at the windows and doors of the houses, who kept shaking their skirts at us and who were otherwise markedly insolent in their demeanor, but supposing this con duct to be instigated by their well-known and perhaps natural prejudices, I ascribed to it no unusual significance. On reaching the edge of the town I halted a moment, and there heard quite distinctly the sound of artillery firing in an unceasing roar. Concluding from this that a battle was in progress, I now felt confident that the women along the street had received intelligence from the battle-field by the "grape vine telegraph," and were in raptures over some good news, while I as yet was utterly ignorant of the actual situation. Moving on, I put my head downward toward the pommel of my saddle and listened intently, trying to locate and interpret the sound, continuing in this position till we had crossed Mill Creek, about half a mile from Winchester. The result of my efforts in the interval was the conviction that the travel of the sound was increasing too rapidly to be accounted for by my own rate of motion, and that therefore my army must be falling back.

At Mill Creek, my escort fell in behind, and we were going ahead at a regular pace, when, just as we made the crest of the rise beyond the stream, there burst upon our view the appalling spectacle of a panic-stricken army—hundreds of slightly wounded men, throngs of others unhurt but utterly demoralized, and baggage-wagons by the score, all pressing to the rear in hopeless confusion, telling only too plainly that a disaster had occurred at the front. On accosting some of the fugitives, they assured me that the army was broken up, in full retreat, and that all was lost; all this with a manner true to that peculiar indifference that takes possession of panic stricken men. I was greatly disturbed by the sight, but at once sent word to Colonel Edwards, commanding the brigade in Winchester, to stretch his troops across the valley, near Mill Creek, and stop all fugitives, directing also that the transportation be passed through and parked on the north side of the town.

As I continued at a walk a few hundred yards farther, thinking all the time of Longstreet's telegram to Early, "Be ready when I join you and we will crush Sheridan," I was fixing in my mind what I should do. My first thought was to stop the army in the suburbs of Winchester as it came back, form a new line, and fight there; but as the situation was more maturely considered a better conception prevailed. I was sure the troops had confidence in me, for heretofore we had been successful; and as at other times they had seen me present at the slightest sign of trouble or distress, I felt that I ought to try now to restore their broken ranks, or, failing in that, to share their fate because of what they had done hitherto. . . .

For a short distance I traveled on the road, but soon found it so blocked with wagons and wounded men that my progress was impeded, and I was forced to take to the adjoining fields to make haste. When most of the wagons and wounded were past I returned to the road, which was thickly lined with unhurt men, who, having got far enough to the rear to be out of danger, had halted, without any organization, and began cooking coffee, but when they saw me they abandoned their coffee, threw up their hats, shouldered their muskets, and as I passed along turned to follow with enthusiasm and cheers. To acknowledge this exhibition of feeling I took off my hat, and with Forsyth and O'Keefe rode some distance in advance of my escort, while every mounted officer who saw me galloped out on either side of the pike to tell the men at a distance that I had come back. In this way the news was spread to the stragglers off the road, when they, too, turned their faces to the front and marched toward the enemy, changing in a moment from the depth of depression to the extreme of enthusiasm. I already knew that even in the ordinary condition of mind enthusiasm is a potent element with soldiers, but what I saw that day convinced me that if it can be excited from a state of despondency its power is almost irresistible. I said nothing except to remark, as I rode among those on the road: "If I had been with you this morning this disaster would not have happened. We must face the other way; we will go back and recover our camp."

My first halt was made just north of Newtown, where I met a chaplain digging his heels into the sides of his jaded horse, and making for the rear with all possible speed. I drew up for an instant, and inquired of him how matters were going at the front. He replied, "Everything is lost; but all will be right when you get there"; yet notwithstanding this expression of confidence in me, the parson at once resumed his breathless pace to the rear. At Newtown I was obliged to make a circuit to the left, to get round the village. I could not pass through it, the streets were so crowded, but, meeting on this detour Major McKinley, of Crook's staff, he spread the news of my return through the motley throng there.

When nearing the Valley pike, just south of Newtown I saw about three-fourths of a mile west of the pike a body of troops, which proved to be Ricketts's and Wheaton's divisions of the Sixth Corps had halted a little to the right and rear of these; but I did not stop, desiring to get to the extreme front. Continuing on parallel with the pike about midway between Newtown and Middletown I crossed to the west of it, and a little later came up in rear of Getty's division of the Sixth Corps. When I arrived this division and the cavalry were the only troops in the presence of and resisting the enemy; they were apparently acting as a rear guard at a point about three miles north of the line we held at Cedar Creek when the battle began. General Torbert was the first officer to meet me, saying as he rode up, "My God! I am glad you've come." Getty's division, when I found it, was about a mile north of Middletown, posted on the reverse slope of some slightly rising ground, holding a barricade made with fence-rails, and skirmishing slightly with the enemy's pickets.

Jumping my horse over the line of rails I rode to the crest of the elevation, and there taking off my hat, the men rose up from behind their barricade with cheers of recognition. An officer of the Vermont brigade, Colonel A.S. Tracy, rode out to the front, and joining me, informed me that General Louis A. Grant was in command there, the regular division commander, General Getty, having taken charge of the Sixth Corps in place of Ricketts, wounded early in the action, while temporarily commanding the corps. I then turned back to the rear of Getty's division, and as I came behind it a line of regimental flags rose up out of the ground, as it seemed, to welcome me. They were mostly the colors of Crook's troops, who had been stampeded and scattered in the surprise of the morning. The color-bearers having withstood the panic, had formed behind the troops of Getty. . . . At the close of this incident I crossed the little narrow valley, or depression, in rear of Getty's line, and dismounting on the opposite crest, established that point as my headquarters. In a few minutes some of my staff joined me, and the first directions I gave were to have the Nineteenth Corps and the two divisions of Wright's corps brought to the front, so they could be formed on Getty's division, prolonged to the right, for I had already decided to attack the enemy from that line as soon as I could get matters in shape to take the offensive. Crook met me at this time, and strongly favored my idea of attacking, but said, however, that most of his troops were going. . .

All this had consumed a good deal of time, and I concluded to visit again the point to the east of the Valley pike, from where I had first observed the enemy, to see what he was doing. Arrived there, I could plainly see him getting ready for attack, and Major Forsyth now suggested that it would be well to ride along the line of battle before the enemy as sailed us, for although the troops had learned of my return, but few of them had seen me. Following his suggestion I started in behind the men, but when a few paces had been taken I crossed to the front and, hat in hand, passed along the entire length of the infantry line; and it is from this circumstance that many of the officers and men who then received me with such heartiness have since supposed that that was my first appearance on the field. But at least two hours had elapsed since I reached the ground, for it was after mid-day when this incident of riding down the front took place, and I arrived not later, certainly, than half-past 10 o'clock.

—*Personal Memoirs of P. H. Sheridan*

XXXII.6

"The Valley Will Have Little in It for Man or Beast"

After Cedar Creek Sheridan was master of the Valley. He had already embarked on a policy of systematic destruction; now he carried that through almost without opposition. Early, to be sure, did put up a stiff fight at Middletown, on November 9, but without effect. In December, again, Rosser tried to prevent the destruction of the Virginia Central Rail way, but again in vain. There was little fighting during the winter, but late in February

1865 Sheridan occupied Staunton and Charlottesville, breaking up the railways leading to the west. Meantime the Valley had suffered the fate of Georgia and South Carolina.

Here is an extract from one of Sheridan's reports to Grant.

Woodstock, October 7, 1861 9 P. M.

I have the honor to report my command at this point to night. I commenced moving back from Port Republic, Mount Crawford, Bridgewater, and Harrisonburg yesterday morning. The grain and forage in advance of these points up to Staunton had previously been destroyed. In moving back to this point the whole country from the Blue Ridge to the North Mountains has been made untenable for a rebel army. I have destroyed over 2,000 barns filled with wheat, hay, and farming implements; over seventy mills filled with flour and wheat; have driven in front of the army over 4,000 head of stock, and have killed and have issued to the troops not less than 3,000 sheep. This destruction embraces the Luray Valley and Little Fort Valley, as well as the main valley. A large number of horses have been obtained, a proper estimate of which I cannot now make. Lieut. John R. Meigs, my engineer officer, was murdered beyond Harrisonburg, near Dayton. For this atrocious act all the houses within an area of five miles were burned. Since I came into the Valley, from Harper's Ferry up to Harrisonburg, every train, every small party, and every straggler has been bushwacked by people, many of whom have protection papers from commanders who have been hitherto in this valley. From the vicinity of Harrisonburg over 400 wagon-loads of refugees have been sent back to Martinsburg; most of these people were Dunkers and had been conscripted. The people here are getting sick of the war; heretofore they have had no reason to complain, because they have been living in great abundance. I have not been followed by the enemy up to this point, with the exception of a small force of rebel cavalry that showed themselves some distance behind my rear guard to-day. A party of 100 of the Eighth Ohio Cavalry, which I had stationed at the bridge over the North Shenandoah, near Mount

Jackson, was attacked by McNeill, with seventeen men; report they were asleep, and the whole party dispersed or captured. I think that they will all turn up; I learn that fifty-six of them have reached Winchester. McNeill was mortally wounded and fell into our hands. This was fortunate, as he was the most daring and dangerous of all the bushwackers in this section of the country. . . . To-morrow I will continue the destruction of wheat, forage, etc., down to Fisher's Hill. When this is completed the Valley, from Winchester up to Staunton, ninety two miles, will have but little in it for man or beast. In previous dispatches I have used "lower Valley" when I should have said "upper Valley," or, in other words, in my last dis patch I intended to say that the grain and forage from Staunton up to Lexington had been sent to Richmond, and that the grain and forage from Staunton to Strasburg had been left for the winter-ing of Early's army. Yesterday Colonel Powell cap-tured a guerrilla camp on the mountains, with ten wagons and teams.

P.H. SHERIDAN
Major-General
LIEUTENANT-GENERAL GRANT
    —*War of the Rebellion . . . Official Records*

XXXIII

LEE AND LINCOLN

Space does not allow us the luxury of portraits of all the distinguished or interesting leaders, military and civilian, of the Union and Confederate causes. We must content ourselves with a presentation of the two men who, at the time and since, seemed to symbolize the two sections and causes, and who, in the end, came to be the common and cherished possession of both. It is one of the happier features of an otherwise tragic war that it left, on the whole, so little bitterness; the sectional animosities of the postwar years were rather a product of Reconstruction than of war itself. It is particularly interesting that the leading figure on each side came to be held in affection by both: this is a circumstance not common in the history of civil wars.

Condemned by the South and, for that matter, by a substantial part of the North during his own lifetime, Lincoln came eventually to be a completely national figure, transcending section and even time. Lee was always admired, even in the North, and Northern opinion found it possible to respect his decision to go with his state while it respected, too, those Southerners like Thomas and Farragut who remained loyal to the old flag.

Since the war there has developed both a Lincoln and a Lee legend. With Lincoln the legend is almost inextricable from fact, nor is this altogether deplorable. With Lee there was less for the mythmakers to work on; while the Lee legend grows, the facts of his career are available and familiar. With Lincoln the difficulty is to separate fact and myth; with Lee to penetrate behind

the deadly oratory
Of twenty thousand Lee Memorial Days*
to reality.

---

* From *John Brown's Body* in *The Selected Works of Stephen Vincent Benét*, published by Rinehart and Company, Inc. Copyright 1927, 1928 by Stephen Vincent Benét.

That the proud and affectionate recollections of Americans should have worked on both men is a matter of gratification and good fortune. If a nation is to have heroes, it would be difficult to find better ones than these two protagonists of the cause of the Union and the cause of State rights.

Lincoln and Lee represent, in a sense, two persistent currents in American history and two strains in the American character. Just as historical legend has insisted on the Puritan and the Cavalier in the founding of America and this despite evidence to the contrary—so it has insisted on the contrast of frontier democracy and plantation aristocracy, a contrast, too, that exists in the realm of legend rather than of history. In Lincoln Americans have seen a symbol of equality and freedom; in Lee a symbol of the Cavalier spirit and chivalry. For a wonder both men fitted their legends. In apotheosizing Lincoln and Lee the American people apotheosized what was best in their character rather than what was most typical.

We do not attempt here biographies of either of these leaders; that, after all, is superfluous, for there are biographies enough, and memoirs and volumes of tributes. Our concern is the war, and the relation of these men to the war. Nor do we approach either Lincoln or Lee afresh. Almost every chapter of our history has said something about one or both of them; they do not come to us as strangers. We present them for themselves, to be sure, and as vehicles of much of the character of the contenders, but we present them in relation to the larger contest. It will be sufficient, therefore, if we introduce the chroniclers as they tell their stories.

There is an inescapable difference in these presentations. We have already seen Lee in action: the story of the Army of Northern Virginia is in a sense the story of Lee, and it is enough here to present a few glimpses of the man. He was, as Benét has said, "the prop and pillar of a state," but that role we have already seen him play. With Lincoln the situation is different. Lincoln's character can never cease to interest us, but we must be concerned with what he did, as head of the state, as well as with what he was. We have, designedly, neglected the political scene somewhat in our survey of the war; we present here some aspects of important political chapters in which Lincoln played a commanding role, notably emancipation.

XXXIII.I

Robert E. Lee Goes With His State

One of the momentous decisions of the war was a personal one—the decision of R. E. Lee that he could not raise his hand against his own people. No officer in the United States Army had a more brilliant record or a more distinguished career than Lee when, at the age of fifty-four, he resigned from the army to go with his state. He had performed brilliantly a number of difficult engineering assignments, fought gallantly in the Mexican War, served as Superintendent of the West Point Military Academy, and dealt effectively with Indian outbreaks along the Mexican border. Recalled to Washington early in 1861 he was informally offered command of the field-forces of the United States. With deep spiritual anguish he refused this offer, resigned his commission, and accepted instead command of the military forces of Virginia. Shortly after he was appointed general in the Confederate Army.

These two letters explain his decision.

A. "My Relatives, My Children, My Home"

To his Sister, Mrs. Anne Marshall.
Arlington, Virginia
April 20, 1861

My Dear Sister: I am grieved at my inability to see you. . . . I have been waiting for a 'more convenient sea son,' which has brought to many before me deep and lasting regret. Now we are in a state of war which will yield to nothing. The whole South is 'in a state of revolution, into which Virginia, after a long struggle, has been drawn; and though I recognize no necessity for this state of things, and would have forborne and pleaded to the end for redress of grievances, real or supposed, yet in my own person I had to meet the question whether I should take part against my native State.

With all my devotion to the Union and the feeling of loyalty and duty of an American citizen, I have not been able to make up my mind to raise my hand against my relatives, my children, my home. I have therefore resigned my com mission in the Army, and save in defense of my native State, with the sincere hope that my poor services may never be needed, I hope I may never be called on to draw my sword. I know you will blame me; but you must think as kindly of me as you can, and believe that I have endeavoured to do what I thought right.

To show you the feeling and struggle it has cost me, I send you a copy of my letter of resignation. I have no time for more. May God guard and protect you and yours, and shower upon you everlasting blessings, is the prayer of your devoted brother,

—R. E. Lee

B. "I Never Desire Again to Draw My Sword"

To General Scott.

Arlington, Virginia
April 20, 1861

General: Since my interview with you on the 18th inst. I have felt that I ought no longer to retain my commission in the Army. I therefore tender my resignation, which I request you will recommend for acceptance. It would have been presented at once but for the struggle it has cost me to separate myself from a service to which I have devoted the best years of my life, and all the ability I possessed.

During the whole of that time more than a quarter of a century—I have experienced nothing but kindness from my superiors and a most cordial friendship from my comrades. To no one, General, have I been as much indebted as to your self for uniform kindness and consideration, and it has always been my ardent desire to merit your approbation. I shall carry to the grave the most grateful recollections of your kind consideration, and your name and fame shall always be dear to me.

Save in defense of my native State, I never desire again to draw my sword.

Be pleased to accept my most earnest wishes for the continuance of your happiness and prosperity, and believe me, most truly yours,

R. E. LEE

—LEE, *Recollections and Letters of General Robert E. Lee*

XXXIII.2

"A SPLENDID SPECIMEN OF AN ENGLISH GENTLEMAN"

Garnet Wolseley was a young lieutenant colonel in the British Army when, in 1862, he slipped away from a tour of duty in Canada to visit the Army of Northern Virginia. We have already enjoyed his portrait of Stonewall Jackson. Lee he admired even more than Jackson and, characteristically, his admiration found expression in extending to Lee the title "English gentleman," which he assumed to be the highest accolade. It was Lord Wolseley who discovered George Henderson and encouraged him to write his classic biography of Stonewall Jackson.

Having presented our letters to the Adjutant-General, we were in turn presented to the Commander-in-Chief. He is a strongly built man, about five feet eleven in height, and apparently not more than fifty years of age. His hair and beard are nearly white; but his dark brown eyes still shine with all the brightness of youth, and beam with a most pleasing expression. Indeed, his whole face is kindly and benevolent in the highest degree. In manner, though sufficiently conversible, he is slightly reserved; but he is a person that, wherever seen, whether in a castle or a hovel, alone or in a crowd, must at once attract attention as being a splendid specimen of an English gentleman, with one of the most rarely handsome faces I ever saw. He had had a bad fall during the Maryland expedition, from which he was not yet recovered, and which still crippled his right hand considerably.

We sat with him for a long time in his tent, conversing upon a variety of topics, the state of affairs being of course the leading one. He talked most freely about the battle of Antietam, and

assured us that at no time during that day's fight had he more than thirty-five thousand men engaged. You have only to be in his society for a very brief period to be convinced that whatever he says may be implicitly relied upon, and that he is quite incapable of departing from the truth under any circumstances. . . .

In visiting the headquarters of the Confederate generals, but particularly those of General Lee, any one accustomed to see European armies in the field cannot fail to be struck with the great absence of all the pomp and circumstance of war in and around their encampments. Lee's headquarters consisted of about seven or eight pole tents, pitched with their backs to a stake fence, upon a piece of ground so rocky that it was unpleasant to ride over it—its only recommendation being a little stream of good water which flowed close by the General's tent. In front of the tents were some three or four wheeled wagons; drawn up without any regularity, and a number of horses roamed loose about the field. The servants, who were of course slaves, and the mounted soldiers' called "couriers," who always accompany each general of division in the field, were unprovided with tents, and slept in or under the waggons.

Waggons, tents, and some of the horses, were marked U.S., showing that part of that huge debt in the North has gone to furnishing even the Confederate generals with camp equipments. No guard or sentries were to be seen in the vicinity; no crowd of aides-de-camp loitering about, making them selves agreeable to visitors, and endeavouring to save their generals from receiving those who have no particular business. A large farm-house stands close by, which, in any other army, would have been the general's residence, pro tem.: but as no liberties are allowed to be taken with personal property in Lee's army, he is particular in setting a good example him self. His staff are crowded together two and three in a tent: none are allowed to carry more baggage than a small box each, and his own kit is but very little larger. Every one who approaches him does so with marked respect, although there is none of that bowing and flourishing of forage-caps which occurs in the presence of European generals: and whilst all honour him and place implicit faith in his courage and ability, those with whom he is most intimate feel for him the affection of sons to a father. Old General Scott was correct in saying that when Lee joined the Southern cause, it was worth as much as the accession of 20,000 men to the "rebels."

Since, then, every injury that it was possible to inflict, the Northerners have heaped upon him. His house on the Pamunky river was burnt to the ground and the slaves carried away, many of them by force; whilst his residence on the Arlington Heights was not only gutted of its furniture, but even the very relics of George Washington were stolen from it and paraded in triumph in the saloons of New York and Boston. Notwithstanding all these personal losses, however, when speaking of the Yankees, he neither evinced any bitterness of feeling, nor gave utterance to a single violent expression, but alluded to many of his former friends and companions amongst them in the kindest terms. He spoke as a man proud of the victories won by his country, and confident of ultimate success under the blessing of the Almighty, whom he glorified for past successes, and whose aid he invoked for all future operations. He regretted that his limited supply of tents and available accommodation would prevent him from putting us up, but he kindly placed at our disposal horses, or a two horsed wagon, if we preferred it, to drive about in.

—[Wolseley], "A Month's Visit to the Confederate Headquarters"

XXXIII.3

"It is Well War Is So Terrible, Or We Should Get Too Fond of it"

Here is another of those little scenes that reveal character: Lee watching the repulse of the Federals at Fredericksburg. General Pendleton, who tells the story, was a West Pointer who had abandoned the army for the Church, was rector of Grace Church in Lexington, Virginia, when he joined the Rockbridge Artillery, and rose to be chief of artillery of the Army of Northern Virginia

From prominent points in our line almost the entire scene could be taken in by the eye. And at one of these, the most commanding, where we had a few powerful guns, General Lee remained much of the day, observing the field; only too indifferent, as was his wont, to danger from the large, numerous, and well-aimed missiles hurled especially thither from the enemy's heavy batteries across the Rappahannock. Seldom, in all the wars of the world, has a spectacle been presented like that which, from this central elevation, we looked upon. More than one hundred thousand blue-coated men in the open plain, with every military appliance, in battle order, and moving in their respective subdivisions to attack our line. Although our numbers were certainly not half those of the enemy, there was misgiving, probably, in no officer or man as to the result.

Events in one quarter of the field, as it lay before us, attracted peculiar interest, and gave occasion to one of those characteristic remarks of General Lee which told at once of his capacity for enjoying the excitements of action, and of the good feeling and strong principle that kept it under control. A large force advanced rapidly to charge our right. Stonewall Jackson was there, and that he would promptly hurl them back little doubt was entertained. Still no such assault can be witnessed without earnest interest, if not concern. Nor was the shock received on our side without loss. There fell the heroic General Gregg, of the gallant and now vengeance-suffering State of South Carolina. Presently, however, as was anticipated, the spirited charge was reversed, and blue figures by thousands were seen recrossing, "double quick," with faces to the rear, the space they had traversed, and hundreds of gray pursuers hastening their speed. While younger spectators near us gave expression to their feelings by shouts, clapping of hands, &c., the gratified yet considerate and amiable commander turned to myself, and with beaming countenance said, "*It is well war is so terrible, or we should get too fond of it.*"

Not long after an incident occurred which made us shudder for our beloved chief. One of our large guns on that eminence, having to be plied continuously against another portion of the enemy's line, which was advancing to charge that part of our defences held by the good and gallant Georgian, General Tom Cobb, and being, like much hastily-cast Southern ordnance, of insufficient tenacity, finally burst with prodigious violence. None, wonderfully and happily, were struck by its fragments. And, remarkably, those who stood nearest, of whom the individual relating it to you was one, within a little over arm's length, although considerably jarred by the shock, proved to be really in less danger than others farther off. General Lee was standing perhaps fifty feet in the rear, and a large piece of the cannon, weighing, we estimated, about a third of a ton, fell just beyond him. He thus very narrowly escaped death. Like himself, however, he only looked upon the mass calmly for a moment, and then, without a syllable expressive of surprise or concern, continued the business occupying him at the time.

—PENDLETON, "Personal Recollections of General Lee"

XXXIII.4

DR. PARKS'S BOY VISITS LEE'S HEADQUARTERS

Here is a charming vignette of Lee on the road to Gettysburg. It comes from Leighton Parks, the small boy who stood wide-eyed looking at Lee and his lieutenants. Written 40 years later, it is undoubtedly bathed in nostalgia. Yet though the conversations are suspect, the episode itself rings true enough. The Elizabethtown referred to was a small Maryland village, no longer on the map.

Before the year was out we learned that the Union troops had again been driven back to Washington, and, soon after, that Lee was crossing the river at Williamsport. The report proved true. First came the cavalry. I had never supposed so many horses were to be found in the world as I now saw slowly passing through the street of Elizabethtown. They kept straight on to the north. I asked many of the soldiers where they were going. The poor fellows knew nothing; many of them were too ignorant to know what it meant to have crossed the Potomac. Had they not crossed many rivers? What was one more than another? But the officers laughed gaily and said: "New York." Why not? What could prevent them? Was not the Army of the Potomac huddled about the defenses of Washington? "Had not Bobby Lee stolen a march on the commanding general, whoever that might be at the moment?" they added with a laugh. Indeed, the darkest hour of the war had come to the North.

So the troops passed on, thousand after thousand. The artillery followed the cavalry; then came the infantry. The impression made by the sight of so many horses was repeated by the hosts of men. It was not only the multitude that impressed those who saw that march; it was also the splendid discipline of the army. They were different from the corps we had seen the year before. These men were well clad and shod, and they came through the town with flags flying and bands playing "Dixie," "Dixie," all day long, with now and then a change to "Maryland, my Maryland" or the "Bonnie Blue Flag." We became as tired of these as we had of "Yankee Doodle" or "The Star-Spangled Banner." (But both armies marched to the tune of "The Girl I Left Behind Me.") They had the air of men who were used to conquer; they believed in the men who led them, and they did not doubt that when they saw the enemy they would drive them before them again. It was a sight such as few have seen even of those who took part in the war. Sixty thousand men, it is said, passed through Elizabethtown on the way to Gettysburg, and I can well believe it. Day after day an unbroken line passed on due north, and at night the rumble of the wagons made sleep impossible for nervous people. And who was not nervous?

Soon after the Confederates began to enter the town I met a friend of mine, the son of Dr. Doyle,

737

who told me that his father had just been sent for to see Lee, and that I might go too if I hurried. It is needless to say that I ran as fast as my small legs could carry me, and we found the doctor just starting. Dr. Doyle was a man who had been in communication with the enemy from the beginning of the war, but had so far managed to escape the fate of many innocent men. Two of his sons had been arrested a short time before, and were lying in the jail when their friends arrived and set them free.

The doctor was in his old gig, and, being an immense man, left no room for any one else in it, so we two boys sat on the springs behind. It was on the Williamsport pike, about half a mile from the town, that we met General Lee. He had dismounted and was standing by his horse, a small sorrel mare, which, I was told, it was his custom to ride on the march. His staff was brilliant in gold lace, but he was very simply dressed. No one could have seen that man without being greatly impressed with the dignity of his bearing and the beauty of his face. His hair at this time was almost entirely white, and those who had seen him the year before said he had aged greatly in the short space of time which had elapsed since the battle of Antietam. I could not help thinking of Washington as I looked at that calm, sad face. It has been said since by those who were near him that he had no expectation of conquering the North, and that, at the most, he only hoped to win a great battle on Northern soil in order to affect public opinion in Europe, and lead to the recognition of the Southern Confederacy. However that may be, there was nothing about his bearing which looked like a great hope.

Dr. Doyle drove straight to where he was standing and announced himself as one who was sure of his welcome. General Lee came at once to the gig and thanked him politely for having come so promptly, and began at once to ask about the roads. I was astonished at the familiarity which he showed with the country, and yet he evidently wished to have his map, which he held in his hand, confirmed by an eye witness. His questions were like those of a lawyer to a witness. What roads ran into the Lightersburg pike? Did the Cavetown pike cross the mountain? What sort of crossing was it? Could cannon be easily brought over it? His right flank, then, was protected by the Blue Ridge until he reached Gettysburg? And on his return should he come that way? Were there good roads running to the river west of the one on which he now stood? Could artillery be moved over them? Was the valley well wooded and watered all the way to Gettysburg? To all of which the answer was "Yes."

Lee had been speaking in a low tone, leaning on the shaft of the gig, with his head under the hood of it, so that we, looking in through the curtain, could see and hear every thing. Suddenly Lee saw us and said: "Doctor, are these your boys?"

"One of them is," said the doctor "The other is the son of Dr. Parks. You must have known his father in the old army."

"Is it possible!" said Lee.

Then we were called down and made our bows, and Lee said something that I could not hear; but the doctor answered, "No danger," and then added something at which Lee smiled and said, "Would you boys like to get on that horse?" pointing to his own little mare.

Of course we said, "Yes," and each in turn was lifted by General Lee up to the horse's back. I suspect that that attention was suggested by Dr. Doyle in order to divert our minds from what we had just heard. When we got back to town, he said to me: "Now run home, my boy, and tell your mother that you have seen General Lee and all that he said to you—in fact, all you can remember to have heard him say. It will interest her."

So home I ran, swelling with importance, and told my mother all the questions that General Lee had asked and what Dr. Doyle had said. Of course my mother saw at once the importance of the conversation, and charged me to keep it perfectly quiet. Which I did.

A day or two after this a friend of the family who had been very kind to me asked me if I should not like to go out to General Lee's headquarters?

"To-morrow," he said, "you will see a sight that you will be able to tell as long as you live, for Lee's generals are to meet him, and the army is to move."

I boldly asked if he would lend me his horse, and he laughed and consented. So the next morning, dressed in white jacket and trousers, I started off on a brown horse, carrying a basket of raspberries to one of Lee's staff whom my mother had known since he was a lad. I remember my costume from the fact that some of the berries melted, and before I was aware of it they had made a stain on my trousers which no amount of rubbing would remove. This troubled me a good deal because I thought General Lee might think I did not know how to ride; and as I had made up my mind to ask him to let me accompany the army in some capacity not very clear to me, this gave me considerable anxiety. However, I reached the camp without further accident and found Colonel Taylor, to whom I was accredited.

Lee's headquarters were in a hickory grove about three miles from Williamsport. The grove was on the top of a small hill, and near enough to the pike for the general to see the troops as they marched by.

When I reached the camp, Colonel Taylor told me that General Lee was away, but that he would probably return before long. Indeed, it was not many minutes before we heard the trampling of horses and the guard turning out, and, on going to the door of the tent, I saw a splendid sight. First there was Lee himself riding a superb iron-gray horse, and with him were Longstreet, Ewell, and A. P. Hill. Colonel Taylor led me to General Lee and said: "General, this gentleman has brought me some raspberries, and I have asked him to take snack with us."

Lee's back was toward me when the colonel spoke, and I was startled to see how severe he looked as, wheeling sharply, he glanced quickly to right and left and then looked down. Then he smiled very pleasantly and remarked: "I have had the pleasure of meeting your friend before." And then, to my great surprise, this severe-looking man

stooped down and, lifting me, kissed me. After this the generals and Colonel Taylor and I went into a large tent for "snack."

I do not remember anything that was said during the meal, nor what we had to eat. I suppose I was a good deal excited, and I know that there was a deal of laughing—I fear at my expense; for they—not Lee, but the others—asked me a great many questions, and then laughed at the answers. I suppose it was a relief to these men, who were carrying such a heavy burden, to have a child to chaff.

After luncheon we went to Lee's tent, and the general took me on his knee and talked to me until, some one having taken his attention, Hill beckoned me to come to him, which I did gladly; for, though Lee was gentle, I could not help standing in awe of him in a way that I did not of the others.

When I had been with him for a little while, Longstreet said: "Come, Hill, you've had him long enough; pass him over." So I was dragged over to Longstreet's knee and had my face well rubbed by his great brown beard. And he whispered in my ear that he had a pony he thought would carry my weight, if I should like to join his staff.

But before I could express my joy, Lee suddenly said, "Well, gentlemen," and immediately Colonel Taylor made me a sign. So I got up and said good-by; and I thought then, and think now, that they were sorry to have me go, for I suppose I brought a new element into their life. One of them—Hill, I think—called to a servant to "bring the captain's horse," at which the man grinned and untied the horse from a tree near by and led him to the front of the tent.

This placed me in a most embarrassing situation, for while I could ride very well for a boy, I was in the habit of mounting my steed by the aid of a fence. Still, I determined to do my best, and, stretching up my leg as high as it would go, managed to touch the stirrup with my toe; but, alas! when I attempted to mount into the saddle I descended to the ground, with my feet very wide apart and my jacket somewhat marked by contact with the horse's flanks. This was greeted with a good-natured laugh, which determined me to mount or die in the attempt. But I was saved either alternative, for before I had time to try again I was lifted lightly into the saddle by Lee himself, who smiled and said: "Give him time, and he'll do for the cavalry yet."

—Parks, "What a Boy Saw of the Civil War"

XXXIII.5

"A Sadness I Had Never Before Seen upon His Face"

We have already seen something of Lee during and after Gettysburg, and Colonel Fremantle has given us an unforgettable picture of Lee rallying his stricken troops with the assurance that all would come right in the end. Here is perhaps a more intimate picture of Lee the night after the battle. It comes from General John Imboden, who protected the Confederate right in the advance on Gettysburg, and was detached to cover the Confederate retreat after the battle.

When night closed the struggle, Lee's army was repulsed. We all knew that the day had gone against us, but the full extent of the disaster was only known in high quarters. The carnage of the day was generally understood to have been frightful, yet our army was not in retreat, and it was surmised in camp that with to-morrow's dawn would come a renewal of the struggle. All felt and appreciated the momentous consequences to the cause of Southern independence of final defeat or victory on that great field.

It was a warm summer's night; there were few camp-fires and the weary soldiers were lying in groups on the luxuriant grass of the beautiful meadows, discussing the events of the day, speculating on the morrow, or watching that our horses did not straggle off while browsing. About 11 o'clock a horseman came to summon me to General Lee. I promptly mounted and, accompanied by Lieutenant George W. McPhail, an aide on my staff, and guided by the courier who brought the message, rode about two miles toward Gettysburg to where half a dozen small tents were

pointed out, a little way from the roadside to our left, as General Lee's headquarters for the night. On inquiry I found that he was not there, but had gone to the headquarters of General A. P. Hill, about half a mile nearer to Gettysburg. When we reached the place indicated, a single flickering candle, visible from the road through the open front of a common wall tent, exposed to view Generals Lee and Hill seated on camp stools with a map spread upon their knees. Dismounting, I approached on foot. After exchanging the ordinary salutations General Lee directed me to go back to his headquarters and wait for him. I did so, but he did not make his appearance until about 1 o'clock, when he came riding alone, at a slow walk, and evidently wrapped in profound thought.

When he arrived there was not even a sentinel on duty at his tent, and no one of his staff was awake. The moon was high in the clear sky and the silent scene was unusually vivid. As he approached and saw us lying on the grass under a tree, he spoke, reined in his jaded horse, and essayed to dismount. The effort to do so betrayed so much physical exhaustion that I hurriedly rose and stepped forward to assist him, but before I reached his side he had succeeded in alighting, and threw his arm across the saddle to rest, and fixing his eyes upon the ground leaned in silence and almost motionless upon his equally weary horse,—the two forming a striking and never-to-be-forgotten group. The moon shone full upon his massive features and revealed an expression of sadness that I had never before seen upon his face. Awed by his appearance I waited for him to speak until the silence became embarrassing, when, to break it and change the silent current of his thoughts, I ventured to remark, in a sympathetic tone, and in allusion to his great fatigue:

"General, this has been a hard day on you."

He looked up, and replied mournfully:

"Yes, it has been a sad, sad day to us;" and immediately relapsed into his thoughtful mood and attitude. Being unwilling again to intrude upon his reflections, I said ho more. After perhaps a minute or two, he suddenly straightened up to his full height, and turning to me with more animation and excitement of manner than I had ever seen in him before, for he was a man of wonderful equanimity, he said in a voice tremulous with emotion:

"I never saw troops behave more magnificently than Pickett's division of Virginians did to-day in that grand charge upon the enemy. And if they had been supported as they were to have been,—but, for some reason not yet fully explained to me, were not,—we would have held the position and the day would have been ours." After a, moment's pause he added in a loud voice, in a tone almost of agony, "Too bad! *Too bad!* Oh! Too Bad!"

I shall never forget his language, his manner, and his appearance of mental suffering. In a few moments all emotion was suppressed, and he spoke feelingly of several of his fallen and trusted officers; among others of Brigadier Generals Armistead, Garnett, and Kemper of Pickett's division.

—Imboden, "The Confederate Retreat from Gettysburg"

XXXIII.6

Lee and Traveller Review the Army of Northern Virginia

This picture of a gala military review comes from August 1863, while the army was recuperating after Gettysburg. It is given us by Lee's son, Captain Robert E. Lee, Jr.

During this period of rest, so unusual to the Army of Northern Virginia, several reviews were held before the commanding general. I remember being present when that of the Third Army Corps, General A. P. Hill commanding, took place. Some of us young cavalrymen, then stationed near the Rappahannock, rode over to Orange Court House to see this grand military pageant. From all parts of the army, officers and men who could get leave came to look on, and from all the surrounding country the people, old and young, ladies and children, came in every pattern of vehicle and on horseback, to see twenty thousand of that "incomparable infantry" of the Army of Northern Virginia pass in review before their great commander.

The General was mounted on Traveller, looking very proud of his master, who had on sash and sword, which he very rarely wore, a pair of new cavalry gauntlets, and, I think, a new hat. At any rate, he looked unusually fine, and sat his horse like a perfect picture of grace and power. The infantry was drawn up in column by divisions, with their bright muskets all glittering in the sun, their battle-flags standing straight out before the breeze, and their bands playing, awaiting the inspection of the General, before they broke into column by companies and marched past him in review.

When all was ready, General Hill and staff rode up to General Lee, and the two generals, with their respective staffs, galloped around front and rear of each of the three divisions standing motionless on the plain. As the cavalcade reached the head of each division, its commanding officer joined in and followed as far as the next division, so-that there was a continual infusion of fresh groups into the original one all along the lines.

Traveller started with a long lope, and never changed his stride. His rider sat erect and calm, not noticing anything but the gray lines of men whom he knew so well. The pace was very fast, as there were nine good miles to go, and the escort began to become less and less, dropping out one by one from different causes as Traveller raced along without a check.

When the General drew up, after this nine-mile gallop, under the standard at the reviewing-stand, flushed with the exercise as well as with pride in his brave men, he raised his hat and saluted. Then arose a shout of applause and admiration from the entire assemblage, the memory of which to this day moistens the eye of every old soldier.

—Lee, *Recollections and Letters of General Robert E. Lee*

XXXIII.7

"He Looked as Though He Was the Monarch of the World"

We have already learned how Lee tried to lead the counter-charge to close up the gap torn in his lines on the morning of the Battle of the Wilderness, May 6, 1864. Here Colonel Oates, whom we have met before, recalls for us his glimpse of Lee as the Alabamians closed up the gap.

At about 2 o'clock A.M. on the 6th we began to move, and progressed so slowly along the devious neighborhood road that it was daylight when the head of the column reached the Plank Road, about two miles in rear of where the fighting ceased the previous evening and where, just at this moment, it recommenced with great fury. As we hurried to the front we passed quite a number of wounded Confederates lying by the side of the road, and among them Generals Cook, of Georgia, and Kirkland, of North Carolina. In anticipation that his troops would be relieved early the next morning, Hill had not prepared to receive the attack which was made on him.

Longstreet's column reached the scene of action none too soon. Hancock was just then turning Hill's right and driving his men from their position, although they were manfully con testing every inch of ground. Anderson's Georgians was the first brigade of Field's division to engage the enemy. Benning's and the Texas Brigade got into action next on the right or south side of the Plank Road, and were temporarily re pulsed. We met General Benning, brought out on a litter severely wounded. Colonel Perry then formed Law's brigade, as it came up in double quick, to the left of the Plank Road with the Fourth Alabama's right resting upon it and the Fifteenth on the left of the brigade and of the line.

To reach our position we had to pass within a few feet of General Lee. He sat his fine gray horse "Traveler," with the cape of his black cloak around his shoulders, his face flushed and full of animation. The balls were flying around him from two directions. His eyes were-on the fight then going on south of the Plank Road between Kershaw's division and the flanking column of the enemy. He had just returned from attempting to lead the Texas Brigade in a second charge, when those gallant men and their officers refused to allow him to do so. My friend Col. Van H. Manning, of the Third Arkansas, then in command of the brigade, did that himself, fell severely wounded while leading the charge, and was taken prisoner.

A group of General Lee's staff were on their horses just in rear of him. He turned in his saddle and called to his chief of staff in a most vigorous tone, while pointing with his finger across the road, and said: "Send an active young officer down there." I thought him at that moment the grandest specimen of manhood I ever beheld. He looked as though he ought to have been and was the monarch of the world. He glanced his eye down on the "ragged rebels" as they filed around him in quick time to their place in line, and inquired, "What troops are these?" And was answered by some private in the Fifteenth, "Law's Alabama brigade." He exclaimed in a strong voice, "God bless the Alabamians!" The men cheered and went into line with a whoop. The advance began.

—OATES, *The War Between the* Union and *the Confederacy*

XXXIII.8

"The Field Resounded with Wild Shouts of Lee, Lee, Lee"

There are altogether, as we pointed out in our chapter on the Wilderness, three "Lee to the Rear" episodes. The third, and best authenticated, is that of May 12, when Hancock broke through the salient, overran Johnson's division, and threatened the whole Confederate line. We give here Colonel Gibson's account of the crisis.

A little after dawn of the 12th [May 1864], I was aroused from a deep sleep by Frank George, one of

General Gordon's orderlies, and was told by him that the Yankees had broke through our works and captured Johnson's division; and when I started to say something, he told me not to talk loud, the enemy were very close to us.

I immediately aroused up two or three men near me and told them to arouse the regiment, and tell the men to fall in as quickly and quietly as possible, without any rattling of canteens, as we were near the enemy. . . . The men fell in line about as soon as I could get mounted, and the staff officer came up a few minutes after, and guided us towards the right, and then towards the left, and after we had marched some two or three hundred yards and had come in sight of the line of unoccupied earthworks to our left, he pointed out a little farmhouse some ten or twelve hundred yards distant, and some four or five hundred yards, apparently, in rear of these works extended, as the headquarters of General Lee. He led us some hundred yards or more almost parallel to these unoccupied works, and then stopped, rather closer than the regulations required, as I thought, to a fine looking body of Confederates, dressed in nice, clean uniforms, that contrasted very strongly with the clothing of those of my brigade.

In the rear of these well-dressed troops I saw four mounted men among them; recognized General Robert E. Lee and Major-General John B. Gordon. General Lee rode towards my brigade, and as soon as I had fronted the men I turned towards him saluting for my orders. He paid no attention to me, but wheeled his horse to the right, passed through the vacancy between the brigades, took off his hat and rode Traveler grandly to the front.

He had scarcely got a dozen paces in front of our brigades when General Gordon and an officer on his left, whom I took to be his adjutant, trotted quickly after General Lee, and Gordon, as soon as he reached him 8eized Traveler by the right cheek of his bit, stopped him, and said to General Lee: "You must not expose yourself; your life is too valuable to the army and to the Confederacy for you to risk it so wantonly; we are Georgians, we are

Virginians, we need no such encouragement." At this some of our soldiers called out, "No, No," Gordon continuing, said: "There is not a soldier in the Confederate army that would not gladly lay down his life to save you from harm;" but the men did not respond to this last proposition.

While Gordon was speaking his adjutant rode around the heads of the horses of the two generals and facing his horse in a direction opposite that of General Lee's began to tug at Traveler's bit or bridle rein. Looking through an aperture in our breastworks I saw a body of the enemy coming from our left, slowly, and cautiously approaching us.

I called out to General Lee to come back, the enemy were approaching, and that we could not fight while he was in our front. A number of our men, especially those of Company A, called out: "Come back, General Lee; we can't fight while you are in our front;" and some members of Company A turned their right shoulders to General Lee and their backs to me, but I immediately brought these men into line by a "steady, front!" . . .

On looking out again for the enemy I noticed that they had drawn very close to our earthworks. I called out to General Lee "To come back, and come quick; that the enemy were dose upon us, and that my men could not fire on the enemy without shooting him." A number of my men called out: "Come back, General Lee; we won't fight as long as you are before us; come back."

The decided call of the men seemed to produce a greater impression on General Lee than the eloquence of Gordon, and my curt suggestions. As Traveler could not be easily turned around with a mounted officer on either side of him, facing in opposite directions, the adjutant let go Traveler's bridle, Gordon turned him around to the right, and proudly started to lead him back, and as he was doing so, I called out: "Three cheers for General Lee and 'Old' Virginia," but forgot to add Gordon's name to the list, which were given with a will. Before the two generals reached the intervening space between the brigades, Gordon let go his hold of Lee's bridle and dropped behind a short space,

Lee as soon as he reached the line of the brigades, turned his horse to the right, close up to mine, and Gordon and his adjutant rode up to the line of the Georgia Bngade.

When General Gordon, amid repeated shouts of "Lee, Lee to the rear!" had approached within eight or ten paces of our line, he found the interval between our two brigades blocked up. A mounted officer had stationed himself on the left of Gordon's brigade, General George Evans commanding. I had remained on the extreme right flank of Early's brigade, where I had placed myself when Lee rode to the front, and the intervening space had been crowded by men of Evans' brigade. Gordon let go his hold of Traveler's bridle, and reined up his horse to fall in behind Lee, and as he did so a member of the Warren Rifles ran forward, seized Lee's horse by the bndle reins, and amid redoubled shouts of "Lee, Lee, Lee to the rear! Lee to the rear!" led him up to the crowd and guided him through the crowders, and I backed my horse to the left to give a freer passage to the nders, and they passed through in single file, and the field of coming carnage resounded with wild shouts of "Lee, Lee, Lee!"

—Account by Colonel J. Catlett Gibson

XXXIII.9

LEE BIDS FAREWELL TO THE ARMY OF NORTHERN VIRGINIA

This moving document needs no introduction. It is relevant, however, to add a word about Lee after the war.

Deeply convinced that the only hope for the South lay in a sincere acceptance of the verdict of Appomattox he devoted himself to healing the wounds of war and training up a generation of young men who might work for the reconstruction of their section. In June 1865 he set an example to others by applying for a presidential pardon; it is mortifying to record that the pardon was never granted. In September 1865 Lee accepted the Presidency of Washington College (now Washington and Lee University), at Lexington, Virginia, and as President inaugurated a series of interesting reforms in the direction of what we would now call progressive education. Stricken with angina pectoris, he died on October 12, 1870, and was buried in Lexington.

In Benét's fine phrase, Lee had known "such glamour as can wear sheer triumph out"; if the cause for which he so valorously fought did not triumph, who can doubt that the admiration and affection in which he came to be held, North as well as South, represented a triumph that has few parallels in history?

Headquarters, Army of Northern Virginia, April 10, 1865

After four years of arduous service, marked by unsurpassed courage and fortitude, the Army of Northern Virginia has been compelled to yield to overwhelming numbers and resources. I need not tell the survivors of so many hard fought battles, who have remained steadfast to the last, that I have consented to this result from no distrust of them; but, feeling that valour and devotion could accomplish nothing that could compensate for the loss that would have attended the continuation of the contest, I have determined to avoid the useless sacrifice of those whose past services have endeared them to their countrymen. By the terms of the agreement, officers and men can return to their homes and remain there until exchanged. You will take with you the satisfaction that proceeds from the consciousness of duty faithfully performed; and I earnestly pray that a merciful God will extend to you His blessing and protection. With an increasing admiration of your constancy and devotion to your country, and a grateful remembrance of your kind and generous consideration of myself, I bid you an affectionate farewell.

—R. E. LEE, General, *Recollections and Letters of General Robert E. Lee*

XXXIII.10

NATHANIEL HAWTHORNE CALLS ON PRESIDENT LINCOLN

From 1853 to 1860 Hawthorne had been in England; when he returned to his own country he was bewildered and saddened at the sectional conflict and the war. In the spring of 1862 he visited Lincoln with a delegation from Massachusetts, was disgusted by some of the politicians and lobbyists he saw about the capital, and wrote a caustic article on his observations for the *Atlantic Monthly*, "Chiefly about War Matters." The editor was so offended that he added a footnote. "We are compelled to omit two or three pages, in which the author describes the interview, and gives his ideas of the personal appearance and deportment of the President. The sketch . . . lacks reverence, and it pains us to see a gentleman of ripe age . . . falling into the characteristic and most ominous fault of Young America." It is difficult now to understand what it was that worried editor J.T. Fields in this piece, on the whole so perceptive.

The article as Hawthorne originally wrote it appeared in his *Tales, Sketches, and Other Papers.*

Nine o'clock had been appointed as the time for receiving the deputation, and we were punctual to the moment; but not so the President, who sent us word that he was eating his breakfast and would come as soon as he could. His appetite, we were glad to think, must have been a pretty fair one; for we waited about half an hour in one of the antechambers, and then were ushered into a reception-room, in one corner of which sat the Secretaries of War and of the Treasury, expecting, like ourselves, the termination of the Presidential breakfast. During this interval there were several new additions to our group, one or two of whom were in a working garb, so that we formed a very miscellaneous collection of people, mostly unknown to each other, and without any common sponsor, but all with an equal right to look our head servant in the face.

By and by there was a little stir on the staircase and in the passage-way, and in lounged a tall, loosejointed figure, of an exaggerated Yankee port and demeanor, whom (as being about the homeliest man I ever saw, yet by no means repulsive or disagreeable) it was impossible not to recognize as Uncle Abe.

Unquestionably, Western man though he be, and Kentuckian by birth, President Lincoln is the essential representative of all Yankees, and the veritable specimen, physically, of what the world seems determined to regard as our characteristic qualities. It is the strangest and yet the fittest thing in the jumble of human vicissitudes, that he, out of so many millions, unlooked for, unselected by any intelligible process that could be based upon his genuine qualities, unknown to those who chose him, and unsuspected of what endowments may adapt him for his tremendous responsibility, should have found the way open for him to fling his lank personality into the chair of state,—where, I presume, it was his first impulse to throw his legs on the council-table and tell the Cabinet Ministers a story. There is no describing his lengthy awkwardness nor the uncouthness of his movement; and yet it seemed as if I had been in the habit of seeing him daily, and had shaken hands with him a thousand times in some village street; so true was he to the aspect of the pattern American, though with a certain extravagance which, possibly, I exaggerated still further by the delighted eagerness with which I took it in. If put to guess his calling and livelihood, I should have taken him for a country schoolmaster as soon as anything else. He was dressed in a rusty black frockcoat and pantaloons, unbrushed, and worn so faithfully that the suit had adapted itself to the curves and angularities of his figure, and had grown to be an outer skin of the man. He had shabby slippers on his feet. His hair was black, still unmixed with gray, stiff, somewhat bushy, and had apparently been acquainted with neither brush nor comb that morning, after the disarrangement of the pillow; and as to a night-cap, Uncle Abe probably knows nothing of such effeminacies. His complexion is dark and sallow, betokening, I fear, an insalubrious atmosphere around the White House; he has thick black eyebrows and an impending brow; his nose is large, and the lines about his mouth are very strongly defined.

The whole physiognomy is as coarse a one as you would meet anywhere in the length and breadth of the States; but withal, it is redeemed, illuminated, softened, and brightened by a kindly though serious look out of his eyes, and an expression of homely sagacity, that seems weighted with rich results of village experience. A great deal of native sense; no bookish cultivation, no refinement; honest at heart, and thoroughly so, and yet, in some sort, sly,—at least, endowed with a sort of tact and wisdom that are akin to craft, and would impel him, I think, to take an antagonist in flank, rather than to make a bull-run at him right in front. But, on the whole, I like this sallow, queer, sagacious visage, with the homely human sympathies that warmed it; and, for my small share in the matter, would as lief have Uncle Abe for a ruler as any man whom it would have been practicable to put in his place.

Immediately on his entrance the President accosted our member of Congress, who had us in charge, and, with a comical twist of his face, made some jocular remark about the length of his breakfast. He then greeted us all round, not waiting for an introduction, but shaking and squeezing everybody's hand with the utmost cordiality, whether the individual's name was announced to him or not. His manner towards us was wholly without pretense, but yet had a kind of natural dignity, quite sufficient to keep the forwardest of us from clapping him on the shoulder and asking him for a story.

—HAWTHORNE, *Tales, Sketches, and Other Papers*

XXXIII.11

JOHN HAY LIVES WITH "THE TYCOON" IN THE WHITE HOUSE

Fresh from Brown University John Hay entered the law office of his uncle, Milton Hay, in Springfield, Illinois. Next door was the office of Lincoln and Herndon, and inevitably Lincoln came to know the young man. A mutual friend, John Nicolay, whom Lincoln had selected as his private secretary, suggested that Hay should go along as assistant private secretary, and Lincoln amiably agreed. For Hay it was the beginning of a distinguished career which led, in the end, to the Secretaryship of State.

While in the White House Hay kept a diary, and it is from this and from his letters to Nicolay that these vivacious extracts are taken

November 13 [1861]. I wish to record what I consider a portent of evil to come. The President, Governor Seward, and I, went over to McClellan's house tonight. The servant at the door said the General was at the wedding of Col. Wheaton at General Buell's, and would soon return. We went in, and after we had waited about an hour, McC. came in and without paying any particular attention to the porter, who told him the President was waiting to see him, went up stairs, passing the door of the room where the President and Secretary of State were seated. They waited about half-an hour, and sent once more a servant to tell the General they were there, and the answer coolly came that the General had gone to bed.

I merely record this unparalleled insolence of epaulettes without comment. It is the first indication I have yet seen of the threatened supremacy of the military authorities.

Coming home I spoke to the President about the matter but he seemed not to have noticed it specially, saying it was better at this time not to be making points of etiquette & personal dignity.

July 18, 1863. Today we spent 6 hours deciding on Court Martials, the President, Judge Holt, & I. I was amused at the eagerness with which the President caught at any fact which would justify him in saving the life of a condemned soldier. He was only merciless in cases where meanness or cruelty were shown.

Cases of cowardice he was specially averse to punishing with death. He said it would frighten the poor devils too terribly, to shoot them. On the case of a soldier who had once deserted & reinlisted he indorsed, "Let him fight instead of shooting him."

One fellow who had deserted & escaped after conviction into Mexico, he sentenced, saying, "We will condemn him as they used to sell hogs in Indiana, as they run."

TO J. G. NICOLAY.

Executive Mansion, Washington,
August 7, 1863

This town is as dismal now as a defaced tombstone. Every body has gone, I am getting apathetic & write blackguardly articles for the *Chronicle* from which West extracts the dirt and fun & publishes the dreary remains. The Tycoon is in fine whack, I have rarely seen him more serene & busy. He is managing this war, the draft, foreign relations, and planning a reconstruction of the Union, all at once. I never knew with what tyrannous authority he rules the Cabinet, till now. The most important things he decides & there is no cavil. I am growing more and more firmly convinced that the good of the country absolutely demands that he should be kept where he is till this thing is over. There is no man in the country, so wise, so gentle and so firm. I believe the hand of God placed him where he is.

29 September, 1863. . . . Today came to the Executive Mansion as assembly of cold-water men & cold-water women to make a temperance speech at the Tycoon & receive a response. They filed into the East Room looking blue & thin in the keen autumnal air; Cooper, my coachman, who was about half tight, gazing at them with an air of complacent contempt and mild wonder. Three blue-skinned damsels did Love, Purity, & Fidelity in Red, White & Blue gowns. A few invalid soldiers stumped along in the dismal procession. They made a long speech at the Tycoon in which they called Intemperance the cause of our defeats. He could not see it, as the rebels drink more & worse whisky than we do. They filed off drearily to a collation of cold water & green apples, & then home to mulligrubs.

June 5, 1864. For a day or two the House has been full of patriots on the way to Baltimore who wish to pay their respects & engrave on the expectant mind of the Tycoon their images, in view of future contingencies. Among the genuine delegations have come some of the bogus & the irregular ones. Cuthbert Bullitt is here with Louisiana in his trousers pocket. He has passed thro' New York & has gotten considerably stampeded by the talk of the trading pettifoggers of politics there. He feels uneasy in his seat.

The South Carolina delegation came in yesterday. The Pres^t says "Let them in." "They are a swindle," I said. "They won't swindle me," quoth the Tycoon. They filed in: a few sutlers, cotton-dealers, and Negroes, presented a petition & retired.

Florida sends two delegations: neither will get in. Each attacks the other as unprincipled tricksters.

—Dennett, ed., *Lincoln and the Civil War in the Diaries and Letters of John Hay*

———— XXXIII.12 ————

"We Shall Nobly Save or Meanly Lose the Last, Best Hope of Earth"

Lincoln's own plan for dealing with the slave problem was compensated emancipation. Again and again he presented this to the country, to the border states, to delegations who came to plead with him. There was never much chance that It would have worked, even had Congress adopted it; even when the Confederacy was palpably collapsing, the border states refused to accept the plan.

This eloquent appeal for compensated emancipation was addressed to Congress in the annual message of December 1, 1862.

This plan is recommended as a means, not in exclusion of, but additional to, all others for restoring and preserving the national authority throughout the Union. The subject is presented exclusively in its economical aspect. The plan would, I am confident, secure peace more speedily and maintain it more permanently than can be done by force alone, while all it would cost, considering amounts and manner of payment and times of payment, would be easier paid than will be the additional cost of the war if we rely solely upon force. It is much, very much, that it would cost no blood at all.

The plan is proposed as permanent constitutional law. It cannot become such without the concurrence of, first, two thirds of Congress, and afterwards three fourths of the States. The requisite three fourths of the States will necessarily include seven of the slave States. Their concurrence, if obtained, will give assurance of their severally adopting emancipation at no very distant day upon the new constitutional terms. This assurance would end the struggle now and save the Union forever. . . .

Fellow-citizens, *we* can not escape history. We of this Congress and this administration will be remembered in spite of ourselves. No personal significance or insignificance can spare one or another of us. The fiery trial through which we pass will light us down in honor or dishonor to the latest generation. We *say* we are for the Union. The world will not forget that we say this. We know how to save the Union. The world knows we do know how to save it. We, even *we here*, hold the power and bear the responsibility. In *giving* freedom to the *slave* we *assure* freedom to *the free*—honorable alike in what we give and what we preserve. We shall nobly save or meanly lose the last, best hope of earth. Other means may succeed; this could not fail. The way is plain, peaceful, generous, just—a way which if followed the world will forever applaud and God must forever bless.

—LINCOLN, Annual Message of December 1, 1862

XXXIII.13

LINCOLN'S CONDOLENCE LETTERS

People who saw Lincoln during the Civil War often wrote of his expression of extraordinary sorrow. One witness of the Gettysburg Address wrote of "the inexpressible sadness of his face." Whitman said Lincoln's expression was one of "deep latent sadness." He wrote: "None of the artists or pictures have caught the deep though subtle and indirect expression of this man's face. There is something else there. One of the great portrait painters of two or three centuries ago is needed."

Lincoln bore the tremendous responsibility of guiding the government through its most difficult time. It required the decision to go to war, resulting in the deaths of more than 600,000 men. Lincoln also suffered from personal tragedies within his own home. His beloved 11-year-old son Willie died in 1862. Many of his personal friends were killed in battle, or had sons killed in the war. When it came to grief, Lincoln spoke from experience.

His most famous letter on the subject of grief was to Mrs. Lydia Bixby, whom Lincoln was told had lost five sons in the war. Recent scholarship, however, has revealed that not all of the Bixby boys died. One returned home safely and two may have deserted. Lincoln wrote another letter of condolence to Fanny McCullough, whose father, William McCullough, was killed in battle.

Washington, November 21, 1864

Dear Madam:

I have been shown in the files of the War Department a statement of the Adjutant general of Massachusetts that you are the mother of five sons who have died gloriously on the field of battle. I feel how weak and fruitless must be any words of mine which should attempt to beguile you from the grief of a loss so overwhelming, but I cannot refrain from tendering to you the consolation that may be found in the thanks of the Republic that they died to save. I pray that the heavenly Father may assuage the anguish of your bereavement, and leave you only the cherished memory of the loved and lost, and the solemn pride that must be yours to have laid so costly a sacrifice upon the altar of freedom.

—ABRAHAM LINCOLN

Executive Mansion
Washington, December 23, 1862

Dear Fanny:

It is with deep grief that I learn of the death of your kind and brave Father; and, especially that it is affecting your young heart beyond what is common in such cases. In this sad world of ours, sorrow comes to all; and, to the young, it comes with bitterest agony, because it takes them unawares. The older have learned ever to expect it. I am anxious to afford some alleviation of your present distress. Perfect relief is not possible, except with time. You can not now realize that you will ever feel better. Is not this so? And yet it is a mistake. You are sure to be happy again. To know this, which is certainly true, will make you some less miserable now. I have had experience enough to know what I say; and you need only to believe it, to feel better at once. The memory of your dear Father, instead of an agony, will yet be a sad, sweet feeling in your heart, of a purer and holier sort than you have known before.

Please present my kind regards to your afflicted mother.

Your sincere friend, A. LINCOLN

XXXIII.14

LINCOLN AND HAY FOLLOW THE ELECTION RETURNS

It is almost inconceivable to us, now, that Lincoln should not have been re-elected in 1864. Yet the prospects, in the summer of that year, were dim. Grant was getting nowhere in the Wilderness or at Petersburg; Sherman did not take Atlanta until September and then started on what many critics were pleased to call a "retreat." Fremont was nominated by a group of disgruntled abolitionists and War Democrats, and on August 29 the Democrats nominated McClellan on a platform declaring that the war was a failure. As late as August 23 Horace Greeley wrote that Lincoln's defeat was inevitable and called for another candidate to save the Union. And on August 23 Lincoln presented his Cabinet with a folded sheet of paper, and asked them to sign on the blank side; the other side contained this statement:

> "This morning as for some days past, it seems exceedingly probable that this administration will not be re-elected. Then it will be my duty to so cooperate with the President-elect as to save the Union between the election and the inauguration; as he will have secured his election on such ground that he cannot possibly save it afterward."

Yet in the end the tide turned. Atlanta fell and Sherman marched triumphantly to the sea; Farragut won at Mobile Bay; Grant whittled away Lee's army in front of Petersburg.

The election returns of 1864 gave Lincoln 2,216,067, McClellan 1,808,725 votes, and Lincoln's electoral vote was 212, McClellan's 21.

Once more it is Hay who tells the story of Lincoln and the election.

Nov. 8, 1864. The house has been still and almost deserted today. Everybody in Washington, not at home voting, seems ashamed of it and stays away from the President.

I was talking with him to-day. He said, "It is a little singular that I, who am not a vindicthe man, should have always been before the people for election in canvasses marked for their bitterness; always but once; when I came to Congress it was a quiet time. But always besides that the contests ill which I have been prominent have been marked with great rancor."

At noon Butler sent a despatch simply saying, "The quietest city ever seen."

Butler was sent to New York by Stanton. The President had nothing to do with it. Thurlow Weed was nervous about his coming, thought it would harm us and even as late as Sunday wrote saying that Butler's presence was on the whole injurious, in spite of his admirable General Order.

Hoffman sent a very cheering despatch giving a rose coloured estimate of the forenoon's voting in Baltimore. "I shall be glad if that holds," said the President, "because I had rather feared that in the increased vote over that on the Constitution, the increase would rather be against us."

During the afternoon few despatches were received.

At night, at 7 o'clock we started over to the War Depart ment to spend the evening. Just as we started we received the first gun from Indianapolis, showing a majority of 8,000 there, a gain of 1,500 over Morton's vote. The vote itself seemed an enormous one for a town of that size and can only be accounted for by considering the great influx since the war of voting men from the country into the State centres where a great deal of Army business is done. There was less significance in this vote on account of the October victory which had disheartened the enemy and destroyed their incentive to work.

The night was rainy, steamy and dark. We splashed through the grounds to the side door of the War Department where a soaked and smoking sentinel was standing in his own vapor with his huddled-up frame covered with a rubber cloak. In side a half-dozen idle orderlies, up-stairs the clerks of the telegraph. As the President entered they handed him a despatch from Forney claiming ten thousand Union majority in Philadelphia. "Forney is a little excitable." Another comes from Felton, Baltimore giving us "15,000 in the city, 5,000 in the state. All Hail, Free Maryland." That is superb. A message from Rice to Fox, followed instantly by one from Sumner to Lincoln, claiming Boston by 5,000, and Rice's & Hooper's elections by majorities of 4,000 apiece. A magnificent advance on the chilly dozens of 1862.

Eckert came in shaking the rain from his cloak, with trousers very disreputably muddy. We sternly demanded an explanation. He had slipped, he said, & tumbled prone, crossing the street. He had done it watching a fellow-being ahead and chuckling at his uncertain footing.

Which reminded the Tycoon, of course. The President said, "For such an awkward fellow, I am pretty sure-footed. It used to take a pretty dextrous man to throw me. I remember, the evening of the day in 1858, that decided the contest for the Senate between Mr. Douglas and myself, was something like this, dark, rainy and gloomy. I had been reading the returns, and had ascertained that we had lost the Legislature and started to go home. The path had been worn hog-back & was slippery. My foot slipped from under me, knocking the other one out of the way, but I recovered myself & lit square, and I said to myself, 'It's a slip and not a fall.' "

The President sent over the first fruits to Mrs. Lincoln. He said, "She is more anxious than I."

We went into the Secretary's room. Mr. Welles and Fox soon came in. They were especially happy over the election of Rice, regarding it as a great triumph for the Navy Department. Says Fox, "There are two fellows that have been especially malignant to us, and retribution has come upon them both. Hale and Winter Davis."

"You have more of that feeling of personal resentment than I," said Lincoln. "Perhaps I may have too little of it, but I never thought it paid. A man has not time to spend half his life in quarrels. If any man ceases to attack me, I never remember the past against him. It has seemed to me recently that Winter Davis was growing more sensible to his own true interests and has ceased wasting his time by attacking me. I hope for his own good he has. He has been very malicious against me but has only injured himself by it. His conduct has been very strange to me. I came here, his friend, wishing to continue so. I had heard nothing but good of him; he was the cousin of my intimate friend Judge

Davis. But he had scarcely been elected when I began to learn of his attacking me on all possible occasions. It is very much the same with Hickman. I was much disappointed that he had failed to be my friend. But my greatest disappointment of all has been with Grimes. Before I came here, I certainly expected to rely upon Grimes more than any other one man in the Senate. I like him very much. He is a great strong fellow. He is a valuable friend, a dangerous enemy. He carries too many guns not to be respected in any point of view. But he got wrong against me, I do not clearly know how, and has always been cool and almost hostile to me. I am glad he has always been the friend of the Navy and generally of the Administration."

Despatches kept coming in all the evening showing a splen did triumph in Indiana, showing steady, small gains all over Pennsylvania, enough to give a fair majority this time on the home vote. Guesses from New York and Albany which boiled down to about the estimated majority against us in the city, 35,000, and left the result in the State still doubtful.

A despatch from Butler was picked up & sent by Sanford, saying that the City had gone 35,000 McC. & the State 40,000. This looked impossible. The State had been carefully canvassed & such a result was impossible except in view of some monstrous and undreamed of frauds. After a while another came from Sanford correcting former one & giving us the 40,000 in the State.

Sanford's despatches all the evening continued most jubilant: especially when he announced that most startling majority of 80,000 in Massachusetts.

General Eaton came in and waited for news with us. I had not before known that he was with us. His denunciations of Seymour were especially hearty and vigorous.

Towards midnight we had supper, provided by Eckert. The President went awkwardly and hospitably to work shoveling out the fried oysters. He was most agreeable and genial all the evening in fact. Fox was abusing the coffee for being so hot— saying quaintly, it kept hot all the way down to the bottom of the cup as a piece of ice staid cold till you finished eating it.

We got later in the evening a scattering despatch from the West, giving us Michigan, one from Fox promising Missouri certainly, but a loss in the first district from that miserable split of Knox & Johnson, one promising Delaware, and one, too good for ready credence, saying Raymond & Dodge & Darling had been elected in New York City.

Capt. Thomas came up with a band about half-past' two, and made some music and a small hifalute.

The President answered from the window with rather unusual dignity and effect & we came home.

W. H. L[amon] came to my room to talk over the Chief Justiceship; he goes in for Stanton & thinks, as I am inclined to think, that the President cannot afford to place an enemy in a position so momentous for good or evil.

He took a glass of whiskey and then, refusing my offer of a bed, went out &, rolling himself up in his cloak, lay down at the President's door; passing the night in that attitude of touching and dumb fidelity, with a small arsenal of pistols and bowie knives around him. In the morning he went away leaving my blankets at my door, before I or the President were awake.

—DENNETT, ed., *Lincoln and the Civil War in the Diaries and Letters of John Hay*

—————— XXXIII.15 ——————

LINCOLN REPLIES TO A SERENADE

On November 10, two days after the election, when the returns were in, Lincoln was serenaded at the White House by some enthusiastic countrymen. He took the occasion to make one of the more thoughtful of his short addresses, one which pointed the significance of the election as a commentary on democracy in wartime.

It has long been a grave question whether any government, not too strong for the liberties of its peo-

ple can be strong enough to maintain its existence in great emergencies. On this point the present rebellion brought our republic to a severe test, and a presidential election occurring in regular course during the rebellion, added not a little to the strain.

If the loyal people united were put to the utmost of their strength by the rebellion, must they not fail when divided and partially paralyzed by a political war among themselves? But the election was a necessity. We cannot have free government without elections; and if the rebellion could force us to forego or postpone a national election, it might fairly claim to have already conquered and ruined us. The strife of the election is but human nature practically applied to the facts of the case. What has occurred in this case must ever recur in similar cases. Human nature will not change. In any future great national trial, compared with the men of this, we shall have as weak and as strong, as silly and as wise, as bad and as good. Let us, therefore, study the incidents of this as philosophy to learn wisdom from, and none of them as wrongs to be revenged. But the election, along with its incidental and undesirable strife, has done good too. It has demonstrated that a people's government can sustain a national election in the midst of a great civil war. Until now, it has not been known to the world that this was a possibility. It shows that, even among candidates of the same party, he who is most devoted to the Union and most opposed to treason can receive most of the people's votes. It shows, also, to the extent yet known, that we have more men now than we had when the war began. Gold is good in its place, but living, brave, patriotic men are better than gold.

But the rebellion continues, and now that the election is over, may not all having a common interest reunite in a common effort to save our common country? For my own part, I have striven and shall strive to avoid placing any obstacle in the way. So long as I have been here I have not willingly planted a thorn in any man's bosom. While I am deeply sensible to the high compliment of a reelection, and duly grateful, as I trust, to almighty God for having directed my countrymen to a right conclusion, as I think, for their own good, it adds nothing to my satisfaction that any other man may be disappointed or pained by the result.

May I ask those who have not differed with me to join with me in this same spirit toward those who have? And now let me close by asking three hearty cheers for our brave soldiers and seamen and their gallant and skilful commanders.

—*Complete Works of Abraham Lincoln*

XXXIII.16

LINCOLN VISITS THE COLORED SOLDIERS AT CITY POINT

Lincoln got to the army as often as possible, and some times to the embarrassment of officers and soldiers alike; Justice Oliver Wendell Holmes once recalled the occasion when he had cried out to the tall, absent-minded President, "Get down, you damn fool," and John Hay tells us of the time when Lincoln waited patiently for McClellan who had gone up to bed and refused to see him. Probably no visit that Lincoln ever paid to his soldiers was more gratifying than this one that General Porter describes.

On Tuesday, June 21 [1864], a white river-steamer arrived at the wharf, bringing President Lincoln, who had embraced this opportunity to visit for the first time the armies under General Grant's immediate command. As the boat neared the shore, the general and several of us who were with him at the time walked down to the wharf, in order that the general in-chief might meet his distinguished visitor and extend a greeting to him as soon as the boat made the landing. As our party stepped aboard, the President came down from the upper deck, where he had been standing, to the after-gang way, and reaching out his long, angular arm, he wrung General Grant's hand vigorously, and held it in his for some time, while he uttered in rapid words his congratulations and expressions of appreciation of the great task which had been accomplished since he and the general had parted in Washington.

The group then went into the after-cabin. General Grant said: "I hope you are very well, Mr. President."

"Yes, I am in very good health," Mr. Lincoln replied; "but I don't feel very comfortable after my trip last night on the bay. It was rough, and I was considerably shaken up. My stomach has not yet entirely recovered from the effects."

An officer of the party now saw that an opportunity had arisen to make this scene the supreme moment of his life, in giving him a chance to soothe the digestive organs of the Chief Magistrate of the nation. He said: "Try a glass of champagne, Mr. President. That is always a certain cure for sea-sickness."

Mr. Lincoln looked at him for a moment, his face lighting up with a smile, and then remarked: "No, my friend; I have seen too many fellows sea-sick ashore from drinking that very stuff." This was a knockdown for the officer, and in the laugh at his expense Mr. Lincoln and the general both joined heartily.

General Grant now said: "I know it would be a great satisfaction for the troops to have an opportunity of seeing you, Mr. President; and I am sure your presence among them would have a very gratifying effect. I can furnish you a good horse, and will be most happy to escort you to points of interest along the line."

Mr. Lincoln replied: "Why, yes; I had fully intended to go out and take a look at the brave fellows who have fought their way down to Petersburg in this wonderful campaign, and I am ready to start at any time."

General Grant presented to Mr. Lincoln the officers of the staff who were present, and he had for each one a cordial greeting and a pleasant word. There was a kindliness in his tone and a hearty manner of expression which went far to captivate all who met him. The President soon stepped ashore, and after sitting awhile at headquarters mounted the large bay horse "Cincinnati," while the general rode with him on "Jeff Davis," Three of us of the staff accompanied them, and the scenes encountered in visiting Butler's and Meade's commands were most interesting. Mr. Lincoln wore a very high black silk hat and black trousers and frock-coat. Like most men who had been brought up in the West, he had good command of a horse, but it must be acknowledged that in appearance he was not a very dashing rider. On this occasion, by the time he had reached the troops he was completely covered with dust, and the black color of his clothes had changed to Confederate gray. As he had no-straps, his trousers gradually worked up above his ankles, and gave him the appearance of a country farmer riding into town wearing his Sunday clothes. A citizen on horseback is always an odd sight in the midst of a uniformed army, and the picture presented by the President bordered upon the grotesque.

However, the troops were so lost in admiration of the man that the humorous aspect did not seem to strike them. The soldiers rapidly passed the word along the line that "Uncle Abe" had joined them, and cheers broke forth from all the commands, and enthusiastic shouts and even words of familiar greeting met him on all sides.

After a while General Grant said: "Mr. President, let us ride on and see the colored troops, who behaved so handsomely in Smith's attack on the works in front of Petersburg last week."

"Oh, yes," replied Mr. Lincoln; "I want to take a look at those boys. I read with the greatest delight the account given in Mr. Dana's despatch to the Secretary of War of how gallantly they behaved. He said they took six out of the sixteen guns captured that day. I was opposed on nearly every side when I first favored the raising of colored regiments; but they have proved their efficiency, and I am glad they have kept pace with the white troops in the recent assaults. When we wanted every able-bodied man who could be spared to go to the front, and my opposers kept objecting to the Negroes, I used to tell them that at such times it was just as well to be a little color-blind. I think, general, we can say of the black boys what a country fellow who was an old-time abolitionist in Illinois said when he went to a theater in Chicago and saw Forrest playing *Othello*. He was not very well up in Shakspere, and didn't know that the tragedian was a white man who had blacked up for the purpose. After the play was over the folks who had invited him to go to the show wanted to know what he thought of the actors, and he said: "Wall, layin' aside all sectional prejudices and any partiality I may have for the race, derned ef I don't think the nigger held his own with any on 'em.' " The Western dialect employed in this story was perfect.

The camp of the colored troops of the Eighteenth Corps was soon reached, and a scene now occurred which defies description. They beheld for the first time the liberator of their race—the man who by a stroke of his pen had struck the shackles from the limbs of their fellow-bondmen and proclaimed liberty to the enslaved. Always impressionable, the enthusiasm of the blacks now knew no limits. They cheered, laughed, cried, sang hymns of praise, and shouted in their Negro dialect, "God bless Massa Linkum!" "De Lord save Fader Abraham!" "De day ob jubilee am come, shuah." They crowded about him and fondled his horse; some of them kissed his hands, while others ran off crying in triumph to their comrades that they had touched his clothes. The President rode with bared head; the tears had started to his eyes, and his voice was so broken by emotion that he could scarcely articulate the words of thanks and congratulation which he tried to speak to the humble and devoted men through whose ranks he rode. The scene was affecting in the extreme, and no one could have witnessed it unmoved.

—PORTER, *Campaigning with Grant*

XXXIII. 17

"WITH MALICE TOWARD NONE"

Comment on Lincoln's noble second Inaugural Address is as superfluous as comment on his Gettysburg Address, It is, however, relevant to remark that the magnanimous policy which he here suggested for reconstruction was repudiated by Congress during his lifetime and after his death, and that this repudiation embittered sectional relations for half a century.

Fellow countrymen: At this second appearing to take the oath of the presidential office there is less occasion for an extended address than there was at the first. Then a statement somewhat in detail of a course to be pursued seemed fitting and proper. Now, at the expiration of four years, during which public declarations have been constantly called forth on every point and phase of the great contest which still absorbs the attention and engrosses the energies of the nation, little that is new could be presented. The progress of our arms, upon which all else chiefly depends, is as well known to the public as to myself, and it is, I trust, reasonably satisfactory and encouraging to all. With high hope for the future, no prediction in regard to it is ventured.

On the occasion corresponding to this four years ago all thoughts were anxiously directed to an impending civil war. All dreaded it, all sought to avert it. While the inaugural address was being delivered from this place, devoted altogether to *saving* the Union without war, insurgent agents were in the city seeking to *destroy* it without war— seeking to dissolve the Union and divide effects by negotiation. Both parties deprecated war, but one of them would *make* war rather than let the nation survive, and the other would *accept* war rather than let it perish, and the war came.

One eighth of the whole population was colored slaves, not distributed generally over the Union, but localized in the southern part of it. These slaves constituted a peculiar and power ful interest. All knew that this interest was somehow the cause of the war. To strengthen, perpetuate, and extend this interest was the object for which the insurgents would rend the Union even by war, while the government claimed no right to do more than to restrict the territorial enlargement of it. Neither party expected for the war the magnitude or the duration which it has already attained. Neither anticipated that the *cause* of the conflict might cease with or even before the conflict itself should cease. Each looked for an easier triumph and a result less fundamental and astounding. Both read the same Bible and pray to the same God, and each invokes His aid against the other. It may seem strange that any men should dare to ask a just God's assistance in wringing their bread from the sweat of other men's faces, but let us judge not,

that we be not judged. The prayers of both could not be answered. That of neither has been answered fully. The Almighty has His own purposes. "Woe unto the world because of offenses; for it must needs be that offenses come, but woe to that man by whom the offense cometh." If we shall suppose that American slavery is one of those offenses which, in the providence of God, must needs come, but which, having continued through His appointed time, He now wills to remove, and that He gives to both North and South this terrible war as the woe due to those by whom the offense came, shall we discern therein any departure from those divine attributes which the believers in a living God always ascribe to Him? Fondly do we hope, fervently do we pray, that this mighty scourge of war may speedily pass away. Yet, if God wills that it continue until all the wealth piled by the bondsman's two hundred and fifty years of unrequited toil shall be sunk, and until every drop of blood drawn with the lash shall be paid by another drawn with the sword, as was said three thousand years ago, so still it must be said, "The judgments of the Lord are true and righteous altogether."

With malice toward none, with charity for all, with firmness in the right as God gives us to see the right, let us strive on to finish the work we are in, to bind up the nation's wounds, to care for him who shall have borne the battle and for his widow and his orphan, to do all which may achieve and cherish a just and lasting peace among ourselves and with all nations.

—Lincoln, "Second Inaugural Address"

XXXIII. 18

Lincoln Is Assassinated

Lincoln had gone to Richmond the day after the Confederates had evacuated it—calling, while there, on Mrs. Pickett—and then had returned to Washington in time to make a memorable address on reconstruction. On the evening of April 14 he went to Ford's Theater to see Laura Keene in an English comedy, *Our American Cousin*. John Wilkes Booth, brother of the more famous Edwin Booth, had concocted a plot to assassinate all the principal officers of the government; a Southern sympathizer, he thought that this might undo the work of the Union armies end save the South. Entering Lincoln's box he sent a ball through the President's head; then leaped to the stage, shouting, *"Sic semper tyrannis!"* and made good his escape.

The moving story of Lincoln's death is told by the sorrowing Gideon Welles.

I had retired to bed about half past-ten on the evening of the 14th of April, and was just getting asleep when Mrs. Welles, my wife, said some one was at our door. Sitting up in bed, I heard a voice twice call to John, my son, whose sleeping-room was on the second floor directly over the front entrance. I arose at once and raised a wondow, when my messenger, James Smith, called to me that Mr. Lincoln, the President, had been shot, and said Secretary Seward and his son, Assistant Secretary Frederick Seward, were assasinated. James was much alarmed and excited. I told him his story was very incoherent and improbable, that he was associating men who were not together and liable to attack at the same time. "Where," I inquired, "was the President when shot?" James said he was at Ford's Theatre on 10th Street. "Well," said I, "Secretary Seward is an invalid in bed in his house yonder on 15th Street." James said he had been there, stopped in at the house to make inquiry before alarming me,

I immediately dressed myself, and, against the earnest remonstrance and appeals of my wife, went directly to Mr. Seward's, whose residence was on the east side of the square, mine being on the north. James accompanied me. As we were crossing 15th Street, I saw four or five men in earnest consultation, standing under the lamp on the corner by St. John's Church. Before I had got half across the street, the lamp was suddenly extinguished and the knot of persons rapidly dispersed. For a moment, and but a moment I was disconcerted to find myself in darkness, but recollecting that it was late and about tune for the moon to rise, I proceeded on, not having lost five steps, merely making a pause without stopping. Hurrying forward into 15th Street, I found it pretty full of people, especially so near the residence of Secretary Seward, where there were many soldiers as well as citizens already gathered.

Entering the house, I found the lower hall and office full of persons, and among them most of the foreign legations, all anxiously inquiring what truth there was in the horrible rumors afloat. I replied that my object was to ascertain the facts. Proceeding through the hall to the stairs, I found one, and I think two, of the servants there holding the crowd in check. The servants were frightened and appeared relieved to see me. I hastily asked what truth there was in the story that an assassin or assassins had entered the house and assaulted the Secretary. They said it was true, and that Mr. Frederick was also badly injured. They wished me to go up, but no others. . . . As I entered, I met Miss Fanny Seward, with whom I exchanged a-single word, and proceeded to the foot of the bed. Dr. Verdi and, I think, two others were there. The bed was saturated with blood. The Secretary was lying on his back, the upper part of his head covered by a cloth, which extended down over his eyes. His mouth was open, the lower jaw dropping down. I exchanged a few whispered words with Dr. V. Secretary Stanton, who came after but almost simultaneously with me, made inquiries in a louder tone till admonished by a word from one of the physicians. We almost immediately withdrew and went into the adjoining front room, where lay Frederick Seward. His eyes were open but he did not move them, nor a limb, nor did he speak' Doctor White, who was in attendance, told me he was unconscious and more dangerously injured than his father.

As we descended the stairs, I asked Stanton what he had heard in regard to the President that was reliable. He said the President was shot at Ford's Theatre, that he had seen a man who was present and witnessed the occurence. I said I would go immediately to the White House. Stanton told me the President was not there but was at the theatre. "Then," said I, "let us go immediately there." . . .

The President had been carried across the street from the theatre, to the house of a Mr. Peterson. We entered by ascending a flight of steps above the basement and passing through a long hall to the rear, where the President lay extended on a bed, breathing heavily. Several surgeons were present, at least six, I should think more. Among them I was glad to observe Dr. Hall, who, however, soon left. I inquired of Dr. H., as I entered, the true condition of the President. He replied the President was dead to all intents, although he might live three hours or perhaps longer.

The giant sufferer lay extended diagonally across the bed, which was not long enough for him. He had been stripped of his clothes. His large arms, which were occasionally exposed, were of a size which one would scarce have expected from his spare appearance. His slow, full respiration lifted the clothes with each breath that he took. His features were calm and striking. I had never seen them appear to better advantage than for the first hour, perhaps, that I was there. After that, his right eye began to swell and that part of his face became discolored.

Senator Sumner was there, I think, when I entered. If not he came in soon after, as did Speaker Colfax, Mr. Secretary McCulloch, and the other members of the Cabinet, with the exception of Mr. Seward. A double guard was stationed at the door and on the sidewalk, to repress the crowd, which was of course highly excited and anxious. The room was small and overcrowded. The surgeons and members of the Cabinet were as many as should have been in the room, but there were many more, and the hall and other rooms in the front or main house were full. One of these rooms was occupied by Mrs. Lincoln and her attendants, with Miss Harris. Mr. Dixon and Mrs. Kinney came to her about twelve o'clock. About once an hour Mrs. Lincoln would repair to the bedside of her dying husband and with lamentation and tears remain until overcome by emotion.

(April 15.) A door which opened upon a porch or gallery, and also the windows, were kept open for fresh air. The night was dark, cloudy, and damp, and about six it began to rain. I remained in the room until then-without sitting or leaving it, when, there being a vacant chair which some one left at the foot of the bed, I occupied it for nearly two hours, listening to the heavy groans, and witnessing the wasting life of the good and great man who was expiring before me.

About 6 A.M. I experienced a feeling of faintness and for the first time after entering the room a little past eleven, I left it and the house, and took a short walk in the open air. It was a dark and gloomy morning, and rain set in before I returned to the house, some fifteen minutes [later]. Large groups of people were gathered every few rods, all anxious and solicitous. Some one or more from each group stepped forward as I passed, to inquire into the condition of the President, and to ask if there was no hope. Intense grief was on every countenance when I replied that the President could survive but a short time. The colored people especially—and there were at this time more of them, perhaps, than of whites—were overwhelmed with grief. . . .

A little before seven, I went into the room where the dying President was rapidly drawing near the closing moments. His wife soon after made her last visit to him. The death-struggle had begun. Robert, his son, stood with several others at the head of the bed. He bore himself well, but on two occasions gave way to overpowering grief and sobbed aloud, turning his head and leaning on the shoulder of Senator Sumner. The respiration of the President became suspended at intervals, and at last entirely ceased at twenty-two minutes past seven. . . .

I went after breakfast to the Executive Mansion. There was a cheerless cold rain and everything seemed gloomy. On the Avenue in front of the White House were several hundred colored people, mostly women and children, weeping and wailing their loss. This crowd did not appear to diminish through the whole of that cold, wet day; they seemed not to know what was to be their fate since their great benefactor was dead, and their hopeless grief affected me more than almost anything else, though strong and brave men wept when I met them.

—*Diary of Gideon Welles*

XXXIV

THE SUNSET OF THE CONFEDERACY

And so we come to the last chapter of the history of the war, a chapter which none can read without emotion. It is a long and ragged chapter, embracing action in Tennessee, the Carolinas, and Virginia over a period of five months. But it has a coherent pattern—the pattern of Confederate disintegration and collapse.

The closing month of 1864 saw the Confederacy in desperate straits. Sheridan had Swept up the Valley, shattering Early's army and closing the-door on that storehouse for Lee's army. Thomas destroyed Hood at Nashville, and the pitiful remnants of the once mighty Army of Tennessee were limping into Alabama and Mississippi. Sherman had taken Savannah and turned northward to spread ruin through South Carolina. Grant was hammering at the Petersburg lines, and Lee thrust in vain against the iron ring that the Union commander had forged around him. The blockade, too, was ever tighter. Mobile had fallen in August; Fort Fisher, the last Confederate port, was captured in January. At the beginning of 1865 only two Confederate armies were still in the field as fighting forces: Johnston's forces in the Carolinas, and Lee's Army of Northern Virginia. All through the winter months of 1865 these were decimated by battle, disease, and desertion. With spring came the final blows. Sherman pursued Johnston into North Carolina and shattered him at Bentonville; Sheridan rode down from the Valley to join Grant south of Petersburg. Lee abandoned the city he had held for nine grim months, gave up Richmond, and fled along the Appomattox toward the west. It was the end.

In a sense it is true that the Confederacy was not beaten on the battlefield until the very end of the war when, in all theaters of operation, the Union forces held a two-to-one numerical superiority, and enjoyed the inestimable advantage of continuous reinforcement. To this day it is argued that the Confederates succumbed not to the armed might of the North but to other forces. There were enough men to fill the depleted ranks—so it is

asserted; there was food enough for the hungry soldiers, and clothing enough in the warehouses; there were arms and munitions sufficient for the needs of the armed forces; there was everything but the will to continue the fight.

But this argument begs the crucial question—why the will to fight had been fatally weakened by 1865? Why did state officials connive with draft evasion? Why did the armies melt away by desertion? Why did the commissary, the transportation system, the economy itself, collapse? A comprehensive answer to these questions would involve a review of the whole war, but a simple answer is not wholly unsatisfactory: these things failed because the Federal armies had overrun most of the South, because they had destroyed so much of the war potential, because they had laid waste the land, killed and wounded the soldiers. The South did not lose because morale was low; morale was low because the South was palpably losing.

The accounts of the collapse of the Confederacy which we include here ten their own story and require little introduction or explanation. What we are witnessing, here, is the working out of the grand strategy that Grant formulated in 1864. Once that strategy had been planned, and backed up with the immense resources available to the North, there was no hope for the South except perhaps in war-weariness and a change of administration in the North. Hood's ambitious attempt to achieve a vast flanking movement against the Union armies was foredoomed to failure; after Atlanta there was nothing left to oppose Sherman; sooner or later the combined armies in Virginia were bound to break Lee's defenses and force him to evacuate Richmond.

Yet to the end two possibilities glimmered in the imaginations of some of the last-ditch Confederates. Lee might have broken away from Petersburg, joined Johnston somewhere in western Virginia or North Carolina, and fought out a last campaign there. Or Lee and Johnston might have encouraged their soldiers to make good their escape and wage a long guerrilla warefare against the invader. Neither possibility had anything to offer. Even had Lee and Johnston joined forces there is no likelihood that they could have opposed successfully the' combined armies of Sherman and Grant—or, for that matter, either of them. And guerrilla warfare would have condemned the South to months and possibly years of devastating warfare without advancing in any way the cause of Southern independence.

Lee and Johnston recognized this, and were realistic enough to know, too, when the end had come. President Davis was less realistic. As late as April 4 he issued an address to the people of the Confederacy asserting that "nothing was now needed to render our triumph certain but the exhibition of our unquenchable resolve." Even after the surrender of Lee, Davis wanted to hold out but was dissuaded by Johnston and Beauregard and by some of his civilian advisers. None can doubt, now, that these were right in their conclusion that the verdict of Appomattox was final.

XXXIV. I

THOMAS ANNIHILATES HOOD AT NASHVILLE

It will be remembered that after Atlanta Hood moved into western Georgia with a view of striking at Sherman's communications. By November Sherman gave up what appeared to be a futile pursuit, and turned eastward. Hood and Davis then conceived an ambitious but visionary plan to recover Tennessee and Kentucky and help Lee in Virginia. Hood was to strike northward across the Tennessee, destroy Sherman's communications, advance into Kentucky, and with such recruits as rallied to his banner, move eastward into Virginia. For this proposed campaign Hood had some 40,000 effectives.

The first part of the operation went according to plan. By the end of October Hood's army was at Florence, Alabama, and on November 19 it began its forward movement across the Tennessee. As yet neither Thomas nor Schofield were strong enough to oppose Hood, but reinforcements were on the way. On November 29 Hood caught up with Schofield at Spring Hill, just south of Franklin; that night while Hood was asleep Schofield escaped through the Confederate lines to Franklin where he threw up entrenchments and awaited the Confederate advance. Hood came up next day, and hurled his divisions against the Union entrenchments in a series of assaults as gallant as those of Gettysburg. He was unable to break Schofield's lines, however, and Franklin proved a costly defeat, Confederate losses running to some 6,000.

After Franklin Schofield withdrew to Nashville, where Thomas was rapidly building up a force strong enough to take the offensive. Hood followed, and on December 2 had his army in position south and east of the city, astride the Franklin Pike and the railroad to Chattanooga. The reinforcements which Grant had arranged for were coming in rapidly, and within a few days Thomas had a force of close to 50,000 men to deal with about half that number under Hood. Grant wanted Thomas to attack at once, but Thomas was, as usual, deliberate; quite rightly he was determined to mount and equip his cavalry before undertaking an offensive which—so he hoped—would require a pursuit. By December 8 Thomas was ready for action; then bad weather intervened and he delayed. Meantime—as General Wilson tells us—Grant had become impatient to the point of ordering Logan to proceed to Nashvtlle to supersede Thomas. On the fourteenth the weather cleared, and Thomas moved out for the kill. Nashville was perhaps the most complete victory of the entire war, for it utterly destroyed Hood's army. Wilson pursued the stricken remnants across the Tennessee; Hood resigned; and the Army of Tennessee was no more.

This account of the battle is by Thomas' brilliant young cavalry commander, General James Wilson.

On December 9, as a result of daily conferences, Thomas ordered me to break camp at Edgefield, to recross the Cumber land with my entire force, and to take position within the defenses of Nashville between the Hillsboro and Harding turn pikes so as to be ready to join in the attack against Hood the next day. But a heavy rain setting in about the time the movement should have begun my orders were countermanded till further notice. Rain, snow, and sleet in abundance followed by intense cold covered the ground that night with such a glare of snow and ice as to render it impossible to move cavalry not especially rough-shod for the occasion. In fact, neither infantry nor cavalry could have made any progress whatever over a battlefield so undulating and broken and so covered with ice and frozen snow as was that which separated our lines from those of the enemy. There cannot be the slightest doubt that the prevailing conditions made it necessary to suspend operations and were a full justification for every hour of delay that followed this remarkable storm. It was at its greatest intensity when Grant telegraphed positive orders directing Thomas to attack the enemy without further delay,

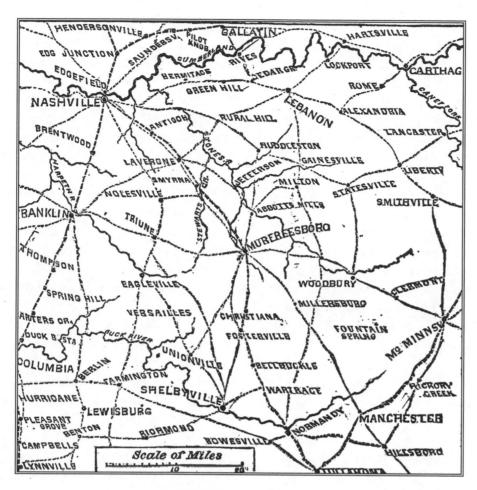

FRANKLIN AND NASHVILLE

and it was after it had spent its full force that Thomas, on the evening of December 10, invited his corps commanders to his headquarters for the purpose of reciting his orders, making known his reply, and asking their views as to the action he had taken entirely on his own responsibility in the emergency then at hand. . . .

As the others were withdrawing Thomas asked me to remain for further conference, and this I did with great pleasure. As soon as we were alone he said, with much feeling:

"Wilson, the Washington authorities treat me as if I were a boy. They seem to think me incapable of planning a campaign or of fighting a battle, but if they will just let me alone till thawing weather begins and the ground is in condition for us to move at all I will show them what we can do. I am sure my plan of operations is correct, and that we shall lick the enemy, if he only stays to receive our attack." . . .

Everything was astir, breakfast was over, and the cavalry corps ready to move out by daylight the next morning [December 15], but, owing to a dense fog which followed the change in the weather, the cavalry as well as the infantry was compelled to delay the advance till half past eight, by which time it had cleared sufficiently to enable each organization to move against the enemy as directed. In spite, however, of every precaution, McArthur's division of Smith's corps, instead of marching to its position on the left by my rear, as Smith had promised, deliberately crossed my front, thereby delaying not only my advance but the advance of the rest of the army till nearly ten o'clock. Had the enemy been specially alert, this unnecessary delay might have greatly deranged our plan of attack. As it was it cost the entire army an hour and a half, which, in the short days of December, could ill be spared, and might have been of inestimable value in our operations of that afternoon.

Simultaneously with the advance of the infantry, the cavalry moved out as directed, though Hatch's division was further delayed after beginning its march by the fact that McArthur's infantry still blocked its way. Finally having got a clear road, it advanced rapidly under the cover of a strong line of skirmishers. Brushing away the enemy's pickets, it soon encountered Ector's brigade of infantry on the farther side of Richland Creek, strongly entrenched on commanding ground.

Without a moment's hesitation, Stewart's brigade threw itself headlong against the enemy, broke through his line, and drove him rapidly beyond Harding's House. . . .

Having by this brilliant operation cleared his front and put the enemy's cavalry to flight, Hatch pushed his first brigade by flank rapidly to the left to join his second brigade. This done, the division found itself on the flank of a four-gun battery, posted in a redoubt which formed the left of the enemy's position. Sending his own battery "I," First Illinois Light Artillery, still farther to the right to a position from which it could enfilade the enemy's entrenchments. Hatch threw forward Coon's brigade, dismounted, broke through the enemy's infantry, and captured the redoubt with four guns. Turning the captured guns upon the enemy occupying a higher hill farther on, Hatch promptly threw forward his second brigade, supported by his first, and swept over a second redoubt, capturing four guns and two hundred and fifty prisoners. This operation was conducted in sight of the infantry, which had never seen dismounted cavalry assault a fortified position before. To men less brave and determined than these dismounted horsemen it would have seemed like madness to attack such

entrenchments, but armed with magazine carbines the strong line of skirmishers made light of the work before them. In spite of the steep acclivity and of the withering fire both of artillery and musketry, the dismounted cavalrymen swept over the next redoubt and, putting the enemy to flight, captured still another four-gun battery which the enemy abandoned in the valley beyond. It was now almost dark, and the cavalrymen, having been fighting on foot swinging on a long radius from hill to hill, over rough and muddy ground, had become exceedingly fatigued. Besides, night was at hand, and Hatch was, therefore, directed to bring forward his horses and bivouac on the Hillsboro turnpike, connecting with Schofield's right and covering it from the enemy. . . .

The cavalry operations still farther to our right had been equally successful. Croxton's brigade and Johnson's division, although delayed by McArthur's infantry, had found the enemy posted behind Richland Creek, but, pressing him vigorously in front and flank, they brushed him quickly out of the way. Croxton, after following him several miles, also turned to the left, skirmishing heavily with the enemy, and finally went into bivouac near the sixth mile post on the Hillsboro turnpike. Both he and Johnson had swept everything before them, thus making it easy to concentrate the entire mounted force within supporting distance of each other on the left and rear of the enemy's position.

From this condensed account, it will be seen that the cavalry corps had driven back the enemy's entire left wing an average of over four miles, and had placed itself in a position from which it was enabled to renew the attack against the enemy's left and rear the next day with deadly effect. . . .

Shortly after dawn of the 16th, the enemy drove in Hammond's pickets and took possession of the Granny White pike. This was the initial movement of the day, but Hammond, a gallant soldier, realizing the importance of that turnpike, without waiting for orders threw out the dismounted men of his entire brigade, drove the enemy back in turn, and regained firm possession of the turnpike. . . .

But by noon our skirmishers, not less than four thousand in number, had pushed their way slowly through the underbrush and woods up the hills in a curved line from Schofield's right, across the Granny White pike, to a position parallel with the enemy's line and facing Nashville. There was no longer any uncertainty as to which flank we ought to be on, for all was now going well. Led and directed by the gallant officers, the men of the two divisions, skirmishing heavily, pressed the enemy steadily back from the start at every point.

In the midst of the heaviest fighting, one of our detachments captured a courier from Hood, carrying a dispatch to Chalmers, directing him "for God's sake to drive the Yankee cavalry from our left and rear or all is lost." Regarding this dispatch as of the first importance, I sent it at once to Thomas without even making a copy of it. Having already informed both Thomas and Schofield by courier of my success and of the steady progress my troopers were making, I sent three staff officers, one after the other, urging Schofield to attack the enemy in front and finish up the day's work with victory. But nothing whatever was done as yet from the right of the infantry line to support my movement.

Finally, fearing that nothing would be done, and that night would come on again before the enemy could be shaken out of his position, by the efforts of the dismounted cavalry alone, I rode around the enemy's left flank to Thomas's headquarters, which I found on the turnpike about two miles from my own. This was between three and four o'clock, and, as it was a cloudy, rainy day, it was already growing dark. Thomas and Schofield were standing together on the reverse side of a small hill, over the top of which the enemy's line on a still higher elevation could be plainly seen less than a mile away. What was of still more importance was that my dismounted men, with their guidons fluttering in the air, flanked and covered by two—batteries of horse artillery, were in plain sight moving against the left and rear of the enemy's line. Shots from their batteries aimed too high but passing over the enemy's heads were

falling in front of Schofield's corps. And yet he gave no orders to advance.

Pointing out the favorable condition of affairs, I urged Thomas, with ill-concealed impatience, to order the infantry forward without further delay. Still the stately chieftain was unmoved. Apparently doubting that the situation could be as I represented it, he lifted his field glasses and coolly scanned what I clearly showed him. It was a stirring sight, and, gazing at it, as I thought, with unnecessary deliberation, he finally satisfied himself. Pausing only to ask me if I was sure that the men entering the left of the enemy's works above us were mine, and receiving the assurance that I was dead certain of it, he turned to Schofield and as calmly as if on parade directed him to move to the attack with his entire corps.

Fully realizing that the crisis was now on, I galloped as rapidly as my good gray, Sheridan, could carry me back to my own command, but when I reached its front the enemy had already broken and was in full but disorderly retreat by the only turnpike left in his possession. This was shortly after 4 P.M.

The dismounted troopers had closed in upon the enemy's entrenchments and entered them from the rear before the infantry reached them in front. They had captured fifteen more field guns, thus bringing their score up to twenty-seven for the two days, and had picked up several hundred prisoners. . . . It was now raining heavily, mist was gathering, and dark was closing down like a pall over both victor and vanquished. . . .

Meanwhile, the Confederate commander had committed his final and fatal mistake and had lost out forever. His flank was turned and taken in reverse and his line was irretrievably broken. The most he could hope to do now was to save his army by flight from total destruction and capture. And in this his most potent allies were darkness, rain, snow, sleet, mud, and rising rivers, all of which he was to have in succession for the next two weeks. With the beginning of darkness he was in full retreat along the two turn pikes and we were thundering at his heels.

—WILSON, *Under the Old Flag*

"The Last Chance of the Confederacy"

Sherman had entered Savannah on December 21, 1864, and then turned north, through the heart of South Carolina. Against his army of veterans Hardee—now in command of Confederate forces in Georgia and South Carolina—could oppose only delaying actions. Columbia fell on February 18, 1865, and that same day the Confederates evacuated Charleston. By the beginning of March Sherman was into North Carolina, moving on Fayetteville and striking toward Raleigh, the capital of the state.

Meantime Grant had decided to open up communications with Sherman by water, and provide him with a convenient Atlantic port for a supply base. Wilmington was the last major port of the Confederacy. It was commanded by Fort Fisher, and after a desperate struggle Federal amphibious forces captured this fort—and Wilmington—in mid-January. New Bern, at the mouth of the Neuse River and with direct railroad connections to Goldsboro and Raleigh, was equally important. Burnside had seized this place in 1862; now Schofield came on from Tennessee to direct an advance along the Neuse to ward Goldsboro and an eventual junction with Sherman coming up from the south.

One of Lee's first acts as commander in chief of the Confederate armies had been to restore Joseph Johnston to command of an armies opposing Sherman. Johnston sent Bragg to hold Schofield and on March 8-10 there was sharp fighting west of the great Dover Swamp. Bragg retired on Goldsboro, and Johnston prepared to move out to attack Sherman before his army and Schofield's could link up. Sherman's Grand Army of the West was strung out in several columns along many miles of road, and it was Johnston's plan to strike its vanguard. The opportunity came at Bentonville on March 19. It was "the last chance of the Confederacy"—and not a very good one. Actually even had Johnston succeeded in breaking Slocum's advance divisions, his position would still have been hopeless, for Sherman and Schofield together could muster some 90,000 to his own 35,000.

Alexander McClurg, who tells the story of the Battle of Bentonville, was a Chicago bookdealer who had helped organize the Crosby Guards at the beginning of the war, fought at Perryvale, Chickamauga, and Chattanooga, and marched with Sherman to the sea and through the Carolinas, as chief of staff to General J. C. Davis. He later became one of America's famous booksellers and publishers.

General Sherman had himself been marching for several days with the left and exposed wing, and on the night of the 18th his headquarters, as well as those of General Slocum, who commanded the left wing, had been pitched within the lines of the Fourteenth Army Corps. On the morning of the 19th . . . when the strains of Old Hundred had ceased, and the men had had their accustomed breakfast of coffee and hardtack, varied here and there with a piece of cold chicken or ham, or a baked sweet potato, foraged from the country, the regiments of the first division—General W. P. Carlin's—of the Fourteenth Corps filed out upon the road, and began the advance. This was about seven o'clock. For the first time almost in weeks, the sun was shining, and there was promise of a beautiful day; and the men strode on vigorously and cheerily.

They found in their front, as they always did, the enemy's cavalry, watching their movements and opposing their advance. But there was of course "nothing but cavalry," and the men pressed on, light-hearted, anticipating the rest they should have at Goldsboro, and then the last march toward Richmond and home. But the cavalry in front were stubborn. They did not yield a foot of ground before it was wrested from them. They were inclined to fight; and the old-expression of the Atlanta campaign was brought out for use again: "They don't drive worth a damn." Even the organized parties of for agers, the historical "bummers" of Sherman's army, men who generally made short work of getting through a thin curtain of cavalry, when chickens and pigs and corn and sweet potatoes were on the other side,—even these renowned troopers fell back, dispirited, behind our skirmishers, and lined the road sides.

At length the whole of the first brigade—General H. C. Hobart's—was deployed and pushed vigorously forward; but still the resistance of the enemy was determined and the advance slow. It began to be evident that they had some reason for this unusual opposition. Ten o'clock came, and we had gained but five miles. General Hobart was hotly engaged. The second brigade—Colonel

George P. Buell's—was ordered to make a detour to the left, and take the enemy's line in the flank; but meanwhile our own right flank was be coming exposed to a similar fate, as the enemy overlapped us in that direction, and the third brigade—Lieutenant Colonel Miles's—was deployed on the right of the first.

Thus the whole of General Cacrlin's division was now deployed and in line of battle; yet everywhere it found the enemy in front strong and stubborn. The right and left of our line were ordered to advance and develop his strength. They did advance right gallantly, but they soon encountered a strong line of infantry. This was pressed back several hundred yards, after severe fighting; and our men dashed, all unprepared, against a line of earthworks, manned with infantry and strengthened with artillery. The enemy opened upon them such a destructive fire that they were compelled to fall back, with severe loss. Many men and officers and two regimental commanders had fallen, and the whole line was severely shattered; but very important information had been gained. Observations and the reports of prisoners captured left little reason to doubt that General Johnston's whole army was in position in our immediate front, and the persistent fighting of the cavalry had been intended to give time for ample preparation.

It was now about half past one o'clock, and Generals Slocum and Davis were together in consultation, in the woods to the left of the road, when a deserter from the enemy was sent to them by General Carlin. . . . This man told a straight but startling story. It was to the effect that General Johnston's whole army, consisting of over thirty thousand men, had by night marches been concentrated in our immediate front, and was strongly entrenched. He said that General Johnston, accompanied by Generals Hardee and Cheatham and Hoke, had just ridden around among his troops, in the highest spirits, and that he had heard him address a portion of them, telling them that "at last the long-wished-for opportunity had occurred;" that they were "concentrated and in position, while General Sherman's army was scattered over miles of country, separated by almost impassable roads.". . .

The news had come none too soon, for our little command was again preparing to attack. . . . Two divisions and a brigade, with a battery of artillery,—in all, less than ten thousand men,—were face to face with an overwhelming force of the enemy, who had chosen their own ground, strengthened it with field-works, and placed their artillery in position. Confident and prepared, they awaited the order to advance, while we were deceived and surprised.

It was certain that they would lose no time, but attack at once and in overwhelming numbers. Up to this time General Slocum had shared the belief of General Sherman that the force in our front was inconsiderable. He was now thoroughly undeceived, and he went energetically to work to prepare for the most vigorous defensive fighting possible. Every precaution was taken, and the men all along our line were in the act of throwing up hasty field-works, when the attack came upon us like a whirlwind. . . .

Almost immediately I met masses of men slowly and doggedly falling back along the road, and through the fields and open woods on the left of the road. They were retreating, and evidently with good cause; but there was nothing of the panic and rout so often seen on battlefields earlier in the war. They were retreating, but they were not demoralized. Minie-balls were whizzing in every direction, although I was then far from the front line as I had left it only a short time before. Pushing on through these retreating men, and down the road, I met two pieces of artillery,—a section of the 19th Indiana baffery, and was dashing past it, when the lieutenant in command called out, "For Heaven's sake, don't go down there! I am the last man of the command. Everything is gone in front of you. The lieutenant commanding my battery and most of the men and horses are killed, and four guns are captured. These two guns are all we have left."

Checking my horse, I saw the rebel regiments in front in full view, stretching through the fields to the left as far as the eye could reach, advancing rapidly, and firing as they came. Everything seemed hopeless on our centre and left; but in the swampy woods on the right of the road our line seemed still to be holding its position. An overwhelming force had struck Carlin's entire division and Robinson's brigade, and was driving them off the field. The onward sweep of the rebel lines was like the waves of the ocean, resistless. . . . General Morgall's division, on the right, had also been heavily as sailed; but it was better situated, and not being at this time out-flanked, it held its position.

One of Morgan's brigades,—that of General Pearing,—being in reserve, had not been engaged. When the left first began to give way, General Davis sent Colonel Litchfield to Fearing, with instructions to hold his brigade in readiness to march in any direction. A few moments later, when the left was falling back, and the rebel line was sweeping after them in hot pursuit, General Davis came plunging through the swamp on his fiery white mare toward the reserve. "Where is that brigade, Litchfield?"

"Here it is, sir, ready to march." It was in column of regiments, faced to the front.

Ordering it swung around to the left, General Davis shouted, "Advance upon their flanks, Fearing! Deploy as you go! Strike them wherever you find them! Give them the best you've got, and we'll whip them yet!" All this was uttered with an emphasis and fire known only upon the field of battle.

The men caught up the closing words, and shouted back, "Hurrah for old Jeff! We'll whip 'em yet!" as they swung off through the woods at a rattling pace. Officers and men, from General Fearing down, were alike inspired with the spirit of their commander, and "We'll whip them yet!" might well be considered their battle-cry. They struck the successful enemy with resistless impetuosity, and were quickly engaged in a desperate conflict. Upon this movement, in all probability, turned the fortunes of the day. It was the right thing, done at the right time.

Seeing at once that, as Fearing advanced, his right flank must in turn become exposed, General

Davis sent to General Slocum, begging for another brigade to move in upon Fearing's right and support him. Portunately, Coggswell's fine brigade of the Twentieth Corps arrived not long after upon the field, and it was ordered to report to General Davis for that purpose. . . . It was splendidly done. The men of these two brigades—Fearing's and Coggswell's seemed to divine that upon them had devolved the desperate honor of stemming the tide of defeat, and turning it into victory; and magnificently they responded. Finer spirit and enthusiasm could not be shown by troops, and it is no wonder that, after a fierce and bloody contest, the flushed and victorious troops of the enemy, thus taken in the flank, gave way, and in their turn fell back in confusion. So stunned and bewildered were they by this sudden and unexpected attack that their whole line with drew from all the ground they had gained, and apparently reentered their works.

And now there was a lull along the whole front, which gave invaluable time for the re-formation of our shattered lines. . . .

To the surprise of every one, a full hour was allowed by the enemy for these new dispositions; and was about five o'clock before their long line was again seen emerging from the pine woods and swampy thickets in front, and sweeping across the open fields. As soon as they appeared, our artillery opened upon them with most destructive effect. Still they pressed gallantly on, but only to be met with a well-delivered fire from our infantry, securely posted behind hastily improvised field-works, such as our troops were then well skilled in throwing up in a very brief time, and of which they had dearly learned the value. Attack after attack was gallantly met and repulsed, and the golden opportunity of the enemy upon our left was lost. . . .

Morgan's whole division was now stretched out over such an extent of ground that all his troops were in the front line, and he had no men left for a second line or a reserve. As all old troops were wont to do at that time, when in the presence of the enemy, they had at once fallen to build such field works as could be hastily thrown up with rails and light timber. As one of their officers expressed it, they had often attacked works, but they had rarely had the pleasure of fighting behind them themselves, and they rather enjoyed the prospect. They were there, and they meant to stay. Their skirmishers were heavily engaged from the time they took position, and they found the enemy in front in force, and shielded by well-constructed works. They were fighting more or less severely until about half-past four o'clock in the after noon, when the enemy attempted to carry their position by assault. The charge was desperate and persistent, and the roar of musketry, as it rolled up from that low wood, was incessant. For half an hour it con-tinued, and the commander of the corps, General Davis, sat uneasily on his horse, a short distance in the-rear, and listened to it. . . .

After a while, a slight cessation was noticed in the firing; and by direction of General Davis, I rode forward toward the line to ascertain definitely how matters stood. The ground was swampy, and here and there were openings through the trees, while generally bushes and thickets obstructed the view. I had gone but a few rods, when I caught a glimpse through a vista, obliquely to the left, of a column of men moving to the right, straight across my path and directly in the rear of our line, though out of sight of it. They looked like rebels, and my sharp-sighted orderly, Batterson, said they were "rebs;" but the view was obscured by smoke, and the idea that the enemy could be in that position was pre-posterous. I hesitated but a moment, and pressed on. A hundred yards further through the bushes, and I broke out suddenly into a large, nearly circu-lar, open space, containing perhaps half an acre. Here the view was not a cheerful one. On the opposite side of the opening, at perhaps twenty-five yards' distance, was a body of unmistakably rebel troops, marching by the flank in column of fours, toward the right. Beyond the column, under a wide-spreading tree, dismounted, stood a group of Confederate officers, whose appearance and uni-forms indicated high rank. . . .

Mitchell's brigade had already discovered the intruders in their rear, who at first were thought by them to be reinforcements. . . . Fortunately, all was now quiet in front, and General Morgan quickly got his men to the reverse of their own works. In other words, they were now in front of their works, and prepared to sustain an attack from the rear. . . .

The enemy attacked vigorously, but instead of taking Morgan by surprise, he found him ready. Again the struggle was sharp and bloody, but brief. Nothing could stand that day before the veterans of the old second division. Truly they were enjoying the novelty of fighting behind works. Hardee was repulsed, with severe loss. . . .

Considering the great disaster which was imminent, and which was averted, it is not too much to claim for this engagement that it was one of the most decisive of the lesser battles of the war. When Johnston, with skillful strategy, and with wonderful celerity and secrecy, massed his scattered troops near the little hamlet of Bentonsville, and placed them, unknown to his great adversary, in a strong position directly across the road upon which two "light divisions," as he expressed it, were marching, he proposed to himself nothing less than to sweep these two divisions from the field, in the first furious onset; and then, hurrying on with flushed and victorious troops, to attack, in deep column and undeployed, the two divisions of the Twentieth Corps, which, through heavy and miry roads, would be hastening to the assistance of their comrades. These divisions he expected to crush easily, while General Sherman and the right wing were many miles from the field. Then, with half his army destroyed, with supplies exhausted, and far from any base, he believed General Sherman and his right wing only would no longer be a match for his elated and eager troops.

Never before, in all the long struggle, had for-tune and circumstance so united to favor him, and never before had hope shone so brightly. If Sherman's army were destroyed, the Confederacy would be inspired with new spirit, and ultimate success would be at last probable. Doubtless such dreams as these flitted through General Johnston's mind on that Sunday morning, when his well-laid plans seemed so sure of execution. With what a sad and heavy heart he turned at night from the hard-fought field, realizing that the last great opportunity was lost, we can only imagine. As the sun went down that night, it undoubtedly carried with it, in the mind of General Johnston, at least, the last hopes of the Southern Confederacy.

—McClurg, "The Last Chance of the Confederacy"

XXXIV.3

"Now Richmond Rocked in Her High Towers to Watch the Impending Issue"

With the failure of the attack on Fort Stedman Lee's position became critical. On March 26 he notified President Davis that Richmond must be abandoned. He himself could not give up Petersburg at once; it took time to collect supplies for an army on the move, and to make the necessary dispositions. Yet every hour that he stayed on in the trenches of Petersburg the situation became more dangerous. Already Grant had issued orders for a general assault on the twenty ninth; already Sheridan had come on from the Valley to the north bank of the James; already Lincoln and Sherman had arrived at City Point to witness the grand climax of the campaign and plan for armistice and peace.

By the end of March Grant had pushed his lines across the Weldon Railroad and the Quaker road and along the White Oak road toward Five Forks. On the twenty-ninth Lee struck at the Federals at Gravelly Run, but failed to break through. If the Federal line extended farther west, it could curve northward and cut off Lee's retreat along the Appomattox. This was precisely what Grant was planning. On the twenty-ninth Grant sent Sheridan to Five Forks via Dinwiddie Court House, and Lee started Fitzhugh Lee and Pickett after him. Pickett and Fitz Lee entrenched at Five Forks; then the two generals went off to a shad bake. At four in the afternoon of April 1 Sheridan struck. It was the greatest disaster that the Army of Northern Virginia ever knew; it was the Waterloo of the Confederacy.

George Alfred Townsend, with whose remarkable literary talents we are already familiar, is once again our historian.

We must start with the supposition that our own men far outnumbered the Rebels. The latter were widely separated from their comrades before Petersburg, and the adjustment of our infantry as well as the great movable force at Sheridan's dis-

posal, renders it doubtful that they could have returned. At any rate they did not do so, whether from choice or necessity, and it was a part of our scheme to push them back into their entrenchments. This work was delegated to the cavalry entirely, but, as I have said before, mounted carbineers, are no match for stubborn, bayoneted infantry. So when the horsemen were close up to the Rebels, they were dismounted, and acted as infantry to all intents. A portion of them, under Gregg and Mackenzie, still adhered to the saddle, that they might be put in rapid motion for flanking and charging purposes; but fully five thousand indurated men, who had seen service in the Shenandoah and elsewhere, were formed in line of battle on foot, and by charge and deploy essayed the difficult work of pressing back the entire Rebel column. This they were to do so evenly and ingeniously, that the Rebels should go no farther than their works, either to escape east ward or to discover the whereabouts of Warren's forces, which were already forming. Had they espied the latter they might have become so discouraged as to break and take to the woods; and Sheridan's object was to capture them as well as to rout them. So, all the afternoon, the cavalry pushed them hard, and the strife went on uninterruptedly and terrifically. . . .

A colonel with a shattered regiment came down upon us in a charge. The bayonets were fixed; the men came on with a yell; their gray uniforms seemed black amidst the smoke; their preserved colors, torn by grape and ball, waved yet defiantly; twice they halted, and poured in volleys, but came on again like the surge from the fog, depleted, but determined; yet, in the hot faces of the carbineers, they read a purpose as resolute, but more calm, and, while they pressed along, swept all the while by scathing volleys, a group of horsemen took them in flank. It was an awful instant; the horses recoiled; the charging column trembled like a single thing, but at once the Rebels, with rare organization, fell into a hollow square, and with solid sheets of steel defied our centaurs. The horsemen rode around them in vain; no charge could break the shining squares, until our dismounted carbineers poured in their volleys afresh, making gaps in the spent ranks, and then in their wavering time the cavalry thundered down. The Rebels could stand no more; they reeled and swayed, and fell back broken and beaten. And on the ground their colonel lay, sealing his devotion with his life.

Through wood and brake and swamp, across field and trench, we pushed the fighting defenders steadily. For a part of the time, Sheridan himself was there, short and broad, and active, waving his hat, giving orders, seldom out of fire, but never stationary, and close by fell the long yellow locks of Custer, sabre extended, fighting like a Viking, though he was worn and haggard with much work. At four o'clock the Rebels were behind their wooden walls at Five Forks, and still the cavalry pressed them hard, in feint rather than solemn effort, while a battalion dismounted, charged squarely upon the face of their breastworks which lay in the main on the north side of the White Oak road. Then, while the cavalry worked round toward the rear, the infantry of Warren, though commanded by Sheridan, prepared to take part in the battle.

The genius of Sheridan's movement lay in his disposition of the infantry. The skill with which he arranged it, and the difficult manaeuvres he projected and so well executed, should place him as high in infantry tactics as he has heretofore shown himself superior in cavalry. The infantry which had marched at 2l/2 P.M. from the house of Boisseau, on the Boydtown plank-road, was drawn up in four battle lines, a mile or more in length, and in the beginning facing the White Oak road obliquely; the left or pivot was the division of General Ayres, Crawford had the center and Griffin the right. These advanced from the Boydtown plank-road, at ten o'clock, while Sheridan was thundering away with the cavalry, mounted and dismounted, and deluding the Rebels with the idea that he was the sole attacking party; they lay concealed in the woods behind the Gravelly Run meeting-house, but their left W&S not a half-mile distant from the Rebel works, though their right reached so far off that a novice would have criticized the position sharply. Little by little, Sheridan, extending his lines, drove the whole Rebel force into their breastworks; then he dismounted the mass of his cavalry and charged the works straight in the front, still thundering on their flank. At last, every Rebel was safe behind his intrenchments. Then the signal W&S given, and the concealed infantry, many thousand strong, sprang up and advanced by echelon to the right. Imagine a great barndoor shutting to, and you have the movement, if you can also imagine the door itself, hinge and all, moving forward also. This was the door:—

AYRES—CRAWFORD—GRIFFIN.

Stick a pin through Ayres and turn Griffin and Crawford forward as you would a spoke in a wheel, but move your pin up also a very little. In this way Ayres will advance, say half a mile, and Griffin, to describe a quarter revolution, will move through a radius of four miles. But to complicate this movement by echelon, we must imagine the right when half was advanced cutting across the centre and reforming, while Crawford became the right and Griffin the middle of the line of battle. Warren was with Crawford on this march. Gregory commanded the skirmishers. Ayres was so close to the Rebel left that he might be said to hinge upon it; and at 6 o'clock the whole corps column came crash upon the full flank of the astonished Rebels. Now came the pitch of the battle.

We were already on the Rebel right in force, and thinly in their rear. Our carbineers were making feint to charge in direct front, and our infantry, four deep, hemmed in their entire left. All this they did not for an instant note, so thorough was their confusion; but seeing it directly, they, so far from giving up, concentrated all their energy and fought like fiends. They had a battery in position, which belched incessantly, and over the breastworks their musketry made one unbroken roll, while against Sheridan's prowlers on their left, by skirmish and sortie, they stuck to their sinking for tunes, so as to win unwilling applause from mouths of wisest censure.

It was just at the coming up of the infantry that Sheridan's little band was pushed the hardest. At one time, indeed, they seemed about to undergo extermination; not that they wavered, but that they were so vastly overpowered. It will remain to the latest time a matter of marvel that so paltry a cavalry force could press back sixteen thousand infantry; but when the infantry blew like a great barndoor—the simile best applicable—upon the enemy's left, the victory that was to come had passed the region of strategy and resolved to an affair of personal courage. We had met the enemy; were they to be ours? To expedite this consummation every officer fought as if he were the forlorn hope. Mounted on his black pony, the same which he rode at Winchester, Sheridan galloped every where, his flushed face all the redder, and his plethoric, but nervous figure all the more ubiquitous. He galloped once straight down the Rebel front, with but a handful of his staff. A dozen bullets whistled for him together; one grazed his arm, at which a faithful orderly rode; the black pony leaped high, in fright, and Sheridan was untouched, but the orderly lay dead in the field, and the saddle dashed afar empty. . . .

The fight, as we closed upon the Rebels, was singularly free from great losses on our side, though desperate as any contest ever fought on the continent. One prolonged roar of rifle shook the afternoon; we carried no artillery, and the Rebel battery, until its capture, raked us like an irrepressible demon, and at every foot of the entrenchments a true man fought both in front and behind. The birds of the forest fled afar; the smoke ascended to heaven; locked in so mad a frenzy, none saw the sequel of the closing day. Now Richmond rocked in her high towers to watch the impending issue, but soon the day began to look gray, and a pale moon came tremulously out to watch the meeting squadrons. Imagine along a line of a full mile, thirty thousand men struggling for life and prestige; the woods gathering about them—but yesterday the

home of hermit hawks and chipmonks—now ablaze with bursting shells, and showing in the dusk the curl of flames in the tangled grass, and, rising up the boles of the pine trees, the scaling, scorching tongues. Seven hours this terrible spectacle had been enacted, but the finale of it had almost come.

It was by all account in this hour of victory when the modest and brave General Winthrop of the first brigade, Ayres division, was mortally wounded. He was riding along the breastworks, and in the act as I am assured, of saving a friend's life, was shot through to the left lung. He fell at once, and his men, who loved him, gathered around and took him tenderly to the rear, where he died before the stretcher on which he lay could be deposited beside the meeting-house door. On the way from the field to the hospital he wandered in mind at times, crying out, "Captain Weaver how is that line? Has the attack succeeded?" . . .

At seven o'clock the Rebels came to the conclusion that they were outflanked and whipped. They had been so busily engaged that they were a long time finding out how desperate were their circumstances; but now, wearied with persistent assaults in front, they fell back to the left, only to see four close lines of battle waiting to drive them across the field, decimated. At the right the horsemen charged them in their vain attempt to fight "out," and in the rear straggling foot and cavalry began also to assemble; slant fire, cross fire, and direct fire, by file and volley rolled in perpetually, cutting down their bravest officers and strewing the fields with bleeding men; groans resounded in the intervals of exploding powder, and to add to their terror and despair, their own artillery, captured from them, threw into their own ranks, from its old position, ungrateful grape and canister, enfilading their breastworks, whizzing and plunging by air line and ricochet, and at last bodies of cavalry fairly mounted their intrenchments, and charged down the parapet, slashing and trampling them, and producing inexplicable confusion. They had no commanders, at least no orders, and looked in vain for some guiding hand to lead them out of a toil into which they had fallen so bravely and so blindly. A few more volleys, a new and irresistible charge, a shrill and warning command to die or surrender, and, with a sullen and tearful impulse, five thousand muskets are flung upon the ground, and five thousand hot, exhausted, and impotent men are Sheridan's prisoners of war.

—TOWNSEND, *Campaigns of a Non-Combatant*

XXXIV.4

"THE MOST SUPERB SOLDIER IN ALL THE WORLD" FALLS AT FIVE FORKS

One by one, in that last bitter year, the Army of Northern Virginia was losing its most dashing leaders. Jeb Stuart had fallen at Yellow Tavern, Robert Rodes at Winchester, Stephen Ramseur at Cedar Creek, General John Pegram, one of the youngest and most brilliant of brigadiers, in the fighting at Petersburg. A. P. Hill, to whom both Jackson and Lee called on their deathbeds, fell the day after Five Forks. One of the most heartbreaking of the losses of Five Forks was that of young William Pegram, the "boy" colonel of artillery—he was just twenty-three—who was admired and beloved as Pelham and Stuart and Ramseur had been.

The tragic event is here recorded by Pegram's adjutant, Gordon McCabe; after the war McCabe became one of the nation's great schoolmasters.

April 1st [1865]. Had nothing to eat, so parched some corn taken from horses' feed. Henry Lee, an old University friend of ours and Ass't Adj't. Gen'l Payne's Brigade, afterwards sent us some meat and bread. At 10 o'clk. we put 3 guns, 1 of Elleff's and Early's section, in position in the centre, and Ellett's other 3 on the right commanding a field. Soon afterwards the enemy's cavalry appeared in front of our right at the distance of 800 yds. We could plainly see them and their pennons flying in the wind. We opened at once with our guns. I told one of the gunners to fire on their colours, on which they were forming. He made a splendid shot, bursting a shell just in front of the colours. The whole line fell back into the woods, but their skirmishers occupied the yard of the Gillem House,

and we continued to give them an occasional shot. Skirmishing now broke out in the centre and Col. P[egram] and myself rode down to our guns there. The skirmishing was quite heavy, and Col. ordered Lt. Early to dismount, but he wouldn't, so I wouldn't. We fired a few rounds and the skirmishing soon died out. Col. and myself went back to the right, where we expected the attack to be made. We lay down at the foot of a tree, as everything was now quiet, and he soon fell asleep.

At about 4 1/2 the enemy attacked him, and we mounted and rode rapidly to the centre. When we reached our guns the enemy were only 30 yds. from them, and the infantry fire terrific beyond anything I have ever seen. We were the only mounted officers at that point. The officers, Lts. Hollis and Early, were as cool as on parade, and the men were serving their guns with a precision and rapidity beyond all praise. Pickett's Divn. were fighting well too. We had not been in the battery very long, when Col. P. riding between Lt. Early's guns reeled out of his saddle, shot through his left arm and left side. He cried out, 'Oh, Gordon, I'm mortally wounded, take me off the field.' His last order was, 'Fire your canister low.' I put him on a stretcher and sent him to the rear, and then went back among the guns to give the order. I ran back to the stretcher, and he took my hand and gave me a message for his mother and sisters. He begged me to remain with him, wh. I intended anyhow to do. When I got him to the ambulance, our skirmishers were falling back, square in our rear, and a line of battle pressing them. We were now completely enveloped, our left having been turned and the enemy in our rear. Our guns were carried within 3 minutes, Lt. Early killed and Lt. Hollis captured and the whole line rolled up.

The rout now became general, with the exception of Corse's Brigade, which had not been heavily engaged. This brigade opened to the right and left and let the rout pass through, and then closed up and came off with their integrity of organization unimpaired. I took Col. in my arms and made the ambulance drive between 2 parallel lines-of-battle of the enemy for 4 or 5 hundred yds. I carried him to Ford's Depot on S. S. R. R. about 10 miles from the field. While in the ambulance we prayed together and he was perfectly resigned to die. At about 10 o'clk we reached Ford's and I obtained a bed for him at a Mr Pegram's. I had given him morphine in small quantities until he was easier, and he soon fell into a doze. The enemy advanced on the place about 12 o'clk, and I was left alone with him. I sent off our sabres, horses, spurs, etc. as I felt sure that we w'd be captured. I shall never forget that night of watching. I could only pray. He breathed heavily through the night, and passed into a stupor. I bound up his wounds as well as I knew how and moistened his lips with water. At about Sunday morning April 2nd, he died as gently as possible.

Thus died the truest Christian, the most faithful friend and the most superb soldier in all the world. He was, indeed, my Jonathon, pure in heart, brave in deed, chivalric until it bordered on Quixotism, generous and utterly unselfish, he was the Havelock of the Army of Northern Virginia. I laid him out, helped to dig his grave, buried him in a blanket, and then read the Episcopal service over him.

—GORDON, *Memories and Memorials of William Gordon McCabe*

XXXIV.5

THE CONFEDERATES ABANDON RICHMOND

After Five Forks the abandonment of Richmond was inevitable. To give President Davis time to move government offices and archives Lee clung to his lines at Petersburg for an other day. Early on the morning of April 2 Grant assaulted the Confederate lines, carrying the first line of entrenchments. Lee retired to the suburbs of the city; Grant attacked and carried Forts Gregg and Whitworth—the last strongholds. A final assault was planned for the morning of the third, but that night Lee's army slipped away and began the race to the west. Meantime the Confederate government had evacuated Richmond; on the morning of the third the capital was formally surrendered to General Weitzel, and

Federal troops moved in to restore order and put out the flames that were threatening to destroy the city.

We have here three descriptions of the evacuation of Richmond and its occupation by the Federals. The first* comes from the brilliant Constance Cary, later Mrs. Burton Harrison, whose husband was private secretary to President Davis. The second account is by a Yankee—Lieutenant R. B. Prescott, who was one of the first of the conquerors to enter the stricken city. The third was written by 14-year-old Frances Caldern de la Barca Hunt, whose family and friends seemed to be torn from her as the city collapsed around her, and for whom surrender came as sad relief.

A. "A Great Burst of Sobbing All Over the Church"

Grace Street, Richmond, April 4, 1865
My Precious Mother and Brother:

I write you this jointly, because I can have no idea where Clarence is. Can't you imagine with what a heavy heart I begin it—? The last two days have added long years to my life. I have cried until no more tears will come, and my heart throbs to bursting night and day. When I bade you good-bye, dear, and walked home alone, I could not trust myself to give another look after you. All that evening the air was full of farewells as if to the dead. Hardly anybody went to bed. We walked through the streets like lost spirits till nearly daybreak. My dearest mother, it is a special Providence that has spared you this! Your going to nurse poor Bert at this crisis has saved you a shock I never can forget. With the din of the enemy's wagon trains, bands, trampling horses, fifes, hurrahs and cannon ever in my ears, I can hardly write coherently. As you desired, in case of trouble, I left our quarters and came over here to be under my uncle's wing. In Aunt M.'s serious illness the house is overflowing; there was not a room or a bed to give me, but that made no difference, they insisted on my staying all the same. Up under the roof there was a lumber-room with two windows and I paid an old darkey with some wrecks of food left from our housekeeping, to clear it out, and scrub floor and walls and

---

* Reprinted from *Recollections Grave and Gay* by Mrs. Burton Harrison; copyright 1911 by Charles Scribner's Sons, 1939 by Fairfax Harrison; used by permission of the publishers.

windows, till all was absolutely clean. A cot was found and some old chairs and tables—our own bed linen was brought over, and here I write in comparative comfort, so don't bother about me!

Hardly had I seemed to have dropped upon my bed that dreadful Sunday night—or morning rather—when I was wakened suddenly by four terrific explosions, one after the other, making the windows of my garret shake. It was the blowing up, by Admiral Semmes, by order of the Secretary of the Navy, of our gunboats on the James, the signal for an all-day carnival of thundering noise and flames. Soon the fire spread, shells in the burning arsenals began to explode, and a smoke arose that shrouded the whole town, shutting out every vestige of blue sky and April sunshine. Flakes of fire fell around us, glass was shattered, and chimneys fell, even so far as Grace Street from the scene. . . .

Edith and I . . . set out for the Capital Square, taking our courage in both hands. Looking down from the upper end of the square, we saw a huge wall of fire blocking out the horizon. In a few hours no trace was left of Main, Cary, and Canal Streets, from 8th to 18th Streets, except tottering walls and smouldering ruins. The War Department was sending up jets of flame. Along the middle of the streets smouldered a long pile, like skeet-sweepings, of papers torn from the different departments' archives of our beloved Government, from which soldiers in blue were picking out letters and documents that caught their fancy. The Custom House was the sole building that defied the fire amongst those environing the Square. The marble Statesman on the Monument looked upon queer doings that day, inside the enclosure from which all green was soon scorched out, or trampled down by the hoofs of cavalry horses picketted at intervals about it. Mr. Reed's Church, Mrs. Stanard's house, the Prestons' house, are all burned; luckily the Lee house and that side of Franklin stand uninjured. General Lee's house has a guard camped in the front yard.

We went on to the head-quarters of the Yankee General in charge of Richmond, that day of doom, and I must say were treated with perfect courtesy and consideration. We saw many people

we knew on the same errand as ourselves. We heard stately Mrs.—and the—were there to ask for food, as their families were starving. Thank God, we have not fallen to that! Certainly, her face looked like a tragic mask carved out of stone.

A courteous young lieutenant . . . was sent to pilot us out of the confusion, and identify the house, over which a guard was immediately placed. Already the town wore the aspect of one in the Middle Ages smitten by pestilence. The streets filled with smoke and flying fire were empty of the respectable class of inhabitants, the doors and shutters of every house tight closed. . . .

The ending of the first day of occupation was truly horrible. Some Negroes of the lowest grade, their heads turned by the prospect of wealth and equality, together with a mob of miserable poor whites, drank themselves mad with liquor scooped from the gutters. Reinforced, it was said, by convicts escaped from the penitentiary, they tore through the streets, carrying loot from the burnt district. (For days after, even the kitchens and cabins of the better class of darkies displayed handsome oil paintings and mirrors, rolls of stuff, rare books, and barrels of sugar and whiskey.) One gang of drunken rioters dragged coffins sacked from undertakers, filled with spoils from the speculators' shops, howling so madly one expected to hear them break into the Carmagnole. Thanks to our trim Yankee guard in the basement, we felt safe enough, but the experience was not pleasant.

Through all this strain of anguish ran like a gleam of gold the mad vain hope that Lee would yet make a stand some where—that Lee's dear soldiers would give us back our liberty.

Dr. Minnegerode has been allowed to continue his daily services and I never knew anything more painful and touching than that of this morning when the Litany was *sobbed* out by the whole congregation.

A service we went to the same evening of the old Monumental I never shall forget. When the rector prayed for 'the sick and wounded soldiers and all in distress of mind or body,' there was a brief pause, filled with a sound of weeping all over the church. He then gave out the hymn: 'When gathering clouds around I view.' There was no organ and a voice that started the hymn broke down in tears. Another took it up, and failed likewise. I, then, with a tremendous struggle for self-control, stood up in the corner of the pew and sang alone. At the words, 'Thou Saviour see'st the tears I shed,' there was again a great burst of crying and sobbing all over the church. I wanted to break down dreadfully, but I held on and carried the hymn to the end. As we left the church, many people came up and squeezed my hand and tried to speak, but could not. Just then a splendid military band was passing, the like of which we had not heard in years. The great swell of its triumphant music seemed to mock the shabby broken spirited congregation defiling out of the gray old church buried in shadows, where in early Richmond days a theatre with many well-known citizens was burned! That was one of the tremendous moments of feeling I experienced that week.

—HARRISON, *Recollections Grave and Gay*

B: "The Poor Colored People Thanked God that Their Sufferings Were Ended"

Every moment the light we had seen over Richmond on starting became more and more brilliant. Above it hung great clouds of heavy smoke, and as we drew nearer there arose a confused murmur now swelling into a loud roar and then subsiding, and again swelling into a great tumult of excited voices, while at frequent intervals short, sharp explosions were heard as of the discharge of field artillery. Weary, breathless, hungry, begrimed with dust and perspiration, but eager and excited, we pushed on, and at half-past six o'clock in the morning I stood with about two-thirds of my men on the summit of a hill and looked down upon the grandest and most appalling sight that my eyes ever beheld. Richmond was literally a sea of flame, out of which the church steeples could be seen protruding here and there, while over all hung a canopy of dense black smoke, lighted up now and then by the bursting shells from the numerous arsenals scattered throughout the city. I waited here until the strag-

glers of my command had come up, then marched down the hill until we came to a little creek, crossed by a few planks which alone separated us from the city. Two mounted cavalry-men stood upon this bridge who said that they had been sent there by General Weitzel with orders to allow no one to cross the bridge until he came up. So there was nothing to do but to wait.

The men stacked arms and threw themselves upon the ground. While resting, a rebel iron-clad lying in the James River in full sight blew up with a terrific crash, scattering fragments of iron and timbers all about us, but fortunately no one was hurt. In a few moments more a carriage appeared coming from the city, and stopped directly before us. Beckoning me to approach, the occupant asked if I was in command of the men lying about, and on being answered in the affirmative, he said that he was the mayor of Richmond, and that he wished to make a formal surrender of the city. At the same time he placed in my hands a large package, containing, I presume, official papers, the city seal, keys and other property. I told him that General Weitzel, commanding the department, would be present in a short time and that he would be a proper person to treat with. Even while we were speaking the general and his staff appeared at the top of the hill, and the mayor rode forward to meet him. The whole party shortly returned, and General Weitzel ordered me to follow him into the city.

This I did, but we had not advanced many rods before the smoke became so thick as to make it impossible to see even a few feet in advance, and for this reason, I suppose, I missed the general, he turning to the right towards the upper part of the city, and I to the left towards the river. We had not gone far before I discovered that I had become separated from him and was uncertain how to proceed, when on a lamp-post at a corner I read the words, "Main Street." Thinking this would at least conduct us to the central part of the city and assist in finding the capitol grounds, I turned into it.

The scene that met our eyes here almost baffles description. Pandemonium reigned supreme.

Two large iron-clads near by in the river exploded with a deafening crash, the concussion sweeping numbers of people off their feet. The street we were in was one compact mass of frenzied people, and it was only with the greatest difficulty that we were able to force our way along. Had they been hostile our lives would not have been worth a moment's purchase.

But the poor colored people hailed our appearance with the most extravagant expression of joy. They crowded into the ranks and besought permission to carry the soldiers' knapsacks and muskets. They clapped them on the back, hung about their necks, and "God bless you," and "Thank God, the Yankees have come," resounded on every side. Women, emaciated, barefoot, with but one scanty skirt made from old bags, fell on their knees in the street, and with clasped hands and streaming eyes thanked God that their sufferings were ended at last. Others with little children, wretched little skeletons, clinging to their scanty skirts and crying with hunger and fright, pressed into the ranks and begged most piteously for food. One woman, I distinctly remember, with three little pale, starved girls clinging about her, herself barefoot, bareheaded, thinly and miserably clad, seized my arm with a vise-like grip, and begged for the love of God, for just a morsel for her starving children. They had tasted nothing since Sunday morning, and then only a spoonful of dry meal. I gave her the contents of my haversack, and one man in the ranks, a great, rough, swearing fellow, poured into her lap his entire three days' rations of pork and hard bread, thrust a ten dollar greenback, all the money he possessed, into her hand, swearing like a pirate all the while as a means of relief to his overcharged feelings, their intensity being abundantly evident by the tears which coursed rapidly down his cheeks. . .

The gutters literally ran whiskey. The members of the City Council, foreseeing the mischief that would ensue should the liquor shops be sacked, had rolled all the barrels to the curbstone, knocked in their heads, and emptied their contents into the gutters. The poisonous flood rolled like a river of death rapidly on into the sewers, while the atmosphere fairly reeked with its unsavory odor. The rougher element of the population, white and black alike, were dipping up the vile stuff with their hands, and pouring it down their throats. The shrill whistle of locomotives sounded loud and frequent in the near distance, as train after train hurried away bearing frantic citizens with what valuables they had time to secure. Bands of thieves and rascals of every degree, broken loose from the penitentiary, were entering the stores on either side the street and stealing whatever they could lay their hands upon, while the entire black population seemed out of doors and crazy with delight. Tumult, violence, riot, pillage, every where prevailed, and as if these were not enough to illustrate the horrors of war, the roar of the flames, the clanging of bells, and general uproar and confusion were sufficient to appal the stoutest heart.

Fearing violence from some unexpected source in the midst of such fearful scenes, I looked about for some avenue of escape into a less crowded street, where I could more easily keep the soldiers apart from the populace, but none presented itself. At length the heat became so great that we could proceed no further. Our hair and beards were scorched, our clothing smoked, the air we breathed was like a furnace blast, and many of the men, weighed down as they were with musket, knapsacks, blanket, ammunition, and other accoutrements, were well-nigh exhausted. Three fire engines were burning in the street immediately before us. On the sidewalk near by lay the bodies of three young girls burnt to a crisp. People jumped from the windows of burning buildings; others with wildly waving arms shrieked for help, not daring to take the fatal leap.

On a lamp-post just at my right, I read the words "Fourteenth Street," and turning to a citizen who stood in a porch on the corner, I asked him to direct me to the capitol.

"Turn right up here," he said, "go straight on for two or three streets, and you will see it just on your left." He also added that General Early, at the head of a body of Confederate cavalry, had passed along only a moment before, and with out-stretched hand showed us through the smoke the rearmost rank. . . .

The same tumultuous scenes just described were visible throughout the city. The spacious capitol grounds afforded the only spot of refuge, and these were crowded with women and children, bearing in their arms and upon their heads their most cherished possessions. Piles of furniture lay scattered in every direction, and about them clustered the hungry and destitute family groups, clinging to each other with the energy of despair. One of the most touching sights amid these accumulated horrors, was that of a little girl—a toddling infant—holding her kitten tightly under her arm, a dilapidated rag doll in one hand and grasping her mother's gown with the other, as they sought shelter from the showers of cinders, under the capitol steps.

The constant explosion of ammunition in the arsenals seemed almost like a battle. Many citizens were killed by the flying fragments. Many were burned to death. In one house seventeen people perished from the flames. The sick, the aged, helpless and infirm, left to themselves in the general panic, could only pray for deliverance, which came to them when the flames had stifled their prayers in death.

Seven hundred and fifty thousand loaded shells in the arsenals, exploding from the heat, tore their way through houses, ploughed up the streets and the gardens, and spread death and destruction on every hand. The whole city jarred and vibrated with horrid sounds, while warehouses, stores, mills, bridges, depots, and dwellings went down by scores and hundreds. The streets leading to the railroad stations were filled with a frantic mob, pushing, struggling, cursing, trampling each other without mercy in their efforts to get away with what plunder they could carry. No troops of either army were in sight, only rebel stragglers, whose long familiarity with similar scenes rendered them, no doubt, the only cool-headed and indifferent spectators of these appalling sights. Over and above all the terrible roar of the conflagration as it leaped from building to building, from street to street, filled the whole city with its scorching breath, and lent added horrors to the scene.

—PRESCOTT, "The Capture of Richmond"

C. "Night Came and with It Came Sorrow and Sadness."

April 2nd 1865. Today is the Sabbath and a very beautiful day it is. It is too beautiful for the impending evil that I felt hovering over us. Flory & I went to church . . . guards were stationed at the church taking up every body that had not a pass. When we came home there were great many rumors afloat, among those were the one which we often here about, Richmond being evacuated, but we did not believe it as usual.

Night came and with it came sorrow and sadness. Cousin Charlie came home and said he would have to go away that night. And then Cousin Willie came and he had to go in the morning. The time came for the sad parting—all was confusion within and without. . . . I retired with a heavy heart for two of my best loved cousins had gone. Perhaps we may never meet again on this earth where nothing but sorrow and sadness reign supreme.

April 3rd 1865. This morning I was awakened from my restless slumber by a loud explosion. I was scared half to death. I thought the Yankees had commenced to bombard the city & they would continue to do all day, but I soon found out . . . our troops were blowing up the magazine to keep the Yankees from getting it. . . . Richmond evacuated it, I cannot realize it. . . . All Cory St. is burnt and Maine is on fire, it is spreading rapidly: almost every minute Flory & I are running out to see if the Yankees are coming and if we see them we run as fast as our feet can carry us.

April 4th. All is very quiet today. The Yankees are behaving very well considering it is them. . . . I am just as restless as I can be. The negroes of Richmond are delighted. We have no school now and don't know when we will have any. . . . Old Abe has just gotten into the city, & they are firing salutes in honor of his arrival. . . . He first went to the president's house & after leaving, rode around to take a view of Richmond & then went back to the gunboat to stay all night. We have just gotten the evening whig [the local newspaper], it said "that there were from 600 to 800 houses burned". . . . The work of destruction went on until three or four o'clock, then the mastery of the flames were obtained and Richmond was saved from utter desolation. . . .

April 10, 1865. Last night heard cannonading and [they] said it was either for the capture of General Lee & His army or for Peace. This morning we heard it again. . . . I went round to Mrs. Hughes . . . and there I heard the dreadful news that General Lee had surrendered & then they told me that we were going to have Peace in a very short time. I was pleased but yet I was sad.

—Frances Caldern de la Barca Hunt

XXXIV.6

THE WHITE FLAG AT APPOMATTOX

On the night of April 2-3, Lee withdrew from Petersburg along the northern bank of the little Appomattox; at the same time Mahone abandoned his lines at Bermuda Hundred, and Ewell retreated from north of the James. The objective of Lee's army was Danville, where there were abundant supplies and from which he might yet hope to link up with Johnston; if he were cut off from Danville he hoped to make Lynchburg and the Valley. Grant, however, was hot in pursuit, Sheridan's cavalry in the lead. Lee planned to concentrate and provision his forces at Amelia Court House, some 30 miles west of Petersburg; when he got there, on April 4 and 5, however, he found no supplies, and a day was lost in for aging for provisions.

Meantime Sheridan's cavalry had reached Jetersville, west of Amelia Court House. Lee turned north, planning to swing around Sheridan and get to Farmville. Meade's infantry came up, however, and at Sayler's Creek inflicted a heavy defeat on the shattered Confederates. By the seventh Lee's army was reduced to two infantry and one cavalry corps, and had lost most of its wagon trains. This diminished force reached Farmville on that day, when it was once again required to fight. That night Lee resumed his retreat toward Lynchburg, but Sheridan raced ahead to Appomattox Court House and blocked his advance.

Already some of his officers were advising surrender, but Lee determined on one final try. He instructed Gordon to move against Sheridan; if he should find only cavalry he was to fight; if he found an army in front of him, he was to abandon the attempt to break through.

Early on the morning of the ninth the dauntless Gordon moved out to the attack. Only Sheridan's cavalry was in front of him, and he assailed it with fury; for a moment he was, miraculously, successful. Then, about 9 a.m. the Union V and XXIV Corps reached the battlefield, and Gordon with drew.

Already Grant had opened discussions looking to the surrender of the Army of Northern Virginia. With the failure of Gordon to break through, Lee was now ready to discuss surrender.

We give here Joshua Chamberlain's description of the fighting on the morning of the ninth, and the "white flag, earnestly borne, like a wraith of morning mist." Chamberlain we have met in the fighting at Fredericksburg and Gettysburg. A clergyman, and professor at Bowdoin College, he enlisted as lieutenant colonel in the 20th Maine, fought in over 20 engagements, was six times wounded, received the Congressional Medal of Honor for his gallantry, and in the Appomattox campaign commanded two brigades of the V Army Corps. After the war he served as Governor of Maine and President of Bowdoin College.

The darkest hours before the dawn of April 9, 1865, shrouded the Fifth Corps sunk in feverish sleep by the roadside six miles away from Appomattox Station on the Southside Road. Scarcely is the first broken dream begun when a cavalryman comes splashing down the road and vigorously dismounts, pulling from his jacket-front a crumpled note. The sentinel standing watch by his commander, worn in body but alert in every sense, touches your shoulder. "Orders, sir, I think." You rise on elbow, strike a match, and with smarting, streaming eyes read the brief, thrilling note, sent back by Sheridan to us infantry commanders. Like this, as I remember: "I have cut across the enemy at Appomattox Station, and captured three of his trains. If you can possibly push your infantry up here to-night, we will have great results in the morning."

Ah, sleep no more. The startling bugle notes ring out "The General"—"To the march." Word is sent for the men to take a bite of such as they have for food: the promised rations will not be up till noon, and by that time we shall be perhaps too far away for such greeting. A few try to eat, no matter what. Meanwhile, almost with one foot in the stirrup, you take from the hands of the black boy a tin plate of nondescript food and a dipper of miscalled coffee;—all equally black, like the night around. You eat and drink at a swallow; mount, and get to the head of the column before you shout the "Forward." They are there—the men: shivering to their senses as if risen out of the earth, but something in them not of it. Now sounds the "Forward," for the last time in our long drawn strife. And they move—these men—sleepless, supperless, breakfastless, sore-footed, stiffjointed, sense-benumbed, but with flushed faces pressing for the front.

By sunrise we have reached Appomattox Station, where Sheridan has left the captured trains. A staff officer is here to turn us square to the right, to the Appomattox River, cutting across Lee's retreat. Already we hear the sharp ring of the horse-artillery, answered ever and anon by heavier field guns; and drawing nearer, the crack of cavalry carbines; and unmistakably, too, the graver roll of musketry of opposing infantry. There is no mistake. Sheridan is square across the enemy's front, and with that glorious cavalry alone is holding at bay all that is left of the proudest army of the Confederacy. It has come at last,—the supreme hour. No thought of human wants or weakness now: all for the front; all for the flag, for the final stroke to make its meaning real—these men of the Potomac and the James, side by side, at the double in time and column, now one and now the other in the road or the fields beside. One striking feature I can never forget,—Birney's black men abreast with us, pressing forward to save the white man's country.

We did not know exactly what was going on. We did know that our cavalry had been doing splendid work all night, and in fact now was holding at bay Lee's whole remaining army. . . .

I was therefore in about the middle of our Fifth Corps column. The boom of the battle thickened ahead of us. We were intent for the front. Suddenly I am accosted by a cavalry officer dashing out of rough wood road leading off to our right. "General, you command this column?"

"Two brigades of it, sir; about half the First Division, Fifth Corps."

"Sir, General Sheridan wishes you to break off from this column and come to his support. The rebel infantry is pressing him hard. Our men are falling back. Don't wait for orders through the regular channels, but act on this at once."

Of course I obey, without question. . . .

Sharp work now. Pushing through the woods at cavalry speed, we come out right upon Sheridan's battle flag gleaming amidst the smoke of his batteries in the edge of the open field. Weird-looking flag it is: fork-tailed, red and white, the two bands that composed it each charged with a star of the contrasting color; two eyes sternly glaring through the cannon-cloud. Beneath it, that storm-center spirit, that form of condensed energies, mounted on the grim charger, Rienzi, that turned the battle of the Shenandoah,—both, rider and steed, of an unearthly shade of darkness, terrible to look upon, as-if masking some unknown powers.

Right before us, our cavalry, Devins' division, gallantly stemming the surges of the old Stonewall brigade, desperate to beat its way through. I ride straight to Sheridan. A dark smile and impetuous gesture are my old orders. Forward into double lines of battle, past Sheridan, his guns, his cavalry, and on for the quivering crest! For a moment it is a glorious sight: every arm of the service in full play,—cavalry, artillery, infantry; then a sudden shifting scene as the cavalry, disengaged by successive squadrons, rally under their bugle-calls with beautiful precision and promptitude, and sweep like a storm-cloud beyond our right to close in on the enemy's left and complete the fateful envelopment.

Ord's troops are now square across the Lynchburg Pike. Ayres and Bartlett have joined them on their right, and all are in for it sharp. In this new front we take up the battle. Gregory follows in on my left. It is a formidable front we make. The scene darkens. In a few minutes the tide is turned; the incoming wave is at flood; the barrier recedes. In truth, the Stonewall men hardly show their well-proved mettle. They seem astonished to see before them these familiar flags of their old

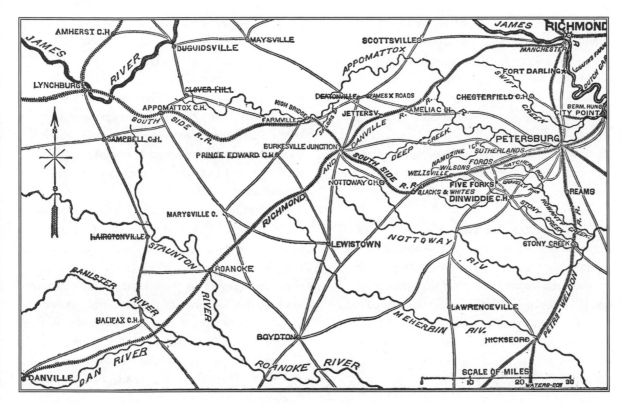

PETERSBURG TO APPOMATTOX

antagonists, not having thought it possible that we could match our cavalry and march around and across their pressing columns.

Their last hope is gone,—to break through our cavalry be fore our infantry can get up. Neither to Danville nor to Lynchburg can they cut their way; and close upon their rear, five miles away, are pressing the Second and Sixth Corps of the Army of the Potomac. It is the end! They are now giving way, but keep good front, by force of old habit. Halfway up the slope they make a stand, with what perhaps they think a good omen,—behind a stone wall. I try a little artillery on them, which directs their thoughts towards the crest behind them, and stiffen my lines for a rush, anxious for that crest myself. My intensity may have seemed like excitement. For Griffin comes up, quizzing me in his queer way of hitting off our weak points when we get a little too serious; accusing me of mistaking a blooming peach tree for a rebel flag, where I was dropping a few shells into a rallying crowd. I apologize—I was a lit-

tle near-sighted, and hadn't been experienced in long-range fighting. But as for peaches, I was going to get some if the pits didn't sit too hard on our stomachs. . . .

But now comes up Ord with a positive order: "Don't expose your lines on that crest. The enemy have massed their guns to give it a raking fire the moment you set foot there." I thought I saw a qualifying look as he turned away. But left alone, youth struggled with prudence. My troops were in a bad position down here. I did not like to be "the under dog." It was much better to be on top and at least know what there was beyond. So I thought of Grant and his permission to "push things" when we got them going; and of Sheridan and his last words as he rode away with his cavalry, smiting his hands together—"Now smash 'em, I tell you; smash 'em!" So we took this for orders, and on the crest we stood. One booming cannon-shot passed close along our front, and in the next moment all was still.

We had done it,—had "exposed ourselves to the view of the enemy." But it was an exposure that worked two ways. For there burst upon our vision a mighty scene, fit cadence of the story of tumultuous years. Encompassed by the cordon of steel that crowned the heights about the Court House, on the slopes of the valley formed by the sources of the Appomattox, lay the remnants of that far-famed counter part and companion of our own in momentous history,—the Army of Northern Virginia—Lee's army! . . .

It was hilly, broken ground, in effect a vast amphitheater, stretching a mile perhaps from crest to crest. On the several confronting slopes before us dusky masses of infantry suddenly resting in place; blocks of artillery, standing fast in a column or mechanically swung into park; clouds of cavalry small and great, slowly moving, in simple restlessness,—all without apparent attempt at offense or defence, or even military order.

In the hollow is the Appomattox,—which we had made the dead-line for our baffled foe, for its whole length, a hundred miles; here but a rivulet that might almost be stepped over dry-shod, and at the road crossing not thought worth while to bridge. Around its edges, now trodden to mire, swarms an indescribable crowd: worn-out soldier struggling to the front; demoralized citizen and denizen, white, black, and all shades between,—following Lee's army, or flying before these suddenly confronted terrible Yankees pictured to them as demon-shaped and bent; animals, too, of all forms and grades; vehicles of every description and non-description,—public and domestic, four-wheeled, or two, or one,—heading and moving in every direction, a swarming mass of chaotic confusion.

All this within sight of every eye on our bristling crest. Had one the heart to strike at beings so helpless, the Appomattox would quickly become a surpassing Red Sea horror. But the very spectacle brings every foot to an instinctive halt. We seem the possession of a dream. We are lost in a vision of human tragedy. But our light-twelve Napoleon guns come rattling up behind us to go into battery; we

catch the glitter of the cavalry blades and brasses beneath the oak groves away to our right, and the ominous closing in on the fated foe. . . .

Watching intently, my eye was caught by the figure of a horseman riding out between those lines, soon joined by an other, and taking a direction across the cavalry front towards our position. They were nearly a mile away, and I curiously watched them tilt lost from sight in the nearer broken ground and copses between.

Suddenly rose to sight another form, close in our own front,—a soldierly young figure, a Confederate staff officer undoubtedly. Now I see the white flag earnestly borne, and its possible purport sweeps before my inner vision like a wraith of morning mist. He comes steadily on, the mysterious form in gray, my mood so whimsicalty sensitive that I could even smile at the material of the flag,—wondering where in either army was found a towel, and one so white. But it bore a mighty message,—that simple emblem of homely service, wafted hitherward above the dark and crimsoned streams that never can wash themselves away.

The messenger draws near, dismounts; with graceful salutation and hardly suppressed emotion delivers his message: "Sir, I am from General Gordon. General Lee desires a cessation of hostilities until he can hear from General Grant as to the proposed surrender."

What word is this! so long so dearly fought for, so feverishly dreamed, but ever snatched away, held hidden and aloof; now smiting the senses with a dizzy flash! "Surrender?"

We had no rumor of this from the messages that had been passing between Grant and Lee, for now these two days, be hind us. "Surrender?" It takes a moment to gather one's speech. "Sir," I answer, "that matter exceeds my authority. I will send to my superior. General Lee is right. He can do no more." All this with a forced calmness, covering a tumult of heart and brain. I bid him wait a while, and the message goes up to my corps commander, General Griffin, leaving me mazed at the boding change.

Now from the right come foaming up in cavalry fashion the two forms I had watched from away beyond. A white flag again, held strong aloft, making straight for the little group beneath our battle-flag, high borne also,—the red Maltese cross on a field of white, that had thrilled hearts long ago. I see now that it is one of our cavalry staff in lead,—indeed I recognize him, Colonel Whitaker of Custer's staff; and, hardly keeping pace with him, a Confederate staff officer. Without dismounting, without salutation, the cavalryman shouts: "This is unconditional surrender! This is the end!" Then he hastily introduces his companion, and adds: "I am just from Gordon and Longstreet. Gordon says 'For God's sake, stop this infantry, or hell will be to pay!' I'll go to Sheridan," he adds, and dashes away with the white flag, leaving Longstreet's aide with me.

I was doubtful of my duty. The flag of truce was in, but I had no right to act upon it without orders. There was still some firing from various quarters, lulling a little where the white flag passed near. But I did not press things quite so hard. Just then a last cannon-shot from the edge of the town plunges through the breast of a gallant and dear young officer in my front line,—Lieutenant Clark, of the 185th New York,—the last man killed in the Army of the Potomac, if not the last in the Appomattox lines. Not a strange thing for war,—this swift stroke of the mortal; but coming after the truce was in, it seemed a cruel fate for one so deserving to share his country's joy, and a sad peace-offering for us all.

Shortly comes the order, in due form, to cease firing and to halt. There was not much firing to cease from; but "halt," then and there? It is beyond human power to stop the men, whose one word and thought and action through crimsoned years had been but forward. They had seen the flag of truce, and could divine its outcome. But the habit was too strong; they cared not for points of direction, it was forward still,—forward to the end; forward to the new beginning; forward to the Nation's second birth!

—CHAMBERLAIN, *The Passing of the Armies*

GENERAL LEE SURRENDERS AT APPOMATTOX

The story of the surrender needs no further introduction. As early as April 7 Grant had suggested to Lee the propriety of surrender, in order to avoid further bloodshed. Lee, as we have seen, was not yet ready to give up. But when he found his sadly decimated army surrounded, on the ninth, he knew that the end had come. "There is nothing left for me to do but go and see General Grant," said Lee, "and I would rather die a thousand deaths." But there was no alternative; that afternoon Lee rode Traveller to the McLean house in Appomattox Court House and accepted Grant's terms of surrender.

We give here Colonel Charles Marshall's account of the famous scene in the McLean house.

We struck up the hill towards Appomattox Court House. There was a man named McLean who used to live on the first battle field of Manassas, at a house about a mile from Manassas Junction. He didn't like the war, and having seen the first battle of Manassas, he thought he would get away where there wouldn't be any more fighting, so he moved down to Appomattox Court House. General Lee told me to go for ward and find a house where he could meet General Grant, and of all people, whom should I meet but McLean. I rode up to him and said, "Can you show me a house where General Lee and General Grant can meet together?" He took me into a house that was all dilapidated and that had no furniture in it. I told him it wouldn't do.

Then he said, "Maybe my house will do!" He lived in a very comfortable house, and I told him I thought that would suit. I had taken the orderly along with me, and I sent him back to General Lee and Babcock, who were coming on behind. I went into the house and sat down, and after a while General Lee and Babcock came in. Colonel Babcock told his orderly that he was to meet General Grant, who was coming on the road, and turn him in when he came along. So General Lee, Babcock and myself sat down in McLean's parlour and talked in the most friendly and affable way.

In about half an hour we heard horses, and the first thing I knew General Grant walked into the room. There were with him General Sheridan, General Ord, Colonel Badeau, General Porter, Colonel Parker, and quite a number of other officers whose names I do not recall.

General Lee was standing at the end of the room opposite the door when General Grant walked in. General Grant had on a sack coat, a loose fatigue coat, but he had no side arms. He looked as though he had had a pretty hard time. He had been riding and his clothes were somewhat dusty and a little soiled. He walked up to General Lee and Lee recognized him at once. He had known him in the Mexican war. General Grant greeted him in the most cordial manner, and talked about the weather and other things in a very friendly way. Then General Grant brought up his officers and introduced them to General Lee.

I remember that General Lee asked for General Lawrence Williams, of the Army of the Potomac. That very morning General Williams had sent word by somebody to General Lee that Custis Lee, who had been captured at Sailor Creek and was reported killed, was not hurt, and General Lee asked General Grant where General Williams was, and if he could not send for him to come and see him. General Grant sent somebody out for General Williams, and when he came, General Lee thanked him for having sent him word about the safety of his son.

After a very free talk General Lee said to General Grant: "General, I have come to meet you in accordance with my letter to you this morning, to treat about the surrender of my army, and I think the best way would be for you to put your terms in writing."

General Grant said: "Yes; I believe it will."

So a Colonel Parker, General Grant's Aide-de-Camp, brought a little table over from a corner of the room, and General Grant wrote the terms and conditions of surrender on what we call field note paper, that is, a paper that makes a copy at the same time as the note is written. After he had written it, he took it over to General Lee.

General Lee was sitting at the side of the room; he rose and went to meet General Grant to take that paper and read it over. When he came to the part in which only public property was to be surrendered, and the officers were to retain their side arms and personal baggage, General Lee said: "That will have a very happy effect."

General Lee then said to General Grant: "General, our cavalrymen furnish their own horses; they are not Government horses, some of them may be, but of course you will find them out—any property that is public property, you will ascertain that, but it is nearly all private property, and these men will want to plough ground and plant corn."

General Grant answered that as the terms were written, only the officers were permitted to take their private property, but almost immediately he added that he supposed that most of the men in the ranks were small farmers, and that the United States did not want their horses. He would give orders to allow every man who claimed to own a horse or mule to take the animal home.

General Lee having again said that this would have an excellent effect, once more looked over the letter, and being satisfied with it, told me to write a reply. General Grant told Colonel Parker to copy his letter, which was written in pencil, and put it in ink. Colonel Parker took the table and carried it back to a corner of the room, leaving General Grant and General Lee facing each other and talking together. There was no ink in McLean's inkstand, except some thick stuff that was very much like pitch, but I had a screw boxwood inkstand that I always carried with me in a little satchel that I had at my side, and I gave that to Colonel Parker, and he copied General Grant's letter with the aid of my inkstand and my pen.

There was another table right against the wall, and a sofa next to it. I was sitting on the arm of the sofa near the table, and General Sheridan was on the sofa next to me. While Colonel Parker was copying the letter, General Sheridan said to me, "This is very pretty country."

I said, "General, I haven't seen it by daylight. All my observations have been made by night and I haven't seen the country at all myself."

He laughed at my remark, and while we were talking I heard General Grant say this: "Sheridan, how many rations have you?"

General Sheridan said: "How many do you want?" and General Grant said, "General Lee has about a thousand or fifteen hundred of our people prisoners, and they are faring the same as his men, but he tells me his haven't anything. Can you send them some rations?"

"Yes," he answered They had gotten some of our rations, having captured a train.

General Grant said: "How many can you send?" and he replied "Twenty-five thousand rations."

General Grant asked if that would be enough, and General Lee replied "Plenty; plenty; an abundance;" and General Grant said to Sheridan "Order your commissary to send to the Confederate Commissary twenty-five thousand rations for our men and his men."

After a while Colonel Parker got through with his copy of General Grant's letter and I sat down to write a reply. I began it in the usual way: "I have the honor to acknowledge the receipt of your letter of such a date," and then went on to say the terms were satisfactory.

I took the letter over to General Lee, and he read it and said: "Don't say, 'I have the honor to acknowledge the receipt of your letter of such a date'; he is here; just say, 'I accept these terms.' "

Then I wrote:—

Headquarters of the Army of Northern
Virginia
April 9, 1865

I received your letter of this date containing the terms of the surrender of the Army of Northern Virginia proposed by you. As they are substantially the same as those expressed in your letter of the 8th instant, they are accepted. I will proceed to designate the proper officers to carry the stipulations into effect.

Then General Grant signed his letter, and I turned over my letter to General Lee and he signed it. Parker handed me General Grant's letter, and I handed him General Lee's reply, and the surrender was accomplished. There was no theatrical display about it. It was in itself perhaps the greatest tragedy that ever occurred in the history of the world, but it was the simplest, plainest, and most thoroughly devoid of any attempt at effect, that you can imagine.

The story of General Grant returning General Lee's sword to him is absurd, because General Grant proposed in his letter that the officers of the Confederate Army should retain their side-arms. Why, in the name of common sense, any body should imagine that General Lee, after receiving a letter which said that he should retain his side-arms, yet should offer to surrender his sword to General Grant, is hard to understand. The only thing of the kind that occurred in the whole course of the transaction—which occupied perhaps an hour—was this: General Lee was in full uniform. He had on the handsomest uniform I ever saw him wear; and he had on a sword with a gold, a very handsome gold and leather, scabbard that had been presented to him by English ladies. General Grant excused himself to General Lee towards the close of the conversation between them, for not having his side arms with him; he told him that when he got his letter he was about four miles from his wagon in which his arms and uniform were, and he said that he had thought that General Lee would rather receive him as he was, than be detained, while he sent back to get his sword and uniform. General Lee told him he was very much obliged to him and was very glad indeed that he hadn't done it.

—Sir FREDERICK MAURICE, ed., *An Aide-de-Camp of Lee*

XXXIV.8

"The Whole Column Seemed Crowned with Red"

The day after the surrender Grant rode over to Lee's headquarters to discuss with him the formalities of surrender; later that day Meade rode over to pay his respects. Already the leaders of the grand armies were binding up the wounds of war, taking the road to reunion. Formal surrender was arranged for the twelfth, and General Chamberlain was designated to receive it on behalf of Grant. Grant, Meade, and Sheridan had all left Appomattox by that day, but Lee stayed on to the bitter end, though he did not witness the actual stacking of arms.

The description of that ceremony comes, appropriately enough, from Chamberlain himself.

It was now the morning of the 12th of April. I had been ordered to have my lines formed for the ceremony at sunrise. It was a chill gray morning, depressing to the senses. . . . We formed along the principal street, from the bluff bank of the stream to near the Court House on the left,—to face the last line of battle, and receive the last remnant of the arms and colors of that great army which ours had been created to confront for all that death can do for life. . . .

Our earnest eyes scan the busy groups on the opposite slopes, breaking camp for the last time, taking down their little shelter-tents and folding them carefully as precious things, then slowly forming ranks as for unwelcome duty. And now they move. The dusky swarms forge forward into gray columns of march. On they come, with the old swinging route step and swaying battle-flags. In the van, the proud Confederate ensign—the great field of white with canton of star-strewn cross of blue on a field of red, the regimental battle-flags with the same escutcheon following on, crowded so thick, by thinning out of men, that the whole column seemed crowned with red. At the right of our line our little group mounted beneath our flags, the red Maltese cross on a field of white, erewhile so bravely borne through many a field more crimson than itself, its mystic meaning now ruling all.

The momentous meaning of this occasion impressed me deeply. I resolved to mark it by some token of recognition, which could be no other than a salute of arms. Well aware of the responsibility assumed, and of the criticisms that would follow, as the sequel proved, nothing of that kind could move me in the least. The act could be defended, if needful, by the suggestion that such a salute was not to the cause for which the flag of the Confederacy stood, but to its going down before the flag of the Union. My main reason, however, was one for which I sought no authority nor asked forgiveness. Before us in proud humiliation stood the embodiment of manhood: men whom neither toils and sufferings, nor the fact of death, nor disaster, nor hopelessness could bend from their resolve; standing, before us now, thin, worn, and famished, but erect, and with eyes looking level into ours, waking memories that bound us together as no other bond,—was not such manhood to be welcomed back into a Union so tested and assured?

Instruction had been given; and when the head of each division column comes opposite our group, our bugle sounds the signal and instantly our whole line from right to left, regiment by regiment in succession, gives the soldier's salutation, from the "order arms" to the old "carry"—the marching salute. Gordon at the head of the column, riding with heavy spirit and downcast face, catches the sound of shifting arms, looks up, and, taking the meaning, wheels superbly, making with himself and his horse one uplifted figure, with profound salutation as he drops the point of his sword to the boot toe; then facing to his own command, gives word for his successive brigades to pass us with the same position of the manual,—honor answering honor. On our part not a sound of trumpet more, nor roll of drum; not a cheer, nor word nor whisper of vainglorying, nor motion of man standing again at the order, but an awed stillness rather, and breath-holding, as if it were the passing of the dead!

As each successive division masks our own, it halts, the men face inward toward us across the road, twelve feet away; then carefully "dress" their line, each captain taking pains for the good appearance of his company, worn and half starved as they were. The field and staff take their positions in the intervals of regiments; generals in rear of their commands. They fix bayonets, stack arms; then, hesitatingly, remove cartridge boxes and lay them down. Lastly,—reluctantly, with agony of expression,—they tenderly fold their flags, battle-worn and torn, blood-stained, heart-holding colors, and lay them down; some frenziedly rushing from the ranks, kneeling over them, clinging to them, pressing them to their lips with burning tears. And only the Flag of the Union greets the sky!

What visions thronged as we looked into each other's eyes! Here pass the men of Antietam, the Bloody Lane, the Sunken Road, the Cornfield, the Burnside-Bridge; the men whom Stonewall Jackson on the second night at Fredericksburg begged Lee to let him take and crush the two corps of the Army of the Potomac huddled in the streets in darkness and confusion; the men who swept away the Eleventh Corps at Chancellorsville; who left six thousand of their companions around the bases of Culp's and Cemetery Hills at Gettysburg; these survivors of the terrible Wilderness, the Bloody-Angle at Spottsylvania, the slaughter pen of Cold Harbor, the whirl pool of Bethesda Church!

Here comes Cobb's Georgia Legion, which held the stone wall on Marye's Heights at Fredericksburg, close before which we piled our dead for breastworks so that the living might stay and live.

Here too come Gordon's Georgians and Hoke's North Carolinians, who stood before the terrific mine explosion at Petersburg, and advancing retook the smoking crater and the dismal heaps of dead—ours more than theirs—huddled in the ghastly chasm.

Here are the men of McGowan, Hunton, and Scales, who broke the Fifth Corps lines on the White Oak Road, and were so desperately driven back on that forlorn night of March 31st by my thrice-decimated brigade.

Now comes Anderson's Fourth Corps, only Bushrod Johnson's Division left, and this the remnant of those we fought so fiercely on the Quaker Road two weeks ago, with Wise's Legion, too fierce for its own good.

Here passes the proud remnant of Ransom's North Carolinians which we swept through Five Forks ten days ago,—and all the little that was left of this division in the sharp passages at Sailor's Creek five days thereafter.

Now makes its last front A. P. Hill's old Corps, Heth now at the head, since Hill had gone too far forward ever to return: the men who poured destruction into our division at Shepardstown Ford, Antietam, in 1862, when Hill reported the Potomac running blue with our bodies; the men who opened the desperate first day's fight at Gettysburg, where with standing them so stubbornly our Robinson's Brigades lost 1185 men, and the Iron Brigade alone 1153,—these men of Heth's Division here too losing 2850 men, companions of these now looking into our faces so differently.

What is this but the remnant of Mahone's Division, last seen by us at the North Anna? its thinned ranks of worn, bright-eyed men recalling scenes of costly valor and ever remembered history.

Now the sad great pageant—Longstreet and his men! What shall we give them for greeting that has not already been spoken in volleys of thunder and written in lines of fire on all the river-banks of Virginia? Shall we go back to Gaines' Mill and Malvern Hill? Or to the Antietam of Maryland, or Gettysburg of Pennsylvania?—deepest graven of all. For here is what remains of Kershaw's Division, which left 40 per cent. of its men at Antietam, and at Gettysburg with Barksdale's and Semmes' Brigades tore through the Peach Orchard, rolling up the right of our gallant Third Corps, sweeping over the proud batteries of Massachusetts—Bigelow and Philips,—where under the smoke we saw the earth brown and blue with prostrate bodies of horses and men, and the tongues of overturned cannon and caissons pointing grim and stark in the air.

Then in the Wilderness, at Spottsylvania and thereafter, Kershaw's Division again, in deeds of awful glory, held their name and fame, until fate met them at Sailor's Creek, where Kershaw himself, and Ewell, and so many more, gave up their arms and hopes,—all, indeed, but manhood's honor.

With what strange emotion I look into these faces before which in the mad assault on Rives' Salient, June 18, 1864, I was left for dead under their eyes! It is by miracles we have lived to see this day,—any of us standing here.

Now comes the sinewy remnant of fierce Hood's Division, which at Gettysburg we saw pouring through the Devil's Den, and the Plum Run gorge; turning again by the left our stubborn Third Corps, then swarming up the rocky bastions of Round Top, to be met there by equal valor, which changed Lee's whole plan of battle and perhaps the story of Gettysburg.

Ah, is this Pickett's Division?—this little group left of those who on the lurid last day of Gettysburg breasted level cross fire and thunderbolts of storm, to be strewn back drifting wrecks, where after that awful, futile, pitiful charge we buried them in graves a furlong wide, with name unknown!

Met again in the terrible cyclone-sweep over the breast works at Five Forks; met now, so thin, so pale, purged of the mortal,—as if knowing pain or joy no more. How could we help falling on our knees, all of us together, and praying God to pity and forgive us all!

—CHAMBERLAIN, *The Passing of the Armies*

XXXIV.9

THE LAST WILL AND TESTAMENT OF J. REB

For the defeated Confederacy, the Union victory was a bitter pill. Four years of sacrifice and gallantry seemed pointless. Like veterans of all war, the men who fought it had been transformed by the experience. Civilians who had enlisted as boys left the army as men marked by the trauma of combat. In contrast to the North, Southern soldiers could not find solace in the triumph of their cause.

John Sergeant Wise was a teenage lieutenant in the defeated Confederate army. Upon Lee's surrender, he returned to Richmond by train, he recalled many years later in his book *The End of an Era*. One sympathetic Union soldier insisted on slipping him some money.

Relatives provided Wise with a home and new clothes. "When I looked in the glass," he wrote, "instead of confronting a striking young officer, I beheld a mere insignificant bit of an eighteen-year-old boy. I had received a great setback in manhood." He composed the following will the next day for his former self—a strapping Rebel officer.

I, J. Reb, being of unsound mind and bitter memory, and aware that I am dead, do make public and declare the following to be my political last will and testament.

I give, device, and bequeath all my slaves to Harriet Beecher Stowe.

I direct that all my shares in the venture of secession shall be cancelled, provided I am released from my unpaid subscription to the stock of said enterprise.

My interest in the civil government of the Confederacy I bequeath to any freak museum that may hereafter be established.

My sword, my veneration for General Robert E. Lee, his subordinate commanders and his peerless soldiers, and my undying love for my old comrades, living and dead, I set apart as the best I have, or shall ever have to bequeath to my heirs forever.

And now, being dead, having experienced a death to Confederate ideas and anew birth unto allegiance to the Union, I depart, with a vague but not definite hope of joyful resurrection, and of a new life, upon lines somewhat different from those of the last eighteen years. I see what has been pulled down very clearly. What is to be built up in its place I know not. It is a mystery; but death is always mysterious. AMEN.

—JOHN WISE

XXXIV.10

THE STARS AND STRIPES ARE RAISED OVER FORT SUMTER

When the Confederate forces evacuated Charleston in February 1865, and Union troops entered, the first thought of the captors was to hold a ceremonial reraising of the flag over the fort. The event was set for April 14, the anniversary of the surrender four years before, and the flag was hoisted by Robert Anderson, who was in command in 1861.

This moving scene is described by Mary Cadwalader Jones, daughter of a well-known Philadelphia attorney, and granddaughter of Horace Binney.

On March 18, 1865, Edwin M. Stanton, Lincoln's last Secretary of War, wrote to brevet Major General Robert Anderson:

"I have the pleasure of communicating to you the inclosed order of the President, directing the flag of the United States to be raised and planted upon the ruins of Fort Sumter by your hands, on the 14th day of April next, the fourth anniversary of the evacuation of that post by the United States forces under your command."

It was my good fortune to be there. . . .

Sailing from New York in the end of February, 1865, we landed at Hilton Head and reached Charleston by way of Savannah in the last days of March or beginning of April. To one who had never seen the actual effects of war, the city was a melancholy spectacle. Our bombardment had left its marks everywhere, even on church steeples and on gravestones in the cemeteries. One heavy Parrott gun, called by our men the "Swamp Angel" which had been planted in a marsh five miles inland, did a great deal of damage before she burst, and was looked upon by the Charlestonians with a mixture of wrath and amazement.

Every one who could possibly get away had left the city before our troops entered it; the streets were deserted except for our sentries, strolling soldiers and sailors, and bands of Negroes who had floated down on flatboats from distant plantations, many of them never having seen a large town

before in their lives. Almost without exception the house and body servants had stuck to their masters and mistresses; these were field hands, and they gaped and laughed like careless children. As their new freedom did not feed them, they lived chiefly on the good-natured charity of our troops and at night camped in the empty cotton warehouses, with the natural result of frequent fires.

Heavy cloth-of-gold roses hung over garden walls and on the porches of closely-shuttered houses; occasionally an old servant would creep furtively from a back door; but there was no sign of ordinary everyday life—the men were all at the war and the women and children either away or in hiding. It had been different in the less aristocratic Savannah, which the Federal troops had occupied since December; when I walked about there, always with an officer or an orderly, the girls would run up their high steps and turn their backs sharply on the hated blue uniform, but if I looked round quickly after I had gone a little farther I usually caught them gazing eagerly at the back of my frock. Fashions were four years old in the Confederacy; it was worth while to run the blockade for rifles or quinine, but not for furbelows. Charleston was, however, too proud and too sad to care about fashions.

The ceremony was to be at noon punctually; four or five thousand people wanted to go, and there was no regular communication between Sumter and the town. The big visiting steamship ferried her own passengers, and the boats belonging to the blockading squadron plied busily to and fro, as temporary landings and steps had been put up on all sides of the fort walls. The entire management was in the hands of the Navy, and everything went like clockwork.

The ceremony began with a short prayer by the old army chaplain who had prayed when the flag was hoisted over Fort Sumter on December 27, 1860. Next a Brooklyn clergyman read parts of several Psalms, expecting the company to read alternate verses, as in church; but that was not very effective, because if any copies were printed, there were not enough of them to go round. Then

Sergeant Hart, who had held up the flag when its staff was shot through in the first attack, came forward quietly and drew the selfsame flag out of an ordinary leather mail bag. We all held our breath for a second, and then we gave a queer cry, between a cheer and a yell; nobody started and nobody led it; I never heard anything like it before or since, but I can hear it now. It stopped suddenly, for we saw that a couple of the sailors who had been in the first fight were fastening the flag to its new halyards with a little wreath of laurel on top. General Anderson stood up, bareheaded, took the halyards in his hands, and began to speak. At first I could not hear him, for his voice came thickly, but in a moment he said clearly, "I thank God that I have lived to see this day," and after a few more words he began to hoist the flag It went up slowly and hung limp against the staff, a weather-beaten, frayed, and shell-torn old flag, not fit for much more work, but when it had crept clear of the shelter of the walls a sudden breath of wind caught it, and it shook its folds and flew straight out above us, while every soldier and sailor instinctively saluted.

I don't know just what we did next, but I remember looking on either side of me and seeing my father's eyelids brimming over and that Admiral Dahlgren's lips were trembling. I think we stood up, somebody started "The Star-Spangled Banner," and we sang the first verse, which is all that most people know. But it did not make much difference, for a great gun was fired close to us from the fort itself, followed, in obedience to the President's order, "by a national salute from every fort and battery that fired upon Fort Sumter." The measured, solemn booming came from Port Moultrie, from the batteries on Sullivan and Folly Islands, and from Fort Wagner. . . . When the forts were done it was the turn of the fleet, and all our warships from the largest—which would look tiny today—down to the smallest monitor, fired and fired in regular order until the air was thick and black with smoke and one's ears ached with the overlapping vibrations.

—JONES, *Lantern Slides*

XXXIV.11

"BOW DOWN, DEAR LAND, FOR THOU HAST FOUND RELEASE"

In July 1865 Harvard College held commemoration services for Harvard men who had given their lives to the preservation of the Union. Altogether 138 Harvard men had been killed, or died, in the Union armies and 64 in the Confederate armies. James Russell Lowell, then a Professor at Harvard College, was called on to write an appropriate ode. "The ode itself," he said later, "was an improvisation . . . the whole thing came out of me with a rush." It is, by common consent, the finest of Lowell's poems, and probably the most noble and moving poem to come out of the Civil War.

> . . . Bow down, dear Land, for thou hast found
>   release!
>   Thy God, in these distempered days,
>   Hath taught thee the sure wisdom of His ways,
> And through thine enemies hath wrought thy
>   peace!
>   Bow down in prayer and praise!
> No poorest in thy borders but may now
> Lift to the juster skies a man's enfranchised brow.
> O Beautiful! my Country! ours once more!
> Smoothing thy gold of war-dishevelled hair
> O'er such sweet brows as never other wore,
>   And letting thy set lips,
>   Freed from wrath's pale eclipse,
> The rosy edges of their smile lay bare,
> What words divine of lover or of poet
> Could tell our love and make thee know it,
> Among the Nations bright beyond compare?
>   What were our lives without thee?
>   What all our lives to save thee?
>   We reck not what we gave thee;
>   We will not dare to doubt thee,
> But ask whatever else, and we will dare!

—JAMES RUSSELL LOWELL, "Ode Recited at the Harvard Commemoration," July 31, 1865

APPENDIX A

RECONSTRUCTING THE NATION

When the shooting stopped on the battlefield, many of the most bitterly contested issues that had led to the Civil War remained in dispute. Union armies had prevented the Confederate states from seceding, but military might alone could not resolve the deep societal differences that had led to the schism that existed between North and South.

The terms under which the United States integrated the South back into the Union helped determine the long-term impact of the Civil War. Reconstruction was a long, difficult struggle that embraced a wide spectrum of issues—land, labor, education, civil rights and more. Real changes took place, and some of those changes met stiff resistance.

"Reconstruction" is the term applied to what happened after the Civil War. But other labels might have been "Restoration" or even "Revolution." Would what came to be known as Reconstruction amount to no more than an edict that simply restored the states back into the Union? Or would it be a more involved process that implied a broader reshaping of the South? Or, further still, would it be a fundamental transformation of Southern society writ large, as some radical Republicans sought?

The debate over Reconstruction began during the war. As early as December 1863, Lincoln issued a Proclamation of Amnesty and Reconstruction, offering a full pardon and restoration of property (except for slaves) for those engaged in the rebellion by simply swearing loyalty to the Union. Any state where 10 percent of the population who voted in the 1860 election made this pledge could return to the Union. It was a moderate approach aimed at rewarding Southern Unionists who remained loyal to the federal government.

Congress, however, wanted to go much further. On July 2, 1864, Congress passed the Wade-Davis Bill, requiring much stricter requirements for readmittance to the Union. The legisla-tion required that half a rebellious state's population swear that they did not support secession (a very difficult threshold to accomplish in 1864), and it called for legal safeguards for freed slaves. Lincoln issued a pocket veto and the bill expired. But the parameters of the debate for a reconstituted Union were set, with a moderate approach under the authority of the government's executive branch on one side, and a radical revolution directed by the legislative branch on the other.

After the election of 1864, Lincoln signaled a shift in his position, favoring a limited enfranchisement of African Americans but relatively generous terms of amnesty. When Lincoln was assassinated, however, Andrew Johnson became the president. After Lincoln's first term, Johnson had been selected as Lincoln's vice-presidential running-mate for the 1864 election in order to broaden Lincoln's appeal to Southern Unionists. Johnson was a Unionist from Tennessee who represented the non-slaveholding Southern yeoman class. But while he despised the slaveholding Southern aristocracy, his policies demonstrated little concern for the rights of African Americans.

Reconstruction is often divided into two periods: Presidential Reconstruction from 1865 to 1867, and Congressional Reconstruction from 1867 to 1877. Johnson out-lined his approach in May 1865. He offered a pardon to all south-ern whites, with the exception of planters with 20 slaves or more. These planters could get an individual pardon if they applied for one. Johnson supported the restitution of all property to Southerners, but this excluded slaves. He called for state con-ventions to reconstitute state governments. No requirements were placed on the conventions, other than they free the slaves and repudiate secession. None of the conventions dealt with the issue of black suffrage or the rights of freed slaves. In fact, some of the new state governments passed "black codes" that effectively reimposed a slavelike status on African Americans. Johnson then announced that Reconstruction was complete.

But Congress did not agree. Dominated by radical Republicans, Congress refused to acknowledge the legitimacy of the new state governments. Johnson and Congress were in constant conflict. Johnson vetoed the Freedmen's Bill and various civil rights bills. This discord was one of the reasons Congress pushed so hard to pass the Fourteenth Amendment. Republicans wanted to remove the issue of "equality before the law" from the realm of politics and into the Constitution as a basic right.

In 1867, Congress passed the Reconstruction Act, overriding a veto by Johnson. It nullified the existing governments in the South, called for new governments, created five military districts, and barred Confederates from holding office. The way was paved for Republicans and former slaves to get involved in the Reconstruction of the South. The battles with Johnson continued, culminating with an 11-week impeachment trial that fell one vote short of ousting Johnson.

Despite the Republicans' sweeping Reconstruction legislation, the impeachment of Johnson and the election of President Ulysses S. Grant, the effort to revolutionize Southern society fell apart very quickly. By 1870, many of the former Confederate states had been readmitted into the Union but were under the control of conservative Democrats. In 1876, only South Carolina, Louisiana and Florida were still under Republican control. Once Democrats regained control of their states, they reversed Republican efforts to strengthen schools and protect civil rights for freed slaves.

Several things contributed to the Republican collapse. Some of the most important and strident Republican leaders died—Thaddeus Stevens in 1868 and Charles Sumner in 1874—and the new generation of leaders did not share their radical vision. Scandal after scandal in the Grant administration undermined Republican credibility. Instead of being saviors of the nation, Republican politicians were seen as self-serving and corrupt. Economic depression, triggered by the Panic of 1873, put 3 million people out of work. Northern citizens simply lost interest in righting the South's wrongs. A new ethos emerged of putting the issues of the war behind the nation. Disillusionment had set in and there was a desire for sectional reconciliation and harmony.

With the election of 1876, a deal was struck in the presidential race. The Democrats agreed to let the Republican Rutherford B. Hayes become president on the condition that federal troops be removed from the South. The agreement ended Reconstruction. Many of the issues, particularly those regarding civil rights, remained unresolved.

The historical treatment of Reconstruction has gone through different interpretations. For decades a Southern interpretation dominated. It was perhaps best exemplified by the D. W. Griffith film The Birth of a Nation. Republican Reconstruction figures were portrayed as corrupt; African Americans as unready for freedom and childlike; and the Ku Klux Klan as protectors of Southern womanhood.

This oversimplified and one-sided perspective contained elements of truth, but it overlooked the commitment the nation had made to the protection of equal rights and due process. That commitment would serve as the basis of the Civil Rights movement of the 1950s and '60s. The nation had been consolidated into a centralized, expansive industrial state. The Civil War and Reconstruction brought experiences and meaning to the ideals of freedom, democracy and liberty, even if they also sometimes reflected the underside of intolerance, inequality and violence toward those outside one's own community.

APPENDIX A.I
THE DESTRUCTION OF THE SOUTH

At the conclusion of the Civil War much of the South was in a state of ruin and confusion: cities were devastated, towns sacked, fields lay fallow, and the economy in shambles. Thousands of people died of starvation. For millions of people, the main goal in the immediate months after the war was survival. With buildings destroyed, railroads ripped out of the ground, farms plundered and bridges demolished, no capital to reinvest in the economy and its labor system turned on its head, Southerners were confronted with a future gloomier than any Americans had ever before faced on such a large scale .

Myrta Lockett Avary recalled how even the wealthiest and most prestigious Southerners had become destitute. Sidney Andrews was a New England journalist who visited the Carolinas and Georgia shortly after the war. He wrote articles about what he found for newspapers in Boston and Chicago. In the South the post-Civil War years would be hard ones dedicated to rebuilding a demolished economy and healing a wounded society.

A. "Prominent Citizens Became Piesellers"

We did anything and everything we could to make a living. Prominent citizens became piesellers. Colonel Cary, of General Magruder's staff, came home to find his family desperately poor, as were all respectable folks. He was a brave soldier, an able officer—before the war, principal of a male academy at Hampton. Now he did not know to what he could turn his hand for the support of himself and family. He walked around his place, came in, and said to his wife: "My dear, I have taken stock of our assets. You pride yourself on your apple pies. We have an apple tree and a cow. I will gather the apples and milk the cow, and you will make the pies, and I will go around and sell them."

Armed with pies, he met his aforetime antagonists at Camp Grant and conquered them quite. The pies were delicious; the seller was a soldier, an officer of distinction, in hard luck; and the men at Camp Grant were soldiers too. There was sharp demand and good prices; only the elite—officers of rank—could afford to indulge in these confections. Well it was that Yankee mothers had cultivated in their sons an appetite for pies. One Savannah lady made thirty dollars selling pies to Sherman's soldiers; in Georgia's aristocratic "city by the sea" highbred dames stood at basement windows selling cakes and pies to whoever would buy.

Colonel Cary had thrifty rivals throughout Dixie. A once-rich Planter near Columbia made a living by selling flowers; a Charleston aristocrat peddled tea by the pound and molasses by the quart to his former slaves. General Stephen Elliott sold fish and oysters which he caught with his own hands. His friend, Captain Stoney, did likewise. Gentlemen of position and formerly of wealth did not pause to consider whether they would be discredited by pursuing occupations quite as humble. Men of high attainments, without capital, without any basis upon which to make a new start in life except "grit," did whatever they could find to do and made merry over it.

For months after the surrender, Confederates were passing through the country to their homes, and hospitality was free to every ragged and footsore soldier; the poor best the larder of every mansion afforded was at the command of the grayjacket. How diffidently proud men would ask for bread, their empty pockets shaming them! When any man turned them off with cold words, it was not well for his neighbors to know; for so he was like to have no more respectable guests. The soldiers were good

company, bringing news from far and wide. Most were cheerful, glad they were going home, undaunted by long tramps ahead. The soldier was used to hard marches. Now that his course was set toward where loved ones watched for his coming, life had its rosy outlook that turned to gray for some who reached the spot where home had stood to find only a bank of ashes. Reports of country through which they came were often summed up: "White folks in the fields, Negroes flocking to towns. Freedmen's Bureau offices everywhere thronged with blacks."

A man who belonged to the crippled squad, not one of whom had a full complement of arms and legs, told this story: As four of them were limping along near Lexington, they noticed a gray-headed white man in rough, mud-stained clothes turning furrows with a plow and behind him a white girl dropping corn. Taking him for a hired man, they hallooed: "Hello, there!" The man raised his head. "Say," they called, "can you tell us where we can get something to eat?" He waved them towards a house where a lady who was on the porch asked them to have a seat and wait while she had food cooked.

They had an idea that she prepared with her own hands the dinner to which they presently sat down, of hot hoecakes, buttermilk, and a little meat so smothered in lettuce leaves that it looked a great deal. When they had cleared up the table, she said: "I am having more bread cooked if you can wait a few minutes. I am sorry we have not more meat and milk. I know this has been a very light repast for hungry men, but we have entertained others this morning, and we have not much left. We hate to send our soldiers hungry from the door; they ought to have the best of everything when they have fought so long and bravely and suffered so much." The way she spoke made them proud of the arms and legs they didn't have.

Now that hunger was somewhat appeased, they began to note surroundings. The dwelling was that of a military man, and a man of piety and culture. A lad running in addressed the lady as Mrs.

Pendleton and said something about "where General Pendleton is plowing."

They stumbled to their crutches! and in blushing confusion humble apologies, all the instincts of the soldier shocked at the liberties they had taken with an officer of such high grade and at the ease of manner with which they had sat at his table to be served by his wife. They knew their host for William Nelson Pendleton, late brigadier general, C.S.A., chief of artillery of the Army of Northern Virginia, a fighting preacher. She smiled when they blundered out the excuse that they had mistaken him for a day laborer.

"The mistake has been made before," she said. "Indeed, the General is a day laborer in his own field, and it does not mortify him in the least now that all our people have to work. He is thankful his strength is sufficient, and for the help that the schoolboys and his daughters give him." She put bread into their haversacks and sent them on their way rejoicing. The day laborer and his plow were close to the roadside, and as they passed, they drew themselves up in line and brought all the hands they had to their ragged caps in salute.

Doctor Robert G. Stephens, of Atlanta, tells me of a Confederate soldier who, returning armless to his Georgia home, made his wife hitch him to a plow which she drove; and they made a crop. A Northern missionary said in 1867, to a Philadelphia audience, that he had seen in North Carolina a white mother hitch herself to a plow which her eleven-year-old son drove, while another child dropped into the furrows seeds Northern charity had given.

—Myrta Lockett Avary, *Dixie After the War*

B. "In the Heart of Destruction"

Columbia, S. C., September 12, 1865—Columbia is in the heart of Destruction. Being outside of it, you can only get in through one of the roads built by Ruin. Being in it, you can only get out over one of the roads walled by Desolation. You go north thirty-two miles and find the end of one railroad; southeast thirty miles and find the end of another; south forty-five miles and find the end of a third;

southwest fifty miles and meet a fourth; and northwest twenty-nine miles and find the end of still another. Sherman came in here, the papers used to say, to break up the railroad system of the seaboard states of the Confederacy. He did his work so thoroughly that half a dozen years will nothing more than begin to repair the damage, even in this regard.

Certain bent rails are the first thing one sees to indicate the advent of his army. They are at Branchville. I looked at them with curious interest. "It passes my comprehension to tell what became of our railroads," said a traveling acquaintance; "one week we had passably good roads, on which we could reach almost any part of the state, and the next week they were all gone,—not simply broken up, but gone; some of the material was burned, I know, but miles and miles of iron have actually disappeared, gone out of existence." Branchville, as I have already said, was flanked, and the army did not take it in the line of march, but some of the boys paid a visit.

At Orangeburg there is ample proof that the army passed that way. About one third of the town was burned. I found much dispute as to the origin of the fire; and while certain fellows of the baser sort loudly assert that it was the work of the Yankee, others of the better class express the belief that it originated with a resident who was angry at the Confederate officers. Thereabouts one finds plenty of railroad iron so bent and twisted that it can never again be used. The genius which our soldiers displayed in destroying railroads seems remarkable. How effectually they did it, when they undertook the work in earnest, no pen can make plain. "We could do something in that line, we thought," said an ex-Confederate captain, "but we were ashamed of ourselves when we saw how your men could do it."

We rode over the road where the army marched. Now and then we found solitary chimneys, but on the whole comparatively few houses were burned, and some of those were fired, it is believed, by persons from the Rebel army or from the neighboring locality. The fences did not escape so well, and most of the planters have had these to build during the summer. This was particularly the case near Columbia. Scarcely a tenth of that destroyed appears to have been rebuilt, and thousands of acres of land of much richness lie open as a common.

There is a great scarcity of stock of all kinds. What was left by the Rebel conscription officers was freely appropriated by Sherman's army, and the people really find considerable difficulty, not less in living than in traveling. Milk, formerly an article much in use, can only be had now in limited quantities; even at the hotels we have more meals without than with it. There are more mules than horses, apparently; and the animals whether mules or horses, are all in ill condition and give evidence of severe overwork.

Columbia was doubtless once the gem of the state. It is as regularly laid out as a checkerboard—the squares being of uniform length and breadth and the streets of uniform width. What with its broad streets, beautiful shade trees, handsome lawns, extensive gardens, luxuriant shrubbery, and wealth of flowers, I can easily see that it must have been a delightful place of residence. No South Carolinian with whom I have spoken hesitates an instant in declaring that it was the most beautiful city on the continent; and, as already mentioned, they charge its destruction directly to General Sherman.

It is now a wilderness of ruins. Its heart is but a mass of blackened chimneys and crumbling walls. Two thirds of the buildings in the place were burned, including, without exception, everything in the business portion. Not a store, office, or shop escaped; and for a distance of three fourths of a mile on each of twelve streets there was not a building left. . . .

Every public building was destroyed, except the new and unfinished Statehouse. This is situated on the summit of tableland whereon the city is built, and commands an extensive view of the surrounding country, and must have been the first building seen by the victorious and on-marching Union army. From the summit of the ridge, on the oppo-

site side of the river, a mile and a half away, a few shells were thrown at it, without doing any particular damage. With this exception, it was unharmed, though the workshops, in which were stored many of the architraves, caps, sills, etc., were burned—the fire, of course, destroying or seriously damaging their contents. The poverty of this people is so deep that there is no probability that it can be finished, according to the original design, during this generation at least.

The ruin here is neither half so eloquent nor touching as that at Charleston. This is but the work of flame, and might have mostly been brought about in time of peace. Those ghostly and crumbling walls and those long-deserted and grass-grown streets show the prostration of a community—such prostration as only war could bring.

—SIDNEY ANDREWS, *The South Since the War*

APPENDIX A.2

"EDUCATION MUST BECOME UNIVERSAL"

The Republican Congress created the Bureau of Refugees, Freedmen, and Abandoned Lands in March 1865 to help alleviate conditions for the 4 million African Americans who had escaped from slavery, had been granted freedom or were about to be freed at the conclusion of the Civil War. Almost all of the slaves were illiterate. Having gained their freedom, many also lost their means for survival. They did not have property, training or experience in a free economy.

The Freedmen's Bureau went about the task of establishing schools to teach freed slaves how to read, write and receive other basic education. The bureau also provided food, set up courts to protect emancipated slaves' civil rights, and founded savings banks. From 1865 to 1872 the bureau spent more than $6 million on education and $15 million for food; it provided medical assistance for more than 500,000 people.

But as this 1868 Congressional Report on the Freedmen's Bureau makes clear, the agency made significant accomplishments in the face of a hostile political environment. The report's conclusion that military enforcement would be necessary to perpetuate the agency's program proved correct. When Reconstruction ended and the military was withdrawn, white hostility pushed back many of the bureau's gains.

When our armies entered the South two facts became apparent: first, a surprising thirst for knowledge among the negroes; second, a large volunteer force of teachers for their instruction.

Without delay schools were successfully established and the earliest efforts to impart knowledge found the freedmen ready for its reception. Teachers of character and culture were ready from the first. To some extent the army had carried its own instructors. Negro servants of officers studied at the campfires of fellow servants. Chaplains of colored troops became instructors. In the campaigns of 1864 and 1865 the Christian Commission employed 50 teachers in colored camps and regiments.

At the close of the war it is believed that 20,000 colored soldiers could read intelligently, and a much larger number were learning their first lessons.

Really wonderful results had been accomplished through the disinterested efforts of benevolent associations working in connection with the government. But arrangements were soon made to give, on a larger scale, systematic and impartial aid to all of them. This consisted in turning over for school use temporary government buildings no longer needed for military purposes, and buildings seized from disloyal owners; also transportation for teachers, books, and school furniture, with quarters and rations for teachers and superintendants when on duty.

Schools were taken in charge by the Bureau, and in some States carried on wholly (in connection with local efforts) by use of the "refugees and freemen's fund." Teachers came under the general direction of the assistant commissioners, and protection through the department commanders was given to all engaged in the work.

Superintendants of schools for each State were appointed July 12, 1865, whose duty it was "to work as much as possible in connection with State officers who may have had school matters in charge, and to take cognizance of all that was being done to educate refugees and freedmen, secure protection to schools and teachers, promote method and efficiency, and to correspond with the benevolent agencies which were supplying his field."

The total number of pupils January 1, 1866, in all the colored schools, as near as could be ascertained, was 90,589; teachers, 1,314; schools, 740.

Whenever our troops broke through the lines of the enemy, schools followed. At Hampton, Beaufort, North Carolina, Roanoke Island, and New Orleans, they were soon in operation. A very efficient system was instituted for Louisiana in the early part of 1864, by Major General Banks, then in command of that State. It was supported by a military tax upon the whole population. Schools were opened in Savannah, Georgia, on the entrance of General Sherman, in December, 1864, and 500 pupils were at once enrolled. Ten intelligent colored persons were the first teachers, and nearly $81,000 were immediately contributed by the negroes for their support. This work was organized by the Secretary of the American Tract Society, Boston. Two of the largest of these schools were in "Bryan's slave mart," where platforms occupied a few days before with bondmen for sale became crowded with children learning to read.

At the end of the school year, July 1, 1866, it was found that while complete organization had not been reached, the schools in nearly all the States were steadily gaining in numbers, attainment, and general influence.

The official reports of superintendants gave 975 schools, 1,405 teachers, and 90,778 pupils. But these figures were not a true exhibit of the actual increase. They did not include many schools which failed to report. It was estimated that in all the different methods of teaching there had been, during the preceding six months, 150,000 freedmen and their children earnestly and successfully occupied in study.

Some change of sentiment had, at this time, been observed among the better classes of the South; those of higher intelligence acknowledging that education must become universal. Still, multitudes bitterly opposed the schools. Teachers were proscribed and ill-treated; school-houses were burned; many schools could not be opened, and others, after a brief struggle, had to be closed. Nevertheless, the country began to feel the moral power of this movement. Commendations came from foreign lands, and the universal demand of good men was that the work should go on.

As showing the desire for education among the freedmen, we give the following facts: When the collection of the general tax for colored schools was suspended in Louisiana by military order, the consternation of the colored population was intense. Petitions began to pour in. I saw one from the plantations across the river, at least thirty feet in length, representing ten thousand negroes. It was affecting to examine it, and note the names and marks [X] of such a long list of parents, ignorant themselves, but begging that their children might be educated, promising that from beneath their present burdens, and out of their extreme poverty, they would pay for it.

In September, 1865, J. W. Alvord, the present general superintendant, was appointed "Inspector of Schools." He traveled through nearly all the States lately in insurrection, and made the first general report to the Bureau on the subject of education, January 1, 1866.

Extracts from this report give the condition of the freedmen throughout the whole South. He says, "The desire of the freedmen for knowledge has not been overstated. This comes from several causes.

"1. The natural thirst for knowledge common to all men.

"2. They have seen power and influence among white people always coupled with learning; it is the sign of that elevation to which they now aspire.

"3. Its mysteries, hitherto hidden from them in written literature, excite to the special study of books.

"4. Their freedom has given wonderful stimulus to all effort, indicating a vitality which augurs well for their whole future condition and character.

"5. But, especially, the practical business of life now upon their hands shows their immediate need of education.

"This they all feel and acknowledge; hence their unusual welcome of and attendance upon schools is confined to no one class or age. Those advanced in life throw up their hands at first in despair, but a little encouragement places even these as pupils at the alphabet.

"Such as are in middle life, the laboring classes, gladly avail themselves of evening and Sabbath-schools. They may be often seen during the intervals of toil, when off duty as servants, on steamboats, along the railroads, and when unemployed in the streets in the city, or on plantations, with some fragment of a spelling-book in their hands, earnestly at study.

"Regiments of colored soldiers have nearly all made improvement in learning. In some of them, where but few knew their letters at first, nearly every man can now read, and many of them write. In other regiments one-half or two-thirds can do this.

"Even in hospitals I discovered very commendable efforts at such elementary instruction.

"But the great movement is among children of the usual school age. Their parents, if at all intelligent, encourage them to study. Your officers add their influence, and it is a fact, not always true of children, that among those recently from bondage, the school-house, however rough and uncomfortable, is of all places the most attractive. A very common punishment for misdemeanor is the threat of being kept at home for a day. The threat, in most cases, is sufficient."

The report goes on to say, "Much opposition has been encountered from those who do not believe in the elevation of the negro. A multitude of facts might be given. It is the testimony of all superintendants that if military power should be withdrawn, our schools would cease to exist.

"This opposition is sometimes ludicrous as well as inhuman. A member of the legislature, in session while I was at New Orleans, was passing one of the schools with me, having at the time its recess, the grounds about the building being filled with children. He stopped and looked intently, then earnestly inquired 'Is this a school?' 'Yes,' I replied. 'What!

of niggers?' 'These are colored children, evidently,' I answered. 'Well! Well!' said he, and raising his hands, 'I have seen many an absurdity in my lifetime, but this is the climax of absurdities!' I am sure he did not speak from effect, but as he felt. He left me abruptly, and turned the next corner to take his seat with legislators similarly prejudiced."

The act of July 16, 1866, enlarged the powers of the Bureau in regard to education. It sanctioned co-operation with private benevolent associations, and with agents and teachers accredited by them. It directed the Commissioner to "hire or provide, by lease, buildings for purposes of education whenever teachers and means of instruction, without cost to the government, should be provided." And, also, that he should "furnish such protection as might be required for the safe conduct of such schools."

The schools, on the passage of this act, assumed in all respects a more enlarged and permanent character. Schools in the cities and larger towns began to be graded. Normal or high schools were planned, and a few came into existence. The earliest of these were at Norfolk, Charleston, New Orleans and Nashville.

Industrial schools for girls, in which sewing, knitting, straw-braiding, etc., were taught, were encouraged. School buildings, by rent or construction, were largely provided, and new stimulus was given to every department.

The freedmen, in view of new civil rights, and what the Bureau had undertaken for them, had gained an advanced standing, with increasing self-respect and confidence that a vastly improved condition was within their reach.

Up to this time it had been questioned, whether colored children could advance rapidly into the higher branches, but it was found that 23,727 pupils were in writing, 12,970 in geography, 31,692 in arithmetic, and 1,573 in higher branches; and that out of 1,430 teachers of the day and night schools, 458 were colored persons.

The January report stated that "the actual results reached since these schools commenced, both in numbers and in advancement, were surpris-

ing." At the end of the school year, July 1, 1867, it could be said, "We look back with astonishment at the amount accomplished. Such progress as is seen under auspices admitted to be unfavorable; the permanency of the schools, scarcely one failing when once commenced; the rapid increase of general intelligence among the whole colored population, are matters of constant remark by every observer. Thus far this educational effort, considered as a whole, has been eminently successful. The country and the world are surprised to behold a depressed race, so lately and so long in bondage, springing to their feet and entering the lists in hopeful competition with every rival."

Reports from all the States show that there are 1,839 day and night schools, 2,087 teachers, and 111,442 pupils. By adding industrial schools, and those "within the knowledge of the superintendant," the number will be 2,207 schools, 2,442 teachers, and 130,735 pupils.

Sabbath-schools also show much larger numbers during the past year, the figures being 1,126 schools and 80,647 pupils; and if we add those "not regularly reported," the whole number of Sabbath-schools will be 1,468, with 105,786 pupils; totals, schools of all kinds, as reported, 3,695; pupils, 238,342. Of these schools 1,086 are sustained wholly or in part by the freedmen, and 391 of the buildings in which these schools are held are owned by themselves; 699 of the teachers in the day and night schools are colored and 1,388 white; 28,068 colored pupils have paid tuition, the average amount per month being $12,720.96, or a fraction over 45 cents per scholar. Only 8,743 pupils were free before the war.

As showing the progress of the Schools, it will be observed that 42,879 pupils are now in writing, 23,957 in geography, 40,454 in arithmetic, and 4,661 in higher branches. Twenty-one normal or high schools are in operation, with 1,821 pupils, the schools having doubled in number during the last year with three times the number of pupils. Of these schools not many are far advanced, but they are intended to be what their name implies.

There are now 35 industrial schools, giving instruction to 2,124 pupils in the various kinds of female labor, not including 4,185 in the day schools, who are taught needle-work. The average daily attendance in all the above schools has been nearly 75 per cent of the enrollment.

There are now connected with these schools 44 children's temperance societies, called the "Vanguard of Freedom," having, in the aggregate, 3,000 members. These societies are constantly increasing, and doing much to train children in correct moral habits.

Education in thrift and economy is effected through the influence of the "Freedmen's Savings and Trust Company," chartered by Congress, and placed under the protection of this Bureau. Twenty branches of this institution, located in as many of the central cities and larger towns of the Southern States, are now in operation. Six of these banks have, at this time (January 1,1868), on deposit an average of over $50,000 each, the whole amount now due depositors at all the branches being $585,770.17. Four times this amount has been deposited and drawn out for use in important purchases, homesteads etc. Both the business and the influence of the banks are rapidly increasing. Multitudes of these people never before had the first idea of saving for future use. Their former industry was only a hard, profitless task, but under the instructions of the cashiers the value of money is learned, and they are stimulated to earn it.

—Congressional Report on the
Freedman's Bureau

APPENDIX A.3

FIRST RECONSTRUCTION ACT

When Vice President Andrew Johnson ascended to the executive office after Lincoln's assassination, he sought to continue Lincoln's relatively lenient Reconstruction policy of creating provisional state governments in the former Confederate states. But as Johnson had little interest in protecting—much less enhancing—the rights of blacks in the South, his only requirement was that these states abolish slavery and repudiate secession. As a result, several states imposed strict new black codes that virtually re-created the slave status of many African Americans. Some states decided to repeal, rather than repudiate, secession. Johnson accepted these actions.

But Congress howled. With the victory of radical Republicans in the 1866 election, Congress imposed a much harsher policy calling for military control over the former Confederate states. In order to be readmitted into the Union, state conventions were required in which delegates were elected by universal male suffrage, with the exception of anyone who participated in the Confederate war effort. As a result, state conventions consisted almost entirely of freed slaves and newly arrived citizens from the North, derisively known as "carpetbaggers." Johnson vetoed the act, saying it was unconstitutional. Congress overrode the veto.

A flurry of vetoes and override votes ensued concerning civil rights, reconstruction policy and presidential authority. Relations between Johnson and Congress rapidly deteriorated. In the summer of 1867 Johnson dismissed Secretary of War Edwin Stanton while Congress was in recess. Republicans accused Johnson of violating the Tenure of Office Act, which Johnson had vetoed but was passed with an override vote by Congress. On February 24, 1868, the House of Representatives resolved to impeach Johnson. Two weeks later the impeachment was presented to the Senate. On May 16, 1868, the Senate voted 35-19 to impeach Johnson, one vote shy of the required two-thirds majority for conviction.

Whereas no legal State governments or adequate protection for life or property now exists in the rebel States of Virginia, North Carolina, South Carolina, Georgia, Mississippi, Alabama, Louisiana, Florida, Texas, and Arkansas; and whereas it is necessary that peace and good order should be enforced in said States until loyal and republican State governments can be legally established: therefore,

Be it enacted by the Senate and House of Representatives of the United States of America in Congress assembled, That said rebel States shall be divided into military districts and made subject to the military authority of the United States as in hereinafter prescribed, and for that purpose Virginia shall constitute the first district; North Carolina and South Carolina the second district; Georgia, Alabama, and Florida the third district; Mississippi and Arkansas the fourth district; and Louisiana and Texas the fifth district.

Section 2. And be it further enacted, That it shall be the duty of the President to assign to the command of each of said districts an officer of the army, not below the rank of brigadier-general, and to detail a sufficient military force to enable such officer to perform his duties and enforce his authority within the district to which he is assigned.

Section 3. And be it further enacted, That it shall be the duty of each officer assigned as aforesaid, to protect all persons in their rights of person and property, to suppress insurrection, disorder, and violence, and to punish, or cause to be punished, all disturbers of the public peace and criminals; and to this end he shall allow local civil tribunals to take jurisdiction of and to try offenders, or, when in his judgment it may be necessary for the trial of offenders, he shall have power to organize military commissions or tribunals for that purpose, and all interference under color of State authority with the exercise of military authority under this act, shall be null and void.

Section 4. And be it further enacted, That all persons put under military arrest by virtue of this act shall be tried without unnecessary delay, and no cruel or unusual punishment shall be inflicted, and no sentence of any military commission or tribunal hereby authorized, affecting the life or liberty of any person, shall be executed until it is approved by the officer in command of the district, and the laws and regulations for the government of the army shall not be affected by this act, except in so far as they conflict with its provisions: Provided, That no sentence of death under the provisions of this act shall be carried into effect without the approval of the President.

Section 5. That when the people of any one of said rebel States shall have formed a constitution of government in conformity with the Constitution of the United States in all respects, framed by a convention of delegates elected by the male citizens of said State twenty-one years old and upward, of whatever race, color, or previous condition, who have been resident in said State for one year previous to the day of such election, except such as may be disfranchised for participation in the rebellion or for felony at common law, and when such constitution shall provide that the elective franchise shall be enjoyed by all such persons as have the qualifications herein states for electors of delegates, and when such constitution shall be ratified by a majority of the persons voting on the question of ratification who are qualified as electors for delegates, and when such constitution shall have been submitted to Congress for examination and approval, and Congress shall have approved the same, and when said State, by a vote of its legislature elected under said constitution, shall have adopted the amendment to the Constitution of the United States said State shall be declared entitled to representation in Congress, and senators and representatives shall be admitted therefrom on their taking the oath prescribed by law, and then and thereafter the preceding sections of this act shall be inoperative in said States: Provided, That no person excluded from the privilege of holding office by said proposed amendment to the Constitution of the United States, shall be eligible to election as a member of the convention to frame a constitution for any of said rebel States, nor shall any such person vote for members of such convention.

—United States Congress

─────── APPENDIX A.4 ───────

Constitutional Amendments

The United States passed three landmark amendments to the Constitution immediately following the Civil War. All three guaranteed the rights of citizenship to African Americans, and the Fourteenth Amendment expanded the rights of all Americans.

In January 1865 Congress passed legislation for the Thirteenth Amendment to the Constitution banning slavery from the United States. Northern states quickly approved the amendment, but to secure ratification by three-quarters of the states, at least some Southern states needed to approve it. Ratification by legislatures in former Confederate states became a condition for restoring relations with the Union. The amendment received final ratification on December 6, 1865, ensuring the freedom of more than 4 million African American slaves from bondage.

Recalling Supreme Court Chief Justice Roger B. Taney's ruling in the Dred Scott decision that blacks—whether free or enslaved—would not be considered as citizens, Congress initiated the Fourteenth Amendment defining citizenship and guaranteeing the equal protection of laws. The immediate effect of the amendment was thus to secure the civil rights of the freedmen. The long-term impact of the equal protection clause, however, embraced a wider range of constituencies (such as women and corporations) and had much broader implications on a spectrum of legal issues.

The second, third and fourth sections of the Fourteenth Amendment were specifically directed at reshaping the South and punishing those who had assisted the Confederate war effort. The second section gives Southern states the choice of either accepting African-American voters or losing seats in the House of Representatives, thus all but compelling them to enfranchise former slaves. The third section wiped out the South's former political leadership by banning former Confederate leaders from taking public office without swearing an oath in support of the Constitution. Finally, the fourth section disavowed Confederate war debt, validated the United States war debt, and disallowed all claims for loss of property, including slaves.

In early 1869 the Republican Congress initiated the Fifteenth Amendment, which enfranched African-American men. Many former Confederate states had already given former slaves the right to vote in their new state constitutions, but radical Republicans were concerned that when the Reconstruction period ended, the new state governments would retract that right. The immediate effect of the amendment was to enfranchise African Americans in the North. Nevertheless, Republican fears were well founded as Southern Democrats imposed a series of obstacles for African-American voters in the late 1800s, including the poll tax, highly restrictive registration laws, literacy and property qualifications, and other loopholes. In many parts of the Deep South, African Americans were effectively barred from voting until the Civil Rights movements in the 1960s.

A. Thirteenth Amendment

Section 1. Neither slavery nor involuntary servitude, except as a punishment for crime whereof the party shall have been duly convicted, shall exist within the United States, or any place subject to their jurisdiction.

Section 2. Congress shall have the power to enforce this article by appropriate legislation.

—UNITED STATES CONGRESS

B. Fourteenth Amendment

Section 1. All persons born or naturalized in the United States, and subject to the jurisdiction thereof, are citizens of the United States and of the State wherein they reside. No state shall make or enforce any law which shall abridge the privileges or immunities of citizens of the United States; nor shall any State deprive any person of life, liberty, or property, without due process of law; nor deny to any person within its jurisdiction the equal protection of the laws.

Section 2. Representatives shall be apportioned among the several States according to their respective numbers, counting the whole number of persons in each State, excluding Indians not taxed. But when the right to vote at any election for the choice of electors for President and Vice-President of the United States, Representatives in Congress, the Executive and Judicial officers of a State, or the members of the Legislature thereof, is denied to any of the male inhabitants of such State, being twenty-one years of age, and citizens of the United States, or in any way abridged, except for participation in rebellion, or other crime, the basis of representation therein shall be reduced in the proportion which the number of such male citizens shall bear to the whole number of male citizens twenty-one years of age in such State.

Section 3. No person shall be a Senator or Representative in Congress, or elector of President and Vice-President, or hold any office, civil or military, under the United States, or under any State, who, having previously taken an oath, as a member of Congress, or as an officer of the United States, or as a member of any State, to support the Constitution of the United States, shall have engaged in insurrection or rebellion against the same; or given aid or comfort to the enemies thereof. But Congress may by a vote of two-thirds of each House, remove such disability.

Section 4. The validity of the public debt of the United States, authorized by law, including debts incurred for payment of pensions and bounties for services in suppressing insurrection or rebellion, shall not be questioned. But neither the United States nor any State shall assume or pay any debt or obligation incurred in aid of insurrection or rebellion against the United States, or any claim for the loss or emancipation of any slave; but all such debts, obligations, and claims shall be held illegal and void.

Section 5. The congress shall have the power to enforce, by appropriate legislation, the provisions of this article.

—UNITED STATES CONGRESS

C. Fifeteenth Amendment

Section 1. The right of citizens of the United States to vote shall not be denied or abridged by the United States or by any State on account of race, color, or previous condition of servitude.

Section 2. The Congress shall have power to enforce this article by appropriate legislation.

—UNITED STATES CONGRESS

— APPENDIX A.5 —
"THE END OF THE WHITE MAN'S GOVERNMENT"

The New Orleans Tribune was the first daily newspaper published by African Americans. In the wake of the Civil War, it served as a voice for freed slaves. The November 22, 1867, editorial shows that despite resentments of how the federal military had implemented Reconstruction policies, renewed federal initiatives to enfranchise and empower African Americans offered hope that freed slaves—who represented more than 35 percent of the total population in the South—might gain political power.

After three years' hesitation and delay the National Government concluded at last to take the right step for reconstruction. Every way was first tried except the sound and logical one. The first attempt at reconstruction was through military power. Provisional officers, taken from the army, were appointed as governors and mayors; provost marshals and freedmen's bureau agents were intrusted with the supervision of affairs in the country parishes. They understood very little of the politi-

cal situation. Governor Shepley discarded the propositions of the Free State Committee. Provost marshals showed the rebels more courtesy and granted them more favors than they did to poor but devoted Union men. Agents of the Freedmen's Bureau might have been designated as planters' agents. They took more trouble to procure hands for the owners of large plantations than to protect the freed people and defend their rights. We still recollect Gen. Banks' order on "small-pox passes," by which, under the absurd plea of preventing the spreading of small-pox, the colored people were placed under a law of exception as far as their movements were concerned. They were not allowed to change plantations, they could not leave a place and hunt for work—which is the natural right of all free laborers—unless they first obtained a pass from their former employer, who, of course, refused to give them any. The hypocritical "small-pox passes" remain on Gen. Banks' record, as one of the most flagrant failures to understand and to establish freedom.

The pro-slavery spirit inspired the act of the military administration. The military was not the power to understand civil liberty; generals used to arbitrary command, felt better disposed in favor of the common laborers. They were, moreover, unwilling to take the responsibility of any important change. And after Butler—who was an exception to the rule—had left us, they did, perhaps unconsciously, as much as they could for the slave power, and as little as they could for the cause of liberty and the rights of man.

At last, however, the military government relinquished its hold. The Convention of 1864 assembled, and under the Constitution they framed, a civil government having its legislative, its executive, and judicial officers, was inaugurated. The attempt was made under the inspiration of the military, and could be, of course, but a continuance of the same errors already made. A very small number of the people of a small number of parishes was called upon to vote. The representatives of the old Union minority of white men met at the City Hall, and ignoring the change of the times, believing themselves the legitimate successors of King Cotton, they made an oligarchical Constitution, nearly as bad, for it was as partial as that of 1852. They forgot through pride and presumption, that they had no power by themselves to uphold the white union oligarchy thus created. The fact is that the very day when military rule came to an end, and the qualified voters—the white voters—under the Constitution of 1864 went to the polls, the Union oligarchs were put aside and rebel officers reinstated in their stead. It did not take great power of intellect to foresee the result. The Union and subsequently the *Tribune* warned our white friends, at the time, of the evident fate in store for them. Still they kept up their illusions; for could they listen to a black organ? The dullest among them believed himself smarter than any colored man in the land; and down they went, having consummated their own ruin. Gov. Wells vindicated our forebodings. He promptly turned them out of office; and then they could see whether the black organ had seen things correctly or not. From that day they began to call again at our office; they said they were ready retrieve their faults, and to proclaim universal suffrage. But the golden opportunity had passed away, they had been blind at the opportune time; they had played in their enemies hands. And rebels showed at the Mechanics' Institute how they intended to treat them.

This was the end of the Union white man's government. Since the eventful day of the 30th of July, 1866, we have lived under the grasp of the rebel oligarchy, restored to power. But congress has finally given us the means of relief. After governments of minorities, we are at last enabled to organize a government of the people. Let us hope that the Convention of 1867 will have more foresight, a sounder judgment and more liberalism than had the Convention of 1864. They have to work in the interest of the whole people and secure the rights of all classes of citizens, of whatever race or color, unless they want to see the fabric they will attempt to build up crumble to pieces, and partake of the fate of the government erected in 1864.

—*The New Orleans Tribune*

APPENDIX A.6
BLACK PARLIAMENT IN SOUTH CAROLINA

White Southerners despised the new terms of Reconstruction. They called Northerners who held office in the new state governments "carpetbaggers," a term suggesting that they had no stake in Southern society. Everything they owned could be hastily packed up into a carpetbag suitcase. Southern whites who cooperated with the new governments were dubbed "scalawags." The spectacle of African Americans voting for public office and holding elected positions shocked white Southerners. Their very presence fostered resentment and complaints of "Negro rule."

James S. Pike was an antislavery Republican from Maine. He had worked for many years as a Washington correspondent for Horace Greeley's *New York Tribune*. Lincoln named Pike as minister to Holland in 1861. Pike visited South Carolina during Reconstruction and wrote *The Prostrate State,* which vividly described the harshness of Reconstruction policies on the state. The following excerpt offers a tragicomic description of the state legislature in session.

Yesterday, about 4 P.M., the assembled wisdom of the state, whose achievements are illustrated on that theater, issued forth from the statehouse. About three-quarters of the crowd belonged to the African race. They were of every hue, from the light octoroon to the deep black. They were such a looking body of men as might pour out of a market house or a courthouse at random in any Southern state. Every Negro type and physiognomy was here to be seen, from the genteel servingman to the roughhewn customer from the rice or cotton field. Their dress was as varied as their countenances. There was the secondhand black frock coat of infirm gentility, glossy and threadbare. There was the stovepipe hat of many ironings and departed styles. There was also to be seen a total disregard of the proprieties of costume in the coarse and dirty garments of the field, the stub jackets and slouch hats of soiling labor. In some instances rough woolen comforters embraced the neck and hid the absence of linen. Heavy brogans and short, torn trousers it was impossible to hide. The dusky tide flowed out into the littered and barren grounds and, issuing through the coarse wooden fence of the inclosure, melted away into the street beyond. These were the legislators of South Carolina.

We will enter the House of Representatives. Here sit one hundred and twenty-four members. Of these, twenty-three are white men, representing the remains of the old civilization. These are good-looking, substantial citizens. They are men of weight and standing in the communities they represent. They are all from the hill country. The frosts of sixty and seventy winters whiten the heads of some among them. There they sit, grim and silent. They feel themselves to be but loose stones, thrown in to partially obstruct a current they are powerless to resist. They say little and do little as the days go by. They simply watch the rising tide and mark the progressive steps of the inundation. They hold their places reluctantly. They feel themselves to be in some sort martyrs, bound stoically to suffer in behalf of all that still great element in the state whose prostrate fortunes are becoming the sport of an unpitying fate. Grouped in a corner of the commodious and well-furnished chamber, they stolidly survey the noisy riot that goes on in the great black Left and Center, where the business and debates of the House are conducted and where sit the strange and extraordinary guides of the fortunes of a once proud and haughty state. In this crucial trial of his pride, his manhood, his prejudices, his spirit, it must be said of the Southern Bourbon of the Legislature that he comports himself with a dignity, a reserve, and a decorum is upon him. He is gloomy, disconsolate, hopeless. The grayheads of this generation openly profess that they look for no relief. They see no way of escape. The recovery of influence, of position, of control in the state, is felt by them to be impossible. They accept their position with a stoicism that promises no reward here or hereafter. They are the types of a conquered race. They staked all and lost all. Their lives remain; their property and their children do not. War, emancipation, and grinding taxation have consumed them. Their struggle now is against complete confiscation. They endure, and wait for the night.

This dense Negro crowd they confront do the debating, the squabbling, the lawmaking, and create all the clamor and disorder of the body. These twenty-three white men are but the observers, the enforced auditors, of the dull and clumsy imitation of a deliberative body whose appearance in their present capacity is at once a wonder and a shame to modern civilization.

Deducting the twenty-three members referred to, who comprise the entire strength of the opposition, we find one hundred and one remaining. Of this one hundred and one, ninety-four are colored, and seven are their white allies. . . .

One of the things that first strike a casual observer in this Negro assembly is the fluency of debate, if the endless chatter that goes on there can be dignified with the term. The leading topics of discussion are all well understood by the members, as they are of a practical character and appeal directly to the personal interests of every legislator as well as to those of his constituents. When an appropriation bill is up to raise money to catch and punish the Ku Klux, they know exactly what it means. They feel it in their bones. So too with educational measures. The free school comes right home to them; then the business of arming and drilling the black militia—they are eager on this point. Sambo can talk on these topics and those of kindred character and their endless ramifications day in and day out. There is no end to his gush and babble. The intellectual level is that of a bevy of fresh converts at a Negro camp meeting. Of course this kind of talk can be extended indefinitely. It is the doggerel of debate and not beyond the reach of the lowest parts. Then the Negro is imitative in the extreme. He can copy like a parrot or a monkey, and he is always ready for a trial of his skill. He believes he can do anything and never loses a chance to try and is just as ready to be laughed at for his failure as applauded for his success. He is more vivacious than the white, and being more volatile and good-natured, he is correspondingly more irrepressible. His measure of language in his imitations is at times ludicrous beyond measure. He notoriously loves a joke or an anecdote and will burst into a broad guffaw on the smallest provocation. He breaks out into an incoherent harangue on the floor just as easily, and being without practice, discipline, or experience and wholly oblivious of Lindley Murray or any other restraint on composition, he will go on repeating himself, dancing as it were to the music of his own voice, forever. He will speak half a dozen times on one question and every time say the same things without knowing it. He answers completely to the description of a stupid speaker in Parliament given by Lord Derby on one occasion; it was said of him that he did not know what he was going to say when he got up, he did not know what he was saying while he was speaking, and he did not know what he had said when he sat down.

But the old stagers admit that the colored brethren have a wonderful aptness at legislative proceedings. They are quick as lightning at detecting points of order, and they certainly make incessant and extraordinary use of their knowledge. No one is allowed to talk five minutes without interruption, and one interruption is the signal for another and another until the original speaker is smothered under an avalanche of them. Forty questions of privilege will be raised in a day. At times nothing goes on but alternating questions of order and of privilege. The inefficient colored friend who sits in the Speaker's chair cannot suppress this extraordinary element of the debate. Some of the blackest members exhibit a pertinacity of intrusion in raising these points of order and questions of privilege that few white men can equal. Their struggles to get the floor, their bellowings and physical contortions, baffle description. The Speaker's hammer plays a perpetual tattoo, all to no purpose. The talking and the interruptions from all quarters go on with the utmost license. Every one esteems himself as good as his neighbor and puts in his oar, apparently as often for riot and confusion as for anything else. It is easy to imagine what are his ideas of propriety and dignity among a crowd of his own color, and these are illustrated without reserve. The Speaker orders a member whom he has discov-

ered to be particularly unruly to take his seat. The member obeys and, with the same motion he sits down, throws his feet on his desk, hiding himself from the Speaker by the soles of his boots. In an instant he appears again on the floor. After a few experiences of this sort, the Speaker threatens, in a laugh, to call "the gemman" to order. This is considered a capital joke, and a guffaw follows. The laugh goes round, and then the peanuts are cracked and munched faster than ever, one hand being employed in fortifying the inner man with this nutriment of universal use while the other enforces the views of the orator. This laughing propensity of the sable crowd is a great cause of disorder. They laugh as hens cackle—one begins and all follow.

But underneath all this shocking burlesque upon legislative proceedings, we must not forget that there is something very real to this uncouth and untutored multitude. It is not all sham nor all burlesque. They have a genuine interest and a genuine earnestness in the business of the assembly which we are bound to recognize and respect unless we would be accounted shallow critics. They have an earnest purpose, born of a conviction that their position and condition are not fully assured, which lends a sort of dignity to their proceedings. The barbarous, animated jargon in which they so often indulge is on occasion seen to be so transparently sincere and weighty in their own minds that sympathy supplants disgust. The whole thing is a wonderful novelty to them as well as to observers. Seven years ago these men were raising corn and cotton under the whip of the overseer. Today they are raising points of order and questions of privilege. They find they can raise one as well as the other. They prefer the latter. It is easier and better paid. Then, it is the evidence of an accomplished result. It means escape and defense from old oppressors. It means liberty. It means the destruction of prison walls only too real to them. It is the sunshine of their lives. It is their day of jubilee. It is their long-promised vision of the Lord God Almighty.

—JAMES SHEPHERD PIKE, *The Prostrate State*

APPENDIX A.7

"A Full Pardon"

On December 25, 1868, Andrew Johnson issued an amnesty proclamation pardoning everyone who participated in the Confederate war effort and restoring their full rights as citizens. The amnesty was similar to Lincoln's 1863 Proclamation of Amnesty and Reconstruction. The restoration of citizenship rights went contrary to Congress's Reconstruction program. Armed with the ability to vote, Southerners used their restored political authority against the state governments established by the federal governments.

[W]hereas, the authority of the Federal Government having been re-established in all the States and Territories within the jurisdiction of the United States,. . . and that a universal amnesty and pardon for participation in said rebellion extended to all who have borne any part therein will tend to secure permanent peace, order, and prosperity throughout the land, and to renew and fully restore confidence and fraternal feeling among the whole people, and their respect for and attachment to the National Government, designed by its patriotic founders for the general good:

Now, therefore, be it known that I, Andrew Johnson,. . . hereby proclaim and declare unconditionally, and without reservation, to all and to every person who directly or indirectly participated in the late resurrection or rebellion, a full pardon and amnesty for the offence of treason against the United States, or of adhering to their enemies during the late civil war, with restoration of all rights, privileges, and immunities under the constitution and the laws which have been made in pursuance thereof.

In testimony whereof, I have signed these presents with my hand, and have caused the seal of the United States to be hereunto affixed.

—Andrew Johnson

APPENDIX A.8

The Ku Klux Klan

Reacting against the enfranchisement of African Americans, Southern whites formed several secret organizations during the era of Reconstruction to undermine federal policies and intimidate African Americans. The most notorious and largest group was the Ku Klux Klan, founded in 1866 in Pulaski, Tennessee. These organizations murdered, whipped, and terrorized African Americans who attempted to exercise their newfound rights as citizens.

The documents below provide descriptions of the impact of the Ku Klux Klan. The first entry is an account provided by Ben Johnson of Durham, South Carolina, when he was interviewed at the age of 85 for the Federal Writers' Project's *Slave Narratives*. The following document was a letter presented by African-American residents in Frankfort, Kentucky. It was one of several formal complaints brought to Congress alerting the federal government to the extent of terrorism that was being inflicted on them, and it cites 64 specific incidents in which more than 50 African Americans were murdered by the Ku Klux Klan or mobs.

Congress responded to the rising violence by making violent abuse of civil and political rights a federal crime and directing the military to crack down on Klan activities. Hundreds of people were arrested, leading to a decline in terrorism. The end of Reconstruction in 1877, however, prompted a resurgence in lynchings. One hundred or more African Americans were lynched every year for the last 20 years of the 19th century. Violence against African Americans was typically used as a way to intimidate them from attempting to elevate their suppressed status in society.

A. "I Shook Hands with Bob 'fore they Hung Him"

I never will forgit when they hung Cy Guy. They hung him for a scandalous insult to a white woman, and they comed after him a hundred strong.

They tries him there in the woods, and they scratches Cy's arm to git some blood, and with that blood they writes that he shall hang 'tween the heavens and earth till he am dead, dead, dead, and that any nigger what takes down the body shall be hunged too.

Well, sir, the next morning there he hung, right over the road, and the sentence hanging over his head. Nobody'd bother with that body for four days, and there it hung, swinging in the wind, but the fourth day the sheriff comes and takes it down.

There was Ed and Cindy, who 'fore the war belonged to Mr. Lynch, and after the war he told 'em to move. He gives 'em a month, and they ain't gone, so the Ku Kluxes gits 'em,

It was on a cold night when they comed and drugged the niggers outen bed. They carried 'em down in the woods and whup them, then they throws 'em in the pond, their bodies breaking the ice. Ed come out and come to our house, but Cindy ain't been seed since.

Sam Allen in Caswell County was told to move, and after a month the hundred Ku Klux come a-toting his casket, and they tells him that his time has come and iffen he wants to tell his wife goodbye and say his prayers hurry up.

They set the coffin on two chairs, and Sam kisses his old woman who am a-crying, then he kneels down side of his bed with his head on the pillow and his arms throwed out in front of him.

He sets there for a minute and when he riz he had a long knife in his hand. 'Fore he could be grabbed he done kill two of the Ku Kluxes with the knife, and he done gone outen the door. They ain't catch him heither, and the next night when they comed back, 'termined to git him, they shot another nigger by accident. . . .

I know one time Miss Hendon inherits a thousand dollars from her pappy's state, and that night she goes with her sweetheart to the gate, and on her way back to the house she gits knocked in the head with a axe. She screams, and her two nigger servants, Jim and Sam, runs and saves her, but she am robbed.

Then she tells the folkses that Jim and Sam am the guilty parties, but her little sister swears that they ain't, so they gits out of it.

After that they finds out that it am five mens—Atwater, Edwards, Andrews, Davis, and Markham. The preacher comes down to where they am hanging to preach their funeral, and he stands there while lightning plays round the dead men's heads and the wind blows the trees, and he preaches such a sermon as I ain't never heard before.

Bob Boylan falls in love with another woman, so he burns his wife and four young-uns up in their house.

The Ku Kluxes gits him, of course, and they hangs him high on the old red oak on the Hillsboro road. After they hunged him, his lawyer says to us boys, "Bury him good, boys, just as good as you'd bury me iffen I was dead."

I shook hands with Bob 'fore they hunged him, and I helped to bury him too, and we bury him nices, and we all hopes that he done gone to glory.

—BEN JOHNSON, SLAVE NARRATIVES

B. Frankfort, Kentucky, Congressional Petition

To the Senate and house of Representatives in Congress assembled: We the Colored Citizens of Frankfort and vicinity to this day memorialize your honorable bodies upon the condition of affairs now existing in this the state of Kentucky.

We would respectfully state that life, liberty and property are unprotected among the colored races of this state. Organized Bands of desperate and lawless men mainly composed of soldiers of the late Rebel armies, Armed disciplined and disguised and bound by Oath and secret obligations, have by force terror and violence subverted all civil society among Colored people, thus utterly rendering insecure the safety of persons and property overthrowing all those rights which are the primary basis and objects of the government which are expressly guaranteed to us by the Constitution of the United States as amended; We believe you are not familiar with the description of the Ku Klux Klans riding nightly over the country going from County to County and in the County towns spreading terror wherever they go, by robbing whipping ravishing and killing our people without provocation, compelling Colored people to brake the ice and bathe in the Chilly waters of the Kentucky River.

The Legislature has adjourned they refused to enact any laws to suppress Ku Klux disorder. We regard them as now being licensed to continue their dark and bloody deeds under cover of the dark night. They refuse to allow us to testify in the state Courts where a white man is concerned. We find their deeds are perpetrated only upon Colored men and white Republicans. We also find that for our services to the Government and our race we have become the special object of hatred and persecution at the hands of the Democratic party. Our people are driven from their homes in great numbers having no redress only the U.S. Courts which is in many cases unable to reach them. We would state that we have been law abiding citizens, pay our tax and in many parts of the state our people have been driven from the poles, refused the right to vote. Many have been slaughtered while attempting to vote, we ask how long is this state of things to last.

We appeal to you as law abiding citizens to enact some laws that will protect us. And that will enable us to exercise the rights of citizens. We see that the senator from this state denies there being organized Bands of desperaders in the state for information we lay before you an number of violent acts occurred during his Administration. Although he [Governor John. W.] Stevenson says half Dozen instances of violence did occur these are not more than one half the acts that have occured. The Democratic party has here a political organization composed only of Democrats not a single Republican can join them where many of these acts have been committed it has been proven that they were the men, don with Armies from the State Arsenal. We pray you will take steps to remedy these evils.

Don by a Committee of Grievances appointed at a meeting of all the Colored Citizens of Frankfort & vicinity.

Mar. 25, 1871

Henry Marrs, Teacher colored school
Henry Lynn, Livery stable keeper
N. N. Trumbo, Grocer
Samuel Damsey
B. Smith
B. T. Crampton, Barber

1. A mob visited Harrodsburg in Mercer County to take from jail a man named Robertson, Nov. 14, 1867.
2. Smith attacked and whipped by regulation in Zelun County Nov. 1867.
3. Colored school house burned by incendiaries in Breckinridge Dec. 24, 1867.
4. A Negro Jim Macklin taken from jail in Frankfort and hung by mob January 28, 1868.
5. Sam Davis hung by mob in Harrodsburg May 28, 1868.
6. Wm. Pierce hung by a mob in Christian July 12, 1868.
7. Geo. Roger hung by a mob in Bradsfordville Martin County July 11, 1868.
8. Colored school Exhibition at Midway attacked by a mob July 31, 1868.
9. Seven person ordered to leave their homes at Standford, Ky. Aug. 7, 1868.
10. Silas Woodford age sixty badly beaten by disguised mob. Mary Smith Curtis and Margaret Mosby also badly beaten, near Keene Jessemine County Aug. 1868.
11. Cabe Fields shot—and killed by disguised men near Keene Jessamine County Aug. 3, 1868.
12. James Gaines expelled from Anderson by Ku Klux Aug. 1868.
13. James Parker killed by Ku Klux Pulaski, Aug. 1868.
14. Noah Blankenship whipped by a mob in Pulaski County Aug. 1868.
15. Negroes attacked robbed and driven from Summerville in Green County Aug. 21, 1868.
16. William Gibson and John Gibson hung by a mob in Washington County Aug. 1868.
17. F. H. Montford hung by a mob near Cogers landing in Jessamine County Aug. 28, 1868.
18. Wm. Glasgow killed by a mob in Warren Country Sep. 5, 1868.
19. Negro hung by a mob Sep. 1868.
20. Two Negros beaten by Ku Klus in Anderson county Sept. 11, 1868.
21. Mob attacked house of Oliver Stone in Fayette county Sept. 11, 1868.

22. Mob attacked Cumins house in Pulaski County. Cumins his daughter and a man named adams killed in the attack Sept. 18, 1868.

23. U. S. Marshall Meriwether attacked captured and beatened with death in Larue County by mob Sept. 1868.

24. Richardson house attacked in Conishville by mob and Crasban killed Sept. 28 1868.

25. Mob attacks Negro cabin at hanging forks in Lincoln County. John Mosteran killed & Cash & Coffey killed Sept. 1869.

26. Terry Laws & James Ryan hung by mob at Nicholasville oct. 26, 1868.

27. Attack on Negro cabin in Spencer County—a woman outraged Dec. 1868.

28. Two negroes shot by Ku Klux at Sulphur Springs in Union County Dec. 1868.

29. Negro shot at Morganfield Union Country, Dec. 1868.

30. Mob visited Edwin Burris house in Mercer County, January, 1869.

31. William Parker whipped by Ku Klux in Lincoln County Jan. 20/69.

32. Mob attacked and fired into house of Jesse Davises in lincoln County Jan. 20, 1868.

33. Spears taken from his room at Harrodsburg by disguise men Jan. 19, 1869.

34. Albert Bradford killed by disguise men in Scott County, Jan. 20, 1869.

35. Ku Klux whipped boy at Standford March 12, 1869.

36. Mob attacked Frank Bournes house in Jessamine County. Roberts killed March 1869.

37. Geo Bratcher hung by mob on sugar creek in Garrard County March 30, 1869.

38. John Penny hung by a mob at Nevada Mercer county May 29, 1869.

39. Ku Klux whipped Lucien Green in Lincoln county June 1869.

40. Miller whipped by Ku Klux in madison country July 2d, 1869.

41. Chas Henderson shot and his wife killed by mob on silver creek Madison county July 1869.

42. Mob decoy from Harrodsburg and hangs Geo Bolling July 17, 1869.

43. Disguise band visited home of I. C. Vanarsdall and T. J. Vanarsdall in Mercer county July 18/69.

44. Mob attack Ronsey's house in Casey country three men and one woman Killed July 1869.

45. James Crowders hung by mob near Lebanon Merion county Aug. 9, 1869

46. Mob tar and feather a citizen of Cynthiana in Harrison county Aug. 1869.

47. Mob whipped and bruised a Negro in Davis county Sept. 1869.

48. Ku Klux burn colored meeting-house in Carrol county Sept. 1869.

49. Ku Klux whipped a negro at John Carmins's farm in Fayette county Sept. 1869.

50. Wiley Gevens killed by Ku Klux at Dixon Webster county Oct. 1869.

51. Geo. Rose killed by Ku Klux near Kirkville in Madison county Oct. 18, 1869.

52. Ku Klux ordered Wallace Sinkhorn to leave his home near Parkville Boyle county Oct. 1869.

53. Man named Shepherd shot by mob near Parksville Oct. 1869.

54. Regulator killed Geo Tanehly in Lincoln county Nov. 2d. 1869.

55. Ku Klux attacked Frank Searcy house in madison county one man shot Nov. 1869.

56. Searcy hung by mob madison county at Richmond Nov. 4th, 1869.

57. Ku Klux killed Robt. Mershon daughter shot Nov. 1869.

58. Mob whipped Pope Hall and Willett in Washington county Nov. 1869.

59. Regulators whipped Cooper in Pulaski County Nov. 1869.

60. Ku Klux ruffians outraged negroes in Hickman county Nov. 20, 1869.

61. Mob take two Negroes from jail Richmond Madison county one hung one whipped Dec. 12, 1869.
62. Two Negroes killed by mob while in civil custody near Mayfield Graves county Dec. 1869.
63. Allen Cooper killed by Ku Klux in Adair county Dec. 24th, 1869.
64. Negroes whipped while on Scott's farm in Franklin county Dec. 1869.

—COLORED CITIZENS OF FRANKFORT AND VICINITY

APPENDIX A.9
"WE HAD ONLY OUR IGNORANCE"

With the end of Reconstruction in the South, the protections and opportunities provided to freed slaves evaporated. Southern white Democratic state governments passed laws sharply restricting the newfound rights of African Americans and segregated blacks from white society. Plantation owners found new ways to bound their former slaves as miserably paid workers through sharecropping and other arrangements. For all practical purposes, many African Americans found themselves in virtually the same position they had occupied before their emancipation. This personal story of one anonymous former Georgia slave, which was published in the *Independent* magazine, illustrates the chicanery, corruption and brutality that characterized black-white relations in the post-Reconstruction South.

I am a Negro and was born some time during the war in Elbert County, Ga., and I reckon by this time I must be a little over forty years old. My mother was not married when I was born, and I never knew who my father was or anything about him. Shortly after the war my mother died, and I was left to the care of my uncle. All this happened before I was eight years old, and so I can't remember very much about it. When I was about ten years old my uncle hired me out to Captain. . . . I was told that the Captain wanted me for his house-boy, and that later on he was going to train me to be his coachman. To be a coachman in those days was considered a post of honor, and young as I was, I was glad of the chance.

But I had not been at the Captain's a month before I was put to work on the farm, with some twenty or thirty other Negroes men, women and children. From the beginning the boys had the same tasks as the men and women. There was no difference. We all worked hard during the week, and would frolic on Saturday nights and often on Sundays. And everybody was happy. The men got $3 a week and the women $2. I don't know what the children got. Every week my uncle collected my money for me, but it was very little of it that I ever saw. My uncle fed and clothed me, gave me a place to sleep, and allowed me ten or fifteen cents a week for "spending change," as he called it.

I must have been seventeen or eighteen years old before I got tired of that arrangement, and felt that I was man enough to be working for myself and handling my own wages. . . . Unknown to my uncle or the Captain I went off to a neighboring plantation and hired myself out to another man. The new landlord agreed to give me forty cents a day and furnish me one meal. I thought that I was doing fine. Bright and early one Monday morning I started for work, still not letting the others know anything about it. But they found it out before sundown. The Captain came over to the new place and brought some kind of officer of the law. The officer pulled out a long piece of paper from his pocket and read it to my new employer. When this was done I heard my new boss say:

"I beg your pardon, Captain. I didn't know this nigger was bound out to you, or I wouldn't have hired him."

"He certainly is bound out to me," said the Captain. "He belongs to me until he is twenty-one, and I'm going to make him know his place."

So I was carried back to the Captain's. That night he made me strip off my clothing down to my waist, had me tied to a tree in his backyard, ordered his foreman to give me thirty lashes with a buggy whip across my bare back, and stood by until it was done. After that experience the Captain made me stay on his place night and day, but my uncle still continued to "draw" my money.

I was a man nearly grown before I knew how to count from one to one hundred. I was a man nearly grown before I ever saw a colored school teacher. I never went to school a day in my life. To-day I can't write my own name, though I can read a little. I was a man nearly grown before I ever rode on a railroad train, and then I went on an excursion from Elberton to Athens. What was true of me was true of hundreds of other Negroes around me—'way off there in the country, fifteen or twenty miles from the nearest town.

When I reached twenty-one the Captain told me I was a free man, but he urged me to stay with him. He said he would treat me right, and pay me as much as anybody else would. The Captain's son and I were about the same age, and the Captain said that, as he had owned my mother and uncle during slavery, and as his son didn't want me to leave them (since I had been with them so long), he wanted me to stay with the old family. And I stayed. I signed a contract—that is, I made my mark for one year. The captain was to give me $3.50 a week, and furnish me a little house on the plantation—a one-room log cabin similar to those used by his other laborers.

During that year I married Mandy. For several years Mandy had been the house-servant for the Captain, his wife, his son and his three daughters, and they all seemed to think a good deal of her. As an evidence of their regard they gave us furniture, which cost about $25, and we set up housekeeping in one of the Captain's two-room shanties. I thought I was the biggest man in Georgia. Mandy still kept her place in the "Big House" after our marriage. We did so well for the first year that I renewed my contract for the second year, and the third, fourth and fifth year I did the same thing.

Before the end of the fifth year the Captain had died, and his son, who had married some two or three years before, took charge of the plantation. Also, for two or three years, this son had been serving at Atlanta in some big office to which he had been elected. I think it was in the Legislature or

something of that sort anyhow, all the people called him Senator. At the end of the fifth year the Senator suggested that I sign up a contract for ten years; then, he said, we wouldn't have to fix up papers every year. I asked my wife about it; she consented; and so I made a ten-year contract.

Not long afterward the Senator had a long, low shanty built on his place. A great big chimney, with a wide, open fireplace, was built at one end of it, and on each side of the house, running lengthwise, there was a row of flames or stalls just large enough to hold a single mattress. . . . They looked for all the world like stalls for horses. . . . Nobody seemed to know what the Senator was fixing for.

All doubts were put aside one bright day in April when about forty able-bodied Negroes, bound in iron chains, and some of them handcuffed, were brought out to the Senator's farm in three big wagons. They were quartered in the long, low shanty, and it was afterward called the stockade. This was the beginning of the Senator's convict camp. These men were prisoners who had been leased by the Senator from the State of Georgia at about $200 each per year, the State agreeing to pay for guards and physicians, for necessary inspection, for inquests, all rewards for escaped convicts, the cost of litigation and all other incidental camp expenses. When I saw these men in shackles, and the guards with their guns, I was scared nearly to death. I felt like running away, but I didn't know where to go. And if there had been any place to go to, I would have had to leave my wife and child behind.

We free laborers held a meeting. We all wanted to quit. We sent a man to tell the Senator about it. Word came back that we were all under contract for ten years and that the Senator would hold us to the letter of the contract, or put us in chains and lock us up—the same as the other prisoners. It was made plain to us by some white people we talked to that in the contracts we had signed we had all agreed to be locked up in a stockade at night or at any other time that our employer saw fit; further, we learned that we could not lawfully break our contract for any reason and go and hire ourselves to somebody else without the consent of our employer; and, more than that, if we got mad and ran away, we could be run down by bloodhounds, arrested without process of law, and be returned to our employers, who, according to the contract, might beat us brutally or administer any other kind of punishment that he thought proper.

In other words, we had sold ourselves into slavery—and what could we do about it? The white folks had all the courts, all the guns, all the hounds, all the railroads, all the telegraph wires, all the newspapers, all the money, and nearly all the land, and we had only our ignorance, our poverty and our empty hands. We decided that the best thing to do was to shut our mouths, say nothing, and go back to work. And most of us worked side by side with those convicts during the remainder of the ten years.

But this first batch of convicts was only the beginning. Within six months another stockade was built, and twenty or thirty other convicts were brought to the plantation, among them six or eight women! The Senator had bought an additional thousand acres of land, and to his already large cotton plantation he added two great big saw-mills and went into the lumber business. Within two years the Senator had in all nearly 200 Negroes working on his plantation about half of them free laborers, so called, and about half of them convicts. The only difference between the free laborers and the others was that the free laborers could come and go as they pleased, at night that is, they were not locked up at night, and were not, as a general thing, whipped for slight offenses.

The troubles of the free laborers began at the close of the ten-year period. To a man, they all wanted to quit when the time was up. To a man, they all refused to sign new contracts—even for one year, not to say anything of ten years. And just when we thought that our bondage was at an end we found that it had really just begun. Two or three years before, or about a year and a half after the Senator had started his camp, he had established a large store, which was called the commissary. All of us free laborers were compelled to buy our supplies—food, clothing, etc. from the store. We never used any money in our dealings at the commissary, only tickets or orders, and we had a general settlement once each year, in October. In this store we were charged all sorts of high prices for goods, because every year we would come out in debt to our employer. If not that, we seldom had more than $5 or $10 coming to us and that for a whole year's work. Well, at the close of the tenth year, when we kicked and meant to leave the Senator, he said to some of us with a smile (and I never will forget that smile—I can see it now):

"Boys, I'm sorry you're going to leave me. I hope you will do well in your new places—so well that you will be able to pay me the little balances which most of you owe me."

Word was sent out for all of us to meet him at the commissary at 2 o'clock. There he told us that, after we had signed what he called a written acknowledgment of our debts, we might go and look for new places. The store-keeper took us one by one and read to us statements of our accounts. According to the books there was no man of us who owed the Senator less than $100; some of us were put down for as much as $200. I owed $165, according to the bookkeeper. These debts were not accumulated during one year, but ran back for three and four years, so we were told in spite of the fact that we understood that we had had a full settlement at the end of each year. But no one of us would have dared to dispute a white man's word— o, no; not in those days. Besides, we fellows didn't care anything about the amounts we were after getting away; and we had been told that we might go, if we signed the acknowledgments. We would have signed anything, just to get away. So we stepped up, we did, and made our marks.

That same night we were rounded up by a constable and ten or twelve white men, who aided him, and we were locked up, every one of us, in the Senator's stockades. The next morning it was explained to us by the two guards appointed to watch us that, in the papers we had signed the day before, we had not only made acknowledgment of our indebtedness, but that we had also agreed to work for the Senator until the debts were paid by hard labor. And from that day forward we were treated just like convicts. Really we had made ourselves lifetime slaves, or peons, as the laws called us. But, call it slavery, peonage, or what not, the truth is we lived in a hell on earth what time we spent in the Senator's peon camp.

I lived in that camp, as a peon, for nearly three years. My wife fared better than I did, as did the wives of some of the other Negroes, because the white men about the camp used these unfortunate creatures as their mistresses. When I was first put in the stockade, my wife was still kept for a while in the "Big House," but my little boy, who was only nine years old, was given away to a Negro family across the river in South Carolina, and I never saw or heard of him after that. When I left the camp, my wife had had two children by some one of the white bosses, and she was living in fairly good shape in a little house off to herself.

But the poor Negro women who were not in the class with my wife fared about as bad as the helpless Negro men. Most of the time the women who were peons or convicts were compelled to wear men's clothes. Sometimes, when I have seen them dressed like men, and plowing or hoeing or hauling logs or working at the blacksmith's trade, just the same as men, my heart would bleed and my blood would boil, but I was powerless to raise a hand. It would have meant death on the spot to have said a word. Of the first six women brought to the camp, two of them gave birth to children after they had been there more than twelve months and the babies had white men for their fathers!

The stockades in which we slept were, I believe, the filthiest places in the world. They were cesspools of nastiness. During the three years that I was there I am willing to swear that a mattress was never moved after it had been brought there, except to turn it over once or twice a month. No

sheets were used, only dark-colored blankets. Most of the men slept every night in the clothing that they had worked in all day. Some of the worst characters were made to sleep in chains. The doors were locked and barred each night, and tallow candles were the only lights allowed. Really the stockades were but little more than cow sheds, horse stables or hog pens. . . .

But I didn't tell you how I got out. I didn't get out—they put me out. When I had served as a peon for nearly three years—and you remember that they claimed that I owed them only $165— when I had served for nearly three years, one of the bosses came to me and said that my time was up. He happened to be the one who was said to be living with my wife. He gave me a new suit of overalls, which cost about seventy-five cents, took me in a buggy and carried me across the Broad River into South Carolina, set me down and told me to "git." I didn't have a cent of money, and I wasn't feeling well, but somehow I managed to get a move on me. I begged my way to Columbia. In two or three days I ran across a man looking for laborers to carry to Birmingham, and I joined his gang. I have been here in Birmingham district since they released me, and I reckon I'll die either in a coal mine or an iron furnace. It don't make much difference which. Either is better than a Georgia peon camp. And a Georgia peon camp is hell itself.

—Anonymous, *Independent Magazine*

——— APPENDIX A.10 ———
"THE UNEDUCATED NEGRO WAS TOO WEAK"

Controversy and fraud marked the 1876 presidential election between Republican Rutherford B. Hayes and Democrat Samuel J. Tilden. A special commission was formed to resolve 20 disputed electoral votes. On a strictly partisan 8-7 vote, the commission assigned all the disputed votes to Hayes, meaning he would win the electoral vote 185-184. Infuriated Democrats threatened to contest the election but instead struck a deal with

Hayes and the Republicans. In exchange for removing troops from the South, naming a Southerner to the cabinet, and allocating federal aid to the South, the Southern Democrats agreed to support the commission's finding. As a result, Democrats regained state political control throughout the region. Former South Carolina governor Daniel Chamberlain wrote about the fall of the Republican Party in South Carolina to William Lloyd Garrison in June 1877.

Dear Mr. Garrison. . .

Your prophecy is fulfilled, and I am not only overthrown, but as a consequence I am now a citizen of New York. It seems to me a remarkable experience indeed, though I hope I do not egotistically exaggerate it, for I am sure it will soon be forgotten by most men in the press and hurry of new events. Why I write this line now and send it to Boston when I know you are in Europe, is because I feel like putting on record my main reflections on my experiences of the last three years. . . .

First, then, my defeat was inevitable under the circumstances of time and place which surrounded me. I mean here exactly that the uneducated negro was too weak, no matter what his numbers, to cope with the whites.

We had lost too, the sympathy of the North, in some large measure, though we never deserved it so certainly as in 1876 in South Carolina.

The Presidential contest also endangered us and doubtless defeated us. The hope of electing Tilden incited our opponents, and the greed of office led the defeated Republicans under Hayes to sell us out. There was just as distinct a bargain to do this at Washington as ever existed which was not signed and sealed on paper. And the South is not to be blamed for it, if anybody is; but rather those leaders, like Evarts, who could never see their Constitutional obligations towards the South until the offices were slipping away from their party.

So the end came, but not as you expected. . . .

—Daniel Chamberlain

APPENDIX A.11

"A General Reestablishment of Order"

When President Rutherford B. Hayes delivered his first annual message to Congress in December 1877, all of the conditions in the political agreement between the Republicans and the Democrats had been accomplished. The Reconstruction Era ended, and a century-long dominance of segregationist Democratic state governments in the South had been initiated. Hayes—who was a decorated Civil War veteran and radical Republican who voted for Johnson's impeachment—emphasized the need for North and South to continue the reconciliation of differences. Hayes praised the progress that had been made in the South in reestablishing its economy, political stability and judicial system.

To complete and make permanent the pacification of the country continues to be, and until it is fully accomplished must remain, the most important of all our national interests. The earnest purpose of good citizens generally to unite their efforts in this endeavor is evident. It found decided expression in the resolutions announced in 1876 by the national conventions of the leading political parties of the country. There was a widespread apprehension that the momentous results in our progress as a nation marked by the recent amendments to the Constitution were in imminent jeopardy; that the good understanding which prompted their adoption, in the interest of a loyal devotion to the general welfare, might prove a barren truce, and that the two sections of the country, once engaged in civil strife, might be again almost as widely severed and disunited as they were when arrayed in arms against each other.

The course to be pursued, which, in my judgment, seemed wisest in the presence of this emergency, was plainly indicated in my inaugural address. It pointed to the time, which all our people desire to see, when a genuine love of our whole country and of all that concerns its true welfare shall supplant the destructive forces of the mutual animosity of races and of sectional hostility. Opinions have differed widely as to the measures best calculated to secure this great end. This was to be expected. The measures adopted by the Administration have been subjected to severe and varied criticism. Any course whatever which might have been entered upon would certainly have encountered distrust and opposition. These measures were, in my judgment, such as were most in harmony with the Constitution and with the genius of our people, and best adapted, under all the circumstances, to attain the end in view. Beneficent results, already apparent, prove that these endeavors are not to be regarded as a mere experiment, and should sustain and encourage us in our efforts. Already, in the brief period which has elapsed, the immediate effectiveness, no less than the justice, of the course pursued is demonstrated, and I have an abiding faith that time will furnish its ample vindication in the minds of the great majority of my fellow-citizens. The discontinuance of the use of the Army for the purpose of upholding local governments in two States of the Union was no less a constitutional duty and requirement, under the circumstances existing at the time, than it was a much-needed measure for the restoration of local self-government and the promotion of national harmony. The withdrawal of the troops from such employment was effected deliberately, and with solicitous care for the peace and good order of society and the protection of the property and persons and every right of all classes of citizens.

The results that have followed are indeed significant and encouraging. All apprehension of danger from remitting those States to local self-government is dispelled, and a most salutary change in the minds of the people has begun and is in progress in every part of that section of the country once the theater of unhappy civil strife, substituting for suspicion, distrust, and aversion, concord, friendship, and patriotic attachment to the Union. No unprejudiced mind will deny that the terrible and often fatal collisions which for several years have been of frequent occurrence and have agitated and alarmed the public mind have almost entirely ceased, and that a spirit of mutual forbearance and hearty national interest has succeeded. There has been a general reestablishment of order and of the orderly administration of justice. Instances of remaining lawlessness have become of rare occurrence; political turmoil and turbulence have disappeared; useful industries have been resumed; public credit in the Southern States has been greatly strengthened, and the encouraging benefits of a revival of commerce between the sections of the country lately embroiled in civil war are fully enjoyed. Such are some of the results already attained, upon which the country is to be congratulated. They are of such importance that we may with confidence patiently await the desired consummation that will surely come with the natural progress of events. . . .

—Rutherford B. Hayes

— APPENDIX B —
DOCUMENTS OF
LASTING INFLUENCE

With all of the attention given to the great battles and legendary military leaders of the Civil War, it is easy to overlook the other less dramatic—but no less important—events that took place during the conflict. Landmark legislation, diplomatic positions, and far-reaching legal precedents were all established during the Civil War as a direct result of the war.

The documents below reflect some of those events, and they serve as an appendix to this volume. The first three entries are pieces of wartime legislation forged after the sudden departure of Southern Democrats from Congress. Freed from the need to compromise with Southern interests, Northern Republicans were able to pass significant measures to hasten the nation's westward development.

The fourth document, Declaration of the People of Virginia, was one of the first steps in the creation of the state of West Virginia, something that would probably never have happened if not for Virginia's secession. A series of diplomatic pronouncements concerning French and Austrian intrusions in Mexico in the early 1860s follow. The Civil War gave European powers the opportunity to reassert their ambitions in Latin America. Once the war ended, however, the American government was quick to reaffirm its commitment to the Monroe Doctrine whereby the United States called for an end to European influence in the Americas.

Finally, Lincoln's decision to suspend the writ of habeas corpus as a military measure forced the nation to define the limits of military power in a democracy. Ex parte Milligan and ex parte Merryman were both landmark decisions that helped establish boundaries for the use of the military in a nation based on individual rights and the superiority of civil authority.

— APPENDIX B.1 —
HOMESTEAD ACT

Prior to the Civil War, Southern congressmen blocked homesteading legislation that would provide for the free distribution of public lands, mostly located west of the Mississippi River. Southern states feared that the availability of free land would sap their strength by weakening their already precarious political power base as people swarmed westward and formed new non-slaveholding states.

The Republicans, however, strongly favored colonizing the West. Giving away free land was very appealing to the Northern public. In March 1860, Congress passed a compromise homestead bill that President James Buchanan vetoed. In the 1860 election, Lincoln pledged his strong support for homesteading. When the Southern states seceded, there was little opposition to a liberal homesteading act. Congress passed the Homestead Act on May 20, 1862.

The Homestead Act placed nearly 2 billion acres in escrow for the landless. An opportunity unparalleled in world history, the legislation provided land for free to anyone willing to work. Horace Greeley praised the act as the opportunity to "give every poor man a home." Within 18 months, settlers had claimed more than 1.2 million acres.

The Homestead Act hastened the development of the Midwestern prairie states and helped confirm the United States as a land of unprecedented opportunity. The legislation, however, did not work entirely as planned. Many of the urban and immigrant families for whom it was intended did not have the money, equipment or experience needed to succeed as farmers. In many cases, speculators acquired large tracts of land for their own future enrichment.

Be it enacted, That any person who is the head of a family, or who has arrived at the age of twenty-one years, and is a citizen of the United States, or who shall have filed his intention to become such, as required by the naturalization laws of the United States, and who has never borne arms against the United States Government or given aid and comfort to its enemies, shall, from and after the first of January, 1863, be entitled to enter one quarter-section or a less quantity of unappropriated public lands, upon which said person may have filed a pre-emption claim, or which may, at the time the application is made, be subject to pre-emption at one dollar and twenty-five cents, or less, per acre; or eighty acres or less of such unappropriated lands, at two dollars and fifty cents per acre, to be located in a body, in conformity to the legal subdivisions of the public lands, and after the same shall have been surveyed: Provided, That any person owning or residing on land may, under the provisions of this act, enter other land lying contiguous to his or her said land, which shall not, with the land so already owned and occupied exceed in the aggregate one hundred and sixty acres.

Sec. 2. That the person applying for the benefit of this act shall, upon application to the register of the land office in which he or she is about to make such entry, make affidavit before the said register or receiver that he or she is the head of a family, or is twenty-one or more years of age, or shall have performed service in the Army or Navy of the United States, and that he has never borne arms against the Government of the United States or given aid and comfort to its enemies, and that such application is made for his or her exclusive use and benefit, and that said entry is made for the purpose of actual settlement and cultivation, and not, either directly or indirectly, for the use or benefit of any other person or persons whomsoever, and upon filing the said affidavit with the register or receiver, and on payment of ten dollars, he or she shall

thereupon be permitted to enter the quantity of land specified: Provided, however, that no certificate shall be given or patent issue therefor until the expiration of five years from the date of such entry—or if he be dead, his widow, or in case of her death, his heirs or devisee; or in case of a widow making such entry, her heirs or devisee, in case of her death—shall prove by two credible witnesses that he, she, or they have resided upon or cultivated the same for the term of five years immediately succeeding the time of filing the affidavit aforesaid, and shall make affidavit that no part of said land has been alienated, and that he has borne true allegiance to the Government of the United States; then in such cases he, she, or they, if at that time a citizen of the United States, shall be entitled to a patent, as in other cases provided for by law: And provided, further, That in case of the death of both father and mother, leaving an infant child or children under twenty-one years of age, the right and fee shall inure to the benefit of said infant child or children; and the executor, administrator, or guardian may, at any time within two years after the death of the surviving parent, and in accordance with the laws of the State in which such children for the time being have their domicile, sell said land for the benefit of said infants, but for no other purpose; and the purchaser shall acquire the absolute title by the purchase, and be entitled to a patent from the United States, on payment of the office fees and sum of money herein specified.

—United States Congress

———— APPENDIX B.2 ————

PACIFIC RAILWAY ACT

Advocates of railroads broached the idea of a transcontinental railroad as early as the 1840s. The rapid growth of California after gold was discovered there in 1848 brought the issue to national attention. Although there was general agreement that a railroad spanning the continent was needed, sectional rivalries prevented agreement on what path the line should take.

Congress authorized a survey of various routes in 1853 under the direction of Secretary of War Jefferson Davis. Hoping to secure land for a southern route, senators from the South helped arrange the Gadsden Purchase of nearly 30,000 square miles from Mexico in 1853. Northerners, however, favored a northern route.

The secession of the Southern states cleared the way for a northern pathway, and in 1862 the first Pacific Railway Act, authorizing the transcontinental railroad, was passed. Generous government assistance was provided through land grants. Two years later a second Pacific Railway Act doubled the land grants and provided that the government have a second instead of a first mortgage on the railroad property. Lincoln, a staunch advocate of railroads and infrastructure improvements, hoped to take the train to California when his term ended.

The Central Pacific Railway was charged with building the line eastward and the Union Pacific Railway westward. After the war, work on the railroad took on a greater sense of urgency. General Grenville M. Dodge, who had proved his talents as Sherman's engineer in the Atlanta campaign, was made chief engineer of the Union Pacific and was largely responsible for the rapid and efficient construction of the road. The two lines met at Promontory Point, Utah, in 1869, an event of national importance.

An Act to aid in the Construction of a Railroad and Telegraph Line from the Missouri River to the Pacific Ocean

Be it enacted, That Walter S. Burgess together with five commissioners to be appointed by the Secretary of the Interior . . . and hereby created and erected into body corporate by the name of "The Union Pacific Railroad Company". . . ; and said corporation is hereby authorized and empowered to lay out, locate, construct, furnish, maintain and enjoy a continuous railroad and telegraph . . . from a point on the one hundredth meridian of longitude west from Greenwich, between the south margin of the valley of the Republican River and the north margin of the valley of the Platte River, to the western boundary of Nevada Territory, upon the route and terms hereinafter provided. . . .

Sec. 2. That the right of way through the public lands be granted to said company for the construction of said railroad and telegraph line; and the right is hereby given to said company to take from the public lands adjacent to the line of said road, earth, stone, timber, and other materials for the construction thereof; said right of way is granted to said railroad to the extent of two hundred feet in width on each side of said railroad when it may pass over the public lands, including all necessary grounds for stations, buildings, workshops, and depots, machine shops, switches, side tracks, turn tables, and water stations. The United States shall extinguish as rapidly as may be the Indian titles to all lands falling under the operation of this act. . . .

Sec. 3. That there be granted to the said company, for the purpose of aiding in the construction of said railroad and telegraph line, and to secure the safe and speedy transportation of mails, troops, munitions of war and public stores thereon, every alternative section of public land, designated by odd numbers, to the amount of five alternate sections per mile on each side of said railroad, on the line thereof, and within the limits of ten miles on each side of said road . . . Provided that all mineral lands shall be excepted from the operation of this act; but where the same shall contain timber, the timber thereon is granted to said company. . . .

Sec. 5 That for the purposes herein mentioned the Secretary of Treasury shall . . . in accordance with the provisions of this act, issue to said company bonds of the United States of one thousand dollars each, payable in thirty years after date, paying six per centum per annum interest . . . to the amount of sixteen of said bonds per mile for each section of forty miles; and to secure the repayment to the United States . . . of the amount of said bonds . . . the issue of said bonds . . . shall ipso facto constitute a first mortgage on the whole line of the railroad and telegraph. . . .

Sec. 9. That the Leavenworth, Pawnee and Western Railroad Company of Kansas are hereby authorized to construct a railroad and telegraph line . . . upon the same terms and conditions in all respects as are provided [for the construction of the Union Pacific Railroad]. . . . The Central Pacific Railroad Company of California are hereby authorized to construct a railroad and telegraph line from the Pacific coast to the eastern boundaries of California, upon the same terms and conditions in all respects [as provided for the Union Pacific Railroad].

Sec. 10. . . . The Central Pacific Railroad Company of California after completing its road across said State, is authorized to continue the construction of said railroad and telegraph through the Territories of the United States to the Missouri River upon the terms and conditions provided in this act in relation to the Union Pacific Railroad Company, until said roads shall meet and connect. . . .

Sec. 11. That for three hundred miles of said road most mountainous and difficult of construction, to wit: one hundred and fifty miles westerly from the eastern base of the Rocky Mountains, and one hundred and fifty miles eastwardly from the western base of the Sierra Nevada mountains . . . the bonds to be issued to aid in the construction thereof shall be treble the number per mile hereinbefore provided; and between the sections last named of one hundred and fifty miles each, the bonds to be issued to aid in the construction thereof shall be double the number per mile first mentioned.

—UNITED STATES CONGRESS

APPENDIX B.3
MORRILL ACT

The Morrill Act, which granted public lands for the support of agricultural and industrial education, is one of the most important pieces of legislation passed on behalf of education in the nation's history. Jonathan B. Turner, a University of Illinois professor, began the movement for a nationally endowed college of agricultural and industrial arts in 1850. Justin S. Morrill, senator from Vermont, latched onto the idea on the belief that the scientific study of farming would reduce wasteful use of farmland and provide opportunities to farmers' sons who could not otherwise afford a college education.

Congress passed a bill submitted by Morrill in 1859, but President James Buchanan vetoed it because he questioned the constitutionality of giving public lands to the states for resale. The measure, however, was very popular, particularly in the northeast. Morrill resubmitted the legislation after the Civil War erupted. Congress approved it in June 1862. Lincoln signed it on

July 2, 1862. Because the program was slow to take hold and many schools struggled financially, Congress passed the Hatch Act of 1887 to secure more financial assistance.

Under the terms of the acts, about 13 million acres of public land were given to states to establish mechanical and agricultural colleges, or to expand existing colleges and universities. The Morrill Act provided a tremendous stimulus to the movement for establishing state universities. It led directly to the creation of 69 land-grant colleges.

An Act donating Public Lands to the several States and Territories which may provide Colleges for the Benefit of Agriculture and the Mechanic Arts.

Be it enacted by the Senate and House of Representatives of the United States of America in Congress assembled, That there be granted to the several States, for the purposed hereinafter mentioned, an amount of public land, to be apportioned to each State a quantity equal to thirty thousand acres for each senator and representative in Congress to which the States are respectively entitled by the apportionment under the census of 1860; Provided, That no mineral lands shall be selected or purchased under the provisions of this act.

Sec. 2 And be it further enacted, That the land aforesaid, after being surveyed, shall be apportioned to the several States in sections or subdivisions of sections, not less than one quarter of a section; and whenever there are public lands in a State subject to sale at private entry at one dollar and twenty-five cents per acre, the quantity to which said State shall be entitled shall be selected from such lands within the limits of such State, and the Secretary of the Interior is hereby directed to issue to each of the States in which there is not the quantity of public lands subject to sale at private entry at one dollars and twenty-five cents per acre; to which said State may be entitled under the provisions of this act, land scrip to the amount in acres for the deficiency of its distributive share: said scrip to be sold by said States and the proceeds thereof applied to the uses and purposed prescribed in this act, and for other use or purpose whatsoever. . . .

Sec. 4 And be it further enacted, That all moneys derived from the sale of the lands aforesaid by the States to which the lands are apportioned, and from the sale of land scrip hereinbefore provided for, shall be invested in stocks of the United States, or of the States, or some other safe stocks, yielding not less than five per centum upon the par value of said stocks; and that the moneys so invested shall constitute a perpetual fund, the capital of which shall remain forever undiminished, (except so far as may be provided in section fifth of this act,) and the interest of which shall be inviolably appropriated, by each State which may take and claim the benefit of this act, to the endowment, support, and maintenance of at least one college where the leading object shall be, without excluding other scientific and classical studies, and including military tactics, to teach such branches of learning as are related to agriculture and mechanic arts, in such manner as the legislatures of the State may respectively prescribe, in order to promote the liberal and practical education of the industrial classes in the several pursuits and professions in life.

Sec. 5. No State while in a condition of rebellion or insurrection against the government of the United States shall be entitled to the benefit of this Act.

—United States Congress

—— APPENDIX B.4 ——
West Virginia Becomes A State

When Virginia seceded from the Union on April 17, 1861, residents of its western counties immediately called meetings to oppose the action. For decades, fierce differences had existed between Virginians living east and those living west of the Allegheny Mountains. Few citizens of the western region owned slaves. They had little in common with the landed gentry of eastern Virginia. The region's major roads and rivers connected the area's economy and culture more to their northern neighbors, Ohio and Pennsylvania, than to the rest of the state. Virginia's decision to join the Confederacy worsened the intrastate rift.

At the same time, Virginia's western counties were an early battleground because of the strategic importance of the Ohio River and the Baltimore & Ohio Railroad. In July, 1861, General George B. McClellan won a series of victories in the Alleghenies, securing the region for the Union.

While McClellan prepared for his campaign, pro-Union citizens summoned a general convention to take action and divide the Old Dominion. Delegates from 26 counties convened at Wheeling on June 11, 1861. The delegates approved The Declaration of the People of Virginia, reprinted here, on June 17.

Over the next two months the illegal convention passed laws reorganizing the government of Virginia and voted to create a new state with its capital at Wheeling. Delegates authorized a reorganized legislature, elected a governor, and called for a constitutional convention. The convention formed a new constitution that was ratified on April 3, 1862, by voters who had taken the oath of allegiance to the Union. Congress admitted West Virginia as a state. Although Lincoln considered vetoing the bill because of its questionable legality, he finally approved it. On June 20, 1863, West Virginia formally entered the Union.

Similar to the situation in Missouri, the Civil War ripped West Virginia apart as guerrillas and bushwhackers engaged in bitter combat in the rugged mountain state. About 25,000 men from West Virginia fought in the Union army, while an estimated 15,000 joined the Confederate army. It took decades for the wounds of bitter partisan warfare and the state's dissolution to heal.

Declaration of the People of Virginia Represented in Convention in Wheeling, June 17, 1861

The true purpose of all government is to promote the welfare and provide for the protection and security of the governed, and when any form of organization of government proves inadequate for, or subversive of this purpose, it is the right, it is the duty of the latter to alter or abolish it. The Bill of Rights of Virginia, framed in 1776, reaffirmed in 1830, and again in 1851, expressly reserves this right to the majority of her people, and the existing Constitution does not confer upon the General Assembly the power to call a Convention to alter its provisions, or to change the relations of the Commonwealth, without the previously expressed consent of such a majority. The act of the General Assembly, calling the Convention which assembled at Richmond in February last, was therefore a usurpation; and the Convention thus called has not only abused the powers nominally intrusted to it, but, with the connivance and active aid of the Executive, has usurped and exercised other powers, to the manifest injury of the people, which, if permitted, will inevitably subject them to a military despotism.

The Convention, by its pretended ordinances, has required the people of Virginia to separate from and wage war against the Government of the United States, and against the citizens of neighboring States, with whom they have heretofore maintained friendly, social, and business relations:

It has attempted to subvert the union founded by Washington and his co-patriots in the purer days of the Republic, which has conferred unexampled prosperity upon every class of citizens and upon every section of the country:

It has attempted to transfer the allegiance of the people to an illegal confederacy of rebellious States, and required their submission to its pretended edicts and decrees:

It has attempted to place the whole military force and military operations of the commonwealth under the control and direction of such Confederacy, for offensive as well as defensive purposes:

It has, in conjunction with the state Executive, instituted wherever their usurped power extends, a reign of terror, intended to suppress the free expression of the will of the people, making elections a mockery and a fraud:

The same combination, even before the passage of the pretended Ordinance of Secession, instituted war by the seizure and appropriation of the property of the Federal Government, and by organizing and mobilizing armies, with the avowed purpose of capturing or destroying the Capital of the Union.:

They have attempted to bring the allegiance of the people of the United States into direct conflict with their subordinate allegiance to the State, thereby making obedience to their pretended Ordinance treason against the former.

We, therefore, the delegates here assembled in Convention to devise such measures and take such action as the safety and welfare of the loyal citizens of Virginia may demand, having mutually considered the premises, and viewing the great concern the deplorable condition to which this once happy Commonwealth must be reduced, unless some regular adequate remedy is speedily adopted, and appealing to the Supreme Ruler of the Universe for the rectitude of our intentions, do hereby in the name and on the behalf of the good people of Virginia, solemnly declare, that the preservation of their dearest rights and liberties, and their security in person and property, imperatively demand the reorganization of the Government of the Commonwealth, and that all acts of said Convention and Executive, tending to separate this Commonwealth from the United States, or to levy and carry on war against them, are without authority and void; and the offices of all who adhere to the said Convention and Executive, whether legislative, executive, or judicial, are vacated.

—PEOPLE OF VIRGINIA

APPENDIX B.5

OUSTING THE FRENCH FROM MEXICO

The Civil War gave Napoleon III an opportunity to bring the New World back into the European balance of power and to reestablish European authority in North America.

When the Mexican Congress suspended all payments on foreign debts in July 1861, France, Spain and Great Britain signed an agreement for joint intervention. In 1862, they took possession of Mexican custom houses. Spain and Great Britain reached an agreement with Mexico and withdrew their forces, leaving France in control of the situation.

The French Army defeated the Mexican Army, captured Mexico City, and organized a provisional government that promptly voted to establish an empire. The new government invited Archduke Maximilian of Austria to the throne.

Secretary of State William Seward watched this violation of the Monroe Doctrine with deep disapproval, but did not want to antagonize the French fearing Napoleon III could join the Confederacy as an ally. The dispatch of March 3, 1862, sets forth the American position on intervention and assumes the honorable intentions of the signatories of the convention of 1861. The success of the Union army emboldened the government's position and in 1864 the House of Representatives staked a bolder position, but the Senate rejected the House's resolution of April 4, 1864.

After the war, Seward assumed a hostile position to the maintenance of a French regime in Mexico. The dispatch of April 16, 1866, made clear that the United States would not tolerate Austrian military support to Emperor Maximilian. French troops were withdrawn from Mexico the following year and Maximilian was shot in June.

A. Seward to Adams, March 3, 1862

Department of State
Washington, March 3, 1862

Sir:

We observe indications of a growing opinion in Europe that the demonstrations which are being made by Spanish, French, and British forces against Mexico are likely to be attended with a revolution in that country which will bring in a monarchical government there, in which the crown will be assumed by some foreign prince.

This country is deeply concerned in the peace of nations, and aims to be loyal at the same time in all its relations, as well to the allies as to Mexico. The President has therefore instructed me to submit his views on the new aspect of affairs to the parties concerned. He has relied upon the assurances given to this government by the allies that they were seeking no political objects and only a redress of grievances. He does not doubt the sincerity of the allies, and his confidence in their good faith, if it could be shaken, would be reinspired by explanations apparently made in their behalf that the governments of Spain, France, and Great Britain are not intending to intervene and will not intervene to effect a change of the constitutional form of government now existing in Mexico, or to produce any political change there in opposition to the will of the Mexican people. Indeed, he understands the allies to be unanimous in declaring that the proposed revolution in Mexico is moved only by Mexican citizens now in Europe.

The president, however, deems it his duty to express to the allies, in all candor and frankness, the opinion that no monarchical government which could be founded in Mexico, in the presence of foreign navies and armies in the waters and upon the soil of Mexico, would have any prospect of security or permanency. Secondly, that the instability of such a monarchy there would be enhanced if the throne should be assigned to any person not of Mexican nativity. That under such circumstances the new government must speedily fall unless it could draw into its support European alliances, which, in fact, make it the beginning of a permanent policy of armed European monarchical intervention injurious and practically hostile to the most general system of government on the continent of America, and this would be the beginning rather than the ending of revolution in Mexico.

These views are grounded upon some knowledge of the political sentiments and habits of society in America.

In such a case it is not to be doubted that the permanent interests and sympathies of this country would be with the other American republics. It is not intended on this occasion to predict the course of events which might happen as a consequence of the proceeding contemplated, either on this continent or in Europe. It is sufficient to say that, in the president's opinion, the emancipation of this continent from European control has been the principal feature in its history during the last century. It is not probable that a revolution in the contrary direction would be successful in an immediately succeeding century, while population in America is so rapidly increasing, resources so rapidly developing, and society so steadily forming itself upon principles of democratic American government. Nor is it necessary to suggest to the allies the improbability that European nations could steadily agree upon a policy favorable to such a counter-revolution as one conducive to their own interests, or to suggest that, however studiously the allies may act to avoid lending the aid of their land and naval forces to domestic revolutions in Mexico, the result would nevertheless be traceable to the presence of those forces there, although for a different purpose, since it may be deemed certain that but for their presence there no such revolution could probably have been attempted or even conceived.

The Senate of the United States has not, indeed, given its official sanction to the precise measures which the President has proposed for lending our aid to the existing government in Mexico, with the approval of the allies, to relieve it from its present embarrassments. This, however, is only a question of domestic administration. It would be very erroneous to regard such a disagreement as indicating any serious difference of opinion in this government or among the American people in their cordial good wishes for the safety, welfare, and stability of the republican system of government in that country.

I am, sir, your obedient servant,

—WILLIAM H. SEWARD

B. House Resolution on French Intervention in Mexico, April 4, 1864

Resolved. That the Congress of the United States are unwilling, by silence, to leave the nations of the world under the impression that they are indifferent spectators of the deplorable events now transpiring in the Republic of Mexico; and they therefore think fit to declare that it does not accord with policy of the United States to acknowledge a monarchical government, erected on the ruins of any republican government in America, under the auspices of any European power.

—UNITED STATES CONGRESS

C. Seward to Motley, April 16, 1866

Mr. Seward to Mr. Motley
Department of State

Washington, April 16, 1866

Sir:

I have had the honor to receive your despatch of the 27th of March, No. 155, which brings the important announcement that a treaty, called a "military supplementary convention," was ratified on the 15th of that month between the Emperor of Austria and the Prince Maximilian, who claims to be an emperor in Mexico.

You inform me that it is expected that about one thousand volunteers will be shipped (under this treaty) from Trieste to Vera Cruz very soon, and that at least as many more will be shipped in autumn.

I have heretofore given you the President's instructions to ask for explanations, and, conditionally, to inform the government of Austria that the despatch of military expeditions by Austria under such an arrangement as the one which seems now to have been consummated would be regarded with serious concern by the United States.

The subject has now been further considered in connexion with the official information thus recently received. The time seems to have arrived when the attitude of this government in relation to Mexican affairs should be once again frankly and distinctly made known to the Emperor of Austria, and all other powers whom it may directly concern. The United States, for reasons which seem to them to be just, and to have their foundation in the laws of nations, maintain that the domestic republican government with which they are in relations of friendly communication is the only legitimate government existing in Mexico; that a war has for a period of several years been waged against that republic by the government of France; which war began with a disclaim of all political or dynastic designs that that war has subsequently taken upon itself, and now distinctly wears the character of an European intervention to overthrow that domestic republican government, and to erect in its stead a European, imperial, military despotism by military force. The United States, in view of the character of their own political institutions, their proximity and intimate relations towards Mexico, and their just influence in the political affairs of the American continent, cannot consent to the accomplishment of that purpose by the means described. The United States have therefore addressed themselves, as they think, reasonably to the government of France, and have asked that its military forces, engaged in that objectionable political invasion, may desist from further intervention and be withdrawn from Mexico.

A copy of the last communication upon this subject, which was addressed by us to the government of France, is herewith transmitted by your special information. This paper will give you the true situation of the question. It will also enable you to satisfy the government of Vienna that the United States must be no less opposed to military intervention for political objects hereafter in Mexico by the government of Austria, than they are opposed to any further intervention of the same character in that country by France.

You will, therefore, at as early a day as may be convenient, bring the whole case, in a becoming manner, to the attention of the imperial royal government. You are authorized to state that the United States sincerely desire that Austria may find it just and expedient to come upon the same ground of non-intervention in Mexico which is maintained by the United States, and to which they have invited France.

You will communicate to us the answer of the Austrian government to this proposition.

This government could not but regard as a matter of serious concern the despatch of any troops from Austria for Mexico while the subject which you are thus directed to present to the Austrian government remains under consideration.

I am, sir, your obedient servant,

—WILLIAM H. SEWARD

—— APPENDIX B.6 ——

EX PARTE MERRYMAN

The writ of habeas corpus protects individuals from unlawful imprisonment, requiring that an accused be informed of the crime he or she has been alleged to commit. The U.S. Constitution guarantees this protection "unless when in Cases of Rebellion or Invasion the public safety may require" its suspension. According to the Constitution, only Congress can suspend the writ of habeas corpus.

In the spring of 1861, however, Congress was not in session. Impatient for the legislature to reconvene and confronted by rebellious activity all around and within Washington, D.C., Lincoln took it upon himself on April 27 to suspend the writ of habeas corpus in the corridor between the Capitol and Philadelphia.

Southern sympathizers were very active in Maryland; one of the most active was John Merryman, of Baltimore, who participated in antiwar riots. Merryman was arrested in May and imprisoned in Fort McHenry by military order. He applied for a writ of habeas corpus. As no probable cause was shown for his arrest, Supreme Court Chief Justice Roger B. Taney ordered that Merryman be released. General George Cadwalader refused. Taney cited him for contempt of court, and the general refused to accept Taney's writ of contempt.

Faced with the standoff between executive and judicial authority, Taney filed his historic opinion in the case of ex parte Merryman—a U.S. circuit court decision as Taney was sitting as justice for the Maryland circuit court. Taney repudiated the authority of the president to suspend the writ of habeas corpus. Although Merryman was released and the case eventually dropped, Lincoln and the military ignored Taney's opinion against the executive's ability to suspend the writ of habeas corpus. Lincoln authorized the military repeatedly to suspend the writ of habeas corpus throughout the war. "Must I shoot a simpleminded soldier boy who deserts, while I must not touch a hair of a wily agitator who induces him to desert?" Lincoln wrote in an 1863 letter in which he also professed his own distaste at having to take the measure. In all, more than 10,000 suspects were imprisoned during the Civil War without the benefit of a habeas corpus hearing.

Ex parte Merryman raised fundamental constitutional issues concerning the protection of a person's rights. Lincoln was sharply criticized in the North, particularly by Democrats, for his decision, which many deemed unconstitutional. The final determination of the constitutionality of his actions was not made until after the war in ex parte Milligan.

The application in this case for a writ of habeas corpus is made to me under the 14th section of the Judiciary Act of 1789, which renders effectual for the citizen the constitutional privilege of the writ of habeas corpus. That act gives to the Courts of the United States, as well as to each justice of the Supreme Court, and to every District Judge, power to grant writs of habeas corpus for the purpose of an inquiry into the cause of commitment. The petition was presented to me at Washington, under the impression that I would order the prisoner to be brought before me there, but as he was confined in Fort McHenry, at the City of Baltimore, which is in my circuit, I resolved to hear it in the latter city, as obedience to the writ, under such circumstances, would not withdraw Gen. Cadwalader who had him in charge from the limits of his military command. . . .

A copy of the warrant or order, under which the prisoner was arrested, was demanded by his counsel, and refused. And it is not alleged in the return that any specific act, constituting an offence against the laws of the United States, has been charged against him upon oath; but he appears to have been arrested upon general charges of treason and rebellion, without proof, and without giving the names of the witnesses, or specifying the act, which in judgment of the military officer, constituted the crime. And having the prisoner thus in custody on these vague and unsupported accusations, he refuses to obey the writ of habeas corpus, upon the ground that he is duly authorized by the President to suspend it.

The case, then, is simply this: A military officer residing in Pennsylvania issues an order to arrest a citizen of Maryland, upon vague and indefinite charges, without any proof, so far as appears. Under this order his house is entered in the night; he is seized as a prisoner, and conveyed to Fort McHenry, and there kept in close confinement. And when a habeas corpus is served on the commanding officer, requiring him to produce the prisoner before a justice of the Supreme Court, in order that he may examine into the legality of the imprisonment, the answer of the officer is that he is authorized by the President to suspend the writ of habeas corpus at his discretion, and, in the exercise of that discretion, suspends it in this case, and on that ground refuses obedience to the writ.

As the case comes before me, therefore, I understand that the President not only claims the right to suspend the writ of habeas corpus himself, at his discretion, but to delegate that discretionary power to a military officer, and to leave it to him to determine whether he will or will not obey judicial process that may be served upon him.

No official notice has been given to the Courts of Justice, or to the public, by proclamation or otherwise, that the President claimed this power and had exercised it in the matter stated in the return. And I certainly listened to it with some surprise, for I had supposed it to be one of those points of constitutional law upon which there was no difference of opinion, and that it was admitted on all

hands that the privilege of the writ could not be suspended except by act of Congress. . . .

The clause in the Constitution which authorizes the suspension of the privilege of the writ of habeas corpus is in the ninth section of the first article. . . .

This article is devoted to the legislative Department of the United States, and has not the slightest reference to the Executive Department. . .

The power of legislation granted by this latter clause is by its word carefully confined to the specific objects before enumerated. But as this limitation was unavoidably somewhat indefinite, it was deemed necessary to guard more effectively certain great cardinal principles essential to the liberty of the citizen and to the rights and equality of the States by denying to Congress, in express terms, any power of legislation over them. It was apprehended, it seems, that such legislation might be attempted under the pretext that it was necessary and proper to carry into execution the powers granted; and it was determined that there should be no room to doubt, where rights of such vital importance were concerned, and accordingly this clause is immediately followed by an enumeration of certain subjects to which the powers of legislation shall not extend; and the great importance which the framers of the Constitution attached to the privilege of the writ of habeas corpus to protect the liberty of the citizen, is proved by the fact that its suspension, except in cases of invasion and rebellion, is first in the list of prohibited power; and even in these cases the power is denied and its exercise prohibited unless the public safety shall require it. It is true that in the cases mentioned Congress is of necessity to judge whether the public safety does or does not require it; and its judgment is conclusive. But the introduction of these words is a standing admonition to the legislative body of the danger of suspending it and of the extreme caution they should exercise before they give the government of the United States such power over the liberty of a citizen.

It is the second Article of the Constitution that provides for the organization of the Executive

Department, and enumerates the powers conferred on it, and prescribes its duties. And if the high power over the liberty of the citizens not claimed was intended to be conferred on the President, it would undoubtedly be found in plain words in this article. But there is not a word in it that can furnish the slightest ground to justify the exercise of the power. . . .

With such provisions in the Constitution, expressed in language too clear to be misunderstood by anyone, I can see no ground whatever for supposing that the President in any emergency or in any state of things can authorize the suspension of the privilege of the writ of habeas corpus, or arrest a citizen except in aid of the judicial power. He certainly does not faithfully execute the laws if he takes upon himself the legislative power by suspending the writ of habeas corpus—and the judicial power, also, by arresting and imprisoning a person without due process of law. Nor can any argument be drawn from the nature of sovereignty, or the necessities of government for self-defence, in times of tumult and danger. The Government of the United States is one of delegated and limited powers. It derives its existence and authority altogether from the Constitution, and neither of its branches—executive, legislative, or judicial—can exercise any of the powers of government beyond those specified and granted. . . .

To guide me to a right conclusion, I have Commentaries on the Constitution of the United States of the late Mr. Justice Story . . . and also the clear and authoritative decision of [the Supreme] Court, given more than half a century since, and conclusively establishing the principles I have above stated. Mr. Story, speaking in his Commentaries of the habeas corpus clause in the Constitution says:

"It is obvious that cases of a peculiar emergency may arise, which may justify, nay, even require, the temporary suspension of any right to the writ. . . . Hitherto no suspension of the writ has ever been authorized by Congress since the establishment of the Constitution. It would seem, as the

power is given to Congress to suspend the writ of habeas corpus in cases of rebellion or invasion, that the right to judge whether the exigency had arisen must exclusively belong to that body".
Commentaries, section 1,336.

And Chief Justice Marshall, in delivering the opinion of the Supreme Court in the case ex parte Bollman and Swartwout, uses this decisive language, in 4 Cranch, 101:

"If at any time the public safety should require the suspension of the powers vested by this act in the courts of the United States, it is for the Legislature to say so. That question depends on political considerations, on which the Legislature is to decide. Until the legislative will be expressed, this court can only see its duty, and must obey the laws."

But the documents before me show that the military authority in this case has gone far beyond the mere suspension of privilege of the writ of habeas corpus. It has, by force of arms, thrust aside the judicial authorities and officers to whom the Constitution has confided the power and duty of interpreting and administering the laws, and substituted a military government in its place, to be administered and executed by military officers. . . .

The Constitution provides, as I have before said, that "no person shall be deprived of life, liberty, or property without due process of law". It declares that "the right of the people to be secure in their persons, houses, papers, and effects against unreasonable searches and seizures shall not be violated, and no warrant shall issue but upon probable cause, supported by oath or affirmation, and particularly describing the place to be searched and the persons or things to be seized." It provides that the party accused shall be entitled to a speedy trial in a court of justice.

And these great and fundamental laws, which Congress itself could not suspend, have been disregarded and suspended, like the writ of habeas corpus, by a military order, supported by force of arms. Such is the case now before me; and I can only say that if the authority which the Constitution has confided to the judiciary department and judicial officers may thus upon any pretext or under any circumstances be usurped by the military power at its discretion, the people of the United States are no longer living under a Government of laws, but every citizen holds life, liberty, and property at the will and pleasure of the army officer in whose military district he may happen to be found.

In such a case my duty was too plain to be mistaken. I have exercised all the power which the Constitution and laws confer on me, but that power has been resisted by a force too strong for me to overcome. It is possible that the officer who had incurred this grave responsibility may have misunderstood his instructions, and exceeded the authority intended to be given him. I shall therefore order all the proceedings in this case, with my opinion, to be filed and recorded in the Circuit Court of the United States for the District of Maryland, and direct the clerk to transmit a copy . . . to the President of the United States. It will then remain for that high officer, in fulfillment of his constitutional obligation to "take care that the laws be faithfully executed" to determine what measure he will take to cause the civil process of the United States to be respected and enforced.

—Justice Roger B. Taney

APPENDIX B.7

Ex Parte Milligan

On March 3, 1863, Congress authorized President Lincoln to suspend the writ of habeas corpus in a questionable attempt to settle the constitutional dispute. Six months later, Lincoln used this authority to suspend the writ in cases where officers held persons for offenses against military service.

Military authorities arrested Lambdin Milligan, one of the most notorious Copperheads in Indiana, in October 1864. Milligan was charged with disloyal practices. A military court found him guilty of treason and sentenced him to hang. Milligan challenged the jurisdiction of the military to try a civilian. The case found its way to the Supreme Court after President Andrew Johnson had restored the writ of habeas corpus.

The landmark decision of the Supreme Court, rendered by Lincoln's friend Justice David Davis, is one of the most notable in U.S. history. It eloquently reasserts the principle of the superiority of the civil over the military. Not only did it condemn military tribunals where the civil courts were open but, by implication, also raised serious doubts as to the legality of the congressional reconstruction.

The Court concluded that Milligan's trial was unconstitutional. The case delimits the executive branch's unilateral supplanting of local civilian authority in the absence of actual hostilities and restrains the use of military authority to combat political crime.

The importance of the main question presented by this record cannot be overstated; for it involves the very framework of the government and the fundamental principles of American liberty.

During the late wicked rebellion, the temper of the times did not allow that calmness in deliberation and discussion so necessary to a correct conclusion of a purely judicial question. *Then*, considerations of safety were mingled with the exercise of power; and feelings and interests prevailed which are happily terminated. Now, that the public safety is assured, this question, as well as all others, can be discussed and decided without passion or the admixture of any element not required to form a legal judgment. We approach the investigation of this case, fully sensible of the magnitude of the inquiry and the necessity of full and cautious deliberation. . . .

The controlling question in the case is this: Upon the facts stated in Milligan's petition, and the exhibits filed, had the military commission mentioned in it jurisdiction, legally, to try and sentence him? Milligan, not a resident of one of the rebellious states, or a prisoner of war, but a citizen of Indiana for twenty years past, and never in the military or naval service, is, while at his home, arrested by the military power of the United States, imprisoned, and, on certain criminal charges preferred against him, tried, convicted, and sentenced to be hanged by a military commission, organized under the direction of the military commander of the military district of Indiana. Had this tribunal the legal power and authority to try and punish this man?

No graver question was ever considered by this court, nor one which more nearly concerns the rights of the whole people; for it is the birthright of every American citizen when charged with crime, to be tried and punished according to law. The power of punishment is alone through the means which the laws have provided for that purpose, and if they are ineffectual, there is an immunity from punishment no matter how great the offender the individual may be, or how much his crimes may have shocked the sense of justice of the country, or endangered its safety. By the protection of the law human rights are secured; withdraw that protection, and they are at the mercy of wicked rulers, or the clamor of an excited people. If there was law to justify this military trial, it is not our province to interfere; if there was not, it is our duty to declare the nullity of the whole proceedings. The decision of this question does not depend on argument or judicial precedents, numerous and highly illustrative as they are. These precedents inform us of the extent of the struggle to preserve liberty, and to relieve those in civil life from military trials. The founders of our government were familiar with the history of that struggle, and secured in a written Constitution every right which the people had wrested from power during a contest of ages. By that Constitution and the laws authorized by it this question must be determined. The provisions of that instrument on the administration of criminal justice are too plain and direct to leave room for misconstruction or doubt of their true meaning. Those applicable to this case are found in that clause of the original Constitution which says, "That the trial of all crimes, except in case of impeachment, shall be by jury"; and in the fourth, fifth, and sixth articles of the amendments. . . .

Time has proven the discernment of our ancestors; for even these provisions, expressed in such plain English words, that it would seem the ingenuity of man could not evade them, are *now*, after the elapse of more than seventy years, sought to be avoided. . . . The Constitution of the United States is a law for rulers and people, equally in war and in peace, and covers with the shield of its protection all classes of men, at all times, and under all circumstances. No doctrine involving more pernicious consequences was ever invented by the wit of man

than that any of its provisions can be suspended during any of the great exigencies of government. Such a doctrine leads directly to anarchy or despotism, but the theory of necessity on which it is based is false; for the government, within the Constitution, has all the powers granted to it which are necessary to preserve its existence; as has been happily proved by the result of the great effort to throw off its just authority.

Have any of the rights guaranteed by the Constitution been violated in the case of Milligan? And if so, what are they?

Every trial involves the exercise of judicial power; and from what source did the military commission that tried him derive their authority? Certainly no part of the judicial power of the country was conferred on them; because the Constitution expressly vests it "in one Supreme Court and such inferior courts as the Congress may from time to time ordain and establish," and it is not pretended that the commission was a court ordained and established by Congress. They cannot justify on the mandate of the President, because he is controlled by law, and has his appropriate sphere of duty, which is to execute, not to make, the laws; and there is "no unwritten criminal code to which resort can be had as a source of jurisdiction."

But it is said that the jurisdiction is complete under the "laws and usages of war."

It can serve no useful purpose to inquire what those laws and usages are, whence they originated, where found, and on whom they operate; they can never be applied to citizens in states which have upheld the authority of the government, and where the courts are open and their process unobstructed. This court has judicial knowledge that in Indiana the federal authority was always unopposed, and its courts always open to hear criminal accusations and redress grievances; and no usage of war could sanction a military trial there for any offense whatever of a citizen in civil life, in nowise connected with the military service. Congress could grant no such power; and to the honor of our national legislature be it said, it has never been provoked by the state of the country even to attempt its exercise. One of the plainest constitutional provisions was, therefore, infringed when Milligan was tried by a court not ordained and established by Congress, and not composed of judges appointed during good behavior.

Why was he not delivered to the circuit court of Indiana to be proceeded against according to law? No reason of necessity could be urged against it; because Congress had declared penalties against the offenses charged, provided for their punishment, and directed that court to hear and determine them. And soon after this military tribunal was ended, the circuit court met, peacefully transacted its business, and adjourned. It needed no bayonets to protect it, and required no military aid to execute its judgments. It was held in a state, eminently distinguished for patriotism, by judges commissioned during the rebellion who were provided with juries, upright, intelligent, and selected by a marshal appointed by the president. The government had no right to conclude that Milligan, if guilty, would not receive in that court merited punishment; for its records disclose that it was constantly engaged in the trial of similar offenses, and was never interrupted in its administration of criminal justice. If it was dangerous, in the distracted condition of affairs, to leave Milligan unrestrained of his liberty, because he "conspired against the government, afforded aid and comfort to rebels, and incited the people to insurrection," the *law* said, arrest him, confine him closely, render him powerless to do further mischief; and then present his case to the grand jury of the district, with proofs of his guilt, and, if indicted, try him according to the course of the common law. If this had been done, the Constitution would have been vindicated, the law of 1863 enforced, and the securities for personal liberty preserved and defended.

Another guarantee of freedom was broken when Milligan was denied a trial by jury. The great minds of the country have differed on the correct interpretation to be given to the various provisions of the federal Constitution; and judicial decision

has been often invoked to settle their true meaning; but until recently no one ever doubted that the right of trial by jury was forfeited in the organic law against the power of attack. It is *now* assailed; but if it can be expressed in words, and language has any meaning, *this right*—one of the most valuable in a free country—is preserved to every one accused of crime who is not attached to the army, or navy, or militia in actual service. . . .

It is claimed that martial law covers with its broad mantle the proceedings of this military commission. The proposition is this: that in a time of war the commander of an armed force (if, in his opinion, the exigencies of the country demand it, and of which he is to judge) has the power, within the lines of his military district, to suspend all civil rights and their remedies, and subject citizens as well as soldiers to the rule of his will; and in the exercise of his lawful authority cannot be restrained, except by his superior officer or the President of the United States.

If this position is sound to the extent claimed, then when war exists, foreign or domestic, and the country is subdivided into military departments for mere convenience, the commander of one of them can, if he chooses, within his limits, on the plea of necessity, with the approval of the Executive, substitute military force for, and to the exclusion of, the laws, and punish all persons, as he thinks right and prospect, without fixed or certain rules.

The statement of this proposition shows its importance; for, if true, republican government is a failure, and there is an end of liberty regulated by law. Martial law, established on such a basis, destroys every guarantee of the Constitution, and effectually renders the "military independent of, and superior to, the civil power,"—the attempt to do which by the king of Great Britain was deemed by our fathers such an offense, that they assigned it to the world as one of the causes which impelled them to declare their independence. Civil liberty and this kind of martial law cannot endure together; the antagonism is irreconcilable; and, in the conflict, one or the other must perish.

This nation, as experience has proved, cannot always remain at peace, and has no right to expect that it will always have wise and humane rulers, sincerely attached to the principles of the Constitution. Wicked men, ambitious of power, with hatred of liberty and contempt of law, may fill the place once occupied by Washington and Lincoln; and if this right is conceded, and the calamities of war again befall us, the dangers to human liberty are frightful to contemplate. If our fathers had failed to provide for just such a contingency, they would have been false to the trust reposed in them. They knew—the history of the world told them—the nation they were founding, be its existence short or long, would be involved in war; how often or how long continued, human foresight could not tell; and that unlimited power, wherever lodged at such a time, was especially hazardous to freemen. For this, and other equally weighty reasons, they secured the inheritance they had fought to maintain, by incorporating in a written Constitution the safeguards which time had proved were essential to its preservation. Not one of these safeguards can the President or Congress, or the judiciary disturb except the one concerning the writ of habeas corpus.

It is essential to the safety of every government that, in a great crisis like the one we have just passed through, there should be a power somewhere of suspending the writ of habeas corpus. In every war, there are men of previously good character, wicked enough to counsel their fellow-citizens to resist the measures deemed necessary by a good government to sustain its just authority and overthrow its enemies; and their influence may lead to dangerous combinations. In the emergency of the times, an immediate public investigation according to law may not be possible; and yet the peril to the country may be too imminent to suffer such persons to go at large. Unquestionably, there is then an exigency which demands that the government, if it should see fit, in the exercise of a proper discretion, to make arrests, should not be required to produce the persons arrested in answer to a writ of habeas

corpus. The Constitution goes no further. It does not say after a writ of habeas corpus is denied a citizen, that he shall be tried otherwise than by the course of the common law; it had intended this result, it was easy by use of direct words to have accomplished it. The illustrious men who framed that instrument were of unlimited power; they were full of wisdom, and the lessons of history informed them that a trial by an established court, assisted by an impartial jury, was the only sure way of protecting the citizen against oppression and wrong. Knowing this, they limited the suspension to one great right, and left the rest to remain forever inviolable. But, it is insisted that the safety of the country in time of war demands that this broad claim for martial law shall be sustained. If this were true, it could be well said that a country, preserved at the sacrifice of all the cardinal principles of liberty, is not worth the cost of preservation. Happily, it is not so.

It will be borne in mind that this is not a question of the power to proclaim martial law, when war exists in a community and the courts and civil authorities are overthrown. Nor is it a question what rule a military commander, at the head of his army, can impose on states in rebellion to cripple their resources and quell the insurrection. The jurisdiction claimed is much more extensive. The necessities of service, during the late rebellion, required that the loyal states should be placed within the limits of certain military districts and commanders appointed in them; and, it is urged, that this, in a military sense, constituted them the theatre of military operations; and as in this case, Indiana had been and was again threatened with invasion by the enemy, the occasion was furnished to establish martial law. The conclusion does not follow from the premises. If armies were collected in Indiana, they were to be employed in another locality, where the laws were obstructed and the national authority disputed. On *her* soil there was no hostile foot; if once invaded, that invasion was at an end, and with it all pretext for martial law. Martial law cannot arise from a *threatened* invasion. The necessity must be actual and present; the invasion real, such as effectually closes the courts and deposes the civil administration.

It is difficult to see how the safety of the country required martial law in Indiana. If any of her citizens were plotting treason, the power of arrest could secure them, until the government was prepared for their trial, when the courts were open and ready to try them. It was as easy to protect witnesses before a civil as a military tribunal; and as there could be no wish to convict, except on sufficient legal evidence, surely an ordained and established court was better able to judge of this than a military tribunal composed of gentlemen not trained to the profession of the law.

It follows, from what has been said in this subject, that there are occasions when martial rule can be properly applied. If, in foreign invasion or civil war, the courts are actually closed, and it is impossible to administer criminal justice according to law, then, on the theatre of active military operations, where war really prevails, there is a necessity to furnish a substitute for the civil authority, thus overthrown, to preserve the safety of the army and society; and as no power is left but the military, it is allowed to govern by martial rule until the laws can have their free course. As necessity creates the rule, so it limits its duration, if this government is continued *after* the courts are reinstated, it is a gross usurpation of power. Martial rule can never exist where the courts are open, and in the proper and unobstructed exercise of their jurisdiction. It is also confined to the locality of actual war. Because, during the late rebellion it could have been overturned and the courts driven out, it does not follow that it should obtain in Indiana, where that authority was never disputed, and justice was always administered. . . .

—Justice David Davis

BIBLIOGRAPHY

CHAPTER I. DARKENING CLOUDS

1. Abraham Lincoln Is Nominated in the Wigwam. Murat Halstead, *Caucuses of 1860.* Columbus, OH, 1860. Pp. 141–154.
2. "First Gallant South Carolina Nobly Made the Stand."
   A. South Carolina Ordinance of Secession. Frank Moore, ed., *The Rebellion Record: A Diary of American Events, with Documents, Narratives, Illustrative Incidents, Poetry, etc.* New York, 1861. I, p. 2.
   B. South Carolina Declaration of Causes of Secession. *Ibid.*, pp. 3 ff.
3. "She Has Left Us in Passion and Pride." Oliver Wendell Holmes, "Brother Jonathan's Lament for Sister Caroline," *Poems.* Boston: Ticknor & Fields, 1862.
4. Lincoln Refuses to Compromise on Slavery.
   A. Letter to E. B. Washburne. Nicolay and Hay, eds., *The Complete Works of Abraham Lincoln.* New York: The Century Co., 1894. I, p. 658. (By permission of Appleton-Century-Crofts, Inc.)
   B. Letter to James T. Hale. *Ibid.*, p. 664.
   C. Letter to W. H. Seward. *Ibid.*, p. 668.
5. Mayor Fernando Wood Recommends the Secession of New York.* Fernando Wood, in Henry Steele Commager, *Documents of American History, Volume I.* New York: Appleton-Century-Crofts, Inc., 1949. Pp. 374–376.
6. Lincoln Is Inaugurated.
   A. Herndon Describes the Inauguration. William H. Herndon and Jesse W. Weik, *Herndon's Lincoln: The True Story of a Great Life.* Chicago: Belford, Clark & Co., 1889. III, pp. 493-497.
   B. The Public Man Attends the Inauguration. Allen Thorndike Rice, ed., "The Diary of a Public Man," *North American Review*, CXXIXX (1879), pp. 382–385.
7. "We Are Not Enemies But Friends." Abraham Lincoln, "First Inaugural Address," in James D. Richardson, ed., *A Compilation of the Messages and Papers of the Presidents, 1789–1902.* New York, 1904. VI, pp. 5–12.
8. Mr. Lincoln Hammers Out a Cabinet. Harriet A. Weed, ed., *The Autobiography of Thurlow Weed.* Boston: Houghton Mifflin Co., 1893. Pp. 605–607.
9. Seward Tries to Take Charge of the Lincoln Administration.
   A. Memorandum from Secretary Seward. Nicolay and Hay, eds., *The Complete Works of Abraham Lincoln.* New York: The Century Co., 1894. I, p. 29. (By permission of Appleton-Century-Crofts, Inc.)
   B. Reply to Secretary Seward's Memorandum. *Ibid.*, p. 30.
10. The Confederacy Organizes at Montgomery. T. C. DeLeon, *Four Years in Rebel Capitals.* Mobile, AL: The Gossip Printing Co., 1890, 1892. Pp. 23–27.
11. Constitution of the Confederate States of America.* In Jerome Agel, ed., *Words That Made America Great: Nearly 200 Timeless Documents That Define the American Character from the Nation's Beginning to Today.* New York: Random House, 1997. Pp. 201–210.
12. A War Clerk Describes Davis and His Cabinet. John B. Jones, *A Rebel War Clerk's Diary at the Confederate States' Capital.* Philadelphia: J. B. Lippincott Co., 1866. I, pp. 36–40.
13. Sam Houston Refuses to Go with His State.* Sam Houston, in Henry Steele Commager, ed., *Fifty Basic Civil War Documents.* Malabar, FL: Robert E. Kreiger Publishing Company, 1982. Pp. 25–28.
14. Inaugural Address of Jefferson Davis.* Jefferson Davis, in Henry Steele Commager, ed., *Fifty Basic Civil War Documents.* Malabar, FL: Robert E. Kreiger Publishing Company, 1982. Pp. 29–32.

CHAPTER II. THE CONFLICT PRECIPITATED

1. Mrs. Chesnut Watches the Attack on Fort Sumter. Mary Boykin Chesnut, *A Diary from Dixie,*

* Denotes a selection that is new to this edition

Isabella D. Martin and Myrta
Lockett Avary, eds. New York:
D. Appleton & Co., 1905. Pp.
32–40. (By permission of
Appleton-Century-Crofts, Inc.)

2. Abner Doubleday Defends Fort
Sumter. Abner Doubleday,
*Reminiscences of Forts Sumter and
Moultrie, 1860-1861*. New York:
Harper & Bros., 1876. Pp.
142–173, *passim*.

3. "The Heather Is on Fire."
A. An Indiana Farm Boy Hears
the News. Oscar Osburn
Winther, ed., *With Sherman to
the Sea, Journal of Theodore
Upson*. Baton Rouge, LA.:
Louisiana State University
Press, 1943. Pp. 9–11. (By per-
mission of Louisiana State
University Press.)
B. "There Is But One Thought—
The Stars and Stripes."
Charles Chauncey Binney, *The
Life of Horace Binney*.
Philadelphia: J. B. Lippincott
Co., 1903. Pp. 330–333. (By
permission of Marie Sorchan
Binney.)
C. "One Great Eagle-Scream."
G. W. Bacon and E. W.
Howland, eds., *Letters of a
Family During the War for the
Union, 1861–1865*. New
Haven, CT: Privately printed,
1899. I, pp. 66–71.

4. "The Spirit of Virginia Cannot Be
Crushed." Lyon G. Tyler, *Letters
and Times of the Tylers*. Richmond,
1884. II, pp. 641–642, pp.
651–652.

5. "I Am Filled with Horror at the
Condition of Our Country." J. G.
de Roulhac Hamilton, ed., *The
Correspondence of Jonathan Worth*.
Raleigh, NC: North Carolina
Historical Commission, 1909. I,
pp. 145–148. (By permission of
State of North Carolina
Department of Archives and
History.)

6. A Northern Democrat Urges
Peaceful Separation. John Bigelow,
ed., *Letters and Literary Memorials of
Samuel J. Tilden*. New York: Harper
& Bros., 1908. I, pp. 157–159. (By
permission of Harper & Bros.)

7. "The Race of Philip Sidneys Is Not
Extinct." George William Curtis,
ed., *The Correspondence of John
Lothrop Morley*. New York: Harper
& Bros., 1889. II, pp. 40–43.

8. The Supreme Court Upholds the
Constitution. *Prize Cases*, 67
United States Supreme Court
Reports 635 (1863).

CHAPTER III. THE GATHERING
OF THE HOSTS

1. "Our People Are All United".
Arney Robinson Childs, ed., *The
Private Journal of Henry William
Ravenel, 1859-1887*. Columbia,
SC.: University of South Carolina
Press, 1947. Pp. 65–67. (By permis-
sion of University of South
Carolina Press.)

2. Southern Ladies Send Their Men
Off to War. Testimony of Mrs.
Mary A. Ward, *Report of the
Committee of the Senate upon the
Relations between Labor and Capital,
and Testimony Taken by the
Committee*. Washington, DC: U. S.
Government Printing Office,
1885. IV, pp. 331–332.

3. The North Builds a Vast Army
Overnight. Edward Dicey, *Six
Months in the Federal States*.
London and Cambridge:
Macmillan, 1863. II, pp. 5–12.

4. Northern Boys Join the Ranks.
A. Warren Goss Enlists in the
Union Army. Warren Lee
Goss, *Recollections of a Private,
A Story of the Army of the
Potomac*. New York: Thomas
Y. Crowell Co., 1890.
Pp. 1–5.
B. Lieutenant Favill Raises a
Company and Gets a
Commission. Josiah Marshall
Favill, *The Diary of a Young
Officer*. Chicago: R. R.
Donnelley & Sons, 1909. Pp.
42 ff.
C. "We Thought the Rebellion
Would Be Over Before Our
Chance Would Come."
Michael H. Fitch, *Echoes of the
Civil War as I Hear Them*. New
York: R. F. Fenno & Co., 1905.
Pp. 17–20. (By permission of
Mr. H. C. Fenno.)

5. Baltimore Mobs Attack the Sixth
Massachusetts. Frederic Emory,
"The Baltimore Riots," in *The
Annals of the War, Written by
Leading Participants North and
South, Originally Published in the
Philadelphia Weekly Times*.
Philadelphia: The Times
Publishing Co., 1879. Pp. 775 ff.

6. Frank Wilkeson Goes South with
Blackguards, Thieves, and Bounty
Jumpers. Frank Wilkeson,
*Recollections of a Private Soldier in
the Army of the Potomac*. New
York: G. P. Putnam's Sons, 1887.
Pp. 1–11.

7. Supplying the Confederacy with
Arms and Ammunition. E. P.
Alexander, *Military Memoirs of a
Confederate*. New York: Charles
Scribner's Sons, 1907. Pp. 52–54.
(By permission of Charles
Scribner's Sons.)

8. How the Army of Northern
Virginia Got Its Ordnance. Col.
William Allan, "Reminiscences of
Field Ordnance Service with the
Army of Northern Virginia—
1863–5," *Southern Historical Society
Papers, XIV* (1886), pp. 138–145.

9. Secretary Benjamin Recalls the
Mistakes of the Confederate
Congress. Sir Frederick Maurice,
ed., *An Aide-de-Camp of Lee,
Papers of Charles Marshall*. Boston:
Little, Brown & Co., 1927. Pp.
14–18. (By permission of Sir
Frederick Maurice.)

10. Northern Ordnance. Comte de
Paris, *History of the Civil War in
America*. Philadelphia: Porter &
Coates, 1875. I, 298–301.

CHAPTER IV. BULL RUN AND
THE PENINSULAR CAMPAIGN

1. A Confederate Doctor Describes
the Victory at First Bull Run.
Letter of Dr. J. C. Nott, in Frank
Moore, ed., *The Rebellion Record*.
New York, 1862. II, pp. 93–94.

2. "Bull Run Russell" Reports the
Rout of the Federals. William
Howard Russell, *My Diary North
and South*. London: Bradbury &
Evans, 1863. II, pp. 210 254.

3. Stonewall Jackson Credits God
with the Victory. Mary Anna
Jackson, *Life and Letters of General
Thomas J. Jackson*. New York:
Harper & Bros., 1891. Pp. 177–178.

4. "The Capture of Washington
Seems Inevitable". Allen
Thorndike Rice, ed., "A Page of
Political Correspondence,
Unpublished Letters of Mr.
Stanton to Mr. Buchanan," *North
American Review, CXXIX* (1879),
pp. 482–483.

5. McClellan Opens the Peninsular
Campaign. George B. McClellan,

McClellan's Own Story. New York: Charles L. Webster & Co., 1887, pp. 352–353.

6. General Wool Takes Norfolk. Egbert L. Viele, "A Trip with Lincoln, Chase, and Stanton," *Scribner's Monthly,* XVI (1878), pp. 819–822.

7. The Army of the Potomac Marches to Meet McClellan. [Sallie Putnam], *Richmond During the War, Four Years of Personal Observation by a Richmond Lady.* New York: G. W. Carleton, 1867. Pp. 119–120.

8. R. E. Lee Takes Command. General Evander M. Law, "The Fight for Richmond," *Southern Bivouac,* II (April 1867), pp. 649 ff.

9. "Beauty" Stuart Rides Around McClellan's Army. John Esten Cooke, *Wearing of the Gray; Being Personal Portraits, Scenes, and Adventures of the War.* New York: E. B. Treat & Co., 1867. Pp. 179 ff.

10. Oliver Norton Fights Like a Madman at Gaines' Mill. Oliver Willcox Norton, *Army Letters, 1861–1865.* Chicago: Privately printed, 1903. Pp. 92 ff.

11. The End of Seven Days.
   A. The Federals Are Forced Back at White Oak Swamp. Thomas L. Livermore, *Days and Events, 1860–1866.* Boston: Houghton Mifflin Co., 1920. Pp. 86–90. (By permission of U. W. Harris Livermore Estate.)
   B. Captain Livermore Fights at Malvern Hill. *Ibid.,* pp. 94–98.

12. Richard Auchmuty Reviews the Peninsular Campaign. E. S. A., ed., *Letters of Richard Tylden Auchmuty, Fifth Corps Army of the Potomac.* Privately printed, n.p., n.d. Pp. 68–72.

CHAPTER V. STONEWALL JACKSON AND THE VALLEY CAMPAIGN

1. Dick Taylor Campaigns with Jackson in the Valley. Richard Taylor, *Destruction and Reconstruction: Personal Experiences of the Late War.* New York: D. Appleton & Co., 1879, 1900. Pp. 44–59.

2. Taylor's Irishmen Capture a Battery at Port Republic. Richard Taylor, *Destruction and Reconstruction.* New York: D. Appleton & Co., 1879, 1900. Pp. 72–76.

3. Colonel Wolseley Visits Stonewall Jackson. [Col. Garnet Wolseley], "A Month's Visit to Confederate Headquarters," in *Blackwood's Edinburgh Magazine,* XCIII (January–June 1863), p. 21.

4. Henry Kyd Douglas Remembers Stonewall Jackson. Henry Kyd Douglas, *I Rode with Stonewall.* Chapel Hill, NC: University of North Carolina Press, 1940. Pp. 234–235, pp. 103–121, *passim,* p. 196. (By permission of University of North Carolina Press.)

CHAPTER VI. SECOND BULL RUN AND ANTIETAM

1. "Who Could Not Conquer With Such Troops as These?" R. L. Dabney, *Life and Campaigns of Lt. Gen. Thomas J. Jackson.* New York: Blelock & Co., 1866. Pp. 516–518.

2. Jackson Outsmarts and Outfights Pope at Manassas. [John Hampden Chamberlayne], "Narrative by a Rebel Lieutenant," in Frank Moore, ed., *The Rebellion Record.* New York, 1863. V, pp. 402–404.

3. Pope Wastes His Strength on Jackson. D. H. Strother, "Personal Recollections of the War," *Harper's New Monthly Magazine,* XXXV (1867), pp. 713 ff.

4. Longstreet Overwhelms Pope at Manassas. Alexander Hunter, *Johnny Reb and Billy Yank.* New York: The Neale Publishing Co., 1905. Pp. 244–245.

5. "Little Mac" Is Reappointed to Command.
   A. "To Fight Is Not His Forte". *Diary of Gideon Welles, Secretary of the Navy Under Lincoln and Johnson.* Boston: Houghton Mifflin Co., 1911. I, pp. 107–108. (By permission of Houghton Mifflin Company.)
   B. General Sherman Explains Why He Cannot Like McClellan. M. A. De Wolfe Howe, ed., *Home Letters of General Sherman.* New York: Charles Scribner's Sons, 1909. Pp. 314–316. (By permission of Charles Scribner's Sons.)
   C. "Little Mac's A-Coming". Oliver Willcox Norton, *Army Letters, 1861–1865.* Chicago: Privately printed, 1903. Pp. 101–102.

6. McClellan "Saves His Country" Twice. George B. McClellan, *McClellan's Own Story.* New York: Charles L. Webster & Co., 1887. Pp. 308–660, *passim.*

7. McClellan Finds the Lost Order. *Letter of the Secretary of War, Organization of the Army of the Potomac, and of its Campaigns in Virginia and Maryland under the command of Maj. Gen. George B. McClellan, from July 26,1861 to November 7, 1862.* Washington DC: Government Printing Office, 1864. Pp. 88–189.

8. McClellan Forces Turner's Gap and Crampton's Gap. D. H. Strother, "Personal Recollections of the War. By a Virginian," *Harper's New Monthly Magazine,* XXXVI (1868), pp. 275–278.

9. The Bloodiest Day of the War. D. H. Strother, "Personal Recollections of the War. By a Virginian," *Harper's New Monthly Magazine,* XXVI (1868), pp. 281–284.

10. Hooker Hammers the Confederate Left—In Vain.
    A. Wisconsin Boys Are Slaughtered in the Cornfield. Rufus R. Dawes, *Service with Sixth Wisconsin Volunteers.* Marietta, OH: E. R. Alderman & Sons, 1890. Pp. 90–92.
    B. McLaws to the Rescue of Hood. James A. Graham, "Twenty-Seventh Regiment," in Walter Clark, ed., *Histories of the Several Regiments and Battalions from North Carolina in the Great War 1861–65.* Raleigh, NC: North Carolina Historical Commission, n.d. II, pp. 433–437.

11. The Desperate Fighting along Bloody Lane.
    A. Thomas Livermore Puts on His War Paint. Thomas L Livermore, *Days and Events, 1860–1866.* Boston: Houghton Mifflin Co., 1920). Pp. 137-141, 146. (By permission of U. W. Harris Livermore Estate.)
    B. General Gordon Is Wounded Five Times at Antietam. General John B. Gordon, *Reminiscences of the Civil War.* New York: Charles Scribner's Sons, 1903. Pp. 81–90. (By permission of Charles Scribner's Sons.)

12. "The Whole Landscape Turns Red" at Antietam. David L. Thompson, "With Burnside at Antietam," in *Battles and Leaders of the Civil War*. New York: The Century Co., 1884, 1887, 1888. II, pp. 661–662.

CHAPTER VII. FREDERICKSBURG AND CHANCELLORSVILLE

1. Lincoln Urges McClellan to Advance. Lincoln to McClellan, in *The War of the Rebellion . . . Official Records*. Ser. I, vol. XIX, pt. 1, pp. 13 ff.
2. Burnside Blunders at Fredericksburg.
   A. The Yankees Attack Marye's Heights. William M. Owen, "A Hot Day on Marye's Heights," in *Battles and Leaders of the Civil War*. New York: The Century Co., 1884, 1888. III, pp. 97–99.
   B. The Irish Brigade Is Repulsed on Marye's Hill. J. B. Polley, *A Soldier's Letters to Charming Nellie*. New York: The Neale Publishing Co., 1908. Pp. 88 ff.
   C. The 5th New Hampshire to the Rescue. Captain John R. McCrillis, in William Child, *A History of the Fifth Regiment New Hampshire Volunteers, in the American Civil War, 1861–1865*. Bristol, NH: R. W. Musgrove, 1893. I, pp. 155–157.
3. The Gallant Pelham at Fredericksburg. John Esten Cooke, *Wearing of the Gray; Being Personal Portraits, Scenes, and Adventures of the War*. New York: E. B. Treat Co., 1867. Pp. 133–134, 137–138.
4. Night on the Field of Fredericksburg. General J. L. Chamberlain, "Night on the Field of Fredericksburg," in W. C. King and W. P. Derby, eds., *Camp-Fire Sketches and Battle-Field Echoes*. Springfield, MA: W. C. King & Co., 1887. Pp. 127–130.
5. Lincoln Appoints Hooker to the Command of the Army. Lincoln to Hooker, in *The War of the Rebellion . . . Official Records*. Ser. I, vol. XL, p. 4.
6. Lee Whips Hooker at Chancellorsville. Charles Fessenden Morse, *Letters Written During the Civil War, 1861–1865*.

Boston: Privately printed, 1898. Pp. 127–138.
7. Pleasonton Stops the Confederates at Hazel Grove. Alfred Pleasonton, "The Successes and Failures of Chancellorsville," in *Battles and Leaders of the Civil War*. New York: The Century Co., 1884. III, pp. 177–181.
8. Stuart and Anderson Link Up at Chancellorsville. Heros von Borcke, *Memoirs of the Confederate War for Independence*. London, 1866. II, pp. 234–241.
9. Lee Loses His Right Arm. Rev. James P. Smith, "Stonewall Jackson's Last Battle," in *Battles and Leaders of the Civil War*. New York: The Century Co., 1884, 1888. III, pp. 211–214.

CHAPTER VIII. HOW THE SOLDIERS LIVED: EASTERN FRONT

1. Theodore Winthrop Recalls a Typical Day at Camp Cameron. Theodore Winthrop, *Life in the Open Air, and Other Papers*. Boston: Ticknor & Fields, 1863. Pp. 271–276.
2. Abner Small Paints a Portrait of a Private in the Army of the Potomac. Harold A. Small, ed., *The Road to Richmond; The Civil War Memoirs of Major Abner R. Small of the Sixteenth Maine Volunteers. Together with the Diary which he kept when he was a Prisoner of War*. Berkeley CA: University of California Press, 1939. Pp. 192–193, pp. 196–197. (By permission of University of California Press.)
3. Life with the Thirteenth Massachusetts. Charles E. Davis, *Three Years in the Army: The Story of the Thirteenth Massachusetts Volunteers*. Boston: Estes & Lauriat, 1894. pp. 3–99, *passim*. (By permission of L. C. Page & Company, Inc.)
4. Minutiae of Soldier Life in the Army of Northern Virginia. Carlton McCarthy, *Detailed Minutiae of Soldier Life in the Army of Northern Virginia, 1861-1865*. Richmond VA: Carlton McCarthy & Co., 1882. Pp. 16–28.
5. Inventions and Gadgets Used by the Soldiers. John D. Billings, *Hardtack and Coffee, or, The Unwritten Story of Army Life*.

Boston: George M. Smith & Co., 1887. Pp. 272 ff.
6. Hardtack and Coffee. John D. Billings, *Hardtack and Coffee, or, The Unwritten Story of Army Life*. Boston: George M. Smith & Co., 1887. Pp. 110 ff.
7. "Starvation, Rags, Dirt, and Vermin." Randolph Abbott Shotwell, "Three Years in Battle," J. G. de Roulhac Hamilton, ed., *The Papers of Randolph Abbott Shotwell*. Raleigh, NC: North Carolina Historical Commission, 1929. I, pp. 314–316. (By permission of State of North Carolina Department of Archives and History.)
8. Voting in the Field.
   A. Electioneering in the Camps. R. G. Plumb, ed., "James A. Leonard, Letters of a Fifth Wisconsin Volunteer," *Wisconsin Magazine of History*, III (1919–1920) pp. 63–64. (By permission of State Historical Society of Wisconsin.)
   B. President Lincoln Needs the Soldier Vote. Letter of Lincoln to General Sherman. Nicolay and Hay, eds., *The Complete Works of Abraham Lincoln*. New York: The Century Co., 1894. II, pp. 577–578. (By permission of Appleton-Century-Crofts, Inc.)
9. Red Tape, North and South.
   A. Dunn Browne Has Trouble with the War Department. [Samuel Fiske], *Mr. Dunn Browne's Experiences in the Army*. Boston: Nichols & Noyes, 1866. Pp. 372–375.
   B. A Confederate Lieutenant Complains That Red-Tapeism Will Lose the War. Randolph Abbott Shotwell, "Three Years in Battle," J. G. de Roulhac Hamilton, ed., *The Papers of Randolph Abbott Shotwell*. Raleigh, NC: North Carolina Historical Cornmission, 1929. I, pp. 382–385. (By permission of State of North Carolina Department of Archives and History.)
10. The Confederates Get Religion.
    A. Religion in the Confederate Army. Benjamin W. Jones, *Under the Stars and Bars; A History of the Surry Light*

Artillery. Richmond, VA: Everett Waddey Co., 1909. Pp. 80 ff.

B. John Dooley Describes Prayer Meetings. Joseph T. Durkin ed., *John Dooley, Confederate Soldier: His War Journal.* Washington, DC: Georgetown University Press, 1945. P. 58. (By permission of Georgetown University Press.)

CHAPTER IX. INCIDENTS OF ARMY LIFE: EASTERN FRONT

1. How It Feels to Be Under Fire. Frank Holsinger, "How Does One Feel Under Fire?" in *War Talks in Kansas . . . Kansas Commandery of the Military Order of the Loyal Legion of the United States.* Kansas City, MO: Franklin Hudson Publishing Co., 1906. I, pp. 301–304. (By permission of Kansas Commandery, Military Order of the Loyal Legion of the United States.)

2. Fitz John Porter Views the Confederates from a Balloon. George Alfred Townsend, *Campaigns of a Non-Combatant, And His Romaunt Abroad During the War.* New York: Blelock & Co., 1866. Pp. 115–118.

3. Stuart's Ball Is Interrupted by the Yankees. Heros von Borcke, *Memoirs of the Confederate War for Independence.* London, 1866, I, pp. 193–198.

4. Foreigners Fight in the Northern Army. George B. McClellan, *McClellan's Own Story.* New York: Charles L. Webster & Co., 1887. Pp. 141–145.

5. With "Extra Billy" Smith at York. Robert Stiles, *Four Years Under Marse Robert.* New York: The Neale Publishing Co., 1903. Pp. 202–206.

6. Blue and Gray Fraternize on the Picket Line. Alexander Hunter, *Johnny Reb and Billy Yank.* New York: The Neale Publishing Co., 1905. Pp. 429–431.

7. Life With the Mosby Guerrillas. John W. Munson, *Reminiscences of a Mosby Guerrilla.* Boston: Moffat, Yard & Co., 1906. Pp. 21 ff.

8. Rebel and Yankee Yells. J. Harvie Dew, "The Yankee and Rebel Yells," *Century Illustrated Magazine,* XLIII (April 1892), pp. 954–955.

9. Women Among the Ranks.
   A. Letters of Sarah Rosetta Wakeman, alias Private Lyons Wakeman.* Lauren Cook Burgess, *An Uncommon Soldier: The Civil War Letters of Sarah Rosetta Wakeman, alias Pvt. Lyons Wakeman, 153rd Regiment, New York State Volunteers, 1862–1864.* New York: Oxford University Press, 1994. Pp. 18–19, p. 53, p. 58.
   B. Exploits of Mrs. Major Belle Reynolds.* *Peoria Daily Transcript,* "An Unprecedented Military Appointment," April 22, 1862; "Major Belle Reynolds", May 19, 1862; "Mrs. Major Belle Reynolds Again—An Un-expected Family Difficulty", May 22, 1862.

CHAPTER X. FROM FORT DONELSON TO STONES RIVER

1. Grant Wins His Spurs at Belmont. Eugene Lawrence, "Grant on the Battle-Field," *Harper's New Monthly Magazine,* XXXIX (1869), p.212.

2. U. S. Grant Becomes Unconditional Surrender Grant. [Ulysses S. Grant], *Personal Memoirs of U. S. Grant.* New York: Charles L. Webster & Co., 1885. I, pp. 296–313.

3. With the Dixie Grays at Shiloh. Dorothy Stanley, ed., *The Autobiography of Sir Henry Morton Stanley.* Boston and New York: Houghton Mifflin Co., 1909. Pp. 187–200. (By permission of Houghton Mifflin Company.)

4. An Illinois Private Fights at the Hornet's Nest. Leander Stillwell, *The Story of a Common Soldier of Army Life in the Civil War, 1861–1865.* 2nd ed.; Kansas City, MO: Franklin Hudson Publishing Co., 1920. Pp. 42–52.

5. The Orphan Brigade Is Shattered at Stones River. L. D. Young, *Reminiscences of a Soldier in the Orphan Brigade.* Paris, KY: Privately printed, n.d. Pp. 47–51.

CHAPTER XI. THE STRUGGLE FOR MISSOURI AND THE WEST

1. Cotton Is King at the Battle of Lexington. Samuel Phillips Day,

Down South. London: Hurst & Blackett, Publishers, 1862. II, pp. 181—188.

2. Guerrilla Warfare in Missouri. Col. William Monks, "A History of Southern Missouri and Northern Arkansas," in William E. Connelley, *Quantrill and the Border Wars.* Cedar Rapids, IA: The Torch Press, 1910. Pp. 213–217.

3. The Tide Turns at Pea Ridge. Franz Sigel, "The Pea Ridge Campaign," in *Battles and Leaders of the Civil War.* New York: The Century Co., 1884–1887. I, pp. 327–329.

4. The Confederates Scatter after Pea Ridge. William Watson, *Life in the Confederate Army; Being the Observations and Experiences of an Alien in the South during the American Civil War.* New York: Scribner & Welford, 1888. Pp. 320–339, *passim.*

5. Quantrill and His Guerrillas Sack Lawrence. Narrative by Gurdon Grovenor, in William E. Connelley, *Quantrill and the Border Wars.* Cedar Rapids, IA: The Torch Press, 1910. Pp. 362–365.

6. Colonel Bailey Dams the Red River. Letter from Rear Admiral Porter to Gideon Welles, May 16, 1864, in W. J. Tenney, *The Military and Naval History of the Rebellion.* New York: D. Appleton & Co., 1865. Pp. 513–514.

7. Price Invades the North and Is Defeated at Westport. Wiley Britton, "Resumé of Military Operations in Missouri and Arkansas, 1864–65," in *Battles and Leaders of the Civil War.* New York: The Century Co., 1884, 1887, 1888. IV, pp. 375–377.

CHAPTER XII. HOW THE SOLDIERS LIVED: WESTERN FRONT

1. John Chipman Gray Views the Western Soldier. Worthington C. Ford, ed., *War Letters, 1862–1865, of John Chipman Gray and John Codman Ropes.* Boston: Houghton Mifflin Co., 1927. Pp. 364–366. (By permission of Massachusetts Historical Society.)

2. A Wisconsin Boy Complains of the Hardships of Training. Chauncey H. Cooke, "Letters of a Badger Boy in Blue: Into the Southland," *Wisconsin Magazine of History,* IV (1920–1921), pp.

209–210. (By permission of State Historical Society of Wisconsin.)

3. Religion and Play in the Army of the Tennessee. Jenkin Lloyd Jones, *An Artilleryman's Diary.* Madison, WI: Wisconsin Historical Commission, 1914. Pp. 166–210, *passim.* (By permission of Wisconsin Historical Commission.)

4. The Great Revival in the Army of Tennessee. Mary A. H. Gay, *Life in Dixie During the War.* 3rd ed., Atlanta, GA: Charles P. Boyd, 1892. Pp. 79–86.

5. From Reveille to Taps. Brevet Major George Ward Nichols, *The Story of the Great March, from the Diary of a Staff Officer.* New York: Harper & Bros., 1865. Pp. 48–55.

6. An Indiana Boy Reassures His Mother about Morals in the Army. Oscar Osburn Winther, ed., *With Sherman to the Sea, Journal of Theodore Upson.* Baton Rouge, LA: Louisiana State University Press, 1943. Pp. 102–105. (By permission of Louisiana State University Press.)

7. Graft and Corruption in the Confederate Commissary. William Watson, *Life in the Confederate Army.* New York: Scribner & Welford, 1888. Pp. 164–166.

8. The Soldiers Get Paid and the Sutler Gets the Money. Charles Beneulyn Johnson, *Muskets and Medicine, or Army Life in the Sixties.* Philadelphia: F. A. Davis Co., 1917. Pp. 197–200. (By permission of P. A. Davis Company.)

9. Song and Play in the Army of Tennessee.
   A. Theatricals in the Army.* "Theatricals in the Army," *The Southern Illustrated News,* May 7, 1864.
   B. Good Cheer in the Ranks. Bromfield L. Ridley, *Battles and Sketches of the Army of Tennessee.* Mexico, MO: Missouri Printing & Publishing Co., 1906. Pp. 461–463.

CHAPTER XIII. INCIDENTS OF ARMY LIFE: WESTERN FRONT

1. Mark Twain Recalls a Campaign That Failed. Mark Twain, "The Private History of a Campaign That Failed," *Century Magazine,* XXXI (December 1885), pp. 194 ff.

2. Major Connolly Loses Faith in the Chivalry of the South. "Major Connolly's Letters to His Wife, 1862–1865," *Transactions of the Illinois State Historical Society for the year 1928.* ("Publications of the Illinois State Historical Library," No. 35.) Springfield, IL., 1928. Pp. 220–224. (By permission of Illinois State Historical Society.)

3. The Great Locomotive Chase in Georgia. William Pittenger, "The Locomotive Chase in Georgia," *Century Magazine,* XIV (May 1888), pp. 141–146.

4. A Badger Boy Meets the Originals of Uncle Tom's Cabin. Chauncey H. Cooke, "Letters of a Badger Boy in Blue: Into the Southland," *Wisconsin Magazine of History,* IV (1920–1921), pp. 324–325, pp. 328–329. (By permission of State Historical Society of Wisconsin.)

5. The Confederates Escape in the Teche Country. John William De Forest, "Forced Marches," *Galaxy,* V (1868), pp. 708 ff.

6. General Wilson Raises His Cavalry the Hard Way. James Harrison Wilson, *Under the Old Flag: Recollections of Military Operations in the War for the Union, the Spanish War, the Boxer Rebellion, etc.* New York: D. Appleton & Co., 1912. II, pp. 32–34. (By permission of Appleton-Century-Crofts, Inc.)

CHAPTER XIV. THE PROBLEM OF DISCIPLINE

1. Thomas Wentworth Higginson Explains the Value of Trained Officers. T. W. Higginson, "Regular and Volunteer Officers," *Atlantic Monthly,* XIV (September 1864), pp. 348–357.

2. "It Does Not Suit Our Fellows to Be Commanded Much." Charles F. Johnson, *The Long Roll; being a Journal of the Civil War, as set down during the years 1861–1863 by Charles F. Johnson, sometime of Hawkins Zouaves.* East Aurora, NY: The Roycrofters, 1911. Pp. 63–64.

3. Conduct Unbecoming an Officer.* Robert C. Murphy, William S. Rosecrans and Ulysses S. Grant, in Thomas P. Lowry, *Tarnished Eagles: The Courts-Martial of Fifty Union Colonels and Lieutenant Colonels.* Mechanicsburg, PA: Stackpole

Books, 1997. Pp. 176–181.

4. A Camp of Skulkers at Cedar Mountain. George Alfred Townsend, *Campaigns of a Non-Combatant, And His Romaunt Abroad During the War.* New York: Blelock & Co., 1866. Pp. 264–265.

5. "The Army Is Becoming Awfully Depraved." Charles W. Wills, *Army Life of an Illinois Soldier.* Washington, DC: Globe Printing Co., 1906. Pp. 135–136, p.209.

6. Robert Gould Shaw Complains That War Is a Dirty Business. Letter of Robert Gould Shaw, in Lydia Minturn Post, ed., *Soldiers' Letters from Camp, Battle-field and Prison.* Published for the U. S. Sanitary Commission. New York: Bunce & Huntington, 1865. Pp. 249 ff.

7. The Yankee Invaders Pillage and Burn.
   A. "The Soldiers Delight in Destroying Everything." "Civil War Letters of Francis Edwin Pierce," in Blake McKelvey, ed., *Rochester in the Civil War.* Rochester, NY: Rochester Historical Society Publications, 1944. Pp. 160–161. (By permission of Rochester Historical Society.)
   B. The Yankees Sack Sarah Morgan's Home. Sarah Morgan Dawson, *A Confederate Girl's Diary,* Warrington Dawson, ed. Boston: Houghton Mifflin Co., 1913. Pp. 174–202, *passim.* (By permission of Mr. Warrington Dawson.)
   C. Grierson's Raiders on a Rampage. Mrs. W. F. Smith, ed., "The Yankees in New Albany: Letter of Elizabeth Jane Beach, July 29, 1864," *The Journal of Mississippi History,* II (1940), pp. 42–48. (By permission of Mississippi Historical Society.)
   D. "Oh, Earth, Behold the Monster!"* Henrietta Lee, in Andrew Carrol, ed., *Letters of a Nation: A Collection of Extraordinary American Letters.* New York: Broadway Books, 1997. Pp. 122–124.

8. Punishments in the Union and Confederate Armies.
   A. Punishments in the Army of the Potomac. Frank Wilkeson, *Recollections of a Private Soldier in the Army of the Potomac.*

New York: G. P. Putnam's Sons, 1887. Pp. 30–36.

B. Punishments in the Army of Northern Virginia. Joseph T. Durkin, ed., *John Dooley, Confederate Soldier: His War Journal*. Washington, DC: Georgetown University Press, 1945. Pp. 73–74, p. 83. (By permission of Georgetown University Press.)

9. Executing Deserters.

A. General Sheridan Executes Two Deserters at Chattanooga. Washington Gardner, "Civil War Letters of Washington Gardner," *Michigan History Magazine*, I (1917), pp. 8–9. (By permission of Michigan Historical Commission.)

B. Executing Deserters from the Confederate Army. Spencer Glasgow Welch, *A Confederate Surgeon's Letters to his Wife—by Spencer Glasgow Welch, Surgeon 13th South Carolina Volunteers, McGowan's Brigade*. New York and Washington: The Neale Publishing Co., 1911. Pp. 44–45, pp. 79–80.

10. General Lee Discusses the Problem of Discipline.

A. The Need for Punishment as a Deterrent. Robert E. Lee, in Douglas Southall Freeman, ed., *Lee's Confidential Dispatches. . . to Jefferson Davis and the War Department of the Confederate States of America, 1862–1865*. New York: G. P. Putnam's Sons, 1915. Pp. 154–158. (By permission of Mr. W. W. De Renne.)

B. "We Cannot Escape the Disgrace that Attends These Evildoers."* Robert E. Lee, in Richard B. Harwell, ed., *The Confederate Reader: How the South Saw the War*. New York: Dover Publications, 1989. Pp. 331–333.

11. Sex in the Civil War.* Thomas P. Lowry, *The Story the Soldiers Wouldn't Tell: Sex in the Civil War*. Mechanicsburg, PA: Stackpole Books, 1994. P. 29.

CHAPTER XV. GREAT BRITAIN AND THE AMERICAN CIVIL WAR

1. Henry Ravenel Expects Foreign Intervention.

Arney Robinson Childs, ed., *The Private Journal of Henry William Ravenel, 1859-1887*. Columbia, SC: University of South Carolina Press, 1947. P. 59. (By permission of University of South Carolina Press.)

2. *Blackwood's Edinburgh Magazine* Rejoices in the Break-Up of the Union. "Democracy Teaching by Example," *Blackwood's Edinburgh Magazine*, XC (October 1861), pp. 401–402.

3. George Ticknor Explains the War to His English Friends. Anna Ticknor and George S. Hillard, eds., *Life, Letters, and Journals of George Ticknor*. Boston: Osgood, 1876. II, pp. 446–448.

4. Captain Wilkes Seizes Mason and Slidell. D. Macneill Fairfax, "Captain Wilkes's Seizure of Mason and Slidell," in *Battles and Leaders of the Civil War*. New York: The Century Co., 1884, 1887, 1888. II, pp. 135–141.

5. "Shall It Be Love, or Hate, John?" James Russell Lowell, "Jonathan to John," *Poems*, many editions.

6. Palmerston and Russell Discuss Intervention. Spencer Walpole, *The Life of Lord John Russell*. London: Longmans, Green & Co., 1889. II, pp. 349–350; and E. D. Adams, *Great Britain and the American Civil War*. New York: Longmans, Green & Co., 1925. II, pp. 43–44. (By permission of Longmans, Green & Co., Inc.)

7. "An Error, the Most Singular and Palpable." John Morley, *The Life of William Ewart Gladstone*. New York: The Macmillan Co., 1903. II, pp. 81–83. (By permission of The Macmillan Company and Mr. Guy E. Morley.)

8. The English Press Condemns the Emancipation Proclamation.

9. Manchester Workingmen Stand by the Union.

A. "We Are Truly One People". Address to President Lincoln by the Working-Men of Manchester, in Frank Moore, ed., *The Rebellion Record*. New York, 1864. VI, p. 344.

B. "An Instance of Sublime Christian Heroism". Lincoln's Reply to the Working-Men of Manchester, in Nicolay and Hay, eds., *The Complete Works of Abraham Lincoln*. New York: The Century Co., 1894. II,

pp. 301–302. (By permission of Appleton-Century-Crofts, Inc.)

10. Richard Cobden Rejoices in the Emancipation Proclamation. Edward L. Pierce, contributor, "Letters of Richard Cobden to Charles Sumner," *American Historical Review*, II (1896–1897), pp. 308–309. (By permission of American Historical Association.)

11. English Aristocrats Organize for Southern Independence. Goldwin Smith, *Letter to a Whig Member of the Southern Independence Association*. London, 1864. Pp. 28–31.

12. "The Reasons Why Great Britain is Averse to Recognise Us."* *The Southern Illustrated News*, October 4, 1862.

13. Minister Adams Points Out That This Is War. Great Britain. Parliament. *Accounts and Papers. State Papers, North America* (1864) 62: 17–18.

CHAPTER XVI. SONGS THE SOLDIERS SANG

1. "Dixie". by Daniel E. Emmett.

2. "The Bonnie Blue Flag". Harry McCarthy.

3. "John Brown's Body". Thomas B. Bishop (?).

4. "All Quiet Along the Potomac". Ethel Lynn Beers.

5. "Marching Along". William Batchelder Bradbury.

6. "Maryland! My Maryland!" James R. Randall.

7. The Battle Hymn of the Republic.

A. Writing "The Battle Hymn of the Republic." Julia Ward Howe, *Reminiscences, 1819–1899*. Boston: Houghton Mifflin Co., 1899. Pp. 273–276.

B. "The Battle Hymn of the Republic". Julia Ward Howe.

C. "The Battle Hymn of the Republic" in Libby Prison. Laura E. Richards and Maud Howe Elliott, *Julia Ward Howe, 1819–1910*. Boston: Houghton Mifflin Co., 1916. I, 188–189. (By permission of Houghton Mifflin Company.)

8. "We Are Coming, Father Abraham". James Sloan Gibbons.

9. "The Battle-Cry of Freedom". George F. Root.

10. "Tramp, Tramp, Tramp". George F. Root.
11. "Just Before the Battle, Mother". George F. Root.
12. "Tenting Tonight". Walter Kittredge.
13. "Marching Through Georgia". Henry Clay Work.
14. Mister, Here's Your Mule.
    A. "Mister, Here's Your Mule". (Author Unknown).
    B. "Do They Miss Me in the Trenches?" J. W. Naff.
    C. "We Are the Boys of Potomac's Ranks." (Author Unknown).
    D. "Goober Peas". A. Pender.
    E. "Grafted into the Army". Henry Clay Work.
15. "Lorena". H. D. L. Webster (?).
16. "When Johnny Comes Marching Home". Patrick S. Gilmore(?).

Bibliographical Note

It is impossible to give satisfactory bibliographical listings for particular Civil War songs. These songs appear, for the most part, in variant forms in a great miscellany of collections. It can rarely be said that any one form is the correct one. In some cases the authorship of popular songs is unknown, in many cases it is in dispute. We have thought it most helpful, therefore, merely to list the most useful of the many volumes of Civil War songs—altogether almost one hundred were published during or after the war—from which our own selection has been drawn.

American War Songs; published under supervision of the National Committee for the Preservation of Existing Records of the National Society of the Colonial Dames of America. Philadelphia: Privately printed, 1925. 202 pp.

Bill, Ledyard, ed., *Lyrics, Incidents, and Sketches of the Rebellion.* 2nd ed.; New York: C. A. Alvord, 1864. Part I, Lyrics of the War. 100 pp.

Browne, Francis Fisher, ed., *Bugle-echoes; a Collection of Poems of the Civil War, Northern and Southern.* New York: White, Stokes & Allen, 1886, 336 pp.

Collection of War Songs of the South. Atlanta: Franklin Printing & Publishing Co., 1895. Cover title: "Southern War Songs."

Davidson, Nora F. M., comp., *Cullings from the Confederacy.* Washington,

DC: Rufus H. Darby Printing Co., 1903. 163 pp.

Duganne, Augustine J. H., *Ballads of the War.* New York: J. Robbins, 1862.

Eggleston, [George Cary], *American War Ballads and Lyrics: a Collection of Songs and Ballads of the Colonial Wars, the Revolution, the War of 1812–15, the War with Mexico, and the Civil War.* New York: G. P. Putnam's Sons, 1889. 2 vols.

Fagan, William Long, ed., *Southern War Songs, Camp-Fire, Patriotic and Sentimental.* New York: M. T. Richardson & Co., 1890. 389 pp.

Hewes, George Whitfield, *Ballads of the War.* New York: Carleton, 1862. 147 pp.

Hubner, Charles W., ed., *War Poets of the South and Confederate Camp-Fire Songs.* Atlanta: U. P. Byrd, 1896. 207 pp.

Mason, Emily V., ed., *The Southern Poems of the War.* Baltimore: J Murphy & Co., 1867. 456 pp.

Miles, Dudley, H., ed., *Poetry and Eloquence of Blue and Gray.* Foreword by William P. Trent, with an appendix "Songs of the War Days" edited by Jeanne Robert Foster. (F. T. Miller, ed., *The Photographic History of the Civil War, Vol. IX.*) New York: The Review of Reviews Co., 1911. 352 pp.

Moore, Frank, ed., *The Civil War in Song and Story, 1860–1865.* New York: P. F. Collier, 1889. 560 pp.

——, ed., *Lyrics of Loyalty.* New York: G. P. Putnam, 1864. 336 pp.

——, ed., *Songs and Ballads of the Southern People, 1861–1865.* New York: D. Appleton & Co., 1886.

Our National War Songs: a Complete Collection of Grand Old War Songs, Battle Songs, National Hymns, Memorial Hymns, Decoration Day Songs . . . Chicago: S. Brainard's Sons Co., [cop. 1892]. 223 pp.

Putnam, Sallie A. Brock, ed., *The Southern Amaranth, a Carefully Selected Collection of Poems Growing out of and in Reference to the Late War.* New York: G. S. Wilcox, 1869. 651 pp.

Simms, William Gilmore, ed., *War Poetry of the South.* New York: Richardson & Co., 1867. 482 pp.

War Songs of the Blue and the Gray, As Sung by the Brave Soldiers of the Union and Confederate Armies in Camp, on the March, and in Garrison; with a preface by Prof. Henry L.

Williams. New York: Hurst & Co., 1905. 215 pp.

Wharton, H. M., ed., *War Songs and Poems of the Southern Confederacy, 1861–1865; a collection of the most popular and impressive songs and poems of war times . . .* Philadelphia: n.p. 1904, 412 pp.

CHAPTER XVII. POEMS OF THE CIVIL WAR

1. Poet Laureate of the South.
   A. Ethnogenesis.* Henry Timrod, "Ethnogenesis," in *The Poems of Henry Timrod*, Paul H. Haynes, ed. (New York, 1873), pp. 100–104.
   B. Carolina.* Henry Timrod, "Carolina," in *Civil War Poetry: An Anthology,* Paul Negri, ed. (Mineola, NY: Dover Publications, 1997), pp. 9–10.
   C. Ode at Magnolia Cemetery.* Henry Timrod, "Carolina," in *Civil War Poetry: An Anthology,* Paul Negri, ed. (Mineola, NY: Dover Publication, 1997), p. 10.
2. The Death of Slavery.* William Cullen Bryant, "The Death of Slavery," in *Civil War Poetry: An Anthology,* Paul Negri, ed. (Mineola, NY: Dover Publications, 1997), pp. 9–10.
3. Barbara Frietchie.* John Greenleaf Whittier, "The Barbara Frietchie," in *Civil War Poetry: An Anthology,* Paul Negri, ed. (Mineol, NY: Dover Publications, 1997), pp. 24–26.
4. "Oh, Mother, Look Down From Heav'n On Me."
   A. The Drummer Boy of Shiloh.* Will "Shakespeare" Hays, "The Drummer Boy of Shiloh," in *The Confederate Reader: How the South Saw the War*, Richard B. Harwell, ed. (Mineola NY: Dover Publications, 1989), p. 77.
   B. Little Giffen.* Francis Orrery Ticknor, "Little Giffen," in *Civil War Poetry: An Anthology,* Paul Negri, ed. (Mineola, NY: Dover Publications, 1997), pp. 33–34.
   C. Killed at the Ford.* Henry Wadsworth Longfellow, "Killed at the Ford," in *Civil War Poetry: An Anthology,* Paul

Negri, ed. (Mineola, NY: Dover Publications, 1997), pp. 58–59.

D. Vigil Strange I Kept on the Field One Night.* Walt Whitman, "Vigil Strange I Kept on the Field One Night," in *Civil War Poetry: An Anthology*, Paul Negri, ed. (Mineola, NY: Dover Publications, 1997), p. 89.

E. Come Up From the Fields Father.* Walt Whitman, "Come Up From the Fields Father," in *Whitman: Poetry and Prose*, Justin Kaplan, ed., (New York: Library of America, 1982), pp. 436–438.

F. Dirge for a Soldier.* George Henry Boker, "Dirge for a Soldier," in *Civil War Poetry: An Anthology*, Paul Negri, ed. (Mineola, NY: Dover Publications, 1997), p. 77.

5. The Honored General.
A. Lee to the Rear.* John Reuben Thompson, "Lee to the Rear," in *Civil War Poetry: An Anthology*, Paul Negri, ed. (Mineola, NY: Dover Publications, 1997), pp. 56–58.

B. Robert E. Lee.* Julia Ward Howe, "Robert E. Lee," in *Civil War Poetry: An Anthology*, Paul Negri, ed. (Mineola, NY: Dover Publications, 1997), p. 2.

6. O Captain! My Captain!* Walt Whitman, "O Captain! My Captain!" in *Civil War Poetry: An Anthology*, Paul Negri, ed. (Mineola, NY: Dover Publications, 1997), pp. 95–96.

7. Driving Home the Cows.* Kate Putnam Osgood, "Driving Home the Cows," in *Civil War Poetry: An Anthology*, Paul Negri, ed. (Mineola, NY: Dover Publications, 1997), pp. 116–117.

8. The Artilleryman's Vision.* Walt Whitman, "The Artilleryman's Vision," in *Civil War Poetry: An Anthology*, Paul Negri, ed. (Mineola, NY: Dover Publications, 1997), pp. 94–95.

9. The Conquered Banner.* Abram Joseph Ryan, "The Conquered Banner," in *Civil War Poetry: An Anthology*, Paul Negri, ed. (Mineola, NY: Dover Publications, 1997), pp. 103–104.

10. The Blue and the Gray.* Francis Miles Finch, "The Blue and The Gray," in *The American Reader:*

Words That Moved a Nation, Diane Ravitch, ed., (New York: Harper Collins, 1990), p. 159.

CHAPTER XVIII. GETTYSBURG

1. General Lee Decides to Take the Offensive. *The War of the Rebellion . . . Official Records.* Ser. I, vol. XXVII, pt. III, pp. 868–869; ser. I, vol. XXVII, pt. III, pp. 880–882; ser. I, vol. XXVII, pt II, p. 305.

2. General Lee Invades Pennsylvania. Letter of William S. Christian, in Frank Moore, ed., *The Rebellion Record.* New York, 1864. VII, p. 325.

3. The Armies Converge on Gettysburg. Henry J. Hunt, "The First Day at Gettysburg," in *Battles and Leaders of the Civil War.* New York. The Century Co., 1884, 1888. III, pp. 271 ff.

4. Buford and Reynolds Hold Up the Confederate Advance. Major Joseph G. Rosengarten, "General Reynolds' Last Battle," in *The Annals of the War, Written by Leading Participants North and South . . . in the Philadelphia Weekly Times.* Philadelphia: The Times Publishing Co., 1879. Pp. 62–64.

5. A Boy Cannoneer Describes Hard Fighting on the First Day. Augustus Buell, "The Cannoneer," in *Recollections of Service in the Army of the Potomac. By "A Detached Volunteer" in the Regular Artillery.* Washington: The National Tribune, 1890. Pp. 63–73, *passim*.

6. The Struggle for Little Round Top.
A. General Warren Seizes Little Round Top. "Reminiscences of the 140th Regiment, New York Volunteer Infantry, by Porter Farley," Blake McKelvey, ed., *Rochester in the Civil War.* Rochester, NY: Rochester Historical Society, 1944. Pp. 218–223. (By permission of Rochester Historical Society.)

B. Colonel Oates Almost Captures Little Round Top. William C. Oates, *The War Between the Union and the Confederacy and Its Lost Opportunities, with a history of the 15th Alabama Regiment and the forty-eight battles in which it was engaged.* New York: The Neale Publishing Co., 1905.

Pp. 21–211, p. 212, pp. 218–221.

C. The 20th Maine Saves Little Round Top. Theodore Gerrish, *Army Life: A Private's Reminiscences of the Civil War.* Portland, ME: Hoyt, Fogg & Donham, 1882. Pp. 104–111.

7. High Tide at Gettysburg.
A. Alexander Gives the Signal to Start. Letter from E. P. Alexander to the Rev. J. Wm. Jones, *Southern Historical Society Papers*, IV (1877), pp. 102–109, passim.

B. Armistead Falls Beside the Enemy's Battery. James Longstreet, *From Manassas to Appomattox: Memoirs of the Civil War in America.* 2nd ed., rev.; Philadelphia: J. B. Lippincott Co., 1903. Pp. 391–394. (By permission of Mrs. Helen Dortch Longstreet.)

C. "The Crest Is Safe". Frank Aretas Haskell, *The Battle of Gettysburg.* ("Wisconsin History Commission Reprints," No. 1.) Wisconsin History Commission, November 1908. Pp. 107 ff. (By permission of Wisconsin Historical Commission.)

D. "All This Will Come Right in the End". [Arthur J. L. Fremantle], "The Battle of Gettysburg and the Campaign in Pennsylvania," *Blackwood's Edinburgh Magazine*, XC1V (1863), pp. 380–382.

8. General Lee Offers to Resign after Gettysburg. *The War of the Rebellion . . . Official Records.* Ser. I, vol. LI, pt. II, pp. 752–753, vol. XXIX, pt. II, pp. 639–640.

9. "Bells Are Ringing Wildly." *War Letters of William Thompson Lusk.* New York: Privately printed, 1911. Pp. 284–285.

10. A Far From Glorious Fourth.* Andrew Carrol, ed., *Letters of a Nation: A Collection of Extraordinary American Letters.* New York: Broadway Books, 1997. Pp. 124–125.

11. "A New Birth of Freedom." Abraham Lincoln, "The Gettysburg Address," November 19, 1863, in Nicolay and Hay, eds., *The Complete Works of Abraham Lincoln.* New York: The Century Co., 1894. II, p. 439. (By

permission of Appleton-Century-Crofts, Inc.)

CHAPTER XIX. VICKSBURG AND PORT HUDSON

1. "Onward to Vicksburg." Edgar L. Erickson, ed., "With Grant at Vicksburg—From the Civil War Diary of Captain Charles E. Wilcox," *Journal of the Illinois State Historical Society*, XXX (January 1938), pp. 463–497, *passim*. (By permission of Illinois State Historical Society.)

2. A Union Woman Suffers through the Siege of Vicksburg. George W. Cable, ed., "A Woman's Diary of the Siege of Vicksburg. Under Fire from the Gunboats," *Century Illustrated Magazine*, VII (1885), pp. 767–775.

3. Hotel de Vicksburg.* *Southern Punch*, August 22, 1863.

4. Vicksburg Surrenders. U. S. Grant, "The Vicksburg Campaign," in *Battles and Leaders of the Civil War*. New York: The Century Co., 1884, 1888. III, pp. 530–536.

5. General Banks Takes Port Hudson.
   A. Eating Mules at Port Hudson. *Port Hudson—Its History from an Interior Point of View, as Sketched from the Diary of an Officer*. St Francisville, LA: 1938. (By permission of Mr. Elrie Robinson.)
   B. Blue and Gray Fraternize after the Surrender at Port Hudson. *Ibid*.

6. "The Father of Waters Again Goes Unvexed to the Sea." Letter of Lincoln to James C. Conkling, in Nicolay and Hay, eds., *The Complete Works of Abraham Lincoln*. New York: The Century Co., 1894. II, pp. 398–399. (By permission of Appleton-Century-Crofts, Inc.)

7. General Morgan Invades the North.
   A. Morgan's Cavalrymen Sweep Through Kentucky. "Journal of Lieutenant-Colonel Alston," Frank Moore, ed., *The Rebellion Record*. New York, 1864. VII, pp. 358–360.
   B. Morgan's Raid Comes to an Inglorious End. James Bennett McCreary, "The Journal of My Soldier Life," *Register of the Kentucky State Historical Society*, XXXIII (July 1935), pp. 198–200. (By permission of Kentucky State Historical Society.)

CHAPTER XX. PRISONS, NORTH AND SOUTH

1. Abner Small Suffers in Danville Prison. Harold A. Small, ed., *The Road to Richmond; The Civil War Memoirs of Major Abner R. Small of the Sixteenth Maine Volunteers. Together with the Diary which he kept when he was a Prisoner of War*. Berkeley, CA: University of California Press, 1939. Pp. 171–176 (By permission of University of California Press.)

2. Suffering in Andersonville Prison. Eliza Frances Andrews, *The War-Time Journal of a Georgia Girl, 1864–1865*. New York: D. Appleton & Co., 1908. Pp. 76–79.

3. The Bright Side of Libby Prison. Frank E. Moran, "Libby's Bright Side: A Silver Lining in the Dark Cloud of Prison Life," in W. C. King and W. P. Derby, eds., *Camp-Fire Sketches and Battle-Field Echoes*. Springfield, MA.: W. C. King & Co., 1887. Pp. 180–181, 183–185.

4. The Awful Conditions at Fort Delaware. Randolph Abbott Shotwell, "Three Years in Battle," J. G. de Roulhac Hamilton, ed., *The Papers of Randolph Abbott Shotwell*. Raleigh, NC: North Carolina Historical Commission, pp. 1931. II, pp. 149–182, *passim*. (By permission of State of North Carolina Department of Archives and History.)

5. The Privations of Life in Elmira Prison. Marcus B. Toney, *The Privations of a Private*. Nashville, TN: Methodist Episcopal Church South, 1905. Pp. 93–104, *passim*.

CHAPTER XXI. BEHIND THE LINES: THE NORTH

1. Washington as a Camp. Noah Brooks, "Washington in Lincoln's Time,'" *Century Illustrated Magazine*, XXVII (November 1894), pp. 140–141. (By permission of Appleton-Century-Crofts, Inc.)

2. Walt Whitman Looks Around in Wartime Washington. Emory Halloway, ed., *The Uncollected Poetry and Prose of Walt Whitman*. New York: Doubleday, Page & Co., 1921. II, pp. 21 ff. (By permission of Doubleday & Company, Inc.)

3. Matthew Brady's "The Dead at Antietam."* *The New York Times*, October 21, 1862, p. 5.

4. Anna Dickinson Sees the Draft Riots in New York City. Anna Elizabeth Dickinson, *What Answer?* Boston: Ticknor & Fields, 1868. Pp. 243–256.

5. The Army of Lobbyists and Speculators. Régis de Trobriand, *Four Years with the Army of the Potomac*. Trans. by George K. Dauchy. Boston: Ticknor & Co., 1889. Pp. 134–136.

6. Charles A. Dana Helps Stop Frauds in the War Department. Charles A. Dana, *Recollections of the Civil War*. New York: D. Appleton & Co., 1898. Pp. 161–164. (By permission of Appleton-Century-Crofts, Inc.)

7. Colonel Baker Outwits Bounty Jumpers and Brokers. LaFayette C. Baker, *The Secret Service in the Late War*. Philadelphia: John E. Potter & Co., 1874. Pp. 249–267, *passim*.

8. Doings in Nevada.* Mark Twain, in Louis J. Budd, ed., *Mark Twain: Collected Tales, Sketches, Speeches, & Essays, 1852-1890*. New York: Library of America, 1992. Pp. 67–68.

9. Confederate Plots Against the North.
   A. A Confederate Plan to Seize Johnson's Island Is Frustrated. Hon. H. B. Brown, "The Lake Erie Piracy Case," The Green Bag, XXI (April 1909), Pp. 143–147.
   B. Confederates Raid Vermont.* John W. Headley, *Confederate Operations in Canada and New York, 1906*, in Philip Van Doren Stern, ed., *Secret Missions of the Civil War*. New York: Outlet Book Company, 1959, Pp. 242–246.
   C. The Confederates Attempt to Burn New York. John W. Headley, *Confederate Operations in Canada and New York*. New York: The Neale Publishing Co., 1906. Pp. 274–277.

10. War Weariness.
   A. A Sense of Infinite Weariness.* Nathaniel

Hawthorne, in Louis P. Masur, *The Real War Will Never Get in the Books: Selections from Writers During the Civil War.* New York: Oxford University Press, 1993. Pp. 177–178.

B. New-Jersey Peace Resolutions.* Henry Steele Commager, *Documents of American History, Volume I.* New York: Appleton-Century-Crofts, Inc., 1949. Pp. 427–428.

C. Protest of the New-Jersey Soldiers.* *Ibid*, p. 428.

11. Election of 1864.* Henry Brook Adams, in Louis P. Masur, *The Real War Will Never Get in the Books: Selections from Writers During the Civil War.* New York: Oxford University Press, 1993. Pp. 17.

CHAPTER XXII. BEHIND THE LINES: THE SOUTH

1. A War Clerk Suffers Scarcities in Richmond. John B. Jones, *A Rebel War Clerk's Diary at the Confederate States Capital.* Philadelphia: J. B. Lippincott Co., 1866. Vols I and II, *passim.*

2. Mr. Eggleston Recalls When Money Was Plentiful. George Cary Eggleston, *A Rebel's Recollections.* New York, 1874. Pp. 78–84, pp. 100–109.

3. Jews in the Confederacy.* Richard B. Harwell, ed., *The Confederate Reader: How the South Saw the War.* Mineola, NY: Dover Publications, 1989. Pp. 287–289.

4. Parthenia Hague Tells How Women Outwitted the Blockade. Parthenia Antoinette Hague, *A Blockaded Family: Life in Southern Alabama During the Civil War.* Boston: Houghton, Mifflin Co., 1888. Pp. 37–42, 100–105.

5. The Confederates Burn Their Cotton. Sarah Morgan Dawson, *A Confederate Girl's Diary,* Warrington Dawson, ed. Boston: Houghton Mifflin Co., 1913. Pp. 16–18. (By permission of Mr. Warrington Dawson.)

6. "The Yankees Are Coming." Testimony of Mrs. Mary A. Ward, *Report of the Committee of the Senate upon the Relations between Labor and Capital, and Testimony Taken by the Committee.* Washington, DC: Government

Printing Office, 1885. IV, pp. 334–336.

7. "The Lives Which Women Have Lead Since Troy Fell." Kate Mason Rowland and Mrs. Morris L. Croxall, eds., *The Journal of Julia LeGrand, New Orleans, 1862–1863.* Richmond, VA: Everett Waddey Co., 1911. Pp. 51–54.

8. "They Must Reap the Whirlwind." M. A. De Wolfe Howe, ed., *Home Letters of General Sherman.* New York: Charles Scribner's Sons, 1909. Pp. 268–269. (By permission of Charles Scribner's Sons.)

9. "I Do Want to See You So Much."* Loulie Gilmer, in Emmy E. Werner, *Reluctant Witnesses: Children's Voices from the Civil War.* Boulder, CO: Westview Press, 1998. P. 20.

10. "They Are Intelligent on All Subjects but that of Negro Slavery, on This They Are Mad."* *Geographical Reader of the Dixie Children,* in Erik Bruun and Jay Crosby, eds., *Our Nation's Archive: The History of the United States in Documents.* New York: Black Dog & Leventhal, 1999. P. 353.

11. Resistance at Home.
   A. President Davis Quells a Food Riot in Richmond.* Henry Steele Commager and Allan Nevis, *Eyewitness to America: A Documentary History of the United States from Its Discovery to Modern Times.* New York: Barnes & Noble Books, 1996. Pp. 703–705.
   B. Deaths from Starvation Have Absolutely Occurred.* Ira Berlin, Barbara J. Fields, Steven F. Miller, Joseph Reidy, Leslie S. Rowland, eds., *Free At Last: A Documentary History of Slavery, Freedom, and the Civil War.* Edison, NJ: The Blue & Grey Press, 1992. Pp. 148–151.

12. Georgia's Governor Laments Davis' Despotism. Joseph E. Brown. Ulrich B. Phillips, ed., "The Correspondence of Robert Toombs, Alexander H. Stephens, and Howell Cobb," *Annual Report of the American Historical Society for the year of 1911.* Washington DC: Government Printing Office, 1913, II, pp. 605–606. (By permission of American Historical Society.)

13. Peace at Any Price. J.G. de Roulhac Hamilton, ed., *The Correspondence of Jonathan Worth.* Raleigh, NC: North Carolina Historical Commission, 1909. I, pp. 257–258. (By permission of State of North Carolina Department of Archives and History.)

14. "The Man Who Held His Conscience Higher Than Their Praise." James Petigru Carson, *Life, Letters and Speeches of James Louis Petigru, The Union Man of South Carolina.* Washington, DC: W. H. Loudermilk & Co., 1920 P. 487.

CHAPTER XXIII. HOSPITALS, SURGEONS AND NURSES

1. George Townsend Describes the Wounded on the Peninsula. George Alfred Townsend, *Campaigns of a Non-Combatant, And His Romaunt Abroad During the War.* New York: Blelock & Co., 1866. Pp. 103–118.

2. The Sanitary Commission to the Rescue. Katherine Wormeley, *The Other Side of the War: With the Army of the Potomac. Letters from the Headquarters of the United States Sanitary Commission during the Peninsular Campaign in Virginia in 1862.* Boston: Ticknor & Co., 1889. Pp. 102–111.

3. Clara Barton Surmounts the Faithlessness of Union Officers. Wiliam E. Barton, *The Life of Clara Barton, Founder of the American Red Cross.* Boston: Houghton Mifflin Co., 1922. I, pp. 277–279. (By permission of Mr. Bruce Barton.)

4. Susan Blackford Nurses the Wounded at Lynchburg. Charles Minor Blackford, ed., *Letters from Lee's Army; or, Memoirs of Life In and Out of the Army in Virginia During the War Between the States. Compiled by Susan Leigh Blackford from original and contemporaneous memoirs, correspondence and diaries.* New York: Charles Scribner's Sons, 1947. Pp. 259–261. (By permission of Charles Scribner's Sons.)

5. Cornelia Hancock Nurses Soldiers and Contrabands. Henrietta Stratton Jaquette, ed., *South After Gettysburg, Letters of Cornelia Hancock from the Army of the Potomac, 1863–1865.* Philadelphia:

University of Pennsylvania Press, 1937. Pp. 8–12, pp. 31–32. (By permission of University of Pennsylvania Press.)

6. The Ghastly Work of the Field Surgeons.
   A. The Heartlessness of the Surgeons. Charles Sterling Underhill, ed., "Your Soldier Boy Samuel"—*Civil War Letters of Lieut. Samuel Edmund Nichols, Amherst '65 of the 37th Regiment Massachusetts Volunteers.* Privately printed, 1929. Pp. 50–52. (By permission of Mrs. I. S. Underhill.)
   B. The Horrors of the Wilderness. Augustus C. Brown, *The Diary of a Line Officer.* New York: Privately printed, 1906. Pp. 43–44.

7. *Hospital Sketches.** Louisa May Alcott, in Louis P. Masur, *The Real War Will Never Get in the Books: Selections from Writers During the Civil War.* New York: Oxford University Press, 1993. Pp. 33–37.

8. The Regimental Hospital. Charles Beneulyn Johnson, *Muskets and Medicine, or Army Life in the Sixties.* Philadelphia: F. A. Davis Co., 1917. Pp. 129–134. (By permission of F. A. Davis Company.)

CHAPTER XXIV. THE AFRICAN-AMERICAN EXPERIENCE

1. "You Debauched a Young Negro Girl."* Thomas P. Lowry, *The Story the Soldiers Wouldn't Tell: Sex in the Civil War.* Mechanicsburg, PA: Stackpole Books, 1994. Pp. 165–166.

2. No Choice But Escape.
   A. "The Alligators Preferred Dog Flesh to Personal Flesh."* Ira Berlin, Barbara J. Fields, Steven F. Miller, Joseph Reidy, Leslie S. Rowland, eds. *Free At Last: A Documentary History of Slavery, Freedom, and the Civil War.* Edison, NJ: The Blue & Grey Press, 1992. Pp. 51–52.
   B. Confederate Officer Tracks Down Runaway Slaves.* *Ibid.*, pp. 144–145.

3. The Proclamation and the Negro Army.* Frederick Douglass, in Louis P. Masur, *The Real War Will Never Get in the Books: Selections from Writers During the Civil War.*

New York: Oxford University Press, 1993. Pp. 115–116.

4. Black Soldiers Serve Bravely.
   A. "Unequaled Coolness & Bravery."* Ira Berlin, Barbara J. Fields, Steven F. Miller, Joseph Reidy, Leslie S. Rowland, eds. *Free At Last: A Documentary History of Slavery, Freedom, and the Civil War.* Edison, NJ: The Blue & Grey Press, 1992. Pp. 439–441.
   B. "Silencing the 'Jeers and Taunts.'"* *Ibid.*, pp. 489–492.

5. The Reverend James T. Ayers Recruits Negro Soldiers in Tennessee. John Hope Franklin, ed., *The Diary of James T. Ayers.* Springfield, IL: Illinois State Historical Society, 1947. Pp. 19–24. (By permission of John Hope Franklin and Illinois State Historical Library.)

6. Standing Up for the Rights of Black Soldiers.
   A. "Are We Soldiers, or Are We Labourers?"* in Virginia M. Adams, ed., *On the Altar of Freedom: A Black Soldier's Civil War Letters from the Front.* New York: Warner Books by arrangement with The University of Massachusetts, 1991. Pp. 118–121.
   B. Hannah Johnson to Abraham Lincoln.* Andrew Carrol, ed., *Letters of a Nation: A Collection of Extraordinary American Letters.* New York: Broadway Books, 1997. Pp. 117–118.
   C. Black Regiment Petitions Government for Redress.* Ira Berlin, Barbara J. Fields, Steven F. Miller, Joseph Reidy, Leslie S. Rowland, eds., *Free At Last: A Documentary History of Slavery, Freedom, and the Civil War.* Edison, NJ: The Blue & Grey Press, 1992. Pp. 228–229.

7. Hardships of an Unequal Freedom.
   A. Contrabands Experience Hardships.* *Ibid.*, pp. 180–182.
   B. "A Sense of Disgust Must Be Awakened."* *Ibid.*, pp. 113–115.

8. The Fate of Black Soldiers—And Those Left Behind
   A. "The Whole Government Gives Cheer to Me."* *Ibid.*, pp. 480–482.
   B. "I Am in Too Much Trouble."* *Ibid.*, p. 464.

C. "I Wish That His Back Had Been as Deeply Scarred."* *Ibid.*, pp. 115–116.

9. "If We Are Regarded as an Evil Here."* *Ibid.*, pp. 38–42.

10. "A Great Desire for Knowledge."* Charlotte Forten, "Life on the Sea Islands," *Atlantic Monthly,* 13 (May and June 1864). Pp. 587–596.

11. Tennessee Petition.* Ira Berlin, Barbara J. Fields, Steven F. Miller, Joseph Reidy, Leslie S. Rowland, eds. *Free At Last: A Documentary History of Slavery, Freedom, and the Civil War.* Edison, NJ: The Blue & Grey Press, 1992. Pp. 497–505.

CHAPTER XXV. A WAR FOR EMANCIPATION

1. Slavery, the Cornerstone of the Confederacy.* Henry Steele Commager, ed., *Fifty Basic Civil War Documents.* Malabar, FL: Robert E. Kreiger Publishing Company, 1982. Pp. 15–17.

2. "This Imbecile Pro-slavery Government Does Try Me So."* Louis P. Masur, *The Real War Will Never Get in the Books: Selections from Writers During the Civil War.* New York: Oxford University Press, 1993. Pp. 43–44, p. 47.

3. The Problem of Contrabands.
   A. General Butler's "Contrabands". Henry Steele Commager, *Documents of American History, Volume I.* New York: Appleton-Century-Crofts, Inc., 1949. Pp. 396–397.
   B. Frémont's Proclamation on Slaves. *Ibid.*, pp. 397–398.

4. Messages to Congress on Compensated Emancipation.
   A. The Gradual Abolishment of Slavery.* *Ibid.*, pp. 402–403.
   B. "We Cannot Escape History."* *Ibid.*, pp. 403–405.

5. "My Paramount Object is to Save the Union."
   A. "The Prayer of Twenty Millions". Greeley to Lincoln, in Frank Moore, ed., *The Rebellion Record.* New York, 1871. XX, p. 480.
   B. "I Would Save the Union". Lincoln to Greely, *Ibid.*

6. Lincoln Becomes the Great Emancipator.
   A. Secretary Chase Recalls a Famous Cabinet Meeting. J. W. Shuckers, *The Life and*

Public Services of Salmon Portland Chase. New York: D. Appleton & Co., 1874. Pp. 453–455.

B. "Forever Free". Abraham Lincoln, "The Emancipation Proclamation," in James D. Richardson, ed., *Messages and Papers of the Presidents*. New York, 1904. VI, pp. 157 ff.

7. Reactions to the Emancipation Proclamation.
   A. The Day of Jubilee Comes.* Louis P. Masur, *The Real War Will Never Get in the Books: Selections from Writers During the Civil War*. New York: Oxford University Press, 1993. Pp. 113–114.
   B. Illinois State Legislature Opposes Emancipation Proclamation.* Henry Steele Commager, *Documents of American History, Volume I*. New York: Appleton-Century-Crofts, Inc., 1949. P. 421.
   C. Kentucky Union Officer Objects to Emancipation.* Ira Berlin, Barbara J. Fields, Steven F. Miller, Joseph Reidy, Leslie S. Rowland, eds., *Free At Last: A Documentary History of Slavery, Freedom, and the Civil War*. Edison, NJ: The Blue & Grey Press, 1992. Pp. 82–83.
   D. Jefferson Davis Replies to the Emancipation Proclamation.* Henry Steele Commager, ed., *Fifty Basic Civil War Documents*. Malabar, FL: Robert E. Kreiger Publishing Company, 1982. Pp. 79–81.
   E. A Note on the Emancipation.* *The Southern Illustrated News*, October 11, 1862.

8. A War for Liberty.* Andrew Carrol, ed., *Letters of a Nation: A Collection of Extraordinary American Letters*. New York: Broadway Books, 1997. Pp. 120–121.

9. Arming Slaves in the Confederate Army.* Ira Berlin, Barbara J. Fields, Steven F. Miller, Joseph Reidy, Leslie S. Rowland, eds. *Free At Last: A Documentary History of Slavery, Freedom, and the Civil War*. Edison, NJ: The Blue & Grey Press, 1992. Pp. 164–165.

10. "Abolitionists Were the Only Traitors."

A. "The Country Was Formed for the White, Not for the Black Man."* John Wilkes Booth, in Nicholas N. Kittire and Eldon D. Wedlock, Jr., eds., *The Tree of Liberty: A Documentary History of Rebellion and Political Crime in America*. Baltimore: The John Hopkins University Press. P. 201.

B. Emancipation Arrives in Texas.* David Colbert, ed., *Eyewitness to the American West*. New York: Penguin Group, 1998. P. 155.

11. "The Work of the Abolitionist Is Not Done."* Diane Ravitch, ed., *The American Reader: Words That Moved a Nation*. New York: HarperCollins Publishers, 1990. Pp. 155–156.

CHAPTER XXVI. THE COAST AND INLAND WATERS

1. The *Merrimac* and the *Monitor*.
   A. The *Minnesota* Fights for Her Life in Hampton Roads, "Report of Captain Van Brunt," in Frank Moore, ed., *The Rebellion Record*. New York, 1863. IV, pp. 267–268.
   B. The *Monitor* Repels the *Merrimac*. S. D. Greene to His Parents, March 14, 1862, in Lydia Minturn Post, ed., *Soldiers' Letters from Camp, Battle-field and Prison*. New York: Bunce & Huntington, 1865. Pp. 109-113.

2. Commodore Farragut Captures New Orleans. Susan Perkins, ed., *Letters of Capt. Geo. Hamilton Perkins, U. S. N. . . . Also a Sketch of His Life*. Concord, NH: Privately printed, 1886. Pp. 67–71.

3. New Orleans Falls to the Yankees.
   A. Julia LeGrand Describes the Surrender of New Orleans. Kate Mason Rowland and Mrs. Morris L. Croxall, eds., *The Journal of Julia LeGrand, New Orleans, 1862–1863*. Richmond, VA: Everett Waddey Co., 1911. Pp. 39–43.
   B. General Butler Outrages the Moral Sentiment of the World. General Butler's Order No. 28, in Frank Moore, ed.,

The Rebellion Record. New York, 1863. V, p. 136.

C. Palmerston Protests Butler's Proclamation, Palmerston to Charles Francis Adams, *Proceedings of the Massachusetts Historical Society* (Boston), XLV (1911–1912), p.257. (By permission of Massachusetts Historical Society.)

D. "A More Impudent Proceeding Cannot Be Discovered." Sarah Agnes Wallace and Frances Elma Gillespie, eds., *The Journal of Benjamin Moran, 1857-1865*. Chicago: University of Chicago Press, 1949. II, pp. 1027–1029. (By permission of University of Chicago Press.)

4. Ellet's Steam Rams Smash the Confederate Fleet at Memphis, Alfred W. Ellet, "Ellet and His Steam-Rams at Memphis," in *Battles and Leaders of the Civil War*. New York: The Century Co., 1884–1887. I, pp. 453–459

5. Attack and Repulse at Battery Wagner. "The Attack on Fort Wagner. New York 'Tribune' Account," in Frank Moore, ed., *The Rebellion Record*. New York, 1864, VII, pp. 211–214.

6. Farragut Damns the Torpedoes at Mobile Bay. John C. Kinney, "Farragut at Mobile Bay," in *Battles and Leaders of the Civil War*. New York: The Century Co., 1884, 1887, 1888. IV, pp. 382 ff.

7. Lieutenant Cushing Torpedoes the *Albemarle*. W. B. Cushing, "The Destruction of the 'Albemarle,'" in *Battles and Leaders of the Civil War*. New York: The Century Co., 1884, 1887, 1888. IV, pp. 634–637.

8. The Confederates Repulse an Attack on Fort Fisher.. William Lamb, "The Defence of Fort Fisher, North Carolina," *Papers of the Military Historical Society of Massachusetts* (Boston), IX (1912), pp. 361–368. (By permission of Military Historical Society of Massachusetts.)

9. "It Beat Anything in History." Augustus Buell, "The Cannoneer." *Recollections of Service In the Army of the Potomac. By "A Detached Volunteer, in the Regular Artillery"*. Washington, DC: The National Tribune, 1890. Pp. 328–333.

CHAPTER XXVII. THE BLOCKADE AND THE CRUISERS

1. The United States Navy Blockades the Confederacy. Horatio L. Wait, "The Blockade of the Confederacy," *The Century Illustrated Magazine*, XXXIV (1898), pp. 94–920, *passim*. (By permission of Appleton-Century-Crofts, Inc.)
2. The *Robert E. Lee* Runs the Blockade. John Wilkinson, *The Narrative of a Blockade-Runner*. New York: Sheldon & Co., 1877. Pp. 162–171.
3. The *Rob Roy* Runs the Blockade out of Havana. William Watson, *The Adventures of a Blockade Runner; or, Trade in Time of War*. London: T. Fisher Unwin, 1892. Pp. 141–159.
4. Blockade-Runners Supply Charleston. W. F. G. Peck, "Four Years Under Fire at Charleston," *Harper's New Monthly Magazine*, XXXI (1865), p. 364.
5. Confederate Privateers Harry Northern Merchantmen.
   A. The *Ivy* Prowls Outside New Orleans. Letter of M. Repard, in *New Orleans Delta*, May 26, 1861, in William Morrison Robinson, Jr., The Confederate Privateers. New Haven, CT: Yale University Press, 1928. Pp. 45–46. (By permission of Yale University Press.)
   B. The *Jefferson Davis* Takes a Prize off Delaware. Captain Fitfield, in *The Charleston Mercury*, July 23, 1861, *Ibid.*, pp. 67–69.
6. The *Georgia* Fires the *Bold Hunter*. James Morris Morgan, *Recollections of a Rebel Reefer*. London: Constable & Co., Ltd., 1918. Pp. 154–156. Boston: Houghton Mifflin Co., 1917. (By permission of Mrs. Daniel Hunter Wallace.)
7. The *Kearsarge* Sinks the *Alabama* off Cherbourg. John McIntosh Kell, *Recollections of a Naval Life, including the Cruises of the Confederate States Steamers "Sumter" and "Alabama."* New York: The Neale Publishing Co., 1900. Pp. 244–251.

CHAPTER XXVIII. CHICKAMAUGA AND CHATTANOOGA

1. The Federals Oppose Hood with Desperation. James R. Carnahan, "Personal Recollections of Chickamauga," in *Sketches of War History, 1861-65 . . . Ohio Commandery of the Military Order of the Loyal Legion of the United States.* Cincinnati: Robert Clarke & Co., 1888. I, pp. 410–417.
2. Thomas Stands Like a Rock at Chickamauga.
   A. Longstreet Breaks the Federal Line. Daniel H. Hill, in "Chickamauga—The Great Battle of the West," in *Battles and Leaders of the Civil War*. New York: The Century Co., 1884, 1888. III, pp. 657–660.
   B. Thomas Holds the Horseshoe Ridge. Gates P. Thruston, "The Crisis at Chickamauga." *Ibid.*, III, pp. 663–664.
3. Chattanooga under Siege. W. F. G. Shanks, "Chattanooga, And How We Held It," *Harper's New Monthly Magazine*, XXXVI (1867–1868), pp. 142–146, pp. 148–149.
4. Hooker Wins the "Battle above the Clouds." Joseph G. Fullerton, "The Army of the Cumberland at Chattanooga," in *Battles and Leaders of the Civil War*. New York: The Century Co., 1884, 1888. III, pp. 721–723.
5. The Army of the Cumberland Carries Missionary Ridge.
   A. "First One Flag, Then Another, Leads". William A. Morgan, "Hazen's Brigade at Missionary Ridge," in *War Talks in Kansas . . . Commandery of Kansas, Military Order of the Loyal Legion of the United States*. Kansas City, MO: Franklin Hudson Publishing Co., 1906. I, pp. 271–275. (By permission of Kansas Commandery, Military Order of the Loyal Legion of the United States.)
   B. "Amid the Din of Battle 'Chickamauga' Could Be Heard". "Major Connolly's Letters to His Wife, 1862–1865," *Transactions of the Illinois State Historical Society*. ("Publications of the Illinois State Historical Library," No. 35.) Springfield IL: 1928. Pp. 298–303. (By permission of Illinois State Historical Society.)
6. "The Disaster Admits of No Palliation." Braxton Bragg to Jefferson Davis, in *The War of the Rebellion . . . Official Records*. Ser. I, vol. LII, pt. II, pp. 745–746.
7. Burnside Holds Out at Knoxville. Henry S. Burrage, "Burnside's East Tennessee Campaign," *Papers of the Military Historical Society of Massachusetts* (Boston), VIII (1910), pp. 574–595, *passim*. (By permission of Military Historical Society of Massachusetts.)

CHAPTER XXIX. ATLANTA AND THE MARCH TO THE SEA

1. General Sherman Takes Command. John Chipman Gray to John Ropes, in Roland Gray, "Memoir of John Chipman Gray," *Proceedings of the Massachusetts Historical Society* (Boston), XLIX (1915–1916), pp. 393–394. (By permission of Massachusetts Historical Society.)
2. Sherman Marches from Chattanooga to Atlanta. W. T. Sherman, "The Grand Strategy of the War of the Rebellion," *Century Illustrated Magazine*, XIII (February 1888), pp. 593–595.
3. Johnston Halts Sherman at New Hope Church. Joseph E. Johnston, *Narrative of Military Operations, Directed, During the Late War Between the States*. New York: D. Appleton & Co., 1874. Pp. 326–331.
4. Joe Johnston Gives Way to Hood.
   A. President Davis Removes General Johnston before Atlanta. Jefferson Davis, *Rise and Fall of the Confederate Government*. New York: D. Appleton & Co., 1881. II, pp. 556–557.
   B. General Johnston Justifies Himself. Letter from Johnston to Maury, Dabney H. Maury, *Recollections of a Virginian*. New York: Charles Scribners Sons, 1897. Pp. 146–148.
5. Hardee Wins and Loses the Battle of Atlanta. Richard S. Tuthill, "An Artilleryman's Recollections of the Battle of Atlanta," in *Military Essays and Recollections . . . Military Order of the Loyal Legion, Illinois Commandery*. Chicago: A. C. McClurg & Co., 1891. I, pp. 302–306.
6. "You Might as Well Appeal against the Thunder-Storm." [William T. Sherman], *Memoirs of General William T. Sherman*. New York:

D. Appleton & Co., 1875. II, pp. 125–127.

7. Child's Diary of the Atlanta Siege.* Emmy E. Werner, *Reluctant Witnesses: Children's Voices from the Civil War*. Boulder, CO: Westview Press, 1998. Pp. 106–116.

8. Sherman Marches from Atlanta to the Sea. [William T. Sherman], *Memoirs of General William T. Sherman*. New York: D. Appleton & Co., 1875. II, pp. 178 ff.

9. Sherman's "Bummers."
   A. A Good Word for the Bummers. Henry O. Dwight, "How We Fight at Atlanta," *Harper's New Monthly Magazine*, XXIX (1864), p. 666.
   B. "We Were Proud of Our Foragers". Daniel Oakey, "Marching Through Georgia and the Carolinas," in *Battles and Leaders of the Civil War*. New York: The Century Co., 1884, 1887, 1888. IV, pp. 672–673.

10. "The Heavens Were Lit Up with Flames from Burning Buildings." Dolly Sumner Lunt, *A Woman's Wartime Journal . . . With an introduction and Notes by Julian Street*. New York: The Century Co., 1918. Pp. 20–32, *passim*. (By permission of Mrs. L. D. Bolton.)

11. Eliza Andrews Comes Home through the Burnt Country. Eliza Frances Andrews, *The War-Time Journal of a Georgia Girl*. New York: D. Appleton & Co., 1908. Pp. 32–33, p. 38.

12. The Burning of Columbia.
    A. "A Scene of Shameful Confusion". Brevet Major George Ward Nichols, Aide-de-Camp to General Sherman, *The Story of the Great March, from the Diary of a Staff Officer*. New York: Harper & Bros., 1865. Pp. 160–166.
    B. Major Hitchcock Explains the Burning of Columbia. M. A. De Wolfe Howe, ed., *Marching with Sherman, Passages from the Letters and Campaign Diaries of Henry Hitchcock*. New Haven, CT: Yale University Press, 1927. Pp. 265–270. (By permission of Yale University Press.)

13. General Sherman Thinks His Name May Live. M. A. De Wolfe Howe, ed., *Home Letters of General Sherman*. New York: Charles

Scribner's Sons, 1909. Pp. 324–327. (By permission of Charles Scribner's Sons.)

CHAPTER XXX. THE WILDERNESS

1. U. S. Grant Plans His Spring Campaign. [Ulysses S. Grant], *Personal Memoirs of U. S. Grant*. New York: Charles L. Webster & Co., 1886. II, pp. 127 ff.

2. Colonel Porter Draws a Portrait of General Grant. General Horace Porter, *Campaigning with Grant*. New York: The Century Co., 1897. Pp. 13–16, pp. 248–250.

3. Private Goss Describes the Battle of the Wilderness. Warren Lee Goss, *Recollections of a Private. A Story of the Army of the Potomac*. New York: Thomas Y. Crowell & Co., 1890. Pp. 268–277.

4. "Texans Always Move Them." R. C. ——, of 'Hood's Texas Brigade,' "Gen. Lee at the 'Wilderness,'" in *The Land We Love*, V (1868), pp. 484–486.

5. "Their Dead and Dying Piled Higher Than the Works." Robert Stiles, *Four Years Under Marse Robert*. New York: The Neale Publishing Co., 1910. Pp. 253–255, pp. 263–264.

6. Spotsylvania and the Bloody Angle. General Horace Porter, *Campaigning with Grant*. New York: The Century Co., 1897. Pp. 101–111.

7. "These Men Have Never Failed You on Any Field." General John B. Gordon, *Reminiscences of the Civil War*. New York: Charles Scribner's Sons, 1903. Pp. 275–281. (By permission of Charles Scribner's Sons.)

8. Grant Hurls His Men to Death at Cold Harbor. William C. Oates, *The War Between the Union and the Confederacy and Its Lost Opportunities*. New York: The Neale Publishing Co., 1905. Pp. 365–368.

CHAPTER XXXI. THE SIEGE OF PETERSBURG

1. Grant's Army Crosses the James. "Grant's Report covering operations of all armies of the U.S. from March, 1864 to May, 1865," in *The War of the Rebellion . . . Official Records*.

Ser. I, vol. XXXVI, pt. I, pp. 22–25.

2. Beauregard Holds the Lines at Petersburg. G. T. Beauregard, "Four Days of Battle at Petersburg," in *Battles and Leaders of the Civil War*. New York: The Century Co., 1884, 1887, 1888, IV, pp. 540–544.

3. "A Hurricane of Shot and Shell." Captain Augustus C. Brown, *The Diary of a Line Officer*. New York: Privately printed, 1906. Pp. 77–82.

4. The Mine and the Battle of the Crater. John S. Wise, *The End of an Era*. Boston: Houghton Mifflin Co., 1899. Pp. 357–366.

5. Lee Stops Hancock at the Gates of Richmond. [Richard Corbin], "Letters of a Confederate Officer to His Family in Europe during the Last Year of the War of Secession," reprinted by William Abbatt, *Magazine of History*, Extra No. 24, 1913. Pp. 57–62.

6. The Iron Lines of Petersburg. George D. Harmon, ed., "Letters of Luther Rice Mills—a Confederate Soldier," *North Carolina Historical Review*, IV (July 1927), pp. 303–308. (By permission of State of North Carolina Department of Archives and History.)

CHAPTER XXXII. THE VALLEY IN 1864

1. V.M.I. Boys Fight at New Market. John S. Wise, "The West Point of the Confederacy," *Century Illustrated Magazine*, XXXVII (1888–1889), pp. 464–470.

2. General Hunter Devastates the Valley. General J. D. Imboden, "Fire, Sword, and the Halter," in *The Annals of the War, Written by Leading Participants North and South . . . in the Philadelphia Weekly Times*. Philadelpha: The Times Publishing Co., 1879. Pp. 177–181.

3. General Ramseur Fights and Dies for His Country. Letters of Ramseur to his fiancée and wife, Ramseur Manuscripts, University of North Carolina. (By permission of Messrs. Paul W. Schenck, Jr., and David Schenck.)

4. Early Surprises the Federals at Cedar Creek. Captain S. E. Howard, "The Morning Surprise at Cedar Creek," in *Civil War Papers . . . Massachusetts*

Commandery, *Military Order of the Loyal Legion of the United States.* Boston: Printed for the Commandery, 1900. II pp. 417–422. (By permission of Massachusetts Commandery, Military Order of the Loyal Legion of the United States.)

5. Sheridan Rides down the Valley Pike to Victory and Fame. [Philip H. Sheridan], *Personal Memoirs of P. H. Sheridan.* New York: Charles L. Webster & Co., 1888. II, pp. 68–86.

6. "The Valley Will Have Little in It for Man or Beast." Letter of General Sheridan, in *The War of the Rebellion . . . Official Records,* Ser. I, vol. XLIII, pt. 1, pp. 30–31.

CHAPTER XXXIII. LEE AND LINCOLN

1. Robert E. Lee Goes with His State.
   A. "My Relatives, My Children, My Home". Lee to his sister, Mrs. Anne Marshall, in Robert E. Lee [Jr.], *Recollections and Letters of General Robert E. Lee,* New York: Doubleday, Page & Co., 1904. Pp. 25–26. (By permission of Doubleday & Company, Inc.)
   B. "I Never Desire Again to Draw My Sword". Lee to General Scott, *Ibid.,* pp. 24–25.

2. "A Splendid Specimen of an English Gentleman." [Col. Garnet Wolseley], "A Month's Visit to the Confederate Headquarters," *Blackwood's Edinburgh Magazine,* XCIII (January–June 1863), p. 18, pp. 20–21.

3. "It Is Well War Is So Terrible or We Should Get Too Fond of It." W. N. Pendleton, "Personal Recollections of General Lee," *Southern Magazine,* XV (1874), pp. 620–621.

4. Dr. Parks's Boy Visits Lee's Headquarters. Leighton Parks, "What a Boy Saw of the Civil War; with Glimpses of General Lee," *Century Illustrated Magazine,* LXX (1905), pp. 258–264. (By permission of Appleton-Century-Crofts, Inc.)

5. "A Sadness I Had Never Before Seen upon His Face." J. D. Imboden, "The Confederate Retreat from Gettysburg," in *Battles and Leaders of the Civil War.* New York: The Century Co., 1884,

1888. III, pp. 420–421.

6. Lee and Traveller Review the Army of Northern Virginia. Robert E. Lee [Jr.], *Recollections and Letters of General Robert E. Lee.* New York: Doubleday, Page & Co., 1904. Pp. 106–107. (By permission of Doubleday & Company, Inc.)

7. "He Looked as Though He Was the Monarch of the World." William C. Oates, *The War Between the Union and the Confederacy and Its Lost Opportunities.* New York: The Neale Publishing Co., 1905. Pp. 343–344.

8. "The Field Resounded with Wild Shouts of Lee, Lee, Lee." Account by Colonel J. Catlett Gibson, in *Southern Historical Society Papers,* XXI (1903), pp. 200–203. (By permission of Southern Historical Society.)

9. Lee Bids Farewell to the Army of Northern Virginia. Robert E. Lee [Jr.], *Recollections and Letters of General Robert E. Lee.* New York: Doubleday, Page & Co., 1904. Pp. 153–154. (By permission of Doubleday & Company, Inc.)

10. Nathaniel Hawthorne Calls on President Lincoln. Nathaniel Hawthorne, *Tales, Sketches, and Other Papers,* many editions.

11. John Hay Lives with "The Tycoon" in the White House. Tyler Dennett, ed., John Hay, *Lincoln and the Civil War in the Diaries and Letters of John Hay.* New York: Dodd, Mead & Co., 1939. Pp. 34–35, pp. 68–69, p. 76, p. 96, p. 185. (By permission of Dodd, Mead & Company, Inc.)

12. "We Shall Nobly Save or Meanly Lose the Last, Best Hope of Earth." Abraham Lincoln, "Annual Message of Dec. 1, 1862," in James D. Richardson, ed., *Messages and Papers of the Presidents.* New York, 1904. VI, pp. 126 ff.

13. Lincoln's Condolence Letters.* Abraham Lincoln. Letter to Lydia Bixby in *Lincoln: Speeches, Letters, Miscellaneous Writings, Presidential Messages and Proclamations.* Don E. Fehrenbacher, ed., (New York, Library of America, 1989), p. 644. Letter to Fanny McCullough, in Andrew Carrol, ed., *Letters of a Nation: A Collection of Extraordinary American Letters.* New York: Broadway Books, 1997. P. 368.

14. Lincoln and Hay Follow the

Election Returns. Tyler Dennett, ed., John Hay, *Lincoln and the Civil War in the Diaries and Letters of John Hay.* New York: Dodd, Mead & Co., 1939. Pp. 232–236. (By permission of Dodd, Mead & Company, Inc.)

15. Lincoln Replies to a Serenade. Nicolay and Hay, eds., *The Complete Works of Abraham Lincoln.* New York: The Century Co., 1894. II, pp. 595–596. (By permission of Appleton-Century-Crofts, Inc.)

16. Lincoln Visits the Colored Soldiers at City Point. General Horace Porter, *Campaigning with Grant.* New York: The Century Co., 1897. Pp. 216–220.

17. "With Malice Toward None." Abraham Lincoln, "Second Inaugural Address," in James D. Richardson, ed., *Messages and Papers of the Presidents.* New York, 1904. VI, pp. 276–277.

18. Abraham Lincoln Is Assassinated. *Diary of Gideon Welles.* Boston: Houghton Mifflin Co., 1911. II, pp. 283 ff. (By permission of Houghton Mifflin Company.)

CHAPTER XXXIV. THE SUNSET OF THE CONFEDERACY

1. Thomas Annihilates Hood at Nashville. James Harrison Wilson, *Under the Old Flag; Recollections of Military Operations in the War for the Union, the Spanish War, the Boxer Rebellion, etc.* New York: D. Appleton & Co., 1912. II, pp. 99–121, *passim.* (By permission of Appleton-Century-Crofts, Inc.)

2. "The Last Chance of the Confederacy." Alexander C. McClurg, "The Last Chance of the Confederacy," *Atlantic Monthly,* L (September 1882), pp. 389 ff.

3. "Now Richmond Rocked in Her High Towers to Watch the Impending Issue." George Alfred Townsend, *Campaigns of a Non-Combatant, And His Romaunt Abroad During the War.* New York: Blelock & Co., 1866. Pp. 318–326.

4. "The Most Superb Soldier in All the World" Falls at Five Forks. Armistead Churchill Gordon, *Memories and Memorials of William Gordon McCabe.* Richmond, VA: Old Dominion Press, Inc., 1925. I, pp. 164–166. (By permission of Mr.

W. Gordon McCabe II and Brigadier General E. R. Warner McCabe.)

5. The Confederates Abandon Richmond.
    A. "A Great Burst of Sobbing All Over the Church" in Mrs. Burton Harrison, *Recollections Grave and Gay*. New York: Charles Scribner's Sons, 1916. Pp. 210–219. (By permission of Charles Scribner's Sons.)
    B. "The Poor Colored People Thanked God That Their Sufferings Were Ended". R. B. Prescott, "The Capture of Richmond," *Civil War Papers . . . Massachusetts Commandery, Military Order of the Loyal Legion of the United States*. Boston: Printed for the Commandery, 1900. I, pp. 64–70. (By permission of Massachusetts Commandery, Military Order of the Loyal Legion of the United States.)
    C. "Night Came and with it Came Sorrow and Sadness."* Frances Calden de la Barca Hunt, in Emmy E. Werner, *Reluctant Witnesses: Children's Voices from the Civil War*. Boulder, CO: Westview Press, 1998. Pp. 135–136.
6. The White Flag at Appomattox. Joshua Lawrence Chamberlain, *The Passing of the Armies, An Account of the Final Campaign of the Army of the Potomac, Based upon Personal Reminiscences of the Fifth Army Corps*. New York: G. P. Putnam's Sons, 1915. Pp. 230–242.
7. General Lee Surrenders at Appomattox. Sir Frederick Maurice, ed., *An Aide-de-Camp of Lee; being the Papers of Colonel Charles Marshall*. Boston: Little, Brown & Co., 1927. Pp. 268–274. (By permission of Sir Frederick Maurice.)
8. "The Whole Column Seemed Crowned with Red." Joshua Lawrence Chamberlain, *The Passing of the Armies, An Account of the Final Campaign of the Army of the Potomac, Based upon Personal Reminiscences of the Fifth Army Corps*. New York: G. P. Putnam's Sons, 1915. P. 248, pp. 258–265.
9. The Last Will and Testament of J. Reb.* Emmy E. Werner, *Reluctant Witnesses: Children's Voices from the Civil War*. Boulder, CO: Westview Press, 1998. Pp. 142–143.
10. The Stars and Stripes Are Raised over Fort Sumter. Mary Cadwalader Jones, *Lantern Slides*. Boston: Privately printed, 1937. (By permission of Mrs. Max Farrand.)
11. "Bow Down, Dear Land, for Thou Hast Found Release." James Russell Lowell, "Ode Recited at the Harvard Commemoration," *Poems*, many editions.

APPENDIX A: RECONSTRUCTING THE NATION

1. The Destruction of the South.
    A. "Prominent Citizens Became Piesellers."* Henry Steele Commager and Allan Nevis, *Eyewitness to America: A Documentary History of the United States from Its Discovery to Modern Times*. New York: Barnes & Noble Books, 1996. Pp. 808–811.
    B. "In the Heart of Destruction."* *Ibid*, Pp. 806–808.
2. "Education Must Become Universal."* "Congressional Report on the Freedmen's Bureau," in Paul F. Boller, Jr., and Ronald Story, *A More Perfect Union: Documents in U.S. History, Volume II*. Boston: Houghton Mifflin Company, 1984. Pp. 12–17.
3. First Reconstruction Act.* Henry Steele Commager, *Documents of American History, Volume II*. New York: Appleton-Century-Crofts, Inc., 1949. Pp. 30–31.
4. Constitutional Amendments.
    A. Thirteenth Amendment.* United States Congress. U.S. Constitution.
    B. Fourteenth Amendment.* United States Congress. *Ibid*.
    C. Fifteenth Amendment.* United States Congress. *Ibid*.
5. "The End of the White Man's Government."* Erik Bruun and Jay Crosby, eds., *Our Nation's Archive: The History of the United States in Documents*. New York: Black Dog & Leventhal, 1999. Pp. 390–391.
6. Black Parliament in South Carolina.* Henry Steele Commager and Allan Nevis, *Eyewitness to America: A Documentary History of the United*

States from Its Discovery to Modern Times. New York: Barnes & Noble Books, 1996. Pp. 812–816.
7. "A Full Pardon."* Nicholas N. Kittire and Eldon D. Wedlock, Jr., eds., *The Tree of Liberty: A Documentary History of Rebellion and Political Crime in America*. Baltimore: The Johns Hopkins University Press. P. 216.
8. The Ku Klux Klan.
    A. "I Shook Hands with Bob 'fore They Hung Him."* Noel Rae, ed., *Witnessing America: The Library of Congress Book of Firsthand Accounts of Life in America 1600–1900*. New York: Penguin Books, 1996. Pp. 432–434.
    B. Frankfort, Kentucky, Congressional Petition.* Erik Bruun and Jay Crosby, eds., *Our Nation's Archive: The History of the United States in Documents*. New York: Black Dog & Leventhal, 1999. Pp. 407–409.
9. "We Had Only Our Ignorance."* Ronald Takaki, ed., *A Larger Memory: A History of Our Diversity, With Voices*. Boston: Little, Brown and Company, 1998. Pp. 102–111.
10. "The Uneducated Negro Was Too Weak."* Erik Bruun and Jay Crosby, eds., *Our Nation's Archive: The History of the United States in Documents*. New York: Black Dog & Leventhal, 1999. Pp. 417–418.
11. "A General Reestablishment of Order."* Paul F. Boller, Jr., and Ronald Story, *A More Perfect Union: Documents in U.S. History, Volume II*. Boston: Houghton Mifflin Company, 1984. Pp. 19–21.

APPENDIX B: DOCUMENTS OF LASTING INFLUENCE

1. Homestead Act.* Henry Steele Commager, ed., *Fifty Basic Civil War Documents*. Malabar, FL: Robert E. Kreiger Publishing Company, 1982. Pp. 128–130.
2. Pacific Railway Act.* *Ibid*., pp. 130–132.
3. Morrill Act.* *Ibid*., pp. 132–134.
4. West Virginia Becomes a State.* *Ibid*., pp. 106–109.
5. Ousting the French from Mexico.
    A. Seward to Adams.* *Ibid*. pp. 96–101.

B. House Resolution of French Intervention in Mexico.* *Ibid.*
C. Seward to Motley.* *Ibid.*
6. Ex Parte Merryman.* *Ibid.*, pp. 109–114.
7. Ex Parte Milligan.* *Ibid.*, pp. 114–121.

Selections quoted from *John Brown's Body,* in *The Selected Works of Stephen Vincent Benét,* published by Rinehart and Company, Inc. Copyright 1927, 1928 by Stephen Vincent Benét, reprinted by permission of Brandt & Brandt.

Statistical table on page 84 from *Numbers and Losses of the Civil War* by Thomas L. Livermore, published by Houghton Mifflin Company. Copyright 1900, reprinted by permission of U. W. Harris Livermore Estate.

Map of The Civil War, 1861–1865, from *The Growth of the American Republic* by S. E. Morison and H. S. Commager. Copyright 1930, 1937, 1942, 1950 by Oxford University Press, Inc., reprinted by permission of Oxford University Press, Inc., and S. E. Morison.

Three maps, The Campaigns in Tennessee and Kentucky, The Strategic Position of Missouri, and Chattanooga and Its Approaches, from *The Mississippi Valley in the Civil War* by John Fiske, published by Houghton, Mifflin & Co. Copyright 1900, reprinted by permission of Houghton Mifflin Company.

INDEX

Abner Doubleday Defends Fort Sumter, 69–71

Abner Small Paints a Portrait of a Private in the Army of the Potomac, 207–208

Abner Small Suffers in Danville Prison, 461–463

"Abolitionists Were the Only Traitors", 582–583

Abraham Lincoln is Nominated in the Wigwam, 39–42

Adams, Charles Francis, quoted, 371–372

Adams, Henry Brook, quoted, 498

African-American experience, 539–563

Alcott, Louisa May, quoted, 533–536

Alexander, Edward P., quoted, 98–99, 425–427

Alexander Gives the Signal to Start, 425–427

Allan, William, quoted, 99–101

"The Alligators Preferred Dog Flesh to Personal Flesh", 541

"All Quiet Along the Potomac" (song), 375–376

"All This Will Come Right in the End", 433–434

Alston, Colonel, quoted, 456–459

"Amid the Din of Battle 'Chickamauga' Could Be Heard", 649–652

Anderson, Robert, Battle of Chancellorsville, 195–202

Andersonville Prison, 463–464

Andrews, Eliza, quoted, 463–464, 677–679

Andrews, Sidney, quoted, 790–791

Anna Dickinson Sees the Draft Riots in New York City, 480–483

Antietam (Sharpsburg), Battle of, 159–181, 227–229; photographic exhibit of, 477–479

Appomatox (Virginia), surrender, 775–781

"Are We Soldiers, or are We Labourors?" 550–551

The Armies Converge on Gettysburg, 408–411

Arming Slaves for the Confederate Army, 582

Armistead Falls Beside the Enemy's Battery, 428–429

Arms and ammunitions supplies, 98–99

"The Army is Becoming Awfully Depraved", 333–335

The Army of Lobbyists and Speculators, 483–484

The Army of the Cumberland Carries Missionary Ridge, 647–652

The Army of the Potomac Marches to Meet McClellan, 116

"The Artilleryman's Vision" (poem), 401

Atlanta, Battle of, 665–671

Atlanta, Sherman's march from, 657–682

Attack and Repulse at Battery Wagner, 600–602

Auchmuty, Richard, quoted, 128–130

Avary, Myrta Lockett, quoted, 788–790

The Awful Conditions at Fort Delaware, 466–469

A Badger Boy Meets the Originals of Uncle Tom's Cabin, 319–320

Baker, Lafayette C., 486–489

Baltimore Mobs Attack the Sixth Massachusetts, 93–96

Banks, General, Fall of Port Hudson, 454–455

"Barbara Frietchie" (poem), 393–394

Barton, Clara, quoted, 526–527

"The Battle-Cry of Freedom" (song), 380–381

"The Battle Hymn of the Republic" (song), 377–379

Beach, E. J., quoted, 340–342

Beauregard, P. G. T., quoted, 703–706

Beauregard Holds the Lines at Petersburg, 703–706

"Beauty" Stuart Rides Around McClellan's Army, 119–123

Beers, Ethyl Lynn, song by, 375–376

Behind the Lines: The North, 473–498; The South, 499–519

"Bells Are Ringing Wildly", 437

Benjamin, Judah P., quoted, 101–102

Benson, William, quoted, 552–553

Bentonville (North Carolina), Battle of, 762–766

Berry, Carrie, quoted, 669–671

Billings, John D., quoted, 216–220

Binney, Horace, quoted, 72–73

Bishop, Thomas B., song by, 375

Bixby, Lydia, Lincoln's letter to, 748

Blackford, Susan, quoted, 527–528

Black Parliament in South Carolina, 799–801

Black Regiment Petitions Government for Redress, 552–553

Black Soldiers Serve Bravely, 543–545

Blackwood's Edinburgh Magazine *Rejoices in the Break-up of the Union*, 352–354

Blockade, the, 617–634

Blockade Runners Supply Charleston, 627–628

The Bloodiest Day of the War, 166–170

Blue and Gray Fraternize on the Picket Line, 237–238

"The Blue and the Gray" (poem), 402–403

Boker, George Henry, poetry of, 397–398

"The Bonnie Blue Flag" (song), 374–375

Booth, John Wilkes: Lincoln's assassination, 754–756; quoted, 582–583

Bounty jumping, 96–98, 486–489

"Bow Down, Dear Land, for Thou Hast Found Release", 786

A Boy Cannoneer Describes Hard Fighting on the First Day, 413–417

Bradbury, William Batchelder, song by, 376–377

Brady, Matthew, photographic exhibit by, 477–479

Bragg, Braxton, quoted, 652–653

The Bright Side of Libby Prison, 464–466

Brisbin, James B., quoted, 544–545

Britton, Wiley, quoted, 280–282

Brooks, Noah, quoted, 473–475

Brown, Augustus, quoted, 532–533, 706–708

Brown, H. B., quoted, 490–491

Brown, Joseph E., quoted, 517–518

Bryant, William Cullen, poetry of, 392–393

Buell, Augustus, quoted, 413–417, 613–615

Buford and Reynolds Hold Up the Confederate Advance, 411–413

Bull Run, Battles of: First Bull Run, 105–113; Second Bull Run, 145–159

"Bull Run Russell" Reports the Route of the Federals, 108–112

"Bummers", 674–675

The Burning of Columbia, 679–681

Burnside Blunders at Fredericksburg, 185–190

Burnside Holds Out at Knoxville, 653–656

Burrage, Henry S., quoted, 653–656

Butler, Benjamin: proclamation of, 595–596; quoted, 568–569

Camp Cameron, 205–207

A Camp of Skulkers at Cedar Mountain, 333

Captain Livermore Fights at Malvern Hill, 126–128

Captain Wilkes Seizes Mason and Slidell, 356–358

The Capture of Washington Seems Inevitable, 113

Carnahan, James R., quoted, 636–638

"Carolina" (poem), 391

Cary, Constance, Constance (Cary), quoted, see Harrison

Casualties, medicine and, 521–538

Cedar Creek (Virginia), attack on, 726–728

Chamberlain, Daniel, quoted, 809–810

Chamberlain, Joshua L., quoted, 192–194, 775–779, 783–784

Chamberlayne, John Hampden, 147–149

Chancellorsville, Battle of, 195–204

Charles A. Dana Helps Stop Frauds in the War Department, 484–486

Chase, S. P., quoted, 575–577

Chattanooga, Battle of, 262–264, 635–652; Lookout Mountain, 645–646; Missionary Ridge, 647–652

Chattanooga Under Siege, 642–645

Chesnut, Mary Boykin, quoted, 65–69

Child, Lydia Maria, quoted, 567–568

Child's Diary of Atlanta Siege, 669–671

Christian, William S., quoted, 407–408

Clara Barton Surmounts the Faithlessness of Union Officers, 526–527

Cobden, Richard, quoted, 367–368

Colonel Bailey Dams the Red River, 277–280

Colonel Baker Outwits Bounty Jumpers and Brokers, 486–489

Colonel Oates Almost Captures Little Round Top, 419–422

Colonel Porter Draws a Portrait of General Grant, 685–687

Colonel Wolseley Visits Stonewall Jackson, 140–141

Colored Citizens of Frankfort and Vicinity, quoted, 803–806

Columbia (South Carolina), burning of, 679–681

"Come Up From the Fields Father" (poem), 396–397

Commodore Farragut Captures New Orleans, 592–594

Conduct Unbecoming an Officer, 331–333

Confederacy: collapse of, 757–786; Constitution, 56–57; organization of at Montgomery Alabama, 54–56

The Confederacy Organizes at Montgomery, 54–56

A Confederate Doctor Describes the Victory at First Bull Run, 106–108

A Confederate Lieutenant Complains that Red-Tapeism Will Lose the War, 224–225

Confederate Officer Tracks Down Runaway Slaves, 541–542

A Confederate Plan to Seize Johnson's Island is Frustrated, 490–491

Confederate Plots Against the North, 490–494

Confederate Privateers Harry Northern Merchantmen, 628–629

The Confederates Abandon Richmond, 770–775

Confederates Attempt to Burn New York, 493–494

The Confederates Burn Their Cotton, 509–510

The Confederates Escape in the Teche Country, 320–323

The Confederates Get Religion, 225–226

Confederates Raid Vermont, 491–493

The Confederates Repulse an Attack on Fort Fisher, 610–613

The Confederates Scatter after Pea Ridge, 272–275

Conkling, James C., Lincoln's letter to, 455–456

Connolly, James A., quoted, 309–311, 649–652

"The Conquered Banner" (poem), 402

Constitution: amendments, 796–798; Confederacy, 56–57; United States, 80–81

Constitutional Amendments, 796–798

Constitution of the Confederate States of America, 56–57

Contrabands Experience Hardships, 553–554

Cooke, Chauncey, quoted, 284–285, 319–320

Cooke, John Esten, quoted, 119–123, 190–191

Corbin, Richard, quoted, 711–712

Cornelia Hancock Nurses Soldiers and Contrabands, 528–531

Cotton is King at the Battle of Lexington, 265–267

"The Country Was Formed for the White, Not for the Black Man", 582–583

"The Crest is Safe", 429–433

Crittenden Compromise, 44–45

Curtis, S. R., quoted, 554

Cushing, William B., quoted, 608–609

Dabney, Robert, quoted, 146–147

Dana, Charles A., quoted, 484–486

Danville Prison, 461–463

Davis, Charles E., quoted, 209–212

Davis, David, quoted, 824–828

Davis, President Jefferson: Cabinet, 58–59; Emancipation Proclamation, reply to, 580; food riot, Richmond, 515–516; Inaugural address, 61–63; quoted, 663–665; removal of Joe Johnston, 663–665

Dawes, Rufus R., 171–173

Dawson, Sarah, quoted, 337–340, 509–510

Day, Samuel P., quoted, 265–267

The Day of Jubilee Comes, 578

"The Death of Slavery" (poem), 392–393

Deaths from Starvation Have Absolutely Occurred, 516–517

De Forest, John, quoted, 320–323

DeLeon, Thomas Cooper, quoted, 54–56

The Desperate fighting Along Bloody Lane, 175–179

Destruction of the South, 788–791

Dew, J. Harvie, quoted, 240–241

Dickinson, Anna, quoted, 480–483

Dick Taylor Campaigns with Jackson in the Valley, 132–138

"Dirge for a Soldier" (poem), 397–398

"The Disaster Admits of No Palliation", 652–653

Discipline problem, 325–350

"Dixie" (song), 373–374

Documents, influential, 813–828

Doings in Nevada, 489–490

Dooley, John, quoted, 226, 345–346

"Do They Miss Me in the Trenches?" (song), 384

Doubleday, Abner, quoted, 69–71
Douglas, Henry Kyd, quoted, 141–144
Douglass, Frederick, quoted, 542–543,
    578, 584–585
Dr. Parks's Boy Visits Lee's Headquarters,
    737–740
Draft riots, New York City, 480–483
"Driving Home the Cows" (poem),
    400
"The Drummer Boy of Shiloh" (poem),
    394–395
*Dunn Brown has Trouble with the War
    Department,* 223
Dwight, Henry, quoted, 674

Early Surprises the Federals at Cedar Creek,
    726–728
Education Must Become Universal,
    791–795
Eggleston, George Cary, quoted,
    503–505
18th Virginia Infantry Regiment, 582
Election of 1864, 498
Electioneering in the Camps, 222
*Eliza Andrews Comes Home Through the
    Burnt Country,* 677–679
Ellet, Alfred W., quoted, 597–599
*Ellet's Steam Rams Smash the Confederate
    Fleet at Memphis,* 597–599
Elmira Prison, 469–471
Emancipation, 565–585
Emancipation Arrives in Texas, 583
Emancipation Proclamation: Great
    Britain, opinion, 363–365, 367–368;
    Negro Army and, 542–543; quote
    from, 577; reactions to, 577–581
Emmett, Daniel Decatur, song by, 373–374
Emory, Frederick, quoted, 93–96
The End of Seven Days, 125–128
"The End of the White Man's Government",
    798–799
*English Aristocrats Organize for Southern
    Independence,* 368–369
*The English Press Condemns the
    Emancipation Proclamation,* 363–365
"An Error, the Most Singular and Palpable",
    362–363
Etheredge, Richard, quoted, 552–553
"Ethnogenesis" (poem), 389–391
Executing Deserters, 346–347
*Executing Deserters from the Confederate
    Army,* 347
Ex Parte Merryman, 821–824
Ex Parte Milligan, 824–828

Fairfax, Donald Macneill, 356–358
A Far From Glorious Fourth, 437–438
Farley, Porter, quoted, 417–419
Farragut, David A.: Mobile Bay, attack
    on, 602–608; New Orleans, capture of,
    592–594
*Farragut Damns the Torpedoes at Mobile
    Bay,* 602–608

*The Fate of the Black Soldier—And Those
    Left Behind,* 554–556
"The Father of Waters Again Goes Unvexed
    to the Sea",* 455–456
Favill, Lieutenant, quoted, 90–91
*The Federals Are Forced Back at White Oak
    Swamp,* 125–126
*The Federals Opposed Hood With
    Desperation,* 636–638
"The Field Resounded with Wild Shouts of
    Lee, Lee, Lee",* 742–744
Fifteenth Amendment, 798
Finch, Francis Mules, poetry of, 402–403
*First Gallant South Carolina Nobly Made
    the Stand,* 42–43
"First One Flag, Then Another, Leads",
    647–649
First Reconstruction Act, 795–796
Fiske, Samuel (Dunn Brown), quoted, 223
Fitch, Michael, quoted, 92–93
Fitfield, Captain, quoted, 629
*Fitz John Porter Views the Confederates
    from a Balloon,* 229–231
Five Forks (Virginia), Battle of, 769–770
Foreigners Fight in the Northern Army,
    233–235
"Forever Free",* 577
Fort Delaware, 466–469
Forten, Charlotte, quoted, 558–559
Fort Fisher, attack on, 610–615
Fort Sumter, attack on, 65–71
Fort Wagner, attack on, 600–602
Fourteenth Amendment, 797–798
Frankfort, Kentucky, Congressional
    Petition, 803–806
*Frank Wilkeson Goes South with
    Blackguards, Thieves, and Bounty
    Jumpers,* 96–98
Fraud, War Department, 484–486
Fredericksburg, Battle of, 183, 185–194
Freedmen's Bureau, 791–795
Freemantle, Arthur J. L., quoted,
    433–434
Frémont, J. C., quoted, 569–570
Frémont's Proclamation on Slaves,
    569–570
From Reveille to Taps, 289–292
Fullerton, Major Joseph, quoted, 645–646
"A Full Pardon",* 802

Gaines' Mill, Battle of, 123–124
The Gallant Pelham at Fredericksburg,
    190–191
Gay, Mrs., quoted, 289
General Banks Takes Port Hudson,
    454–455
*General Butler Outrages the Mortal
    Sentiment of the World,* 595
General Butler's "Contrabands", 568–569
*General Gordon is Wounded Five Times at
    Antietam,* 177–179
General Hunter Devastates the Valley,
    719–721

General Johnston Justifies Himself,
    664–665
General Lee Decides to Take the Offensive,
    406–408
*General Lee Discusses the Problem of
    Discipline,* 347–349
General Lee Invades Pennsylvania,
    407–408
*General Lee Offers to Resign After
    Gettysburg,* 435–436
General Lee Surrenders at Appomatox,
    779–781
General Morgan Invades the North,
    456–460
*General Ramseur Fights and Dies for His
    Country,* 721–726
"A General Reestablishment of Order",
    810–811
*General Sheridan Executes Two Deserters at
    Chattanooga,* 346–347
*General Sherman Explains Why He Cannot
    Like McClellan,* 158
General Sherman Takes Command,
    658–659
*General Sherman Thinks His Name May
    Live,* 681–682
General Warren Seizes Little Round Top,
    417–419
*General Wilson Raises His Cavalry the
    Hard Way,* 324
General Wool Takes Norfolk,
    115–116
Geographical Reader of the Dixie Children,
    quoted, 514
*George Ticknor Explains the War to his
    English Friends,* 354–355
*George Townsend Describes the Wounded on
    the Peninsula,* 521–523
The Georgia Fires the Bold Hunter,
    629–631
*Georgia's Governor Laments Davis'
    Despotism,* 517–518
Gerrish, Theodore, quoted, 422–424
Gettysburg, Battle of, 405–438; Little
    Round Top, 417–424
"Gettysburg Address" (Lincoln), 438
The Ghastly Work of the Field Surgeons,
    531–533
Gibbons, James Sloan, song by, 379–380
Gibson, Colonel, quoted, 742–744
Gilmer, Loulie, quoted, 513
Gilmore, Patrick S., song by, 387
Gladstone, William Ewart, quoted,
    362–363
Glover, Martha, quoted, 556
"Goober Peas" (song), 385
Good Cheer in the Ranks, 298–300
Gooding, James Henry, quoted,
    550–551
A Good Word for the Bummers, 674
Gordon, John B., quoted, 177–179
Gordon, Lee, quoted, 696–699
Goss, Warren, quoted, 89–90, 687–690

The Gradual Abolishment of Slavery,
570–571
Graft and Corruption in the Federal Army,
294–295
"Grafted into the Army" (song), 385
Graham, James, quoted, 173–175
Grant, Ulysses S.: Belmont, attack,
245–247; Fort Donelson, surrender,
247–252; Murphy, R. C., indictment
of, 331–333; Petersburg, Siege of,
701–714; quoted, 450–454, 684–685,
702–703; Vicksburg, surrender of,
450–454; Wilderness campaign,
683–700
Grant Hurls His Men to Death at Cold
Harbor, 699–700
Grant's Army Crosses the James,
702–703
Grant Wins His Spurs at Belmont,
245–247
Gray, John Chipman, quoted, 283–284,
658–659
Great Britain, 351–372
"A Great Burst of Sobbing All Over the
Church", 770–772
"A Great Desire for Knowledge",
558–559
The Great Locomotive Chase in Georgia,
312–318
The Great Revival in the Army of
Tennessee, 288–289
Greeley, Horace, quoted, 574
Green, S. Dana, quoted, 590–591
Grier, Justice, Prize Cases, 80–81
Grierson's Raiders on a Rampage,
340–342
Grovenor, Gurdon, 275–277
Guerrilla Warfare in Missouri, 268–270

Hague, Parthenia, quoted, 507–509
Hale, James T., letter from Lincoln, 45
Halstead, Murat, quoted, 39–42
Hancock, Cornelia, quoted, 528–531
Hannah Johnson to Abraham Lincoln,
551–552
Hardee Wins and Loses the Battle of
Atlanta, 665–668
Hardships of an Unequal Freedom,
553–554
Hardtack and Coffee, 217–220
Harrison, Constance (Cary), quoted,
770–772
Haskell, Frank, quoted, 429–433
Hawthorne, Nathaniel, quoted, 495–496,
744–746
Hay, John, quoted, 746–747, 749–751
Hayes, Rutherford B., quoted, 810–811
Hays, Will "Shakespeare," poetry of,
394–395
Headley, John W., quoted, 491–494
The Heartlessness of the Surgeons,
531–532
The Heather Is on Fire, 71–75

"The Heavens Were Lit Up with Flames
from Burning Buildings", 675–677
"He Looked as Though He Was the
Monarch of the World", 742
Henry Kyd Douglas Remembers Stonewall
Jackson, 141–144
Henry Ravenel Expects Foreign Intervention,
352
Herndon, William Henry, quoted, 47–48
Herndon Describes the Inauguration,
47–48
Higginson, Thomas Wentworth, quoted,
326–330, 545–549
High Tide at Gettysburg, 424–438
Hill, D. H., quoted, 639–640
Hitchcock, Henry, quoted, 680–681
Holmes, Oliver Wendell, poetry of, 43–44
Holsinger, Frank, quoted, 227–229
Homestead Act, 813–814
"The Honored General" (poetry),
398–399
Hood, General: Chattanooga, Battle of,
636–638; Nashville (Tennessee), Battle
of, 758–761; New Hope Church,
engagement at, 661–663; Second Bull
Run, 171–173
Hooker, Joe: appointment to Command
of the Army, 194–195;
Chancellorsville, Battle of, 195–198;
Chattanooga, Battle of, 645–646;
Second Bull Run, 170–175
Hooker Hammers the Confederate Left—In
Vain, 170–175
Hooker Wins the "Battle Above the Clouds",
645–646
Hope, Samuel E., quoted, 541–542
Hornet's Nest (Shiloh, Battle of),
257–262
The Horrors of the Wilderness, 532–533
Hospital Sketches, 533–536
Hotel de Vicksburg, 449–450
Houston, Sam, quoted, 59–61
Howard, Captain, quoted, 726–728
Howe, Julia Ward: poem by, 399; song by,
377–379
How it Feels to be Under Fire, 227–229
How the Army of Northern Virginia Got its
Ordnance, 99–101
Hunt, Frances Caldern de la Barca, quoted, 774–775
Hunt, General, quoted, 408–411
Hunter, Alexander, quoted, 152–156,
237–238
Hunter, David, quoted, 581–582
"A Hurricane of Shot and Shell",
706–708

I Am Filled with Horror at the Condition of
Our Country, 77–78
"I Am in Too Much Trouble", 556
"I Do Want to See You So Much", 513
"If We Are Regarded as Evil Here",
557–558

An Illinois Private Fights at the Hornet's
Nest, 257–262
Illinois State Legislature Opposes
Emancipation Proclamation, 579
Imboden, John, quoted, 719–721,
740–741
Inaugural Address of Jefferson Davis,
61–63
An Indiana Boy Reassures His Mother
About Morals in the Army, 293–294
"I Never Desire Again to Draw My Sword",
734
"An Instance of Sublime Christian
Heroism", 366–367
"In the Heart of Destruction", 790–791
Inventions and Gadgets Used by the Soldiers,
216–217
The Irish Brigade is Repulsed on Marye's
Hill, 188–190
The Iron Lines of Petersburg, 712–714
"I Shook Hands with Bob 'fore they Hung
Him", 802–803
"It Beat Anything in History", 613–615
"It Does Not Suit Our Fellows to Be
Commanded Much", 330–331
"It is Well War Is So Terrible, or We
Should Get Too Fond of It",
736–737
The Ivy Prowls Outside New Orleans,
628–629
"I Wish That His Back Had Been as Deeply
Scarred", 556
"I Would Save the Union", 574–575

Jackson, Thomas J. ("Stonewall"),
131–144; death of, 202–204; Douglas,
Henry Kid, on, 141–144; First Bull
Run, 112; Port Republic, attack,
138–140; Second Bull Run, 146–152;
Taylor, Richard, campaign with,
132–138; Wolseley, Garnet, visit from,
138–140
Jackson Outsmarts and Outfights Pope at
Manassas, 147–149
Jefferson Davis Replies to the Emancipation
Proclamation, 580
The Jefferson Davis Takes a Prize Off
Delaware, 629
Jews in the Confederacy, 505–507
Joe Johnston Gives Way to Hood, 663–665
"John Brown's Body" (song), 375
John Chipman Gray Views the Western
Soldier, 283–284
John Dooley Describes Prayer Meetings,
226
John Hay Lives with "The Tycoon" in the
White House, 746–747
Johnson, Andrew, quoted, 802
Johnson, Ben, quoted, 802–803
Johnson, Charles, quoted, 295–297,
330–331, 536–538
Johnson, Hannah, quoted, 551–552
Johnson, Octave, quoted, 541

Johnson's Island, planned seizure of, 490–491

Johnston, J. B., quoted, 661–665

Johnston Halts Sherman at New Hope Church, 661–663

Jones, Reverend Doctor Charles Colcock, quoted, 540

Jones, Jenkin, quoted, 285–288

Jones, John Beauchamp, quoted, 58–59, 499–503, 515–516

Jones, Reverend John W., quoted, 225–226

Jones, Mary Cadwalader, quoted, 785–786

Julie LeGrand Describes the Surrender of New Orleans, 594–595

"Just Before the Battle, Mother" (song), 381–382

The Kearsarge Sinks the Alabama *Off Cherbourg*, 631–634

Kell, John, quoted, 631–634

Kentucky Union Officer Objects to Emancipation, 579–580

"Killed at the Ford" (poem), 395–396

Kinney, John, quoted, 602–608

Kittredge, Walter, song by, 382

Knoxville, Battle of, 653–656

The Ku Klux Klan, 802–806

Lamb, William, quoted, 610–613

"The Last Chance of the Confederacy", 762–766

The Last Will and Testament of J. Reb, 784

Law, Evander M., quoted, 117–119

Lawrence, Eugene, quoted, 245–247

Lawrence (Kansas), massacre, 275–277

Lee, Henrietta, quoted, 342–343

Lee, Robert E.: Appomatox (Virginia), surrender, 775–781; Chancellorsville, Battle of, 195–204; discipline,discussion of problem of, 347–349; Gettysburg, Battle of, 406–413, 435–436; poetry, as subject of, 398–399; portraits, 733–744; quoted, 734–735, 744; resignation from army to go with his state, 734–735; Seven Pines, Battle of, 117–119

Lee, Robert E., Jr., quoted, 741

Lee and Traveller Review the Army of Northern Virginia, 741

Lee Bids Farewell to the Army of Northern Virginia, 744

Lee Loses His Right Arm, 202–204

Lee Stops Hancock at the Gates of Richmond, 711–712

"Lee to the Rear" episodes, 691–693, 696–699, 742–744

"Lee to the Rear" (poem), 398–399

Lee Whips Hooker at Chancellorsville, 195–198

LeGrand, Julia, quoted, 512, 594–595

Leonard, James A., quoted, 222

Letters of Sarah Rosetta Wakeman, alias Private Lyons Wakeman, 241–243

Lexington (Missouri), Battle of, 265–267

Libby Prison, 464–466

Lieutenant Cushing Torpedoes the Albemarle, 608–609

Lieutenant Favill Raises a Company and Gets a Commission, 90–91

Life with the Mosby Guerrillas, 238–240

Life with the Thirteenth Massachusetts, 209–212

Lincoln, President Abraham, see also Emancipation Proclamation; assassination of, 754–756; Bixby, Lydia, letter to, 748; Cabinet, selection of, 51–52; compensated emancipation, plea for, 747–748; Conkling, James C., letter to, 455–456; 1894 election, 498; emancipation, messages to Congress, 570–573; "First Inaugural Address," 50–51; "Gettysburg Address," 438; Horace Greeley, letter to, 574–575; inauguration, 47–49; Johnson, Hannah, letter from, 551–552; Manchester workingmen, correspondence, 365–367; McClellan George B., letter to, 184–185; nomination of, 39–42; poem about, 51–52; portraits, 744–756; Second Inaugural Address, 753–754; Seward's attempt to take charge of administration, 52–54; Sherman, General, letter to, 222; slavery, letters on, 44–45

Lincoln and Hay Follow the Election Returns, 749–751

Lincoln Appoints Hooker to the Command of the Army, 194–195

Lincoln Becomes the Great Emancipator, 575–577

Lincoln is Assassinated, 754–756

Lincoln is Inaugurated, 47–49

Lincoln Refuses to Compromise on Slavery, 44–45

Lincoln Replies to a Serenade, 751–752

Lincoln's Condolence Letters, 748

Lincoln Urgers McClellan to Advance, 184–185

Lincoln Visits the Colored Soldiers at City Point, 752–753

"Little Giffen" (poem), 395

"Little Mac" is Reappointed to Command, 157–159

"Little Mac's A-Coming", 158–159

Little Round Top (Gettysburg), 417–424

Livermore, Thomas: Antietam (Sharpsburg), Battle of, 175–177; quoted, 125–128; statistics by, 84

"The Lives Which Women Have Lead Since Troy Fell", 512

Longfellow, Henry Wadsworth, poetry of, 395–396

Longstreet, James, quoted, 428–429

Longstreet Breaks the Federal Line, 639–640

Longstreet Overwhelms Pope at Manassas, 152–156

Lookout Mountain, 645–646

"Lorena" (song), 386

Lowell, James Russell, poetry of, 358–360, 786

Lunt, Dolly, quoted, 675–677

Lusk, William Thompson, quoted, 437

Major Connolly Loses Faith in the Chivalry of the South, 309–311

Major Fernando Wood Recommends the Secession of New York, 45–47

Major Hitchcock Explains the Burning of Columbia, 680–681

Malvern Hill, Battle of, 126–128

Manassas, Battles of, *see* Bull Run

Manchester Workingmen Stand by the Union, 365–367

"The Man Who Held His Conscience Higher Than Their Praise", 519

"Marching Along" (song), 376–377

"Marching Through Georgia" (song), 382–383

March to the Sea, 657–682

Mark Twain Recalls a Campaign that Failed, 301–309

Marshall, Charles, quoted, 779–781

Marye's Heights, attack on, 185–190

"Maryland! My Maryland!" (song), 377

Matthew Brady's "The Dead at Antietam", 477–479

McCabe, Gordon, quoted, 769–770

McCarthy, Carlton, quoted, 212–216

McCarthy, Harry, song by, 374–375

McClellan, George B.: Antietam Campaign, 158–162; appointment to Army of Potomac, 157–159; 1894 election, 498; letters to his wife, 158–162; Lincoln, letter from, 184–185; Peninsular Campaign, 119–123, 158–162; quoted, 113–114, 233–235; Special Order 191, 163

McClellan Finds the Lost Order, 163

McClellan Forces Turner's Gap and Crampton's Gap, 164–166

McClellan Opens the Peninsular Campaign, 113–114

McClellan "Saves His Country" Twice, 158–162

McClurg, Alexander, quoted, 762–766

McCreary, James B., quoted, 459–460

McCrillis, John, quoted, 188–190

McLaws to the Rescue of Hood, 173–175

Medicine, 521–538

Memphis (Tennessee), Battle of, 597–599

The Merrimac and the Monitor, 588–591

Messages to Congress on Compensated Emancipation, 570–573

Michelbacher, Rabbi Maximilian, quoted, 505–507

Mills, Luther Rice, quoted, 712–714

The Mine and the Battle of the Crater, 708–710

Mining, gold and silver, 489–490
Minister Adams Points Out That This is War, 371–372
The Minnesota Fights for Her Life in Hampton Roads, 588–590
Minutiae of Soldier Life in the Army of Northern Virginia, 212–216
Missionary Ridge, 647–652
Missouri, Guerrilla warfare, 268–270
"Mister, Here's Your Mule" (song), 383–384
Mobile Bay, attack on, 602–608
The Monitor Repels The Merrimac, 590–591
Monks, Colonel, quoted, 268–270
Montgomery, Alabama, organization of Confederacy, 54–56
Moran, Benjamin, quoted, 596
Moran, Frank, quoted, 464–466
"A More Impudent Proceeding Cannot Be Discovered", 596
Morgan, James, quoted, 629–631
Morgan, William, quoted, 647–649
Morgan's Cavalrymen Sweep Through Kentucky, 456–459
Morgan's Raid Comes to an Inglorious End, 459–460
Morrill Act, 816–817
Morse, Charles, quoted, 195–198
Mosby Guerrillas, 238–240
"The Most Superb Soldier in All the World" Falls at Five Forks, 769–770
Motley, John Lothrop, quoted, 79–80
Mr. Eggleston Recalls When Money Was Plentiful, 503–505
Mr. Lincoln Hammers Out a Cabinet, 51–52
Mrs. Chesnut Watches the Attack on Fort Sumter, 65–69
Mrs. Major Belle Reynolds, 243–244
Mundy, Marcellus, quoted, 579–580
Munson, John, quoted, 238–240
Murphy, R. C., indictment of, 331–333
"My Paramount Object is to Save the Union", 573–575
"My Relatives, My Children, My Home", 734

Naff, J. W., song by, 383–384
Nashville (Tennessee), Battle of, 758–761
Nathaniel Hawthorne Calls on President Lincoln, 744–746
Naval power, 587–615; blockade, the, 617–634
Nevada, mining, 489–490
"A New Birth of Freedom", 438
New Hope Church, engagement at, 661–663
New Jersey Peace Resolutions, 496–497
New Market (Virginia), Battle of, 715–719
New Orleans, capture of, 592–596
New Orleans Falls to the Yankees, 594–596

The New Orleans Tribune, 798–799
New York, recommended secession of, 45–47
New York City: attempt to burn, 493–494; draft riots, 480–483
New York Tribune, 600–602
Nichols, George Ward, quoted, 289–292, 679–680
Nichols, Samuel, quoted, 531–532
"Night came and with It Came Sorrow and Sadness", 774–775
Night on the Field of Fredericksburg, 192–194
No Choice But Escape, 541–542
Northern Boys Join the Ranks, 89–93
A Northern Democrat Urges Peaceful Separation, 78–79
Northern Ordnance, 102–104
Norton, Oliver, quoted, 123–124, 158–159
A Note on the Emancipation Proclamation, 581
Nott, J. C., quoted, 106–108
"Now Richmond Rocked in Her High Towers to Watch the Impending Issue", 766–769

Oakey, Daniel, quoted, 674–675
Oates, William, quoted, 419–422, 699–700, 742
"O Captain! My Captain!" (poem), 399–400
"Ode" (poem), 391
"Oh, Earth, behold the monster!", 342–343
"Oh Mother, Look Down From Heav'n On Me" (poetry), 394–398
Oliver Norton Fights Like a Madman at Gaines' Mill, 123–124
"Onward to Vicksburg", 440–444
The Orphan Brigade is Shattered at Stones River, 262–264
Osgood, Kate Putnam, poetry of, 400
O'Sullivan, John L., quoted, 78–79
Our People Are All United, 84–85
Ousting the French From Mexico, 818–821
Owen, William, quoted, 185–188

Pacific Railway Act, 814–816
Palmerston, Viscount, quoted, 360–362
Palmerston and Russell Discuss Intervention, 360–362
Palmerston Protests Butler's Proclamation, 595–596
Paris, Comte de, quoted, 102–104
Parks, Leighton, quoted, 737–740
Parthenia Hague Tells How Women Outwitted the Blockade, 507–509
Peace at any Price, 518–519
Pea Ridge campaign, 270–272
Peck, W. F. G., quoted, 627–628
Pendleton, General, quoted, 736–737
Peninsular Campaign, 113–130, 158–162; wounded, 521–523

Pennsylvania, invasion of, 407–408
Perkins, George H., 592–594
Petersburg, Siege of, 701–714
Petrigru, James Louis, 519
Phisterer, Frederick, statistics by, 84
Pickett, George E., quoted, 437–438
Pierce, Francis Edwin, quoted, 337
Pike, James Shepherd, quoted, 799–801
Pittenger, William, quoted, 312–318
Pleasonton, General, quoted, 198–200
Pleasonton Stops the Confederates at Hazel Grove, 198–200
Poems of the Civil War, 389–403
Poet Laureate of the South, 389–391
Polley, J. B., quoted, 188–190
"The Poor Colored People Thanked God that their Sufferings were Ended", 772–774
Pope, General, Second Bull Run, 147–152
Pope Wastes His Strength on Jackson, 149–152
Porter, David D., quoted, 277–280
Porter, Fitz John, quoted, 229–231
Porter, Horace, quoted, 685–687, 694–696, 752–753
Port Hudson, Fall of, 454–455
Port Republic, attack, 138–140
"The Prayer of Twenty Millions", 574
Prescott, R. B., quoted, 772–774
President Davis Quells a Food Riot in Richmond, 515–516
President Lincoln Needs the Soldier, 222
Price Invades the North and is Defeated at Westport, 280–282
Prisons, 461–471
Private Goss Describes the Battle of the Wilderness, 687–690
The Privations of Life in Elmira Prison, 469–471
Prize Cases, 80–81
The Problem of Contrabands, 568–570
The Proclamation and the Negro Army, 542–543
"Prominent Citizens Became Piesellers", 788–790
Protest of the New Jersey Soldiers, 497–498
The Public Man Attends the Inauguration, 48–49
Punishments in the Army of Northern Virginia, 345–346
Punishments in the Army of the Potomac, 344–345
Punishments in the Union and Confederate Armies, 343–346
Putnam, Sallie, quoted, 117

Quantrill and His Guerrillas Sack Lawrence, 275–277

R. E. Lee Takes Command, 117–119
The Race of Philip Sidneys is Not Extinct, 79–80

Railroads: Georgia locomotive chase, 312–318; Morgan raid, 456–460

Ramseur, Stephen Dodson, quoted, 721–726

Randall, James R., song by, 377

Ravenel, Henry William, quoted, 84–85, 352

Reactions to the Emancipation Proclamation, 577–581

The Reasons Why Great Britain is Averse to Recognize Us, 370–371

Rebel and Yankee Yells, 240–241

Rebellion Record, 42–43

Reconstruction, 787–811

Recruiting companies, 89–93

Red River dams, 277–280

Red Tape, North and South, 223–225

The Regimental Hospital, 536–538

Religion and Play in the Army of the Tennessee, 285–288

Religion in the Confederate Army, 225–226

Repard, M., quoted, 628–629

Resistance at Home, 515–517

Reynolds, Belle, letters regarding, 243–244

Reynolds, John, Battle of Gettysburg, 411–413

Rice, Spotswood, quoted, 555–556

Richard Auchmuty Reviews the Peninsular Campaign, 128–130

Richard Cobden Rejoices in the Emancipation Proclamation, 367–368

Richmond: abandonment of, 770–775; attack on, 766–769; food riot, 515–516

Ridley, Bromfield, quoted, 298–300

Riots: Baltimore, 93–96; draft riots, New York City, 480–483; food riot, Richmond, 515–516

Robert E. Lee Goes With His State, 734–735

"Robert E. Lee" (poem), 399

The Robert E. Lee Runs the Blockade, 622–624

Robert Gould Shaw Complains That War is a Dirty Business, 335–336

The Rob Roy Runs the Blockade Out of Havana, 624–627

Root, George F., songs by, 380–382

Rosecrans, William S., quoted, 331–332

Rosengarten, Joseph, quoted, 411–413

Russell, Earl, quoted, 360–362

Russell, William Howard, quoted, 108–112

Ryan, Abram Joseph, poetry of, 402

"*A Sadness I Had Never Before Seen Upon His Face*", 740–741

Sam Houston Refuses to Go with His State, 59–61

The Sanitary Commission to the Rescue, 524–526

"*A Scene of Shameful Confusion*", 679–680

Secession: New York, recommended, 45–47; South Carolina, 42–43; Texas, 59–61; Virginia, 75–76

Secretary Benjamin Recalls the Mistakes of the Confederate Congress, 101–102

Secretary Chase Recalls a Famous Cabinet Meeting, 575–577

"*A Sense of Disgust Must be Awakened*", 554

A Sense of Infinite Weariness, 495–496

Seven Days Battle, 123–128

Seven Pines, Battle of, 117–119

Seward, William H.: Lincoln, letter from, 45; Lincoln administration, attempt to take charge of, 52–54; quoted, 818–821

Seward Tries to Take Charge of the Lincoln Administration, 52–54

Sex in the Civil War, 350

"*Shall It Be Love, or Hate, John?*" (poem), 358–360

Shanks, W. F. G., quoted, 642–645

Shaw, Robert Gould, 335–336

"*She Has Left Us in Passion and Pride*" (Holmes), 43–44

Sheridan, P. H.: execution of deserters, 346–347; quoted, 728–732

Sheridan Rides Down the Valley Pike to Victory and Fame, 728–731

Sherman, General William T.: Atlanta, and march to sea, 657–682; letter to his wife, 513; Lincoln, letter from, 222; quoted, 158, 659–661, 668–669, 671–674, 681–682

Sherman Marches from Atlanta to the Sea, 671–674

Sherman Marches From Chattanooga to Atlanta, 659–661

Sherman's "Bummers", 674–675

Shiloh (Pittsburg Landing), Battle of, 252–257; Hornet's Nest, 257–262

Shotwell, Randolph Abbott, quoted, 220–221, 224–225, 466–469

Sigel, Franz: quoted, 270–272; Valley campaigns, 715–721

Silencing the "Jeers and Taunts", 544–545

Slavery, The Cornerstone of the Confederacy, 566–567

Small, Abner, quoted, 207–208, 461–463

Smith, Goldwin, quoted, 368–369

Smith, Reverend James Power, quoted, 202–204

Soldiers, lives of: Eastern front, 205–244; Western front, 283–300

"*The Soldiers Delight in Destroying Everything*", 337

The Soldiers Get Paid and the Sutler Gets the Money, 295–297

Song and Play in the Army of Tennessee, 297–300

Songs the Soldiers Sang, 373–387

South Carolina, secession, 42–43

Southern Illustrated News, 297–298, 449–450, 581; editorial, 370–371

Southern Ladies Send Their Men Off to War, 85–87

Special Order 191, 163

The Spirit of Virginia Cannot Be Crushed, 75–76

"*A Splendid Specimen of an English Gentleman*", 735–736

Spotsylvania and the Bloody Angle, 694–696

Standing Up for the Rights of Black Soldiers, 549–553

Stanley, Henry Morgan, quoted, 252–257

Stanton, Edward M., quoted, 113

The Stars and Stripes are Raised over Fort Sumter, 785–786

"*Starvation, Rags, Dirt, and Vermin*", 220–221

Stephens, Alexander, quoted, 566–567

Stiles, Robert, quoted, 235–236, 692–693

Stillwell, Leander, quoted, 257–262

Stokes, Reverend T. J., quoted, 288–289

Stonewall Jackson Credits God with the Victory, 112

Strother, David, quoted, 149–152, 164–170

The Struggle for Little Round Top, 417–424

Strunke, Elias D., quoted, 544

Stuart, J. E. B.: Chancellorsville, Battle of, 195–202; Peninsular Campaign, 119–123

Stuart and Anderson Link up at Chancellorsville, 200–202

Stuart's Ball is Interrupted by the Yankees, 231–232

Suffering in Andersonville Prison, 463–464

Supplying the Confederacy with Arms and Ammunition, 98–99

The Supreme Court Upholds the Constitution, 80–81

Susan Blackford Nurses the Wounded at Lynchburg, 527–528

Taney, Roger B., quoted, 821–824

Taylor, Richard, quoted, 132–140

Taylor, W. H., quoted, 347–349

Taylor's Irish Men Capture a Battery at Port Republic, 138–140

Tennessee Petition, 559–563

"*Tenting Tonight*" (song), 382

"*Texans Always Move Them*", 691–692

Texas, secession, 59–61

Texas brigade, 691–692

Theatricals in the Army, 297–298

"*Their Dead and Dying Piled Higher than the Works*", 692–693

Theodore Winthrop Recalls a Typical Day at Camp Cameron, 205–207

"*These Men Have Never Failed You on Any Field*", 696–699

They Are Intelligent on All Subjects but that of Negro Slavery, on This They Are Mad, 514

"They Must Reap the Whirlwind", 513

Thirteenth Amendment, 797

Thirteenth Massachusetts, 209–212

"This Imbecile Pro-slavery Government Does Try Me So", 567–568

Thomas Annihilates Hood at Nashville, 758–761

Thomas Holds the Horseshoe Ridge, 640–642

Thomas Livermore Puts on His War Paint, 175–177

Thomas Stands Like a Rock at Chattanooga, 638–642

Thomas Wentworth Higginson Celebrates Life in a Black Regiment, 545–549

Thomas Wentworth Higginson Explains the Value of Trained Officers, 326–330

Thompson, David, quoted, 179–181

Thompson, John Reuben, poetry of, 398–399

Thruston, Gates P., quoted, 640–642

Ticknor, Francis Orrery, poetry of, 395

Ticknor, George, quoted, 354–355

The Tide Turns at Pea Ridge, 270–272

Timrod, Henry, poetry of, 389–391

"To Fight is Not His Forte", 157–158

Toney, Marcus, quoted, 469–471

Townsend, George Alfred, quoted, 333, 521–523, 766–769

"Tramp, Tramp, Tramp" (song), 381

Trobriand, Régis de, quoted, 483–484

Turner, Reverend Henry M., quoted, 557–558

Tuthill, Richard, quoted, 665–668

Twain, Mark, quoted, 301–309, 489–490

The 20th Maine Saves Little Round Top, 422–424

Tyler family, correspondence, 75–76

U. S. Grant Becomes Unconditional Surrender Grant, 247–252

U. S. Grant Plans his Spring Campaign, 684–685

"The Uneducated Negro Was Too Weak", 809–810

"Unequaled Coolness and Bravery", 544

A Union woman Suffers Through the Siege of Vicksburg, 445–449

The United States Navy Blockades the Confederacy, 618–622

Upson, Theodore, quoted, 71–73, 293–294

Valley campaigns, 715–732

"The Valley Will Have Little in it for Man or Beast", 731–732

Van Brunt, Captain, quoted, 588–590

Vermont, raid of, 491–493

Vicksburg, Siege of, 440–454

Vicksburg campaign, 439–440

Vicksburg Surrenders, 450–454

Viele, Egbert Ludovicus, quoted, 115–116

"Vigil Strange I Kept on the Field One Night" (poem), 396

Virginia: ordnance, 99–101; secession, 75–76

V.M.I. Boys Fight at New Market, 715–719

Von Borcke, Heros, quoted, 200–202, 231–232

Voting in the Field, 222

Wait, Horatio, quoted, 618–622

Wakeman, Sarah Rosetta, quoted, 241–243

Walt Whitman Looks Around in Wartime Washington, 475–477

A War Clerk Describes Davis Amid His Cabinet, 58–59

A War Clerk Suffers Scarcities in Richmond, 499–503

Ward, Mary A., quoted, 85–87, 510–511

A War for Liberty, 581–582

Warren, G. K., Little Round Top (Gettysburg), 417–419

Warren Goss Enters in the Union Army, 89–90

War Weariness, 495–497

Washburne, E. B., letter from Lincoln, 44–45

Washington as a Camp, 473–475

Watson, William, quoted, 272–275, 294–295, 624–627

"We Are Coming, Father Abraham" (song), 379–380

We are not Enemies but Friends, 50–51

"We Are the Boys of Potomac's Ranks" (song), 384–385

"We Are Truly One People", 365–366

Webster, H. D. L., song by, 386

"We Cannot Escape History", 571–573

Weed, Thurlow, quoted, 51–52

"We Had Only Our Ignorance", 806–809

Welch, A., quoted, 347

Welles, Gideon, quoted, 157–158, 754–756

"We Shall Nobly Save or Meanly Lose the Last, Best Hope of Earth", 747–748

Westport (Missouri), raid of, 280–282

West Virginia Becomes a State, 817–818

We Thought the Rebellion Would Be Over Before Our Chance Would Come, 92–93

"We Were Proud of Our Foragers", 674–675

"When Johnny Comes Marching Home" (song), 387

The White Flag at Appomattox, 775–779

White Oak Swamp, Battle of, 125–126

Whitman, Walt: poetry of, 396–397, 399–401; quoted, 475–477

Whittier, John Greenleaf, poetry by, 393–394

"Who Could Not Conquer with Such Troops as These?", 146–147

"The Whole Column Seemed Crowned with Red", 783–784

"The Whole Government Gives Cheer to Me", 555–556

"The Whole Landscape Turns Red" at Antietam, 179–181

Wilcox, Charles, quoted, 440–444

Wild, Edward A., quoted, 556

Wilderness, Battle of, 687–690, 742–744

Wilderness campaign, 683–700

Wilkeson, Frank, quoted, 96–98, 344–345

Wilkinson, John, quoted, 622–624

Wills, Charles, quoted, 333–335

Wilson, Harrison, quoted, 324

Wilson, James, quoted, 758–761

Winthrop, Theodore, quoted, 205–207

A Wisconsin Boy Complains of the Hardships of Training, 284–285

Wisconsin Boys are Slaughtered in the Cornfield, 171–173

Wise, John, quoted, 708–710, 715–719, 784

With "Extra Billy" Smith at York, 235–236

"With Malice Toward None", 753–754

With the Dixie Grays at Shiloh, 252–257

Wolseley, Garnet, quoted, 140–141, 735–736

Women Among the Ranks, 241–244

Wood, Fernando, quoted, 45–47

Wool, General, 115–116

Woolsey, Jane Stuart, quoted, 74–75

Work, Henry Clay, songs by, 382–385

"The Work of the Abolitionists Is Not Done", 584–585

Wormeley, Katharine, quoted, 524–526

Worth, Jonathan, quoted, 77–78, 518–519

The Yankee Invaders Pillage and Burn, 336–343

"The Yankees Are Coming", 510–511

The Yankees Attack Marye's Heights, 185–188

The Yankees Sack Sarah Morgan's Home, 337–340

"You Debauched a Young Negro Girl", 540

"You Might as Well Appeal Against the Thunder-Storm", 668–669

Young, Lieutenant L.D., 262–264